GO!

with Microsoft®

Access 2007

Comprehensive First Edition

**Shelley Gaskin, Carolyn McLellan,
Susan Dozier, and Kris Townsend**

PEARSON

Prentice
Hall

Upper Saddle River, New Jersey

This book is dedicated to my students, who inspire me every day, and to my husband, Fred Gaskin.
—Shelley Gaskin

I dedicate this book to my daughters Megan, Rachel, and Mandy; my mother, who always believed in me and encouraged me to become a teacher; and my sister Debbie, who was my first student and is an inspiration to me. It is a true testimony of friendship that Susan remains a faithful and loving friend through our joint venture in writing this book.
—Carolyn McLellan

I dedicate this book to my truest blessings on earth—my loving husband, Richard; and my six wonderful children Jennifer, Amanda, Ricky, Emily, Heather, and Jonathan. I thank my God for the friendship and inspiration Carolyn has given to me.
—Susan Dozier

This book is dedicated to the students at Spokane Falls Community College. Their adventures, joys, and frustrations guide my way.
—Kris Townsend

Library of Congress Cataloging-in-Publication Data

Go! with. Microsoft Access comprehensive / Shelley Gaskin ... [et al.].
    p. cm.
Includes index.
ISBN 0-13-232762-7
1. Microsoft Access. 2. Database management. I. Title: Microsoft Access comprehensive. II. Gaskin, Shelley.
QA76.9.D3G685 2008
005.75'65--dc22

2007044460

Vice President and Publisher: Natalie E. Anderson
Associate VP/Executive Acquisitions Editor, Print: Stephanie Wall
Executive Acquisitions Editor, Media: Richard Keaveny
Product Development Manager: Eileen Bien Calabro
Editorial Project Manager: Sarah Parker McCabe
Development Editor: Jennifer Lynn
Editorial Assistant: Terenia McHenry
Executive Producer: Lisa Strite
Content Development Manager: Cathi Profitko
Media Project Manager: Alana Coles
Production Media Project Manager: Lorena Cerisano
Director of Marketing: Margaret Waples
Senior Marketing Manager: Tori Olson-Alves
Marketing Assistants: Angela Frey, Kathryn Ferranti
Senior Sales Associate: Rebecca Scott

Senior Managing Editor: Cynthia Zonneveld
Associate Managing Editor: Camille Trentacoste
Production Project Manager: Mike Lackey
Production Editor: GGS Book Services
Photo Researcher: GGS Book Services
Operations Specialist: Natacha Moore
Senior Art Director: Jonathan Boylan
Cover Photo: Courtesy of Getty Images, Inc./Marvin Mattelson
Composition: GGS Book Services
Project Management: GGS Book Services
Cover Printer: Phoenix Color
Printer/Binder: RR Donnelley/Willard

Microsoft, Windows, Word, PowerPoint, Outlook, FrontPage, Visual Basic, MSN, The Microsoft Network, and/or other Microsoft products referenced herein are either trademarks or registered trademarks of Microsoft Corporation in the U.S.A. and other countries. Screen shots and icons reprinted with permission from the Microsoft Corporation. This book is not sponsored or endorsed by or affiliated with Microsoft Corporation.

Credits and acknowledgments borrowed from other sources and reproduced, with permission, in this textbook are as follows or on the appropriate page within the text.

Page 2: Gunter Marx © Dorling Kindersley; page 114: Greg Nicholas; pages 216 and 708: PhotoEdit Inc.; page 332: Getty Images, Inc.—PhotoDisc; page 430: Helena Smith © Rough Guides; page 520: Dorling Kindersley Media Library; page 612: Andrea Gingerich; page 800: The Stock Connection; pages 880 and 952: Getty Images Inc.—Stone Allstock; page 1026: M. Eric Honeycutt.

10 9 8 7 6 5 4 3 2 1
ISBN-10: 0-13-232762-7
ISBN-13: 978-0-13-232762-6

Contents in Brief

Table of Contents

Chapter 10 Administering Databases 879

Letter from the Editor

Dear Instructors and Students,

The primary goal of the *GO!* Series is two-fold. The first goal is to help instructors teach the course they want in less time. The second goal is to provide students with the skills to solve business problems using the computer as a tool, for both themselves and the organization for which they might be employed.

The *GO!* Series was originally created by Series Editor Shelley Gaskin and published with the release of Microsoft Office 2003. Her ideas came from years of using textbooks that didn't meet all the needs of today's diverse classroom and that were too confusing for students. Shelley continues to enhance the series by ensuring we stay true to our vision of developing quality instruction and useful classroom tools.

But we also need your input and ideas.

Over time, the *GO!* Series has evolved based on direct feedback from instructors and students using the series. *We are the publisher that listens.* To publish a textbook that works for you, it's critical that we continue to listen to this feedback. It's important to me to talk with you and hear your stories about using *GO!* Your voice can make a difference.

My hope is that this letter will inspire you to write me an e-mail and share your thoughts on using the *GO!* Series.

Stephanie Wall
Executive Editor, *GO!* Series
stephanie_wall@prenhall.com

GO! System Contributors

We thank the following people for their hard work and support in making the GO! System all that it is!

Additional Author Support

Coyle, Diane	Montgomery County Community College
Fry, Susan	Boise State
Townsend, Kris	Spokane Falls Community College
Stroup, Tracey	Amgen Corporation

Instructor Resource Authors

Arnold, Linda	Harrisburg Area Community College
Bankowski, Hellene	Philadelphia University
Behrens, Sharon	Northeast Wisconsin Technical College
Bowen, Lynn	Valdosta Technical College
Davidson, Spring	University of Delaware
Faix, Dennis	Harrisburg Area Community College
Flomberg, Howard	Metropolitan State College of Denver
Fry, Susan	Boise State University
Hearn, Barbara	Community College of Philadelphia
Le Grand, M. Kate	Broward Community College
St. John, Steve	Tulsa Community College
Weber, Sandra	Gateway Technical College

Super Reviewers

Alexander, Christine	
Fry, Susan	Boise State
Hayes, Darren	Pace University
Lamoureaux, Jackie	Central New Mexico State
Yoxheimer, Eric	Harrisburg Area Community College

Technical Editors

Allen, Lindsey
Bates, Lee Ann
Daley, Bill
Snyder, Janice

Student Reviewers

Allen, John	Asheville-Buncombe Tech Community College
Alexander, Steven	St. Johns River Community College
Alexander, Melissa	Tulsa Community College
Bolz, Stephanie	Northern Michigan University
Berner, Ashley	Central Washington University
Boomer, Michelle	Northern Michigan University
Busse, Brennan	Northern Michigan University
Butkey, Maura	Central Washington University
Christensen, Kaylie	Northern Michigan University
Connally, Brianna	Central Washington University
Davis, Brandon	Northern Michigan University
Davis, Christen	Central Washington University
Den Boer, Lance	Central Washington University
Dix, Jessica	Central Washington University
Moeller, Jeffrey	Northern Michigan University
Downs, Elizabeth	Central Washington University
Erickson, Mike	Ball State University
Gadomski, Amanda	Northern Michigan University
Gyselinck, Craig	Central Washington University
Harrison, Margo	Central Washington University
Heacox, Kate	Central Washington University
Hill, Cheretta	Northwestern State University
Innis, Tim	Tulsa Community College
Jarboe, Aaron	Central Washington University
Klein, Colleen	Northern Michigan University
Moeller, Jeffrey	Northern Michigan University
Nicholson, Regina	Athens Tech College
Niehaus, Kristina	Northern Michigan University
Nisa, Zaibun	Santa Rosa Community College
Nunez, Nohelia	Santa Rosa Community College
Oak, Samantha	Central Washington University
Oertii, Monica	Central Washington University
Palenshus, Juliet	Central Washington University
Pohl, Amanda	Northern Michigan University
Presnell, Randy	Central Washington University
Ritner, April	Northern Michigan University
Rodriguez, Flavia	Northwestern State University
Roberts, Corey	Tulsa Community College
Rossi, Jessica Ann	Central Washington University
Shafapay, Natasha	Central Washington University
Shanahan, Megan	Northern Michigan University
Teska, Erika	Hawaii Pacific University
Traub, Amy	Northern Michigan University
Underwood, Katie	Central Washington University
Walters, Kim	Central Washington University
Wilson, Kelsie	Central Washington University
Wilson, Amanda	Green River Community College

Series Reviewers

Abraham, Reni	Houston Community College
Agatston, Ann	Agatston Consulting Technical College
Alexander, Melody	Ball Sate University
Alejandro, Manuel	Southwest Texas Junior College
Ali, Farha	Lander University
Amici, Penny	Harrisburg Area Community College
Anderson, Patty A.	Lake City Community College
Andrews, Wilma	Virginia Commonwealth College, Nebraska University
Anik, Mazhar	Tiffin University
Armstrong, Gary	Shippensburg University
Atkins, Bonnie	Delaware Technical Community College
Bachand, LaDonna	Santa Rosa Community College
Bagui, Sikha	University of West Florida
Beecroft, Anita	Kwantlen University College
Bell, Paula	Lock Haven College
Belton, Linda	Springfield Tech. Community College
Bennett, Judith	Sam Houston State University
Bhatia, Sai	Riverside Community College
Bishop, Frances	DeVry Institute—Alpharetta (ATL)
Blaszkiewicz, Holly	Ivy Tech Community College/Region 1
Branigan, Dave	DeVry University
Bray, Patricia	Allegany College of Maryland
Brotherton, Cathy	Riverside Community College
Buehler, Lesley	Ohlone College
Buell, C	Central Oregon Community College
Byars, Pat	Brookhaven College
Byrd, Lynn	Delta State University, Cleveland, Mississippi
Cacace, Richard N.	Pensacola Junior College
Cadenhead, Charles	Brookhaven College
Calhoun, Ric	Gordon College
Cameron, Eric	Passaic Community College
Carriker, Sandra	North Shore Community College
Cannamore, Madie	Kennedy King
Carreon, Cleda	Indiana University—Purdue University, Indianapolis
Chaffin, Catherine	Shawnee State University
Chauvin, Marg	Palm Beach Community College, Boca Raton
Challa, Chandrashekar	Virginia State University
Chamlou, Afsaneh	NOVA Alexandria
Chapman, Pam	Wabaunsee Community College
Christensen, Dan	Iowa Western Community College
Clay, Betty	Southeastern Oklahoma State University
Collins, Linda D.	Mesa Community College
Conroy-Link, Janet	Holy Family College
Cosgrove, Janet	Northwestern CT Community
Courtney, Kevin	Hillsborough Community College
Cox, Rollie	Madison Area Technical College
Crawford, Hiram	Olive Harvey College
Crawford, Thomasina	Miami-Dade College, Kendall Campus
Credico, Grace	Lethbridge Community College
Crenshaw, Richard	Miami Dade Community College, North
Crespo, Beverly	Mt. San Antonio College
Crossley, Connie	Cincinnati State Technical Community College
Curik, Mary	Central New Mexico Community College
De Arazoza, Ralph	Miami Dade Community College
Danno, John	DeVry University/Keller Graduate School
Davis, Phillip	Del Mar College
DeHerrera, Laurie	Pikes Peak Community College
Delk, Dr. K. Kay	Seminole Community College
Doroshow, Mike	Eastfield College
Douglas, Gretchen	SUNYCortland
Dove, Carol	Community College of Allegheny
Driskel, Loretta	Niagara Community College
Duckwiler, Carol	Wabaunsee Community College
Duncan, Mimi	University of Missouri-St. Louis
Duthie, Judy	Green River Community College
Duvall, Annette	Central New Mexico Community College
Ecklund, Paula	Duke University
Eng, Bernice	Brookdale Community College
Evans, Billie	Vance-Granville Community College
Feuerbach, Lisa	Ivy Tech East Chicago
Fisher, Fred	Florida State University
Foster, Penny L.	Anne Arundel Community College
Foszcz, Russ	McHenry County College
Fry, Susan	Boise State University
Fustos, Janos	Metro State
Gallup, Jeanette	Blinn College
Gelb, Janet	Grossmont College
Gentry, Barb	Parkland College
Gerace, Karin	St. Angela Merici School
Gerace, Tom	Tulane University
Ghajar, Homa	Oklahoma State University
Gifford, Steve	Northwest Iowa Community College
Glazer, Ellen	Broward Community College
Gordon, Robert	Hofstra University
Gramlich, Steven	Pasco-Hernando Community College
Graviett, Nancy M.	St. Charles Community College, St. Peters, Missouri
Greene, Rich	Community College of Allegheny County
Gregoryk, Kerry	Virginia Commonwealth State
Griggs, Debra	Bellevue Community College
Grimm, Carol	Palm Beach Community College
Hahn, Norm	Thomas Nelson Community College
Hammerschlag, Dr. Bill	Brookhaven College
Hansen, Michelle	Davenport University
Hayden, Nancy	Indiana University—Purdue University, Indianapolis
Hayes, Theresa	Broward Community College
Helfand, Terri	Chaffey College
Helms, Liz	Columbus State Community College
Hernandez, Leticia	TCI College of Technology
Hibbert, Marilyn	Salt Lake Community College
Hoffman, Joan	Milwaukee Area Technical College
Hogan, Pat	Cape Fear Community College
Holland, Susan	Southeast Community College
Hopson, Bonnie	Athens Technical College
Horvath, Carrie	Albertus Magnus College
Horwitz, Steve	Community College of Philadelphia
Hotta, Barbara	Leeward Community College
Howard, Bunny	St. Johns River Community
Howard, Chris	DeVry University
Huckabay, Jamie	Austin Community College
Hudgins, Susan	East Central University
Hulett, Michelle J.	Missouri State University
Hunt, Darla A.	Morehead State University, Morehead, Kentucky
Hunt, Laura	Tulsa Community College
Jacob, Sherry	Jefferson Community College

Jacobs, Duane	Salt Lake Community College	Marucco, Toni	Lincoln Land Community College
Jauken, Barb	Southeastern Community	Mason, Lynn	Lubbock Christian University
Johnson, Kathy	Wright College	Matutis, Audrone	Houston Community College
Johnson, Mary	Kingwood College	Matkin, Marie	University of Lethbridge
Johnson, Mary	Mt. San Antonio College	McCain, Evelynn	Boise State University
Jones, Stacey	Benedict College	McCannon, Melinda	Gordon College
Jones, Warren	University of Alabama, Birmingham	McCarthy, Marguerite	Northwestern Business College
Jordan, Cheryl	San Juan College	McCaskill, Matt L.	Brevard Community College
Kapoor, Bhushan	California State University, Fullerton	McClellan, Carolyn	Tidewater Community College
Kasai, Susumu	Salt Lake Community College	McClure, Darlean	College of Sequoias
Kates, Hazel	Miami Dade Community College, Kendall	McCrory, Sue A.	Missouri State University
		McCue, Stacy	Harrisburg Area Community College
Keen, Debby	University of Kentucky	McEntire-Orbach, Teresa	Middlesex County College
Keeter, Sandy	Seminole Community College	McLeod, Todd	Fresno City College
Kern-Blystone, Dorothy Jean	Bowling Green State	McManus, Illyana	Grossmont College
		McPherson, Dori	Schoolcraft College
Keskin, Ilknur	The University of South Dakota	Meiklejohn, Nancy	Pikes Peak Community College
Kirk, Colleen	Mercy College	Menking, Rick	Hardin-Simmons University
Kleckner, Michelle	Elon University	Meredith, Mary	University of Louisiana at Lafayette
Kliston, Linda	Broward Community College, North Campus	Mermelstein, Lisa	Baruch College
		Metos, Linda	Salt Lake Community College
Kochis, Dennis	Suffolk County Community College	Meurer, Daniel	University of Cincinnati
Kramer, Ed	Northern Virginia Community College	Meyer, Marian	Central New Mexico Community College
Laird, Jeff	Northeast State Community College	Miller, Cindy	Ivy Tech Community College, Lafayette, Indiana
Lamoureaux, Jackie	Central New Mexico Community College	Mitchell, Susan	Davenport University
Lange, David	Grand Valley State	Mohle, Dennis	Fresno Community College
LaPointe, Deb	Central New Mexico Community College	Monk, Ellen	University of Delaware
		Moore, Rodney	Holland College
Larson, Donna	Louisville Technical Institute	Morris, Mike	Southeastern Oklahoma State University
Laspina, Kathy	Vance-Granville Community College		
Le Grand, Dr. Kate	Broward Community College	Morris, Nancy	Hudson Valley Community College
Lenhart, Sheryl	Terra Community College	Moseler, Dan	Harrisburg Area Community College
Letavec, Chris	University of Cincinnati	Nabors, Brent	Reedley College, Clovis Center
Liefert, Jane	Everett Community College	Nadas, Erika	Wright College
Lindaman, Linda	Black Hawk Community College	Nadelman, Cindi	New England College
Lindberg, Martha	Minnesota State University	Nademlynsky, Lisa	Johnson & Wales University
Lightner, Renee	Broward Community College	Ncube, Cathy	University of West Florida
Lindberg, Martha	Minnesota State University	Nagengast, Joseph	Florida Career College
Linge, Richard	Arizona Western College	Newsome, Eloise	Northern Virginia Community College Woodbridge
Logan, Mary G.	Delgado Community College		
Loizeaux, Barbara	Westchester Community College	Nicholls, Doreen	Mohawk Valley Community College
Lopez, Don	Clovis-State Center Community College District	Nunan, Karen	Northeast State Technical Community College
Lord, Alexandria	Asheville Buncombe Tech	Odegard, Teri	Edmonds Community College
Lowe, Rita	Harold Washington College	Ogle, Gregory	North Community College
Low, Willy Hui	Joliet Junior College	Orr, Dr. Claudia	Northern Michigan University South
Lucas, Vickie	Broward Community College	Otieno, Derek	DeVry University
Lynam, Linda	Central Missouri State University	Otton, Diana Hill	Chesapeake College
Lyon, Lynne	Durham College	Oxendale, Lucia	West Virginia Institute of Technology
Lyon, Pat Rajski	Tomball College		
MacKinnon, Ruth	Georgia Southern University	Paiano, Frank	Southwestern College
Macon, Lisa	Valencia Community College, West Campus	Patrick, Tanya	Clackamas Community College
		Peairs, Deb	Clark State Community College
Machuca, Wayne	College of the Sequoias	Prince, Lisa	Missouri State University-Springfield Campus
Madison, Dana	Clarion University		
Maguire, Trish	Eastern New Mexico University	Proietti, Kathleen	Northern Essex Community College
Malkan, Rajiv	Montgomery College	Pusins, Delores	HCCC
Manning, David	Northern Kentucky University	Raghuraman, Ram	Joliet Junior College
Marcus, Jacquie	Niagara Community College	Reasoner, Ted Allen	Indiana University—Purdue
Marghitu, Daniela	Auburn University	Reeves, Karen	High Point University
Marks, Suzanne	Bellevue Community College	Remillard, Debbie	New Hampshire Technical Institute
Marquez, Juanita	El Centro College	Rhue, Shelly	DeVry University
Marquez, Juan	Mesa Community College	Richards, Karen	Maplewoods Community College
Martyn, Margie	Baldwin-Wallace College	Richardson, Mary	Albany Technical College

Rodgers, Gwen	Southern Nazarene University
Roselli, Diane	Harrisburg Area Community College
Ross, Dianne	University of Louisiana in Lafayette
Rousseau, Mary	Broward Community College, South
Samson, Dolly	Hawaii Pacific University
Sams, Todd	University of Cincinnati
Sandoval, Everett	Reedley College
Sardone, Nancy	Seton Hall University
Scafide, Jean	Mississippi Gulf Coast Community College
Scheeren, Judy	Westmoreland County Community College
Schneider, Sol	Sam Houston State University
Scroggins, Michael	Southwest Missouri State University
Sever, Suzanne	Northwest Arkansas Community College
Sheridan, Rick	California State University-Chico
Silvers, Pamela	Asheville Buncombe Tech
Singer, Steven A.	University of Hawai'i, Kapi'olani Community College
Sinha, Atin	Albany State University
Skolnick, Martin	Florida Atlantic University
Smith, T. Michael	Austin Community College
Smith, Tammy	Tompkins Cortland Community Collge
Smolenski, Bob	Delaware County Community College
Spangler, Candice	Columbus State
Stedham, Vicki	St. Petersburg College, Clearwater
Stefanelli, Greg	Carroll Community College
Steiner, Ester	New Mexico State University
Stenlund, Neal	Northern Virginia Community College, Alexandria
St. John, Steve	Tulsa Community College
Sterling, Janet	Houston Community College
Stoughton, Catherine	Laramie County Community College
Sullivan, Angela	Joliet Junior College
Szurek, Joseph	University of Pittsburgh at Greensburg
Tarver, Mary Beth	Northwestern State University
Taylor, Michael	Seattle Central Community College
Thangiah, Sam	Slippery Rock University
Thompson-Sellers, Ingrid	Georgia Perimeter College
Tomasi, Erik	Baruch College

Toreson, Karen	Shoreline Community College
Trifiletti, John J.	Florida Community College at Jacksonville
Trivedi, Charulata	Quinsigamond Community College, Woodbridge
Tucker, William	Austin Community College
Turgeon, Cheryl	Asnuntuck Community College
Turpen, Linda	Central New Mexico Community College
Upshaw, Susan	Del Mar College
Unruh, Angela	Central Washington University
Vanderhoof, Dr. Glenna	Missouri State University-Springfield Campus
Vargas, Tony	El Paso Community College
Vicars, Mitzi	Hampton University
Villarreal, Kathleen	Fresno
Vitrano, Mary Ellen	Palm Beach Community College
Volker, Bonita	Tidewater Community College
Wahila, Lori (Mindy)	Tompkins Cortland Community College
Waswick, Kim	Southeast Community College, Nebraska
Wavle, Sharon	Tompkins Cortland Community College
Webb, Nancy	City College of San Francisco
Wells, Barbara E.	Central Carolina Technical College
Wells, Lorna	Salt Lake Community College
Welsh, Jean	Lansing Community College Nebraska
White, Bruce	Quinnipiac University
Willer, Ann	Solano Community College
Williams, Mark	Lane Community College
Wilson, Kit	Red River College
Wilson, Roger	Fairmont State University
Wimberly, Leanne	International Academy of Design and Technology
Worthington, Paula	Northern Virginia Community College
Yauney, Annette	Herkimer County Community College
Yip, Thomas	Passaic Community College
Zavala, Ben	Webster Tech
Zlotow, Mary Ann	College of DuPage
Zudeck, Steve	Broward Community College, North

About the Authors

Shelley Gaskin, Series Editor, is a professor of business and computer technology at Pasadena City College in Pasadena, California. She holds a master's degree in business education from Northern Illinois University and a doctorate in adult and community education from Ball State University. Dr. Gaskin has 15 years of experience in the computer industry with several Fortune 500 companies and has developed and written training materials for custom systems applications in both the public and private sector. She is also the author of books on Microsoft Outlook and word processing.

Carolyn McLellan is the Dean of the Division of Information Technology and Business at Tidewater Community College in Virginia Beach, Virginia. She has an M.A. degree in Secondary Education from Regent University and a B.S. degree in Business Education from Old Dominion University. She taught for Norfolk Public Schools for 17 1/2 years in Business Education and served as a faculty member at Tidewater Community College for eight years teaching networking, where she developed over 23 new courses and earned the Microsoft Certified Trainer and Microsoft Certified System Engineer industry certifications. In addition to teaching, Carolyn loves to play volleyball, boogie board at the beach, bicycle, crochet, cook, and read.

Susan N. Dozier is a faculty member of the IT/Business Division of Tidewater Community College. She holds degrees from Virginia Tech and Old Dominion University. She has over 20 years of teaching experience in the Information Technology field and has been awarded a Microsoft Office Specialist Master Certificate.

Kris Townsend is an Information Systems instructor at Spokane Falls Community College in Spokane, Washington, where he teaches computer applications, Internet programming, and digital forensics. Kris received his B.A. in Education and his B.A. in Business from Eastern Washington University with majors in Mathematics and Management Information Systems, respectively. He received his M.A. in Education from City University with an emphasis in Educational Technology. Kris has also worked as a public school teacher and as a systems analyst for a public school assessment department. In addition to teaching and authoring, Kris enjoys working with wood, snowboarding, and camping. He commutes to work by bike and enjoys long road rides in the Palouse country south of Spokane.

Visual Walk-Through of the *GO!* System

The *GO!* System is designed for ease of implementation on the instructor side and ease of understanding on the student. It has been completely developed based on professor and student feedback.

The *GO!* System is divided into three categories that reflect how you might organize your course— **Prepare**, **Teach**, and **Assess**.

Prepare

NEW

Transition Guide

New to *GO!*–We've made it quick and easy to plan the format and activities for your class.

Syllabus Template

Includes course calendar planner for 8-,12-, and 16-week formats.

GO!

Because the GO! System was designed and written by instructors like yourself, it includes the tools that allow you to Prepare, Teach, and Assess in your course. We have organized the GO! System into these three categories that match how you work through your course and thus, it's even easier for you to implement.

To help you get started, here is an outline of the first activities you may want to do in order to conduct your course.

There are several other tools not listed here that are available in the GO! System so please refer to your GO! Guide for a complete listing of all the tools.

Prepare
1. Prepare the course syllabus
2. Plan the course assignments
3. Organize the student resources

Teach
4. Conduct demonstrations and lectures

Assess
5. Assign and grade assignments, quizzes, tests, and assessments

PREPARE

1. Prepare the course syllabus
A syllabus template is provided on the IRCD in the **go07_syllabus_template** folder of the main directory. It includes a course calendar planner for 8-week, 12-week, and 16-week formats. Depending on your term (summer or regular semester) you can modify one of these according to your course plan, and then add information pertinent to your course and institution.

2. Plan course assignments
For each chapter, an Assignment Sheet listing every in-chapter and end-of-chapter project is located on the IRCD within the **go01_gotoffice2007intro_instructor_resources_by_chapter** folder. From there, navigate to the specific chapter folder. These sheets are Word tables, so you can delete rows for the projects that you choose not to assign or add rows for your own assignments—if any. There is a column to add the number of points you want to assign to each project depending on your grading scheme. At the top of the sheet, you can fill in the course information.

Transitioning to GO! Office 2007   Page 1 of 1

GO! with Microsoft Office 2007 Introductory
SAMPLE SYLLABUS (16 weeks)

I. COURSE INFORMATION

Course No.:	Semester:
Course Title:	Credits:
Course Hours:	

Instructor:	Office:
Office Hours:	
Email:	Phone:

II. TEXT AND MATERIALS
Before starting the course, you will need the following:

> GO! with Microsoft Office 2007 Introductory by Shelley Gaskin, Robert L. Ferrett, Alicia Vargas, Suzanne Marks ©2007, published by Pearson Prentice Hall. ISBN 0-13-167990-6

> Storage device for saving files (any of the following: multiple diskettes, CD-RW, flash drive, etc.)

III. WHAT YOU WILL LEARN IN THIS COURSE
This is a hands-on course where you will learn to use a computer to practice the most commonly used Microsoft programs including the Windows operating system, Internet Explorer for navigating the Internet, Outlook for managing your personal information and the four most popular programs within the Microsoft Office Suite (Word, Excel, PowerPoint and Access). You will also practice the basics of using a computer, mouse and keyboard. You will learn to be an intermediate level user of the Microsoft Office Suite.

Within the Microsoft Office Suite, you will use Word, Excel, PowerPoint, and Access. Microsoft Word is a word processing program with which you can create common business and personal documents. Microsoft Excel is a spreadsheet program that organizes and calculates accounting-type information. Microsoft PowerPoint is a presentation graphics program with which you can develop slides to accompany an oral presentation. Finally, Microsoft Access is a database program that organizes large amounts of information in a useful manner.

Assignment Sheet

One per chapter. Lists all possible assignments; add to and delete from this simple Word table according to your course plan.

GO! with Microsoft Office 2007 Introductory

Assignment Sheet for GO! with Microsoft Office 2007 Introductory
Chapter 5

Instructor Name: _____
Course Information: _____

Do This (✓ when done)	Then Hand in This — Check each Project for the elements listed on the Assignment Tag. Attach the Tag to your Project.	Submit Printed Formulas	By This Date	Possible Points	Your Points
Study the text and perform the steps for Activities 5.1 – 5.11	Project 5A Application Letter				
Study the text and perform the steps for Activities 5.12 – 5.23	Project 5B Company Overview				
End-of-Chapter Assessments					
Complete the Matching and Fill-in-the-Blank questions	As directed by your instructor				
Complete Project 5C	Project 5C Receipt Letter				
Complete Project 5D	Project 5D Marketing				
Complete Project 5E	Project 5E School Tour				
Complete Project 5F	Project 5F Scouting Trip				
Complete Project 5G	Project 5G Contract				
Complete Project 5H	Project 5H Invitation				
Complete Project 5I	Project 5I Fax Cover				
Complete Project 5J	Project 5J Business Running Case				
Complete Project 5K	Project 5K Services				
Complete Project 5L	Project 5L Survey Form				
Complete Project 5M	Project 5M Press Release				

Copyright © 2008 Pearson Prentice Hall   Page 1 of 1

File Guide to the GO! Supplements

Tabular listing of all supplements and their file names.

NEW

Assignment Planning Guide

Description of GO! assignments with recommendations based on class size, delivery mode, and student needs. Includes examples from fellow instructors.

GO! with Microsoft Office 2007 Introductory
Assignment Planning Guide

Planning the Course Assignments

For each chapter in GO!, an Assignment Sheet listing every in-chapter and end-of-chapter project is located on the IRCD. These sheets are Word tables, so you can delete rows for the projects that you will not assign, and then add rows for any of your own assignments that you may have developed. There is a column to add the number of points you want to assign to each project—depending on your grading scheme. At the top of the sheet, you can fill in your course information.

Additionally, for each chapter, student Assignment Tags are provided for every project (including Problem Solving projects)—also located on the IRCD. These are small scoring checklists on which you can check off errors made by the student, and with which the student can verify that all project elements are complete. For campus classes, the student can attach the tags to his or her paper submissions. For online classes, many GO! instructors have the student include these with the electronic submission.

Deciding What to Assign

Front Portion of the Chapter—Instructional Projects: The projects in the front portion of the chapter, which are listed on the first page of each chapter, are the instructional projects. Most instructors assign all of these projects, because this is where the student receives the instruction and engages in the active learning.

End-of-Chapter—Practice and Critical Thinking Projects: In the back portion of the chapter (the gray pages), you can assign on a prescriptive basis; that is, for students who were challenged by the instructional projects, you might assign one or more projects from the two *Skills Reviews*, which provide maximum prompting and a thorough review of the entire chapter. For students who have previous software knowledge and who completed the instructional projects easily, you might assign only the *Mastery Projects*.

You can also assign prescriptively by Objective, because each end-of-chapter project indicates the Objectives covered. So you might assign, on a student-by-student basis, only the projects that cover the Objectives with which the student seemed to have difficulty in the instructional projects.

The five Problem Solving projects and the You and GO! project are the authentic assessments that pull together the student's learning. Here the student is presented with a "messy real-life situation" and then uses his or her knowledge and skill to solve a problem, produce a product, give a presentation, or demonstrate a procedure. You might assign one or more of the Problem

GO! Assignment Planning Guide   Page 1 of 1

Student Data Files

Online Study Guide for Students

Interactive objective-style questions based on chapter content.

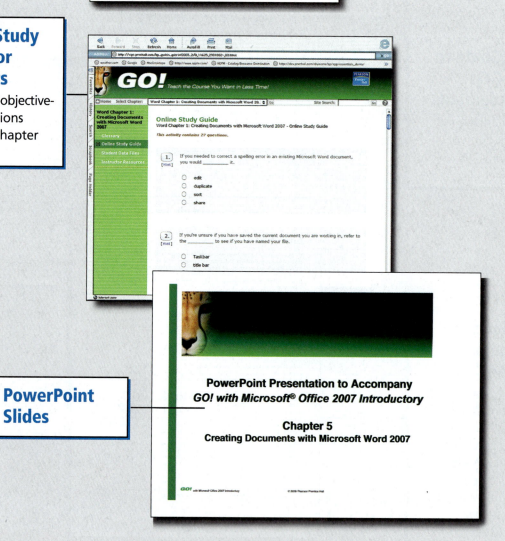

PowerPoint Slides

Teach

Student Textbook

Word 2007

5 chapterfive

Creating Documents with Microsoft Word 2007

OBJECTIVES
At the end of this chapter you will be able to:

OUTCOMES
Mastering these objectives will enable you to:

1. Create and Save a New Document
2. Edit Text
3. Select, Delete, and Format Text
4. Print a Document

PROJECT 5A
Create, Edit, Save, and Print a Document

5. Navigate the Word Window
6. Add a Graphic to a Document
7. Use the Spelling and Grammar Checker
8. Preview and Print Documents, Close a Document, and Close Word
9. Use the Microsoft Help System

PROJECT 5B
Navigate the Word Window and Check Your Work

Word   237

NEW

Music School Records

Music School Records was created to launch young musical artists with undiscovered talent in jazz, classical, and contemporary music. The creative management team searches internationally for talented young people, and has a reputation for mentoring and developing the skills of its artists. The company's music is tailored to an audience that is young, knowledgeable about music, and demands the highest quality recordings. Music School Records releases are available in CD format as well as digital downloads.

Getting Started with Microsoft Office Word 2007

A word processor is the most common program found on personal computers and one that almost everyone has a reason to use. When you learn word processing you are also learning skills and techniques that you need to work efficiently on a personal computer. You can use Microsoft Word to perform basic word processing tasks such as writing a memo, a report, or a letter. You can also use Word to complete complex word processing tasks, such as those that include sophisticated tables, embedded graphics, and links to other documents and the Internet. Word is a program that you can learn gradually, and then add more advanced skills one at a time.

Visual Summary

Shows students upfront what their projects will look like when they are done.

Project Summary

Stated clearly and quickly in one paragraph.

NEW

File Guide

Clearly shows students which files are needed for the project and the names they will use to save their documents.

Objective

The skills the student will learn are clearly stated at the beginning of each project and color coded to match projects listed on the chapter opener page.

Teachable Moment

Expository text is woven into the steps—at the moment students need to know it—not chunked together in a block of text that will go unread.

NEW

Screen Shots

Larger screen shots.

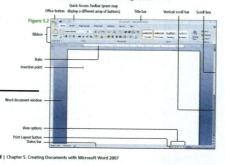

Steps

Color coded to the current project, easy to read, and not too many to confuse the student or too few to be meaningful.

GO! | Sequential Pagination

No more confusing letters and abbreviations.

---

5 Press Enter two more times.

In a business letter, insert two blank lines between the date and the inside address, which is the same as the address you would use on an envelope.

6 Type **Mr. William Hawken** and then press Enter.

The wavy red line under the proper name *Hawken* indicates that the word has been flagged as misspelled because it is a word not contained in the Word dictionary.

7 On two lines, type the following address, but do not press Enter at the end of the second line:

123 Eighth Street
Harrisville, MI 48740

Note — Typing the Address

Include a comma after the city name in an inside address. However, for mailing addresses on envelopes, eliminate the comma after the city name.

8 On the **Home tab**, in the **Styles group**, click the **Normal** button.

The Normal style is applied to the text in the rest of the document. Recall that the Normal style adds extra space between paragraphs; it also adds slightly more space between lines in a paragraph.

9 Press Enter. Type **Dear William:** and then press Enter.

This salutation is the line that greets the person receiving the letter.

10 Type **Subject: Your Application to Music School Records** and press Enter. Notice the light dots between words, which indicate spaces and display when formatting marks are displayed. Also, notice the extra space after each paragraph, and then compare your screen with Figure 5.6.

The subject line is optional, but you should include a subject line in most letters to identify the topic. Depending on your Word settings, a wavy green line may display in the subject line, indicating a potential grammar error.

GO! | Microsoft Procedural Syntax

All steps are written in Microsoft Procedural Syntax to put the student in the right place at the right time.

Note — Space Between Lines in Your Printed Document

The Cambria font, and many others, uses a slightly larger space between the lines than more traditional fonts like Times New Roman. As you progress in your study of Word, you will use many different fonts and also adjust the spacing between lines.

2 From the **Office** menu, click **Close**, saving any changes if prompted to do so. Leave Word open for the next project.

Another Way | **To Print a Document**

To Print a document:

• From the Office menu, click Print to display the Print dialog box (to be covered later), from which you can choose a variety of different options, such as printing multiple copies, printing on a different printer, and printing some but not all pages.

• Hold down Ctrl and then press P. This is an alternative to the Office menu command, and opens the Print dialog box.

• Hold down Alt, press F, and then press P. This opens the Print dialog box.

End You have completed Project 5A

End-of-Project Icon

All projects in the *GO! Series* have clearly identifiable end points, useful in self-paced or on-line environments.

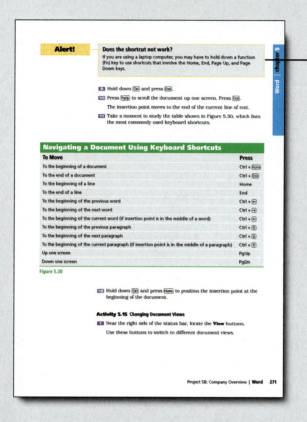

Alert box
Draws students' attention to make sure they aren't getting too far off course.

Another Way box
Shows students other ways of doing tasks.

More Knowledge box
Expands on a topic by going deeper into the material.

Note box
Points out important items to remember.

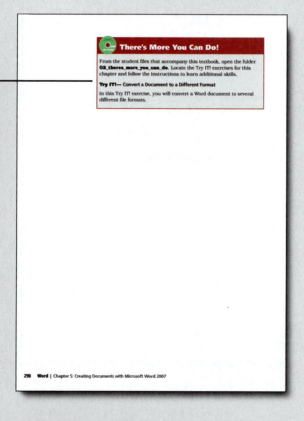

NEW

There's More You Can Do!
Try IT! exercises that teach students additional skills.

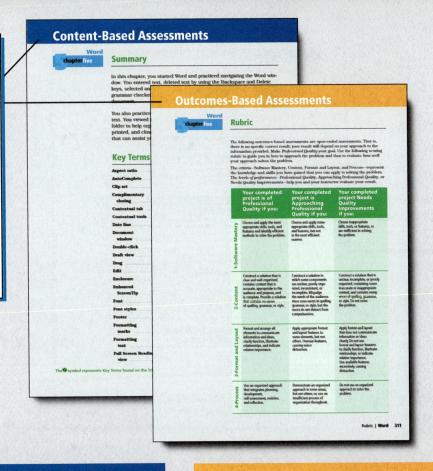

End-of-Chapter Material

Take your pick! Content-based or Outcomes-based projects to choose from. Below is a table outlining the various types of projects that fit into these two categories.

Content-Based Assessments
(Defined solutions with solution files provided for grading)

Project Letter	Name	Objectives Covered
N/A	Summary and Key Terms	
N/A	Multiple Choice	
N/A	Fill-in-the-blank	
C	Skills Review	Covers A Objectives
D	Skills Review	Covers B Objectives
E	Mastering Excel	Covers A Objectives
F	Mastering Excel	Covers B Objectives
G	Mastering Excel	Covers any combination of A and B Objectives
H	Mastering Excel	Covers any combination of A and B Objectives
I	Mastering Excel	Covers all A and B Objectives
J	Business Running Case	Covers all A and B Objectives

Outcomes-Based Assessments
(Open solutions that require a rubric for grading)

Project Letter	Name	Objectives Covered
N/A	Rubric	
K	Problem Solving	Covers as many Objectives from A and B as possible
L	Problem Solving	Covers as many Objectives from A and B as possible.
M	Problem Solving	Covers as many Objectives from A and B as possible.
N	Problem Solving	Covers as many Objectives from A and B as possible.
O	Problem Solving	Covers as many Objectives from A and B as possible.
P	You and GO!	Covers as many Objectives from A and B as possible
Q	GO! Help	Not tied to specific objectives
R	* Group Business Running Case	Covers A and B Objectives

* This project is provided only with the *GO! with Microsoft Office 2007 Introductory* book.

Objectives List

Most projects in the end-of-chapter section begin with a list of the objectives covered.

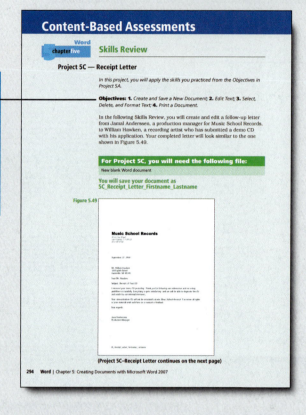

Content-Based Assessments

Word
chapter five   **Skills Review**

Project 5C — Receipt Letter

In this project, you will apply the skills you practiced from the Objectives in Project 5A.

Objectives: 1. Create and Save a New Document; **2.** Edit Text; **3.** Select, Delete, and Format Text; **4.** Print a Document.

In the following Skills Review, you will create and edit a follow-up letter from Jamal Anderssen, a production manager for Music School Records, to William Hawken, a recording artist who has submitted a demo CD with his application. Your completed letter will look similar to the one shown in Figure 5.49.

For Project 5C, you will need the following file:
New blank Word document

You will save your document as
5C_Receipt_Letter_Firstname_Lastname

Figure 5.49

(Project 5C–Receipt Letter continues on the next page)

294   **Word** | Chapter 5: Creating Documents with Microsoft Word 2007

End of Each Project Clearly Marked

Clearly identified end points help separate the end-of-chapter projects.

Content-Based Assessments

Word
chapter five   **Skills Review**

(Project 5C–Receipt Letter continued)

14. Save the changes you have made to your document. Press Ctrl + A to select the entire document. On the **Home tab**, in the **Font group**, click the **Font button arrow**. Scroll as necessary, and watch Live Preview change the document font as you point to different font names. Click to choose **Tahoma**. Recall that you can type T in the Font box to move quickly to the fonts beginning with that letter. Click anywhere in the document to cancel the selection.

15. Select the entire first line of text—*Music School Records*. On the Mini toolbar, click the **Font button arrow**, and then click **Arial Black**. With the Mini toolbar still displayed, click the **Font Size button arrow**, and then click **20**. With the Mini toolbar still displayed, click the **Bold** button.

16. Select the second, third, and fourth lines of text, beginning with *2620 Vine Street* and ending with the telephone number. On the Mini toolbar, click the **Font button arrow**, and then click **Arial**. With the Mini toolbar still displayed, click the **Font Size button arrow**, and then click **10**. With the Mini toolbar still displayed, click the **Italic** button.

17. In the paragraph beginning *Your demonstration*, select the text *Music School Records*. On the Mini toolbar, click the **Italic** button, and then click anywhere to deselect the text.

18. Click the **Insert tab**. In the **Header & Footer group**, click the **Footer** button,

and then click **Edit Footer**. On the **Design tab**, in the **Insert group**, click the **Quick Parts** button, and then click **Field**. In the **Field** dialog box, under **Field names**, scroll down and click to choose **FileName**, and then click **OK**. Double-click anywhere in the document to leave the footer area.

19. Click the **Page Layout tab**. In the **Page Setup group**, click the **Margins** button to display the Margins gallery. At the bottom of the **Margins gallery**, click **Custom Margins** to display the **Page Setup** dialog box. Near the top of the **Page Setup** dialog box, click the **Layout tab**. Under **Page**, click the **Vertical alignment arrow**, click **Center**, and then click **OK**.

20. From the **Office** menu, point to the **Print arrow**, and then click **Print Preview** to make a final check of your letter. Follow your instructor's directions for submitting this file. Check your *Chapter Assignment Sheet* or *Course Syllabus* or consult your instructor to determine if you are to submit your assignments on paper or electronically. To submit electronically, go to Step 22, and then follow the instructions provided by your instructor.

21. On the **Print Preview tab**, in the **Print group**, click the **Print** button. Collect your printout from the printer and submit it as directed.

22. From the **Office** menu, click **Exit Word**, saving any changes if prompted to do so.

End You have completed Project 5C

296   **Word** | Chapter 5: Creating Documents with Microsoft Word 2007

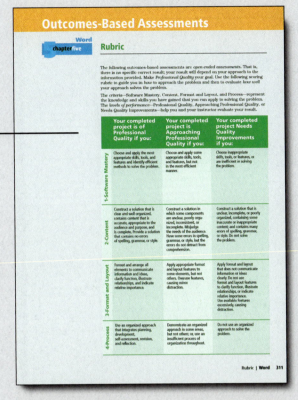

NEW

Rubric

A matrix that states the criteria and standards for grading student work. Used to grade open-ended assessments.

GO! with Help

Students practice using the Help feature of the Office application.

NEW

You and GO!

A project in which students use information from their own lives and apply the skills from the chapter to a personal task.

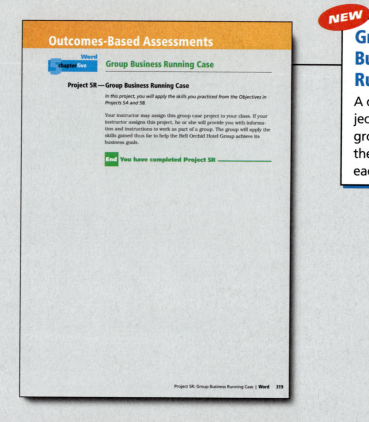

Outcomes-Based Assessments

Word
chapter five — **Group Business Running Case**

Project 5R — Group Business Running Case

In this project, you will apply the skills you practiced from the Objectives in Projects 5A and 5B.

Your instructor may assign this group case project to your class. If your instructor assigns this project, he or she will provide you with information and instructions to work as part of a group. The group will apply the skills gained thus far to help the Bell Orchid Hotel Group achieve its business goals.

End **You have completed Project 5R**

Project 5R: Group Business Running Case | **Word** **319**

NEW

Group Business Running Case

A continuing project developed for groups that spans the chapters within each application.

Student Resource CD-ROM

See readme file on this CD-ROM for usage instructions.

PEARSON
Prentice Hall

Technical Support:
http://247.prenhall.com

disc
COMPACT
DIGITAL DATA

©2008 Pearson Prentice Hall
Upper Saddle River, NJ 07458
0-13-221718-X

GO!
with Microsoft®

Office 2007
Introductory

www.prenhall.com/go

Student CD includes:

- Student Data Files
- There's More You Can Do!
- Business Running Case
- You and *GO!*

Companion Website

An interactive Web site to further student leaning.

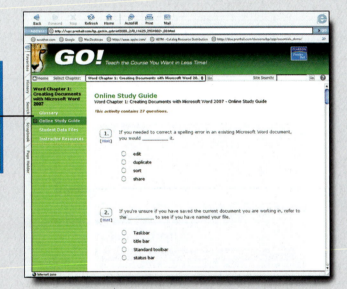

Online Study Guide

Interactive objective-style questions to help students study.

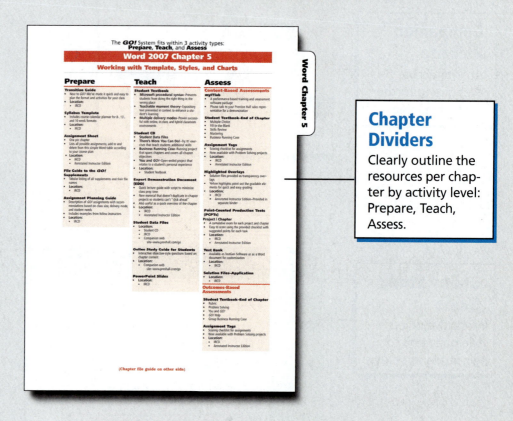

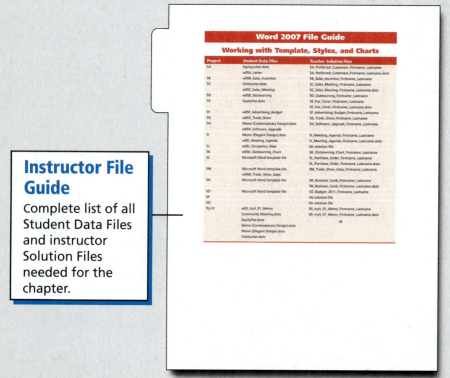

Annotated Instructor Edition

The Annotated Instructor Edition contains a full version of the student textbook that includes tips, supplement references, and pointers on teaching with the *GO!* instructional system.

Chapter Dividers

Clearly outline the resources per chapter by activity level: Prepare, Teach, Assess.

Instructor File Guide

Complete list of all Student Data Files and instructor Solution Files needed for the chapter.

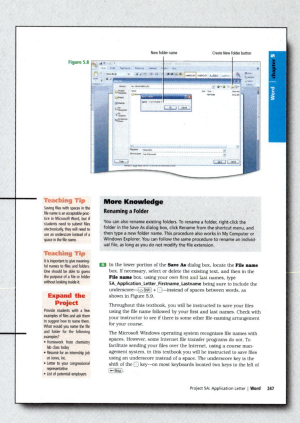

Helpful Hints, Teaching Tips, Expand the Project

References correspond to what is being taught in the student textbook.

NEW

Full-Size Textbook Pages

An instructor copy of the textbook with traditional Instructor Manual content incorporated.

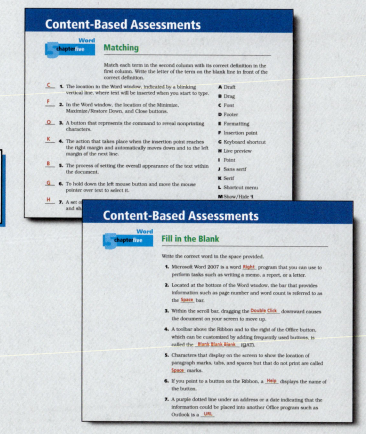

End-of-Chapter Concepts Assessments contain the answers for quick reference.

Rubric

A matrix to guide the student on how they will be assessed is reprinted in the Annotated Instructor Edition with suggested weights for each of the criteria and levels of performance. Instructors can modify the weights to suit their needs.

Assignment Tags

Scoring checklist for assignments. Now also available for Problem-Solving projects.

NEW

GO! with Microsoft® Office 2007

Assignment Tags for GO! with Office 2007
Word Chapter 5

Name:		Project:	5A
Professor:		Course:	

Task	Points	Your Score
Center text vertically on page	2	
Delete the word "really"	1	
Delete the words "try to"	1	
Replace "last" with "first"	1	
Insert the word "potential"	1	
Replace "John W. Diamond" with "Lucy Burrows"	2	
Change entire document to the Cambria font	2	
Change the first line of text to Arial Black 20 pt. font	2	
Bold the first line of text	2	
Change the 2nd through 4th lines to Arial 10 pt.	2	
Italicize the 2nd through 4th lines of text	2	
Correct/Add footer as instructed	2	
Circled information is incorrect or formatted incorrectly		
Total Points	**20**	**0**

Name:		Project:	5B
Professor:		Course:	

Task	Points	Your Score
Insert the file w05B_Music_School_Records	4	
Insert the Music Logo	4	
Remove duplicate "and"	2	
Change spelling and grammar errors (4)	8	
Correct/Add footer as instructed	2	
Circled information is incorrect or formatted incorrectly		
Total Points	**20**	**0**

Name:		Project:	5C
Professor:		Course:	

Task	Points	Your Score
Add four line letterhead	2	
Insert today's date	1	
Add address block, subject line, and greeting	2	
Add two-paragraph body of letter	2	
Add closing, name, and title	2	
In subject line, capitalize "receipt"	1	
Change "standards" to "guidelines"	1	
Insert "quite"	1	
Insert "all"	1	
Change the first line of text to Arial Black 20 pt. font	2	
Bold the first line of text	1	
Change the 2nd through 4th lines to Arial 10 pt.	1	
Italicize the 2nd through 4th lines of text	1	
Correct/add footer as instructed	2	
Circled information is incorrect or formatted incorrectly		
Total Points	**20**	**0**

Name:		Project:	5D
Professor:		Course:	

Task	Points	Your Score
Insert the file w05D_Marketing	4	
Bold the first two title lines	2	
Correct spelling of "Marketting"	2	
Correct spelling of "geners"	2	
Correct all misspellings of "allready"	2	
Correct grammar error "are" to "is"	2	
Insert the Piano image	4	
Correct/add footer as instructed	2	
Circled information is incorrect or formatted incorrectly		
Total Points	**20**	**0**

Highlighted Overlays

Solution files provided as transparency overlays. Yellow highlights point out the gradable elements for quick and easy grading.

Music School Records

2620 Vine Street
Los Angeles, CA 90028
323-555-0028

[20 point Arial Black, bold and underline]

[10 point Arial, italic]

September 12, 2009

Mr. William Hawken
123 Eighth Street
Harrisville, MI 48740

[Text vertically centered on page]

[Body of document changed to Cambria font, 11 point]

Dear William:

Subject: Your Application to Music School Records

Thank you for submitting your application to Music School Records. Our talent scout for Northern Michigan, Catherine McDonald, is very enthusiastic about your music, and the demo CD you submitted certainly confirms her opinion. [Word "really" deleted]

We discuss our applications from **potential** clients during the **first** week of each month. We will have a decision for you by the second week of October.

[Words "try to" deleted]

Yours Truly,

Lucy Burroughs

Point-Counted Production Tests (PCPTs)

A cumulative exam for each **project**, **chapter**, and **application**. Easy to score using the provided checklist with suggested points for each task.

GO! with Microsoft® Office 2007 Introductory

***Point-Counted Production Test—Project
for GO! with Microsoft® Office 2007 Introductory
Project 5A***

Instructor Name: _____
Course Information: _____

1. Start Word 2007 to begin a new blank document. Save your document as 5A_Cover_Letter_Firstname_Lastname Remember to save your file frequently as you work.

2. If necessary, display the formatting marks. With the insertion point blinking in the upper left corner of the document to the left of the default first paragraph mark, type the current date (you can use AutoComplete).

3. Press Enter three times and type the inside address:

   Music School Records
   2620 Vine Street
   Los Angeles, CA 90028

4. Press Enter three times, and type Dear Ms. Burroughs:

   Press Enter twice, and type Subject: Application to Music School Records

   Press Enter twice, and type the following text (skipping one line between paragraphs):

   I read about Music School Records in Con Brio magazine and I would like to inquire about the possibility of being represented by your company.

   I am very interested in a career in jazz and am planning to relocate to the Los Angeles area in the very near future. I would be interested in learning more about the company and about available opportunities.

   I was a member of my high school jazz band for three years. In addition, I have been playing in the local coffee shop for the last two years. My demo CD, which is enclosed, contains three of my most requested songs.

   I would appreciate the opportunity to speak with you. Thank you for your time and consideration. I look forward to speaking with you about this exciting opportunity.

5. Press Enter three times, and type the closing Sincerely, Press enter four times, and type your name.

6. Insert a footer that contains the file name.

7. Delete the first instance of the word *very* in the second body paragraph, and insert the word modern in front of *jazz*.

Copyright © 2008 Pearson Prentice Hall   Page 1 of 1

Test Bank

Available as TestGen Software or as a Word document for customization.

Chapter 5: Creating Documents with Microsoft Word 2007

Multiple Choice:

1. With word processing programs, how are documents stored?

   A. On a network

   B. On the computer

   C. Electronically

   D. On the floppy disk

Answer: C   **Reference:** Objective 1: Create and Save a New Document   **Difficulty:** Moderate

2. Because you will see the document as it will print, _____ view is the ideal view to use when learning Microsoft Word 2007.

   A. Reading

   B. Normal

   C. Print Layout

   D. Outline

Answer: C   **Reference:** Objective 1: Create and Save a New Document   **Difficulty:** Moderate

3. The blinking vertical line where text or graphics will be inserted is called the:

   A. cursor.

   B. insertion point.

   C. blinking line.

   D. I-beam.

Answer: B   **Reference:** Objective 1: Create and Save a New Document   **Difficulty:** Easy

**Solution Files–
Application
and PDF
format**

 Music School Records

Music School Records discovers, launches, and develops the careers of young artists in classical, jazz, and contemporary music. Our philosophy is to not only shape, distribute, and sell a music product, but to help artists create a career that can last a lifetime. Too often in the music industry, artists are forced to fit their music to a trend that is short-lived. Music School Records does not just follow trends, we take a long-term view of the music industry and help our artists develop a style and repertoire that is fluid and flexible and that will appeal to audiences for years and even decades.

The music industry is constantly changing, but over the last decade, the changes have been enormous. New forms of entertainment such as DVDs, video games, and the Internet mean there is more competition for the leisure dollar in the market. New technologies give consumers more options for buying and listening to music, and they are demanding high quality recordings. Young consumers are comfortable with technology and want the music they love when and where they want it, no matter where they are or what they are doing.

Music School Records embraces new technologies and the sophisticated market of young music lovers. We believe that providing high quality recordings of truly talented artists make for more discerning listeners who will cherish the gift of music for the rest of their lives. The expertise of Music School Records includes:

- Insight into our target market and the ability to reach the desired audience
- The ability to access all current sources of music income
- A management team with years of experience in music commerce
- Innovative business strategies and artist development plans
- Investment in technology infrastructure for high quality recordings and business services

pagexxxix_top.docx

chapterone

Creating Database Tables

OBJECTIVES

At the end of this chapter you will be able to:

1. Start Access
2. Create a Database and Enter Data Using a Template
3. Modify a Template Table
4. Find, Modify, and Print Records
5. Use the Access Help System and Exit Access

6. Create a New Database and Tables
7. Modify the Table Design
8. Format a Table for Printing

OUTCOMES

Mastering these objectives will enable you to:

PROJECT 1A

Create a Database and Table Using a Template, Modify Records in a Table, and Use the Access Help System

PROJECT 1B

Create, Edit, and Print Access Database Tables

Eastern Cape Inn

Cape Charles is a quiet beach town located in the Eastern Shore area of Virginia, north of Virginia Beach. The Eastern Cape Inn has 20 rooms and is often booked to capacity with returning regular guests who appreciate its comfort, beautiful beachfront location, and the warmth and hospitality of its owners. The dining room, where a full homemade breakfast is served each morning, the expansive porch, and some guest rooms overlook the Chesapeake Bay. Cape Charles is located approximately 200 miles from Washington, DC, Philadelphia, and Baltimore and makes an excellent base for day trips to Williamsburg, Jamestown, and Assateague Island. Several local restaurants serve outstanding fresh seafood, and the tourist area of Virginia Beach is only a short drive away.

Getting Started with Microsoft Office Access 2007

Individuals, small businesses, and large corporations need ways to organize and to keep track of information. For example, an individual might need a way to organize information about a stamp collection, including the date of issue, purchase price, and current value of each stamp. Both small and large corporations need methods to track inventories, to maintain accurate customer lists, and to generate customized mailings. Microsoft Access is a program that can help individuals and businesses keep track of information.

Project 1A Guest Rooms

In Activities 1.1 through 1.13, you will create a database to store information about guests who visit Eastern Cape Inn. You will add new guest information to the database and print a table, a form, and a report. Your printouts will look similar to Figure 1.1.

For Project 1A, you will need the following file:

New blank Access database

You will save your database as
1A_Guests_Firstname_Lastname

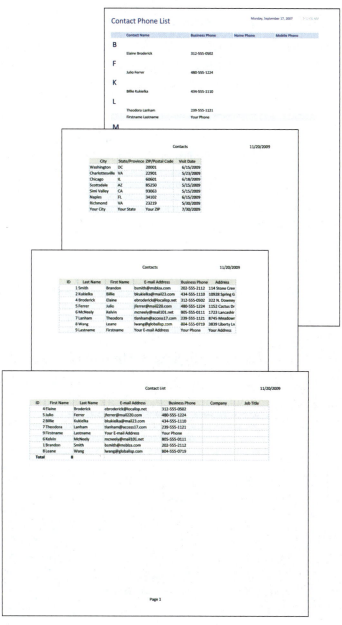

Figure 1.1
Project 1A—Guests

Objective 1
Start Access

Microsoft Office Access 2007 is a database program. A ***database*** is a collection of ***data***—facts about people, events, things, or ideas—related to a particular topic or purpose. Data that has been organized in a useful manner is referred to as ***information***. An example of a database is an address book. Data in the address book might include names, addresses, phone numbers, and birthdays. You would not keep a list of DVDs in your address book because the data is not related to addresses; you would create another database. Databases, such as the ones you will work with in Access, include not only the data but also tools for organizing the data in a way that is useful to you.

Activity 1.1 Starting Access

When you start Access 2007, the Getting Started with Microsoft Office Access page displays. From this page, you can create a new database, open an existing database, or view featured content from Microsoft Office Online.

Alert!

Do you see a Welcome to Microsoft Office 2007 window?

If this is the first time you have opened a program in Microsoft Office 2007, you will see a Welcome to Microsoft Office 2007 window with Privacy Options selected. Click to clear the check box to the left of any option you do not desire, and then click OK to close the window.

1 On the left side of the Windows taskbar, point to and then click the **Start** button [start].

2 From the displayed **Start** menu, locate the Access program, and then click **Microsoft Office Access 2007**.

Organizations and individuals store computer programs in a variety of ways. The Access program might be located under All Programs or Microsoft Office or on the main Start menu.

Note — Comparing Your Screen with the Figures in This Textbook

Your screen will match the figures shown in this textbook if you set your screen resolution to 1024 × 768. At other resolutions, your screen will closely resemble, but not match, the figures shown. To view your screen's resolution, on the Windows desktop, right-click in an empty area, click Properties, and then click the Settings tab.

3 Take a moment to study the elements of the Getting Started with Microsoft Office Access screen as shown in Figure 1.2 and described in the table in Figure 1.3.

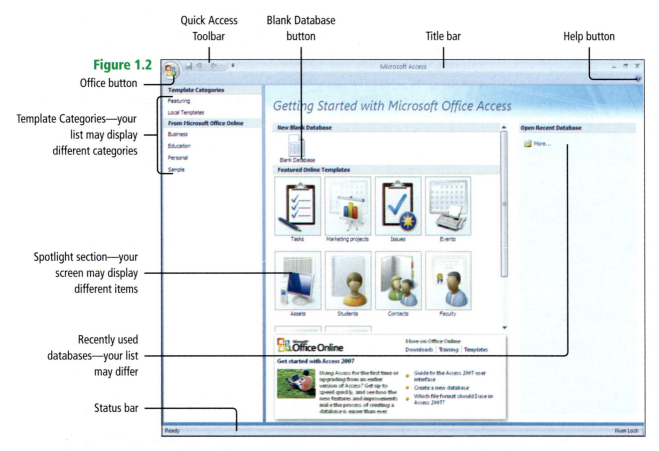

Figure 1.2

Quick Access Toolbar

Blank Database button

Title bar

Help button

Office button

Template Categories—your list may display different categories

Spotlight section—your screen may display different items

Recently used databases—your list may differ

Status bar

Getting Started with Microsoft Office Access Screen Elements

Screen Element	Description
Blank Database button	Enables you to create a new database.
Help button	Displays the Access Help window.
Office button	Displays a list of commands related to tasks you can do *with* a database, such as opening, saving, managing, e-mailing, or printing.
Quick Access Toolbar	Displays buttons used to perform frequently used commands with a single click, including Save, Print, and Undo. For commands that *you* use frequently, you can add additional buttons to the Quick Access Toolbar.
Recently used databases	Enables you to browse for a database on your computer or on the network, or open a database that has been used recently.
Spotlight area	The middle area of the screen that displays when Featuring is selected under Template Categories. This area changes based on your selection under Template Categories.
Status bar	A horizontal bar at the bottom of the window that displays indicators and buttons related to Access.
Template Categories	A list of templates that can be used to create databases.
Title bar	Displays the name of the program. The Minimize, Maximize/Restore Down, and Close buttons are grouped on the right side of the title bar.

Figure 1.3

Objective 2
Create a Database and Enter Data Using a Template

You create a new database using a **template**—a ready-to-use database that has been created by Microsoft to help you quickly create your own database. A template gives you a starting point for your database. You can use the template database as it is or customize it to suit your needs. You can add or modify the text and design, add a company logo or images, or delete text and other content that do not apply. You can use the templates that are included with the Access program or download templates for Microsoft Office Online.

Activity 1.2 Creating a Database Using a Template

1 In the **Template Categories** pane, under **Template Categories**, click **Local Templates**.

The Spotlight area displays templates that do not have to be downloaded from Microsoft.

2 In the **Spotlight** area, click the **Contacts** database, and then compare your screen with Figure 1.4.

Near the right side of the window, Access suggests a file name and a storage location for your database.

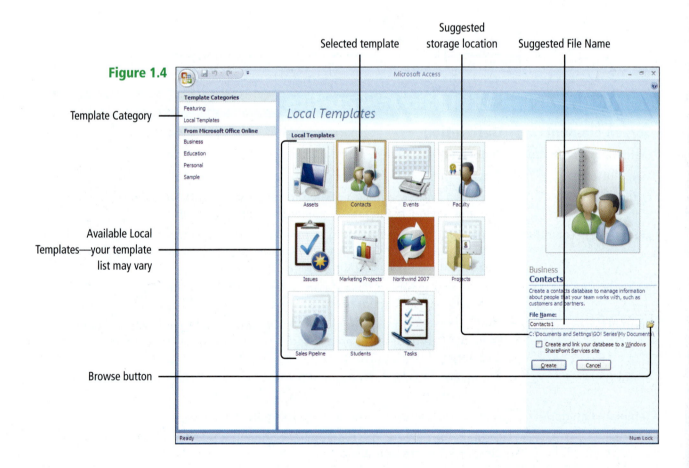

Figure 1.4

3 To the right of the **File Name** box, click the **Browse** button 📁. On the left side of the **File New Database** dialog box, click **My Computer** to view a list of the drives available to you, as shown in Figure 1.5.

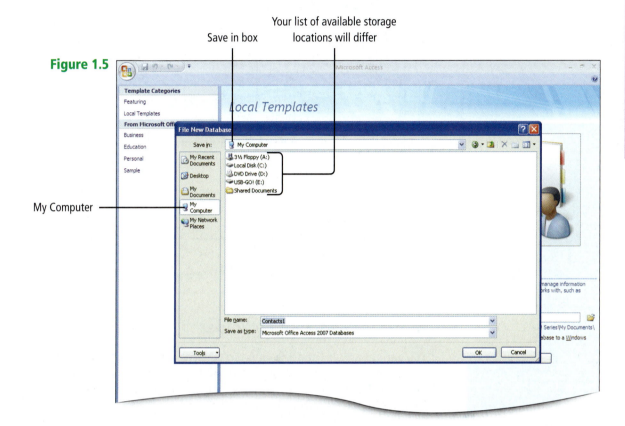

Save in box

Your list of available storage locations will differ

Figure 1.5

My Computer

4 Double-click the drive on which you will be saving your folders and projects for this chapter—for example, a USB flash drive that you have connected, a shared drive on a network, or the drive designated by your instructor or lab coordinator. If necessary, navigate to a folder that has been designated by your instructor.

5 In the **File New Database** dialog box, click the **Create New Folder** button 📁. In the displayed **New Folder** dialog box, in the **Name** box, type **Access Chapter 1** as shown in Figure 1.6, and then click **OK**.

The new folder name displays in the Save in box, indicating that the folder is open and ready to save your database file.

Figure 1.6

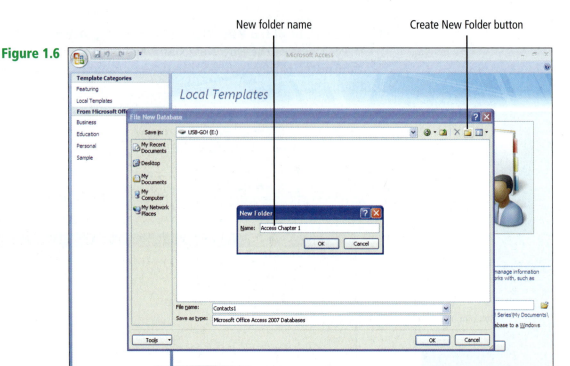

Note — Renaming a Folder

You can rename existing folders. To rename a folder, in the File New Database dialog box, right-click the folder. From the displayed shortcut menu, click Rename, type a new folder name, and then press [Enter]. This procedure also works in My Computer or Windows Explorer.

6 In the lower portion of the **File New Database** dialog box, locate the **File name** box. If necessary, select or delete the existing text. Then, in the **File name** box, using your own first and last name, type **1A_Guests_Firstname_Lastname** as shown in Figure 1.7.

Throughout this textbook, you will be instructed to save your files by using the file name followed by your first and last name. Check with your instructor to see whether there is some other file-naming arrangement for your course.

The Microsoft Windows operating system recognizes file names with spaces. However, some Internet file transfer programs do not. To facilitate sending your files over the Internet by using a course management system, in this textbook you will be instructed to save files by using an underscore instead of a space. The underscore is created by holding down the [⇧ Shift] key and then pressing [-], which is usually located two keys to the left of the [←Bksp] key.

Underscore characters in file name

Figure 1.7

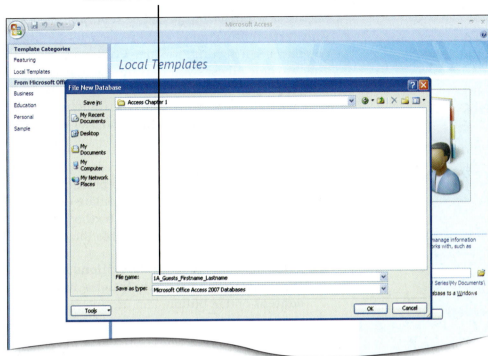

7 In the lower portion of the **File New Database** dialog box, click **OK**, or press Enter.

8 In the pane at the right side of the window, click the **Create** button, and then compare your screen with Figure 1.8.

Your database is saved with the new file name in the *Access Chapter 1* folder on the storage device that you selected. The new database file name also displays in the title bar. The database is automatically opened and ready for you to enter data. If you download a template from Microsoft Office Online, you click the Download button instead of the Create button.

The message bar is reserved for messages about files you are trying to open and displays a Security Alert Warning.

Database name in title bar

Figure 1.8

Message bar with security warning

Contact List form is open and ready for data entry

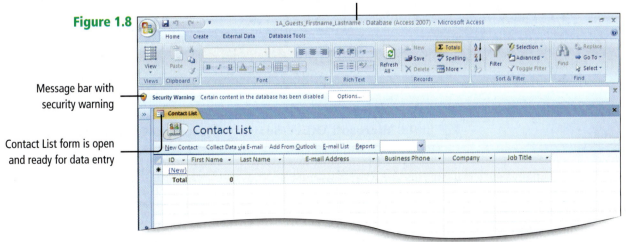

Activity 1.3 Enabling Database Content

Microsoft Windows has sensitive security precautions. Depending on your version of Windows and the security settings on your computer, you may see a security warning every time you open an Access database. This warning advises you that the file may not be safe if it contains code that was intended to harm your computer, and that the file does not have a ***digital signature***—an electronic signature that can be used to authenticate the identity of the sender of a message or the signer of a document.

Because database objects are interconnected and may contain macros, this security warning displays as a precaution. ***Macros*** are programs within Access that are used to automate commands and manage databases. The databases used in this textbook are safe to open. Each time you see this security warning, enable the content.

1 In the message bar, click the **Options** button. In the displayed **Microsoft Office Security Options** dialog box, click the **Enable this content** option button, and then compare your screen with Figure 1.9.

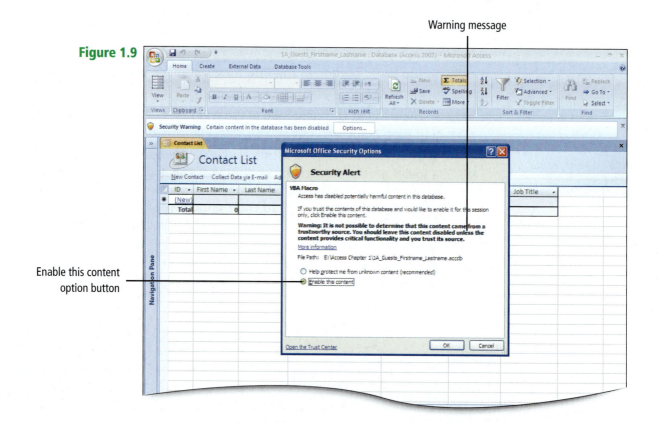

Warning message

Figure 1.9

Enable this content option button

2 In the **Microsoft Office Security Options** dialog box, click **OK**. After a moment, the message bar closes.

Activity 1.4 Navigating the Database Window

When you open a database, the view may differ depending on how you or someone else saved that database. Being able to efficiently navigate the Database window will increase your productivity when creating or modifying the database.

1 Take a moment to study the elements of the **Database** window shown in Figure 1.10 and described in the table in Figure 1.11.

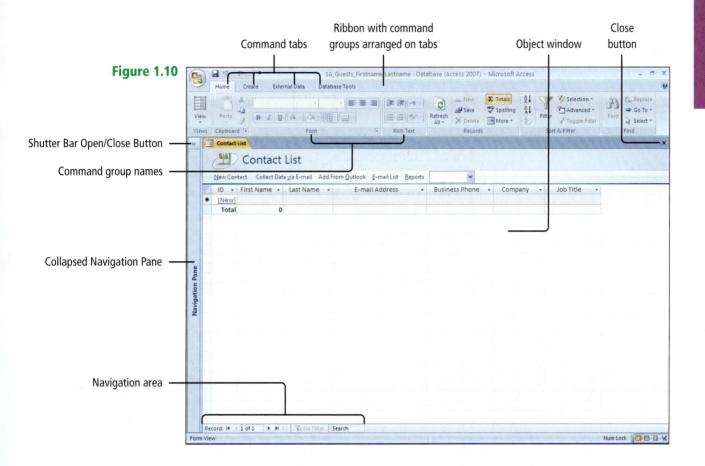

Figure 1.10

Microsoft Access Database Window Elements	
Screen Element	**Description**
Close button	Closes the current object—indicated by an orange tab—but does not close the database or exit Access.
Command group names	Contains groups of related command buttons associated with the selected command tab.
Command tab	Each tab displays the commands most relevant for a particular task. The most commonly used commands are grouped in the Home tab.
Navigation area	Displays buttons that enable you to move to different records in the displayed object.
Navigation Pane	Displays the database objects; from here, you open the database objects to display in the object window at the right.

(Continued)

(Continued)

Object window	Displays the open object.
Ribbon with command groups arranged on tabs	The area just under the title bar, in which commands are grouped on tabs for performing related database tasks.
Shutter Bar Open/Close button	Expands and collapses the Navigation Pane. If the Navigation Pane is collapsed, arrows point to the right (Open). If the Navigation Pane is expanded, arrows point to the left (Close).

Figure 1.11

2 On the **Navigation Pane**, click the **Shutter Bar Open/Close** button
 ⟩⟩ to expand the Navigation Pane, and then compare your screen with Figure 1.12.

You can open database **objects**—the components in the database, such as tables, forms, and reports—from the Navigation Pane. The Navigation Pane divides the database objects into categories and then divides the objects in each category into groups.

The default group name—Contacts Navigation—displays as the menu title at the top of the Navigation Pane. This is a custom group name created by the designers of the template. Because this database was created by using a template and a custom group name, each object is displayed as a **shortcut**—an icon with an arrow in it.

Database objects
represented as shortcuts

Figure 1.12

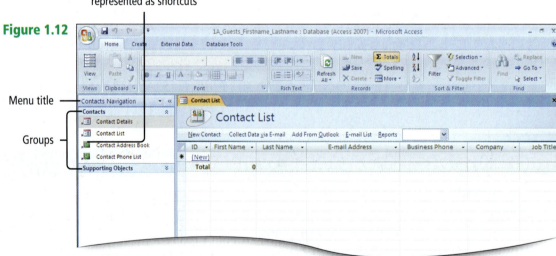

Menu title

Groups

3 Click the **Shutter Bar Open/Close** button ⟨⟨ to collapse the **Navigation Pane**, which becomes a small vertical strip at the left side of the window, increasing the size of the object window.

4 Click the **Shutter Bar Open/Close** button ⟩⟩ to expand the **Navigation Pane**. Alternatively, click anywhere on the collapsed Navigation Pane to expand it.

5 On the **Navigation Pane**, click **Contacts Navigation**, which is the menu title, to display a list as shown in Figure 1.13.

The Categories section displays the predefined and custom categories for the open database. The check mark indicates the current category. The Groups section displays predefined or custom groups that reside in the selected category. The groups change as you select different categories. When you select different categories or groups, the menu title changes also.

Figure 1.13

Categories

Groups within the
selected category

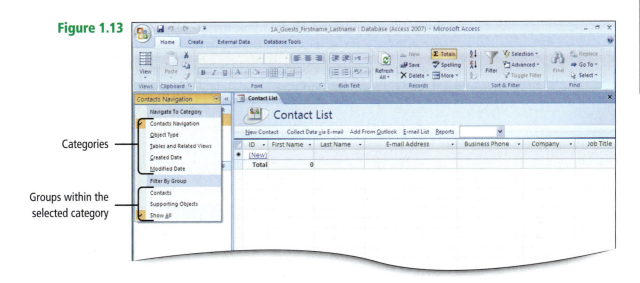

6 From the displayed list, click **Object Type**.

The menu title changes to *All Access Objects*, which indicates that all of the objects in the database are displayed in the Navigation Pane. The icons representing the objects are not shortcuts because this is a predefined group.

7 On the **Navigation Pane**, click **All Access Objects**, which is the menu title. Notice that the **Groups** section now displays different options. Take a moment to examine the brief explanation of each database object in the table in Figure 1.14.

Microsoft Access Database Objects

Object	Description
Tables	Contain the data.
Queries	Retrieve data from one or more tables to answer a question.
Forms	Display data from the table in a visually attractive format that can be used to enter data.
Reports	Display data from one or more tables in a formatted manner for printing and publication.

Figure 1.14

Recall that a database contains objects. By selecting an object in the Groups section, you can limit the objects displayed in the Navigation Pane. The other objects are not deleted from the database; they are just not displayed in the Navigation Pane.

8 From the displayed list, click **Created Date** to group all Access objects by the date created.

You may forget the name of an object but remember the approximate date you created it. This grouping method enables you to find the object based on the created date.

9 On the **Navigation Pane**, click the menu title—**All Dates**—and then compare your screen with Figure 1.15.

If you have many objects in a database, you can view objects created today, yesterday, on a specific day of the week, or on other dates.

Figure 1.15

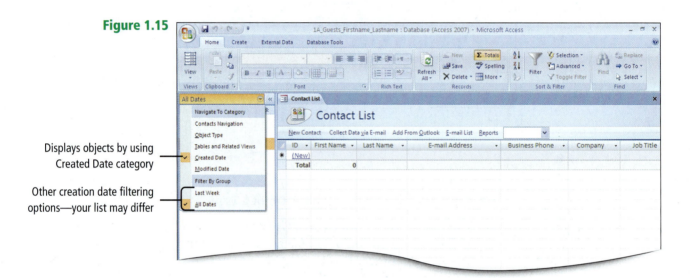

Displays objects by using Created Date category

Other creation date filtering options—your list may differ

10 From the displayed list, click **Tables and Related Views**. Notice that all of the objects are grouped under **Contacts**, which is the name of the table used in this database.

Data is stored in the table. Forms, queries, and reports are objects that view the data in the table. When these objects are opened, the table is read, and the objects are updated to display the current data. If you have more than one table in a database, grouping by Tables and Related Views will help you determine the table that was used to create other objects.

11 Using the technique you just practiced, categorize the objects by **Object Type**. Notice that the opened **Contact List** is displayed under **Forms**.

The Navigation Pane again displays all Access objects grouped by object type. Whenever you open an existing database, you should display all Access objects—the last person who used the database may have changed how the objects are arranged on the Navigation Pane, and Access saves the Navigation Pane with the view that is in effect when the database is closed.

Activity 1.5 Entering Data into the Database

Tables are the foundation on which an Access database is built because all of the data in an Access database is stored in one or more tables. Each table contains data about only one subject. The designers of the Contacts database template created the Contacts table to hold all the data. Using the Contacts table, the designers created the other objects you see in the Navigation Pane, such as the Contact List form, which is another method by which you can view data from—or enter data into—the Contacts table. In this activity, you will use the Contact List form to enter data into the Contacts table.

1 **Collapse** ⟪ the **Navigation Pane**, and then compare your screen with Figure 1.16.

The Contact List form was designed to look similar to a table, where data is displayed in rows and columns. In Form view, you can edit fields, add and delete data, and search for data. The name of the form is displayed in a tab on the tab row.

In Access, each column in a table contains a category of data called a ***field***. Field names display at the top of each column of a table. Each row contains a ***record***—all of the data pertaining to one person, place, thing, event, or idea. In this form, each record consists of the data related to one guest.

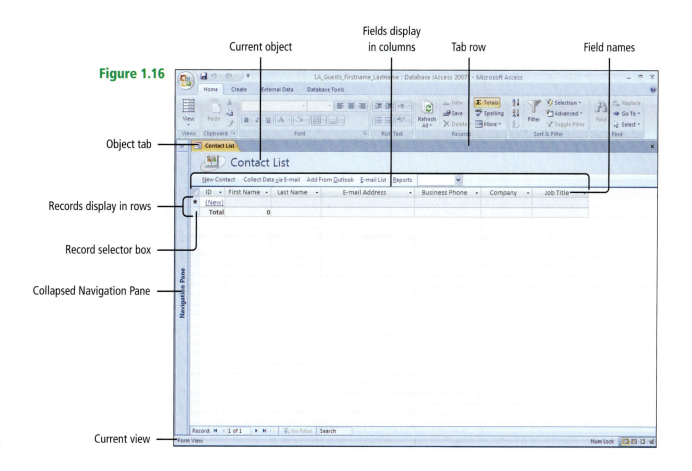

Figure 1.16

2 Click in the box under **First Name** to place the *insertion point*—a blinking vertical line that indicates where text will be typed—in the *field box*—the intersection of a column and row.

The First Name field is the current field as indicated by the orange background. You are ready to enter the data for the first record.

3 In the **First Name** field box, type **Brandon** and then press Tab or Enter to move to the next field. Notice that a small pencil icon 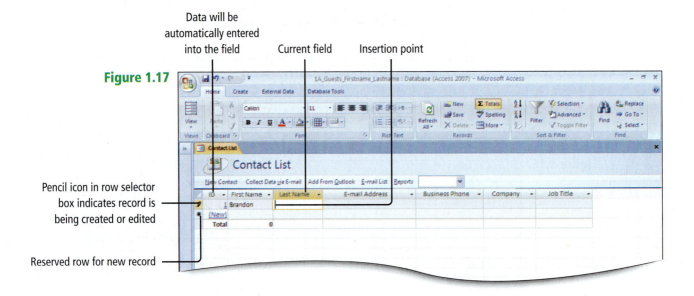 displays in the record selector box to the left of *1* in the ID field, indicating that the record is being created or edited. Compare your screen with Figure 1.17.

The first field—ID—contains the number *1*. The designers of this form configured the ID field to automatically fill with sequential numbers. The record is highlighted in blue, and the *current field*— the field in which you are ready to enter data—is white with a blinking insertion point.

Data will be automatically entered into the field

Current field

Insertion point

Figure 1.17

Pencil icon in row selector box indicates record is being created or edited

Reserved row for new record

4 In the **Last Name** field box, type **Smith** and then press Tab to move to the **E-mail Address** field. In the **E-mail Address** field box, type **bsmith@msblza.com** and then press Tab to move to the **Business Phone** field.

5 In the **Business Phone** field box, type **202-555-2112** and then press Tab three times to move to the next record.

Eastern Cape Inn does not keep data about a person's company name or job title, so those fields will be left empty. Notice that the designers of this database form have included a Total line to keep track of the total number of guests entered into the database. You have completed one record, so the current total is *1*. On the second row, under ID, *(New)* is highlighted. The asterisk (*) in the record selector box indicates that this row is reserved for a new record.

6 In the **ID** field box, type **56** and then press Tab to move to the **First Name** field.

Because this field was designed to automatically insert a sequential number, Access ignores your attempt to type 56 into the field. If your computer is equipped with a sound card and the volume is turned on, you may hear a sound that signifies you tried to do something that Access will not allow.

7 In the **First Name** field box, type **Bill** and then press Tab to move to the **Last Name** field. Notice that the ID for the second record changed from (New) to 2.

8 In the **Last Name** field box, type **Kukielka** and then press Tab. In the **E-mail Address** field box, type **bkukielka@mail23.com** and then press Tab. In the **Business Phone** field box, type **434-555-1110** and then press Tab four times to move to the **First Name** field on the New Record row.

9 Using the techniques you have just practiced, enter the following records, and then compare your screen with Figure 1.18. After typing the last record, press Tab three times to move to the new record row. Do not be concerned if you make typing errors; you will practice correcting errors later in this project.

First Name	Last Name	E-mail Address	Business Phone
Zachary	Juras	zjuras@citycom.net	303-555-0829
Elaine	Broderick	ebroderick@localisp.net	312-555-0502
Julio	Ferrer	jferrer@mail220.com	480-555-1224
Kelvin	McNeely	kmcneely@mail101.net	805-555-0111
Theodora	Lanham	tlanham@access17.com	239-555-1121
Leane	Wang	lwang@globalisp.com	804-555-0719

Figure 1.18

Eight records entered

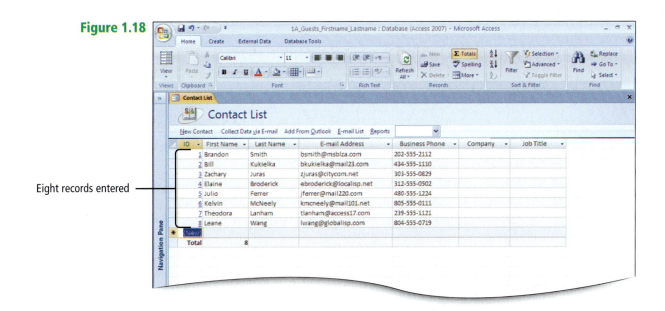

Objective 3
Modify a Template Table

You entered data using a form—a different view of the table. Even though it looks as though the data is stored in the form, it is actually stored in the table. After entering a complete record and moving to the next row, the record is saved in the underlying table—the *Contacts* table. In Activities 1.6 and 1.7, you will open the underlying table and modify it by renaming, adding, and hiding fields. A template is a starting point; you can then modify the template to suit your needs.

Activity 1.6 Hiding Fields in a Template Table

Before modifying fields in the underlying table, you must open the table.

1 Expand ⟩ the **Navigation Pane** to display all of the Access objects in the database.

2 On the **Navigation Pane**, under **Tables**, point to the **Contacts** table, and then *double-click*—click the left mouse button two times in rapid succession. Alternatively, *right-click*—click the right mouse button one time—while the pointer is on the Contacts table, and then from the shortcut menu, click Open. Compare your screen with Figure 1.19. Notice the table displays the records you entered in the Contact List form.

When you right-click an object icon, that object becomes the current object, and a shortcut menu displays. A *shortcut menu* is a list of context-related commands that displays when you right-click a screen element or object.

The Contacts table opens in *Datasheet view*—a window that displays data in rows and columns. In Datasheet view, you can edit fields, add and delete data, and search for data. The name of the table is displayed in an orange tab.

Figure 1.19

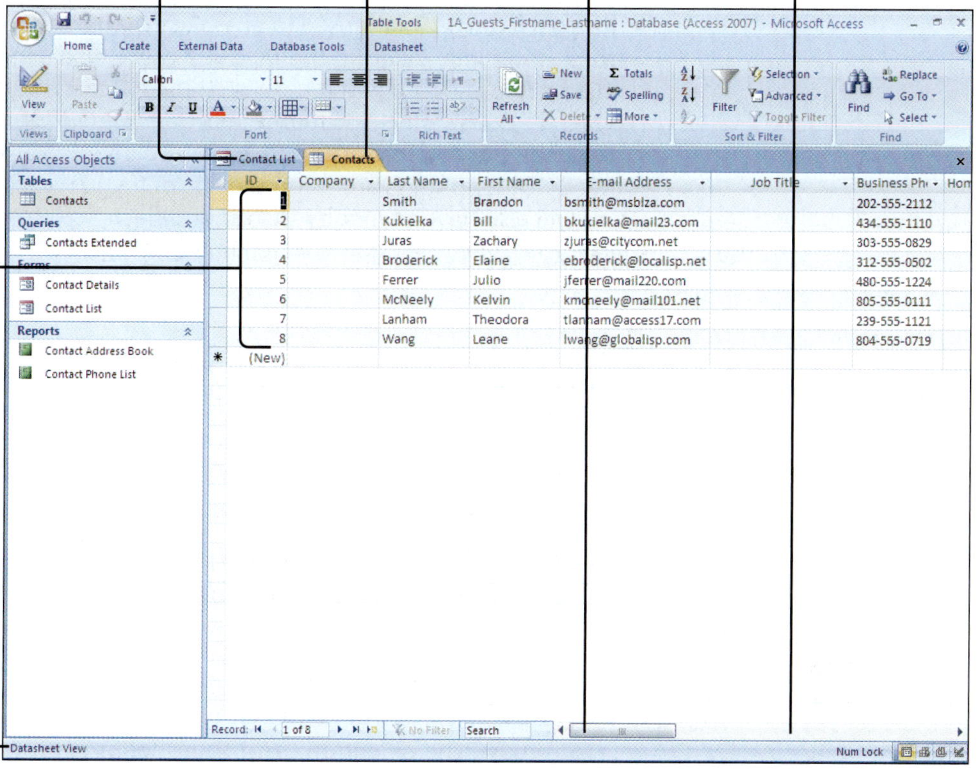

Contact List form tab

Contacts table—the current object

Horizontal scroll box

Horizontal scroll bar

Eight records that were entered in the Contact List form are stored in this table

ID	Company	Last Name	First Name	E-mail Address	Job Title	Business Phi	Hom
1		Smith	Brandon	bsmith@msblza.com		202-555-2112	
2		Kukielka	Bill	bkukielka@mail23.com		434-555-1110	
3		Juras	Zachary	zjuras@citycom.net		303-555-0829	
4		Broderick	Elaine	ebroderick@localisp.net		312-555-0502	
5		Ferrer	Julio	jferrer@mail220.com		480-555-1224	
6		McNeely	Kelvin	kmcneely@mail101.net		805-555-0111	
7		Lanham	Theodora	tlanham@access17.com		239-555-1121	
8		Wang	Leane	lwang@globalisp.com		804-555-0719	
(New)							

Current view

Datasheet View

3 Collapse « the **Navigation Pane**. *Drag* the horizontal scroll box to the right until you see the last fields. To drag, click the object you want to move, hold down the left mouse button, and then move the mouse in the specified direction. Notice that the table has many more fields that are in a different order than those displayed in the form you used to enter the data.

You can modify any of the objects that are included in a template. Because this chapter deals with tables, you will practice modifying the template for the table.

4 If necessary, scroll to the left, and then move the mouse pointer to the **Job Title** field name box to display the ↓ pointer. Click one time to select the entire field.

The selected Job Title field displays with an orange border, and all record selector boxes are also orange.

5 On the **Home tab**, in the **Records group**, click the **More** button. From the displayed list, click **Hide Columns**. Alternatively, right-click the field name, and then from the shortcut menu, click Hide Columns.

The Job Title field is hidden from view and will not print. It has not been deleted from the table. In a template, hiding, rather than deleting, fields is a good technique to use if you wish to use the other objects that were created from the table.

Deleting fields in a database template can cause adverse effects

If a field from a table is used in an object that is dependent on—created from—the table, deleting the field will cause errors in the dependent objects. Recall that when a form is opened, Access reads the underlying table. If Access cannot locate the Job Title field in the table, *#Name?* will display in all the records for this field. Before deleting a field in a table, ensure that no other objects are using that field. If you want to delete the field, you will also have to modify the other objects so that the error will not display. The same rule applies to renaming fields.

6 Locate and then click the **Company** field name to select the field. Using the technique you just practiced, hide the column.

7 If necessary, drag the horizontal scroll box to the right so that you can see the **Home Phone**, **Mobile Phone**, and **Fax Number** fields. Move the mouse pointer to the **Home Phone** field name box to display the ⬇ pointer. Keeping the pointer in the field name boxes, drag to the right to the **Fax Number** field name box to select the three fields. Compare your screen with Figure 1.20.

An orange border displays around the three fields. If you select the wrong number of fields, click on the datasheet in an unselected area to remove the selection, and then begin again.

Three fields selected

Figure 1.20

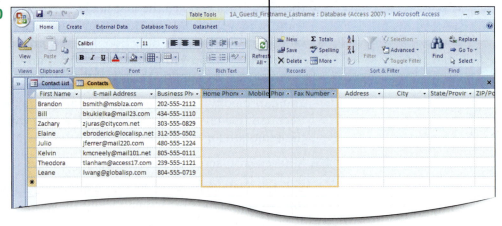

8 Hide the selected columns.

Selecting multiple columns that are **_contiguous_**—located next to one another—is a good technique when you want to perform the same action on the columns.

9 Using the techniques you just practiced, hide the **Country/Region**, **Web Page**, **Notes**, and **Attachment** fields.

The Attachment field looks like a paper clip. Do not be concerned about the Add New Field column. Like the New Record row, this column is reserved for creating a new field and will not print if the field contains no data.

10 On the **tab row**, click the **Contact List form tab** to make the form current. Notice that the fields you hid in the underlying table—Home Phone, Mobile Phone, and Fax Number—are not hidden in the form.

On the **tab row**, **Close** ☒ the Contact List form, leaving the Contacts table current.

More Knowledge
To Unhide Columns

To unhide columns or to determine which fields are hidden, on the Home tab, in the Records group, click the More button. From the displayed list, click Unhide Columns. In the Unhide Columns box, all the field names are displayed with check boxes. If the check box is selected, the field displays. If the check box is not selected, the field is hidden. To unhide a field, select the check box for the field name, and then click the Close button.

Activity 1.7 Adding Fields and Data in a Template Table

1 If necessary, scroll to the right to display the last column in the table. Point to **Add New Field**, right-click, and then from the displayed shortcut menu, click **Rename Column**.

2 With the insertion point in the **field name** box, type **Visit Date** and then press [Enter] to create the field. If necessary, drag the horizontal scroll box to the right to see the **Visit Date** field, which is displayed to the right of the **ZIP/Postal Code** field.

The insertion point is positioned in an empty field name box to the right of the Visit Date field so that you can continue to enter field names.

3 Using the techniques you practiced in Activity 1.5, enter the following data for the first record in the Contacts table. Do not be concerned if the data does not completely display in the field. When you finish typing the *Visit Date* for the first record, you can either press [Tab] six times to move to the **Address** field for the second record or click in the Address field box for the second record.

Additional data has been entered for the first record. The date will display as 6/15/2009.

ID	Address	City	State/Province	ZIP/Postal Code	Visit Date
1	114 Stone Creek Dr.	Washington	DC	20001	6/15/09

4 Enter the following data for the second record. Press ⎋Tab⎋ after entering the ZIP/Postal Code to move the insertion point to the **Visit Date** field for Record 2.

ID	Address	City	State/Province	ZIP/Postal Code
2	10928 Spring Green Rd.	Charlottesville	VA	22901

The Date Picker ▦ displays to the right of the Visit Date field for Record 2. Because you entered a date in the field for the first record, Access has identified this field as a Date field.

Clicking ▦ opens a calendar from which you can choose a date instead of typing the date in the field. This is convenient when you want to schedule an event and must see the day of the week. To enter the date in the field, click the date. If the field is empty, the calendar will display the current month. If the field box contains a date, the calendar will display the month and year for the data in the field box. The Today button will insert the current date into the field.

5 Click ▦ to open the calendar, and then compare your screen with Figure 1.21.

Next month button

Figure 1.21

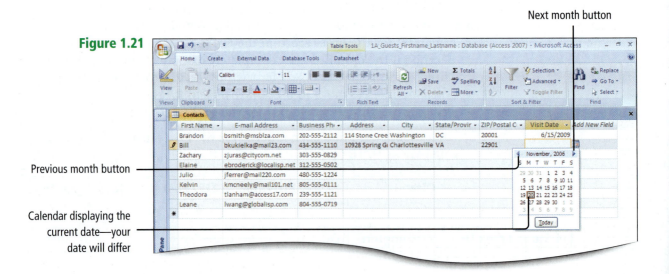

Previous month button

Calendar displaying the current date—your date will differ

6 Click any date to insert that date in the field. Experiment with the Date Picker to insert a date from another month. Then insert the current date by clicking the **Today** button. When you are finished, select the entire date—drag across the entire date. With the date selected, type **5/23/09** and then click in the **Address** field for **Record 3**.

7 Enter the following data for Records 3 through 8. Do not press Tab after entering the Visit Date for Record 8.

ID	Address	City	State/Province	ZIP/Postal Code	Visit Date
3	1173 Salina Dr.	Denver	CO	80012	7/21/09
4	322 N. Downey St.	Chicago	IL	60601	6/18/09
5	1152 Cacts Dr.	Scottsdale	AZ	85250	5/15/09
6	1723 Lancashire Ct.	Simi Valley	CA	93063	5/15/09
7	8745 Meadowridge Ln.	Naples	FL	34102	6/15/09
8	3839 Liberty Ln.	Richmond	VA	23219	5/30/09

Objective 4
Find, Modify, and Print Records

Data in a database is usually **dynamic**—changing. Records can be created, deleted, and edited in a table; and the table can be printed to show the existing records.

Activity 1.8 Adding Records in a Template Table and Checking Spelling

In Activity 1.5, you added records to the table by using the Contact List form. In this activity, you will add records directly into the Contacts table. You can use a form or a table to enter data into a database; however, the data is actually stored in the table.

1 On the **Home tab**, in the **Records group**, click the **New** button. Alternatively, click in the first field in the empty row at the bottom of the table, or you can hold down Ctrl and press +.

The insertion point moves to the first field in the empty row at the end of the table. The New button is dimmed if the insertion point is already located on the New Record row. If the table contains hundreds of records, using the New button is a more efficient way to quickly move to the end of the table.

2 Press Tab one time to move to the **Last Name** field, and then type your last name. Continue entering data in all the fields by using your own information. Using the **Date Picker**, type the current date for the **Visit Date** field, and then press Tab to save the record. Compare your screen with Figure 1.22.

Figure 1.22

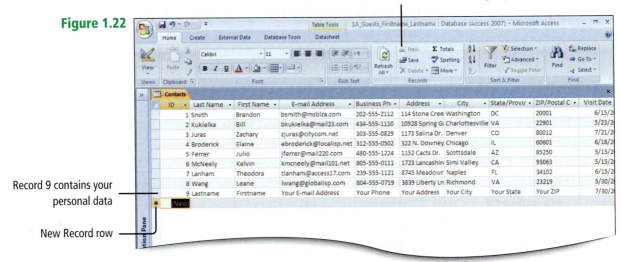

Record 9 contains your personal data

New Record row

3 Take a moment to study the Datasheet view navigation buttons as shown in Figure 1.23.

Figure 1.23

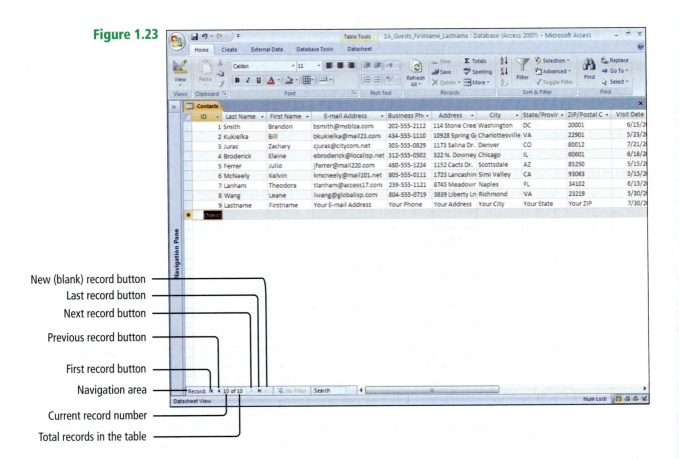

New (blank) record button
Last record button
Next record button
Previous record button
First record button
Navigation area
Current record number
Total records in the table

4 In the navigation area, click the **First record** button. Experiment with the other navigation buttons, but do not enter a new record.

When you are finished, click the **First record** button.

The insertion point is blinking in the ID field to the left of *1*, and the data is highlighted.

5 On the **Home tab**, in the **Records group**, click the **Spelling** button. Alternatively, press ⌨F7⌨. Compare your screen with Figure 1.24.

The Spelling dialog box displays, and *Kukielka* is highlighted because it is not in the Office dictionary. Many proper names will be *flagged*—highlighted—by the spelling checker. Take a moment to review the options in the Spelling dialog box; these are described in the table in Figure 1.25.

Word not in dictionary

Figure 1.24

Highlighted word in the table

Suggested alternatives—none could be found in the dictionary

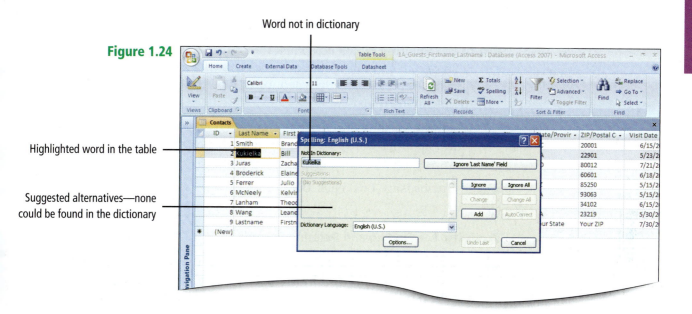

Spelling Dialog Box Buttons

Button	Action
Ignore 'Last Name' Field	Ignores any words in the selected field.
Ignore	Ignores this one occurrence of the word but continues to flag other instances of the word.
Ignore All	Discontinues flagging any instance of the word anywhere in the table.
Change	Changes the identified word to the word highlighted under Suggestions.
Change All	Changes every instance of the word in the table to the word highlighted under Suggestions.
Add	Adds the word to a custom dictionary, which can be edited. This option does not change the built-in Office dictionary.
AutoCorrect	Adds the flagged word to the AutoCorrect list, which will subsequently correct the word automatically if misspelled in any objects typed in the future.
Options	Displays the Access Options dialog box.
Undo Last	Undoes the last change.

Figure 1.25

6 In the **Spelling** dialog box, click the **Ignore 'Last Name' Field** button. Most proper names will be flagged by the spelling checker because these names do not display in the dictionary that is included with Microsoft Office.

Cacts, which displays in the Address field, is flagged by the spelling checker. In the Spelling dialog box under Suggestions, *Cactus* is highlighted.

7 In the **Spelling** dialog box, click the **Change** button to change the word from *Cacts* to *Cactus*.

Meadowridge, which displays in the Address field, is flagged as a misspelled word.

8 In the **Spelling** dialog box, click the **Ignore** button. If any other data is flagged, correct or ignore as necessary. If a suggestion does not display for an incorrectly typed word, type the correct data to replace the highlighted text.

When the spelling checker has completed checking the table and has found no other words missing from its dictionary, a message displays stating *The spelling check is complete*.

9 In the message box, click **OK**.

Activity 1.9 Finding and Deleting Records

1 In the table, in the **Last Name** field, click in the record containing your last name—Record 9. On the **Home tab**, in the **Find group**, click the **Find** button. Alternatively, hold down Ctrl, and then press F.

The Find and Replace dialog box displays with the Find tab current.

2 In the **Find and Replace** dialog box, in the **Find What** box, type **Juras**

The Look In box displays *Last Name* because you clicked in the Last Name field before you clicked the Find button.

3 In the **Find and Replace** dialog box, click the **Look in box arrow**. Notice that Access can search for the data in the entire Contacts table instead of only the Last Name field. Leaving the entry as **Last Name**, click the **Look in box arrow** one time to close the list, and then click the **Find Next** button. Compare your screen with Figure 1.26.

If Access did not locate Record 3, ensure that you typed *Juras* correctly in the Find What box. If you misspelled *Juras* in the table, type the misspelled version in the Find What box.

Figure 1.26

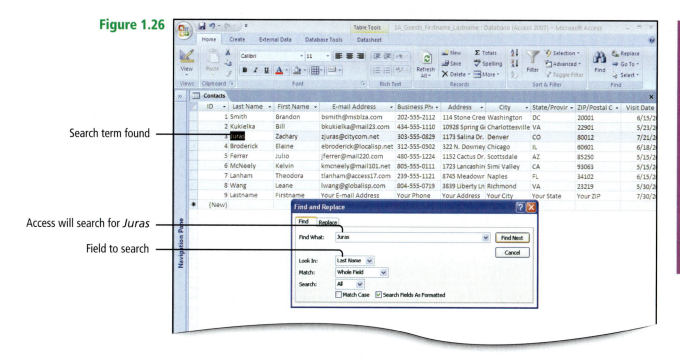

Search term found

Access will search for *Juras*

Field to search

---

4 In the **Find and Replace** dialog box, click **Cancel** to close the dialog box.

The table displays with *Juras* selected in Record 3. Even though you can locate this record easily in the table because there are only a few records, keep in mind that most database tables contain many more records. Using the Find button is an efficient way to locate a record in the table.

5 Point to the orange **Record Selector** box for the *Juras* record until the ➡ pointer displays. Click one time to ensure that the entire record is selected, and then compare your screen with Figure 1.27.

Delete button   Delete button arrow   Selected record

Figure 1.27

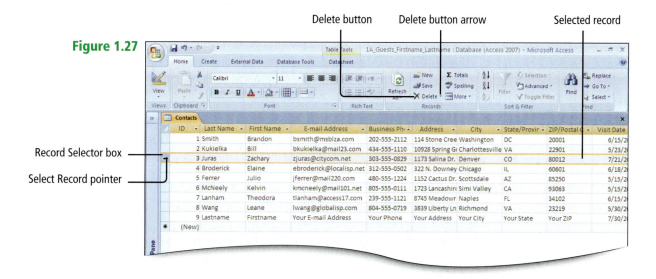

Record Selector box

Select Record pointer

6 On the **Home tab**, in the **Records group**, click the **Delete** button, and then compare your screen with Figure 1.28. Notice that Access displays a message stating that you are about to delete one record and will be unable to undo the Delete operation.

Figure 1.28

Record with ID 3 is not displayed

Warning message

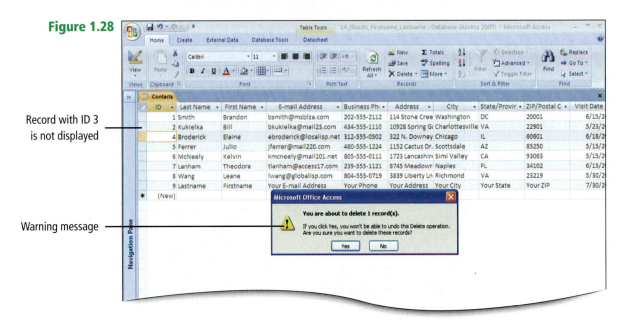

Another Way

To Delete Records in a Table

There are three other methods to delete selected records in a table:

- On the Home tab, in the Records group, click the Delete button arrow, and then click Delete Record.
- On the selected record, right-click and then click Delete Record.
- From the keyboard, press Delete.

---

7 In the message box, click **Yes** to confirm the deletion.

The record holding information for *Juras* no longer displays in the table, has been permanently deleted from the table, and will no longer display in any other objects that were created using the Contacts table. The record of ID 4—Elaine Broderick—is now Record 3 and is the current record.

More Knowledge

Why the ID Field Data Did Not Renumber Sequentially

The designers of this database table template made the ID field a special field called the ***primary key field***. When data is entered into a primary key field, it is unique data and can never be used again within the same field in the table.

Activity 1.10 Finding and Modifying Records

When data changes, you must locate and modify the record with the data. Recall that you can move among records in a table using the navigation buttons at the bottom of the window and that you can use the Find button to locate specific data. Other navigation methods include using keys on the keyboard and using the Search box in the navigation area.

1 Take a moment to review the table in Figure 1.29, which lists the key combinations you can use to navigate within an Access table.

Key Combinations for Navigating a Table

Keystroke	Movement
↑	Moves the selection up one record at a time.
↓	Moves the selection down one record at a time.
Page Up	Moves the selection up one screen at a time.
PgDn	Moves the selection down one screen at a time.
Ctrl + Home	Moves the selection to the first field in the table or the beginning of the selected field.
Ctrl + End	Moves the selection to the last field in the table or the end of the selected field.
Tab	Moves the selection to the next field in the table.
⇧ Shift + Tab	Moves the selection to the previous field in the table.
Enter	Moves the selection to the next field in the table.

Figure 1.29

2 On the keyboard, press ↓ to move the selection down one record. Record 4—*Julio Ferrer*—is now the current record.

If you are using a laptop computer, you may have to hold down a function (Fn) key to use shortcuts that involve the Home, End, Page Up, and Page Down keys.

3 On the keyboard, hold down Ctrl, and then press Home to move to the first field of the first record in the table—*1* in the ID field.

4 In the navigation area, click the **Next record** button ▶ four times to navigate to Record 5—*Kelvin McNeely*. In the **E-mail Address** field for Record 5, click to the right of **mail101.net** to make the field current. On the keyboard, hold down Ctrl, and then press Home to move the insertion point to the beginning of the current field—before *kmcneely@mail101.net*. Press Delete one time to remove the letter *k* from the beginning of the e-mail address.

Because the field was current, this key combination moved the insertion point to the beginning of the field, rather than the first field in the table.

5 In the navigation area, click in the **Search** box. In the **Search** box, type **b**

Record 1 is selected, and the letter *B* in *Brandon* is highlighted. Search found the first occurrence of the letter *b*. It is not necessary to type capital letters in the Search box; Access will locate the words regardless of capitalization.

6 In the **Search** box, continue by typing **i**

Record 2 is selected, and the letters *Bi* in *Bill* are highlighted. Search found the first occurrence of the letters *bi*. This is the record that needs to be modified. It is not necessary to type an entire word in the Search box to locate a record containing that word.

7 In the field box, click to the left of the letter *B*, and then press ⌈Ctrl⌉ + ⌈End⌉ to move the insertion point to the end of Bill. Type **ie** to change the first name from *Bill* to *Billie*. Press ⌈↓⌉ to move to the next record and save the change.

If you must edit part of a name, drag through letters or words to select them. You can then type the new letters or words over the selection to replace the text without having to press ⌈Delete⌉ or ⌈←Bksp⌉.

Recall that the Small Pencil icon 🖉 in the Record Selector box means that the record is being edited and has not yet been saved.

8 Expand ⌈»⌉ the **Navigation Pane**. Under **Forms**, double-click **Contact List** to open the form, and then collapse ⌈«⌉ the **Navigation Pane**. Compare your screen with Figure 1.30 and notice the changed e-mail address for Kelvin McNeely, the corrected spelling of Billie Kukielka's first name, the deleted record—ID of 3—and the new record displaying your information.

The form does not display the records in the same order as the table—the records are sorted alphabetically by the Last Name field. Recall that a form is another way of displaying data that exists in a table.

The form does not contain the additional fields and data you created in the table. To display the fields in the form, you would have to change the design of the form. The Delete button cannot be used to remove a field from a form.

Figure 1.30

Fields were edited in the table

Record for Juras—ID 3—deleted from table

Created this record in table

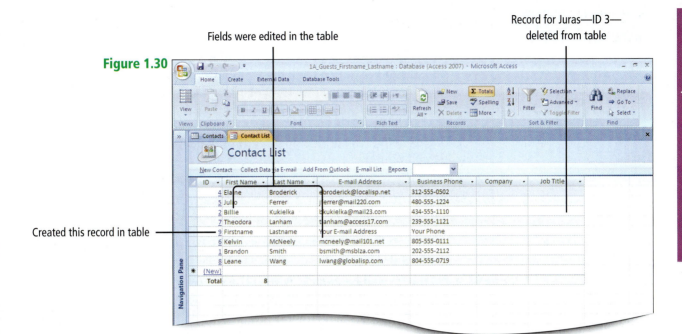

9 In the navigation area, click the **Last record** button ▶| to move to the last record. Click the **ID** number for this record.

The Contact Details form opens, displaying data for this record. This form was also based on the Contacts table.

10 In the **Contact Details** form, click the **Close** button ☒.

Activity 1.11 Printing the Table and a Report

1 Check your *Chapter Assignment Sheet* or *Course Syllabus* or consult your instructor to determine whether you are to submit your assignments on paper or electronically, for example, by using your college's learning management system. If you are directed to submit an electronic printout of this table and report, you can do so by using the *Save As PDF or XPS* command from the Office menu, and then move to Step 6.

2 At the top left corner of the screen, click the **Office** button 🔘, and then click **Print**. In the displayed **Print** dialog box, click **OK**.

Using the Print dialog box, you can select a variety of different options, such as printing multiple copies, selecting a different printer, printing some but not all pages, and printing selected records.

3 On the **tab row**, click the **Contacts tab** to make the table current. Using the technique you just practiced, **Print** the table.

The Add New Field column, the New Record row, and the hidden fields do not print. The table will print on two pages, and not all of the data will be displayed.

Access provides several methods to print an object:

- Click the Office button, click the Print button arrow, and then click Quick Print. The object will print a single copy on the default printer.
- Click the Office button, click the Print arrow, and then click Print Preview. On the Print Preview tab, in the Print group, click the Print button, which will print a single copy of the entire object on the default printer.
- Press Ctrl + P. This is an alternative to the Office button Print command, and displays the Print dialog box.
- On the Navigation Pane, click the object to select it. Click the Office button, and then click Print to display the Print dialog box, which prints a single copy of the entire object on the default printer without opening the object.
- On the Navigation Pane, click the object to select it. Click the Office button; point to Print; and then click Print, Quick Print, or Print Preview.

4 Expand ⟩⟩ the **Navigation Pane**. Under **Reports**, double-click **Contact Phone List** to open the report. Using the techniques you just practiced, **Print** the report.

Recall that a report is a visually attractive format of the table that can contain all or part of the data in a table.

5 Collect your printouts from the printer, and then submit them as directed.

6 On the **tab row**, right-click any object tab. From the shortcut menu, click **Close All**. If prompted, click **Yes** to save changes.

All the objects are closed, and the Navigation Pane is expanded. Access will reopen the database displaying the Navigation Pane as it is displayed when you close the database.

Objective 5
Use the Access Help System and Exit Access

As you work with Access, you can get assistance by using the Help feature. You can choose a topic or search for information, and Help will provide you with information and step-by-step instructions for performing tasks. The easiest way to use Help is to search for information in the Help window.

Activity 1.12 Using Help to Find Access Information

In this activity, you will use Help to add a command to the Quick Access Toolbar. As you use Access, you will discover buttons—commands—that you want to have readily available. If you are able to make changes to the software on your computer, you should add frequently used buttons to the Quick Access Toolbar. Examples include Print, Print Preview, and Open.

1 On the right side of the Ribbon, click the **Help** button 🔵. Alternatively, press F1. Compare your screen with Figure 1.31.

The first time you use the Help feature, the online Help window displays in a default location and size on your screen. You can resize or reposition the Help window. To resize, move the pointer over a corner of the Help window until you see the double-headed arrow, and then drag the corner until the window is the size you desire. To move the Help window, move the pointer to the title bar and drag the window to the desired location. Access will maintain the changes you make to the Help window.

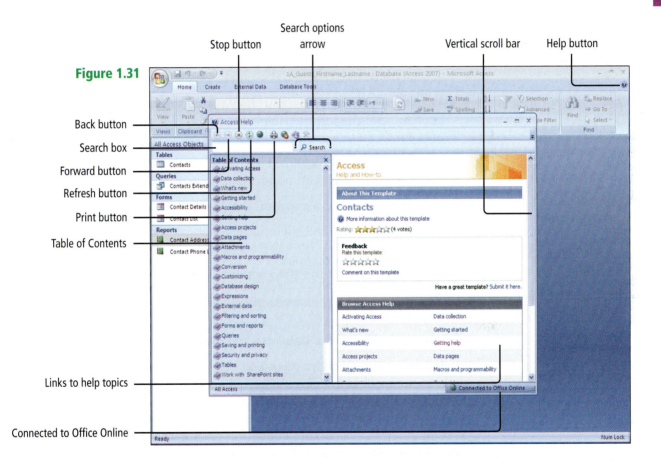

Figure 1.31

Alert!

Do you see a Not Connected message?

If your computer is not connected to the Internet, a Not Connected message displays under the Search box. The help you receive will be from the help files that are stored with the Access program on your computer. If you are connected to the Internet, you have access to the most up-to-date help files at Microsoft Online.

2 In the Search box, type **quick access toolbar** and then press [Enter].

If no Internet connection is available, the program will search only the Help files that are installed on your computer.

Alert!

Were there no results found matching "quick access toolbar"?

If no results are found matching *quick access toolbar*, in the Access Help window, to the right of the Search box, click the Search button arrow, and then click Access Help.

3 On the displayed list, point to and then click **Customize the Quick Access Toolbar**. The Help window displays information about customizing the Quick Access Toolbar.

4 Under **What do you want to do?**, click **Add a command to the Quick Access Toolbar directly from the Ribbon**. The Help window scrolls down to the selected section.

5 Take a moment to read about how to add items to the Quick Access Toolbar, and then in the Help window, scroll down to display the end of the information.

Most Help windows will have topics listed under *See Also* that may relate to the search you performed.

6 If you want to print a copy, on the Access Help toolbar, click the

Print button 🖶 , and then in the displayed **Print** dialog box, click **Print**.

7 On the title bar for the **Help** window, click the **Close** button [X] to exit Help.

Activity 1.13 Closing the Database and Exiting Access

When you move to another record or close an Access table, any changes made to the records are saved automatically. If you change the design of the table or change the Datasheet view layout, such as adjusting column widths, you will be prompted to save your changes when you change views or when you close the table. After closing the table, close the database. If you do not need to create any other databases, exit Access.

1 In the upper left corner of your screen, click the **Office** button

🔘 , and then click **Close Database** to close the database.

The database window closes, and the Getting Started window displays.

2 On the **Microsoft Access** title bar, click the **Close** button [X] to exit the Access program. Alternatively, click the Office button, and then click Exit Access. A third way to exit Access is to press [Alt] + [F] + [X].

More Knowledge

Viewing Keyboard Shortcuts

You can locate the key combinations for keyboard shortcuts using the Control key by moving the pointer over a button. Key combinations are also listed on menus. For example, to exit Access, hold down the Alt key, and then press the underlined letter combination to use the keyboard shortcut. The keyboard shortcuts using the Alt key are displayed by pressing and then releasing the Alt key when a program is open.

End **You have completed Project 1A** ——————————

Project 1B Inventory

In Activities 1.14 through 1.25, you will create a new database for Debra Chandler-Walker and Derek Walker, owners of Eastern Cape Inn. The database will contain one table with inventory information and another table with suppliers for the bed and breakfast. Your completed tables will look similar to those in Figure 1.32.

For Project 1B, you will need the following file:

New blank Access database

You will save your database as
1B_Inventory_Firstname_Lastname

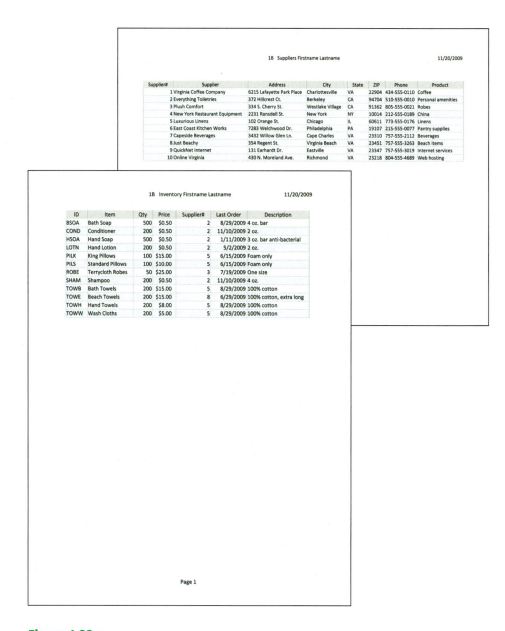

Figure 1.32
Project 1B—Inventory

Objective 6
Create a New Database and Tables

Like an architect creates a blueprint before beginning to build a new house, when creating a new database, it is a good idea to plan your database on paper. First, you need to determine what data you need to store. Second, you need to determine how you will use the information. For Eastern Cape Inn, you might need to keep track of not only the type of toiletries provided for guests, but also the contact information of your suppliers. After you know what data you need to track, you need to think about the kinds of questions the database should be able to answer for you. For example, at Eastern Cape Inn, you might want to know: Which items are needed for the rooms? How many items are on hand? What is the cost per item? Or who supplies the items?

Activity 1.14 Creating a New Database

1 **Start** Access. In the **Getting Started** window, under **New Blank Database**, click the **Blank Database** button. On the right side of the screen, under **Blank Database**, notice that a name is displayed in the **File Name** box.

If this is the first database you have created, the file name will be *Database1*; the second database will be named *Database2*. When you exit Access, reopen it, and create a new database, the numbering of the file name will begin at *1* again, provided you have not saved a database with the default name. These are not descriptive names of a database—database names should refer to the data within them.

2 In the **File Name** box, select the text, and then using your own name type **1B_Inventory_Firstname_Lastname** Recall that you should type underscores between the words.

When text is selected or highlighted, you can type over it, which deletes the selected text and replaces it with the text you type. To select the file name, double-click the file name—double-clicking a single word selects that word.

3 At the right of the **File Name** box, click the **Browse** button 📂. Navigate to the drive on which you are saving your folders and projects for this chapter, and open the *Access Chapter 1* folder. Then, in the lower right corner of the **File New Database** dialog box, click **OK**.

The storage location is under the File Name box, and the file name has an extension of *.accdb* as shown in Figure 1.33.

Figure 1.33

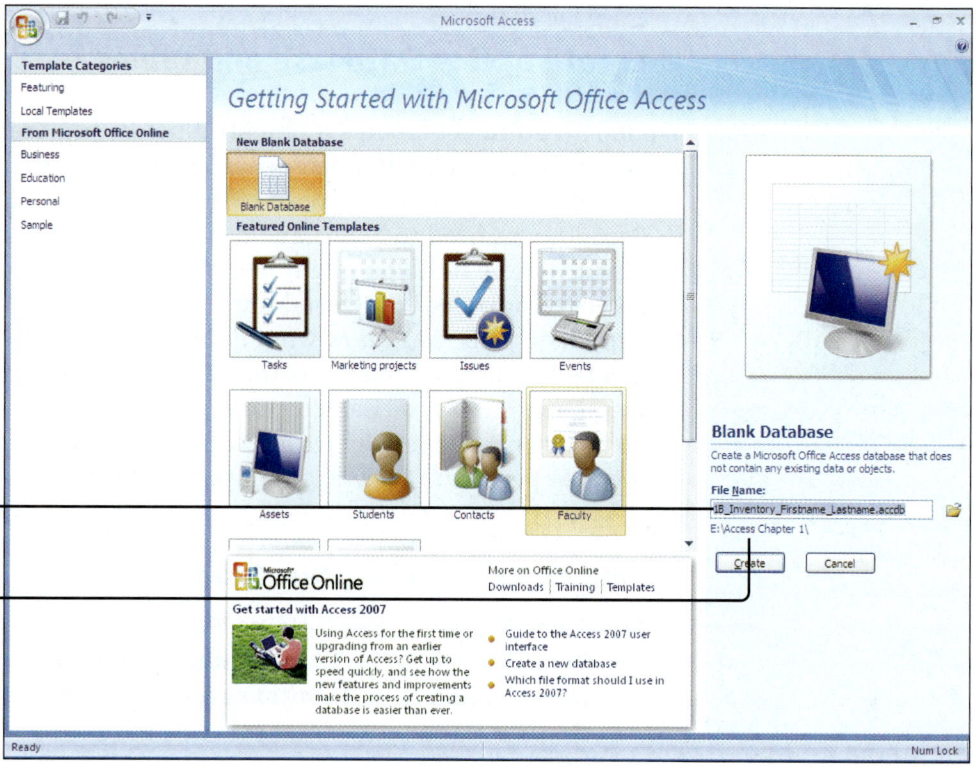

Figure 1.33

File name with .accdb extension

Storage location—yours may differ

4 In the **Blank Database** area, click the **Create** button to save and open the database.

The database is open and ready for you to enter data into a table using Datasheet view, and the Add New Field column is selected. Because you are creating this database, a security message does not display—the database is trusted to be safe.

Activity 1.15 Creating Fields in a New Table in Datasheet View

If you were to buy an address book to keep track of the suppliers for Eastern Cape Inn, it would be useless until you filled it in with names, addresses, and phone numbers. Likewise, a new database is not useful until you **populate**, or fill, a table with data.

The quickest and least-controlled way to create a table is in Datasheet view, entering data and naming fields as you go. Access will apply some table settings based on the data that you enter. You might use this method when you must set up a basic table and enter data quickly. You can then switch to *Design view*—a view that displays more options for field modifications—to refine your basic table. You must refine the table design before entering a lot of data because changing the settings may affect the data that has already been entered.

1 Take a moment to study the elements of the window as shown in Figure 1.34.

The ID field is automatically created by Access. By default, Access creates this field for all new datasheets and sets the data type for the field to AutoNumber, which sequentially numbers each record.

The Navigation Pane is grouped by tables and displays one table named *Table1*. On the title bar, notice Table Tools. Because a new, empty table is the current object, **contextual tools** named *Table Tools* display, and a **contextual tab** is added next to the standard tabs on the Ribbon. Contextual tools enable you to perform specific commands related to the current or selected object. The contextual tools display one or more contextual tabs that contain related groups of commands that you may need while working with an object. Contextual tools display only when needed for the current or selected object. When the object is no longer current or selected, the contextual tools no longer display.

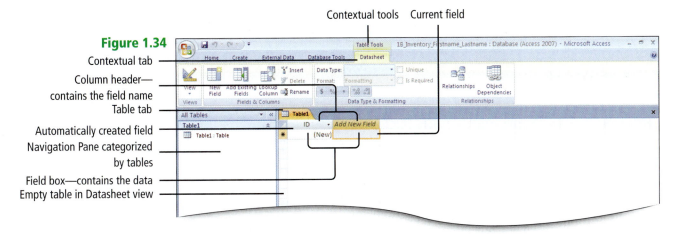

Figure 1.34

Contextual tab

Column header—contains the field name

Table tab

Automatically created field

Navigation Pane categorized by tables

Field box—contains the data

Empty table in Datasheet view

Contextual tools   Current field

2 On the **Navigation Pane**, click the **Shutter Bar Open/Close** button

[«] to collapse the Navigation Pane. Click the **Add New Field** column to make the field current—the field is outlined in orange.

Recall that the Add New Field column is available in case you decide to add another field to the table and that it will not print unless you type data into the field box for a record.

3 On the **Datasheet tab**, in the **Fields & Columns group**, click the **Rename** button.

The insertion point displays in the column header. It is helpful to plan your database on paper first, deciding on field names and the types of data that will be entered into the fields. Recall that fields—the columns in your table—are categories that describe each piece of data stored in the table.

4 Type **Item** and then press [Tab] to move to the third field. Alternatively, press [→] to move to the next field.

5 Add the following field names, pressing [Tab] after the last field name. Do not be concerned if the field name does not completely display or if you misspell a field name—you will correct these items later in this project.

Quantity
Cost Per Item
Last Order
Description

6 Compare your screen with Figure 1.35. Notice that there are six field names, and the insertion point is positioned in an empty field name box. Under the field names, on the first row in the **Record Selector** box, notice the ⟨*⟩—this symbol shows the location to enter a new record.

To the right of each field name is a Sort & Filter arrow that enables you to change the display of the field.

Field names

Figure 1.35

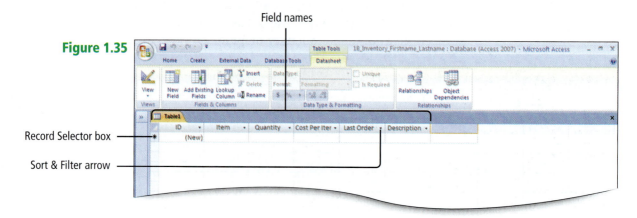

Record Selector box

Sort & Filter arrow

7 Under **ID**, click in the field box containing *(New)*, and then compare your screen with Figure 1.36. Alternatively, press ⟨Tab⟩.

The Record Selector box and the column header are orange, indicating that this field box is the current field box. When you begin typing, data will be entered into the current field box.

Figure 1.36

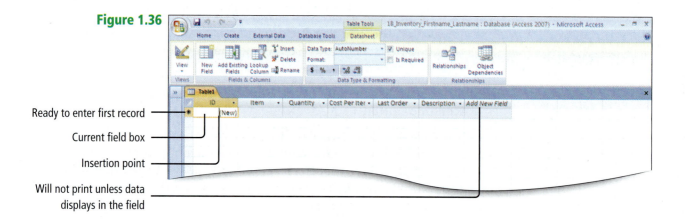

Ready to enter first record

Current field box

Insertion point

Will not print unless data displays in the field

8 On the **Datasheet tab**, in the **Data Type & Formatting group**, click the **Data Type arrow**, and then click **Text**.

You will enter an ID for the field instead of letting Access automatically number each record.

Activity 1.16 Adding the First Record to a Table in Datasheet View

Each row in the table represents a record. In this activity, you will enter the first record in Datasheet view to begin populating the table.

1 In the **ID** field, type **LOTN** and then press [Tab] or [Enter] to move the insertion point to the field box under **Item**. Alternatively, click in the field box.

2 In the **Item** field, type **Hand Lotion** and then press [Tab] to move to the next field. In the **Quantity** field box, type **200** and then press [Tab]. In the **Cost Per Item** field box, type **.50** and then press [Tab].

Recall that in the Record Selector box, the small pencil icon indicates that the record is being created or edited, and the [*] indicates an empty record.

Note — Correcting Typing Errors

Use the [←Bksp] key to remove characters to the left, and the [Delete] key to remove characters to the right. You can also select the text you want to replace, and then type the correct information. If you have *not* moved to the next record, which saves the record, you can press [Esc] to exit from the record being edited.

3 In the **Last Order** field box, type **5/2/09** and then press [Tab]. In the **Description** field box, type **2 oz.** and then press [Tab]. Compare your screen with Figure 1.37.

The first record is saved in the table automatically when you move the insertion point to another record. Under Cost Per Item, the number you entered displays as 0.5, and the date displays four digits for the year. These fields were formatted based on the data you entered.

Datasheet tab   .50 displays as 0.5

Figure 1.37

First record entered

Insertion point blinking in first field of second record

Date formatted by Access

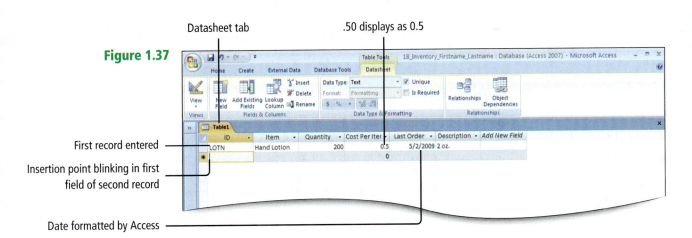

4 On the Quick Access Toolbar, click the **Save** button.

The Save As dialog box displays. Under Table Name, a suggested name of *Table1* is selected. Yours may differ depending on the number of tables you have attempted to create in this database.

5 In the **Save As** dialog box, under **Table Name**, using your first and last name, type **1B Inventory Firstname Lastname** and then compare your screen with Figure 1.38.

You should save a table as soon as you have entered the field names and one record. Every object that you create in a database should be saved with a name that reflects the data within that object. The table name does not require underscores between the words unless you attach only the table to an e-mail message.

Figure 1.38

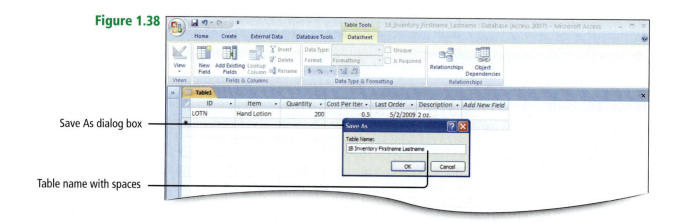

Save As dialog box

Table name with spaces

6 In the **Save As** dialog box, click **OK**. Notice that the table tab displays the saved table name.

More Knowledge

Renaming a Table

To change the name of a table, expand the Navigation Pane. Right-click the table name, and then from the displayed shortcut menu, click Rename. Type the new name or edit it as you would any selected text. To rename a table, the table must be closed.

Activity 1.17 Changing Data Types

As you add each item to the record, Access determines the *data type*—a characteristic that defines the kind of data that can be entered into a field, such as numbers, text, or dates. Access determines the data type based on the data you enter into a field. Each field can contain only one data type. You should enter the data for the first record before saving the table; otherwise, Access will assign a data type of Text to every field.

1 In the first record, click in the **Item** field box.

2 On the **Datasheet tab**, in the **Data Type & Formatting group**, move the mouse pointer to **Data Type** to display a **ScreenTip**, and then compare your screen with Figure 1.39.

A *ScreenTip* is a short description that displays when you hold the mouse pointer over an object. The ScreenTip displays a definition of a data type.

Data Type box

Figure 1.39

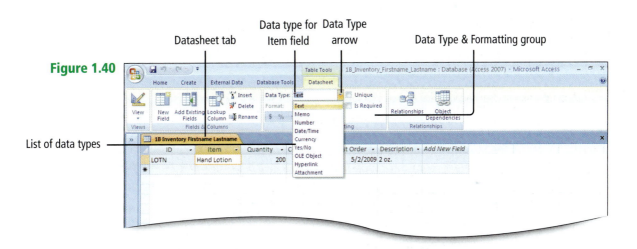

ScreenTip

3 Notice the box next to **Data Type**, which contains *Text*. To the right of **Text**, click the **Data Type arrow** to display a list of data types, as shown in Figure 1.40. Take a moment to study the table in Figure 1.41 that describes all 11 possible data types.

Some data types display only in certain views or with certain fields.

Data type for Data Type
Item field arrow

Datasheet tab   Data Type & Formatting group

Figure 1.40

List of data types

Data Types

Data Type	Description	Example
Text	Text or combinations of text and numbers; also, numbers that are not used in calculations. Limited to 255 characters or length set on field, whichever is less. Access does not reserve space for unused portions of the text field. This is the default data type.	An inventory item, such as towels, or a phone number or postal code that is not used in calculations and that may contain characters other than numbers.
Memo	Lengthy text or combinations of text and numbers that can hold up to 65,535 characters depending on the size of the database.	Description of a product.

(Continued)

(*Continued*)

Number	Numeric data used in mathematical calculations with varying field sizes.	A quantity, such as 500.
Date/Time	Date and time values for the years 100 through 9999.	An order date, such as 11/10/2009 3:30 p.m.
Currency	Monetary values and numeric data that can be used in mathematical calculations involving data with one to four decimal places. Accurate to 15 digits on the left side of the decimal separator and to four digits on the right side. Use this data type to store financial data and when you do not want Access to round values.	An item price, such as $8.50.
Yes/No	Contains only one of two values—Yes/No, True/False, or On/Off. Access assigns 1 for all Yes values and 0 for all No values.	Whether an item was ordered—Yes or No.
OLE Object	An object created by programs other than Access that is linked to or embedded in the table. *OLE* is an abbreviation for *object linking and embedding*, a technology for transferring and sharing information among programs. Stores up to two gigabytes of data (the size limit for all Access databases). Must have an OLE server registered on the server that runs the database. Should usually use Attachment data type instead.	A graphics file, such as a picture of a product, a sound file, a Word document, or an Excel spreadsheet stored as a bitmap image.
Hyperlink	Web or e-mail addresses.	An e-mail address, such as dwalker@ eastcapeinn.com, or a Web page, such as http://www.eastcapeinn.com.
Attachment	Any supported type of file—images, spreadsheet files, documents, or charts. Similar to e-mail attachments.	Same as OLE Object.
AutoNumber	Available in Design view. A unique sequential or random number assigned by Access as each record is entered that cannot be updated.	An inventory item number, such as 1, 2, 3, or a randomly assigned employee number, such as 3852788.
Lookup Wizard	Available in Design view. Not really a data type, but will display in the list of data types. Links to fields in other tables to display a list of data instead of having to manually type the data.	Link to another field in another table.

Figure 1.41

Note — Change the Data Type Before Entering Additional Records

Changing a field's data type after you enter data in a table causes a potentially lengthy process of data conversion when you save the table, especially if the table contains a large amount of data. If the data type for data already stored in a field conflicts with the data type to which you change, you may lose some data.

4 Click **Text**. In the first record, click in the **ID** field box. On the **Datasheet tab**, in the **Data Type & Formatting group**, locate the **Unique** check box. Point to **Unique** to display the **ScreenTip**.

No two records can contain the same data in this field. Setting a field as *unique* helps to ensure the accuracy of data entry. For example, if you had a field containing Social Security numbers, you should designate this field as a unique field. If you try to type the same Social Security number for two different records, you will receive an error message. You can designate one or more fields as unique. Because this field was automatically created by Access to ensure that each record had a unique number, the check box is selected.

5 Press Tab to move to the **Item** field box. Alternatively, click in the Item field box. In the **Data Type & Formatting group**, notice that Access assigned a **Data Type** of **Text**, which is correct.

When you tab to a field box containing data, the data is highlighted. You can type over the data to replace it. If you press a character on the keyboard, you might inadvertently change the existing data. When you click in a field box containing data, the insertion point blinks where you click, and you can edit the data without typing over the entire entry.

6 In the first record, click in the **Quantity** field box. In the **Data Type & Formatting group**, notice that Access assigned a **Data Type** of **Number**, which is correct.

Because you typed a number in this field, Access assigns the Number data type. If an incorrect data type is applied to the field, click the Data Type arrow, and then click the correct data type. Numeric data aligns at the right side of the field box, and text aligns at the left side of the field box.

7 In the **Data Type & Formatting group**, click the **Format arrow** to display a list of numeric formats as shown in Figure 1.42. Take a moment to study the table in Figure 1.43, which describes the numeric formats.

Use the Format arrow to specify how data displays and prints. For example, you can specify the number of decimal places that should be displayed in a number. There are also buttons under the Format box that you can use to quickly format a number.

Data type is Number   Format arrow

Figure 1.42

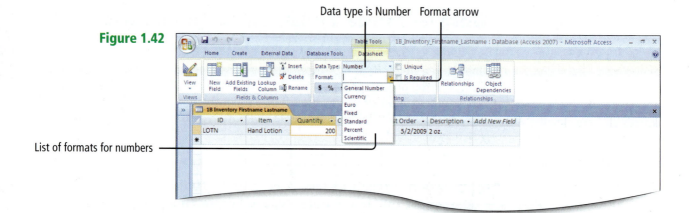

List of formats for numbers

Numeric Formats

Format	Description	Data Entered	Data Displays As
General Number	Displays the number as entered, except for numbers less than one—this is the default format.	3456.789 −3456.789 $213.21 .50	3456.789 −3456.789 $213.21 0.5
Currency	Uses the thousand separator, a $ symbol, and rounds the decimal places to two digits.	3456.789 −3456.789 .50	$3,456.79 ($3,456.79) $0.50
Euro	Uses the euro symbol (€), regardless of the default currency symbol.	3456.789 −3456.789 .50	€ 3,456.79 (€ 3,456.79) € 0.50
Fixed	Displays at least one digit, and you can set the number of decimal places.	3456.789 −3456.789 3.56645 .50	3456.79 −3456.79 3.57 0.50
Standard	Uses the thousand separator, and you can set the number of decimal places.	3456.789 −3456.789 3.56645 .50	3,456.79 −3,456.79 3.57 0.50
Percent	Multiplies the value by 100, and appends a percent sign (%). You can set the number of decimal places.	3 .50	300% 50%
Scientific	Uses standard scientific notation.	3456.789 −3456.789 .50	3.46E+03 −3.46E+03 5.00E−01

Figure 1.43

8 Experiment with the different formats by clicking each option and then viewing how the data is displayed in the datasheet. When you are finished, change the format to **General Number**.

9 In the first record, click in the **Cost Per Item** field box. In the **Data Type & Formatting group**, notice that Access assigned a **Data Type** of **Number**. Click the **Data Type arrow**, and then from the displayed list, click **Currency**. When a message box displays, click **Yes**. Compare your screen with Figure 1.44.

Because this is a monetary value, the correct data type is currency. The data now displays as *$0.50*. The data type of currency ensures accuracy if this field is used in a calculation. The format of currency displays a dollar symbol on the left side of the number.

Data type is Currency   Format is Currency

Figure 1.44

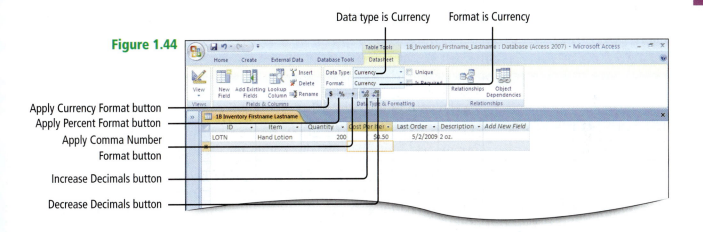

Apply Currency Format button
Apply Percent Format button
Apply Comma Number
Format button
Increase Decimals button
Decrease Decimals button

10 In the first record, click in the **Cost Per Item** field, and experiment with the different format buttons by clicking each button, and then viewing how the data is displayed in the datasheet. When you are finished, change the **Data Type** to **Currency**, change the **Format** to **Currency**, and ensure that only two digits display to the right of the decimal point.

11 In the first record, click in the **Last Order** field box. In the **Data Type & Formatting group**, notice that Access assigned a **Data Type** of **Date/Time**. Click the **Format arrow**. Take a moment to study the table in Figure 1.45 that describes the date and time formats.

Date/Time Formats

Format	Description	Data Entered	Data Displays As
General Date	If the value is a date only, no time is displayed. If the value is a time only, no date is displayed. This setting is a combination of Short Date and Long Time. This is the default format for dates.	5/2/09 5:39 PM	5/2/2009 5:39:00 PM

(Continued)

Long Date	Displays day of week along with the date.	5/2/09	Saturday, May 02, 2009
Medium Date	Displays the day, the month, and the year separated by a hyphen (-).	5/2/09	02-May-09
Short Date	Displays the month, date, and year separated by a slash (/).	5/2/09	5/2/2009
Long Time	Displays the hour, minutes, and seconds separated by a colon with AM or PM appended.	5:39 PM	5:39:00 PM
Medium Time	Displays the hour and minutes separated by a colon with AM or PM appended.	5:39 PM	5:39 PM
Short Time	Shows time using 24-hour clock, also known as military time.	5:39 PM	17:39

Figure 1.45

12 Experiment by selecting different date/time formats without changing the data in the field. When you are finished, click **Short Date**.

The date displays as 5/2/2009. Your date format may differ—date formats are controlled by your computer settings.

13 In the first record, click in the **Description** field box. Because you entered a few characters, Access assigned a **Data Type** of **Text**. Using the techniques you have just practiced, change the **Data Type** to **Memo**.

Recall that a text field can contain up to 255 characters and a memo field can contain up to 65,535 characters. Because some of the descriptions of inventory items may exceed 255 characters, the memo data type is more appropriate. The Format arrow is dimmed—unavailable—because there are no formats for a memo field or a text field.

14 Press Tab to move to the new record row. Alternatively, click in the first field on the new record row or press ↓.

The changes to the first record are saved, and you are ready to type the remaining records. Even though the record is saved, the changes you made to the data types and formats are not saved—these represent changes to the *database structure*. The database structure includes field names, data types, data formats, and other settings that define the database.

15 On the Quick Access Toolbar, click the **Save** button 🖫. Compare your screen with Figure 1.46.

Because you previously saved this table, the Save As dialog box does not display. The table is saved with the same name. If you close the table without saving changes to the database structure, a message displays asking if you wish to save the new design.

Figure 1.46

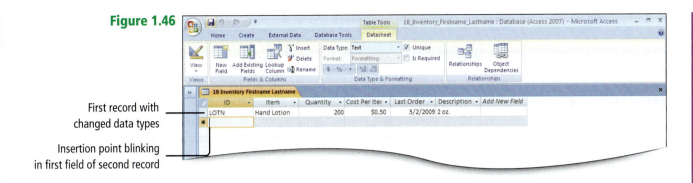

First record with changed data types

Insertion point blinking in first field of second record

Activity 1.18 Creating Additional Records in a Table in Datasheet View

After you have created the fields and the first record, changed data types, and saved the table, you are ready to enter additional records.

1 If necessary, on the second row in the **ID** field, click to display the insertion point. Type **BSOA** and then press Tab to move to the next field box. In the **Item** field, type **Bath Soap** and then press Tab. In the **Quantity** field, type **500** and then press Tab. In the **Cost Per Item** field, type **.5** and then press Tab. Compare your screen with Figure 1.47.

Notice that the amount you typed in the Cost Per Item field has been formatted as *$0.50*—the field is formatted as currency. To save time when entering data in a field that has been formatted as currency—or a field with a data type of number and specified decimal places—you do not have to type the zeros on the right side of the decimal on the right side of the *significant digit*. A significant digit is a number other than 0. If the amount is $10.00, you need to type only *10*. If the amount is $8.05, you must type *8.05*. If the amount is $8.50, type *8.5*.

The Date Picker icon displays on the right of the Last Order field. Recall that clicking the Date Picker opens a calendar from which you can choose a date.

Figure 1.47

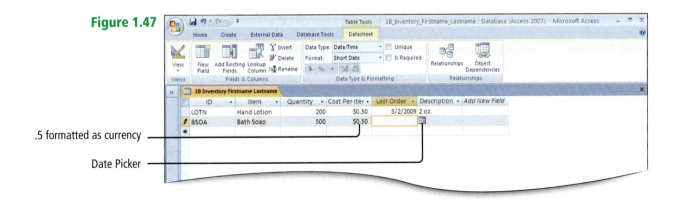

.5 formatted as currency

Date Picker

2 On the second row, in the **Last Order** field box, type **8/29/9** and then press Tab.

Recall that this field has a data type of *Date/Time* and is formatted as *Short Date*. The date may display as 8/29/2009 or as 8/29/09 depending upon the regional settings of your computer.

3 In the **Description** field for the second record, type **4 oz. bar** and then press ⟨Tab⟩ to move to the next record. Alternatively, click in the first field of the third row.

4 Continue entering the records shown in the following list. Do not be concerned if the data does not completely display in the column. Do not be concerned if you type the records out of order. When you have entered the last field of the last record, press ⟨Tab⟩ to save the record, and then compare your screen with Figure 1.48.

Item#	Item	Quantity	Cost Per Item	Last Order	Description
TOWB	Bath Towels	200	15	8/29/9	100% cotton
SHAM	Shampoo	200	.5	11/10/9	4 oz.
COND	Conditioner	200	.5	11/10/9	2 oz.
PILK	King Pillows	100	15	6/15/9	Foam only
PILS	Standard Pillows	100	10	6/15/9	Foam only
ROBE	Terrycloth Robes	50	25	7/19/9	One size
TOWH	Hand Towels	200	8	8/29/9	100% cotton
TOWW	Wash Cloths	200	5	8/29/9	100% cotton
HSOA	Hand Soap	500	.5	1/11/9	3 oz. bar anti-bacterial
TOWE	Beach Towels	200	15	6/29/9	100% cotton, extra long

Figure 1.48

12 records added to the table

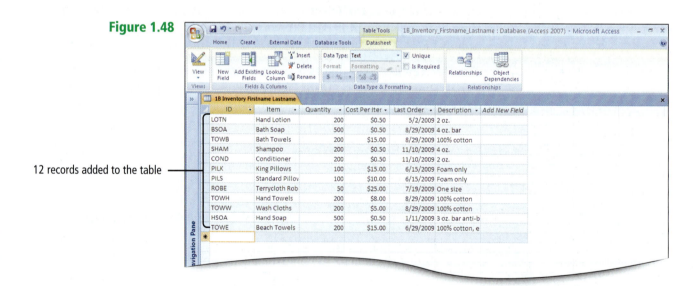

5 On the Ribbon, click the **Home tab**. In the first record, click in the **ID** field—*LOTN*. Using the techniques you practiced in Project 1A, use the spelling checker to correct any errors in the table.

6 On the **Home tab**, in the **Views group**, click the **View** button, and then compare your screen with Figure 1.49. Notice the field names and the data types.

Objects in an Access database have different views. You created the table in Datasheet view. You could also create the structure of the table in Design view and then switch to Datasheet view to enter the records. Because you are viewing the table in Design view, the Design tab displays on the Ribbon. Recall that contextual tabs will display the tools needed to work with a specific object.

On the Design tab, the View button has changed. If you click the View button, you would display the table in Datasheet view. Additional view buttons are located on the right side of the status bar.

Figure 1.49

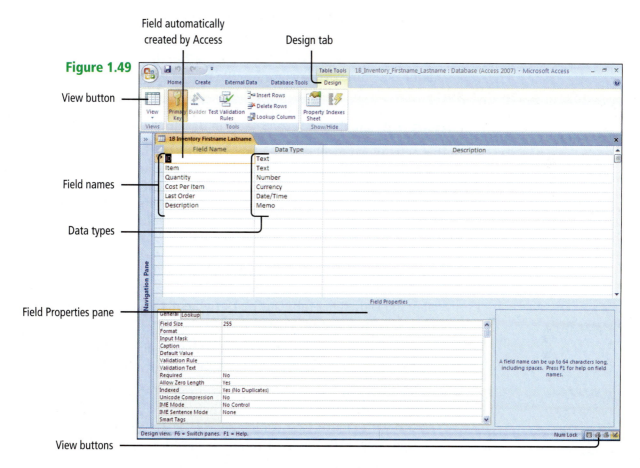

Field automatically created by Access

Design tab

View button

Field names

Data types

Field Properties pane

View buttons

7 Locate the field named **Last Order**, and then click in the associated **Description** box. In the **Field Properties** pane, next to **Format**, notice the Format type—**Short Date**.

Formats are stored as a property of the field.

8 In the **Description** box for the **Last Order** field, type **Date this item was last ordered**

9 On the **Design tab**, in the **Views group**, click the **View** button. Alternatively, click the Datasheet View button on the right side of the status bar. You can also click the View button arrow, and then from the displayed list, select Datasheet View; or on the tab row, right-click the table tab, and then click Datasheet View. In the displayed message box, click **Yes** to save the table.

Anytime you make changes to the structure of the table—you added a description to a field—you will be prompted to save the changes when switching views or closing the table.

10 In the first record, click in the **Last Order** field. Notice that the description you typed displays on the left side of the status bar. Also notice that the records are now in alphabetical order by the ID.

The ID field was automatically created by Access and is the primary key field. By default, the records will be sorted by the primary key field when saved.

11 On the **tab row**, click the **Close** button ☒ to close the *1B Inventory* datasheet. Alternatively, right-click the table tab, and from the displayed shortcut menu, click Close.

Recall that closing the table does not close the database. Notice the database name displays in the title bar.

Activity 1.19 Creating a Second Table in Design View

In this activity, you will create a table to keep track of Eastern Cape Inn suppliers. Creating a table in Design view gives you the most control over the characteristics of the table and the fields. Most database designers use Design view, setting the data types and formats before entering any records. Design view is a good way to create a table when you know exactly how you want to set up your fields.

1 On the Ribbon, click the **Create tab**. In the **Tables group**, click the **Table** button to open an empty table in Datasheet view and to display the Datasheet tab. On the **Datasheet tab**, in the **Views group**, click the **View** button to switch to Design view.

The Save As dialog box displays. Whenever you create an object and switch views, you will be prompted to save the object.

2 In the displayed **Save As** dialog box, under **Table Name**, type **1B Suppliers Firstname Lastname** and then click **OK**. Compare your screen with Figure 1.50, which shows the *1B Suppliers* table open in Design view, with the Design tab displayed.

Notice an ID field has already been created by Access. Recall that the *1B Inventory* table also displayed this field. Access automatically adds this first field to every table you create. Notice the key icon next to the field name, which indicates that this field is the primary key field. The primary function of a primary key field is to ensure that each record is unique. A secondary function of a primary key is to link tables together to perform tasks. Recall that the ID field in the *1B Inventory* table was unique. Access sets a unique property for the primary key field, which prevents duplicate records within the same table. Good database design dictates that every table should have a primary key field. In a table, you can have multiple unique fields, but you should have only *one* primary key field.

Consider a database for the Department of Motor Vehicles that keeps track of the license plates that have been distributed to customers. Because each license plate number is unique to each customer, the license plate should be the primary key field for that database. No two employees should have the same employee number, so the employee number field should be designated the primary key field in a database of employees with employee numbers. If a data entry clerk tried to enter an employee number for a person and typed an existing number into a new record, an error message would display.

If your table has a **natural primary key**—data that cannot be used more than one time, such as an employee number or license plate number—you should designate that field as the primary key field. If your table does not have a natural primary key, then use the automatically created primary key field, which uses a data type of AutoNumber. Recall that AutoNumber will assign the number *1* to the first record, the number *2* to the second record, and so on. You can rename a primary key field.

Figure 1.50

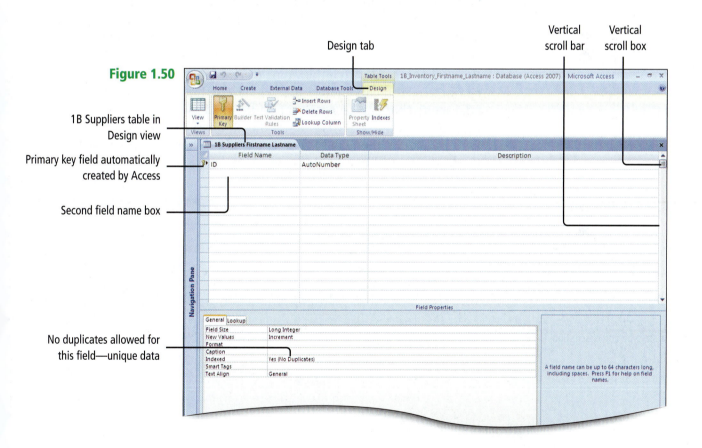

Design tab

Vertical scroll bar

Vertical scroll box

1B Suppliers table in Design view

Primary key field automatically created by Access

Second field name box

No duplicates allowed for this field—unique data

3 Under **Field Name**, under **ID**, click in the empty field name box, type **Name** and then press Tab.

A message displays stating that *Name* is a reserved word and that you might receive an error when referring to this field. You should avoid using reserved words as field or object names. To see a list of reserved words, you can click the Help button and, in the search box, type *reserved words*.

4 In the message box, click **OK** to close the message. Alternatively, click Cancel. In the field name box, double-click **Name** to select the text. Type **Supplier** and then press (Tab) to move to the **Data Type** box.

5 Click the **Data Type arrow** to display a list of data types.

In Design view, all the data types are displayed. In Datasheet view, the list depends on the data entered in the field and does not display Lookup Wizard.

6 From the displayed list, click **Text**, and then press (Tab) to move to the **Description** box. In the **Description** box, type **Supplier's Name**

Field names should be short; use the description field to display more information about the contents of the field.

7 At the bottom of the screen, in the **Field Properties** pane, locate **Field Size**, and then click to the right of **255**. Compare your screen with Figure 1.51.

Field properties are characteristics or attributes of a field that control how the field will display and how the data can be entered in the field. Using this portion of the screen, you can define properties for each field that you create. When you click in any of the property boxes, a description of the property displays to the right. Field properties change depending on the data type of the field.

Recall that a field with a data type of Text can store up to 255 characters. You can change the field size to limit the number of characters that can be entered into the field to ensure accuracy. For example, if you use the two-letter state abbreviations for a state field, limit the size of the field to two characters. When entering a state in the field, you will be unable to type more than two characters.

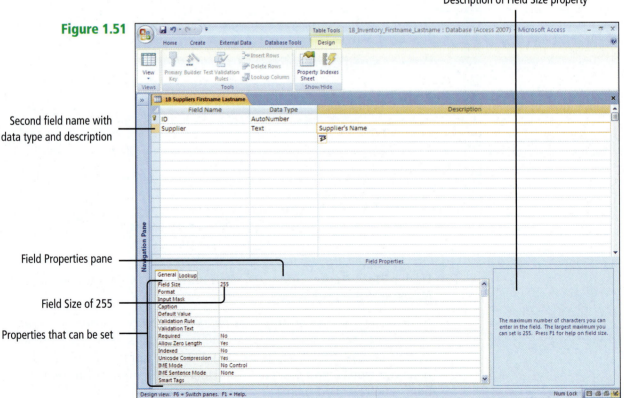

Description of Field Size property

Figure 1.51

Second field name with data type and description

Field Properties pane

Field Size of 255

Properties that can be set

8 Click in the third **Field Name** box, type **Address** and then press [Tab] two times to move to the **Description** box. Type **Enter street address only** and then press [Tab] to move to the fourth **Field Name** box.

Because Text is the default data type, you do not have to select it if it is the correct data type for the field.

9 In the fourth **Field Name** box, type **City** and then press [Tab] three times to move to the next **Field Name** box. Alternatively, press [↓] one time.

The data type for this field is Text, and because the field name is descriptive, no description is necessary.

10 In the fifth **Field Name** box, type **State** and then press [Tab] to move to the **Data Type** box. Press [F6] to move to the **Field Properties** pane. Alternatively, click in the Field Size property box.

Pressing [F6] while in the Data Type column moves the insertion point to the first field property box in the Field Properties pane.

11 With the **Field Size** property of *255* selected, type **2** to change the field size to two characters, and then press [F6] to move back to the top pane.

Pressing [F6] toggles between the top pane and Field Properties pane.

Because the data in the State field will be the state's two-letter abbreviation, changing the field size to 2 will ensure that only two characters can be typed in this field. This does not ensure that the correct two letters will be typed, because you could type *VI* for Virginia instead of *VA* and the data will be accepted because it contains only two characters.

12 Click in the sixth **Field Name** box, and then type **ZIP** Press [Tab] two times to move to the **Description** box, and then type **5-digit ZIP code** Under **Field Properties** and using the techniques you have just practiced, change the **Field Size** property to **5**

The data type of Text is appropriate for this field even though the data is numbers. Recall that a data type of Text can contain text and numbers. You should only use a data type of Number if the number can be used in a calculation. You would not use a ZIP code in a calculation. Other examples of numeric data that should use a data type of text are Social Security numbers, employee numbers, phone numbers, and office numbers.

13 Click in the seventh **Field Name** box, and then type **Phone** Press [Tab] two times to move to the **Description** box, type **Enter as ###-###-####** and then change the **Field Size** property to **12**

14 Click in the eighth **Field Name** box—use the vertical scroll box if necessary—and then type **Product** Press [↓] to move to the ninth **Field Name** box.

15 In the ninth **Field Name** box, type **Del Charge** and then press [Tab] to move to the **Data Type** box. Press [C] to change the data type to **Currency**, press [Tab] to move to the **Description** box, and then type **Charge for Delivery**

You can type the first letter of a data type to select it instead of displaying the list of data types. To select the Number data type, press N. To select the Percent data type, press P.

16 In the **Field Properties** pane, click in the **Format** property box next to **Currency**. To the right of Currency, click the **arrow** to display the formatting options for this field. Compare your screen with Figure 1.52.

The formatting options are the same as those that displayed in Datasheet view for a number. Also, there is no Field Size property, which is a property for a Text data type. The field properties change based on the field data type. The Del Charge format type should be Currency.

Figure 1.52

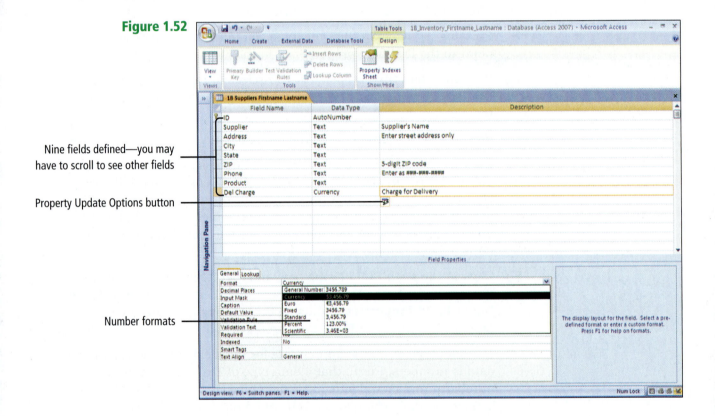

Nine fields defined—you may have to scroll to see other fields

Property Update Options button

Number formats

17 In the **Description** column, under **Charge for Delivery**, click the **Property Update Options** button ⓩ.

You probably noticed that this button displayed after typing in a description for a field. If a field with the same name exists in other tables in the same database, you can add the same description to those fields by clicking Update Status Bar Text everywhere that the field is used.

18 Click anywhere in the **Design view** window to close the Property Update Options list.

Activity 1.20 Creating Records in the Second Table

After the structure of the table has been created, switch to Datasheet view to enter the records in the table.

1 On the **Design tab**, in the **Views group**, click the **View** button to switch to **Datasheet** view. In the message box, click **Yes** to save the table.

2 Click in the **Supplier** field on the first row, and then type **Virginia Coffee Company**

Supplier's Name displays on the left side of the status bar. You typed this in the Description box in Design view for this field. Typing a description helps you to remember what should be entered in a field or how it should be formatted. Do not be concerned if all of your data does not display in the field. Recall that the data type for the ID field is AutoNumber, so as you start typing in another field, the number automatically displays in the ID field.

3 Press Tab to move to the **Address** field, type **6215 Lafayette Park Place** and then notice the description in the status bar. Press Tab to move to the **City** field, and then type **Charlottesville** Notice that in the status bar, no description displays because you did not enter a description for this field.

4 Press Tab to move to the **State** field, and then type **Virginia** Notice that Access allows you to type only *Vi* because you set the field size to 2.

5 Press ←Bksp one time to delete the letter *i*, and then type **A** Press Tab to move to the **ZIP** field, and then type **22904-6215** Notice that you can type only the first five digits of the ZIP code because you set the field size to 5. Also notice that the *5-digit ZIP code* description displays in the status bar.

6 Press Tab to move to the **Phone** field, and then type **434-555-0110**

The *Enter as ###-###-####* description displays in the status bar. This description reminds you how to format the phone number as you type. You also set a field size of 12 so that you can enter up to 12 characters in this field.

7 Press Tab to move to the **Product** field, and then type **Coffee** Press Tab to move to the **Del Charge** field, type **4.5** and then press Tab to move to the next row.

Recall that the Del Charge field is formatted as Currency and that you do not have to type zeros that are to the right of the significant digit in a decimal.

8 Using the techniques you have just practiced, enter the records shown in the following list. Do not be concerned if the data does not completely display in the field. Type the data on one line instead of multiple lines as shown in the table. When you are finished, correct any spelling errors, and then compare your screen with Figure 1.53.

Supplier	Address	City	State	Zip	Phone	Product	Del Charge
Everything Toiletries	372 Hillcrest Ct.	Berkeley	CA	94704	510-555-0010	Personal amenities	10
Plush Comfort	334 S. Cherry St.	Westlake Village	CA	91362	805-555- 0021	Robes	25
New York Restaurant Equipment	2231 Ransdell St.	New York	NY	10014	212-555-0189	China	50.95
Luxurious Linens	102 Orange St.	Chicago	IL	60611	773-555-0176	Linens	36.25
East Coast Kitchen Works	7283 Welchwood Dr.	Philadelphia	PA	19107	215-555-0077	Pantry supplies	16
Capeside Beverages	3432 Willow Glen Ln.	Cape Charles	VA	23310	757-555-2112	Beverages	15
Just Beachy	354 Regent St.	Virginia Beach	VA	23451	757-555-3263	Beach items	0
QuickNet Internet	131 Earhardt Dr.	Eastville	VA	23347	757-555-3019	Internet service	0
Online Virginia	430 N. Moreland Ave.	Richmond	VA	23218	804-555-4689	Web hosting	0

Figure 1.53

Ten records entered

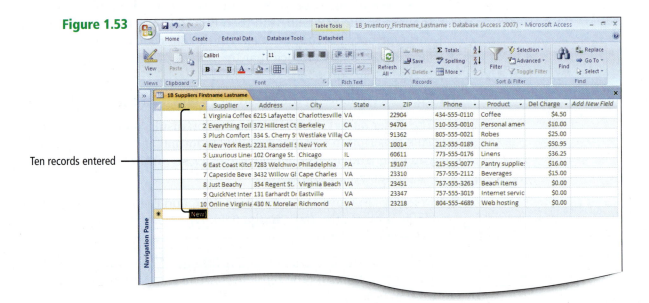

Objective 7
Modify the Table Design

Table design should be carefully planned before entering records in the table, especially when setting data types. There will be times that you must modify the design by designating a primary key field, adding fields, deleting fields, and renaming fields. Design changes can be made in Datasheet view or Design view, but Design view provides more options.

Activity 1.21 Changing the Primary Key

Recall that the function of a primary key is to prevent duplicate records in the same table and to link tables. Although you can create a table without designating a field as a primary key field, good database design dictates that every table should have a primary key field that is unique for each record. In this activity, you will designate a field as the primary key field that differs from the field Access created as the primary key field.

1 Switch the **1B Suppliers** table to **Design** view. Under **Field Name**, click in the second field name box—**Supplier**. On the **Design tab**, in the **Tools group**, click the **Primary Key** button. Alternatively, right-click, and then from the shortcut menu, click Primary Key. Compare your screen with Figure 1.54.

The primary key icon is removed from the ID field and placed in the Row Selector box for the Supplier field. Recall that you can have only one primary key field in a table.

Primary key button

Figure 1.54

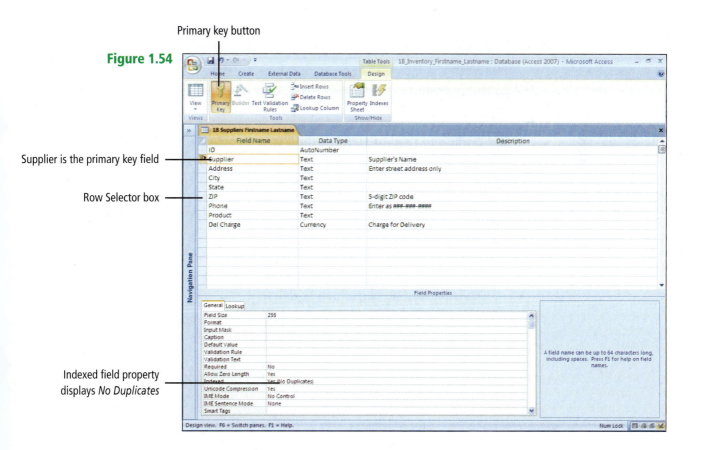

Supplier is the primary key field

Row Selector box

Indexed field property displays *No Duplicates*

2 Switch to **Datasheet** view. In the displayed message box, click **Yes** to save the design change. Notice that the records are in alphabetical order by the Supplier—the new primary key field. In the new record row, click in the **Supplier** field box, type **Just Beachy** and then press ↓.

A message displays, indicating that you cannot enter a record that has the same primary key text—*Just Beachy*—as another record. Recall that a primary key field is unique for every record. If no message displays, you may have spelled the name of the supplier differently from the way it displays in the table.

3 In the displayed message box, click **OK**. In the new record, position the insertion point to the right of *Beachy*, drag to the left until *Just Beachy* is highlighted, and then press Delete. Press ↓.

Another message displays, indicating that the primary key field cannot contain a **null value**—be empty. A primary key field must contain data to ensure that the record is a unique record.

4 In the displayed message box, click **OK**. In the **Supplier** field for the new record, press Esc.

Press Esc in a field to cancel the entry for that field. Press Esc two times to cancel an entry for a field and to cancel the record—this must be done before the record is saved.

Activity 1.22 Deleting, Adding, and Moving Fields in Datasheet View and Design View

In this activity, you will delete, add, and move fields in Design view and in Datasheet view.

1 Switch to **Design** view. In the **Field Name** column, to the left of the **Del Charge** field, point to the **Row Selector** box to display the

→ pointer. Click one time to select the field.

2 On the **Design tab**, in the **Tools group**, click the **Delete Rows** button. Alternatively, press Delete. You can also right-click the selected row, and then from the shortcut menu, click Delete Rows.

A message displays indicating that this field and all of the data in the field will be permanently deleted.

3 In the displayed message box, click **Yes** to delete the field, and then compare your screen with Figure 1.55.

Figure 1.55

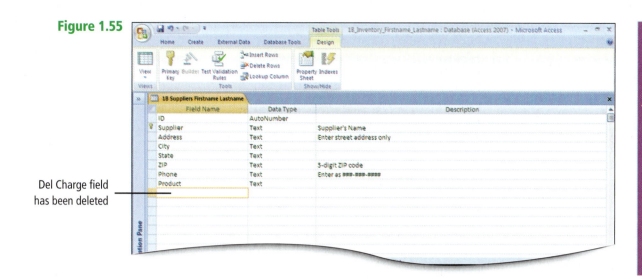

Del Charge field
has been deleted

4 Click the **Shutter Bar Open/Close** button ⟩⟩ to expand the **Navigation Pane**. Right-click the **1B Inventory** table. From the displayed shortcut menu, click **Design View**. Collapse ⟨⟨ the **Navigation Pane**.

When you double-click a table in the Navigation Pane, it opens in Datasheet view. If you want to open it directly into Design view, use the shortcut menu. Both tables are open. The *1B Inventory* table is current and displays in Design view.

5 In the **Field Name** column, locate the **Description** field name, and then click anywhere in the box.

6 On the **Design tab**, in the **Tools group**, click the **Insert Rows** button. Alternatively, right-click, and then from the shortcut menu, click Insert Rows.

A new row is inserted above the Description field. Recall that a row in Design view is a field.

7 In the empty **Field Name** box, type **Good Quality** and then press Tab to move to the **Data Type** column. Click the **Data Type arrow** to display the list of data types, and then click **Yes/No** to set the data type for this field. Compare your screen with Figure 1.56.

A new field has been created in the *1B Inventory* table.

Figure 1.56

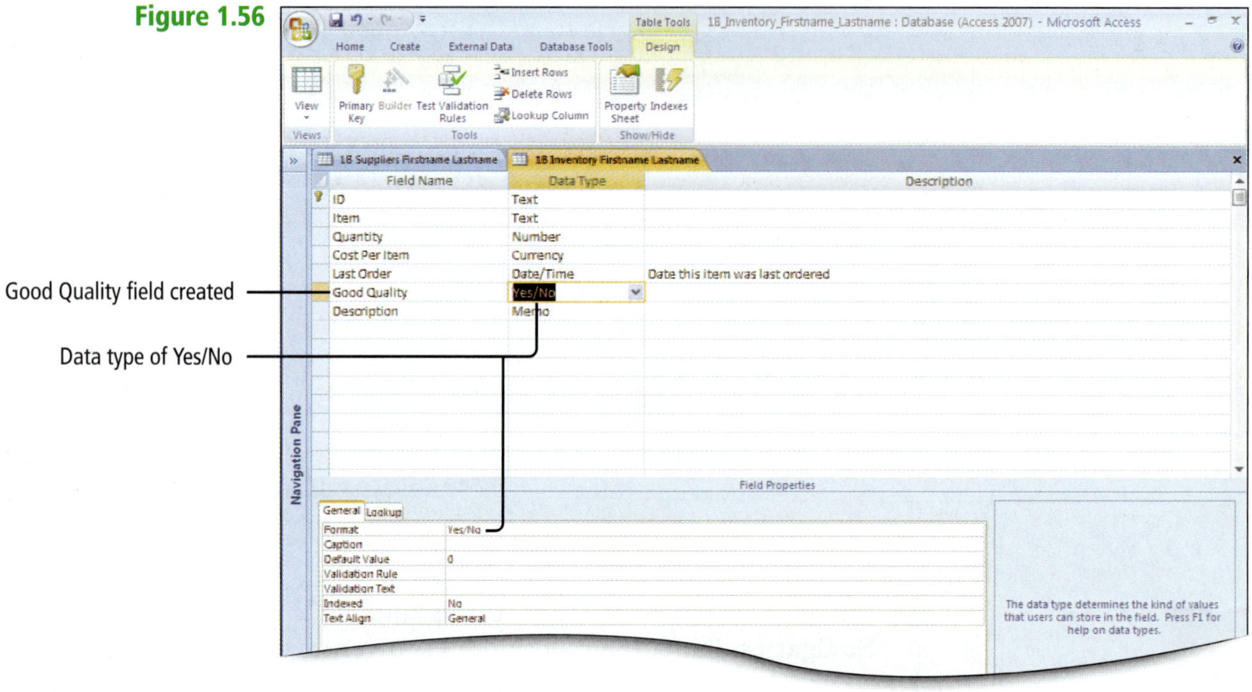

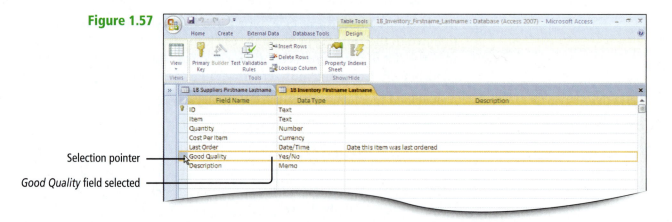

Good Quality field created ——

Data type of Yes/No ——

---

8 Switch the *1B Inventory* table to **Datasheet** view. In the displayed message box, click **Yes** to save the design change.

The Good Quality field displays to the left of the Description field. A check box is displayed in the field. To indicate yes, click in the check box.

9 Switch the *1B Inventory* datasheet to **Design** view. In the **Field Name** column, locate **Good Quality**, and then click the **Row Selector** box to select the field. Point to the **Row Selector** box to display the ⬚ pointer, and then compare your screen with Figure 1.57.

Figure 1.57

Selection pointer ——

Good Quality field selected ——

10 Drag the field up until you see a dark horizontal line between *Item* and *Quantity*, and then release the mouse button. Compare your screen with Figure 1.58.

The Good Quality field is moved after the Item field and before the Quantity field. If you move a field to the wrong position, select the field again, and then drag it to the correct position; or on the Quick Access Toolbar, click the Undo button to place the field back in its previous position.

Figure 1.58

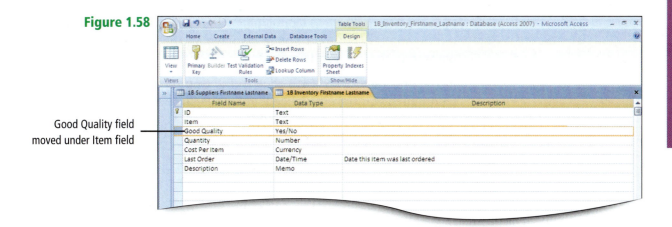

Good Quality field
moved under Item field

11 Switch the *1B Inventory* table to **Datasheet** view. In the displayed message box, click **Yes** to save the design change. Notice that the Good Quality field is moved between Item and Quantity.

12 In the **Good Quality** field, click to select the check boxes for all fields except *King Pillows* and *Standard Pillows*.

Because the pillows are of poor quality, leaving the check box empty is the equivalent of *No*.

13 At the top of the *1B Inventory* table, point to **Description** until the ⬇ pointer displays, and then click one time to select the column. On the Ribbon, click the **Datasheet tab**, and then, in the **Fields & Columns group**, click **Insert**. Alternatively, right-click the selected field and, from the shortcut menu, click Insert Column.

A new field is inserted to the left of the Description field. When you insert a field in Datasheet view, first select the field that will display to the right of the new field. An advantage of adding a field in Design view is that you name the field and set the data type when you insert the field.

14 Double-click **Field1**—the name of your field may differ if you have been experimenting with adding fields—to select the field name. Type **Supplier#** and then press Enter to save the field name.

15 On the first record, click in the empty **Supplier#** field box. In the **Data Type & Formatting group**, click the **Data Type arrow**, and then click **Number**.

You have set the data type for the Supplier# field to Number. Recall that the default format for a Number data type is General Number. Because this field will be used to link to the *1B Suppliers* ID field, which has a data type of AutoNumber, this field must use a data type of Number, even though it will not be used in a calculation.

16 Select the **Supplier#** column. With the ↖ pointer on **Supplier#**, drag to the left until you see a dark vertical line between *Cost Per Item* and *Last Order*. Release the mouse button to move the Supplier# field between the Cost Per Item field and the Last Order field.

As you drag the column, a dark line displays between columns to indicate where the field will display when you release the mouse button. A small rectangular shape displays on the tail of the selection pointer as the column is moved.

17 In the first record—*BSOA*—click in the **Supplier#** field. Using the techniques you have practiced, enter the supplier number for each record shown in the following list, pressing ↓ after each entry to move to the next record.

Item#	Supplier#
BSOA	2
COND	2
HSOA	2
LOTN	2
PILK	5
PILS	5
ROBE	3
SHAM	2
TOWB	5
TOWE	8
TOWH	5
TOWW	5

18 Select the **Good Quality** column. On the **Datasheet tab**, in the **Fields & Columns group**, click the **Delete** button. Alternatively, right-click the selected column, and from the shortcut menu, click Delete Column. In the displayed message box, click **Yes** to delete the field. Compare your screen with Figure 1.59.

The Good Quality field is deleted from the *1B Inventory* table, and the Supplier# field is populated with data.

Figure 1.59

Supplier# field moved between
Cost Per Item and Last Order fields

Supplier# field
populated with data

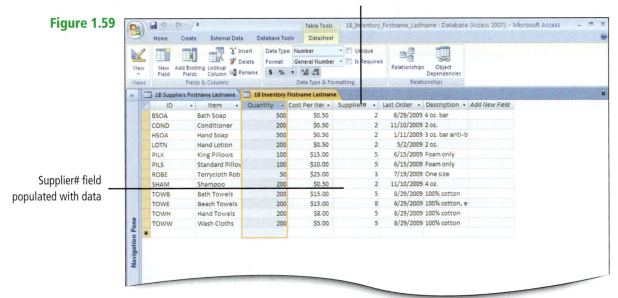

Activity 1.23 Renaming a Field in Datasheet View and Design View

In this activity, you rename fields in Datasheet view and in Design view.

1 At the top of the *1B Inventory* table, click **Cost Per Item** to select the field. On the **Datasheet tab**, in the **Fields & Columns group**, click the **Rename** button. Type **Price** and then press Enter to save the new field name.

Alternatively, double-click a field name to select it, and then type over the selected name; or right-click a field name, and from the shortcut menu, click Rename Column.

2 Switch the *1B Inventory* datasheet to **Design** view. Under **Field Name**, double-click **Quantity** to select the field name. Type **Qty** and then press Enter to save the new field name.

3 Switch the *1B Inventory* datasheet to **Datasheet** view, saving the table when prompted. Compare your screen with Figure 1.60.

Recall that a view is a way of looking at the table. Any changes made in one view will display in the other view.

Figure 1.60

Renamed fields

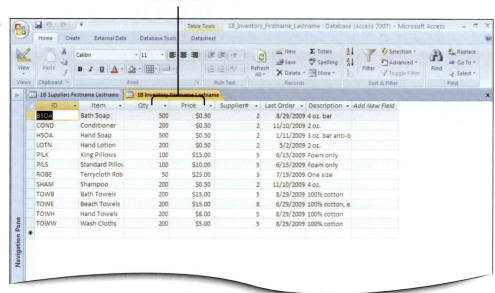

4 On the **tab row**, click the **1B Suppliers tab** to make the *1B Suppliers* table current. Using any of the renaming techniques you just practiced, change the name of the **ID** field to **Supplier#** and make this field the **primary key** field.

5 On the Quick Access Toolbar, click the **Save** button to save changes made to the *1B Suppliers* table. Click the **1B Inventory tab** to make it current, and **Save** changes to the table.

Objective 8
Format a Table for Printing

You should always use the Print Preview command to determine if a table will print on one page or if you must adjust column widths, margins, or the direction the data displays on the page.

Activity 1.24 Changing Column Widths

Although a printed table does not look as professional or formal as a report, there are times when you may want to print your table to use as a quick reference or for proofreading.

1 Be sure that your **1B Inventory** table is open in **Datasheet** view.

Notice that all of the columns are the same width regardless of the width of data that is entered in the field or the field size that was set. If you print the table as currently displayed, some of the data in the Item and Description fields will not be fully displayed. Sometimes the column is not wide enough to display the field name. Thus, it is recommended that you widen the columns to display all of the data and field names.

2 In the column heading row, point to the border between **Item** and **Qty** to display the ✛ pointer, and then compare your screen with Figure 1.61.

Pointer indicating you
can adjust column width

Figure 1.61

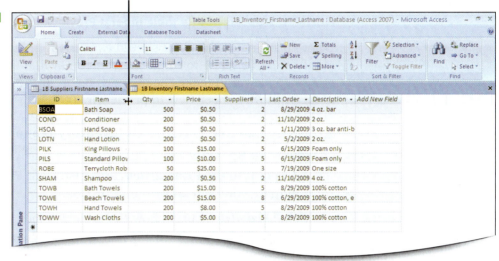

3 With the ✛ pointer positioned as shown in Figure 1.61, double-click the boundary between these two field names.

The column width on the left—the *Item* field—widens to fully display all the data in the field. Double-clicking the right column boundary will increase or decrease the width of the column to fit its contents.

4 Point to the right border of **Supplier#**, and then double-click.

The Supplier# column decreases in width—it is as wide as the field name, which is the widest entry in this column. You can also drag the border to the left or right to adjust the column width. Adjusting the size of columns does not change the data contained in the records—it changes only your *view* of the data.

5 Using the technique you just practiced, adjust each of the column widths so that they are just wide enough to display the data and field name. If necessary, use the horizontal scroll bar to scroll to view all of the columns.

Another Way ── **To Change All of the Column Widths at Once**

In the column headings area, drag to select all of the columns and then double-click any one of the borders to adjust all of the columns to the width required to display the data and field names.

6 **Save** 💾 the changes to the *1B Inventory* table. On the **tab row**, click the **1B Suppliers tab** to make the table current. Switch to **Datasheet** view. Using the techniques you just practiced, adjust all of the column widths in the *1B Suppliers* table, and then **Save** 💾 the design changes. Use the horizontal scroll bar to view columns on the right side.

Activity 1.25 Viewing a Table in Print Preview and Printing a Table

Before printing a table, you should examine it in Print Preview. If adjustments must be made to the table, you can switch back to Datasheet view or Design view and make the changes before printing the table. A table must be in Datasheet view to preview it.

1 On the **tab row**, click the **1B Inventory tab** to make it the current object. In the upper left corner of your screen, click the **Office** button 🔵, point to the **Print arrow**, and then click **Print Preview**. Compare your screen with Figure 1.62.

Print Preview displays how the table will look when printed. Even though the table is hard to read, you can see how all of the fields and data will display on the printed page. The Ribbon displays the Print Preview *program tab*, which replaces the standard set of tabs when you switch to certain authoring modes or views, including Print Preview. Print Preview displays the entire page and enables you to see what the table will look like when printed.

Print Preview tab   1B Inventory in Print Preview

Figure 1.62

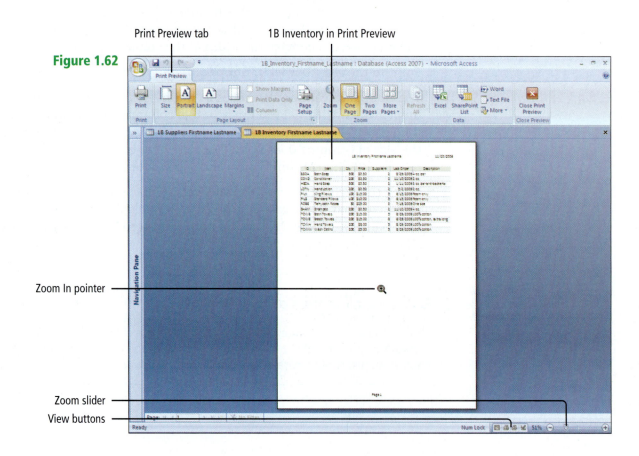

Zoom In pointer

Zoom slider

View buttons

2 Move your mouse until the **Zoom In** pointer 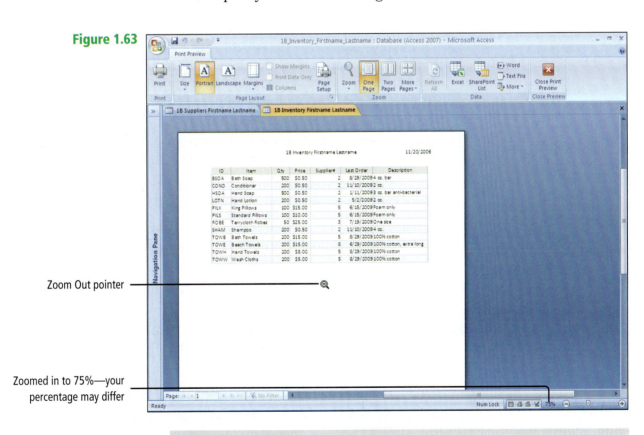 displays at the top of the table, and then click one time. Notice that the **Zoom In** pointer changes to the **Zoom Out** pointer and that you can see all of the data in the table.

You can move the Zoom In pointer to a specific location on the table and click to zoom in on that section. On the right side of the status bar, the Zoom slider displays *100%*. To **zoom** means to increase or to decrease the viewing area of the screen. You can **zoom in** to look closely at a particular section of a table or **zoom out** to see a whole page on the screen.

3 Drag the **Zoom slider** to the left or right until **75%** (or a percentage close to 75%) displays. Alternatively, click the Zoom In button or the Zoom Out button on the Zoom slider until you get near 75%. Compare your screen with Figure 1.63.

Figure 1.63

Zoom Out pointer

Zoomed in to 75%—your percentage may differ

Note — Zoom Percentages

Using the Zoom In or Zoom Out pointers enables only two views, a larger view and a smaller view. The percentages vary depending upon your screen size and resolution. Before using the Zoom slider, clicking the Zoom In pointer displays the object at 100%. Zooming to 100% displays the object in the approximate size it will be when it is printed. When you use the Zoom slider to zoom in or zoom out, the percentages associated with the Zoom In and Zoom Out pointers change. When you reopen the object, the default values for your screen size and resolution will again be associated with these pointers.

4 At the bottom of the window, locate the navigation area, which displays *1* in the **Page** box, and the right-pointing arrow—the **Next** button—is dimmed, which indicates that the table will print on one page.

In Print Preview, the navigation buttons are used to navigate from one page to the next, rather than from one record to the next.

Note — Headers and Footers in Access Objects

A **header** displays at the top of every page, and a **footer** displays at the bottom of every page. The headers and footers in Access *tables* and *queries* are controlled by Access; you cannot add, delete, or edit the information. The name of the object displays in the center of the header area with the current date on the right, which is why adding your own name to the object name is helpful to identify your paper or electronic results. The page number displays in the center of the footer area. The headers and footers in Access *forms* and *reports* can be changed.

---

5 Check your *Chapter Assignment Sheet* or your *Course Syllabus* or consult your instructor to determine whether you are to submit your assignments on paper or electronically. To print on paper, in the **Print group**, click the **Print** button, and then click **OK**. To create an electronic printout, from the **Office** menu [icon], point to **Save As**, and then click **PDF or XPS**. Navigate to the location where you are saving your electronic printouts, and then click **Publish**.

6 On the **Print Preview tab**, in the **Close Preview group**, click the **Close Print Preview** button to display the *1B Inventory* table in **Datasheet** view. On the **tab row**, click the **Close** button [×] to close the *1B Inventory* table. If prompted to save changes to the layout, click **Yes**.

7 Using the technique you just practiced, view the **1B Suppliers** table in **Print Preview**.

8 In the navigation area, in the **Page** box, *1* displays. Notice that the **Next** button is dark—active—indicating that the table will print on multiple pages.

If at all possible, a table should be printed on one page for readability.

9 In the navigation area, click the **Next Page** button [▶].

Page 2 displays, and the Next button is dimmed, indicating there are no more pages.

10 In the navigation area, click the **First Page** button [◄] to display the first page of the table.

11 On the **Print Preview tab**, in the **Page Layout group**, click the **Landscape** button, and then compare your screen with Figure 1.64.

By default, Access prints in *portrait orientation*—the printed page is taller than it is wide. By changing to *landscape orientation*, the printed page is wider than it is tall. Switching to landscape orientation is the first step you should take to print the table on one page. Before adjusting margins, you should always select the page orientation to ensure the margin settings will be correct.

Print Preview tab

Figure 1.64

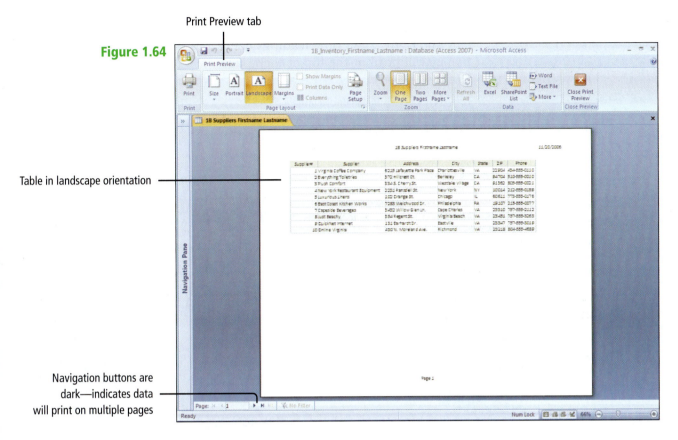

Table in landscape orientation

Navigation buttons are dark—indicates data will print on multiple pages

12 In the **Page Layout group**, click the **Margins** button to display a list of margins as shown in Figure 1.65.

List of margins

Figure 1.65

Margins button

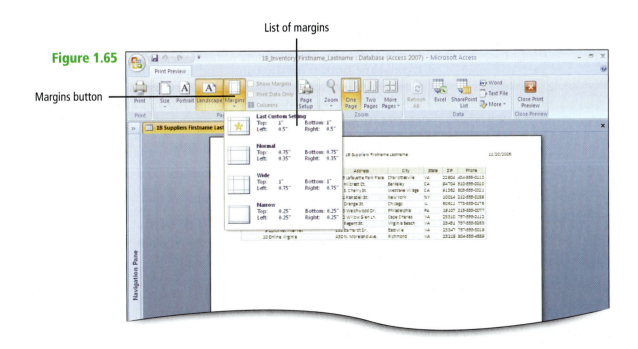

13 Experiment by selecting different margin settings. When you are finished, in the **Page Layout group**, in the bottom right corner, click the **Dialog Box Launcher** to display the **Page Setup** dialog box, and then compare your screen with Figure 1.66.

The Print Options tab of the Page Setup dialog box displays. By default, all Access objects have 1-inch margins for the top, bottom, left, and right. The Print Headings check box is selected—the field names will print at the top of each page.

Dialog Box Launcher

Figure 1.66

Default margins

Will print field names

14 Change the **top** margin to **1.5** and then change the **bottom** margin to **.75** Change the **left** margin to **.75** and the **right** margin to **.75**

15 In the **Page Setup** dialog box, click the **Page tab**.

Under Orientation, Landscape is selected because you clicked the Landscape button on the command tab. To print your table using a printer other than the default printer, select the printer on the Page tab. The Page Setup dialog box gives you more control over the display of the printed document.

16 In the **Page Setup** dialog box, click **OK**.

The table displays with the new margins, and the **Next Page arrow** ▶ indicates there is no further data.

17 On the **Print Preview tab**, in the **Page Layout group**, click the **Margins** button. Notice the margins you set are displayed under **Last Custom Setting**. Press Esc to close the listing. Compare your screen with Figure 1.67.

You can use the custom margin settings with other objects in the database. The navigation arrows are dimmed—inactive—because all of the fields and all of the records display on one page.

If all of the fields in the table do not display on one page, open the Page Setup dialog box and reduce the size of the left and right margins until the table prints on one page.

Figure 1.67

Top margin of 1.5″

Right margin of .75″

Page orientation is landscape

Left margin of .75″

Bottom margin of .75″

Navigation arrows are inactive—the table will print on one page

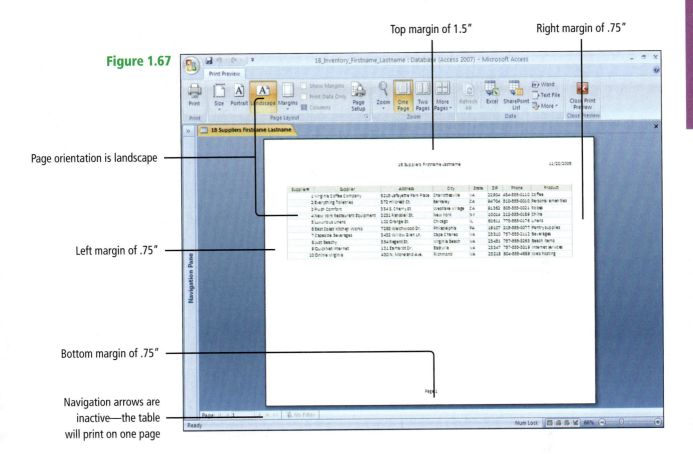

Note — Print Settings Are Not Saved with the Table

Any changes you make to print settings are not saved with the table. Each time you open the table and print, you must check the page orientation, margins, and other print parameters to ensure that the data will print as you intend.

18 Check your *Chapter Assignment Sheet* or *Course Syllabus* or consult your instructor to determine whether you are to submit the table on paper or as an electronic printout. To print on paper, in the **Print group**, click the **Print** button, and then click **OK**. To create an electronic printout, from the **Office** menu, point to **Save As**, and then click **PDF or XPS**. Navigate to the location where you are saving your electronic printouts, and then click **Publish**.

19. On the **tab row**, click the **Close** button ☒ to close the *1B Suppliers* table. Expand 〉〉 the **Navigation Pane**.

20. Click the **Office** button 🔲, and then click **Close Database**.

Click the **Office** button 🔲, and then click the **Exit Access** button.

End **You have completed Project 1B** ——————————

There's More You Can Do!

From My Computer, navigate to the student files that accompany this textbook. In the folder **02_theres_more_you_can_do**, locate and open the folder for this chapter. Open and print the instructions for this project, which are provided to you in Adobe PDF format.

Try It! 1—Saving a Database That Was Created with a Previous Version of Access

In this Try It! project, you will open a database that was created with Access 2003 and save it in the Access 2007 file format.

Content-Based Assessments

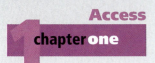

Summary

In this chapter, you started Access and practiced navigating the Access window. You created a database using a template, which had the database structure predefined, and entered records into the database using both a form and the underlying table. You practiced navigating among the records, finding records, and modifying records in addition to hiding fields in the underlying table. The spelling checker tool and Help were demonstrated; and you printed the template table, form, and report.

You then created a database and created two tables in the database using Datasheet view and Design view. You changed data types, data formats and data properties; and set the primary key field. You practiced deleting, adding, modifying, and renaming fields in both Datasheet view and Design view. You changed the column widths to display the longest entry in the field. Finally, you displayed the tables in Print Preview, changed margins and page orientation, and printed the tables.

Key Terms

Content-Based Assessments

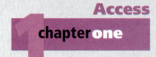
Matching

Match each term in the second column with its correct definition in the first column by writing the letter of the term on the blank line in front of the correct definition.

_____ **1.** A collection of data.

_____ **2.** Facts about people, events, things, or ideas.

_____ **3.** Data that has been organized in a useful manner.

_____ **4.** A ready-to-use database structure that has been created by Microsoft to help you quickly create your own database.

_____ **5.** The components in the database, such as tables, forms, and reports.

_____ **6.** An electronic signature that can be used to authenticate the identity of the sender of a message or the signer of a document.

_____ **7.** The foundation on which an Access database is built.

_____ **8.** The field in which you are ready to enter data.

_____ **9.** A list of context-related commands that displays when you right-click a screen element or object.

_____ **10.** A view that displays data in rows and columns.

_____ **11.** A term that describes columns that are located next to one another.

_____ **12.** The term used to describe that data in a database is usually changing.

_____ **13.** Tools that enable you to perform specific commands related to the current or selected object.

_____ **14.** In the number data type entry of 9.120, the zero is not needed in the data. The digits 9, 1, and 2 are the _____ digits.

_____ **15.** To increase or to decrease the screen view.

A Contextual tools

B Contiguous

C Current field

D Data

E Database

F Datasheet view

G Digital signature

H Dynamic

I Information

J Objects

K Shortcut menu

L Significant

M Tables

N Template

O Zoom

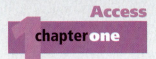

Fill in the Blank

Write the correct word in the space provided.

1. Programs within Access that are used to automate commands and manage databases are called _____.

2. In a table of guest data, the last name of the guest would be a _____.

3. All of the data pertaining to one particular person or thing comprises a(n) _____.

4. A shortcut menu is a list of context-related commands that displays when you _____-_____ a screen element or object.

5. If you run the spelling checker on a table and a data item is high-lighted, it is _____ by the spelling checker.

6. Because Social Security numbers are unique, you should designate that data as the _____ _____ _____.

7. A new database is not useful unless you _____ it with data.

8. When you hold the mouse pointer over an object, a short description called a _____ displays.

9. The cost of an item should have a field _____ _____ selected as currency.

10. The _____ structure includes field names, data types, data formats, and other settings that define the database.

11. Most database designers use _____ _____ to set the data types and formats before entering any records.

12. To change the size of a field, select the field size from the _____ Properties pane.

13. The primary key field cannot be empty. It cannot contain a _____ _____.

14. To look closely at a particular section of a report, you would _____ _____.

15. By changing to _____ orientation, the printed page is wider than it is tall.

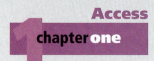

Access

chapter one

Skills Review

Project 1C — Activities

In this project, you will apply the skills you practiced from the Objectives in Project 1A.

Objectives: 1. *Start Access;* **2.** *Create a Database and Enter Data Using a Template;* **3.** *Modify a Template Table;* **4.** *Find, Modify, and Print Records;* **5.** *Use the Access Help System and Exit Access.*

In the following Skills Review, you will create a database to store information about the activities available for the guests who visit Eastern Cape Inn. You will add new activity information to the database and print a table, a form, and a report. Your printouts will look similar to Figure 1.68.

For Project 1C, you will need the following file:

Events database template

You will save your database as
1C_Activities_Firstname_Lastname

Figure 1.68

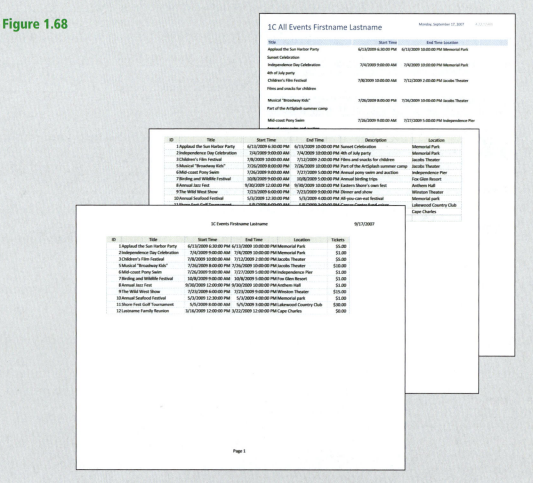

(Project 1C–Activities continues on the next page)

Content-Based Assessments

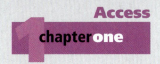
Skills Review

(Project 1C– Activities continued)

1. On the left side of the Windows taskbar, point to and then click the **Start** button. From the displayed **Start** menu, locate the **Access** program, and then click **Microsoft Office Access 2007**.

2. In the **Template Categories** pane, under **Template Categories**, click **Local Templates**. In the **Spotlight** area, click **Events**.

3. To the right of the **File Name** box, click the **Browse** button. In the **File New Database** dialog box, at the right edge of the **Save in** box, click the **Save in arrow** to view a list of the drives available to you.

4. Navigate to the drive on which you will be saving your folders and projects for this chapter. Navigate to the *Access Chapter 1* folder. In the lower portion of the **File New Database** dialog box, locate the **File name** box. If necessary, select or delete the existing text. In the **File name** box, using your own first and last name, type **1C_Activities_Firstname_Lastname** Click **OK**. In the pane at the right side of the window, click the **Create** button.

5. In the message bar, click the **Options** button. In the displayed **Microsoft Office Security Options** dialog box, click the **Enable this content** option button, and then click **OK**.

6. On the **Navigation Pane**, click the **Shutter Bar Open/Close** button to expand the **Navigation Pane**. On the **Navigation Pane**, click the menu title **Events Navigation**. From the displayed list, click **Object Type**. In the **Navigation Page**, under **Tables**, right-click **Events**. From the displayed shortcut menu, click **Rename**. Type **1C Events Firstname Lastname** and then press Enter to rename the table.

7. On the **Navigation Pane**, under **Forms**, right-click **Event List**, and then click **Rename**. Type **1C Event List Firstname Lastname** press Enter, and then double-click the **1C Event List** form. Click the **Navigation Pane**, click the **Shutter Bar Open/Close** button to collapse the **Navigation Pane**. Click the **Attachment** field name to select the field. On the **Home tab**, in the **Records group**, click the **More** button. From the displayed list, click **Hide Columns**.

8. Click in the box under **Title**. In the **Title** field box, type **Applaud the Sun Harbor Party** Press Tab to move to the next fied. In the **Start Time** field box, type **6/13/2009 6:30 PM** and then press Tab to move to the **End Time** field.

9. In the **End Time** field box, type **6/13/2009 10:00 PM** (Note: Access automatically formats the time with a place for seconds.) Press Tab to move to the **Description** field. In the **Description** field box, type **Sunset Celebration** and then press Tab to move to the **Location** field.

10. In the **Location** field box, type **Memorial Park** You will not be entering data in the last field. Press Tab three times to move to the next record.

11. Enter the following records. After typing the last record, press Tab two times to move to the new record row.

Title	Start Time	End Time	Description	Location
Independence Day Celebration	7/4/2009 9:00 AM	7/4/2009 10:00 PM	4th of July party	Memorial Park
Children's Festival	7/8/2009 10:00 AM	7/12/2009 2:00 PM	Films and snacks for children	Jacobs Theater

(Project 1C– Activities continues on the next page)

Content-Based Assessments

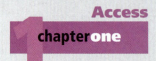

Skills Review

(Project 1C– Activities continued)

Festive Flamenco	7/18/2009 8:00 PM	7/18/2009 10:00 PM	Delightful mix of traditional and new flamenco	Jacobs Theater
Musical "Broadway Kids"	7/26/2009 8:00 PM	7/26/2009 10:00 PM	Part of the ArtSplash summer camp	Jacobs Theater
Mid-coast Pony Swim	7/26/2009 9:00 AM	7/27/2009 5:00 PM	Annual pony swim and auction	Independence Pier
Birding and Wildlife Festival	10/8/2009 9:00 AM	10/8/2009 5:00 PM	Annual birding trip	Fox Glen Resort
Annual Jazz Fest	9/30/2009 12:00 PM	9/30/2009 10:00 PM	Eastern Shore's own fest	Anthem Hall
The Wild West Show	7/23/2009 6:00 PM	7/23/2009 9:00 PM	Dinner and show	Winston Theater
Annual Seafood Festival	5/3/2009 12:30 PM	5/3/2009 4:00 PM	All-you-can-eat festival	Memorial Park
Shore Fest Golf Tournament	5/5/2009 8:00 AM	5/5/2009 3:00PM	Cancer Center fundraiser	Lakewood Country Club

12. On the **tab row**, right-click the **1C Event List** tab. From the shortcut menu, click **Close**. If prompted, click **Yes** to save changes. Expand the **Navigation Pane** to display all of the Access objects in the database. On the **Navigation Pane**, under **Tables**, double-click the **1C Events** table.

13. Collapse the **Navigation Pane**. If necessary, drag the horizontal scroll box to the right until you see the last field. Move the mouse pointer over the **Attachment** field name box to display the ⬇ pointer. Click one time to select the entire field. On the **Home tab**, in the **Records group**, click the **Delete button arrow**. From the **Delete** button list, click **Delete Column** to remove the column. In the message box, click **Yes** to remove the **Attachment** field. In the message box, click **Yes** to remove the field and all its indexes.

14. Click the **Description** field name to select the field. On the **Home tab**, in the **Records group**, click the **More** button. From the displayed list, click **Hide Columns**.

15. Move the mouse pointer to **Add New Field**, right-click to display the shortcut menu, and then click **Rename Column**. Type **Tickets** and then press Enter to create the field. Add the following data to the **Events** table:

(Project 1C– Activities continues on the next page)

Content-Based Assessments

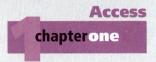

Access

chapter one

Skills Review

(Project 1C– Activities continued)

ID	Tickets
1	$5.00
2	$1.00
3	$5.00
4	$20.00
5	$10.00
6	$1.00
7	$1.00
8	$1.00
9	$15.00
10	$1.00
11	$30.00

16. On the **Home tab**, in the **Records group**, click the **New** button. The New button is dimmed if your insertion point is already located on the New Record row. Press ⟨Tab⟩ one time to move to the **Title** field, and then, substituting your own last name, type **Lastname Family Reunion** Continue entering data in all the fields for a week-long, free reunion at Cape Charles. In the **Start Time** field, use the **Date Picker** to enter the current date. Enter **12:00 PM** for the starting time. Press ⟨Tab⟩ to save the record.

17. On the **Home tab**, in the **Records group**, click the **Spelling** button. Correct any errors.

18. In the **Events** table, click in the **Title** field. On the **Home tab**, in the **Find group**, click the **Find** button. In the **Find and Replace** dialog box, in the **Find What** box, type **Festive Flamenco** and then click the **Find Next** button. In the **Find and Replace** dialog box, click **Cancel** to close the dialog box. Point to the orange **Record Selector** box for the *Festive Flamenco* record until the pointer displays. Click one time to select the entire record. On the **Home tab**, in the **Records group**, click the **Delete button arrow**. From the **Delete** button list, click **Delete Record**. In the message box, click **Yes** to confirm the deletion.

19. In the navigator area, click in the **Search** box. In the **Search** box, type **c** In the **Search** box, continue by typing **h** Click in the field with *Children's Festival* to the right of *Children's*. Press ⟨Spacebar⟩, and then type **Film** Press ⟨↓⟩ to move to the next record and save the change. Adjust all column widths to display all field names and data. Check your *Chapter Assignment Sheet* or your *Course Syllabus* or consult your instructor to determine whether you are to submit the printed pages that are the results of this project. If you are to submit your assignments on paper, follow Steps 20 to 22.

20. Click the **Office** button, point to the **Print** button, and then click **Print Preview**. From the **Print Preview tab**, in the **Page Layout group**, click **Landscape** orientation. To print on paper, in the **Print group**, click the **Print** button, and then click **OK**. To create an electronic printout, from the **Office** menu, point to **Save As**, and then click **PDF or XPS**. Navigate to the location where you are saving your electronic printouts, and then click **Publish**. In the **Close Preview group**, click **Close Print Preview**.

(Project 1C–Activities continues on the next page)

Content-Based Assessments

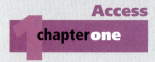
Skills Review

(Project 1C–Activities continues)

21. Expand the **Navigation Pane**. Double-click **1C Event List** to make the form current. Compare your screen with Figure 1.68. Adjust column widths to display all field names and data. Click the **Office** button, point to the **Print** button, and then click **Print Preview**. From the **Print Preview tab**, in the **Page Layout group**, click **LandsCape** orientation. To print on paper, in the **Print group**, click the **Print** button, and then click **OK**. To create an electronic printout, from the **Office** menu , point to **Save As**, and then click **PDF or XPS**. Navigate to the location where you are saving your electronic printouts, and then click **Publish**. **Close** the **Print Preview** window.

22. Under **Reports**, right-click **All Events**, and then click **Rename**. Type **1C All Events Firstname Lastname press** Enter, and then, double-click **All Events** to open the report. On the **Home tab**, in the **Views group**, point to the **View** button, and then select **Layout View**. Drag to select the **All Events** title, and then type **1C All Events Firstname Lastname Save** the form. Compare your screen with Figure 1.68. To print on paper, click the **Office** button, point to the **Print** button, and then click **Quick Print**. To create an electronic printout, from the **Office** menu , point to **Save As**, and then click **PDF or XPS**. Navigate to the location where you are saving your electronic printouts, and then click **Publish**.

23. On the **tab row**, right-click any of the object tabs. From the shortcut menu, click **Close All**. If prompted, click **Yes** to save changes.

24. On the right side of the Ribbon, click the **Help** button. Maximize the Access **Help** window. In the **Search** box, type **templates** and then press Enter. On the displayed list, point to and then click **Create a new database**. In the right pane of the **Help** window, drag the vertical scroll box down to display the end of the information.

25. On the **Help** window title bar, click the **Close** button to exit Help.

26. Click the **Office** button, and then click **Close Database** to close the database. On the **Microsoft Access** title bar, click the **Close** button to exit the Access program.

End You have completed Project 1C —————————————————————

Access

chapter one

Skills Review

Project 1D — Employees

In this project, you will apply the skills you practiced from the Objectives in Project 1B.

Objectives: 6. *Create a New Database and Tables;* **7.** *Modify the Table Design;* **8.** *Format a Table for Printing.*

In the following Skills Review, you will create a new database to be used at Eastern Cape Inn. The database will contain one table with employee information and another table with work schedules for the employees. Your completed tables will look similar to the ones shown in Figure 1.69.

For Project 1D, you will need the following file:
New blank Access database

You will save your database as
1D_Employees_Firstname_Lastname

Figure 1.69

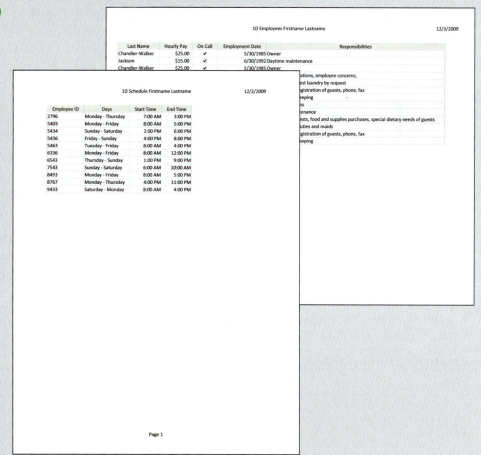

(Project 1D–Employees continues on the next page)

Content-Based Assessments

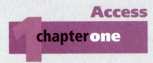
(Project 1D–Employees continued)

1. **Start** Access. In the **Getting Started** window, under **New Blank Database**, click the **Blank Database** button. In the **File Name** box, with the text selected and using your own information, type **1D_Employees_Firstname_Lastname**

2. At the right of the **File Name** box, click the **Browse** button. Navigate to the *Access Chapter 1* folder. Then, in the lower right corner of the **File New Database** dialog box, click **OK**. In the **New Access Database** portion of the screen at the bottom right corner, click the **Create** button to save and open the database.

3. On the **Navigation Pane**, click the **Shutter Bar Open/Close** button to collapse the Navigation Pane.

4. Click the **ID** field column header. On the **Datasheet tab**, in the **Fields and Columns group**, click the **Rename** button. Type **Employee ID** and then press Tab. From the **Datasheet tab**, in the **Data Type & Formatting group**, click the **Data Type arrow**, and then click **Text**. Click the **Add New Field** column header. On the **Datasheet tab**, in the **Fields and Columns group**, click the **Rename** button. Type **Last Name** and then press Tab to move to the third field. Add the following field names, pressing Tab after each field name:

   First Name
   Position
   Pay Rate
   Phone
   Hire Date

5. On the first row, under **Employee ID**, type **1807** and then press Tab to move to the next field. On the first row, under **Last Name**, type **Chandler-Walker** and then press Tab to move to the next field. Under **First Name**, type **Debra** and then press Tab. Under **Position**, type **Owner** and then press Tab. Under **Pay Rate**, type **25** and then press Tab. Under **Phone**, type **(757) 555-0057** and then press Tab. Under **Hire Date**, type **5/30/1985** and then press Tab.

6. On the Quick Access Toolbar, click the **Save** button. In the **Save As** dialog box, under **Table Name** and using your first and last name, type **1D Employees Firstname Lastname** Click **OK**.

7. Under the **Pay Rate** field, click in the first record, and then change the **Data Type** to **Currency**. Click in the **Hire Date** field, and notice the Data Type is **Date/Time**. On the **Datasheet tab**, under **Data Type and Formatting**, click the **Format button arrow**, and then click **Short Date**. Be sure **Text** is selected for the **Data Type** of all of the other fields.

8. On the Quick Access Toolbar, click the **Save** button. If necessary, under **Employee ID** in the second row, click to display the insertion point, and then type the following:

Employee ID	Last Name	First Name	Position	Pay Rate	Phone	Hire Date
2796	Jackson	Emanuel	Maintenance	15	(757) 555-2331	6/30/1992

(Project 1D–Employees continues on the next page)

Content-Based Assessments

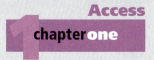

(Project 1D–Employees continued)

9. Continue entering the records shown in the following list:

Employee ID	Last Name	First Name	Position	Pay Rate	Phone	Hire Date
3241	Chandler-Walker	Derek	Owner	25	(757) 555-0057	5/30/1985
5403	Amerline	Dominique	Manager	20	(757) 555-1221	10/1/1986
5434	Oreda	Maria	Laundress	7	(757) 555-9998	2/27/2000
5436	Macintosh	Caleb	Front Desk Clerk	8	(757) 555-7422	1/1/1998
5463	Wright	Janet	Maid	7	(757) 555-9964	3/1/2000
6336	Rosenthall	Louis	Gardener	12	(757) 555-7654	4/1/1998
6543	Cheney	Victor	Maintenance	12	(757) 555-5432	6/1/1994
7543	Matteson	Bradley	Cook	15	(757) 555-1987	1/15/1997
8493	Brondello	Elena	Housekeeping Manager	12	(757)555-8965	6/30/1992
8767	Johnson	Michael	Front Desk Clerk	8	(757) 555-6545	1/1/1990
9433	Rangle	Arlene	Maid	7	(757) 555-7655	3/1/1998

10. In the first record, click in the **Employee ID** field. Click the **Home tab**, and then in the **Records group**, click the **Spelling** button to check the spelling in the table and correct any errors.

11. On the **Home tab**, in the **Views group**, click the **View** button, and then click **Design View**. Locate the field named **Pay Rate**, and then click in the **Description** box associated with this field. Type **Hourly rate - overtime may be required**

12. On the status bar, click the **Datasheet View** button. In the message box, click **Yes** to save the table. On the **tab row**, click the **Close** button to close the *1D Employees* table.

13. Click the **Create tab**. In the **Tables group**, click **Table** to open an empty table in **Datasheet** view and display the **Datasheet tab**. On the **Datasheet tab**, in the **Views group**, click the **View** button to switch to **Design** view. In the **Save As** dialog box, under **Table Name**, type 1D Schedule Firstname Lastname and then click **OK**.

14. In the first field name box, select **ID**, and then type **Employee ID** Press [Tab] to move to the **Data Type** column. Click the **Data Type arrow** to display a list of data types. From the **Data Type** list, click **Text**, and then press [Tab] to move to the **Description** box. In the **Description** box, type **Employee's ID** In the **Field Properties** section, locate **Field Size**, select **255**, and then type **4** to change the field size to four characters. Press [F6] to move back to the top part of the window.

15. Click in the second **Field Name** box, type **Days** and then press [Tab] two times to move to the **Description** box. Type **Days/Nights of the week** Click in the third **Field Name** box and type

(Project 1D–Eastern Cape Inn Employees continues on the next page)

Content-Based Assessments

Skills Review

(Project 1D—Employees continued)

Start Time Press ⟨Tab⟩ to move to the **Data Type** column. Display the **Data Type arrow**, click **Date/Time**, and then press ⟨Tab⟩. In the **Description** box, type **Time employee starts work** In the **Field Properties** section, click **Format**, click the **arrow**, and then select **Medium Time**. Press ⟨F6⟩. In the fourth **Field Name** box, type **End Time** and then select the same data type and format as selected for *Start Time*. In the **Description** box, type **Time employee finishes work** and then press ⟨Tab⟩ to move to the next **Field Name** box. On the **Design tab**, in the **Views group**, click the **View** button to switch to **Datasheet** view. In the message box, click **Yes** to save the table.

16. Click in the **Employee ID** field on the first row, and then type **8767** Press ⟨Tab⟩ to move to the **Days** field, and then type **Monday - Thursday** Press ⟨Tab⟩ to move to the **Start Time** field, and then type **4:00 PM** Press ⟨Tab⟩ to move to the **End Time** field, and then type **11:00 PM**

17. Enter the records shown in the following list, and then correct any spelling errors.

Employee ID	Days	Start Time	End Time
2796	Monday – Thursday	7:00 AM	3:00 PM
5403	Monday – Friday	8:00 AM	5:00 PM
5434	Sunday – Saturday	2:00 PM	6:00 PM
5436	Friday – Sunday	4:00 PM	8:00 PM
5463	Tuesday – Friday	8:00 AM	4:00 PM
6336	Monday – Friday	8:00 AM	12:00 PM
6543	Thursday – Sunday	1:00 PM	9:00 PM
7543	Sunday – Saturday	6:00 AM	10:00 AM
8493	Monday – Friday	8:00 AM	5:00 PM
9433	Saturday – Monday	8:00 AM	4:00 PM

18. On the **Navigation Pane**, click the **Shutter Bar Open/Close** button to expand the **Navigation Pane**. On the **Navigation Pane**, click the menu title. From the displayed list, click **Object Type**. Right-click the **1D Employees** table. From the displayed shortcut menu, click **Design View**. Collapse the **Navigation Pane**. In the **Field Name** column, locate the *Hire Date* field name and click anywhere in the box. On the **Design tab**, in the **Tools group**, click **Insert Row**. In the empty **Field Name** box, type **On Call** and then press ⟨Tab⟩ to move to the **Data Type** column. Click the **Data Type arrow** to display the list of data types, and then click **Yes/No**. Press ⟨Tab⟩ to move to the Description box, and then type **Available if needed** Click the **Save** button.

19. In the **Field Name** column, locate **On Call**, and then click in the **Row Selector** box to select the row. Move the mouse to the **Row Selector** box to display the ▯ pointer. Drag the field up until you see a dark horizontal line between *Pay Rate* and *Phone*, and then release the mouse

(Project 1D—Employees continues on the next page)

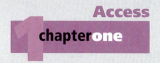
(Project 1D–Employees continued)

button. Switch the *1D Employee* table to **Datasheet** view, and then save your changes when prompted. In the **On Call** field, click the check box for all fields except the *Laundress*, the *Gardener*, and the *Cook*.

20. At the top of the *1D Employees* table, point to **Pay Rate** until the ⬇ pointer displays, and then click one time to select the column. Click the **Datasheet tab**, and then, in the **Fields and Columns group**, click **Insert**. Double-click **Field1** to select the field name. Type **Responsibilities** On the first record under *Responsibilities*, click in the empty field box. On the **Datasheet tab**, in the **Data Type and Formatting group**, click the **Data Type arrow**, and then click **Memo**.

21. Select the **Responsibilities** column. With the ⬉ pointer on **Responsibilities**, drag to the right until you see a black vertical line between *Hire Date* and *Add New Field*, and then release the mouse button. In the first record—*Employee ID 1807*—click in the **Responsibilities** field. Enter the data shown in the following list, pressing ⬇ after each entry to move to the next record.

Employee ID	Responsibilities
1807	Owner
2796	Daytime maintenance
3241	Owner
5403	Day-to-day operations, employee concerns, guest satisfaction
5434	Guest linens, guest laundry by request
5436	Welcome and registration of guests, phone, fax
5463	General housekeeping
6336	Lawn and gardens
6543	Nighttime maintenance
7543	Breakfast for guests, food and supplies purchases, special dietary needs of guests
8493	Housekeeping duties and maids
8767	Welcome and registration of guests, phone, fax
9433	General housekeeping

22. At the top of the *1D Employees* table, click the **Pay Rate** column header to select the field. On the **Datasheet tab**, in the **Fields and Columns group**, click **Rename**. Type **Hourly Pay** and then press Enter to save the new field name.

23. Switch the *1D Employees* datasheet to **Design** view. Under **Field Name**, select **Hire Date**. Type **Employment Date** and then press Enter. **Save** the table.

(Project 1D–Employees continues on the next page)

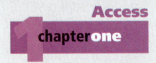

(Project 1D–Employees continued)

24. Open the **1D Schedule** table in **Datasheet** view. In the column heading row, point to the border between *Days* and *Start Time* to display the  pointer. Double-click the boundary between the two field names. Adjust all column widths so that they are just wide enough to display the data and field name.

25. Check your *Chapter Assignment Sheet* or your *Course Syllabus* or consult your instructor to determine whether you are to submit the printed page that is the result of this project. If you are required to turn in printouts, click the **Office** button, point to **Print**, and then click **Print Preview**. To print on paper, in the **Print group**, click the **Print** button, and then click **OK**. To create an electronic printout, from the **Office** menu 🗔 , point to **Save As**, and then click **PDF or XPS**. Navigate to the location where you are saving your electronic printouts, and then click **Publish**. On the **Print Preview tab**, in the **Close Preview group**, click the **Close Print Preview** button to display the *1D Schedule* table in **Datasheet** view. To submit electronically, follow the directions provided by your instructor. On the **tab row**, click the **Close** button to close the *1D Schedule* table. If prompted to save changes to the layout, click **Yes**.

26. Switch the **1D Employees** table to **Datasheet** view. Select the **Employee ID**, right-click the selection, and then click **Hide Columns**. Use the same technique to hide the **First Name**, **Position**, and **Phone** columns. Adjust all column widths to display field names and data.

27. Check your *Chapter Assignment Sheet* or *Course Syllabus* or consult your instructor to determine whether you are to submit the printed page that is the result of this project. If you are required to turn in printouts, on the **Print Preview tab**, in the **Page Layout group**, click the **Dialog Box Launcher**. Change the left and right margins to **.35** Use the default settings for the top and bottom margins. In the **Page Setup** dialog box, click the **Page tab**, and then under **Orientation**, click **Landscape**. Click **OK**. To print on paper, in the **Print group**, click the **Print** button, and then click **OK**. To create an electronic printout, from the **Office** menu 🗔 , point to **Save As**, and then click **PDF or XPS**. Navigate to the location where you are saving your electronic printouts, and then click **Publish**.

28. Redisplay the hidden fields. On the **tab row**, click the **Close** button to close the *1D Employees* table. Expand the **Navigation Pane**.

29. From the **File** menu, click **Close Database**, and then from the **File** menu, click the **Exit Access** button.

End **You have completed Project 1D** ────────────────────

Mastering Access

Project 1E — Antiques

In this project, you will apply the skills you practiced from the Objectives in Project 1A.

Objectives: 1. *Start Access;* **2.** *Create a Database and Enter Data Using a Template;* **3.** *Modify a Template Table;* **4.** *Find, Modify, and Print Records.*

In the following Mastering Access project, you will use a template to create a database of the antique shops around Cape Charles. Your completed table will look similar to the one in Figure 1.70.

For Project 1E, you will need the following file:

Contacts database template

You will save your database as
1E_Antiques_Firstname_Lastname

Figure 1.70

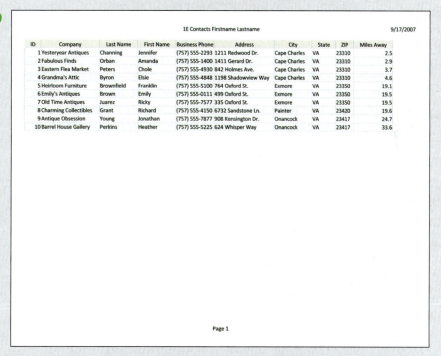

1E Contacts Firstname Lastname   9/17/2007

ID	Company	Last Name	First Name	Business Phone	Address	City	State	ZIP	Miles Away
1	Yesteryear Antiques	Channing	Jennifer	(757) 555-2293	1211 Redwood Dr.	Cape Charles	VA	23310	2.5
2	Fabulous Finds	Orban	Amanda	(757) 555-1400	1411 Gerard Dr.	Cape Charles	VA	23310	2.9
3	Eastern Flea Market	Peters	Chole	(757) 555-4930	842 Holmes Ave.	Cape Charles	VA	23310	3.7
4	Grandma's Attic	Byron	Elsie	(757) 555-4848	1198 Shadowview Way	Cape Charles	VA	23310	4.6
5	Heirloom Furniture	Brownfield	Franklin	(757) 555-5100	764 Oxford St.	Exmore	VA	23350	19.1
6	Emily's Antiques	Brown	Emily	(757) 555-0111	499 Oxford St.	Exmore	VA	23350	19.5
7	Old Time Antiques	Juarez	Ricky	(757) 555-7577	335 Oxford St.	Exmore	VA	23350	19.5
8	Charming Collectibles	Grant	Richard	(757) 555-4150	6732 Sandstone Ln.	Painter	VA	23420	19.6
9	Antique Obsession	Young	Jonathan	(757) 555-7877	908 Kensington Dr.	Onancock	VA	23417	24.7
10	Barrel House Gallery	Perkins	Heather	(757) 555-5225	624 Whisper Way	Onancock	VA	23417	33.6

Page 1

(Project 1E–Antiques continues on the next page)

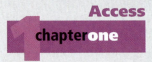

Mastering Access

(Project 1E–Antiques continued)

1. **Start** Access. From the **Template Categories**, click **Local Templates**, and then select the **Contacts** database. **Save** the database as **1E_Antiques_Firstname_Lastname** In response to the Security Alert, enable content. In the **Navigation Pane**, under **Tables**, right-click **Contacts**. From the displayed shortcut menu, click **Rename**. Type **1E Contacts Firstname Lastname** and then press [Enter] to rename the table.

2. Close the **Contact List** form, and then open the **1E Contacts** table. Delete the following fields: **Home Phone**, **Mobile Phone**, **Fax Number**, **Country/Region**, **Web Page**, **Notes**, and **Attachment**. Hide the **E-mail Address** field and the **Job Title** field. Select the **ID** column, and then change the data type from AutoNumber to **Number**. Enter the following data:

ID	Company	Last Name	First Name	Business Phone	Address	City	State/ Province	ZIP/ Postal Code
1	Yesteryear Antiques	Channing	Jennifer	(757) 555-2293	1211 Redwood Dr.	Cape Charles	VA	23310
2	Fabulous Finds	Orban	Amanda	(757) 555-1400	1411 Gerard Dr.	Cape Charles	VA	23310
3	Eastern Flea Market	Peters	Chole	(757) 555-4930	842 Holmes Ave.	Cape Charles	VA	23310
4	Grandma's Attic	Byron	Elsie	(757) 555-4848	1198 Shadowview Way	Cape Charles	VA	23310
5	Heirloom Furniture	Brownfield	Franklin	(757) 555-5100	764 Oxford St.	Exmore	VA	23350
6	Emily's Antiques	Brown	Emily	(757) 555-0111	499 Oxford St.	Exmore	VA	23350
7	Old Time Antiques	Juarez	Ricky	(757) 555-7577	335 Oxford St.	Exmore	VA	23350
8	Charming Collectibles	Grant	Richard	(757) 555-4150	6732 Sandstone Ln.	Painter	VA	23420
9	Antique Obsession	Young	Jonathan	(757) 555-7877	908 Kensington Dr.	Onancock	VA	23417
10	Barrel House	Perkins	Heather	(757) 555-5225	624 Whisper Way	Onancock	VA	23417

(Project 1E–Antiques continues on the next page)

Mastering Access

(Project 1E–Antiques continued)

3. Add a new field to the table design. Name it **Miles Away** Set the data type to **Number**, and use the **General Number** format. Set the **Field Size** to **Single** and **Decimal Places** to **1**. In the **Description** field, type **Miles from downtown Cape Charles** and then populate the table with the following data:

ID	Miles Away
1	2.5
2	2.9
3	3.7
4	4.6
5	19.1
6	19.5
7	19.5
8	19.6
9	24.7
10	33.6

4. Click in the **Search** box, and then type **bar** This will locate the record containing Barrel House in the **Company** field. In the field with **Barrel House**, click to the left of *Barrel*. Press End to move the insertion point to the end of the field, insert a space, and then type **Gallery** Press ↓.

5. Rename the **State/Province** field to **State** and then rename the **ZIP/Postal Code** field to **ZIP** Adjust the column widths so that all field names and data are displayed. **Save** the table.

6. Check your *Chapter Assignment Sheet* or *Course Syllabus* or consult your instructor to determine whether you are to submit the printed page that is the result of this project. If you are required to turn in printouts, from the **Print Preview tab**, in the **Page Layout group**, click **Landscape**. Click **Margins**, and then select **Normal**. If you are instructed to submit this result, create a paper or electronic printout.

7. **Close** the table, expand the **Navigation Pane**, **Close** the database, and **Exit** Access.

End **You have completed Project 1E** ————————————

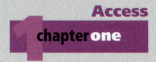

Mastering Access

Project 1F—Food Orders

In this project, you will apply the skills you practiced from the Objectives in Project 1B.

Objectives: 6. *Create a New Database and Tables;* **7.** *Modify the Table Design;* **8.** *Format a Table for Printing.*

In the following Mastering Access project, you will create a new database for the Eastern Cape Inn Dining Room. The Walkers, owners of the inn, open their dining room to guests, local residents, and tourists of Cape Charles for delicious evening meals. The database will contain one table with a category of food items and another table with food brokers. Your completed tables will look similar to those in Figure 1.71.

For Project 1F, you will need the following file:

New blank Access database

You will save your database as
1F_Food_Orders_Firstname_Lastname

Figure 1.71

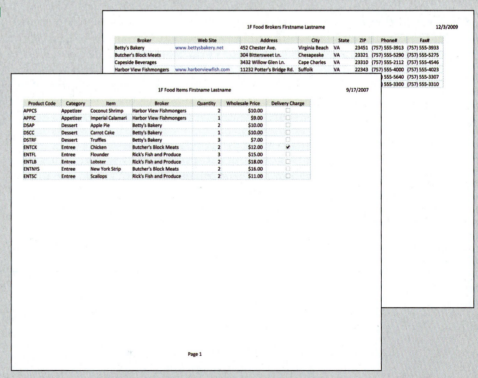

(Project 1F—Food Orders continues on the next page)

Content-Based Assessments

Mastering Access

(Project 1F—Food Orders continued)

1. **Start** Access, and then open a **Blank Database**. Navigate to the *Access Chapter 1* folder, and then save the database as **1F_Food_Orders_Firstname_Lastname**

2. Make the **Add New Field** column current. **Rename** the field **Category** and then press Tab. Add the following field names, pressing Tab after each field name:

   Item
   Delivery Date
   Quantity
   Unit Cost
   Broker

3. Click in the field box under **Category**. Type **Appetizer** and then press Tab to move to the next field. Under **Item**, type **Coconut Shrimp** and then press Tab. Under **Delivery Date**, type **5/11/2009** and then press Tab. Under **Quantity**, type **2** and then press Tab. Under **Unit Cost**, type **10** and then press Tab. Under **Broker**, type **Harbor View Fishmongers** and then press Tab. **Save** the table as **1F Food Items Firstname Lastname**

4. Change the **ID** field data type to **Text**. In the datasheet under **ID**, change the data to **APPCS** and then press Tab. Change the **Unit Cost** field data type to **Currency**. Change the **Delivery Date** field format to **Medium Date**.

5. Enter the records shown in the following list, and then run the spelling checker to correct any errors in the table:

ID	Category	Item	Delivery Date	Quantity	Unit Cost	Broker
APPIC	Appetizer	Imperial Calamari	11-May-09	1	9	Harbor View Fishmongers
ENTSC	Entree	Scallops	18-May-09	2	11	Rick's Fish and Produce
ENTFL	Entree	Flounder	25-May-09	3	15	Rick's Fish and Produce
ENTLB	Entree	Lobster	11-May-09	2	18	Rick's Fish and Produce
ENTCK	Entree	Chicken	18-May-09	2	12	Butcher's Block Meats
ENTNYS	Entree	New York Strip	11-May-09	2	16	Butcher's Block Meats
DSAP	Dessert	Apple Pie	11-Jun-09	2	10	Betty's Bakery
DSCC	Dessert	Carrot Cake	18-May-09	1	10	Betty's Bakery
DSTRF	Dessert	Truffles	25-May-09	3	7	Betty's Bakery

6. Create a new table, and then switch to **Design** view. **Save** the table as **1F Food Brokers Firstname Lastname**

7. Create the following fields: **Broker** as a **Text** field with **Food broker's name** as the description; **Address** as a **Text** field; **City** as a **Text** field; **State** as a **Text** field; **ZIP** as a **Text** field with **5-digit zip code** as the description; **Phone#** as a **Text** field with **Business Phone Number, include Area Code** as the description; and **Fax#** as a **Text** field.

(Project 1F—Food Orders continues on the next page)

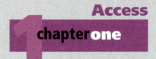
(Project 1F–Food Orders continued)

8. Change the **State** field **Field Size** property from 255 to **2** and then change the **ZIP** field **Field Size** property from 255 to **5** Switch to **Datasheet** view, saving changes when prompted. Populate the table with the following information:

Broker	Address	City	State	ZIP	Phone#	Fax#
Rick's Fish and Produce	6007 Wexford Rd.	Cape Charles	VA	23310	(757) 555-3300	(757) 555-3310
Harbor View Fishmongers	11232 Potter's Bridge Rd.	Suffolk	VA	22343	(757) 555-4000	(757) 555-4023
Betty's Bakery	452 Chester Ave.	Virginia Beach	VA	23451	(757) 555-3913	(757) 555-3933
Butcher's Block Meats	304 Bittersweet Ln.	Chesapeake	VA	23321	(757) 555-5290	(757) 555-5275
Lee's Farm Produce	788 Bennet Dr.	Norfolk	VA	23510	(757) 555-5640	(757) 555-3307
Capeside Beverages	3432 Willow Glen Ln.	Cape Charles	VA	23310	(757)-555-2112	(757) 555-4546

9. Switch the *1F Food Brokers* table to **Design** view. Make the **Broker** field the primary key field, and then select and delete the **ID** field.

10. Display the *1F Food Items* table in **Design** view; insert a new field above the *Broker* field. Name the field **Delivery Charge** and then change the **Data Type** to **Yes/No**. Move the **Broker** field between the *Item* and *Delivery Date* fields.

11. Switch the *1F Food Items* table to **Datasheet** view, and then save changes when prompted. In the **ENTCK** record, click to select the **Delivery Charge** field check box.

12. Switch to the *1F Food Brokers* table, and then switch to **Datasheet** view. Select the **Phone#** field, and then use the shortcut menu to insert a column. Change the field name of the new field to **Web Site** and then press ⏎ to save the field name. On the first record under **Web Site**, click in the empty field box, and then change the **Data Type** to **Hyperlink**. Move the **Web Site** column between the *Broker* and *Address* fields. Enter the records shown in the following list:

Broker	Web Site
Lee's Farm Produce	www.leesfarmproduce.com
Betty's Bakery	www.bettysbakery.net
Harbor View Fishmongers	www.harborviewfish.com

(Project 1F–Food Orders continues on the next page)

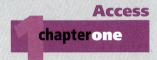

Mastering Access

(Project 1F–Food Orders continued)

13. Switch to the *1F Food Items* table, and then delete the **Delivery Date** field. Change the **Unit Cost** field name to **Wholesale Price** and then switch to **Design** view. Change the **ID** field name to **Product Code** and then press Enter. Switch to **Datasheet** view.

14. Adjust all of the columns in both tables to the width required to display the data and field names. Check your *Chapter Assignment Sheet* or *Course Syllabus* or consult your instructor to determine whether you are to submit the printed page that is the result of this project. On the **Print Preview tab**, in the **Page Layout group**, click the **Margins** button. From the gallery, click **Normal**. Change the print orientation to **Landscape**. If you are instructed to submit this result, create a paper or electronic printout. Repeat this procedure with the *1F Food Brokers* table.

15. **Close** and **Save** the tables, expand the **Navigation Pane**, **Close** the database, and **Exit** Access.

End You have completed Project 1F ——————————————————————

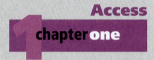

Mastering Access

Project 1G — Business Clients

In this project, you will apply the following Objectives found in Projects 1A and 1B.

Objectives: 1. *Start Access;* **6.** *Create a New Database and Tables;* **7.** *Modify the Table Design;* **8.** *Format a Table for Printing.*

In the following Mastering Access project, you will create a database that consists of a table of business clients in the Cape Charles area. Dominique Amerline, manager of Eastern Cape Inn, wants to organize business clients in Cape Charles who have expressed an interest in using the newly constructed conference room at the inn. Your completed table will look similar to the one in Figure 1.72.

For Project 1G, you will need the following file:

New blank Access database

You will save your database as
1G_Business_Clients_Firstname_Lastname

Figure 1.72

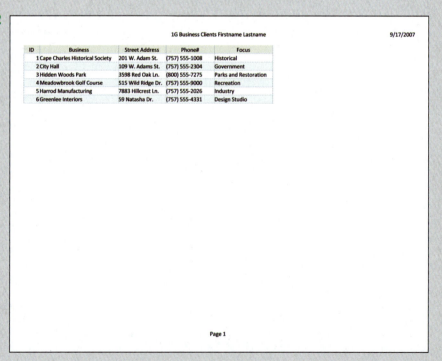

(Project 1G–Business Clients continues on the next page)

Content-Based Assessments

(Project 1G–Business Clients continued)

1. **Start** Access, and then open a **Blank Database**. Navigate to the *Access Chapter 1* folder, and then save the database as **1G_Business_Clients_Firstname_Lastname**

2. Switch to **Design** view. Name the table **1G Business Clients Firstname Lastname** For the **ID** field, change the **Data Type** to **Number**. Click in the field name below **ID**, type **Business** and then press ⬇. Add the following field names, pressing ⬇ after the each field name: **Street Address Phone#** and **Focus** Click in the **Description** box for **Focus**, and then type **Type of Business**

3. Switch to **Datasheet** view. Populate the table with the following data:

ID	Business	Street Address	Phone#	Focus
1	Cape Charles Historical Society	201 W. Adams St.	(757) 555-1008	Historical
2	City Hall	109 W Adams St.	(757) 555-2304	Government
3	Hidden Woods Park	3598 Red Oak Ln.	(800) 555-7275	Parks and Restoration
4	Meadowbrook Golf Course	515 Wild Ridge Dr.	(757) 555-9000	Recreation
5	Harrod Manufacturing	7883 Hillcrest Ln.	(757) 555-2026	Industry
6	Greenlee Interiors	59 Natasha Dr.	(757) 555-4331	Design Studio

4. Adjust all of the columns to the width required to display the data and field names. **Save** the table. On the **Print Preview tab**, in the **Page Layout group**, click the **Margins** button. From the gallery, click **Normal**. Change print orientation to **Landscape**. If you are instructed to submit this result, create a paper or electronic printout.

5. **Close** the table, expand the **Navigation Pane**, **Close** the database, and **Exit** Access.

 End **You have completed Project 1G** ——————————————————

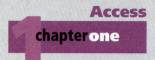

Access

chapterone

Mastering Access

Project 1H—Attractions

In this project, you will apply the following Objectives found in Projects 1A and 1B.

Objectives: 1. *Start Access;* **6.** *Create a New Database and Tables;* **4.** *Find, Modify, and Print Records.*

In the following Mastering Access project, you will create a new database of the attractions that can be found in the city of Virginia Beach. Eastern Cape Inn maintains a listing for the guests who plan a day excursion to Virginia Beach. One table will list the museums, and another table will list the shopping establishments of the area. Your completed tables will look similar to those in Figure 1.73.

> ### For Project 1H, you will need the following file:
>
> New blank Access database

You will save your database as
1H_Attractions_Firstname_Lastname

Figure 1.73

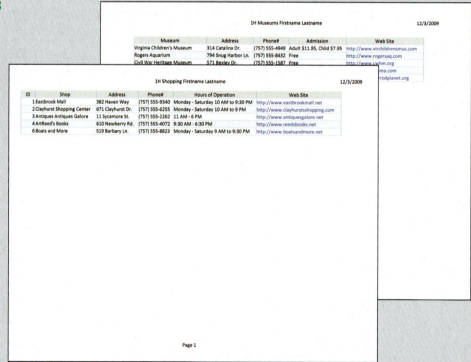

(Project 1H–Attractions continues on the next page)

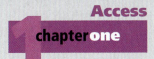

Mastering Access

(Project 1H–Attractions continued)

1. **Start** Access, and then create a new database. Navigate to the *Access Chapter 1* folder, and then **save** the database as **1H_Attractions_Firstname_Lastname**

2. Create a table in **Datasheet** view. Enter the following field names:

   Museum
   Address
   Phone#
   Hours of Operation
   Admission
   Web Site

3. Set the **Data Type** for the **ID** field to **Number**. Set the **Data Type** for the **Hours of Operation** field to **Memo**.

4. Enter the following data:

ID	Museum	Address	Phone#	Hours of Operation	Admission	Web Site
1	Virginia Children's Museum	314 Catalina Dr.	(757) 555-4949	9 AM - 5 PM daily, EST, to Memorial Day, 9 AM - 7 PM, daily, EST Memorial Day - Labor Day.	Adult $11.95, Child $7.95	http://www. virchildrensmus .com
2	Rogers Aquarium	794 Snug Harbor Ln.	(757) 555-8432	Memorial Day Weekend - Labor Day Weekend, Monday - Saturday 10 AM - 5 PM, Sunday Noon - 5 PM. Labor Day Weekend - Memorial Day Weekend, Tuesday-Saturday 10 AM - 5 PM, Sunday Noon - 5 PM. Closed Monday.	Free	http://www. rogersaq.com
3	Civil War Heritage Museum	571 Bexley Dr.	(757) 555-1587	Monday - Saturday 10 AM - 5 PM. Sunday Noon - 5 PM.	Free	http://www. cwhm.org
4	Virginia Museum of Modern Art	689 W. 54th St.	(757) 555-0000	Tuesday - Friday 10 AM 5 PM. Saturday 10 AM 4 PM. Sunday Noon 4 PM. Closed Monday.	Free	http://www. vmma.com
5	Harrod Planetarium	390 Bancroft Ln.	(757) 555-4067	Tuesday 7 PM, reservations suggested.	Free	http://www. harrodplanet. org

(Project 1H–Attractions continues on the next page)

Content-Based Assessments

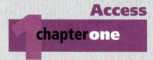
(Project 1H–Attractions continued)

5. Run the **spelling checker**. **Save** the table as **1H Museums Firstname Lastname**

6. Create a second table for this database. Set the **Data Type** for the **ID** field to **Number**, and then set the **Data Type** for the **Hours of Operation** field to **Memo**. Enter the following field names and data:

ID	Shop	Address	Phone	Hours of Operation	Web Site
1	Eastbrook Mall	382 Haven Way	(757) 555-9340	Monday - Saturday 10 AM - 9:30 PM.	http://www. eastbrookmall.net
2	Clayhurst Shopping Center	671 Clayhurst Dr.	(757) 555-6255	Monday - Saturday 10 AM - 9 PM.	http://www. clayhurstsshopping.com
3	Antiques Antiques Galore	11 Sycamore St.	(757) 555-2262	11 AM - 6 PM.	http://www. antiquesglaore.net
4	ArtReed's Books	610 Newberry Rd.	(757) 555-4072	9:30 AM – 6:30 PM.	http://www. reedsbooks.net
5	Fun in the Sun	8721 Boulevard Pl.	(757) 555-0964	10 AM - 9 PM.	http://www. funinthesun.com
6	Boats and More	519 Barbary Ln.	(757) 555-8823	Monday - Saturday 9 AM - 9:30 PM.	http://www. boatsandmore.net

7. Run the **spelling checker**. **Save** the table as **1H Shopping Firstname Lastname**

8. Use **Find and Replace** to locate the *Fun in the Sun* shop. **Delete** the entire record for this entry. **Save** the table.

9. Adjust the column widths so that all field names and data are displayed. **Print Preview** the *1H Shopping* table, and then select **Landscape** orientation and **Normal** margins. If you are instructed to submit this result, create a paper or electronic printout.

10. In the *1H Museums* table, hide the **ID** and the **Hours of Operation** fields. Adjust the column widths so that all field names and data are displayed. **Print Preview** the *1H Museums* table, and then select **Landscape** orientation. If you are instructed to submit this result, create a paper or electronic printout.

11. **Close** and **Save** the tables, expand the **Navigation Pane**, **Close** the database, and **Exit** Access.

End   **You have completed Project 1H**

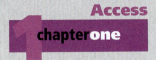

Mastering Access

Project 1I—Dining Out

In this project, you will apply all the skills you practiced from the Objectives in Projects 1A and 1B.

In the following Mastering Access project, you will create a database of the restaurants in the Cape Charles region. Eastern Cape Inn maintains a listing for the guests who plan to dine out during their visits. You will use a template to which you will add two tables. Your completed tables will look similar to Figure 1.74.

For Project 1I, you will need the following file:

Contacts database template

**You will save your database as
1I_Dining_Out_Firstname_Lastname**

Figure 1.74

Restaurant	Last Name	First Name	E-mail Address	Business Phone
Blue Heron Seafood	Your Lastname	Your Firstname		(757) 555-3123
Clamdigger Café	Masters	George	gmasters@clamdiggercafe.net	(757) 555-2092
Corey's Seafood	Brigs	Lewis	coreysseafood@quicklsp.net	(757) 555-2305
Della's	McFarland	Swanie	dellas@mail101.net	(757) 555-1541
Garfield Inn and Restaurant	Porter	Maray	garfield@garfieldinn.net	(757) 555-7400
Italian Bistro	Anders	Paul		(757) 555-7831
Java Café	Engle	Mike		(757) 555-1880
Ray's Lobster Pound	Kline	LD		(757) 555-5759
Soup and More	Combs	Wanda		(757) 555-1212
Wildfire Grill	Fischer	Scott		(757) 555-3005

1I Contacts Firstname Lastname   9/17/2007

State	Zip	Web Site
VA	2	http://www.blueheronseafood.net
VA	2	http://www.clamdiggercafe.net
VA	2	http://www.coreysseafood.com
VA	2	http://www.dellasrest.net
VA	2	http://www.garfieldinnandrest.net
VA	2	http://www.italbistro.com
VA	2	http://www.javacafe.net

1I Restaurants Firstname Lastname   9/17/2007

Restaurant	Type	Cuisine	Specialty	Address	City
Blue Heron Seafood	Fine Dining	Seafood Bistro	Crab Cakes	8215 Auburn Ridge	Cape Charles
Clamdigger Cafe	Casual	Seafood	Stuffed Flounder and Clams	4112 Marshall Dr.	Exmore
Corey's Seafood	Casual	Seafood	Steamed Crabs and Homemade Chili	918 Auburn Rd.	Cape Charles
Della's	Fine Dining	Seafood	Local Fish	8742 Whitecliff Way	Cape Charles
Garfield Inn and Restaurant	Fine Dining	American	Ice Cream	5333 Clairborne St.	Onancock
Italian Bistro	Casual	Homemade Italian	Lasagna	563 W 54th St.	Nassawadox
Java Cafe	Casual	Coffee, Sandwiches, and Desserts	Cappuccino and Chocolate Torte	2447 Appleton Dr.	Cape Charles
Ray's Lobster Pound	Casual	Seafood	Lobster	3324 Franklin Rd.	Machipongo
Soup and More	Casual	Southern Homestyle	Sandwiches and Soups	590 Meadowlark Rd.	Cape Charles
Wildfire Grill	Casual	American	Shrimp Quesadillas	619 Rosalind Ct.	Cape Charles

1I Restaurants Firstname Lastname   9/17/2007

Page 1

(Project 1I–Dining Out continues on the next page)

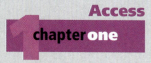
(Project 1I–Dining Out continued)

1. **Start** Access. In the **Template Categories** pane, click **Local Templates**, and then select the **Contacts** database. Navigate to the *Access Chapter 1* folder, and then **save** the database as **1I_Dining_Out_Firstname_Lastname** In response to the Security Warning, select **Enable this content**. Enter the following data in the **Contact List** form:

ID	First Name	Last Name	E-mail Address	Business Phone	Company
1	Paul	Anders		(757) 555-7831	Italian Bistro
2	Lewis	Brigs	coreysseafood@quickisp.net	(757) 555-2305	Corey's Seafood
3	Wanda	Combs		(757) 555-1212	Soup and More
4	Mike	Engle		(757) 555-1880	Java Cafe
5	Scott	Fischer		(757) 555-3005	Wildfire Grill
6	LD	Kline		(757) 555-5759	Ray's Lobster Pound
7	George	Masters	gmasters@clamdiggercafe.net	(757) 555-2092	Clamdigger Cafe
8	Swanie	McFarland	dellas@mail101.net	(757) 555-1541	Della's
9	Maray	Porter		(757) 555-7400	Garfield Inn and Restaurant
10	Your Firstname	Your Lastname		(757) 555-3123	Blue Heron Seafood

2. Close the **Contact List** form. Rename the **Contacts** table to **1I Contacts Firstname Lastname** In the **1I Contacts** table, hide all nonpopulated fields. Change the primary key field from ID to **Company**. Hide the **ID** field. **Rename** the **Company** field **Restaurant** Adjust column widths to display all field names and data.

3. Create a table for the following restaurant data. Name the table **1I Restaurants Firstname Lastname** Include the field names as listed. Set the **Restaurant** field the primary key field. Determine appropriate data types and field sizes. Run the **spelling checker** on your entries.

Restaurant	Type	Cuisine	Specialty	Address	City	State	Zip	Web Site
Italian Bistro	Casual	Homemade Italian	Lasagna	563 W. 54th St.	Nassa-wadox	VA	23413	http://www. italbistro.com
Corey's Seafood	Casual	Seafood	Steamed Crabs and Homemade Chili	918 Auburn Rd.	Cape Charles	VA	23310	http://www. coreysseafood. com
Soup and More	Casual	Southern Homestyle	Sandwiches and Soup	590 Meadowlark Rd.	Cape Charles	VA	23310	http://www. soupandmore.net
Java Cafe	Casual	Coffee, Sandwiches, and Desserts	Coffee, Sandwiches, and Desserts	2447 Appleton Dr.	Cape Charles	VA	23310	http://www. javacafe.net

(Project 1I–Dining Out continues on the next page)

Content-Based Assessments

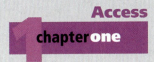

Mastering Access

(Project 1I–Dining Out continued)

Wildfire Grill	Casual	American	Shrimp Quesadillas	619 Rosalind Ct.	Cape Charles	VA	23310	http://www. wildfiregrill.net
Ray's Lobster Pound	Casual	Seafood	Lobster	3324 Franklin Rd.	Machipongo	VA	23405	http://www. rayslobsterpound. com
Clamdigger Cafe	Casual	Seafood	Stuffed Flounder and Clams	4112 Marshall Dr.	Exmore	VA	23350	http://www. clamdiggercafe.net
Della's	Fine Dining	Seafood	Local Fish	8742 White- cliff Way	Cape Charles	VA	23310	http://www. dellasrest.net
Garfield Inn and Restaurant	Fine Dining	American	Ice Cream	5333 Clair- borne St.	Onan- cock	VA	23417	http://www. garfieldinnandrest. net
Blue Heron Seafood	Fine Dining	Seafood Bistro	Crab Cakes	8215 Auburn Ridge	Cape Charles	VA	23310	http://www. blueheronseafood. net

4. Change the field size for the **State** field to **2** Adjust all column widths to display all field names and data. **Save** the table.

5. In the *Contacts* table, use **Find and Replace** to locate *Garfield Inn and Restaurant*. Add **garfield@garfieldinn.net** as the e-mail address. **Save** the table.

6. Go to Access **Help**. In the **Search** box, type **print** and then click **Search**. From the displayed list, locate **Print with landscape orientation**, and then read the information. **Close** the **Help** window.

7. If you are instructed to submit this result, create a paper or electronic printout of the *1I Restaurants* table in **Landscape** orientation and with **Normal** margins. This table will print on two pages. **Print** the *1I Contacts* table in **Portrait** orientation and with **Normal** margins. If you are instructed to submit this result, create a paper or electronic printout.

8. **Close** and **Save** the tables, expand the **Navigation Pane**, **Close** the database, and **Exit** Access.

End **You have completed Project 1I**

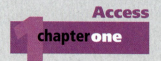

Business Running Case

Project 1J — Business Running Case

In this project, you will apply the skills you have practiced from the Objectives in Projects 1A and 1B.

From My Computer, navigate to the student files that accompany this textbook. In the folder **03_business_running_case**, locate and open the folder for this chapter. Open and print the instructions for this project, which are provided to you in Adobe PDF format. Follow the instructions and use the skills you have gained thus far to assist the brother and sister team of Michael and Kristen Landry in meeting the challenges of owning and running their business.

End **You have completed Project 1J** ————————————

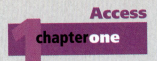

Access

Rubric

The following outcomes-based assessments are *open-ended assessments*. That is, there is no specific correct result; your result will depend on your approach to the information provided. Make *Professional Quality* your goal. Use the following scoring rubric to guide you in *how* to approach the problem and then to evaluate *how well* your approach solves the problem.

The *criteria*—Software Mastery, Content, Format and Layout, and Process—represent the knowledge and skills you have gained that you can apply to solving the problem. The *levels of performance*—Professional Quality, Approaching Professional Quality, or Needs Quality Improvement—help you and your instructor evaluate your result.

	Your completed project is of Professional Quality if you:	Your completed project is Approaching Professional Quality if you:	Your completed project Needs Quality Improvements if you:
Software Mastery	Choose and apply the most appropriate skills, tools, and features and identify efficient methods to solve the problem.	Choose and apply some appropriate skills, tools, and features, but not in the most efficient manner.	Choose inappropriate skills, tools, or features, or are inefficient in solving the problem.
Content	Construct a solution that is clear and well organized, contains content that is accurate, appropriate to the audience and purpose, and is complete. Provide a solution that contains no errors of spelling, grammar, or style.	Construct a solution in which some components are unclear, poorly organized, inconsistent, or incomplete. Misjudge the needs of the audience. Have some errors in spelling, grammar, or style, but the errors do not detract from comprehension.	Construct a solution that is unclear, incomplete, or poorly organized, containing some inaccurate or inappropriate content; and contains many errors of spelling, grammar, or style. Do not solve the problem.
Format and Layout	Format and arrange all elements to communicate information and ideas, clarify function, illustrate relationships, and indicate relative importance.	Apply appropriate format and layout features to some elements, but not others. Overuse features, causing minor distraction.	Apply format and layout that do not communicate information or ideas clearly. Do not use format and layout features to clarify function, illustrate relationships, or indicate relative importance. Use available features excessively, causing distraction.
Process	Use an organized approach that integrates planning, development, self-assessment, revision, and reflection.	Demonstrate an organized approach in some areas, but not others; or, use an insufficient process of organization throughout.	Do not use an organized approach to solve the problem.

Outcomes-Based Assessments

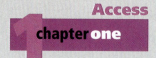

Problem Solving

Project 1K—DVD Collection

In this project, you will construct a solution by applying any combination of the skills you practiced from the Objectives in Projects 1A and 1B.

For Project 1K, you will need the following file:

New blank Access database or Microsoft Access template

You will save your database as
1K_DVD_Collection_Firstname_Lastname

In addition to the dining room and the expansive porch where guests can gather to enjoy each other's company, Eastern Cape Inn has a family recreation room with a state-of-the-art entertainment center. There is a collection of DVDs provided for the guests. You may use items from the following sample, or you may use DVDs from your personal collection.

You can assist the manager of the inn by creating a database to organize this collection. Create a table in Microsoft Access that will list the DVD by title, genre (for example, Comedy, Mystery, Romance, Science Fiction, and so on), rating, and year of release. Check the table for spelling errors. Adjust the column widths so that all field names and data are displayed. Save the database as **1K_DVD_Collection_Firstname_Lastname** and then if you are instructed to submit this result, create a paper or electronic printout.

Sample data:

Title	Genre	Rating	Release
Napoleon Dynamite	Comedy	PG	2004
Love Actually	Romantic Comedy	R	2004
Paycheck	Action/Suspense	PG-13	2002
Elf	Comedy	PG	2003
The Count of Monte Cristo	Action/Suspense	PG-13	2002
The Interpreter	Suspense	PG-13	2004
Star Wars III: Revenge of the Sith	Action	PG-13	2005
Aviator	Historical Fiction	PG-13	2004
Spiderman	Action	PG-13	2002
The Phantom of the Opera	Musical	PG-13	2004
The Princess Bride	Action/Comedy	PG	1987
The Patriot	Action	R	2000
Harry Potter and the Chamber of Secrets	Children's	PG	2002

End **You have completed Project 1K** ———————————————

Outcomes-Based Assessments

Access

chapter one

Problem Solving

Project 1L—Maintenance

In this project, you will construct a solution by applying any combination of the skills you practiced from the Objectives in Projects 1A and 1B.

For Project 1L, you will need the following file:

New blank Access database or Microsoft Access template

You will save your database as
1L_Maintenance_Firstname_Lastname

Mr. Dominique Amerline is the manager of Eastern Cape Inn. In this project, you will create a database table of items that require a regular maintenance schedule. Include items such as painting walls, replacing light bulbs, sanding and refinishing the hardwood floors, opening and closing the pool, cleaning the fireplace and chimney, washing windows, repairing window screens, and so on. Include fields to list such things as the dates of maintenance, cost, and time involved. You may create your table with or without a template. Use a variety of data types, but be sure to use them appropriately. Check the table for spelling errors. Adjust the column widths so that all field names and data are displayed. Save the database as **1L_Maintenance_Firstname_Lastname** and then if you are instructed to submit this result, create a paper or electronic printout.

End **You have completed Project 1L** ——————

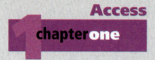

Problem Solving

Project 1M—Food Inventory

In this project, you will construct a solution by applying any combination of the skills you practiced from the Objectives in Projects 1A and 1B.

For Project 1M, you will need the following file:

New blank Access database or Microsoft Access template

You will save your database as
1M_Food_Inventory_Firstname_Lastname

Chef Bradley Matteson needs to keep a food inventory for the kitchen at Eastern Cape Inn. In this project, you will create a table to list the items needed to prepare a full breakfast for 20 guests. In addition to listing the foods and the amount of each item in stock, you should consider special dietary needs, purchase costs, and seasonal availability (fresh or frozen). A Yes/No check box data type will let the chef know whether there is sufficient inventory or whether he needs to schedule a delivery of an item. You may create your table with or without a template. Use a variety of data types, but be sure to use them appropriately. Check the table for spelling errors. Adjust the column widths so that all field names and data are displayed. Save the database as **1M_Food_Inventory_Firstname_Lastname** and then if you are instructed to submit this result, create a paper or electronic printout.

End **You have completed Project 1M** ———————————

Outcomes-Based Assessments

Access
chapter one

Problem Solving

Project 1N — Beach Equipment

In this project, you will construct a solution by applying any combination of the skills you practiced from the Objectives in Projects 1A and 1B.

For Project 1N, you will need the following file:

New blank Access database or Microsoft Access template

You will save your database as
1N_Beach_Equipment_Firstname_Lastname

The owners of Eastern Cape Inn want to provide all the beach extras for their guests. The inn prides itself on having an extensive collection of beach supplies. This includes items such as bicycles, beach chairs, umbrellas, volleyball sets, and boogie boards. You can assist the manager of the inn by creating a database to track this collection. Create a table in Microsoft Access that lists the items. Include information such as whether a guest has checked out the item, the name of the guest, checkout time, and time returned. You may create your table with or without a template. Check the table for spelling errors. Adjust the column widths so that all field names and data are displayed. Save the database as **1N_Beach_Equipment_Firstname_Lastname** and then if you are instructed to submit this result, create a paper or electronic printout.

End You have completed Project 1N —————

Outcomes-Based Assessments

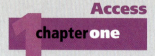
Project 10 — Books

In this project, you will construct a solution by applying any combination of the skills you practiced from the Objectives in Projects 1A and 1B.

For Project 10, you will need the following file:

New blank Access database or Microsoft Access template

**You will save your database as
10_Books_Firstname_Lastname**

Eastern Cape Inn has a small library of classic and contemporary novels. If a guest wants to check out a book for those rainy days, late nights, or sunny afternoons on the beach, the library is the room to visit. Create a table in Microsoft Access that will list the book by title, author, and genre (Mystery, Romance, Biography, and Science Fiction). You might want to add fields that list the number of pages, type of cover (hard or soft), and a check box for indicating whether or not the book is checked out. List at least 10 titles that would be available in the library. You may create your table with or without a template. Check the table for spelling errors. Adjust the column widths so that all field names and data are displayed. Save the database as **10_Books_Firstname_Lastname** and then if you are instructed to submit this result, create a paper or electronic printout.

End You have completed Project 10 ————————————

Outcomes-Based Assessments

 You and *GO!*

Project 1P — You and *GO!*

In this project, you will construct a solution by applying any combination of the Objectives found in Projects 1A and 1B.

From My Computer, navigate to the student files that accompany this textbook. In the folder **04_you_and_go**, locate and open the folder for this chapter. Open and print the instructions for this project, which are provided to you in Adobe PDF format. Follow the instructions to create a table of your insured household items.

 End **You have completed Project 1P** ——————————

GO! with Help

Project 1Q — *GO!* with Help

The Access Help system is extensive and can help you as you work. In this project, you will view information about getting help as you work in Access.

1 **Start** Access. On the right side of the Ribbon, click the **Microsoft Office Access Help** button. In the **Type words to search for** box, type **help** Click the **Search arrow**.

2 In the displayed **Search** drop-down list, click **Access Help**. Maximize the displayed window, and at the top of the window, click the **Show Table of Contents** link. Click **Getting help**. Scroll through and read all the various ways you can get help while working in Access.

3 If you want, print a copy of the information by clicking the **Print** button at the top of Access Help window. If you are instructed to submit this result, create a paper or electronic printout.

4 Close the **Help** window, and then **Exit** Access.

 End **You have completed Project 1Q** ——————————

2 chaptertwo

Sorting, Filtering, and Querying Databases

OBJECTIVES

At the end of this chapter you will be able to:

1. Open and Rename an Existing Database
2. Sort Records
3. Filter Records
4. Open, Edit, Sort, and Print an Existing Query
5. Create Table Relationships and a Simple Query

6. Create a Select Query
7. Specify Criteria in a Query
8. Specify Compound Criteria in a Query

OUTCOMES

Mastering these objectives will enable you to:

Project 2A
Display Specified Records in a Database

Project 2B
Retrieve Information from a Database

Laurel County Community College

Laurel County Community College (LCCC) is located in eastern Pennsylvania and serves urban, suburban, and rural populations. The college offers this diverse area a broad range of academic and vocational programs, including associate degrees, certificate programs, and noncredit continuing education and personal development courses. LCCC makes positive contributions to the community through cultural and athletic programs and partnerships with businesses and nonprofit organizations. The college also provides industry-specific training programs for local businesses through its economic development center.

Sorting, Filtering, and Querying a Database

A well-designed database is a collection of data that can be converted into meaningful, useful information. People who gather data usually want to extract information from the database based on some question. For example, if you have a database with data about your DVD collection, you may want to display a listing of all of the comedy DVDs or all of the live concert DVDs. When you extract that information, you will probably want to display it in a certain order; for example, in alphabetical order by the title of the DVD or in order by the DVD release date. In this chapter, you will extract data from the database and turn it into meaningful, useful information that can be used to make decisions.

Project 2A Athletic Events

Laurel County Community College uses sorting techniques, filters, and queries to locate information about the data in its databases. In Activities 2.1 through 2.13, you will assist Pavel Linksz, vice president of student services, in locating information about the game schedules of the athletic teams. Your results will look similar to those in Figure 2.1.

For Project 2A, you will need the following file:

a02A_Athletic_Events

You will save your database as
2A_Athletic_Events_Firstname_Lastname

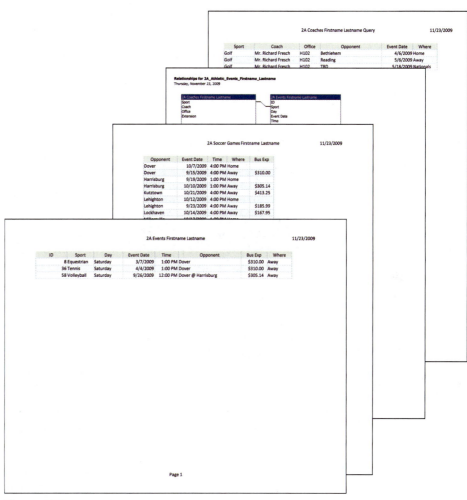

Figure 2.1
Project 2A—Athletic Events

Objective 1
Open and Rename an Existing Database

When you open a database for editing, you may need to preserve the original database. That way, if you encounter problems while editing a copy of the database, the original database is still intact, and the original objects and the data in them can be retrieved.

Activity 2.1 Opening and Renaming an Existing Database

In this activity, you will open an existing database and save it with another name.

1 **Start** Access. Click the **Office** button 🗔 , and then click **Open**. Alternatively, under Open Recent Database, click More.

2 On the left side of the **Open** dialog box, click **My Computer**, and then navigate to the location where the student data files for this textbook are saved. Locate and then click to select **a02A_Athletic_Events**. In the lower right corner of the **Open** dialog box, click **Open**. Alternatively, double-click the file name.

The a02A_Athletic_Events database opens, and a Security Warning message displays in the message bar.

Note — Using File Extensions

The computer you are using may be set to display file extensions. If so, this file name will display as *02A_Athletic_Events.accdb*. The *.accdb* extension indicates that this file is a Microsoft Access 2007 database file. Older versions of Access database files have an extension of *.mdb*.

3 Click the **Office** button 🗔 , point to the **Save As arrow**, and then under **Save the database in another format**, click **Access 2007 Database**. In the **Save As** dialog box, click **My Computer** to view a list of the available drives. Navigate to the drive on which you will be saving your folders and projects for this chapter.

4 In the **Save As** dialog box, click the **Create New Folder** button 🗀 . In the displayed **New Folder** dialog box, in the **Name** box, type **Access Chapter 2** and then click **OK**.

5 In the **Save As** dialog box, locate the **File name** box. Using your own first and last name, type **2A_Athletic_Events_Firstname_Lastname** as shown in Figure 2.2.

Figure 2.2

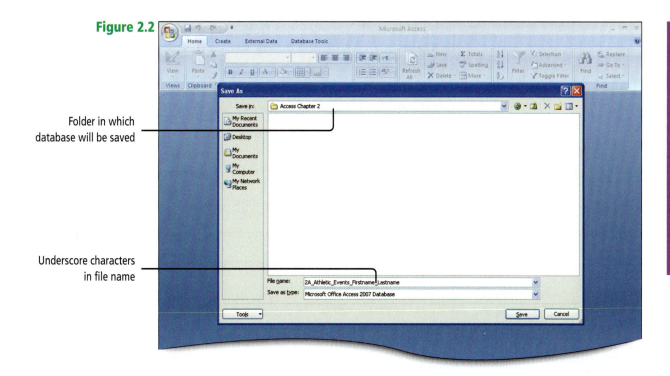

Folder in which database will be saved

Underscore characters in file name

6 In the **Save As** dialog box, click the **Save** button, or press Enter.

Your database is saved on the storage device that you selected, and it is saved in the *Access Chapter 2* folder with the new file name. The new file name also displays in the title bar. The original file remains unchanged.

7 In the message bar, click the **Options** button. In the displayed **Microsoft Office Security Options** dialog box, click the **Enable this content** option button, and then click **OK**.

The message bar closes, and the security warning no longer displays. Recall that every time you open a database, a security warning displays in the message bar.

8 Click the **Office** button 🔘, and then click **Close Database**. In the **Getting Started with Microsoft Office Access** window, under **Open Recent Database**, click **2A_Athletic_Events** to reopen the database. Notice that the **Security Warning** again displays.

Using the Enable Content button disables the Security Alert for the database for the time that you have the database open. When you close the database and reopen it, you must enable the content again.

Activity 2.2 Adding a File Location to Trusted Locations

In this activity, you will add the location of your database files for this chapter and the location of the student data files to the *Trust Center*—a security feature that checks documents for macros and digital signatures. When you open any database from a location displayed in the Trust Center, no security warning will display. You should not designate the My Documents folder as a trusted location because others may try to gain access to this known folder.

1 In the message bar, click the **Options** button. In the **Microsoft Office Security Options** dialog box, in the lower left corner, click **Open the Trust Center**.

2 In the **Trust Center** window, in the left pane, click **Trusted Locations**, and then compare your screen with Figure 2.3.

The right pane displays the locations that are trusted sources. A *trusted source* is a person or organization that you know who will not send you databases with malicious code. Under Path and User Locations, there is already an entry. A *path* is the location of a folder or file on your computer or storage device.

Figure 2.3

Location on computer for Access Wizard databases

Trusted locations

Information about selected path

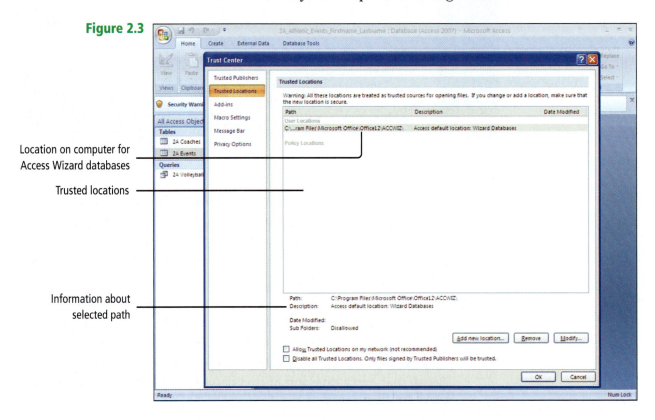

3 In the **Trusted Locations** pane, at the lower right, click **Add new location**. In the **Microsoft Office Trusted Location** dialog box, click **Browse**. In the **Browse** dialog box, navigate to where you saved your *Access Chapter 2* folder, double-click **Access Chapter 2**, and then click **OK**. Compare your screen with Figure 2.4.

The Microsoft Office Trusted Location dialog box displays the path to a trusted source of databases. Notice that you can trust any subfolders in the *Access Chapter 2* folder.

Figure 2.4

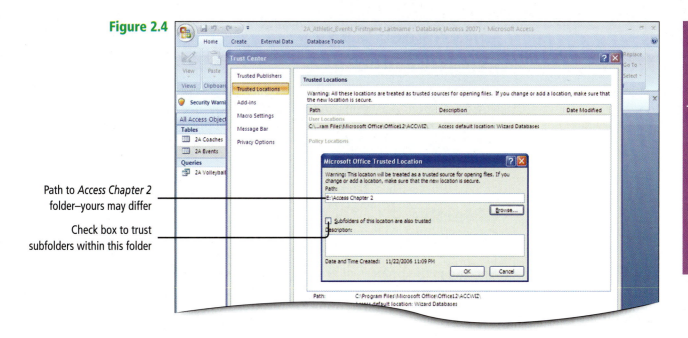

Path to *Access Chapter 2* folder—yours may differ

Check box to trust subfolders within this folder

4 In the **Microsoft Office Trusted Location** dialog box, under **Description**, using your own first and last name, type **Databases created by Firstname Lastname** and then click **OK**.

The Trusted Locations pane displays the path of the *Access Chapter 2* folder. You will no longer receive a security warning when you open databases from this location.

5 Using the technique you just practiced, add the location of your student data files to the Trust Center. For the description, type **Student data files created for GO! Series**

You should add to the Trust Center only locations that you know are secure locations. If other people have access to the databases and can change the information in the database, the location is not secure.

6 At the lower right corner of the **Trust Center** dialog box, click **OK**. In the displayed **Microsoft Office Security Options** dialog box, click **OK**.

The message bar no longer displays—you opened the database from a trusted location.

7 Click the **Office** button , and then click **Close database**. In the **Getting Started** window, under **Open Recent Database**, click **2A_Athletic_Events**.

The database opens, and the message bar with the Security Alert does not display. Using the Trust Center button is an efficient way to open databases that are saved in one location.

More Knowledge

Remove a Trusted Location

Click the Office button [icon], and then click the Access Options button. In the Access Options dialog box, in the left pane, click Trust Center. In the right pane, click the Trust Center Settings button, and then click Trusted Locations. Under Path, click the trusted location that you want to remove, and then click the Remove button.

Objective 2
Sort Records

Sorting is the process of arranging data in a specific order based on the value in a field. For example, a company might want to display specific product data according to the delivery date or by the supplier's name.

Initially, records in an Access table display in the order in which they were entered. If you change the primary key field from the ID field that Access automatically generates, then the records display in order based on the new primary key field.

You can sort data in either *ascending order* or *descending order*. Ascending order sorts text alphabetically (A to Z) and sorts numbers from the lowest number to the highest number. Descending order sorts text in reverse alphabetical order (Z to A) and sorts numbers from the highest number to the lowest number.

Activity 2.3 Sorting Records in Ascending and Descending Order

Laurel County Community College (LCCC) sponsors athletic teams that compete with other community colleges in eastern Pennsylvania. The president of LCCC, Diane Gilmore, likes to attend as many events as possible. She cannot attend athletic events on Wednesdays because she has meetings. If Ms. Gilmore cannot attend or if more than one event is scheduled for the same date, she asks other administrators to attend on her behalf. In this activity, you will sort records in the Athletic Events database to group the events by team, day of the week, and event date.

1 On the **Navigation Pane**, under **Tables**, right-click **2A Events**. From the displayed shortcut menu, click **Rename**. Click to the right of *2A Events*, and then press [Spacebar] one time. Using your own first and last name, type **Firstname Lastname** and then press [Enter] to rename the table *2A Events Firstname Lastname*.

Note — Naming Conventions

A ***naming convention*** is a set of rules that an organization uses to standardize the naming of objects. Many organizations require that all table names begin with *tbl*; for example, *tblEvents*. A query might be named qryVolleyballgames. Another common naming convention is not to have spaces in object names. If an Access database will be used with other database management systems, you should contact the database administrator to see whether there are naming conventions so that you do not have to rename all of your objects at a later date.

2 Double-click **2A Events Firstname Lastname** to display the table in Datasheet view. Collapse ⟪ the **Navigation Pane**. Notice that the table is sorted in ascending order by the ID number.

Recall that Access creates a primary key field named ID with a data type of AutoNumber to ensure that no duplicate records are entered in a table. Each sporting event has a unique ID number. This is the order that the records were entered into the table. By default, Access sorts tables by the primary key field.

3 In the **Sport** field, click in any record. On the **Home tab**, in the **Sort & Filter group**, click the **Ascending** button ⬆. Compare your screen with Figure 2.5.

The records display in alphabetical order by Sport. To sort records, first, click in any record in the field (column) on which you want to sort. A sort icon displays next to the Sort & Filter arrow in the field name box for Sport. Because the same sport names are now grouped, you can quickly scroll the length of the datasheet to see which teams have the greatest number of scheduled events. Changing the sort order does not change the value in the ID field. Sorting changes only the way the data in the table is displayed. On the Home tab, in the Sort & Filter group, the Clear All Sorts button is active—this button is active only when a sort has been applied to a field.

Figure 2.5

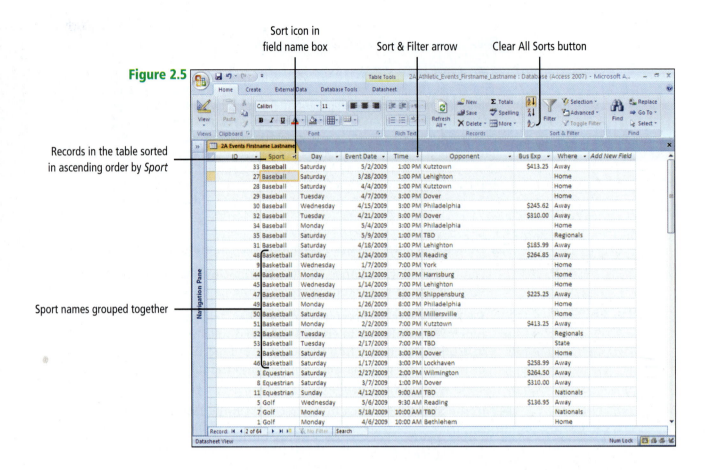

Sort icon in field name box

Sort & Filter arrow

Clear All Sorts button

Records in the table sorted in ascending order by *Sport*

Sport names grouped together

4 On the **Home tab**, in the **Sort & Filter group**, click the **Clear All Sorts** button to remove the sort from the Sport field. In the **Day** field, click in any record in the field. In the **Sort & Filter group**, click the **Descending** button .

The records in the table are sorted in reverse alphabetical order by Day. Because Wednesday begins with the letter *W*, all events scheduled for Wednesday display first. You can scroll down to see the grouping by days.

5 Using the technique you just practiced, click the **Clear All Sorts** button , and then sort the **Event Date** field, displaying the dates in order from the earliest date to the latest date. If necessary, scroll down to locate duplicate dates, starting with *3/28/2009*. Compare your screen with Figure 2.6.

You can see that on 3/28/2009, there is a tennis match scheduled for 3:00 PM and a baseball game scheduled for 1:00 PM.

Figure 2.6

Sorted in ascending
order by Event Date

Events scheduled
for the same date

ID	Sport	Day	Event Date	Time	Opponent	Bus Exp	Where	Add New Field
9	Basketball	Wednesday	1/7/2009	7:00 PM	York		Home	
2	Basketball	Saturday	1/10/2009	3:00 PM	Dover		Home	
44	Basketball	Monday	1/12/2009	7:00 PM	Harrisburg		Home	
45	Basketball	Wednesday	1/14/2009	7:00 PM	Lehighton		Home	
46	Basketball	Saturday	1/17/2009	3:00 PM	Lockhaven	$258.99	Away	
47	Basketball	Wednesday	1/21/2009	8:00 PM	Shippensburg	$225.25	Away	
48	Basketball	Saturday	1/24/2009	5:00 PM	Reading	$264.85	Away	
49	Basketball	Monday	1/26/2009	8:00 PM	Philadelphia		Home	
50	Basketball	Saturday	1/31/2009	3:00 PM	Millersville		Home	
51	Basketball	Monday	2/2/2009	7:00 PM	Kutztown	$413.25	Away	
52	Basketball	Tuesday	2/10/2009	7:00 PM	TBD		Regionals	
53	Basketball	Tuesday	2/17/2009	7:00 PM	TBD		State	
3	Equestrian	Saturday	2/27/2009	2:00 PM	Wilmington	$264.50	Away	
8	Equestrian	Saturday	3/7/2009	1:00 PM	Dover	$310.00	Away	
6	Tennis	Saturday	3/28/2009	3:00 PM	Harrisburg	$305.14	Away	
27	Baseball	Saturday	3/28/2009	1:00 PM	Lehighton		Home	
28	Baseball	Saturday	4/4/2009	1:00 PM	Kutztown		Home	
36	Tennis	Saturday	4/4/2009	1:00 PM	Dover	$310.00	Away	
1	Golf	Monday	4/6/2009	10:00 AM	Bethlehem		Home	
29	Baseball	Tuesday	4/7/2009	3:00 PM	Dover		Home	
37	Tennis	Tuesday	4/7/2009	3:00 PM	Philadelphia		Home	
38	Tennis	Saturday	4/11/2009	1:00 PM	Kutztown	$413.25	Away	
11	Equestrian	Sunday	4/12/2009	9:00 AM	TBD		Nationals	
30	Baseball	Wednesday	4/15/2009	3:00 PM	Philadelphia	$245.62	Away	
39	Tennis	Wednesday	4/15/2009	3:00 PM	Harrisburg		Home	
31	Baseball	Saturday	4/18/2009	1:00 PM	Lehighton	$185.99	Away	
32	Baseball	Tuesday	4/21/2009	3:00 PM	Dover	$310.00	Away	

Record: 1 of 64

Datasheet View

Another Way — **To Sort Records in a Table**

Access provides three other methods for sorting table records:

- In any record, right-click in the field you want to use for the sort, and then click the sort method.
- In any field name, right-click and then click the sort method.
- In the field name box, click the Sort & Filter arrow, and then, from the sort and filter list, click the sort method.

6 In the **Sort & Filter group**, click the **Clear All Sorts** button.

Clearing all sorts does not remove the sort from the primary key field.

Activity 2.4 Sorting Records on Multiple Fields

Pavel Linksz would like to compare the home and away games to ensure that LCCC teams have an equal number of home and away games among opponents. He would like to first display away games and then home games for each opponent. Access enables you to sort on two or more fields in a table.

1 Using the techniques you practiced in Activity 2.3, sort the **Where** field in **Ascending** order. Scroll down to display the data in the **Where** field and to verify the data is sorted in ascending order.

The field displays Away games, then Home games, then Nationals, then Regionals, and then finally State.

2 With the **Where** field still sorted, click anywhere in the **Opponent** field, and then sort the field in **Ascending** order. Scroll down to display the records under *Opponent* for *Philadelphia*, and then compare your screen with Figure 2.7.

When you sort by multiple fields, it is important to sort the fields in the correct order. The field used for the major grouping—in this instance, Opponent—should be sorted last. Access first sorted this table by the Where field—the first field you selected—grouping the records by Away, Home, and so on. Then, Access sorted the Opponent field—the second field—which regrouped the records and displayed them in alphabetical order. Within each Opponent name, the records are in ascending order by the Where field.

Figure 2.7

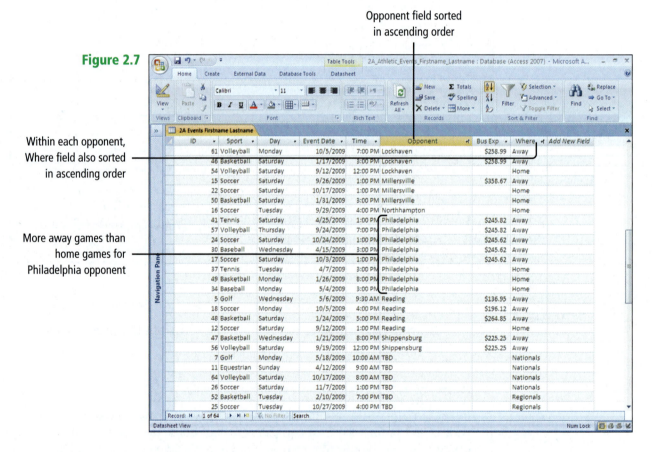

Opponent field sorted in ascending order

Within each opponent, Where field also sorted in ascending order

More away games than home games for Philadelphia opponent

3 In the **Sort & Filter group**, click the **Clear All Sorts** button.

Objective 3
Filter Records

Filtering records in a table displays only a portion of the total records—a *subset*—based on matching specific values. Filters are commonly used to provide a quick answer, and the result is generally not saved for future use. However, if you close a table that has a filter applied, when the table is reopened—even if the database has been closed—the records will display with the filter applied.

Activity 2.5 Filtering by Data in One Field

Because the president cannot attend events scheduled on Wednesdays, Pavel Linksz would like to view only the records for events scheduled for that day of the week, without having to sort or scroll through the table. In addition, Pavel Linksz is an avid volleyball and baseball fan and wants to display the schedules for these games.

1 In the **Day** field name box, click the **Sort & Filter arrow**, and then compare your screen with Figure 2.8.

At the top of the displayed list are sorting options. At the bottom of the list, all of the data that appears in the field is displayed with a check mark in each check box. A check mark indicates that any record containing the data in that field will be displayed.

Sort & Filter arrow   Sorting options

Figure 2.8

Filtering options

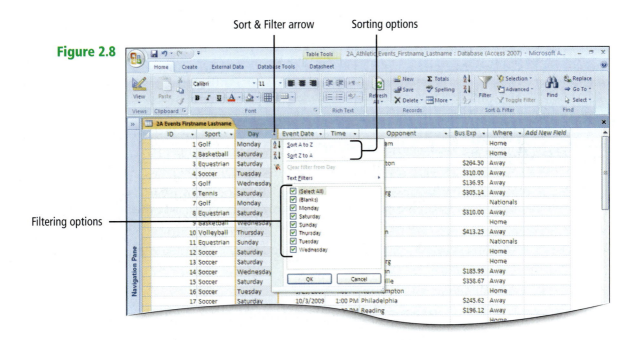

2 In the list, click to clear the **(Select All)** check box, which removes the check marks from all of the check boxes. Next to **Wednesday**, select the check box, and then click **OK**. Compare your screen with Figure 2.9.

Twelve records that match the value Wednesday display. A filter icon displays next to the Sort & Filter arrow in the field name box for Day. In the status bar, *Filtered* displays to indicate that a filter has been applied. In the navigation area, a Filtered button displays and is active. On the Home tab, in the Sort & Filter group, the Toggle Filter button is active and has an orange background.

Figure 2.9

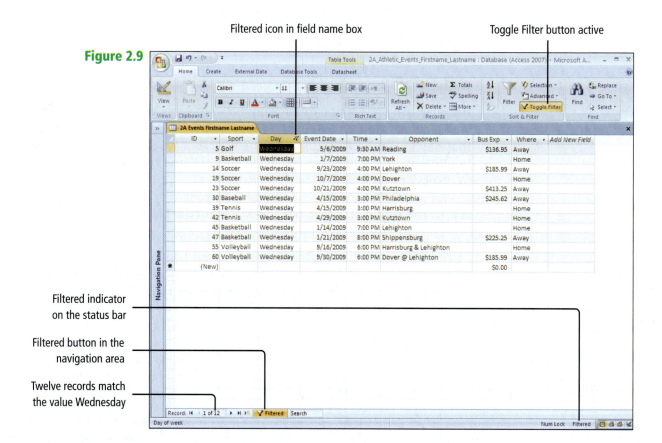

Filtered icon in field name box

Toggle Filter button active

Filtered indicator on the status bar

Filtered button in the navigation area

Twelve records match the value Wednesday

Another Way

To Filter by Selection

Click in the field in a text box containing the data by which you want to filter; for example, in the Day field, click in any record containing Wednesday. On the Home tab, in the Sort & Filter group, click the Selection button. From the displayed list, click Equals "Wednesday", Does Not Equal "Wednesday", Contains "Wednesday", or Does Not Contain "Wednesday".

Note — Toggle Filter Button and Filtered Buttons

On the Home tab, in the Sort & Filter group, the Toggle Filter button applies or removes a filter. In the navigation area, the Filtered button also applies or removes a filter. If no filter has been created, the buttons are inactive—they are unavailable. After a filter is created, these buttons become active. Because they are *toggle buttons*—buttons that are used to perform a task and then cancel the same task—the ScreenTip that displays for these buttons will alternate between Apply Filter, when a filter has been created but not applied, and Remove Filter, when a filter has been applied.

3 On the **Home tab**, in the **Sort & Filter group**, click the **Toggle Filter** button to display all of the records. Alternatively, click the Filtered button in the navigation area.

The Toggle Filter button is still active because a filter has been created for this table. In the navigation area, the Filtered button displays as *Unfiltered*. Removing a filter changes only the records that display. The filter is saved with the table and can be reapplied.

4 In the navigation area, click the **Unfiltered** button to reapply the filter to redisplay the 12 filtered records.

5 Using the technique you just practiced, display all of the records. In the **Sport** field name box, click the **Sort & Filter arrow**. In the displayed list, click to clear the **(Select All)** check box, click to select the **Volleyball** check box, and then click **OK**.

Twelve records display for only volleyball games. The filter icon displays in the field name box for Sport and does not display in the Day field name box. The first filter is not saved.

Alert!

Do two records display instead of 12?

If only two records display for Volleyball games on Wednesday, you may not have displayed all of the records before applying the filter on the Sport field.

6 In the **Sport** field name box, point to the filter icon to display the ScreenTip of *Sport equals "Volleyball"*.

If a filter icon is displayed next to the field name, displaying the ScreenTip is a fast way to determine the data used to create the filter.

7 In the navigation area, click the **Filtered** button to remove the filter and redisplay all of the records.

The filter is removed from the displayed records but is not deleted from the table.

8 In the **Sport** field name box, click the **Sort & Filter arrow**. From the displayed list, click **Clear filter from Sport**.

The filter is deleted from the table and cannot be reapplied unless it is re-created. The Toggle Filter button is inactive—if you point to the button, a ScreenTip of Toggle Filter displays. In the navigation area, No Filter is inactive. All 64 records display.

9 In the **Sport** field name box, click the **Sort & Filter arrow**, and then click **Sort A to Z**. Click the **Sort & Filter arrow** again, and then click to clear the **(Select All)** check box. Click to select the **Baseball** and **Volleyball** check boxes, and then click **OK**. Compare your screen with Figure 2.10.

The Sport field is filtered to display only Baseball and Volleyball games, and the field is sorted in ascending order. A sort icon and a filter icon display in the Sport field name box. When you select the sort order, the list closes, and the field displays using the specified sort order. You must reopen the list to apply a filter to the field. If you apply a filter first, you must click OK and then reopen the list to apply a sort order; otherwise, the filter is ignored, and only the sort is applied.

Sort icon   Filtered icon

Figure 2.10

Sorted in ascending order

Filtered for two sports

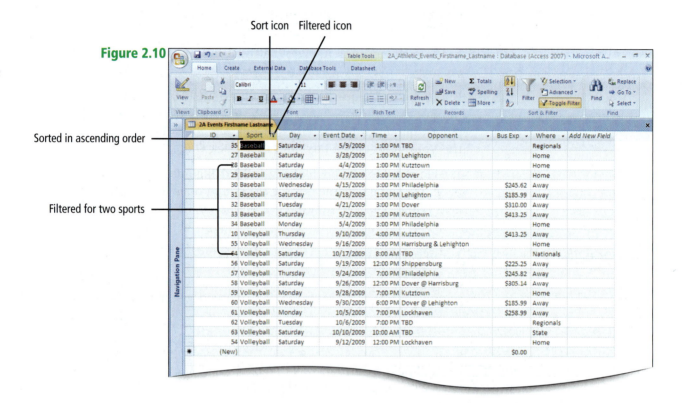

10 Using the techniques you have practiced, click the **Clear All Sorts** button [icon], and then clear the filter from the **Sport** field.

Another Way

To Filter by Form

On the Home tab, in the Sort & Filter group, click the Advanced button, and then click Filter by Form. A Filter by Form object displays that looks like a datasheet; field names display, but there is no data under the field names. You can type the value—for example, Baseball—under the field name or select the value from a list. To filter by a second value in the same field, click the Or tab, which displays a duplicate datasheet, and then enter the second value—for example, Volleyball—under the field. On the Home tab, in the Sort & Filter group, click the Toggle Filter button.

Activity 2.6 Filtering by Data in More than One Field

There is a great rivalry between LCCC and Delaware. Pavel Linksz, vice president of student services, plans activities for the weekend away games between these two schools to ensure that the student body travels to these games to support the LCCC athletes.

1 In the **Opponent** field name box, click the **Sort & Filter arrow**. Notice there are three entries for Dover—*Dover, Dover @ Harrisburg,* and *Dover @ Lehighton.*

2 From the displayed **Sort & Filter** list, point to **Text Filters**, and then compare your screen with Figure 2.11.

Instead of selecting the colleges from the list, you can display text filters to refine your filter. *Equals* means the text box must contain the exact data you enter for the filter. *Contains* means the text box can contain other data in addition to the data you enter for the filter. Other options are also displayed.

Three different listings for Dover

Figure 2.11

Text filters list

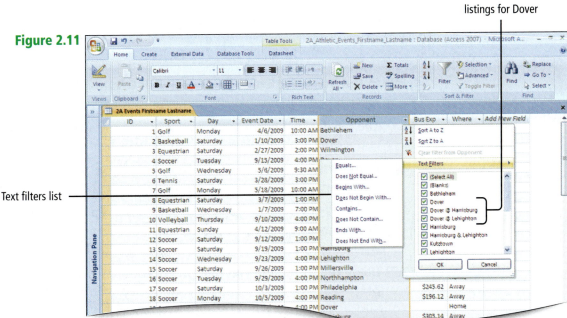

3 From the displayed **Text Filters** list, click **Contains**. In the **Custom Filter** dialog box, in the **Opponent contains** box, type **dover** and then compare your screen with Figure 2.12.

Like the searches you performed in Chapter 1, the text entered in the Custom Filter dialog box is not case sensitive. Access will find all occurrences of Dover, regardless of capitalization.

Figure 2.12

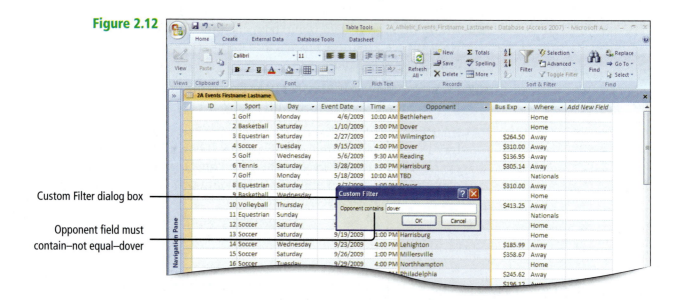

Custom Filter dialog box

Opponent field must contain—not equal—dover

---

4 In the **Custom Filter** dialog box, click **OK**. Notice that the last two records are for *Dover @ Harrisburg* and *Dover @ Lehighton*.

The ten games scheduled between LCCC and Dover are displayed, and a filter icon displays in the Opponent field name box.

5 In the **Where** field name box, click the **Sort & Filter arrow**. Using the techniques you practiced in Activity 2.5, select only **Away** games, and then click **OK**.

The six away games between LCCC and Dover are displayed, and a filter icon displays in the Opponent and the Where field name boxes.

6 Using the technique you just practiced, filter the **Day** by selecting **Saturday**, and then compare your screen with Figure 2.13.

Three records match the filter criteria you have applied—games are against *Dover*, games are *away*, and games are on *Saturday*.

Filtered Day field–*Saturday*   Filtered Opponent field–*Dover*   Filtered Where field–*Away*

Figure 2.13

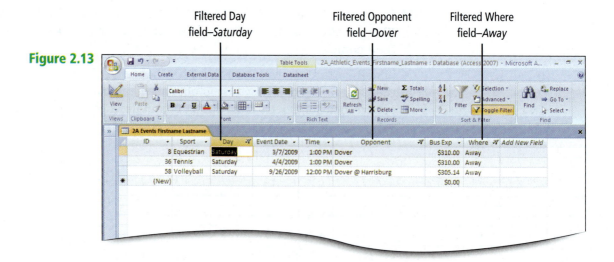

7 Display the table in **Print Preview**, and then change the page orientation to **Landscape**. If you are instructed to submit this result, create a paper or electronic printout. **Close** the Print Preview window.

8 On the **Home tab**, in the **Sort & Filter group**, click the **Advanced** button, and then click **Clear All Filters**.

If you have multiple filters applied, you can delete them from the table at one time by using the Advanced button. Clearing filters deletes them from the table—to reapply, you have to re-create the filters. Removing filters does not delete the filters from the table— the data is displayed without the filter being applied, but you can reapply the filter without having to re-create it.

Note — Removing Filters from a Table

After a filter is created, it becomes part of the table until it is replaced with another filter. The active Toggle Filter button in the Home tab, the Filter icons in the field name boxes, the Filtered button in the navigation area, and the Filtered indicator on the status bar are visual indications that a filter has been created and is still an active part of the table. To ensure that a filter does not become a permanent part of the table, do not save the table when you close it; or, clear all filters before closing the table. If a filter is saved with a table, it might be applied without the individual who is using the database being aware that the displayed data is a subset of the entire table. For this reason, use filters to answer quick questions. If a filter is useful and needs to be used again, create it as a query so that it can be saved and applied to the data when necessary.

Objective 4
Open, Edit, Sort, and Print an Existing Query

A *query* is a question formed in a manner that Access can interpret. The question that is asked may be simple or complex. For example, you might ask, "What is the complete schedule for volleyball games?" Unless a query has already been set up to ask this question, you must create a new one. When it comes to answering questions, queries offer more flexibility than sorts and filters because you can limit the fields that are included in the results, use more than one table, include calculated fields, and save the query for future use. To limit the records that display, you set *criteria*—conditions that identify the specific records for which you are looking.

Activity 2.7 Opening and Modifying an Existing Query

Queries are database objects used to sort, search, and limit the data that displays—these are the actions that change data into meaningful information. You can also perform calculations using a query. To *query* is to ask a question. For example, you could create a query to determine how many volleyball games are held on Saturday. You could create another query to determine which games were against Luzerne. When you locate specific information in a database by using a query, you are *extracting* information from the database.

1 Expand » the **Navigation Pane**, click the **All Access Objects** menu title, and then click **Tables and Related Views**. Compare your screen with Figure 2.14.

The Navigation Pane is categorized by tables. In each table section, the related objects are displayed. Under *2A Events*—the table—the *2A Volleyball Games query* object displays. Objects have different icons to help you determine the object type. By displaying the Navigation Pane in *Tables and Related Views*, you can easily determine the tables that were used to create other Access objects. The Tables and Related Views category groups the objects by tables and their related objects. For example, a query that is based upon a table will be grouped with that table. The *2A Events* table was used to create the *2A Volleyball Games* query.

2A Volleyball Games query was created using the *2A Events* table

No related objects for the *2A Coaches* table

Figure 2.14

Icon for a table

Categorized by Tables and Related Views

Icon for a query

2 On the **Navigation Pane**, double-click **2A Volleyball Games** to display the query results in Datasheet view, and then collapse « the **Navigation Pane**.

After a query has been created and saved, you can open the query. Opening an existing query causes the query to *run*. When a query is run, Access looks at the records in the table or tables you included in the query, locates the records that match specified criteria (if any), and displays those records in Datasheet view. The query is always run against current data, presenting the most up-to-date data.

3 Take a moment to review the records that display, and then compare your screen with Figure 2.15.

This query responds to the question: *What is the schedule for volleyball games?* Recall that the *2A Events* table displayed 64 events; you can click the 2A Events table tab to verify this information. The number of records in the query is less than the number of records in the *2A Events* table because criteria is entered as part of the query.

Figure 2.15

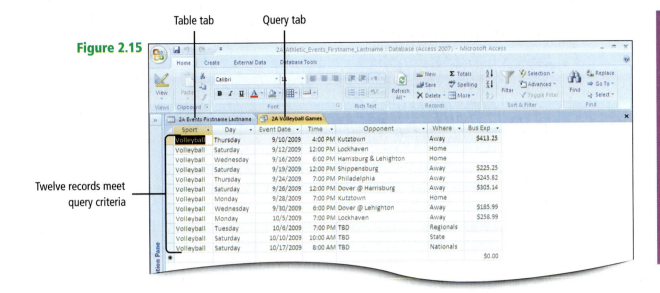

Table tab

Query tab

Twelve records meet query criteria

4 With the *2A Volleyball Games* query current, on the **Home tab**, in the **Views group**, click the **View** button, and then compare your screen with Figure 2.16.

The **Query Datasheet view** displays the results of the query; the **Query Design view** displays how the query was formed, including the tables/queries and the fields used and the criteria specified. Recall that the tabs on the Ribbon change to display contextual command tabs that are used with the current view of the object—Design—which are grouped under contextual tools—Query Tools.

The top portion of the query window—the **Query design workspace**—displays a **field list**, a box listing the field names in the table used to create the query—the *2A Events* table. The lower portion of the window is the **design grid** and includes seven field names. Under the Sport field, *"Volleyball"* displays on the Criteria row. Because of this criteria, the query results are restricted to display only volleyball events. The design grid is used to specify the field names and the criteria for the query.

Seven fields included
in the query design   Query design workspace

Figure 2.16

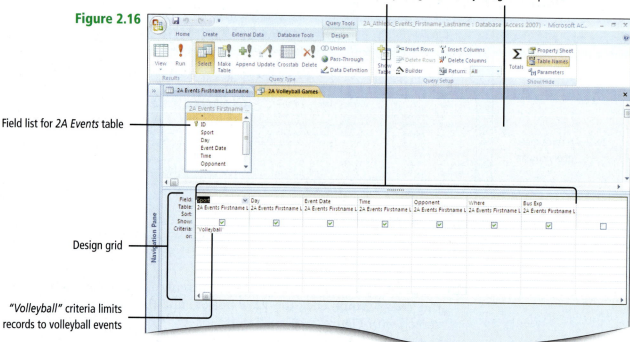

Field list for *2A Events* table ——

Design grid ——

"*Volleyball*" criteria limits
records to volleyball events

Another Way — **To Open a Query in Design View**
To open a query directly in Design view, on the Navigation Pane, right-click the query object, and then click Design View.

5 In the design grid, under **Sport**, select **"Volleyball"**—including the quotation marks—and then press Delete. Type **soccer** and then click in any empty box in the design grid. Compare your screen with Figure 2.17.

Access inserts quotation marks (") around *soccer* because the Sport field has a data type of Text. Access uses the quotation marks to indicate that data is text and not numbers. Like search and filters, criteria is not case sensitive.

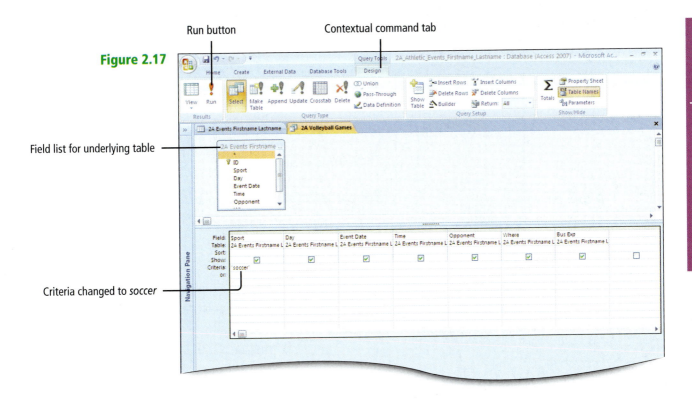

Run button   Contextual command tab

Figure 2.17

Field list for underlying table

Criteria changed to *soccer*

▶ 6   On the **Design tab**, in the **Results group**, click the **Run** button. Alternatively, in the Results group, click the View button to run the query. Switching to Datasheet view will run the query.

The results of the query in Datasheet view display 16 records, all with the sport of soccer.

Alert!

Are one or more fields missing in Datasheet view?

If a field is missing in Datasheet view, you may have inadvertently clicked in the Show row, which will clear the check box. Switch to Design view, click in the Show row under the field that does not display to select the check box, and then view the query results.

▶ 7   On the **Home tab**, in the **Views group**, click the **View** button to switch to Design view.

▶ 8   In the design grid, point to the **selection bar** above the **Day** field until the ⬇ pointer displays, as shown in Figure 2.18.

Figure 2.18

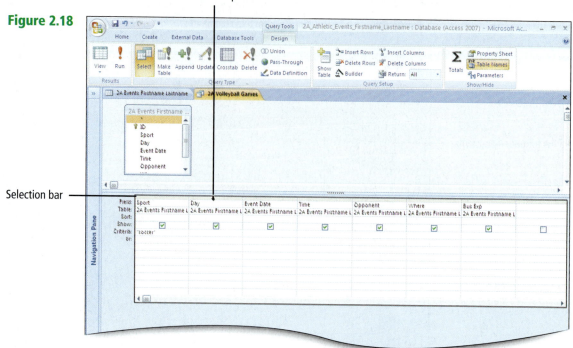

Selection bar

9 Click to select the **Day** field, and then press Delete. Alternatively, with the field selected, on the Home tab, in the Records group, click the Delete button.

The Day field is removed from the design grid, and the Event Date field moves to the second column in the design grid. In a query, you can delete fields in Design view only.

10 On the **Design tab**, in the **Results group**, click the **Run** button.

The results display the soccer games *without* the day of the week. The Day field is deleted from the query only; it is not deleted from the underlying table.

11 Switch to **Design** view. Using the technique you just practiced, in the design grid, select the **Opponent column**. Then, point to the **selection bar** at the top of the **Opponent column** to display the pointer. Drag to the left until a black vertical line displays between the **Sport** field and the **Event Date** field, and then release the mouse button. Compare your screen with Figure 2.19.

To rearrange fields in the query, first select the field you want to move, and then drag it to a new position in the design grid.

Drag using the selection
pointer to move the field

Figure 2.19

Opponent is in the
second field position

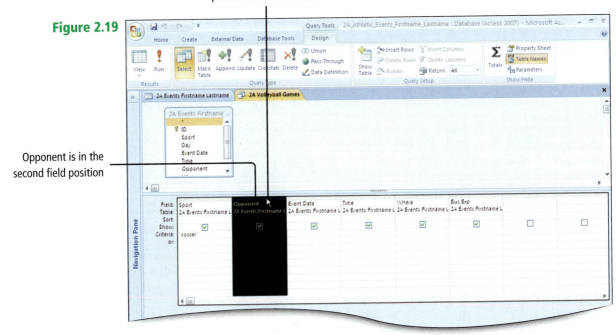

12 **View** the query results. Notice that the **Opponent** field displays to the right of the **Sport** field.

You can run the query by clicking the Run button or the View button on the Design tab, or by clicking the View button on the Home tab.

13 On the **tab row**, click the **Close** button ✕ to close the query. In the displayed message box, click **Yes** to save changes to the query design. The *2A Events* table is now current.

You did not change any of the data in the underlying table. Every Sport displays, the Day field displays, and the Opponent field is in its original position. The query changes only the view of the data using the underlying table.

14 Expand ⟩⟩ the **Navigation Pane**. Using the technique you practiced in Activity 2.3, **Rename** *2A Volleyball Games* to **2A Soccer Games Firstname Lastname** Collapse ⟨⟨ the **Navigation Pane**.

An object must be closed before you can rename it. Recall that an object should be named to reflect the contents of that object. If you open a query named *Volleyball Games*, you would expect to see data about volleyball games, not soccer games.

Activity 2.8 Adding a Record in the Underlying Table

Records cannot be added to a query; you can only extract information from the underlying table. Advanced queries, however, can be used to add records to a table—the data is still stored in the table, not the query. In this activity, you will add a record to the underlying table and view the updated query.

1 With the *2A Events* table as the current object, in the navigation area, click the **New (blank) record** button ▶❋.

This positions the insertion point in the ID field on a blank record—Record 65.

2 Press Tab to move to the **Sport** field. Using the techniques you practiced in Chapter 1, enter the following data in the fields for Record 65.

Sport	Day	Event Date	Time	Opponent	Bus Exp	Where
Soccer	Wednesday	10/14/09	4 pm	Lockhaven	167.95	Away

Because the ID field has a data type of AutoNumber, the ID field is populated when you start typing in another field.

3 On the **tab row**, click the **Close** button ✕ to close the table. If prompted to save changes to the table, click **Yes**.

4 Expand ➤ the **Navigation Pane**, and then double-click **2A Soccer Games** to open the query in Datasheet view. Collapse ◀ the **Navigation Pane**. If necessary, scroll down until the last record is displayed, and then compare your screen with Figure 2.20.

The record you entered in the *2A Events* table displays in the query. Every time you open a query, Access runs the query using the underlying table. An advantage of saving a query is that as you add records to the underlying table, the query will always display the updated information without you having to re-create the query.

Figure 2.20

New record displays in query ⸺

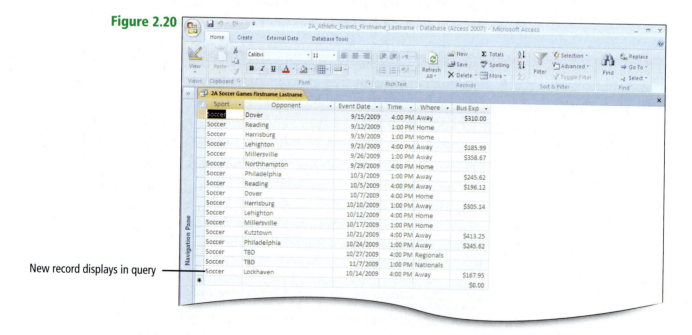

5 Switch to **Design** view. Under **Sport** in the **Show row**, clear the check box, and then compare your screen with Figure 2.21.

By default, all fields in the design grid display in the results. You can hide a column from the results by removing the check mark from the Show check box for a field. You can also hide a field in Datasheet view by right-clicking the field and then clicking Hide Columns. Because this query displays only the sport of soccer, the results do not need to display the redundant data in the Sport field.

Check mark will display the field and its data

Figure 2.21

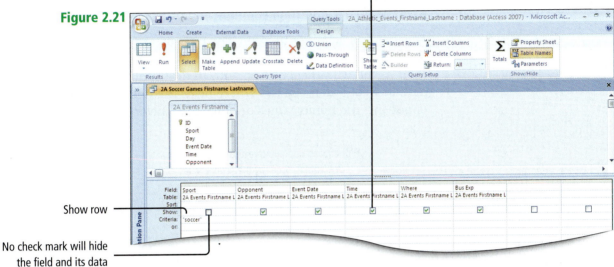

Show row

No check mark will hide the field and its data

6 **Run** the query.

The Sport field is hidden from the display. You do not want to remove the Sport field from the design grid because you have criteria entered for this field. If you remove the Sport field from the design grid, there will be no criteria, and all the records will display.

Activity 2.9 Sorting an Existing Query

You can sort the results of a query either in Datasheet view or Design view. Because query results are formatted like a table in Datasheet view, the process for sorting query results is similar to sorting in the table. You can sort records in ascending or descending order.

If you add a sort order to the design grid of a query, it remains as a permanent part of the query. If you use the Sort button in Datasheet view, it will *override*—take the place of—the sort order of Design view and can be saved as part of the query, but the sort order will not display in the design grid in Design view.

1 Switch to **Design** view. In the design grid, under **Event Date**, click in the **Sort row** to display an arrow. Click the **arrow**, and from the displayed list, click **Ascending**. **Run** the query.

The results display the soccer games sorted by Event Date, with the earliest date—9/12/2009—displayed first and the latest date—11/7/2009—displayed last.

2 Switch to **Design** view. Under **Event Date** in the **Sort row**, click the **Sort arrow** next to Ascending. If the arrow is not displayed, under **Event Date**, click in the **Sort row**. Click **(not sorted)** to remove the sort. Alternatively, with Ascending selected, press Delete.

The records will revert to the original sort order, in ascending order by ID, the primary key field.

3 Using the technique you just practiced, sort the **Opponent** field in **Ascending** order, and then sort the **Where** field in **Descending** order. **Run** the query, and then compare your screen with Figure 2.22.

Access sorts from left to right. The records are sorted first in ascending order by the Opponent field, the leftmost field. The records are then sorted within each opponent, in descending order—reverse alphabetical order—by the Where field, the rightmost field. For each opponent, the home games are displayed before the away games.

Within each opponent, records are sorted in descending order by the *Where* field

Figure 2.22

Records are sorted in ascending order, first by the leftmost field—*Opponent*

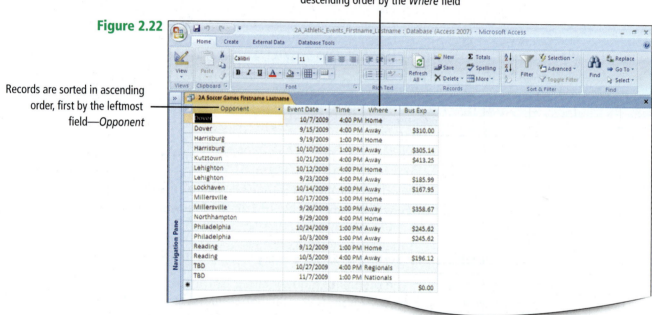

Activity 2.10 Printing a Query

1 On the **Quick Access Toolbar**, click the **Save** button ▢ to save the changes to the query design.

2 Using the techniques you practiced in Chapter 1, adjust all of the column widths to display all of the data in the fields and all of the field names. View the query in **Print Preview** to ensure that the query will print on one page even if you do not have to submit a printed copy. The query should print on one page in **Portrait** orientation.

3 If you are instructed to submit this result, create a paper or electronic printout. **Close** the Print Preview window.

4 On the **tab row**, click the **Close** button ⊠ to close the *2A Soccer Games* query. In the displayed message box, click **Yes** to save changes to the layout of the query.

Objective 5
Create Table Relationships and a Simple Query

Access databases are ***relational databases***—the tables in the database can relate to or connect to other tables through common fields. A relational database avoids redundant data, helps reduce errors, and saves space. Each table in a database contains information about one subject. For example, in the 2A Athletic Events database, one table contains data about the team events at LCCC, and the second table contains data about the coaches. Each table has a primary key field, which ensures that the same record is not recorded more than one time in the table.

When you have a database full of different tables, you need a method of connecting the data in those tables to create and display meaningful, useful information. To do this, you define relationships. A ***relationship*** is an association that is established between two tables using ***common fields***—fields that contain the same data in more than one table.

Activity 2.11 Creating Table Relationships

In this activity, you will create a relationship between the *2A Coaches* table and the *2A Events* table. To identify which coach is responsible for each team, you must connect the data in the tables with a common field. The common field is Sport—which displays in both tables. To create a relationship, the two connected fields must have the same data type and the same field size, but they do not have to have the same field name. For example, in the *2A Coaches* table, the common field name could be Sport; and in the *2A Events* table, the common field name could be Team.

1 Expand ⟩⟩ the **Navigation Pane**. Click **All Tables**, and then from the displayed list, click **Object Type** to group the objects by type.

2 **Rename** the *2A Coaches* table to **2A Coaches Firstname Lastname** Open the **2A Events** table, and then open the **2A Coaches** table, both in Datasheet view. Collapse ⟨⟨ the **Navigation Pane**. In **2A Coaches**, notice there are no duplicates in the **Sport** field. Switch to **Design** view, and notice that **Sport** is the primary key field. Switch to **Datasheet** view. Recall that the primary key field contains unique data that can never be used again within the same field, ensuring that each record is unique.

3 On the **tab row**, click the **2A Events tab** to make the table current. Notice there are *many* instances of the same sport.

4 On the **tab row**, right-click either **object tab**. From the shortcut menu, click **Close All**.

The tables close, but the database remains open. To create relationships between tables, the tables must be closed.

5 On the Ribbon, click the **Database Tools tab**. In the **Show/Hide group**, click the **Relationships** button, and then compare your screen with Figure 2.23.

A Relationships tab displays on the tab row, and the Show Table dialog box displays. The Show Table dialog box displays the tables and queries in the database that you can use to create a relationship. Even though all of the tables in the database are listed, the tables must meet the requirements for creating a relationship—they must share a common field with the same data type and field size.

Relationships tab

Figure 2.23

Show Table dialog box

List of available tables in alphabetical order

Note — If the Show Table Dialog Box Does Not Display

If the Show Table dialog box does not display, on the Ribbon, click the Design tab. In the Relationships group, click the Show Table button.

6 In the **Show Table** dialog box with the **2A Coaches** table selected, click **Add**. Notice that the field list for the *2A Coaches* table is added to the **Relationships** window.

7 In the **Show Table** dialog box, double-click the **2A Events** table.

The *2A Events* field list is added to the Relationships window. You may be unable to see the field list—it may have been inserted under the Show Table dialog box. Double-clicking adds the field list to the Relationships window without clicking the Add button.

8 **Close** the **Show Table** dialog box, and then compare your screen with Figure 2.24.

Figure 2.24

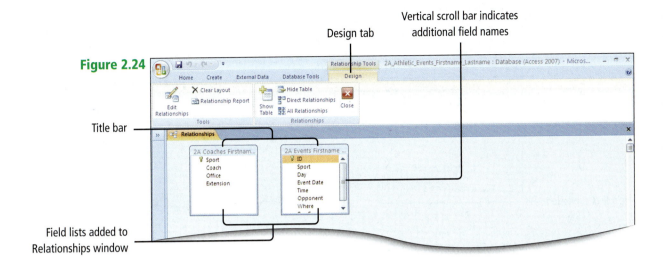

Design tab

Vertical scroll bar indicates additional field names

Title bar

Field lists added to Relationships window

Alert!

Are there more than two tables in the Relationships window?

If you add one of the tables more than once, you must remove it from the Relationships window. Click the title bar for the duplicate field list to make it current. On the Design tab, in the Relationships group, click Hide Table. Alternatively, right-click the field list, and then click Hide Table. To clear all of the field lists from the Relationships window, on the Design tab, in the Tools group, click Clear Layout.

---

9 In the **2A Events** field list, position the mouse pointer over the lower edge of the field list to display the ⊥ pointer, and then drag downward to display the entire field list.

Because you can now view the entire list, the scroll bar on the right is removed. Expanding the field list enables you to see all of the available fields without having to scroll.

10 In the **2A Events** field list, position your mouse pointer over the right edge of the field list to display the ↔ pointer, and then drag to the right to display the entire name in the title bar. Point to the title bar of the **2A Events** field list that you just resized, and then drag it to the right, approximately 1 inch, to make room to expand the 2A Coaches field list.

11 Using the techniques you just practiced, expand the **2A Coaches** field list to display the entire table name. Compare your screen with Figure 2.25.

Figure 2.25

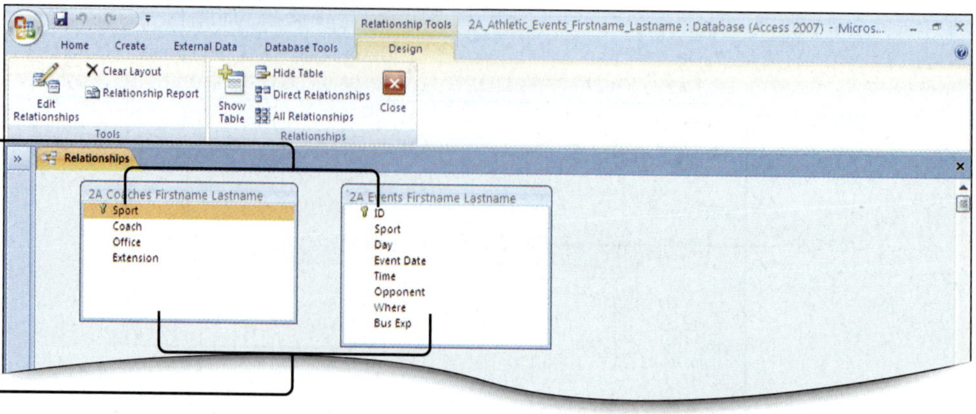

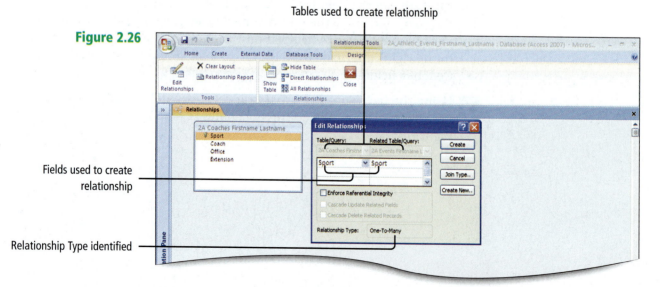

Primary key fields

Field lists expanded

12 In the **2A Coaches** field list, point to **Sport**—the primary key field—and drag to the right to the **2A Events** field list until the [icon] points to **Sport**, and then release the mouse button. Compare your screen with Figure 2.26.

The Edit Relationships dialog box displays. As you drag, a small graphic displays to indicate that you are dragging the Sport primary key from the *2A Coaches* table to the Sport field in the *2A Events* table. Each record in the *2A Coaches* table can be related to *many* records in the *2A Events* table. Sport is referred to as the ***foreign key field*** in the *many* table—the *2A Events* table. The foreign key field is the field that is included in the related table so that it can be joined with the primary key field in another table. It links the two tables.

In the *2A Coaches* table, Sport is the primary key field—ensuring that a sport can be in the table only one time. In the *2A Events* table, each scheduled event includes the name of the sport. Because a single coach is responsible for a team with *many* events, the sport displays *many* times in the *2A Events* table. The relationship between each coach and the team event is known as a ***one-to-many relationship***—*one* coach is responsible for *many* team events. This is the most common type of relationship in Access.

Tables used to create relationship

Figure 2.26

Fields used to create relationship

Relationship Type identified

Note — Using AutoNumber Fields in a Relationship

To create a relationship using an AutoNumber data type in one table to a foreign key field in a second table, the foreign key data type must be set to Number, and the field size property must be set to long integer, which includes whole numbers from -2,147,483,648 through 2,147,483,647.

13 In the **Edit Relationships** dialog box, click **Create**, and then compare your screen with Figure 2.27.

A *join line*—the line connecting the primary key field to the foreign key field—displays between the two field lists.

Foreign key field

Figure 2.27

Primary key field

Join line connecting Sport fields

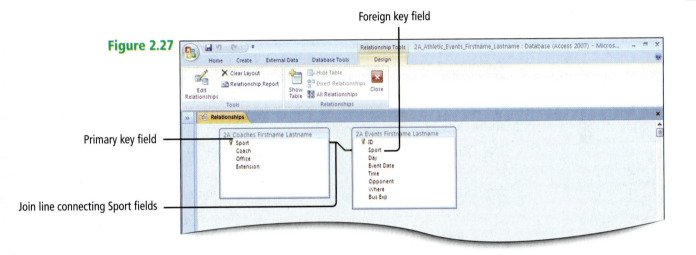

14 On the **Design tab**, in the **Tools group**, click **Relationship Report**. Compare your screen with Figure 2.28, which displays a report of the relationships you just created in Print Preview view.

Relationships Report object tab

Figure 2.28

Print Preview program tab

Relationships object tab

Database name

Current date—yours will differ

Field lists with join line

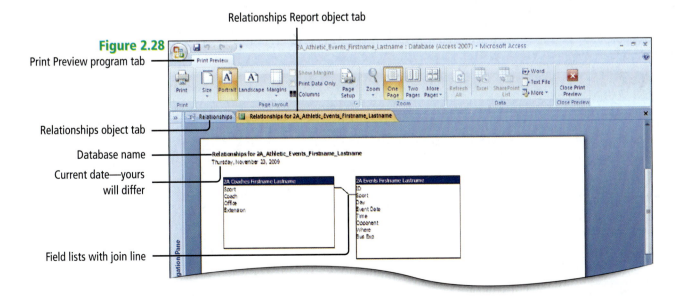

15 If you are instructed to submit this result, create a paper or electronic printout. **Close** the Print Preview window.

16 On the **tab row**, click the **Close** button ☒, and then click **Yes** when prompted to save the report. In the displayed **Save As** dialog box,

click **OK** to accept the default report name. Expand ⟩⟩ the **Navigation Pane**, and notice that the relationships report displays under **Reports**.

17 On the **tab row**, click the **Close** button ☒ to close the Relationships window. If a message displays asking whether you want to save the layout of the relationships, click **Yes**. On the **Navigation Pane**,

under **Tables**, click **2A Coaches** to select the table. Collapse ⟨⟨ the **Navigation Pane**.

Saving the layout of the relationships preserves the way the field lists display in the Relationships window.

Activity 2.12 Creating a Simple Query Using Joined Tables

One advantage of creating a relationship between tables is that you can create a query using fields from both tables. Access uses the join line to find related data in the tables.

1 On the Ribbon, click the **Create tab**, which you can use to create all of the objects in a database.

2 On the **Create tab**, in the **Other group**, click the **Query Wizard** button.

A *wizard* is a guide that presents each step as a dialog box in which you choose what you want to do and how you want the results to look.

3 In the displayed **New Query** dialog box, click **Simple Query Wizard**, and then click **OK**. Compare your screen with Figure 2.29.

The Simple Query Wizard dialog box displays the first step in creating a query. In this dialog box, you can select the tables or queries, along with the fields, that will be used to create a query. *Table: 2A Coaches* is displayed in the Tables/Queries box. If another table is listed in the Tables/Queries box, click the arrow, and then click Table: 2A Coaches.

Figure 2.29

Add Field button   Add All Fields button

Tables/Queries that can be selected for query

Available Fields in the Selected Table/Query

Remove Field button

Remove All Fields button

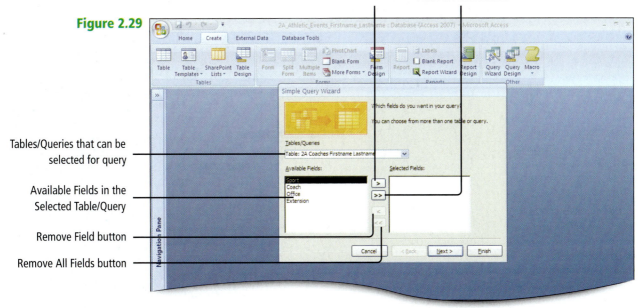

4 In the **Simple Query Wizard** dialog box, under **Available Fields**, click **Sport**, and then click the **Add Field** button ⟩. Alternatively, under Available Fields, double-click the field name to add it to Selected Fields.

The Sport Field displays under Selected Fields and will be used in the query.

5 Click the **Add All Fields** button ⟩⟩.

Under Selected Fields, all of the fields from the *2A Coaches* table are displayed and will be used in the query. Clicking the Add All Fields button is a more efficient way to use all of the fields from a table in a query. If you want to use most of the fields, but not all, click Add All Fields, and then remove the few fields that should not be included in the query.

6 Under **Selected Fields**, click **Extension**, and then click the **Remove Field** button ⟨ so the Extension field will not be used in the query.

7 Click the **Tables/Queries arrow**, and then compare your screen with Figure 2.30.

Figure 2.30

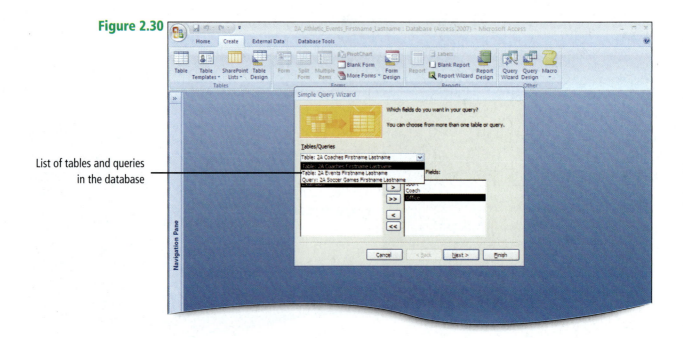

List of tables and queries
in the database

8 From the displayed list, click **Table: 2A Events**.

Under Available Fields, a list of fields for the *2A Events* table displays. Under Selected Fields, the fields from the *2A Coaches* table display.

9 Using the techniques you just practiced, add the following fields to the **Selected Fields** list in the order given: **Opponent**, **Event Date**, and **Where**. Compare your screen with Figure 2.31.

Figure 2.31

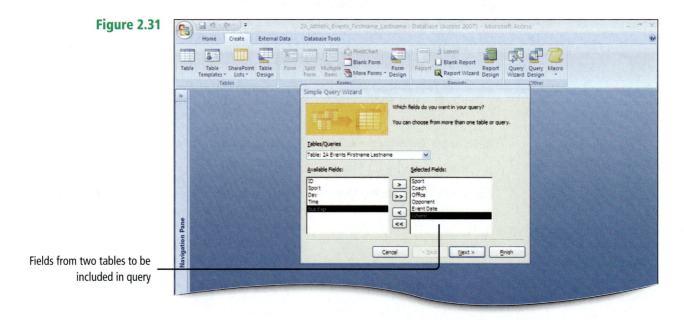

Fields from two tables to be
included in query

10 In the **Simple Query Wizard** dialog box, click **Next** to move to the next step.

The next dialog box enables you to show every field of every record (for the fields you selected in the previous step) or to summarize the data. Use a summary when you want to calculate a numeric field or count the number of records.

11 Click **Next** to accept the default of Detail.

The next dialog box displays the default title of *2A Coaches Firstname Lastname Query* and enables you to open the query to view information. If you need to make further modifications to the simple query, click the *Modify the query design* option button.

12 Click **Finish** to accept the default name and to view the query results in Datasheet view.

Every sporting event is listed—65 records—with the related coach's name.

13 On the Ribbon, click the **Home tab**, switch to **Design** view, and then compare your screen with Figure 2.32.

The field lists for the *2A Coaches* and *2A Events* tables with the join line display. The tables are joined because you created a relationship between the tables. Access used the Sport field to extract information from both fields. Using the Query Wizard to create a Simple Query is only one way to create a query. After creating the query, you can refine the query by adding criteria in the design grid.

Related tables
used in query

Table used
for field

Figure 2.32

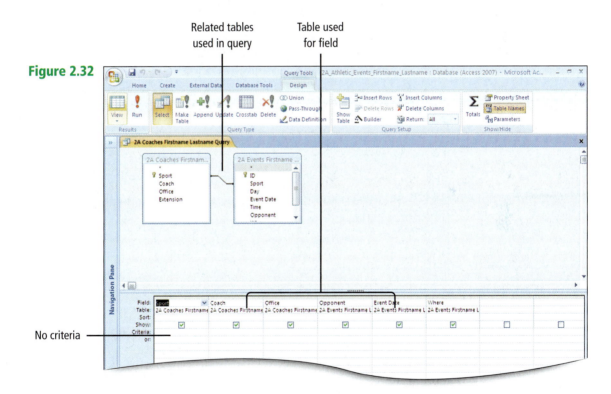

No criteria

More Knowledge

Create Table Relationships When You Create a Query

When you create a query, you select the tables from which to extract data. If the primary key and the foreign key fields share the same field name, Access automatically creates a relationship between the tables in the query design window. Having the same field name is not a requirement for primary key and foreign key fields, but it is the preferred method for some database administrators. If the fields do not share the same name, you must create the join line between the two tables in Design view.

Creating table relationships in this manner does not save the layout of the table relationships and does not enable you to print a table relationships report. If a relationship will be used frequently, it should be created in the relationships window before creating the query.

Activity 2.13 Printing Selected Records from a Query

1 Switch to **Datasheet** view. Scroll down until the three records for the sport of **Golf** are displayed. Click in the **record selector** box for the first Golf record—the Opponent is *Bethlehem*—and then drag down until the ➡ pointer displays in the record selector box for the third Golf event—the Opponent is *TBD*. Release the mouse, and then compare your screen with Figure 2.33.

Figure 2.33

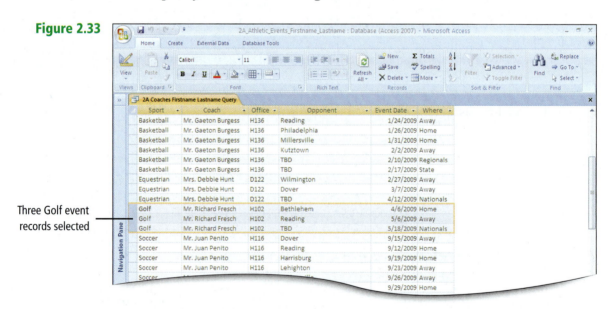

Three Golf event records selected

2 Hold down [Ctrl], and then press [P] to display the **Print** dialog box.

3 In the **Print** dialog box, under **Print Range**, click the **Selected Record(s)** option button, and then compare your screen with Figure 2.34.

Default printer—yours will differ

Figure 2.34

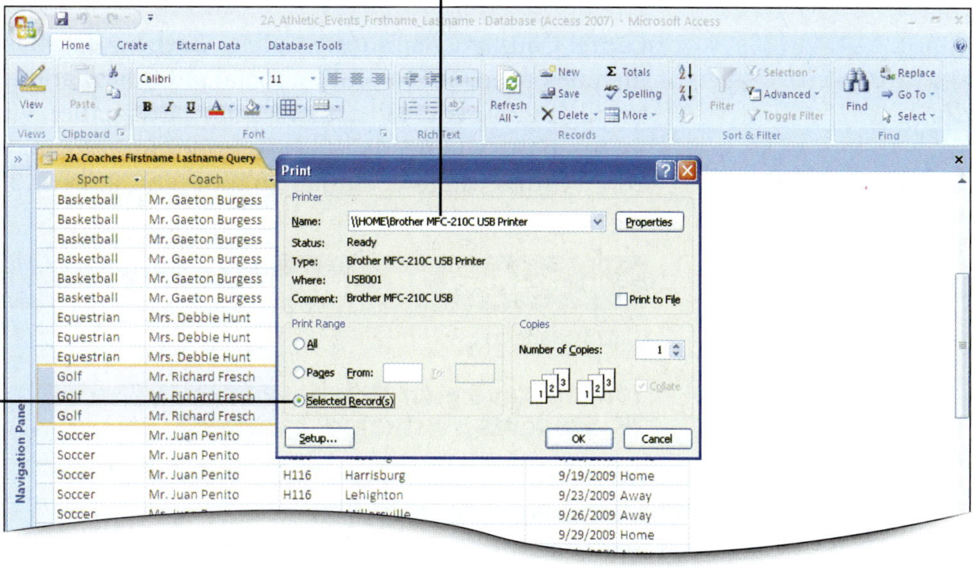

Will print the three *Golf*
records, which are selected
in the datasheet

4 In the **Print** dialog box, click the **Setup** button. In the **Page Setup** dialog box, under **Margins**, change the **Left** margin to **.5** and the **Right** margin to **.5** and then click **OK**. If you are instructed to submit this result, create a paper or electronic printout.

Another Way ── **To Print Selected Records**

An alternative to printing selected records is to filter the field, which displays only those records matching the filter criteria, print the filtered datasheet, and then remove or clear the filter.

5 On the **tab row**, click the **Close** button ☒ to close the query. If a message displays asking you to save the changes to the design of the query, click **Yes**. Expand ☒ the **Navigation Pane** so that when you reopen the database, the Navigation Pane will be expanded. **Close** the database, and then **Exit** Access.

6 Check your Chapter Assignment Sheet or Course Syllabus or consult your instructor to determine whether you are to submit your assignments on paper or electronically using your college's course information management system.

End **You have completed Project 2A** ────────────

Project 2B Students

Laurel County Community College keeps a database of students that includes scholarship and financial aid information. In Activities 2.14 through 2.24, you will assist Michael Schaeffler, vice president of instruction, who needs to extract relevant information from the database. Your results will look similar to those in Figure 2.35.

For Project 2B, you will need the following file:

a02B_Students

You will save your database as
2B_Students_Firstname_Lastname

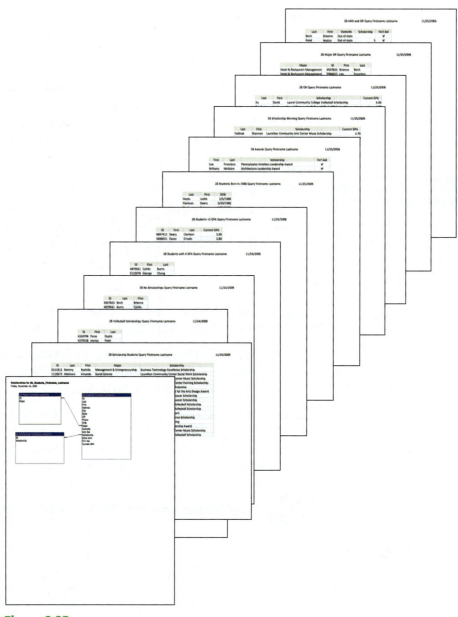

Figure 2.35
Project 2B—Students

Objective 6
Create a Select Query

A *select query* obtains its data from one or more tables, from existing queries, or from a combination of the two. The results of the query are displayed in Datasheet view. The select query is a subset of data that is used to answer specific questions. You can create a select query by using a wizard or using Design view.

Activity 2.14 Creating Multiple Table Relationships

In Project 2A, you created a relationship between two tables before creating a query. In this activity, you will create multiple relationships between tables.

1 **Start** Access. Click the **Office** button 🔲 , and then click **Open**. Navigate to the location where you have saved the student data files that accompany this text, and then double-click **a02B_Students** to open the database. Click the **Office** button 🔲 , point to the **Save As arrow**, and then under **Save the database in another format**, click **Access 2007 Database**. In the **Save As** dialog box, navigate to your **Access Chapter 2** folder. In the **File name** box, select the existing file name. Using your own first and last name, type **2B_Students_Firstname_Lastname** and then click **Save**.

Because you added the location of the student data files and the Access Chapter 2 folder to Trusted Locations, the message bar and Security Warning do not display.

2 Using the technique you practiced in Project 2A and your own first and last name, **Rename** all tables by adding **Firstname Lastname** to the end of each table name. For example, *2B Majors* should be renamed as *2B Majors Firstname Lastname*.

3 On the **Navigation Pane**, double-click **2B Students**. In Datasheet view, scroll to the right to view all of the fields in the table, noting the data in the **Major** and **Scholarship** fields. Compare your screen with Figure 2.36.

Before creating a query, you should view the tables and the data in the tables. Both the Major and Scholarship fields display codes.

Figure 2.36

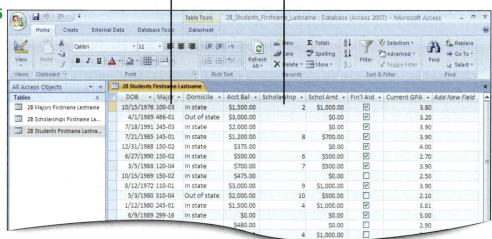

4 On the **Navigation Pane**, double-click **2B Majors** to open the table in Datasheet view. Notice the ID that corresponds to the Major. Locate the major that is associated with an **ID** of **100-01**, which is the code used to represent a **Finance** major.

5 On the **tab row**, click the **2B Students tab** to make the table current. In the navigation area, in the **Search** box, type **100-01** Scroll to the left until you see the **Last** field.

Access finds the first occurrence of 100-01 and selects the record. *Paras Gupta—Record 17—*is majoring in *Finance.*

6 Scroll to the right until the **Scholarship** field is displayed for the selected record. On the **Navigation Pane**, double-click **2B Scholarships** to open the table. Notice the ID that corresponds to the Scholarship.

ID 5 is the code used to represent the Laurel Community College Volleyball Scholarship.

7 On the **tab row**, click the **2B Students tab** to make the table current. Using the techniques you practiced in Project 2A, create a **filter** to display only those records that have a **Scholarship** code of **5**. Scroll to the left to display the **Last** field, and then compare your screen with Figure 2.37.

Three students are receiving a volleyball scholarship, including Paras Gupta.

Figure 2.37

Three students with a
Scholarship code of 5

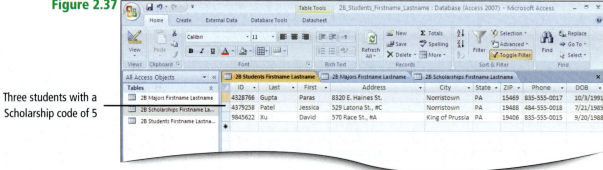

8 On the **Home tab**, in the **Sort & Filter group**, click the **Advanced** button, and then click **Clear All Filters** to remove the filters from the table. **Close** all tables, saving changes if prompted, but do not close the database.

You extracted information from the database by opening all the tables to see the related fields and performed a search and created a filter. Recall that you can create a relationship between tables, use the relationship to create a query, and extract information without having to manually search the tables for the data.

9 On the Ribbon, click the **Database Tools tab**, and then in the **Show/Hide group**, click the **Relationships** button. In the displayed **Show Table** dialog box, click **Close**. If the Show Table dialog box did not display, continue to the next step.

10 On the **Navigation Pane**, click to select the **2B Majors** table. Hold down ⬆ Shift, and then click **2B Students** to select all three tables. Drag the selected tables to the right to the **Relationships** window.

11 Using the techniques you practiced in Activity 2.11, expand each field list to display all of the fields and the entire table name. Pointing to the title bars of the field lists, drag the field lists until they are positioned as displayed in Figure 2.38.

Figure 2.38

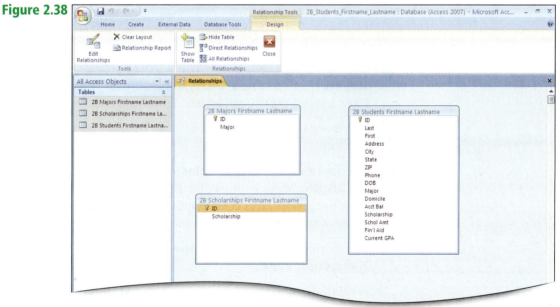

12 In the **2B Majors** field list, drag the **ID** field to the **2B Students** field list, point to the **Major** field, and release the mouse. In the displayed **Edit Relationships** dialog box, click **Create**.

A join line displays between the 2B Majors field list and the 2B Students field list.

13 Using the technique you just practiced, create a relationship between the *2B Scholarships* **ID** field and the *2B Students* **Scholarship** field, and then compare your screen with Figure 2.39.

A join line displays between the 2B Scholarships field list and the 2B Students field list.

Figure 2.39

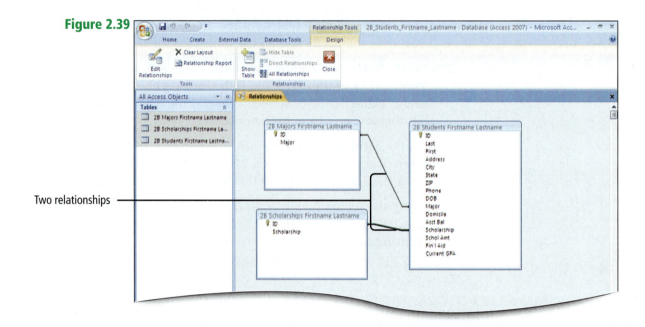

Two relationships

14 On the **Design tab**, in the **Tools group**, click the **Relationship Report** button. If necessary, to display all three field lists, in the Page Layout group, click the Landscape button.

15 If you are instructed to submit this result, create a paper or electronic printout.

16 On the **tab row**, click the **Close** button ⊠ to close the **Relationships for 2B_Students** window. In the displayed message box, click **Yes** to save the report, and then click **OK** to save the report with the default name. On the **tab row**, click the **Close** button ⊠ to close the **Relationships** window, and then collapse ⊠ the **Navigation Pane**.

A relationships report has been created that displays the relationships you established, and the relationships are saved with the database.

Activity 2.15 Creating a Select Query in Design View

In Activity 2.12, you created a select query using the Query Wizard. You can create a select query using the Query Wizard and then switch to Design view to refine your query, or you can create a select query in Design view. In this activity, you will create a select query in Design view to display student IDs, names, majors, and scholarships.

1 On the Ribbon, click the **Create tab**, and then in the **Other group**, click the **Query Design** button.

A query object is created with a tab named *Query1*. The Show Table dialog box displays. Recall that the top part of the Query window is the Query design workspace and the lower part of the window is the Query design grid.

2 Using the technique you practiced in Activity 2.14 to select multiple objects, from the **Show Table** dialog box, add all three tables to the **Query design workspace**, and then **Close** the **Show Table** dialog box. Expand the field lists to display all of the fields and the table names. Rearrange the field lists as shown in Figure 2.40. In the **2B Students** field list, point to **ID**. Drag the ID field down to the design grid in the first column in the field box, and then compare your screen with Figure 2.40.

Rearranging the field lists has no effect on the query; it is easier to see the related fields and the join lines. In the first column of the design grid, *ID* displays in the field box, and *2B Students* displays in the Table box. Because each field list contains a field named ID, the Table box clarifies from which table the ID field will be extracted.

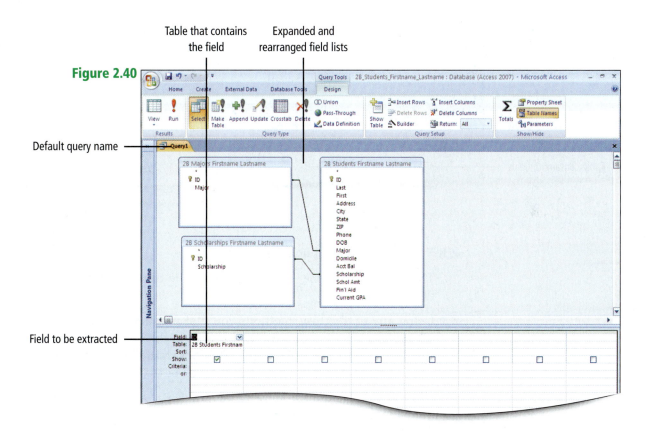

Figure 2.40

Table that contains the field

Expanded and rearranged field lists

Default query name

Field to be extracted

3 In the **2B Students** field list, double-click **Last**.

The Last—last name—field from the *2B Students* table is inserted into the second column in the design grid.

4 In the design grid, in the third column, click in the **Table** box. Click the **Table box arrow**, and from the displayed list, click **2B Students**.

In the design grid, in the third column, click in the **Field** box. Click the **Field box arrow**, and then compare your screen with Figure 2.41.

A list of fields for the *2B Students* table displays. If you had not first selected a table in the Table box, a list would display with the table name followed by the field name for each field in each table— you would not be able to see the field names because the entries would be too lengthy. If there is only one table in the Query design workspace, you do not have to select the table first.

List of fields in the *2B Students* table

Figure 2.41

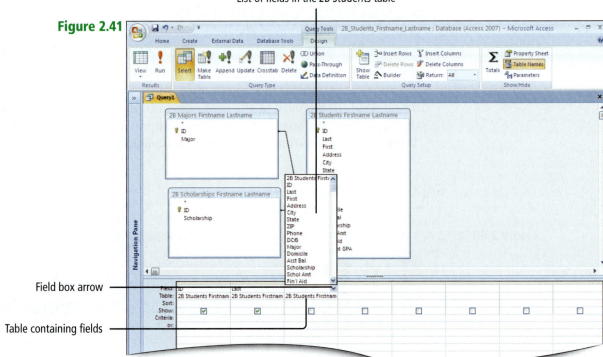

Field box arrow

Table containing fields

5 From the displayed field list, click **First**.

The First—first name—field displays in the third column of the design grid.

6 Using any of the three methods you just practiced, from the **2B Majors** field list, add the **Major** field to the fourth column of the design grid. Then, from the **2B Scholarships** field list, add the **Scholarship** field to the fifth column of the design grid. Compare your screen with Figure 2.42.

Figure 2.42

Three fields from the *2B Students* table

One field from the *2B Scholarships* table

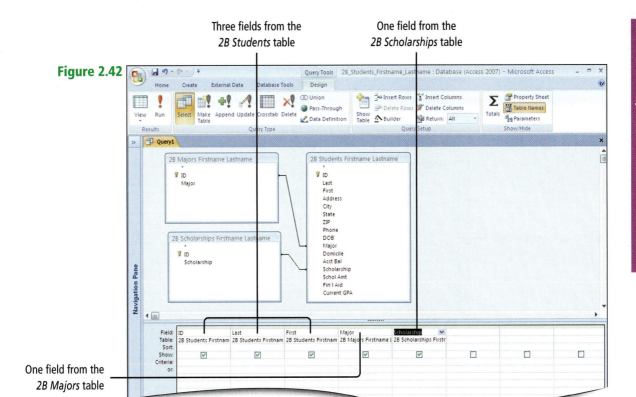

One field from the *2B Majors* table

7 On the **Design tab**, in the **Results group**, click the **Run** button. Alternatively, on the Design tab, in the Results group, click the View button; or in the status bar, click the Datasheet view button. Compare your screen with Figure 2.43.

Of the 28 students in the *2B Students* table, 16 have scholarships. If you needed to display all of the students, even the students who do not have scholarships, you would need a code in the Scholarship field with a corresponding value in the *2B Scholarships* table or to create a query that displays empty fields. The primary key field controls the data that displays in a query involving related tables.

Because you established a relationship between the *2B Students* and *2B Scholarships* tables, Access used the Scholarship code, the foreign key field, in the *2B Students* table (for example, 5) to find the same value in the ID field—the primary key field—and then found the corresponding scholarship name in the *2B Scholarships* table. The same is true for the major; Access used the Major code, the foreign key field, in the *2B Students* table (for example, 100-03) to find the same value in the ID field—the primary key field—and then found the name of the Major in the *2B Majors* table.

You might question why the major and scholarship names were not entered in the *2B Students* table. By separating the major and scholarship information into separate tables, you can later add fields to these two tables that deal specifically with the major or scholarship. For example, you might add contact information for each scholarship or the classes that are required for each major.

Majors—not codes—
are displayed

Scholarship names—not
codes—are listed

Figure 2.43

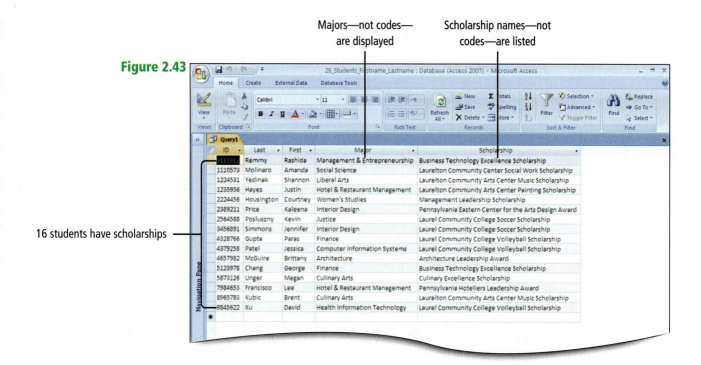

16 students have scholarships

8 On the **tab row**, click the **Close** button ![x] to close the query. In the displayed message box, click **Yes** to save the changes to the design of the query. In the displayed **Save As** dialog box in the **Query Name** box, replace the default name with **2B Scholarship Students Query**

Firstname Lastname and then click **OK**. Expand ![»] the **Navigation Pane**, which displays the saved query.

9 On the **Navigation Pane**, select the query. Click the **Office** menu

![icon] , point to **Print**, and then click **Print Preview**. On the **Print Preview tab**, in the **Page Layout group**, click the **Landscape** button to display the query on one page. If you are instructed to submit this result, create a paper or electronic printout. **Close** the Print Preview window. Recall that page orientation is not saved with the object.

More Knowledge

Using the * from the Field List

The first entry in every field list is an asterisk (*). If you drag the * down into the design grid, all of the fields in the table will be added to the design grid; however, you will not see the individual field names, which means that you cannot add criteria to the individual field names. You might use this method if you want to display all of the fields from one table and selected fields from another table.

Objective 7
Specify Criteria in a Query

Recall that you use queries to locate information in an Access database. These queries are based on criteria that you specify as part of the query. Recall that criteria are conditions that identify the specific records for which you are looking. By using criteria, you are able to pose more specific questions; and, therefore, you will get more specific results. By using criteria, you can limit the results to display only those students receiving a volleyball scholarship, for example, or limit the display to those students whose grade point averages are 3.5 or higher.

Activity 2.16 Specifying Text Criteria in a Query

In this activity, you will specify criteria in the query so that only the records of students receiving a volleyball scholarship display.

1 Collapse « the **Navigation Pane**. On the Ribbon, click the **Create tab**, and then in the **Other group**, click the **Query Design** button. In displayed **Show Table** dialog box, click the **Queries tab**, and then double-click **2B Scholarship Students Query** to add the query to the Query design workspace. **Close** the **Show Table** dialog box. Expand the **2B Scholarship Students Query** field list to display the entire query name.

Because you created a query in Activity 2.15 that extracted all the scholarship students from the database, you are using that query to create another query.

2 Using any of the techniques you practiced in Activity 2.15—dragging, double-clicking, or selecting from the field box arrow list—add the following fields, in the order listed, to the design grid: **ID**, **First**, **Last**, and **Scholarship**.

Alert!

Are there more than four fields displayed in the design grid?
If you double-click a field name two times, it will be added to the design grid in two separate columns. To remove columns, click anywhere in the column. On the Design tab, in the Query Setup group, click the Delete Columns button.

3 In the design grid, in the **Criteria row**, under the **Scholarship** field, type **laurel community college volleyball scholarship** Compare your screen with Figure 2.44. The Scholarship column has been widened in Figure 2.44 to display the entire criteria. You will see only the last characters you typed.

The Criteria row is where you specify the condition or conditions that will limit the results of the query to your exact specifications.

Criteria in Scholarship field

Figure 2.44

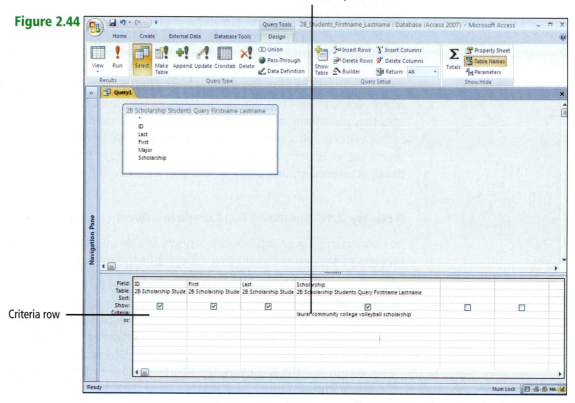

Criteria row

Note — Widen Columns in the Design Grid

Widen a column in the design grid using the same techniques you used in a table. In the selection bar at the top of the column, point to the right border of a column, and then double-click to widen the column and fully display the contents on the criteria row. You can also drag the right border to the desired width.

4 On the **Design tab**, in the **Results group**, click the **Run** button to display the results of the query. Compare your screen with Figure 2.45.

Three records display that meet the criteria—records that have *Laurel Community College Volleyball Scholarship* in the Scholarship field.

Figure 2.45

Three records extracted that match criteria

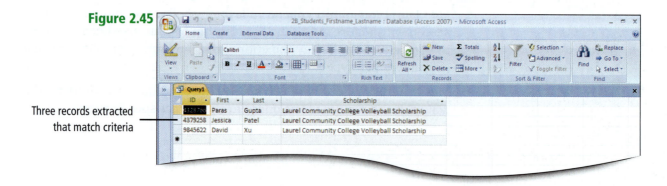

Alert!

Do your query results differ?

If you mistype the criteria or enter it under the wrong field, no records will display. This indicates that no records in the table match the criteria as you entered it. To correct this, return to Design view and re-examine the query design. Verify that the criteria is typed on the Criteria row under the correct field and that it is spelled and spaced correctly. Then, rerun the query.

5 Click the **Save** button 🖫. In the displayed **Save As** dialog box, name the query **2B Volleyball Scholarships Query Firstname Lastname** and then click **OK**.

Activity 2.17 Hiding Fields in the Query Results

Not every field included in the Query design grid has to display in the results; there will be times when you want to prevent some fields from displaying. For example, in the last query, all of the records display the name of the scholarship, which is redundant, especially because you named the query *2B Volleyball Scholarships Query*.

1 With **2B Volleyball Scholarships Query** open, switch to **Design** view.

2 In the design grid, on the **Show row**, notice that, by default, the check box is selected for every field to display—show—in the results.

3 In the design grid, in the **Show row**, under the **Scholarship** field, clear the check box. Compare your screen with Figure 2.46.

Figure 2.46

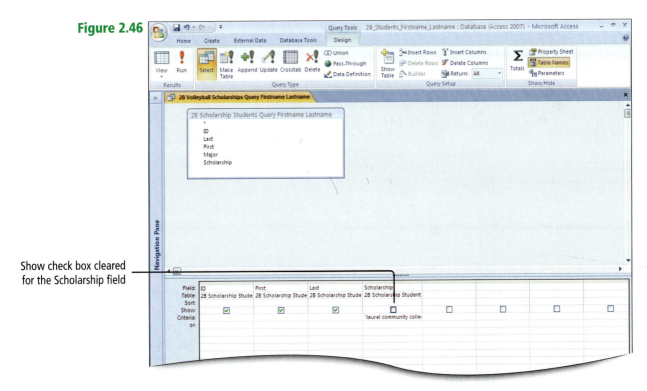

Show check box cleared for the Scholarship field

4 **Run** the query.

The query results display the same three records, but the Scholarship field no longer displays. The Scholarship field is included in the criteria to extract specific records, but it is not necessary to display the field in the results. Clear the Show check box to avoid cluttering the query results with redundant data.

5 If you are instructed to submit this result, create a paper or electronic printout.

6 Close ☒ the query, saving changes, but do not close the database.

Activity 2.18 Finding Empty Fields

At times, you may want to locate records where specific data is missing. For example, you might want to display the students who do not have scholarships. To locate these records, use ***is null***—empty—as criteria for the Scholarship field. You can also locate records that have data entered in a field by using ***is not null***—not empty—as criteria.

1 On the Ribbon, click the **Create tab**, and then in the **Other group**, click the **Query Design** button. In the displayed **Show Table** dialog box, double-click **2B Students**, and then click **Close**.

2 Expand the **2B Students** field list to display all of the fields and the table name. From the **2B Students** field list, add, in the order given, the following fields to the design grid: **ID**, **Last**, **First**, and **Scholarship**.

3 In the **Criteria row**, under the **Scholarship** field, type **is null** and then press ⏎. Compare your screen with Figure 2.47.

Access changed the criteria to *Is Null*. The criteria *Is Null* examines the field and searches for records that do not have any values entered in the Scholarship field.

Figure 2.47

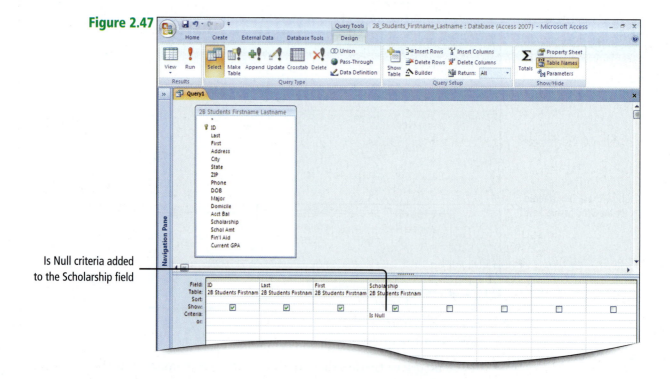

Is Null criteria added to the Scholarship field

Note — Access Sometimes Alters Criteria

If you press Enter or click in another column or row in the Query design grid, after you have added the criteria, you can see how Access alters the criteria so that it can interpret what you typed. At times, Access may capitalize a letter or add quotation marks or other symbols to clarify the criteria. At other times, there is no change, such as when a number is added as criteria for a number or currency field. Pressing Enter after the criteria is added does not affect the query results. It is used in this text to help you understand how the program behaves.

4 Under the **Last** field, click in the **Sort row**, click the **Sort arrow**, and then click **Ascending**. **Run** the query to display the results, and then compare your screen with Figure 2.48.

Twelve students do not have scholarships—the Scholarship field is empty for these students.

Records sorted in ascending order by Last field

Scholarship field empty for 12 records

Figure 2.48

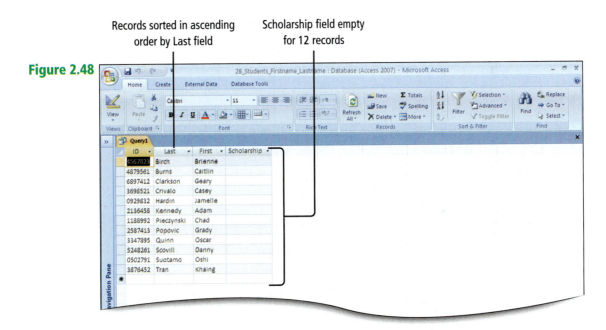

5 Using the technique you practiced in Activity 2.17, hide the **Scholarship** field from results, and then **Run** the query. **Save** the query as **2B No Scholarships Query Firstname Lastname**

6 If you are instructed to submit this result, create a paper or electronic printout.

7 **Close** ☒ the query, but do not close the database.

Activity 2.19 Specifying Numeric Criteria in a Query

In this activity, you will specify criteria so that only those students with a 4.0 GPA—grade point average—will display.

1 Using the techniques you just practiced in this project, create a new query in **Query Design**. Add the **2B Students** table to the Query design workspace. Expand the field list. From the **2B Students** field list, add the following fields, in the order specified, to the design grid: **ID**, **First**, **Last**, and **Current GPA**.

2 Click in the **Sort row** under **Last**, click the **arrow**, and then click **Ascending**. In the **Criteria row**, under **Current GPA**, type **4.0** and then press Enter. Compare your screen with Figure 2.49.

Access removed the decimal point and zero from the criteria. You should include a decimal point only if you are looking for a specific number that includes decimals—for example, 3.95. Unlike a text field, Access does not add quotation marks around criteria entered for a field with a data type of Number or Currency.

Sort in ascending order by Last name

Figure 2.49

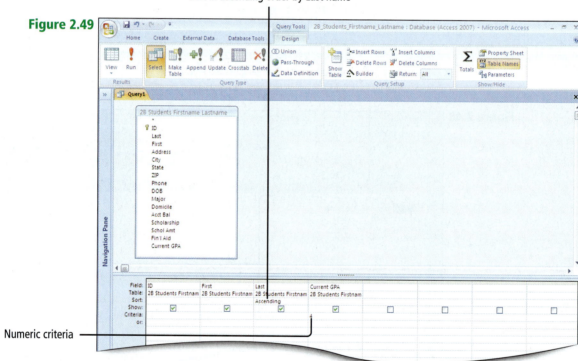

Numeric criteria

Note — Criteria for Currency Data Types

When entering currency values as criteria in the design grid, do not type the dollar sign or comma. Only include the decimal point if you are looking for a specific amount that includes cents—for example, 1456.98.

3 **Run** the query to display the results.

The records are sorted in ascending order by the last name, and six students have a 4.00 GPA. It is good practice to view the results of a query, displaying all of the fields to ensure that you have extracted the correct records; then you can hide fields with redundant data.

4 Hide the **Current GPA** field, and then **Run** the query. **Save** 🖫 the query as **2B Students with 4 GPA Query Firstname Lastname**

Because database object names cannot contain periods, you typed 4 GPA instead of 4.00 GPA.

5 If you are instructed to submit this result, create a paper or electronic printout.

6 **Close** ☒ the query, but do not close the database.

Activity 2.20 Using Comparison Operators in a Query

Comparison operators are symbols that Access uses to compare the value in the field with the value given after the comparison operator. All records that meet the condition are displayed in the results. If no comparison operator is specified, equal (=) is assumed. For example, in Activity 2.19, you created a query to display only records of students who have a GPA of 4. The comparison operator of ⬚ was assumed, and Access displayed only records that had entries equal to the number specified—4.

In this activity, you will specify criteria in the query to display records from the *2B Students* table for students who have a GPA that is greater than 3.8 and then less than 3.0. You will also display records of students born between specific dates.

1 Expand ⬚ the **Navigation Pane**. Under **Queries**, click **2B Students with 4 GPA Query** to select the query. Click the **Office** button ⬚, and then point to **Save As**. Under **Save the current database object**, click **Save Object As**. In the displayed **Save As** dialog box, under **Save '2B Students with 4 GPA Query . . .' to:**, type **2B Students GPA Query Firstname Lastname** and then click **OK**.

Because this query will use the same fields as the query you created in Activity 2.19, it is easier to create a copy of that query and then make changes to it. Both queries display on the Navigation Pane, and the newly saved query is open in Datasheet view.

2 Collapse ⬚ the **Navigation Pane**. Switch to **Design** view. In the design grid, under **Current GPA**, in the **Show row**, select the **Show** check box. Take a moment to study the comparison operators as described in the table in Figure 2.50.

Access Comparison Operators

Operator	Description	Example	Displays Records with
=	Equal to. If no operator included in criteria, equal is assumed.	="McLellan" =200	Text value of McLellan. Numeric value of 200.
>	Greater than.	>300 >7/19/09	Values greater than 300. Dates later than 7/19/09.
>=	Greater than or equal to.	>=300	Values greater than or equal to 300.
<	Less than.	<200	Values less than 200.
<=	Less than or equal to.	<=200	Values less than or equal to 200.
<>	Not equal to.	<>"McLellan" <>15	Anything but text value of McLellan or numeric value of 15.
Between . . . And . . .	The two values and all the values between them.	Between 200 And 300	Numbers from 200 to 300, inclusive.
In ()	Included in a set of values.	In("VA", "PA")	Either VA or PA.
Is Null	Field is empty.	Is Null	Records with no value in the field.
Is Not Null	Field is not empty.	Is Not Null	Records with a value in the field.
" "	Text or memo fields that have no characters.	=""	Records with no characters in the field.
Like	Matches a pattern; used with wildcards.	Like "M*"	Any text values that begin with M.

Figure 2.50

3 In the **Criteria row**, under **Current GPA**, select **4**, type **>3.8** and then press Enter. Compare your screen with Figure 2.51.

Figure 2.51

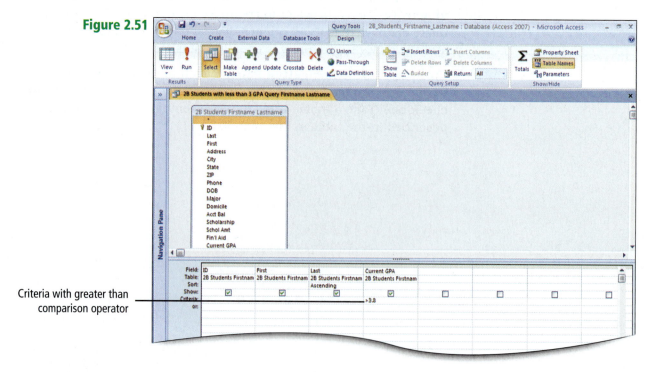

Criteria with greater than comparison operator

4 **Run** the query to display the results. Notice there are no records with a GPA of 3.80.

Fourteen records display, and each student has a GPA greater than 3.8.

5 Switch to **Design** view. In the **Criteria row**, under **Current GPA**, select the existing criteria, type **>=3.8** and then **Run** the query.

Sixteen students have a GPA of 3.8 or higher. The criteria included a comparison operator for greater than or equal to 3.8. Students who have a GPA of 3.80 are displayed in the results.

6 Switch to **Design** view. In the **Criteria row**, under **Current GPA**, select the existing criteria, type **<3** and then **Run** the query. Notice that eight students have a GPA of less than 3.00. **Save** 🔲 the query.

7 If you are instructed to submit this result, create a paper or electronic printout.

8 **Close** ☒ the query, but do not close the database.

9 **Create** a new query in **Query Design**. Add the **2B Students** table to the Query design workspace, and then expand the field list. Add the following fields, in the order specified, to the design grid: **Last**, **First**, and **DOB**. **Sort** the **DOB** field in **Ascending** order.

10 In the **Criteria row**, under **DOB**, type **between 1/1/88 and 12/31/88** and then press [Enter]. Compare your screen with Figure 2.52, which has been widened to fully display the criteria.

This criteria instructs Access to look in the DOB field, which stands for Date Of Birth, for values that begin with 1/1/1988 and end with 12/31/1988. Depending on your computer settings, the year may be displayed with two digits or four digits. Both the beginning and ending dates will be included in the query results if the dates exist in the field. Access capitalizes *Between* and *And*. Access also places # symbols around both dates, which identifies these values as dates.

Figure 2.52

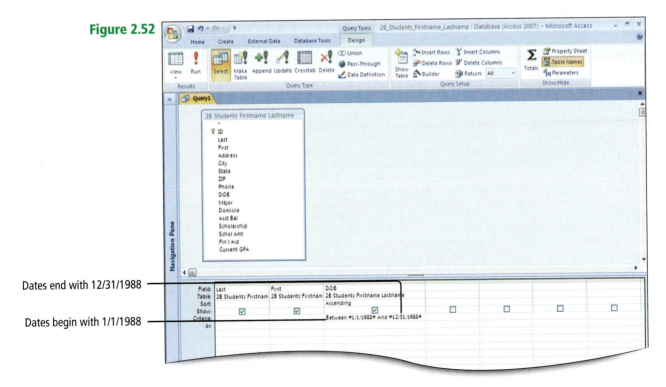

Dates end with 12/31/1988

Dates begin with 1/1/1988

11 **Run** the query. Notice that six students have birth dates between the dates you specified in the criteria. **Save** 💾 the query as **2B Students Born in 1988 Query Firstname Lastname**

There are no records with a DOB of 1/1/1988 in the table. There is one student who was born on 12/31/1988.

12 If you are instructed to submit this result, create a paper or electronic printout. **Close** ✕ the query, but do not close the database.

Activity 2.21 Using a Wildcard in Query and Rearranging Fields

When you are unsure of the particular character or set of characters to include in the criteria, you can use special characters known as wildcard characters in place of the characters in the criteria. **Wildcard characters** in a query serve as a placeholder for one or more unknown characters in your criteria.

Use the asterisk (*) wildcard character to represent one or more characters. For example, if you use the * wildcard in the criteria Do*, the results would return Doe, Door, Doreen, Dozier, and so on. In this activity, you will use the asterisk (*) wildcard to specify criteria so that only the students with a last name starting with the letter *P* display in the results.

1 **Create** a new query in **Query Design**. Add the **2B Students** table to the Query design workspace, and expand the field list. Add the following fields, in the order specified, to the design grid: **Last**, **First**, **Address**, **City**, **State**, and **ZIP**. **Sort** the **Last** field in **Ascending** order and the **First** field in **Ascending** order.

2 In the **Criteria row**, under **Last**, type **p*** and then press Enter. Compare your screen with Figure 2.53.

The wildcard character * is used as a placeholder for one or more characters—the last name must begin with *p* followed by one or more characters. The text entered for criteria is not case sensitive; you can type the letter in lowercase or uppercase. When you press Enter, *Like* is added by Access to the beginning of the criteria. This is used to compare a sequence of characters to test whether the data matches a pattern.

Figure 2.53

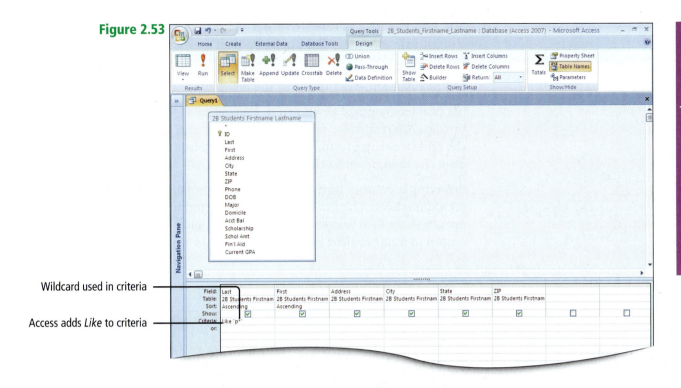

Wildcard used in criteria

Access adds *Like* to criteria

Note — Parentheses in Criteria

Access adds quotation marks to text criteria to identify the text as a string of characters. Parentheses are used by Access in programming code and in calculations. If parentheses are part of the criteria for a text field, you must type the quotation marks as part of the criteria—Access will not automatically insert the quotation marks. An example is using an area code of *(804)* as criteria with the * wildcard character. If the area code is stored in the table within parentheses, you must enter "*(804)**" to find all the records that have a telephone number starting with the area code of 804.

3 **Run** the query.

Five records display with the last names of students beginning with *P*. The records are sorted in ascending order by the Last field. If any of the last names had duplicate values, the records would be sorted in ascending order by First name within the Last names.

4 Switch to **Design** view. In the **Criteria row**, under **Last**, select and then delete the existing text of **Like "p*"**. In the **Sort row**, under **First**, change the sort to **(not sorted)**, and then press Enter. Alternatively, double-click in the Sort row to select the sort method, and then press Delete.

5 In the design grid, point to the **selection bar** above **Address** until the ⬇ pointer displays, and then click one time to select the column.

6 On the **Design tab**, in the **Query Setup group**, click the **Delete Columns** button. Alternatively, right-click the selected column, and then click Cut; or with the column selected, press Delete.

The Address field is removed from the design grid. Recall that you cannot delete a query field in Datasheet view.

7 In the **2B Students** field list, click **Fin'l Aid** to select the field. Point to **Fin'l Aid** and drag down to the design grid on top of **City** until the ⬛ pointer displays as shown in Figure 2.54. Release the mouse button. Alternatively, select the City field; and on the Design tab, in the Query Setup group, click the Insert Columns button, and then drag the field down to the empty column.

Selecting a column in the design grid is similar to selecting a column on a datasheet. The Fin'l Aid field is inserted into the design grid, and the City field moves to the right. Dragging a field into the grid on top of another field is an efficient way to insert fields.

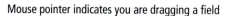
Mouse pointer indicates you are dragging a field

Figure 2.54

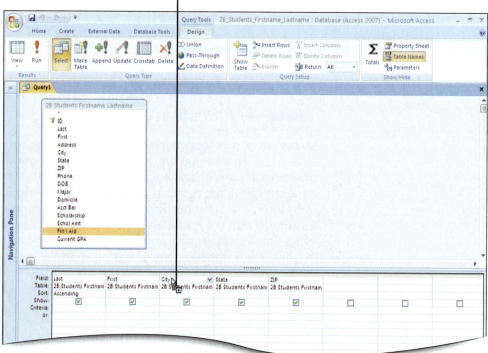

8 In the design grid, point to the **selection bar** above **City** until the ⬇ pointer displays. Click and drag to the right to select the **City**, **State**, and **ZIP** columns, and then press Delete.

9 On the **Design tab**, in the **Query Setup group**, click the **Show Table** button. Alternatively, right-click in the Query design workspace—not on a field list—and from the shortcut menu, click Show Table. In the **Show Table** dialog box, double-click **2B Scholarships**, and then click **Close**. Expand the **2B Scholarships** field list.

The *2B Scholarships* field list is added to the Query design workspace and is joined to the *2B Students* table. Recall that you created the relationship between these tables. The ID field in the *2B Scholarships* table—primary key field—and the Scholarship field in the *2B Students* table—foreign key field—are the common fields.

10 In the **2B Scholarships** field list, double-click **Scholarship** to add the field to the fourth column in the design grid.

11 Point to the **selection bar** above **Scholarship** to display the 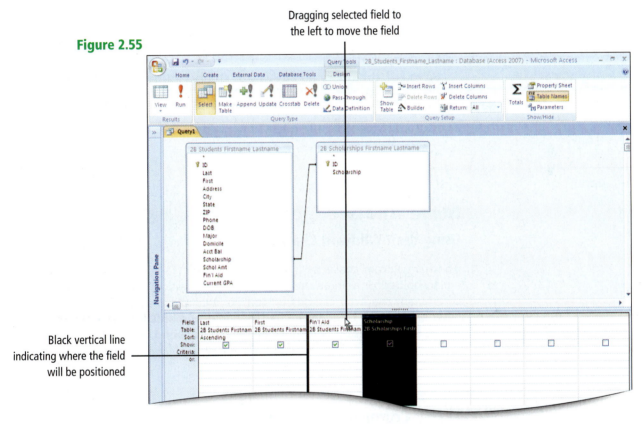 pointer. Drag to the left until a vertical black line displays between the **First** and **Fin'l Aid** columns, as shown in Figure 2.55, and then release the mouse button.

The black vertical line displays where the dragged field will be placed after the mouse button is released. Moving fields in the Query design grid is similar to moving fields in a datasheet.

Dragging selected field to the left to move the field

Figure 2.55

Black vertical line indicating where the field will be positioned

12 Using the technique you just practiced, drag the **Last** field to the right of the **First** field. Alternatively, drag the First field to the left of the Last field. Verify that the fields display in this order: First, Last, Scholarship, and Fin'l Aid.

13 In the **Criteria row**, under **Scholarship**, type ***award** and then press Enter.

Access changes the criteria to *Like "*award"*. The * can be used at the beginning or the end of the criteria. The position of the wildcard character determines the location of the unknown characters. Here you will extract records that have *award* at the end of the Scholarship field.

The * can also be used in the middle of criteria. For example, *a*a*
extracts records for data that starts with *a* and ends with *a*. You can
also have two asterisks; for example, **a** extracts records for data
that have *a* between the first and last characters.

Note — Structured Query Language

Structured Query Language (SQL) is a language used in querying, updating, and managing relational databases. The term *Like* is used in SQL to
compare string expressions. In Access, the term **expression** is a synonym for
formula. A **string expression** looks at a sequence of characters and compares them to the criteria in a query.

---

14 **Run** the query. Notice that three students are receiving Scholarships
that have the word *Award* at the end of the scholarship name.

Save 🖫 the query as **2B Awards Query Firstname Lastname**

15 If you are instructed to submit this result, create a paper or electronic
printout. **Close** ✕ the query, but do not close the database.

More Knowledge
Using the ? Wildcard Character

Another wildcard character is the question mark (?). Each question mark is
a placeholder for a single character. For each question mark included in the
criteria, any character can be inserted. For example, if *b?d* is entered as the
criteria, the query could locate bad, bed, bid, and bud. If *b??d* is entered as
the criteria, the results could include band, bird, bond, and bled.

Objective 8
Specify Compound Criteria in a Query

Sometimes it is necessary to specify multiple conditions; this is called
compound criteria. Three types of **logical operators** are used in
compound criteria—AND, OR, and NOT. Logical operators are used to
enter criteria for the same field or different fields.

Activity 2.22 Using AND in a Query

Compound criteria using the AND logical operator will display records
that meet all parts of the criteria. In this activity, you will create a query
that displays scholarship students with a GPA that is less than 3.0.

1 Take a moment to study the logical operators as described in the
table in Figure 2.56.

Access Logical Operators

Operator	Description	Example	Displays Records with
AND	All criteria must be true.	>=5 AND <=10 (Criteria in different fields)	Values between 5 and 10, inclusive—similar to Between . . . And . . .
		<3 AND "Award" (Criteria in different fields)	Value less than 3 and text of Award.
OR	Either criteria must be true.	"Volleyball" OR "Soccer"	Either Volleyball or Soccer.
NOT	Not true.	NOT Like "Do*"	All values except those beginning with Do—similar to <>.

Figure 2.56

2 **Create** a new query in **Query Design**. In the **Show Table** dialog box, on the **Tables tab**, add **2B Students** to the Query design workspace. Click the **Queries tab**, add **2B Scholarship Students Query** to the Query design workspace, and then expand both field lists. From the **2B Scholarship Students Query** field list, add the following fields, in the order specified, to the design grid: **Last**, **First**, and **Scholarship**. From the **2B Students** field list, add the **Current GPA** field to the design grid in the fourth column. **Sort** the **Current GPA** field in **Descending** order.

Alert!

Is the 2B Scholarship Students query field list not displaying the Last and First fields?

If the 2B Scholarship Students Query field list does not display the Last and First fields, you may have added the 2B Scholarships *table* instead of the *query*. If that is the case, right-click the 2B Scholarships field list, and then click Remove Table. Right-click in a blank area of the Query design workspace, and then click Show Table. In the Show Table dialog box, click the Queries tab, and then add 2B Scholarship Students Query to the Query design workspace.

3 In the **Criteria row**, under **Scholarship**, type **laurel*** and then press Enter. In the **Criteria row**, under **Current GPA**, type **<3** and then compare your screen with Figure 2.57.

Entering criteria on the same Criteria row in two different fields creates an AND condition. The Scholarship *must* begin with laurel *AND* the Current GPA *must* be less than 3.00—both criteria must be true to extract the records.

Figure 2.57

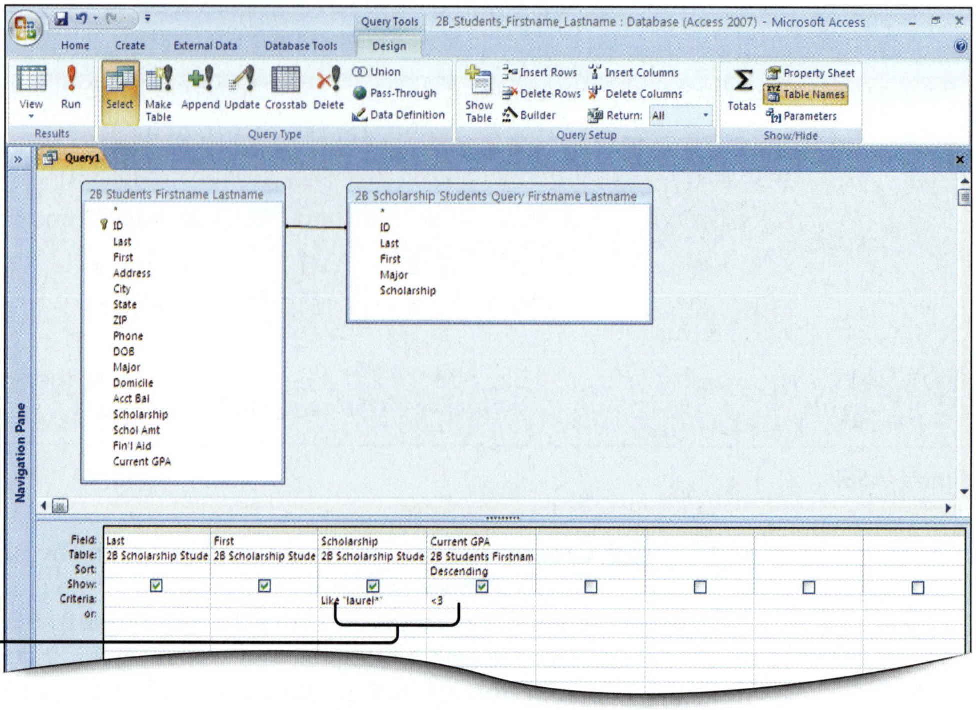

Criteria for Scholarship AND criteria for Current GPA

4 **Run** the query. Notice that two records match both criteria—the Scholarship starts with *laurel* AND the Current GPA is less than 3.

Save 💾 the query as **2B Scholarship Warning Query Firstname Lastname**

5 If you are instructed to submit this result, create a paper or electronic printout. **Close** ❌ the query, saving changes if prompted, but do not close the database.

Activity 2.23 Using OR in a Query

Use the OR condition to specify multiple criteria for a single field or multiple criteria on different fields when you want to extract the records that meet either condition.

1 Expand 》 the **Navigation Pane**. Under **Queries**, click **2B Scholarship Warning Query** to select the query. Click the **Office** button 🔘, and then point to **Save As**. Under **Save the current database object**, click **Save Object As**. In the displayed **Save As** dialog box, under **Save '2B Scholarship Warning Query . . .' to:**, type **2B OR Query Firstname Lastname** and then click **OK**.

2 Collapse 《 the **Navigation Pane**, and then switch to **Design** view. In the **Criteria row**, under **Current GPA**, select **<3**, and then press [Delete]. In the **or row**, under **Current GPA**, type **<3** and then compare your screen with Figure 2.58.

Entering criteria on the Criteria row and then entering different criteria on the or row creates an OR condition. The Scholarship *can* begin with laurel *OR* the Current GPA *can* be less than 3—only one of the criteria must be true to extract the records.

Criteria for Scholarship OR criteria for Current GPA

Figure 2.58

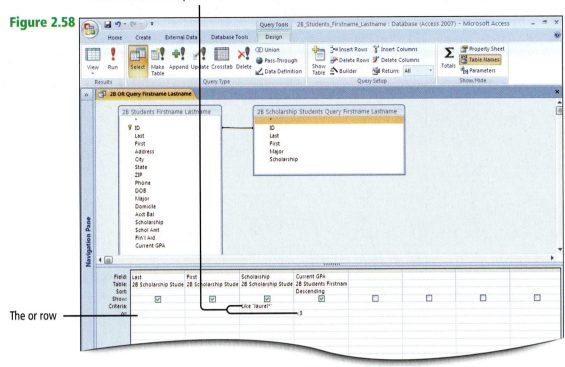

The or row

3 **Run** the query. Notice that ten records match either criteria—the Scholarship starts with *laurel* OR the Current GPA is less than 3.00.

Record 10 displays a Scholarship that starts with *Pennsylvania*. The Scholarship criteria was not met. However, the Current GPA for record 10 is *2.10*, which matches the second criteria. Only one of the criteria in an OR condition must be true to extract the records. Record 1 matches the Scholarship criteria but does not match the Current GPA criteria—one criteria of the OR condition is true, so the record is displayed in the results.

4 If you are instructed to submit this result, create a paper or electronic printout. **Close** ✕ the query, and **Save** the changes to the query design. Do not close the database.

5 **Create** a new query in **Query Design**. Add the **2B Students** table to the Query design workspace, and then expand the field list. Add the following fields, in the order specified, to the design grid: **ID**, **First**, **Last**, and **Major**. **Sort** the **Major** field in **Ascending** order.

6 In the **Criteria row**, under **Major**, type **120-04** and then press ↓. In the **or row**, under **Major**, type **299*** and then press Enter. Compare your screen with Figure 2.59.

Use the OR condition in one field by typing the first criteria on the Criteria row and the second criteria on the or row in the same column. If you have a third criteria for an OR condition, type the criteria in the same column in the row under the or row.

Figure 2.59

Two criteria for Major

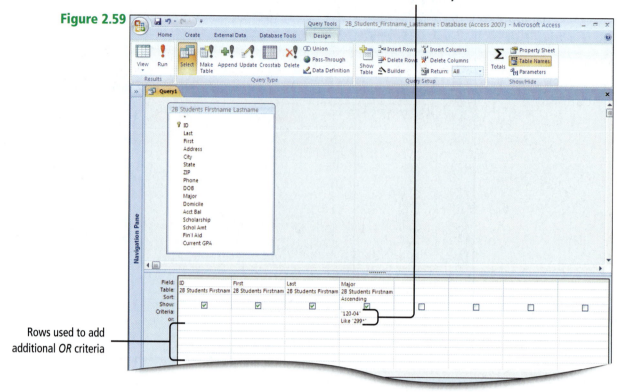

Rows used to add additional *OR* criteria

---

7 **Run** the query. Notice that six records match *either* criteria—the Major is equal to 120-04 OR the Major begins with 299. The records are sorted in ascending order by the Major field.

Another Way — **To Use the OR Logical Operator**

You can type multiple criteria for the same field on the Criteria row. For example, type *120-04 or 299**. The results will be the same as if you typed the first criteria on the Criteria row and the second criteria on the or row. You can use this same technique using the AND logical operator when you want to display a range of numbers from the same field.

---

8 Switch to **Design** view. **Sort** the **Last** field in **Ascending** order. **Run** the query. Look carefully at the sort order of the **Last** and **Major** fields.

The Last names are in ascending order, but the Major field is no longer in ascending order—the last three records are not in ascending order by Major. The intention was to sort by the Major field. If there are multiple records with the same major, those records should be sorted by the Last name field. Access sorts from left to right, so the field that should be sorted first needs to be to the left of the field that is sorted second.

9 Switch to **Design** view. Move the **Major column** to the left of the **ID column**, and then **Run** the query. Notice that the records are sorted first by Major and then by Last name.

10 Switch to **Design** view. On the **Design tab**, in the **Query Setup group**, click the **Show Table** button. In the **Show Table** dialog box, double-click **2B Majors** to add the field list to the Query design workspace, and then expand the **2B Majors** field list.

11 In the **2B Majors** field list, drag the **Major** field down into the design grid on top of the **ID** field.

The Major field from *2B Majors* is inserted between the Major field from *2B Students* and the ID field from *2B Students*.

12 **Run** the query, and then compare your screen with Figure 2.60.

The name of the major is displayed in the second column. Because the design grid contains two field names that are the same—Major— Access includes the table name before the field name in the column heading. You should keep this in mind as you design your related tables and ensure that all fields have unique names if you will use those fields in other database objects.

Duplicate field names
from different tables

Figure 2.60

13 Switch to **Design** view. In the design grid, under **Major** for *2B Students*—the first column—in the **Show row**, clear the check box. **Run** the query.

You used the Major code from the *2B Students* table to select majors of 120-04 and majors starting with 299, which is less typing than entering the entire major name. You then used the related table— *2B Majors*—to display the name of the major. Access extracts the code from the *2B Students* table, matches the code with the record in the *2B Majors* field, and extracts the name of the major.

Because you are now displaying only one of the Major fields in the results, Access does not include the table name in the column heading.

14 **Save** the query as **2B Major OR Query Firstname Lastname**

15 Unless you have been instructed to submit your database electronically, **Print** the query. **Close** ✕ the query, but do not close the database.

Activity 2.24 Using AND and OR in a Query

You can use both the AND and OR logical operators in a query. In this activity, you will extract records displaying out-of-state students who have either a scholarship or who are receiving financial aid.

1 **Create** a new query in **Query Design**. Add the **2B Students** table to the Query design workspace, and expand the field list. Add the following fields, in the order specified, to the design grid: **Last**, **First**, **Domicile**, **Scholarship**, and **Fin'l Aid**. **Sort** the **Last** field in **Ascending** order.

2 In the **Criteria row**, under **Domicile**, type **out of state** In the **Criteria row**, under **Scholarship**, type **is not null** In the **or row**, under **Domicile**, type **out of state** In the **or row**, under **Fin'l Aid**, type **yes** and then press Enter. Compare your screen with Figure 2.61.

Recall that the criteria of *is not null* looks for a field that contains data—is not empty. The criteria for the Fin'l Aid field will extract records that have the check box selected. You can also type *True* instead of Yes. If you want to extract records where the check box is cleared, the criteria would be *No* or *False*.

Think of the criteria entered on the Criteria row as one condition and the criteria entered on the or row as another condition. These two conditions are joined with the OR logical operator, so only one of the conditions needs to be true for the record to be extracted. If Access finds a match on the first condition, it will not check the second condition. If the first condition is not met—false—then Access will evaluate the second condition.

In this query, Access will look for students who are out of state AND have a scholarship. If the criteria is true, Access will not look at the or row. OR, if the criteria is false, Access will look for students who are out of state AND who have financial aid.

Figure 2.61

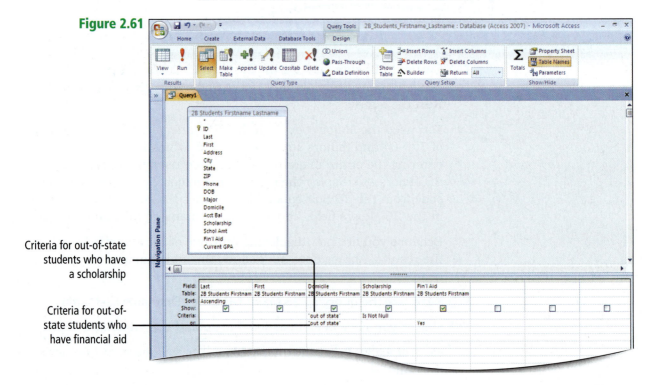

Criteria for out-of-state students who have a scholarship

Criteria for out-of-state students who have financial aid

3 **Run** the query, and then compare your screen with Figure 2.62. Notice that five records match the criteria.

When criteria contains multiple AND or OR logical operators, Access first evaluates the AND conditions. After all the AND conditions are evaluated, Access then evaluates the OR conditions.

Out of state and has financial aid—second AND condition

Figure 2.62

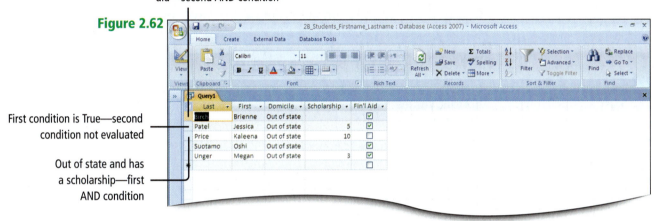

First condition is True—second condition not evaluated

Out of state and has a scholarship—first AND condition

4 **Save** 🖫 the query as **2B AND and OR Query Firstname Lastname**

A query name should be descriptive of the query results. In this project, you have saved some of the queries, including this one, with a name that reflects the technique used to create the query. As you create other queries, you can use these already created queries as examples, opening them in Design view to display the criteria.

5 If you are instructed to submit this result, create a paper or electronic printout.

6 **Close** ✕ the query, and expand 》 the **Navigation Pane**.

7 On the **Navigation Pane**, click the **Navigation Pane arrow** ⊙, and then click **Tables and Related Views**.

The objects are grouped by tables. Under each table, the objects that were created using the table are displayed. Some queries display more than one time under a different table name. If you create a query using two related tables, the query displays under both table names. Before modifying objects, it is a good idea to display the Navigation Pane by Tables and Related Views so that you will know the other objects that may be affected by any changes you make to a related object.

8 **Close** the database, and **Exit** Access.

End **You have completed Project 2B**

There's More You Can Do!

From My Computer, navigate to the student files that accompany this textbook. In the folder **02_theres_more_you_can_do**, locate and open the folder for this chapter. Open and print the instructions for this project, which are provided to you in Adobe PDF format.

Try It! 1—Creating a Top Value Query

In this Try It! project, you will create a top value query to locate records that contain the top values in a field.

Try It! 2—Creating a Top Value Query for Grouped Records

In this Try It! project, you will create a top value query to display the bottom values of records that have been grouped by a specific category.

Content-Based Assessments

Summary

In this chapter, you opened and renamed an existing database, and sorted and filtered records. You joined tables together to create table relationships and created select queries using the Query Wizard and Query Design. You then practiced extracting specific information from a database by adding criteria to a query.

Key Terms

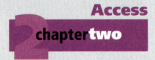

Matching

Match each term in the second column with its correct definition in the first column by writing the letter of the term on the blank line in front of the correct definition.

—— **1.** The process of arranging data in a specific order based on the value in a field.

—— **2.** The order that sorts text in reverse alphabetical order (Z to A) and sorts numbers from the highest number to the lowest number.

—— **3.** A process used to display only a portion of the total records in a table based on matching specific values.

—— **4.** Buttons that are used to perform a task and then undo the same task.

—— **5.** Database objects used to sort, search, and limit the data that displays.

—— **6.** An association that is established between two tables using common fields.

—— **7.** The field that is included in the related table so that it can be joined with the primary key field in another table.

—— **8.** The line connecting the primary key field to the foreign key field. It displays between the two field lists.

—— **9.** A guide that presents each step as a dialog box in which you choose what you want to do and how you want the results to look.

—— **10.** A security feature that checks documents for macros and digital signatures.

—— **11.** Conditions that identify the specific records for which you are looking.

—— **12.** The language used in querying, updating, and managing relational databases.

—— **13.** In Access, the term that is a synonym for *formula*.

—— **14.** A formula that looks at a sequence of characters and compares them to the criteria in a query.

—— **15.** The characters * and ?.

A Criteria

B Descending

C Expression

D Filtering

E Foreign key field

F Join line

G Queries

H Relationship

I Sorting

J String expression

K Structured Query Language (SQL)

L Toggle buttons

M Trust Center

N Wildcard characters

O Wizard

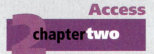

Fill in the Blank

Write the correct word in the space provided.

1. _____ order sorts text alphabetically (A to Z) and sorts numbers from the lowest number to the highest number.

2. Filtering records in a table displays only a portion of the total records or a(n) _____ based on matching specific values.

3. To _____ is to ask a question.

4. When you locate specific information in a database by using a query, you are _____ information from the database.

5. When a query is _____, Access looks at the records in the table or tables you have included in the query, finds the records that match specified criteria (if any), and displays those records in Datasheet view.

6. The _____ _____ view displays the results of the query; the _____ _____ view displays how the query was formed.

7. Access databases are _____ databases, which means the tables in the databases can relate or connect to other tables through common fields.

8. Because a single coach is responsible for a team with many events, the relationship between each coach and the team event is known as a(n) _____-_____-_____ relationship.

9. A(n) _____ query obtains its data from one or more tables, from existing queries, or from a combination of the two.

10. A(n) _____ is the location of a folder or file on your computer or storage device.

11. The comparison operator for greater than or equal to is keyed as _____.

12. When you are unsure of the particular character or set of characters to include in the criteria, you can use _____ characters in place of the characters in the criteria.

13. A(n) _____ expression looks at a sequence of characters and compares them to the criteria in a query.

14. You can specify more than one condition—criteria—in a query; this is called _____ _____.

15. The three types of logical operators used in compound criteria are _____, _____, and _____.

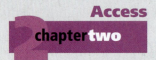

Skills Review

Project 2C—Cultural Events

In this project, you will apply the skills you practiced from the Objectives in Project 2A.

Objectives: 1. *Open and Rename an Existing Database;* **2.** *Sort Records;* **3.** *Filter Records;* **4.** *Open, Edit, Sort, and Print an Existing Query;* **5.** *Create Table Relationships and a Simple Query.*

Laurel County Community College uses sorting techniques, filters, and queries to locate information about the data in its databases. In the following Skills Review, you will assist Pavel Linksz, vice president of student services, in locating information about the cultural events scheduled for students of the college. Your results will look similar to those in Figure 2.63.

For Project 2C, you will need the following file:

a02C_Cultural_Events

**You will save your database as
2C_Cultural_Events_Firstname_Lastname**

Figure 2.63

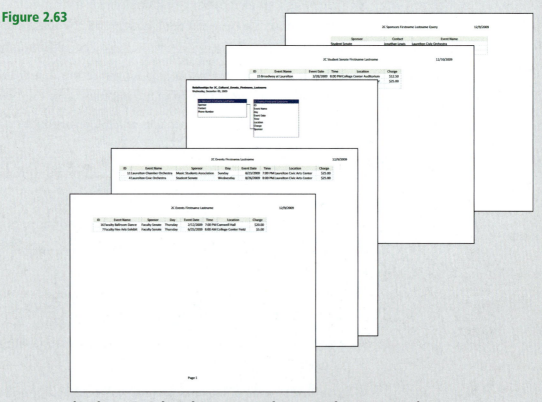

(Project 2C–Cultural Events continues on the next page)

Content-Based Assessments

(Project 2C–Cultural Events continued)

1. **Start** Access. Click the **Office** button, and then click **Open**. In the **Open** dialog box, click the **Look in arrow**, and then navigate to the location where the student data files for this textbook are saved. Locate and select **a02C_Cultural_Events**. Click **Open**.

2. Click the **Office** button, point to the **Save As arrow**, and then under **Save the database in another format**, click **Access 2007 database**. In the **Save As** dialog box, navigate to the **Access Chapter 2** folder. In the **File name** box, using your own first and last name, type 2C_Cultural_Events_Firstname_Lastname and then click **Save**.

3. If necessary, expand the **Navigation Pane**. On the **Navigation Pane**, under **Tables**, right-click **2C Events**, and then click **Rename**. Click to the right of **2C Events**, and then press Spacebar one time. Using your own first and last name, type **Firstname Lastname** and then press Enter.

4. Double-click **2C Events** to display the table in Datasheet view. Collapse the **Navigation Pane**. Point to any **field name**, and then right-click. From the shortcut menu, click **Unhide Columns**. In the **Unhide Columns** dialog box, select the check box for **ID**, and then click **Close**.

5. Click the **Sponsor** field name to select the column, and then point to the selected **Sponsor** field name. When the ↘ pointer displays, drag the **Sponsor column** to the left until a black vertical line displays between **Event Name** and **Day**, and then release the mouse button. With the **Sponsor** field still selected, hold down ⇧Shift, and then click the **Day** field name to select both columns. On the **Home tab**, in the **Sort & Filter group**, click the **Ascending** button. Click in any record to cancel the selection of the Sponsor and Day fields.

6. In the **Sponsor** field name box, click the **Sort & Filter arrow**. In the list, click to clear the **(Select All)** check box to remove the check marks from all of the check boxes. Next to **Faculty Senate**, select the check box, and then click **OK**. In the **Day** field name box, click the **Sort & Filter arrow**. In the displayed list, click to clear the **(Select All)** check box to clear all the check boxes. Next to **Thursday**, select the check box, and then click **OK**. The two events sponsored by the Faculty that are scheduled on Thursday will display. Adjust all of the columns to the width required to display the data and field names.

7. Change the page orientation to **Landscape**, and then if you are instructed to submit this result, create a paper or electronic printout. On the **Home tab**, in the **Sort & Filter group**, click the **Advanced** button, and then click **Clear All Filters**.

8. In the **Sponsor** field name box, click the **Sort & Filter arrow**, and then click the **(Select All)** check box to remove the check marks from all of the check boxes. Next to **Music Students Association**, click the check box. Next to **Student Senate**, click the check box, and then click **OK** to display the records for these two sponsors.

9. In the **Event Name** field name box, click the **Sort & Filter arrow**, point to **Text Filters**, and then click **Contains**. In the **Custom Filter** dialog box, in the **Event Name contains** box, type **Laurelton** and then click **OK**. In the **Location** field name box, click the **Sort & Filter arrow**. Select only the **Laurelton Civic Arts Center** check box. Adjust all of the columns to the width required to display the data and field names.

(Project 2C–Cultural Events continues on the next page)

(Project 2C–Cultural Events continued)

10. Display the table in **Print Preview** and then change the page orientation to **Landscape**. Select **Margins** and click **Normal**. If you are instructed to submit this result, create a paper or electronic printout. If you are saving a PDF file, change the **File name** to 2C Events Laurelton Firstname Lastname On the **Home tab**, in the **Sort & Filter group**, click the **Advanced** button, and then click **Clear All Filters**.

11. Expand the **Navigation Pane**, and then click the **All Access Objects** menu title. From the displayed list, click **Tables and Related Views**. Double-click the **2C International Students Association query**, and then collapse the **Navigation Pane**. On the **Home tab**, in the **Views group**, click the **View** button. In the design grid under **Sponsor**, select "**International Students Association**"—including the quotation marks—and then press Delete. Type **Student Senate** and then click in any empty box in the design grid.

12. **Run** the query. On the **Home tab**, in the **Views group**, click the **View** button to switch to **Design** view. In the design grid, point to the **selection bar** above the **Day** field until the ↓ pointer displays. Click to select the **Day** field, and then press Delete. In the design grid, select the **Sponsor column**. Then, point to the **selection bar** at the top of the **Sponsor column** to display the ⇖ pointer. Drag to the left until a black vertical line displays between the **Event Name** field and the **Event Date** field, and then release the mouse button. View the query results. On the **tab row**, click the **Close** button to close the query. In the displayed message box, click **Yes**. Expand the **Navigation Pane**. Rename *2C International Students Association* to **2C Student Senate Firstname Lastname**

13. Collapse the **Navigation Pane**. With the **2C Events** table as the current object, in the navigation area, click the **New (blank) record** button. Press Tab to move to the **Event Name** field. Enter the following data in the fields for **Record 17**.

Event Name	Sponsor	Day	Event Date	Time	Location	Charge
Mock United Nations Debate	Student Senate	Wednesday	9/23/2009	6:00 PM	Camwell Hall	

14. On the **tab row**, click the **Close** button to close the table. When prompted to save changes to the table, click **Yes**. Expand the **Navigation Pane**, and then double-click **2C Student Senate** to open the query in Datasheet view. Collapse the **Navigation Pane**. Switch to **Design** view. Under **Sponsor** in the **Show row**, click to clear the check box. **Run** the query.

15. With the **2C Student Senate** query as the current object, switch to **Design** view. In the design grid, under **Event Date**, click in the **Sort row**, click the **arrow**, and then from the displayed list, click **Ascending**. **Run** the query. Adjust the column widths to display all of the data in the fields and all of the field names. On the **Quick Access Toolbar**, click the **Save** button to save the changes to the query design. Open the query in **Print Preview**. Change the page orientation to **Landscape** even if you do not have to submit a printed copy.

16. If you are instructed to submit this result, create a paper or electronic printout. **Close** Print Preview. On the **tab row**, click the **Close** button to close the **2C Student Senate query**.

(Project 2C–Cultural Events continues on the next page)

Content-Based Assessments

(Project 2C–Cultural Events continued)

17. Expand the **Navigation Pane**. On the **All Tables** menu, click the **arrow**. From the displayed list, click **Object Type**. Rename *2C Sponsors* as **2C Sponsors Firstname Lastname** Open **2C Events**, and then open **2C Sponsors**. Collapse the **Navigation Pane**.

18. In **2C Sponsors**, notice there are no duplicates in the **Sponsor** field. Switch to **Design** view, and notice that Sponsor is the primary key field. Switch to **Datasheet** view. On the **tab row**, click the **2C Events tab** to make the table current. Notice there are *many* instances of the same sponsor. On the **tab row**, right-click either **object tab**. From the shortcut menu, click **Close All**.

19. From the **Database Tools tab**, in the **Show/Hide group**, click the **Relationships** button. In the **Show Table** dialog box, select the **2C Sponsors** table, and then click **Add**. In the **Show Table** dialog box, double-click the **2C Events** table. **Close** the **Show Table** dialog box.

20. In the **2C Events** field list, position the mouse pointer over the lower edge of the field list to display the ⊥ pointer, and then drag downward to display the entire field list. In the **2C Events** field list, position your mouse pointer over the right edge of the field list to display the ↔ pointer, and then drag to the right to display the entire name in the title bar. Expand the **2C Sponsors** field list to display all of the field names and to display the entire name of the table, and drag the tables apart, if necessary. In the **2C Sponsors** field list, point to **Sponsor**, drag to the left to the **2C Events** field list until the ⬚ points to **Sponsor**, and then release the mouse button. In the **Edit Relationships** dialog box, click **Create**. On the **Design tab**, in the **Tools group**, click **Relationship Report**.

21. If you are instructed to submit this result, create a paper or electronic printout.

22. On the **tab row**, click the **Close** button, and then click **Yes** when prompted to save the report. In the displayed **Save As** dialog box, click **OK** to accept the default report name. On the **tab row**, click the **Close** button to close the Relationships window. If a message displays asking if you want to save the layout of the relationships, click **Yes**.

23. On the Ribbon, click the **Create tab**. On the **Create tab**, in the **Other group**, click **Query Wizard**. In the displayed **New Query** dialog box, if necessary, click **Simple Query Wizard**, and then click **OK**. In the **Simple Query Wizard** dialog box, under **Available Fields**, click the **Add All Fields** button. Under **Selected Fields**, with **Phone#** selected, click the **Remove Field** button. Click the **Tables/Queries arrow**, and from the displayed list, click **Table: 2C Events**. Add the **Event Name** field to the **Selected Fields** list. In the **Simple Query Wizard** dialog box, click **Next**. Click **Next** to accept the default of **Detail**, and then click **Finish** to accept the default name and to view the query results in Datasheet view. Adjust column widths.

24. Click in the **record selector** box for the first **Student Senate** record, and then drag down until the ➡ pointer displays in the **Record Selector** box for the third **Student Senate** event. Release the mouse. Display the table in **Print Preview** and then change the page orientation to **Landscape**. Click **Print**. In the displayed **Print** dialog box, under **Print Range**, click the **Selected Record(s)** option button. In the **Print** dialog box, click the **Setup** button. In the **Page Setup** dialog box, under **Margins**, change the **Left** margin to **2** and the **Right** margin to **2** Be sure **Print Headings** is selected, and then click **OK**.

(Project 2C–Cultural Events continues on the next page)

Access

chapter two

Skills Review

(Project 2C—Cultural Events continued)

25. If you are instructed to submit this result, create a paper or electronic printout. **Close** the Print Preview window. On the **tab row**, click the **Close** button to close the query. If a message displays asking you to save the changes to the design of the query, click **Yes**. Expand the **Navigation Pane**, **Close** the database, and **Exit** Access.

 You have completed Project 2C ————————————————————————

Content-Based Assessments

Access
chapter two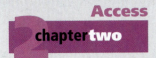

Skills Review

Project 2D — Classes

In this project, you will apply the skills you practiced from the Objectives in Project 2B.

Objectives: 6. *Create a Select Query;* **7.** *Specify Criteria in a Query;* **8.** *Specify Compound Criteria in a Query.*

Laurel County Community College keeps a database of class schedules for the fall, winter, and summer terms. In this Skills Review, you will be assisting Michael Schaeffler, vice president of instruction, who needs to extract relevant information from the database. Your results will look similar to those in Figure 2.64.

For Project 2D, you will need the following file:

For Project 2D, you will need the following file:

a02D_Classes

You will save your database as
2D_Classes_Firstname_Lastname

Figure 2.64

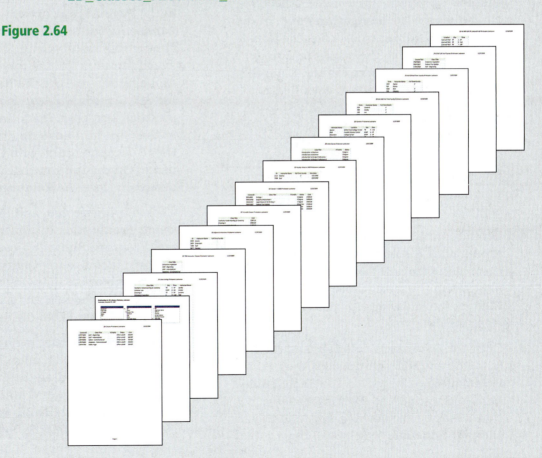

(Project 2D–Classes continues on the next page)

Content-Based Assessments

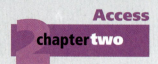

(Project 2D–Classes continued)

1. **Start** Access. Click the **Office** button, and then click **Open**. Navigate to the location where you have saved the student data files that accompany this text, and double-click **a02D_Classes** to open the database.

2. Click the **Office** button, and point to the **Save As arrow**. Under **Save the database in another format**, click **Access 2007 database**. In the **Save As** dialog box, navigate to the *Access Chapter 2* folder. In the **File name** box, using your own first and last name, type **2D_Classes_Firstname_Lastname** and then click **Save**.

3. Rename all tables by adding your **Firstname Lastname** to the end of each table name. On the **Navigation Pane**, double-click **2D Classes** to open the table in Datasheet view. Collapse the **Navigation Pane**. In the **Course ID** field name box, click the **Sort & Filter arrow**. From the displayed **Sort & Filter** list, point to **Text Filters**. From the displayed **Text Filters** list, click **Begins With**. In the **Custom Filter** dialog box, in the **Course ID begins with** box, type **CONT** and then click **OK**. Adjust all of the columns to the width required to display the data and field names. If you are instructed to submit this result, create a paper or electronic printout.

4. On the **Home tab**, in the **Sort & Filter group**, click the **Advanced** button, and then click **Clear All Filters** to delete the filters from the table. **Close** the **2D Classes** table, saving changes, but do not close the database.

5. Click the **Database Tools tab**, and then in the **Show/Hide group**, click the **Relationships** button. In the **Show Table** dialog box, select the **2D Classes** table, if necessary. Hold down ⇧ Shift, and then click **2D Schedule** to select all three

tables. Click **Add**, and then **Close** the **Show Table** dialog box. Expand each field list to display all of the fields and the entire table name. In the **2D Classes** field list, drag the **Course ID** field to the **2D Schedule** field list, point to the **Course Title** field, and release the mouse. In the displayed **Edit Relationships** dialog box, click **Create**. Create a relationship between the **2D Instructors ID** field and the **2D Schedule Instructor Name** field. Arrange the tables so that they are adjacent in order of 2D Classes, 2D Schedule, and 2D Instructors.

6. On the **Design tab**, in the **Tools group**, click the **Relationship Report** button. If necessary, to show all three field lists, in the **Page Layout group**, click the **Landscape** button. If you are instructed to submit this result, create a paper or electronic printout. On the **tab row**, click the **Close** button to close the **Relationships for 2D_Classes** window. In the displayed message box, click **Yes** to save the report. In the displayed **Save As** dialog box, click **OK** to save the report with the default name. On the **tab row**, click the **Close** button to close the **Relationships** window.

7. Click the **Create tab**, and then in the **Other group**, click the **Query Design** button. From the **Show Table** dialog box, add all three tables to the **Query design workspace** in the following order: **2D Classes**, **2D Schedule**, and **2D Instructors**. Close the **Show Table** dialog box.

8. Expand the field lists to display all of the fields and the table names. In the **2D Classes** field list, drag the **Class Title** field down to the design grid in the first column in the field box. In the **2D Schedule** field list, double-click **Day**. In the design grid,

(Project 2D–Classes continues on the next page)

Content-Based Assessments

Skills Review

(Project 2D–Classes continued)

in the third column, click in the **Table** box. Click the **Table box arrow**, and from the displayed list, click **2D Schedule**. In the design grid, in the third column, click in the **Field** box. Click the **Field box arrow**. From the displayed field list, click **Time**. From the **2D Instructors** field list, add the **Instructor Name** field to the fourth column of the design grid. On the **Sort row**, under the **Class Title** field, click the **Sort arrow**, and then click **Ascending**.

9. On the **Design tab**, in the **Results group**, click the **Run** button. On the **tab row**, right-click the **query tab**, and then click **Save**. In the displayed **Save As** dialog box, in the **Query Name** box, replace the default name with **2D Class Listing Firstname Lastname** and then click **OK**. Expand the **Navigation Pane**, which displays the saved query. Adjust all of the columns to the width required to display the data and field names.

10. If you are instructed to submit this result, create a paper or electronic printout. **Close** the query. **Save** changes.

11. Collapse the **Navigation Pane**. Click the **Create tab**, and then in the **Other group**, click the **Query Design** button. In the displayed **Show Table** dialog box, click the **Queries tab**, and then double-click **2D Class Listing** to add the query to the Query design workspace. **Close** the **Show Table** dialog box. Expand the **2D Class Listing** field list to display the entire query name. Add the following fields, in the order listed, to the design grid: **Class Title** and **Instructor Name**. In the **Criteria row**, under the **Instructor Name** field, type **TBD** In the **Show row**, under the **Instructor Name** field, clear the check box. On the **Design tab**, in the **Results group**, click

Run to display the list of classes with instructors to be determined. On the **Quick Access Toolbar**, click the **Save** button. In the displayed **Save As** dialog box, in the **Query Name** text box, type **2D TBD Instructor Classes Firstname Lastname** and then click **OK**. If you are instructed to submit this result, create a paper or electronic printout. **Close** the query.

12. Click the **Create tab**, and then in the **Other group**, click the **Query Design** button. In the displayed **Show Table** dialog box, double-click **2D Instructors**, and then click **Close**. Expand the field list to display all of the fields and the table name. From the **2D Instructors** field list, add, in the order given, the following fields to the design grid: **ID**, **Instructor Name**, **Office#**, and **Full Time Faculty**. In the **Criteria row** under the **Office#** field, type **is null** and then press Enter. On the **Sort row**, under the **Instructor Name** field, click the **Sort arrow**, and then click **Ascending**. Hide the **Office#** field from the results, and then **Run** the query. The query results display the instructors who have adjunct status. **Save** the query as **2D Adjunct Instructors Firstname Lastname** If you are instructed to submit this result, create a paper or electronic printout. **Close** the query.

13. **Create** a new query in **Query Design**. Add the **2D Classes** table to the Query design workspace. Expand the field list. From the **2D Classes** field list, add the following fields, in the order specified, to the design grid: **Class Title**, **# Credits**, and **Cost**. In the **Sort row** under **Class Title**, click the **Sort arrow**, and then click **Ascending**. In the **Criteria row**, under **Credits**, type **3** and then press Enter. Hide the **# Credits** field from the results, and then **Run** the query. Adjust all of the columns to the width required to

(Project 2D–Classes continues on the next page)

(Project 2D–Classes continued)

display the data and field names. The query should display 3-credit classes. **Save** the query as **2D 3-Credit Classes Firstname Lastname** If you are instructed to submit this result, create a paper or electronic printout. **Close** the query.

14. **Create** a new query in **Query Design**. Add the **2D Classes** table to the Query design workspace. Expand the field list. From the **2D Classes** field list, add the following fields, in the order specified, to the design grid: **Course ID**, **Class Title**, **# Credits**, **Status**, and **Cost**. Sort the **Course ID** field in **Ascending** order. In the **Criteria row**, under **Cost**, type **>=400** and then press Enter. **Run** the query to display the classes that cost at least $400. Adjust all of the columns to the width required to display the data and field names. **Save** the query as **2D Classes $400 Firstname Lastname** If you are instructed to submit this result, create a paper or electronic printout. **Close** the query.

15. **Create** a new query in **Query Design**. Add the **2D Instructors** table to the Query design workspace. Expand the field list. From the **2D Instructors** field list, add the following fields, in the order specified, to the design grid: **ID**, **Instructor Name**, **Full Time Faculty**, and **Hire Date**. Sort the **Hire Date** field in **Ascending** order.

16. In the **Criteria row**, under **Hire Date**, type **between 1/1/1999 and 12/31/1999** and then press Enter. **Run** the query to display the results. **Save** the query as **2D Faculty Hired in 1999 Firstname Lastname** If you are instructed to submit this result, create a paper or electronic printout. **Close** the query.

17. **Create** a new query in **Query Design**. Add the **2D Classes** table to the Query design workspace. Expand the field list. From the **2D Classes** field list, add the following fields, in the order specified, to the design grid:

Class Title, **# Credits**, and **Status**. Sort the **Class Title** field in **Ascending** order. In the **Criteria row**, under **Class Title**, type **intro*** and then press Enter. **Run** the query to display the results. The result will display the introductory classes. Adjust all of the columns to the width required to display the data and field names. **Save** the query as **2D Intro Classes Firstname Lastname** If you are instructed to submit this result, create a paper or electronic printout. **Close** the query.

18. **Create** a new query in **Query Design**. Add the **2D Instructors** and **2D Schedule** tables to the Query design workspace. Expand the field lists. From the **2D Instructors** field list, add **Instructor Name** to the first column in the design grid. From the **2D Schedule** field list, add the following fields, in the order specified, to the design grid: **Day**, **Time**, and **Location**. Select the **Location column**, and then point to the selection bar above

Location to display the ⇩ pointer. Drag to the left until a vertical black line displays between **Instructor Name** and **Day**, and then release the mouse button. Sort the **Instructor Name** field and the **Location** field in **Ascending** order. In the **Criteria row**, under **Location**, type ***Center** and then press Enter. **Run** the query to display the results. The listing displays the instructors teaching at centers. Adjust all of the columns to the width required to display the data and field names. **Save** the query as **2D Centers Firstname Lastname** If you are instructed to submit this result, create a paper or electronic printout. **Close** the query.

19. **Create** a new query in **Query Design**. Add the **2D Schedule** and **2D Instructors** tables to the Query design workspace. Expand both field lists. From the **2D Schedule** field list, add the **Term** field to the first column in

(Project 2D–Classes continues on the next page)

Content-Based Assessments

Skills Review

(Project 2D–Classes continued)

the design grid. From the **2D Instructors** field list, add the **Instructor Name** field and the **Full Time Faculty** field to the design grid. Sort the **Instructor Name** in **Ascending** order. In the **Criteria row**, under **Term**, type **F*** and then press Enter. In the **Criteria row**, under **Full Time Faculty**, type **yes** and then press Enter. **Run** the query to display the results. This result displays only those full-time instructors who are teaching the fall semester. **Save** the query as **2D Fall AND Full Time Faculty Firstname Lastname** If you are instructed to submit this result, create a paper or electronic printout. **Close** the query.

20. Expand the **Navigation Pane**. Under **Queries**, click **2D Fall AND Full Time Faculty Query** to select the query. Click the **Office** button, and then point to **Save As**. Under **Save the current database object**, click **Save Object As**. In the displayed **Save As** dialog box, under **Save '2D Fall AND Full Time Faculty. . .' to:**, type **2D Fall OR Full Time Faculty Firstname Lastname** and then click **OK**. Collapse the **Navigation Pane**, and then switch to **Design** view. In the **Criteria row**, under the **Full Time Faculty**, select **yes** and then press Delete. In the **or row**, under **Full Time Faculty**, type **Yes Run** the query to display the results. This query displays all of the faculty who are teaching the fall semester or who have a status of full time. **Save** the query as **2D Fall OR Full Time Faculty Firstname Lastname** If you are instructed to submit this result, create a paper or electronic printout. **Close** the query.

21. **Create** a new query in **Query Design**. Add the **2D Schedule** and **2D Classes** tables to the Query design workspace. Expand both field lists. From the **2D Schedule** field list, add the **Course Title** field to the first column in the design grid. From the **2D Classes** field list, add the **Class Title** field, and then sort this field in **Ascending** order. In the **Criteria row**, under **Course Title**, type **CONT* OR PROF*** and then press Enter. **Run** the query to display both the continuing education and professional development classes listed in the schedule. **Save** the query as **2D CONT OR PROF Classes Firstname Lastname** If you are instructed to submit this result, create a paper or electronic printout. **Close** the query.

22. **Create** a new query in **Query Design**. Add the **2D Schedule** table to the Query design workspace. Expand the field list. From the **2D Schedule** field list, add the following fields, in the order specified, to the design grid: **Location**, **Day**, and **Time**. In the **Criteria row**, under **Location**, type **Camwell Hall** In the **Criteria row**, under **Day**, type **TR** In the **or row**, under **Location**, type **Camwell Hall** In the **or row**, under **Day**, type **W Run** the query to display the results. The query displays the classes LCCC offers on Wednesday and Thursday at Camwell Hall. **Save** the query as **2D W AND OR TR Camwell Hall Firstname Lastname** If you are instructed to submit this result, create a paper or electronic printout.

23. **Close** the query, saving changes if prompted. Expand the **Navigation Pane**, **Close** the database, and **Exit** Access.

End **You have completed Project 2D**

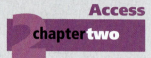

Content-Based Assessments

Mastering Access

Project 2E — Training Programs

In this project, you will apply the skills you practiced from the Objectives in Project 2A.

Objectives: 1. *Open and Rename an Existing Database;* **2.** *Sort Records;* **3.** *Filter Records;* **4.** *Open, Edit, Sort, and Print an Existing Query;* **5.** *Create Table Relationships and a Simple Query.*

Laurel County Community College uses sorting techniques, filters, and queries to locate information about the data in its databases. In the following Mastering Access project, you will help Kesia Toomer, vice president of administration and development, locate information about the industry-specific training programs for local businesses that are offered through the economic development center of LCCC. Your results will look similar to those in Figure 2.65.

> **For Project 2E, you will need the following file:**
>
> a02E_Training_Programs
>
> **You will save your database as**
> **2E_Training_Programs_Firstname_Lastname**

Figure 2.65

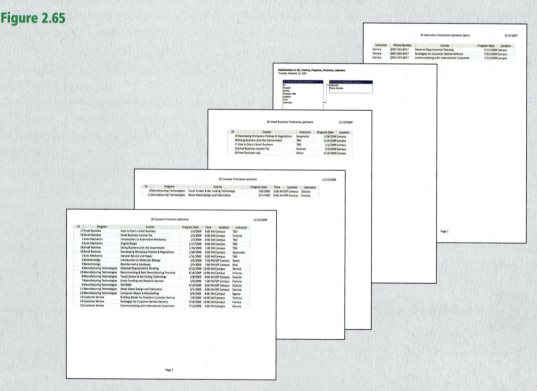

(Project 2E–Training Programs continues on the next page)

Content-Based Assessments

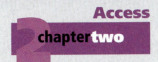
(Project 2E–Training Programs continued)

1. **Start** Access. Locate and open the student data file **a02E_Training_Programs**. **Save** this file as **2E_Training_Programs_Firstname_Lastname**

2. **Rename 2E Courses** to **2E Courses Firstname Lastname** and then open the table in **Datasheet** view. Unhide the **ID** field.

3. Drag the **Time column** to the left between **Program Date** and **Location**. Select both the **Program Date** and **Time** field name boxes, and then sort the fields in **Ascending** order. Adjust all of the columns to the width required to display the data and field names. Change the page orientation to **Landscape**, adjust margins to **Normal**, and then if you are instructed to submit this result, create a paper or electronic printout.

4. Filter the **Location** field so that the table displays only those courses that are offered Off Campus. Filter the **Time** field to include only morning classes. If you are instructed to submit this result, create a paper or electronic printout. If you are saving a PDF file, change the **File name** to **2E Courses Morning Firstname Lastname** Then, click **Clear All Filters**.

5. Open the **2E Manufacturing Technologies** query in **Design** view. In the design grid under **Program**, delete "**Manufacturing Technologies**". Type **Small Business** and then click in any empty box in the design grid. Delete the **Time** field. Drag the **Instructor** field to the left to position it between the **Course** field and the **Program Date** field. View the query. **Close** the query, and **Save** changes. Rename **2E Manufacturing Technologies** to **2E Small Business Firstname Lastname**

6. To the **2E Courses** table, add a new record with the following data:

Program	Course	Program Date	Time	Location	Instructor
Small Business	Small Business Law	2/16/2009	7:00 PM	Campus	Oliver

7. **Close** the table, and **save** changes. Open the **2E Small Business** query in **Design** view. Under **Program** in the **Show row**, clear the check box. Sort the **Course** field in **Ascending** order. **Run** the query. Open the query in **Print Preview** to ensure that it will print on one page even if you do not have to submit a printed copy. If you are instructed to submit this result, create a paper or electronic printout. **Close** and **Save** changes to the query.

8. **Rename 2E Instructors** as **2E Instructors Firstname Lastname** Open **2E Courses**, and then open **2E Instructors**. View the contents of each table. **Close** both tables. Create a relationship between the **2E Courses** and the **2E Instructors** tables, joining the **Instructor** field from each table. Click **Relationship Report**. If you are instructed to submit this result, create a paper or electronic printout. **Close** and **Save** changes to the report using the default name. **Close** the **Relationships** window.

9. **Create** a query using the **Simple Query Wizard**. Add all fields from the **2E Instructors** table. From the **2E Courses** table, add **Course**, **Program Date**, and **Location**, in this order. Accept the wizard's default options and query name. Sort the query by **Instructor** in **Ascending** order. Select all three records that have **Ferrera** listed as **Instructor**. In the **Print** dialog box,

(Project 2E–Training Programs continues on the next page)

(Project 2E–Training Programs continued)

click the **Selected Record(s)** option button. In the **Print** dialog box, click the **Setup** button. Under **Margins**, change the **Left** margin to **0.5** and the **Right** margin to **0.5** and then click **OK**. If you are instructed to submit this result, create a paper or electronic printout.

10. **Close** and **Save** changes to the query. Expand the **Navigation Pane**, **Close** the database, and **Exit** Access.

End **You have completed Project 2E** ─────────────────────

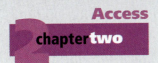

Mastering Access

Project 2F—Economic Development Center

In this project, you will apply the skills you practiced from the Objectives in Project 2B.

Objectives: 6. *Create a Select Query;* **7.** *Specify Criteria in a Query;* **8.** *Specify Compound Criteria in a Query.*

The economic development center on the campus of Laurel County Community College offers training programs for the local businesses. In this Mastering Access project, you will be assisting Kesia Toomer, vice president of administration and development, who needs to extract relevant information from the database. Your results will look similar to those in Figure 2.66.

For Project 2F, you will need the following file:

a02F_Economic_Development_Center

**You will save your database as
2F_Economic_Development_Center_Firstname_Lastname**

Figure 2.66

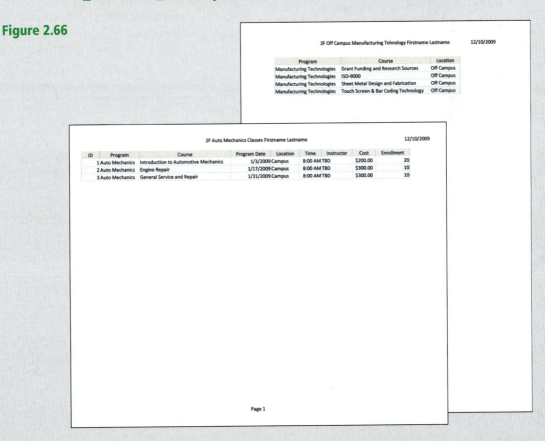

(Project 2F—Economic Development Center continues on the next page)

Content-Based Assessments

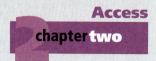

(Project 2F—Economic Development Center continued)

1. **Start** Access. Locate and open the student data file **a02F_Economic_Development_Center**. **Save** this file as 2F_Economic_Development_Center_Firstname_Lastname **Rename** the tables by adding your **Firstname Lastname** to the end of each table name.

2. Click the **Create tab**, and then in the **Other group**, click the **Query Design** button. Add the **2F Training** table to the Query design workspace. Select and drag all fields from the table down to the design grid. In the **Criteria row**, under the **Program** field, type **Auto Mechanics** and then **Run** the query. **Save** the query as **2F Auto Mechanic Classes Firstname Lastname** If you are instructed to submit this result, create a paper or electronic printout. View the query in **Print Preview**, and then make adjustments to print the query on one page. **Print** the query. **Close** the **Print**

    Preview window. **Close** and **Save** changes to the query.

3. **Create** another query using the **2F Training** table. Add the **Program**, **Course**, and **Location** fields to the design grid. Sort the **Course** field in **Ascending** order. For **Criteria**, under the **Program** field, type **Manufacturing Technologies** and under the **Location** field, type **Off Campus** **Run** the query, and then **Save** the query as **2F Off Campus Manufacturing Technology Firstname Lastname** If you are instructed to submit this result, create a paper or electronic printout. View the query in **Print Preview**, and then make adjustments to print the query on one page. **Close** the **Print Preview** window.

4. **Close** the query, expand the **Navigation Pane**, **Close** the database, and **Exit** Access.

End **You have completed Project 2F**

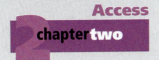

Mastering Access

Project 2G — Class Schedule

In this project, you will apply the following Objectives found in Projects 2A and 2B.

Objectives: 1. *Open and Rename an Existing Database;* **2.** *Sort Records;* **3.** *Filter Records;* **6.** *Create a Select Query;* **7.** *Specify Criteria in a Query.*

In the following Mastering Access project, you will create a select query to help Michael Schaeffler, vice president of instruction for Laurel County Community College, plan the schedule for the summer semester. Your results will look similar to those in Figure 2.67.

For Project 2G, you will need the following file:

a02G_Class_Schedule

You will save your database as
2G_Class_Schedule_Firstname_Lastname

Figure 2.67

2G Summer Classes Firstname Lastname Query   12/10/2009

Term	Location	Course Title
SU09	Camwell Hall	Introduction to Business
SU09	Camwell Hall	Federal Tax Update
SU09	Camwell Hall	Principles of Finance
SU09	Chester Building	Safety Inspection
SU09	College Center	Golf - Intermediate
SU09	College Center	Golf - Beginning
SU09	College Center	Introduction to Hospitality Administration
SU09	College Center	Food and Beverage Management

2G Courses Firstname Lastname   12/10/2009

ID	Term	Course Title	Section#	Day	Time	Instructor Name	Location	Room#
30	SU09	Emissions Inspection	01	S	9 - 12A	TBD	TBD	TBD
13	SU09	Federal Tax Update	01	S	2 - 5P	Fortuna	Camwell Hall	1020
7	SU09	Food and Beverage Management	01	TR	1 - 4P	Eisenstein	College Center	B10
27	SU09	Golf - Beginning	01	S	1 - 4P	TBD	College Center	B10
28	SU09	Golf - Intermediate	01	TR	7 - 8P	TBD	College Center	L401
14	SU09	Introduction to Business	01	TR	9 - 11A	Fortuna	Camwell Hall	920
8	SU09	Introduction to Hospitality Administration	01	MWF	3 - 4P	Eisenstein	College Center	E20
26	SU09	Nursing II	01	MWF	8 - 9A	Santora	Medical Sciences Bldg	520
31	SU09	Portfolio Development	01	TR	9 - 11A	Zieziula	McNeil Technology Center	2105
12	SU09	Principles of Finance	01	TR	1 - 3P	Ferrera	Camwell Hall	800
6	SU09	Safety Inspection	01	S	9 - 12A	Chawich	Chester Building	222
21	SU09	Women in History	01	T	7 - 10A	Kanamalla	Social Sciences Building	LL3

Page 1

(Project 2G—Class Schedule continues on the next page)

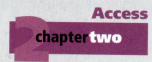

Access

chapter two   Mastering Access

(Project 2G–Class Schedule continued)

1. **Start** Access. Locate and open the student data file **a02G_Class_Schedule**. **Save** this file as **2G_Class_Schedule_Firstname_Lastname** **Rename 2G Courses** to **2G Courses Firstname Lastname** and then open the table in **Datasheet** view.

2. Sort the **Course Title** field in **Ascending** order. Filter the **Term** field so that the table displays only those courses that are offered **SU09**. If you are instructed to submit this result, create a paper or electronic print-out. Make adjustments to print the table on one page. Close **Print Preview**, and then click **Clear All Filters**. **Close** and **save** changes to the table.

3. **Create** a new query using the **Simple Query Wizard**. Add the following fields to

the **Selected Fields** list in the order given: **Term**, **Location**, and **Course Title**. In the **Simple Query Wizard** dialog box, click **Next**. Select **Modify the query design**. Name the query **2G Summer Classes Firstname Lastname Query** Click **Finish**.

4. Sort **Location** in **Ascending** order. In the **Criteria row**, under the **Term** field, type **SU09 Run** the query. If you are instructed to submit this result, create a paper or electronic printout.

5. **Close** and **Save** changes to the query. Expand the **Navigation Pane**, **Close** the database, and **Exit** Access.

End **You have completed Project 2G** ————————————————

Access

chapter two

Mastering Access

Project 2H — Cultural Programs

In this project, you will apply the following Objectives found in Projects 2A and 2B.

Objectives: 1. *Open and Rename an Existing Database;* **2.** *Sort Records;* **6.** *Create a Select Query.*

In the following Mastering Access project, you will assist Pavel Linksz, vice president of student services, in locating information about the cultural programs scheduled for the community. He wants to advertise the fall offerings. Your results will look similar to those in Figure 2.68.

For Project 2H, you will need the following file:

a02H_Cultural_Programs

You will save your database as
2H_Cultural_Programs_Firstname_Lastname

Figure 2.68

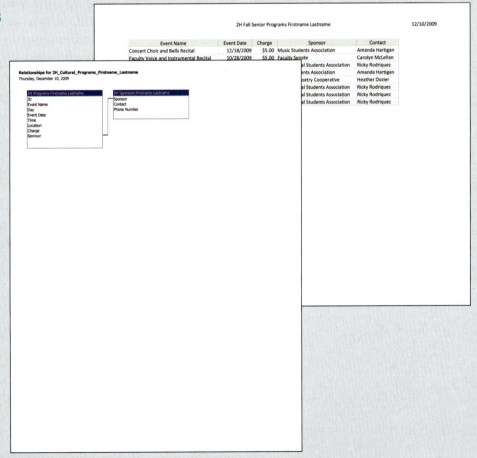

(Project 2H—Cultural Programs continues on the next page)

Content-Based Assessments

(Project 2H–Cultural Programs continued)

1. **Start** Access. Locate and open the student data file **a02H_Cultural_Programs**. **Save** this file as 2H_Cultural_Programs_ Firstname_Lastname **Rename** the two tables by adding your **Firstname Lastname** to the end of the table names.

2. Click the **Database Tools tab**, and then in the **Show/Hide group**, click the **Relationships** button. Add the **2H Programs** table and the **2H Sponsors** table. Create a relationship between the **Sponsor** fields of each table.

3. **Create** a **Relationship Report**. If you are instructed to submit this result, create a paper or electronic printout. On the **tab row**, **Close** the **Relationships for 2H_ Cultural_Programs** window. In the displayed message box, click **Yes** to save the report and accept the default name. **Close** the **Relationships** window.

4. **Create** a new query in **Query Design**. Add the **2H Programs** and the **2H Sponsors** tables to the Query design workspace. From the **2H Programs** field list, add the following fields, in the order specified, to the design grid: **Event Name**, **Event Date**, and **Charge**. From the **2H Sponsors** field list, add **Sponsor** and **Contact**.

5. Sort the **Event Name** field in **Ascending** order. In the criteria row under **Event Date**, create a criteria that will display all of the events after 9/1/2009.

6. **Run** the query. **Save** the query as 2H Fall Senior Programs Firstname Lastname

7. If you are instructed to submit this result, create a paper or electronic print-out. View the query in **Print Preview**, make adjustments to print the query on one page, and then print the query. After printing, **Close** the **Print Preview** window. **Close** the query.

8. **Close** the database, expand the **Navigation Pane**, and **Exit** Access.

End **You have completed Project 2H**

Content-Based Assessments

Mastering Access

Project 2I — Retention

In this project, you will apply all the skills you practiced from the Objectives in Projects 2A and 2B.

Diane Gilmore, president of Laurel County Community College, wants to encourage all of the deans of the different programs to improve student retention from the fall semester to the spring semester. She wants to offer financial aid to those students who have high account balances. In the following Mastering Access project, you will create queries to extract the student information for the different deans to use in mailings to advertise the spring classes and to offer advice on financial aid. Your results will look similar to Figure 2.69.

For Project 2I, you will need the following file:

a02I_Retention

**You will save your database as
2I_Retention_Firstname_Lastname**

Figure 2.69

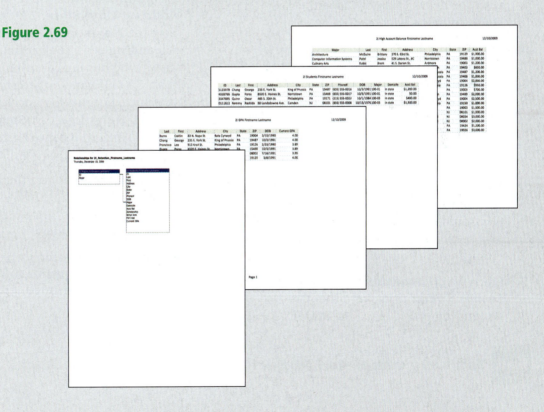

(Project 2I—Retention continues on the next page)

Access
chapter two

Mastering Access

(Project 2I–Retention continued)

1. **Start** Access. Locate and open the student data file **a02I_Retention**. **Save** this file as **2I_Retention_Firstname_Lastname** Rename both tables by adding your **Firstname Lastname** to the end of the table names.

2. **Create** a relationship between the **2I Students** table and the **2I Majors** table. From the **2I Majors** table, join the **ID** field with the **Major** field of the **2I Students** table.

3. Prepare a **Relationship Report**. Submit your report electronically or in print form as directed. If you are to turn in a paper copy, click the **Print** button. Click the **Close** button to close the **Relationships for 2I_Retention** window. **Save** the report with the default name. **Close** the **Relationships** window.

4. Rename the **2I GPA** query as **2I GPA Firstname Lastname** and then open the query in **Design** view. Sort the **Last** field in **Ascending** order. Create criteria that will display all students with a DOB after **1/1/1990** and with a GPA greater than or equal to **3 Run** the query. In Print Preview, change the page orientation to **Landscape**, and then if you are instructed to submit this result, create a paper or electronic printout. Close **Print Preview**, and then close the query. **Save** the changes to the query.

5. Open the **2I Students** table. Select the **Last** and **First** fields, and then sort in **Ascending** order. Filter the **Major** field so

the table displays only those students who have majors of **100-01** and **100-03**. In Print Preview, change the page orientation to **Landscape**, adjust margins to **Normal**, and then if you are instructed to submit this result, create a paper or electronic printout. **Print** only page one of the sorted and filtered table. Close **Print Preview**, and then click **Clear All Filters**. **Close** the table, saving your changes.

6. **Create** a query using **Query Design**. Add the **2I Students** and **2I Majors** tables to the Query design workspace. From the **2I Majors** table, add the **Major** field to the first column in the design grid. From the **2I Students** table, add the following field names in the order listed: **Last**, **First**, **Address**, **City**, **State**, **ZIP**, and **Acct Bal**. Sort the **Major** and **Last** fields in **Ascending** order. Select only in-state students who have account balances greater than $500.00 and out-of-state students who have account balances greater than $1,000. **Run** the query. **Save** the query as **2I High Account Balance Firstname Lastname**

7. In Print Preview, change the page orientation to **Landscape**, and then if you are instructed to submit this result, create a paper or electronic printout. **Close** the **Print Preview** window.

8. **Close** the query, saving when prompted. Expand the **Navigation Pane**, **Close** the database, and **Exit** Access.

End **You have completed Project 2I**

Content-Based Assessments

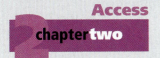 **Access**

 Business Running Case

Project 2J — Business Running Case

In this project, you will apply the skills you have practiced from the Objectives in Projects 2A and 2B.

From My Computer, navigate to the student files that accompany this textbook. In the folder **03_business_running_case**, locate and open the folder for this chapter. Open and print the instructions for this project, which are provided to you in Adobe PDF format. Follow the instructions and use the skills you have gained thus far to assist the brother and sister team of Michael and Kristen Landry in meeting the challenges of owning and running their business.

 End You have completed Project 2J _____

Outcomes-Based Assessments

Rubric

The following outcomes-based assessments are *open-ended assessments*. That is, there is no specific correct result; your result will depend on your approach to the information provided. Make *Professional Quality* your goal. Use the following scoring rubric to guide you in *how* to approach the problem and then to evaluate *how well* your approach solves the problem.

The *criteria*—Software Mastery, Content, Format and Layout, and Process—represent the knowledge and skills you have gained that you can apply to solving the problem. The *levels of performance*—Professional Quality, Approaching Professional Quality, or Needs Quality Improvement—help you and your instructor evaluate your result.

	Your completed project is of Professional Quality if you:	Your completed project is Approaching Professional Quality if you:	Your completed project Needs Quality Improvements if you:
Software Mastery	Choose and apply the most appropriate skills, tools, and features and identify efficient methods to solve the problem.	Choose and apply some appropriate skills, tools, and features, but not in the most efficient manner.	Choose inappropriate skills, tools, or features, or are inefficient in solving the problem.
Content	Construct a solution that is clear and well organized, contains content that is accurate, appropriate to the audience and purpose, and is complete. Provide a solution that contains no errors of spelling, grammar, or style.	Construct a solution in which some components are unclear, poorly organized, inconsistent, or incomplete. Misjudge the needs of the audience. Have some errors in spelling, grammar, or style, but the errors do not detract from comprehension.	Construct a solution that is unclear, incomplete, or poorly organized, containing some inaccurate or inappropriate content; and contains many errors of spelling, grammar, or style. Do not solve the problem.
Format and Layout	Format and arrange all elements to communicate information and ideas, clarify function, illustrate relationships, and indicate relative importance.	Apply appropriate format and layout features to some elements, but not others. Overuse features, causing minor distraction.	Apply format and layout that does not communicate information or ideas clearly. Do not use format and layout features to clarify function, illustrate relationships, or indicate relative importance. Use available features excessively, causing distraction.
Process	Use an organized approach that integrates planning, development, self-assessment, revision, and reflection.	Demonstrate an organized approach in some areas, but not others; or, use an insufficient process of organization throughout.	Do not use an organized approach to solve the problem.

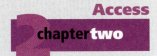

Problem Solving

Project 2K—Schedule

In this project, you will construct a solution by applying any combination of the skills you practiced from the Objectives in Projects A and B.

For Project 2K, you will need the following file:

a02K_Schedule

**You will save your database as
2K_Schedule_Firstname_Lastname**

Susan Jones is an entering freshman student at Laurel County Community College. She plans to major in management and entrepreneurship. She prefers morning classes and does not want to attend classes on Friday or Saturday. She is one of several students who lives out of town and likes to visit her family on weekends.

Susan is meeting with her advisor to put together a schedule of classes for the fall, winter, and summer semesters of her freshman year. Her advisor reminds Susan that she will need to plan for some liberal arts classes and electives in her program of study. Together, they look at the options of classes, schedules, and instructors. There is a new database that the advisor can access. The database has only available tables. The advisor recognizes that a relationship between the tables should be created, so that she can query the fields and print some results to help with Susan's unique requests.

Save the database as **2K_Schedule_Firstname_Lastname** Create relationships and queries that the advisor would use to help Susan plan her freshman year. Save these queries with descriptive names that include your first name and last name in the query title, and begin each saved item with **2K** Submit this project as instructed.

End You have completed Project 2K ———————————

Outcomes-Based Assessments

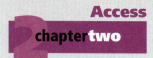

Access

chapter two

Problem Solving

Project 2L — Accounting

In this project, you will construct a solution by applying any combination of the skills you practiced from the Objectives in Projects 2A and 2B.

For Project 2L, you will need the following file:

a02L_Accounting

You will save your database as
2L_Accounting_Firstname_Lastname

It is time to request funding from the legislature. The administrators and faculty of Laurel County Community College know that the Commonwealth of Pennsylvania awards funding to community colleges based on several financial criteria. Diane Gilmore, president of Laurel Community College, will be meeting with representatives of the commonwealth next month. She has asked the finance office to prepare a report for her. She wants answers to the following questions:

- How many students are listed in the sample in table 2L Students?
- What are the account balances for these students?
- What is the amount awarded in scholarships for each student in this sample?

Save the database as **2L_Accounting_Firstname_Lastname** Create filters and queries to help the finance office with the report. Save your queries with descriptive names that include your first name and last name in the query title, and begin each saved item with **2L** Submit this project as instructed.

End **You have completed Project 2L** ——————

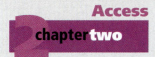

Problem Solving

Project 2M — Student Data

In this project, you will construct a solution by applying any combination of the skills you practiced from the Objectives in Projects 2A and 2B.

For Project 2M, you will need the following file:

a02M_Student_Data

**You will save your database as
2M_Student_Data_Firstname_Lastname**

In this project, you will create queries to help Kesia Toomer, vice president for administration and development at Laurel County Community College. Ms. Toomer wants to extract data from the student data file. She is very concerned with student demographics and personal data. Her goal is to look at the current trends and to use this information to develop new programs at LCCC. She wants to know the answers to the following questions:

- What are the birthdates of the students in each major?
- What is the domicile breakdown by major?
- Which students receive financial aid?

Save the database as **2M_Student_Data_Firstname_Lastname** Save your queries with descriptive names that include your first name and last name in the query title, and begin each saved item with **2M** Submit this project as instructed.

End **You have completed Project 2M** ————————

Outcomes-Based Assessments

Problem Solving

Project 2N — Semester Training

In this project, you will construct a solution by applying any combination of the skills you practiced from the Objectives in Projects 2A and 2B.

> ### For Project 2N, you will need the following file:
>
> a02N_Semester_Training
>
> ### You will save your database as
> ### 2N_Semester_Training_Firstname_Lastname

In this project, you will filter or create queries to extract the data from the Training Program file. The vice president for administration and development at Laurel County Community College, Kesia Toomer, wants to be certain that there is variety in the program offerings each semester. Based on the schedule she has been given, it appears that all of the training is scheduled for the winter or summer semester. Ms. Toomers requires the following:

- Separate listings for the winter and summer semesters
- Charge for each course for each semester
- Listings by location, day, and time for each semester

Save the database as **2N_Semester Training_Firstname_Lastname** Save your queries with descriptive names that include your first name and last name in the query title, and begin each saved item with **2N** Submit this project as instructed.

End **You have completed Project 2N** ———————

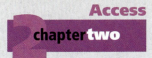

Problem Solving

Project 2O — Teaching Hours

In this project, you will construct a solution by applying any combination of the skills you practiced from the Objectives in Projects 2A and 2B.

For Project 2O, you will need the following file:

a02O_Teaching_Hours

**You will save your database as
2O_Teaching_Hours_Firstname_Lastname**

At Laurel County Community College, the full-time faculty members are required to carry a teaching load of six credit hours a semester. In this project, you will create relationships and queries to help Michael Schaeffler, vice president of instruction at Laurel County Community College, determine the number of hours each full-time faculty member is teaching per semester. He will need to call and inform any of the instructors who are scheduled for fewer than six credit hours for any semester.

Save the database as **2O_Teaching_Hours_Firstname_Lastname** Save your queries with descriptive names that include your first name and last name in the query title, and begin each saved item with **2O** Submit this project as instructed.

End **You have completed Project 2O** ————————————

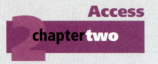 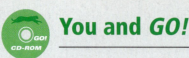

Project 2P — You and *GO!*

In this project, you will construct a solution by applying any combination of the Objectives found in Projects 2A and 2B.

From My Computer, navigate to the student files that accompany this textbook. In the folder **04_you_and_go**, locate and open the folder for this chapter. Open and print the instructions for this project, which are provided to you in Adobe PDF format. Follow the instructions to filter and query the table of your insured household items.

End You have completed Project 2P ——————

GO! with Help

Project 2Q — *GO!* with Help

The Access Help system is extensive and can help you as you work. In this project, you will view information about using wildcards in Access filters and queries.

 1 **Start** Access. On the right side of the Ribbon, click the **Microsoft Office Access Help** button. In the **Access Help** window, in the **Type words to search for** box, type **wildcards** and then click the **Search arrow**.

2 In the displayed **Search list**, click **Access Help**. Click the **Search Access Help** button. Select **Access wildcard character reference**. Maximize the displayed window. Scroll through and view some of the additional characters that can be used as wildcards in Access filters and queries.

3 If you want, print a copy of the information by clicking the **Print** button at the top of the **Access Help** window. Click **Print**.

4 **Close** the **Help** window, and then **Exit** Access.

End You have completed Project 2Q ——————

3 chapterthree

Creating Forms and Reports

OBJECTIVES

At the end of this chapter you will be able to:

1. Create a Form
2. Add, Delete, Edit, and Print Records in a Form
3. Modify the Design of a Form in Layout View
4. Modify the Design of a Form in Design View

5. Create a Report
6. Modify the Design of a Report in Layout View
7. Modify the Design of a Report in Design View
8. Keep Grouped Records Together and Print a Report

OUTCOMES

Mastering these objectives will enable you to:

Project 3A
Create Forms to Enter Data into a Table

Project 3B
Create Reports to Display Database Information

Seattle-Tacoma Job Fair

The Seattle-Tacoma Job Fair is a nonprofit organization that brings together employers and job seekers in the greater Seattle/Tacoma metropolitan area. Each year, the organization holds a number of targeted job fairs and the annual Greater Seattle Job Fair that draws 2,000 employers in more than 70 industries and registers more than 5,000 candidates. Candidate registration is free; employers pay a nominal fee to display and present at the fairs. Candidate resumes and employer postings are managed by a state-of-the-art database system, allowing participants quick and accurate access to job data and candidate qualifications.

Creating Forms and Reports

You can view, enter, modify, and delete data in a table or in an Access form. Forms can be designed to display one record at a time with fields placed in the same order as the paper source document. When the form on the screen matches the pattern of information on the paper form, it is easier to enter new information. When viewing information, it is often easier to view just one record at a time.

Reports are used to summarize data and to display the data in a more professional-looking format. Most reports are created using queries. Reports cannot be used to modify data in an underlying table; they can be used only to view data. In this chapter, you will create and modify forms and reports for the Seattle-Tacoma Job Fair.

Project 3A Job Fair Employers

Janice Strickland is the employer coordinator for the Seattle-Tacoma Job Fair. A database with three tables—an *Employers* table, an *Industries* table, and a *Job Openings* table—tracks the employers who participate in the job fair. A query in the database displays job openings with an annual salary greater than $50,000. In Activities 3.1 through 3.13, you will create forms in the database. Your completed forms will look similar to those in Figure 3.1.

For Project 3A, you will need the following files:

a03A_Job_Fair_Employers
a03A_Logo

You will save your database as
3A_Job_Fair_Employers_Firstname_Lastname

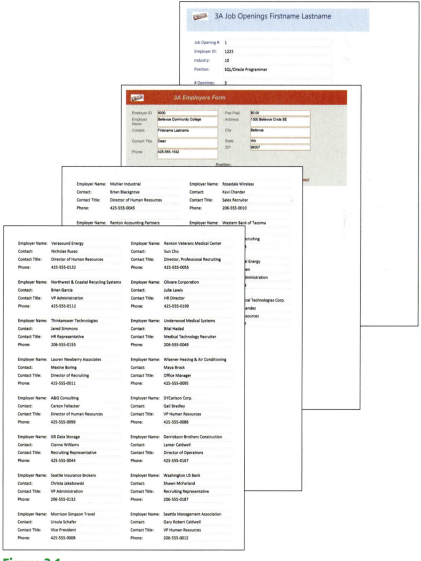

Figure 3.1
Project 3A—Job Fair Employers

Objective 1
Create a Form

A *form* is a database object that can be used to enter or modify data in a table. A form can also be used to view data from a table or query. A form can display all or some of the fields from a table. When a form has been designed to be visually attractive, it makes working with the database more pleasant and more efficient.

Usually, a form is designed to display only one record at a time, making it useful not only to the person who performs the *data entry*—typing in the records—but also to anyone who views the information in the database. For example, the organizers of the Seattle-Tacoma Job Fair can look at information for one employer without seeing the records of all the other employers. A form designed to display one record at a time will help prevent data entry errors.

Activity 3.1 Using the Form Tool to Create a Form

There are several ways to create a form in Access, but the fastest and easiest method is to use the *Form tool*. With a single click of the mouse, all of the fields and records from the underlying table are inserted into the form. Records that you add using the form are automatically added to the underlying table. In this activity, you will create a form using the Form tool, and then use the form to add a new job opening to the underlying table.

1 **Start** Access. Navigate to the location where the student data files for this textbook are saved. Locate and open the **a03A_Job_ Fair_Employers** file. Click the **Office** button 🔳 , and then **Save As** an **Access 2007 Database**. Navigate to the drive on which you will be saving your folders and projects for this chapter. Create a new folder named **Access Chapter 3** and then save the file as **3A_Job_ Fair_Employers_Firstname_Lastname** in the folder.

2 Using the techniques you practiced in Chapter 2, either enable the content or add the **Access Chapter 3** folder to the **Trust Center** to close the message bar.

3 Rename the three tables and one query by adding **Firstname Lastname** to the end of each table and query name—for example, rename *3A Employers* to *3A Employers Firstname Lastname*.

4 Open the **3A Job Openings** table in **Datasheet** view, and then collapse « the **Navigation Pane**. If necessary, scroll to the right until you see all seven fields.

5 On the Ribbon, click the **Create tab**. In the **Forms group**, click the **Form** button, and then compare your screen with Figure 3.2.

Access creates a form based on the current object—the *3A Job Openings* table—and displays it in *Layout view*. In Layout view, you can modify a form with the form running—showing the data from an underlying table or query in a form or report displayed in Layout view—and you can see the data as it displays in Form view. However, you cannot enter data in the form in Layout view. The table does not have to be open to create a form—it can be selected on the Navigation Pane.

The Form tool creates a form with two sections—the **_Form Header section_** and the **_Detail section_**. The Form Header section displays information contained in the **_header_**—a header contains information that displays at the top of every form. The Form tool creates the header section that displays a title based on the underlying table— _3A Job Openings_—and a **_placeholder_** for a company logo or other graphic. A placeholder is an object that can be replaced with another object; in this case, the placeholder is a graphic of a form. The Detail section displays the field names and related text boxes for one record. The Form tool arranges the record in a simple top-to-bottom layout with all the fields in the table aligned in a single column. The data for the first record in the table displays in the fields.

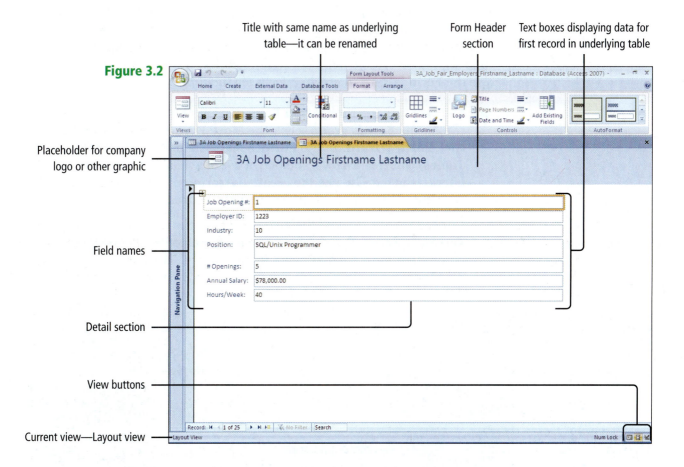

Figure 3.2

Title with same name as underlying table—it can be renamed

Form Header section

Text boxes displaying data for first record in underlying table

Placeholder for company logo or other graphic

Field names

Detail section

View buttons

Current view—Layout view

6 On the **Format tab**, in the **Views group**, click the **View** button to display the form in **Form** view.

When you open a form from the Navigation Pane, it opens in Form view. If you create a form and wish to enter data into the form, you must switch to Form view.

7 Right-click the **3A Job Openings tab** for the form, and then click **Close**. Alternatively, click the Close button ⊠. In the displayed message box, click **Yes** to save the changes to the form. In the **Save As** dialog box, change the form name to **3A Job Openings Form Firstname Lastname** and then click **OK**. On the **tab row**, right-click the **3A Job Openings tab** for the table, and then click **Close**.

Expand ⮞ the **Navigation Pane**.

On the Navigation Pane, *3A Job Openings Form* displays under the Forms category. Adding the word *Form* to the form name will help you when a table and a form with the same name are open, even though the icons on the object tabs are different.

Activity 3.2 Using the Form Wizard to Create a Form

The Form tool creates an instant form in a simple top-to-bottom layout with all the fields aligned in a single column. Using the ***Form Wizard***, you can select the fields from one or more tables or queries, select a form layout, and select a style. To select fields from multiple tables, a relationship should be established between the tables. In this activity, you will use the Form Wizard to create a form for the *Employers* table.

1 Collapse ⮜ the **Navigation Pane**. On the Ribbon, click the **Create tab**. In the **Forms group**, click the **More Forms** button, and then click **Form Wizard**. In the **Form Wizard** dialog box, click the **Tables/Queries arrow** to display a list of available tables and queries that can be used to create the form, and then click **Table: 3A Employers**. Compare your screen with Figure 3.3.

Under Available Fields, the field names for the table displayed in the Tables/Queries box are listed. Recall that all of the fields are displayed in a form created using the Form tool. The Form Wizard enables you to select the fields you want to include in your form.

Figure 3.3

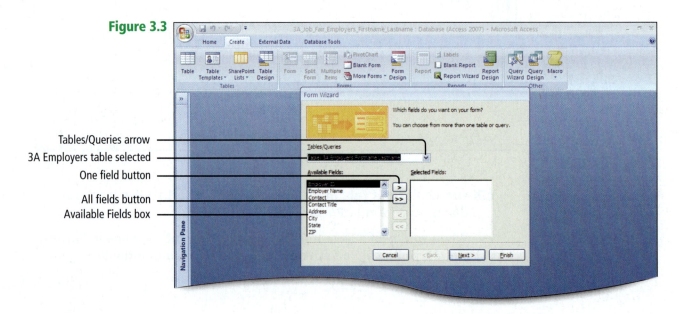

Tables/Queries arrow

3A Employers table selected

One field button

All fields button

Available Fields box

2 Click the **All Fields** button `>>` to select all of the fields and move them to the **Selected Fields** box, and then click **Next**.

The second Form Wizard dialog box enables you to select a layout for your form. When you click an option, the image on the left displays a preview of the layout you have selected.

Note — Including Multiple Tables and Queries on a Form

To include fields from multiple tables and queries on a form, do not click Next after selecting the fields from the first table or query on the first page of the Form Wizard. Instead, click the Tables/Queries list arrow to select another table or query, and then select the fields to include on the form. When you are finished selecting the tables and queries with their associated fields to include on the form, click the Next button.

3 Experiment by clicking different layout options and previewing the layouts. When you are finished, click the **Columnar** option button, and then click **Next**.

The third Form Wizard dialog box enables you to select a style for the form. The style controls the font, font size, font color, and background.

4 Click several of the styles to preview the formatting, and then scroll, if necessary, to click **Flow**. Notice in the preview area, that the label control and text box control have no borders. In this project, it is easier to modify forms when borders display around the controls. In the style box, click **Equity**. Click **Next** to move to the fourth and final Form Wizard dialog box.

The fourth Form Wizard dialog box enables you to name the form, open the form or modify the form, and display help on working with the form.

5 Under **What title do you want for your form**, change the default name to **3A Employers Form Firstname Lastname** and then click **Finish** to close the Wizard and create the form. Compare your screen with Figure 3.4.

The form displays using the layout and style selected in the Form Wizard, and the first record in the underlying table—*3A Employers*—displays in the Detail section. You can enter records in the form in Form view, and the underlying table will be updated.

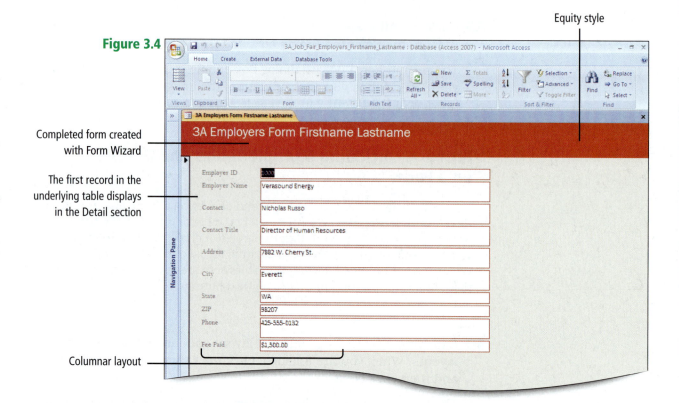

Figure 3.4

Equity style

Completed form created with Form Wizard

3A Employers Form Firstname Lastname

The first record in the underlying table displays in the Detail section

Columnar layout

Employer ID	1000
Employer Name	Verasound Energy
Contact	Nicholas Russo
Contact Title	Director of Human Resources
Address	7882 W. Cherry St.
City	Everett
State	WA
ZIP	98207
Phone	425-555-0132
Fee Paid	$1,500.00

6 **Close** ✕ the **3A Employers Form**, and then expand » the **Navigation Pane**. Under **Forms**, **3A Employers Form** displays. Collapse « the **Navigation Pane**.

Activity 3.3 Using the Blank Form Tool to Create a Form

If the Form tool or Form Wizard does not adequately meet your needs, you can use the **Blank Form tool**—a tool used to create a simple form without any special formatting—to create a form. This can be a quick method to create a form, especially if your form contains only a few fields.

1 On the Ribbon, click the **Create tab**, and in the **Forms group**, click the **Blank Form** button.

A blank form displays in Layout view; and on the right side of the screen, a Field List pane displays.

2 If necessary, in the **Field List** pane, click **Show all tables**, and then click the plus sign (+) to the left of **3A Employers** to display the fields in the table.

3 Drag the **Employer Name** field to any location on the blank form, and then compare your screen with Figure 3.5.

As you drag a field onto the form, an orange border displays on the form, indicating the margins of the form. No matter where you drag the first field on a blank form, the field displays in the upper left corner. An AutoLayout Options button displays below the field. Clicking the AutoLayout Options button enables you to change the layout of the field names and fields on the form.

Figure 3.5

Field List pane

Blank form in Layout view

Displays data in first record from underlying table

AutoLayout Options button

Expanded field list for *3A Employers* table

Collapsed field list for related table

Collapsed field list for other table

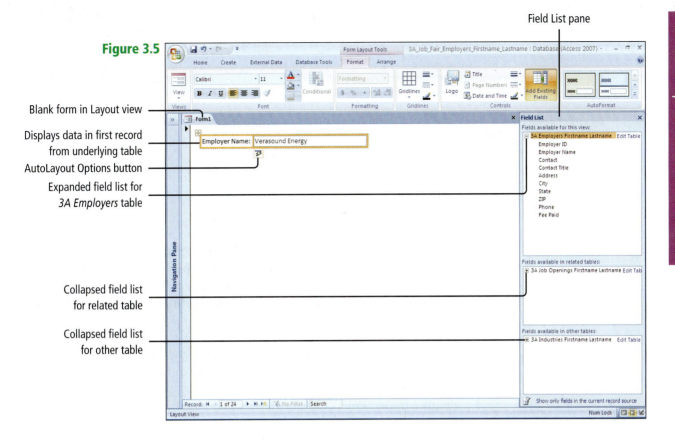

4 Click the **AutoLayout Options** button , and then click **Show in Tabular Layout**. Notice the form displays with the field name at the top, and the data displays directly below the field name. Click the

AutoLayout Options button , and then click **Show in Stacked Layout**. Notice the field name displays at the left, and the data displays to the right of the field name.

5 In the **Field List** pane, click **Contact**, hold down Shift, and then click **Contact Title**. Drag the two selected fields onto the form.

The two fields display at the left margin under the Employer Name field. Recall that you can use Shift to select contiguous objects.

6 Click anywhere in the form to cancel the selection of the two fields. In the **Field List** pane, double-click **Phone**.

You can either drag a field to the form or double-click a field to add it to the form. If the Contact and Contact Title fields had still been selected when you double-clicked, the Phone field would have displayed between those two fields.

7 **Close** the **Field List** pane, and then compare your screen with Figure 3.6.

Four fields display in the Detail section in a simple top-to-bottom layout. All of the fields in the table are aligned in a single column.

Figure 3.6

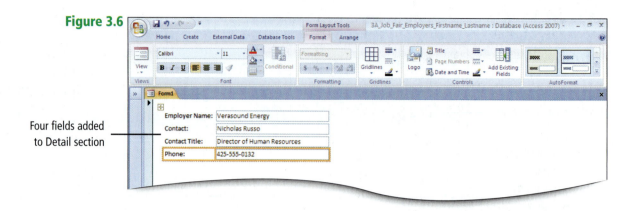

Four fields added
to Detail section

8 **Close** ☒ the form, and in the displayed message box, click **Yes** to save the changes to the design of the form. In the **Save As** dialog box, under **Form Name**, select the text if necessary, type **3A Employers Contact List Form Firstname Lastname** and then click **OK**.

Expand ⟫ the **Navigation Pane**.

On the Navigation Pane, the new form displays under Forms. You can use this form to add or modify records in the underlying table— *3A Employers.* Any modifications to the data in this form will also display in *3A Employers Form*, which is also based on the *3A Employers* table.

Objective 2
Add, Delete, Edit, and Print Records in a Form

Adding, deleting, and editing records using a form helps to prevent data entry errors because the person performing the data entry is looking at only one record at a time. Your database is useful only if the data is accurate—just like your personal address book is useful only if it contains accurate addresses and phone numbers.

Activity 3.4 Adding Records to a Table Using a Form

Forms are based on the table where the records are stored. The data in a form is **bound**—tied—to the data in the underlying table. When a record is created in a form, the new record is added to the underlying table. The reverse is also true—when a record is added to a table, the new record is displayed in the related form. In this activity, you will add a new record to the *3A Job Openings* table using the form you created in Activity 3.1.

1 On the **Navigation Pane**, under **Tables**, double-click **3A Job Openings**. Under **Forms**, double-click **3A Job Openings Form**.

Collapse ⟪ the **Navigation Pane**.

The form is the current object. When you open a form from the Navigation Pane, it displays in Form view. The underlying table does not have to be open to update the data from a form.

2 In the navigation area, click the **Next record** button ▶ two times.

The third record—a position for an *Electrical Engineer*—displays. Use the navigation buttons to move among the records. Recall that in a datasheet, clicking the Next record button moves you down in the datasheet to the next record.

3 In the navigation area, click the **New (blank) record** button ▶✱.

A blank form displays, and in the Job Opening # field, *(New)* displays. Recall that in a datasheet, clicking the New (blank) record button moves the insertion point to the empty row beneath the last record where *(New)* is displayed in the first field.

4 On the form, click in the **Employer ID** field, and then type **1223** Notice that the Job Opening # field is automatically populated with 26.

In the underlying table—*3A Job Openings*—this field has a data type of AutoNumber. By default, the fields in a form inherit the properties of the fields in the underlying table.

5 To move to the next field, press [Tab] or [Enter], or click in the next field. Enter the following data in the fields indicated—do not press [Tab] after the last field—and then compare your screen with Figure 3.7. Notice that the data has been entered for Record 26 but has not been saved.

Industry	10
Position	Security Specialist
# Openings	1
Annual Salary	85000
Hours/Week	40

Data entered in fields
on form for Record 26

Figure 3.7

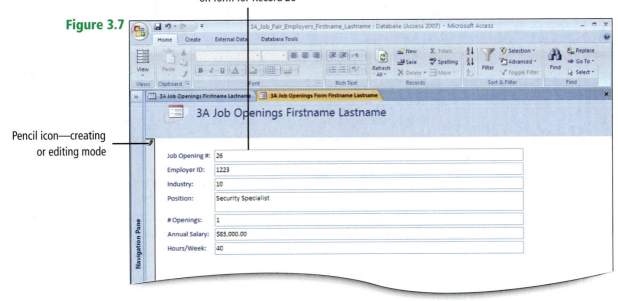

Pencil icon—creating
or editing mode

6 Press Tab or Enter to save the record.

7 On the **tab row**, click the **3A Job Openings tab** to make the table current, and then compare your screen with Figure 3.8. Notice that the table displays in Datasheet view, but Record 26 is not yet displayed.

Object tab for form   Refresh All button

Figure 3.8

Object tab for table

Record 26 is not yet displayed

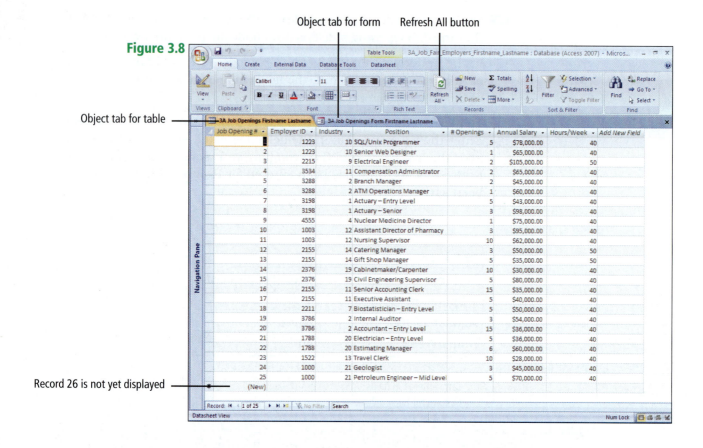

8 On the **Home tab**, in the **Records group**, click the **Refresh All** button. Notice that Record 26 now displays.

If the underlying table is open while adding or editing records in a form, the updates are not immediately displayed. If the table is closed, when you open it, the table automatically displays the update.

Clicking the Refresh All button prompts Access to *synchronize* the objects in the database. To synchronize, Access compares the records in database objects and updates changes. If Access finds a change to data in a form, Access updates the data in the underlying table. If Access finds a change to data in a table, it displays the updated data in the related forms, queries, reports, and other database objects.

Activity 3.5 Deleting Records from a Table Using a Form

In this activity, you will delete two records in the *3A Job Openings* table using the related form.

1 Expand ⟩⟩ the **Navigation Pane**. Under **Queries**, double-click **3A Salary > $50,000** to open the query and make it the current object.

Notice the last record—Position of *Security Specialist*. Collapse ⟨⟨ the **Navigation Pane**. On the **Home tab**, in the **Views group**, click the **View** button to switch to **Design** view, and then locate the criteria used in the creation of the query.

The query uses two tables—*3A Employers* and *3A Job Openings*—and extracts records where the annual salary—Annual Salary—is greater than $50,000. Because the *3A Job Openings* table is one of the underlying tables in this query, any changes to the data in the table will be displayed in the query. Recall that when a query is opened, Access reads the data in the underlying table, and extracts the records based on the fields and criteria used in the query. The new record with the Position of Security Specialist displays in the query because the annual salary is greater than $50,000.

2 Switch to **Datasheet** view. In the navigation area, in the **current record** box, select the displayed text—for example, *1 of 14*. Type **7** and then press Enter.

The current record is Record 7 for *Watson Medical Technologies Corp.* with a Position of *Nuclear Medicine Director*. Typing a record number in the current record box moves the insertion point to that record number. You will delete this record from the *3A Job Openings* table using the related form. It is not possible to delete records in the query object.

3 On the **tab row**, click **3A Job Openings Form** to make the form the current object. In the navigation area, in the **Search** box, type **nuclear** and then compare your screen with Figure 3.9. Alternatively, on the Home tab, in the Find group, click the Find button, and then type **nuclear** in the Find What box.

Record 9 displays. You may have noticed that you needed to type only the first two letters of *nuclear*—*nu*—for Access to find the correct record. Recall that as you type in the Search box, Access finds the first occurrence of the letter *n*. When you type the letter *u*, Access finds the first occurrence of *nu*. You can use the same find and search techniques in a form that you used in a datasheet.

Figure 3.9

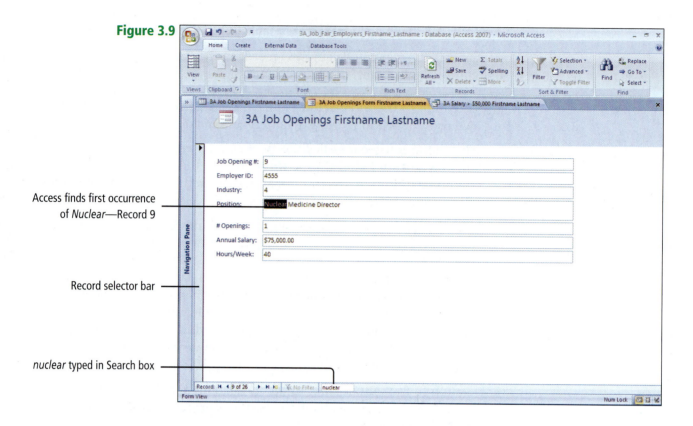

Access finds first occurrence of *Nuclear*—Record 9

Record selector bar

nuclear typed in Search box

4 Click anywhere in the **record selector** bar to select it.

When the record selector bar is selected—highlighted in black—all of the fields in the displayed record are selected. This is similar to the record selector box in a datasheet or table, which selects the entire row (record).

5 In the **Records group**, click the **Delete** button. Alternatively, press Delete or right-click the record selector bar, and then from the short-cut menu, click Cut.

A message displays warning that you are about to delete 1 record(s).

Alert! — **Is the Delete button dimmed?**

If the record selector bar is not selected, the Delete button in the Records group is dimmed—inactive. Either click to select the record selector bar or click the Delete button arrow, and then click Delete Record.

6 In the displayed message box, click **Yes** to delete the record. Notice that the record for *Job Opening # 10* is the current record and is now Record 9.

7 On the **tab row**, click the **3A Job Openings tab** to make the table current, and then compare your screen with Figure 3.10.

In the ninth record position, Access has inserted #*Deleted* in all the fields, which is an indication that the table has not been synchronized with its related objects. Recall that if the table is closed when changes are made to the related form, when you open the table, the record will be deleted and #*Deleted* will not display.

Figure 3.10

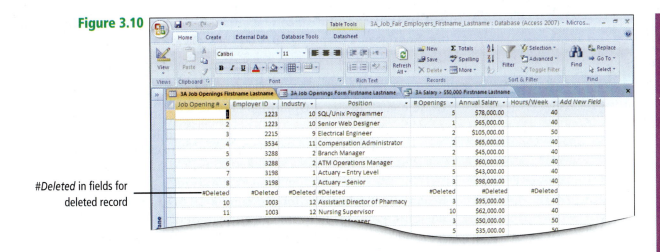

#*Deleted* in fields for
deleted record

8 In the **Records group**, click the **Refresh All** button to synchronize the table with its related objects. Notice that Job Opening # 9 is deleted from the table.

9 On the **tab row**, click the **3A Salary > $50,000 tab** to display the query results. Using the technique you just practiced, synchronize the query with the underlying table to remove the record.

If the query object is closed, you will not see *#Deleted* in the record when you open the query.

10 **Close** the **3A Salary > $50,000** query object, and then **Close** the **3A Job Openings** table object to make *3A Job Openings Form* the current object.

11 Using the techniques you have practiced in this activity, search for the record that has **ATM** as part of the position name in the **Position** field, and notice the salary of *$60,000*. **Delete** Record 6 using the form.

12 Expand » the **Navigation Pane**. Open the **3A Job Openings** table, and notice that the record for *Job Opening # 6* is deleted. Open the **3A Salary > $50,000** query, and notice there is no *Position* for an *ATM Operations Manager*.

Because the underlying table and related query were closed when the record was deleted using the form, both objects do not display *#Deleted* in the fields and you do not have to synchronize the objects. When working with forms, it is rare that the underlying table is also open.

13 **Close** the table and query, and then collapse « the **Navigation Pane**, leaving the form open and current.

Activity 3.6 Editing a Record in a Table Using a Form

In this activity, you will edit a record in the *3A Job Openings* table using the related form.

1 On the **Home tab**, in the **Find group**, click the **Find** button. In the displayed **Find and Replace** dialog box, in the **Find What** box, type

gift Be sure that the **Match** box displays **Any Part of Field** and that the **Search** box displays **All**, and then click **Find Next**.

Record 11 with the Position of Gift Shop Manager displays.

2 In the **Find and Replace** dialog box, click the **Close** button ⊠. Double-click in the **# Openings** field to select **5**, and then type **3**

In the navigation area, click the **Next record** button ▶ to save the changes to this record, and then click the **Previous record** button ◀.

Record 11 displays for Job Opening # 13, and the # Openings field has been changed to 3. Because the annual salary is not greater than $50,000, the query is not affected by the change to this record.

3 Expand ≫ the **Navigation Pane**, and then open the **3A Job Openings** table. Locate the record for **Job Opening # 13**, and notice that the **# Openings** field for this record displays 3, the number you entered in the form.

The data in *3A Job Openings Form* is bound to the data in the *3A Job Openings* table. Whenever you change data in a form, the data is updated in the underlying table. Editing records in a form helps to prevent changing the data in the wrong record because only one record is displayed at a time.

4 In the **3A Job Openings** table, in **Record 1**, in the **Position** field, double-click **Unix** to select the word, type **Oracle** and then press ↓ to save the record.

The record is not saved until the insertion point is positioned in another record. If the pencil icon displays in the record selector box, the record is not saved.

5 On the **tab row**, click **3A Job Openings Form** to make the form the current object. In the navigation area, click the **First record** button ◄◄, and then compare your screen with Figure 3.11.

The first record in the form displays with the change in the position field. If *Unix* displays instead of *Oracle*, use the technique you practiced in Activity 3.5 to synchronize—*Refresh All*—the database objects. The data in the *3A Job Openings* table is bound to the data in the *3A Job Openings Form* object. Whenever you change the data in a table, the data is displayed in the table's related objects.

Figure 3.11

Access | chapter 3

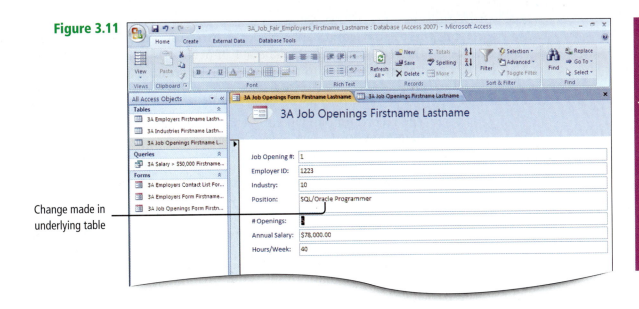

Change made in
underlying table

6 On the **tab row**, right-click the **3A Job Openings tab**, and then click
Close, leaving *3A Job Openings Form* open and current. Collapse ⟪
the **Navigation Pane**.

Activity 3.7 Filtering and Sorting Records in a Form

Like tables, you can filter and sort records in a form. Recall that filtering
records displays a subset of the records, and that filters provide quick
answers to questions. Sorting puts the records in either ascending or
descending order.

1 With *3A Job Openings Form* displayed in **Form** view, click in the
Annual Salary field box. On the **Home tab**, in the **Sort & Filter
group**, click the **Filter** button. From the displayed list, point to
Number Filters, and then click **Greater Than**. Alternatively, right-
click in the field, point to Number Filters, and then click Greater
Than. In the displayed **Custom Filter** dialog box, type **50000.01** and
then click **OK**.

Even though you selected Greater Than, the Custom Filter dialog box
indicates the filter will display records with the Annual Salary
greater than or equal to the value typed in the text box. Because you
want to display salaries greater than $50,000, you must enter
50000.01 so that salaries of $50,000 are not included in the filter.

In the navigation area, the Current Record box indicates that 12
records meet the filter criteria. Just like filtering in tables, the filter
indicators are active—in the Sort & Filter group, the Toggle Filter
button is active; in the navigation area, the Filtered button is active;
and in the status bar, *Filtered* displays.

2 In the navigation area, click the **Next record** button ▶ five times,
observing the data in the **Annual Salary** field.

The records are not sorted by the *Annual Salary* field—they are
sorted by the *Job Opening* # field, which is the primary key field.

3 In the navigation area, click the **First record** button ⏮ to display the record for *Job Opening # 1*. If necessary, click in the **Annual Salary** field box. In the **Sort & Filter group**, click the **Descending** button ⏫.

The record for Job Opening # 3 displays with an annual salary of $105,000.00.

4 In the navigation area, click the **Next record** button ▶ five times, observing the data in the **Annual Salary** field. Click the **Last record** button ⏭, and then compare your screen with Figure 3.12.

The records are arranged in descending order on the Annual Salary field—ranging from $105,000.00 to $54,000.00—and are filtered, displaying only salaries greater than $50,000.00.

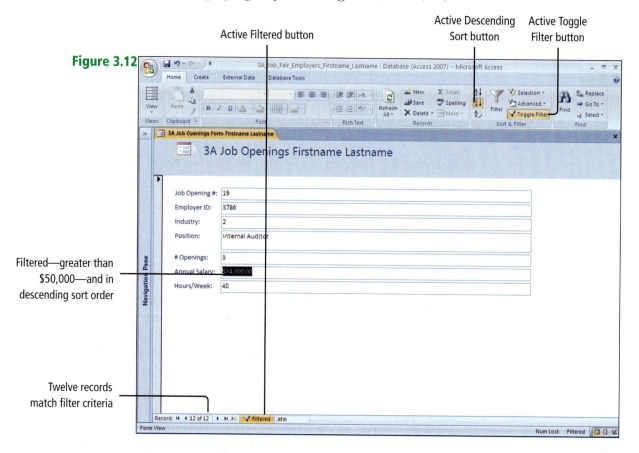

Figure 3.12

Active Filtered button

Active Descending Sort button

Active Toggle Filter button

Filtered—greater than $50,000—and in descending sort order

Twelve records match filter criteria

5 In the **Sort & Filter group**, click the **Advanced** button, and then click **Clear All Filters**. In the **Sort & Filter group**, click the **Clear All Sorts** button ⏬.

Recall that filters and sorts change the way the data displays. When you are finished viewing the filtered forms, you should remove the filter because someone else may open the form and not realize it is only a subset of the records in the database.

6 **Close** ✕ the form, and then expand ⏩ the **Navigation Pane**.

Activity 3.8 Printing a Simple Form

Like other Access objects, forms can be printed. By default, all of the records will print in the selected form layout. In this activity, you will print the records from the form you created using the Blank Form tool. The forms you created using the Form tool and the Form Wizard require further modification before printing.

1 On the **Navigation Pane**, under **Forms**, double-click **3A Employers Contact List Form** to open the form, and then collapse « the **Navigation Pane**.

2 Click the **Office** button 🔘, point to **Print**, and then click **Print Preview**. On the **Print Preview tab**, in the **Zoom group**, click the **Two Pages** button, and then compare your screen with Figure 3.13.

Print Preview displays the form as it will print. In this case, the records display in a single column, and the right half of each page is empty. In the navigation area, the active buttons indicate there are more pages.

Dialog Box Launcher

First two pages display as they would print

Figure 3.13

Active buttons indicate there are more pages

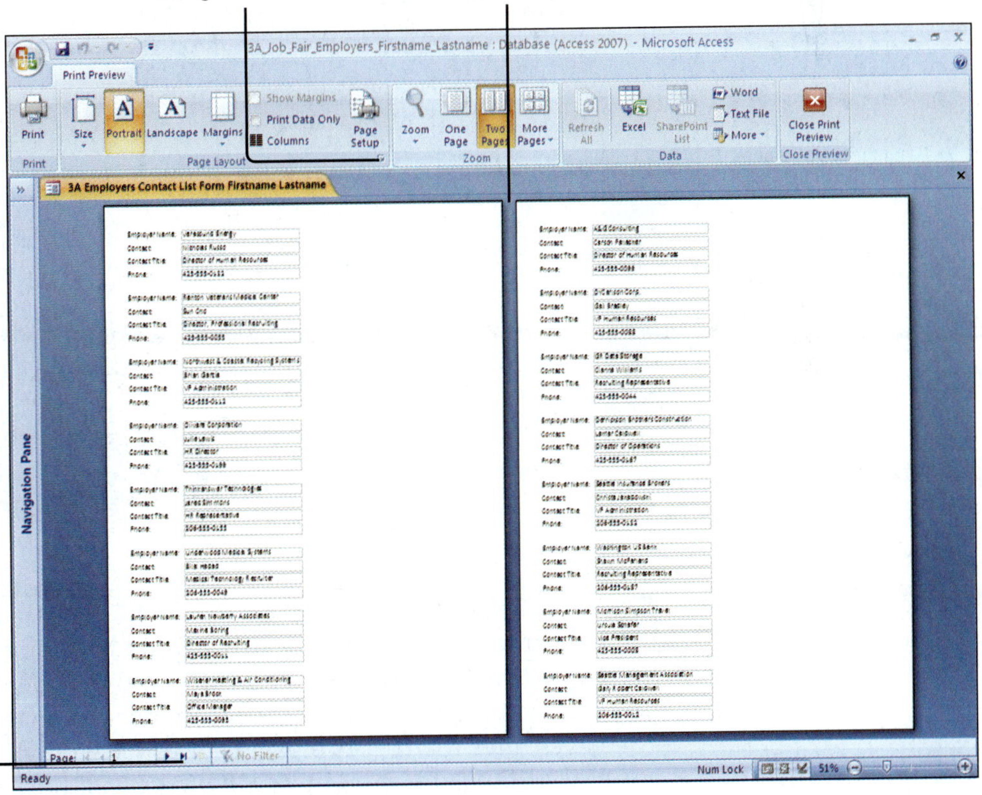

3 In the navigation area, click the **Last Page** button ▶, and notice that three pages will print.

When two pages are being displayed at a time, Access shows the pages in pairs—Page 1 and Page 2, then Page 3 and Page 4, and so on. Because there are only three pages, the third page is displayed by itself.

4 In the **Page Layout group**, click the **Columns** button. Alternatively, in the Page Layout group, click the Dialog Box Launcher to display the Page Setup dialog box, and then click the Columns tab.

The Page Setup dialog box displays with the Columns tab selected. On this page, you can change the number of columns, the row spacing, the column width and height, and the column layout.

5 Under **Grid Settings**, change the **Number of Columns** to **2** and change the **Column Spacing** to **0.05** Under **Column Size**, change the **Width** to **3.9** and then compare your screen with Figure 3.14.

Use two columns to maximize the number of records that display on a page. The space between columns is adjusted to allow for a column width of 3.9 inches so that the entire width of the two columns will print. You may have to experiment with the settings on the Columns tab to ensure that all the data will display when printed.

First record prints in left column; second record prints in right column

Column spacing changed to 0.05 inch

Figure 3.14

Number of columns changed to 2

Column size width changed to 3.9 inches

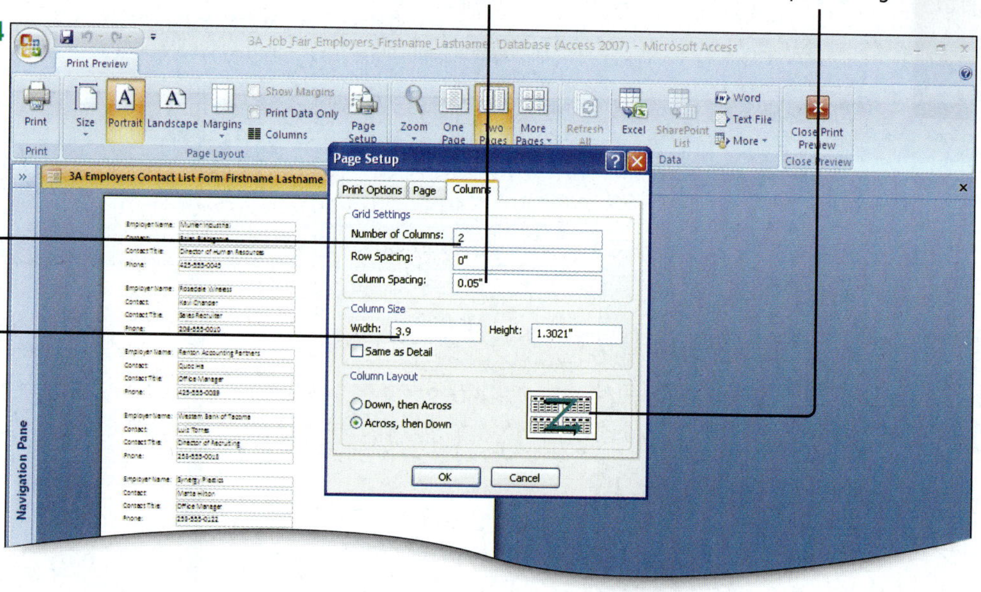

6 In the **Page Setup** dialog box, click **OK**, and then compare your screen with Figure 3.15 to verify that all of the records display on two pages in a two-column layout. In the navigation area, notice that the **Next Page arrow** is inactive, indicating that there are no more pages after the first two pages—if you are previewing one page at a time, the Next Page button will be active if the first page is displayed.

Records are displayed
in two columns | Two Pages button is active

Figure 3.15

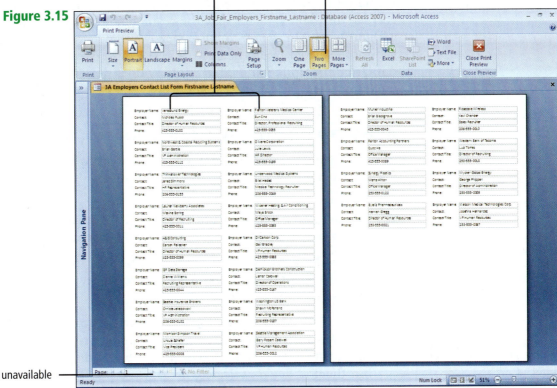

Next Page button is unavailable

7 Drag the **Form Footer section**, bar to the **0.5-inch mark on the vertical ruler**. Click the **Label** button. Position the **label control** at the left side and the bottom of the Form Footer. Drag to the right to **3.0 inches on the horizontal ruler** and then upward approximately **0.25 inches**. Using your own name, type **Designed by: Firstname Lastname** and then press Enter. If you are instructed to submit this result, create a paper or electronic printout. On the **tab row**, click the **Close** button ✕ to close the Print Preview object and the form.

Objective 3
Modify the Design of a Form in Layout View

After you have created a form, you can make further changes. For example, you can rearrange the fields and adjust the field sizes. Access provides three views for forms: Form view, Layout view, and Design view. If you want to view, add, delete, or modify records using the form, use *Form view*. If you want to view, add, delete, or modify field information—such as the placement of fields on the form—use either Layout view or *Design view*.

Layout view is the easiest view to use when modifying a form, and it can be used for almost all changes. Recall that in Layout view, the form is running—you can see the data as it displays in Form view. Because you can see the data, you can view the results of field changes immediately without having to switch to Form view. Design view gives a more detailed view of the structure of the form, and the form is not running—the data from the underlying table or query does not display while making modifications.

Activity 3.9 Inserting a Logo and a Date into a Form

In this activity, you will insert a logo and date into the 3A Employers form in Layout view, and then format the title.

1 Expand ⟩⟩ the **Navigation Pane**. Under **Forms**, double-click **3A Employers Form** to open the form in **Form** view. Collapse ⟨⟨ the **Navigation Pane**. On the **Home tab**, in the **Views group**, click the **View** button to switch to **Layout** view, and then compare your screen with Figure 3.16.

Clicking the View button toggles between Form view and Layout view. Most modifications to the design of a form can be done in Layout view. The record looks similar to the display in Form view, but the first field is selected.

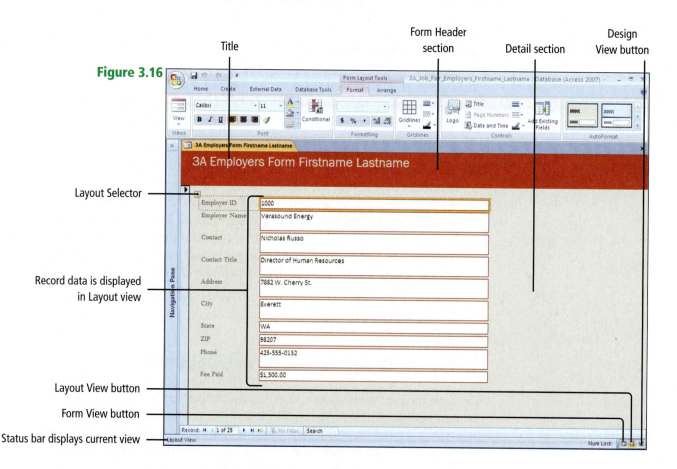

Figure 3.16

Labels: Title, Form Header section, Detail section, Design View button, Layout Selector, Record data is displayed in Layout view, Layout View button, Form View button, Status bar displays current view

3A Employers Form Firstname Lastname

Employer ID	1000
Employer Name	Verasound Energy
Contact	Nicholas Russo
Contact Title	Director of Human Resources
Address	7882 W. Cherry St.
City	Everett
State	WA
ZIP	98207
Phone	425-555-0132
Fee Paid	$1,500.00

2 In the **Form Header section**, click the title—**3A Employers Form**—to select it. On the **Format tab**, in the **Font group**, click the **Font button arrow** `Calibri`, scroll up, and then click **Arial**. Click the **Font Size button arrow** `11`, and then click **18**. Click the **Bold** button `B`, and then click the **Italic** button `I`. Click the **Font Color button arrow** `A`, and under **Standard Colors**, on the second row, click the third color—**Medium Gray 1**. Compare your screen with Figure 3.17.

Figure 3.17

Font changes to title ———

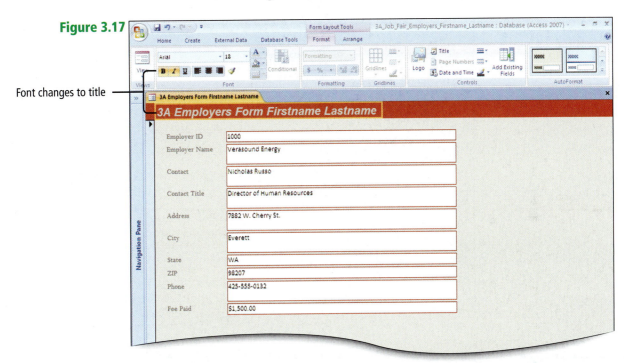

3 On the **Format tab**, in the **Controls group**, click the **Logo** button. In the displayed **Insert Picture** dialog box, navigate to the location where the student data files for this textbook are saved. Locate and double-click **a03A_Logo**.

The Seattle-Tacoma Job Fair logo is inserted on the left side of the title. A *logo* is a graphic or picture used to identify a company or organization.

4 Click anywhere in the title to select it and to display the [pointer icon] pointer. Drag the title to the right and downward until the left edge of the title box aligns with the right edge of the logo, and then compare your screen with Figure 3.18.

All of the objects on a form are contained in boxes that are referred to as *controls*. Controls display data, perform actions, and let you enhance the form by adding objects, such as text boxes, labels, images, and check boxes. Controls can be bound, unbound, or calculated. A *bound control* obtains its data from an underlying table or query—for example, the text box control for the Employer Name field retrieves the data from the Employer Name field in the *3A Employers* table. When you add a field to a form by using the Field

List pane or the Form Wizard, you are creating a bound control. The title in the Form Header section is an example of an **unbound control**, which does not obtain data from an underlying table or query. A **calculated control** obtains its data from an expression or formula, similar to creating a calculated field in a query.

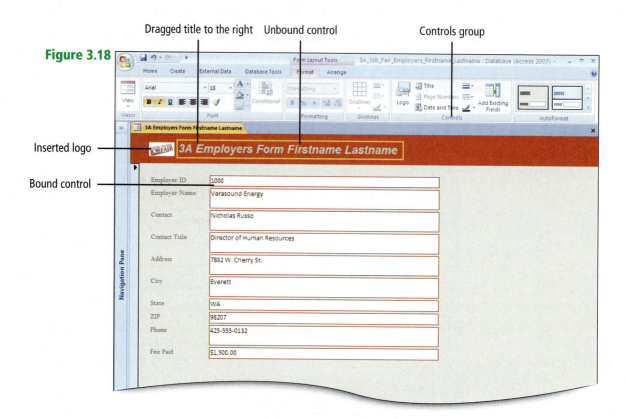

Figure 3.18

Dragged title to the right   Unbound control   Controls group

Inserted logo

Bound control

5 In the **Controls group**, click the **Date and Time** button. In the displayed **Date and Time** dialog box, under **Include Date**, click to select the third option, which displays the current date in the *mm/dd/yyyy* format. Clear the **Include Time** check box, and then compare your screen with Figure 3.19. Under **Sample**, the options you select display as they will be inserted into the form.

Figure 3.19

Date options—your date will differ

Time options—your time will differ

Preview of selected options—your preview will differ

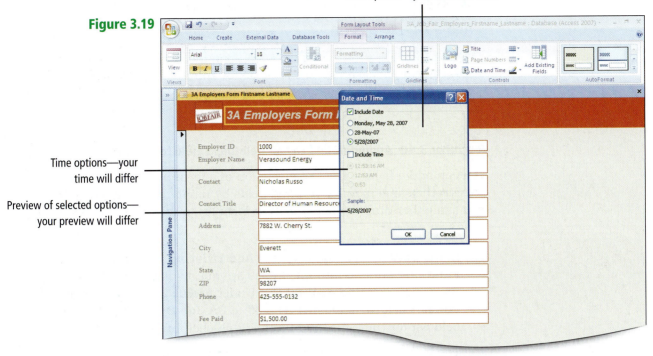

6 In the **Date and Time** dialog box, click **OK**.

The current date is inserted into the form and is aligned at the right side of the Form Header section. It is difficult to see because of the font color. The date is retrieved from the computer's clock and will always display the current date. To insert a fixed date, you must be in Design view.

7 In the **Form Header section**, click the date. Using the techniques you just practiced, change the font to **Arial**, change the font color to

Medium Gray 1, and then add **Bold** emphasis to the date. **Save** the form.

When making changes to a form or report, it is a good idea to frequently save your changes.

More Knowledge

Change the Style of a Form in Layout View

You can easily add or change the style of a form in Layout view. On the Format tab, in the AutoFormat group, click the arrows to scroll through a gallery of style samples. You can also click the More arrow to display the entire gallery. Click the style, and your form will be reformatted.

More Knowledge

Add a Title to a Form

When you create a form using the Blank Form tool, a title is not automatically created. To add a title to a form, on the Format tab, in the Controls group, click the Title button.

Activity 3.10 Adding a Field to and Deleting a Field from a Form

You can add a field to the Detail section of a form by using the Field List pane in the same manner you add fields by using the Blank Form tool. You can either drag the field onto the form or double-click the field in the Field List pane.

1 In the **Controls group**, click the **Add Existing Fields** button. In the **Field List** pane, if multiple tables are not displayed, at the bottom of the pane, click **Show all tables**. Under **Fields available in related tables**, click the plus sign (+) next to **3A Job Openings** to display the field list for the table, and then double-click **Industry**.

The Industry field from the *3A Job Openings* table is inserted under the Fee Paid field in the form. In the Field List pane, the *3A Job Openings* table displays under Fields available for this view.

Alert!

Is the Industry field inserted in another position on the form?

If one of the fields in the record is selected, the Industry field is inserted under the selected field. To correct, click the Undo button to remove the inserted field, click anywhere in the Detail section—not on a field—and then begin again.

2 Using the technique you just practiced, from the **3A Job Openings** table, add the **Position** field to the form under the **Industry** field, and then **Close** ☒ the **Field List** pane.

3 In the **Detail section**, notice the orange border that displays around the **Position** field name and the text box. The orange border indicates that the field name and text box are selected.

4 In the **Font group**, click the **Bold** button ⬛ᴮ . Notice that the field name and data are both displayed in bold. On the **Quick Access Toolbar**, click the **Undo** button ⬛ . Click the field name—**Position**—and notice the dashed border that displays around the Position field name and the text box.

The field name is displayed in a *label control*—a control on a form or report that displays text that is not bound to an underlying table or query; the data from the underlying table is displayed in a *text box control*—a control on a form or report that displays data that is bound to an underlying table or query. The label control is grouped with the text box control as indicated by the dashed line border.

If the label control displaying the field name is deleted, then the related text box control is also deleted from the form.

5 In the **Font group**, click the **Bold** button **B**, and notice that only the field name displays as bold. Click in the **Position text box control**—*Geologist*. Notice that the dashed line border still displays around the label control and the text box control, but the text box control is now selected.

6 In the **Font group**, click the **Font Size button arrow** [11 ▾], and then click **14**. Only the data in the text box control is affected by the font size change.

7 In the navigation area, click the **Next record** button [▶] to display Record 2, and then compare your screen with Figure 3.20.

Formatting and font changes to the form on one record affect the formatting of every record in the form.

Label control—field name is bold   Text box control—font size of 14 for data   Label control and text box control grouped

Figure 3.20

Two fields added to form

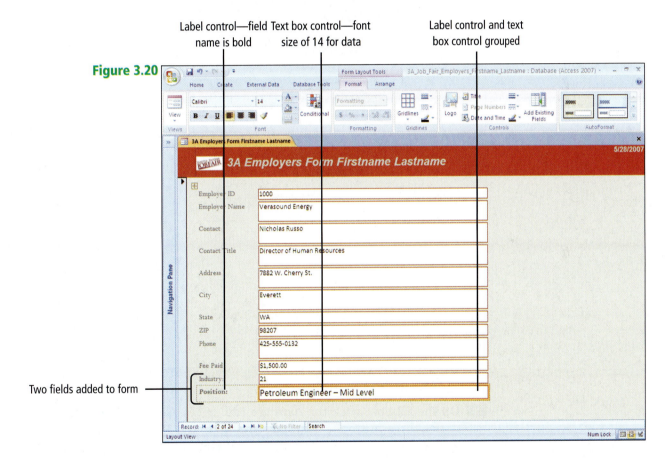

8 Click to select the **Industry label control**, and then press [Delete]. In the navigation area, click the **First record** button [◀] to display Record 1, and then click the **Save** button [💾].

The label control with the field name and text box control with the data are deleted from the form. They are *not* deleted from the underlying table.

Activity 3.11 Moving Fields in a Form

You can use either Layout view or Design view to change the form *layout*—the arrangement of controls on a form. The layout is usually changed to make it easier to view and enter data. Sometimes forms are modified to match an existing paper form used by the organization. For example, Janice Strickland, Employer Coordinator for the Seattle-Tacoma Job Fair, sends prospective employers a paper form to fill out as illustrated in Figure 3.21. Transferring this information from the paper form to the computer database is easier if the layout of the form on the screen matches the layout of the paper form.

Figure 3.21

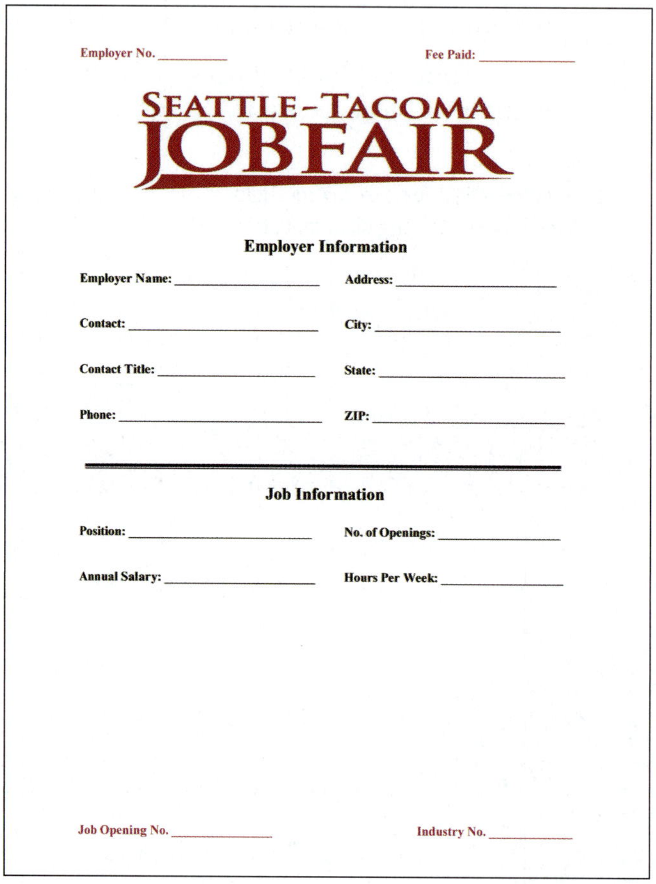

Employer No. _____   Fee Paid: _____

SEATTLE-TACOMA
JOBFAIR

Employer Information

Employer Name: _____   Address: _____

Contact: _____   City: _____

Contact Title: _____   State: _____

Phone: _____   ZIP: _____

Job Information

Position: _____   No. of Openings: _____

Annual Salary: _____   Hours Per Week: _____

Job Opening No. _____   Industry No. _____

1 On the Ribbon, click the **Arrange tab**. In the **Control Layout group**, notice three buttons—**Tabular**, **Stacked**, and **Remove**. In the **Detail section**, click the **Employer ID label control**, and then click the

Layout Selector ✛ to select the columns. Compare your screen with Figure 3.22.

Every column in a form is contained in its own *control layout*—a guide that aligns the controls on a form or report horizontally and vertically to give the form or report a uniform appearance. When you click the Layout Selector, the controls within the control layout are selected. Because of the control layout, when you drag a field from one column to another, the controls align. When you add a new field to a form, its placement is determined by the control layout.

There are two types of control layouts—Tabular and Stacked. In the Control Layout group, the buttons show how the controls are aligned for each type of control layout. In a **tabular control layout**, the controls are arranged in columns and rows, like a datasheet, with label controls—usually field names—across the top and text box controls—usually containing data from the underlying table or query—under the related label controls. In a **stacked control layout**, the controls are arranged vertically, as shown in *3A Employers Form*, with the label control to the left of the text box control.

You can have multiple control layouts of either type on a form. By default, Access creates forms with stacked control layouts when you create a form using the Form tool and Blank Form tool or when you select the columnar layout using the Form Wizard.

Two types of control layouts

Figure 3.22

Layout Selector

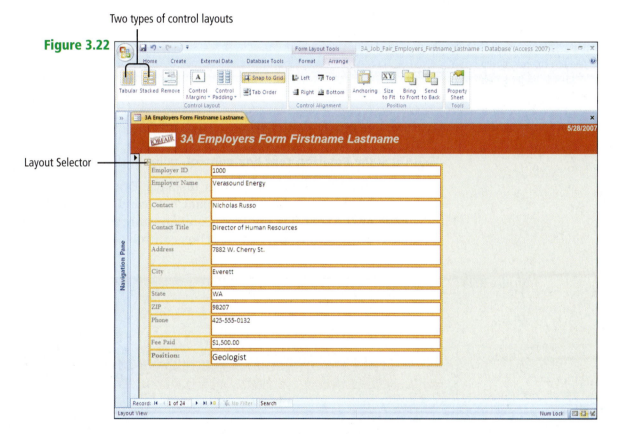

2 In the navigation area, click the **Next record** button ▶ to display Record 2. In the **Detail section**, click in an empty space to deselect the column. In the **Detail section**, click the **Employer Name text box control**.

Point to the left edge of the text box control until the ↔ pointer displays. Drag the left edge of the text box control to the left until there is approximately **.25 inch** of space between **Employer Name:** and the **left edge of the text box control**. Compare your screen with Figure 3.23.

Because these controls are included in the stacked control layout, every text box control in the column is resized. One of the advantages of using a control layout is the uniformity of control sizes, which makes a more visually attractive form.

Figure 3.23

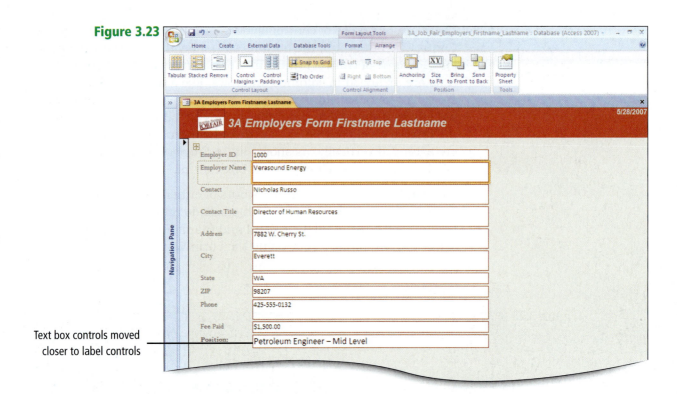

Text box controls moved
closer to label controls

3 Click the **Position text box control**, point to the right edge of the text box control until the ↔ pointer displays. Drag to the left until there is approximately **0.25 inch** of space between **Level** and the **right edge of the text box control**. Compare your screen with Figure 3.24. The width of all of the text box controls is decreased.

Figure 3.24

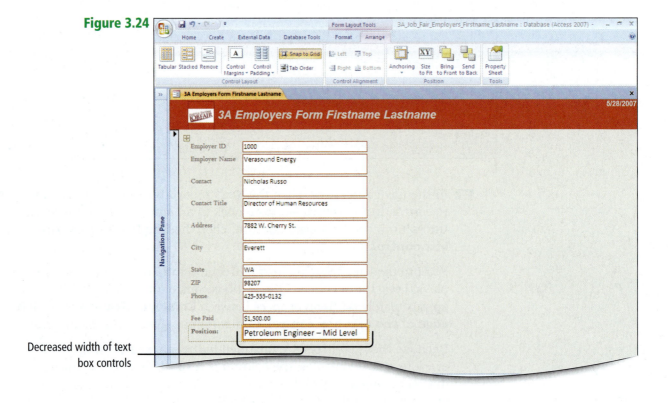

Decreased width of text
box controls

4 **Save** 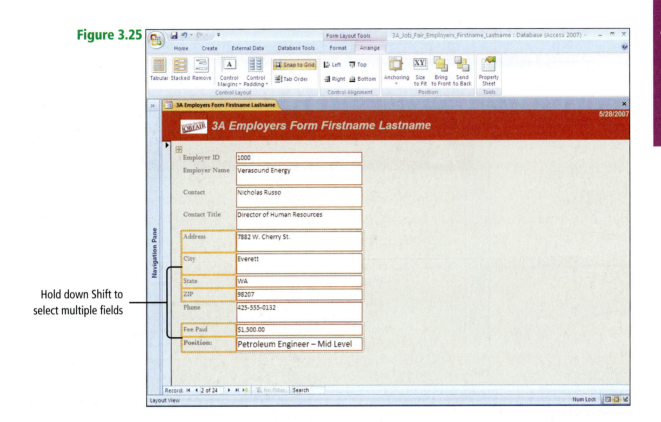 the form. Click the **Address label control**. Holding down ⬆Shift , click the following label controls: **City**, **State**, **ZIP**, **Fee Paid**, and **Position**. Compare your screen with Figure 3.25.

To select multiple contiguous or noncontiguous fields in Layout view, you must hold down ⬆Shift , and then click each control.

Figure 3.25

Hold down Shift to select multiple fields

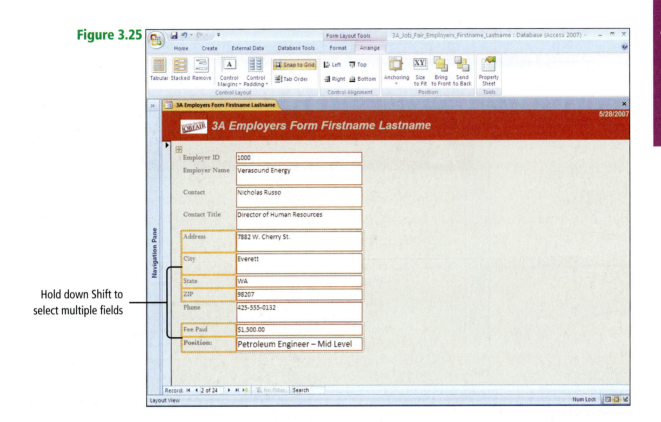

5 In the **Control Layout group**, click the **Stacked** button, and then compare your screen with Figure 3.26.

The controls are moved to the second column, and the second column has its own Layout Selector. The controls are aligned using the stacked control layout.

Stacked control layout

Controls moved to another column

Figure 3.26

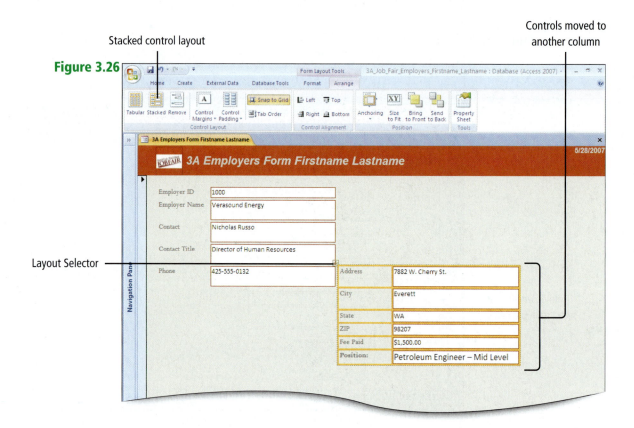

Layout Selector

6 Above the **Address label control**, point to the **Layout Selector** until the pointer displays. Drag upward and slightly to the right, as shown in Figure 3.27, until the top of the **Address label control** aligns with the top of the **Employer ID text box control**, and then release the mouse button.

An advantage of having the controls grouped in one layout is the ability to move all of the controls at one time.

Move Select pointer

Outline displays where controls will display after dragging

Figure 3.27

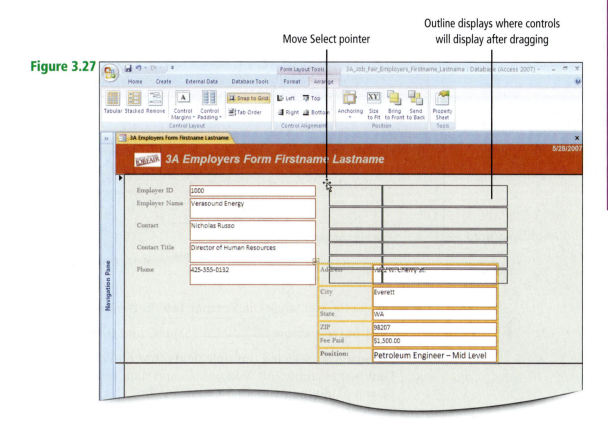

7 With the second column selected, hold down ⇧Shift, and then click the **Employer ID label control**. Still holding down ⇧Shift, above **Employer ID**, click the **Layout Selector** ⊞. Compare your screen with Figure 3.28.

All controls in both columns are selected. Each column in this form has its own Layout Selector.

Figure 3.28

Layout Selectors

Both columns selected

8 On the Ribbon, click the **Format tab**. In the **Font group**, click the **Font button arrow** Calibri ▾ , and then click **Arial**.

Because you selected multiple fields that had different fonts, the Font box is empty. All field names and data in the text boxes are displayed using the Arial font. Changing font characteristics can increase the size of the displayed data. The text in the Position text box control does not entirely display.

9 Click the **Position text box control**. In the **Font group**, click the **Font Size button arrow** 11 ▾ , and then click **12**. **Save** 🖫 the form.

The entire text now displays in the Position text box control. Alternatively, you could have dragged the right edge of the text box control to the right to increase the width of the text box control.

10 Click the **Fee Paid label control** to display the 🔀 pointer. Drag the control upward until a dark orange line displays above the **Address** field controls, and then release the mouse button.

Because the Fee Paid field is part of the second column's stacked layout, it aligns perfectly with the other controls in the column. The fields are aligned to match the layout of the paper form, with the exception of the *Position* field, which extracts the data from the *3A Job Openings* table.

11 Click the **Position label control**. On the Ribbon, click the **Arrange tab**. In the **Control Layout group**, click the **Remove** button.

The Position label control and text box control are both selected and are removed from the stacked control layout in the second column.

12 With both controls selected, point to the **Position label control** or **text box control** to display the ⬚ pointer, and then drag the field downward and to the left as shown in Figure 3.29—do not release the mouse button.

As you drag the controls, an outline of both controls displays where the controls will be placed on the form.

Black line indicates bottom   Controls removed
of Detail section   Move Select pointer from control layout

Figure 3.29

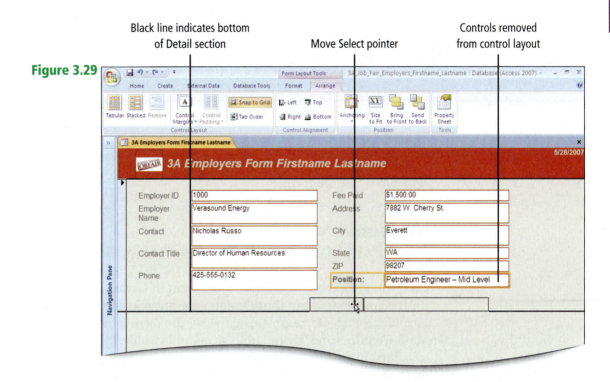

13 Release the mouse button. Click the **Position text box control**, which cancels the label control selection. Notice that there is no broken border around the label control and the text box control, which means the controls are no longer grouped.

14 Drag the **Position text box control** downward and to the left as shown in Figure 3.30. On the Ribbon, click the **Format tab**, and in the **Font group**, click the **Center** button ▤ . Do not be concerned if your controls are not aligned exactly as shown in Figure 3.30.

After removing controls from a control layout, you can select either the label control or the text box control, and then drag the control to another position on the form. If you want to move both controls at the same time, hold down ⇧ Shift, and then click each control to select both controls.

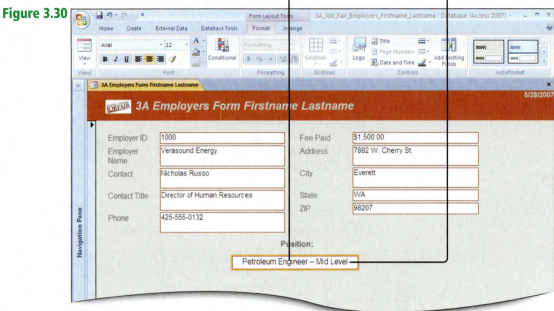

Data in text box control centered

Text box control dragged under label control

Figure 3.30

15 **Save** 💾 the form.

Objective 4
Modify the Design of a Form in Design View

Every modification you made to the form in Layout view can also be done in Design view. Recall that Design view gives a more detailed view of the structure of the form. In Design view, the form is not running, so the data from the underlying table or query is hidden while you are making modifications—to see the effects of changes, you must switch to Layout view or Form view, which is a disadvantage of using Design view. Some tasks cannot be completed in Layout view, such as adding page numbers, footers, labels, images, lines, and rectangles. In Design view, you can also resize form sections.

Activity 3.12 Inserting a Footer into a Form and Aligning Controls

In this activity, you will add a **footer**—information that displays at the bottom of every form or the bottom of every page in a report—to the form. You cannot add a footer in Layout view; however, once a footer is added in Design view, you can format and edit the text in the controls or delete the controls in Layout view.

1 On the **Format tab**, in the **Views group**, click the **View button arrow**, and then click **Design View**. Alternatively, on the status bar, click the Design View button or right-click the object tab, and then click Design View. Compare your screen with Figure 3.31.

In Design view, this form is divided into three sections—Form Header, Detail, and **Form Footer**—designated by a bar called a **section bar**. The Form Footer section is a section of the form that displays information in the footer. Recall that the Form Header section contains information that will display at the top of every form, and the Detail section displays the field names and text boxes.

In Design view, the data from the underlying table is not displayed. Instead, the text box control displays a placeholder—the field name— for the data.

Placeholder for data

Figure 3.31

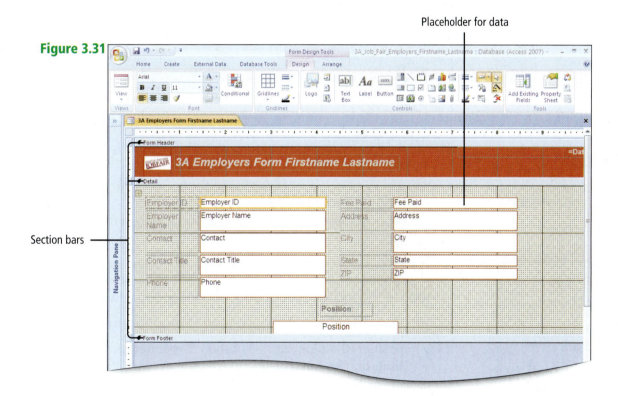

Section bars

2 At the bottom of the form, point to the lower edge of the **Form Footer section** bar to display the ⊞ pointer. Drag downward to the **1-inch mark on the vertical ruler**, and then compare your screen with Figure 3.32.

The Form Footer section is expanded so that you can add the page number to the form. Do not be concerned if your expanded Form Footer section does not exactly match Figure 3.32—it will be adjusted later. The background grid is dotted and divided into 1-inch squares to help you place and align controls on the form. Use the vertical and horizontal rulers to guide the placement of a control on the form.

Horizontal ruler

Grid lines

Figure 3.32

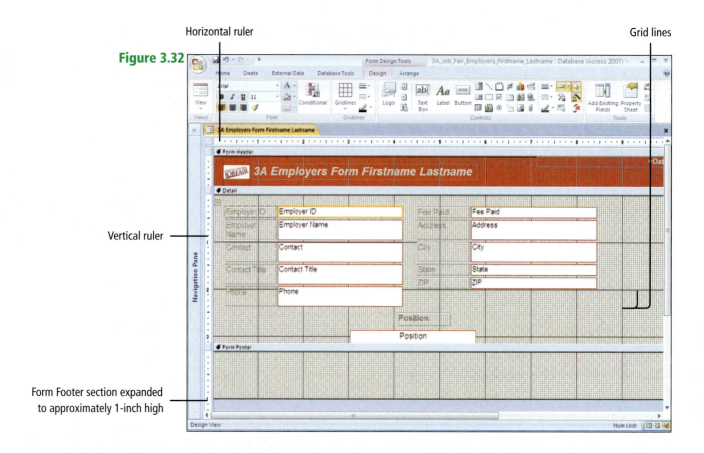

Vertical ruler

Form Footer section expanded to approximately 1-inch high

Alert! — **Are the rulers missing?**

If the horizontal and vertical rulers do not display, on the Arrange tab, in the Show/Hide group, click the Ruler button.

---

3 On the **Design tab**, in the **Controls group**, click the **Label** button. Move the ⌖ pointer down to the **Form Footer section**, and then position the plus sign (+) of the ⁺A pointer at approximately **0.25 inch on the horizontal ruler** and even with the bottom edge of the **Form Footer section** bar. Drag to the right to **3 inches on the horizontal ruler** and then downward approximately **0.25 inch**. Compare your screen with Figure 3.33. If you are not satisfied with your result, click anywhere in the Form Footer section—not in the label control. The control will be removed from the form, and you can begin again.

While you are dragging the ⁺A pointer, the horizontal and vertical rulers indicate the height and width of the label control, and the label control has a dotted outline. When you release the mouse button, the label control is positioned as shown by the white box. This label control is an example of an unbound control.

Figure 3.33

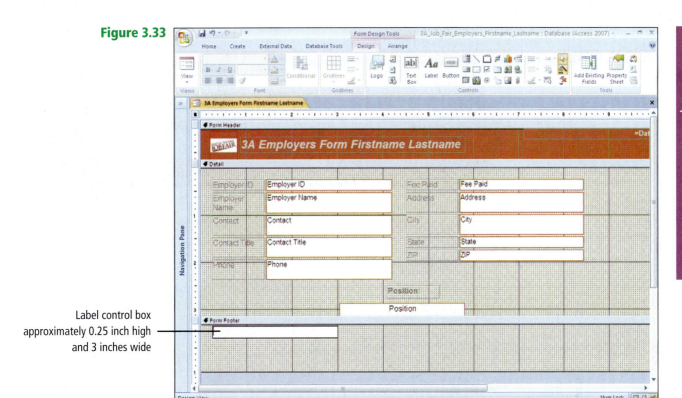

**Label control box
approximately 0.25 inch high
and 3 inches wide**

4 Using your own first and last name, in the label control, type
Designed by: Firstname Lastname and then press Enter. Compare your
screen with Figure 3.34.

Pressing Enter adds the text you typed to the label in the Form Footer
section and selects the label so that it can be formatted. The small
boxes around the edge of the label control are **sizing handles**,
which are used to resize a control and to indicate when a control is
selected. Depending on the number of characters in your name,
Access may adjust the right edge of the label control to accommodate
the length of your name.

Figure 3.34

Label text

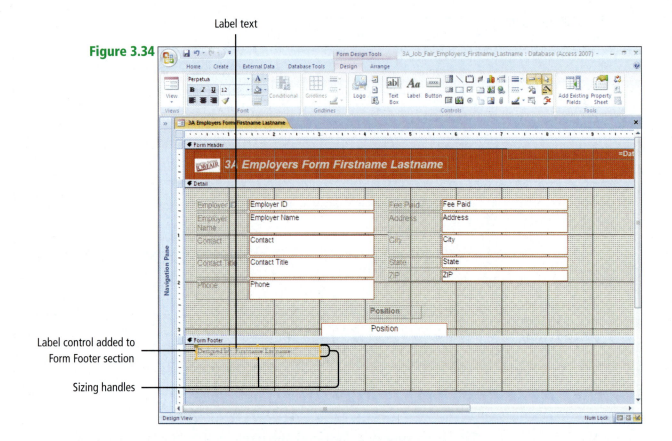

Label control added to Form Footer section

Sizing handles

Alert!

Did the label control disappear?

The label control will disappear from a form if you click any area other than the label control before typing the text.

---

5 With the sizing handles displayed around the label control, on the **Design tab**, in the **Font group**, click the **Font button arrow**

Calibri , scroll up, and then click **Arial**. Click the **Font Color button arrow** A . Under **Standard Colors**, in the sixth row, click the sixth color—**Maroon 5**. In the **Font group**, click the **Bold** button B .

6 On the label control, point to the right middle sizing handle to display the ↔ pointer, and then double-click to adjust the size of the label to fit the text.

7 In the **Form Header section**, click one time to select the **label control for the title**—sizing handles display. Pointing to the selected label control and to the left of your first name, click one more time to enter into the editing mode.

Alert!

Did the Property Sheet display to the right of the form?

If the Property Sheet opens, you double-clicked the Title label control. Close the Property Sheet, and in the Title label control, click one time to enter into the editing mode.

---

8 Select your first name and last name, press ⌦Delete, and then press ⌫Bksp to delete the extra space after *Form*. Press ⏎Enter. In the **Font group**, click the **Center** button 🗉. **Save** 🖫 the form.

The title of the form is changed to *3A Employers Form*. Because you have your name in the Form Footer section, displaying your name in the title is redundant. This does not affect the name of the form as shown in the form tab on the tab row. You can also edit data in controls in Layout view.

9 In the **Form Header section**, if necessary, scroll to the right to display the Date label control. Click the **Date label control** to select it.

Point to the **Date label control** to display the 🖑 pointer, and then drag the label control downward into the **Form Footer section** as shown in Figure 3.35. Change the font color of the **Date label control** to **Maroon 5**.

You cannot drag a control into the Form Footer section in Layout view—you can only drag a control from the Form Header section into the Detail section. The Date label control displays = *Date()*, which is an expression used by Access to retrieve the current date from the computer system. Recall that when you added the label control for the date, you selected the option to display only the date.

Expression to retrieve the computer system's date

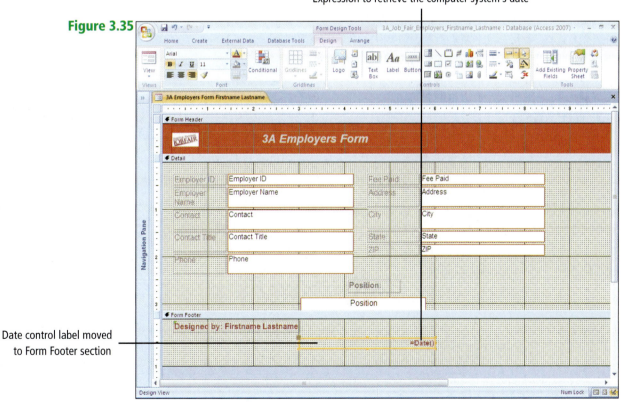

Figure 3.35

Date control label moved to Form Footer section

10 In the **Form Footer section**, if necessary, click to select the **Date label control**. Hold down ⇧Shift, and then in the **Detail section**, click to select the **ZIP text box control**. On the Ribbon, click the **Arrange tab**, and in the **Control Alignment group**, click the **Right** button.

The right edge of the Date label control is aligned with the right edge of the text box controls in the second column in the Detail section.

11 In the **Form Footer section**, click the **Designed by label control**, which cancels the selection of the Date label control and the ZIP text box control. Hold down ⇧Shift, and then click the **Date label control**. In the **Control Alignment group**, click the **Top** button, and then compare your screen with Figure 3.36.

The label control for the date is aligned at the top with the Designed by Firstname Lastname label control. Use the Control Alignment buttons to quickly align controls to make your form more visually attractive. You can also align controls in Layout view.

An Error Checking Options button displays under the Date label control.

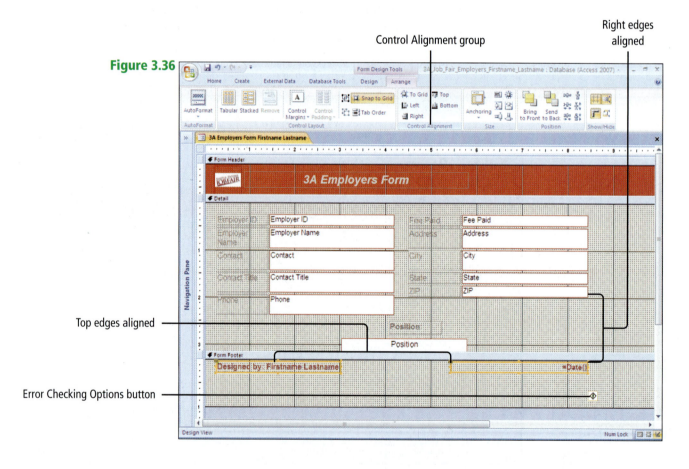

Figure 3.36

12 Point to the **Error Checking Options** button ◈ to display the ScreenTip—Access has determined that the two selected controls are not associated with one another. Click the **Error Checking Options button arrow**, and then click **Dismiss Error**. Alternatively, click anywhere in the Form Footer section to cancel the current selection.

Access recognizes that the two selected fields are not associated with one another and gives you the opportunity to correct the situation if you have made an error.

13 To deselect the two control labels, click in an empty area of the **Form Footer section**. Click the **Designed by label control**. Point to the bottom middle sizing handle until the ⬍ pointer displays. Drag downward approximately **0.25 inch** to increase the height of the label control.

14 With the **Designed by label control** selected, hold down ⬆Shift, and then click the **Date label control**. On the **Arrange tab**, in the **Size group**, click the **Size to Shortest** button ⬒.

Use the Size buttons to adjust the size of selected controls. Size to Shortest compares the selected controls and resizes them to match the size of the control with the shortest height. Size to Tallest resizes to match the size of the control with the tallest height. Size to Widest resizes to match the size of the control with the widest width, and Size to Narrowest resizes to match the size of the control with the narrowest width.

15 To deselect the controls, click in an empty area of the **Form Footer section**. Point to the bottom edge of the **Form Footer section**—not the Form Footer section bar—to display the ✛ pointer. Drag the bottom edge upward until there are approximately **3 dots** between the selected controls and the bottom edge of the Form Footer section. Compare your screen with Figure 3.37.

The height of the Form Footer section is decreased. You cannot adjust the size of a Form section in Layout view.

Figure 3.37

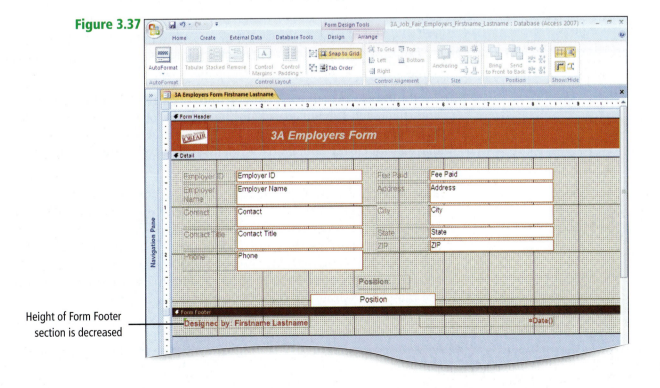

Height of Form Footer section is decreased

16 Reduce the width of the form, if necessary. Scroll to the right and then point to the right edge of the form until the ✛ pointer displays. Drag to the left until the right edge of the form aligns with the **10-inch** mark on the horizontal ruler.

17 **Save** 🖫 the form. On the **status** bar, click the **Form View** button 🖽.

More Knowledge

Add Header and Footer Sections to a Form

When you create a form using the Blank Form tool, the only section created is the Detail section. To display the Header and Footer sections, open the form in Design view. On the Arrange tab, in the Show/Hide group, click the Form Header/Footer button.

Activity 3.13 Changing the Tab Order and Printing a Selected Record

Now that you have arranged the controls on the form to match the paper form used by employers who participate in the Seattle-Tacoma Job Fair, you will enter a record to test the form and then print a sample form for approval.

1 With your *3A Employers Form* in Form view, in the navigation area, click the **New (blank) record** button ▸.

The fields are cleared and ready to accept a new entry. The record number advances to 25, indicating that this will be the 25th record.

2 Click in the **Employer ID** field box, type **6000** and then press Tab four times.

The insertion point is positioned in the State field. The fields are not in a natural order for data entry. The fields should be entered in the same order as they display on the paper form.

3 On the **Home tab**, in the **Views group**, click the **View button arrow**, and then click **Design View**. On the Ribbon, click the **Arrange tab**. In the **Control Layout group**, click the **Tab Order** button. In the displayed **Tab Order** dialog box, under **Section**, click **Detail**, and then compare your screen with Figure 3.38.

Tab order is the order in which the fields on a form are selected when Tab or Enter is pressed. The Tab Order dialog box enables you to change the tab order. The Section box enables you to select the form section that contains the controls for which you want to change the tab order. The Custom Order box displays the controls in the selected section. Under the Section box are instructions for changing the tab order—dragging rows to change the tab order.

Sections in form   Fields in selected section

Figure 3.38

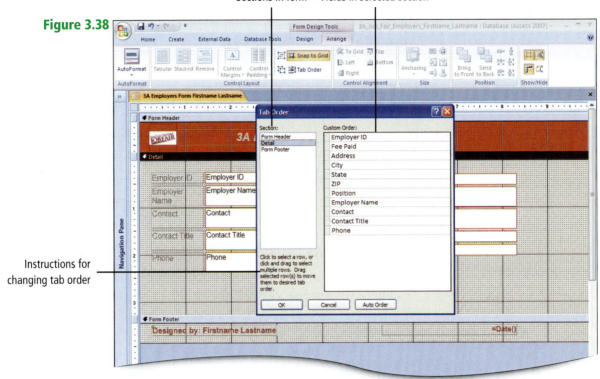

Instructions for
changing tab order

4 In the **Tab Order** dialog box, click **Auto Order**. Notice that the tab order of the fields in the Detail section has changed so that you can enter all the data in the first column and then in the second column.

Using Auto Order is an efficient way to change the tab order if you wish to enter the data in one column before moving to another column.

5 In the **Tab Order** dialog box, click **OK**. On the status bar, click the **Form View** button. In the navigation area, click the **Last record** button. Click in the **Employer Name** field.

Scroll arrows display at the right edge of the field box to indicate that the data in the field might be displayed on more than one line.

6 Enter the following data in the fields for **Record 25**.

Employer Name	Bellevue Community College
Contact	Firstname Lastname
Contact Title	Dean
Phone	425-555-1542
Fee Paid	0
Address	1300 Bellevue Circle SE
City	Bellevue
State	WA
ZIP	98007
Position	Instructor

7 Press ⎀Tab⎀ to save the record and move to a blank form. In the navigation area, click the **Previous record** button ◀, and then compare your screen with Figure 3.39.

Figure 3.39

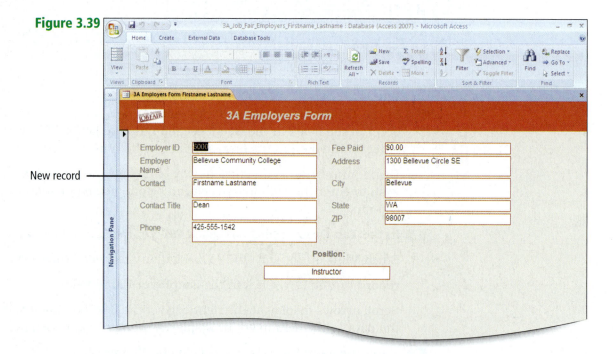

New record

8 **Save** 🖫 the form. With the record for *Bellevue Community College* displayed in the form, click the **Office** button 🖳, point to **Print**, and then click **Print Preview**. Click the **Next Page** button ▶.

The form size exceeds the width of the paper in Portrait view.

9 On the **Print Preview tab**, in the **Page Layout group**, click the **Landscape** button. Notice that the extra page with the column of background color no longer displays.

10 Click the **Last Page** button [▶|]. Notice the footer information at the bottom of the page, and also notice that the title does not display at the top of the page. Click the **First Page** button [|◀] to display Page 1. Notice the title at the top of the page, and also notice that the footer does not display at the bottom of the page.

Forms are used for data entry and are usually not printed. For that reason, when you view a form on the screen, the header and footer information display on every record. When you print all of the records in the form layout, the header information prints only on the first page, and the footer information prints only on the last page.

11 In the **Close Preview group**, click the **Close Print Preview** button. With the form displayed in **Form** view, display the **last record—** *Employer Name of Bellevue Community College.* Click the **record selector** bar. Click the **Office** button [🗔], and then click the **Print** button. In the displayed **Print** dialog box, under **Print Range**, click **Selected Record(s)**, and then click **OK**. If you are required to submit your database electronically, click **Cancel**, and then from the **Office** menu [🗔], point to **Save As**, and then click **PDF or XPS**. In the **Publish as PDF or XPS** dialog box, click **Options**, and then click **Selected records**. Navigate to the location where you are saving your electronic printouts, and then click **Publish**.

Record 25 prints and displays both the header and footer.

12 **Close** [✕] the form, and then expand [»] the **Navigation Pane**.

13 Under **Forms**, double-click **3A Job Openings Form**, and then collapse [«] the **Navigation Pane**. View the form in **Print Preview**, and then click the **Next Page** button. Notice that Page 2 displays the right edges of the controls.

14 In the **Close Preview group**, click the **Close Print Preview** button. Switch the form to **Layout** view. Click the **Job Openings text box control**. Point to the right edge of the text box control until the [↔] pointer displays. Drag to the left until the right edge of the text box control aligns with the right edge of your Lastname in the title. Click the **Title label control**. Point to the right edge of the label control until the [↔] pointer displays. Drag to the left until the right edge of the label control aligns with the right edge of the text box controls in the Detail section. Compare your screen with Figure 3.40.

In order to decrease the right margin of the form, you must first decrease the width of the text box controls in Layout view.

Figure 3.40

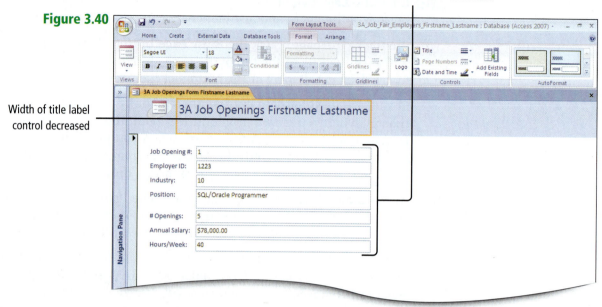

15 View the form in **Print Preview**. A message displays stating that the section width is greater than the page width and that there are no items in the additional space, so some pages may be blank. In the message box, click **OK**. In the navigation area, click the **Next Page** ▶ button. Notice that a small piece of the Form Header background color displays at the top of the page.

16 In the **Close Preview group**, click the **Close Print Preview** button. Switch to **Design** view. Point to the right edge of the form until the ✛ pointer displays. Drag to the left until the right edge of the form aligns with the **6.5 inch** mark on the horizontal ruler.

The width of the form is decreased to fit on one page in Portrait orientation. A regular-sized piece of paper in Portrait orientation has a width of 8.5 inches.

17 Notice that the **Title label control** displays the title on two lines, even though it displays on one line in Layout view. If you were to print the form, the title would display as displayed in Design view. Using the techniques you have practiced, increase the width of the Title label control, dragging the right edge of the control to the right until the entire title displays on one line.

18 On the **Design tab**, in the **Controls group**, click the **Logo** button. In the displayed **Insert Picture** dialog box, navigate to the location where the student data files for this textbook are saved. Locate and double-click **a03A_Logo**.

The Seattle-Tacoma Job Fair logo is inserted on the left side in the Form Header section.

19 **Save** 🖫 the form, and then switch to **Form** view. If you are instructed to submit this result, create a paper or electronic printout of the **first record**—*Position of SQL/Oracle Programmer*—in **Portrait** orientation.

20 **Close** ✕ the form, and then expand » the **Navigation Pane**. **Close** the database, and **Exit** Access.

End **You have completed Project 3A** ——————————

Project 3B Job Openings

Michael Dawson, executive director of the Seattle-Tacoma Job Fair, needs several reports to present to the organizers and participants of the Job Fair. In Activities 3.14 through 3.22, you will create reports in the database. As you create these reports, you will be using some of the same techniques used in creating forms. Your completed reports will look similar to those in Figure 3.41.

For Project 3B, you will need the following files:

a03B_Job_Openings
a03B_Logo

**You will save your database as
3B_Job_Openings_Firstname_Lastname**

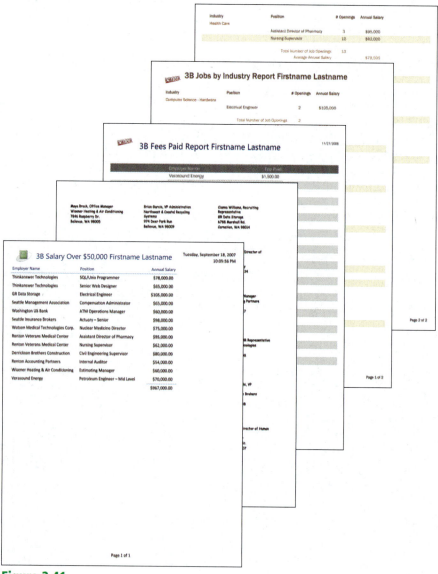

Figure 3.41
Project 3B—Job Openings

Objective 5
Create a Report

A *report* is a database object that can be used to summarize and present data from a table or query in a professional-looking format. When a report is opened, it displays the current data in the underlying table. Reports are usually printed, but they can be displayed on the screen, exported to other programs, or sent in e-mail messages. The tools used to create a report are similar to the tools used to create a form. Reports cannot be used to update data in the underlying tables and queries.

Activity 3.14 Using the Report Tool to Create a Report

There are various ways to create a report in Access, but the fastest and easiest method is to use the *Report tool*. Similar to the Form tool, the Report tool creates a report using all the fields from the underlying table or query. To create a report using multiple tables, a relationship between the tables should first be established, and then a query is created to include the fields from the tables or queries. After creating the report, you can save it and then modify it in Layout view or Design view.

1 Start **Access**. Navigate to the location where the student data files for this textbook are saved. Locate and open the **a03B_Job_Openings** file. **Save As** an **Access 2007 Database**. Navigate to the drive on which you are saving your folders and projects for this chapter, and then save the file as **3B_Job_Openings_Firstname_Lastname** in the **Access Chapter 3** folder.

2 If you did not add the **Access Chapter 3** folder to the Trust Center, enable the content. Rename the three tables and two queries by adding **Firstname Lastname** to the end of each table and query name—for example, rename *3B Employers* to *3B Employers Firstname Lastname*.

3 On the **Navigation Pane**, under **Queries**, click **3B Salary Over $50,000**. On the Ribbon, click the **Create tab**, and then in the **Reports group**, click the **Report** button. Compare your screen with Figure 3.42.

Access creates a report based on the selected object—the *3B Salary Over $50,000 query*—and displays it in Layout view. In Layout view, you can modify a report while the report is running—you can see the data as it displays in Report view. All of the records from the underlying query are displayed using the tabular control layout. Recall that forms are created using the stacked control layout. The dashed lines on the report display the margins for the page.

Figure 3.42

Placeholder for company logo or other graphic

Title with same name as query

Records in tabular control layout—field names display at the top

Margin—represented by dashed line

Date and time

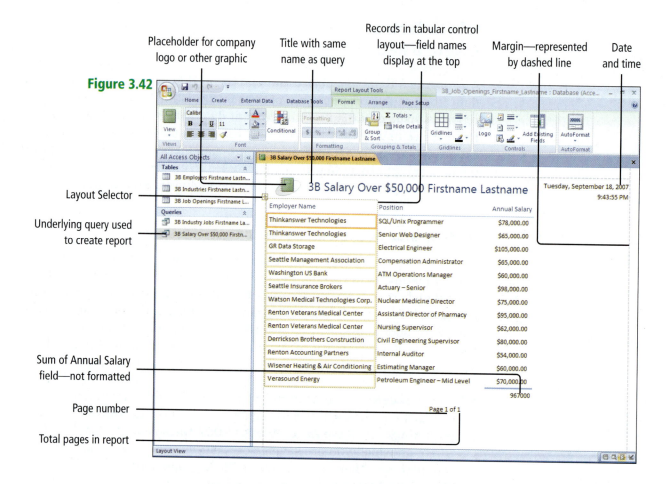

Layout Selector

Underlying query used to create report

Sum of Annual Salary field—not formatted

Page number

Total pages in report

---

4 Collapse `«` the **Navigation Pane**. On the **Format tab**, in the **Views group**, click the **View** button to switch to **Report** view.

When you open a report from the Navigation Pane, it opens in Report view. **Report view** displays the report as it will look when printed. The View button toggles between Report view and Layout view.

5 Switch to **Layout** view. In the **Annual Salary column**, click **967000** to select the sum. Notice that the sum is not formatted. In the **Formatting group**, click the **Apply Currency Format** button `$`.

The Annual Salary sum is formatted with a dollar sign ($), a comma, and two decimal places.

6 In the **Views group**, click the **View button arrow**, and then click **Design View**. Alternatively, on the status bar, click the Design View button. Compare your screen with Figure 3.43.

The Report tool creates a report with five sections. The **Report Header section** displays information that will print at the top of the first page. The Report tool inserts controls for a logo, the title, the date, and the time in the Report Header section. The **Page Header section** displays information that will print at the top of every page. The Report tool inserts label controls for the field names from the underlying query in the Page Header section. The Detail section displays the text box controls for all of the records in the *3B Salary Over $50,000* query. The **Page Footer section** displays information that will print at the bottom of every page. The Report tool inserts a control to print the current page and the total number of pages in the report. The **Report Footer section** displays information that will print at the bottom of the last page. The Report tool inserts a calculated control in the Report Footer section to calculate the sum of the Annual Salary column.

Calculated control

Figure 3.43

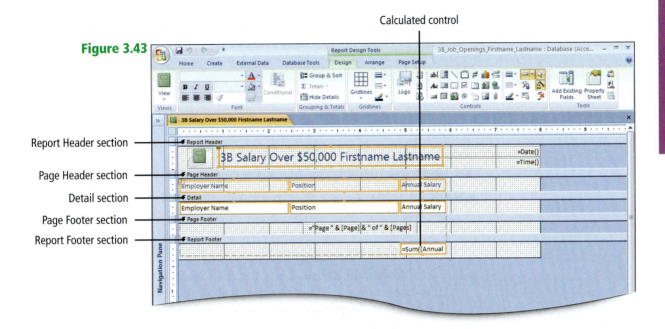

Report Header section

Page Header section

Detail section

Page Footer section

Report Footer section

7 In the **Views group**, click the **View button arrow**, and then click **Print Preview**. Alternatively, on the status bar, click the Print Preview button ; or right-click the report tab, and then click Print Preview; or click the Office button , point to the Print arrow, and then click Print Preview.

The report displays as it will print. Use the zoom pointer, zoom buttons, and Zoom slider to change the amount of data that displays on the screen.

8 In the navigation area, notice that the **Next Page** button is inactive—the report will print on one page. **Save** the report as **3B Salary Over $50,000 Report Firstname Lastname** If you are instructed to submit this result, create a paper or electronic printout.

9 **Close** the report, and then expand the **Navigation Pane**. On the **Navigation Pane**, under **Reports**, **3B Salary Over $50,000 Report** displays.

Activity 3.15 Using the Report Wizard to Create a Report

The Report tool creates an instant report using all the fields in the underlying table or query and displays the records in a tabular layout. Like the Form Wizard, the **Report Wizard** gives you more control in creating a report. Using the Report Wizard, you can select fields from one or more tables or queries, specify grouping and sorting for the data, select the report layout and orientation, and select the style. In this activity, you will create a report using a query based on three related tables to display the job openings grouped by industry and sorted by the position. Your report will display the average annual salary per industry and the total number of positions per industry.

1. On the **Navigation Pane**, under **Queries**, right-click **3B Industry Jobs**, and then click **Design View**.

2. In the design grid, notice the tables and fields that are included in this query. Also, notice that the Industry field and Employer Name field are sorted in ascending order.

   This query has no criteria. It was specifically designed to easily create a report. Most reports use queries as the source of data.

3. **Close** ⊠ the query, and then collapse ⟪ the **Navigation Pane**.

4. On the Ribbon, click the **Create tab**, and in the **Reports group**, click the **Report Wizard** button. Click the **Tables/Queries arrow** to display a list of available tables and queries that can be used to create the report, and then click **Query: 3B Industry Jobs**.

5. Under **Available Fields**, click the **All Fields** button `>>` to move all of the field names to the **Selected Fields** box. Under **Selected Fields**, click **Employer Name**, and then click the **One Field Back** button `<` to move the field to the **Available Fields** box. Compare your screen with Figure 3.44.

Four fields to be displayed in the report

Figure 3.44

Query used to create report

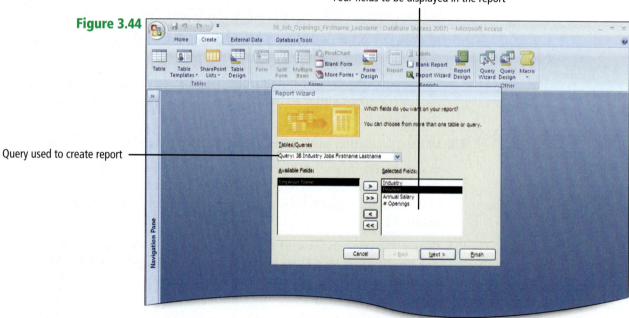

6 Click **Next** to display the second Report Wizard dialog box, which enables you to specify how you want your records grouped. To the left of **Show me more information**, click the ⟩⟩ button.

A Report Wizard Tips dialog box displays stating that the wizard evaluates the relationships between the tables you selected and groups the records in the report based on the relationships. You can choose to have data grouped or ungrouped. A report can have up to four grouping levels.

7 In the **Report Wizard Tips** dialog box, click **Close**, and then compare your screen with Figure 3.45.

On the left side, you can select the table containing the field by which to group the records. This step will format the first level of grouping. Because Industry was the first field you selected for the report, the Report Wizard previews how the report will display if grouped by the Industry field.

Field names

Field used from selected table for grouping

Figure 3.45

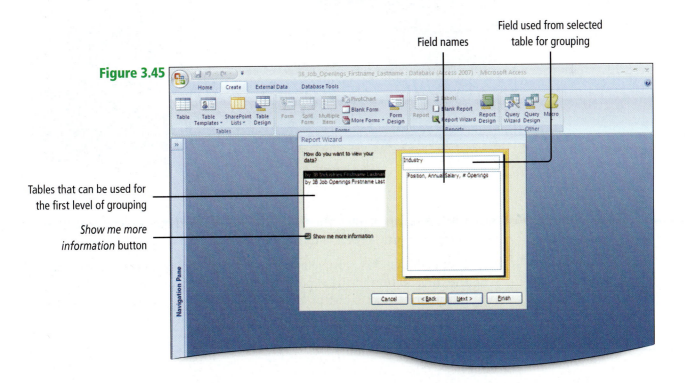

Tables that can be used for the first level of grouping

Show me more information button

8 Under **How do you want to view your data?**, click **by 3B Job Openings**. In the preview box, notice that Access cannot find a unique field by which to group. Click **by 3B Industries**, and then click **Next**.

The third Report Wizard dialog box displays, which enables you to add the second, third, and fourth levels of grouping to the report.

9 Experiment by selecting a field and then clicking the **One Field** button ⟩, and in the preview box, view the results of grouping. Also, experiment by changing the priority of the grouping levels.

When you are finished, click the **One Field Back** button ⟨ as many times as needed to remove all subgrouping levels, and then compare your screen with Figure 3.46.

This report requires only the first level of grouping. The records will be grouped by the Industry field. Because the Industry field is sorted in ascending order in the query, the report will also display the Industry groupings in ascending order.

First level of grouping

Figure 3.46

Fields that can be used
for further grouping

Priority buttons—change
grouping positions

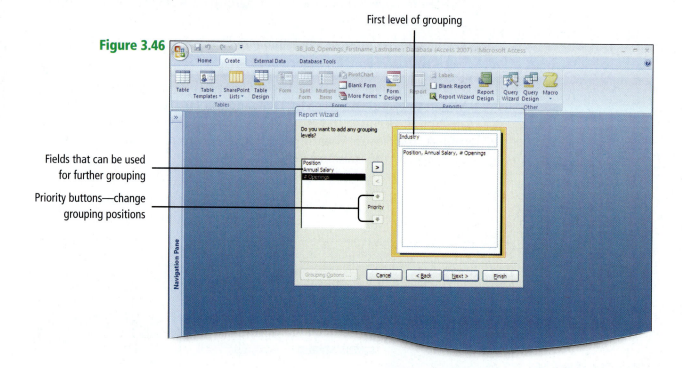

10 Click **Next** to display the fourth Report Wizard dialog box, and then compare your screen with Figure 3.47.

In this dialog box, you select how you want to sort and summarize the information in the report. You can sort up to four fields. The Summary Options button displays because the records are grouped and some of the fields contain numerical or currency data.

Figure 3.47

Used to change the sort from ascending to descending

Select the fields by which to sort

Displays because number or currency fields are included

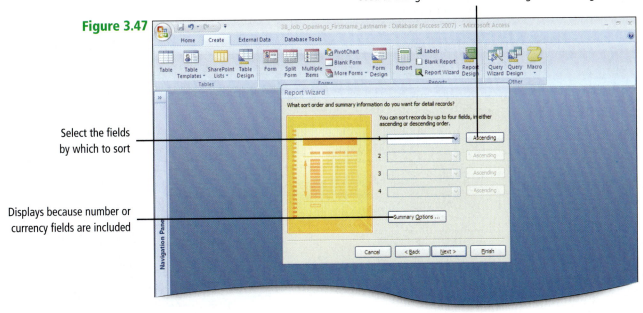

11 Click the **1 box arrow**, and then click **Position**. Notice that the Industry field name you selected for grouping does not display in the list.

This action will cause the records in the report to be sorted alphabetically by the Position field *within* the Industry grouping. Sorting records in a report presents a more organized report.

12 Click the **Summary Options** button, and then compare your screen with Figure 3.48.

The Summary Options dialog box displays. Here you can change the default of displaying the details—each record—and summary information—the results of calculations of fields as shown on the left side of the Summary Options dialog box—to Summary Only. If you sum a field, you can select the check box for *Calculate percent of total for sums*.

Select how you want to summarize the data

Select to display details and summary or only summary information

Currency data type

Figure 3.48

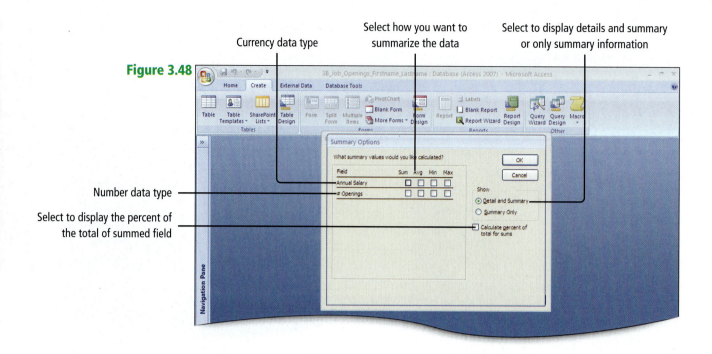

Number data type

Select to display the percent of the total of summed field

13 To the right of **Annual Salary**, select the **Avg** check box. To the right of **# Openings**, select the **Sum** check box. Under **Show**, be sure the **Detail and Summary** option button is selected, and then compare your screen with Figure 3.49.

Annual Salary field will be averaged

Figure 3.49

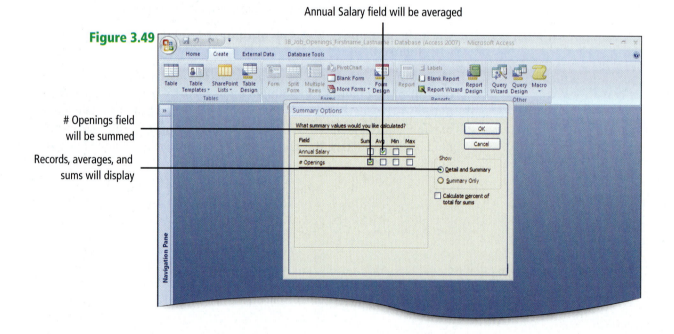

Openings field will be summed

Records, averages, and sums will display

14 Click **OK**, and then click **Next** to display the fifth Report Wizard dialog box, where you select the layout and page orientation. The box on the left displays a preview of the currently selected layout and orientation. Under **Layout**, click each option button, previewing the layout, and then click the **Stepped** option button. Under **Orientation**, be sure **Portrait** is selected, and then at the bottom of the dialog box, be sure the **Adjust the field width so all fields fit on a page** check box is selected. Click **Next** to display the sixth Report Wizard dialog box.

In this step, you select the style and preview the results.

15 Experiment by clicking several styles and preview the style in the box at the left side. When you are finished, click **Trek**, and then click **Next** to display the seventh and final Report Wizard dialog box. Under **What title do you want for your report?**, select the default title, type **3B Jobs by Industry Report Firstname Lastname** and then click **Finish**.

The report is named and displays in Print Preview. This step also saves the report with the name you entered as the report title.

16 Use the vertical scroll bar to examine the data on the first page of the report, and then compare your screen with Figure 3.50.

Each of the specifications you defined in the Report Wizard is reflected in the Print Preview of the report. The records are grouped by Industry, and the positions within each industry grouping are alphabetized. Summary information displays for each grouping.

This report still needs modifications before being printed. The industry names are *truncated*—a condition that occurs when a control in a form or report is not wide enough to display the data, causing some of the ending characters to be cut off—and the summary information is not lined up under the columns being summarized.

 # Openings field summed within each Industry grouping

Annual salary averaged within each Industry grouping

Figure 3.50

Records grouped by Industry

Records sorted by Position within the Industry grouping

Industry name truncated

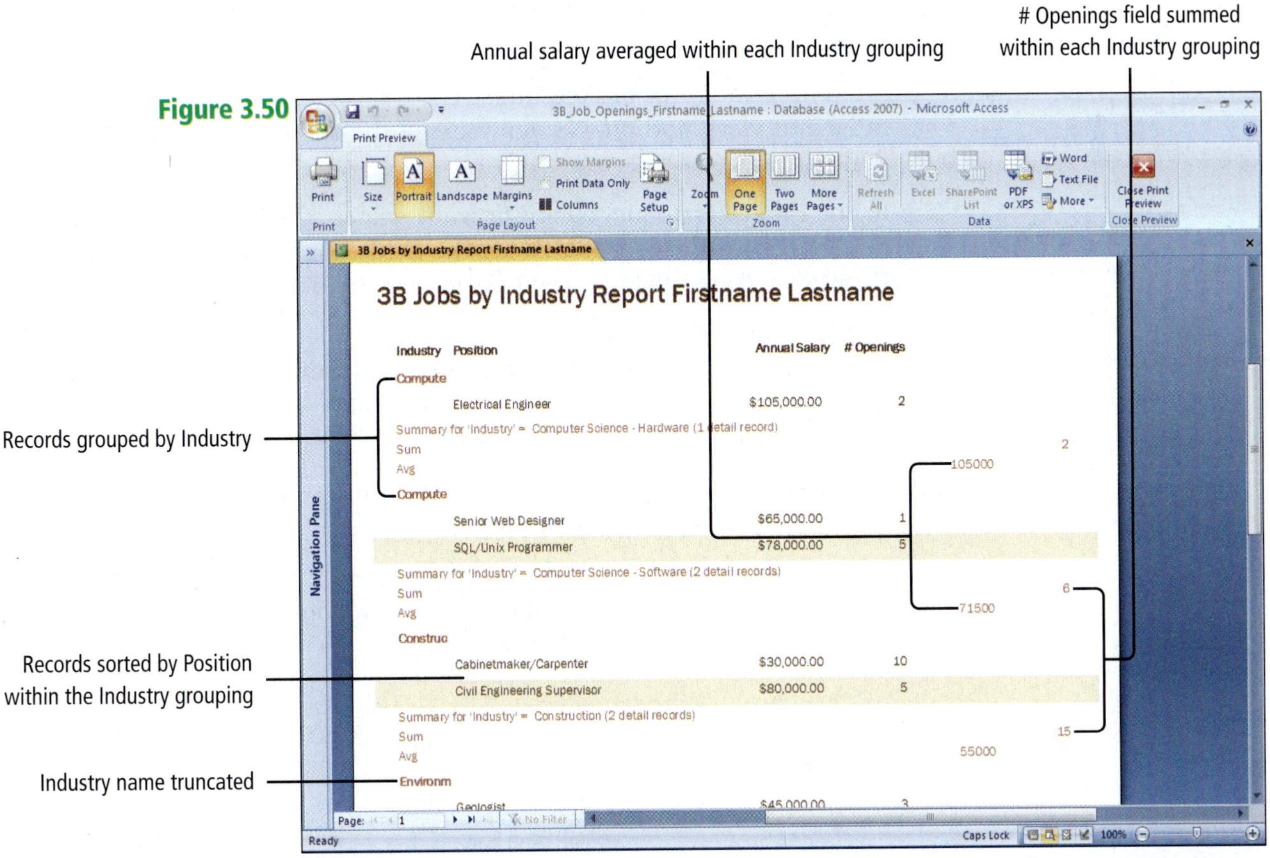

Do the annual salaries display as pound or number signs?

If the data in the Annual Salary column displays as pound or number signs (########), the text box control is not wide enough to display the numeric data. In Layout view, click the text box control and drag the right edge to the right to increase the width of the text box control. After adjusting the width, view the report in Print Preview to ensure the text box control displays numbers instead of ########.

17 In the navigation area, click the **Last Page** button ▶|, and notice the grand total of **130**—the sum of the # Openings column.

The Report Wizard creates a control for grand totals of any fields that are summed.

18 Close ☒ **3B Jobs by Industry Report**, and then expand ≫ the **Navigation Pane**. Under **Reports**, *3B Jobs by Industry Report* displays Collapse ≪ the **Navigation Pane**.

Activity 3.16 Using the Blank Report Tool to Create a Report

If the Report tool or Report Wizard does not adequately meet your needs, you can use the **Blank Report tool** to create a simple report without any special formatting. Similar to the Blank Form tool, this can be a quick method to create a report, especially if your report contains only a few fields.

1 Click the **Create tab**, and then in the **Reports group**, click the **Blank Report** button.

A blank report with broken lines representing the margins displays in Layout view, and on the right side of the screen, the Field List pane displays.

2 In the **Field List** pane, click **Show all tables**. Click the plus sign (**+**) next to **3B Employers** to display the fields in the table. Drag the **Employer Name** field to any location on the blank report.

The Employer Name field displays at the top left corner of the report, and the data from all of the records displays under the field name. As you drag fields onto the report, they will be arranged in tabular control layout.

3 In the **Field List** pane, drag **Fee Paid** onto the report, and then compare your screen with Figure 3.51.

The Fee Paid field displays to the right of the Employer Name field, and the Layout Selector displays above *Employer Name*. This report requires modifications before printing.

Figure 3.51

Displays data for every record from underlying table

Expanded field list for *3B Employers* table

Field List pane

Layout Selector

Tabular control layout

Current view—Layout view

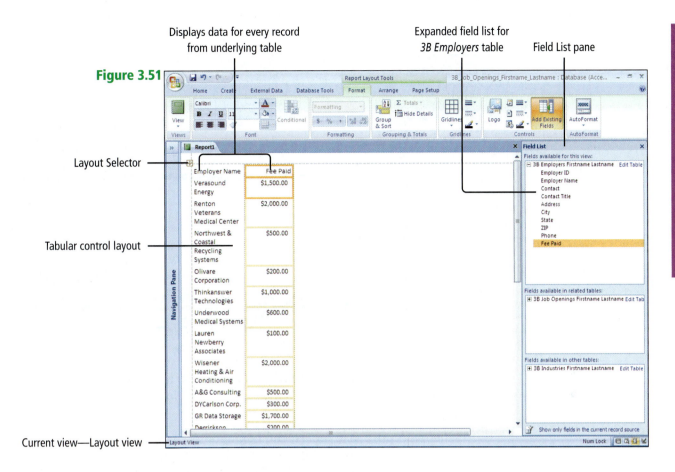

---

4 **Close** the **Field List** pane, and then **Close** the **Report** object. In the displayed message box, click **Yes** to save changes to the design of the report. In the **Save As** dialog box, under **Report Name**, type **3B Fees Paid Report Firstname Lastname** and then click **OK**.

5 Expand the **Navigation Pane**. Under **Reports**, *3B Fees Paid Report* displays.

Activity 3.17 Using the Label Wizard to Create Labels

In this activity, you will create mailing labels for the contacts of the employers who are participating in the Seattle-Tacoma Job Fair. Using the *Label Wizard*, you can quickly and efficiently create labels for a wide variety of standard label sizes.

1 On the **Navigation Pane**, under **Tables**, click **3B Employers**. Click the **Create tab**, and then in the **Reports group**, click the **Labels** button. Compare your screen with Figure 3.52.

You must select or open the underlying table or query before using the Label Wizard. The Label Wizard dialog box displays, enabling you to select the label manufacturer, the product number, and the label type, or you can click the Customize button to specify your own label dimensions.

Figure 3.52

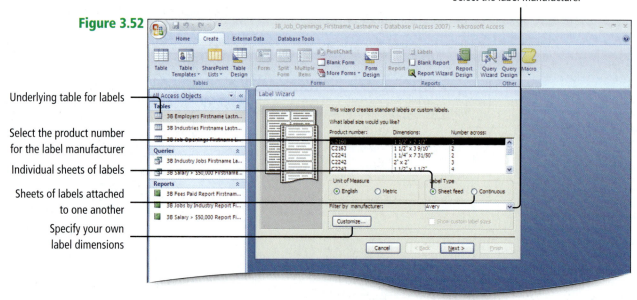

Select the label manufacturer

Underlying table for labels

Select the product number for the label manufacturer

Individual sheets of labels

Sheets of labels attached to one another

Specify your own label dimensions

2 In the **What label size would you like?** box, scroll down, and then under **Product number**, click **J8160**. Click **Next** to display the second Label Wizard dialog box.

When you purchase labels, the box usually displays the label size or a compatible Avery version. In the second dialog box, you can change the appearance of the text that displays in each label, including the font name, font size, font weight, and text color. You can also underline or italicize the text.

3 Click the **Font name arrow** Calibri ▼ , scroll down, and then click **Comic Sans MS**. If your list does not display Comic Sans MS, select any other font name. Click the **Font weight arrow** Font weight: Semi-bold ▼ , and from the displayed list, click **Semi-bold**.

On the left side of the Label Wizard dialog box, a print preview box displays the font changes.

4 Click **Next** to display the third Label Wizard dialog box. Under **Available fields**, double-click **Contact** to add the field to the Prototype label box.

Under Prototype label, the contact field displays as *{Contact}*, and the insertion point is positioned to the right of the field. All field names are enclosed in curly braces because you can also type text into the Prototype label box. The curly braces are used by Access to distinguish the enclosed text as a field, which is bound to the underlying table or query.

5 In the **Prototype label** box, type a comma, and then press Spacebar. Under **Available fields**, double-click **Contact Title**, and then press Enter.

Under Prototype label, *{Contact Title}* displays to the right of *{Contact}*, the comma, and the space. A gray bar displays on the second line of the Prototype label box, and the insertion point is positioned at the beginning of the line.

6 Using the techniques you have just practiced, add the fields to the **Prototype label** box as shown in Figure 3.53.

If you add a field by mistake, select the field, and then press Delete. If you position a field in the wrong place, delete the field, position the insertion point where the field should display, and then add the field to the Prototype label box. You can always click Cancel and begin again.

Fields and text that
will display on label

Figure 3.53

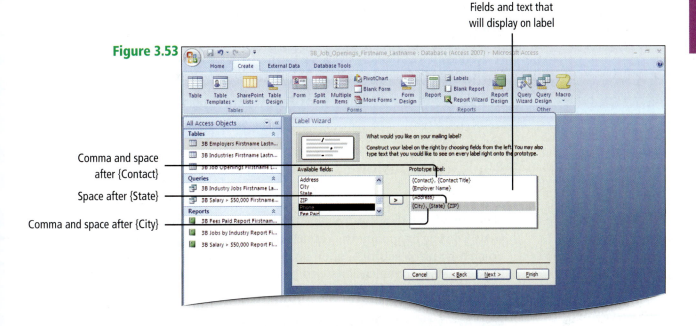

Comma and space
after {Contact}

Space after {State}

Comma and space after {City}

7 Click **Next** to display the fourth Label Wizard dialog box. Under **Available fields**, double-click **ZIP** to sort the labels by the ZIP code.

You can sort by more than one field, including fields that are not added to the label. If two fields are listed in the *Sort by* boxes, the labels sort first by the field listed at the top. If there are multiple records with the same data in the sorted field, the records sort by the field listed second.

8 Click **Next** to display the fifth and final Label Wizard dialog box. Name the report **3B Labels for Employers Firstname Lastname** and then click **Finish**.

The labels display in Print Preview. In the navigation area, the Next Page button is active, indicating that there are more pages.

9 In the **Close Preview group**, click the **Close Print Preview** button. In Design view, drag the **Page Footer section** bar to the **0.25-inch mark on the vertical ruler**. Click the **Label** button. Position the **label control** at the left side and the bottom of the Page Footer. Drag to the right to **2.0 inches on the horizontal ruler** and then upward approximately **0.25 inches**. Using your own name, type **Firstname Lastname** and then press Enter.

10 On the status bar, click the **Print Preview** button. Use the vertical scroll bar to scroll down to display the records on the first page. Notice the labels are sorted by *ZIP*. The labels print across the page and then down. In the navigation area, click the **Last Page** button ⏭. Notice that there are two pages of labels.

11 In the navigation area, click the **First Page** button ⏮. If you are instructed to submit this result, create a paper or electronic printout of the first page of labels only.

Normally, you print the labels on a sheet of labels; however, you can test the layout by first printing on regular paper to see if any adjustments need to be made.

12 In the **Close Preview group**, click the **Close Print Preview** button.

The report displays in Design view. The Label Wizard inserts controls with special commands in the Detail section to create the labels.

13 Close ✕ the **3B Labels for Employers** report.

Objective 6
Modify the Design of a Report in Layout View

Access provides four views for a report: Report view, Layout view, Design view, and Print Preview. To view the report on the screen, use Report view. To view or modify the report, use either the Layout or Design views. To change print settings, such as orientation or margins, use Print Preview. Most modifications can be made in Layout view, which displays the data from the underlying table or query.

Activity 3.18 Adjusting and Formatting Controls in a Report Created Using the Blank Report Tool

In this activity, you will adjust the controls in *3B Fees Paid Report* to make the report more visually attractive.

1 On the **Navigation Pane**, under **Reports**, double-click **3B Fees Paid Report** to open the report in **Report** view. Collapse « the **Navigation Pane**. On the **Home tab**, in the **Views group**, click the **View** button to switch to **Layout** view.

Clicking the View button toggles between Report view and Layout view because most modifications to the design of a report can be done in Layout view. The report looks similar to the display in Report view, but the first field is selected, and the Layout Selector displays above Employer Name.

2 Under **Employer Name**, notice the third record for **Northwest & Coastal Recycling Systems**. Move the pointer to the right edge of the selected column until the ↔ pointer displays, and then drag to the right until the data in the third record displays on one line. Compare your screen with Figure 3.54.

The Employer Name controls are widened so that the data for each record displays on one line. The Fee Paid column moves to the right.

Figure 3.54

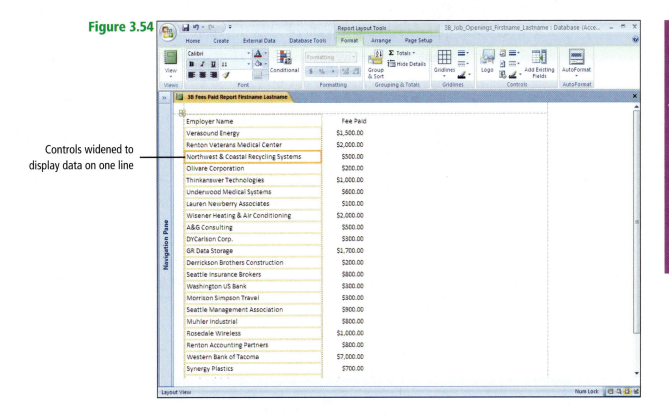

Controls widened to
display data on one line

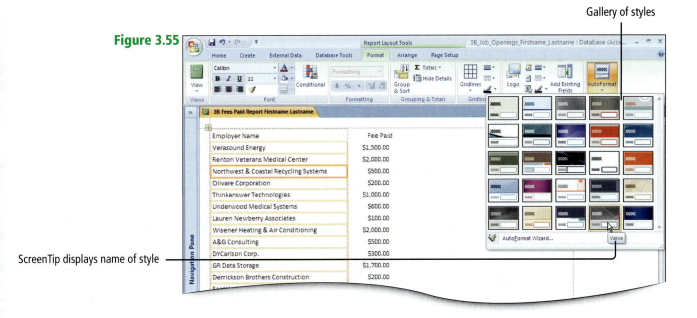

Gallery of styles

Figure 3.55

ScreenTip displays name of style

3 On the **Format tab**, in the **AutoFormat group**, click the

AutoFormat button. In the **fifth row**, point to the **fourth style** to display the **ScreenTip** of *Verve*, and then compare your screen with Figure 3.55.

Clicking the AutoFormat button displays a gallery of styles. These are the same styles you can select when creating a report using the Report Wizard.

4 In the **AutoFormat gallery**, click the **Verve** style. Above **Employer Name**, click the **Layout Selector** ⊞ to select both columns. In the **Font group**, click the **Font Size button arrow** [11 ▾], and then click **10**. After you have selected a style, you can make modifications to the report. The *Verve* style displays the records with alternating colors, which makes it easier to associate the fee paid with the employer name.

5 If necessary, click the **Layout Selector** ⊞. Point to the **Layout Selector** ⊞ until the pointer displays. Drag to the right until the report is centered between the left and right margins of the report as shown in Figure 3.56.

As you drag, there is a gray line above the status bar showing where the fields will be positioned between the margins. You may have to drag several times to position the fields in the center of the page.

Approximately centered
between the margins

Figure 3.56

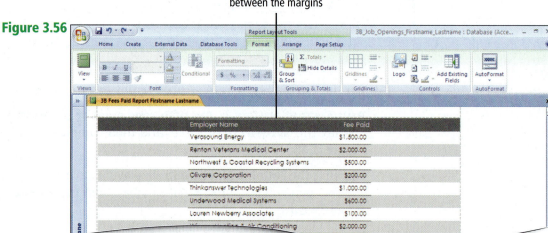

6 **Save** 🖫 the report.

Activity 3.19 Inserting a Title, Logo, Date, Sum, and Page Number into a Report

Like forms, reports can contain a title, logo, date, and page number. Unlike forms, you can insert the page number into a report in Layout view. In this activity, you will add summary information to the report by displaying the total of the Fee Paid column.

1 On the **Format tab**, in the **Controls group**, click the **Title** button 🔲.

A title—*3B Fees Paid Report*—is inserted at the top of the report.

2 In the **Controls group**, click the **Logo** button. In the displayed **Insert Picture** dialog box, navigate to the location where the student data files for this textbook are saved. Locate and double-click **a03B_Logo** to insert the Seattle-Tacoma Job Fair logo to the left of the title. Click the **Title label control**. In the **Font group**, click the **Font Size arrow** 11 , and then click **20**.

3 In the **Controls group**, click the **Date and Time** button . In the **Date and Time** dialog box, under **Include Date**, click the third option button to display the date in the *mm/dd/yyyy* format. Clear the **Include Time** check box, and then click **OK**. These options may already display because you used them on a form.

The date displays in the upper right corner of the report. The title now displays on two lines.

4 In the upper right corner of the report, click the **Date label control**.

Point to the left edge of the **Date label control** until the ↔ pointer displays. Drag to the right until the label control is slightly wider than the date that is displayed within it.

5 Click the **Title label control**. Point to the right edge of the label control until the ↔ pointer displays. Drag to the right until there is approximately **0.5 inch** between the right edge of the Title label control and the Date label control. Compare your screen with Figure 3.57. If you have many characters in your name, you may have to reduce the font size for the title to display it on one line.

The label control for the title is widened to display the title on one line.

Title of report   Current date—yours will differ

Figure 3.57

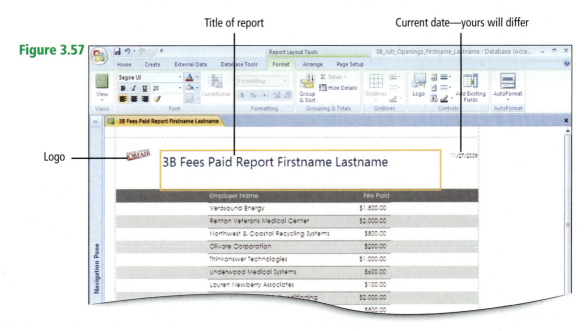

Logo

6 To select the **Fee Paid column**, click anywhere in the column. In the **Grouping & Totals group**, click the **Totals** button, and then click **Sum**. Use the vertical scroll bar to scroll down to the end of the report.

The sum—*25500*—is added at the bottom of the Fee Paid column in a calculated control, and the number is not formatted.

7 Click to select the calculated control displaying **25500**. On the Ribbon, click the **Arrange tab**, and in the **Tools group**, click the **Property Sheet** button. Alternatively, right-click the calculated control, and from the shortcut menu, click Properties. Compare your screen with Figure 3.58. If the Property Sheet does not display for the correct control, close the Property Sheet, and then be sure you select the calculated control before clicking the Property Sheet button.

Property Sheet for selected calculated control

Figure 3.58

Name of the control Access automatically created

Format property box

Selected calculated control

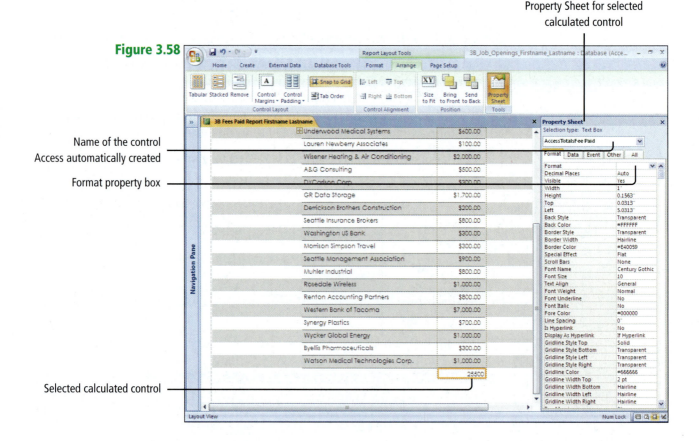

8 In the **Property Sheet**, click the **Format arrow**, and then click **Currency**. **Close** ☒ the **Property Sheet**. On the Ribbon, click the **Format tab**, and then notice the buttons in the **Formatting group**.

The text in the calculated control is formatted using the data type of Currency and displays as *$25,500.00*. You can either format a numeric field by opening the Property Sheet or by displaying the Format tab, and then in the Formatting group, clicking the appropriate Formatting button. If a control needs to be formatted with a data type other than Currency, Percent, or Comma, you must open the Property Sheet.

9 In the **Controls group**, click the **Insert Page Number** button ![icon]. In the displayed **Page Numbers** dialog box, under **Format**, click the **Page N of M** option button. Under **Position**, click the **Bottom of Page [Footer]** option button. Under **Alignment**, be sure **Center** is displayed and the **Show Number on First Page** check box is selected. Click **OK**.

10 Use the vertical scroll bar to scroll down to display the end of the report, and then compare your screen with Figure 3.59.

The page number is added to the bottom of the report and is centered in the Footer section. The page number displays the current page along with the total number of pages in the report.

Figure 3.59

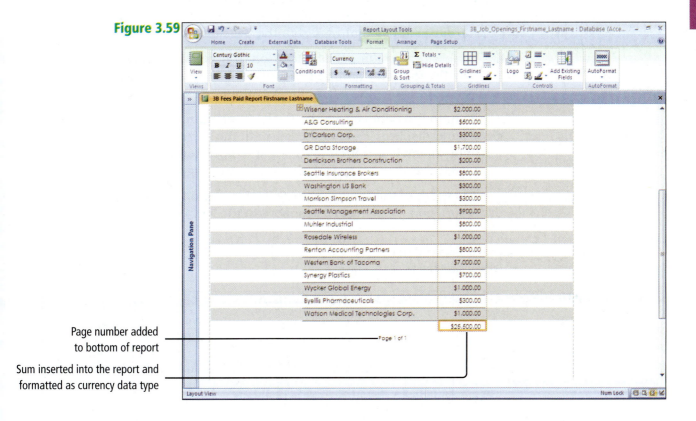

Page number added to bottom of report

Sum inserted into the report and formatted as currency data type

11 In the status bar, click the **Print Preview** button ![icon]. If you are instructed to submit this result, create a paper or electronic printout.

12 **Close** ![X] the **3B Fees Paid Report**, saving changes if prompted.

Activity 3.20 Adjusting Controls in a Report Created with the Report Wizard

In this activity, you will adjust the controls in the *3B Jobs by Industry Report* that was created with the Report Wizard. Although you could adjust the controls in Design view, it is easier doing so in Layout view because you can immediately see the effects of the changes on the displayed data. In Design view, after adjusting a control, you must switch back to Layout view or Report view to see the effects of changes.

1 Expand 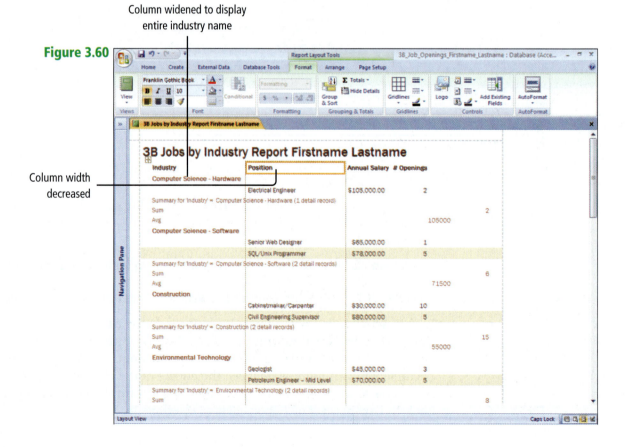► the **Navigation Pane**. Under **Reports**, double-click **3B Jobs by Industry Report** to open the report in **Report** view. Recall that this report needs further modifications before it can be printed.

Collapse ◄ the **Navigation Pane**.

2 On the **Home tab**, in the **Views group**, click the **View** button to switch to **Layout** view. To select the column, click **Industry**. Point to the right edge of the **Industry label control** until the ↔ pointer displays. Drag to the right until the first Industry name—**Computer Science - Hardware**—displays.

The *Industry* column is widened, displaying the entire industry name in each grouping. You can drag the right border anywhere in the column. The other fields are adjusted to fit on the page as indicated by the dashed lines that represent the page margins.

3 To select the column, click **Position**. If necessary, scroll down to display the **Industry** grouping of *Environmental Technology*. Under **Position**, notice the record for **Petroleum Engineer - Mid Level**.

Point to the right edge of the **Position column** until the ↔ pointer displays. Drag to the left until the right edge of the column is approximately **0.5 inch** to the right of **Petroleum Engineer - Mid Level**, and then compare your screen with Figure 3.60.

The width of the *Position* column is decreased, and the *Annual Salary* and *# Openings* fields move to the left.

Column widened to display
entire industry name

Figure 3.60

Column width
decreased

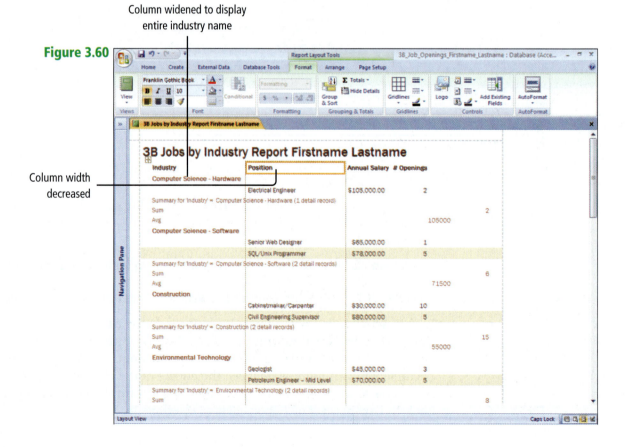

4 To select the text box controls for the column, under **Annual Salary**, click **$105,000.00**. On the **Format tab**, in the **Formatting group**, click the **Decrease Decimals** button two times, and then **Save** the report.

Because the annual salaries do not contain any significant digits—numbers other than 0—to the right of the decimal point, the values are easier to read without them.

5 Select the **# Openings column**. Point to the **# Openings label control** until the pointer displays. Drag the column to the left until a vertical orange line displays to the left of the **Annual Salary column**, and then release the mouse button.

The # Openings column now displays between the Position and Annual Salary columns.

6 In the **Industry** grouping for **Computer Science - Hardware**, under **Electrical Engineer**, click **Summary for 'Industry' = Computer Science – Hardware (1 detail record)**. Be sure that only the summary descriptions are selected as shown in Figure 3.61.

The summary descriptions are automatically inserted by Access when the report is created when summary options are selected in the wizard. The summary descriptions for each grouping are selected.

Figure 3.61

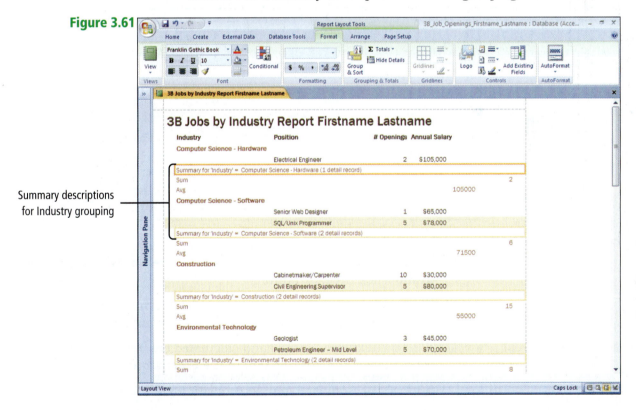

Summary descriptions for Industry grouping

7 With the **summary descriptions** selected, press ⟨Delete⟩ to remove the controls from the report, making the report easier to read. **Save** the report.

8 Notice that the values for the sum and average are not displayed directly under the related columns—# Openings is summed, and Annual Salary is averaged for each grouping. To select the calculated controls for the sum, in the **Industry** grouping for **Computer Science - Hardware**, near the right margin, click **2**. Be sure that you do not click 2 under # Openings.

9 With the **calculated control** for the sum selected, hold down ⇧Shift, and then under **# Openings**, click the **text box control** displaying **2**. Compare your screen with Figure 3.62.

Both the text box controls and calculated controls for the # Openings column are selected. A dotted line represents the margins of the column.

Figure 3.62

Selected text box control ————

Selected calculated control ————

Left margin of column ————

Right margin of column ————

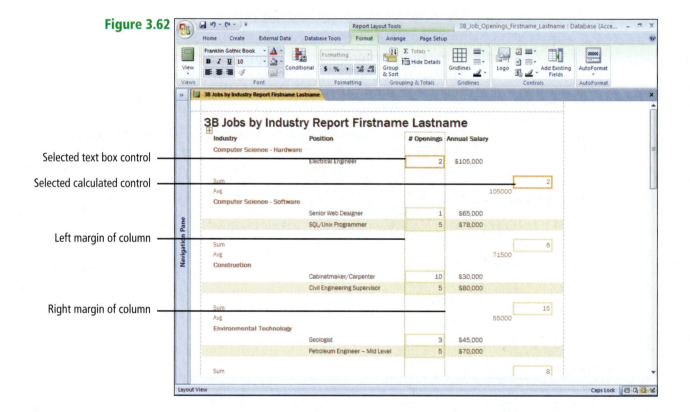

10 On the Ribbon, click the **Arrange tab**. In the **Control Alignment group**, click the **Left** button.

The text box controls and the calculated controls are aligned within the column, and the values in both controls are aligned.

11 With the text box controls and calculated controls selected, on the Ribbon, click the **Format tab**. In the **Font group**, click the **Center** button. Compare your screen with Figure 3.63.

The data in the controls is centered under the # Openings label control.

Figure 3.63

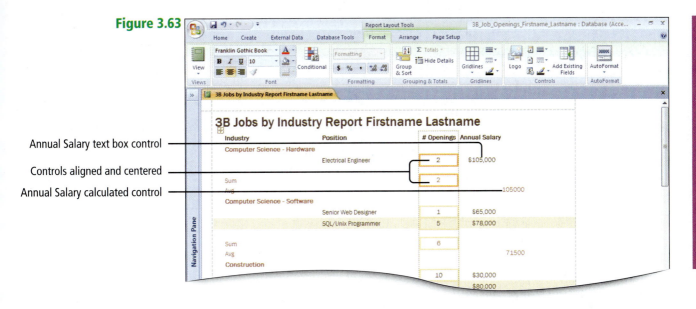

Annual Salary text box control

Controls aligned and centered

Annual Salary calculated control

12 **Save** ![save icon] the report. Using the techniques you have practiced in this project, format the data in the **Annual Salary calculated control** as **Currency** with **no decimal places**, and then align the **Annual Salary calculated control** with the **Annual Salary text box control**.

13 In the **Industry** grouping for **Computer Science - Hardware**, select the **Sum label control**. Click **Sum** one more time to enter into the editing mode. Select the text, type **Total Number of Job Openings** and then press Enter.

The text in the label control is changed to display a better description of the summed data.

14 Using the same technique, change the **Avg label control** text to **Average Annual Salary**

15 With **Average Annual Salary** selected, hold down ⇧Shift, and then click **Total Number of Job Openings** to select both label controls.

Point to either selected label control until the ![pointer icon] pointer displays. Drag the controls to the right until the right edge of the **Total Number of Job Openings label control** is approximately **0.5 inch** to the left of the value—**2**—in the calculated control as shown in Figure 3.64.

Moving the label controls closer to the calculated controls makes the summary information easier to read.

Figure 3.64

Controls aligned

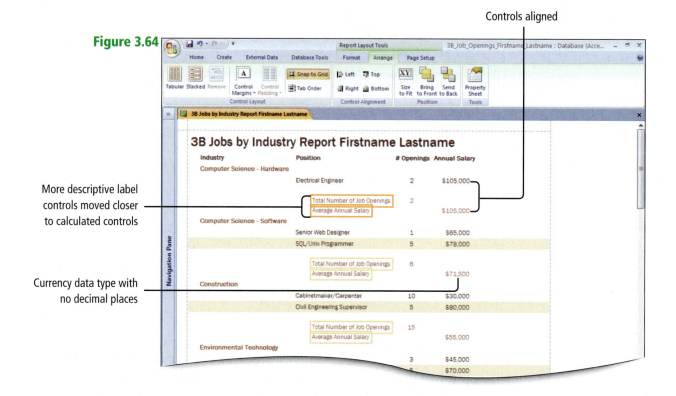

More descriptive label controls moved closer to calculated controls

Currency data type with no decimal places

16 **Save** 💾 the report. On the Ribbon, click the **Format tab**. Using the techniques you practiced in this project, add the Seattle-Tacoma Job Fair logo—**a03B_Logo**—to the top of the report, and then drag the title to the right to display all of the text.

17 Scroll down to display the end of the report, and notice that the **Grand Total label control** and its associated **calculated control** display the value of **130**. Use the techniques you practiced in this activity to change the text in the label control to **Total Number of Job Openings for All Industries** and then align the **Grand Total calculated control** with the **Total Number of Job Openings calculated control** as shown in Figure 3.65. Center the data in the **Grand Total calculated control**.

Calculated controls aligned

Figure 3.65

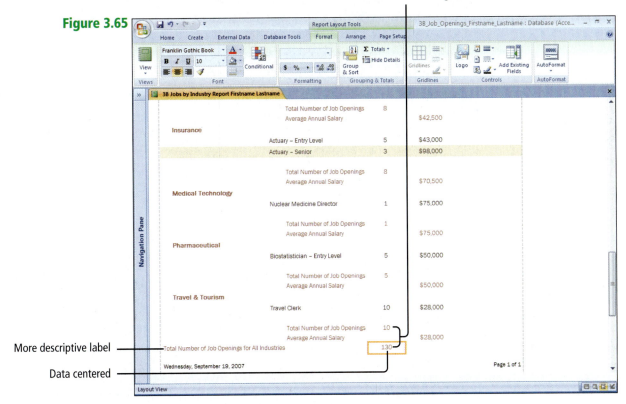

More descriptive label

Data centered

18 Click the **Total Number of Job Openings for All Industries label control**. Holding down ⬆Shift, click **Average Annual Salary**, and then click **Total Number of Job Openings** to select all three label controls. On the Ribbon, click the **Arrange tab**. In the **Control Alignment group**, click the **Right** button. Compare your screen with Figure 3.66, and then **Save** 🖫 the report.

The controls are aligned at the right. Access uses the rightmost edge of the selected controls to align all of the controls at the right.

Figure 3.66

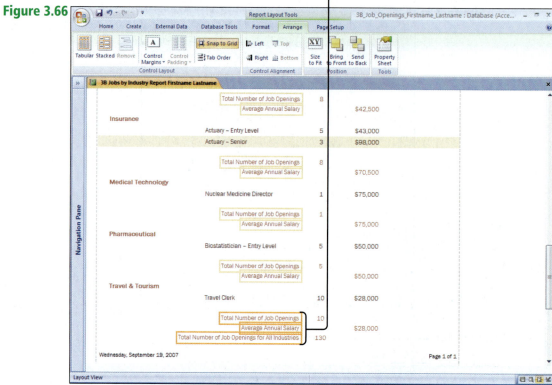

Objective 7
Modify the Design of a Report in Design View

Every modification you made to the report in Layout view can also be done in Design view. Recall that Design view gives a more detailed view of the structure of the report. In Design view, the report is not running, so you cannot see the data from the underlying table or query while you are making modifications. To see the effects of changes, you must switch to Layout view or Report view, which is a disadvantage of using Design view. Some tasks cannot be completed in Layout view, such as directly adding report sections and special controls or resizing report sections.

Activity 3.21 Adding a Control in the Page Footer Section

In this activity, you will add a control to the Page Footer section of the report.

1 On the **tab row**, right-click the **3B Jobs by Industry Report tab**, and then click **Design View**. Compare your screen with Figure 3.67. In the **Industry Footer section**, notice the position of the controls.

In Design view, this report is divided into seven sections—Report Header, Page Header, Industry Header, Detail, Industry Footer, Page Footer, and Report Footer—designated by section bars. The Industry Header section displays the text box control by which the records are grouped. The Industry Footer section displays the summary information—Sum of the # Openings field and Average of the Annual Salary field—for each industry grouping.

Overlapping controls

Figure 3.67

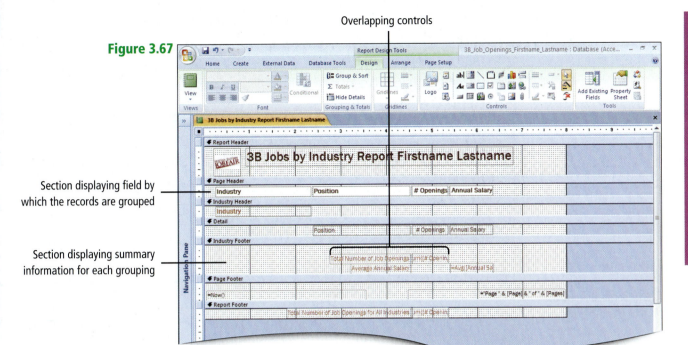

Section displaying field by which the records are grouped

Section displaying summary information for each grouping

2 In the **Page Footer section**, click the calculated control that displays **=Now()**, an expression that retrieves the computer system's date and time. Point to the right middle sizing handle until the ↔ pointer displays. Drag the right edge of the control to the left to the **2-inch mark on the horizontal ruler**.

3 In the **Page Footer section**, click the calculated control that displays the **Page number**. Point to the left middle sizing handle until the ↔ pointer displays. Drag the left edge of the control to the right to the **6-inch mark** on the horizontal ruler.

4 On the **Design tab**, in the **Controls group**, click the **Label (Form Control)** button _Aa_. Move the pointer to the **Page Footer section**, and then position the plus sign (+) of the ⁺A pointer at approximately **3 inches on the horizontal ruler** and even with the bottom edge of the Page Footer section bar. Drag to the right to the **5-inch mark on the horizontal ruler** and then downward approximately **0.25 inch**. Compare your screen with Figure 3.68. If you are not satisfied with the results, click anywhere in the Page Footer section—not in the label control. The control will be removed from the report, and you can begin again.

Figure 3.68

Label (Form Control) button

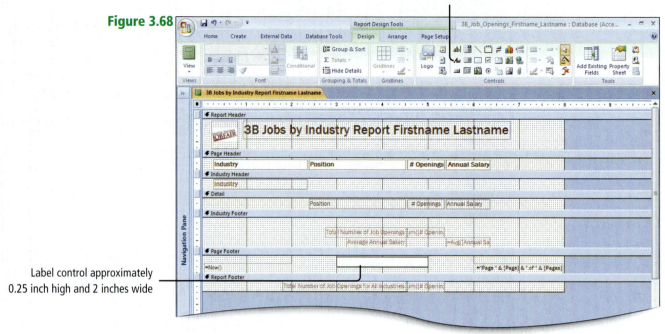

Label control approximately
0.25 inch high and 2 inches wide

5 In the **label control** box, type **Seattle-Tacoma Job Fair** and then press
[Enter]. Click the **Error Checking Options** button ◈, and then click
Ignore Error.

Text is inserted into the label control, the sizing handles display
around the control, and the Error Checking Options button displays.
Recall that the Error Checking Options button warns you that this
control is not associated with any other control. If you do not click
Ignore Error, in Design view, the label control displays a green triangle in the upper left corner; and every time you select the control, the
Error Checking Options button displays.

6 With the newly created label control selected, hold down ⇧Shift, and
then click the **date's calculated control**—*=Now()*—to select both
controls. On the Ribbon, click the **Arrange tab**. In the **Control
Alignment group**, click the **Bottom** button.

Access aligns the bottom edges of the selected controls based on the
bottom-most edge. You do not have to be precise when dragging a
control onto a report—you can use the Control Alignment buttons to
align controls to make the report more professional looking.

7 In the **Page Footer section**, click anywhere in the grid between controls to cancel the selection. Click the **Seattle-Tacoma Job Fair
label control**. On the Ribbon, click the **Design tab**. In the **Controls
group**, click the **Special Effects button arrow** ▭▾. From the displayed list, click **Special Effect: Shadowed**. In the **Font group**,
click the **Center** button ≡. **Save** 🖫 the report. In the **Views
group**, click the **View** button to switch to **Report** view. Scroll down
to display the end of the report, and then compare your screen with
Figure 3.69.

To see the effects of modifications made in Design view, you must switch to Report view or Layout view. If you make many changes in Design view, you can see that you will spend a lot of time going back and forth between views.

Figure 3.69

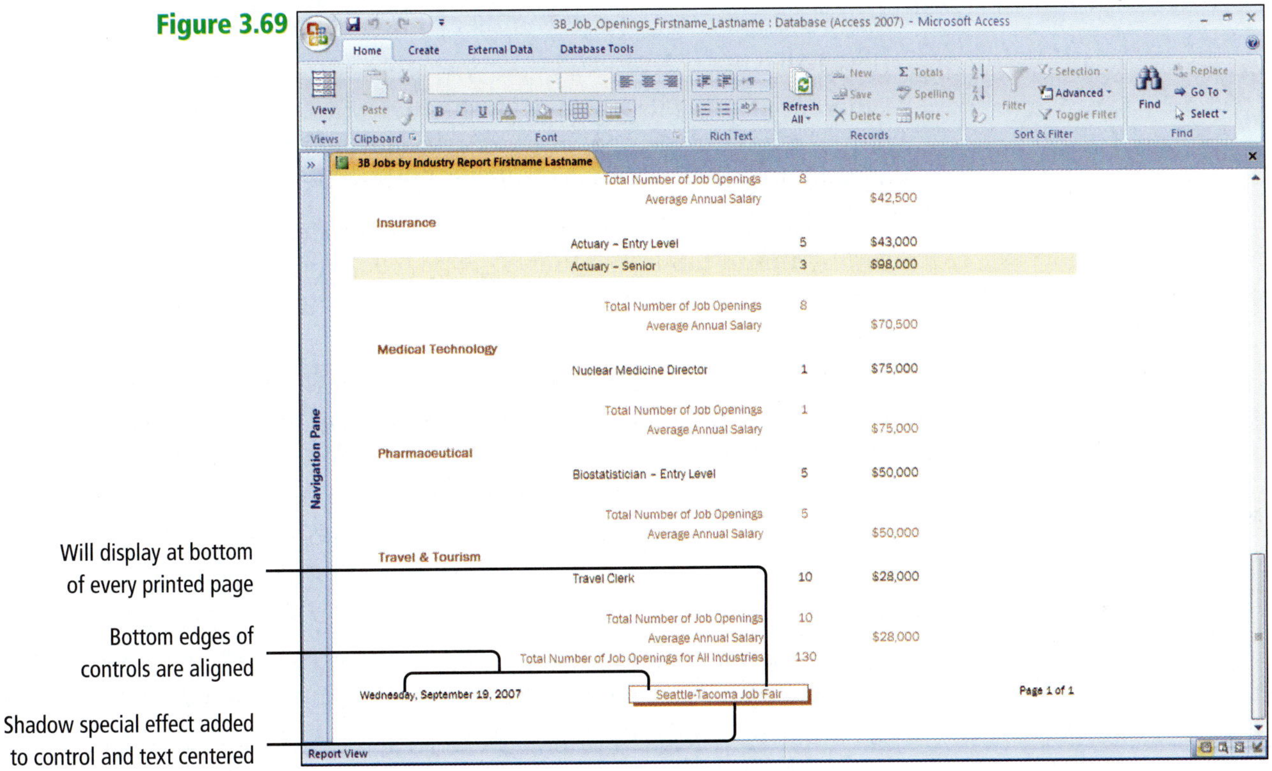

Will display at bottom of every printed page

Bottom edges of controls are aligned

Shadow special effect added to control and text centered

More Knowledge

Add Header Sections and Footer Sections to a Report

When you create a report using the Blank Report tool, the only section created is the Detail section. To display the Header and Footer sections, open the report in Design view. On the Layout tab, in the Show/Hide group, click the Report Header/Footer button and/or the Page Header/Footer button, which are toggle buttons. If you create a report that displays unwanted sections, click the active button to remove the sections from the report.

Objective 8
Keep Grouped Records Together and Print a Report

Before you print a report, examine the report in Print Preview to ensure that all of the labels and data display fully and to make sure the data is properly grouped. Sometimes, a page break occurs in the middle of a group of data, leaving the group header information on one page and the data or summary information on another page.

Activity 3.22 Keeping Grouped Records Together and Printing a Report

You can format the data in a group so that it does not break across a page, unless the data itself exceeds more than the length of the page.

1 On the status bar, click the **Print Preview** button. In the navigation area, click the **Last Page** button. Scroll down until the end of the page displays, and then **zoom in** until you can read the data. Notice that **Total Number of Job Openings**, **Average Annual Salary**, and **Total Number of Job Openings for All Industries** are truncated.

Different printers format text in different ways. Your report may not have the data truncated, or other text may be truncated. It is always a good idea to view a report in Print Preview before printing.

2 In the **Close Preview group**, click the **Close Print Preview** button. On the **Home tab** in the **Views group**, click the **View** button to switch to **Layout** view. Scroll down until the end of the report displays.

3 To select the three label controls, click **Total Number of Job Openings**. Holding down Shift, click **Average Annual Salary**, and then click **Total Number of Job Openings for All Industries**. Point to the left edge of the **Average Annual Salary label control** until the pointer displays. Drag the left edge of the control to the left until it aligns with the letter *T* in **Total Number of Job Openings**.

4 If the top of the report displays, scroll down to the end of the report—do not click in the report or your controls will no longer be selected. With same label controls selected, in the **Font group**, click the **Align Text Right** button to right align the text in all of the label controls. Compare your screen with Figure 3.70.

The width of the label controls is increased, and the data in the label controls is aligned on the right side of the controls.

Figure 3.70

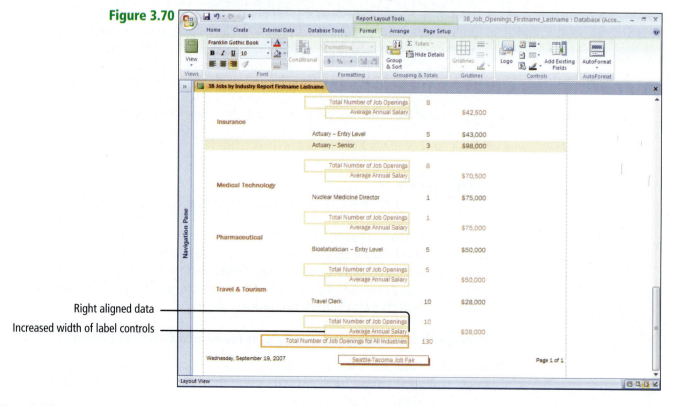

Right aligned data

Increased width of label controls

5 On the status bar, click the **Print Preview** button . Display the last page, and then verify that **Total Number of Job Openings**, **Average Annual Salary**, and **Total Number of Job Openings for All Industries** are not truncated. Scroll through the report to ensure that all of the data is displayed. If any data is truncated, switch to Layout view, and then increase the width of the related control.

6 With **page 2** of the report displayed in **Print Preview**, scroll to the top of the page to see where the second page starts, and then in the navigation area, click the **First Page** button. Scroll down to the end of the page to see where the first page ends.

The report prints on two pages. The data in the Industry grouping for Health Care is split between page 1 and page 2. The second record and the summary information for the Health Care grouping display at the top of page 2.

7 On the **tab row**, right-click the **3B Jobs by Industry Report tab**, and then click **Layout View**. On the Ribbon, click the **Format tab**. In the **Grouping & Totals group**, click the **Group & Sort** button, and then compare your screen with Figure 3.71.

At the bottom of the screen the Group, Sort, and Total pane displays. Group on Industry is selected as indicated by the orange options bar. In this pane, you can control how the records are grouped and sorted and in what sections you want totals to display.

Figure 3.71

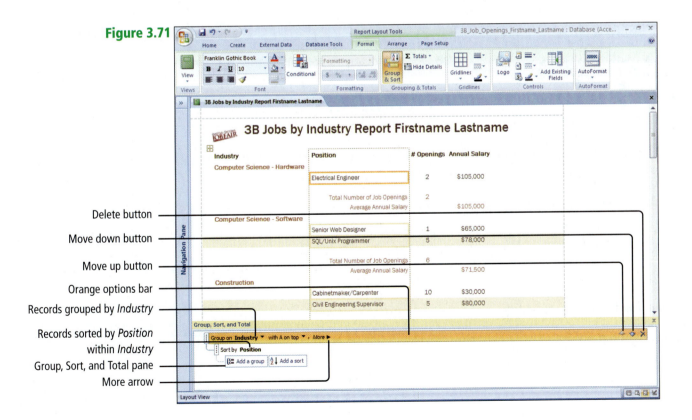

Delete button
Move down button
Move up button
Orange options bar
Records grouped by *Industry*
Records sorted by *Position* within *Industry*
Group, Sort, and Total pane
More arrow

8 In the **Group, Sort, and Total** pane, click the **with A on top arrow**, and then click **with Z on top** to display the groupings in descending order. Click **Sort by Position**, which makes the sorting level active.

Each sorting or grouping level has a number of options that can be set to obtain the results you want.

9 Click **Group on Industry**, and then change the sort back to an ascending sort. Click the **More arrow**, and then compare your screen with Figure 3.72. Take a moment to examine the brief explanation of each setting in the table in Figure 3.73.

The More arrow displays all of the options for the grouping level. The Less arrow hides the options.

Figure 3.72

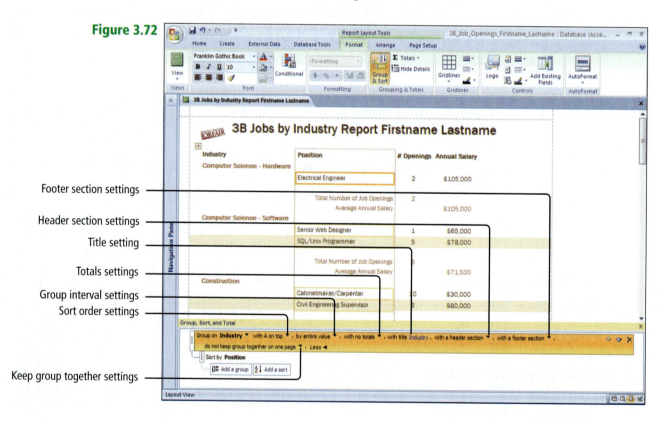

Footer section settings

Header section settings

Title setting

Totals settings

Group interval settings

Sort order settings

Keep group together settings

Group, Sort, and Total Settings

Setting	Description
Sort order	Sorts in ascending or descending order.
Group interval	Determines how the records are grouped together. By default, the entire value is used. You can group on the first character of a text field so that all the data starting with the letter *A* are grouped, all that start with the letter *B* are grouped, and so on. For a date field, you can group by the day, week, month, or quarter. You can also design a custom interval.
Totals	Adds totals to one or more fields and selects whether the totals display in the group header section or the group footer section.
Title	Changes the title of the field being summarized. When selected, a Zoom dialog box displays the current title.
Header section	Adds or removes the header section that precedes each group. When you add a header section, Access moves the grouping field to the header section. When you remove a header section that contains controls other than the grouping field, Access displays a message prompting you to confirm the deletion of the controls.
Footer section	Similar to the header section settings, except the section follows each group.
Keep group together	Determines how groups are laid out on the page when the report is printed.

Figure 3.73

10 On the options bar, click the **do not keep group together on one page arrow**. In the displayed list of settings, click **keep whole group together on one page**.

Keeping the whole group together on one page will sometimes cause more pages to print, with some of the pages having blank space at the bottom. To reduce the number of printed pages, click *keep header and first record together on one page*.

11 To the right of **Group, Sort, and Total**, click the **Close** button **X** to close the pane. Do not click the Delete button in the options bar.

Note — Remove a Grouping or Sort from a Report

To remove a grouping or sort using the Group, Sort, and Total pane, click the Delete button on the right side of the orange options bar. To change grouping levels, select the group, and then click the Move up button or Move down button.

12 On the **tab row**, right-click the **3B Jobs by Industry Report tab**, and then click **Print Preview**. View the bottom of page 1, and then view the top of page 2.

The entire Health Care group has been moved to the top of page 2. Recall that the second record and the summary information for the Health Care group were previously displayed at the top of page 2 and that Health Care and the first record were displayed at the bottom of page 1.

13 If you are instructed to submit this result, create a paper or electronic printout.

14 On the **tab row**, click the **Close** button , and then click **Yes** to save changes to the design of your report. Expand the **Navigation Pane**. **Close** the database, and **Exit** Access.

End You have completed Project 3B ————————————

There's More You Can Do!

From My Computer, navigate to the student files that accompany this textbook. In the folder **02_theres_more_you_can_do**, locate and open the folder for this chapter. Open and print the instructions for this project, which are provided to you in Adobe PDF format.

Try It! 1—Create and Modify a Form That Contains a Datasheet

In this Try It! exercise, you will create and modify a form that contains a datasheet.

Content-Based Assessments

Summary

A form is a tool for either entering or viewing information in a database. Although you can both enter and view information in a table, using a form is easier because it can display one record at a time. The Form tool creates an instant form based on all the fields in the table. The Form Wizard enables you to create a customized form. The Blank Form creates a simple form based on the fields you drag onto the form. Once created, a form can be modified in Layout view or Design view. Layout view is the preferred view to use when modifying a form because the data is displayed in the form and you can immediately see the effects of modifications to a field; however, you may have to switch to Design view when a formatting option is not available in Layout view.

Reports summarize the data tables or queries in a professional-looking manner suitable for printing. You can create a report using the Report tool, the Report Wizard, or the Blank Report tool. In addition, you can use the Label Wizard to create a wide variety of label sizes. Once created, the report can be modified in Layout view or Design view, with Layout view being the preferred view for report modifications. The records in a report can be grouped by a specified field, and the grouped data can be kept together on a page.

Key Terms

The 🌐 symbol represents Key Terms found on the Student CD in the 02_theres_more_you_can_do folder for this chapter.

Content-Based Assessments

Matching

Match each term in the second column with its correct definition in the first column. Write the letter of the term on the blank line in front of the correct definition.

——— **1.** The term for typing in the records in a table or form.

——— **2.** The view in which you can modify a form with the form running.

——— **3.** An object that can be replaced with another object.

——— **4.** To compare and update changes.

——— **5.** Displays the form as it will print.

——— **6.** A graphic or picture used to identify a company or organization.

——— **7.** Does not obtain data from an underlying table or query.

——— **8.** Displays the field name on a form.

——— **9.** A guide that aligns the controls horizontally and vertically to give the form a uniform appearance.

——— **10.** The information that displays at the bottom of every form.

——— **11.** In Design view, divides a form into three sections.

——— **12.** The small boxes around the edge of the label used to resize a control and to indicate when a control is selected.

——— **13.** A database object that can be used to summarize and present data in a professional-looking format from a table or query.

——— **14.** Displays the report as it will look when printed.

——— **15.** Means that part of the text is "cut off."

A Control layout

B Data entry

C Footer

D Label control

E Layout view

F Logo

G Placeholder

H Print Preview view

I Report view

J Report

K Section bar

L Sizing handles

M Synchronize

N Truncated

O Unbound control

Content-Based Assessments

Fill in the Blank

Write the correct word in the space provided.

1. A database object that can be used to enter or modify data in a table is a(n) _____.

2. The fastest and easiest method to create a form in Access is to use the _____ _____.

3. If the Form tool or Form Wizard does not adequately meet your needs, you can use the _____ _____ tool to create a form.

4. The Form tool creates a form with two sections: the _____ _____ section and the _____ section.

5. The _____ _____ guides you through the creation of a form in which you can select fields from multiple tables or queries, select a form layout, and select a style.

6. The field names and data in a form are _____ to the field names in the underlying table.

7. A control that obtains its data from an expression or formula is a(n) _____ control.

8. The field name is displayed in a(n) _____ control; the data from the underlying table is displayed in a(n) _____ _____ control.

9. There are two types of control layouts: _____ and _____.

10. In Design view, a form is divided into three sections: _____ _____, _____, and _____ _____.

11. The fastest and easiest method to create a report in Access is to use the _____ _____.

12. The _____ _____ section displays information that will print at the top of the first page of a report.

13. The _____ _____ section displays information that will print at the bottom of every page of a report.

14. The _____ _____ gives you more control over the creation of a report. You can select fields from multiple tables or queries, specify grouping and sorting, select a report layout and orientation, and select a style.

15. To create labels for a wide variety of standard label sizes, use the _____ _____.

Skills Review

Project 3C — Job Fair Candidates

In this project, you will apply the skills you practiced from the Objectives in Project 3A.

Objectives: 1. *Create a Form;* **2.** *Add, Delete, Edit, and Print Records in a Form;* **3.** *Modify the Design of a Form in Layout View;* **4.** *Modify the Design of a Form in Design View.*

Michael Dawson is the executive coordinator for the Seattle-Tacoma Job Fair. He uses a database of candidates, industries, employers, and job openings to match the candidates' experience and interests with the employment opportunities presented at the fair. In the following Skills Review, you will create forms based on a query in the database that identifies candidates who have indicated on their resumes that they have experience in the industry for which they are seeking employment. Your completed forms will look similar to those in Figure 3.74.

For Project 3C, you will need the following files:

a03C_Job_Fair_Candidates
a03C_Logo

**You will save your database as
3C_Job_Fair_Candidates_Firstname_Lastname**

Figure 3.74

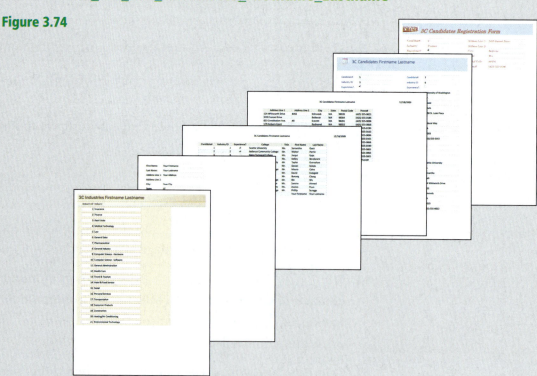

(Project 3C–Job Fair Candidates continues on the next page)

Content-Based Assessments

(Project 3C—Job Fair Candidates continued)

1. **Start** Access. Locate and open the **a03C_Job_Fair_Candidates** file. Click the **Office** button. **Save As** an **Access 2007 Database** in the **Access Chapter 3** folder, and then save the file as **3C_Job_Fair_ Candidates_Firstname_Lastname** Rename the tables and query by adding your **Firstname Lastname** to the end of each table and query name.

2. Open the **3C Candidates** table in **Datasheet** view, and then collapse the **Navigation Pane**. On the Ribbon, click the **Create tab**. In the **Forms group**, click the **Form** button. On the **Format tab**, in the **Views group**, click the **View** button. On the **tab row**, right-click the **3C Candidates tab** for the *table*, and then click **Close**. Right-click the **3C Candidates tab** for the *form*, and then click **Close**. Save the form as **3C Candidates Form Firstname Lastname**

3. Click the **Create tab**, and in the **Forms group**, click **More Forms**, and then click **Form Wizard**. Click the **Tables/Queries arrow**, and then click **Table: 3C Industries**. Click the **All Fields** button to select both fields and display them in the **Selected Fields** box, and then click **Next**. Click the **Tabular** option button, and then click **Next**. Click the **Trek** style, and then click **Next**. Accept the default form title, and then click **Finish**. If you are instructed to submit this result, create a paper or electronic printout and then **Close** the **3C Industries** form.

4. On the **Create tab**, in the **Forms group**, click the **Blank Form** button. In the **Field List** pane, display the **3C Candidates** fields. If the tables in your database are not displayed in the Field List pane, click to show all tables. Drag the **First Name** field to any location on the blank form. Drag the

Last Name field to the blank form below the **First Name label control**. In the **Field List** pane, click **Address Line 1**, hold down ⇧ Shift, and then click **Address Line 2**. Drag the two selected fields onto the form below the **Last Name label control**. In the **Field List** pane, click **City**, hold down ⇧ Shift, and then click **Postal Code**. Drag the three selected fields onto the form below the **Address Line 2 label control**. **Close** the **Field List** pane. **Close** the form, and then save it as **3C Candidates Mailing Info Firstname Lastname**

5. Expand the **Navigation Pane**, and then under **Tables**, double-click **3C Candidates**. Under **Forms**, double-click **3C Candidates Form** to open the form. Collapse the **Navigation Pane**. In the navigation area, click the **New (blank) record** button. On the form, in the **Industry ID** field, type **6** and then press Tab. In the remaining fields, type your personal information. Press Tab to save the record. On the **Home tab**, in the **Records group**, click the **Refresh All** button. Expand the **Navigation Pane**.

6. Open the **3C Candidates Mailing Info** form. In the navigation area, in the **Search** box, type your **Lastname** Click anywhere in the record selector bar. If you are instructed to submit this result, create a paper or electronic printout of the selected record. **Close** the **3C Candidates Mailing Info** form.

7. Under **Queries**, double-click **3C General Sales Candidates** to open the query. View the query, and then collapse the **Navigation Pane**. On the **tab row**, click **3C Candidates Form**. In the navigation area, in the **Current Record** box, select the displayed text, type **6** and then

(Project 3C—Job Fair Candidates continues on the next page)

Skills Review

(Project 3C—Job Fair Candidates continued)

press Enter. Click in the record selector bar. Press Delete. Click **Yes** to delete this record. On the **tab row**, click the **3C Candidates tab**. In the **Records group**, click the **Refresh All** button to synchronize the table with its related objects.

8. On the **tab row**, click the **3C General Sales Candidates tab** to display the query results. Using the technique you just practiced, synchronize the query with the underlying table to remove the record. **Close** the **3C General Sales Candidates** query, and then **Close** the **3C Candidates** table.

9. With the **3C Candidates Form** open and current, click in the **Last Name** field. On the **Home tab**, in the **Find group**, click the **Find** button. In the displayed **Find and Replace** dialog box, in the **Find What** box, type **Perrie** and then click **Find Next**. In the **Find and Replace** dialog box, click the **Close** button. In the **College** field, select **None**, and then type **Bellevue Community College** In the navigation area, click the **Next record** button to save the changes to this record.

10. Expand the **Navigation Pane**, and then open the **3C Candidates** table. Collapse the **Navigation Pane**. Locate the record for **Candidate# 2**, and then notice that the **College** field for this record displays **Bellevue Community College**. Adjust all column widths so that field names and data are displayed. If you are instructed to submit this result, create a paper or electronic printout using **Landscape** orientation. The printout will be two pages.

11. In the **3C Candidates** table, in **Record 12**, in the **Title** field, double-click **Ms.** to select the title, and then type **Mrs.** In the **Last Name** field, double-click **Pyun** to select the

name, type **Lewis** and then press ↓ to save the record.

12. Display the **3C Candidates Form** object in **Form** view, and then click in the **College** field box. On the **Home tab**, in the **Sort & Filter group**, click the **Filter** button. From the displayed list, point to **Text Filters**, and then click **Contains**. In the displayed **Custom Filter** dialog box, type **University** and then click **OK**. Click in the **Last Name** field box, and then in the **Sort & Filter group**, click the **Ascending** button.

13. Click the **Office** button, point to **Print**, and then click **Print Preview**. On the **Print Preview tab**, in the **Zoom group**, click the **Two Pages** button. In the **Page Layout group**, click the **Columns** button. Under **Grid Settings**, change the **Number of Columns** to 2 and change the **Column Spacing** to 0.5" Under **Column Size**, change the **Width** to 3.5 and then click **OK**. If you are instructed to submit this result, create a paper or electronic printout and then **Close** Print Preview.

14. In the **Sort & Filter group**, click the **Advanced** button, and then click **Clear All Filters**. In the **Sort & Filter group**, click the **Clear All Sorts** button. On the **Home tab**, in the **Views group**, click the **View button arrow**, and then click **Design View**. On the **Design tab**, in the **Controls group**, click the **Title** button.

15. Select the title and type **3C Candidates Registration Form** and then press Enter. In the **Font group**, click the **Font button arrow**, and then click **Century**. Click the **Font Size button arrow** and then click **22**. Click the **Bold** button, click the **Italic** button, and then click the **Center** button. Click the **Font Color button arrow**, and under **Standard Colors**, on the first row, pick the sixth color—**Maroon**.

(Project 3C—Job Fair Candidates continues on the next page)

Content-Based Assessments

(Project 3C—Job Fair Candidates continued)

16. On the **Design tab**, in the **Controls group**, click the **Logo** button. In the displayed **Insert Picture** dialog box, locate and double-click **a03C_Logo**. Click anywhere in the logo to select it. Drag the left edge to the left margin and resize the right edge until it aligns with the left edge of the title box.

17. On the **Home tab**, in the **Views group**, click the **View button arrow**, and then click **Layout View**. In the **Controls group**, click the **Add Existing Fields** button. If necessary, at the bottom of the **Field List** pane, click **Click to show all tables**. In the displayed **Field List** pane, under **Fields available in related tables,** click the plus sign (**+**) next to **3C Industries** table to display the field list for the table, and then double-click **Industry**. Close the **Field List** pane.

18. Click the **Industry label control**. Point the mouse in the label control or text box control until the  pointer displays. Drag the grouped controls until a bold orange line displays below the **Industry ID** controls. Release the mouse. Click the **Industry ID text box control**, and then press Delete.

19. Click the **Candidate# label control**, and then above the upper left corner of the control, click the **Layout Selector**. In the **Font group**, click the **Font button arrow**, and then click **Century**. Click the **Font Color button arrow**. In the **Color gallery**, under **Recent Colors**, click the **Maroon (4D50C0)** color. If the color is not displayed under Recent Colors, under Standard Colors, in the first row, click the sixth color—Maroon.

20. On the **Format tab**, in the **Views group**, click the **View button arrow**, and then click **Design View**. Click in the Candidate# text box. Point to the right edge of the

Candidate# **text box control** until the pointer displays. Click and drag the right border of the text box control to the left to the **3.75-inch mark on the horizontal ruler**.

21. Click the **Address Line 1 label control box**. Hold down the ⇧Shift key, and then click the **Address Line 2**, **City**, **State**, **Postal Code**, and **Phone# label control boxes**. On the **Arrange tab**, in the **Control Layout group**, click **Stacked**.

22. Point to the **Layout Selector** button. When the displays, drag the selected label and text control boxes to the **4-inch mark on the horizontal ruler** and vertically aligned with the **Candidate# control boxes**.

23. At the bottom of the form, point to the upper edge of the **Form Footer section** bar, and then drag upward to the **2.5-inch mark on the vertical ruler**.

24. At the bottom of the form, point to the lower edge of the **Form Footer section** bar, and then drag downward to the **0.5-inch mark on the vertical ruler**. On the **Design tab**, in the **Controls group**, click the **Label** button. Move the pointer to the **Form Footer section**, and then position the plus sign (+) of the pointer at approximately **3.0 inches on the horizontal ruler** and even with the bottom edge of the Form Footer section. Drag to the right to **6.0 inches** on the horizontal ruler and then upward approximately **0.25 inch**. Using your own name, type **Graphic Designer: Firstname Lastname** and then press Enter.

25. With the sizing handles displayed around the label control, in the **Font group**, click the **Font button arrow**, and then click **Century**. Click the **Font Color button arrow**. In the **Color gallery**, under **Recent Colors**, click the **Maroon** color. On the

(Project 3C—Job Fair Candidates continues on the next page)

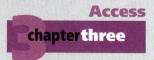

(Project 3C—Job Fair Candidates continued)

right side of the label control, point to the middle sizing handle to display the pointer, and then double-click to adjust the size of the label.

26. In the **Form Footer section**, click to select the **label control**, hold down ⇧Shift, and then in the **Detail section**, click to select the **Last Name text box control**. On the **Arrange tab**, in the **Control Alignment group**, click the **Left** button. Switch to **Form** view. Click the **Office** button, point to the **Print button arrow**, and then click **Print Preview**. In the **Page Layout group**, click **Columns**. In the **Page Setup** dialog box, on the **Columns tab**, change the

Number of Columns to **1** and the **Column Size Width** to **8** Click **OK**. **Close Print Preview**. In the navigation area, select the text in the **Current Record** box. Type **2** and then press Enter. If you are instructed to submit this result, create a paper or electronic printout of only **Record 2**. If you are creating an electronic printout, save the PDF file as **3C Candidates Registration Form Firstname Lastname Close** and **Save** the form. On the **tab row**, right-click the **3C Candidates** table tab, and then click **Close**. Expand the **Navigation Pane**, **Close** the database, and **Exit** Access.

 End You have completed Project 3C ————————————

Skills Review

Project 3D — Employers

In this project, you will apply the skills you practiced from the Objectives in Project 3B.

Objectives: 5. *Create a Report;* **6.** *Modify the Design of a Report in Layout View;* **7.** *Modify the Design of a Report in Design View;* **8.** *Keep Grouped Records Together and Print a Report.*

Janice Strickland, employer coordinator for the Seattle-Tacoma Job Fair, needs several reports to present to the organizers and participants of the job fair. In the following Skills Review, you will create reports in the database. Your completed reports will look similar to those in Figure 3.75.

For Project 3D, you will need the following file:

a03D_Job_Fair_Employers

**You will save your database as
3D_Job_Fair_Employers_Firstname_Lastname**

Figure 3.75

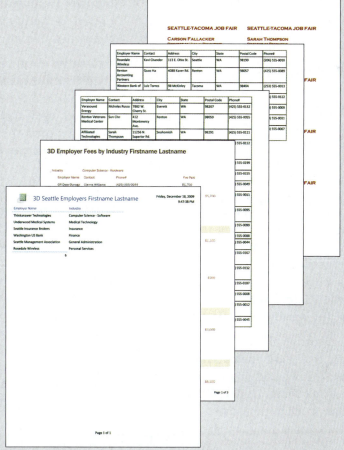

(Project 3D—Employers continues on the next page)

Content-Based Assessments

(Project 3D—Employers continued)

1. **Start** Access. Locate and open the **a03D_Job_Fair_Employers** an file. Click the **Office** button. **Save As** an **Access 2007 Database** in the **Access Chapter 3** folder as 3D_Job_Fair_Employers_Firstname_ Lastname Rename the tables and query by adding your **Firstname Lastname** to the end of each table and query name.

2. On the **Navigation Pane**, under **Queries**, click **3D Seattle Employers**. On the Ribbon, click the **Create tab**, and in the **Reports group**, click the **Report** button. Collapse the **Navigation Pane**. On the status bar, click the **Print Preview** button. In the navigation area, notice the **Next Page** button is inactive—the report will print on one page. If you are instructed to submit this result, create a paper or electronic printout.

3. In the **Close Preview group**, click the **Close Print Preview** button. **Close** the report, and then **Save** the report with the default name.

4. Expand the **Navigation Pane**, and then double-click the **3D Fees** query to view the query results. **Close** the **3D Fees** query. On the Ribbon, click the **Create tab**, and in the **Reports group**, click the **Report Wizard** button. Click the **Tables/Queries list arrow**, and then click **Query: 3D Fees**. Under **Available Fields**, click the **All Fields** button to move all of the field names to the **Selected Fields** box. Under **Selected Fields**, click **Employer ID**, and then click the **One Field Back** button to move the field to the **Available Fields** box.

5. Click **Next**. The records will be grouped on the **Industry** field in the **3D Industries** table. Click **Next**. Do not add any further grouping levels. Click **Next**. Under **What sort order**, in **Box 1**, click the **down**

arrow, and then click **Employer Name**. Be sure the sort button shows **Ascending**.

6. Click the **Summary Options** button, and then to the right of **Fee Paid**, select the **Sum** check box. Under **Show**, be sure the **Detail and Summary** option button is selected, and then click **OK**. Click **Next**.

7. Under **Layout**, click the **Outline** option button. Under **Orientation**, be sure **Portrait** is selected. At the bottom of the dialog box, be sure the **Adjust the field width so all fields fit on a page** check box is selected. Click **Next**.

8. Click **Trek** as the report style, and then click **Next**. Under **What title do you want for your report?**, select the default title text, and then type **3D Employer Fees by Industry Firstname Lastname** Select the option to **Modify the report's design**, and then click **Finish**.

9. In **Design** view, in the **Detail section**, click the **Fee Paid text box control**. With both the **label** and the **text box controls** selected, click the **right sizing handle**, and then drag the controls to the right to the **6.5-inch mark on the horizontal ruler**.

10. In the **Industry Footer section**, click the **Sum text box control**, hold down the ⇧Shift key, and then click in the **Report Footer** on the **Grand Total text box control**. With both controls selected, drag the right sizing handle to the right to the **7.5-inch mark on the horizontal ruler**. On the **Design tab**, in the **Grouping & Totals group**, click the **Group & Sort** button. From the **Group, Sort, and Total** pane, click the **More** button. Click the **do not keep group together on one page arrow**, and then click **keep whole group together**

(Project 3D—Employers continues on the next page)

Content-Based Assessments

(Project 3D—Employers continued)

on one page. On the **Design tab**, in the **Grouping & Totals group**, click the **Group & Sort** button to close the **Grouping** dialog box.

11. On the status bar, click the **Print Preview** button. In the navigation area, click the **Last Page** button, and then notice that the **Fees Paid column** displays a grand total of **$25,600**. In the navigation area, click the **First Page** button. If you are instructed to submit this result, create a paper or electronic printout of only the first page of the report. **Close** the **3D Employer Fees by Industry** report, and then **Save** your changes when prompted.

12. Click the **Create tab**, and then in the **Reports group**, click the **Blank Report** button. In the **Field List** pane, click **Show all tables**. Click the plus sign (**+**) next to **3D Employers** to display the fields in the table. Drag the **Employer Name** field to any location on the blank report. In the **Field List** pane, drag **Contact** onto the report. Double-click each of the following fields in the order given to add them to the report: **Address**, **City**, **State**, **Postal Code**, and **Phone#**. **Close** the **Field List**.

13. Click the **Employer Name label control**, and then above the upper left corner of the control, click the **Layout Selector**. On the **Format tab**, in the **Gridlines group**, click the **Gridlines** button, and then click **Both**. Switch to **Design** view. At the bottom of the report, point to the lower edge of the **Page Footer section** bar, and then drag downward to the **0.5-inch mark on the vertical ruler**.

14. On the **Design tab**, in the **Controls group**, click the **Label** button. Move the pointer down to the **Page Footer section**, and then position the plus sign (**+**) of the pointer at approximately **1.0 inch on the horizontal**

ruler and even with the bottom edge of the Page Footer section. Drag to the right to **3.0 inches on the horizontal ruler** and then upward approximately **0.25 inch**.

15. Using your own name, type **Prepared by: Firstname Lastname** and then press [Enter]. **Save** the report as **3D Employers Contact List Firstname Lastname** Click **Print Preview**. If you are instructed to submit this result, create a paper or electronic printout. **Close** the report.

16. On the **Navigation Pane**, under **Tables**, click to select the **3D Employers** table. Collapse the **Navigation Pane**. On the **Create tab**, in the **Reports group**, click the **Labels** button. In the **What label size would you like?** box, scroll down, and then under **Product number**, click **5843 Badge**.

17. Click **Next**. Under **Text appearance**, click the **Font name arrow**, and then in the displayed list, scroll down and click **Copperplate Gothic Bold**. If your list does not display **Copperplate Gothic Bold**, select any other font name. Click the **Font size arrow**, and then click **14**. Click the **Font weight arrow**, and then from the displayed list, click **Normal**. Click the **Text color ellipses**, and then under **Basic colors**, click the color on the fourth row, first column, and then click **OK**.

18. Click **Next**. Under the **Prototype Label**, type **SEATTLE-TACOMA JOB FAIR** and then press [Enter] two times. Under **Available fields**, double-click **Contact**. Press [Enter], and then under **Available fields**, double-click **Contact Title**. Press [Enter], and then under **Available fields**, double-click **Employer Name**. Press [Enter] two times, and then type **Event Organizer: Firstname Lastname**

19. Click **Next**. Under **Available fields**, double-click **Employer Name** to sort the

(Project 3D—Employers continues on the next page)

Content-Based Assessments

(Project 3D–Employers continued)

labels by Employer. Click **Next**. Name the report **3D Employer Name Tags Firstname Lastname** and then click **Finish**. **Close** Print Preview.

20. Switch to **Layout** view. Click the **Contact Title text box control**. On the **Format tab**, in the **Font group**, click the **Font Size button arrow**, and then click **10**. Using this same procedure, change the **Employer Name** to a font size of **12**, and

then change the **Event Organizer: Firstname Lastname** to a font size of **8**.

21. If you are instructed to submit this result, create a paper or electronic printout of only the first page. **Close** the **3D Employer Name Tags** report, saving changes. Expand the **Navigation Pane**, **Close** the database, and **Exit** Access.

End You have completed Project 3D

Mastering Access

Project 3E—Job Openings

In this project, you will apply the skills you practiced from the Objectives in Project 3A.

Objectives: 1. *Create a Form;* **2.** *Add, Delete, Edit, and Print Records in a Form;* **3.** *Modify the Design of a Form in Layout View;* **4.** *Modify the Design of a Form in Design View.*

In the following Mastering Access project, you will create a form to be used at the Seattle-Tacoma Job Fair. The form will be used by employers to enter job openings. Your completed form and table will look similar to those in Figure 3.76.

For Project 3E, you will need the following files:

a03E_Job_Openings
a03E_Logo

You will save your database as
3E_Job_Openings_Firstname_Lastname

Figure 3.76

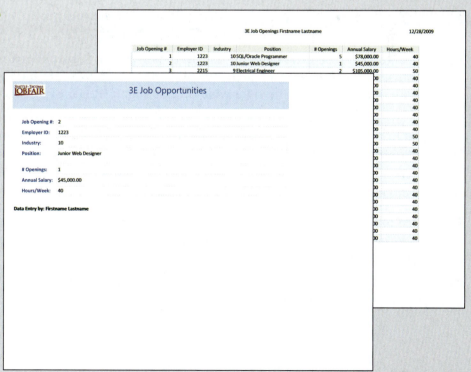

(Project 3E–Job Openings continues on the next page)

Content-Based Assessments

(Project 3E–Job Openings continued)

1. **Start** Access. Locate and open the **a03E_Job_Openings** file. From the **Office** menu, **Save As** an **Access 2007 Database** in the **Access Chapter 3** folder as **3E_Job_Openings_Firstname_ Lastname** Open the **Navigation Pane**. Rename the tables by adding your **Firstname Lastname** to the end of each table name.

2. Select the **3E Job Openings** table, and then collapse the **Navigation Pane**. On the **Create tab**, in the **Forms group**, click the **Form** button. Switch to **Form** view.

3. Add a **New (blank) Record**. For record **Job Opening Number 26**, enter the following data:

Employer ID	1300
Industry	12
Position	Director of Medical Records
# Openings	1
Annual Salary	75000
Hours/Week	40

4. Navigate to **Record 13**, **Gift Shop Manager position**. Click anywhere in the **record selector** bar, and then **Delete** the record.

5. Switch to **Layout** view. On the **Format tab**, in the **Controls group**, click **Title**. Edit the title to read **3E Job Opportunities** and then press Enter. **Center** the title.

6. In **Design** view, click the **Logo** button. In the displayed **Insert Picture** dialog box, locate and then insert the **a03E_Logo**. Click anywhere in the logo to select it. Drag the left edge to the left margin, and then resize the right edge until it aligns with the left edge of the title box.

7. Drag the **Form Footer section** bar to the **0.5-inch mark on the vertical ruler**. Click the **Label** button. Position the **label control** at the left side and the bottom of the Form Footer. Drag to the right to **3.0 inches on the horizontal ruler** and then upward approximately **0.25 inches**. Using your own name, type **Data Entry by: Firstname Lastname** and then press Enter.

8. Add **Bold** formatting to all of the **label controls**.

9. Switch to **Form** view. Click in the **Position** field. Display the **Find and Replace** dialog box. In the **Find What** box, type **Web** and then in the **Match** box, click the **arrow**, and then click **Any Part of Field**. Then, click **Find Next**. In the **Find and Replace** dialog box, click the **Close** button.

10. In the **Position** field, double-click **Senior**, and then type **Junior** In the **Annual Salary** field, select **$65,000.00**, and then type **45000** In the navigation area, click the **Next record** button to save the changes to this record. Click **Previous record** to make the edited record current.

(Project 3E–Job Openings continues on the next page)

Content-Based Assessments

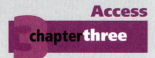
Mastering Access

(Project 3E–Job Openings continued)

11. Click the **record selector** bar. On the **Print Preview tab**, in the **Page Layout group**, click the **Landscape** button. Close **Print Preview**. **Save** the form as **3E Job Opportunities Firstname Lastname** If you are instructed to submit this result, create a paper or electronic printout of the selected record only. **Close** the form.

12. Expand the **Navigation Pane**. Open the **3E Job Openings** table. Adjust all column widths to display all field names and data. If you are instructed to submit this result, create a paper or electronic printout in **Landscape** orientation. **Close** the table, **Close** the database, and **Exit** Access.

End **You have completed Project 3E** ————————————————————

Access

chapter three

Mastering Access

Project 3F—Booth Assignments

In this project, you will apply the skills you practiced from the Objectives in Project 3B.

Objectives: 5. *Create a Report;* **6.** *Modify the Design of a Report in Layout View;* **7.** *Modify the Design of a Report in Design View;* **8.** *Keep Grouped Records Together and Print a Report.*

In the following Mastering Access project, you will prepare a report to help Janice Strickland, employer coordinator for the Seattle-Tacoma Job Fair, when she assigns the booths to the employers for their displays at the fair. Your completed report will look similar to Figure 3.77.

For Project 3F, you will need the following file:

a03F_Booth_Assignments

You will save your database as
3F_Booth_Assignments_Firstname_Lastname

Figure 3.77

(Project 3F–Booth Assignments continues on the next page)

Content-Based Assessments

(Project 3F–Booth Assignments continued)

1. **Start** Access. Locate and open the **a03F_ Booth Assignments** file. From the **Office** menu, **Save As** an **Access 2007 Database** in the **Access Chapter 3** folder as **3F_Booth Assignments_Firstname_ Lastname**

2. Rename the tables by adding your **Firstname Lastname** to the end of each table name.

3. On the **Create tab**, start the **Report Wizard**. Using the **Table: 3F Employer Booth** table as a field source, add the **Section Name** and the **Booth#** fields to the **Selected Fields** box. From the **3F Employers** table, move the **Employer Name** and **Contact** fields to the **Selected Fields** box.

4. Click **Next** two times. Group the report on the **Section Name** field. Click **Next**. Sort on **Employer Name** in **Ascending** order first, and then sort on the **Booth#** field in **Ascending** order.

5. Click **Next**. Choose the **Stepped** layout and **Portrait** orientation. Make certain that the box for **Adjust the field width so all fields fit on a page** is selected. Click

Next, and then click the **Metro** style. Click **Next**, and then name the report 3F Employer Booth Assignments Firstname Lastname Select **Modify the report's design**, and then click **Finish**.

6. In the **Page Footer section**, note the location of the **Text box control** for the **page number**, and then delete the control. From the **Design tab**, in the **Controls group**, click the **Label** button. Draw a **label control** box in the previous location of the **page number control text** box. Type **Report Prepared by: Firstname Lastname** and then **Align Top** the two controls in the **Page Footer section**.

7. Switch to **Layout** view. Select the **Title** of the report, and then delete **Firstname Lastname** from the title. Resize the **Title label control** to the width of the text. Adjust the width of the **Section Name column** to display all of the data.

8. If you are instructed to submit this result, create a paper or electronic printout. **Close** the **3F Employers Booth Assignments** report, **Close** the database, and **Exit** Access.

End **You have completed Project 3F**

Access

chapter three

Mastering Access

Project 3G — Job Postings

In this project, you will apply the following Objectives found in Projects 3A and 3B.

Objectives: 1. *Create a Form;* **2.** *Add, Delete, Edit, and Print Records in a Form;* **3.** *Modify the Design of a Form in Layout View.*

Janice Strickland, employer coordinator, has posted a form on the Web for employers to enter the job openings that they will be advertising at the Seattle-Tacoma Job Fair. In the following Mastering Access project, you will create a form for this purpose. Your completed form will look similar to Figure 3.78.

For Project 3G, you will need the following files:

a03G_Job_Postings
a03G_Logo

You will save your database as
3G_Job_Postings_Firstname_Lastname

Figure 3.78

JOB FAIR 3G JOB POSTINGS

Wednesday, September 19, 2007
9:09:37 PM

INDUSTRY:	Computer Science - Hardware
POSITION:	Electrical Engineer
# OPENINGS:	2
ANNUAL SALARY:	$105,000.00
HOURS/WEEK:	50

Firstname Lastname

(Project 3G–Job Postings continues on the next page)

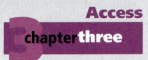

Access

chapter three

Mastering Access

(Project 3G—Job Postings continued)

1. **Start** Access. Locate and open the **a03G_Job_Postings** file. From the **Office** menu, **Save As** an **Access 2007 Database** in the **Access Chapter 3** folder as **3G_Job_Postings_Firstname_Lastname** Rename the tables by adding **Firstname Lastname** to the end of each table name.

2. Open a blank form. From the **3G Industries** table, add the **Industry** field. From the **3G Job Openings** table, add the following fields in the given order: **Position**, **# Openings**, **Annual Salary**, and **Hours/Week**.

3. In **Layout** view, modify the design of the form. Title the form **3G Job Postings** Add the Seattle-Tacoma Job Fair Logo—**a03G_Logo**. Add the **Date and Time** to the form. Accept the default format and the default location of upper right corner.

4. Select all **label controls** and the **title**. Apply the **Perpetua Titling MT** font. Apply **Bold** to the label controls, and then apply the **Maroon** color to all of them. Center the title vertically in the Form Header. Drag the **Date** and **Time** labels to the left until their right sides align at the **8-inch mark on the horizontal ruler**. Decrease the width of the form to 8.25 inches.

5. In **Design** view, in the **Form Footer section**, add a label that contains your **Firstname Lastname** Size the **label control** box to just fit the text. **Center** the label horizontally in the **Form Footer**.

6. In Form view locate the job opening for the **Position** of **Electrical Engineer**, and then if you are instructed to submit this result, create a paper or electronic printout of only that one record in **Landscape** orientation.

7. **Close** the form, saving it as **3G Job Postings Firstname Lastname Close** the database, and then **Exit** Access.

End **You have completed Project 3G**

Mastering Access

Project 3H — Employer Fees

IIn this project, you will apply the following Objectives found in Projects 3A and 3B.

Objectives: 5. *Create a Report;* **6.** *Modify the Design of a Report in Layout View;* **7.** *Modify the Design of a Report in Design View;* **8.** *Keep Grouped Records Together and Print a Report.*

In the following Mastering Access project, you will design a report for Janice Strickland, employer coordinator for the Seattle-Tacoma Job Fair. Ms. Strickland wants to verify, in report documentation, the statistics for the fees that the employers paid to participate in the job fair. Your report will be based on the query found in the database. Your completed report will look similar to Figure 3.79.

For Project 3H, you will need the following files:

a03H_Employer_Fees
a03H_Logo

**You will save your database as
3H_Employer_Fees_Firstname_Lastname**

Figure 3.79

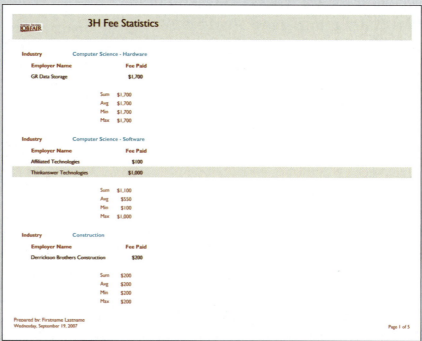

(Project 3H–Employer Fees continues on the next page)

Content-Based Assessments

(Project 3H–Employer Fees continued)

1. **Start** Access. Locate and open the **a03H_Employer_Fees** file. From the **Office** menu, **Save As** an **Access 2007 Database** in the **Access Chapter 3** folder as **3H_Employer_Fees_Firstname_Lastname** Rename the tables and query by adding **Firstname Lastname** to the end of each Ωname.

2. Open the **3H Fees** query. View the results, and then **Close** the query.

3. Create a report using the **Report Wizard**. Base the report on the **3H Fees** query. Select all of the fields from the query. View your data by **3H Employers**. Group by **Industry**. Sort by **Employer Name** in **Ascending** order. In **Summary Options**, for **Fee Paid**, select **Sum**, **Avg**, **Min**, and **Max**. Show **Detail and Summary**. Select **Outline** layout and **Landscape** orientation. All fields should fit on a page. Select the **Solstice** style. Name the report **3H Fee Statistics Firstname Lastname**

4. In **Layout** view, resize the label and text box controls so that all field names and data display. In the **Industry Footer**, delete the **Summary calculated control**. Position the statistic label controls closer to the corresponding text box controls as shown in Figure 3.79.

5. Switch to **Design** view. Select the report title, and then delete **Firstname Lastname**. Position the **Title label control** so that the left side of the control is at the **2-inch mark on the horizontal ruler**. Resize the **title label control** to just fit the text. Add the Seattle-Tacoma Job Fair Logo—**a03H_Logo**. In the **Page Footer section**, add a **label control**. Position it directly above the **calculated text box control** that displays *Now()*. Type **Prepared by: Firstname Lastname** Resize the **label control** to just fit the text.

6. Select all **label controls** and all **calculated controls**, and then change the font color to **Maroon**.

7. Switch to **Layout** view. On the **Format tab**, under **Grouping & Totals**, click the **Group & Sort** button, click **More Options**, and then select **keep whole group together on one page**. If you are instructed to submit this result, create a paper or electronic printout of **Page 1** only in **Landscape** orientation.

8. **Close** the report and **Save** changes. **Close** the database, and then **Exit** Access.

End **You have completed Project 3H**

Content-Based Assessments

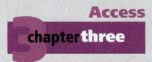
Project 3I—Candidate Registration

In this project, you will apply all the skills you practiced from the Objectives in Projects 3A and 3B.

Janna Sorokin, database manager for the Seattle-Tacoma Job Fair, has been asked to meet with Michael Dawson, the executive director. They need to create forms and reports that will be useful to the candidates during the registration and check-in process at the job fair. Mr. Dawson has suggested that candidate packets be prepared for each individual. The packets will be labeled with the candidate's name. The reports will include a listing by industry of the employer booth numbers. In the following Mastering Access project, you will create these forms and reports. Your completed forms and reports will look similar to those in Figure 3.80.

For Project 3I, you will need the following files:

a03I_Candidate_Registration
a03I_Logo

You will save your database as
3I_Candidate_Registration_Firstname_Lastname

Figure 3.80

(Project 3I–Candidate Registration continues on the next page)

Mastering Access

(Project 3I–Candidate Registration continued)

1. **Start** Access. Locate and open the **a03I_Candidate_Registration** file. From the **Office** menu, **Save As** an **Access 2007 Database** in the **Access Chapter 3** folder as **3I_Candidate_Registration_Firstname_Lastname**

2. Rename the objects by adding your **Firstname Lastname** to the end of each name.

3. Open a blank form. From the **3I Candidates** table, drag the **Last Name** field to any location on the blank form. Drag the **First Name** field to the blank form below the **Last Name label control**. Drag the following fields onto the form in the specified order: **Address Line 1**, **Address Line 2**, **City**, **State**, **Postal Code**, **Phone#**, and **College**.

4. **Save** the form as **3I Registration Form Firstname Lastname**

5. Switch to **Design** view. Add a **Title** to the **3I Registration Form**. Edit the text of the title to **3I Registration Form**. In the **Form Header**, using the **a03I_Logo** file, add the Seattle-Tacoma Job Fair logo. Resize the logo to align with the left edge of the form, and then align the right edge with the left edge of the **Title label control** box.

6. In the **Form Footer**, add a **label control** with the following text: **Job Fair Assistant: Firstname Lastname** Start the control at the left edge of the form and extend it to the **4-inch mark on the horizontal ruler**, and then **Center** the text. Select all **label controls** on the form. Include the **Title** and the **Form Footer label controls**. Format these controls in **Italic** and a standard color of **Brown 4**.

7. Switch to **Form** view. In the navigation area, click the **New (blank) record** button. On the form, type your personal information. If you are instructed to submit this result, create a paper or electronic

printout of only this record. **Save** and **Close** the form.

8. Create a report using the **Report Wizard**. From the **3I Industries** table, add the **Industry** field. From the **3I Employers** table, add the **Employer Name** field. Using the **3I Employer Booth** table, add the **Booth#** field. View by **3I Employer Booth**. Group by **Industry** and then by **Employer Name**. Sort the **Booth#** in **Ascending** order. Use the **Outline** layout and **Portrait** orientation. Choose **Oriel** as the style for this report. Name the report **3I Employer Booth# Firstname Lastname** If you are instructed to submit this result, create a paper or electronic printout of page one only. **Close** the report.

9. In the Navigation Pane, select the **3I Candidates** table. Create labels for the candidates' packets using the **Label Wizard**. Choose label size **L7164**. Use an **8-point Copperplate Gothic Light** font, with a **Font weight** of **Light**, and a **Text color** of **Orange**—row 4, column 2. In the **Prototype label**, type **Seattle-Tacoma Job Fair** and then press Enter. Type **Candidate** and then press Spacebar. Add the **Candidate # field**. Press Enter three times. Add the **First Name** and **Last Name** fields, separated by a space. Sort by **Last Name** and then **First Name**. Name the report **3I Packet Labels Firstname Lastname**

10. Modify the label design. Change the **Font size** of the first four lines to **10** point. In **Report** view, search for the label containing your name. If you are instructed to submit this result, create a paper or electronic printout of only the page that contains your label.

11. **Close** the report and **Save** changes. **Close** the database, and then **Exit** Access.

End **You have completed Project 3I**

Content-Based Assessments

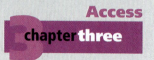
 Business Running Case

Project 3J — Business Running case

In this project, you will apply the skills you have practiced from the Objectives in Projects 3A and 3B.

From My Computer, navigate to the student files that accompany this textbook. In the folder **03_business_running_case**, locate and open the folder for this chapter. Open and print the instructions for this project, which are provided to you in Adobe PDF format. Follow the instructions and use the skills you have gained thus far to assist the brother and sister team of Michael and Kristen Landry in meeting the challenges of owning and running their business.

End **You have completed Project 3J** _____

Outcomes-Based Assessments

Rubric

The following outcomes-based assessments are *open-ended assessments*. That is, there is no specific correct result; your result will depend on your approach to the information provided. Make *Professional Quality* your goal. Use the following scoring rubric to guide you in *how* to approach the problem and then to evaluate *how well* your approach solves the problem.

The *criteria*—Software Mastery, Content, Format and Layout, and Process—represent the knowledge and skills you have gained that you can apply to solving the problem. The *levels of performance*—Professional Quality, Approaching Professional Quality, or Needs Quality Improvement—help you and your instructor evaluate your result.

	Your completed project is of Professional Quality if you:	Your completed project is Approaching Professional Quality if you:	Your completed project Needs Quality Improvements if you:
Software Mastery	Choose and apply the most appropriate skills, tools, and features and identify efficient methods to solve the problem.	Choose and apply some appropriate skills, tools, and features, but not in the most efficient manner.	Choose inappropriate skills, tools, or features, or are inefficient in solving the problem.
Content	Construct a solution that is clear and well organized, contains content that is accurate, appropriate to the audience and purpose, and is complete. Provide a solution that contains no errors of spelling, grammar, or style.	Construct a solution in which some components are unclear, poorly organized, inconsistent, or incomplete. Misjudge the needs of the audience. Have some errors in spelling, grammar, or style, but the errors do not detract from comprehension.	Construct a solution that is unclear, incomplete, or poorly organized, containing some inaccurate or inappropriate content; and contains many errors of spelling, grammar, or style. Do not solve the problem.
Format and Layout	Format and arrange all elements to communicate information and ideas, clarify function, illustrate relationships, and indicate relative importance.	Apply appropriate format and layout features to some elements, but not others. Overuse features, causing minor distraction.	Apply format and layout that does not communicate information or ideas clearly. Do not use format and layout features to clarify function, illustrate relationships, or indicate relative importance. Use available features excessively, causing distraction.
Process	Use an organized approach that integrates planning, development, self-assessment, revision, and reflection.	Demonstrate an organized approach in some areas, but not others; or, use an insufficient process of organization throughout.	Do not use an organized approach to solve the problem.

Problem Solving

Project 3K — Survey

In this project, you will construct a solution by applying any combination of the skills you practiced from the Objectives in Projects 3A and 3B.

For Project 3K, you will need the following files:

a03K_Survey
a03K_Logo

**You will save your database as
3K_Survey_Firstname_Lastname**

The executive director for the Seattle-Tacoma Job Fair, Michael Dawson, wants to evaluate the success of this year's fair. In order to accomplish this goal, he wants to use a survey form. In this project, you will develop an attractive form for the survey. Open the a03K_Survey database, and then save it as **3K_Survey_Firstname_Lastname** Rename all objects by adding your Firstname Lastname to the end of the object name. Set up the survey so that it contains the fields that are found in the *3K Survey* table. The table is not populated with any data at this time. For the survey questions, use the questions in the table *3K Survey Questions*. On the form, enter the questions in label controls. (Hint: Copy and paste from the *3K Survey Questions* table.) List the response below the question. Add the job fair logo if you think it is appropriate. Save your survey as **3K Candidate Survey Firstname Lastname** Enter your personal information and evaluation as the first candidate to respond to the survey.

Mr. Dawson would like to mail the survey to each candidate who attended the fair, so you will need to create mailing labels to place on the survey envelopes. The mailing information for each candidate can be found in the *3K Candidates* table. Add yourself as a candidate. Create a report using the Label Wizard to provide the labels. Sort the labels in the report in postal code order. Save the report of labels as **3K Mailing Labels Firstname Lastname** If you are to submit a printed copy of this project, print your completed survey and your mailing label. If you are to submit your work electronically, follow your instructor's directions. Save the database as **3K_Survey_Firstname_Lastname**

End You have completed Project 3K ————————

Problem Solving

Project 3L—Facility Requests

In this project, you will construct a solution by applying any combination of the skills you practiced from the Objectives in Projects 3A and 3B.

> ### For Project 3L, you will need the following files:
>
> a03L_Facility_Requests
> a03L_Logo

You will save your database as
3L_Facility_Requests_Firstname_Lastname

The employer coordinator for the Seattle-Tacoma Job Fair, Janice Strickland, is organizing this year's fair. She needs to know what facility requests the employers would like to make. In this project, you will prepare a form into which Ms. Strickland can enter the data to accommodate the employers' requests. Open the a03L_Facility_Requests database, and then save it as **3L Facility_Requests_Firstname_Lastname** Rename all objects by adding your Firstname Lastname to the end of the object name. Use the employer request options found in the *3L Facility Options* table. Add the Seattle-Tacoma Job Fair Logo to the Form Header section. Add your Firstname Lastname in the Form Footer section. Adjust all control sizes so that all label and text box controls display the field names and data completely. Save the form as **3L Employer Request Firstname Lastname** If you are instructed to submit this result, create a paper or electronic printout of first page of the form. Save the database as **3L_Facility_Requests_Firstname_Lastname**

End **You have completed Project 3L** ——————

Access
chapterthree

Problem Solving

Project 3M—Job Fair Ad

In this project, you will construct a solution by applying any combination of the skills you practiced from the Objectives in Projects 3A and 3B.

For Project 3M, you will need the following files:

a03M_Job_Fair_Ad
a03M_Logo

**You will save your database as
3M_Job_Fair_Ad_Firstname_Lastname**

In this project, you will create a report that Michael Dawson, the executive director of the Seattle Job Fair, can use as an advertisement article in the area newspapers. Mr. Dawson believes that if he can ask the newspapers to print a report of the industries, companies, positions, and number of openings, then the attendance at the fair will be good. Open the a03M_Job_Fair_Ad database, and then save it as **3M_Job_Fair_Ad_Firstname_Lastname** Rename all objects by adding your Firstname Lastname to the end of all object names. Use the *3M Job Openings*, *3M Employers*, and *3M Industries* tables to create the report. The report should include the Seattle-Tacoma Job Fair logo and your Firstname Lastname. Use appropriate formatting in font size, style, and color. Choose a grouping for the report, and ensure that the groups will be kept together when the report is printed. All field names and data should display on the report. Correct any truncation problems. Save the report as **3M Advertisement Firstname Lastname** If you are instructed to submit this result, create a paper or electronic printout.

End **You have completed Project 3M**

Access

chapter three

Problem Solving

Project 3N — Candidate Participation

In this project, you will construct a solution by applying any combination of the skills you practiced from the Objectives in Projects 3A and 3B.

> **For Project 3N, you will need the following files:**
>
> a03N_Candidate_Participation
> a03N_Logo
>
> **You will save your database as**
> **3N_Candidate_Participation_Firstname_Lastname**

The database manager for the Seattle-Tacoma Job Fair, Janna Sorokin, has created a *3N Candidates* table that contains the personal information of those people who registered for and attended the job fair. Michael Dawson, executive director for the job fair, is interested in the demographics of the candidates who participated in the fair. In this project, you will create any two of the following reports: grouped by candidate's city of residence, industry interest, college attended, or experience.

Open the a03N_Candidate_Participation database, and then save it as **3N_Candidate_Participation_Firstname_Lastname** Rename all objects by adding your Firstname Lastname to the end of each object name. Create two reports of your choosing and format them in a legible and professional manner. Name the reports with appropriate names, beginning with **3N** and ending with Firstname Lastname. Keep grouped records together. If you are instructed to submit this result, create a paper or electronic printout. Save the database as **3N_Candidate_Participation_Firstname_Lastname**

End **You have completed Project 3N** —————————

Problem Solving

Project 30 — Job Fair Planning

In this project, you will construct a solution by applying any combination of the skills you practiced from the Objectives in Projects 3A and 3B.

For Project 30, you will need the following file:

a03O_Job_Fair_Planning

You will save your database as
30_Job_Fair_Planning_Firstname_Lastname

Michael Dawson, Janice Strickland, and Janna Sorokin are all organizers for the upcoming Seattle-Tacoma Job Fair. They are working together to make certain this will be a profitable experience for the cities of Seattle and Tacoma, the employers, and the candidates. The employers are paying fees to help offset the costs of advertising, rental charge of the facility, security personnel, parking attendants, refreshments for candidates, hospitality room for employers, and an Internet connection.

Open the a03O_Job_Fair_Planning database, and then save it as **30_Job_Fair_Planning_Firstname_Lastname** Rename all objects by adding your Firstname Lastname to the end of each object name. Create a report using fields from the *30 Employers* and *30 Estimated Costs* tables. Use the Report Wizard and the Summary feature to compare the total amount of fees paid to the total estimated costs of the job fair. Format your report in an attractive manner, using appropriate fonts, spacing, and design. Add an appropriate title to the report. Include a footer that reflects the fact that you designed the report. In the report footer, add a label box that contains a statement on the estimated profit for the cities of Seattle and Tacoma. Save the report as **30 Job Fair Profits Firstname Lastname** Keep grouped records together. If you are instructed to submit this result, create a paper or electronic printout. Save the database as **30_Job_Fair_Planning_Firstname_Lastname**

End **You have completed Project 30** ————————————

 **Access**
chapter three

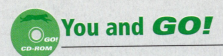 You and **GO!**

Project 3P—You and *GO!*

In this project, you will construct a solution by applying any combination of the Objectives found in Projects 3A and 3B.

From My Computer, navigate to the student files that accompany this textbook. In the folder **04_you_and_go**, locate and open the folder for this chapter. Open and print the instructions for this project, which are provided to you in Adobe PDF format. Follow the instructions to create a form and report for your personal inventory.

End **You have completed Project 3P** ————————————

GO! with Help

Project 3Q—*GO!* with Help

The Access Help system is extensive and can help you as you work. In this project, you will view information about grouping records in an Access report.

1 **Start** Access. On the right side of the Ribbon, click the **Microsoft Office Access Help** button. In the **Type words to search for** box, in the **Access Help** window, type **keep records together** Press `Enter`.

2 In the displayed **Search** list, click **Create a grouped or summary report**. Maximize the displayed window, and then click **Add or modify grouping and sorting in an existing report**. Read the section titled **Change grouping options**, which is about keeping records together in an Access report.

3 If you want, **Print** a copy of the information by clicking the printer button at the top of **Access Help** window.

4 **Close** the Help window, and then **Exit** Access.

End **You have completed Project 3Q** ————————————

4 chapterfour

Enhancing Tables

OBJECTIVES

At the end of this chapter you will be able to:

1. Modify Existing Tables
2. Customize the Navigation Pane
3. Create and Modify Table Relationships
4. Enter Records Using a Subdatasheet

5. Change Data Types
6. Set Field Properties
7. Create Data Validation Rules and Validation Text
8. Create a Lookup Field
9. Attach Files to Records

OUTCOMES

Mastering these objectives will enable you to:

Project 4A
Create Related Tables and Enforce Data Integrity

Project 4B
Format Tables and Validate Data Entry

City of Westland Plains

Westland Plains, Texas, is a city of approximately 800,000 people in the western portion of the second-most populous state in the United States. The city's economy is built around the oil industry, a regional airport serving western Texas and eastern New Mexico, a multilocation medical center, and a growing high-tech manufacturing industry. Westland Plains has a rich cultural history that is kept alive by a number of civic organizations and museums; new culture and traditions are encouraged through the city's Art Council. City residents of all ages enjoy some of the finest parks, recreation areas, and sports leagues in the state.

Enhancing Tables

Access provides tools for enhancing tables and improving data accuracy and data entry. In this chapter, you will redesign an existing table, breaking it down into separate related tables. You will add custom groups to the Navigation Pane and enter data into related tables by using a subdatasheet. You will use the field properties to enhance the table and to improve data accuracy and data entry, including looking up data in another table.

Project 4A City Directory

Joaquin Alonzo, the new City Manager of Westland Plains, has a database of city directory information. This database has three tables that have duplicate information in them. In Activities 4.1 through 4.13, you will redesign the tables, taking advantage of table relationships to avoid entering and storing redundant data. Your completed tables and relationships will look similar to those in Figure 4.1.

For Project 4A, you will need the following files:

a04A_City_Directory
a04A_City_Employees
New blank Word document

You will save your database as
4A_City_Directory_Firstname_Lastname
4A_Navigation_Pane_Firstname_Lastname
4A_City_Employees_Firstname_Lastname

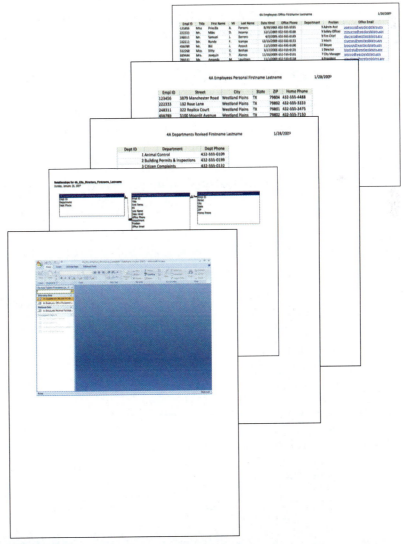

Figure 4.1
Project 4A—City Directory

Objective 1
Modify Existing Tables

A database is most effective when the designers of the database follow the principle that each table in the database should store data about a single subject. When tables are designed improperly, data can be lost, inaccurate, or hard to retrieve. Therefore, it is important to avoid repeating data in more than one table except for the common fields between related tables. Separating tables by subject increases efficiency by having the information about the subject in one table. When corrections are made to the data, the corrections can be made in one table instead of multiple tables, increasing the accuracy of the data. It is easier to add fields and records to a well-designed database that does not include duplicate data.

Activity 4.1 Backing Up a Database

Before modifying the structure of an existing database, it is important to **back up** the database so that a copy of the original database will be available if you need it. It is also important to back up databases regularly to avoid losing data.

1 **Start** Access. Navigate to the location where the student data files for this textbook are saved. Locate and open the **a04A_City_Directory** file.

2 Click the **Office** button , point to **Manage**, and then click **Back Up Database**. In the **Save As** dialog box, navigate to the drive on which you will be saving your folders and projects for this chapter. Create a new folder named **Access Chapter 4** and then compare your screen with Figure 4.2.

Access appends the date to the file name as a suggested name for the backed-up database. Having the date as part of the file name assists you in determining the copy that is the most current.

Figure 4.2

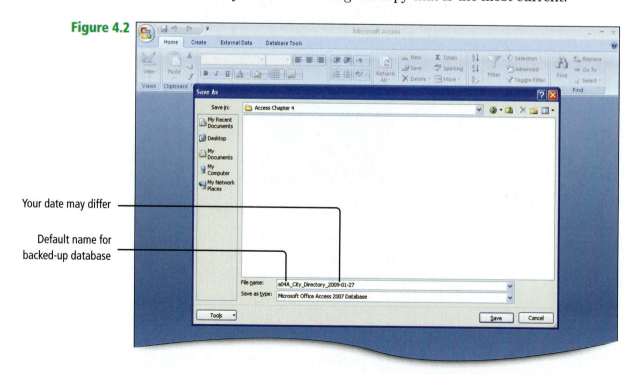

Your date may differ

Default name for backed-up database

3 In the **File name** box, after the date, type **_Firstname_Lastname** In the **Save As** dialog box, click **Save**. Notice that in the middle of the status bar a message displays stating that the database is being backed up. In the title bar, notice that the original database file—not the backed-up file—is open.

4 Click the **Start** button , click **My Computer**, and then navigate to the location of your **Access Chapter 4** folder. Open the folder to verify that the backed-up database exists, but do not open the file. **Close** ⊠ the Access Chapter 4 window.

5 **Save As** an **Access 2007 Database** in your **Access Chapter 4** folder, and then name the database **4A_City_Directory_Firstname_Lastname**

This is another method of making a copy of a database. The original file exists with the original name—the date is not appended to the database name, and the newly saved file is open.

6 If necessary, enable the content or add the Access Chapter 4 folder to the Trust Center to close the message bar.

Activity 4.2 Analyzing the Structure of the Tables

Before modifying the table design, the data and fields should be examined to determine whether tables have been created that use good design techniques. For example, are primary key fields defined? Is data repeated in more than one table? Can the tables be related to one another? In this activity, you will examine the structure of the tables in the 4A_City_Directory database.

1 On the **Navigation Pane**, double-click **4A Departments** to open the table in **Datasheet** view, and then compare your screen with Figure 4.3.

This table stores 37 department names, the names of each department head and administrative assistant, and the department phone number.

Figure 4.3

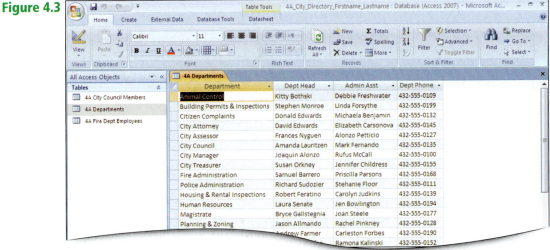

2 Switch to **Design** view. Notice that a primary key field has not been designated for this table. Switch to **Datasheet** view.

Recall that good table design dictates that every table should have a primary key field to ensure that each record is unique.

3 Open the **4A City Council Members** table in **Datasheet** view. Scroll to the right to display all of the fields, noting that the first 10 fields display personal information about the City Council members and the last 4 fields display departmental information about the City Council members. Scroll to the left to display the **Last Name** field, and notice that the first record displays the last name **Fernando** and the second record displays the last name **Lauritzen**.

4 On the **tab row**, click the **4A Departments tab** to make the datasheet current. Notice that in **Record 6**—*City Council*—under **Dept Head**, **Amanda Lauritzen** displays, and under **Admin Asst**, **Mark Fernando** displays.

There is duplication between the two tables. If the City Council president is replaced, you must remember to update the data in both tables.

5 Click the **4A City Council Members tab**. Switch to **Design** view, and then notice that a primary key field has not been designated. Switch to **Datasheet** view.

6 Open the **4A Fire Dept Employees** table, and then scroll to the right to display all of the fields. Notice that this table displays the same field names as those in the *4A City Council Members* table. Switch to **Design** view, and notice that a primary key has not been designated for this table. Switch to **Datasheet** view.

The *4A Fire Department Employees* table and the *4A City Council Members* table both use the same field names. Again, data has been duplicated. Recall that there are 37 departments for the city of Westland Plains. Using the existing structure of this database, there will be 37 separate tables listing all of the employees for each department, and all would use the same field names. If you change the name of a field, you must remember to change the name of the field in all 37 tables.

7 Click the **4A Departments tab** to make the datasheet current. Notice that in **Record 9**—*Fire Administration*—under **Dept Head**, **Samuel Barrero** displays, and under **Admin Asst**, **Priscilla Parsons** displays.

There is duplication between the two tables. If a Fire Department administrative assistant is replaced or the name is modified, you must remember to update the data in both tables.

8 On the **tab row**, right-click any table tab, and then click **Close All**.

Activity 4.3 Copying a Table and Modifying the Structure

In this activity, you will copy the *4A Departments* table, modify the structure by deleting fields and data that are duplicated in other tables, and then designate a primary key field.

1 On the **Navigation Pane**, click **4A Departments**. On the **Home tab**, in the **Clipboard group**, click the **Copy** button 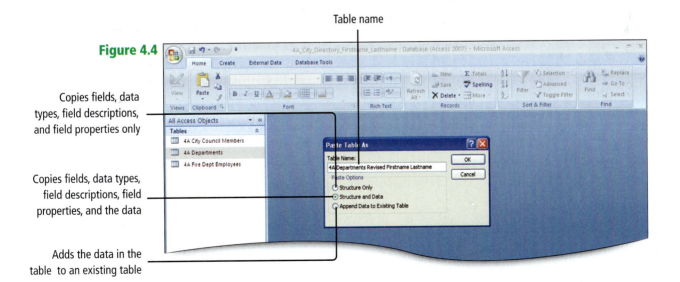. In the **Clipboard group**, click the **Paste** button.

Copy sends a duplicate version of the selected table to the Clipboard, leaving the original table intact. The *Clipboard* is a temporary storage area in Windows. Office can store up to 24 items in the Clipboard. *Paste* moves the copy of the selected table from the Clipboard into a new location. Because two tables cannot have the same name in a database, you must rename the pasted version.

Another Way

To Copy and Paste Tables

There are two other methods to copy and paste selected tables:

- On the Navigation Pane, right-click the table, and from the displayed list, click Copy. To paste the table, right-click the Navigation Pane, and then from the displayed list, click Paste.

- On the Navigation Pane, click the table, hold down Ctrl, and then press C. To paste the table, point to the Navigation Pane, hold down Ctrl, and then press V.

2 In the displayed **Paste Table As** dialog box, under **Table Name**, type **4A Departments Revised Firstname Lastname** and then compare your screen with Figure 4.4.

Under Paste Options, you can copy the structure only, including all the items that are displayed in Design view—field names, data types, descriptions, and field properties. To make an exact duplicate of the table, click Structure and Data. To copy the data from the table into another existing table, click Append Data to Existing Table.

Table name

Figure 4.4

Copies fields, data types, field descriptions, and field properties only

Copies fields, data types, field descriptions, field properties, and the data

Adds the data in the table to an existing table

3 Under **Paste Options**, be sure that the **Structure and Data** option button is selected, and then click **OK**. Notice that the copied table displays on the **Navigation Pane**. Open the **4A Departments Revised** table in **Datasheet** view, and then collapse « the **Navigation Pane**.

The *4A Departments Revised* table is an exact duplicate of the *4A Departments* table. Working with a duplicate table ensures that the original table will be available if needed.

4 Point to the **Dept Head** field name until the ↓ pointer displays. Drag to the right to the **Admin Asst** field name to select both fields. On the **Home tab**, in the **Records group**, click the **Delete** button. In the displayed message box, click **Yes** to permanently delete the fields and the data.

The names of the employees are deleted from this table to avoid having employee data in more than one table. Recall that a table should store data about one subject—this table now stores only departmental data. In addition to removing duplicate data, the fields that you deleted were also poorly designed, combining both the first and last names in the same field.

5 Switch to **Design** view. To the left of **Department**, click the **row selector** box. On the **Design tab**, in the **Tools group**, click the **Insert Rows** button to insert a blank row (field) above the *Department* field.

6 Under **Field Name**, click in the blank field name box, type **Dept ID** and then press Tab. In the **Data Type** box, type **a** and then press Tab. Alternatively, click the Data Type arrow, and then select the AutoNumber data type. In the **Tools group**, click the **Primary Key** button, and then compare your screen with Figure 4.5.

Recall that a primary key field is used to ensure that each record is unique. Because each department has a unique name, you might question why the Department field is not designated as the primary key field. Primary key fields should be data that does not change often. When organizations or companies are reorganized, department names are often changed. Also, if the department name is the primary key field, you may have to retype that department name in the related table that uses the department name as the common field.

Figure 4.5

Field added to table —

Primary key field —

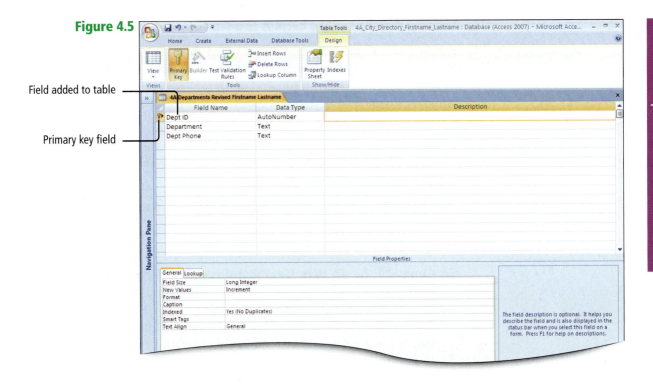

---

7 Switch to **Datasheet** view, and in the displayed message box, click **Yes** to save the table.

Because the *Dept ID* field has a data type of AutoNumber, each record is sequentially numbered.

8 In the datasheet, next to **Department**, click the **Sort and Filter arrow**, and then click **Sort A to Z**.

Sorting the records by the department name makes it easier to locate a department.

9 **Save** the table. **Close** the table, and then expand the **Navigation Pane**.

More Knowledge

Clipboard Size Limitations

Access tables can be very large, depending on the number of fields and records in the table. Although the Office Clipboard can store up to 24 selected items, you might find that you cannot add more items to the Clipboard even if there are fewer than 24 stored items. Access will prompt you to clear items from the Clipboard if there is not enough storage space.

Activity 4.4 Appending Records to a Table

In this activity, you will copy the *4A City Council Members* table to use as the basis for a single employees table. You will then copy the data in the *4A Fire Dept Employees* table and **append**—add on—the data to the new employees table.

1 Using the technique you practiced in Activity 4.3, copy and paste the structure and data of the **4A City Council Members** table, and then save the pasted table as **4A Employees Firstname Lastname**

An exact duplicate of the *4A City Council Members* table is created. The *4A Employees* table will be used to build a table of all employees.

2 Open the **4A Employees** table, and notice the duplicate records that were copied from the *4A City Council Members* table.

3 **Copy** the **4A Fire Dept Employees** table, and then click the **Paste** button. In the **Paste Table As** dialog box, under **Table Name**, type **4A Employees Firstname Lastname** Under **Paste Options**, click the **Append Data to Existing Table** option button, and then click **OK**. With the **4A Employees table** current, in the **Records group**, click the **Refresh All** button, and then compare your screen with Figure 4.6.

The table to which you are appending the records must exist before using the Append option. Clicking the Refresh All button causes Access to refresh or update the view of the table, displaying the newly appended records. The *4A Employees* table displays the two records for the Fire Department employees—last names of *Barrero* and *Parsons*—and the records are arranged in ascending order by the first field. The records still exist in the *4A Fire Dept Employees* table. If all 37 tables existed for the employees for each department, you would repeat these steps until every employee's record is appended to the *4A Employees* table.

Barrero and Parsons
records appended to table

Figure 4.6

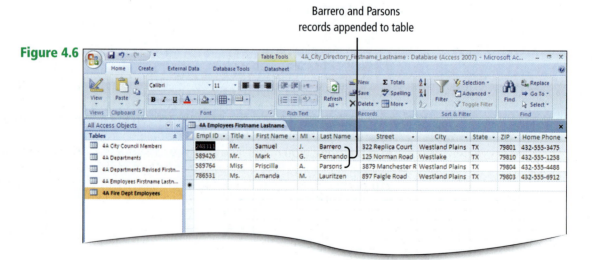

Does a message box display?

If a message box displays stating that the Microsoft Office Access database engine could not find the object, you probably mistyped the name of the table in the Paste Table As dialog box. In the Navigation Pane, note the spelling of the table name to which you are copying the records. In the message box, click OK, and then in the Paste Table As dialog box, under Table Name, correctly type the table name.

4 **Close** [×] the table.

More Knowledge

Appending Records

Access appends all records from the *source table*—the table from which you are copying records—into the *destination table*—the table to which the records are appended—as long as the field names and data types are the same in both tables. Exceptions include:

- If the source table does not have all of the fields that the destination table has, Access will still append the records, leaving the data in the missing fields empty in the destination table.

- If the source table has a field name that does not exist in the destination table or the data type is incompatible, the append procedure will fail.

Before performing an append procedure, carefully analyze the structure of both the source table and the destination table.

Activity 4.5 Splitting a Table into Two Tables

The *4A Employees* table stores personal data and office data about the employees. Although the table contains data about one subject—employees—you will split the table into two separate tables to keep the personal information separate from the office information.

1 Using the technique you practiced, copy and paste the structure and data of the **4A Employees** table, naming the pasted table **4A Employees Personal Firstname Lastname** Repeat the procedure for the **4A Employees** table, naming the pasted table **4A Employees Office Firstname Lastname**

Access creates two exact duplicates of the *4A Employees* table. These tables will be used to split the *4A Employees* table into two separate tables—one storing personal data and the other storing office data.

2 Open the **4A Employees Personal** table, and then collapse [«] the **Navigation Pane**. Scroll to the right to display the **Date Hired**, **Office Phone**, **Position**, and **Office Email** fields. Select all four fields. On the **Home tab**, in the **Records group**, click the **Delete** button. In the displayed message box, click **Yes** to permanently delete the fields and data.

Because these fields contain Office data, they are deleted from the *4A Employees Personal* table. These fields will be stored in the *4A Employees Office* table.

3 Select the **Title**, **First Name**, **MI**, and **Last Name** fields, and then delete the fields.

These fields are stored in the *4A Employees Office* table. You have deleted redundant data from the *4A Employees Personal* table.

4 **Save** 🔲 the table, and then expand ⌐» the **Navigation Pane**. Open the **4A Employees Office** table, and then collapse ⌐« the **Navigation Pane**.

5 Point to the **Street** field name until the ⬇ pointer displays. Drag to the right to the **Home Phone** field name, and then compare your screen with Figure 4.7.

Five fields are selected and will be deleted from this table. This is duplicate data that exists in the *4A Employees Personal* table. The *Empl ID* field is the common field between the two tables.

Duplicate data—stored in 4A
Employees Personal table

Figure 4.7

Common field—4A Employees
Office table and 4A Employees
Personal table

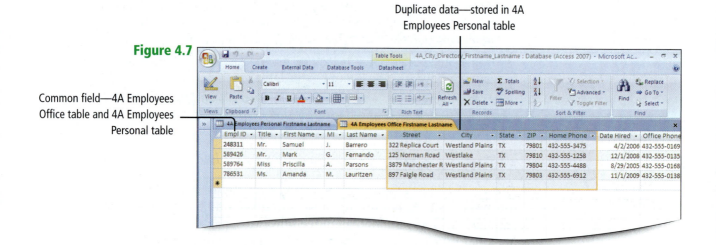

6 Delete the selected fields and data from the table.

The *4A Employees Office* table now stores only office data about the employees and can be linked to the *4A Employees Personal* table through the common field—*Empl ID*.

7 Click in a field to deselect the columns, and then click the **Position** field name. On the Ribbon, click the **Datasheet tab**. In the **Fields & Columns group**, click the **Insert** button.

A blank field is inserted between the *Office Phone* field and the *Position* field.

8 In the **Data Type & Formatting group**, click the **Data Type arrow**, and then from the displayed list, click **Number**. In the displayed message box, click **Yes** to continue. In the **Fields & Columns group**, click the **Rename** button, type **Department** and then press Enter.

Save 🔲 the table.

The Department field will store the department number for the employee.

9 In the first record—**Empl ID** of **248311**—click in the **Department** field. Expand 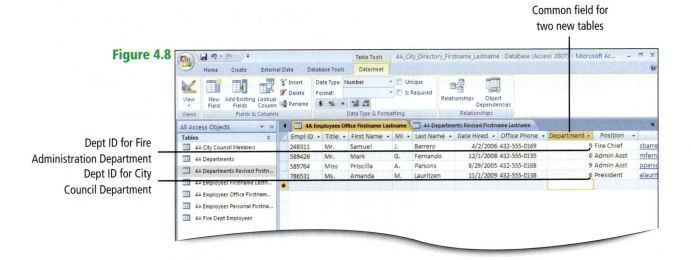 the **Navigation Pane**, and then open the **4A Departments Revised** table.

The *4A Departments Revised* table opens in Datasheet view, and the records are sorted in ascending order by the *Department* field.

10 Locate the record for the **Fire Administration Department**, and notice the **Dept ID** of **9**. On the **tab row**, click the **4A Employees Office tab** to make the table current. In the first record, in the **Department** field, type **9** and then press ⬇ two times. In the third record—**Empl ID** of **589764**—type **9** and then press ⬇ to save the record. Recall that a record is saved when you move to another record in the table.

11 Using the techniques you just practiced, find the **Dept ID** for the **City Council Department**, enter that number in the **Department** field for the second and fourth records in the **4A Employees Office** table, and then compare your screen with Figure 4.8.

The *Department* field is a common field with the *Dept ID* field in the *4A Departments Revised* table and will be used to link the two tables.

Figure 4.8

Common field for two new tables

Dept ID for Fire Administration Department
Dept ID for City Council Department

12 On the **tab row**, right-click any table tab, and then click **Close All**.

Activity 4.6 Appending Records from Another Database

Additional employee records are stored in another database. In this activity, you will open a second database to copy and paste records from tables in the second database to tables in the *4A_City_Directory* database.

1 On the taskbar, click the **Start** button ![start], and then **open Access**. Navigate to the location where the student data files for this textbook are saved. Locate and open the **a04A_City_Employees** file.

Save As an **Access 2007 Database** in your **Access Chapter 4** folder, and then name the database **4A_City_Employees_Firstname_Lastname**

2 In the **4A_City_Employees** database window, on the **Navigation Pane**, right-click **4A Office**, and then click **Copy**. Compare your screen with Figure 4.9.

Each time you start Access, you open an *instance* of it. Two instances of Access are open, and each instance displays in the taskbar.

You cannot open multiple databases in one instance of Access. If you open a second database in the same instance, Access closes the first database. You can, however, open multiple instances of Access that display different databases. The number of times you can start Access at the same time is limited by the amount of your computer's available RAM.

Figure 4.9

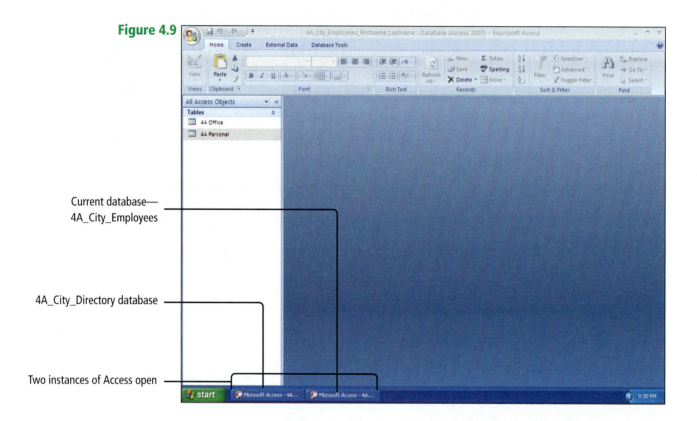

Current database— 4A_City_Employees

4A_City_Directory database

Two instances of Access open

Alert! **Does your taskbar display only one instance of Access?**

If you have multiple programs or files open, there may be only one button on the taskbar for the Access program. If Windows runs out of room on the taskbar, it will group open files, displaying them on one button. If this happens, the button on the taskbar will display a downward-pointing arrow on the right side. When you click the button, the names of the opened files display.

3 On the taskbar, point to each Microsoft Access button to display the ScreenTip, and then click the button for the **4A_City_Directory** database. In the **4A_City_Directory** database window, right-click the **Navigation Pane**, and then click **Paste**—recall that you copied the *4A Office* table. In the **Paste Table As** dialog box, under **Table Name**, type **4A Employees Office Firstname Lastname** being careful to type the table name exactly as it displays in the Navigation Pane. Under **Paste Options**, click the **Append Data to Existing Table** option button, and then click **OK**.

The records from the *4A Office* table in the source database— *4A_City_Employees*—are copied and pasted into the *4A Employees Office* table in the destination database—*4A_City_Directory.*

4 Using the techniques you just practiced, append the records from the **4A Personal** table in the **4A_City_Employees** database to the **4A Employees Personal Firstname Lastname** table in the **4A_City_Directory** database.

5 Make the **4A_City_Employees** database current, and on the title bar for the **4A_City_Employees** database window, click the

Close button ⊠ . In the displayed message box, click **Yes** to exit this instance of Access and to empty the Clipboard.

6 If the 4A_City_Directory database is not current, on the taskbar, click the Microsoft Access button. Open the **4A Employees Personal** table, and then open the **4A Employees Office** table.

Collapse ⟨⟨ the **Navigation Pane**.

7 View the records in both tables, and notice that three records—**Empl ID** of **456789**, **532268**, and **689444**—have been added to each table. If necessary, on the tab row, click the 4A Employees Office tab to make the table current, and then compare your screen with Figure 4.10.

In addition to appending records, you can copy a single record or data in a field from a table in the source database file to a table in the destination database file. Now that you have finished restructuring the database, you can see that it is wise to plan your database before creating the tables and entering data.

Figure 4.10

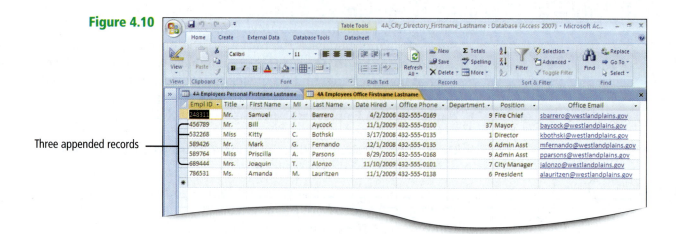

Three appended records

Activity 4.7 Setting a Primary Key

Recall that a primary key is a field—or a set of fields—in a table that provides Access with a unique identifier for each record. Primary key fields can never be empty, or null, and the data should rarely, if ever, change. You should always specify a primary key for a table.

1 Switch the **4A Employees Office** table to **Design** view. With the insertion point in the **Empl ID** field, in the **Tools group**, click the **Primary Key** button. **Save** ⊞ the table. Switch the **4A Employees Personal** table to **Design** view, set the **Empl ID** field as the primary key field, and then **Save** ⊞ the table.

Primary key fields are designated for all of the revised tables in the 4A_City_Directory database.

2 On the **tab row**, right-click any table tab, and then click **Close All**.

Objective 2
Customize the Navigation Pane

By default, the Navigation Pane displays all objects in the database, displays the objects in categories, and divides the categories into groups. For a new Access 2007 database, the default category is Tables and Related Views, and the default group for the category is All Tables. Some objects may display more than one time in the Tables and Related Views category. If an object is based on two tables, the object will display in the groups created for each table. For example, if you create a report that extracts data from two tables, the report displays in the groups for each table. You can customize the Navigation Pane by creating custom categories and groups, by hiding objects and groups, and by setting global options for the Navigation Pane.

Activity 4.8 Creating a Custom Category and Group

You create custom categories and groups when the default categories and groups do not meet your needs for organizing objects on the Navigation Pane. You cannot change or delete the predefined categories. In this activity, you will create a custom category for the restructured tables and then create two groups.

1 Expand ⟫ the **Navigation Pane**, right-click the **Navigation Pane title**—**All Access Objects**—and then point to **View By**. Click **Details**, and notice that the objects are displayed on the Navigation Pane with details about the objects—type of object, the creation date, and the modification date.

This display is useful when you need to see whether a database object has been recently modified.

2 Right-click the **Navigation Pane title**, point to **View By**, and then click **Icon**. Notice that the icon for each displayed object is larger. Right-click the **Navigation Pane title**, point to **View By**, and then click **List** to return the display of the Navigation Pane objects to the default setting.

Changing the view to icon will help someone who has difficulty seeing the smaller objects.

3 Right-click the **Navigation Pane title**, and then click **Navigation Options**. Alternatively, right-click an empty area at the bottom of the Navigation Pane, and then click Navigation Options. In the displayed **Navigation Options** dialog box, click **Add Item**, and then compare your screen with Figure 4.11.

In the Categories pane, a new category name displays. The text is selected so that you can rename the category. You can add a maximum of 10 custom categories to a database. The Move Up and Move Down arrows are used to change the order of the displayed custom categories when you click the Navigation Pane arrow. A custom category cannot be moved above the default categories.

Groups pane with default group name for the custom category

Figure 4.11

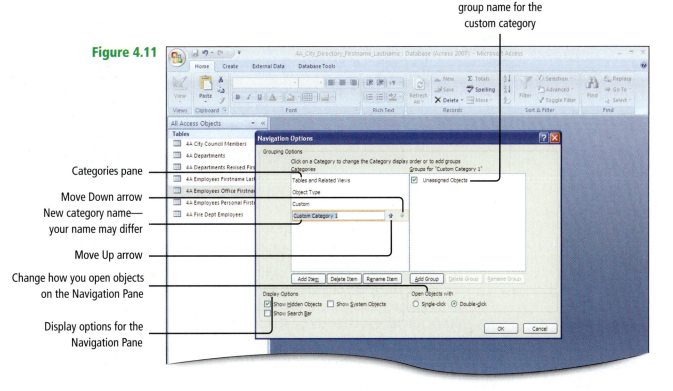

Categories pane

Move Down arrow

New category name— your name may differ

Move Up arrow

Change how you open objects on the Navigation Pane

Display options for the Navigation Pane

4 With the new category name selected and using your own first and last name, type **Revised Tables Firstname Lastname** and then press Enter. If necessary, under Display Options, if Show Hidden Objects is selected, click to clear the check box.

Category and group names should be descriptive of their purposes. After creating a custom category, you create one or more groups for the category. There is no limitation on the number of groups you can create for each category.

5 Under **Groups for "Revised Tables"**, click **Add Group**, type **Personal Data** and then press Enter. Click **Add Group**, type **Directory Data** and then press Enter. To the right of **Directory Data**, click the **Move Up arrow**, and then compare your screen with Figure 4.12.

One new category—*Revised Tables*—is created, and two groups for the category are created. By default, Access creates the *Unassigned Objects* group for a custom category. It contains all of the objects in the open database that can be used to populate the custom group.

Two new groups for
Revised Tables category

Figure 4.12

New category
Default Unassigned
Objects group

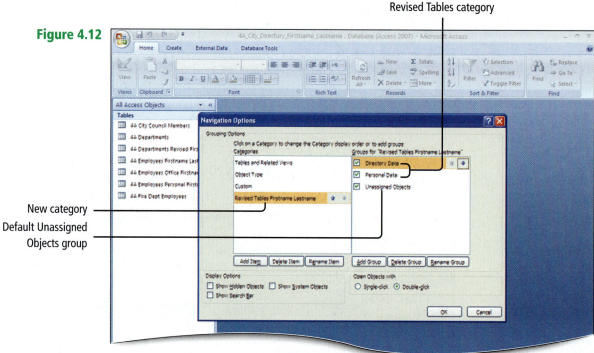

6 Be sure the check boxes next to all of the groups, including the Unassigned Objects group, are selected, and then click **OK**.

If a group is not selected, it will not display as an option when you try to organize the objects on the Navigation Pane. Although the custom category and groups are created, the Navigation Pane still displays All Access Objects by Object Type.

Another Way — **To Create a Custom Group**

On the Navigation Pane, right-click an object for which you want to create a custom group. From the shortcut menu, point to Add to group, and then click New Group. A new group displays on the Navigation Pane, ready for you to give it a name; and the object displays in the group.

7 Click the **Navigation Pane title**, and then click **Revised Tables**. Compare your screen with Figure 4.13. Do not be concerned if your Navigation Pane displays a different highlighted table.

The custom category name displays as the title of the Navigation Pane, the two custom group names display under the custom category name, and the database objects display under the Unassigned Objects group. Each category can be expanded or collapsed.

Figure 4.13

Custom groups

Group expand button

Custom category

Default Unassigned Objects group with database objects

Group collapse button

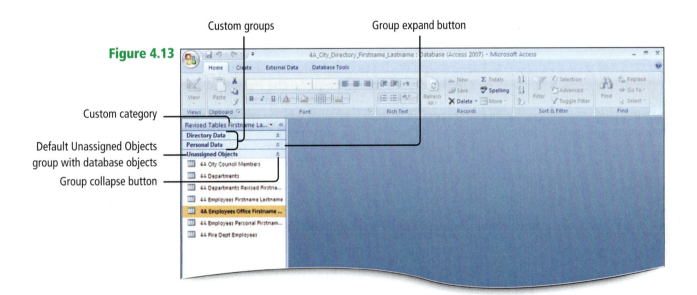

More Knowledge

Deleting a Custom Category or Group

To delete a custom category or group, right-click the Navigation Pane title, and then click Navigation Options. To delete a custom category, in the Categories pane, click the category name, and then click Delete Item. If the custom category contains groups, the groups and shortcuts will be deleted also—the objects will not be deleted.

To delete a custom group, in the Categories pane, click the custom category. In the Groups pane, click the custom group, and then click Delete Group. If the custom group contains shortcuts, the shortcuts will be deleted. The objects that had shortcuts in the deleted custom category or custom group display under Unassigned Objects.

Activity 4.9 Adding Objects to a Custom Group and Hiding a Group

In this activity, you will add objects to the custom groups, hide the Unassigned Objects group, and set *global options*—options that affect multiple items—for the Navigation Pane, which will affect all Navigation Pane categories and groups.

1 On the **Navigation Pane**, under **Unassigned Objects**, right-click **4A Departments Revised**. From the shortcut menu, point to **Add to group**, and then click **Directory Data**.

The *4A Departments Revised* table object displays under *Directory Data*. When you add a database object to a custom group, Access creates a shortcut to that object. You do not move or copy the object itself. If you rename or delete a shortcut in a custom group, those changes do not affect the actual object, only the shortcut.

2 Under **Unassigned Objects**, click **4A Employees Office**. Drag the table to the **Directory Data** group.

Dragging an object is a second method for adding objects to a custom group.

3 Using one of the two techniques you just practiced, add the **4A Employees Personal** table to the **Personal Data** group.

4 Right-click the **Navigation Pane title**, and then click **Navigation Options**. In the displayed **Navigation Options** dialog box, under **Categories**, click **Revised Tables**. Under **Groups for "Revised Tables"**, clear the **Unassigned Objects** check box, and then click **OK**. Alternatively, on the Navigation Pane, right-click the group title, and then click Hide.

The Unassigned Objects group is hidden and does not display on the Navigation Pane. The objects are not deleted from the database. To hide individual objects in a group, right-click the object, and then click Hide in this Group.

5 Right-click the **Navigation Pane title**, and then click **Navigation Options**. At the bottom of the dialog box, under **Display Options**, select the **Show Hidden Objects** check box, select the **Show Search Bar** check box, and then click **OK**. Compare your screen with Figure 4.14.

The Search box is used in a database to quickly find an object that contains a large number of objects. The Unassigned Objects group, which is hidden, displays as semi-transparent icons, and the objects in the hidden group can be opened.

Figure 4.14

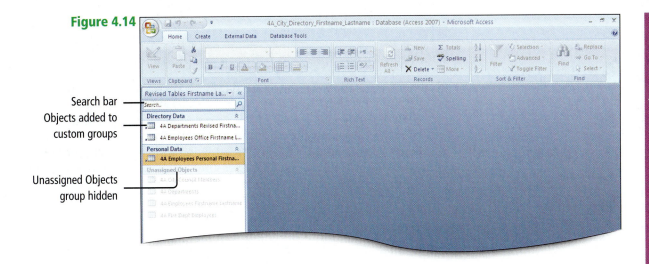

Search bar
Objects added to
custom groups

Unassigned Objects
group hidden

6 If the Search bar does not display, right-click the **Navigation Pane title**, and then click **Search Bar**. In the **Search** box, type **dep** and notice that Access hides any object that does not contain the letters *dep*.

As you enter the search text, the list of groups and objects in the Navigation Pane changes to display only the objects you are trying to locate. If you enter text that is not contained in an object, all of the groups on the Navigation Pane are hidden.

7 To redisplay the groups and objects, on the **Navigation Pane**, to the right of the **Search** box, click the **Clear Search String** button. Alternatively, in the Search box, delete the text.

8 Hold down Alt, and then press PrtScr—the label on your key may vary.

This places a copy of the current window in the Clipboard. Nothing will print at this time. Holding down the Alt key copies only the current window. This will be used to verify that you made changes to the Navigation Pane. If you need to print a copy of the entire desktop, press PrtScr by itself.

9 On the taskbar, click the **Start** button 🏁 start , and then open **Word 2007**. Hold down Ctrl, and then press V—a keyboard shortcut for Paste. Notice that the copy of the Access window displays in the Word document. If you are instructed to submit this result, create a paper or electronic printout.

10 **Save** 💾 the document in your **Access Chapter 4** folder as

4A_Navigation_Pane_Firstname_Lastname and then **Close** ❌ Word.

More Knowledge

The Navigation Pane and Untrusted Databases

By default, if you open an untrusted database, Access blocks potentially harmful content, and the blocked objects display in the Unrelated Objects group. For example, if a query contains a potentially unsafe function, it will display in the Unrelated Objects group on the Navigation Pane. If that query was used to create a form or report, the related form or report cannot be opened from the Navigation Pane. To restore an object to its normal group or to open related objects of a blocked object, the database must be trusted.

Objective 3
Create and Modify Table Relationships

Recall that Access databases are relational databases—the tables in the database can relate to or connect to other tables through common fields. A relational database avoids redundant data, helps to reduce errors, and saves space. To create a relationship, the common fields must have the same data type and same field size, but they do not need to have the same field name. After creating relationships, you can create queries, forms, and reports that display information from several tables. Table relationships work by matching data using the common fields in the tables. For example, you could have four tables relating to employees—one table for personal data, one table for office data, one table for payroll data, and one table for training data. All of these tables are connected to one another through a common field—the employee ID.

Activity 4.10 Creating Table Relationships

You should create relationships before creating other database objects, such as queries, forms, and reports, because when you create another object, Access displays all of the available tables and fields. For example, if you create a query and a relationship is not defined, you must add the tables to the query and then create the join line. In this activity, you will create relationships between the tables in the 4A_City_Directory database.

1 Collapse « the **Navigation Pane**. On the Ribbon, click the **Database Tools tab**. In the **Show/Hide group**, click the **Relationships** button. If the Show Table dialog box does not display, on the Design tab, in the Relationships group, click the Show Table button. Alternatively, right-click an empty area in the Relationships window and then click Show Table.

The Show Table dialog box displays, and the Tables tab is current. The Tables tab displays all of the tables in the database, including the hidden tables.

2 In the **Show Table** dialog box, click **4A Departments Revised**. Holding down [Ctrl], click **4A Employees Office**, and then click **4A Employees Personal**. Notice that three tables are selected. Click **Add**, and then click **Close**.

The three tables are added to the Relationships window. Two field lists display all of the field names. The 4A Employees Office field list displays a vertical scroll bar, indicating that there are more fields than those displayed.

3 Expand all of the field lists so that the entire table name and all of the field names display as shown in Figure 4.15.

Figure 4.15

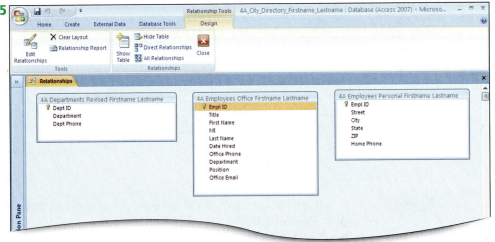

4 In the **4A Departments Revised** field list, click **Dept ID**, and then drag to the right to the **4A Employees Office** field list until the pointer points to **Department**, release the mouse button, and then compare your screen with Figure 4.16.

The Edit Relationships dialog box displays the tables used in the relationship and the common fields. The Department field in the *4A Employees Office* table is the foreign key field, which is used to link to the primary key field—*Dept ID*—in the *4A Departments Revised* table. The relationship type is ***one-to-many***—each record in the *4A Departments Revised* table can be related to *many* records in the *4A Employees Office* table. When you create the relationship, it does not matter if you first click the field on the one side of the relationship or the field on the many side of the relationship before dragging to the other field list.

Tables used to create relationship

Figure 4.16

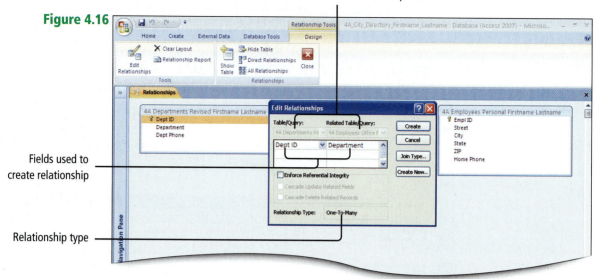

Fields used to create relationship

Relationship type

Are the wrong field names displayed in the Edit Relationships dialog box?

If you released the mouse button on a field other than Department in the 4A Employees Office field list, that field name will be displayed in the Edit Relationships dialog box. To correct this, in the Edit Relationships dialog box, click Cancel, and then re-create the relationship.

5 In the displayed **Edit Relationships** dialog box, select the **Enforce Referential Integrity** check box.

Referential integrity is a concept that prevents *orphan records*—records that reference deleted records in a related table. Enforcing referential integrity ensures that an employee cannot be added to the *4A Employees Office* table if the employee has not been assigned to a valid department. Similarly, it is not possible to delete a department from the *4A Departments Revised* table if there is an employee working in that department in the *4A Employees Office* table. If referential integrity is not enforced and you delete a department record that has a related record in the employees table, the record in the employees table is orphaned because it points to a department record that no longer exists.

6 In the **Edit Relationships** dialog box, click **Create**, and then compare your screen with Figure 4.17.

Recall that the join line displays between the two field lists. On the line, *1* indicates the *one* side of the relationship, and the infinity symbol (∞) indicates the *many* side of the relationship. One department can have many employees, and an employee can be assigned to only one department. These symbols display when referential integrity is enforced.

Figure 4.17

Many side of the relationship

One side of the relationship

Join line

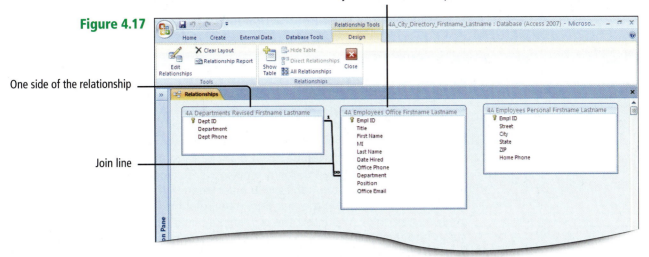

7 In the **4A Employees Office** field list, click **Empl ID**, drag to the right to the **4A Employees Personal** field list until the pointer points to **Empl ID**, and then release the mouse button. In the displayed **Edit Relationships** dialog box, select the **Enforce Referential Integrity** check box, notice the Relationship Type—One-to-One—and then click **Create**.

A join line displays between the two field lists, indicating a one-to-one relationship between the two tables. By enforcing referential integrity in a **one-to-one relationship**, each record in the first table—*4A Employees Personal*—can have only one matching record in the second table—*4A Employees Office*—and each record in the second table can have only one matching record in the first table. This type of relationship is uncommon because the data is usually stored in the same table. A one-to-one relationship can be used to divide a table with many fields, to isolate part of the table for security reasons, or to store a part of the main table.

8 On the **Design tab**, in the **Tools group**, click the **Relationship Report** button. On the **Print Preview tab**, in the **Page Layout group**, click the **Landscape** button. If you are instructed to submit this result, create a paper or electronic printout. To close the **Print Preview** window, on the **tab row**, click the **Close** button, and then click **Yes** to save the relationships report.

9 In the displayed **Save As** dialog box, click **OK** to accept the default report name. Expand the **Navigation Pane**.

The report closes, and its name displays in the Navigation Pane under *Unassigned Objects*. Because the report is a map of the relationships only and not a report containing actual data, it is not associated with any of the tables. If you display All Access Objects on the Navigation Pane, the relationships report will display under the Reports group.

10 **Close** ✕ the Relationships object. If a message displays prompting you to save the layout of the relationships, click **Yes**.

> ## More Knowledge
> ### Create a Many-to-Many Relationship
>
> Consider the relationship between an employees table and an assigned tasks table. A single employee can be given many tasks to perform. Conversely, a single task can be assigned to many employees. To create a *many-to-many relationship* between two tables, you must create a third table—a *junction table*—that breaks down the many-to-many relationship into two one-to-many relationships. You insert the primary key field from each of the two tables into the junction table, which records each instance of the relationship. The primary key fields from the two tables are connected to the foreign key fields in the junction table.

Activity 4.11 Testing Referential Integrity

Recall that enforcing referential integrity in a one-to-many table relationship ensures that an employee cannot be added to the *4A Employees Office* table if a department does not exist in the *4A Departments Revised* table. Also, you will be unable to delete a department from the *4A Departments Revised* table if there is an employee who works in that department stored in the *4A Employees Office* table. In this activity, you will test these two integrity protection features.

1 On the **Navigation Pane**, under **Directory Data**, open the **4A Departments Revised** table, and then open the **4A Employees Office** table. Collapse ⟪ the **Navigation Pane**.

Both tables open in Datasheet view, and the *4A Employees Office* table is the current table.

2 Create a new record by using the following information. Do not press Tab after entering data in the *Office Email* field.

Empl ID	Title	First Name	MI	Last Name	Date Hired	Office Phone	Department	Position	Office Email
332211	Mr.	Randy	F.	Icampo	12/15/09	432-555-0133	50		Intern	ricampo@ westland plains.gov

3 Press Tab to move to the next record, and then compare your screen with Figure 4.18.

A message box displays indicating that you cannot add or change this record because a related record—a record for Department 50—is required in the *4A Departments Revised* table. Enforcing referential integrity prevents you from creating this record because there is no related record for the department.

Figure 4.18

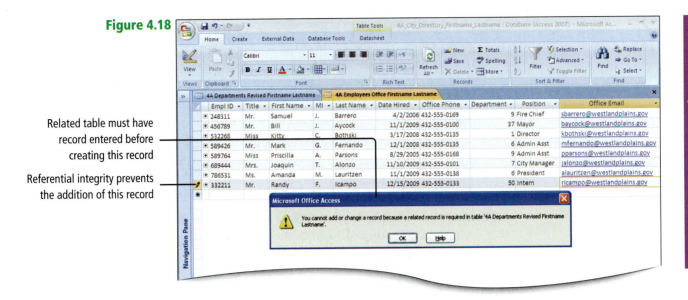

Related table must have record entered before creating this record

Referential integrity prevents the addition of this record

4 In the displayed message box, click **OK**. In the new record, under **Department**, select **50**, type **1**—the Department ID for Animal Control—and then press ↓ to save the record. **Close** ☒ the table.

The *4A Employees Office* table closes, and the *4A Departments Revised* table is current.

5 In the **4A Departments Revised** table, point to the record selector box for the sixth record—**City Council**—and then click to select the record. On the **Home tab**, in the **Records group**, click the **Delete** button.

A message displays stating that the record cannot be deleted or changed because of related records in the *4A Employees Office* table. Referential integrity protects an individual from deleting a record in one table that has related records in another table.

6 In the displayed message, click **OK**. **Close** ☒ the **4A Departments Revised** table.

Activity 4.12 Set and Test Cascade Options

There might be a time that you need to make a change to the primary key field in the table on the *one* side of the relationship. For example, the employee ID may have been incorrectly entered into the database, and it needs to be changed for all records. You also may need to delete a record that has a related record in another table. When referential integrity is enforced, you cannot make these changes. For that reason, Access provides *cascade options*—options that update records in related tables when referential integrity is enforced—that will enable an individual to complete these tasks when referential integrity is enforced. To use Cascade Options, referential integrity must be enforced.

1 On the Ribbon, click the **Database Tools tab**. In **the Show/Hide group**, click the **Relationships** button. Click the **join line** between the **4A Employees Office** field list and the **4A Employees Personal** field list. On the **Design tab**, in the **Tools group**, click the **Edit Relationships** button. Alternatively, right-click the join line, and then click Edit Relationships; or double-click the join line.

2 In the displayed **Edit Relationships** dialog box, select the **Cascade Update Related Fields** check box, and then click **OK**. **Close** the Relationships object, and expand the **Navigation Pane**.

3 Open the **4A Employees Office** table. Recall that this table has a one-to-one relationship with the *4A Employees Personal* table. Collapse the **Navigation Pane**.

4 Locate the record for Empl ID **589764**. Between the record selector box and the Empl ID field, click the plus sign (**+**), and then compare your screen with Figure 4.19.

After you create a relationship between two tables, in Datasheet view, plus signs display next to every record of the table that is the one side of the relationship. Clicking the plus sign displays the **subdatasheet**—record or records from the related table—and changes the plus sign to a minus sign (–). Clicking the minus sign collapses the subdatasheet.

Figure 4.19

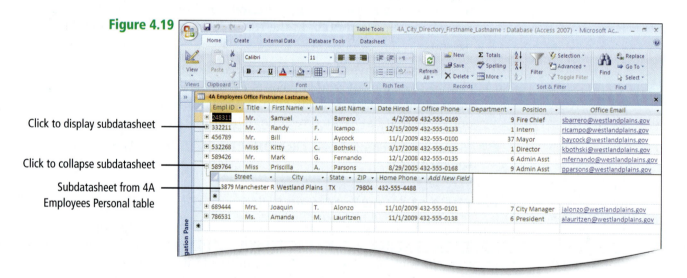

Click to display subdatasheet

Click to collapse subdatasheet

Subdatasheet from 4A Employees Personal table

5 Click the minus sign (–) to collapse the related record. In the **Empl ID** field, select **589764**, type **123456** and then press ↓.

6 Expand the **Navigation Pane**, and then open the **4A Employees Personal** table. Notice that the first record—the **Empl ID**—is changed to **123456**.

The **Cascade Update** option enables you to change a primary key field and updates the records in the related tables.

7 Collapse `«` the **Navigation Pane**. In the **4A Employees Personal** datasheet, click the plus sign (**+**) for the first record.

Because this table and the *4A Employees Office* table are joined with a *one-to-one relationship*, each table displays the subdatasheet for the other table. If tables are joined with a *one-to-many relationship*, the subdatasheet can be displayed only in the table on the *one* side of the relationship.

8 Collapse the subdatasheet for the first record, and then close the open tables. Click the **Database Tools tab**, and then in the **Show/Hide group**, click the **Relationships** button. Double-click the **join line** between the **4A Employees Office** field list and the **4A Employees Personal** field list to display the **Edit Relationships** dialog box.

To edit relationships, the tables must be closed.

9 In the displayed **Edit Relationships** dialog box, select the **Cascade Delete Related Records** check box, and then click **OK**. **Close** `×` the Relationships object. Expand `»` the **Navigation Pane**, open the **4A Employees Personal** table, and then open the **4A Employees Office** table. Collapse `«` the **Navigation Pane**.

10 In the **4A Employees Office** datasheet, locate the record for the **Empl ID** of **589426**, and then select the record. On the **Home tab**, in the **Records group**, click the **Delete** button—do not click a button in the displayed message box. Compare your screen with Figure 4.20.

A message displays stating that deleting this record in this table will cause records in the related tables to also be deleted.

Figure 4.20

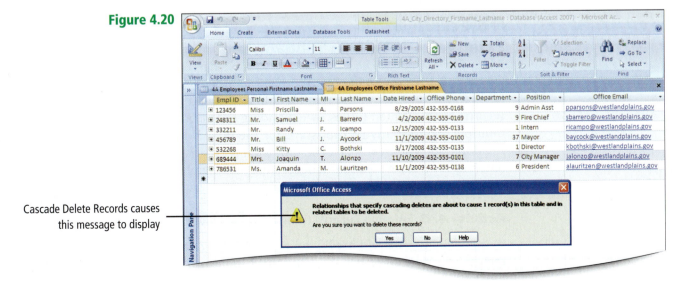

Cascade Delete Records causes this message to display

11 In the displayed message box, click **Yes**. Be sure that the **4A Employees Office** datasheet is current. if necessary. On the **Home tab**, in the **Records group**, click the **Refresh All** button.

Recall that if a table is open and changes are made to fields or records in a related object, the changes are not immediately displayed. Clicking the Refresh All button updates the view of the table, removing the deleted record—the record for Mark Fernando.

The *Cascade Delete* option—an option used when referential integrity is enforced that enables an individual to delete a record in a table and delete all of the related records in related tables—ensures that orphan records are not left in the database.

12 **Close** both tables, and expand ⟩⟩ the **Navigation Pane**.

Objective 4
Enter Records Using a Subdatasheet

One of the advantages of creating relationships is that you can open the table on the *one* side of the relationship and then create or modify records in the related tables by expanding the subdatasheet. If there are multiple one-to-many relationships for the table on the one side of the relationship, when you click the plus sign (+) to display the subdatasheet, an Insert Subdatasheet dialog box displays, where you can select the related table that you want to display as a subdatasheet.

Activity 4.13 Entering Records Using a Subdatasheet

In this activity, you will modify an existing record, and then create a record for a new employee by using the subdatasheets that display in the *4A Departments Revised* table.

1 Open **4A Departments Revised**, and then collapse « the **Navigation Pane**.

2 Under **Department**, locate the record for the **Fire Administration**, and then click the plus sign (**+**) to expand the subdatasheet. In the first record—**Empl ID** of **123456**—select the last four digits of the office phone number—**0168**. Type **5555** and then press ↓.

The Office Phone number is changed in the *4A Employees Office* table, using the subdatasheet that displays in the *4A Departments Revised* table.

3 In the subdatasheet, on the new record row, click in the **Empl ID** field, type **222333** and then press Tab or Enter. Continue entering the data for the new employee by using the following information, and then compare your screen with Figure 4.21.

ID Title	First Name	MI	Last Name	Date Hired	Office Phone	Position	Office Email
Mr.	Mike	D.	Incarno	12/1/09	432-555-0168	Safety Officer	mincarno@ westlandplains.gov

The new record is created in the *4A Employees Office* table by using the subdatasheet in the *4A Departments Revised* table. Recall that the *4A Employees Office* table is linked to the *4A Departments Revised* table, using the common fields of Dept ID and Department. If you open the *4A Employees Office* table and enter the record directly into the table, you must type the correct Dept ID number in the Department field, and you might enter the wrong number. Using the subdatasheet eliminates this error—in the *4A Employees Office* table, the Department field is automatically populated with *9*, the ID for the Fire Administration department.

Figure 4.21

Phone number changed

Subdatasheet for 4A Employees Office table

New record

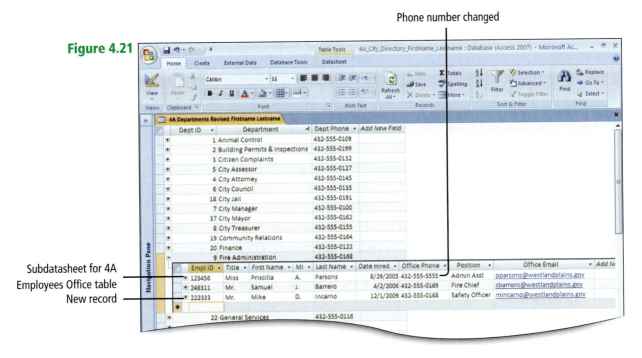

4 In the subdatasheet, expand (**+**) the subdatasheet for the third record—**Empl ID** of **222333**.

The subdatasheet for the *4A Employees Personal* table displays because the table is related to the *4A Employees Office* table, and the insertion point is still positioned in the *4A Employees Office* subdatasheet.

5 In the subdatasheet for the *4A Employees Personal* table, click in the **Street** field, type **132 Rose Lane** and then press Tab or Enter to move to the City field. Continue entering the data for the new employee using the following information, and then compare your screen with Figure 4.22.

City	State	ZIP	Home Phone
Westland Plains	TX	79802	432-555-3333

The new record is created in the *4A Employees Personal* table by using the subdatasheet of the *4A Employees Office* table in the *4A Departments Revised* table. Recall that the *4A Employees Office* table is linked to the *4A Employees Personal* table, using the common fields of Empl ID. If you open the *4A Employees Personal* table and enter the record directly into the table, you must type the correct Empl ID, and you might enter the wrong number. Using the subdatasheet increases data entry accuracy—the Empl ID field in the *4A Employees Personal* table is automatically populated with the correct employee ID of *222333*.

Figure 4.22

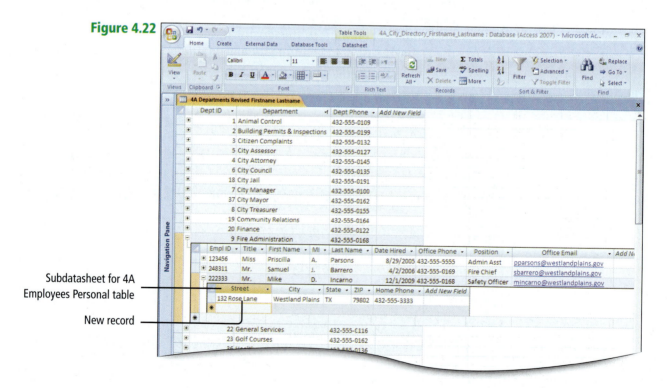

Subdatasheet for 4A Employees Personal table

New record

6 Collapse (–) both subdatasheets. Click the **Office** button, point to the **Print button arrow**, and then click **Print Preview**. Zoom in and be sure that all field names and data display—if data is truncated, switch to Datasheet view and adjust the column widths. If you are instructed to submit this result, create a paper or electronic printout of the table, and then **Close** Print Preview.

7 **Close** the **4A Departments Revised** table, expand the **Navigation Pane**, open **4A Employees Office**, and then open **4A Employees Personal**. Collapse the **Navigation Pane**.

8 In the **4A Employees Personal** table, notice the second record—**Empl ID** of **222333**. This is the record you created in the subdatasheet. Because you entered the record in the subdatasheet, the Empl ID was automatically entered. Adjust column widths to display all of the field names and data. View the table in **Print Preview**. If you are instructed to submit this result, create a paper or electronic printout of the table, and then **Close** Print Preview.

9 Make the **4A Employees Office** table current. Notice the second record—**Empl ID** of **222333**. This record was also created in the subdatasheet. In the **Department** field for this record, notice the **Department** number—**9**. Because you entered the record in the subdatasheet, the Department number was automatically entered. Adjust the column widths, if necessary.

10 View the document in **Print Preview**, and then change the orientation to **Landscape**. On the **Print Preview tab**, in the **Page Layout group**, click the **Margins** button, and then click **Normal**. Notice that all of the fields now display on one page. If you are instructed to submit this result, create a paper or electronic printout of the table, and then **Close** Print Preview.

11 Close the open tables; and, if prompted, **Save** changes. Expand the **Navigation Pane**. **Close** the database, and then **Exit** Access.

End **You have completed Project 4A** ——————————

Project 4B Tasks

Matthew Shoaf, Director of the Information Technology Department, has created a table to keep track of tasks that he has assigned to the employees in his department. In Activities 4.14 through 4.23, you will modify the properties and customize the fields in the table that stores records about assigned tasks. You will add features to the database table that will help to reduce data entry errors and that will make data entry easier, and you will add attachments to records. Your completed table will look similar to the table shown in Figure 4.23.

For Project 4B, you will need the following files:

a04B_Tasks
a04B_WorkOrder_1
a04B_WorkOrder_2

You will save your database as
4B_Tasks_Firstname_Lastname

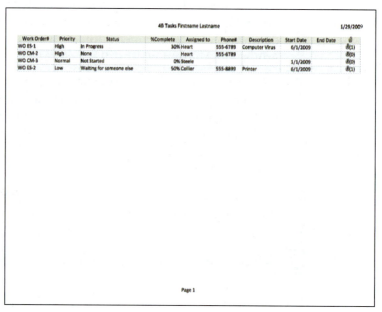

Figure 4.23
Project 4B—Tasks

Objective 5
Change Data Types

Before creating a table, it is important to decide on the data types for the fields in the table. Setting a specific data type helps to ensure that the proper data will be entered into a field; for example, it is not possible to enter text into a field with a Currency data type. Once data is entered into the field, caution must be exercised when changing the data type—data may be truncated or deleted. You can change the data type in either Datasheet view or Design view.

Activity 4.14 Changing Data Types

1 **Start** Access. Navigate to the location where the student data files for this textbook are saved. Locate and open the **a04B_Tasks** file. **Save** the database in the **Access 2007 Database** format in your **Access Chapter 4** folder as 4B_Tasks_Firstname_Lastname

2 If you did not add the Access Chapter 4 folder to the Trust Center, enable the content. On the **Navigation Pane**, under **Tables**, rename **4B Tasks** by adding **Firstname Lastname** to the end of the table name, and then open the **4B Tasks** table. Collapse ⟪ the **Navigation Pane**.

3 Switch to **Design** view. Change the data type for the **%Complete** field to **Number**. Change the data type for the **Description** field to **Memo**. Change the data type for **Start Date** field and **End Date** field to **Date/Time**. **Save** 🖫 the changes, and then compare your screen with Figure 4.24.

The data types are changed to reflect the type of data that will be stored in the fields.

Figure 4.24

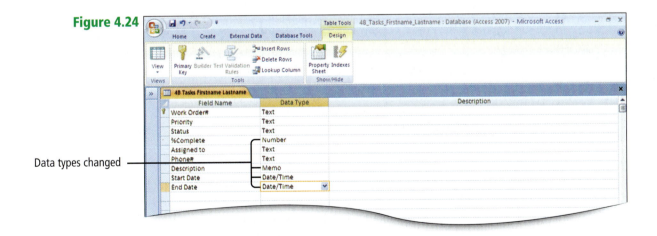

Data types changed

4 Click the **Help** button ![help icon]. In the **Access Help** window, in the search box, type **data type conversion** and then press [Enter]. Under **Searched for: "data type conversion"**, click **Modify or change the data type setting for a field**. On the right side, under **In this article**, click **Restrictions on changing data types**. Compare your screen with Figure 4.25. Take a moment to scroll down, and notice the restrictions that apply when converting from one data type to another data type.

You can find information about Access by using the Help feature.

Access Help window

Figure 4.25

Search term —

Table with conversion
type restrictions —

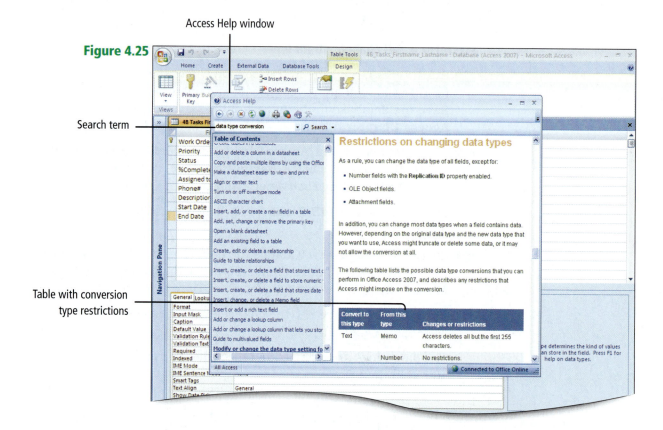

5 **Close** ![X] the Access Help window.

Objective 6
Set Field Properties

A *field property* is an attribute or characteristic of a field that controls the display and input of data. You previously used field properties to change the size of a field and to specify a specific format for data types. Available field properties depend upon the data type.

Activity 4.15 Creating an Input Mask Using the Input Mask Wizard

An *input mask* is a field property that determines the data that can be entered, how the data displays, and how the data is stored. For example, an input mask can require individuals to enter telephone numbers by using a specific format, for example, (757) 555-1212. If you enter the telephone number without supplying an area code, you will be unable to save the record until the area code is entered. Input masks provide ***data validation***—rules that help prevent individuals from entering invalid data—and help ensure that individuals enter data in a consistent manner. By default, you can apply input masks to fields with a data type of Text, Number, Currency, and Date/Time. The Input Mask Wizard can be used to apply input masks to fields with a data type of Text or Date/Time only.

1 Under **Field Name**, click **Phone#**. Under **Field Properties**, click in the **Input Mask** box. At the right side of the Field Properties, notice the description given for this property. In the **Input Mask** box, click the **Build** button [⋯]. Compare your screen with Figure 4.26.

The Build button displays after you click in a field property box so you can further define the property. The Input Mask Wizard starts, which enables you to create an input mask using one of several standard masks that Access has designed, such as Phone Number, Social Security Number, Zip Code, and so on. Clicking in the Try It box enables you to enter data to test the input mask.

Figure 4.26

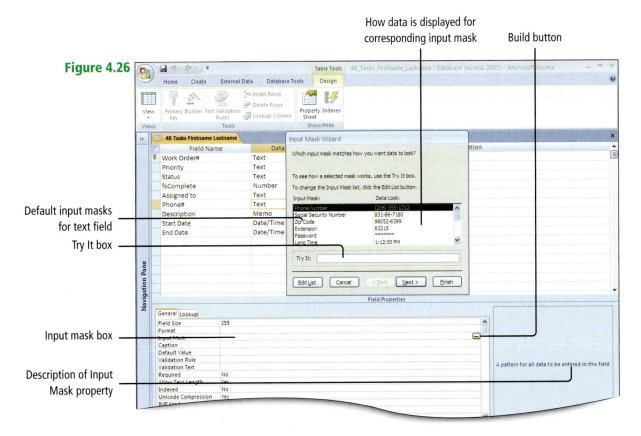

How data is displayed for corresponding input mask

Build button

Default input masks for text field

Try It box

Input mask box

Description of Input Mask property

2 In the displayed **Input Mask Wizard** dialog box, with **Phone Number** selected, click **Next**, and then compare your screen with Figure 4.27. In the **Input Mask Wizard** dialog box, notice the entry in the **Input Mask** box.

A *0* indicates a required digit; a *9* indicates an optional digit or space. The area code is enclosed in parentheses, and a hyphen (-) separates the three-digit prefix from the four-digit number. The exclamation point (!) causes the input mask to fill in from left to right. The Placeholder character indicates that the field will display an underscore character (_) for each digit.

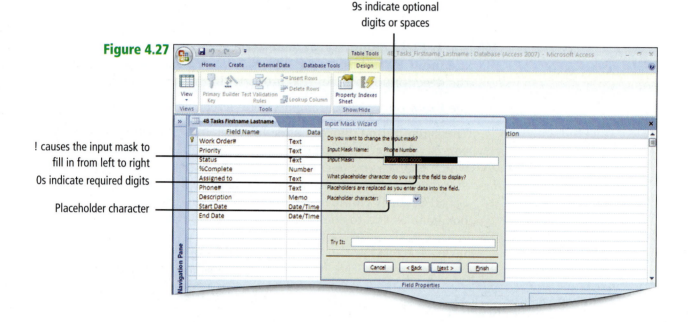

Figure 4.27

9s indicate optional digits or spaces

! causes the input mask to fill in from left to right

0s indicate required digits

Placeholder character

3. In the **Input Mask Wizard** dialog box, click **Back**, and then click **Edit List**.

The Customize Input Mask Wizard dialog box displays, which enables you to edit the default input mask or add an input mask.

4. In the **Customize Input Mask Wizard** dialog box, in the navigation area, click the **New (blank) record** button [ ]. In the **Description** box, type **Local Phone Number** In the **Input Mask** box, type **!000-0000** Click in the **Placeholder** box, and then change _ to # Click in the **Sample Data** box, select the data, and then type **555-1212** Compare your screen with Figure 4.28.

Because tasks are assigned to local personnel, the area code is unnecessary. Instead of displaying an underscore as the placeholder in the field, the number sign (#) displays.

New input mask for
local phone numbers

Figure 4.28

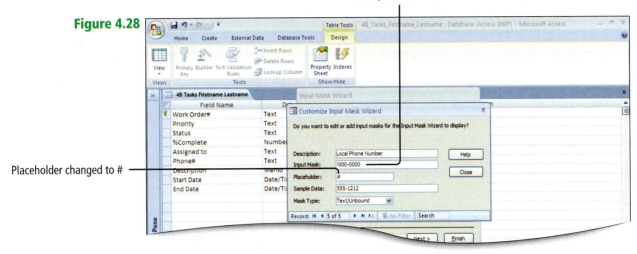

Placeholder changed to #

5 In the **Customize Input Mask Wizard** dialog box, click **Close**.

The newly created input mask for Local Phone Number displays below the input mask for Password.

6 Under **Input Mask**, click **Local Phone Number**, and then click **Next**. Click the **Placeholder character arrow** to display other symbols that can be used as placeholders. Be sure that **#** is displayed as the placeholder character, and then click **Next**.

After creating an input mask to be used with the Input Mask Wizard, you can change the placeholder character for individual fields.

7 The next wizard screen enables you to decide how you want to store the data. Be sure that the **Without the symbols in the mask, like this** option button is selected, as shown in Figure 4.29, and then click **Next**.

Saving the data without the symbols makes the database size smaller.

Figure 4.29

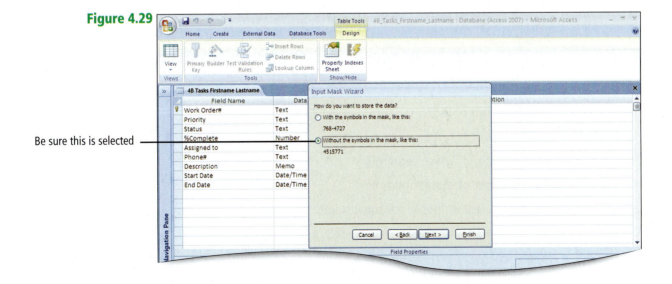

Be sure this is selected

8 In the final wizard screen, click **Finish**. Notice that the entry in the **Input Mask** box displays as **!000-0000;;#**.

Recall that the exclamation point (!) fills the input mask from left to right, and the 0s indicate required digits. The two semicolons (;) are used by Access to separate the input mask into three sections. This input mask has data in the first section—the 0s—and in the third section—the placeholder of #.

The second and third sections of an input mask are optional. The second section, which is not used in this input mask, determines whether the literal characters—in this case, the hyphen (-)—are stored with the data. A *0* in the second section will store the literal characters; a *1* or leaving it blank stores only the characters entered in the field. The third section of the input mask indicates the place-holder character—in this case, the # sign. If you want to leave the fill-in spaces blank instead of using a placeholder, type " "—there is a space between the quotation marks—in the third section.

9 Switch to **Datasheet** view, click **Yes** to save the table, and then in the first row, click the left edge of the **Phone#** field. Notice the input mask of **###-####**. Type **aaa** and notice that Access will not allow a letter entry because the input mask you just created requires numbers in this field.

10 Type **5551212** and notice that Access fills in the phone number from left to right and skips over the hyphen, which increases data entry efficiency. Press Esc to delete the entry. Switch to **Design** view.

11 Take a moment to study the table shown in Figure 4.30, which describes the characters that can be used to create a custom input mask.

Most Common Input Mask Characters

Character	Description
0	Required digit (0 through 9).
9	Optional digit or space.
#	Optional digit, space, plus sign, or minus sign; blank positions are converted to spaces.
L	Required letter (A through Z).
?	Optional letter.
A	Required digit or letter.
a	Optional digit or letter.
&	Any character or space; required.
C	Any character or space; optional.
<	All characters that follow are converted to lowercase.
>	All characters that follow are converted to uppercase.
!	Characters typed into the mask are filled from left to right. The exclamation point can be included anywhere in the input mask.

(Continued)

(*Continued*)	
\	Character that follows is displayed as text. This is the same as enclosing a character in quotation marks.
Password	Creates a password entry box that displays asterisks (∗) as an individual types. Access stores the characters.
" "	Used to enclose displayed text.
.	Decimal separator.
,	Thousands separator.
: ; - /	Date and time separators. Character used depends on your regional settings.

Figure 4.30

Activity 4.16 Creating an Input Mask Using the Input Mask Properties Box

In addition to using the wizard, input masks can be created directly in the Input Mask box. The input mask, however, will not be saved with the Input Mask Wizard. In this activity, you will use the Input Mask Properties box to create a mask that will ensure the Work Order# is entered according to departmental policy. An example of a work order number used by the Information Technology Department is WO CM-46341. WO is an abbreviation for Work Order. CM represents the initials of the person entering the work order data. A hyphen separates the initials from a number assigned to the work order.

1 With the **4B Tasks** table displayed in **Design** view, click in the **WorkOrder#** field. Under **Field Properties**, click in the **Input Mask** box, type **WO >LL-99999** (there is a space after *WO*), and then compare your screen with Figure 4.31.

The letters *WO* and a space will display at the beginning of every Work Order#. The greater than (>) sign converts any text following it to uppercase. Each *L* indicates that a letter (not a number) is required. A hyphen (-) follows the two letters, and the five 9s indicate optional numbers.

Figure 4.31

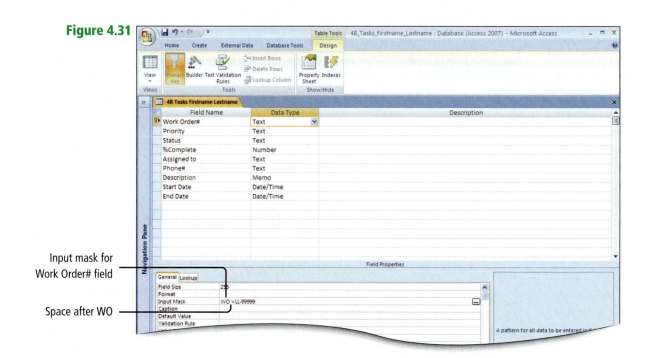

Input mask for
Work Order# field

Space after WO

2 Switch to **Datasheet** view, and then **Save** changes to the table. In the first record under **Work Order#**, type **cm1**

As you type the data, the field automatically displays *WO*—an abbreviation for *Work Order*—and a space. The letters *cm* are automatically capitalized, and the hyphen is inserted before typing 1.

3 Tab to the **Phone#** field, type **5551234** and then press ⬇ to save the record. Switch to **Design** view. If necessary, click in the **Work Order#** field, and notice how Access formatted the input mask.

Access placed quotation marks around WO and the space to indicate text that is displayed in the field. Access inserted a backslash (\) after LL, which forces Access to display the character that immediately follows.

4 Take a moment to study the examples of input masks, as shown in the table in Figure 4.32.

Examples of Input Masks

Input Mask	Sample Data	Description
(000) 000-0000	(206) 555-1212	Must enter an area code because of 0s enclosed in parentheses.
(999) 000-0000!	(206) 555-1212 ( ) 555-1212	Area code is optional because of 9s enclosed in parentheses. Exclamation point causes mask to fill in from left to right.
(000) AAA-AAAA	(206) 555-TELE	Enables you to substitute the last four digits of a U.S. style phone number with letters. Area code is required.
#999	-20 2009	Any positive or negative number of no more than four characters and no thousands separator or decimal places.

(Continued)

(*Continued*)

>L????L?000L0	GREENGR339M3 MAY R 452B7	A combination of required (L) and optional (?) letters and required numbers (0). The greater than (>) sign changes letters to uppercase.
00000-9999	23703- 23703-5100	Required five-digit postal code (0) and optional plus-four section (9).
>L<???????????????	Carolyn Mclellan	Up to 15 letters in which first letter is required and is capitalized; all other letters are lowercase.
ISBN 0-&&&&&&&&&-0	ISBN 0-13-232762-7	A book number with text of ISBN, required first and last digits, and any combination of characters between those digits.
>LL00000-0000	CM23703-1224	Combination of two required letters, all uppercase, followed by five required numbers, a hyphen, and then four required numbers. Could be used with part or inventory numbers.

Figure 4.32

5 Click in the **Start Date** field to make the field current. Under **Field Properties**, click in the **Format** box, and then click the **arrow**. From the displayed list, click **Short Date**. Set the format of **End Date** to **Short Date**.

More Knowledge

Differences Between Input Masks and Display Formats

You can define input masks to control how data is entered into the field and then apply a separate display format to the same data. For example, you can require individuals to enter dates in a format such as 24 Dec. 2009 by using an input mask of DD MMM. YYYY. By using the Format property, you can specify a format of Short Date, which will display the data as 12/24/2009, regardless of how the data was entered. The data will be stored in the table as 24 Dec. 2009 but be displayed as 12/24/2009.

Input masks, by themselves, affect how data is stored and how it is displayed. Field formats affect only how data is displayed. Input masks and field formats can interfere with each other. Always test data entry using the input mask to ensure that data will be displayed properly.

Activity 4.17 Specifying a Required Field

Recall that if a table has a field designated as the primary key field, an entry for the field is *required*; it cannot be left empty. You can set this requirement on other fields in either Design view or Datasheet view. In this activity, you will require an entry in the Status and Start Date fields. Use the Required field property to ensure that a field contains data and is not left blank.

1 Click in the **Status** field, and then under **Field Properties**, click in the **Required** box. Click the **Required arrow**, and then compare your screen with Figure 4.33.

Only Yes and No options display in the list.

Figure 4.33

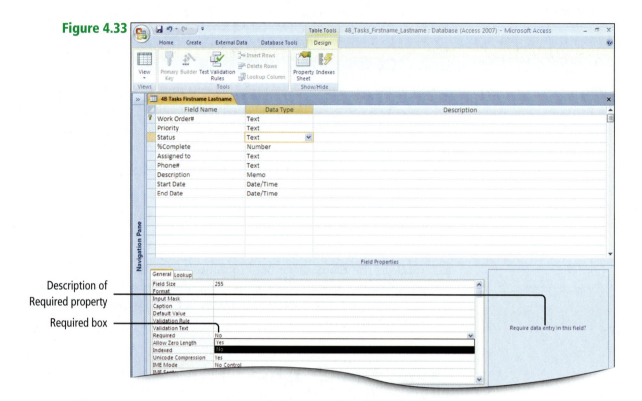

Description of Required property

Required box

2 Click **Yes** to require an individual to enter the status for each record. Switch to **Datasheet** view, and then **Save** the changes to the table.

A message displays stating that data integrity rules have been changed and that existing data may not be valid for the new rules. This message displays whenever you change field properties where data exists in the field. Clicking Yes requires Access to examine the field in every record to see if the existing data meets the new data validation rule. If Access finds data that does not meet the new validation rule, a new message displays that prompts you to keep testing with the new setting. Every record that violates the new validation rule will result in this same message displaying. You also can revert to the prior validation setting and continue testing or cancel testing of the data.

3 In the displayed message box, click **No**. On the Ribbon, click the **Datasheet tab**, and then in the table, click in the **Status** field. On the **Datasheet tab**, in the **Data Type & Formatting group**, notice that the **Is Required** check box is selected.

4 In the table, click in the **Assigned to** field, and then on the **Datasheet tab**, in the **Data Type & Formatting group**, select the **Is Required** check box.

A message displays stating that existing data violates the Required property for the Assigned to field—the field is currently blank.

5 In the displayed message box, click **Cancel**, and then switch to **Design** view. Under **Field Name**, click **Assigned to**. Under **Field Properties**, notice that the **Required** box displays **Yes**. Switch to **Datasheet** view. In the first record, click in the **Status** field, and then type **Not Started** Press Tab two times to move to the **Assigned to** field, type **Joan Steele** and then press ↓. Compare your screen with Figure 4.34.

Required fields

Figure 4.34

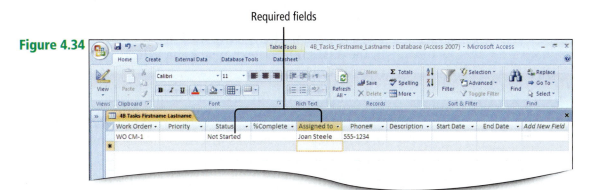

More Knowledge

Allowing Blank Data in a Required Text or Memo Field

By default, all fields except the primary key field can be empty—null. If the Required property for a field is set to Yes, a value must be entered into the field. If data is required, Access will not save the record until a value is entered. You may not have the data to enter into a text or memo field where the Required property is set to Yes. To allow for this situation, you can set the Allow Zero Length property for the field. The Allow Zero Length property setting of Yes enables you to enter zero-length strings in a field. A *zero-length string* is created by typing two quotation marks with no space between them (" "), which indicates that no value exists for a required text or memo field.

Activity 4.18 Setting Default Values for Fields

You can use the Default Value field property to display a value in a field for new records. As you enter data, you can change the *default value* in the field to another value unless a validation rule prohibits it. For example, if all of the employees in the organization live in Texas, set the default value of the state field to TX. If most of the employees in your organization live in the city of Westland Plains, set the default value of the city field to Westland Plains. When entering data, if an employee lives in another city, type the new value over the displayed default value. Setting a default value for fields that contain the same data for multiple records increases the efficiency of data entry.

1 Switch to **Design** view. Under **Field Name**, click the **Priority** field. Under **Field Properties**, click in the **Default Value** box, and then type **Normal** Switch to **Datasheet** view, and then **Save** changes to the table. Notice that the **Priority** field displays *Normal* in the New Record row.

Setting a default value does not change the data in saved records; the default value will display in new records and will be saved only if nothing else is typed in the field.

2 In the second record, click in the **Work Order#** field, type **cm2** and then press Tab or Enter to move to the next field. In the **Priority** field, type **High** and then press Tab. Notice that the new record row displays *Normal* in the Priority field. In the **Status** field, type **Not Started** In the **Assigned to** field, type **Robert Heart** and in the **Phone#** field, type **5556789** Press ↓.

You can type over the displayed default value.

3 Switch to **Design** view, and notice that in the **Default Value** box for the **Priority** field, Access inserted quotation marks around *Normal* because the value is text.

4 Using the technique you just practiced, for the **Status** field, set the **Default Value** property to **Not Started** For the **%Complete** field, set the **Field Size** property to **Single**, set the **Format** property to **Percent**, set the **Decimal Places** property to **0** and then set the **Default Value** property to **0**

5 For the **Start Date** field, set the **Default Value** to **1/1/09** Switch to **Datasheet** view, and then **Save** changes to the table. Compare your screen with Figure 4.35.

The Status field shows a default value of *Not "Started"*. Recall that *Not* is an Access logical operator; therefore, Access excluded the word *Not* from the text expression.

Figure 4.35

Default value for Start Date

Default value of 0, formatted as percent with no decimal places

Not is reserved word

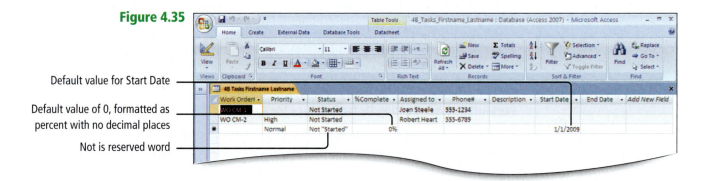

6 Switch to **Design** view. Click in the **Status** field. Under **Field Properties**, in the **Default Value** box, select the text, and then type **"Not Started"** Click in the **Start Date** field, and notice that in the **Default Value** box, Access displays the date as **#1/1/2009#**. Switch to **Datasheet** view, **Save** changes to the table, and then view the default value in the **Status** field.

Inserting quotation marks around *Not Started* informs Access that both words are part of the text expression.

7 Switch to **Design** view.

More Knowledge

Using the Current Date as a Default Value

To use the current date as the default value for a Date/Time field, in the Default Value box, type date().

Activity 4.19 Indexing Fields in a Table

An ***index*** is a special list created in Access to speed up searches and sorting—such as the index at the back of a book. The index is visible only to Access and not to you, but it helps Access find items much faster. You should index fields that you search frequently, fields that you sort, or fields used to join tables in relationships. Indexes, however, can slow down the creation and deletion of records because the data must be added to or deleted from the index.

1 Under **Field Name**, click **Work Order#**. Under **Field Properties**, locate the **Indexed** property box, and notice the entry of **Yes (No Duplicates)**.

By default, primary key fields are indexed. Because Work Order# is the primary key field, the field is automatically indexed, and no duplicate values are permitted in this field.

2 Under **Field Name**, click **Assigned to**. Under **Field Properties**, click in the **Indexed** property box, and then click the displayed **arrow**. Compare your screen with Figure 4.36.

Three options display for the Indexed property—No, Yes (Duplicates OK), and Yes (No Duplicates).

Figure 4.36

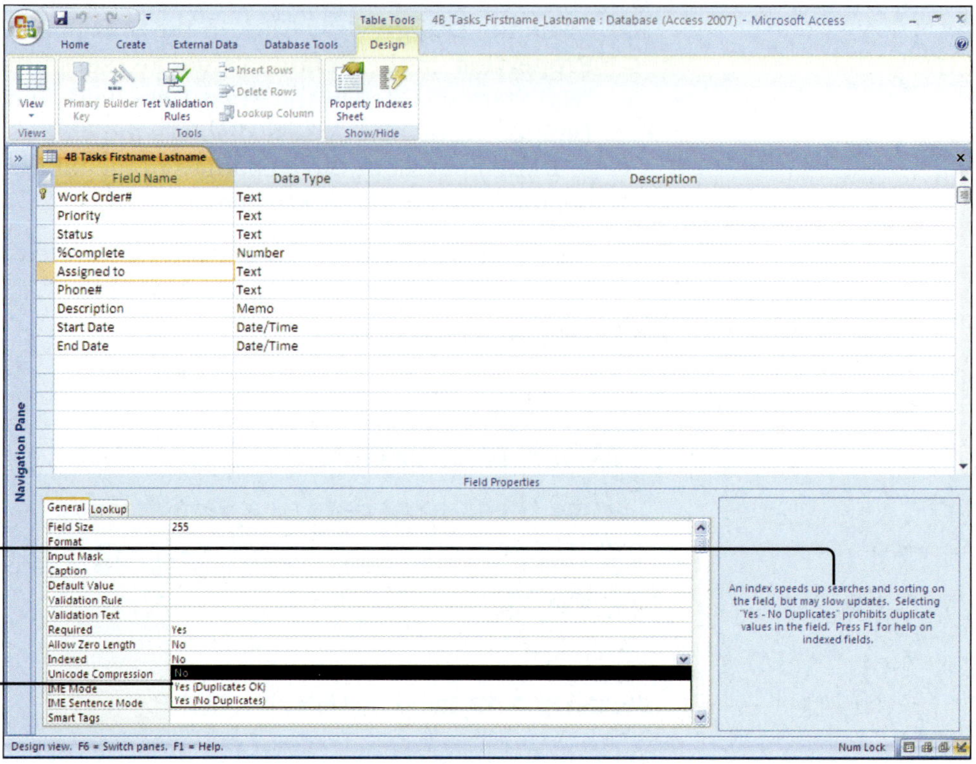

Description of Indexed property

Indexed property options

3 Click **Yes (Duplicates OK)**.

By adding an index to the field and allowing duplicates, you create faster searches and sorts on this field, while allowing duplicate data. Because a person may be assigned more than one task, allowing duplicate data is appropriate.

4 **Save** 🔲 the table design.

5 On the **Design tab**, in the **Show/Hide group**, click the **Indexes** button.

An Indexes dialog box displays the indexes in the current table. Each index can use up to ten fields. Opening the Indexes dialog box is an efficient way to determine the fields that have been indexed in a table.

6 In the **Indexes: 4B Tasks** dialog box, click the **Close** button ⊠.

More Knowledge

About the Caption Property

The Caption property is used to give a name to the field that is used on forms and reports. Many database administrators create field names in tables that are short and abbreviated. In a form or report based on the table, a more descriptive name is desired. The value in the Caption property is used in label controls on forms and reports instead of the field name. If the Caption property is blank, the field name is used in the label control. A caption can contain up to 2,048 characters.

Objective 7
Create Data Validation Rules and Validation Text

You have practiced different techniques to help ensure that data entered into a field is valid. Data types restrict the type of data that can be entered into a field; for example, a Number field accepts numeric values. Field sizes control the number of characters that can be entered into a field. Field properties further control how data is entered into a field, including the use of input masks to require individuals to enter data in a specific way.

Another way to ensure the accuracy of data is by using the Validation Rule property. A *validation rule* is an expression that precisely defines the range of data that will be accepted in a field. An *expression* is a combination of functions, field values, constants, and operators that brings about a result. *Validation text* is the error message that displays when an individual enters a value prohibited by the validation rule.

Activity 4.20 Creating Data Validation Rules and Validation Text

In this activity, you will create data validation rules and validation text for the %Complete field, the Start Date field, and the Priority field.

1 Under **Field Name**, click **%Complete**. Under **Field Properties**, click in the **Validation Rule** box, and then click the **Build** button .

The Expression Builder dialog box displays. The *Expression Builder* is a feature used to create formulas (expressions) in query criteria, form and report properties, and table validation rules.

2 In the upper box of the **Expression Builder** dialog box, type **>=0 and <=1** Alternatively, type the expression in the Validation Rule property box. Compare your screen with Figure 4.37.

The %Complete field has a data type of Number and is formatted as a percent. Recall that the format property changes the way the stored data displays. To change the display of a number to percent, Access multiplies the value by 100 and appends the percent sign (%). Therefore, 100% is stored as 1—Access multiples 1 by 100, resulting in 100. A job that is halfway completed—50%—has the value stored as .5 because .5 times 100 equals 50. Therefore, this validation rule requires that all entries be greater than (>) or equal to 0—0%—and less than (<) or equal to 1—100%.

Figure 4.37

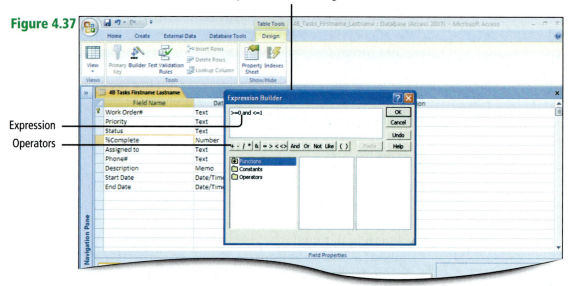

Expression Builder dialog box

Expression

Operators

Another Way

To Use the Expression Builder

When using the Expression Builder to create an expression, you can either type the entire expression or, on the small toolbar in the dialog box, click an existing button, such as the > button, to insert operators in the expression.

---

3 In the **Expression Builder** dialog box, click **OK**, and then switch to **Datasheet** view, saving changes to the table. Click **No** in the message box stating that data integrity rules have been changed.

4 In the new record row, in the **Work Order#** field, type **cm3** and then press [Tab] or [Enter] three times to move to the **%Complete** field. With **0%** selected, type **50** and then press [Tab].

Unlike the validation rule, you can type 50 to represent 50%.

5 Hold down [⇧ Shift], and then press [Tab] to move to the left one field and to select **50%**. Type **110** and then press [Tab]. Compare your screen with Figure 4.38.

A message displays stating that the validation rule prohibits the entry. This message would be very confusing to an individual who might think the only valid entries are between 0 and 1.

Figure 4.38

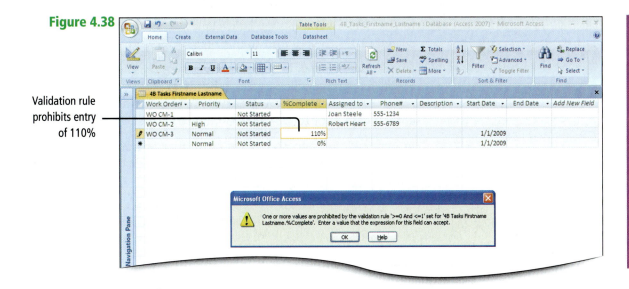

Validation rule
prohibits entry
of 110%

6. In the displayed message box, click **OK**. Under **%Complete**, select **110%**—be sure you include the % sign. Type **.03** and then press Tab. Alternatively, type 3. In the **Assigned to** field, type **Joan Steele** and then press ↓.

Access changes .03 to 3%. Because .03 is greater than 0 and less than 1, the entry is accepted.

7. Switch to **Design** view. Be sure **%Complete** is the current field. Under **Field Properties**, click in the **Validation Text** box. Type **You cannot enter a value less than 0 or greater than 100.**

8. Switch to **Datasheet** view, saving changes to the table. In the third record, in the **%Complete** field, select **3%**, type **110** and then press Tab. Compare your screen with Figure 4.39.

A message displays using the validation text you typed. This message is more helpful to the person entering the data.

Figure 4.39

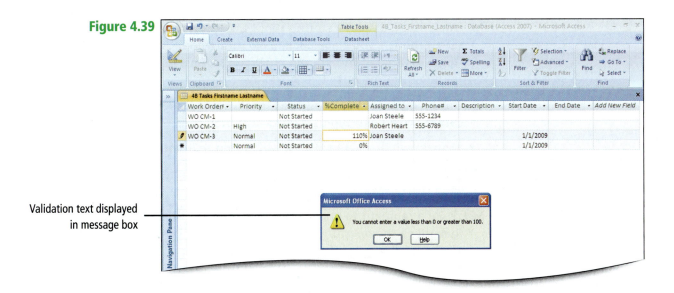

Validation text displayed
in message box

9 In the displayed message box, click **OK**. In the **%Complete** field, select **110%**, type **0** and then press ↓. Switch to **Design** view.

10 Under **Field Name**, click **Start Date** to make the field current. Under **Field Properties**, click in the **Validation Rule** box, and then type **>=1/1/2009** Click in the **Validation Text** box, and then type **You cannot enter a date prior to 1/1/2009.** Compare your screen with Figure 4.40.

In expressions, Access inserts a number or pound sign (#) before and after a date. This validation rule ensures that the person entering data cannot enter a date prior to 1/1/2009.

Figure 4.40

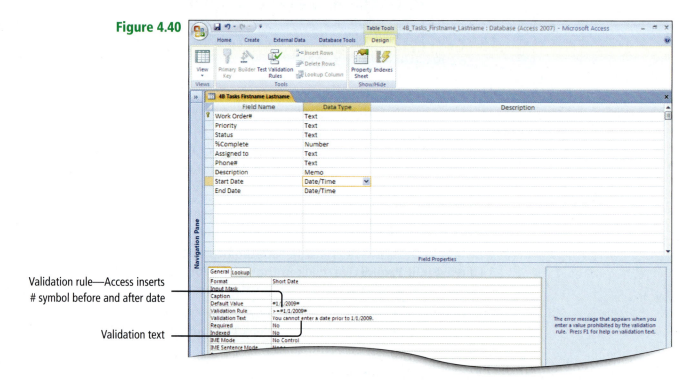

Validation rule—Access inserts # symbol before and after date

Validation text

11 Switch to **Datasheet** view, saving changes to the table.

A message displays stating that data integrity rules have changed. Even though you have clicked No in previous message boxes, in a large database, you should click Yes to have Access check the data in all of the records.

12 In the displayed message box, click **No**. In the first record, in the **Start Date** field, type **12/24/53** and then press Tab.

A message displays with the validation text you entered.

13 In the displayed message box, click **OK**. Change the year—**53**—to **9** and then press ↓.

14 Take a moment to study the table shown in Figure 4.41, which describes the operators that can be used in building expressions.

Operators Used in Expressions

Operator	Function	Example
Not	Tests for values NOT true.	**Not** > 10 (the same as <=10)
In	Tests for values equal to existing members in a list.	**In** ("High","Normal","Low")
Between. . . And	Tests for a range of values.	**Between** 0 **And** 100 (the same as >=0 **And** <=100)
Like	Matches pattern strings in Text and Memo fields.	**Like** "Car∗"
Is Not Null	Requires individuals to enter values in the field. If used in place of the Required field, you can create Validation Text that better describes what should be entered in the field.	**Is Not Null** (the same as setting Required property to Yes)
And	Specifies that all of the entered data must be true or fall within the specified limits.	>=#01/01/2009# **And** <=#03/01/2009# (Date must be between 01/01/2009 and 03/01/2009) Can use And to combine validation rules. For example, **Not** "USA" **And Like** "U∗"
Or	Specifies that one or more pieces of data can be true.	"High" **Or** "Normal" **Or** "Low"
<	Less than.	<100
<=	Less than or equal to.	<=100
>	Greater than.	>0
>=	Greater than or equal to.	>=0
=	Equal to.	=Date()
<>	Not equal to.	<>#12/24/53#

Figure 4.41

15 Switch to **Design** view. Under **Field Name**, click **Priority**. Under **Field Properties**, click in the **Validation Rule** box, and then type: **in ("High","Normal","Low")** Click in the **Validation Text** box, and then type **You must enter High, Normal, or Low.** Compare your screen with Figure 4.42.

The operators are not case sensitive; Access will capitalize the operators when you click in another property box. With the *In* operator, the members of the list must be enclosed in parentheses, and each member must be enclosed in quotation marks and separated from each other by commas. Another way to specify the same validation rule is: "High" Or "Normal" Or "Low".

Figure 4.42

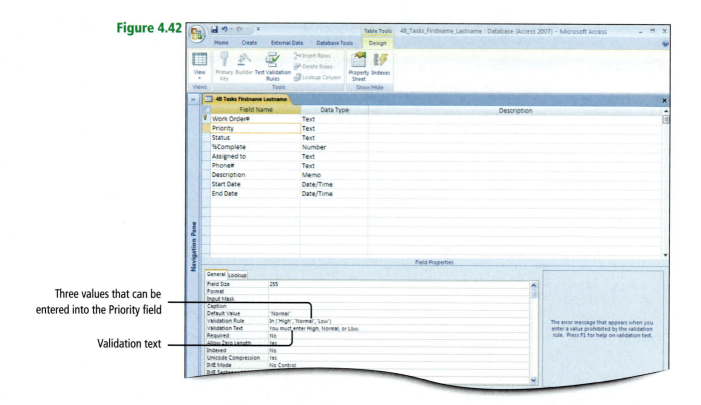

Three values that can be entered into the Priority field

Validation text

16 After verifying the accuracy of your entries into the two property boxes, switch to **Datasheet** view, saving changes to the table. In the displayed message box, click **No** to skip testing of the existing data.

17 In the first record, click in the **Priority** field, type **None** and then press Tab. A message displays with the validation text you entered. Click **OK**, select **None**, type **Low** and then press ↓ to save the record. Switch to **Design** view.

Objective 8
Create a Lookup Field

Creating a *lookup field* can restrict the data entered in a field because the person entering the data selects the data from a list that is retrieved from another table, from a query, or from a list of entered values. The choices can be displayed in a *list box*—a box containing a list of choices—or a *combo box*—a box that is a combination of a list box and a text box. You can create a lookup field by using the Lookup Wizard or manually by setting the field's lookup field properties. Whenever possible, use the Lookup Wizard because it simplifies the process, automatically populates the associated field properties, and creates the needed table relationships.

Activity 4.21 Creating a Lookup Field Based on Data in Another Table

In this activity, you will create a lookup field for the Assigned to field.

1 With the **4B Tasks** table open in **Design** view, in the **Assigned to** field, click in the **Data Type** box, and then click the **Data Type arrow**. From the displayed list of data types, click **Lookup Wizard**.

2 In the first **Lookup Wizard** dialog box, be sure that the **I want the lookup column to look up the values in a table or query** option button is selected.

The first screen of the Lookup Wizard enables you to choose whether you want Access to locate the information from another table or query or whether you would like to type the information to create a list.

3 Click **Next**. There is only one other table in this database from which to choose—4B Employees—and it is selected.

4 Click **Next** to display the third **Lookup Wizard** dialog box. Under **Available Fields**, click **Last Name**, and then click the **Add Field** button ![>] to move the field to the **Selected Fields** box. Move the **First Name** and **Job Title** fields from the **Available Fields** box to the **Selected Fields** box. Compare your screen with Figure 4.43.

Because there might be several people with the same last name, the First Name field and the Job Title field are included.

Figure 4.43

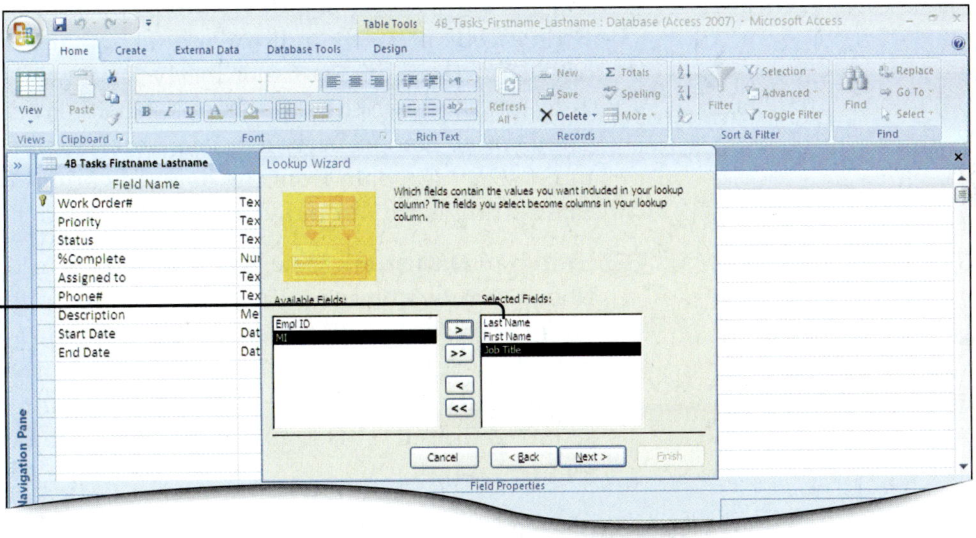

Fields from 4B Employees table

5 Click **Next** to display the fourth **Lookup Wizard** dialog box. In the **1** box, click the **arrow**, and then click **Last Name**. In the **2** box, click the **arrow**, and then click **First Name**. In the **3** box, click the **arrow**, and then click **Job Title**. Leave all three sort orders as **Ascending**.

The list will first display last names in ascending order. If there are duplicate last names, then the duplicate last names will then be sorted by the first name in ascending order. If there are duplicate last names and first names, then those names will be sorted in ascending order by the job title.

6 Click **Next** to display the fifth **Lookup Wizard** dialog box. This screen enables you to change the width of the lookup field and to display the primary key field. Be sure the **Hide key column (recommended)** check box is selected, and then click **Next** to display the sixth and final **Lookup Wizard** dialog box.

The actual data that is stored in the lookup field is the data in the primary key field.

7 Under **What label would you like for your lookup column?**, leave the default of **Assigned to** and be sure that **Allow Multiple Values** is *not* selected.

Because you have already named the field, the default name is appropriate. If you were creating a new field that had not yet been named, a label should be entered on this screen. If you want to allow the selection of more than one last name when the lookup field displays and then store the multiple values, select the Allow Multiple Values check box, which changes the lookup field to a multivalued field. A **multivalued field** holds multiple values, such as a list of people to whom you have assigned a task.

8 Click **Finish**. A message displays stating that the table must be saved before Access can create the needed relationship between the *4B Tasks* table and the *4B Employees* table. Click **Yes**.

9 With the **Assigned to** field selected, under **Field Properties**, click the **Lookup tab**.

The Lookup Wizard populates the Lookup properties boxes. The *Row Source Type* property indicates that the data is retrieved from a Table or Query. The *Row Source* property displays the SQL statement that is used to retrieve the data from the fields in the *4B Employees* table. The *Limit to List* property displays Yes, which means an individual must select the data from the list and cannot type data in the field. If this setting is No, an individual could type a value in the field.

10 Switch to **Datasheet** view, saving changes to the design of the table. Notice that by changing the field to a lookup field, Access deleted the data in the Assigned to field for each record in the table. In the first record, click in the **Assigned to** field, and then click the **arrow** to display a list of Last Names, First Names, and Job Titles that were retrieved from the *4B Employees* table. Compare your screen with Figure 4.44.

Access *looked up* the information in the *4B Employees* table to display the list in the Assigned to field.

Extracted from fields in
4B Employees table

Figure 4.44

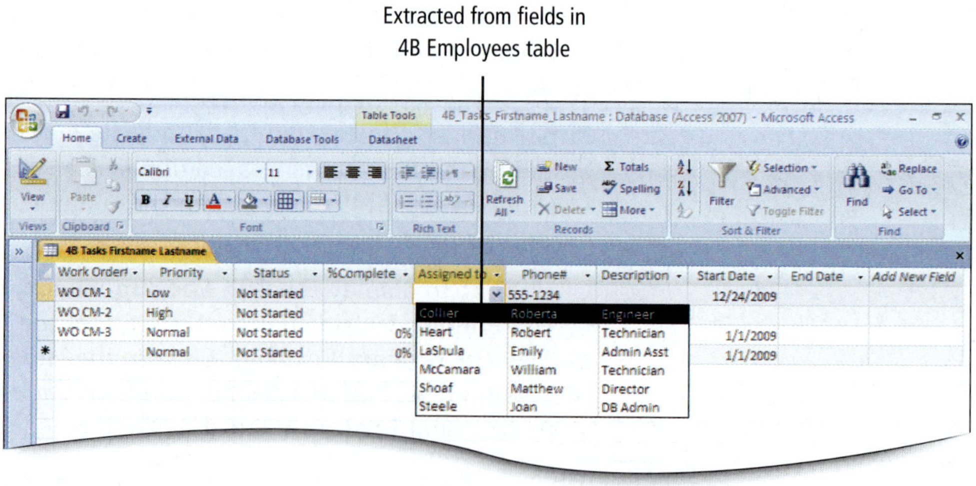

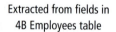

11 From the displayed list, click **Heart**, and then press ⬇.

Even though the datasheet displays *Heart* in the field, the data in the primary key field for the record is actually stored in the field. The primary key field for the *4B Employees* table is Empl ID.

Another Way

To Locate Items in a List

You can locate an entry in a long list faster if you type the first letter of the data for which you are searching. For example, if you are searching for a last name that begins with the letter *M*, when the list displays, type *m* or *M*. The selection will move down to the first entry that begins with the letter.

12 In the second record, in the **Assigned to** field, type **Hart** and then press Tab.

A message displays stating that the text you entered is not an item on the list. You can type a last name only exactly as it displays in the lookup field, or you must select the last name from the displayed list. Recall that the Limit to List property is set to Yes.

13 In the displayed message box, click **OK**, and then from the displayed list, click **Heart**.

14 In the third record, in the **Assigned to** field, display the list, click **Steele**, and then press ⬇ or ⬆ to save the record. Switch to **Design** view.

Activity 4.22 Creating a Lookup Field Based on a List of Values

In this activity, you will create a lookup field for the Status field.

1 With the **4B Tasks** table open in **Design** view, in the **Status** field, click in the **Data Type** box, and then click the **arrow**. From the displayed list of data types, click **Lookup Wizard**.

2 In the first **Lookup Wizard** dialog box, click the **I will type in the values that I want** option button, and then click **Next**. Compare your screen with Figure 4.45.

The second screen enables you to select the number of columns you want to include in the lookup field. The values are typed in the grid, and you can adjust the column width of the displayed list.

Figure 4.45

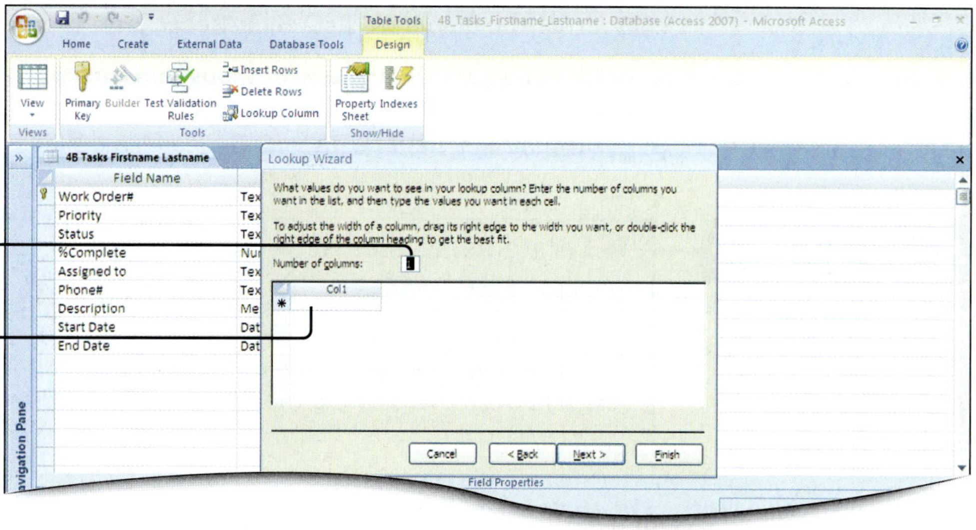

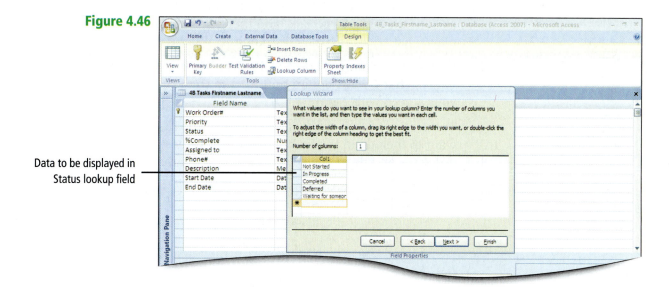

Number of columns to display in the lookup field

Type first item here

3 Be sure the number of columns is **1**. Under **Col1**, click in the first row, type **Not Started** and then press Tab or ↓ to save the first item.

If you mistakenly press Enter, the next dialog box of the wizard displays—if that happens, click the Back button.

4 Type the following data, and then compare your screen with Figure 4.46.

In Progress
Completed
Deferred
Waiting for someone else

Figure 4.46

Data to be displayed in Status lookup field

5 To widen the column, double-click the right edge of **Col1** to adjust the column width, and then click **Next**. In the final dialog box, click **Finish**. With the **Status** field selected, under **Field Properties**, if necessary, click the **Lookup tab**.

The Lookup Wizard populates the Lookup property boxes. The *Row Source Type* property indicates that the data is retrieved from a Value List, a list that you created. The *Row Source* property displays the data you entered in the list. The *Limit to List* property displays No, so an individual can type alternative data in the field.

6 Switch to **Datasheet** view, saving changes to the table. In the first record, click in the **Status** field, and then click the **arrow**. From the displayed list, click **In Progress**, and then press ↓.

Recall that the default value for the Status field is *Not Started*.

Alert!

Is the last item in the list truncated?

If the last item in the list—Waiting for someone else—is truncated, switch to Design view. Select the field. Under Field Properties, on the Lookup tab, click in the List Width box, and then increase the width of the list box by typing a larger number than the one displayed.

7 In the second record, in the **Status** field, select **Not Started**, type **None** and then press ↓ to save the record.

Recall that the Limit to List property setting is set to No, enabling you to type data other than that displayed in the list box. If the purpose of the lookup field is to restrict individuals from entering only certain data, then the Limit to List property setting should be set to Yes.

8 Switch to **Design** view.

Objective 9
Attach Files to Records

The attachment data type can be used to add one or more files to the records in a database. For example, if you have a database for a coin collection, you can attach a picture of each coin and a Word document that contains a description of the coin. Access stores the attached files in their native formats—if you attach a Word document, it is saved as a Word document. By default, fields contain only one piece of data; however, you can attach more than one file by using the attachment data type. As you attach files to a record, Access creates one or more **system tables** to keep track of the multiple entries in the field. You cannot view or work with these system tables.

Activity 4.23 Attaching a Word Document to a Record

In this activity, you will attach a Work Order Report that was created in Word to records in the *4B Tasks* table.

1 With the **4B Tasks** table open in **Design** view, click in the empty field name box under **End Date**, type **Work Order** and then press Tab to move to the **Data Type** box. Click the **Data Type arrow**, click **Attachment**, and then press Enter. Under **Field Properties**, click the **General tab**, and notice that only two field properties—**Caption** and **Required**—are displayed for an Attachment field.

Depending on the data type of a field, different field properties display.

2 Switch to **Datasheet** view, saving changes to the table. If necessary, scroll to the right to display the newly created Attachment field. Notice that the field name of *Work Order* does not display; instead, a paper clip symbol displays. In the first record, *(0)* displays after the paper clip symbol, indicating that there are no attachments for this record.

Because multiple files can be attached to a record, the name of the field displays the paper clip symbol.

3 In the first record, double-click in the **Attachment** field. In the displayed **Attachments** dialog box, click **Add**. Navigate to the location where the student data files for this textbook are saved. In the **Choose File** dialog box, double-click **a04B_WorkOrder_1**, and then compare your screen with Figure 4.47.

The Word document is added to the Attachments dialog box. You can attach multiple files to the same record.

Indicates number of
attachments for this record

Attachment field

Figure 4.47

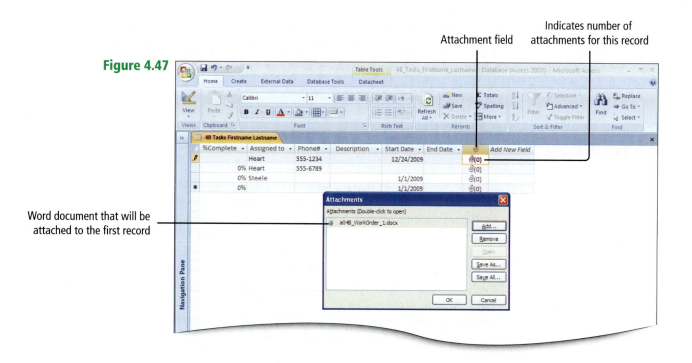

Word document that will be
attached to the first record

4 In the **Attachments** dialog box, click **OK**. Notice that the **Attachment** field now indicates there is **1** attachment for the first record.

5 In the first record, double-click in the **Attachment** field. In the **Attachments** dialog box, click **a04B_WorkOrder_1.docx**, and then click **Open**.

Word opens, and the document displays. You can make changes to the document, and then save it in the database.

6 **Close** ☒ Word. In the **Attachments** dialog box, click **OK**. Press ↓ to save the record.

Note — Saving Changes to an Attached File

When you open an attached file in the program that was used to create it, Access places a temporary copy of the file in a temporary folder on the hard drive of your computer. If you change the file and save changes, Access saves the changes in the temporary copy. Closing the program used to view the attachment returns you to Access. When you click OK to close the Attachments dialog box, Access prompts you to save the attached file again. Click Yes to save the changes to the attached file in the database, or click No to keep the original, unedited version in the database.

To find the location of your temporary folder, start Internet Explorer. On the Tools menu, click Internet Options. On the General tab, click Settings. In the Settings dialog box, the temporary folder path displays in the Temporary Internet Files folder section.

7 If necessary, scroll to the left to display the first field in the table. In the first record, click in the **Work Order#** field, select **CM**, type **es** and then press Tab to move to the Priority field.

The Work Order# should begin with the initials of the person who filled out the work order form. Emily Shula is the Administrative Assistant for the Information Technology Department, so the initials *es* are used. Recall that the Work Order# field is the primary key field, which makes it a required field. An input mask was created that automatically inserts WO, capitalizes the two required letters, and inserts a hyphen after the letters.

8 In the **Priority** field, select **Low**, type **High** and then press Tab or Enter.

Recall that the Priority field has a default value of Normal, and a validation rule—with validation text—was created to ensure that you can enter only High, Normal, or Low.

9 In the **Status** field, press Tab or Enter to move to the %Complete field.

Recall that the Status field has a default value of Not Started, data is required for the field, and the field was changed to a lookup field that displays a list of values from which to choose. Data entered in this field is not limited to the text displayed in the list.

10 In the **%Complete** field, type **30** and then press ⟨Tab⟩ or ⟨Enter⟩ to move to the Assigned to field.

Recall that the %Complete field has a default value of 0 and a validation rule with validation text to limit the entry to numbers from 0 to 1 (0% to 100%).

11 In the **Assigned to** field, press ⟨Tab⟩ or ⟨Enter⟩.

Recall that the Assigned to field is indexed and displays a list of last names from the *4B Employees* table.

12 In the **Phone#** field, change the phone number to **5556789** and then press ⟨Tab⟩.

Recall that the Phone# field has an input mask that was created using the Input Mask Wizard.

13 In the **Description** field, type **Computer Virus** and then press ⟨Tab⟩.

Recall that the Description field is a Memo field.

14 In the **Start Date** field, with the date selected, type **6/1/9** and then press ⟨↓⟩ to save the record. Compare your screen with Figure 4.48.

Recall that the Start Date field has a default value of 1/1/2009 and has a validation rule and validation text requiring that the date be either 1/1/2009 or after 1/1/2009. The field is formatted as short date, so the field displays 6/1/2009.

Figure 4.48

Data for first record ———

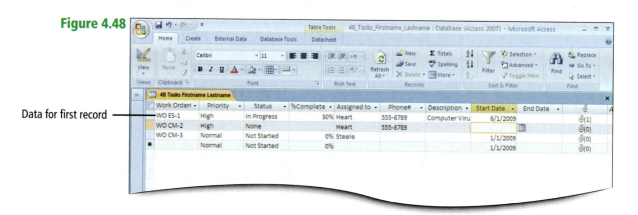

15 Enter the following data for **Record 4**—a new record. Do not enter any data in the End Date field. The attachment is located in the student data files.

Work Order#	Priority	Status	%Complete	Assigned to	Phone#	Description	Start Date	End Date	Attachment
es2	Low	Waiting for someone else	50	Collier	555-8899	Printer	6/1/9		a04B_WorkOrder_2

16 Adjust all column widths, ensuring that all of the field names and all of the field data display. View the table in **Print Preview**, and then change the orientation to **Landscape**. Adjust the margins to display the table on one page, and be sure that the table name, date, and page number display. If you are instructed to submit this result, create a paper or electronic printout.

17 **Close** ☒ the table, saving changes. Expand ☒ the **Navigation Pane**. **Close** the database, and **Exit** Access.

End You have completed Project 4B ———————————

There's More You Can Do!

From My Computer, navigate to the student files that accompany this textbook. In the folder **02_theres_more_you_can_do**, locate and open the folder for this chapter. Open and print the instructions for this project, which are provided to you in Adobe PDF format.

Try It! 1—Modify an Existing Field to Store Rich Text Data

In this Try It! exercise, you will enable a memo field to store data in Rich Text Format.

Try It! 2—Create a Multivalued Lookup Field

In this Try It! exercise, you will create a multivalued lookup field.

Content-Based Assessments

Summary

A well-designed database avoids using tables with redundant data. In this chapter, you examined a poorly designed database and redesigned it to remove redundant data. You copied tables within the database and appended table information from another database. You established a one-to-many relationship and a one-to-one relationship between the database tables to reduce data redundancy and to increase data entry accuracy. Using the established relationships, you entered data into the related tables by opening one table, expanding the subdatasheets, and entering data into the tables. You set referential integrity, cascade update, and cascade delete options to ensure that changes made to one table did not adversely affect the data in other related tables. You customized the Navigation Pane by creating custom groups and displaying the Search box. You also used the Backup feature to create a duplicate of the original database.

Using field properties, you controlled the data that is entered into a field. You practiced changing data types and added an Attachment field. You practiced setting default values, creating input masks, requiring data to be entered into the field, creating validation rules and validation text, and creating lookup fields. In addition, you indexed fields to speed up searches.

Key Terms

The 🌐 symbol represents Key Terms found on the Student CD in the 03_theres_more_you_can_do folder for this chapter.

Content-Based Assessments

Matching

Match each term in the second column with its correct definition in the first column. Write the letter of the term on the blank line in front of the correct definition.

_____ **1.** To make a copy of the original database.

_____ **2.** A temporary storage area in Windows.

_____ **3.** A command that moves the selected table from the Clipboard into a new location.

_____ **4.** Records that reference deleted records in a related table.

_____ **5.** The table that breaks down the many-to-many relationship into two one-to-many relationships.

_____ **6.** The option that enables you to change a primary key field and updates the records in the related tables.

_____ **7.** An attribute or characteristic of a field that controls the display and input of data.

_____ **8.** Determines the data that can be entered, how the data displays, and how the data is stored.

_____ **9.** Rules that help prevent individuals from entering invalid data and help ensure that individuals enter data in a consistent manner.

_____ **10.** Two quotation marks with no space between them, indicating no value exists for a required field.

_____ **11.** A special list created in Access to speed up searches and sorting.

_____ **12.** An expression that precisely defines a range of data that will be accepted in a field.

_____ **13.** The error message that displays when an individual enters a value prohibited by the validation rule.

_____ **14.** A feature used to create formulas in query criteria, form and report properties, and table validation rules.

_____ **15.** A field that holds multiple values, such as a list of people to whom you have assigned a task.

A Back up

B Cascade Update

C Clipboard

D Data validation

E Expression Builder

F Field property

G Index

H Input mask

I Junction table

J Multivalued field

K Orphan records

L Paste

M Validation rule

N Validation text

O Zero-length string

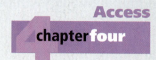

Fill in the Blank

Write the correct word in the space provided.

1. To add one or more records from another source of a table end is to _____ the records.

2. Access will append all records from the _____ table into the _____ table.

3. Each time you start Access, you open a(n) _____ of it.

4. _____ changes affect all Navigation Pane categories.

5. On the join line, the *1* indicates the *one* side of the relationship, and the infinity symbol (∞) indicates the *many* side of the relationship if _____ _____ is enforced.

6. By enforcing referential integrity in a(n) _____ relationship, each record in the first table can have only one matching record in the second table, and each record in the second table can have only one matching record in the first table.

7. To create a many-to-many relationship between two tables, you must create a(n) _____ table that breaks down the many-to-many relationship into two one-to-many relationships.

8. To ensure that orphan records are not left in the database, use the _____ _____ option.

9. To ensure that a field contains data and is not left empty, use the _____ _____ property.

10. To display a value in a field for new records, use the _____ _____ field property.

11. An expression that precisely defines the range of data that will be accepted in a field is called a(n) _____ _____.

12. A combination of functions, field values, constants, and operators that brings about a result is called a(n) _____.

13. To restrict the data entered in a field to a list that is retrieved from another table, query, or list entered by an individual, create a(n) _____ _____.

14. When creating a lookup field, the choices can be displayed in a _____ box or a(n) _____ box.

15. A table that cannot be viewed by an individual but is created by Access to keep track of data is called a(n) _____ table.

Skills Review

Project 4C—Industries

In this project, you will apply the skills you practiced from the Objectives in Project 4A.

Objectives: 1. *Modify Existing Tables;* **2.** *Customize the Navigation Pane;* **3.** *Create and Modify Table Relationships;* **4.** *Enter Records Using a Subdatasheet.*

Joaquin Alonzo, the City Manager of Westland Plains, has a database of the city's industry information. This database has five tables. The Industries table contains summary information from the other four tables. Each update to an individual industry table would require updates to the summary table. In the following Skills Review, you will redesign the tables, taking advantage of table relationships to avoid entering and storing redundant data. Your completed tables and relationships will look similar to those in Figure 4.49.

For Project 4C, you will need the following files:

a04C_Industries
New blank Word document

You will save your database as
4C_Industries_Firstname_Lastname
You will save your document as
4C_Navigation_Pane_Firstname_Lastname

Figure 4.49

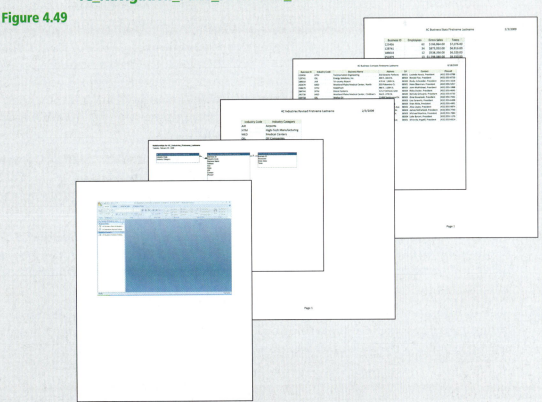

(Project 4C–Industries continues on the next page)

(Project 4C–Industries continued)

1. **Start** Access. Locate and open the **a04C_Industries** file. From the **Office** menu, point to **Manage**, and then click **Back Up Database**. In the **Save As** dialog box, navigate to the drive on which you will be storing your folders and projects for this chapter, and then click **Save** to accept the default name. **Save** the database in the **Access 2007 Database** format in your **Access Chapter 4** folder as 4C_Industries_Firstname_Lastname

2. On the **Navigation Pane**, double-click **4C Industries**. Take a moment to review the contents of the table, and then **Close** the table. On the **Home tab**, in the **Clipboard group**, click the **Copy** button. In the **Clipboard group**, click the **Paste** button.

3. In the displayed **Paste Table As** dialog box, under **Table Name**, type 4C Industries Revised Firstname Lastname Under **Paste Options**, be sure that the **Structure and Data** option button is selected, and then click **OK**. Double-click **4C Industries Revised** to open the table in **Datasheet** view. Collapse the **Navigation Pane**.

4. Point to the **Business #5** field name until the ⬇ pointer displays. Drag to the left to the **Business #1** field name to select the five fields. On the **Home tab**, in the **Records group**, click the **Delete** button. In the displayed message box, click **Yes** to permanently delete the fields and the data.

5. Switch to **Design** view. To the left of **Industry Code**, click the **row selector** box, and then in the **Tools group**, click the **Primary Key** button. **Close** the table, saving any changes, and then expand the **Navigation Pane**.

6. Using the technique you practiced in Step 3, copy and paste the structure and data of the **4C Airports** table, and then **Save** the pasted table as 4C Business Contacts Firstname Lastname

7. On the **Navigation Pane**, click **4C High-Tech Manufacturing**. On the **Home tab**, in the **Clipboard group**, click the **Copy** button, and then click the **Paste** button. In the **Paste Table As** dialog box, under **Table Name**, type 4C Business Contacts Firstname Lastname Under **Paste Options**, click the **Append Data to Existing Table** option button, and then click **OK**. Using the same procedure, append the **4C Medical Centers** table and the **4C Oil Companies** table to the **4C Business Contacts Firstname Lastname** table.

8. Repeat the procedure, copying and pasting the structure and data of the **4C Business Contacts** table, and then naming the pasted table **4C Business Stats Firstname Lastname** One table will contain only contact information, and the other table will contain only statistical information.

9. Open the **4C Business Contacts** table, and then collapse the **Navigation Pane**. Select the **Employees**, **Gross Sales**, and **Taxes** field names. On the **Home tab**, in the **Records group**, click the **Delete** button. In the displayed message box, click **Yes** to permanently delete the fields and data.

10. Click the **Business Name** field name. On the Ribbon, click the **Datasheet tab**. In the **Fields & Columns group**, click the **Insert** button. In the **Fields & Columns group**, click the **Rename** button, type Industry Code and then press Enter. **Save** your work.

(Project 4C–Industries continues on the next page)

Content-Based Assessments

Skills Review

(Project 4C–Industries continued)

11. In the first record—Business ID **189018**—click in the **Industry Code** field. Expand the **Navigation Pane**, and then open the **4C Industries Revised** table. Under **Industry Category**, locate the record for the **Airports**, and notice the **Industry Code** of **AIR**. On the **tab row**, click the **4C Business Contacts tab** to make the table current. In the **Business ID** of **189018**, in the **Industry Code** field, type AIR Locate the **Business ID** of **675234**, and then in the **Industry Code** field, type AIR

12. Using the techniques you just practiced, locate the **Industry Codes** for the **High-Tech Manufacturing**, **Medical Center**, and **Oil Company** Industry Categories. In **Records 3 through 7**, type HTM In **Records 8 through 11**, type MED and then in **Records 12 through 15**, type OIL

13. Switch the **4C Business Contacts** table to **Design** view. With the insertion point in the **Business ID** field, in the **Tools group**, click the **Primary Key** button. **Save** the changes.

14. Open the **4C Business Stats** table, and then collapse the **Navigation Pane**. Select the **Business Name** field, and then press Delete. Click **Yes** to delete the field and data. Scroll to the right to display the **Address**, **City**, **State**, **ZIP**, **Contact**, and **Phone#** fields. Select all six fields, and then on the **Home tab**, in the **Records group**, click the **Delete** button. In the displayed message box, click **Yes** to permanently delete the fields and data.

15. Switch the **4C Business Stats** table to **Design** view, set the **Business ID** field as the primary key field, and then **Save** the changes. On the **tab row**, right-click any table tab, and then click **Close All**.

16. Expand the **Navigation Pane**. Right-click the **Navigation Pane title**, and then click **Navigation Options**. In the displayed **Navigation Options** dialog box, click **Add Item**. With the new category name selected and using your own first and last name, type **My Tables Firstname Lastname** and then press Enter.

17. Under **Groups for "My Tables"**, click **Add Group**, type **Business Contacts** and then press Enter. Click **Add Group**, type **Business Stats** and then press Enter. To the right of **Business Stats**, click the **Move Up arrow**. Be sure the check boxes next to all of the groups, including the Unassigned Objects group, are selected, and then click **OK**. Click the **Navigation Pane title**, and then click **My Tables**.

18. On the **Navigation Pane**, under **Unassigned Objects**, right-click **4C Industries Revised**. From the shortcut menu, point to **Add to group**, and then click **Business Stats**. Under **Unassigned Objects**, drag the **4C Business Stats** table to the **Business Stats** group. Using one of the two techniques you just practiced, add the **4C Business Contacts** table to the **Business Contacts** group.

19. Right-click the **Navigation Pane title**, and then click **Navigation Options**. In the displayed **Navigation Options** dialog box, under **Categories**, click **My Tables**. Under **Groups for "My Tables"**, clear the **Unassigned Objects** check box, and then click **OK**. If necessary, under Display Options, if Show Hidden Objects is selected, clear the option.

(Project 4C–Industries continues on the next page)

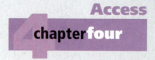

(Project 4C–Industries continued)

20. Hold down Alt, and then press PrtScr to place a copy of the window in the Clipboard. Start **Word 2007**. Hold down Ctrl, and then press V. **Save** the document in your **Access Chapter 4** folder as **4C_Navigation_Pane_Firstname_Lastname** If you are instructed to submit this result, create a paper or electronic printout. **Exit** Word.

21. Collapse the **Navigation Pane**. On the Ribbon, click the **Database Tools tab**. In the **Show/Hide group**, click the **Relationships** button. If the Show Table dialog box does not display, on the Design tab, in the Relationships group, click the Show Table button. From the **Show Table** dialog box, add the **4C Industries Revised**, **4C Business Contacts**, and the **4C Business Stats** tables, and then click **Close**.

22. Expand the field lists to display the entire table name and all of the fields. In the **4C Industries Revised** field list, drag the **Industry Code** field to the right to the **4C Business Contacts** field list until the 🖰 pointer points to **Industry Code**, and then release the mouse button. In the displayed **Edit Relationships** dialog box, select the **Enforce Referential Integrity**, **Cascade Update Related Fields**, and **Cascade Delete Related Records** check boxes. In the **Edit Relationships** dialog box, click **Create**.

23. In the **4C Business Contacts** field list, drag the **Business ID** field to the right to the **4C Business Stats** field list until the 🖰 pointer points to **Business ID**, and then release the mouse button. In the displayed **Edit Relationships** dialog box, select the **Enforce Referential Integrity** check box. Click **Create**.

24. On the **Design tab**, in the **Tools group**, click the **Relationship Report** button. On the **Print Preview tab**, in the **Page Layout group**, click the **Landscape** button. If you are instructed to submit this result, create a paper or electronic printout. To close the **Print Preview** window, on the **tab row**, click the **Close** button, and then click **Yes** to save the report. In the displayed **Save As** dialog box, click **OK** to accept the default report name.

25. Click the **join line** between the **4C Business Contacts** field list and the **4C Business Stats** field list. On the **Design tab**, in the **Tools group**, click the **Edit Relationships** button. In the displayed **Edit Relationships** dialog box, select the **Cascade Update Related Fields** check box and the **Cascade Delete Related Records** check box, and then click **OK**. **Close** the Relationships window, and then expand the **Navigation Pane**.

26. Open the **4C Business Contacts** table. Locate the record for **Business ID 927685**. In the **Business ID** field, select **927685**, type **123456** and then press ↓ to save the record. Locate the record for the **Business ID** of **420943**. Click in the record selector box to select the record. On the **Home tab**, in the **Records group**, click the **Delete** button. In the displayed message box, click **Yes**. **Close** the table.

27. Open **4C Industries Revised**, and then collapse the **Navigation Pane**. Locate the record for the **HTM** in the **Industry Code** field, and then click the plus sign (**+**) to expand the sub-datasheet. In the fourth record—**Business ID** of **123456**—click the plus sign to expand the subdatasheet. In the **Employees** field in the first record, select **59**. Type **62** and then press ↓

(Project 4C–Industries continues on the next page)

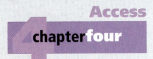

(Project 4C–Industries continued)

to save. Collapse the subdatasheet. In the subdatasheet, on the new record row, click the **Business ID** field, type **284744** and then press ⟨Tab⟩. Continue entering the data for the new industry by using the following information:

Business Name	Address	City	State	ZIP	Contact	Phone #
Dozier Systems	1212 Techway Lane	Westland Plains	TX	88504	Ricky Dozier, President	(432) 555-4645

28. In the subdatasheet, expand the subdatasheet for the new record—**Business ID** of **284744**. In the subdatasheet for the *4C Business Stats* table, click in the **Employees** field, and then type **189** Click in the **Gross Sales** field, and then type **2374963** Click in the **Taxes** field, and then type **15774**

29. Collapse both subdatasheets. If you are instructed to submit this result, create a paper or electronic printout of the table. **Close** the **4C Industries Revised** table. Expand the **Navigation Pane**, open the **4C Business Contacts** table, and then **hide** the **City** and **State** fields. Open the **4C Business Stats** table. Adjust column widths and margins if necessary. If you are instructed to submit this result, create a paper or electronic printout of these tables.

30. **Close** the database, and **Exit** Access.

 You have completed Project 4C ————————————————

Access

Skills Review

Project 4D — Airport Employees

In this project, you will apply the skills you practiced from the Objectives in Project 4B.

Objectives: 5. *Change Data Types;* **6.** *Set Field Properties;* **7.** *Create Data Validation Rules and Validation Text;* **8.** *Create a Lookup Field;* **9.** *Attach Files to Records.*

Joaquin Alonzo, City Manager of Westland Plains, Texas, has created a table to keep track of airport personnel. In the following Skills Review, you will modify the properties and customize the fields in the table that stores records about the employees. You will add features to the database table that will help to reduce data entry errors and that will make data entry easier. You will add attachments to records. Your completed table will look similar to the table shown in Figure 4.50.

> #### For Project 4D, you will need the following files:
>
> a04D_Airport_Employees
> a04D_Service_Award
> Two new blank Word documents

You will save your database as 4D_Airport_Employees_Firstname_Lastname
You will save your documents as 4D_Indexes_Firstname_Lastname 4D_Validation_Firstname_Lastname

Figure 4.50

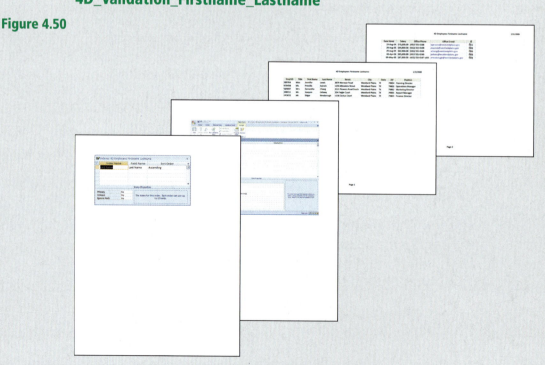

(Project 4D–Airport Employees continues on the next page)

Content-Based Assessments

Skills Review

(Project 4D–Airport Employees continued)

1. **Start** Access. Locate and open the **a04D_Airport_Employees** file. **Save** the database in the **Access 2007 Database** format in your **Access Chapter 4** folder as 4D_Airport_Employees_Firstname_Lastname

2. On the **Navigation Pane**, under **Tables**, rename the **4D Employees** table by adding your **Firstname Lastname** to the end of the table name. Double-click **4D Employees** to open the table. Collapse the **Navigation Pane**.

3. Switch to **Design** view. Change the data type for the **Date Hired** field to **Date/Time**. Change the data type for the **Salary** field to **Currency**. Change the data type for the **Office E-mail** field to **Hyperlink**. **Save** your work. You will see a message box warning that some data may be lost. Click **Yes** to continue.

4. Under **Field Name**, click **Office Phone**. Under **Field Properties**, click in the **Input Mask** box. In the **Input Mask** box, click the **Build** button.

5. In the displayed **Input Mask Wizard** dialog box, with **Phone Number** selected, click **Edit List**. In the **Customize Input Mask Wizard** dialog box, click the **New (blank) record** button. In the **Description** box, type **Phone Number with Extension** In the **Input Mask** box, type **!(999) 000-0000 \X999** Click in the **Placeholder** box, and then change _ to # Click in the **Sample Data** box, and then change **(###) ###-#### x###** to **(432) 555-1234 X236** In the **Customize Input Mask Wizard** dialog box, click **Close**.

6. Under **Input Mask**, scroll down, click **Phone Number with Extension**, and then click **Next**. Be sure that # is displayed as the placeholder character, and then click **Next**. The next wizard screen enables you to decide how you want to store the data. Be sure that the **Without the symbols in the mask, like this** option button is selected, and then click **Next**. In the final wizard screen, click **Finish**.

7. Click in the **Date Hired** field. Under **Field Properties**, click in the **Format** box, and then click the **Format arrow**. From the displayed list, click **Medium Date**. Click in the **Required** box. Click the **Required arrow**, and then click **Yes**.

8. Under **Field Name**, click **State**. Under **Field Properties**, click in the **Default Value** box, and then type **TX** Using the same technique, set the **Default Value** of the **City** field to **Westland Plains**

9. Under **Field Name**, click **Last Name**. Under **Field Properties**, click in the **Indexed** property box, and then click the displayed **arrow**. Click **Yes (Duplicates OK)**. **Save** your work. In the message box, click **Yes** to test the existing data with the new rules. On the **Design tab**, in the **Show/Hide group**, click the **Indexes** button. Hold down Alt, and then press PrtScr. Start **Word 2007**. Press Ctrl + V. **Save** the document in your **Access Chapter 4** folder as **4D_Indexes_Firstname_Lastname** If you are instructed to submit this result, create a paper or electronic printout. **Exit** Word. **Close** Indexes.

10. Under **Field Name**, click **Date Hired**. Under **Field Properties**, click in the **Validation Rule** box, and then click the **Build** button. In the upper box of the **Expression Builder** dialog box, type **<now()** and then click **OK**. Click in the **Validation Text** box, and then type **You cannot enter a date later than or equal to today** Hold down Alt, and then press PrtScr. Start **Word 2007**. Hold down Ctrl, and

(Project 4D–Airport Employees continues on the next page)

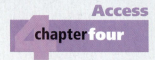
(Project 4D–Airport Employees continued)

then press V. **Save** the document in your **Access Chapter 4** folder as **4D_Validation_Firstname_Lastname** If you are instructed to submit this result, create a paper or electronic printout. **Exit** Word.

11. With the **4D Employees** table open in **Design** view, in the **Position** field, click in the **Data Type** box, and then click the **arrow**. From the displayed list of data types, click **Lookup Wizard**. In the first **Lookup Wizard** dialog box, be sure that **I want the lookup column to look up the values in a table or query** is selected. Click **Next**. There is only one other table in this database from which to choose—4D Positions—and it is selected. Click **Next** to display the third **Lookup Wizard** dialog box. Under **Available Fields**, click **Position**, and then click the **Add Field** button to move the field to the **Selected Fields** box.

12. Click **Next** to display the fourth **Lookup Wizard** dialog box. In the **1** box, click the **arrow**, and then click **Position**. Leave the sort order as **Ascending**. Click **Next** to display the fifth **Lookup Wizard** dialog box. Click **Next** to display the sixth and final **Lookup Wizard** dialog box. Under **What label would you like for your lookup column?**, leave the default of **Position** and be sure that **Allow Multiple Values** is *not* selected. Click **Finish**. Click **Yes**. In the message box, click **Yes** to test the existing data with the new rules.

13. With the **4D Employees** table open in **Design** view, in the **Title** field, click in the **Data Type** box, and then click the **arrow**. From the displayed list of data types, click **Lookup Wizard**. In the first **Lookup Wizard** dialog box, click **I will type in the values that I want** option button, and then click **Next**. Be sure the number of

columns is **1**. Click in the first row under **Col1**, type **Mr.** and then press Tab or ↓ to save the first item. Type the following data: **Mrs.** and **Miss** and **Ms.** and then click **Next**. In the final dialog box, click **Finish**.

14. With the **4D Employees** table open in **Design** view, click in the blank field name box under **Office E-mail**, type **Service Award** and then press Tab to move to the **Data Type** box. Click the **Data Type arrow**, click **Attachment**, and then press Enter.

15. Switch to **Datasheet** view, saving changes to the table. In the first record, double-click in the **Attachment** field. In the displayed **Attachments** dialog box, click **Add**. Navigate to the location where the student data files for this textbook are stored. In the **Choose File** dialog box, double-click **a04D_Service_Award**. In the **Attachments** dialog box, click **OK**.

16. Click the **New (blank) record** button. Type the following data:

Empl ID: **543655**
Title: **Mr.**
First Name: **Edgar**
Last Name: **Newbrough**
Street: **1136 Cactus Court**
City: **Westland Plains**
State: **TX**
ZIP: **79803**
Position: **Finance Director**
Date Hired: **5/09/03**
Salary: **87000**
Office Phone: **(432) 555-0167 X101**
Office E-mail: **enewbrough@ westlandplains.gov**

17. If you are instructed to submit this result, create a paper or electronic printout of the **4D Employees** table in **Landscape** orientation. This table will print on two pages. **Close 4D Employees**. From the

(Project 4D–Airport Employees continues on the next page)

(Project 4D–Airport Employees continued)

Database Tools tab, in the **Analyze group**, click the **Database Documenter** button. In the **Documenter** window, under the **Tables tab**, select the **4D Employees** check box. Click **OK**. **Print** the **Object Definition**. If you are to

submit your work electronically, follow your instructor's directions.

18. Expand the **Navigation Pane**. **Close** the **Object Definition** window. **Close** the database, and **Exit** Access.

End **You have completed Project 4D** ————————————————————

Mastering Access

Project 4E—Arts Council

In this project, you will apply the skills you practiced from the Objectives in Project 4A.

Objectives: 1. *Modify Existing Tables;* **2.** *Customize the Navigation Pane;* **3.** *Create and Modify Table Relationships;* **4.** *Enter Records Using a Subdatasheet.*

In the following Mastering Access project, you will modify tables, create relationships, and enter records in a subdatasheet for the database that contains cultural information about the city of Westland Plains. The database will be used by the arts council. Your completed tables and report will look similar to those in Figure 4.51.

For Project 4E, you will need the following file:

a04E_Arts_Council

You will save your database as
4E_Arts_Council_Firstname_Lastname
You will save your document as
4E_Navigation_Pane_Firstname_Lastname

Figure 4.51

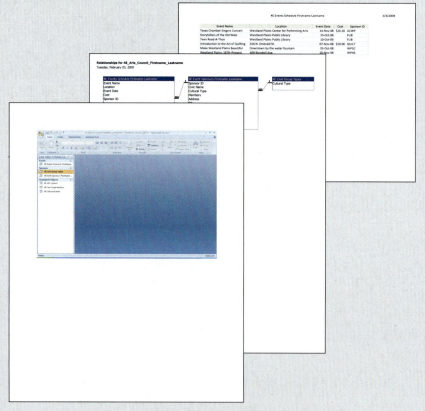

(Project 4E–Arts Council continues on the next page)

Mastering Access

(Project 4E–Arts Council continued)

1. **Start** Access. Locate and open the **a04E_Arts_Council** file. **Save** the database in the **Access 2007 Database** format in your **Access Chapter 4** folder as **4E_Arts_Council_Firstname_Lastname**

2. Right-click the **4E Cultural Events** table. Select **Copy**, and then in the clear area of the **Navigation Pane**, right-click and select **Paste**. In the **Paste Table As** dialog box, in the **Table Name** box, type 4E Events Schedule Firstname Lastname The **Paste Options** should include **Structure and Data**. Click **OK**.

3. Make a second copy of the **4E Cultural Events** table. Name the table **4E Event Sponsors Firstname Lastname** and maintain the **Structure and Data** of the source table.

4. Open the **4E Event Sponsors** table in **Datasheet** view. Select the first four columns beginning with the **Event Name** field through the **Cost** field. Press Delete, and then click **Yes** to delete the fields and data. Switch to **Design** view, and then make the **Sponsor ID** field the **Primary Key** field. **Close** and **Save** the changes to the **4E Event Sponsors** table.

5. Open the **4E Events Schedule** table in **Datasheet** view. Select and delete the following fields: **Civic Name**, **Cultural Type**, **Members**, **Address**, **City**, **St**, **ZIP**, **Contact**, and **Phone#**. **Close** and **Save** the table.

6. Customize the **Navigation Pane** by creating a **Category** named Event Tables Firstname Lastname To this category add two groups named **Events** and **Sponsors** Accept the default settings for **Display Options** and **Open Objects with Double-click**. Click **OK**. Click the **Navigation Pane down arrow**, and then select **Event Tables** as the title for the pane. Move the **4E Events Schedule** table to the **Events** group, and then move the **4E Event Sponsors** and **4E Civic Group Types** tables to the **Sponsors** group. Use the Alt Hold down, and then press PrtScr. **Start** Word 2007. Press Ctrl. **Save** the document as **4E_Navigation_Pane_Firstname_Lastname** If you are instructed to submit this result, create a paper or electronic printout and then **Exit** Word. Collapse the **Navigation Pane**.

7. Create a relationship between the **4E Events Schedule** and the **4E Event Sponsors** tables using **Sponsor ID** as the common field. Select **Enforce Referential Integrity**, **Cascade Update Related Fields**, and **Cascade Delete Related Records**.

8. Create a relationship between the **4E Civic Group Types** table and the **4E Event Sponsors** table using **Cultural Type** as the common field. Check **Enforce Referential Integrity**, **Cascade Update Related Fields**, and **Cascade Delete Related Records**. Adjust all field lists so that all table names and field names display.

9. Create a **Relationship Report**. Accept the default name for the report. If you are instructed to submit this result, create a paper or electronic printout. **Close** the **Relationships** window.

10. Expand the Navigation Pane. Open the **4E Civic Group Types** table in **Datasheet** view. Collapse the Navigation Pane. Under **Cultural Type**, expand the **Service** field. Under **Sponsor ID**, expand **FLIB**. Add the following event:

Event Name	Location	Event Date	Cost
Teen Read-A-Thon	Westland Plains Public Library	10/10/09	

(Project 4E–Arts Council continues on the next page)

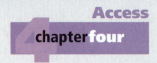

(Project 4E–Arts Council continued)

11. Collapse the subdatasheets. Close the **4E Civic Group Types** table. Open the **4E Events Schedule** table in **Datasheet** view, and then confirm that the new record displays. **Print** the table in **Landscape** orientation. If you are instructed to submit this result, create a paper or electronic printout.

12. **Close** the table. Expand the **Navigation Pane**. **Close** the database, and **Exit** Access.

End **You have completed Project 4E** —————————————————————

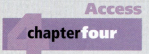

Mastering Access

Project 4F — Library Programs

In this project, you will apply the skills you practiced from the Objectives in Project 4B.

Objectives: 5. *Change Data Types;* **6.** *Set Field Properties;* **7.** *Create Data Validation Rules and Validation Text;* **8.** *Create a Lookup Field;* **9.** *Attach Files to Records.*

Joaquin Alonzo, City Manager, has asked Amanda Hartigan, Deputy Manager for the Quality of Life Division of the city, to improve the library database. In the following Mastering Access project, you will modify the properties and customize the fields in the table that stores records about the Westland Plains Library. You will add features to the database table that will help to reduce data entry errors and that will make data entry easier. You will add attachments to records. Your completed table will look similar to the table shown in Figure 4.52.

> ### For Project 4F, you will need the following files:
>
> a04F_Library_Programs
> a04F_Photo_1
> a04F_Photo_2
> a04F_Photo_3

**You will save your database as
4F_Library_Programs_Firstname_Lastname**

Figure 4.52

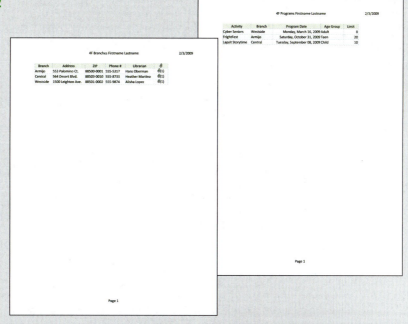

(Project 4F–Library Programs continues on the next page)

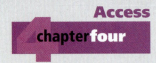

(Project 4F–Library Programs continued)

1. **Start** Access. Locate and open the **a04F_Library_Programs** file. **Save** the database in the **Access 2007 Database** format in your **Access Chapter 4** folder as **4F_Library_Programs_ Firstname_Lastname** Rename the tables by adding your **Firstname Lastname** to the end of each table name.

2. Open the **4F Programs** table in **Design** view. Change the data type of the **Program Date** field to **Date/Time** with a **Format** of **Long Date**. Change the data type of the **Limit** field to **Number** with a **Field Size** of **Integer**.

3. In the **Branch** field data type column, select **Lookup Wizard**. Be sure that **I want the lookup column to look up the values in a table or query** is selected. Click **Next**. There is only one other table in this database from which to choose—4F Branches—and it is selected. Click **Next**. Under **Available Fields**, click **Branch**, and then click the **Add Field** button. Click **Next**. In the **1** box, click the **arrow**, and then click **Branch**. Leave the sort order as **Ascending**. Click **Next** two times. Under **What label would you like for your lookup column?**, accept the default of **Branch**, and then be sure that **Allow Multiple Values** is *not* selected. Click **Finish**, and then **Save** the table.

4. In the **Age Group** field, in the **Validation Rule** box, type **"Child" OR "Teen" OR "Adult"** For the **Validation Text**, type **Entry must be Child, Teen, or Adult.**

5. In the **Limit** field, for the **Validation Rule**, type **<=20** For the **Validation Text**, type **Participation is limited to a maximum of 20.**

6. In the **Activity** field, in the **Field Properties**, click the **Indexed down arrow**, and then select **Yes (Duplicates OK)**. Make it a **Required** field. **Close** the table, saving the changes to the design.

7. Open the **4F Branches** table in **Design** view. Add a **Photo ID** field to the table using an **Attachment** data type.

8. In the **ZIP** field, under **Input Mask**, click the **Build** button. From the **Input Mask Wizard**, under **Input Mask**, select **Zip Code**, and then click **Next**. Accept the default "_" as the place-holder character. Click **Next**. Store the data without the symbols in the mask, click **Next**, and then click **Finish**.

9. Switch to **Datasheet** view, saving the changes to the table design. Populate the table with the following data:

Branch	Address	ZIP	Phone #	Librarian	Attachment
Armijo	553 Palomino Ct.	88500-0001	555-5317	Hans Oberman	a04F_Photo_1.jpg
Westside	1500 Leighton Ave.	88501-0002	555-9874	Alisa Lopez	a04F_Photo_2.jpg
Central	564 Desert Blvd.	88503-0010	555-8733	Heather Martino	a04F_Photo_3.jpg

(Project 4F–Library Programs continues on the next page)

Content-Based Assessments

Mastering Access

(Project 4F–Library Programs continued)

10. Open the **4F Programs** table in **Datasheet** view, and then populate the table with the following data:

Activity	Branch	Program Date	Age Group	Limit
Cyber Seniors	Westside	3/16/09	Adult	8
FrightFest	Armijo	10/31/09	Teen	20
Lapsit Storytime	Central	9/8/09	Child	10

11. Adjust column widths as needed to display all of the data and field names. **Save** the table. If you are instructed to submit this result, create a paper or electronic printout of both tables. **Close** the tables. From the **Database Tools tab**, in the **Analyze group**, click **Database Documenter**. Check both table boxes, and then click **OK**. From the **Print Preview tab**, in the **Print group**, click the **Print** button. If you are to submit your work electronically, follow your instructor's directions.

12. **Close** the database, and **Exit** Access.

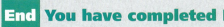

End **You have completed Project 4F** —————————————

Project 4G — Parks and Recreation

In this project, you will apply the following Objectives found in Projects 4A and 4B.

Objectives: 1. *Modify Existing Tables;* **3.** *Create and Modify Table Relationships;* **4.** *Enter Records Using a Subdatasheet;* **6.** *Set Field Properties;* **9.** *Attach Files to Records.*

Yvonne Guillen is the Chair of the Parks & Recreation Commission for Westland Plains, Texas. The database she is using has separate tables that should be combined. In the following Mastering Access project, you will combine these tables into a facilities table. You will modify the existing tables, set field properties to ensure more accurate data entry, and add driving directions to the facilities as an attached document. Your completed work will look similar to Figure 4.53.

For Project 4G, you will need the following files:

a04G_Parks_and_Recreation
a04G_Harris_Park
a04G_Northwest_Recreational_Center

You will save your database as
4G_Parks_and_Recreation_Firstname_Lastname
You will save your document as
4G_Phone_Properties_Firstname_Lastname

Figure 4.53

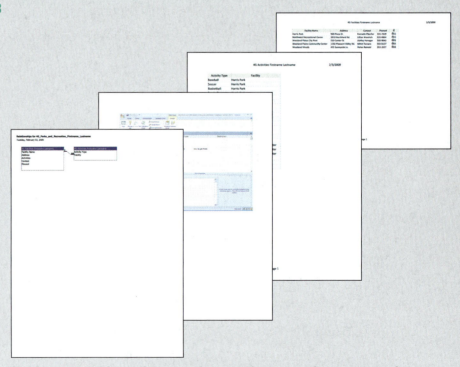

(Project 4G–Parks and Recreation continues on the next page)

Access

chapter four

Mastering Access

(Project 4G– Parks and Recreation continued)

1. **Start** Access. Locate and open the **a04G_Parks_and_Recreation** file. **Save** the database in the **Access 2007 Database** format in your **Access Chapter 4** folder as **4G_Parks_and_Recreation_ Firstname_Lastname** Rename all tables by adding your **Firstname Lastname** to the end of each table name.

2. Select the **4G Community Centers** table. **Copy** and **Paste** the table. Name the table **4G Facilities Firstname Lastname** In the **Paste Table As** dialog box, be sure the **Paste Structure and Data** option is selected. Click **OK**.

3. Select the **4G Parks** table, click the **Copy** button, and then click **Paste**. In the **Table Name** box, type **4G Facilities Firstname Lastname** Under **Paste Options**, select **Append Data to Existing Table**, and then click **OK** to create one table that contains all of the facility information for the Parks and Recreation Department.

4. From the **Database Tools tab**, in the **Show/Hide group**, click **Relationships**. Select the **4G Facilities** and **4G Activities** tables. Create a one-to-many relationship between the **4G Facilities** table **Facility Name** field and the **4G Activities** table **Facility** field. Be sure to check **Enforce Referential Integrity**, **Cascade Update Related Fields**, and **Cascade Delete Related Records**.

5. Create a **Relationship Report**, and if you are instructed to submit this result, create a paper or electronic printout. **Save** the report using the default name. **Close** the report, and then **Close** the Relationships window.

6. Open the **4G Facilities** table in **Design** view. Delete the **Activities** field. This field is no longer needed in this table because the relationship is established.

7. Add a new **Directions** field to the table and use a data type of **Attachment**. In the description box, type **How to get there**

8. Select the **Phone#** field. In the **Input Mask** box, type **!000-0000** Change the field size to **8**. Set the **Field Property** of **Required** to **Yes**. Using the Clipboard and Word, submit a printed copy of the **Phone#** Field Properties if you are requested to do so. **Save** the document as **4G_Phone_ Properties_Firstname_Lastname** Switch to **Datasheet** view. **Save** your changes.

9. Expand the **Westland Woods** record to display the subdatasheet. To the **Activity Type**, add a new record by typing **Camping** Collapse the subdatasheet.

10. In the **Harris Park** record, in the **Attachment** field, double-click, and then from the student data files, attach **a04G_Harris_Park**. Click **OK**.

11. Using the same technique, for the **Northwest Recreational Center**, add the directions that are in the **a04G_ Northwest_Recreational_Center** file.

12. If you are instructed to submit this result, create a paper or electronic printout of the **4G Activities** table and the **4G Facilities** table. Be sure that all field names and data display.

13. **Close** the tables, **Close** the database, and **Exit** Access.

 You have completed Project 4G

Access

chapter four

Mastering Access

Project 4H — Application Tracking

In this project, you will apply the following Objectives found in Projects 4A and 4B.

Objectives: 1. *Modify Existing Tables;* **3.** *Create and Modify Table Relationships;* **5.** *Change Data Types;* **6.** *Set Field Properties;* **7.** *Create Data Validation Rules and Validation Text;* **8.** *Create a Lookup Field;* **9.** *Attach Files to Records.*

In the following Mastering Access project, you will modify an existing table for City Manager Joaquin Alonzo. The database is designed to track the application and permit process for the citizens of Westland Plains. You will create data validation and add lookup tables to assist data entry personnel. You will attach copies of the completed applications. Your completed work will look similar to that in Figure 4.54.

For Project 4H, you will need the following files:

a04H_Application_Tracking
a04H_CofC_Form
a04H_Engcost_Form

You will save your database as
4H_Application_Tracking_Firstname_Lastname

Figure 4.54

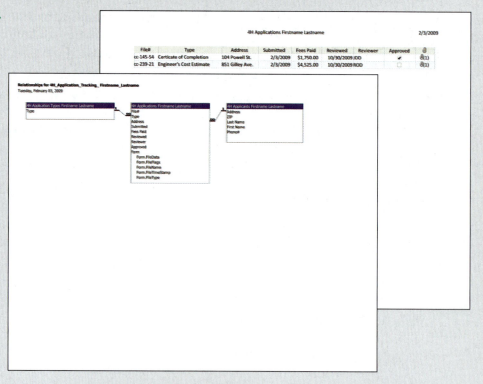

(Project 4H–Application Tracking continues on the next page)

(Project 4H–Application Tracking continued)

1. **Start** Access. Locate and open the **a04H_Application_Tracking** file. **Save** the database in the **Access 2007 Database** format in your **Access Chapter 4** folder as **4H_Application_ Tracking_ Firstname_Lastname** Rename the tables by adding your **Firstname Lastname** to the end of each table name.

2. Open the **4H Applications** table in **Design** view. In the **File#** field, in the **Input Mask** box, click the **Build** button. Click **Edit List**, and then in the **Customize Input Mask Wizard** dialog box, click the **New (blank) record** button. In the **Description** box, type **File#** In the **Input Mask** box, type **LL-000-00** Click in the **Placeholder** box, and then accept the default underscore. In the **Sample Data** box, type **BP12312** and then click **Close**. Click **Finish**. Change the field size to **7**, and then set the **File#** field as the **Primary Key** field.

3. In the **Type** field, set the data type to **Lookup Wizard**. Use the **4H Application Types** table to look up the values. Select the **Type** field, and then sort it in **Ascending** order. Adjust the column width to display all of the field text. Accept the default label of **Type** for the column.

4. Click the **Address** field, and then change the field size to **25**.

5. In the **Submitted** field, set the data type to **Date/Time** with a format of **Short Date**. Add a default that specifies that the date is today's date. Click in the **Required** box, and then click **Yes**.

6. Change the data type of the **Fees Paid** field to **Currency**.

7. Change the data type of the **Reviewed** field to **Date/Time** with a format of **Short Date**.

8. In the **Reviewer** field, change the field size to **3**. In the **Validation Rule** box, type **"ROD" OR "JDD" OR "NDH"** In the **Validation Text** box, type **Authorized Reviewer Only**

9. Change the data type of the **Approved** field to **Yes/No**.

10. Add a new **Form** field with a data type of **Attachment**.

11. **Close** the table and **Save** the design changes.

12. Edit the relationship between the **4H Application Types** table and the **4H Applications** table to include **Enforced Referential Integrity** and **Cascade Update Related Fields**. Create a relationship between the **4H Applications** table and the **4H Applicants** table. Check **Enforce Referential Integrity** and **Cascade Update Related Fields**. Create a **Relationships Report**, and then if you are instructed to submit this result, create a paper or electronic printout of the report in **Landscape** orientation. **Close** the Relationships Report, accepting the default name. **Close** the Relationships window.

13. Open the **4H Applicants** table. Type the following data in the first and third record subdatasheets.

Address	File #	Type	Submitted	Fees Paid
104 Powell St	cc-145-54	Certificate of Completion	Today's Date	1750
851 Gilley Ave	ec-239-21	Engineer's Cost Estimate	Today's Date	4525

(Project 4H–Application Tracking continues on the next page)

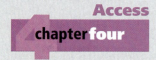

Access

chapter **four**

Mastering Access

(Project 4H–Application Tracking continued)

Reviewed	Reviewer	Approved	Attachment
10/30/09	JDD	Yes	a04H_CofC_Form
10/30/09	ROD	No	a04H_Engcost_Form

14. If you are instructed to submit this result, create a paper or electronic printout of the **4H Applications** table in **Landscape** orientation. **Print** from the Database Documenter.

15. **Close** the table. **Save** changes. **Close** the database, and **Exit** Access.

 End **You have completed Project 4H** ─────────────────────────

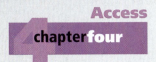

Mastering Access

Project 4I — Health Services

In this project, you will apply all the skills you practiced from the Objectives in Projects 4A and 4B.

Joaquin Alonzo, City Manager, works with the Director of the Westland Plains Health Services to provide a variety of care for the residents of the city. The information about these services is maintained in a database. In the following Mastering Access project, you will modify the tables to eliminate redundancy, create relationships to assist in maintaining accurate records, and set field properties to aid with data entry. Your completed work will look similar to that in Figure 4.55.

> ### For Project 4I, you will need the following files:
>
> a04I_Health_Services
> New blank Word document
> a04I_Badge

You will save your database as
4I_Health_Services_Firstname_Lastname
You will save your document as
4I_Navigation_Pane_Firstname_Lastname

Figure 4.55

(Project 4I–Health Services continues on the next page)

Access

chapter four

Mastering Access

(Project 4I–Health Services continued)

1. **Start** Access. Locate and open the **a04I_Health_Services** file. **Save** the database in the **Access 2007 Database** format in your **Access Chapter 4** folder as **4I_Health_Services_Firstname_Lastname**

2. Select the **4I Services** table. Click **Copy**, and then click **Paste**. Name the table **4I Services Information Firstname Lastname** Be sure **Structure and Data** is selected. Make a second copy of the **4I Services** table, and then name it **4I Directors Information Firstname Lastname** Maintain the structure and data of the original table.

3. Open the **4I Services Information** table. Select and delete the following fields: **Home Phone**, **Address**, **City**, **State**, **ZIP**, **Hire Date**, and **Salary**. **Close** the table, saving changes.

4. Open the **4I Directors Information** table in **Design** view. Select and delete the following fields: **Service**, **Location**, **Office Phone**, and **Fax #**. In the **State** field, set the default value to **TX** In the **Hire Date** field, set the data type to **Date/Time** with a format of **Medium Date**. In the **Salary** field, change the data type to **Currency** with **0** decimal places. In the **ZIP** field, in the **Validation Rule** box, type "88500" OR "88501" OR "88502" In the **Validation Text** box, type **ZIP must be in the Westland Plains area**

5. Set the **Director** field as the **Primary Key** field. Insert a field below the **Director** field. In the **Field Name** box, type **Photo** Change the data type to **Attachment**. Switch to **Datasheet** view. Add the following file to the **Photo** field for Director Lisa Sarewitz: **a04I_Badge**. If you are instructed to submit this result, create a paper or electronic printout of the table.

6. **Close** the table, saving changes.

7. Select the **4I Service Name** table. Click **Copy**, and then click **Paste**. Be sure

Structure and Data is selected. Name the copy of the table **4I Service Codes Firstname Lastname**

8. Open the **4I Service Codes** table in **Design** view. Insert a field above the **Service** field, and in the **Field Name** box, type **Code** Set the data type to **Text** with a field size of **3** Click in the **Input Mask** box, and then type **HS-999**

9. In the **Service** field, set the **Required** property to **Yes**, and then change the field size to **15**

10. Switch to **Datasheet** view. Type the following codes for the Health Services:

Code	Service
101	Dental Clinic
110	Immunizations
103	WIC Program
200	Education

11. Switch to **Design** view, and then set the **Code** field as the **Primary Key** field. **Close** the table, saving changes when prompted.

12. Open the **4I Services Information** table in **Design** view. Click in the **Location** field, and then change the data type to **Lookup Wizard**. Select **I want the lookup column to look up the values in a table or query**. Click **Next**. Select the **Medical Centers** table. Click **Next**. Add **Location** field to **Selected** fields. Click **Next**. Sort the **Location** field in **Ascending** order. Click **Next**. Adjust the column widths to display the medical center names. Accept the default name of **Location** for the lookup field, and do not allow multiple values. Rename the **Service** field to **Service Code**. Change the field size to **3** Switch to **Datasheet** view, and then replace the

(Project 4I–Health Services continues on the next page)

(Project 4I–Health Services continued)

truncated contents of the **Service Code** field with the data in the preceding table. If required, If you are instructed to submit this result, create a paper or electronic printout.

13. **Close** the table, and **Save** your changes.

14. Create a relationship. From the **4I Service Codes** table, join the **Code** field to the **4I Services Information** table **Service Code** field. Create a second relationship. From the **4I Services Information** table, join the **Director** field to the **4I Director Information Director** field. Edit both relationships to **Enforce Referential Integrity**, **Cascade Update Related Fields**, and **Cascade Delete Related Records**. Adjust all field lists to display all table titles and field names.

15. Create a **Relationship Report**. If you are instructed to submit this result, create a paper or electronic printout. **Close** the report, accepting the default name.

16. Customize the **Navigation Pane** by selecting **Navigation Options**. Under **Categories**, click **Add Item**, and then type

Updated Health Services Objects Click **Add Group**, and then type **Services** Click **Add Group**, and then type **Directors** Position **Directors** above **Services**. Click **OK**. In the **Navigation Pane**, select **Updated Health Services Objects**. Move the **4I Director Information** table to the **Directors** group. Move the **4I Services Information** table and the **4I Service Codes** table to the **Services** group. Use the print screen feature to copy a picture of the Navigation Pane into Word. **Save** the Word document as **4I_Navigation_Pane_Firstname_Lastname** If you are instructed to submit this result, create a paper or electronic printout. **Exit** Word.

17. If you are to submit a printed copy of your work, from the **Database Tools tab**, in the **Analyze group**, click **Database Documenter**. From the **Tables tab**, select the **4I Director Information**, **4I Service Codes**, and the **4I Service Information** tables. Click **OK**. Click the **Print** button. **Close** Print Preview.

18. **Close** the database, and **Exit** Access.

End **You have completed Project 4I**

Content-Based Assessments

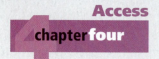

Project 4J — Business Running Case

In this project, you will apply the skills you have practiced from the Objectives in Projects 4A and 4B.

From My Computer, navigate to the student files that accompany this textbook. In the folder **03_business_running_case,** locate and open the folder for this chapter. Open and print the instructions for this project, which are provided to you in Adobe PDF format. Follow the instructions and use the skills you have gained thus far to assist the brother and sister team of Michael and Kristen Landry in meeting the challenges of owning and running their business.

End **You have completed Project 4J** ————————

Rubric

The following outcomes-based assessments are *open-ended assessments*. That is, there is no specific correct result; your result will depend on your approach to the information provided. Make *Professional Quality* your goal. Use the following scoring rubric to guide you in *how* to approach the problem and then to evaluate *how well* your approach solves the problem.

The *criteria*—Software Mastery, Content, Format and Layout, and Process—represent the knowledge and skills you have gained that you can apply to solving the problem. The *levels of performance*—Professional Quality, Approaching Professional Quality, or Needs Quality Improvement—help you and your instructor evaluate your result.

	Your completed project is of Professional Quality if you:	Your completed project is Approaching Professional Quality if you:	Your completed project Needs Quality Improvements if you:
1-Software Mastery	Choose and apply the most appropriate skills, tools, and features and identify efficient methods to solve the problem.	Choose and apply some appropriate skills, tools, and features, but not in the most efficient manner.	Choose inappropriate skills, tools, or features, or are inefficient in solving the problem.
2-Content	Construct a solution that is clear and well organized, contains content that is accurate, appropriate to the audience and purpose, and is complete. Provide a solution that contains no errors of spelling, grammar, or style.	Construct a solution in which some components are unclear, poorly organized, inconsistent, or incomplete. Misjudge the needs of the audience. Have some errors in spelling, grammar, or style, but the errors do not detract from comprehension.	Construct a solution that is unclear, incomplete, or poorly organized, containing some inaccurate or inappropriate content; and contains many errors of spelling, grammar, or style. Do not solve the problem.
3-Format and Layout	Format and arrange all elements to communicate information and ideas, clarify function, illustrate relationships, and indicate relative importance.	Apply appropriate format and layout features to some elements, but not others. Overuse features, causing minor distraction.	Apply format and layout that does not communicate information or ideas clearly. Do not use format and layout features to clarify function, illustrate relationships, or indicate relative importance. Use available features excessively, causing distraction.
4-Process	Use an organized approach that integrates planning, development, self-assessment, revision, and reflection.	Demonstrate an organized approach in some areas, but not others; or, use an insufficient process of organization throughout.	Do not use an organized approach to solve the problem.

Access

chapter four

Problem Solving

Project 4K — Fire Department

In this project, you will construct a solution by applying any combination of the skills you practiced from the Objectives in Projects 4A and 4B.

> **For Project 4K, you will need the following file:**
>
> a04K_Fire_Department

You will save your database as
4K_Fire_Department_Firstname_Lastname

The City Manager for Westland Plains, Texas, is responsible for the operations of the city's fire department. He is working with a database that could be more effective in both storing and retrieving data. Open the **4K_Fire_Department** database. Make a backup copy of the original file. In this project, you will modify the existing tables, add primary key fields, and create a relationship between the tables. Notice that the 4K Administration Staff Directory, 4K Aircraft Rescue Staff Directory, and 4K Fire Prevention Staff Directory all contain the same fields. The Fire Chief wants one directory for the department: **4K_Fire_Department_Firstname_Lastname**

To complete this project:

- Use the copy and append techniques to create a combined directory.

- Add an employee ID field that uses the AutoNumber feature. Set this field as the primary key.

- Create relationships between the directory and the 4K Title and 4K Divisions tables. Ensure consistency by enforcing referential integrity and cascading updates and deletions.

- Set field sizes and change data types to match the data. Set field properties, and create data validation rules and text.

- Create input masks and lookup fields to reduce the number of data entry errors.

- Group your revised tables and reports by customizing the Navigation Pane.

- As you work, rename all revised objects by adding your **Firstname Lastname** to the end of the object name.

If you are instructed to submit this result, create a paper or electronic printout of your table, relationship report, and the Database Documenter generated report. Save the database as **4K_Fire_Department_Firstname_Lastname**

 End **You have completed Project 4K** —————

Problem Solving

Project 4L — City Zoo

In this project, you will construct a solution by applying any combination of the skills you practiced from the Objectives in Projects 4A and 4B.

For Project 4L, you will need the following files:

a04L_Zoo
a04L_Llama

You will save your database as
4L_Zoo_Firstname_Lastname

Amanda Hartigan, Deputy City Manager for the Quality of Life Division of Westland Plains City, Texas, and City Manager Joaquin Alonzo are meeting with the Mayor, Bill J. Aycock, to discuss the funding for the city zoo. The Corporate and Foundation Council provides citizens and corporations with a partnering opportunity to support the city zoo. Amanda has outlined a database to organize the sponsorships.

In this project, you will open the **a04L_Zoo** database and examine the tables. Rename the tables by adding your **Firstname Lastname** to each table name. Modify the 4L Sponsors table and the 4L Sponsored Events table to eliminate redundancy. Create a relationship and report between the 4L Sponsors table and the 4L Sponsored Events table. Change data types and adjust field sizes to match the data. In the 4L Sponsors table, create data validation for sponsor type. In the 4L Sponsors table, use the 4L Sponsor Levels table as a lookup field. To the 4L Sponsor Levels table, add an attachment field. Add the **a04L_Llama** file from the student data files to the Llama record. Save the database as **4L_Zoo_Firstname_Lastname** If you are instructed to submit this result, create a paper or electronic printout of the tables, relationship report, and the Object Definition report.

End **You have completed Project 4L**

Access

chapter four

Problem Solving

Project 4M — Street Repairs

In this project, you will construct a solution by applying any combination of the skills you practiced from the Objectives in Projects 4A and 4B.

> ### For Project 4M, you will need the following files:
>
> a04M_Street_Repairs
> a04M_Work_Request

You will save your database as
4M_Street_Repairs_Firstname_Lastname

In this project, you will examine the database that has been created to help the Deputy City Manager of Development and Infrastructure Services organize and track the constituent work requests for the city street repairs. Rename all of the tables by adding your **Firstname Lastname** to the end of each table name. Open a04M_Work_Request, and then use the data from this document to populate the 4M Work Requests table. Set field sizes and data types to match the data for all table fields. Set the Work Order # field as the primary key field, and then create an input mask to match the field data. For the Type field, create a lookup table using the 4M Repair Types table. In the Repair Team field, create a Lookup Wizard data type using the 4M Repair Teams table. In the Priority field, set the Required property to Yes, and then create a validation rule requiring an entry of 1, 2, or 3. Explain this rule with appropriate validation text. Use today's date as the start date. Add an attachment field, and then add a04M_Work_Request as the attachment. Save the database as **4M_Street_Repairs_Firstname_Lastname** If you are instructed to submit this result, create a paper or electronic printout of the 4M Work Requests table and an Object Definition report.

End **You have completed Project 4M** ————————————————

Outcomes-Based Assessments

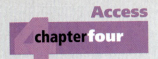

Access

chapter four

Problem Solving

Project 4N—Police Department

In this project, you will construct a solution by applying any combination of the skills you practiced from the Objectives in Projects 4A and 4B.

For Project 4N, you will need the following file:

a04N_Police_Department

**You will save your database as
4N_Police_Department_Firstname_Lastname**

The City Manager of Westland Plains City, Texas, is the governing official over the police department. Joaquin Alonzo holds this position. He has reviewed the database that contains the information about the force and the individual officers. In this project, you will update the database to be more efficient. Before you begin this project, back up the original database. The database contains one table of many fields. Your job is to separate the table into two smaller tables that can be related—personal and professional information.

Change the field sizes and set data types as appropriate. Create validation rules, and then select field properties that will decrease the number of data entry errors. Customize the Navigation Pane, and then place the new tables into appropriately named categories. Enter your own information as the first record in the new database. Use Badge ID of **WP-321** You may choose a Regional Command from the following: Central, Northeast, Southside, or Westside. Choices for Precinct include: First, Second, Third, or Fourth. You may choose your rank from Commander, Sergeant, or Lieutenant. You were hired last month. Save the modified database as **4N_Police_Department_Firstname_Lastname** If you are instructed to submit this result, create a paper or electronic printout of the tables, the relationship report, and an Object Definition report.

End **You have completed Project 4N** _____

Outcomes-Based Assessments

Access
chapter four

Problem Solving

Project 4O — Museums

In this project, you will construct a solution by applying any combination of the skills you practiced from the Objectives in Projects 4A and 4B.

For Project 4O, you will need the following file:

a04O_Museums

**You will save your database as
4O_Museums_Firstname_Lastname**

Mayor Joaquin Alonzo has appointed Amanda Hartigan to the position of Deputy City Manager for the Quality of Life Division. One of Mrs. Hartigan's responsibilities is to oversee the activities of the city's museums. You have been asked to help her revise the database that contains the information about the museums and the upcoming calendar of events.

Open the 4O_Museums database. Examine the two tables. Set field sizes and data types to match the data. In the 4O Museum Events table, index the Event Name, allowing duplicates. Create a relationship between the two tables. Establish referential integrity. Enter an event that you would like to see offered at one of the two museums by using the subdatasheet to enter the event. If you are instructed to submit this result, create a paper or electronic printout of the tables, the relationship report, and an Object Definition report. Save the database as
4O_Museums_Firstname_Lastname

End **You have completed Project 4O** _____

Outcomes-Based Assessments

 You and GO!

Project 4P — You and GO!

In this project, you will construct a solution by applying any combination of the Objectives found in Projects 4A and 4B.

From My Computer, navigate to the student files that accompany this textbook. In the folder **04_you_and_go**, locate and open the folder for this chapter. Open and print the instructions for this project, which are provided to you in Adobe PDF format. Follow the instructions to create a form and report for your personal inventory.

 You have completed Project 4P

GO! with Help

Project 4Q — GO! with Help

The Access Help system is extensive and can help you as you work. In this project, you will view information about creating a multivalued field in an Access table.

1 **Start** Access. On the right side of the Ribbon, click the **Microsoft Office Access Help** button. In the **Type words to search for** box, type **multivalued field** and then press Enter.

2 In the displayed **Results** pane, click **Add or change a lookup column that lets you store multiple values**. Maximize the displayed window. Read the section titled **Using the Lookup Wizard**.

3 If you want, **Print** a copy of the information by clicking the printer button at the top of the **Access Help** window.

4 **Close** the Help window, and then **Exit** Access.

 You have completed Project 4Q

5

chapterfive

Enhancing Queries

OBJECTIVES

At the end of this chapter you will be able to:

1. Create Calculated Fields
2. Use Aggregate Functions
3. Create a Crosstab Query
4. Find Duplicate and Unmatched Records
5. Create a Parameter Query

6. Create a Make Table Query
7. Create an Append Query
8. Create a Delete Query
9. Create an Update Query
10. Modify the Join Type

OUTCOMES

Mastering these objectives will enable you to:

Project 5A
Create Special-Purpose Queries

Project 5B
Create Action Queries and Modify Join Types

Board Anywhere Surf and Snowboard Shop

College classmates Dana Connolly and J.R. Kass grew up in the sun of Orange County, California; but they also spent time in the mountain snow. After graduating with business degrees, they combined their business expertise and their favorite sports to open Board Anywhere, a snowboard and surf shop. The store carries top brands of men's and women's apparel, goggles and sunglasses, and boards and gear. The surfboard selection includes both classic boards and the latest high-tech boards. Snowboarding gear can be purchased in packages or customized for the most experienced boarders. Connolly and Kass are proud to count many of Southern California's extreme sports games participants among their customers.

Enhancing Queries

Queries can do more than extract data from tables and other queries. You can create queries to perform special functions, such as create a new field to calculate numeric fields and to summarize numeric data. For example, a query can be created using existing data in tables with the addition of a field to calculate the total payroll or to sum the amount of goods on hand for an inventory. The results of a query can be displayed in a spreadsheet-like format for easier analysis.

Queries can also be used to find duplicate and unmatched records in tables, which is useful for data integrity. If you want more flexibility in the data that the query extracts from underlying tables, you can create a parameter query, where an individual is prompted for the criteria. Queries can create additional tables in the database, append records to an existing table, delete records from a table, and modify data in a table. This is useful when you do not want to directly modify the data in the tables.

Project 5A **Inventory**

Ali Cardona, Purchasing Manager of Board Anywhere Surf and Snowboard Shop, has a database containing inventory data and supplier data. In Activities 5.1 through 5.10, you will create special-purpose queries to calculate data, summarize and group data, display data in a spreadsheet-like format, and find duplicate and unmatched records. You will also create a query that prompts individuals to enter the criteria. Your completed queries will look similar to the queries shown in Figure 5.1.

For Project 5A, you will need the following file:

a05A_Inventory

**You will save your database as
5A_Inventory_Firstname_Lastname**

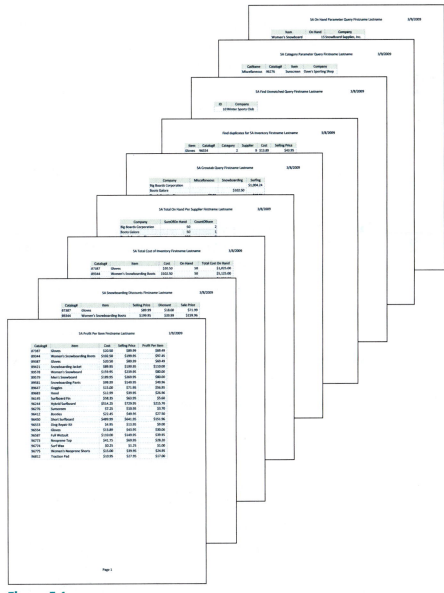

Figure 5.1
Project 5A—Inventory

Objective 1
Create Calculated Fields

Queries can be used to create a **calculated field**—a field that obtains its data by performing a calculation or computation, using a formula. For example, to determine the profit that will be made from the sale of an item, you subtract the cost of the item from the sale price of the item. Another example is to create a calculated field that computes the gross pay for an employee. There are two steps needed to produce a calculated field in a query. In the design grid of the query, in a blank column, type the name of the field that will store the results of the calculated field—the name must be followed by a colon (:). Second, type the **expression**—the formula—that will perform the calculation. *Each field name* used in the expression must be enclosed within *its own pair* of square brackets, []. If you are using a number in the expression—for example, a percentage—type only the number; do not enclose a number in brackets.

Activity 5.1 Creating a Calculated Field Based on Two Existing Fields

In this activity, you will create a calculated field to determine the profit for each item in the inventory database.

1 **Start** Access. Navigate to the location where the student data files for this textbook are saved. Locate and open the **a05A_Inventory** file. Click the **Office** button 🔘 , point to **Save As**, and then click **Access 2007 Database**. In the **Save As** dialog box, navigate to the drive on which you will be saving your folders and projects for this chapter. Create a new folder named **Access Chapter 5** and then save the file as **5A_Inventory_Firstname_Lastname** in the folder.

2 If necessary, enable the content or add the Access Chapter 5 folder to the Trust Center. On the **Navigation Pane**, rename each table by adding **Firstname Lastname** to the end of each table name.

3 On the **Navigation Pane**, double-click **5A Inventory**. If the Field List pane opens, close it. Take a moment to study the fields in the table.

Snowboarding items have a catalog number beginning with *8*; surfing items have a catalog number beginning with *9*. *Cost* is the price the company pays to a supplier for each item. *Selling Price* is what the company will charge its customers for each item. The *Category* field is a Lookup column. If you click in the Category field, and then click the arrow, a list of category numbers and their meanings display.

4 Switch to **Design** view, and then take a moment to study the data structure. Recall that Lookup columns have a data type of Number.

When you are finished, **Close** ❎ the table, and then collapse 🔳 the **Navigation Pane**.

5 On the Ribbon, click the **Create tab**. In the **Other group**, click the **Query Design** button. In the **Show Table** dialog box, double-click **5A Inventory** to add the table to the Query design workspace, and then click **Close**. Expand the field list.

6 From the **5A Inventory** field list, add the following fields, in the order specified, to the design grid: **Catalog#**, **Item**, **Cost**, and **Selling Price**. Recall that you can double-click a field name to add it to the design grid, or you can drag the field name to the field box on the design grid. You can also click in the field box, click the arrow, and click the field name from the displayed list.

7 On the **Design tab**, in the **Results group**, click the **Run** button to display the four fields used in the query, and then compare your screen with Figure 5.2.

Four fields extracted from table

Figure 5.2

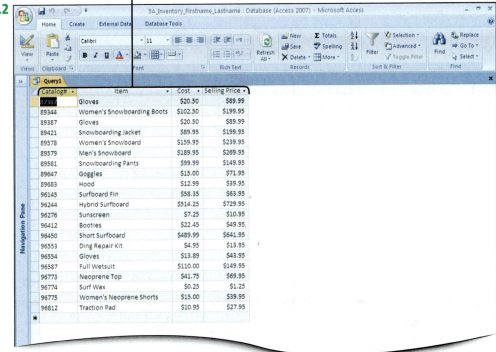

8 Switch to **Design** view. In the **Field row**, right-click in the first empty column—the fifth column—to display a shortcut menu, and then click **Zoom**.

The Zoom dialog box gives you working space so that you can see the expression—formula—as you enter it. The expression can also be entered directly in the empty Field box.

9 In the **Zoom** dialog box, type **Profit Per Item:[Selling Price]-[Cost]** and then compare your screen with Figure 5.3.

The first element of the calculated field—*Profit Per Item*—is the new field name that will display the calculated value. The field name must be unique for the table being used in the query. Following the new field name is a colon (:). A colon in a calculated field separates the new field name from the expression. *Selling Price* is enclosed in square brackets because it is an existing field name from the *5A Inventory* table and contains data that will be used in the calculation.

Following *[Selling Price]* is a minus sign (–), which, in math calculations, signifies subtraction. Finally, *Cost*, an existing field in the *5A Inventory* table, is enclosed in square brackets. This field also contains data that will be used in the calculation.

Figure 5.3

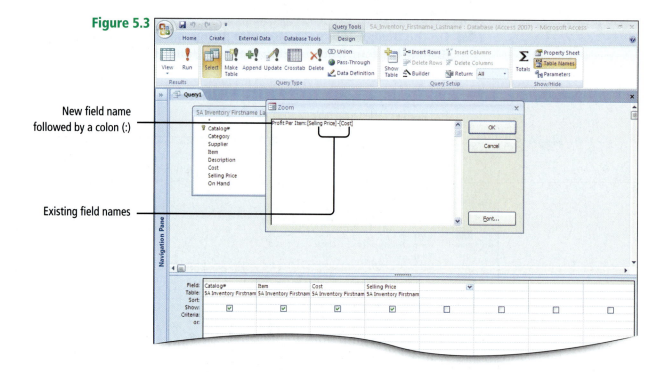

New field name
followed by a colon (:)

Existing field names

Note — Using Square Brackets Around Field Names in Expressions

Square brackets are not required around a field name in an expression if the field name is only one word. For example, if the field name is *Cost*, it is not necessary to type brackets around it—Access will automatically insert the square brackets. If a field name has a space in it, however, you must type the square brackets around the field name. Otherwise, Access will display a message stating that the expression you entered contains invalid syntax.

10 ***Arithmetic operators*** are mathematical symbols used in building expressions. Take a moment to study the arithmetic operators as described in the table in Figure 5.4.

Access Arithmetic Operators

Operator	Description	Example	Result
+	Addition	Cost:[Price]+[Tax]	Adds the value in the Price field to the value in the Tax field and displays the result in the Cost field.
–	Subtraction	Cost:[Price]–[Markdown]	Subtracts the value in the Markdown field from the value in the Price field and displays the result in the Cost field.
* (Note: This is an asterisk, not an *x*.)	Multiplication	Tax:[Price]*.05	Multiplies the value in the Price field by .05 (5%) and displays the result in the Tax field.
/	Division	Average:[Total]/3	Divides the value in the Total field by 3 and displays the result in the Average field.
^	Exponentiation	Required:2^[Bits]	Raises 2 to the power of the value in the Bits field and stores the result in the Required field.
\	Integer division	Average:[Children]\[Families]	Divides the value in the Children field by the value in the Families field and displays the integer portion—the digits to the left of the decimal point—in the Average field.
Mod	Modulo or modulus division	Remainder:[Year] Mod 4	Divides the value in the Year field by 4 and displays the *remainder* in the Remainder field. In the example, if the year is 2009, the answer (Remainder) would be 1-2009 divided by 4, which gives a quotient of 502 with a remainder of *1*.

Figure 5.4

11 In the **Zoom** dialog box, click **OK**, and then **Run** the query. Compare your screen with Figure 5.5.

A fifth column—the calculated field—with a field name of *Profit Per Item* displays. For each record, the value in the *Profit Per Item* field is calculated by subtracting the value in the *Cost* field from the value in the *Selling Price* field.

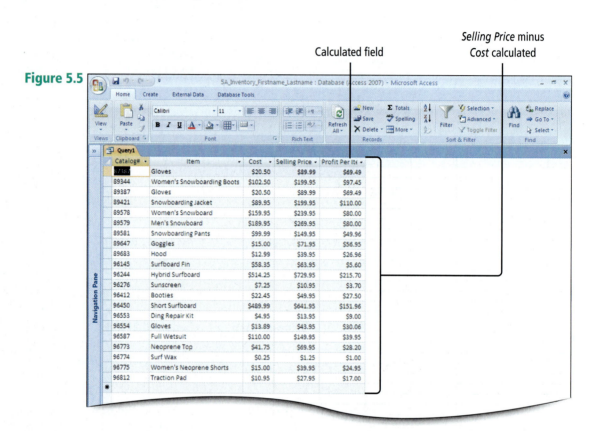

Calculated field

Selling Price minus *Cost* calculated

Figure 5.5

12 Adjust the column width of the *Profit Per Item* field. On the **tab row**, right-click the **Query1 tab**, and then click **Save**. In the **Save As** dialog box, under **Query Name**, type **5A Profit Per Item Firstname Lastname** and then click **OK**. View the query in **Print Preview**, ensuring that the query prints on one page, and then if you are instructed to submit this result, create a paper or electronic printout. **Close** ☒ the query.

Activity 5.2 Creating a Calculated Field Based on One Existing Field and a Number

In this activity, you will calculate the sale prices of each snowboarding item for the annual sale. During this event, all snowboarding supplies are discounted by 20 percent.

1 On the Ribbon, click the **Create tab**. In the **Other group**, click the **Query Design** button. Add the **5A Inventory** table to the Query design workspace, and then **Close** the **Show Table** dialog box. Expand the field list.

2 From the **5A Inventory** field list, add the following fields, in the order specified, to the design grid: **Catalog#**, **Item**, and **Selling Price**.

3 In the **Field row**, right-click in the first empty column—the fourth column—to display a shortcut menu, and then click **Zoom**. In the **Zoom** dialog box, type **Discount:[Selling Price]*.20** and then compare your screen with Figure 5.6.

The value in the *Discount* field is calculated by multiplying the value in the *Selling Price* field by .20—20%. Recall that only field names are enclosed in square brackets.

Figure 5.6

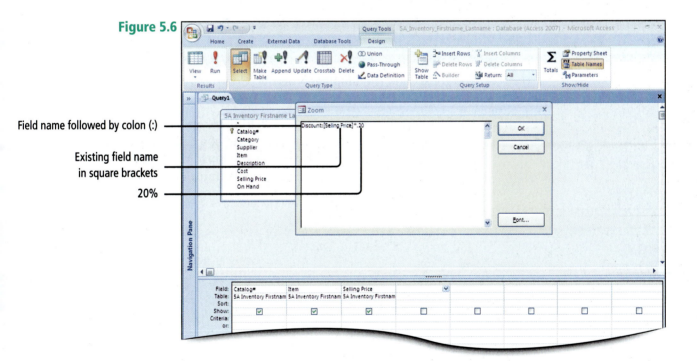

Field name followed by colon (:)

Existing field name in square brackets

20%

4 In the **Zoom** dialog box, click **OK**, and then **Run** the query.

The *Discount* field displays the results of the calculation. The data is not formatted with a dollar sign, and the first record displays a discount of 17.998. When using a number in an expression, the values in the calculated field may not be formatted the same as in the existing field.

5 Switch to **Design** view. On the **Design tab**, in the **Show/Hide group**, click the **Table Names** button.

In the design grid, the Table row no longer displays. If all of the fields in the design grid are from one table, you can hide the Table row. The Table Names button is a toggle button; if you click it again, the Table row displays in the design grid.

6 In the **Field row**, click in the **Discount** field box. On the **Design tab**, in the **Show/Hide group**, click the **Property Sheet** button. Alternatively, right-click in the field box and click Properties, or hold down [Alt] and press [Enter].

The Property Sheet for the selected field—*Discount*—displays on the right side of the screen. In the Property Sheet, under the title of *Property Sheet*, is the subtitle—*Selection type: Field Properties*.

Alert!

Does the Property Sheet display a subtitle of Selection type: Query Properties?

To display the Property Sheet for a field, you must first click in the field; otherwise, the Property Sheet for the query might display. If this occurs, in the Field row, click the Discount field box to change the Property Sheet to this field.

7 In the **Property Sheet**, on the **General tab**, click in the **Format** box, and then click the displayed **arrow**. Compare your screen with Figure 5.7.

A list of possible formats for this field displays. This list is the same as the format list in the properties pane of a table in Design view. A horizontal scroll bar may display at the bottom of the list to indicate that the width of the list is greater than that displayed.

Figure 5.7

Title bar

Property Sheet for the Discount field

Format arrow

List of possible formats

Horizontal scroll bar

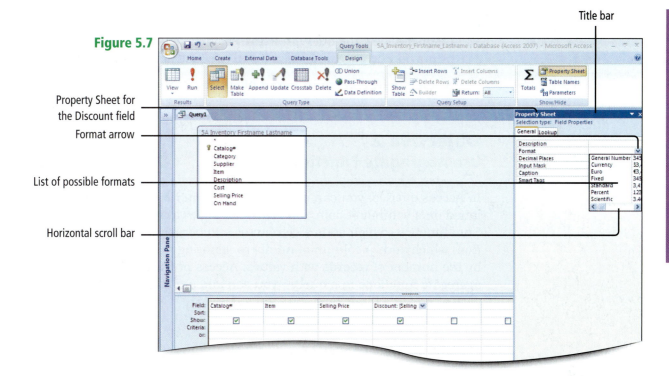

8 In the list of formats, click **Currency**. On the **Property Sheet** title bar, click the **Close** button [×]. **Run** the query to display the results.

The values in the Discount field now display with a dollar sign, and the first record's discount—$18.00—displays with two decimal places.

9 Switch to **Design** view. In the **Field row**, right-click in the first empty column, and then click **Zoom**. In the **Zoom** dialog box, type **Sale Price:[Selling Price]-[Discount]** and then click **OK**. **Run** the query to display the results.

The first record displays a *Sale Price* of *$71.99*. The value in the *Sale Price* field is calculated by subtracting the value in the *Discount* field from the value in the *Selling Price* field. The field names are not case sensitive—you can type a field name in lower case, such as *[selling price]*. Because you used only existing fields in the expression that were formatted as currency, the values in the *Sale Price* field are formatted as currency.

10 Switch to **Design** view. In the design grid, under **Catalog#**, click in the **Criteria** box, type **8*** and then press [Enter].

Recall that the asterisk (*) is a wildcard. In this criteria, Access will extract those records where the catalog number begins with *8* followed by one or more characters. Also, recall that Access formats the criteria. For example, you typed *8**, and Access formatted the criteria as *Like "8*"*.

11 **Run** the query. Notice that only the records with a **Catalog#** beginning with an **8** display—snowboarding items.

12 **Save** 🖫 the query as **5A Snowboarding Discounts Firstname Lastname** View the query in **Print Preview**, ensuring that the query prints on one page, and then if you are instructed to submit this result, create a paper or electronic printout. **Close** ☒ the query.

Objective 2
Use Aggregate Functions

In Access queries, you can use **aggregate functions** to perform a calculation on a column of data and return a single value. Examples are the Sum function, which adds a column of numbers, and the Average function, which adds a column of numbers, ignoring null values, and divides by the number of records with values. Access provides two ways to use aggregate functions in a query—you can add a total row in Datasheet view or create a totals query in Design view.

Activity 5.3 Adding a Total Row to a Query

In this activity, you will create a query and then run the query. In Datasheet view, you will add a Total row to insert an aggregate function in one or more columns without having to change the design of the query.

1 Create a new query in **Query Design**. Add the **5A Inventory** table to the Query design workspace, and then **Close** the **Show Table** dialog box. Expand the field list. From the **5A Inventory** field list, add the following fields, in the order specified, to the design grid: **Catalog#**, **Item**, **Cost**, and **On Hand**.

2 In the **Field row**, right-click in the first empty column, and then click **Zoom**. In the **Zoom** dialog box, type **Total Cost On Hand:[Cost]*[On Hand]**

The value in the *Total Cost On Hand* field is calculated by multiplying the value in the *Cost* field by the value in the *On Hand* field. This field will display the cost of all of the inventory items, not just the cost per item.

3 In the **Zoom** dialog box, click **OK**, and then **Run** the query to display the results in Datasheet view. Adjust the column width of the newly calculated field to display the entire field name, and then compare your screen with Figure 5.8.

If the *Total Cost On Hand* for the first record is not *$1,025.00*, switch to Design view and edit the expression you entered for the calculated field.

Figure 5.8

New field name

Result of Cost * On Hand

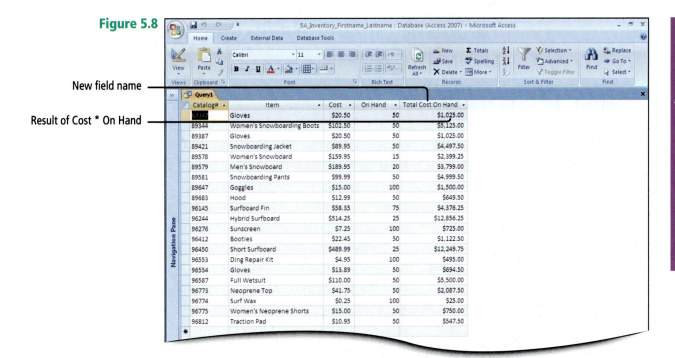

4 On the **Home tab**, in the **Records group**, click the **Totals** button. If necessary, scroll down until the newly created Total row displays. In the **Total row**, under **Total Cost On Hand**, click in the empty box to display an arrow at the left edge. Click the **arrow**, and then compare your screen with Figure 5.9. Take a moment to study the aggregate functions that can be used with both the Total row and the design grid as described in the table in Figure 5.10. Notice that the *Count* function works on more data types than the other functions.

The Total row displays after the New record row. The first field in a Total row contains the word *Total*. The Total row is not a record.

Figure 5.9

Totals button—a toggle button

List of aggregate functions that can be used with this field

Total row

Record navigator bar displays Totals

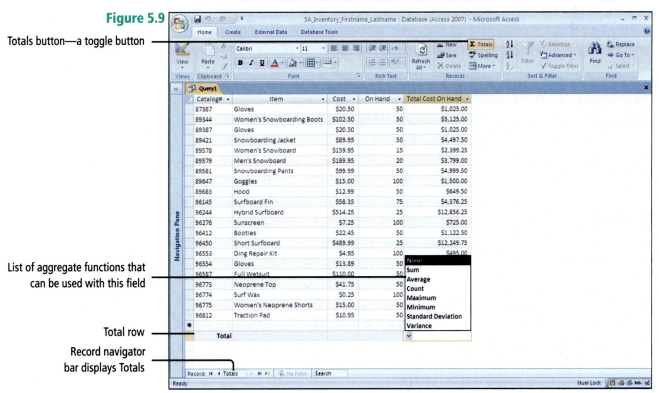

Access Aggregate Functions

Function	Description	Can Be Used with Data Type(s)
Sum	Adds the values in a column.	Currency, Decimal, Number
Average	Calculates the average value for a column, *ignoring null values*.	Currency, Date/Time, Decimal, Number
Count	Counts the number of items in a column, *ignoring null values*.	All data types, except complex repeating scalar data, such as a column of multivalued lists
Maximum	Displays the item with the highest value. Can be used with text data only in Design view. With text data, the highest value is *Z*. Case and null values are ignored.	Currency, Date/Time, Decimal, Number, Text
Minimum	Displays the item with the lowest value. Can be used with text data only in Design view. For text data, the lowest value is *A*. Case and null values are ignored.	Currency, Date/Time, Decimal, Number, Text
Standard Deviation	Measures how widely values are dispersed from the mean value.	Currency, Decimal, Number
Variance	Measures the statistical variance of all values in the column. If the table has less than two rows, a null value is displayed.	Currency, Decimal, Number

Figure 5.10

5 From the displayed list, click **Sum**, and then compare your screen with Figure 5.11.

A sum of $66,449.00 displays, which is the total of all the data in the Total Cost On Hand field.

Summed column

Figure 5.11

Catalog#	Item	Cost	On Hand	Total Cost On Hand
87387	Gloves	$20.50	50	$1,025.00
89344	Women's Snowboarding Boots	$102.50	50	$5,125.00
89387	Gloves	$20.50	50	$1,025.00
89421	Snowboarding Jacket	$89.95	50	$4,497.50
89578	Women's Snowboard	$159.95	15	$2,399.25
89579	Men's Snowboard	$189.95	20	$3,799.00
89581	Snowboarding Pants	$99.99	50	$4,999.50
89647	Goggles	$15.00	100	$1,500.00
89683	Hood	$12.99	50	$649.50
96145	Surfboard Fin	$58.35	75	$4,376.25
96244	Hybrid Surfboard	$514.25	25	$12,856.25
96276	Sunscreen	$7.25	100	$725.00
96412	Booties	$22.45	50	$1,122.50
96450	Short Surfboard	$489.99	25	$12,249.75
96553	Ding Repair Kit	$4.95	100	$495.00
96554	Gloves	$13.89	50	$694.50
96587	Full Wetsuit	$110.00	50	$5,500.00
96773	Neoprene Top	$41.75	50	$2,087.50
96774	Surf Wax	$0.25	100	$25.00
96775	Women's Neoprene Shorts	$15.00	50	$750.00
96812	Traction Pad	$10.95	50	$547.50

Total row ⎯⎯ | **Total** | | | | $66,449.00 |

Note — Applying Aggregate Functions to Multiple Fields

You can apply aggregate functions to more than one field by clicking in the Total row for the field, clicking the arrow, and then clicking the function. The functions for multiple fields can be different functions.

6 **Save** 🖫 the query as **5A Total Cost of Inventory Firstname Lastname** View the query in **Print Preview**, ensuring that the query prints on one page, and then if you are instructed to submit this result, create a paper or electronic printout. **Close** ⊠ the query.

More Knowledge

Removing the Aggregate Function and Removing the Total Row

To remove an aggregate function from a column, on the Total row under the field, click the arrow and then click None. To remove the Total row, on the Home tab, in the Records group, click the Totals button. You cannot cut or delete a Total row; you can only turn it on or off. You can copy a Total row and paste it into another file—for example, an Excel worksheet or a Word document.

Activity 5.4 Creating a Totals Query

A **totals query** calculates subtotals across groups of records. For example, to subtotal the number of inventory items by suppliers, use a totals query to group the records by the supplier and then apply an aggregate function to the On Hand field. In the previous activity, you created a Total row, which applied an aggregate function to one column—field—of data. A totals query is used when you need to apply an aggregate function to some or all of the records in a query. A totals query can then be used as a source for another database object, such as a report.

1 Create a new query in **Query Design**. Add the **5A Suppliers** table and the **5A Inventory** table to the Query design workspace, and then **Close** the **Show Table** dialog box. Expand both field lists. Notice that there is a one-to-many relationship between the tables— *one* supplier can supply *many* items. From the **5A Inventory** field list, add **On Hand** to the first field box in the design grid.

2 On the **Design tab**, in the **Show/Hide group**, click the **Totals** button.

Like the Totals button on the Home tab, this button is a toggle button. In the design grid, a Total row displays under the Table row; and *Group By* displays in the box.

3 In the design grid, in the **Total row**, under **On Hand**, click in the box displaying *Group By* to display the arrow. Click the **arrow**, and then compare your screen with Figure 5.12.

A list of aggregate functions displays. This list displays more functions than the list in Datasheet view, and the function names are abbreviated.

Figure 5.12

Toggle button

Total row

List of aggregate functions

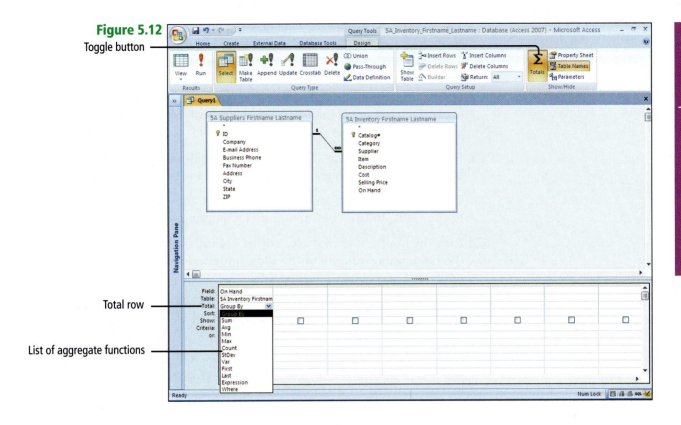

4 From the displayed list, click **Sum**. **Run** the query, and then compare your screen with Figure 5.13.

When you run a totals query, the result—*1160*—of the aggregate function is displayed; the records are not displayed. The name of the function and the field used are displayed in the column heading.

Figure 5.13

Field name displays the function used—*Sum*

Only the sum is displayed in a totals query

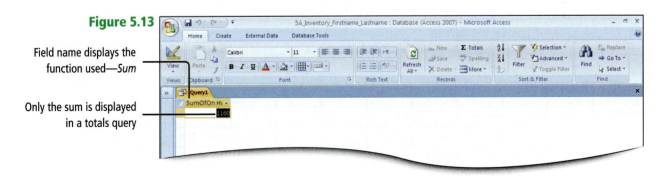

5 Adjust the width of the column to display the entire field name, and then switch to **Design** view. In the **5A Inventory** field list, double-click **Item** to insert the field in the second column in the design grid. In the design grid, under **Item**, click in the **Total row** box, click the displayed **arrow**, and then click **Count**. **Run** the query. Adjust the width of the second column to display the entire field name.

The number of records—*21*—displays. You can include multiple fields in a totals query, but each field in the query must have an aggregate function applied to it. If you include a field but do not apply an aggregate function, the query results will display every record and will not display a single value for the field or fields. The exception to this is when you group records by a category, such as supplier name.

6 Switch to **Design** view. From the **5A Suppliers** field list, drag **Company** to the design grid until the field is on top of **On Hand**.

Company is inserted as the first field, and the *On Hand* field moves to the right. In the *Total* row under *Company*, *Group By* displays.

7 **Run** the query. If necessary, adjust column widths to display all of the field names and all of the data under each field, and then compare your screen with Figure 5.14.

The results display the total number of inventory items on hand from each supplier and the number of individual items purchased from each supplier. By using this type of query, you can identify the supplier that provides the most individual items—Wetsuit Country—and the supplier from whom the company has the most on-hand inventory items—Dave's Sporting Shop.

Figure 5.14

Summed *On Hand* field for each Supplier

Number of inventory items for each Supplier

8 **Save** the query as **5A Total On Hand Per Supplier Firstname Lastname** View the query in **Print Preview**, ensuring that the query prints on one page, and then if you are instructed to submit this result, create a paper or electronic printout. **Close** the query.

Objective 3
Create a Crosstab Query

A **crosstab query** uses an aggregate function for data that is grouped by two types of information and displays the data in a compact, spreadsheet-like format. A crosstab query always has at least one row heading, one column heading, and one summary field. Use a crosstab query to summarize a large amount of data in a small space that is easy to read.

Activity 5.5 Creating a Select Query as the Source for the Crosstab Query

In this activity, you will create a select query displaying suppliers, the category of the inventory item, the inventory item, and the cost per item paid to the supplier. Recall that a select query is the most common type of query, and it extracts data from one or more tables or queries, displaying the results in a datasheet. After creating the select query, you will use the query to create a crosstab query to display the data in a format that is easier to analyze. Because most crosstab queries extract data from more than one table or query, you should first create a select query that contains all of the fields you will use in the creation of the crosstab query.

1 Create a new query in **Query Design**. Add the following tables, in the order specified, to the Query design workspace: **5A Category**, **5A Inventory**, and **5A Suppliers**. In the **Show Table** dialog box, click **Close**. Expand the field lists, rearranging the field lists as needed.

2 In the **5A Suppliers** field list, double-click **Company** to add it to the first field box in the design grid. In the **5A Category** field list, double-click **CatName** to add it to the second field box in the design grid. In the **5A Inventory** field list, double-click **Cost** to add it to the third field box in the design grid. In the design grid, under **Company**, click in the **Sort** box. Click the **arrow**, and then click **Ascending**. Sort the **CatName** field in **Ascending** order.

3 On the **Design tab**, in the **Show/Hide group**, click the **Totals** button. In the design grid, notice a **Total row** displays under the **Table row**. Under **Cost**, click in the **Total** box, click the **arrow**, and then click **Sum**. Compare your screen with Figure 5.15.

Figure 5.15

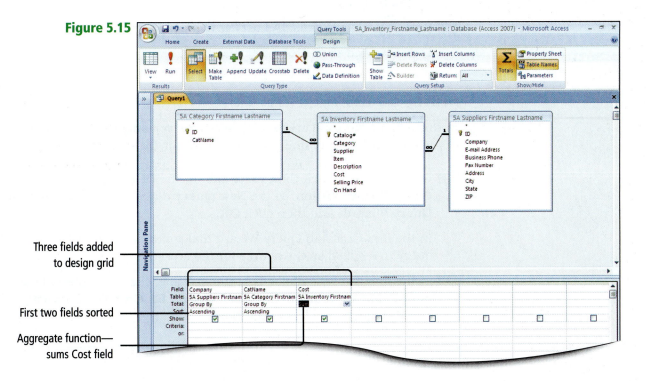

Three fields added to design grid

First two fields sorted

Aggregate function—sums Cost field

4 **Run** the query. In the datasheet, adjust all column widths to display the entire field name and the data for each record, and then compare your screen with Figure 5.16.

The select query groups the totals vertically by company and then by category.

Sum of cost per item sold by the
company within the category

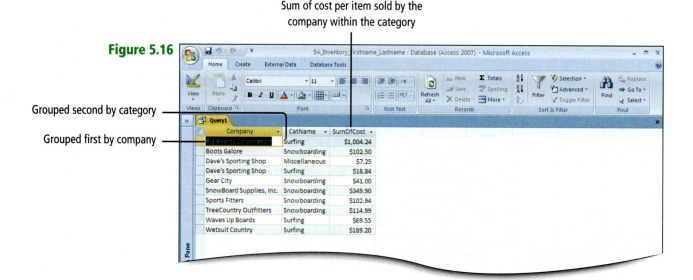

Figure 5.16

Grouped second by category

Grouped first by company

5 Switch to **Design** view. On the **Design tab**, in the **Show/Hide group**, click the **Totals** button to remove the Total row from the design grid.

This select query will be used to create the crosstab query. When you create a crosstab query, you will be prompted to use an aggregate function on a field, so it should not be summed prior to creating the crosstab query.

6 **Save** the query as **5A Cost Per Company and Category Firstname Lastname** and then **Close** the query.

Activity 5.6 Creating a Crosstab Query

In this activity, you will create a crosstab query using the 5A Cost Per Company and Category query as the source for the crosstab query.

1 On the Ribbon, click the **Create tab**. In the **Other group**, click the **Query Wizard** button. In the **New Query** dialog box, click **Crosstab Query Wizard**, and then click **OK**.

In the first Crosstab Query Wizard dialog box, you select the table or query to be used as the source for the crosstab query.

2 In the middle of the dialog box, under **View**, click the **Queries** option button. In the list of queries, click **Query: 5A Cost Per Company and Category**, and then click **Next**.

In the second Crosstab Query Wizard dialog box, you select the fields with data that you want to use as the row headings.

3 Under **Available Fields**, double-click **Company**, and then compare your screen with Figure 5.17.

Company displays under Selected Fields. At the bottom of the dialog box, in the Sample area, a preview of the row headings displays. Each company name will be listed on a separate row, in the first column.

Figure 5.17

Data from Company field populates first column in each row

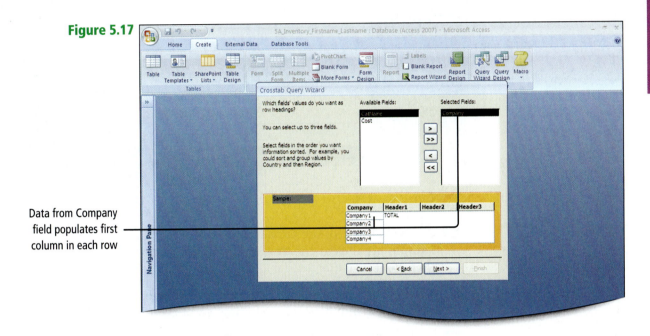

4 In the **Crosstab Query Wizard** dialog box, click **Next**.

In the third dialog box, you select the fields with data that you want to use as column headings.

5 In the displayed list of fields, double-click **CatName**, and then notice in the sample area that the category names display in separate columns. Under **Functions**, click **Sum**, and then compare your screen with Figure 5.18.

This dialog box enables you to apply an aggregate function to one or more fields. The function will add the cost of every item sold by each company for each category. Every row can also be summed.

Figure 5.18

Categories—Snowboarding,
Surfing, Miscellaneous

Cost of items summed per
company, per category

Each row will be summed

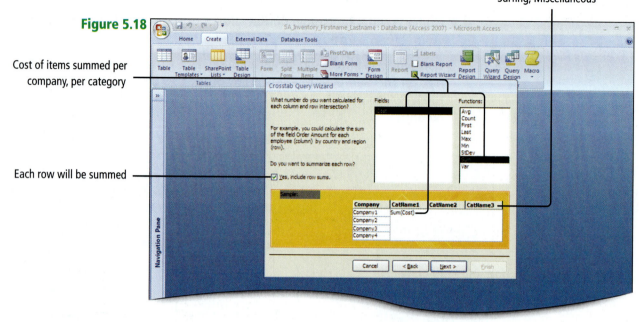

6 On the left side of the **Crosstab Query Wizard** dialog box, above the **Sample** area, clear the **Yes, include row sums** check box, and then click **Next**.

If the check box is selected, a column will be inserted between the first and second column that sums all of the numeric data per row.

7 Under **What do you want to name your query?**, select the existing text, type **5A Crosstab Query Firstname Lastname** and then click **Finish**. Adjust all of the column widths to display the entire field name and the data in each field, and then compare your screen with Figure 5.19. Then take a moment to compare this screen with Figure 5.16, the select query you created with the same extracted data.

The same data is extracted using the select query as shown in Figure 5.16; however, the crosstab query displays the data differently. A crosstab query reduces the number of records displayed as shown by the entry for Dave's Sporting Shop. In the select query, there are two records displayed, one for the Miscellaneous category and one for the Surfing category. The crosstab query combines the data into one record.

Categories—column headings

Cost summed per company, per category

Figure 5.19

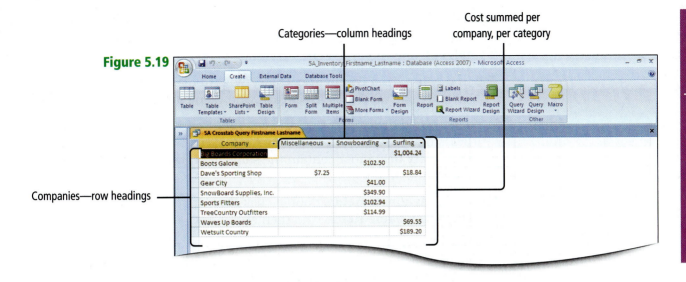

Companies—row headings

Company	Miscellaneous	Snowboarding	Surfing
Big Boards Corporation			$1,004.24
Boots Galore		$102.50	
Dave's Sporting Shop	$7.25		$18.84
Gear City		$41.00	
SnowBoard Supplies, Inc.		$349.90	
Sports Fitters		$102.94	
TreeCountry Outfitters		$114.99	
Waves Up Boards			$69.55
Wetsuit Country			$189.20

Note — Including Row Sums

If you include row sums in a crosstab query, the sum will display in a column between the column for the row headings and the first category column. In the crosstab query created in this activity, the row sums column would display between the Company column and the Miscellaneous column. For Dave's Sporting Shop, the row sum would be $26.09—$7.25 plus $18.84.

8 View the query in **Print Preview**, ensuring that the query prints on one page, and then if you are instructed to submit this result, create a paper or electronic printout. **Close** ☒ the query, saving changes— you adjusted the column widths.

Objective 4
Find Duplicate and Unmatched Records

Even when a table contains a primary key, it is still possible to have duplicate records in a table. For example, the same inventory item can be entered into a table two times, each having a different catalog number. You can use the **Find Duplicates Query Wizard** to locate duplicate records in a table. As databases grow, you may have records in one table that have no matching records in a related table; these are **unmatched records**. For example, there may be a record for a supplier in the Suppliers table, but no inventory items are ordered from that supplier. You can use the **Find Unmatched Query Wizard** to locate unmatched records and then delete the records from the table.

Activity 5.7 Finding Duplicate Records

In this activity, you will find duplicate records in the *5A Inventory* table by using the Find Duplicates Query Wizard.

1 On the **Create tab**, in the **Other group**, click the **Query Wizard** button. In the **New Query** dialog box, click **Find Duplicates Query Wizard**, and then click **OK**.

2 In the first **Find Duplicates Query Wizard** dialog box, in the list of tables, click **Table: 5A Inventory**, and then click **Next**.

The second dialog box displays, enabling you to select the field or fields that may contain duplicate data. If you select all of the fields, then every field must contain the same data, which is not the case for a primary key field.

3 Under **Available fields**, double-click **Item** to move it under **Duplicate-value fields**, and then click **Next**.

The third dialog box displays, enabling you to select one or more fields to display that contain data that will help you distinguish duplicate from nonduplicate records.

4 Under **Available fields**, add the following fields, in the order specified, to the **Additional query fields** box: **Catalog#**, **Category**, **Supplier**, **Cost**, and **Selling Price**. Compare your screen with Figure 5.20.

Fields to help identify
duplicate records

Figure 5.20

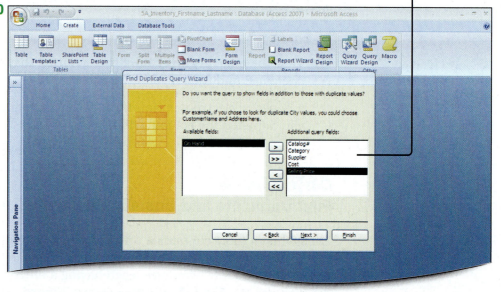

5 Click **Next**. Click **Finish** to accept the suggested query name—*Find duplicates for 5A Inventory Firstname Lastname*—and then compare your screen with Figure 5.21.

Three records display with a duplicate value in the *Item* field. Using the displayed fields, you can determine that the second and third records are duplicates; the *Catalog#* was entered incorrectly for one of the records. By examining the *5A Inventory* table, you can determine that Category 1 is Snowboarding and Category 2 is Surfing. You must exercise care when using the Find Duplicates Query Wizard. If you do not include additional fields to help determine whether the records are duplicates or nonduplicates, you might mistakenly determine that they are duplicates.

Different data in primary key field

Figure 5.21

Duplicate records

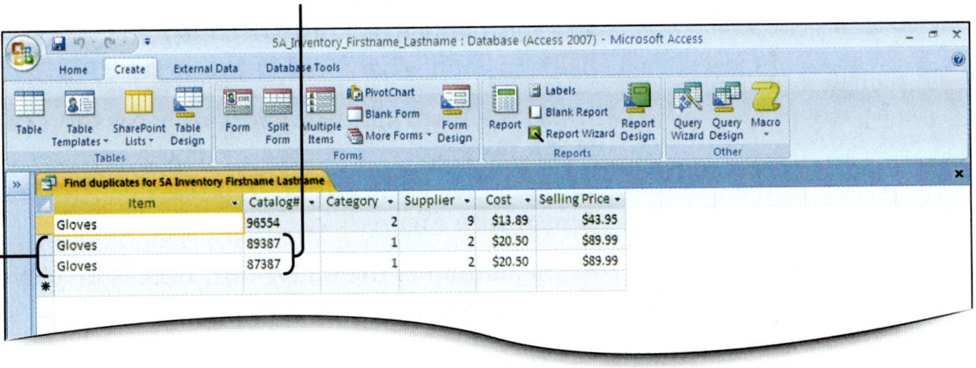

6 Adjust all column widths. View the query in **Print Preview**, ensuring that the query prints on one page, and then if you are instructed to submit this result, create a paper or electronic printout. **Close** ✕ the query, saving changes.

Normally, you would delete the duplicate record, but your instructor needs to verify that you have found the duplicate record by using a query.

More Knowledge
Removing Duplicate Records

If you choose to delete duplicate records, you must first deal with existing table relationships. If the record you want to delete exists in the table on the *many* side of the relationship, you can delete the record without taking additional steps. If the record exists in the table on the *one* side of the relationship, you must first delete the relationship, and then delete the record. You should then re-create the relationship between the tables. You can either manually delete the duplicate records or create a Delete Query to remove the duplicate records.

Activity 5.8 Finding Unmatched Records

In this activity, you will find unmatched records in related tables—
5A Suppliers and *5A Inventory*—by using the Find Unmatched Query Wizard.

1 On the **Create tab**, in the **Other group**, click the **Query Wizard** button. In the **New Query** dialog box, click **Find Unmatched Query Wizard**, and then click **OK**.

2 In the first **Find Unmatched Query Wizard** dialog box, in the list of tables, click **Table: 5A Suppliers**, and then click **Next**.

The second dialog box displays, enabling you to select the related table or query that you would like Access to compare to the first table to find unmatched records.

3 In the list of tables, click **Table: 5A Inventory**, and then click **Next**.

The third dialog box displays, enabling you to select the matching fields in each table.

4 Under **Fields in 5A Suppliers**, if necessary, click **ID**. Under **Fields in 5A Inventory**, if necessary, click **Supplier**. Between the two fields columns, click the button that displays **<=>**, and then compare your screen with Figure 5.22.

At the bottom of the dialog box, Access displays the matching fields of ID and Supplier.

Links common fields

Common field in 5A Inventory table

Figure 5.22

Common field in 5A Suppliers table

Matching fields

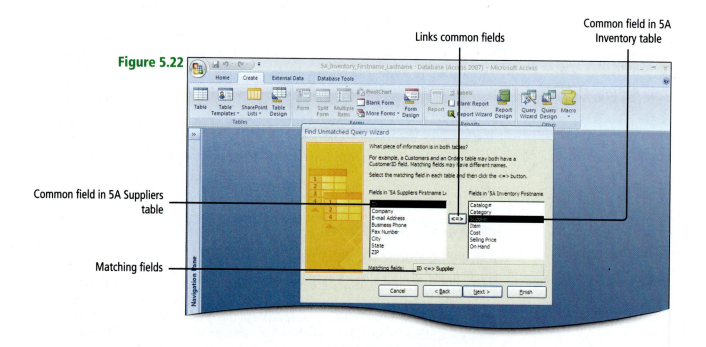

5 Click **Next**. Under **Available fields**, double-click **ID**, and then double-click **Company** to move the field names under **Selected Fields**. Notice that these fields will display in the query results. Click **Next**.

6 In the last dialog box, under **What would you like to name your query?**, type **5A Find Unmatched Query Firstname Lastname** and then click **Finish**. Compare your screen with Figure 5.23.

The query results display one company—*Winter Sports Club*—that has no inventory items in the *5A Inventory* table. Normally, you would either delete the Winter Sports Club record from the *5A Suppliers* table or add inventory items in the related *5A Inventory* for the Winter Sports Club, but your instructor needs to verify that you have located an unmatched record by using a query.

Figure 5.23

Supplier with no inventory items

---

7 Adjust all column widths. View the query in **Print Preview**, ensuring that the query prints on one page, and then if you are instructed to submit this result, create a paper or electronic printout. **Close** ☒ the query, saving changes.

More Knowledge

Finding Unmatched Records in a Table with Multivalued Fields

You cannot use the Find Unmatched Query Wizard with a table that has *multivalued fields*—fields that appear to hold multiple values. If your table contains multivalued fields, you must first create a query, extracting all of the fields except the multivalued fields, and then create the query to find unmatched records.

Objective 5
Create a Parameter Query

A *parameter query* prompts you for criteria before running the query. For example, if you had a database of snowboarding events, you might need to find all of the snowboarding events in a particular state. You can create a select query for a state, but when you need to find information about snowboarding events in another state, you must open the original select query in Design view, change the criteria, and then run the query again. With a parameter query, you can create one query—Access will prompt you to enter the state and then display the results based upon the criteria you enter in the dialog box.

Activity 5.9 Creating a Parameter Query Using One Criteria

In this activity, you will create a parameter query to display a specific category of inventory items. You can enter a parameter anywhere you use text, number, or date criteria.

1 Expand ⌦ the **Navigation Pane**. Under **Tables**, double-click **5A Inventory** to open the table in **Datasheet** view. In any record, click in the **Category** field, and then click the **arrow** to display the list of categories. Take a moment to study the four categories used in this table. Be sure you do not change the category for the selected record. **Close** ⊠ the table, and collapse « the **Navigation Pane**.

2 Create a new query in **Query Design**. Add the **5A Category** table, the **5A Inventory** table, and the **5A Suppliers** table to the Query design workspace, and then **Close** the **Show Table** dialog box. Expand the field lists. From the **5A Category** field list, add **CatName** to the first column in the design grid. From the **5A Inventory** field list, add **Catalog#** and **Item** to the second and third columns in the design grid. From the **5A Suppliers** field list, add **Company** to the fourth column in the design grid.

3 In the **Criteria row**, in the **CatName** field, type **[Enter a Category]** and then compare your screen with Figure 5.24.

The brackets indicate a **parameter**—a value that can be changed—rather than specific criteria. When you run the query, a dialog box will display, prompting you to Enter a Category. The category you type will be set as the criteria for the query. Because you are prompted for the criteria, you can reuse this query without resetting the criteria in Design view.

Figure 5.24

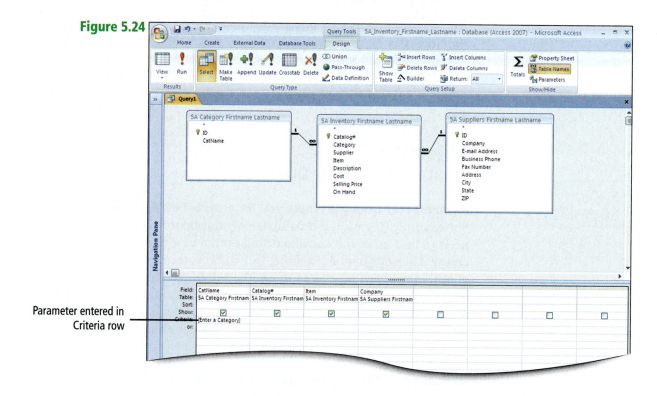

Parameter entered in Criteria row

4 **Run** the query. In the **Enter Parameter Value** dialog box, type **Snowboarding** and then compare your screen with Figure 5.25.

Figure 5.25

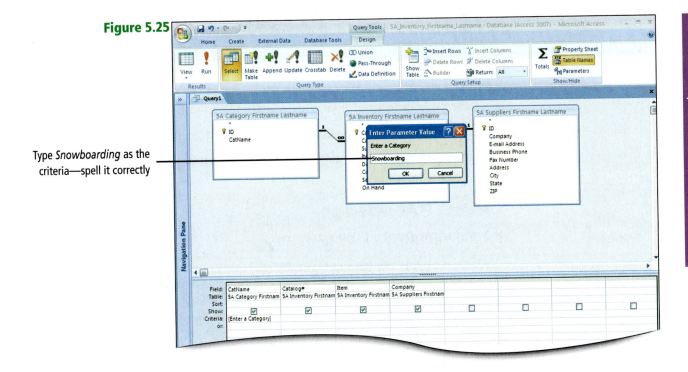

Type *Snowboarding* as the criteria—spell it correctly

Alert!

Does your screen differ?

If the Enter Parameter Value dialog box does not display, you may have typed the parameter incorrectly in the design grid. Common errors include using parentheses or curly braces instead of square brackets around the parameter text, causing Access to interpret the text as specific criteria. When you run the query, there are no records displayed. If you use curly braces, the query will not run. To correct, display the query in Design view, and then correct the parameter entered in the criteria row.

5 In the **Enter Parameter Value** dialog box, click **OK**.

Nine records display where the CatName field is Snowboarding.

6 Adjust all column widths, and **Save** the query as **5A Category Parameter Query Firstname Lastname Close** ☒ the query, and then expand ⟩⟩ the **Navigation Pane**.

7 On the **Navigation Pane**, under **Queries**, double-click **5A Category Parameter Query**. In the **Enter Parameter Value** dialog box, type **Surfing** and then click **OK**.

Eleven items categorized as Surfing display. Recall that when you open a query, Access runs the query so that the most up-to-date data is extracted from the underlying table or query. When you have entered a parameter as the criteria, you will be prompted to enter the criteria every time you open the query.

8 Switch to **Design** view. Notice that the parameter—[Enter a Category]—is stored with the query. Access does not store the criteria entered in the Enter Parameter Value dialog box.

9 **Run** the query, and in the **Enter Parameter Value** dialog box, type **Miscellaneous** being careful to spell it correctly. Click **OK** to display one record. Adjust all column widths.

10 View the query in **Print Preview**, ensuring that the query prints on one page, and then if you are instructed to submit this result, create a paper or electronic printout. **Close** ⊠ the query, saving changes, and then collapse « the **Navigation Pane**.

More Knowledge

Parameter Query Prompts

When you enter the parameter in the criteria row, make sure that the prompt—the text enclosed in the square brackets—is not the same as the field name. For example, if the field name is *Category*, do not enter *[Category]* as the parameter. Because Access uses field names in square brackets for calculations, no prompt will display. If you want to use the field name by itself as a prompt, type a question mark at the end of the prompt; for example, *[Category?]*. You cannot use a period, exclamation mark (!), square brackets ([]), or the ampersand (&) as part of the prompt.

Activity 5.10 Creating a Parameter Query Using Multiple Criteria

In this activity, you will create a parameter query to display the inventory items that fall within a certain range in the On Hand field.

1 Create a new query in **Query Design**. Add the **5A Suppliers** table and the **5A Inventory** table to the Query design workspace, and then **Close** the **Show Table** dialog box. Expand the field lists. From the **5A Inventory** field list, add **Item** and **On Hand** to the first and second columns in the design grid. From the **5A Suppliers** field list box, add **Company** to the third column in the design grid.

2 In the **Criteria row**, right-click in the **On Hand** field, and then click **Zoom**. In the **Zoom** dialog box, type **Between[Type the lower on-hand number:]And[Type the higher on-hand number:]** and then compare your screen with Figure 5.26.

The Zoom dialog box enables you to see the entire parameter. The parameter includes *Between* and *And*, which will display a range of data. Two dialog boxes will display when you run the query. You will be prompted first to enter the lower number and then the higher number.

Zoom dialog box

Figure 5.26

Parameter with two prompts

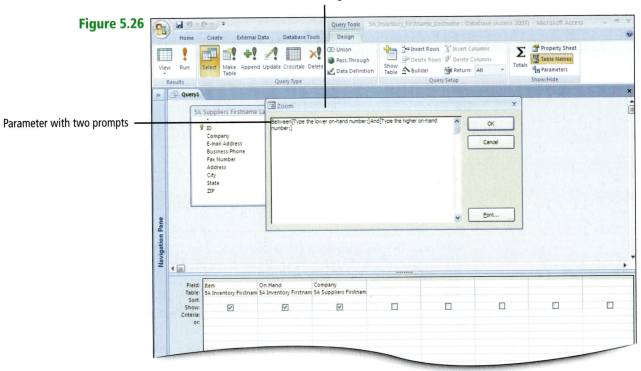

3 After verifying that you have entered the correct parameter, in the **Zoom** dialog box, click **OK**, and then **Run** the query. In the first **Enter Parameter Value** dialog box, type **0** and then click **OK**. In the second **Enter Parameter Value** dialog box, type **20** and then click **OK**. Compare your screen with Figure 5.27.

Two records have on-hand items in the range of 0 to 20. These might be inventory items that need to be ordered.

In the range of 0 to 20

Figure 5.27

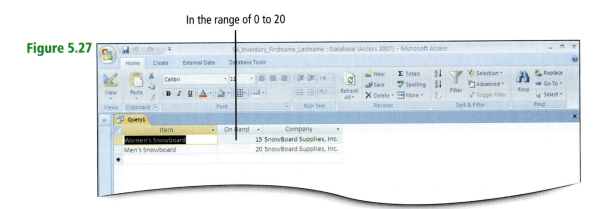

4 Adjust all column widths, and **Save** the query as **5A On Hand Parameter Query Firstname Lastname**

5 View the query in **Print Preview**, ensuring that the query prints on one page, and then if you are instructed to submit this result, create a paper or electronic printout. **Close** ☒ the query.

6 Expand ☒ the **Navigation Pane**. **Close** the database, and **exit** Access.

More Knowledge

Creating a Parameter Query Using Multiple Criteria

When you create a query using more than one field with parameters, the individual sees the prompts in the order that the fields are arranged from left to right in the design grid. When you create a query using more than one parameter in a single field, the individual sees the prompts in the order displayed, from left to right, in the criteria box. If you want the prompts to display in a different order, on the Design tab, in the Show/Hide group, click the Parameters button.

In the Parameter column, type the prompt for each parameter exactly as it was typed in the design grid. Enter the parameters in the order you want the dialog boxes to display when the query is run. In the Data type column, next to each entered parameter, specify the data type by clicking the arrow and displaying the list of data types. Click OK, and then run the query.

End **You have completed Project 5A** ————————

Project 5B **Orders**

Shinpei Kawano, Sales Associate for Board Anywhere Surf and Snowboard Shop, must keep the tables in the database up to date and ensure that the queries display pertinent information. In Activities 5.11 through 5.18, you will create action queries that will create a new table, update records in a table, append records to a table, and delete records from a table. You will also modify the join type of relationships to display different subsets of the data when the query is run. Your completed queries will look similar to the queries shown in Figure 5.28.

For Project 5B, you will need the following files:

a05B_Orders
a05B_Potential_Customers

**You will save your databases as
5B_Orders_Firstname_Lastname
5B_Potential_Customers_Firstname_Lastname**

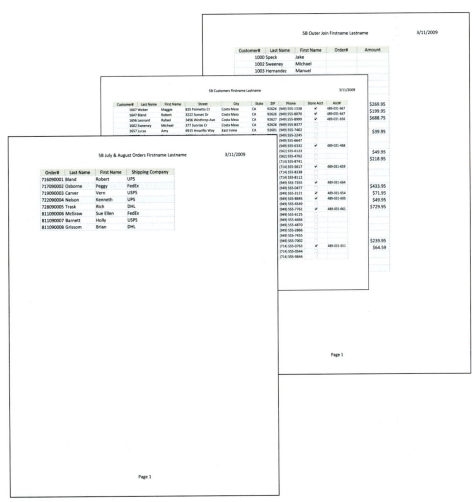

Figure 5.28
Project 5B—Orders

Objective 6
Create a Make Table Query

An *action query* enables you create a new table or change data in an existing table. A *make table query* is an action query that creates a new table by extracting data from one or more tables. Creating a new table from existing tables is useful when you need to copy or back up data. For example, you may wish to create a table that displays the orders for the past month. The orders will not change because the month is in the past. You can extract that data and store it in another table, using the new table as a source for reports or queries. So, why not use a query instead of creating a new table? Extracting data from a large database can take time, and recall that every time you open a query, the underlying tables or queries are read to ensure that the query displays the most up-to-date data. Extracting data and storing it in a new table reduces the time to retrieve *static data*—data that does not change—and creates a convenient backup of the data.

Activity 5.11 Creating a Select Query

In this activity, you will create a select query to extract the fields you wish to store in the new table.

1 **Start** Access. Navigate to the location where the student data files for this textbook are saved. Locate and open the **a05B_Orders** file. Save the database in the **Access 2007 Database** format in your **Access Chapter 5** folder as 5B_Orders_Firstname_Lastname

2 If you did not add the Access Chapter 5 folder to the Trust Center, enable the content. On the **Navigation Pane**, under **Tables**, rename the four tables by adding **Firstname Lastname** to the end of each table name. Take a moment to open each table and observe the data in each. In the **5B Orders** table, make a note of the data type for the **Order#** field and the pattern of data entered in the field. When you are finished, close all of the tables, and collapse « the **Navigation Pane**.

In the *5B Orders* table, the first record contains an Order# of 7-16-09-0001. The first section of the order number is the month of the order, the second section is the day of the month, and the third section is the year. The fourth section is a sequential number. Records with orders for July, August, and September are contained in this table.

Alert!

Action queries and trusted databases

To run an action query, the database must reside in a trusted location, or you must enable the content. If you try running an action query and nothing happens, check the status bar for the following message: *This action or event has been blocked by Disabled Mode*. Either add the storage location to Trusted Locations or enable the content. Then, run the query again.

---

3 **Create** a new query in **Query Design**. From the **Show Table** dialog box, add the following tables, in the order specified, to the Query design workspace: **5B Customers**, **5B Orders**, and **5B Shippers**. **Close** the **Show Table** dialog box, and then expand the field lists. Notice the relationships between the tables.

The *5B Customers* table has a one-to-many relationship with the *5B Orders* table—*one* customer can have *many* orders. The *5B Shippers* table has a one-to-many relationship with the *5B Orders* table—*one* shipper can ship *more* than one order.

4 From the **5B Orders** field list, add **Order#** to the first column of the design grid. From the **5B Customers** field list, add **Last Name** and **First Name**, in the order specified, to the second and third columns of the design grid. From the **5B Shippers** field list, add **Shipping Company** to the fourth column of the design grid.

5 In the design grid, under **Order#**, click in the **Criteria row**, type **"7*"** and then compare your screen with Figure 5.29.

Because this field has a data type of Text, you must type quotation marks around *7**; otherwise, Access will interpret the criteria as numeric data, resulting in a data mistype error when you run the query. Recall that the asterisk is a wildcard that stands for one or more characters—Access will extract the records where the Order# starts with a 7, and it does not matter what the following characters are. The first section of the Order# contains the month the order was placed. You do not need criteria in a select query to convert it to a make table query.

Field added from 5B Shipping table

Figure 5.29

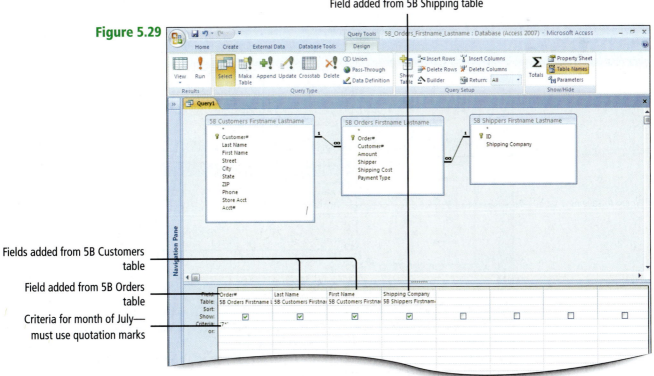

Fields added from 5B Customers table

Field added from 5B Orders table

Criteria for month of July— must use quotation marks

Note — Using Expressions and Aggregate Functions in a Make Table Query

In addition to using criteria in a select query upon which a make table query is based, you can use expressions to create a calculated field; for example, *Total Price:[Unit Price]**[On Hand]*. You can also use aggregate functions; for example, you may want to sum the *On Hand* field.

6 **Run** the query, and notice that five orders were placed in July.

The select query displays the records that will be stored in the new table.

Activity 5.12 Converting a Select Query to a Make Table Query

In this activity, you will convert the select query you just created to a make table query.

1 Switch to **Design** view. On the **Design tab**, in the **Query Type group**, click the **Make Table** button. Notice the dark exclamation point (!) in several of the buttons in the Query Type group—these are action queries. In the **Make Table** dialog box, in the **Table Name** box, type **5B July Orders Firstname Lastname** and then compare your screen with Figure 5.30.

The table name should be a unique table name for the database in which the table will be saved. If it is not, you will be prompted to delete the first table before the new table can be created. You can save a make table query in the current database or in another existing database.

Dark exclamation point designates action query type

New table name

Figure 5.30

Where to save new table

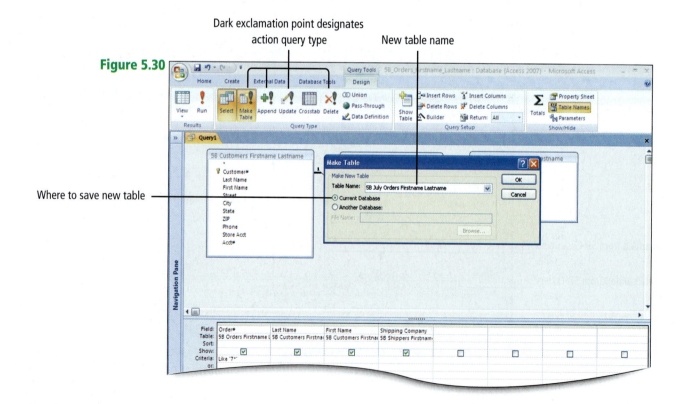

2 In the **Make Table** dialog box, be sure that **Current Database** is selected, and then click **OK**. **Run** the query.

A message displays indicating that *You are about to paste 5 row(s) into a new table* and that you cannot use the Undo command.

3 In the displayed message box, click **Yes**. **Close** ✕ the query, click **Yes** in the message box prompting you to save changes, and then name the query **5B Make Table Query Firstname Lastname**

4 Expand 》 the **Navigation Pane**. Notice that under **Tables**, the new table you created—**5B July Orders**—is displayed. Under **Queries**, the **5B Make Table Query** is displayed.

5 On the **Navigation Pane**, click the title—**All Access Objects**. Under **Navigate To Category**, click **Tables and Related Views**, and then compare your screen with Figure 5.31.

The Navigation Pane is grouped by tables and related objects. Because the 5B Make Table Query extracted records from three tables—*5B Customers*, *5B Orders*, and *5B Shippers*—it is displayed under all three tables. Changing the grouping on the Navigation Pane to Tables and Related Views enables you to easily determine which objects are dependent upon other objects in the database.

Figure 5.31

Icon for make table query

Query extracted records from three tables

Table created with make table query

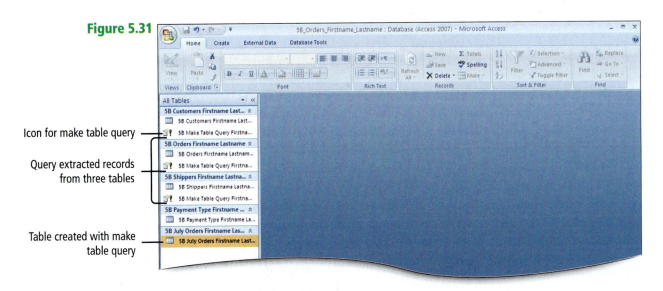

6 On the **Navigation Pane**, double-click **5B July Orders** to open the table in datasheet view. If you click the category title instead of the table, the category will collapse—if that happens, double-click the category title to redisplay the table, and then double-click the table. Notice that the data in the **Order#** field does not display as it did in the **5B Orders** table. Switch to **Design** view.

7 Notice that the **Order#** table has a data type of **Number** and that there is no **Primary Key** field for this table.

Because the data in the Order# field began with a number, when the new table was created, Access assigned a data type of Number to the field. The data type for this field in the *5B Orders* table is Text. When using a make table query to create a new table, the data in the new table does not inherit the field properties or the primary key field setting from the original table.

8 Switch to **Datasheet** view, and then adjust all column widths. **Close** [×] the table, saving changes.

Note — Updating a Table Created with a Make Table Query

The data stored in a table created with a make table query is not automatically updated when records in the original tables are modified. To keep the new table up to date, you must run the make table query periodically to be sure the information is current.

Objective 7
Create an Append Query

An **append query** is an action query that adds new records to an existing table by adding data from another Access database or from a table in the same database. An append query can be limited by criteria. Use an append query when the data already exists and you do not want to manually enter it into an existing table. Like the make table query, you first create a select query and then convert it to an append query.

Activity 5.13 Creating an Append Query for a Table in the Current Database

In this activity, you will create a select query to extract the records for customers who have placed orders in August and then append the records to the *5B July Orders* table.

1 Collapse [«] the **Navigation Pane**. Create a new query in **Query Design**. From the **Show Table** dialog box, add the following tables, in the order specified, to the Query design workspace: **5B Customers**, **5B Orders**, and **5B Shippers**. **Close** the **Show Table** dialog box, and then expand the field lists.

2 From the **5B Customers** field list, add **First Name** and **Last Name**, in the order specified, to the first and second columns of the design grid. From the **5B Orders** field list, add **Order#** and **Shipping Cost**, in the order specified, to the third and fourth columns of the design grid. From the **5B Shippers** field list, add **Shipping Company** to the fifth column of the design grid.

3 In the design grid, under **Order#**, click in the **Criteria row**, type **"8*"** and then press [↓]. Compare your screen with Figure 5.32.

Figure 5.32

Access | chapter 5

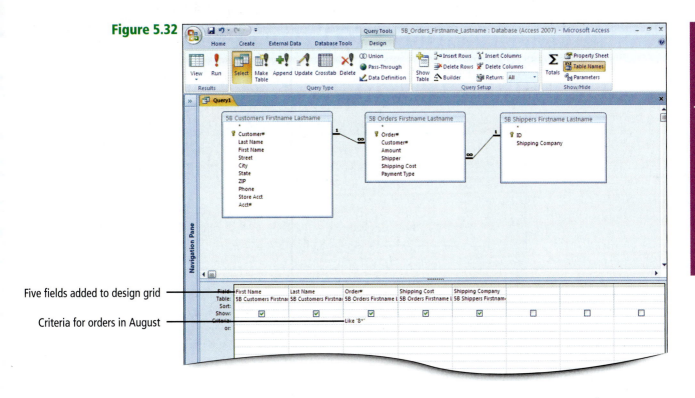

Five fields added to design grid

Criteria for orders in August

4 **Run** the query, and notice that three customers placed orders in August.

5 Switch to **Design** view. On the **Design tab**, in the **Query Type group**, click the **Append** button. In the **Append** dialog box, click the **Table Name arrow**, and from the displayed list, click **5B July Orders**, and then click **OK**. Compare your screen with Figure 5.33.

In the design grid, Access inserts an *Append To* row above the Criteria row. Access compares the fields in the Append query with the fields in the **destination table**—the table to which you are appending the fields—and attempts to match the fields. If a match in field names is found, Access automatically adds the names of the destination fields to the Append To row in the query with brackets around each field name. If no match is found, Access leaves the destination field blank. You can click the box in the Append To row and select a destination field.

Figure 5.33

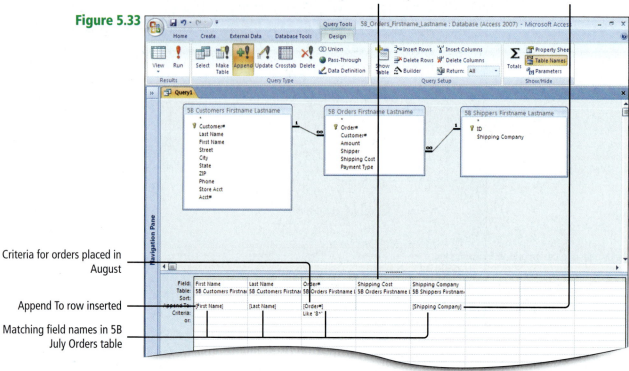

Criteria for orders placed in August

Append To row inserted

Matching field names in 5B July Orders table

6 In the design grid, under **First Name**, click in the **Append To row**, and then click the displayed **arrow**. From the displayed list, click **First Name**, and then press ↓. Alternatively, delete the brackets that display around the field name.

The brackets no longer display around the field name. In order for the append query to run properly, there should not be any brackets around the field names in the Append To row.

7 Using the technique you just practiced, on the **Append To row**, remove the brackets from **[Last Name]**, **[Order#]**, and **[Shipping Company]**.

8 **Run** the query. In the displayed message box, click **Yes** to append the three rows to the *5B July Orders* table.

9 **Close** ✕ the query, and then save it as **5B Append August Orders Firstname Lastname**

10 Expand » the **Navigation Pane**. Notice that **5B Append August Orders** displays under the three tables from which data was extracted.

11 On the **Navigation Pane**, click the title—**All Tables**. Under **Navigate To Category**, click **Object Type** to group the Navigation Pane objects by type. Under **Queries**, notice the icon that displays for **5B Append August Orders**. Recall that this icon indicates the query is an action query.

12 Under **Tables**, double-click **5B July Orders** to open the table in **Datasheet** view, and then compare your screen with Figure 5.34.

Three orders for August are appended to the *5B July Orders* table. Because there is no match in the *5B July Orders* table for the Shipping Cost field in the 5B Append August Orders Query, the field is ignored when the records are appended.

Figure 5.34

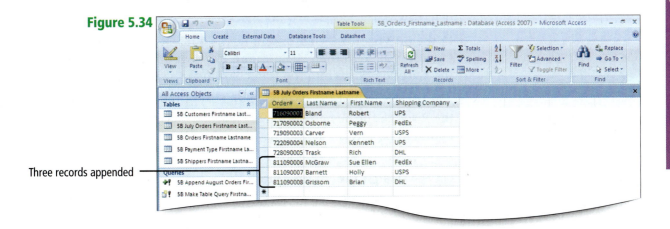

Three records appended

<table>
<tr><th>Order#</th><th>Last Name</th><th>First Name</th><th>Shipping Company</th></tr>
<tr><td>716090001</td><td>Bland</td><td>Robert</td><td>UPS</td></tr>
<tr><td>717090002</td><td>Osborne</td><td>Peggy</td><td>FedEx</td></tr>
<tr><td>719090003</td><td>Carver</td><td>Vern</td><td>USPS</td></tr>
<tr><td>722090004</td><td>Nelson</td><td>Kenneth</td><td>UPS</td></tr>
<tr><td>728090005</td><td>Trask</td><td>Rich</td><td>DHL</td></tr>
<tr><td>811090006</td><td>McGraw</td><td>Sue Ellen</td><td>FedEx</td></tr>
<tr><td>811090007</td><td>Barnett</td><td>Holly</td><td>USPS</td></tr>
<tr><td>811090008</td><td>Grissom</td><td>Brian</td><td>DHL</td></tr>
</table>

13 **Close** ☒ the table. On the **Navigation Pane**, under **Tables**, right-click **5B July Orders**, and then click **Rename**. Rename the table as **5B July & August Orders Firstname Lastname**

14 With **5B July & August Orders** selected, click the **Office** button 🗐 and view the table in **Print Preview**. If you are instructed to submit this result, create a paper or electronic printout of the table, and then **Close** ☒ the Print Preview window.

Activity 5.14 Creating an Append Query for a Table in Another Database

Shinpei Kawano recently discovered that the marketing manager has been keeping a database of persons who have requested information about the Board Anywhere Surf and Snowboard Shop. These names need to be added to the *5B Customers* table so those potential clients can receive catalogs when they are distributed. In this activity, you will create an append query to add the records from the marketing manager's table to the *5B Customers* table.

1 On the Access window title bar, click the **Minimize** button 🔲 . Click the **Start** button ⟦🏁 start⟧ , and then open **Access**. Navigate to the location where the student data files for this textbook are saved. Locate and open the **a05B_Potential_Customers** file. Save the database in the **Access 2007 Database** format in your **Access Chapter 5** folder as **5B_Potential_Customers_Firstname_Lastname**

2 If you did not add the Access Chapter 5 folder to the Trust Center, enable the content. On the **Navigation Pane**, under **Tables**, rename the table by adding **Firstname Lastname** to the end of **5B Potential Customers**. Take a moment to open the table, noticing the fields and field names. When you are finished, **Close** ☒ the table, and collapse ⟦«⟧ the **Navigation Pane**.

The *5B Potential Customers* table in this database contains similar fields to the *5B Customers* table in the 5B_Orders database.

3 Create a new query in **Query Design**. From the **Show Table** dialog box, add the **5B Potential Customers** table to the Query design workspace, and then **Close** the **Show Table** dialog box. Expand the field list.

4 In the **5B Potential Customers** field list, click **Customer#**, hold down ⇧Shift, and then click **Phone** to select all of the fields. Drag the selection down into the first column of the design grid.

Although you could click the asterisk (*) in the field list to add all of the fields to the design grid, it is easier to detect which fields have no match in the destination table when the field names are listed individually in the design grid.

5 On the **Design tab**, in the **Query Type group**, click the **Append** button. In the **Append** dialog box, click the **Another Database** option button, and then click the **Browse** button. Navigate to your **Access Chapter 5** folder, and then double-click **5B_Orders**.

The 5B_Orders database contains the destination table.

6 In the **Append** dialog box, click the **Table Name arrow**, click **5B Customers**, and then compare your screen with Figure 5.35.

Once you select the name of another database, the tables contained in that database display.

Figure 5.35

Destination table

Destination database

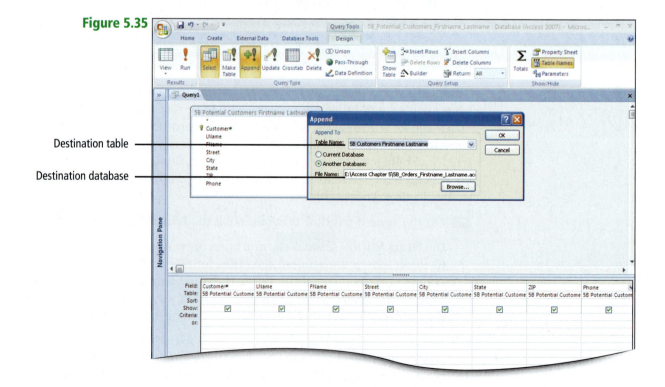

7 Click **OK**. In the design grid, notice that in the **Append To row**, Access found field name matches for all fields, except **LName** and **FName**. In the design grid, under **Customer#**, click in the **Append To row**, and then click the **arrow**. From the displayed list, click **Customer#**.

The brackets no longer display around Customer#. Recall that the brackets must be removed from any field name that displays in the Append To row for the query to run correctly.

8 In the design grid, under **LName**, click in the **Append To row**, click the **arrow**, and then compare your screen with Figure 5.36.

A list displays the field names contained in the *5B Customers* table. If the field names are not exactly the same in the source and destination tables, Access will not designate them as matched fields. A *source table* is the table from which records are being extracted.

Figure 5.36

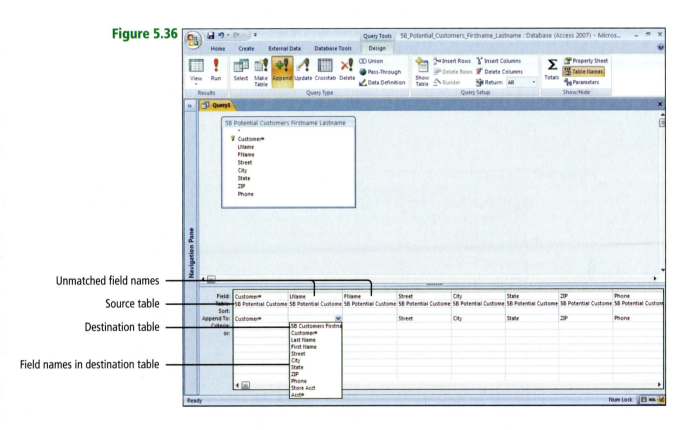

Unmatched field names
Source table
Destination table
Field names in destination table

9 In the displayed list, click **Last Name**. Under **FName**, click in the **Append To row**, and then click the **arrow**. In the displayed list, click **First Name**.

10 **Save** the query as **5B Append to 5B Customers Firstname Lastname** and then **Run** the query. In the displayed message box, click **Yes** to append 8 rows. **Close** the query, and then expand the **Navigation Pane**. **Close** the database, and then **Exit** Access.

To trust or not to trust? That is the question!

When you allow someone else to run an action query that will modify a table in your database, be sure that you can trust that individual. One mistake in the action query could destroy your table. A better way of running an action query that is dependent upon someone else's table is to obtain a copy of the table, place it in a database that you have created, and examine the table for malicious code. Once you are satisfied that the table is safe, you can create the action query to modify the data in your tables. Be sure to make a backup copy of the destination database before running action queries.

11 On the taskbar, click the button for your **5B_Orders** database. If you mistakenly closed the 5B_Orders database, reopen it. On the **Navigation Pane**, under **Tables**, double-click **5B Customers** to open the table in **Datasheet** view. Collapse ⟪ the **Navigation Pane**. Compare your screen with Figure 5.37.

The first eight records—Customer#'s 1000 through 1007—have been appended to the 5B Customers table. The last two fields—Store Acct and Acct#—are blank since there were no corresponding fields in the 5B Potential Customers table.

No matching fields in source table

Figure 5.37

Eight records appended from another database table

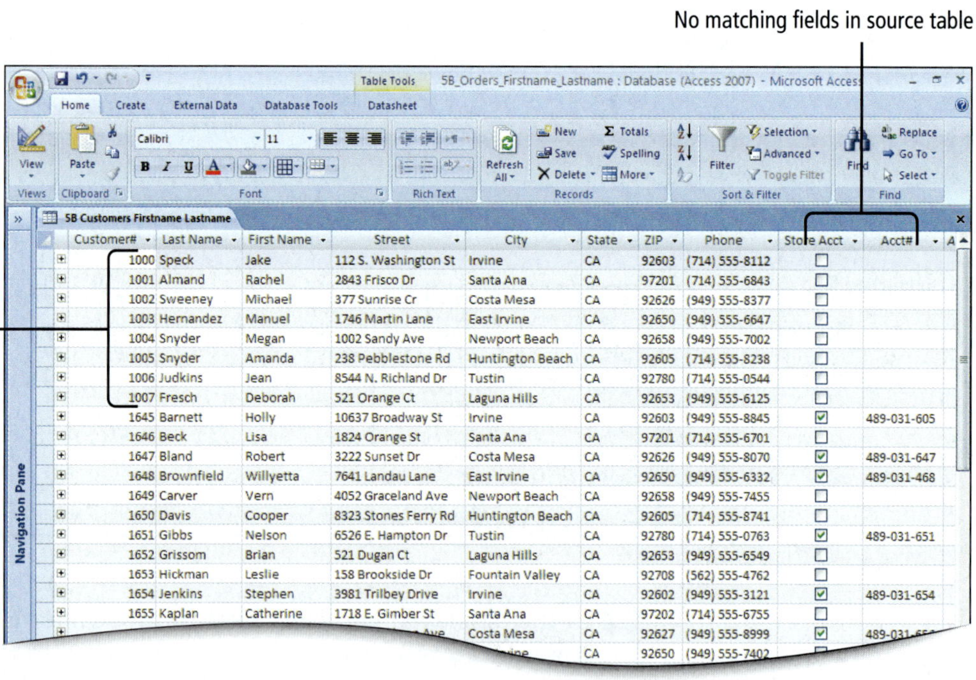

More Knowledge

Running the Same Append Query a Second Time

If you run the same append query a second time with the same records in the source table and no primary key field is involved in the appending of records, you will have duplicate records in the destination table. If a primary key field is part of the record being duplicated, a message will display stating that Access cannot append all of the records due to one of several rule violations. If new records were added to the source table that were not originally appended to the destination table, clicking Yes in the message dialog box will enable those records to be added without adding duplicate records.

Objective 8
Create a Delete Query

A **delete query** is an action query that removes records from an existing table in the same database. When information becomes outdated or is no longer needed, the records should be deleted from your database. Recall that one method you can use to find unnecessary records is to create a Find Unmatched query. Assuming outdated records have a common criteria, you can create a select query, convert it to a delete query, and then delete all of the records at one time rather than deleting the records one by one. Use delete queries only when you need to remove many records quickly. Before running a delete query, you should back up the database.

Activity 5.15 Creating a Delete Query

A competing store has opened in Santa Ana, and the former customers living in that city have decided to do business with that store. In this activity, you will create a select query and then convert it to a delete query to remove records for clients living in Santa Ana.

1 With the **5B Customers** table open in **Datasheet** view, under **City**, click in any row. On the **Home tab**, in the **Sort & Filter group**, click the **Descending** button to arrange the cities in descending alphabetical order.

2 At the top of the datasheet, in the record for **Customer# 1660**, click the **plus (+) sign** to display the subdatasheet. Notice that this customer has placed an order that has been shipped.

3 Display the subdatasheets for the four customers residing in **Santa Ana**, and then compare your screen with Figure 5.38.

All four customers residing in Santa Ana have placed no orders.

Figure 5.38

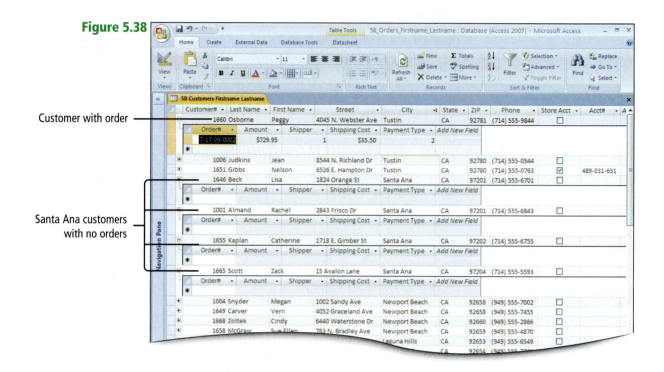

Customer with order

Santa Ana customers
with no orders

4 Collapse all of the subdatasheets by clicking each **minus (–) sign**.

5 On the Ribbon, click the **Database Tools tab**. In the **Show/Hide group**, click the **Relationships** button. On the **Design tab**, in the **Relationships group**, click the **All Relationships** button. Expand the field lists and rearrange the field lists to match the layout displayed in Figure 5.39.

The *5B Customers* table has a one-to-many relationship with the *5B Orders* table, and referential integrity has been enforced. By default, Access will prevent the deletion of records from the table on the *one* side of the relationship if related records are contained in the table on the *many* side of the relationship.

To delete records from the table on the *one* side of the relationship that have related records in the table on the *many* side of the relationship, you must either delete the relationship or enable Cascade Delete Related Records. Because the records for the Santa Ana customers do not have related records in the related table, you will be able to delete the records from the *5B Customers* table, which is on the *one* side of the relationship. If you need to delete records on the *many* side of the relationship, you can do so without changing or deleting the relationship.

Figure 5.39

One-to-many relationship   *Many* side

One side

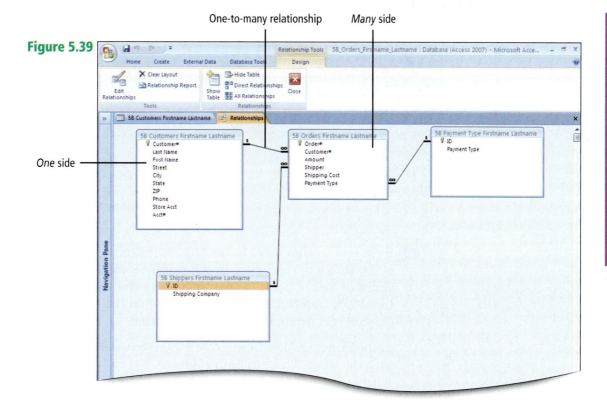

6 On the **tab row**, right-click any tab, and then click **Close All**, saving changes to the table and to the layout of the Relationships window. Create a new query in **Query Design**. Add the **5B Customers** table to the Query design workspace, and then close the **Show Table** dialog box. Expand the field list. From the field list, add **Customer#** and **City**, in the order specified, to the first and second columns in the design grid.

Since you are deleting existing records based on criteria, you need to add only the field that has criteria attached to it—the City field. However, it is easier to analyze the results if you include another field in the design grid.

7 In the design grid, under **City**, click in the **Criteria** row, type **Santa Ana** and then press ⬇.

Access inserts the criteria in quotation marks because this is a Text field.

8 **Run** the query, and then compare your screen with Figure 5.40.

Four records for customers in Santa Ana are displayed. If your query results display an empty record, switch to Design view and be sure that you typed the criteria correctly.

Figure 5.40

Customers living in Santa Ana

9 Switch to **Design** view. In the Query design workspace, to the right of the field list, right-click in the empty space. From the displayed shortcut menu, point to **Query Type** as shown in Figure 5.41, and then click **Delete Query**. Alternatively, on the Design tab, in the Query Type group, click the Delete button.

In the design grid, a Delete row is inserted above the Criteria row with the word *Where* in both columns. Access will delete all records *Where* the City is Santa Ana. If you include all of the fields in the query using the asterisk (*), Access inserts the word *From* in the Delete row, and all of the records will be deleted.

Shortcut menu

Figure 5.41

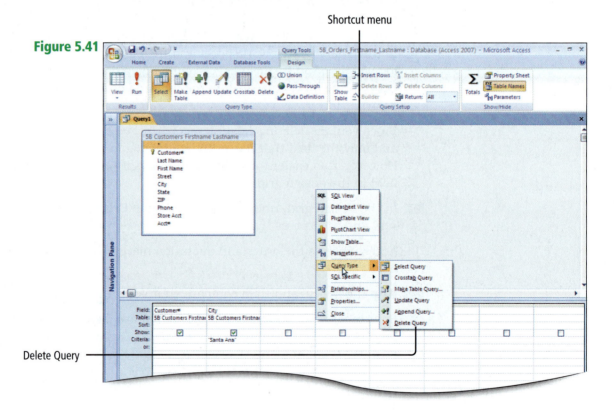

Delete Query

10 Save [icon] the query as **5B Delete Santa Ana Customers Firstname Lastname** and then **Run** the query. In the message box stating that *You are about to delete 4 row(s) from the specified table*, click **Yes**.

11 Close [icon] the query, and then expand [icon] the **Navigation Pane**. Under **Queries**, notice the icon that is associated with a delete query—**5B Delete Santa Ana Customers**. Under **Tables**, open the **5B Customers** table in **Datasheet** view. Notice that the records are still in descending order by the **City** field, and notice that the four records for customers living in **Santa Ana** have been deleted from the table.

12 Collapse [icon] the **Navigation Pane**, leaving the table open for the next activity. On the **Home tab**, in the **Sort & Filter group**, click the **Clear All Sorts** button [icon] to remove the descending sort from the City field.

Objective 9
Create an Update Query

An *update query* is an action query that is used to add, change, or delete data in fields of one or more existing records. Combined with criteria, an update query is an efficient way to change data for a large number of records at one time, and you can change records in more than one table at a time. If you need to change data in a few records, you can use the Find and Replace dialog box. You are unable to use update queries to add records to a table or delete records from a table; you can use them only to change data in existing records. To add records to a table, use an append query. To delete records from a table, use a delete query. You should back up your database before running an update query.

Activity 5.16 Creating an Update Query

The ZIP codes are changing for all of the customers living in Irvine or East Irvine to a consolidated ZIP code. In this activity, you will create a select query to extract the records from the *5B Customers* table for customers living in these cities and then convert the query to an update query so that you change the ZIP codes for all of the records at one time.

1 With the **5B Customers** table open in **Datasheet** view, click in the **City** field in any row. Sort the **City** field in **Ascending** order. Notice that there are four customers living in **East Irvine** with ZIP codes of **92650** and five customers living in **Irvine** with ZIP codes of **92602**, **92603**, and **92604**.

2 Close [icon] the table, saving changes. Create a new query in **Query Design**. Add the **5B Customers** table to the Query design workspace, and then close the **Show Table** dialog box. Expand the field list.

3 In the **5B Customers** field list, double-click **City** to add the field to the first column of the design grid. Then add the **ZIP** field to the second column of the design grid. In the design grid, under **City**, click in the **Criteria row**, and then type **Irvine or East Irvine** Alternatively, type **Irvine** in the Criteria row, and then type **East Irvine** in the or row. **Run** the query.

Nine records display for the cities of Irvine or East Irvine. If your screen does not display nine records, switch to Design view and be sure you typed the criteria correctly. Then run the query again.

4 Switch to **Design** view, and then notice how Access changed the criteria under the **City** field, placing quotation marks around the text and capitalizing *or*. On the **Design tab**, in the **Query Type group**, click the **Update** button.

In the design grid, an Update To row is inserted above the Criteria row.

5 In the design grid, under **ZIP**, click in the **Update To row**, type **92601** and then compare your screen with Figure 5.42.

Figure 5.42

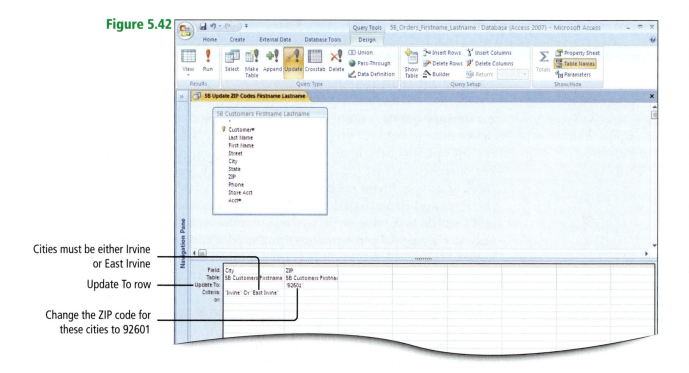

Cities must be either Irvine or East Irvine

Update To row

Change the ZIP code for these cities to 92601

6 **Save** the query as **5B Update ZIP Codes Firstname Lastname** and then **Run** the query. In the message box stating that *You are about to update 9 row(s)*, click **Yes**.

7 **Close** the query, and then expand the **Navigation Pane**. Under **Queries**, notice the icon that is associated with an update query—**5B Update ZIP Codes**. Under **Tables**, open the **5B Customers** table in **Datasheet** view. Notice that the records are still in ascending order by the **City** field, and notice that the nine records for customers living in **East Irvine** and **Irvine** have **ZIP** codes of **92601**.

8 View the table in **Print Preview**. Change the orientation to **Landscape**, and, if necessary, change the margins to ensure that the table prints on one page, with the table name and date at the top of the page and the page number at the bottom. If you are instructed to submit this result, create a paper or electronic printout and then **Close** ⊠ the Print Preview window.

More Knowledge

Other Restrictions for Update Queries

It is not possible to run an update query with these types of table fields:

- Fields that result in calculations because the calculations do not permanently reside in tables.
- Fields that use total queries or crosstab queries as their source.
- AutoNumber fields, which can change only when you add a record to a table.
- Fields in union queries.
- Fields in unique-values or unique-records queries.
- Primary key fields that are common fields in table relationships, unless you set Cascade Update Related Fields. You cannot cascade updates for tables that use a data type of AutoNumber to generate the primary key field.

Objective 10
Modify the Join Type

When multiple tables are included in a query, a *join* helps you extract the correct records from the related tables. The relationship between the tables, based upon common fields, is represented in a query by a join, which is displayed as the join line between the related tables. When you add tables to the Query design workspace, Access creates the joins based on the defined relationships. If you add queries to the Query design workspace or tables where the relationship has not been defined, you can manually create joins between the objects by dragging a common field from one object to the common field in the second object, creating the join between the two objects. Joins establish rules about records to be included in the query results and combine the data from multiple sources on one record row in the query results.

Activity 5.17 Viewing the Results of a Query Using an Inner Join

The default join type is the *inner join*, which is the most common type of join. When a query with an inner join is run, only the records where the common field exists in both related tables are displayed in the query results. All of the queries you have previously run have used an inner join. In this activity, you will view the results of a query that uses an inner join.

1 Collapse ⧏ the **Navigation Pane**. On the Ribbon, click the **Database Tools tab**. In the **Show/Hide group**, click the **Relationships** button, and then notice the relationship between the **5B Customers** table and the **5B Orders** table.

Because referential integrity has been enforced, it is easy to determine that the *5B Customers* table is on the *one* side of the relationship, and the *5B Orders* table is on the *many* side of the relationship. *One* customer can have *many* orders. The common field is Customer#.

2 In the **Relationships** window, double-click the **join line** between the **5B Customers** table and the **5B Orders** table, and then compare your screen with Figure 5.43. Alternatively, right-click the join line, and then click Edit Relationship, or click the line, and then in the Tools group, click the Edit Relationships button.

The Edit Relationships dialog box displays, indicating that referential integrity has been enforced and that the relationship type is *One-to-Many*. Because the relationship has been established for the tables, you can view relationship properties in the Relationships window.

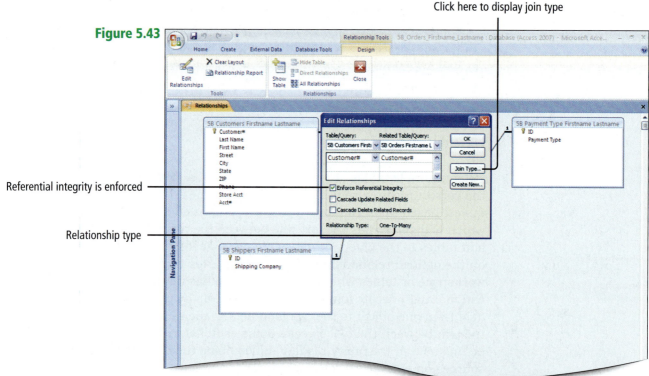

Click here to display join type

Figure 5.43

Referential integrity is enforced

Relationship type

Alert!

Is your Edit Relationships dialog box empty?

If your Edit Relationships dialog box does not display as shown in Figure 5.43, you may have double-clicked near the join line and not on the join line. In the Edit Relationships dialog box, click Cancel, and then try again.

---

3 In the **Edit Relationships** dialog box, click **Join Type**, and then compare your screen with Figure 5.44. In the displayed **Join Properties** dialog box, notice that option **1** is selected—*Only include rows where the joined fields from both tables are equal.*

Option 1 is the default join type, which is an inner join. Options 2 and 3 are outer join types.

Figure 5.44

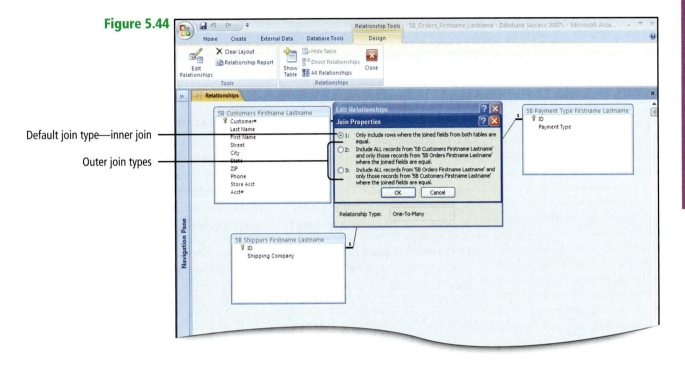

Default join type—inner join

Outer join types

4 In the **Join Properties** dialog box, click **Cancel**. In the **Edit Relationships** dialog box, click **Cancel**. **Close** [×] the Relationships window.

Because the relationships have been established and saved in the database, you should not change the join properties in the Relationships window. You should change join properties in the Query design workspace.

5 Expand [»] the **Navigation Pane**. On the **Navigation Pane**, open the **5B Orders** table and the **5B Customers** table, in the order specified, and then collapse [«] the **Navigation Pane**.

6 With the **5B Customers** table current, on the **Home tab**, in the **Sort & Filter group**, click the **Clear All Sorts** button to remove the ascending sort from the City field. Notice that the records are now sorted by the Customer# field—the primary key field.

7 In the first record, click the **plus (+) sign** to expand the subdatasheet—the related record in the *5B Orders* table—and then notice that **Jake Speck** has no related records—he has not placed any orders. Click the **minus (–) sign** to collapse the subdatasheet.

8 Expand the subdatasheet for **Customer# 1645**, and then notice that **Holly Barnett** has one related record in the *5B Orders* table—she has placed one order. Collapse the subdatasheet.

9 Expand the subdatasheet for **Customer# 1647**, and then notice that **Robert Bland** has two related records in the *5B Orders* table—he has placed *many* orders. Collapse the subdatasheet.

10 On the **tab row**, click the **5B Orders tab** to make the datasheet current, and then notice that **12** orders have been placed. On the **tab row**, right-click any tab, and then click **Close All**, saving changes, if prompted.

11 Create a new query in **Query Design**. From the **Show Table** dialog box, add the **5B Customers** table and the **5B Orders** table, in the order specified, to the Query design workspace, and then close the **Show Table** dialog box. Expand both field lists.

12 From the **5B Customers** field list, add **Customer#**, **Last Name**, and **First Name**, in the order specified, to the design grid. In the design grid, under **Customer#**, click in the **Sort row**, click the **arrow**, and then click **Ascending**. **Run** the query, and then compare your screen with Figure 5.45. There is no record for **Jake Speck**, there is one record for **Customer# 1645**—Holly Barnett—and there are two records for **Customer# 1647**—Robert Bland.

Because the default join type is an inner join, the query results display records only where there is a matching Customer#—the common field—in both related tables, even though you did not add any fields from the *5B Orders* table to the design grid. All of the records display for the table on the *many* side of the relationship—*5B Orders*. For the table on the *one* side of the relationship—*5B Customers*—only those records that have matching records in the related table display. Recall that there were 29 records in the *5B Customers* table and 12 records in the *5B Orders* table.

Figure 5.45

Common field

One corresponding record in 5B Orders table

Many corresponding records in 5B Orders table

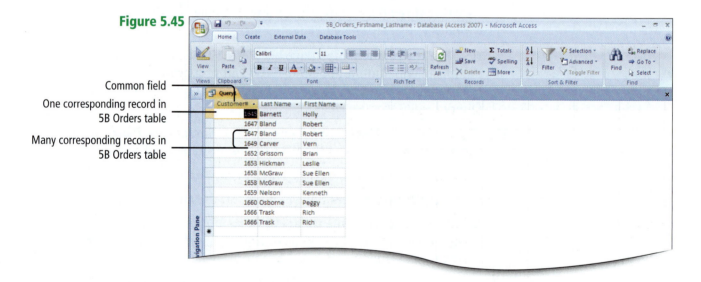

13 Switch to **Design** view. From the **5B Orders** field list, add **Order#** to the fourth column of the design grid, and then add **Amount** to the fifth column of the design grid. **Run** the query to display the results.

The same 12 records display but with two additional fields.

Activity 5.18 Changing the Join Type to an Outer Join

An **outer join** is typically used to display records from both tables, regardless of whether there are matching records. In this activity, you will modify the join type to display all of the records from the *5B Customers* table, regardless of whether the customer has placed an order.

1 Switch to **Design** view. In the Query design workspace, double-click the **join line** to display the **Join Properties** dialog box. Alternatively, right-click the join line, and then click Join Properties. Compare your screen with Figure 5.46.

The Join Properties dialog box displays the tables used in the join and the common fields from both tables. Option 1—inner join type—is selected by default. Options 2 and 3 are two different types of outer joins.

Option 2 is a **left outer join**. Select a left outer join when you want to display all of the records on the *one* side of the relationship, whether or not there are matching records in the table on the *many* side of the relationship. Option 3 is a **right outer join**. Selecting a right outer join will display all of the records on the *many* side of the relationship, whether or not there are matching records in the table on the *one* side of the relationship. This should not occur if referential integrity has been enforced because all orders should have a related customer.

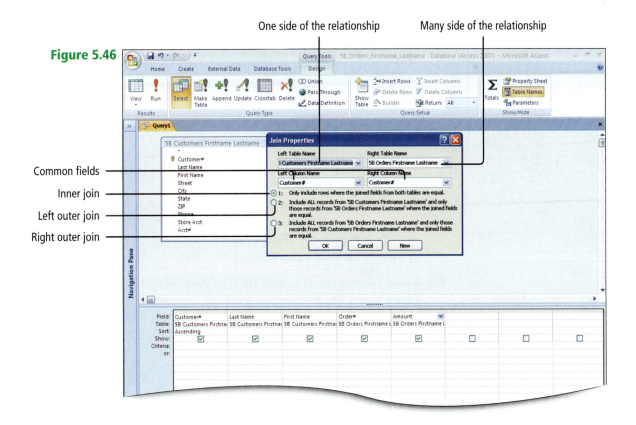

Figure 5.46

2 In the **Join Properties** dialog box, click the option button next to **2**, and then click **OK**. **Run** the query, and then compare your screen with Figure 5.47.

Thirty-two records display. There are 29 records in the *5B Customers* table; however, three customers have two orders, so there are two separate records for each of these customers. If a customer does not have a matching record in the *5B Orders* table, the Order# and Amount fields are left empty in the query results.

Fields blank because there are no
matching records in the 5B Orders table

Figure 5.47

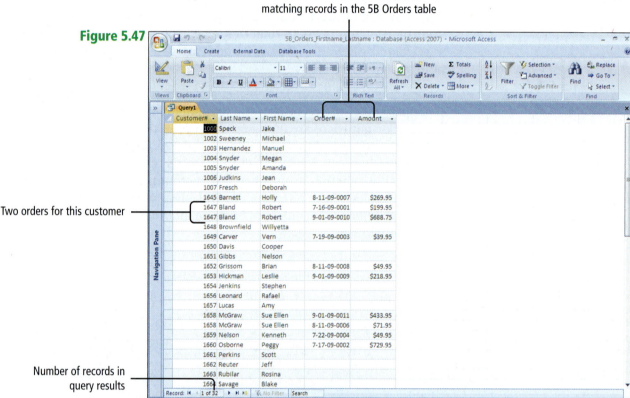

Two orders for this customer

Number of records in
query results

3 **Save** the query as **5B Outer Join Firstname Lastname** View the query in **Print Preview**, ensuring that the table prints on one page, and then if you are instructed to submit this result, create a paper or electronic printout.

4 **Close** the query, and then expand the **Navigation Pane**. **Close** the database, and then **Exit** Access.

More Knowledge

Other Types of Joins

There are two other types of joins: *cross joins* and *unequal joins*. A cross join is not explicitly set in Access 2007. In a cross join, each row from one table is combined with each row in a related table. Cross joins are usually created unintentionally when you do not create a join line between related tables. In fact, the results of the query will probably not make much sense. In the previous query, you would create a cross join by deleting the join line between the *5B Customers* table and the *5B Orders* table. A cross join produces many records; and depending on the number of records in both tables, the cross join can take a long time to run. A cross join using the aforementioned tables would result in 348 displayed records when the query is run (29 customers × 12 orders = 348 records).

An unequal join is used to combine rows from two data sources based on field values that are not equal. The join can be based on any comparison operator, such as greater than (>), less than (<), or not equal to (<>). The results in an unequal join using the not equal to comparison operator are difficult to interpret and can display as many records as those displayed in a cross join. Unequal joins cannot be created in Design view; they can be created only in SQL view.

End **You have completed Project 5B** ———————

 There's More You Can Do!

From the student files that accompany this textbook, open the folder **02_theres_more_you_can_do**. Locate the Try It! Exercises for this chapter and follow the instructions to learn additional skills.

Try It! 1—Creating a Parameter Query Using a Wildcard

In this Try It! exercise, you will use a wildcard when creating a parameter query.

Try It! 2—Creating an Update Query for a Numeric Field

In this Try It! exercise, you will create an update query to change the value in a table's numeric field.

Content-Based Assessments

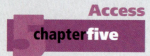

Summary

Queries are powerful database objects that can be created to do more than just extract data from tables and other queries. In this chapter, you created queries for special purposes, such as creating calculated fields, summarizing and grouping data, displaying the data in a spreadsheet-like format for easier analysis, finding duplicate records and unmatched records that might cause problems with the database, and creating prompts to use in dynamic queries. You created action queries to create new tables, append records to tables, delete records from tables, and update data in tables. Finally, you examined the query results based upon the default inner join and an outer join.

Key Terms

Content-Based Assessments

Matching

Match each term in the second column with its correct definition in the first column. Write the letter of the term on the blank line in front of the correct definition.

_____ **1.** A field that obtains its data by performing a calculation or computation, using a formula.

_____ **2.** A formula that performs a calculation.

_____ **3.** A query that calculates subtotals across groups of records.

_____ **4.** A query that uses an aggregate function for data that is grouped by two types of information and then displays the data in a compact, spreadsheet-like format.

_____ **5.** Records in one table that have no matching records in a related table.

_____ **6.** A query that prompts you for criteria before running it.

_____ **7.** An action query that creates a new table by extracting data from one or more tables.

_____ **8.** Data that does not change.

_____ **9.** An action query that adds new records to an existing table by adding data from another Access database or from a table in the same database.

_____ **10.** An action query that removes records from an existing table in the same database.

_____ **11.** An action query that is used to add, change, or delete data in fields of one or more existing records.

_____ **12.** The type of join in which only the records where the common field exists in both related tables are displayed in the query results.

_____ **13.** A join that is typically used to display records from both tables, regardless of whether there are matching records.

_____ **14.** A join in which each row from one table is combined with each row in a related table.

_____ **15.** A join that is used to combine rows from two data sources based on field values that are not equal.

A Append query

B Calculated field

C Cross join

D Crosstab query

E Delete query

F Expression

G Inner join

H Make table query

I Outer join

J Parameter query

K Static data

L Totals query

M Unequal join

N Unmatched records

O Update query

Content-Based Assessments

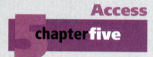
Fill in the Blank

Write the correct word in the space provided.

1. Symbols such as +, −, *, and / are used to build expressions. They are _____ _____.

2. The expression 2^3 returns the value _____.

3. In Access queries, you can use _____ _____ to perform a calculation on a column of data and return a single value.

4. To add a column of numbers and return a single value, use the _____ function.

5. To add a column of numbers, ignoring null values, and divide by the number of records with values, use the _____ function.

6. To summarize a large amount of data in a small space that is easy to read, you should use a(n) _____ query.

7. Use the _____ _____ Query Wizard to locate duplicate records in a table.

8. Use the _____ _____ Query Wizard to locate unmatched records and then delete the records from the table.

9. A value that can be changed is called a(n) _____.

10. A(n) _____ query enables you create a new table or change data in an existing table.

11. When creating an append query, the table to which you are appending the fields is called the _____ table.

12. When creating an append query, the table from which records are being extracted is called the _____ table.

13. _____ establish rules about records to be included in the query results and combine the data from multiple sources on one record row in the query results.

14. To display all of the records on the *one* side of the relationship, whether or not there are matching records in the table on the *many* side of the relationship, select a(n) _____ outer join.

15. To display all of the records on the *many* side of the relationship, whether or not there are matching records in the table on the *one* side of the relationship, select a(n) _____ outer join.

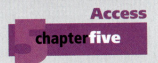

Skills Review

Project 5C—Payroll

In this project, you will apply the skills you practiced from the Objectives in Project 5A.

Objectives: 1. *Create Calculated Fields;* **2.** *Use Aggregate Functions;* **3.** *Create a Crosstab Query;* **4.** *Find Duplicate and Unmatched Records;* **5.** *Create a Parameter Query.*

Shinpei Kawano, Lead Sales Associate of Board Anywhere Surf and Snowboard Shop, has a database containing employee data and payroll data. In the following Skills Review, you will create special-purpose queries to calculate data, summarize and group data, display data in a spreadsheet-like format, and find duplicate and unmatched records. You will also create a query that prompts an individual to enter the criteria. Your completed queries will look similar to the queries shown in Figure 5.48.

> ### For Project 5C, you will need the following file:
>
> a05C_Payroll

You will save your document as 5C_Payroll_Firstname_Lastname

Figure 5.48

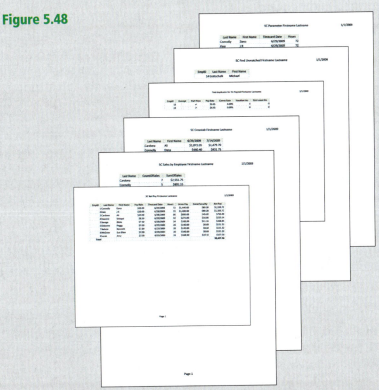

(Project 5C–Payroll continues on the next page)

Content-Based Assessments

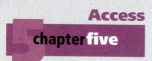
(Project 5C–Payroll continued)

1. **Start** Access. Locate and open the **a05C_Payroll** file. Click the **Office** button. Click **Save As Access 2007 Database**, and then save the database in the **Access Chapter 5** folder as **5C_Payroll_Firstname_Lastname** Rename the tables by adding **Firstname Lastname** to the end of each table name. **Close** the Navigation Pane.

2. On the Ribbon, click the **Create tab**. In the **Other group**, click the **Query Design** button. In the **Show Table** dialog box, select the following three tables—**5C Employees**, **5C Payroll**, and **5C Timecard**. **Add** the tables to the Query design workspace, and then click **Close**. Expand the field lists.

3. From the **5C Employees** field list, add the following fields, in the order specified, to the design grid: **EmpID**, **Last Name**, and **First Name**. From the **5C Payroll** field list, add the **Pay Rate** field. From the **5C Timecard** field list, add the **Timecard Date** and the **Hours** field in this order. In the **Timecard Date** field **Criteria row**, type **6/29/2009**

4. In the **Field row**, right-click in the first empty column to display a shortcut menu, and then click **Zoom**. In the **Zoom** dialog box, type **Gross Pay:[Pay Rate]*[Hours]** and then click **OK**. Press Enter.

5. In the **Field row**, click in the **Gross Pay** field box that you just added. On the **Design tab**, in the **Show/Hide group**, click the **Property Sheet** button. In the **Property Sheet**, on the **General tab**, click in the **Format** box, and then click the displayed **arrow**. In the list of formats, click **Currency**. On the **Property Sheet** title bar, click the **Close** button.

6. In the **Field row**, right-click in the first empty column to display a shortcut menu, and then click **Zoom**. In the **Zoom** dialog box, type **Social Security:[Gross Pay]*0.062** and then click **OK**. Using the technique you just practiced, set a **Currency** format for this field. **Close** the Property Sheet.

7. In the **Field row**, right-click in the first empty column to display a shortcut menu, and then click **Zoom**. In the **Zoom** dialog box, type **Net Pay:[Gross Pay]-[Social Security]** and then click **OK**. **Run** the query to display the payroll calculations.

8. On the **Home tab**, in the **Records group**, click the **Totals** button. In the **Total row**, under **Net Pay**, click in the empty box, and then click the **arrow** at the left edge. From the displayed list, click **Sum**.

9. Adjust column widths to display all field names and all data under each field. On the **tab row**, right-click the **Query1 tab**, and then click **Save**. In the **Save As** dialog box, under **Query Name**, type **5C Net Pay Firstname Lastname** and then click **OK**. View the query in **Print Preview**, ensuring that the query prints on one page, and then if you are instructed to submit this result, create a paper or electronic printout. **Close** the query.

10. Create a new query in **Query Design**. Add the **5C Employees** table and the **5C Sales** table to the Query design workspace, and then **Close** the **Show Table** dialog box. Expand both field lists. From the **5C Employees** field list, add **Last Name** to the first field box in the design grid. From the **5C Sales** table, add **Sales** to both the second and third field boxes.

11. On the **Design tab**, in the **Show/Hide group**, click the **Totals** button. In the design grid, in the **Total row**, under the first **Sales** field, click in the box displaying

(Project 5C–Payroll continues on the next page)

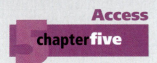

(Project 5C–Payroll continued)

Group By to display the arrow, and then click the **arrow**. From the displayed list, click **Count**. Under the second **Sales** field, click in the box displaying *Group By* to display the arrow, and then click the **arrow**. From the displayed list, click **Sum**. In the design grid, in the **Sort row**, under **Last Name**, click in the box to display the arrow, and then click the **arrow**. From the displayed list, click **Ascending**. **Run** the query to display the total number of sales and the total amount of the sales for each associate.

12. If necessary, adjust column widths to display all field names and all data under each field. **Save** the query as **5C Sales by Employee Firstname Lastname Run** the query. View the query in **Print Preview**, ensuring that the query prints on one page, and then if you are instructed to submit this result, create a paper or electronic printout. **Close** the query.

13. **Create** a new query in **Query Design**. Add the following tables, in the order specified, to the Query design workspace: **5C Employees** and **5C Sales**. In the **Show Table** dialog box, click **Close**. Expand the field lists.

14. From the **5C Employees** table, add the **Last Name** and the **First Name** fields. From the **5C Sales** table, add the **Timecard Date** and **Sales** fields. Save the query as **5C Sales by Date Firstname Lastname** and then **Close** the query.

15. On the Ribbon, click the **Create tab**. In the **Other group**, click the **Query Wizard** button. In the **New Query** dialog box, click **Crosstab Query Wizard**, and then click **OK**. In the middle of the dialog box, under **View**, click the **Queries** option button. In

the list of queries, click **Query: 5C Sales by Date**, and then click **Next**.

16. Under **Available Fields**, double-click **Last Name** and **First Name**. In the **Crosstab Query Wizard** dialog box, click **Next**. In the displayed list of fields, double-click **Timecard Date**. Select an interval of **Date**. Click **Next**. Under **Functions**, click **Sum**. On the left side of the **Crosstab Query Wizard** dialog box, above the **Sample** area, clear the **Yes, include row sums** check box, and then click **Next**.

17. Under **What do you want to name your query?**, select the existing text, type **5C Crosstab Firstname Lastname** and then click **Finish**. Adjust all of the column widths to display the entire field name and the data in each field. The result is a spreadsheet view of total sales by employee by payroll date. View the query in **Print Preview**, ensuring that the query prints on one page, and then if you are instructed to submit this result, create a paper or electronic printout. **Close** the query, saving changes.

18. On the **Create tab**, in the **Other group**, click the **Query Wizard** button. In the **New Query** dialog box, click **Find Duplicates Query Wizard**, and then click **OK**. In the first **Find Duplicates Query Wizard** dialog box, in the list of tables, click **Table: 5C Payroll**, and then click **Next**. Under **Available fields**, double-click **EmpID** to move it under **Duplicate-value fields**, and then click **Next**.

19. Under **Available fields**, add all of the fields to the **Additional query fields** box. Click **Next**. Click **Finish** to accept the suggested query name—*Find duplicates for 5C Payroll Firstname Lastname*. Adjust all

(Project 5C–Payroll continues on the next page)

Content-Based Assessments

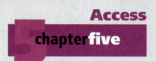
(Project 5C–Payroll continued)

column widths. View the query in **Print Preview**, ensuring that the query prints on one page, and then if you are instructed to submit this result, create a paper or electronic printout. **Close** the query, saving changes.

20. Open the **5C Payroll** table. Locate record **14**, the duplicate record. Click the row selector, and then press Delete. Click **Yes** to confirm the deletion. The employee with *EmpID 13* is now in the *5C Payroll* table only one time. **Close** the table.

21. On the **Create tab**, in the **Other group**, click the **Query Wizard** button. In the **New Query** dialog box, click **Find Unmatched Query Wizard**, and then click **OK**. In the first **Find Unmatched Query Wizard** dialog box, in the list of tables, click **Table: 5C Employees**, and then click **Next**. In the list of tables, click **Table: 5C Payroll**, and then click **Next**. Under **Fields in 5C Employees**, click **EmpID**. Under **Fields in 5C Payroll**, if necessary, click **EmpID**. Click the **<=>** button.

22. Click **Next**. Under **Available fields**, double-click **EmpID**, **Last Name**, and **First Name** to move the field names under **Selected Fields**. Click **Next**. In the last dialog box, under **What would you like to name your query?**, type **5C Find Unmatched Firstname Lastname** and then click **Finish**. The query results display one employee—*Michael Gottschalk*—who took unpaid time off during this pay period.

23. Adjust all column widths. View the query in **Print Preview**, ensuring that the query prints on one page, and then if you are instructed to submit this result, create a

paper or electronic printout. **Close** the query, saving changes.

24. **Create** a new query in **Query Design**. Add the **5C Employees** table and the **5C Timecard** table to the Query design workspace, and then **Close** the **Show Table** dialog box. Expand the field list. From the **5C Employees** field list, add **Last Name** and **First Name** to the first and second columns in the design grid. From the **5C Timecard** field list, add **Timecard Date** and **Hours** to the third and fourth columns in the design grid.

25. In the **Criteria row**, in the **Timecard Date** field, type **[Enter Date]**

26. In the **Criteria row**, right-click in the **Hours** field, and then click **Zoom**. In the **Zoom** dialog box, type **Between[Enter the Minimum Hours]And[Enter the Maximum Hours]** and then click **OK**.

27. **Run** the query. In the **Enter Parameter Value** dialog box, type **6/29/09** In the **Enter Parameter Value** dialog box, click **OK**. Type **60** and then click **OK**. Type **80** and then click **OK**. Three employees have worked between 60 and 80 hours during the pay period for 6/29/09. They have earned vacation hours.

28. Adjust all column widths, and **Save** the query as **5C Parameter Firstname Lastname** View the query in **Print Preview**, ensuring that the query prints on one page, and then if you are instructed to submit this result, create a paper or electronic printout. **Close** the query.

29. Expand the **Navigation Pane, Close** the database, and then **Exit** Access.

End **You have completed Project 5C**

Skills Review

Project 5D — Sale Clearance

In this project, you will apply the skills you practiced from the Objectives in Project 5B.

Objectives: 6. *Create a Make Table Query;* **7.** *Create an Append Query;* **8.** *Create a Delete Query;* **9.** *Create an Update Query;* **10.** *Modify the Join Type.*

Ali Cardona, Purchasing Manager for Board Anywhere Surf and Snowboard Shop, must keep the tables in the database up to date and ensure that the queries display pertinent information. Two of the suppliers, Wetsuit Country and Boots Galore, will no longer provide merchandise for Board Anywhere Surf and Snowboard Shop. This merchandise must be moved to a new discontinued items table. In the following Skills Review, you will create action queries that will create a new table, update records in a table, append records to a table, and delete records from a table. You will also modify the join type of relationships to display different subsets of the data when the query is run. Your completed queries will look similar to the queries shown in Figure 5.49.

> **For Project 5D, you will need the following files:**
>
> a05D_Sale_Clearance
> a05D_Warehouse_Items
>
> **You will save your databases as**
> **5D_Sale_Clearance_Firstname_Lastname**
> **5D_Warehouse_Items_Firstname_Lastname**

Figure 5.49

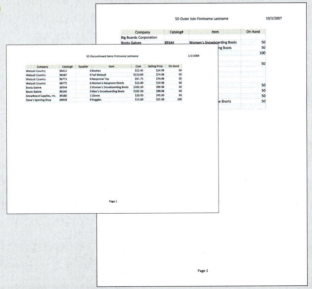

(Project 5D–Sale Clearance continues on the next page)

(Project 5D–Sale Clearance continued)

1. **Start** Access. Locate and open the **a05D_Sale_Clearance** file. Click the **Office** button. Click **Save As Access 2007 Database**, and then save the database in the **Access Chapter 5** folder as 5D_Sale_Clearance_Firstname_Lastname Rename the tables by adding your **Firstname Lastname** to the end of each table name. Collapse the **Navigation Pane**.

2. Create a new query in **Query Design**. From the **Show Table** dialog box, add the following tables, in the order specified, to the Query design workspace: **5D Suppliers** and **5D Inventory**. **Close** the **Show Table** dialog box, and then expand the field lists.

3. From the **5D Suppliers** field list, add **Company** to the first column of the design grid. From the **5D Inventory** field list, add all fields in the field list to the design grid.

4. In the design grid, under **Supplier**, click in the **Criteria** row, type 6 and then **Run** the query. Notice that four items are supplied by *Wetsuit Country*.

5. Switch to **Design** view. On the **Design tab**, in the **Query Type group**, click the **Make Table** button. In the **Make Table** dialog box, in the **Table Name** box, type 5D Discontinued Items Firstname Lastname In the **Make Table** dialog box, be sure that **Current Database** is selected, and then click **OK**. **Run** the query. In the displayed message box, click **Yes** to paste the rows to the new table.

6. **Close** the query, click **Yes** in the message box asking if you want to save changes, and then name the query 5D Wetsuit Country Items Firstname Lastname

7. Create a new query in **Query Design**. From the **Show Table** dialog box, add the following tables, in the order specified, to the Query design workspace: **5D Suppliers** and **5D Inventory**. **Close** the **Show Table** dialog box, and then expand the field lists.

8. From the **5D Suppliers** field list, add **Company** to the first column of the design grid. From the **5D Inventory** field list, add all fields in the field list to the design grid.

9. In the design grid, under **Supplier**, click in the **Criteria row**, type 3 and then **Run** the query. Notice that one item is supplied by *Boots Galore*.

10. Switch to **Design** view. On the **Design tab**, in the **Query Type group**, click the **Append** button. In the **Append** dialog box, click the **Table Name arrow**, and from the displayed list, click **5D Discontinued Items Firstname Lastname**, and then click **OK**.

11. In the design grid, in the **Append To row**, remove any brackets that Access may have placed around the field names. **Run** the query. In the displayed message box, click **Yes** to append one row. **Close** the query, and then save it as 5D Append1 Firstname Lastname

12. On the Access window title bar, click the **Minimize** button. **Start** a second instance of Access. Navigate to the location where the student data files for this textbook are saved. Locate and open the **a05D_Warehouse_Items** file. Save the database in the **Access 2007 Database** format in your **Access Chapter 5** folder as 5D_Warehouse_Items_Firstname Lastname

(Project 5D–Sale Clearance continues on the next page)

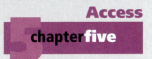

(Project 5D– Sale Clearance continued)

13. Create a new query in **Query Design**. From the **Show Table** dialog box, add the **5D Suppliers** table and the **5D Discontinued Items** table to the Query design workspace, and then close the **Show Table** dialog box. Expand the field lists. From the **5D Suppliers** field list, add **Company** to the first column of the design grid. From the **5D Discontinued Items** field list, add all of the fields to the design grid in the order listed.

14. On the **Design tab**, in the **Query Type group**, click the **Append** button. In the **Append** dialog box, click the **Another Database** option button, and then click the **Browse** button. Navigate to your **Access Chapter 5** folder, and then double-click **5D_Sale_Clearance_Firstname_Lastname**.

15. In the **Append** dialog box, click the **Table Name arrow**, click **5D Discontinued Items**, and then click **OK**. Check the **Append To row**, and remove any brackets that Access may have placed around the field names. **Save** the query as **5D Append2 Firstname Lastname** and then **Run** the query. In the displayed message box, click **Yes** to append 3 rows. **Close** the query. **Close** the database, and then **Exit** this instance of Access. The *5D Discontinued Items* table now contains 8 rows.

16. From the Windows taskbar, click the **5D_Sales_Clearance** database. Create a new query in **Query Design**. Add the **5D Inventory** table to the Query design workspace, and then **Close** the **Show Table** dialog box. Expand the field list. From the field list, add **Catalog#** and **On Hand**, in this order, to the first and second columns in the design grid. In the design grid, under **On Hand**, click in the **Criteria row**, type **0** and then **Run** the query.

17. Switch to **Design** view. In the Query design workspace, right-click in the empty space. From the displayed shortcut menu, point to **Query Type**, and then click **Delete Query**.

18. **Save** the query as **5D Delete Zero Inventory Firstname Lastname** and then **Run** the query. In the message box stating that *You are about to delete 1 row(s) from the specified table*, click **Yes**. **Close** the query. You have removed this item from the inventory.

19. Create a new query in **Query Design**. Add the **5D Discontinued Items** table to the Query design workspace, and then **Close** the **Show Table** dialog box. Expand the field list.

20. In the **5D Discontinued Items** field list, double-click **Catalog#** to add the field to the first column of the design grid. Then add the **Selling Price** field to the second column of the design grid. On the **Design tab**, in the **Query Type group**, click the **Update** button. In the design grid, under **Selling Price**, click in the **Update To row**, and then type **[Selling Price]*0.5**

21. **Save** the query as **5D Discounted Selling Prices Firstname Lastname** and then **Run** the query. In the message box stating that *You are about to update 8 row(s)*, click **Yes**.

22. **Close** the query. Expand the **Navigation Pane**, and then double-click the **5D Discontinued Items** table to open it in **Datasheet** view. Collapse the **Navigation Pane**. Select the **Description column**, and then hide the column. Adjust all column widths. View the table in **Print Preview**, ensuring that the table prints on one page, and then if you are instructed to submit this result, create a paper or electronic printout. **Close** the table, saving changes.

(Project 5D–Sale Clearance continues on the next page)

Skills Review

(Project 5D–Sale Clearance continued)

23. Create a new query in **Query Design**. From the **Show Table** dialog box, add the **5D Suppliers** table and the **5D Discontinued Items** table to the Query design workspace, and then **Close** the **Show Table** dialog box. Expand both field lists. From the **5D Suppliers** table, drag the **ID** field to the **5D Discontinued Items** table **Supplier** field to create a join between the tables.

24. From the **5D Suppliers** field list, add **Company** to the first column in the design grid. From the **5D Discontinued Items** field list, add **Catalog#**, **Item**, and **On Hand**, in this order, to the design grid. In the design grid, under **Company**, click in the **Sort row**, click the **arrow**, and then click **Ascending**. **Run** the query.

25. Switch to **Design** view. In the Query design workspace, double-click the **join line** to display the **Join Properties** dialog box. Click the option button next to **2**, and then click **OK**. **Run** the query. This query displays all of the supplier companies used by the shop, not just those with discontinued items.

26. **Save** the query as **5D Outer Join Firstname Lastname** View the query in **Print Preview**, ensuring that the table prints on one page, and then if you are instructed to submit this result, create a paper or electronic printout. **Close** the query.

27. Expand the **Navigation Pane**, **close** the database, and then **Exit** Access.

End **You have completed Project 5D**

Mastering Access

Project 5E — Surfing Lessons

In this project, you will apply the skills you practiced from the Objectives in Project 5A.

Objectives: 1. *Create Calculated Fields;* **2.** *Use Aggregate Functions;* **3.** *Create a Crosstab Query;* **4.** *Find Duplicate and Unmatched Records;* **5.** *Create a Parameter Query.*

Dana Connolly, one of the owners of Board Anywhere Surf and Snowboard Shop, has a database containing student, instructor, and surfing lesson data. In the following Mastering Access project, you will create special-purpose queries to calculate data, summarize and group data, display data in a spreadsheet-like format, and find duplicate and unmatched records. You will also create a query that prompts an individual to enter the criteria. Your completed queries will look similar to the queries shown in Figure 5.50.

> ### For Project 5E, you will need the following file:
>
> a05E_Surfing_Lessons
>
> **You will save your database as**
> **5E_Surfing_Lessons_Firstname_Lastname**

Figure 5.50

(Project 5E–Surfing Lessons continues on the next page)

Content-Based Assessments

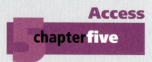

(Project 5E–Surfing Lessons continued)

1. **Start** Access. Locate and open the **a05E_Surfing_Lessons** file. Click the **Office** button. Click **Save As Access 2007 Database**, and then save the database in the **Access Chapter 5** folder as 5E_ Surfing_Lessons_Firstname_Lastname Rename the tables by adding your **Firstname Lastname** to the end of each table name.

2. **Create** a query in **Query Design** using the **5E Surfing Lessons** table and the **5E Students** table. From the **5E Surfing Lessons** table, add the **Instructor** field, the **Lesson Date** field, and the **Duration** field to the first, second, and third columns of the design grid. From the **5E Students** table, add the **Last Name** and **First Name** fields to the fourth and fifth columns.

3. In the sixth column of the design grid, add a calculated field. In the field name row, type **End Time:[Duration]/24+[Lesson Date]** Display the field properties sheet, and then format this field as **Medium Time**. This field will display the time the lesson ends.

4. In the first blank column, in the field name row, add the calculated field **Fees:[Duration]*50** From the field properties sheet, select the **Format** of **Currency**. Surfing lessons cost $50.00 an hour.

5. In the **Instructor** field, in the **Sort row**, click **Ascending**. In the **Lesson Date** field, in the **Sort row**, click **Ascending**. **Run** the query.

6. On the **Home tab**, in the **Records group**, click the **Totals** button. In the **Fees column**, in the **Total row**, click the **down arrow**, and then click **Average**. Adjust field widths as necessary.

7. **Save** the query as **5E Student Lessons Firstname Lastname** View the query in

Print Preview, ensuring that the query prints on one page, and then if you are instructed to submit this result, create a paper or electronic printout. **Close** the query.

8. **Create** a new query using the **Crosstab Query Wizard**. Select the **Query: 5E Student Lessons**. Click **Next**. From the **Available Fields**, add **Instructor** to the **Selected Fields** column. Click **Next**. Double-click **Lesson Date**, and then choose **Date**. Click **Next**. From the **Fields column**, select **Fees**, and then from **Functions**, select **Sum**. Clear the **Yes, include row sums** check box. Click **Next**. Name the query **5E Crosstab Firstname Lastname** Select **Modify the design**, and then click **Finish**.

9. Right-click the **Fees** field name, click **Properties**, and then from the **Property Sheet**, select the **Format** of **Currency**. **Run** the query. This query displays the instructor and his or her amount collected in fees by date. Adjust field widths as necessary.

10. View the query in **Print Preview**, ensuring that the query prints on one page, and then if you are instructed to submit this result, create a paper or electronic printout. **Close** the query, saving changes.

11. Click the **Query Wizard** button. In the **New Query** dialog box, click **Find Duplicates Query Wizard**. Search the **Table: 5E Surfing Lessons**, and select the **Lesson Date** field for duplicate information. Click **Next**. From **Available Fields**, add the **Instructor** and **Duration** fields to the **Additional Query fields column**. Accept the default name for the query. Click **Finish**. The query results show that there are duplicate lesson times. Adjust field widths as necessary.

(Project 5E–Surfing Lessons continues on the next page)

Content-Based Assessments

Access
chapter **five**

Mastering Access

(Project 5E–Surfing Lessons continued)

12. View the query in **Print Preview**, ensuring that the query prints on one page, and then if you are instructed to submit this result, create a paper or electronic printout. **Close** and **Save** the query.

13. Click the **Query Wizard** button. In the **New Query** dialog box, click **Find Unmatched Query Wizard**. Select **Table: 5E Surfing Instructors**. From the **Which table or query contains the related records?** dialog box, choose **Table: 5E Surfing Lessons**. Click **Instructor** as the **Matching** field. Display the one field **Instructor** in the query. Name the query **5E Unmatched Firstname Lastname** and then click **Finish**. Emily is the only instructor who has no students.

14. View the query in **Print Preview**, ensuring that the query prints on one page, and then if you are instructed to submit this result, create a paper or electronic printout. **Close** the query.

15. **Create** a query in **Design** view using the **5E Surfing Lessons** table and the **5E**

Students table. From the **5E Surfing Lessons** table, add the **Instructor** field. From the **5E Students** table, add the **Last Name**, **First Name**, and **Phone#** fields in that order to the design grid. In the **Instructor** field, in the **Criteria row**, type **[Enter Instructor's Name]**

16. **Run** the query. In the **Enter Parameter Value** dialog box, type **Ricardo** and then press Enter. The query displays Ricardo's students and their phone numbers.

17. **Save** the query as **5E Parameter Firstname Lastname** Adjust field widths as necessary.

18. View the query in **Print Preview**, ensuring that the query prints on one page, and then if you are instructed to submit this result, create a paper or electronic printout. **Close** the query.

19. Expand the **Navigation Pane**, **Close** the database, and then **Exit** Access.

End **You have completed Project 5E**

Project 5F—Gift Cards

In this project, you will apply the skills you practiced from the Objectives in Project 5B.

Objectives: 6. *Create a Make Table Query;* **7.** *Create an Append Query;* **8.** *Create a Delete Query;* **9.** *Create an Update Query;* **10.** *Modify the Join Type.*

Shinpei Kawano, Sales Associate for Board Anywhere Surf and Snowboard Shop, has decided to offer gift cards for purchase at the shop. She has a database of the employees and the details of the cards they have sold. In the following Mastering Access project, you will create action queries that will create a new table, update records in a table, append records to a table, and delete records from a table. You will also modify the join type of the relationship to display a different subset of the data when the query is run. Your completed queries will look similar to the queries shown in Figure 5.51.

For Project 5F, you will need the following file:

a05F_Gift_Cards

**You will save your document as
5F_Gift_Cards_Firstname_Lastname**

Figure 5.51

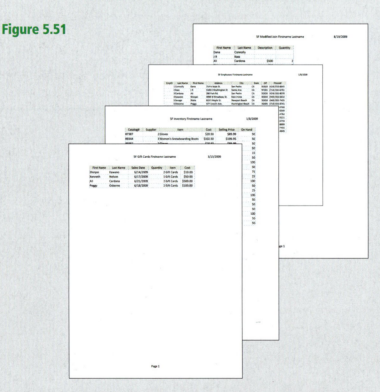

(Project 5F–Gift Cards continues on the next page)

(Project 5F–Gift Cards continued)

1. **Start** Access. Locate and open the **a05F_Gift_Cards** file. Click the **Office** button. Click **Save As Access 2007 Database** in the **Access Chapter 5** folder, and then save as **5F_Gift_Cards_Firstname_Lastname** Rename the tables by adding your **Firstname Lastname** to the end of each table name.

2. Create a new query in **Query Design**. To the Query design workspace, add the **5F Employees**, **5F Sales**, and the **5F Inventory** tables. From the **5F Employees** table, add the **First Name** and **Last Name** fields to the first and second columns of the design grid. From the **5F Sales** table, add the following fields to the design grid in the order specified: **Sales Date** and **Quantity**. From the **5F Inventory** table, add the **Item** and **Cost** fields.

3. In the **Item** field column, in the **Criteria row**, type **Gift Cards** In the **Cost** field column, in the **Criteria row**, type **10 Or 50 Sort** the **Last Name** field in **Ascending** order.

4. On the **Design tab**, click the **Make Table** button. Name the table **5F $10 or $50 Gift Cards Firstname Lastname** Select **Current Database**, click **OK**, and then **Run** the query. **Close** the query, saving it as **5F Make Table Firstname Lastname** Open the **5F $10 or $50 Gift Cards** table to display the two gift card purchases. **Close** the table.

5. Create a new query in **Query Design**. To the Query design workspace, add the **5F Employees**, **5F Sales**, and the **5F Inventory** tables. From the **5F Employees** table, add the **First Name** and **Last Name** fields to the first and second columns of the design grid. From the **5F Sales** table, add the following fields to the design grid in the following order: **Sales Date** and **Quantity**. From the **5F Inventory** table, add the **Item** and **Cost** fields.

6. In the **Item** field column, in the **Criteria row**, type **Gift Cards** In the **Cost** field column, in the **Criteria row**, type **100 Or 500 Sort** the **Last Name** field in **Ascending** order.

7. Click the **Append** button, and then append the records to the **5F $10 or $50 Gift Cards** table. Click **OK**. In the **Append To row**, remove any brackets that Access may have placed around the field names. **Run** the query. Click **Yes** to append two rows. **Close** the query, saving it as **5F Append Firstname Lastname** Open the **5F $10 or $50 Gift Cards** table to display all gift card purchases. **Close** the table, and then rename it **5F Gift Cards Firstname Lastname**

8. View the table in **Print Preview**, ensuring that the table prints on one page, and then if you are instructed to submit this result, create a paper or electronic printout. **Close** the table.

9. Create a new query in **Query Design**. Add the **5F Inventory** table to the Query design workspace. From the **5F Inventory** table, add the **Catalog#** and **Item** fields to the first and second columns of the design grid. In the design grid, under **Item**, click in the **Criteria row**, and then type **Gift Cards**

10. **Run** the query to view the results. Switch to **Design** view, click the **Query Type: Delete** button, and then **Run** the query. Click **Yes** to delete the gift cards from the **5F Inventory** table. The gift cards are not to be counted as inventory items. **Close** and **Save** the query, naming it **5F Delete Firstname Lastname**

11. Open the **5F Inventory** table, and then **hide** the **Description** field. If you are instructed to submit this result, create a paper or electronic printout. **Close** the table. Do not save changes.

(Project 5F–Gift Cards continues on the next page)

Content-Based Assessments

(Project 5F–Gift Cards continued)

12. Create a new query in **Query Design**. Add the **5F Employees** table to the Query design workspace. From the **5F Employees** table, add **Phone#** to the first column of the design grid. In the design grid, under **Phone#**, click in the **Criteria row**, and then type **"(310)*"** **Run** the query to view the results. Switch to **Design** view. Click the **Query Type: Update** button.

13. In the design grid, under **Phone#**, click in the **Update To row**, and then type **"(424)" & Right([Phone#],9)** This concatenation and function will update the area code but maintain the original seven digits of the phone number.

14. **Run** the query. Click **Yes** to update four rows. **Close** the query, saving it as **5F Update Firstname Lastname** Open the **5F Employees** table. View the table in **Print Preview**, ensuring that the table prints on one page, and then if you are instructed to submit this result, create a paper or electronic printout. **Close** the table.

15. Create a new query in **Query Design**. Add the **5F Employees** and **5F Gift Cards**

tables to the Query design workspace. From the **5F Employees** field list, add **First Name** and **Last Name** to the first two columns of the design grid. From the **5F Gift Cards** field list, add **Cost** and **Quantity** field, in this order, to the design grid. In the design grid, click to the left of the **Cost** field name. Type **Description:** and then use the **Property Sheet** to format the field as **Currency** with zero decimal places.

16. From the **5F Employees** field list, click **Last Name**, and then drag to the **5F Gift Cards Last Name** field. Double-click the **join line**, and then select option **2**. **Run** the query to display the results, which include all 14 employees and not just gift card sellers. **Save** the query as **5F Modified Join Firstname Lastname**

17. Unless you are required to submit your database electronically, view the query in **Print Preview**, ensuring that the query prints on one page, and then **Print** the query. **Close** the query.

18. **Close** the database, and then **Exit** Access.

End **You have completed Project 5F**

Mastering Access

Project 5G — Advertisements

In this project, you will apply the following Objectives found in Projects 5A and 5B.

Objectives: 1. *Create Calculated Fields;* **2.** *Use Aggregate Functions;* **3.** *Create a Crosstab Query;* **5.** *Create a Parameter Query.*

J. R. Kass, one of the owners of Board Anywhere Surf and Snowboard Shop, is responsible for all of the advertising for the business. In the following Mastering Access project, you will create special-purpose queries to calculate data, and then summarize and group data for advertising cost analysis. You will also create a query that prompts an individual to enter the criteria for a specific type of advertisement media. Your completed queries will look similar to the queries shown in Figure 5.52.

For Project 5G, you will need the following file:

a05G_Advertisements

You will save your database as
5G_Advertisements_Firstname_Lastname

Figure 5.52

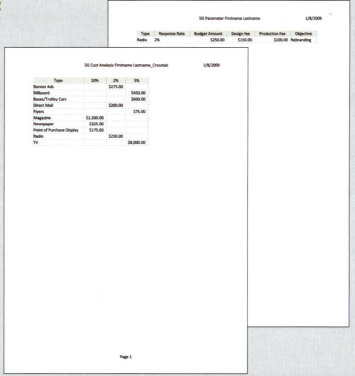

(Project 5G–Advertisements continues on the next page)

(Project 5G–Advertisements continued)

1. **Start** Access. Locate and open the **a05G_Advertisements** file. Click the **Office** button. Click **Save As Access 2007 Database**, and then save the database in the **Access Chapter 5** folder as 5G_Advertisements_Firstname_Lastname Rename the table by adding your **Firstname Lastname** to the end of the table name. Collapse the **Navigation Pane**.

2. Create a new query in **Query Design**. From the **5G Advertisements** table, add the **Type**, **Response Rate**, **Budget Amount**, **Design Fee**, and **Production Fee** fields to the design grid in this order.

3. In the first blank **Field row**, add a calculated field. Type **Cost:[Design Fee]+[Production Fee]** In the next blank field column, add a second calculated field: **Over/Under Budget:[Budget Amount]-[Cost]**

4. **Run** the query. Add a **Total row** to the datasheet. In the **Over/Under Budget** field, in the **Total row**, click the **arrow**. Select **Sum** to display the total amount over or under the budget amount.

5. **Close** the query, saving it as **5G Cost Analysis Firstname Lastname**

6. Create a new query. Click the **Query Wizard** button, and then select **Crosstab Query Wizard**. Select the **Query: 5G Cost Analysis**. For row headings, use **Type**, and for column headings, use **Response Rate**. Select **Cost** for the calculated field,

using the **Sum** function. Do not summarize each row. Accept the default name for this query.

7. Click **Finish** to view the cost in relation to the response rate for each type of advertisement.

8. View the query in **Print Preview**, ensuring that the query prints on one page, and then if you are instructed to submit this result, create a paper or electronic printout. **Close** the query.

9. Create a new query in **Query Design**. From the **5G Advertisements** table, select and add all fields from the field list to the design grid in the order they are listed. In the design grid, under the **Type** field, in the **Criteria row**, type **[Enter Advertisement Media]**

10. **Run** the query. Enter **Radio** as the parameter value. Click **OK**. Adjust column widths to display all field names and data. Save the query as **5G Parameter Firstname Lastname**

11. View the query in **Print Preview**, ensuring that the query prints on one page, and then if you are instructed to submit this result, create a paper or electronic printout. **Close** the query.

12. Expand the **Navigation Pane**, **Close** the database, and then **Exit** Access.

End **You have completed Project 5G**

Project 5H—Contests

In this project, you will apply the following Objectives found in Projects 5A and 5B.

Objectives: 6. *Create a Make Table Query;* **7.** *Create an Append Query;* **8.** *Create a Delete Query;* **9.** *Create an Update Query;* **10.** *Modify the Join Type.*

The Board Anywhere Surf and Snowboard Shop sponsors snowboarding contests for children, teenagers, and adults. The shop allows the public to register either in the store or at its Web site. In the following Mastering Access project, you will create action queries that will create a new table of contest participants, update records in a table by appending the in-store registrations with the online registrations, and delete records of previous contests. You will add a calculated field to update the age of the participant. You will also modify the join type of relationships to display different subsets of the data when the query is run. Your completed queries will look similar to the queries shown in Figure 5.53.

For Project 5H, you will need the following files:

a05H_Contests
a05H_On-Line_Registrations

**You will save your databases as
5H_Contests_Firstname_Lastname
5H_On-Line_Registrations_Firstname_Lastname**

Figure 5.53

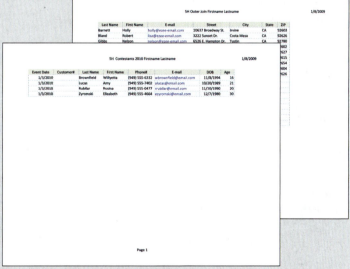

(Project 5H–Contests continues on the next page)

(Project 5H–Contests continued)

1. **Start** Access. Locate and open the **a05H_Contests** file. Click the **Office** button. Click **Save As Access 2007 Database**, and then save the database in the **Access Chapter 5** folder as **5H_Contests_Firstname_Lastname** Rename the table by adding your **Firstname Lastname** to the end of the table name.

2. Create a query in **Query Design**. From the **5H Customers** table, add the following fields to the design grid in the specified order: **Event Date**, **Customer#**, **Last Name**, **First Name**, **Phone#**, **E-mail**, and **DOB**. **Save** the query as **5H In-Store Registrations Firstname Lastname**

3. In the **Event Date** field, in the **Criteria row**, type **Not Null Run** the query to verify that you have selected only the customers who have registered for a snowboarding contest.

4. Switch to **Design** view, and then click the **Make Table** button. Name the table **5H In-Store Contest Registrations Firstname Lastname** and then save it in the **Current Database**. **Run** the query to paste the records into the new table. **Close** the query. **Minimize** this instance of Access.

5. **Start** a second instance of Access. Locate and open the **a05H_On-line_Registrations** file. Click the **Office** button. Click **Save As Access 2007 Database**, and then save the database in the **Access Chapter 5** folder as **5H_On-Line_Registrations_Firstname_Lastname** Rename the table by adding your first and last name to the end of the table name.

6. Create a new query in **Query Design**. Add the **5H Registrations** table to the Query design workspace. Select and add all fields in the field list order to the query design

   grid. Click the **Append** button. In the **Append** dialog box, select **Another Database**. Browse to find the **5H_Contests_Firstname_Lastname** database. From the table name list, select **5H In-Store Contest Registrations**. Click **OK**. Check the **Append To row**, and then remove any brackets that Access may have placed around the field names. **Run** the query. **Close** the query, and then **Save** it as **5H Append Firstname Lastname**

7. **Close** the **5H_On-Line_Registrations** database, and then **Exit** this instance of Access.

8. From the taskbar, click the minimized instance of **Access**. Expand the **Navigation Pane**. Rename the **5H In-Store Contest Registrations** table to **5H Contestants Firstname Lastname** This table now contains both in-store and online registrations.

9. **Copy** the **5H Contestants** table, and then **Paste** it as **5H Contestants 2010 Firstname Lastname** Open this table in **Design** view, and then add a field **Age** in the row below the **DOB** field. Use a data type of **Number** with the default format of **Long Integer**. **Close** the table, saving changes.

10. Create a query in **Query Design**. Add the **5H Contestants 2010** table to the Query design workspace. Select and add all fields to the query design grid. Under the **Event Date** field, in the **Criteria row**, type **<01/01/2010** Click the **Delete Query** button. **Run** the query. Click **Yes** to confirm the deletion of those records of contests prior to January 1, 2010. **Close** the query, saving it as **5H Delete Firstname Lastname**

11. Create a query in **Query Design** to update the **5H Contestants 2010** table to add the

(Project 5H–Contests continues on the next page)

(Project 5H–Contests continued)

correct age to the data. From this table, add the **Age** field to the query design grid. Click the **Update Query** button. Under the **Age** field, in the **Update To row**, type **DateDiff("yyyy",[DOB],[Event Date])** to calculate and update the ages of the contestants. **Run** the query. Click **Yes** to update the table. **Close** the query, saving it as **5H Update Firstname Lastname**

12. Open the **5H Contestants 2010** table in **Datasheet** view. View the table in **Print Preview**, ensuring that the table prints on one page, and then if you are instructed to submit this result, create a paper or electronic printout. **Close** the table.

13. Create a query in **Query Design**. Add the **5H Contestants** and the **5H Customers** tables to the query workspace area. From the **5H Contestants** table, add the following fields in this order: **Last Name**, **First**

Name, and **E-mail**. From the **5H Customers** table, add the **Street**, **City**, **State**, and **ZIP** fields. Modify the **Join Type** by selecting item **2** to include all records from the *5H Contestants* table. **Run** the query. This will display all contestants, whether or not they are in the customer table. This adjustment to the join will provide a means of advertising contests via e-mail or the postal service. Adjust the column widths to display all field names and data. **Save** the query as **5H Outer Join Firstname Lastname**

14. View the query in **Print Preview**, ensuring that the query prints on one page, and then if you are instructed to submit this result, create a paper or electronic printout. **Close** the query. **Close** the database, and then **Exit** Access.

 You have completed Project 5H ———————————————

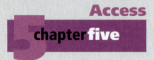

Mastering Access

Project 5I — Ski Trips

In this project, you will apply all the skills you practiced from the Objectives in Projects 5A and 5B.

Dana Connolly and J. R. Kass love to ski. They coordinate day, overnight, and international trips. In the following Mastering Access project, you will create a query to display only the day ski trips. You will append records from the waiting list to the reservations list and then delete them from the waiting list. You will use the Count function and create a new field to calculate the balances. You will display the results of a query in a spreadsheet-like format for easier analysis and find duplicate and unmatched records in tables. You will also create a query that prompts an individual for the criteria based on the name of the ski resort. In addition, you will change the join type of table relationships to display a different subset of the data—the customers not taking ski trips—when the query is run. Your completed queries will look similar to those in Figure 5.54.

For Project 5I, you will need the following file:

a05I_Ski_Trips

You will save your database as
5I_Ski_Trips_Firstname_Lastname

Figure 5.54

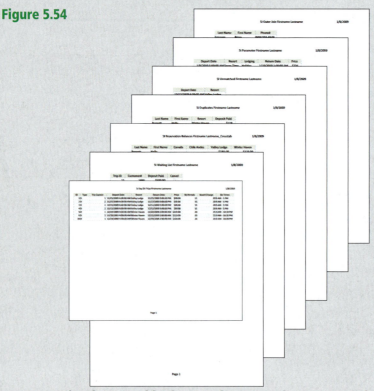

(Project 5I–Ski Trips continues on the next page)

Content-Based Assessments

(Project 5I–Ski Trips continued)

1. **Start** Access. Locate and open the **a05I_ Ski_Trips** file. Click the **Office** button. Click **Save As Access 2007 Database**, and then save the database in the **Access Chapter 5** folder as **5I_Ski_Trips_Firstname_ Lastname** Rename the objects by adding your **Firstname Lastname** to the end of each object name.

2. Create a new query in **Query Design**. From the **5I Ski Trips** table, select all fields except the **Lodging** field, and then drag them into the design grid in the order they are listed. Under the **Type** field, in the **Criteria row**, type **D** and then **Run** the query to verify that only day ski trips are displayed.

3. Switch to **Design** view, and then click the **Make Table** button. Name the new table **5I Day Ski Trips Firstname Lastname** and then save it in the **Current Database**. **Run** the query. Click **Yes** to paste the rows into the new table. **Close** the query, saving it as **5I Make Table Firstname Lastname**

4. Open the **5I Day Ski Trips** table. View the table in **Print Preview**, ensuring that the table prints on one page, and then if you are instructed to submit this result, create a paper or electronic printout. **Close** the table.

5. Create a new query in **Query Design**. From the **5I Waiting List** table, select all fields, and then drag them into the query design grid in the order they are listed. Under the **Trip ID** field, in the **Criteria row**, type **1** and then **Run** the query. View the results to see the waiting list for the trip to *Valley Lodge* on *November 25, 2009*. Switch to **Design** view, and then click **Append**. Append these records to the **5I Reservations** table in the **Current Database**. Review the **Append To row**, and then remove any brackets that Access

may have placed around the field names. **Save** the query as **5I Append Firstname Lastname**

6. **Run** the query, and then click **Yes** to append the records. **Close** the query. **Copy** the query, and then **Paste** it as **5I Delete Firstname Lastname** Open this query in **Design** view. In the **Query Type group**, click **Delete**, and then **Run** the query. Click **Yes** to delete the skiers who were on the waiting list and who have been appended to the reservations list. **Close** the query, and then **Save** changes.

7. Open the **5I Waiting List** table in **Datasheet** view. On the **Home tab**, in the **Records group**, click the **Totals** button. In the **Customer#** field, in the **Total row**, click the **arrow**, and then click **Count**.

8. View the table in **Print Preview**, ensuring that the table prints on one page, and then if you are instructed to submit this result, create a paper or electronic printout. **Close** the table.

9. Create a query in **Query Design**. Add the **5I Customers**, **5I Reservations**, and **5I Ski Trips** tables to the Query design work-space. From the **5I Customers** table, add the **Last Name** and **First Name** fields. From the **5I Reservations** field list, add **Deposit Paid**. From **5I Ski Trips**, add the **Resort** and **Depart Date** fields. In the first empty field column, add a calculated field. Type **Balance:[Price]-[Deposit Paid]**

10. **Run** the query. **Close** the query, saving it as **5I Reservation Balances Firstname Lastname**

11. From the **Create tab**, in the **Other group**, click the **Query Wizard**. Select the **Crosstab Query Wizard**. Select **Query: 5I Reservation Balances**.

(Project 5I–Ski Trips continues on the next page)

(Project 5I–Ski Trips continued)

12. Select **Last Name** and **First Name** for **Available fields**. Click **Resort** for column headings and **Deposit Paid** for the calculated field for each column and row intersection. Select the **Function** of **Sum**. Do not include row summaries. Accept the default name for the query.

13. View the query in **Print Preview**, ensuring that the query prints on one page, and then if you are instructed to submit this result, create a paper or electronic printout. **Close** the query.

14. Click the **Query Wizard**. Select **Find Duplicates Query Wizard**. Search for duplicates in the **Query: 5I Multiple Trips**. Under **Duplicate-value fields**, select **Last Name** and **First Name**. For **Additional query fields**, select **Resort** and **Deposit Paid**. Select the default name for the query and then type **5I Duplicates Firstname Lastname** Click **Finish**. The result displays the records of those customers planning more than one ski trip.

15. View the query in **Print Preview**, ensuring that the query prints on one page, and then if you are instructed to submit this result, create a paper or electronic printout. **Close** the query.

16. Click the **Query Wizard**. Select **Find Unmatched Records**. Select **Table: 5I Ski Trips**, and then select **Table: 5I Reservations** as the tables to search for unmatched records. From the **5I Ski Trips** table, use the **ID** field to match the **5I Reservations Trip ID** field. Include the **Depart Date** and **Resort** fields in the query. Name the query **5I Unmatched Records Firstname Lastname** and then click **Finish** to display the ski trips without skiers. Adjust column widths to display all field names and data.

17. View the query in **Print Preview**, ensuring that the query prints on one page, and then if you are instructed to submit this result, create a paper or electronic printout. **Close** the query.

18. Create a query in **Query Design**. Add the **5I Ski Trips** table to the Query design workspace. Add the **Depart Date**, **Resort**, **Lodging**, **Return Date**, and **Price** to the design grid in the specified order. Under **Resort**, in the **Criteria row**, type **[Enter Resort Name]** and then **Run** the query. In the **Parameter** dialog box, type **Snow Time** and then **Save** the query as **5I Parameter Firstname Lastname** Adjust column widths to display all field names and data.

19. View the query in **Print Preview**, ensuring that the query prints on one page, and then if you are instructed to submit this result, create a paper or electronic printout. **Close** the query.

20. Create a query in **Query Design**. Add the **5I Customers** and the **5I Reservations** tables to the Query design workspace. From **5I Customers**, add **Last Name**, **First Name**, and **Phone#**. From **5I Reservations**, add **Deposit Paid**. In the **Deposit Paid** field, clear the **Show** box, and in the **Criteria row**, type **Is Null** Edit the relationship by selecting item **2**. **Run** the query to show customers who are not taking advantage of the ski trips. **Save** the query as **5I Outer Join Firstname Lastname**

21. View the query in **Print Preview**, ensuring that the query prints on one page, and then if you are instructed to submit this result, create a paper or electronic printout.

22. **Close** the query, **Close** the database, and then **Exit** Access.

 End **You have completed Project 5I**

Access

chapter five

Business Running Case

Project 5J — Business Running Case

In this project, you will apply the skills you have practiced from the Objectives in Projects 5A and 5B.

From My Computer, navigate to the student files that accompany this textbook. In the folder **03_business_running_case**, locate and open the folder for this chapter. Open and print the instructions for this project, which are provided to you in Adobe PDF format. Follow the instructions and use the skills you have gained thus far to assist the brother and sister team of Michael and Kristen Landry in meeting the challenges of owning and running their business.

 End **You have completed Project 5J** —————————

Rubric

The following outcomes-based assessments are *open-ended assessments*. That is, there is no specific correct result; your result will depend on your approach to the information provided. Make *professional quality* your goal. Use the following scoring rubric to guide you in *how* to approach the problem and then to evaluate *how well* your approach solves the problem.

The *criteria*—Software Mastery, Content, Format and Layout, and Process—represent the knowledge and skills you have gained that you can apply to solving the problem. The *levels of performance*—Professional Quality, Approaching Professional Quality, or Needs Quality Improvement—help you and your instructor evaluate your result.

	Your completed project is of Professional Quality if you:	Your completed project is Approaching Professional Quality if you:	Your completed project Needs Quality Improvements if you:
1-Software Mastery	Choose and apply the most appropriate skills, tools, and features and identify efficient methods to solve the problem.	Choose and apply some appropriate skills, tools, and features, but not in the most efficient manner.	Choose inappropriate skills, tools, or features, or are inefficient in solving the problem.
2-Content	Construct a solution that is clear and well organized, contains content that is accurate, appropriate to the audience and purpose, and is complete. Provide a solution that contains no errors of spelling, grammar, or style.	Construct a solution in which some components are unclear, poorly organized, inconsistent, or incomplete. Misjudge the needs of the audience. Have some errors in spelling, grammar, or style, but the errors do not detract from comprehension.	Construct a solution that is unclear, incomplete, or poorly organized, containing some inaccurate or inappropriate content; and contains many errors of spelling, grammar, or style. Do not solve the problem.
3-Format and Layout	Format and arrange all elements to communicate information and ideas, clarify function, illustrate relationships, and indicate relative importance.	Apply appropriate format and layout features to some elements, but not others. Overuse features, causing minor distraction.	Apply format and layout that does not communicate information or ideas clearly. Do not use format and layout features to clarify function, illustrate relationships, or indicate relative importance. Use available features excessively, causing distraction.
4-Process	Use an organized approach that integrates planning, development, self-assessment, revision, and reflection.	Demonstrate an organized approach in some areas, but not others; or, use an insufficient process of organization throughout.	Do not use an organized approach to solve the problem.

Problem Solving

Project 5K — Applicant

In this project, you will construct a solution by applying any combination of the skills you practiced from the Objectives in Projects 5A and 5B.

For Project 5K, you will need the following file:

a05K_Applicant

You will save your database as
5K_Applicant_Firstname_Lastname

The owners of Board Anywhere Surf and Snowboard Shop, Dana Connolly and J. R. Kass, will be expanding their shop and are looking for more employees. In this project, you will create special function queries to assist with their selections from a pool of applicants.

Start by opening the *a05K_Applicant* database, which contains three tables: *5K Applicant*, *5K Interview Schedule*, and *5K Positions*. Create a Find Unmatched Records query to show which applicants have not been scheduled for an interview. Create a Parameter query to locate a particular applicant. Delete the people who have filled the current job offerings from the *5K Applicant* table. Use an aggregate function to count the number of applicants grouped by position. Save your queries by using the query type followed by your first and last names. View the queries in Print Preview, ensuring that the queries print on one page, and then if you are instructed to submit this result, create a paper or electronic printout. Close the queries. Save the database as **5K_Applicant_Firstname_Lastname**

End **You have completed Project 5K** ——————————

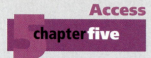

Problem Solving

Project 5L — Ski Apparel

In this project, you will construct a solution by applying any combination of the skills you practiced from the Objectives in Projects 5A and 5B.

For Project 5L, you will need the following file:

a05L_Ski_Apparel

**You will save your database as
5L_Ski_Apparel_Firstname_Lastname**

Ali Cardona is the Purchasing Manager for the Board Anywhere Surf and Snowboard Shop. It is her responsibility to keep the clothing inventory current and fashionable. Using the *a05L_Ski_Apparel* database, you have been asked to help her with this task.

The database consists of a table of clothing for youth, women, and men. Use a make table query to separate the clothing into tables by these groups. Next, separate the inventory into categories of apparel to be considered for purchase (promotional), current fashions (in stock), and discontinued clothing. Create a parameter query to display the number of in-stock items. Update the selling price of the discontinued items to 80% of the cost. Save your queries using the query type followed by your first and last names. View the queries in Print Preview, ensuring that the queries print on one page, and then if you are instructed to submit this result, create a paper or electronic printout. Close the queries. Save the database as **5L_Ski_Apparel_Firstname_Lastname**

End **You have completed Project 5L** ⸺⸺⸺⸺⸺

Problem Solving

Project 5M — Surfboards

In this project, you will construct a solution by applying any combination of the skills you practiced from the Objectives in Projects 5A and 5B.

For Project 5M, you will need the following file:

a05M_Surfboards

You will save your database as
5M_Surfboards_Firstname_Lastname

In this project, you will design queries for special functions. Ali Cardona, Purchasing Manager for Board Anywhere Surf and Snowboard Shop, is stocking the shop with a variety of surfboards and accessories for the upcoming season.

In this project, you will open the *5M_Surfboards* database and create queries to perform special functions. Create a calculated field to compute the potential profit by multiplying the selling price minus the cost by the number on hand for each item. Use an aggregate function to display the total potential inventory value. Check the supplier against the inventory using the Find Unmatched Records query. Create an outer join query using the *5M Suppliers* table and the *5M Inventory* table. Save your queries using the query type followed by your first and last names. View the queries in Print Preview, ensuring that the queries print on one page, and then if you are instructed to submit this result, create a paper or electronic printout. Close the queries. Save the database as **5M_Surfboards_Firstname_Lastname**

End **You have completed Project 5M**

Outcomes-Based Assessments

Access
chapter five

Problem Solving

Project 5N — Shop Promotions

In this project, you will construct a solution by applying any combination of the skills you practiced from the Objectives in Projects 5A and 5B.

For Project 5N, you will need the following file:

a05N_Shop_Promotions

**You will save your database as
5N_Shop_Promotions_Firstname_Lastname**

The owners of Board Anywhere Surf and Snowboard Shop have invited some of Southern California's best extreme sports game participants to the shop to promote certain lines of clothing and gear. These participants will be on hand to answer questions, give demonstrations, and distribute prizes to customers. In this project, you will enhance the database by creating queries to perform special functions.

Open the *a05N_Shop_Promotions* database. Use the Find Duplicates Query Wizard to find any events that may have been scheduled at the same time for the same day. The shop must be closed for remodeling. Use a select query and an update query to select those events that are scheduled after July 31, 2009, and reschedule those events for one week later than each original date. Create a parameter query to display the events that will feature giveaways. Save your queries using the query type, followed by your first and last names. View the queries in Print Preview, ensuring that the queries print on one page, and then if you are instructed to submit this result, create a paper or electronic printout. Close the queries. Save the database as **5N_Shop Promotions_Firstname_Lastname**

End **You have completed Project 5N**

Access

chapter five

Problem Solving

Project 5O — Newsletter

In this project, you will construct a solution by applying any combination of the skills you practiced from the Objectives in Projects 5A and 5B.

For Project 5O, you will need the following file:

a05O_Newsletter

You will save your database as
5O_Newsletter_Firstname_Lastname

The staff of Board Anywhere Surf and Snowboard Shop produces a monthly newsletter. The database uses tables of customers, contestants, and suppliers. Open the *a05O_Newsletter* database, and view these tables. Use a make table query to select mailing information from the *5O Customers* table. Create append queries to add similar fields from both the *5O Contestants* and the *5O Suppliers* tables. Name this new table **5O Distribution List Firstname Lastname** Create a query to locate duplicate address records. Delete those duplicates so there is only one mailing per household. Save your queries using the query type followed by your first and last names. View the queries in Print Preview, ensuring that the queries print on one page, and then if you are instructed to submit this result, create a paper or electronic printout. Close the queries. Save the database as **5O_Newsletter_Firstname_Lastname**

End **You have completed Project 5O** ——————

Outcomes-Based Assessments

 You and *GO!*

Project 5P — You and *GO!*

In this project, you will construct a solution by applying any combination of the Objectives found in Projects 5A and 5B.

From My Computer, navigate to the student files that accompany this textbook. In the folder **04_you_and_go**, locate and open the folder for this chapter. Open and print the instructions for this project, which are provided to you in Adobe PDF format. Follow the instructions to create a form and report for your personal inventory.

 End You have completed Project 5P _____

GO! with Help

Project 5Q — *GO!* with Help

The Access Help system is extensive and can help you as you work. In this project, you will view information about grouping records in an Access report.

1 **Start** Access. On the right side of the Ribbon, click the **Microsoft Office Access Help** button. In the **Type words to search for** box, type **outer join** and then press Enter.

2 In the displayed **Results** pane, click **Join tables and queries**. Maximize the displayed window, and then click **Outer joins**. Read the section titled **How do I use an outer join?**, which describes the steps to change an inner join to an outer join in an Access query.

3 If you want, **Print** a copy of the information by clicking the printer button at the top of **Access Help** window.

4 **Close** the Help window, and then **Close** Access.

 End You have completed Project 5Q _____

chaptersix

Customizing Forms and Reports

OBJECTIVES

At the end of this chapter you will be able to:

1. Create a Form in Design View
2. Change and Add Controls
3. Format a Form
4. Make a Form User Friendly

5. Create a Report in Design View
6. Add Controls to a Report
7. Group, Sort, and Total Records in Design View
8. Create a Crosstab Report

OUTCOMES

Mastering these objectives will enable you to:

PROJECT 6A
Customize Forms

PROJECT 6B
Customize Reports

Wild Islands Breeze

Wild Islands Breeze is a "quick, casual" franchise restaurant chain with headquarters in Jacksonville, Florida. The founders wanted to create a restaurant where the flavors of the Caribbean islands would be available at reasonable prices in a bright, comfortable atmosphere. The menu features fresh food and quality ingredients in offerings like grilled chicken skewers, wrap sandwiches, fruit salads, mango ice cream, smoothies, and coffee drinks. All 150 outlets offer wireless Internet connections, making Wild Islands Breeze the perfect place for groups and people who want some quiet time.

Customizing Forms and Reports

Forms provide you with a way to enter, edit, and display data from underlying tables. You have created forms using the Form button, the Form Wizard, and the Blank Form button. Forms can also be created in Design view. Access provides tools that can enhance the visual appearance of forms; for example, adding color, backgrounds, borders, or instructions to the person using the form. Forms can also be used to manipulate data from multiple tables if a relationship exists between the tables.

Reports display data in a professional-looking format. You have created reports using the Report tool, the Report Wizard, and the Blank Report tool. Like forms, reports can also be created in Design view and can be enhanced using Access tools. Most reports are based on queries, but they can also be based on tables.

Project 6A **Franchises**

Victoria Kiddoe, President, and James McKinnon, Vice President of Franchising, want to create robust forms to match their needs for Wild Islands Breeze. For example, the forms can include color and different types of controls and can manipulate data from several tables. In Activities 6.1 through 6.10, you will customize your forms to make them easier to use and more attractive.

For Project 6A, you will need the following files:

a06A_Franchises
a06A_Logo
a06A_Background

You will save your database as
6A_Franchises_Firstname_Lastname

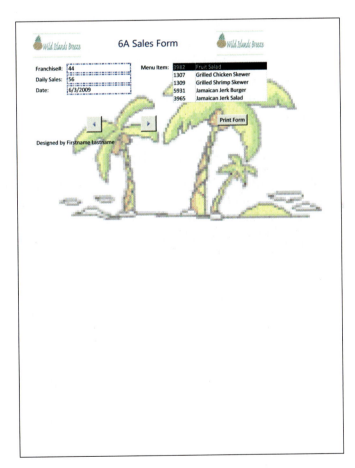

Figure 6.1
Project 6A—Franchises

Objective 1
Create a Form in Design View

You usually create a form using the Form tool, the Blank Form tool, or the Form Wizard, and then modify the form in Design view to suit your needs. Use Design view to create a form when these tools do not meet your needs, or if you want more control in the creation of a form. Creating or modifying a form in Design view is a common technique when additional controls, such as combo boxes or images, need to be added to the form.

Activity 6.1 Creating a Form in Design View

In this activity, you will create a form in Design view that will enable employees to enter the daily sales data for each franchise of Wild Islands Breeze.

1 **Start** Access. Navigate to the location where the student data files for this textbook are saved. Locate and open the **a06A_Franchises** file. Click the **Office** button , point to **Save As**, and then click **Access 2007 Database**. In the **Save As** dialog box, navigate to the drive on which you will be saving your folders and projects for this chapter. Create a new folder named **Access Chapter 6** and then save the database as **6A_Franchises_Firstname_Lastname** in the folder.

2 Enable the content or add the Access Chapter 6 folder to the Trust Center. On the **Navigation Pane**, rename each table by adding **Firstname Lastname** to the end of each table name.

3 On the **Navigation Pane**, double-click **6A Sales** to open the table in **Datasheet** view. Take a moment to examine the fields in the table. In any record, click in the **Franchise#** field, and then click the **arrow**. This field is a Lookup field—the values are looked up in the *6A Franchises* table. The Menu Item field is also a Lookup field—the values are looked up in the *6A Menu Items* table.

4 **Close** the table, and then collapse the **Navigation Pane**. On the Ribbon, click the **Create tab**. In the **Forms group**, click the **Form Design** button.

The design grid for the Detail section displays.

5 On the **Design tab**, in the **Tools group**, click the **Property Sheet** button. Compare your screen with Figure 6.2. Notice that the *Selection type* box displays *Form*—this is the Property Sheet for the entire form.

Every object on a form, including the form, itself, has an associated *Property Sheet* that can be used to further enhance the object. *Properties* are characteristics that determine the appearance, structure, and behavior of an object. This Property Sheet displays the properties that affect the appearance and behavior of the form. The left column displays the property name, and the right column displays the property setting. Some of the text in the property setting boxes is truncated.

Figure 6.2

Property Sheet for form

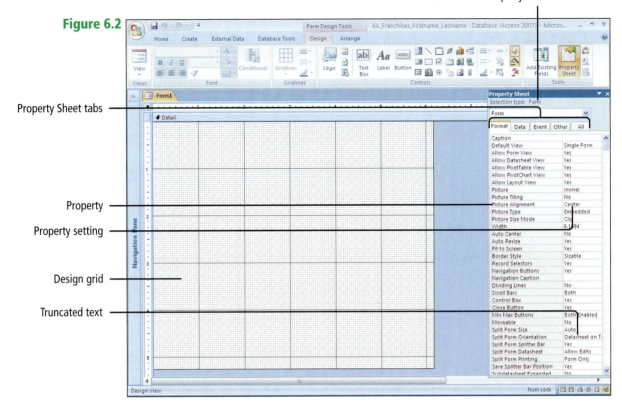

Property Sheet tabs

Property

Property setting

Design grid

Truncated text

6 If necessary, on the **Property Sheet**, click the **Format tab**, and then scroll down in the Property Sheet to display the **Split Form Orientation** property box. Point to the left edge of the **Property Sheet** until the ↔ pointer displays. Drag to the left until the setting in the **Split Form Orientation** property box—**Datasheet on Top**—displays entirely.

7 On the **Property Sheet**, click the **Data tab**. Click the **Record Source property setting box arrow**, and then click **6A Sales**.

The *Record Source property* enables you to specify the source of the data for a form or a report. The property setting can be a table name, a query name, or an SQL statement.

Another Way — **To Set the Record Source for a Form**

On the Property Sheet for the form, click the Data tab. In the Record Source property setting box, click the Build button, which displays a Query Builder window and the Show Table dialog box. Add the objects from the Show Table dialog box, and then drag the appropriate fields down into the design grid. A query will be created that is used in the form.

8 **Close** ✕ the **Property Sheet**. On the **Design tab**, in the **Tools group**, click the **Add Existing Fields** button, and then compare your screen with Figure 6.3.

The Field List for the record source—6A Sales—displays.

Figure 6.3

Field List for 6A Sales

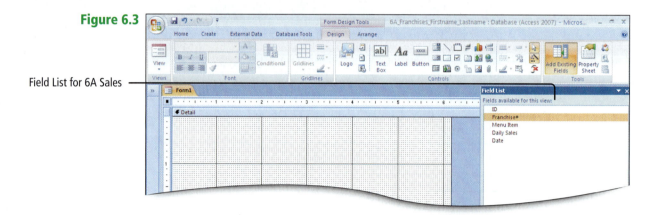

9 In the **Field List**, click **Franchise#**. To select multiple fields, hold down ⇧ Shift, and then click **Date**. Drag the selected fields onto the design grid until the top of the arrow of the ⌖ pointer is **three dots** below the bottom edge of the Detail section bar and aligned with the **1.5-inch mark on the horizontal ruler** as shown in Figure 6.4, and then release the mouse button.

Drag the fields to where the text box controls should display. If you drag to where the label controls should display, the label controls and text box controls will overlap. If you move the controls to an incorrect position, click the Undo button.

Figure 6.4

1.5-inch mark

Detail section bar

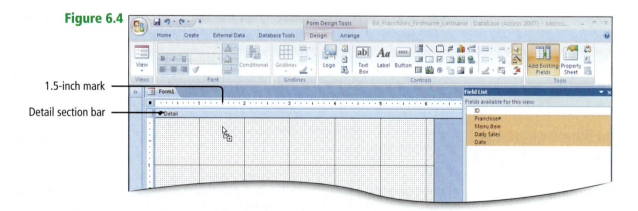

Another Way — **To Add Fields to a Form**

In the Field List, double-click each field name to add the fields to the form. It is not possible to select all the fields and then double-click. Alternatively, in the Field List, right-click a field name, and then click Add Field to View.

10 **Close** ☒ the **Field List**. **Save** 💾 the form as **6A Sales Form Firstname Lastname**

11 Click the **Franchise# combo box control**, and notice that there is no Layout Selector ✥ for the column. On the Ribbon, click the **Arrange tab**. In the **Detail** section, hold down ⇧ Shift, and then click the label controls and text box controls for each field. With all controls selected, in the **Control Layout group**, click the **Stacked** button.

When you create a form in Design view, the controls are not automatically grouped in a stacked or tabular layout. Grouping the controls makes it easier to format the controls and keeps the controls aligned.

12 **Save** 💾 the form.

More Knowledge

Horizontal and Vertical Spacing Between Controls

If the controls on a form are not grouped in a tabular or stacked layout, you can change the spacing between the controls. With the controls selected, on the Arrange tab, in the Position group, click the appropriate button to control spacing. Buttons include Make Horizontal Spacing Equal, Increase Horizontal Spacing, Decrease Horizontal Spacing, Make Vertical Spacing Equal, Increase Vertical Spacing, and Decrease Vertical Spacing.

Activity 6.2 Adding Sections to the Form

The only section that is automatically added to a form when it is created in Design view is the Detail section. In this activity, you will add a Form Header section and a Form Footer section.

1 Switch to **Form** view, and notice that the form displays only the data. There is no header section with a logo or name of the form.

2 Switch to **Design** view. On the Ribbon, click the **Arrange tab**. In the **Show/Hide group**, click the **Form Header/Footer** button 🖼.

Two sections—the Form Header and the Form Footer—are added to the form. Sections can be added only in Design view.

3 On the Ribbon, click the **Design tab**. In the **Controls group**, click the **Logo** button. Navigate to the location where the student data files for this textbook are saved. Locate and double-click **a06A_Logo** to insert the logo in the Form Header section. On the selected logo, point to the right middle sizing handle until the ↔ pointer displays. Drag to the right until the right edge of the logo is aligned with the **1.25-inch mark on the horizontal ruler**.

4 In the **Controls group**, click the **Title** button 🖼. In the label control for the title, click to the right of Form. Delete the space and your first name and last name, and then press Enter. With the label control for the title selected, hold down Ctrl, and then press ↓ **nine times**. Alternatively, drag the label control downward until the label control is approximately centered between the top and bottom edges of the logo control. Compare your screen with Figure 6.5.

The name of the form is inserted as a title into the Form Header section, and the label control is centered between the top edge and bottom edge of the logo control. Hold down the Ctrl key, and then press an arrow key in the direction you wish to move the selected controls.

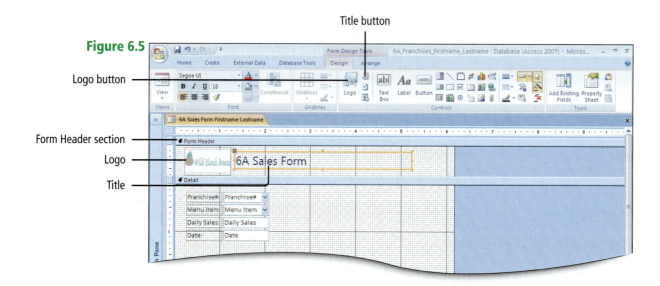

Figure 6.5

Title button

Logo button

Form Header section

Logo

Title

5 Scroll down until the **Form Footer** section bar displays. Point to the top of the **Form Footer** section bar until the ✛ pointer displays. Drag upward until the top of the Form Footer section bar aligns with the **2-inch mark on the vertical ruler**.

The height of the Detail section is decreased. Extra space at the bottom of the Detail section will cause blank space to display between records if the form is printed.

6 In the **Controls group**, click the **Label** button. Point to the **Form Footer** section until the plus sign (**+**) of the ⁺A pointer aligns with the bottom of the **Form Footer** section bar and with the left edge of the **Date label control**. Drag downward to the bottom of the **Form Footer** section and to the right to the **3-inch mark on the horizontal ruler**. Using your own first name and last name, type **Designed by Firstname Lastname** and then compare your screen with Figure 6.6.

Label button

Figure 6.6

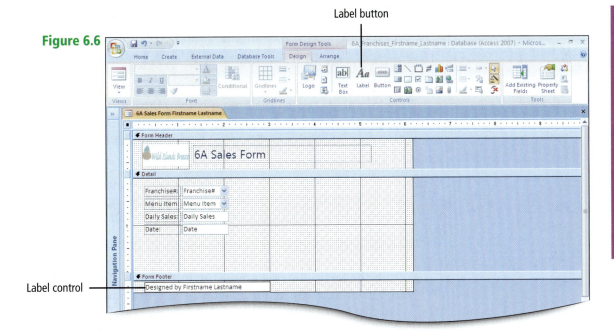

Label control

7 Press Enter. With the label control in the Form Footer section selected, hold down ⇧ Shift, and then click the **Date label control**. On the Ribbon, click the **Arrange tab**. In the **Control Alignment group**, click the **Left** button. **Save** 🖫 the form, and then switch to **Form** view.

The Form Header section displays the logo and the title of the form. The Form Footer section displays the label control that is aligned with the label controls in the Detail section. Both the Form Header and Form Footer sections display on every form page.

More Knowledge

Adding Sections to a Form

If you add a Logo, Title, or Date & Time control to a form, the Form Header section is automatically created. The Date & Time control can also add a Form Footer section to the form. If you add a Page Number control to a form, a Page Header section will be created.

Objective 2
Change and Add Controls

A *control* is an object, such as a label or text box, in a form or report that enables individuals to view or manipulate information stored in tables or queries. You have worked with label controls, text box controls, and, earlier in the chapter, logo controls; but there are more controls that can be added to a form. By default, when you create a form, Access uses the same object type as that in the underlying table or query. More controls are available in Design view than in Layout view.

Activity 6.3 Changing Controls on a Form

In this activity, you will change a combo box control to a list box control.

1 Click the **Menu Item field arrow**.

Because the underlying table—*6A Sales*—designated this field as a lookup field, Access inserted a combo box control for this field instead of a text box control. The Franchise# field is also a combo box control. A *combo box* enables individuals to select from a list or to type a value.

2 Switch to **Design** view. In the **Detail** section, click the **Menu Item label control**. On the Ribbon, click the **Arrange tab**, and then in the **Control Layout group**, click the **Remove** button.

Recall that the Remove button is used to remove a field from a stacked or tabular layout—it does not delete the field or remove it from the form. If fields are in the middle of a stacked layout column and are removed from the layout, the remaining fields in the column will display over the removed field. To avoid the clutter, first move the fields that you want to remove from the layout to the bottom of the column.

3 Click the **Undo** button [icon]. Point to the **Menu Item label control** until the [icon] pointer displays. Drag downward until a thin orange line displays on the bottom edges of the **Date** controls.

Alert!

Did the control stay in the same location?

In Design view, the orange line that indicates the location where controls will be moved is much thinner than—and not as noticeable as—the line in Layout view. If you drag downward too far, Access will not move the selected fields.

---

4 In the **Control Layout group**, click the **Remove** button to remove the Menu Item field from the stacked layout. With the **Menu Item label control** selected, hold down ⇧Shift, and then click the **Menu Item combo box control**. Point to the selected controls, and then drag to the right and upward until the **Menu Item label control** is aligned with the **Franchise#** controls and with the **3-inch mark on the horizontal ruler**. Compare your screen with Figure 6.7.

Figure 6.7

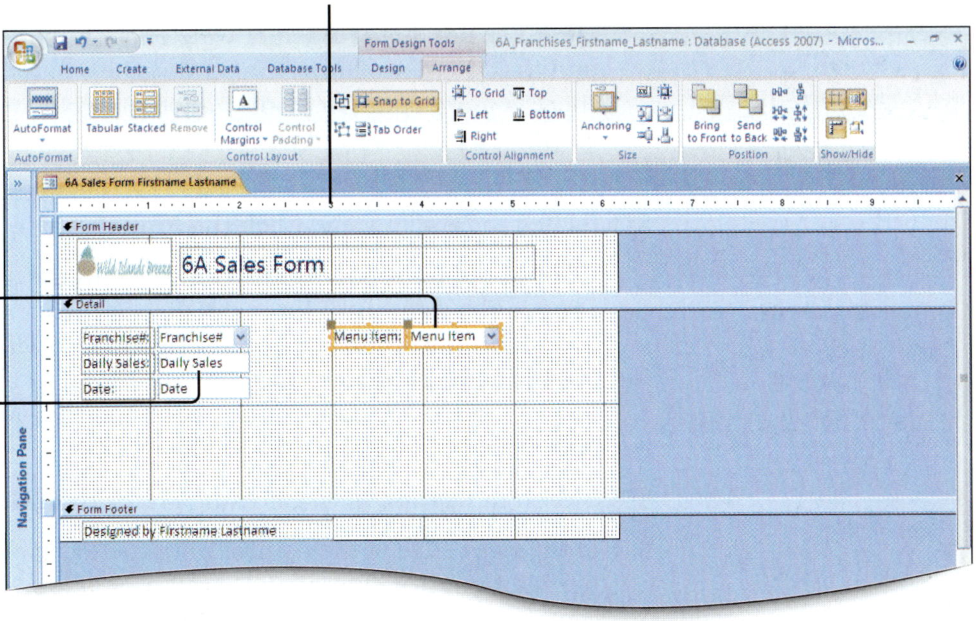

3-inch mark

Combo box control

Text box control

5 With the **Menu Item controls** selected, in the **Control Layout group**, click the **Stacked** button. Click anywhere in the **Detail** section to deselect the second column.

The Menu Item controls display in the second column and are grouped in a stacked layout. Recall that a stacked layout keeps the controls aligned and makes it easier to edit and move the controls.

6 Right-click the **Menu Item combo box control**. From the shortcut menu, click **Change To**, and then click **List Box**.

A *list box* enables individuals to select from a list but does not enable individuals to type anything that is not in the list. Based on the data in the underlying table or query, Access displays the control types to which you can change a field. The control type can be changed in Design view only.

Another Way ── **To Create a List Box or Combo Box by Using a Wizard**

To manually add a list box or combo box to a form, display the form in Design view. On the Design tab, in the Controls group, click either the List Box button or the Combo Box button. Click the form where you wish the control to display. A wizard displays, prompting you for the location of the values. The control can be populated by looking up data in a table or query, by typing values that seldom change, or by creating an unbound control that finds the data in a record on the form.

If you populate the control by looking up the data or by typing a list of values, you are prompted to select one of two options. Click *Remember the value for later use* to create an unbound control—Access will retain the selected value until an individual changes it or closes the form, but the data will not be written to the underlying table. Click *Store that value in this field* to create a bound control, and then select the field to which to bind the control. Finally, type a label for the control, which is displayed next to the control.

7 **Save** 💾 the form, and then switch to **Form** view. Notice the **Menu Item list box control** is not wide enough to display both columns and that there are horizontal and vertical scroll bars to indicate there is more data. To display another problem, click the **Franchise# combo box arrow**, and then notice that some of the city names are truncated. Press Esc.

8 Switch to **Design** view. Click the **Franchise# combo box**, and then point to the right edge of the control until the ↔ pointer displays. Drag to the right until the right edge of the control aligns with the **2.75-inch mark on the horizontal ruler**. Switch to **Form** view, click the **Franchise# arrow**, and then be sure that all of the city names display—if they do not, return to Design view and increase the width of the combo box control.

9 Switch to **Layout** view. Click the **Menu Item list box control**. Point to the right edge of the control until the ↔ pointer displays. Drag to the right until the horizontal scroll bar no longer displays in the combo box and all of the Menu Item *1307* displays—release the mouse button to display the resized list box.

10 **Save** 💾 the form, and switch to **Design** view.

More Knowledge

Validate or Restrict Data in Forms

When you design tables, set field properties to ensure the entry of valid data by using input masks, validation rules, and default values. Any field in a form created with a table having these properties inherits the validation properties from the underlying table. Setting these properties in the table is the preferred method; however, you can also set the properties on controls in the form. If conflicting settings occur, the setting on the bound control in the form will override the field property setting in the table.

Activity 6.4 Adding Controls to a Form

In this activity, you will add an image control and button controls to the form. An *image control* enables individuals to insert an image into any section of a form or report. A *button control* enables individuals to add a command button to a form or report that will perform an action when the button is clicked.

1 On the **Design tab**, in the **Controls group**, click the **Image** button 🖼. Move the mouse pointer down into the **Form Header** section. Align the plus sign (+) of the 🖼 pointer with the bottom of the **Form Header** section bar and with the **5-inch mark on the horizontal ruler** as shown in Figure 6.8.

Image control button

Figure 6.8

5-inch mark

Mouse pointer

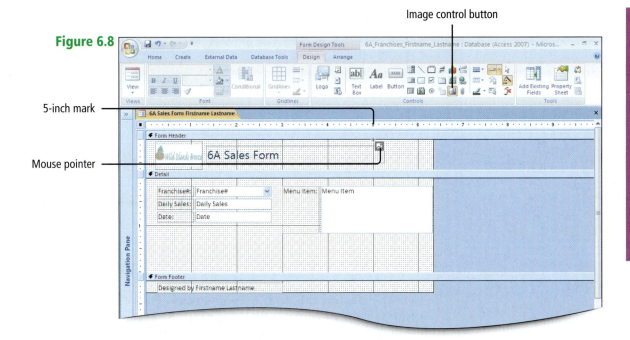

2 Drag downward to the top of the **Detail** section bar and to the right to the **6.25-inch mark on the horizontal ruler**. In the displayed **Insert Picture** dialog box, navigate to the location where the student data files for this textbook are saved. Locate and double-click **a06A_Logo** to insert the picture in the Form Header section. Do not be concerned that the logo on the left side and the image on the right side are different sizes.

Recall that using the logo control inserts the logo in a predetermined location—the left side—of the Form Header section. The image control is used to insert a picture anywhere in the form.

3 Click the **title's label control**. Point to the right edge of the label control until the ↔ pointer displays. Drag to the left until there are **two dots** between the right edge of the label control and the left edge of the image control. On the **Design tab**, in the **Font group**, click the **Center** button ≣. Switch to **Form** view, and then compare your screen with Figure 6.9.

The title is centered between the logo on the left and the image on the right, but the logo and the image are not the same height and width.

Figure 6.9

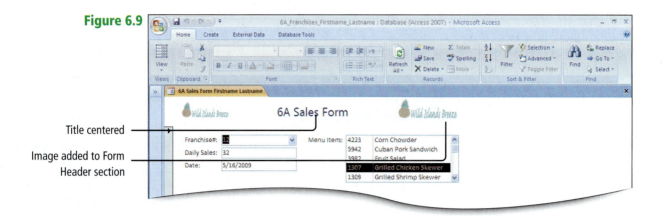

Title centered

Image added to Form
Header section

4 Switch to **Design** view, and then click the **image control**—the Wild Islands Breeze image on the right side in the Form Header section. On the **Design tab**, in the **Tools group**, click the **Property Sheet** button. If necessary, on the **Property Sheet**, click the **Format tab**, and then compare your screen with Figure 6.10. Notice the Width and Height property settings.

The Width property setting is 1.25 inches—yours may differ. The Height property setting is .625 inches—yours may differ.

Property Sheet for
selected image control

Figure 6.10

Image control

Width property
setting—yours may differ

Height property
setting—yours may differ

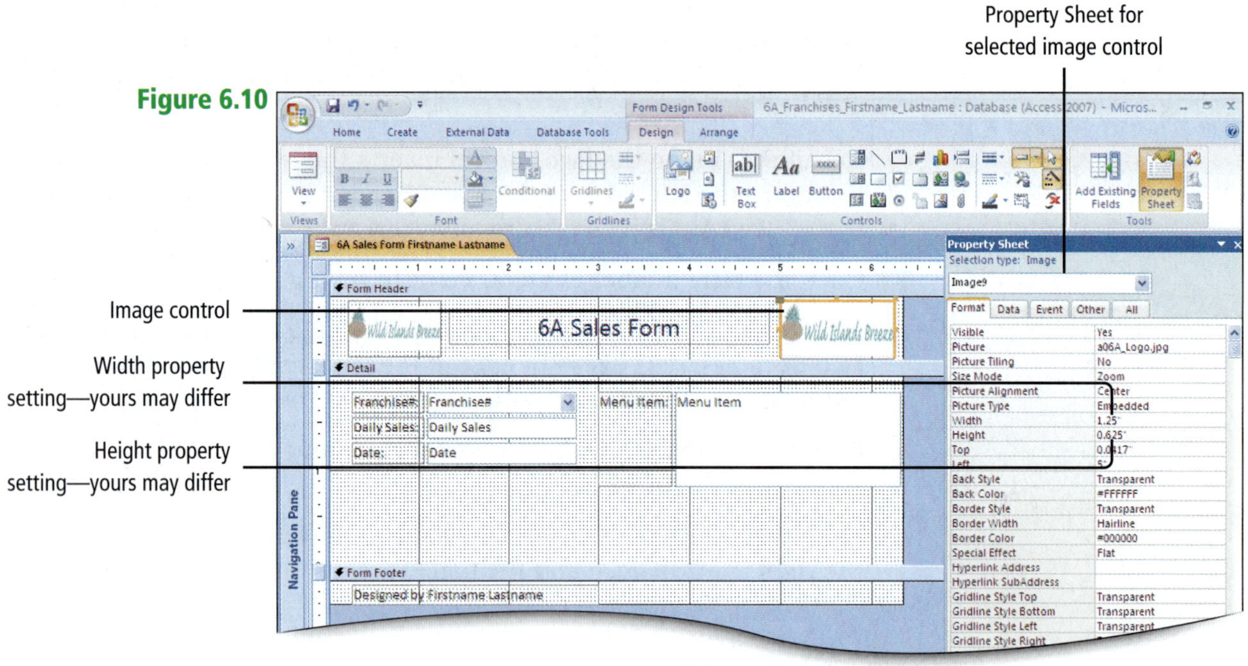

5 If necessary, change the Width property setting to **1.25** and then change the Height property setting to **.625** In the **Form Header** section, on the left side, click the **logo control**, and then notice that the Property Sheet for the logo control displays. On the **Property Sheet**, change the **Width** property setting to **1.25** and then change the **Height** property setting to **.625**

The width and height of the two controls are the same.

6 On the Ribbon, click the **Arrange tab**. With the logo control selected, hold down ⇧Shift, and then click the **image control**. In the **Control Alignment group**, click the **Bottom** button. Click the **title's label control**. Point to the left middle sizing handle until the ↔ pointer displays. Drag to the right until there are **two dots** between the right edge of the logo control and the left edge of the title's label control.

The logo control and the image control are aligned at the bottom, and the title's label control is resized.

7 **Close** ✕ the **Property Sheet**. On the Ribbon, click the **Design tab**, and then in the **Controls group**, click the **Button** button. Move the mouse pointer down into the **Detail** section. Align the plus sign (**+**) of the ⌗ pointer with the **1.5-inch mark on the vertical ruler** and the **1.5-mark on the horizontal ruler**, and then click. Compare your screen with Figure 6.11.

The Command Button Wizard dialog box displays. The first dialog box enables you to select an action for the button based on the selected category.

Button control button

Figure 6.11

Command Button
Wizard dialog box

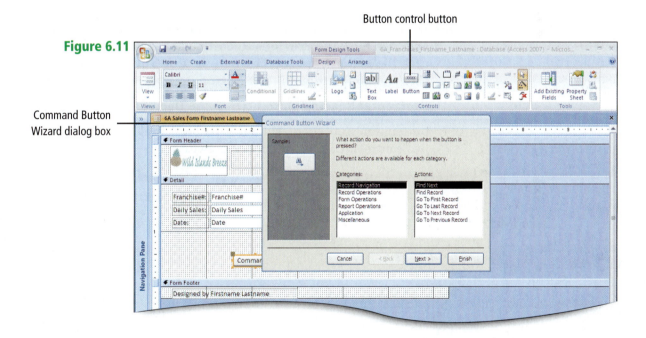

8 Take a moment to click the different categories to display the actions associated with the category. When you are finished, under **Categories**, click **Record Navigation**. Under **Actions**, click **Go To Previous Record**, and then click **Next**.

The second Command Button Wizard dialog box displays, which enables you to select what will display on the button—either text or a picture. If you select picture, navigate to a location on your computer where pictures are saved, and then select any picture. If you select text, accept the default text or type new text. A preview of the button displays on the left side of the dialog box.

9 Next to **Picture**, be sure **Go to Previous** is selected, and then click **Next**.

The third Command Button Wizard dialog box displays, which enables you to name the button. If you need to refer to the button later—usually in creating macros—a meaningful name is helpful. The buttons created with the Command Button Wizard are linked to macros—programs—that cannot be run or edited in previous versions of Access.

10 In the text box, type **btnPrevRecord** and then click **Finish**.

When creating controls that can later be used in programming, it is a good idea to start the name of the control with an abbreviation of the type of control—btn—and then a descriptive abbreviation of the purpose of the control.

11 Using the techniques you have just practiced, add a **button control** to the right of the Previous Record button control. Under **Categories**, click **Record Navigation**. Under **Actions**, click **Go to Next Record**. For **Picture**, click **Go to Next**, and then name the button **btnNextRecord** Do not be concerned if the button controls are not exactly aligned.

12 With the **Next Record button control** selected, hold down ⇧ Shift, and then click the **Previous Record button control**. On the Ribbon, click the **Arrange tab**, and then in the **Control Alignment group**, click the **Top** button. In the **Position group**, click either the **Increase Horizontal Spacing** button ⊞ or the **Decrease Horizontal Spacing** button ⊞ until there is approximately **1 inch** of space between the two controls. Compare your screen with Figure 6.12.

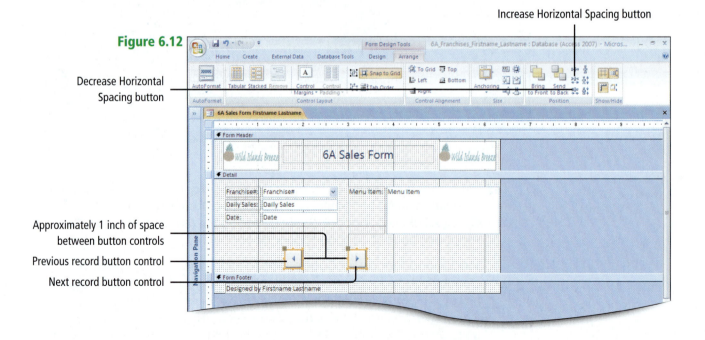

Figure 6.12

Decrease Horizontal Spacing button

Increase Horizontal Spacing button

Approximately 1 inch of space between button controls

Previous record button control

Next record button control

13 Save 🖫 the form, and then switch to **Form** view. Experiment by clicking the **Next Record** button and the **Previous Record** button, and notice in the navigation area that you are displaying different records.

14 Switch to **Design** view. On the **Design tab**, in the **Controls group**, click the **Button** button. Align the plus sign (**+**) of the ⊞ pointer with the **1.5-inch mark on the vertical ruler** and with the **5-inch mark on the horizontal ruler**, and then click.

15 In the **Command Button Wizard** dialog box, under **Categories**, click **Form Operations**. Under **Actions**, click **Print Current Form**, and then click **Next**. Click the **Text** option button to accept *Print Form*, and then click **Next**. Name the button **btnPrtForm** and then click **Finish**.

You will use this button to print one form when you are finished formatting the form.

16 Save 🖫 the form.

Objective 3
Format a Form

There are several methods you can use to modify the appearance of a form. Each section and control on a form has properties. Some properties can be modified by using buttons in the groups on a tab or by changing the property setting on the Property Sheet.

Activity 6.5 Adding a Background Color

In this activity, you will modify the background color of the Form Header section, the Form Footer section, and the Detail section of the *6A Sales Form*. The background color is a property setting for each section; there is no background color property setting for the entire form. Property settings can also be changed in Layout view.

1 With **6A Sales Form** open in **Design** view, click the **Form Header** section bar.

The darkened bar indicates that the entire Form Header section of the form is selected.

2 On the **Design tab**, in the **Font group**, click the **Fill/Back Color button arrow** 🖌▾. Under **Standard Colors**, on the third row, click the seventh color—**Green 2**.

The background color for the Form Header section changes to a light shade of green.

3 Double-click the **Form Footer** section bar to display the Property Sheet for the Form Footer section. On the **Property Sheet**, click in the **Back Color** property setting box—it displays #FFFFFF. Click the **Build** button ⋯.

The color palette displays. #FFFFFF is a code used by Access to represent the color white. You can select an Access Theme Color, a Standard Color, a Recent Color, or click More Colors to select shades of colors.

4 Click **More Colors**. In the displayed **Colors** dialog box, click the **Custom tab**.

All colors use varying shades of Red, Green, and Blue.

5 In the **Colors** dialog box, click **Cancel**. On the **Property Sheet**, click the **Back Color property setting arrow**.

A list of color schemes display. These colors also display on the color palette under Access Theme Colors.

6 From the displayed list, experiment by clicking on different color schemes and viewing the effects of the background color change. You will have to click the property setting arrow each time to select another color scheme. When you are finished, click the **Build** button ![...]. Under **Standard Colors**, on the third row, click the seventh color—**Green 2**—and then press Enter.

You can change the background color either by using the Fill/Back Color button in the Font group or by changing the Back Color property setting on the Property Sheet. The code used by Access to represent Green 2 is #E6EDD7.

Another Way — **To Add a Background Color**

Open the form in Layout view. To select a section, click in an empty area of the section. On the Home tab or on the Format tab, in the Font group, click the Fill/Back Color button.

---

7 Using one of the techniques you have just practiced, change the background color of the **Detail** section to **Green 2**. Switch to **Form** view, and then compare your screen with Figure 6.13.

Figure 6.13

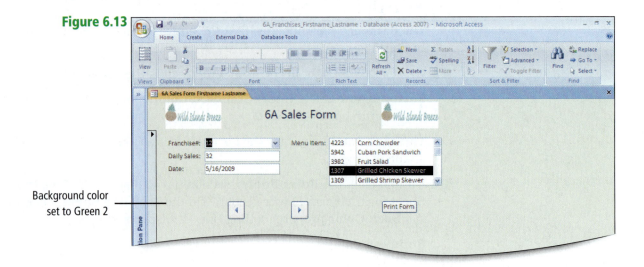

Background color set to Green 2

8 **Save** 🖫 the form, and then switch to **Design** view. **Close** ✕ the **Property Sheet**.

More Knowledge
Adding a Background Color to Controls

Background colors can also be added to controls. First, click the control or controls to which you want to add a background color. If you want to use color schemes, open the Property Sheet, and then click the Back Color property setting arrow. If you want to use the color palette, click the Home tab or Format tab. In the Font group, click the Fill/Back Color button.

Activity 6.6 Adding a Background Picture to a Form

In this activity, you will add a picture to the background of *6A Sales Form*.

1 With **6A Sales Form** open in **Design** view, locate the **Form selector** as shown in Figure 6.14.

The **Form selector** is the box where the rulers meet, in the upper left corner of a form in Design view. Use the Form selector to select the entire form.

Figure 6.14

Form Selector ———

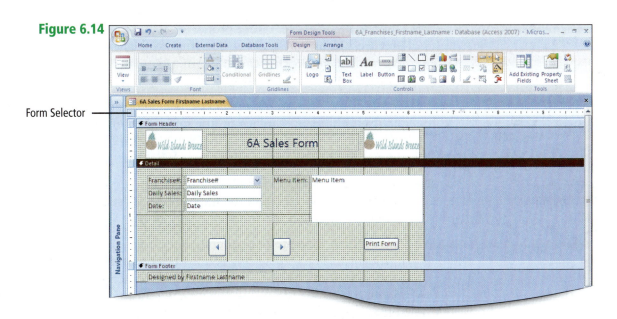

2 Double-click the **Form selector** to open the Property Sheet for the form.

3 On the **Property Sheet**, on the **Format tab**, click in the **Picture** property setting box. Click the **Build** button 🔳. Navigate to the location where the student data files for this textbook are saved. Locate and double-click **a06A_Background** to insert the picture in the center of the form, and then compare your screen with Figure 6.15.

Centered picture

Figure 6.15

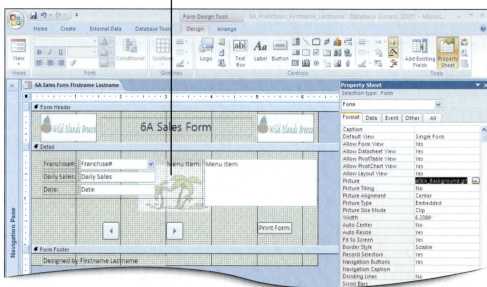

4 On the **Property Sheet**, click in the **Picture Tiling** property setting box. Click the **arrow**, and then click **Yes**.

Tiling creates a 1-inch square of a picture that is repeated across and down the form.

5 Change the **Picture Tiling** property setting to **No**. Click in the **Picture Alignment** property setting box, click the **arrow**, and then experiment by clicking the different alignment options. When you are finished, click **Form Center**.

The ***Picture Alignment property*** determines where the background picture for a form displays on the form. Center places the picture in the center of the page when the form is printed. Form Center places the picture in the center of the form when the form is printed.

6 Click in the **Picture Size Mode** property setting, and then click the **arrow** to display the options. Experiment by selecting the different options. When you are finished, click **Zoom**.

The ***Picture Size Mode property*** determines the size of the picture in the form. The Clip setting retains the original size of the image. The Stretch setting stretches the image both vertically and horizontally to match the size of the form—the image may be distorted. The Zoom setting adjusts the image to be as large as possible without distorting the image. Both Stretch Horizontal and Stretch Vertical can distort the image. If you have a background color and set the Picture Type property setting to Stretch, the background color will not display.

7 **Close** ☒ the **Property Sheet**, **Save** 🖫 the form, and then switch to **Layout** view. Compare your screen with Figure 6.16.

Figure 6.16

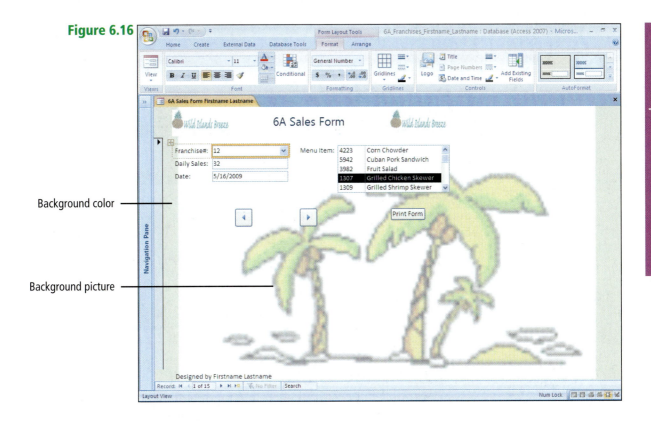

Background color ——

Background picture ——

Activity 6.7 Modifying the Borders of Controls

In this activity, you will modify the borders of some of the controls on *6A Sales Form*. There are related property settings on the Property Sheet.

1 With **6A Sales Form** open in **Layout** view, click the **Franchise# combo box control**. Holding down ⇧Shift, click the **Daily Sales text box control**, and then click the **Date text box control**. On the **Format tab**, in the **Controls group**, notice the buttons that are used to modify borders—Line Thickness [≡▾], Line Type [▦▾], and Line Color [✎▾]. Compare your screen with Figure 6.17.

To modify the borders of controls, be sure to use the buttons in the Controls group. Similar buttons are displayed in the Gridlines group—they are used to modify the gridlines that display in Design view or if you choose to display gridlines in Layout view.

Line Thickness button

Figure 6.17

Line Type button

Line Color button

Selected controls

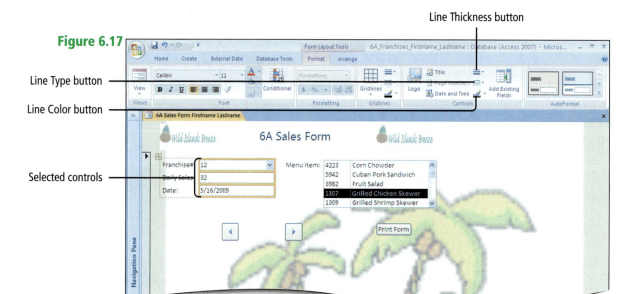

2 On the **Format tab**, in the **Controls group**, click the **Line Type** button [icon]. Point to each line type to display the **ScreenTip**. The second line type—**Solid**—is the default line type. Click the last line type—**Dash Dot Dot**—and then switch to **Form** view to display the results. Notice that the borders of the three controls display a line type of Dash Dot Dot.

You can review the results in Layout view, but you would have to deselect the three controls. Because you will change other border property settings, by switching to Form view, the controls will remain selected.

3 Switch to **Layout** view. Notice that the three controls are still selected—if they are not, use the technique you have practiced to select them again. On the **Format tab**, in the **Controls group**, click the **Line Thickness** button [icon]. Point to each line thickness to display the **ScreenTip**. The first line thickness—Hairline—is the default line thickness. Click the third line type—**2 pt**.

4 In the **Controls group**, click the **Line Color button arrow** [icon] to display the color palette. Under **Access Theme Colors**, point to each color to display the **ScreenTip**, and then on the second row, click the eighth color—**Access Theme 8**. Switch to **Form** view to display the results.

The borders of the three controls display a line thickness of 2 points, and the color of the borders is a darker shade. A *point* is 1/72 of an inch.

5 Switch to **Layout** view. With the three controls still selected, on the Ribbon, click the **Arrange tab**. In the **Tools group**, click the **Property Sheet** button, and then compare your screen with Figure 6.18. Notice the properties that are associated with the buttons with which you changed the borders of the selected controls.

Because multiple items on the form are selected, the Property Sheet displays *Selection type: Multiple selection.* You changed the property settings of the controls by using buttons, and the Property Sheet displays the results of those changes. You can also select multiple controls, open the Property Sheet, and make the changes to the properties. The Property Sheet displays more settings than those available through the use of buttons.

Figure 6.18

Border Style—related to Line Type button

Border Width—related to Line Thickness button

Border Color—related to Line Color button

6 **Close** ✕ the **Property Sheet**, and then **Save** 🖫 the form. Switch to **Form** view.

More Knowledge

Adding Borders to Label Controls

By default, the border style—line style—of a Label control is transparent, effectively hiding the border from the display. Because borders display around bound controls that contain data, it is recommended that you do not add borders to label controls so that individuals can easily distinguish the control that holds data.

Objective 4
Make a Form User Friendly

To make forms easy to use, you can add instructions that display on the status bar while data is being entered and custom **ControlTips** that display when an individual pauses the mouse pointer over a control on a form. Additionally, you can change the tab order of the fields on a form. *Tab order* refers to the order in which the fields are selected when the [Tab] key is pressed. By default, the tab order is created based on the order in which the fields are added to the form.

Activity 6.8 Adding a Message to the Status Bar

When you created tables, you added a description to the field, and the description displayed in the status bar of the Access window. If a description is included for a field in the underlying table of a form, the text of the description will also display in the status bar when an individual clicks in the field on the form. In this activity, you will add a description to the Daily Sales field in the *6A Sales* table, and then *propagate*—disseminate or apply—the changes to *6A Sales Form*. You will also add status bar text to a field on a form using the Property Sheet of the control.

1 With **6A Sales Form** open in **Form** view, click in the **Daily Sales** field. On the left side of the status bar, *Form View* displays—there is no text that helps an individual enter data.

2 **Close** ✕ the form, and then expand » the **Navigation Pane**. Under **Tables**, right-click **6A Sales**, and then from the shortcut menu, click **Design View**. In the **Daily Sales** field, click in the **Description** box. Type **How many items were sold?** and then press Enter. Compare your screen with Figure 6.19.

A ***Property Update Options button*** displays in the Description box for the Date field. When you make changes to the design of a table, Access displays this button, which enables individuals to update the Property Sheet for this field in all objects that use this table as the record source.

Description entered

Figure 6.19

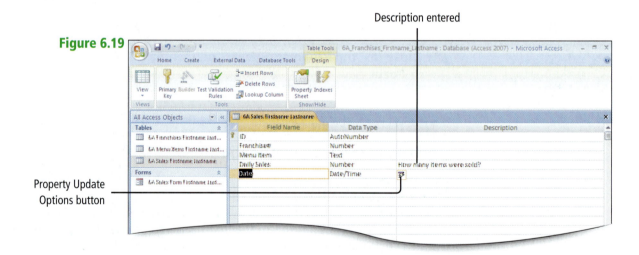

Property Update Options button

3 Click the **Property Update Options** button ⧉, and then click **Update Status Bar Text everywhere Daily Sales is used**. In the displayed **Update Properties** dialog box, under **Update the following objects?**, notice that only one object—*Form: 6A Sales Form*—displays, and it is selected. In the **Update Properties** dialog box, click **Yes**.

The changes in the Description field in the table will be propagated to *6A Sales Form*. If multiple objects use the *6A Sales* table as the underlying object, you can propagate the change to all of the objects.

4 **Close** ⊠ the table, saving changes, and then open the **6A Sales** table in **Datasheet** view. On any record, click in the **Daily Sales** field, and then notice the text—*How many items were sold?*—that displays on the left side of the status bar.

5 **Close** ⊠ the table. On the **Navigation Pane**, under **Forms**, double-click **6A Sales Form** to open it in Form view. Collapse ⟪ the **Navigation Pane**. Click in the **Daily Sales** field, and then notice that on the left side of the status bar, *How many items were sold?* displays.

Access propagated the change made in the underlying table to the form.

6 Switch to **Design** view. Click the **Daily Sales text box control**. On the **Design tab**, in the **Tools group**, click the **Property Sheet** button.

7 On the **Property Sheet**, click the **Other tab**. Locate the **Status Bar Text** property, and notice the setting *How many items were sold?*

When Access propagated the change to the form, it populated the Status Bar Text property setting. The **Status Bar Text property** enables individuals to add descriptive text that will display in the status bar for a selected control.

8 In the **Detail** section, click the **Date text box control**, and then notice that the **Property Sheet** changes to display the properties for the **Date** text box control. Click in the **Status Bar Text** property setting box, type **Enter date of sales report** and then press [Enter].

You do not have to enter a description for the field in the underlying table for text to display in the status bar when a field is selected in a form. Access does not display a Property Update Options button to propagate changes to the underlying table, and the text will not be added to the Description box for the field in the table.

9 **Save** 🖫 the form, and then switch to **Form** view. Click in the **Date** field, and then compare your screen with Figure 6.20.

The status bar displays the text you entered in the Status Bar Text property setting box.

Figure 6.20

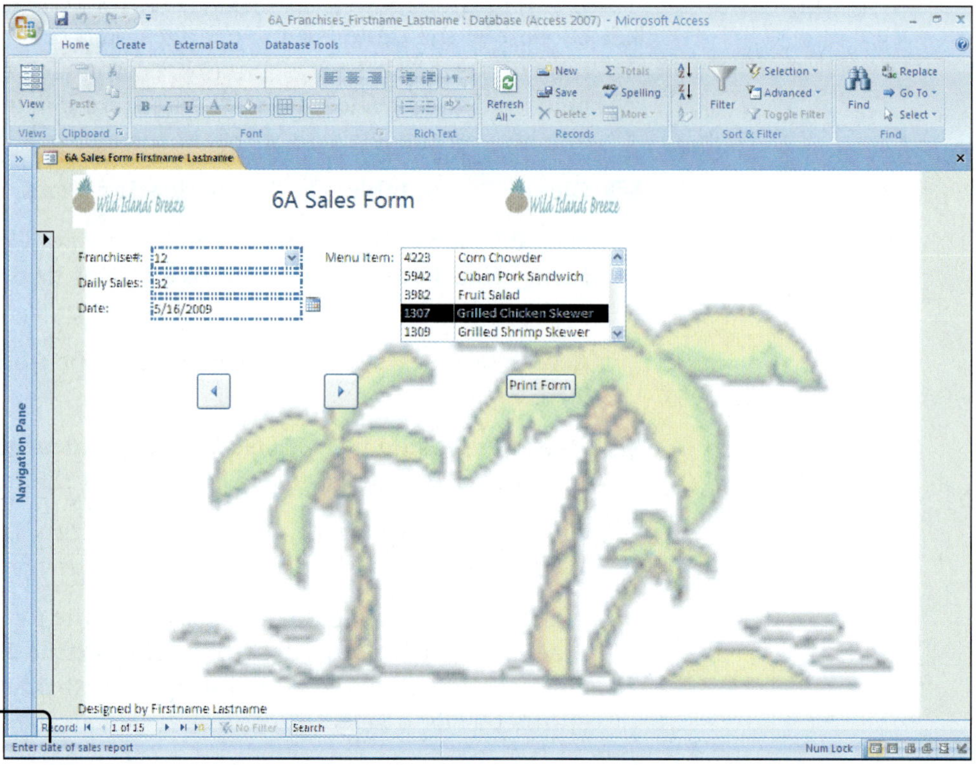

Entered in Status Bar Text property setting box

10 Switch to **Design** view.

More Knowledge

Conflicting Field Description and Status Bar Text Property Setting

When you create a form, the fields inherit the property settings from the underlying table. You can change the Status Bar Text property setting for the form, and it will override the setting that is inherited from the table. If you later change field properties in Table Design view, the Property Update Options button displays—you must manually propagate those changes to the table's related objects; propagation is not automatic. An exception to this are Validation Rules—changes are automatically propagated.

Activity 6.9 Creating Custom ControlTips

Another way to make a form easier to use is to add custom ControlTips to objects on the form. A **ControlTip** is similar to a ScreenTip and temporarily displays descriptive text while the mouse pointer is paused over the control. This method is somewhat limited because most individuals press Tab or Enter to move from field to field, and thus do not see the ControlTip. However, a ControlTip is a useful tool in a training situation when an individual is learning how to use the data entry form. In this activity, you will add a ControlTip to the Print Form button control.

1 With **6A Sales Form** open in **Design** view and the **Property Sheet** displayed, click the **Print Form** button. Notice the **Property Sheet**

displays *Selection type: Command Button* and the Selection type box displays *btnPrtForm*, the name you gave to the button when you added it to the form. If necessary, click the **Other tab** to make it current.

2 Click in the **ControlTip Text** property setting box, type **Prints the selected record** and then press Enter. Compare your screen with Figure 6.21.

Property Sheet for selected button

Figure 6.21

ControlTip property setting

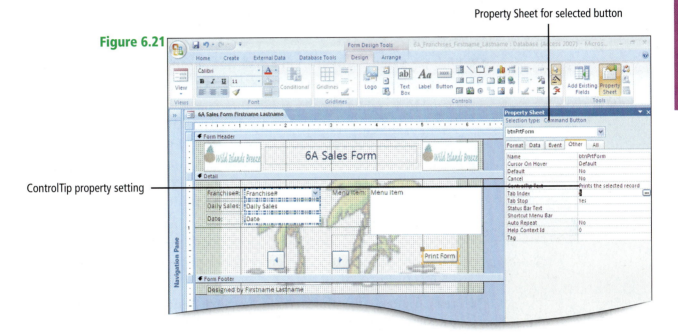

3 **Close** ✕ the **Property Sheet**, **Save** 💾 the form, and then switch to **Form** view. Point to the **Print Form** button, and then compare your screen with Figure 6.22.

A ControlTip displays the message you typed for the ControlTip Text property setting.

Figure 6.22

ControlTip

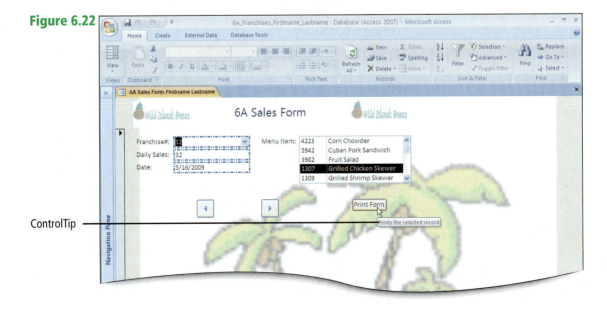

4 Leave *6A Sales Form* open in Form view for the next activity.

Activity 6.10 Changing the Tab Order

You can customize the order in which you enter data on a form by changing the tab order. Recall that tab order refers to the order in which the fields are selected each time Tab is pressed. As you press Tab, the *focus* of the form changes. Focus refers to the object that is selected and currently being acted upon. When you press Tab, the focus changes from one control to another control.

1 With **6A Sales Form** open in **Form** view, in the navigation area, click the **New (blank) record** button [icon]. If necessary, click in the Franchise# combo box. Press Tab three times, and then notice that the insertion point moves from field to field, ending with the **Menu Item** list box, although there is no insertion point for a list box.

2 Press Tab, and then notice that the focus changes to the **Previous Record** button. Press Enter, and then notice that **Record 15** displays. The focus is still on the **Previous Record** button—the button displays with a darker border. Press Enter again.

Because the focus is still on the Previous Record button, pressing Enter causes the button to perform an action—displaying the previous record—Record 14.

3 Press Tab to change the focus to the **Next Record** button. Press Enter, and then notice that *Record 15* displays. Press Tab to move the focus to the **Print Form** button, and then press Enter.

Because the focus is on the Print Form button, the Print dialog box displays.

4 In the **Print** dialog box, click **Cancel**. Switch to **Layout** view. Although you will be making tab order changes in Layout view, you can also make the changes in Design view.

5 On the Ribbon, click the **Arrange tab**. In the **Control Layout group**, click the **Tab Order** button, and then compare your screen with Figure 6.23.

The Tab Order dialog box displays. Under Section, Detail is selected. Under Custom Order, the fields and controls display in the order they were added to the form. To the left of each field name or button name is a row selector button.

As you rearrange fields on a form, the tab order does not change from the original tab order. This can make data entry chaotic because the focus is changed in what appears to be an illogical order. The Auto Order button will change the tab order based on the position of the controls in the form from left to right and top to bottom.

Figure 6.23

Row selector box

Field names

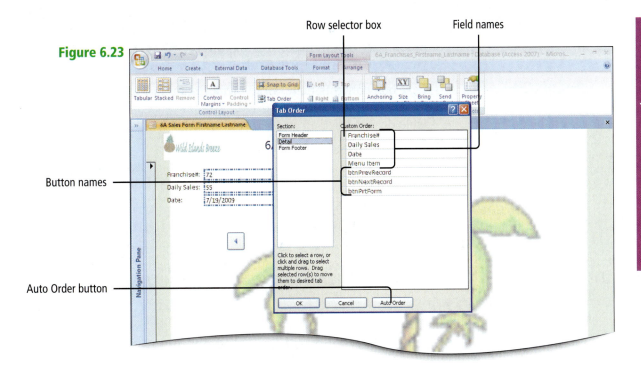

Button names

Auto Order button

---

6 To the left of **Menu Item**, click the **row selector** box. Point to the **row selector** box until the ⬚ pointer displays. Drag upward until a dark horizontal line displays between **Franchise#** and **Daily Sales**.

The Menu Item field will now receive the focus after the Franchise# field.

Alert! | **Did the field stay in the same location?**

You must point to the row selector box before dragging the field. If you point to the field name, the field will not be moved.

---

7 In the **Tab Order** dialog box, click **OK**. **Save** 🖫 the form, and then switch to **Form** view. In the navigation area, click the **Last Record** button ▷|. When the Menu Item field has the focus, it is easier to see it on a blank record. In the navigation area, click the **New (blank) record** button ▷✲.

The insertion point displays in the Franchise# field.

8 Press Tab. Even though it is difficult to see, the focus changes to the **Menu Item** list box. Press Tab again, and then notice that the focus changes to the **Daily Sales** text box.

Before allowing individuals to enter data into a form, you should always test the tab order to ensure that the data will be easy to enter.

9 Switch to **Design** view. In the **Detail** section, right-click the **Daily Sales text box control**, click **Property Sheet**, and then compare your screen with Figure 6.24.

Text box controls have three properties relating to tab order: Tab Index, Tab Stop, and Auto Tab. Combo box controls and list box controls do not have an Auto Tab property.

Property Sheet for Daily Sales text box control

Figure 6.24

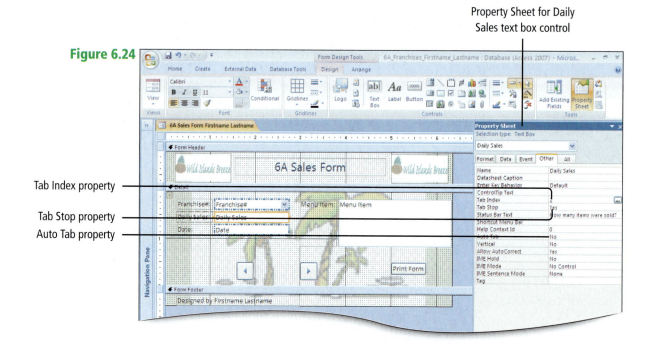

Tab Index property

Tab Stop property

Auto Tab property

10 On the **Property Sheet**, click in the **Tab Index** property setting box, which displays 2. Click the **Build** button ⬚.

Tab Index settings begin with 0. Franchise# has a Tab Index setting of 0, which indicates that this field has the focus when the form is opened. Menu Item has a Tab Index setting of 1—it will receive the focus when Tab is pressed one time. Daily Sales has a Tab Index setting of 2—it will receive the focus when Tab is pressed the second time.

11 In the **Tab Order** dialog box, click **Cancel**. On the **Property Sheet**, notice that the **Tab Stop** property setting is **Yes**, which means individuals can press Tab to move to this field.

The Auto Tab property setting is No. It should be changed to Yes only when a text field has an input mask. Recall that an input mask controls how the data is entered into a field; for example, the formatting of a phone number.

12 In the **Detail** section, click the **Franchise# combo box control**, and then on the **Property Sheet**, notice the settings for the **Tab Index** and **Tab Stop** properties.

The Tab Index setting is 0, which means this field has the focus when the form page is displayed—it is first on the tab order list. The

Tab Stop setting is Yes. Because an input mask cannot be applied to a combo box, there is no Auto Tab property. The Auto Tab property applies only to a text box control.

13 In the **Detail** section, click the **Previous Record** button control. On the **Property Sheet**, click in the **Tab Stop** property setting box, click the **arrow**, and then click **No**.

Changing the Tab Stop property setting to No means that the focus will not be changed to the button by pressing Tab.

14 **Save** 🖫 the form, and then switch to **Form** view. In the navigation area, click the **Last record** button ▸ . Press Tab **three times**, watching the focus change from the Franchise# field to the Date field. Press Tab one time, and then compare your screen with Figure 6.25.

Because the Tab Stop property setting for the Previous Record button control was changed to No, the button does not receive the focus by pressing the Tab key.

Focus is on Next Record button

Figure 6.25

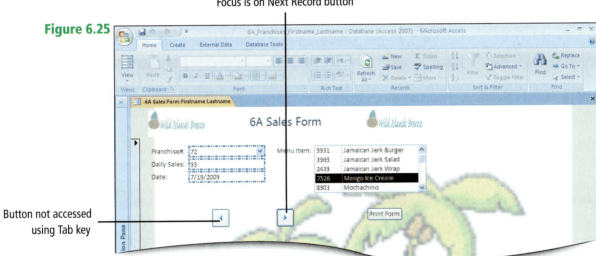

Button not accessed using Tab key

15 In the **Detail** section, click the **Previous Record** button.

The previous record displays—you can still use the button by clicking on it.

16 Switch to **Design** view. Using the techniques you have just practiced, for the **Next Record** button and the **Print Form** button, change the **Tab Stop** property setting to **No**.

17 **Close** ☒ the **Property Sheet**. **Save** 🖫 the form, and then switch to **Form** view. Test the tab order by pressing Tab, making sure that the focus does not change to the Next Record button or the Print Form button.

When the focus is on the Date field, pressing the Tab key moves the focus to the Franchise# field in the next record.

18 Navigate to **Record 5**—Franchise# 44. Unless, you are required to submit your database electronically, in the **Detail** section, click the **Print Form** button. In the **Print** dialog box under **Print Range**, click **Selected Record(s)**, and then click **OK**. If you are instructed to submit this result as an electronic printout, select the record using the selector bar, and then from the **Office** menu, point to **Save As** and click **PDF or XPS**. Navigate to the folder where you store your electronic printouts. Click the **Options** button, click **Selected records**, and then click **OK**. Click **Publish**.

19 **Close** ☒ the form, and then expand the **Navigation Pane**. **Close** the database, and then **Exit** Access.

More Knowledge

Changing the Tab Order for a Form in Datasheet View

When you change the tab order in Form Design view, Access will rearrange the fields in the form's Datasheet view to match the tab order.

End **You have completed Project 6A** ————————————

Project 6B WIB

The corporate office of Wild Islands Breeze (WIB) maintains a database about the franchises, including daily sales of menu items per franchise, the franchise owners, and franchise fees and payments. Reports are often run to summarize data in the tables or queries. Creating customized reports will help the owners and officers of the company view the information in the database in a meaningful way. In Activities 6.11 through 6.18, you will create customized reports. Your completed reports will look similar to those shown in Figure 6.26.

For Project 6B, you will need the following files:

a06B_WIB
a06B_Logo

You will save your database as
6B_WIB_Firstname_Lastname

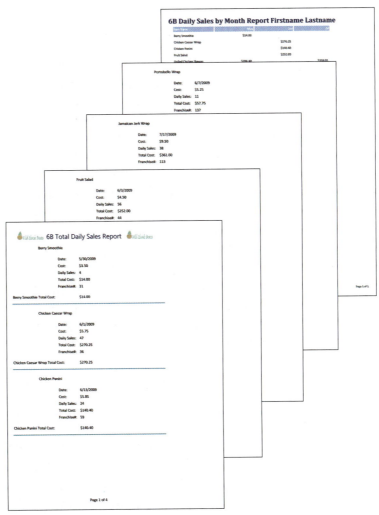

Figure 6.26
Project 6B—WIB

Objective 5
Create a Report in Design View

You usually create a report using the Report tool, the Blank Report tool, or the Report Wizard, and then modify the report in Design view to suit your needs. Use Design view to create a report when these tools do not meet your needs or if you want more control in the creation of a report. Creating or modifying a report in Design view is a common technique when additional controls, such as calculated controls, need to be added to the report or properties need to be changed.

Activity 6.11 Creating a Report in Design View

Creating a report with the Report tool, the Blank Report tool, or the Report Wizard is the easiest way to start the creation of a customized report, but you can also create a report from scratch in Design view. Once you understand the sections of a report and how to manipulate the controls within the sections, it is easier to modify a report that has been created using the report tools.

1 **Start** Access. Navigate to the location where the student data files for this textbook are saved. Locate and open the **a06B_WIB** file. Save the database in the **Access 2007 Database** format in your **Access Chapter 6** folder as 6B_WIB_Firstname_Lastname

2 If you did not add the *Access Chapter 6* folder to the Trust Center, enable the content. On the **Navigation Pane**, rename the tables and queries by adding **Firstname Lastname** to the end of each table and query name. Open **6B Total Daily Sales Query**. Switch to **Design** view, and then notice the underlying tables that were used in the creation of the query. Notice the calculated field—*Total Cost*.

Recall that a calculated field contains the field name, followed by a colon, and then an expression. In the expression, the existing field names must be enclosed in square brackets. The Total Cost was calculated by multiplying the value in the Cost field by the value in the Daily Sales field.

3 When you are finished, **Close** ⊠ the query, and collapse « the **Navigation Pane**. On the Ribbon, click the **Create tab**. In the **Reports group**, click the **Report Design** button. When the design grid displays, scroll down to display all of the report sections.

Three sections are included in the blank design grid: the Page Header section, the Detail section, and the Page Footer section. Recall that a page header displays at the top of every printed page, and the page footer displays at the bottom of every printed page.

4 On the **Design tab**, in the **Tools group**, click the **Property Sheet** button to display the Property Sheet for the report.

5 On the **Property Sheet**, click the **Data tab**. Click the **Record Source property setting box arrow**, and then compare your screen with Figure 6.27. If necessary, increase the width of the Property Sheet.

As with forms, the Record Source property setting is used to select the underlying table or query for the report.

Figure 6.27

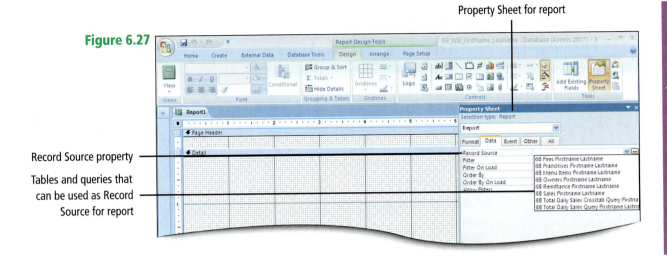

Property Sheet for report

Record Source property

Tables and queries that can be used as Record Source for report

6. From the displayed list of tables and queries, click **6B Total Daily Sales Query**, and then **Close** ✕ the **Property Sheet**.

6B Total Daily Sales Query is the record source—underlying query—for this report.

7. On the **Design tab**, in the **Tools group**, click the **Add Existing Fields** button to display the fields in 6B Total Daily Sales Query.

8. In the **Field List**, click **Date**. Hold down ⇧Shift, and then click **Franchise#** to select all of the fields.

9. Drag the selected fields into the **Detail** section of the design grid until the top of the arrow of the 🔳 pointer is **three dots** below the bottom edge of the **Detail** section bar and aligned with the **3-inch mark on the horizontal ruler**, and then compare your screen with Figure 6.28.

As with forms, drag the fields to where the text box controls should display.

3-inch mark   Text box controls

Figure 6.28

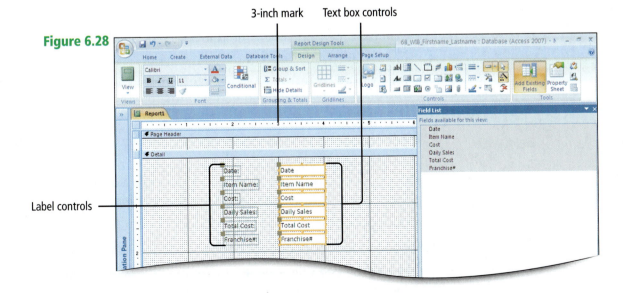

Label controls

10 With the label controls and text box controls for the fields selected, on the Ribbon, click the **Arrange tab**. In the **Control Layout group**, click the **Stacked** button to group the fields together for easier formatting.

11 Close ⊠ the **Field List**, and then **Save** 🖫 the report as **6B Total Daily Sales Report Firstname Lastname**

Activity 6.12 Modifying the Sections of a Report

By default, a report created in Design view includes a Page Header section and a Page Footer section. Reports can also include a Report Header section and a Report Footer section. In this activity, you will add the Report Header and Report Footer sections and hide the Page Header section. Recall that a Report Header displays at the top of the first printed page of a report, and the Report Footer displays at the bottom of the last printed page of a report.

1 On the **Arrange tab**, in the **Show/Hide group**, click the **Report Header/Footer** button 🖫. Notice that the **Report Header** section displays at the top of the design grid. Scroll down to display the **Report Footer** section.

2 Scroll up to display the **Report Header** section. On the Ribbon, click the **Design tab**. In the **Controls group**, click the **Logo** button. Locate and double-click **a06B_Logo** to insert the logo in the Report Header section. On the selected logo, point to the right middle sizing handle until the ↔ pointer displays. Drag to the right until the right edge of the logo is aligned with the **1.25-inch mark on the horizontal ruler**.

3 On the **Design tab**, in the **Controls group**, click the **Title** button 🖫. In the **title's label control**, click to the right of **Report**, delete the space and Firstname Lastname, and then press ⏎. On the **title's label control**, point to the right middle sizing handle until the ↔ pointer displays, and then double-click to adjust the size of the label control to fit the text. Alternatively, drag the right middle sizing handle to the left.

4 With the label control for the title selected, hold down ⌃, and then press ↓ **nine times**.

Use ⌃ and the arrow keys to slightly move controls. The label control for the title is centered between the top and bottom edges of the logo control.

5 Scroll down until the **Page Footer** section bar displays. Point to the top edge of the **Page Footer** section bar until the ➕ pointer displays. Drag upward until the top of the **Page Footer** section bar aligns with the **2.25-inch mark on the vertical ruler**.

This prevents extra blank space from printing between the records.

6 Scroll up until the **Report Header** section displays. Point to the top edge of the **Detail** section bar until the ➕ pointer displays. Drag upward until the top edge of the **Detail** section bar aligns with the bottom edge of the **Page Header** section bar, and then compare your screen with Figure 6.29.

The Page Header and Page Footer sections are paired together. Likewise, the Report Header and Report Footer sections are paired together. You cannot remove only one section of the pair. If you wish to remove one section of a paired header/footer, decrease the height of the section. Alternatively, set the Height property for the section to 0. Because there is no space in the Page Header section, nothing will print at the top of every page. To remove both of the paired header/footer sections, on the Arrange tab, in the Show/Hide group, click the active Page Header/Footer button.

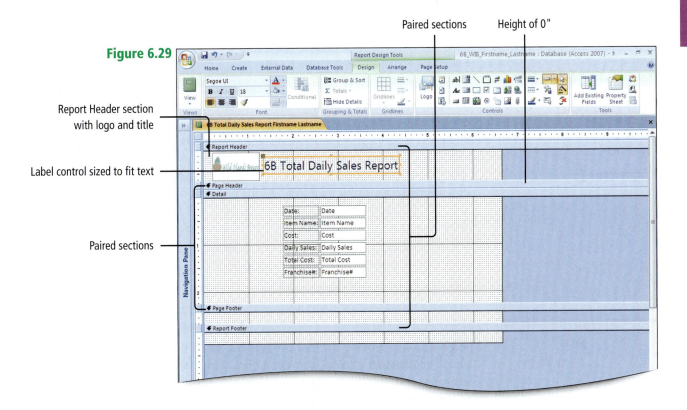

Figure 6.29

Paired sections

Height of 0"

Report Header section with logo and title

Label control sized to fit text

Paired sections

Note — Removing Sections with Controls

If you try to delete a section using the buttons on the Arrange tab, in the Show/Hide group, Access displays a message warning you that deleting the paired sections will also delete all of the controls in them and that you cannot undo the action. Click Yes to remove the sections from the report, along with any controls in them. Click No to cancel the removal of the sections. In addition, you will be unable to change the height of a section containing controls to less than the height required to display the controls.

7 **Save** the report.

Objective 6
Add Controls to a Report

Reports are not used to manipulate data in the underlying table or query, so they contain fewer types of controls. You can add label controls, text box controls, images, hyperlinks, or calculated controls to a report.

Activity 6.13 Add Label and Text Box Controls to a Report

In this activity, you will add controls to the report that will contain the page number, the date, and your first name and last name.

1 On the **Design tab**, in the **Controls group**, click the **Insert Page Number** button. In the displayed **Page Numbers** dialog box, under **Format**, click **Page N of M**. Under **Position**, click **Bottom of Page [Footer]**, and then click **OK**.

A text box control displays in the center of the Page Footer section. The control displays an expression that will display the page number. Every expression begins with an equal sign (=). "Page" is enclosed in quotation marks. Access interprets anything enclosed in quotation marks as text and will display it exactly as it is typed within the quotation marks, including the space. The & symbol *concatenates*—links or joins—strings. A *string* is a series of characters. The word *Page* followed by a space will be concatentated—joined—to the string that follows the & symbol.

[Page] is a reserved name that retrieves the current page number. This is followed by another & symbol that concatenates the page number to the next string—"of". The & symbol continues concatenation of [Pages], a reserved name that retrieves the total number of pages in the report.

2 **Save** the report. On the **Design tab**, in the **Views group**, click the **View button arrow**, and then click **Print Preview**. On the **Print Preview tab**, in the **Zoom group**, click the **Two Pages** button. Notice at the bottom of each page the format of the page number.

3 In the **Close Preview group**, click the **Close Print Preview** button.

4 On the **Design tab**, in the **Controls group**, click the **Label (Form Control)** button. Point to the **Report Footer** section until the plus sign (+) of the pointer aligns with the bottom edge of the **Report Footer** section bar and with the left edge of the **Report Footer** section. Drag downward to the bottom of the **Report Footer** section and to the right to the **3-inch mark on the horizontal ruler**. Using your own first name and last name, type **Submitted by Firstname Lastname** and then compare your screen with Figure 6.30.

Figure 6.30

Label button

Text box control for page number

Label control

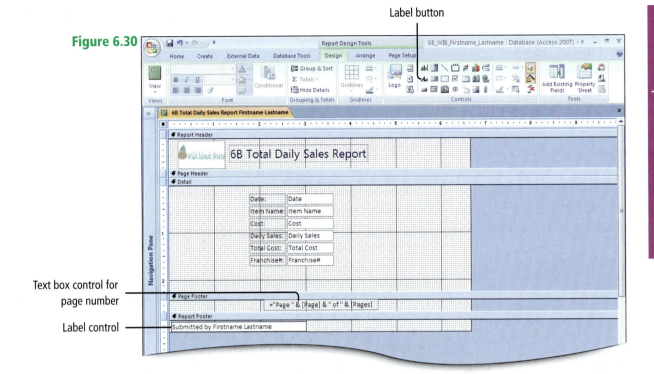

5 Press Enter, and then **Save** the report. On the **Design tab**, in the **Controls group**, click the **Date & Time** button. In the **Date and Time** dialog box, under **Include Date**, click the third option button—displays the date as mm/dd/yyyy. Clear the **Include Time** check box, and then click **OK**.

A text box control with an expression for the current date displays in the Report Header section.

6 Click the **Date text box control**, and then point to the selected text box control until the pointer displays. Drag the text box control downward into the **Report Footer** section until the right edge of the text box control aligns with the **6-inch mark on the horizontal ruler**.

7 **Save** the report, and then switch to **Layout** view. Notice that, for the first record, the data for the **Item Name** field is truncated. In the first record, click the **Item Name text box control**, which displays truncated *Berry Smoothie*. Point to the right edge of the **Item Name text box control** until the pointer displays. Drag to the right approximately **1 inch**. Because no ruler displays in Layout view, you will have to estimate the distance to drag.

Because the controls are in a stacked layout, the widths of all of the text box controls are increased.

8 Scroll down, observing the data in the **Item Name** field. Ensure that all of the data displays. If the data is truncated in a record, use the technique you just practiced to increase the width of the text box control until all of the data displays.

9 Switch to **Design** view. Point to the right edge of the design grid until the ⊕ pointer displays. If necessary, drag to the left until the right edge of the design grid aligns with the **6-inch mark on the horizontal ruler**. **Save** 🖫 the report.

The width of the report page is decreased, which will enable the report to fit with the margins of paper in portrait orientation.

More Knowledge
Adding a Hyperlink to a Report

Add a hyperlink to a report in Design view by clicking the Insert Hyperlink button in the Controls group and then specifying the target. To test the hyperlink, in Design view, right-click the hyperlink, click Hyperlink, and then click Open Hyperlink. The hyperlink is active—jumps to the target—in Design view, Report view, and Layout view. The hyperlink is not active in Print Preview view. If the report is exported to another Office application, the hyperlink is active when it is opened in that application. An application that can *export* data can create a file in a format that another application under-stands, enabling the two programs to share the same data.

Activity 6.14 Adding an Image Control and a Line Control to a Report

1 In the **Report Header** section, right-click the **logo control**. From the displayed shortcut menu, click **Copy**. Right-click anywhere in the **Report Header** section, and then from the shortcut menu, click **Paste**.

A copy of the image displays on top and slightly to the left of the original logo control.

2 Point to the selected logo until the ⟨↖⟩ pointer displays. Drag to the right until the left edge of the outlined control aligns with the **4.5-inch mark on the horizontal ruler**. If necessary, hold down Ctrl, and then press → or ← until there are **three dots** between the right edge of the title's label control and the left edge of the image control.

Recall that when you created a form in Design view, you clicked the Image button and selected the location in the header section. You then had to change the properties of the image to match the size of the image in the logo control. Because you copied the original image from the logo, the images are the same size.

3 With the image control on the right selected, hold down ⟨⇧ Shift⟩, and then click the **logo control**. On the Ribbon, click the **Arrange tab**. In the **Control Alignment group**, click the **Bottom** button, and then compare your screen with Figure 6.31.

Both the logo control and the image control are aligned along the bottom edges.

Figure 6.31

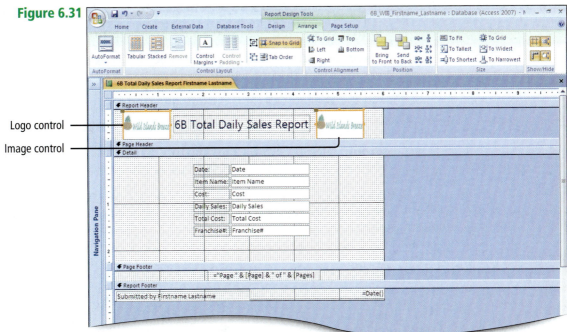

Logo control

Image control

4 On the Ribbon, click the **Design tab**. In the **Controls group**, click the **Line** button ☒. Point to the **Detail** section until the middle of the plus sign (**+**) of the ☒ pointer aligns with the **2-inch mark on the vertical ruler** and the **0-inch mark on the horizontal ruler** as shown in Figure 6.32.

A *line control* enables an individual to insert a line in a form or report.

Line button

Figure 6.32

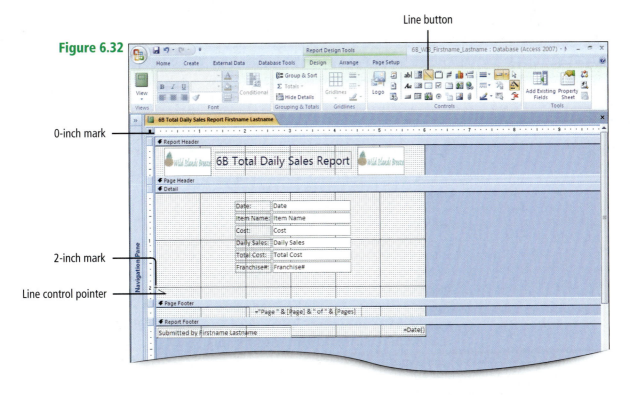

0-inch mark

2-inch mark

Line control pointer

5 Hold down Shift, drag to the right to the **6-inch mark on the horizontal ruler**, and then release the mouse button.

An orange line control displays. Holding down the Shift key ensures that the line will be straight.

6 On the **Design tab**, in the **Controls group**, click the **Line Thickness** button ≡▾, and then click the third line—**2 pt**. In the **Controls group**, click the **Line Color button arrow** ▾. Under **Standard Colors**, on the sixth row, click the ninth color—**Aqua Blue 5**.

7 **Save** 🖫 the report, and then switch to **Report** view. Compare your screen with Figure 6.33. Notice the horizontal line that displays between the records.

Figure 6.33

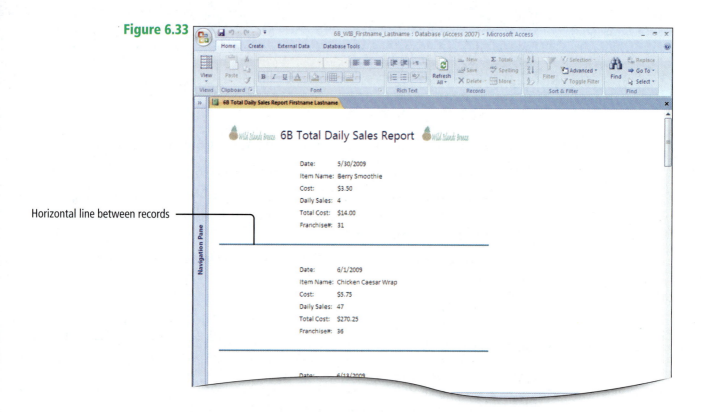

Horizontal line between records

8 Switch to **Design** view.

Objective 7
Group, Sort, and Total Records in Design View

Although it is much easier to create a report that is grouped and sorted using the Report Wizard, the same tasks can be completed in Design view. If a report has been created that was not grouped, you can modify the report in Design view to include grouping and summary data. Calculated controls are often added to reports to display summary information in reports with grouped records.

Activity 6.15 Adding a Grouping and Sort Level to a Report

In this activity, you will add a grouping and sort order to the report, and then move a control from the Detail section to the Header section.

1 On the **Design tab**, in the **Grouping & Totals group**, click the **Group & Sort** button, and then compare your screen with Figure 6.34.

The Group, Sort, and Total Pane displays at the bottom of the screen. Because no grouping or sorting has been applied to the report, two buttons relating to these functions display in the Group, Sort, and Total Pane.

Figure 6.34

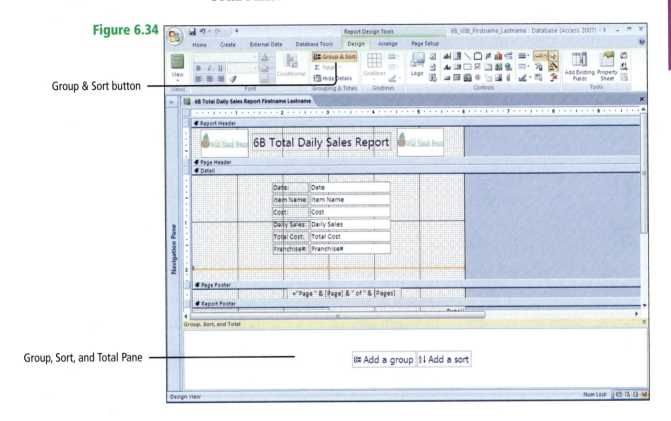

Group & Sort button

Group, Sort, and Total Pane

2 In the **Group, Sort, and Total Pane**, click the **Add a group** button. A list of fields that are used in the report displays as shown in Figure 6.35.

Figure 6.35

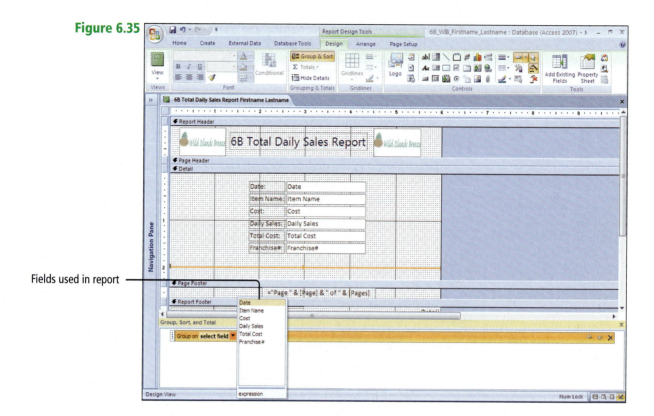

Fields used in report

3 From the displayed list, click **Item Name**.

An empty Item Name Header section is inserted above the Detail Section. The report will be grouped by the Item Name, and the Item Names will be sorted in ascending order.

4 In the **Detail** section, click the **Item Name text box control**. Point to the selected text box control until the [pointer] pointer displays. Drag downward until a thin orange line displays at the bottom of the **Franchise#** controls.

The text box control for this field will be moved to the Item Name Header section in the report. Recall that moving the controls to the bottom of the stacked layout makes it easier to remove the controls from the stacked layout.

5 On the Ribbon, click the **Arrange tab**. In the **Control Layout group**, click the **Remove** button.

The label control and the text box control for the Item Name field are removed from the stacked layout.

6 Point to the selected **Item Name text box control** until the [pointer] pointer displays. Drag the selected control upward into the **Item Name Header** section until the left edge of the dotted control aligns with the **1-inch mark on the horizontal ruler**.

The controls for the Item Name are moved from the Detail section to the Item Name Header section. Because the report is being grouped by this field, the controls should be moved out of the Detail section.

7 In the **Item Name Header** section, click the **Item Name label control**, and then press Delete. Compare your screen with Figure 6.36.

Because the records are grouped by the data in the Item Name field, the name of the field is unnecessary.

Figure 6.36

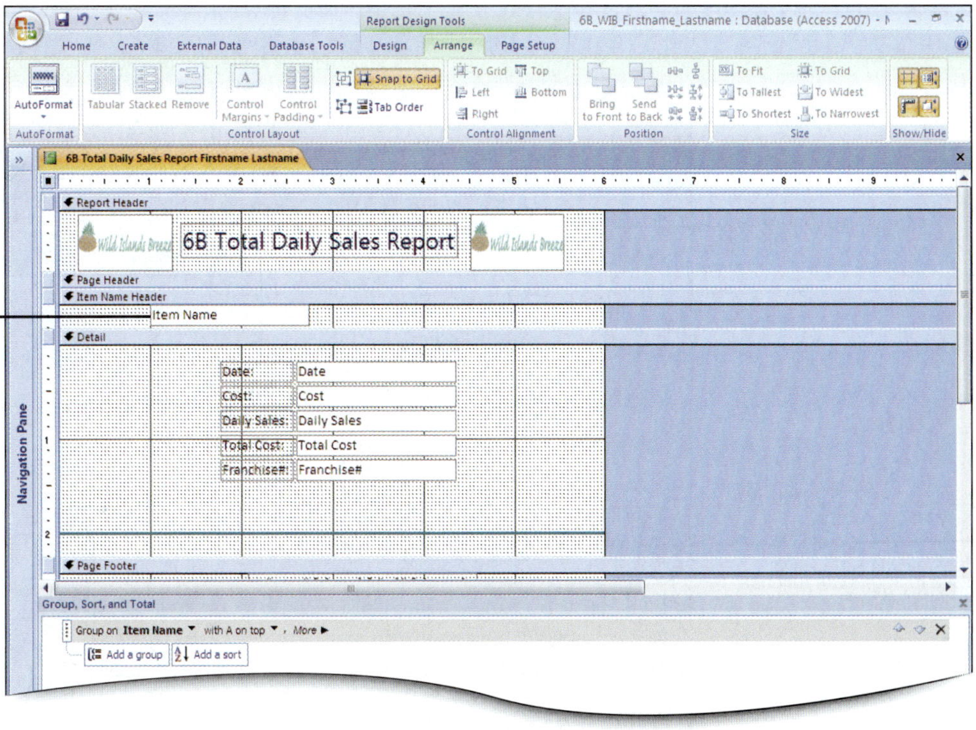

Item Name text box control moved from Detail section

8 **Save** the report, and then switch to **Report** view. Scroll down, noticing the grouping of records, until the grouping for **Grilled Chicken Skewer** displays. Notice that there are two records, one for Franchise# 102 and another for Franchise# 12. For these two records, notice the dates.

9 Switch back to **Design** view. In the **Group, Sort, and Total Pane**, click the **Add a sort** button, and then click **Date**. Notice that the Date will be sorted from oldest to newest.

10 **Save** the report, and then switch to **Report** view. Scroll down until the **Grilled Chicken Skewer** grouping displays. Within the grouping, the two records are arranged in order by the date with the oldest date listed first.

11 Switch to **Design** view, and then **Close** ⊠ the **Group, Sort, and Total Pane**. Be sure to click the Close button and not the Delete button.

Activity 6.16 Adding Calculated Controls to a Report

1 In the **Detail** section, click the **Total Cost text box control**. On the **Design tab**, in the **Grouping & Totals group**, click the **Totals** button, and then compare your screen with Figure 6.37.

A list of *aggregate functions*—functions that group and perform calculations on multiple fields—displays. Before selecting the Totals button, the field that will be used in the aggregate function must be selected. If you wish to perform aggregate functions on multiple fields, you must select each field individually, and then select the aggregate function to apply to the field.

List of aggregate functions

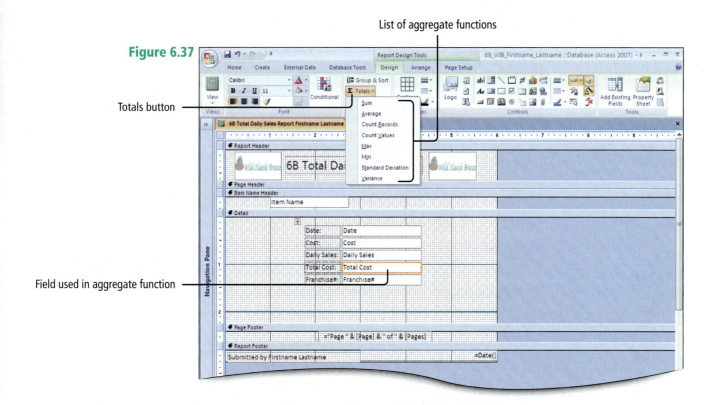

Figure 6.37

Totals button

Field used in aggregate function

2 In the displayed list of aggregate functions, click **Sum**, and then compare your screen with Figure 6.38.

The Item Name Footer section is added to the Report. A calculated control is added to the section that contains the expression that will display the sum of the Total Cost field for each grouping. Recall that an expression begins with an equal sign (=). The Sum function adds or totals numeric data. The items that are t*Sum*. Field names are included in square brackets.

Figure 6.38

Calculated control

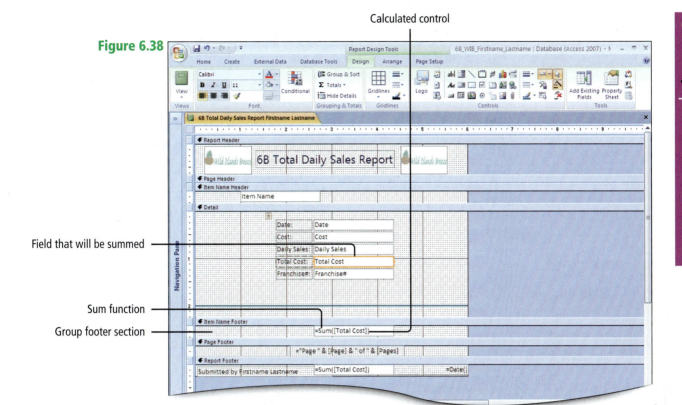

Field that will be summed

Sum function

Group footer section

3 **Save** 🖫 the report, and then switch to **Report** view. Notice that for the first grouping—Banana Smoothie—which only contains one record, the sum of the grouping displays below the horizontal line. Scroll down to the **Grilled Chicken Skewer** grouping, and then notice that the total for the grouping—**$644.40**—displays below the horizontal line for the second record in the grouping.

The placement of the horizontal line is distracting in the report, and there is no label attached to the grouping total.

4 Switch to **Design** view. On the **Design tab**, in the **Controls group**, click the **Text Box** button. Point to the **Item Name Footer** section until the plus sign (**+**) of the 🔲 pointer aligns with the bottom edge of the **Item Name Footer** section bar and with the **0.5-inch mark on the horizontal ruler**. Drag downward to the bottom of the **Item Name Footer** section and to the right to the **2.5-inch mark on the horizontal ruler**.

5 Type **=[Item Name] & " Total Cost:"** ensuring that you include a space between the quotation mark and *Total* and that *Item Name* is enclosed in square brackets. Compare your screen with Figure 6.39.

Because a field name is included in the description of the total, a text box control must be used. This binds the control to the Item Name field in the underlying query, which makes this control a bound control. If you wish to insert only string characters as a description—for example, Total Cost—add a label control, which is an unbound control.

Figure 6.39

Text box button

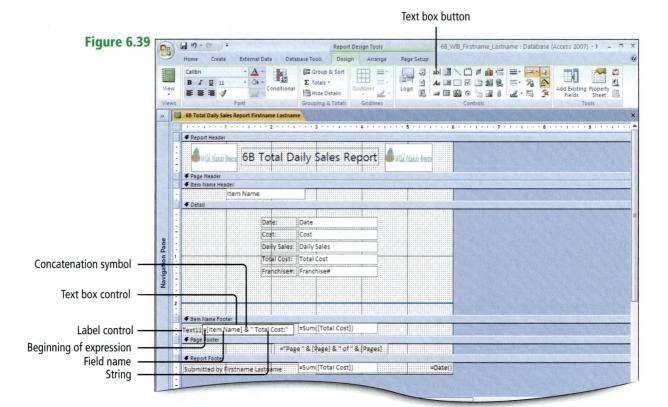

Concatenation symbol

Text box control

Label control
Beginning of expression
Field name
String

6. In the **Item Name Footer** section, click the **label control** that displays to the left of the text box control where you typed the expression. Press Delete to delete the text box control's associated label control.

The data in the text box control is descriptive and does not require an additional label control.

7. In the **Item Name Footer** section, click the **text box control** that contains the expression you typed. Point to the left middle sizing handle until the ↔ pointer displays. Drag to the left until the left edge of the text box control aligns with the left edge of the design grid. With the text box control selected, hold down ⇧Shift. In the **Item Name Footer** section, click the **calculated control** for the sum. On the Ribbon, click the **Arrange tab**. In the **Control Alignment group**, click the **Bottom** button to align both controls at the bottom.

8. Point to the top of the **Page Footer** section bar until the ⊕ pointer displays. Drag downward to the top of the **Report Footer** section bar to increase the height of the Item Name Footer section.

9. In the **Detail** section, click the **line control**. Point to the line control until the ⬚ pointer displays. Drag downward into the **Item Name Footer** section under the controls until there are approximately **three dots** between the text box controls and the line control.

The line control is moved from the Detail section to the Item Name Footer section.

10 Point to the top of the **Item Name Footer** section bar until the ⊕ pointer displays. Drag upward until approximately **three dots** display between the **Franchise#** controls and the top edge of the **Item Name Footer** section bar. Compare your screen with Figure 6.40.

The height of the Detail section is decreased.

Figure 6.40

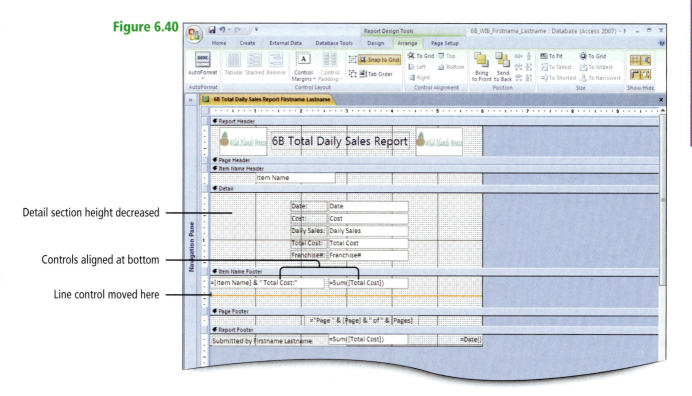

Detail section height decreased

Controls aligned at bottom

Line control moved here

11 **Save** 🔳 the report, and then switch to **Report** view. Scroll down until the **Grilled Chicken Skewer** grouping displays, and then compare your screen with Figure 6.41.

The report is easier to read with the horizontal line moved to the grouping footer section and with an explanation of the total for the grouping.

Figure 6.41

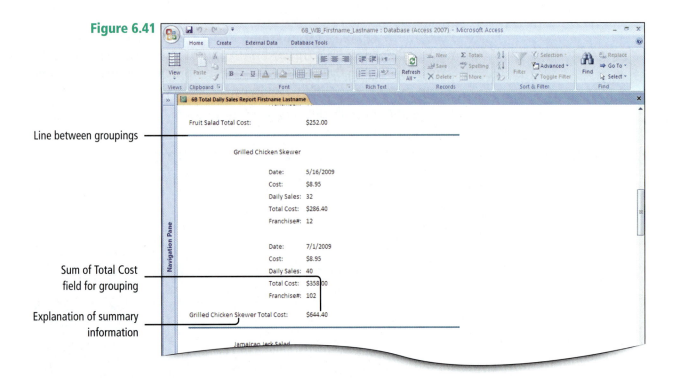

Line between groupings ———

Sum of Total Cost field for grouping ———

Explanation of summary information ———

12 Hold down Ctrl, and then press End to move to the end of the report. Notice the sum of **$2,384.40**. Switch to **Design** view. In the **Report Footer** section, notice the calculated control—displays **=Sum([Total Cost])**.

By default, when you insert an aggregate function into a report, a calculated control for the grand total is inserted in the Report Footer section. The control is aligned with the text box control that is being used in the aggregate function. If the Report Footer section is not tall enough and multiple aggregate functions are used, the controls will display on top of one another.

13 Point to the bottom of the **Report Footer** section—not the section bar—until the ⬍ pointer displays. Drag downward approximately **1 inch**.

14 Click the label control that displays **Submitted by Firstname Lastname**. Hold down ⇧ Shift, and then click the text box control that displays the **Date** expression. On the Ribbon, click the **Arrange tab**. In the **Control Alignment group**, click the **Bottom** button. In the **Size group**, click the **To Tallest** button.

The two controls are aligned at the bottom edges of the controls and are the same height.

15 Point to either of the selected controls until the ⬚ pointer displays. Drag downward until the bottom edges of the controls align with the bottom edge of the Report Footer section, and then compare your screen with Figure 6.42.

The controls are moved to the bottom of the Report Footer section to increase readability and to make space to insert a label control for the grand total.

Figure 6.42

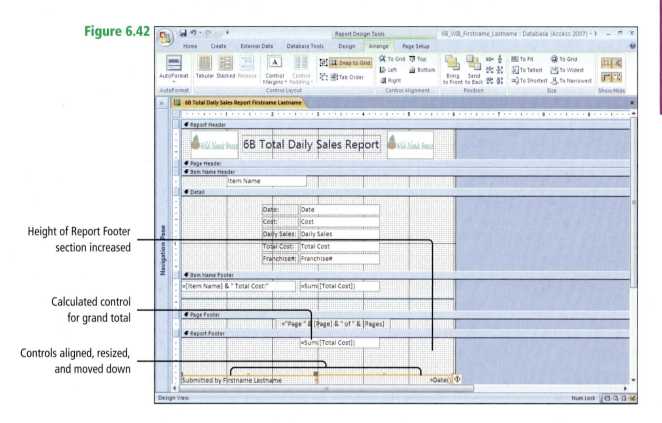

Height of Report Footer section increased

Calculated control for grand total

Controls aligned, resized, and moved down

16 On the Ribbon, click the **Design tab**. Use the techniques you have practiced to add a **label control** in the Report Footer section to the left of the calculated control—the left edge of the control should be aligned with the **0-inch mark on the horizontal ruler**. In the label control, type **Grand Total for Cost of All Items:** Align the label control with the calculated control and be sure that the controls are the same height. Compare your screen with Figure 6.43.

Figure 6.43

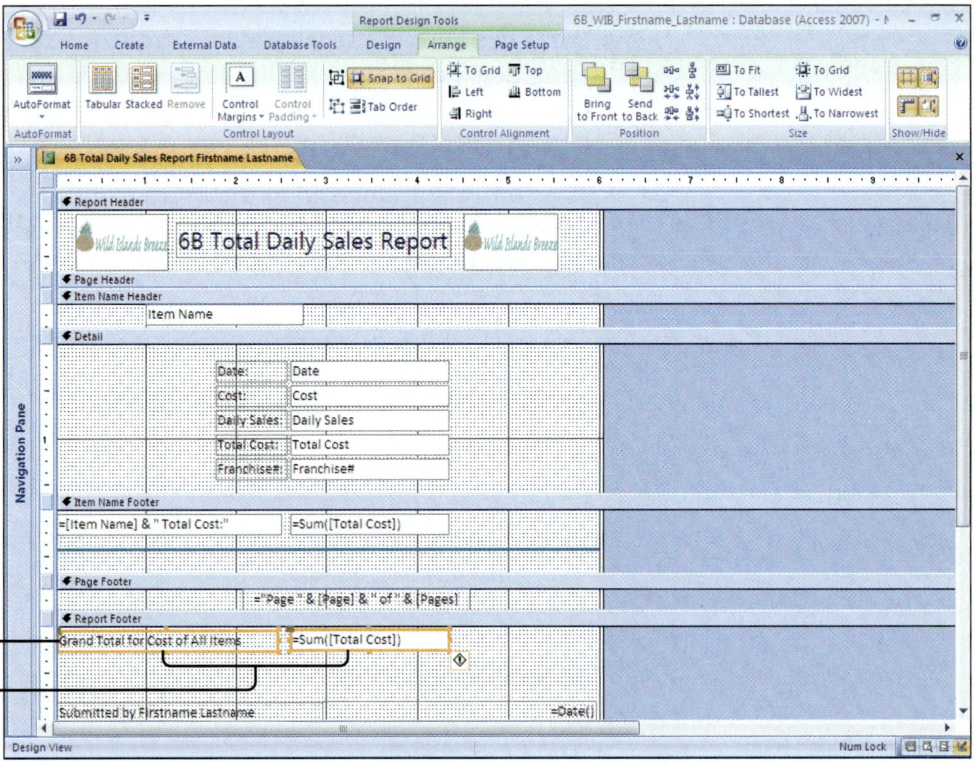

Label control ——————

Controls aligned and same size ——————

Alert! ——— **Does your control display with two boxes?**

If your control displays with two boxes—one that displays text and a number; for example Test35, and one that displays Unbound—you selected the Text Box button instead of the Label (Form Control) button. If that happens, click the Undo button, and then begin again.

---

17 **Save** [💾] the report, and then switch to **Report** view. Hold down Ctrl, and then press End to move to the end of the report. Notice that the grand total is now easier to distinguish because a description of the control has been added and the other controls are moved down.

18 Switch to **Print Preview** view. If necessary, on the **Print Preview tab**, in the **Zoom group**, click the **Two Pages** button. Look at the bottom of Page 1 and the top of Page 2, and notice that the grouping breaks across two pages. In the navigation area, click the **Next Page** button [▶] to display Pages 3 and 4. Groupings are split between these pages.

For a more professional-looking report, avoid splitting groupings between pages.

19 In the **Close Preview group**, click the **Close Print Preview** button. Switch to **Design** view. On the **Design tab**, in the **Grouping & Totals group**, click the **Group & Sort** button.

20 In the displayed **Group, Sort, and Total Pane**, on the **Group on Item Name** bar, click **More**. Click the **do not keep group together on one page arrow**, and then click **keep whole group together on one page**. Close ☒ the **Group, Sort, and Total Pane**—do not click the Delete button.

21 **Save** 🖫 the report, and then switch to **Print Preview** view. In the navigation area, click the buttons to display pages in the report, and then notice that groupings are no longer split between pages. Also notice that more blank space displays at the bottom of some pages.

22 If you are instructed to submit this result, create a paper or electronic printout. On the **Print Preview tab**, in the **Close Preview group**, click the **Close Print Preview** button. **Close** ☒ the report, and then expand ⟩⟩ the **Navigation Pane**.

More Knowledge

Formatting a Report

You can add a background picture to a report or change the background color of a report using the same techniques you used in forms.

Objective 8
Create a Crosstab Report

Recall that a **crosstab query** uses an aggregate function for data that is grouped by two types of information and displays the data in a compact, spreadsheet-like format. A **crosstab report** uses a crosstab query as the record source and displays calculated data grouped by two different types of information.

Activity 6.17 Creating a Crosstab Report

In this activity, you will create a crosstab report for Wild Islands Breeze that displays the data from the 6A Total Daily Sales Crosstab Query that has already been created.

1 On the **Navigation Pane**, under **Queries**, double-click **6B Total Daily Sales Crosstab Query**. Take a moment to study the data in the query as shown in Figure 6.44.

The data is grouped by Item Name and Month. The sum function calculates the total daily sales for each item per month.

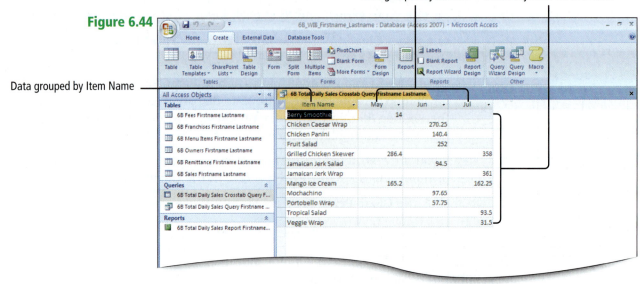

Figure 6.44

Data grouped by Item Name

Data grouped by Months

Aggregate function sums total daily sales for each item

2 **Close** [×] the query, and then collapse [«] the **Navigation Pane**.

3 On the Ribbon, click the **Create tab**. In the **Reports group**, click the **Report Wizard** button.

4 Because the crosstab query was selected on the Navigation Pane, in the **Report Wizard** dialog box, in the **Tables/Queries** box, **Query: 6B Total Daily Sales Crosstab Query** displays. If it does not display, click the Tables/Queries arrow, and then click Query: 6B Total Daily Sales Crosstab Query.

5 Under **Available Fields**, notice there are more months than those that were displayed in 6B Total Daily Sales Crosstab Query.

Because there was data for the months of May, June, and July only, the other months were hidden from the display in the query. Recall that to hide a column in Datasheet view, right-click the column header, and then from the shortcut menu, click Hide Columns.

6 Under **Available Fields**, double-click each field name, in the order specified, to add the field names to the Selected Fields box: **Item Name**, **May**, **Jun**, and **Jul**.

7 In the **Report Wizard** dialog box, click **Next**. Because no grouping levels will be used, click **Next**.

8 To sort the records within the report by Item Name, click the **arrow** next to the **1** box. From the displayed list, click **Item Name**. Leave the sort order as **Ascending**, and then click **Next**.

9 Under **Layout**, be sure the **Tabular** option button is selected. Under **Orientation**, be sure the **Portrait** option button is selected, and then click **Next**.

10 In the style box, select **Office**, and then click **Next**. For the title of the report, type **6B Daily Sales by Month Report Firstname Lastname** and then click **Finish**. Compare your screen with Figure 6.45.

The report displays in Print Preview. Because the column headings are hard to see and some of the data in the Item Name column is truncated, the report needs some modifications.

Figure 6.45

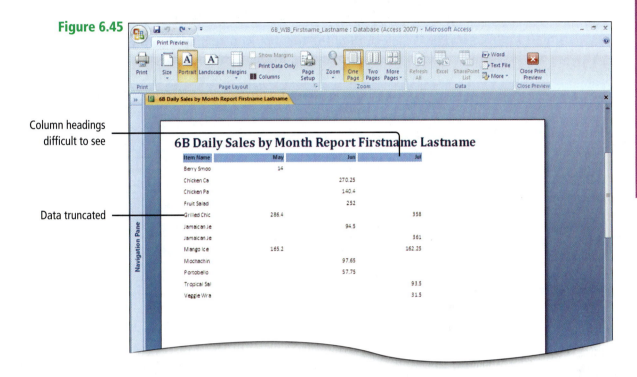

Column headings difficult to see

Data truncated

Activity 6.18 Modifying a Crosstab Report

In this activity, you will modify controls in the Crosstab Report to make the report easier to read.

1 On the **Print Preview tab**, in the **Close Preview group**, click the

Close Print Preview button. If the Field List displays, Close ☒ it. In the **Page Heade**r section, notice that a background color has been added to each of the label controls.

2 Click anywhere in an empty area of the report to deselect the Item Name column. To select all of the controls in the **Page Header** section, hold down ⇧Shift, and then click each label control. On the **Design tab**, in the **Font group**, click the **Font Color button arrow**. Under **Standard Colors**, on the first row, click the first color—**White**.

3 Save ☐ the report, and then switch to **Layout** view.

Alert!

Did the data in the Item Name column disappear?

If there is no data in the Item name column, you probably did not deselect the Item Name controls before selecting the label controls in the Page Header section. To correct this, switch to Design view. In the Detail section, click the Item Name text box control. On the Design tab, in the Font group, click the Font Color button arrow. Under Standard Colors, on the first row, click the second color—Black.

4 In the **Item Name** column, select any **text box control**. Point to the right edge of the control until the ⟷ pointer displays. Drag to the right approximately **1.5 inches**. If some data in the column is still truncated, repeat the procedure until all of the data displays.

5 To select all of the text box controls, in the **May** column, click **14**. Holding down ⇧Shift, in the **Jun** column, click a **text box control**. Still holding down ⇧Shift, in the **Jul** column, click a **text box control**; and then compare your screen with Figure 6.46.

Figure 6.46

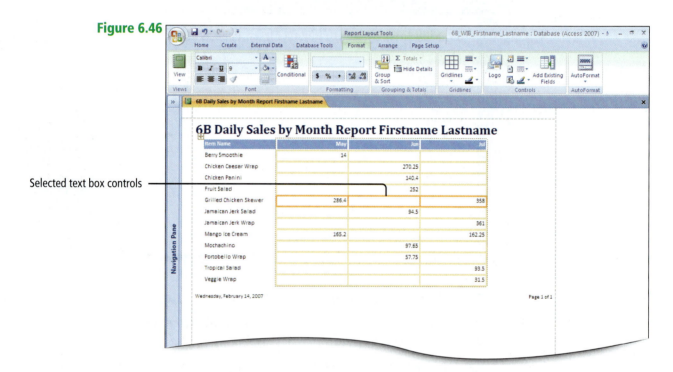

Selected text box controls

6 On the Ribbon, click the **Arrange tab**. In the **Tools group**, click the **Property Sheet** button. Notice that the selection type is *Multiple selection*.

7 On the **Property Sheet**, click the **Format tab**. Click the **Format property setting arrow**. From the displayed list, click **Currency**, and then **Close** ✕ the **Property Sheet**.

8 **Save** 🖫 the report, and then switch to **Print Preview** view. If you are instructed to submit this result, create a paper or electronic printout. On the **Print Preview tab**, in the **Close Preview group**, click the **Close Print Preview** button.

9 **Close** ✕ the report, and then expand » the **Navigation Pane**. **Close** the database, and then **Exit** Access.

End **You have completed Project 6B** ——————————

There's More You Can Do!

From My Computer, navigate to the student files that accompany this textbook. In the folder **02_theres_more_you_can_do**, locate and open the folder for this chapter. Open and print the instructions for this project, which are provided to you in Adobe PDF format.

Try It! 1—Hide Duplicate Items in a Report

In this Try It! project, you will sort a report and then hide duplicate values that display in two fields.

Try It! 2—Add a Background Graphic to a Report

In this Try It! project, you will add a background picture to a report.

Access

chapter six

Summary

Forms are database objects that are used to interact with the data in tables. In the first project, you created a form in Design view, added sections to the form, and modified the sections. You changed a combo box control to a list box control, and moved controls around on the form. In addition to label controls, you inserted an image control and command button controls. You formatted forms by adding a background color, adding a background picture, and modifying control borders. Finally, you made a form more user friendly, by adding a message to the status bar for fields, creating custom ControlTips, and changing the tab order.

Reports are database objects that are used to present data from tables or queries in a professional-looking format. Reports are usually created using queries as the record source. In the second project, you created a report in Design view and modified the sections of the report. You added text box controls to the report that contained expressions. You concatenated strings and field names to build expressions. You also added an image control and a line control to a report. In Design view, you added grouping and sorting levels to the report. You then added calculated controls that used aggregate functions. Finally, you created a report based on a crosstab query and a report based on a parameter query, adding the parameter criteria as a subtitle in the report.

Key Terms

Content-Based Assessments

Matching

Match each term in the second column with its correct definition in the first column. Write the letter of the term on the blank line in front of the correct definition.

_____ **1.** Characteristics that determine the appearance, structure, and behavior of an object.

_____ **2.** Displays the properties that affect the appearance and behavior of the object.

_____ **3.** The property setting can be a table name, a query name, or an SQL statement.

_____ **4.** Enables an individual to insert an image into any section of a form or report.

_____ **5.** Enables an individual to add a command button to a form or report that will perform an action when the button is clicked.

_____ **6.** The box where the rulers meet, in the upper left corner of a form in Design view.

_____ **7.** The measurement equal to 1/72 of an inch.

_____ **8.** Text that displays when an individual pauses the mouse pointer over a control on a form.

_____ **9.** Refers to the order in which the fields are selected when the [Tab] key is pressed.

_____ **10.** To spread, disseminate, or apply.

_____ **11.** A button that enables an individual to update the Property Sheet for a field in all objects that use this table as the record source.

_____ **12.** Refers to the object that is selected and currently being acted upon.

_____ **13.** A series of characters.

_____ **14.** To enable two programs to share the same data.

_____ **15.** A control that enables an individual to insert a line in a form or a report.

A Button control

B ControlTip

C Export

D Focus

E Form selector

F Image control

G Line control

H Point

I Propagate

J Properties

K Property Sheet

L Property Update Options button

M Record Source property

N String

O Tab order

Content-Based Assessments

Fill in the Blank

Write the correct word in the space provided.

1. Every object on a form, including the form itself, has an associated _____ _____ that can be used to further enhance the object.

2. The property that enables you to specify the source of the data for a form or a report is the _____ _____ property.

3. An object, such as a label or text box, in a form or report that enables an individual to view or manipulate information stored in tables or queries is called a(n) _____.

4. A box that enables an individual to select from a list or to type in a value is a(n) _____ _____.

5. A box that enables an individual to select from a list but does not enable the individual to type anything not in the list is a(n) _____ _____.

6. The process of creating a 1-inch square of a picture that is repeated across and down the form is called _____.

7. The property that determines where the background picture for a form displays on the form is the _____ _____ property.

8. The property that determines the size of the picture in the form is the _____ _____ _____ property.

9. In the Picture Size Mode property, the setting that stretches the image both vertically and horizontally to match the size of the form is the _____ setting.

10. To convert a point size setting to inches, divide the point size by _____.

11. The property that enables an individual to add descriptive text that will display in the status bar for a selected control is the _____ _____ _____ property.

12. The & symbol _____ strings.

13. Functions that group and perform calculations on multiple fields are _____ functions.

14. A query that uses an aggregate function for data that is grouped by two types of information and displays the data in a compact, spreadsheet-like format is a(n) _____ query.

15. A report that uses a crosstab query as the record source and displays calculated data grouped by two different types of information is a(n) _____ report.

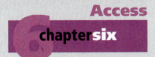

Skills Review

Project 6C—Party Orders

In this project, you will apply the skills you practiced from the Objectives in Project 6A.

Objectives: 1. *Create a Form in Design View;* **2.** *Change and Add Controls;* **3.** *Format a Form;* **4.** *Make a Form User Friendly.*

Martin Famosa, Vice President of Marketing for the Wild Islands Breeze franchise restaurant chain, wants to expand the chain's offering to include party trays for advance order and delivery. In the following project, you will create a form to use for the data entry of these party order items. Your completed form will look similar to the one in Figure 6.47.

> ### For Project 6C, you will need the following files:
>
> a06C_Party_Orders
> a06C_Logo
> a06C_Pineapple

You will save your database as
6C_Party_Orders_Firstname_Lastname

Figure 6.47

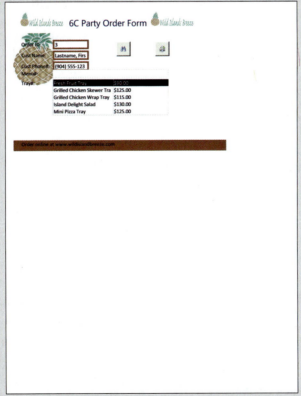

(Project 6C–Party Orders continues on the next page)

(Project 6C–Party Orders continued)

1. **Start** Access. Locate and open the **a06C_ Party_Orders** file. Save the database in the **Access 2007 Database** format in your **Access Chapter 6** folder as **6C_Party_ Orders_Firstname_Lastname**

2. Double-click **6C Orders** to open the table in **Datasheet** view. Take a moment to examine the fields in the table. In any record, click in the **Tray#** field, and then click the **arrow**. This field is a Lookup field in the *6C Trays* table. In any record, click in the **Menu#** field, and then click the **arrow**. This field is a Lookup field in the *6C Menu Items* table. **Close** the table, and then collapse the **Navigation Pane**.

3. On the Ribbon, click the **Create tab**. In the **Forms group**, click the **Form Design** button. On the **Design tab**, in the **Tools group**, click the **Property Sheet** button. On the **Property Sheet**, click the **Data tab**. Click the **Record Source property setting box arrow**, and then click **6C Orders**. **Close** the **Property Sheet**.

4. On the **Design tab**, in the **Tools group**, click the **Add Existing Fields** button. In the **Field List**, click **Order ID**, hold down ⇧ Shift, and then click **Menu#**. Drag the selected fields onto the design grid until the top of the ⬚ pointer arrow is aligned with the **0.25-inch mark on the vertical ruler** and aligned with the **2-inch mark on the horizontal ruler,** and then release the mouse button. **Close** the **Field List**.

5. On the Ribbon, click the **Arrange tab**. With all of the controls still selected, in the **Control Layout group**, click the **Stacked** button. Drag the left edge of the selected text box controls to the **0.5-inch mark on the horizontal ruler**. **Save** the form as 6C Order Form Firstname Lastname

6. On the **Arrange tab**, in the **Show/Hide group**, click the **Form Header/Footer**

button. Click the **Design tab**. In the **Controls group**, click the **Logo** button. Navigate to the location where the student data files for this textbook are saved. Locate and double-click **a06C_Logo** to insert the logo in the Form Header section. On the selected logo, point to the right middle sizing handle until the ↔ pointer displays. Drag to the right until the right edge of the logo is aligned with the **1.5-inch mark on the horizontal ruler**.

7. In the **Controls group**, click the **Title** button. In the label control for the title, select and replace the text with **6C Party Order Form** and then press Enter. Drag the label control downward until the label control is approximately centered between the top and bottom edges of the logo control. Drag the left edge of the title to align it with the **1.5- inch mark on the horizontal ruler**. Drag the right edge of the title to align it with the **4- inch mark on the horizontal ruler**. With the title selected, on the **Design tab**, in the **Font group**, click the **Center** button.

8. Scroll down until the **Form Footer** section bar displays. Point to the top of the **Form Footer** section bar until the ⊕ pointer displays. Drag upward until the top of the Form Footer section bar aligns with the **3- inch mark on the vertical ruler**. In the **Controls group**, click the **Label** button. Point to the **Form Footer** section until the plus sign (+) of the ⁺A pointer aligns with the bottom of the **Form Footer** section bar and the **0.25-inch mark on the horizontal ruler**. Drag downward to the bottom of the **Form Footer** section and to the right to the **3.25-inch mark on the horizontal ruler**. Type **Order online at www.wildislandbreeze. com** and then press Enter.

(Project 6C–Party Orders continues on the next page)

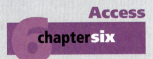

Access

chapter six

Skills Review

(Project 6C–Party Orders continued)

9. With the label control in the Form Footer section selected, hold down ⇧Shift, and then click the **Logo control** and the **Menu# label** control. On the Ribbon, click the **Arrange tab**. In the **Control Alignment group**, click the **Align Left** button, and then **save** the form.

10. Click and hold the **Tray# label control** until the 🕏 pointer displays. Drag downward until a thin orange line displays on the bottom edges of the **Menu#** controls. With the **Tray# label control** selected, hold down ⇧Shift, and then click the **Menu# label control**.

11. On the **Arrange tab**, in the **Control Layout group**, click the **Remove** button to remove the *Menu#* field and the *Tray#* field from the stacked layout. Right-click the **Tray# combo box control**. From the shortcut menu, point to **Change To**, and then click **List Box**.

12. **Save** the form, and then switch to **Form** view. Notice that the **Tray# list box control** is not wide enough to display all columns and that there are horizontal and vertical scroll bars to indicate there is more data. Click the **Menu# combo box arrow**, and then notice that some of the menu item names and prices are truncated. Press Esc.

13. Switch to **Design** view. Click the **Menu# combo box**. Point to the right edge of the control until the ↔ pointer displays. Drag to the right until the right edge of the control aligns with the **4.5-inch mark on the horizontal ruler**. Switch to **Form** view, click the **Menu# arrow**, and then be sure that all of the menu items display.

14. Switch to **Layout** view. Click the **Tray# list box control**. Point to the right edge of

the control until the ↔ pointer displays. Drag to the right until the right edge aligns with the right edge of the Menu# text box control. **Save** the form, and then switch to **Design** view.

15. On the **Design tab**, in the **Controls group**, click the **Image** button. Move the mouse pointer into the **Form Header** section.

Align the plus sign (+) of the 🖼 pointer with the bottom of the **Form Header** section bar and with the **4-inch mark on the horizontal ruler**.

16. Drag downward to the top of the **Detail** section bar and to the right to the **5.25-inch mark on the horizontal ruler**. In the displayed **Insert Picture** dialog box, navigate to the location where the student data files for this textbook are saved. Locate and double-click **a06C_Logo** to insert the picture in the Form Header section.

17. Click the **image control**—the Wild Islands Breeze image on the right side in the Form Header section. On the **Design tab**, in the **Tools group**, click the **Property Sheet** button. If necessary, on the **Format tab**, change the **Width** property setting to **1.25** and then change the **Height** property setting to **.625** In the **Form Header** section, click the **logo control**, and then notice that the Property Sheet for the logo control displays. On the **Property Sheet**, change the **Width** property setting to **1.25** and then change the **Height** property setting to **.625**

18. On the Ribbon, click the **Arrange tab**. With the logo control selected, hold down ⇧Shift, and then click the **image control**. In the **Control Alignment group**, click the **Top** button.

19. **Close** the **Property Sheet**. On the Ribbon, click the **Design tab**, and then in the

(Project 6C–Party Orders continues on the next page)

Skills Review

(Project 6C–Party Orders continued)

Controls group, click the **Button** button. Move the mouse pointer down into the **Detail** section. Align the plus sign (**+**) of the pointer with the **0.25-inch mark on the vertical ruler** and the **3-inch mark on the horizontal ruler**, and then click.

20. Under **Categories**, click **Record Navigation**. Under **Actions**, click **Find Record**, and then click **Next** two times. In the text box, type **btnFindRecord** and then click **Finish**.

21. Using the techniques you have just practiced, add a **button control** to the right of the Tray# list box control. Under **Categories**, click **Form Operations**. Under **Actions**, click **Print Current Form**. Under **Picture**, click **Printer**, and then name the button **btnPrtForm** Click **Finish**.

22. With the **Print Current Form button control** selected, hold down ⇧Shift, and then click the **Find Record button control**. On the Ribbon, click the **Arrange tab**, and then in the **Control Alignment group**, click the **Top** button. In the **Position group**, click the **Decrease Horizontal Spacing** button until the right edge of the Print Current Form button control is aligned with the right edge of the Menu# text box control.

23. Switch to **Layout** view. Click in the **Form Footer** section. On the **Format tab**, in the **Font group**, click the **Fill/Back Color** button. Under **Standard Colors**, in the sixth row, click the tenth color—**Brown 5**.

24. Switch to **Design** view, and then locate the **Form selector**. Double-click the **Form selector** to open the Property Sheet for the form. On the **Property Sheet**, on the **Format tab**, click in the **Picture** property setting box, and then click the **Build** button. Navigate to the location where the

student data files for this textbook are saved. Locate and double-click **a06C_Pineapple** to insert the picture in the form. Click in the **Picture Alignment** property setting box, click the **arrow**, and then click **Form Center**.

25. **Close** the **Property Sheet**, and then **save** the form. Switch to **Layout** view, click the **Order ID text box control**, and then holding down ⇧Shift, click the **Cust Name text box control**, and the **Cust Phone# text box control**. On the **Format tab**, in the **Controls group**, click the **Line Type** button. Click the second line type—**Solid**. On the **Format tab**, in the **Controls group**, click the **Line Thickness** button. Click the fourth line type—**3 pt**. In the **Controls group**, click the **Line Color button arrow**. Under **Standard Colors**, in the sixth row, click the tenth color—**Brown 5**.

26. Switch to **Form** view, and then click in the **Cust Phone#** text box control. On the left side of the status bar, *Form View* displays—there is no text that helps an individual enter data. **Close** the form, **save** your changes, and expand the **Navigation Pane**.

27. Under **Tables**, right-click **6C Orders**, and then from the shortcut menu, click **Design View**. In the **Cust Phone#** field, click in the **Description** box. Type **Include area code for 10-digit dialing.** and then press Enter. Click the **Property Update Options** button, and then click **Update Status Bar Text everywhere Cust Phone# is used**. In the displayed **Update Properties** dialog box, under **Update the following objects?**, notice that only one object—*Form: 6C Order Form*—displays, and it is selected. In the **Update Properties** dialog box, click **Yes**. **Close** the table, saving changes.

28. On the **Navigation Pane**, under **Forms**, double-click **6C Order Form** to open it in

(Project 6C–Party Orders continues on the next page)

(Project 6C–Party Orders continued)

Form view. Collapse the **Navigation Pane**. Click in the **Cust Phone#** field, and then notice that on the left side of the status bar, *Include area code for 10-digit dialing* displays. Switch to **Design** view. Click the **Cust Phone# text box control**. On the **Design tab**, in the **Tools group**, click the **Property Sheet** button. On the **Property Sheet**, click the **Other tab**. Locate the **Status Bar Text** property, and then notice the setting of *Include area code for 10-digit dialing*.

29. With **6C Order Form** open in **Design** view and the **Property Sheet** displayed, click the **Print Form** button. Notice that the **Property Sheet** displays *Selection type: Command Button* and the **Selection type** box displays *btnPrtForm*, the name you gave to the button when you added it to the form. On the **Other tab**, click in the **ControlTip Text** property setting box, type **Prints the Current Form** and then press [Enter]. **Close** the **Property Sheet**, **save** the form, and then switch to **Form** view. Point to the **Print Form** button to display the ControlTip.

30. Switch to **Design** view. In the **Detail** section, click the **Order ID text box control**, hold down [⇧ Shift], and then click the **Find Record button control** and the **Print Current Form button control**. On the **Design tab**, in the **Tools group**, click the **Property Sheet** button. If necessary, on the **Property Sheet**, click the **Other tab**. On

the **Property Sheet**, click in the **Tab Stop** property setting box, click the **arrow**, and then click **No**. Click the **Cust Name text box control**. Click in the **Tab Index** property setting box, and then type **0 Close** the **Property Sheet**.

31. Switch to **Form** view. Click the **Find Record** button. In the **Find and Replace** dialog box, in the **Find What** box, type **Gonzalez, Ricardo** Click **Find Next**. **Close** the Find and Replace dialog box. In the **Cust Name** text box, type your **Lastname, Firstname** replacing Ricardo's name with yours. Press [Tab]. In the Cust Phone# field, enter your phone number, and then press [Enter]. **Save** the form.

32. If you are instructed to submit this result, create a paper or electronic printout. Click the **Print Current Form** button. In the **Print** dialog box, select the **Selected Record(s)** option button, and then click **OK**. From the **Database Tools tab**, in the **Analyze group**, click the **Database Documenter** button. In the **Documenter** window, under the **Forms tab**, select the **6C Order Form** check box, and then click **OK**. **Print** the **Object Definition**. If you are to submit your work electronically, follow your instructor's directions.

33. **Close** the form, expand the **Navigation Pane**, **Close** the database, and then **Exit** Access.

End **You have completed Project 6C**

Skills Review

Project 6D — Catering

In this project, you will apply the skills you practiced from the Objectives in Project 6B.

Objectives: 5. *Create a Report in Design View;* **6.** *Add Controls to a Report;* **7.** *Group, Sort, and Total Records in Design View;* **8.** *Create a Crosstab Report.*

The individual restaurants of Wild Islands Breeze each maintain a database about the orders that are placed for the catering entity of the business. Reports are run to summarize data in the tables or queries. Creating customized reports will help the managers of each location view the information in the database in a meaningful way. In this project, you will create customized reports. Your completed reports will look similar to those shown in Figure 6.48.

For Project 6D, you will need the following files:

a06D_Catering
a06D_Logo

You will save your database as
6D_Catering_Firstname_Lastname

Figure 6.48

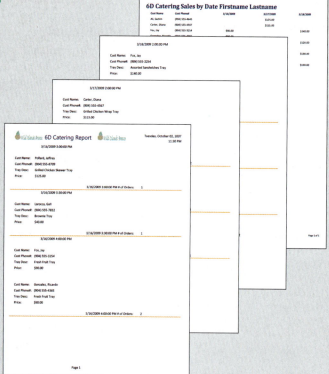

(Project 6D–Catering continues on the next page)

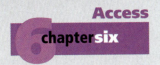
(Project 6D–Catering continued)

1. **Start** Access. Locate and open the **a06D_Catering** file. Save the database in the **Access 2007 Database** format in your **Access Chapter 6** folder as **6D_Catering_ Firstname_Lastname**

2. On the **Navigation Pane**, double-click the **6D Catering Orders** query. Collapse the **Navigation Pane**. View the data, and then **Close** the query. On the Ribbon, click the **Create tab**. In the **Reports group**, click the **Report Design** button. On the **Design tab**, in the **Tools group**, click the **Property Sheet** button to display the Property Sheet for the report. On the **Property Sheet**, click the **Data tab**. Click the **Record Source arrow**. From the displayed list of tables and queries, click **6D Catering Orders**, and then **Close** the **Property Sheet**.

3. On the **Design tab**, in the **Tools group**, click the **Add Existing Fields** button to display the fields in *6D Catering Orders* query. In the **Field List**, click **Pickup Time**. Hold down ⇧ Shift, and then click **Price** to select all of the fields. Drag the selected fields into the **Detail** section of the design grid until the top of the arrow of the pointer is aligned with the **0.25-inch mark on the vertical ruler** and aligned with the **1.5-inch mark on the horizontal ruler**.

4. With the label controls and text box controls for the fields selected, on the Ribbon, click the **Arrange tab**. In the **Control Layout group**, click the **Stacked** button. **Close** the **Field List**, and then **Save** the report as **6D Catering Report Firstname Lastname**

5. On the **Arrange tab**, in the **Show/Hide group**, click the **Report Header/Footer** button. On the Ribbon, click the **Design tab**. In the **Controls group**, click the **Logo**

(Project 6D–Catering continues on the next page)

button. Locate and double-click **a06D_Logo** to insert the logo in the Report Header section. On the selected logo, point to the right middle sizing handle until the ↔ pointer displays. Drag to the right until the right edge of the logo is aligned with the **1.5-inch mark on the horizontal ruler**.

6. On the **Design tab**, in the **Controls group**, click the **Title** button. In the **title's label control**, click to the right of **Report**, delete the space and Firstname Lastname, and then press Enter. On the **title's label control**, point to the right middle sizing handle until the ↔ pointer displays, and then double-click to adjust the size of the label control to fit the text. With the label control for the title selected, hold down Ctrl, and then press ↓ 11 times.

7. Scroll down until the **Page Footer** section bar displays. Point to the top edge of the **Page Footer** section bar until the ✛ pointer displays. Drag upward until the top of the **Page Footer** section bar aligns with the **1.5-inch mark on the vertical ruler**.

8. Scroll up until the **Report Header** section displays. Point to the top edge of the **Detail** section bar until the ✛ pointer displays. Drag upward until the top edge of the **Detail** section bar aligns with the bottom edge of the **Page Header** section bar. **Save** the report.

9. On the **Design tab**, in the **Controls group**, click the **Insert Page Number** button. In the displayed **Page Numbers** dialog box, under **Format**, click **Page N**. Under **Position**, click **Bottom of Page [Footer]**, and then click **OK**.

10. On the **Design tab**, in the **Controls group**, click the **Label** button. Point to the **Report Footer** section until the plus sign (**+**) of the

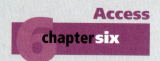
(Project 6D–Catering continued)

pointer aligns with the bottom edge of the **Report Footer** section bar and with the left edge of the **Report Footer** section, and then click. Using your own first name and last name, type **Catering Manager: Firstname Lastname** Press Enter.

11. On the **Design tab**, in the **Controls group**, click the **Date & Time** button. In the **Date and Time** dialog box, under **Include Date**, click the first option button. Under **Include Time**, click the second option button, and then click **OK**. **Save** the report.

12. Switch to **Layout** view. Notice that for the first record, the data for the **Tray Desc** field is truncated. In the first record, click the **Tray Desc text box control**, point to the right edge of the **Tray Desc text box control** until the ↔ pointer displays. Drag to the right until all of the text displays—*Grilled Chicken Skewer Tray*.

13. Switch to **Design** view. In the **Report Header** section, right-click the **logo control**. From the displayed shortcut menu, click **Copy**. Right-click anywhere in the **Report Header** section, and then from the shortcut menu, click **Paste**. Point to the selected logo, and then drag to the right until the left edge of the outlined control aligns with the **4-inch mark on the horizontal ruler**. With the image control on the right selected, hold down Shift, and then click the **logo control**. On the Ribbon, click the **Arrange tab**. In the **Control Alignment group**, click the **Bottom** button.

14. On the **Design tab**, in the **Grouping & Totals group**, click the **Group & Sort** button. In the **Group, Sort, and Total Pane**, click the **Add a group** button. From the displayed list, click **Pickup Time**. Click the **by quarter arrow**, and then click **by entire value**. Click the **do not keep group**

(Project 6D–Catering continues on the next page)

together on one page arrow, and then click **keep whole group together on one page**. In the **Group, Sort, and Total Pane**, click the **Add a sort** button, and then click **Cust Name. Close** the **Group, Sort, and Total Pane**.

15. In the **Detail** section, click the **Pickup Time text box control**. Drag downward until a thin orange line displays at the bottom of the **Price** controls.

16. On the Ribbon, click the **Arrange tab**. In the **Control Layout group**, click the **Remove** button. Point to the selected **Pickup Time text box control,** and then drag the selected control upward into the **Pickup Time Header** section until the left edge of the dotted control aligns with the **1.5-inch mark on the horizontal ruler**. In the **Pickup Time Header** section, click the **Pickup Time label control**, and then press Delete.

17. In the **Detail** section, click the **Tray Desc text box control**. On the **Design tab**, in the **Grouping & Totals group**, click the **Totals** button. In the displayed list of aggregate functions, click **Count Records**. In the **Pickup Time Footer** section, select the calculated **Count text box control**, and then holding down Shift, select from the **Report Footer** section the calculated **Count text box control**. Align the left edges with the **6-inch marker on the horizontal ruler**.

18. On the **Design tab**, in the **Controls group**, click the **Text Box** button. Point to the **Pickup Time Footer** section until the plus sign (+) of the pointer aligns with the bottom edge of the **Pickup Time Footer** section bar and with the **3.5-inch mark on the horizontal ruler**. Drag downward to the bottom of the **Pickup Time Footer** section and to the right to the **6-inch mark on the horizontal ruler**.

(Project 6D–Catering continued)

Type =[Pickup Time] & " # of Orders:" In the **Pickup Time Footer** section, click the **label control** that displays to the left of the text box control, and then press Delete to delete the text box control's associated label control.

19. In the **Pickup Time Footer** section, click the **text box control** that contains the expression you typed. With the text box control selected, hold down ⇧Shift. In the **Pickup Time Footer** section, click the **calculated control** for the count. On the Ribbon, click the **Arrange tab**. In the **Control Alignment group**, click the **Bottom** button to align both controls at the bottom.

20. Switch to **Report** view. Hold down Ctrl, and then press End to move to the end of the report. Notice the count of 12. Switch to **Design** view. In the **Report Footer** section, notice the calculated control—displays =Count(*). Point to bottom of the **Report Footer** section, and then drag downward approximately **1 inch**.

21. Click the label control that displays **Catering Manager**. Hold down ⇧Shift, and then click the text box control that displays the **Count** expression. On the Ribbon, click the **Arrange tab**. In the **Control Alignment group**, click the **Bottom** button. In the **Size group**, click the **To Tallest** button.

22. Point to either of the selected controls, and then drag downward until the bottom edges of the controls align with the bottom edge of the **Report Footer** section.

23. Use the techniques you have practiced to add a label control in the **Report Footer** section to the left of the calculated control—the left edge of the control should be aligned

with the **4.5-inch mark on the horizontal ruler**. In the **label control**, type Total # of Orders: Align the label control with the calculated control and then be sure that the controls are the same height.

24. On the Ribbon, click the **Design tab**. In the **Controls group**, click the **Line** button. Point to the **Pickup Time Footer** section until the middle of the plus sign (**+**) of the pointer aligns with the top of the **Page Footer** section bar and the **0-inch mark on the horizontal ruler**. Hold down ⇧Shift, drag to the right to the **8-inch mark on the horizontal ruler**, and then release the mouse button. On the **Design tab**, in the **Controls group**, click the **Line Thickness** button, and then click the fourth line—**3 pt**. In the **Controls group**, click the **Line Color button arrow**. Under **Standard Colors**, on the first row, click the tenth color—**Brown**. **Save** the report.

25. Adjust the margins or report width as needed. If you are instructed to submit this result, create a paper or electronic printout. On the **Print Preview tab**, in the **Close Preview group**, click the **Close Print Preview** button. **Close** the report, and then expand the **Navigation Pane**.

26. On the **Navigation Pane**, under **Queries**, double-click **6D Catering_Crosstab**. Take a moment to study the data in the query. **Close** the query, and then collapse the **Navigation Pane**.

27. On the Ribbon, click the **Create tab**. In the **Reports group**, click the **Report Wizard** button. Click the **Tables/Queries arrow**, and then click **Query: 6D Catering _Crosstab**. Under **Available Fields**, click the **All Fields** button to add all of the field names to the **Selected Fields** box.

(Project 6D–Catering continues on the next page)

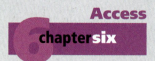

(Project 6D–Catering continued)

28. In the **Report Wizard** dialog box, click **Next**. Because no grouping levels will be used, click **Next**.

29. To sort the records within the report by Customer Name, click the **arrow** next to the **1** box. From the displayed list, click **Cust Name**. Leave the sort order as **Ascending**, and then click **Next**.

30. Under **Layout**, be sure the **Tabular** option button is selected. Under **Orientation**, be sure the **Portrait** option button is selected. Be sure the **Adjust the field width so all fields fit on a page** check box is selected. Click **Next**.

31. In the style box, click **Office**, and then click **Next**. For the title of the report, type **6D Catering Sales by Date Firstname Lastname** Select **Modify the report's design**, and then click **Finish**.

32. Switch to **Layout** view. In the **Cust Name column**, point to the right edge of any **text**

box control, and then drag to the right until all of the data displays.

33. Click anywhere in an empty area of the report to deselect the **Cust Name column**. To select all of the controls in the **Page Header** section, hold down ⇧Shift, and then click each label control. On the **Format tab**, in the **Font group**, click the **Fill/Back color button arrow**. Under **Standard Colors**, on the first row, click the first color—**White**.

34. **Save** the report, and then switch to **Print Preview** view. If you are instructed to submit this result, create a paper or electronic printout. On the **Print Preview tab**, in the **Close Preview group**, click the **Close Print Preview** button.

35. **Close** the report, and then expand the **Navigation Pane**. **Close** the database, and then **Exit** Access.

End **You have completed Project 6D**

Mastering Access

Project 6E — Promotions

In this project, you will apply the skills you practiced from the Objectives in Project 6A.

Objectives: 1. *Create a Form in Design View;* **2.** *Change and Add Controls;* **3.** *Format a Form;* **4.** *Make a Form User Friendly.*

In the following project, you will create a form that will be used to enter the data for the promotions that are offered to guests of the Wild Islands Breeze restaurant franchise. Your task includes designing a form that will be attractive and provide data entry ease for the staff. Your completed form will look similar to the one in Figure 6.49.

For Project 6E, you will need the following files:
a06E_Promotions
a06E_Logo
a06E_Dollar

You will save your database as
6E_Promotions_Firstname_Lastname

Figure 6.49

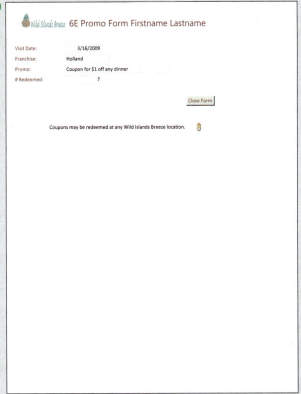

(Project 6E–Promotions continues on the next page)

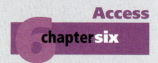

(Project 6E–Promotions continued)

1. **Start** Access. Locate and open the **a06E_Promotions** file. Save the database in the **Access 2007 Database** format in your **Access Chapter 6** folder as 6E_Promotions_Firstname_Lastname

2. On the **Create tab**, in the **Forms group**, click the **Form Design** button. Display the **Property Sheet**. On the **Data tab**, click the **Record Source property setting box arrow**, and then click **6E Promo Results**. **Close** the **Property Sheet**.

3. In the **Tools group**, click **Add Existing Fields**. In the **Field List**, display the fields for the *6E Promo Results* table, and then select all of the fields. Drag the selected fields onto the design grid until the top of the arrow of the pointer is aligned with the **0.25-inch mark on the vertical ruler** and aligned with the **1-inch mark on the horizontal ruler**. **Close** the **Field List**.

4. With all of the text box controls selected, display the **Property Sheet**, and then click the **Format tab**. In the **Left** property box, type 1.5 Click in the **Detail** section. Select the **Franchise text box control**, and then drag the right edge to the **2.75-inch mark on the horizontal ruler**. Select the **Promo text box control**, and in the **Property Sheet**, on the **Format tab**, click in the **Width** property box, and then type 3 **Save** the form as 6E Promo Form Firstname Lastname

5. On the **Arrange tab**, in the **Show/Hide group**, display the form header and footer. On the **Design tab**, in the **Controls group**, click the **Logo** button, and then insert the **a06E_Logo**. Widen the selected logo to the **1.5-inch mark on the horizontal ruler**.

6. In the **Controls group**, add a **Title**, and then accept the default title. Center the label control between the top and bottom edges of the logo control. With the title

selected, select all of the label controls. On the **Design tab**, in the **Font group**, change the color to **Brown**— the tenth color in the first row under Standard colors.

7. Scroll down until the **Form Footer** section bar displays. Point to the top of the **Form Footer** section bar until the ⊹ pointer displays. Drag upward until the top of the Form Footer section bar aligns with the **2.5-inch mark on the vertical ruler**.

8. In the **Controls group**, click the **Label** button. Point to the **Form Footer** section until the plus sign (+) of the ⁺A pointer aligns with the bottom of the **Form Footer** section bar and with the **1-inch mark on the horizontal ruler**. Drag downward to the bottom of the **Form Footer** section and to the right to the **4-inch mark on the horizontal ruler**. Type Coupons may be redeemed at any Wild Islands Breeze location. Press Enter.

9. On the **Design tab**, in the **Controls group**, click the **Image** button. Move the mouse pointer down into the **Form Footer** section. Align the plus sign (+) of the pointer with the top of the **Form Footer** section and with the **5.25-inch mark on the horizontal ruler**.

10. Drag downward to the bottom of the **Form Footer** section and to the right to the **5.5-inch mark on the horizontal ruler**. Locate and insert the file **a06E_Dollar**.

11. **Close** the **Property Sheet**. On the **Design tab**, in the **Controls group**, click the **Button** button. Move the mouse pointer down into the **Detail** section. Align the plus sign (+) of the pointer with the **1.75-inch mark on the vertical ruler** and the **5-inch mark on the horizontal ruler**, and then click.

(Project 6E–Promotions continues on the next page)

Content-Based Assessments

(Project 6E–Promotions continued)

12. Under **Categories**, click **Form Operations**. Under **Actions**, click **Close Form**, and then click **Next**. Select the **Text** radio button, and then click **Next**. In the text box, type **btnCloseForm** and then click **Finish**. With the button selected, in the **Font group**, change the **Font Color** to **Brown**.

13. If you are instructed to submit this result, create a paper or electronic printout of **record 10**. From the **Database Tools tab**, in the **Analyze group**, click the **Database Documenter** button. In the **Documenter** window, under the **Forms tab**, click the **6E Promo** form check box, and then click **OK**. **Print** the **Object Definition**. If you are to submit your work electronically, follow your instructor's directions.

14. Click the **Close Form** button, saving changes. Expand the **Navigation Pane**. **Close** the database, and then **Exit** Access.

End **You have completed Project 6E** ————————————————

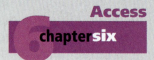

Access

chapter **six**

Mastering Access

Project 6F—Promotional Results

In this project, you will apply the skills you practiced from the Objectives in Project 6B.

Objectives: 5. *Create a Report in Design View;* **6.** *Add Controls to a Report;* **7.** *Group, Sort, and Total Records in Design View;* **8.** *Create a Crosstab Report.*

In the following project, you will create a report that will display the promotions that are offered to guests of the Wild Islands Breeze restaurant franchise. You will also create a crosstab report that will summarize the results of the promotions. Creating customized reports will help the managers of each location view the information in the database in a meaningful way. Your completed reports will look similar to those shown in Figure 6.50.

For Project 6F, you will need the following files:

a06F_Promotional_Results
a06F_Logo

**You will save your database as
6F_Promotional_Results_Firstname_Lastname**

Figure 6.50

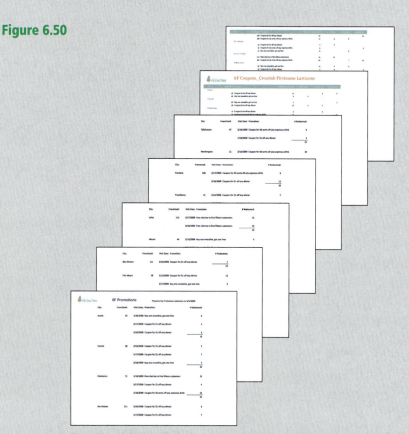

(Project 6F–Promotional Results continues on the next page)

(Project 6F–Promotional Results continued)

1. **Start** Access. Locate and open the **a06F_Promotional Results** file. Save the database in the **Access 2007 Database** format in your **Access Chapter 6** folder as **6F_Promotional_Results_Firstname Lastname**

2. Open the **6F Coupons** query. Switch to **Design** view, and then notice the underlying tables that were used in the creation of the query. **Close** the query, and then collapse the **Navigation Pane**.

3. On the **Create tab**, open a new report in **Report Design**. On the **Design tab**, display the **Property Sheet**. On the **Data tab**, click the **Record Source property setting box arrow**, and then click **6F Coupons**. **Close** the **Property Sheet**.

4. From the **Field List**, select all fields. Drag the selected fields into the **Detail** section of the design grid until the top of the pointer is aligned with the **0.25-inch mark on the vertical ruler** and the **1.5-inch mark on the horizontal ruler**. With the controls selected, on the **Arrange tab**, click the **Tabular** button. **Close** the **Field List**, and then **Save** the report as **6F Promotions Firstname Lastname**

5. On the **Design tab**, click the **Group & Sort** button. Click the **Add a group** button, and then from the displayed list, click **City**. Apply **Keep whole group together on one page**. Click the **Add a sort** button, and then click **Visit Date**. **Close** the **Group, Sort, and Total Pane**.

6. In the **Detail** section, select the **City text box control** and the **Franchise# text box control**. Right-click the selection, and then click **Properties**. On the **Format tab**, in the **Hide Duplicates** property box, click the **down arrow**, and then select **Yes**. **Close** the **Property Sheet**.

7. Align the top of the **Page Footer** section bar with the **0.5-inch mark on the vertical ruler**. Drag the **Detail** section bar upward until the top edge of the **Detail** section bar aligns with the bottom edge of the **City Header** section bar.

8. In the **Detail** section, click the **#Redeemed text box control**. On the **Design tab**, click the **Totals** button. From the list of aggregate functions, click **Sum**. Point to the top edge of the **Report Footer** section bar, and then drag up to the bottom of the **Page Footer** section bar.

9. On the **Design tab**, click the **Logo** button, and then insert the **a06F_Logo**. Widen the selected logo to the **1.5-inch mark on the horizontal ruler**.

10. In the **Controls group**, add a **Title**. Click to the right of **Promotions**, delete the space and Firstname Lastname, and then press Enter. Adjust the size of the label control to fit the text. Click and drag the control until the left edge of the control aligns with the **2.5-inch mark on the horizontal ruler** and the bottom edge of the control aligns with the **0.5-inch mark on the vertical ruler**.

11. On the **Design tab**, click the **Label** button. Point to the **Report Footer** section until the plus sign (+) of the pointer aligns with the bottom edge of the **Report Footer** section bar and with the **3-inch mark on the horizontal ruler**. Click and type **Total # Redeemed Coupons**

12. Click the **Date & Time** button. Under **Include Date**, click the first option button. Do not **Include Time**. In the **Report Header** section, click the **Date text box control** two times. Position the insertion point between the equal sign and the *D*.

(Project 6F–Promotional Results continues on the next page)

(Project 6F–Promotional Results continued)

Type **"Prepared by Firstname Lastname on "&** and then press Enter. With the **Date** text box still selected, hold down ⇧ Shift, and then click the **Title text box control**. On the **Arrange tab**, click **Bottom**.

13. Switch to **Layout** view, and then adjust all controls to fit the data. In **Design** view, adjust the report width to **9 inches**. Move the **Total # Redeemed Coupons label control** to the right, aligning its right edge at the **5.5-inch mark on the horizontal ruler**. **Save** the report. If you are instructed to submit this result, create a paper or electronic printout in **Landscape** orientation. **Close** the report.

14. Expand the **Navigation Pane**. Under **Queries**, double-click the **6F Coupons_ Crosstab** query. Take a moment to study the data in the query. **Close** the query, and then collapse the **Navigation Pane**.

15. **Create** a report using the **Report Wizard**. From the **Query: 6F Coupons_Crosstab**, select all of the fields. Under **Do you want to add any grouping or levels?**, select **City**. **Sort** the records within the report by **Franchise#** in **Ascending** order. Under **Layout**, be sure the **Stepped** option button is selected. Under **Orientation**, click the **Landscape** option button. Be sure the

Adjust the field width so all fields fit on a page check box is selected. In the style box, click **Civic**. For the title of the report, accept the default. Select **Modify the report's design**, and then click **Finish**.

16. Switch to **Layout** view. Select the **City label control**. Drag to the right to widen the column to display all data. Repeat these steps to display all labels and data in the report.

17. Switch to **Design** view. On the **Design tab**, click the **Logo** button. Insert the **a06F_Logo** and widen it to the **1.5-inch mark on the horizontal ruler**. Select the **Title text box control**, and then drag it until the left edge of the control aligns with the **2-inch marker on the horizontal ruler**. Click at the end of the text in the **Title text box control**. Type a space and then type your first and last name.

18. In the **Page Footer** section, delete the **page number control**. Reduce the report width to **9 inches**.

19. **Save** the report. If you are instructed to submit this result, create a paper or electronic printout. **Close** the report.

20. Expand the **Navigation Pane**, **Close** the database, and then **Exit** Access.

End **You have completed Project 6F**

Content-Based Assessments

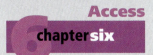
Mastering Access

Project 6G — Wireless

In this project, you will apply the following Objectives found in Projects 6A and 6B.

Objectives: 1. *Create a Form in Design View;* **2.** *Change and Add Controls;* **3.** *Format a Form;* **4.** *Make a Form User Friendly;* **8.** *Create a Crosstab Report.*

Martin Famosa, Vice President of Marketing for Wild Islands Breeze Franchises, keeps a database on the wireless usage per franchise on a monthly basis. The individual restaurants report the number of customers using the wireless connections and the average length of usage per customer. In this project, you will design a form for the data entry of this data and design a report that can be used by Mr. Famosa to plan next year's marketing strategies. Your completed work will look similar to the form and report in Figure 6.51.

> ### For Project 6G, you will need the following files:
>
> a06G_Wireless
> a06G_Logo
>
> **You will save your database as**
> **6G_Wireless_Firstname_Lastname**

Figure 6.51

(Project 6G–Wireless continues on the next page)

Content-Based Assessments

Access
chapter six

Mastering Access

(Project 6G–Wireless continued)

1. **Start** Access. Locate and open the **a06G_Wireless** file. Save the database in the **Access 2007 Database** format in your **Access Chapter 6** folder as **6G_Wireless_Firstname_Lastname** Collapse the **Navigation Pane**.

2. Create a form in **Form Design**. For the **Record Source**, use the **6G Wireless Usage** table. Select all of the fields, and then drag them onto the design grid until the top of the arrow is aligned with the **1-inch mark on the horizontal ruler** and the **0.25-inch mark on the vertical ruler**. **Save** the form as **6G Wireless Usage Firstname Lastname**

3. With all controls still selected, on the **Arrange tab**, click the **Stacked** button. Click the **Form Header/Footer** button.

4. On the **Design tab**, click the **Logo** button. Locate and double-click **a06G_Logo**. Widen the selected logo to the **1.5-inch mark on the horizontal ruler**.

5. Click the **Title** button. In the label control for the title, click to the left of *Firstname*. Delete the space and your first name and last name, and then press Enter. Double-click the right edge of the title label control to just fit the text. Center the label control between the top and bottom edges of the logo control.

6. Click the **Button** button. In the **Detail** section, align the plus sign (+) 📷 with the **0.5-inch mark on the vertical ruler** and the **2.5-inch mark on the horizontal ruler**, and then click. Under **Categories**, click **Record Operations**. Under **Actions**, click **Add New Record**, and then click **Next**. Next to **Picture**, be sure **Go to New** is selected, and then click **Next**. In the text box, type **btnNewRecord** and then click

Finish. With the **New Record** button selected, click the **Property Sheet** button. Click the **Other tab**, click in the **Tab Stop** property setting box, click the **arrow**, and then click **No**. **Close** the **Property Sheet**.

7. Click the **Label** button. In the **Form Footer** section, align the plus sign (+) 📷 pointer with the bottom of the **Form Footer** section bar and the left edge of the form. Click and type **Created by Firstname Lastname** and then press Enter.

8. Switch to **Form** view. Click the **New Record** button. From the list of **Franchises**, select **Charleston SC**. In the **Wireless Month text box control**, select the date on which this project is due. In the **# of Customers text box control**, type **757** In the **Avg Minutes text box control**, type **25**. Click the **Record Selector bar**.

9. If you are instructed to submit this result, create a paper or electronic printout of the new, selected record only. **Close** the form and **Save** changes.

10. **Create** a report using the **Report Wizard**. From the **Query: 6G Wireless_Crosstab**, select all fields. Do not add any grouping levels. **Sort** records within the report by **City**, in **Ascending** order. Use a **Tabular** layout and a **Landscape** orientation. Select a style of **Trek**. Title your report as **6G Wireless Usage by Month Firstname Lastname**

11. Switch to **Layout** view. Adjust control widths to display all field names and data.

12. If you are instructed to submit this result, create a paper or electronic printout. **Close** the report and **Save** changes.

13. Expand the **Navigation Pane**, **Close** the database, and then **Exit** Access.

End **You have completed Project 6G**

Project 6H—Ads

In this project, you will apply the following Objectives found in Projects 6A and 6B.

Objectives: 1. *Create a Form in Design View;* **3.** *Format a Form;* **5.** *Create a Report in Design View;* **6.** *Add Controls to a Report;* **7.** *Group, Sort, and Total Records in Design View.*

In the following project, you will create a form. Martin Famosa, Vice President of Marketing, will use this form to enter the details of the advertising contracts for the Wild Islands Breeze franchise restaurant chain. You will also design a report to group, sort, and total this data. Your completed form and report will look similar to those in Figure 6.52.

For Project 6H, you will need the following files:

a06H_Ads
a06H_Logo

**You will save your database as
6H_Ads_Firstname_Lastname**

Figure 6.52

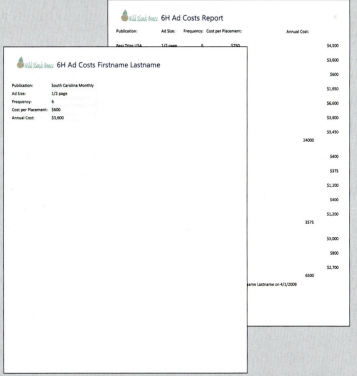

(Project 6H–Ads continues on the next page)

Access

chaptersix

Mastering Access

(Project 6H–Ads continued)

1. **Start** Access. Locate and open the **a06H_Ads** file. Save the database in the **Access 2007 Database** format in your **Access Chapter 6** folder as **6H_Ads_Firstname_Lastname**

2. Open the **6H Annual Ad Costs** query, and then view the data. **Close** the query. Collapse the **Navigation Pane**. **Create** a form in **Form Design**. For the **Record Source**, use the **6H Annual Ad Costs** query. Select all of the fields, and then drag them onto the design grid. Align the top of the **arrow** of the pointer with the **0.25-inch mark on the vertical ruler** and the **1-inch mark on the horizontal ruler**.

3. With all controls selected, on the **Arrange tab**, click the **Stacked** button. **Save** the form as **6H Ad Costs Firstname Lastname** Click the **Form Header/Footer** button.

4. On the **Design tab**, click the **Logo** button. Locate and double-click **a06H_Logo**. Widen the selected logo to the **1.5-inch mark on the horizontal ruler**. Click the **Title** button. Use the default title for the form. Center the label control between the top and bottom edges of the logo control. Drag the top of the **Form Footer** section bar to the **2-inch mark on the vertical ruler**.

5. Switch to **Layout** view. Navigate to **record 10**. Click the **Publication text box control**, and then drag the right edge to display the data. **Save** the form. Click the **Record Selector bar**. If you are instructed to submit this result, create a paper or electronic printout of record 10 only. **Close** the form.

6. **Create** a report using **Report Design**. For the **Record Source**, use the **6H Ad Costs** table. Select all fields except the *ID* field, and then drag them to the **Detail** section design grid. Align the top of the **arrow** of

the pointer with the **0.25-inch mark on the vertical ruler** and the left edge of the report.

7. On the **Arrange tab**, click the **Tabular** button. Drag the top of the **Page Footer** section bar upward to the **0.5-inch mark on the vertical ruler**. **Close** the **Field List**, and then **save** the report as **6H Ad Costs Report Firstname Lastname**

8. On the **Arrange tab**, in the **Show/Hide group**, display the report header and footer. On the **Design tab**, in the **Controls group**, click the **Logo** button, and then insert the **a06H_Logo**. Widen the selected logo to the **1.5-inch mark on the horizontal ruler**.

9. Click the **Title** button. In the label control for the title, click to the left of *Firstname*. Delete the space and your first name and last name, and then press Enter. Size the title label control to just fit the text. Center the label control between the top and bottom edges of the logo control

10. Click the **Text box** button. Point to the **Report Footer** section until the plus sign (+) pointer aligns with the bottom edge of the **Report Footer** section bar and with the **3.5-inch marker on the horizontal ruler**. Drag downward to the bottom of the **Report Footer** section and to the right to the **6.5-inch mark on the horizontal ruler**. Using your own first name and last name, type **="Prepared by Firstname Lastname on " & Date()** Press Enter. Select the corresponding label control and delete it. Drag the top of the Report Footer up to the bottom of the Page Footer.

11. Click the **Text box** button. Point to the **Report Footer** section until the plus sign (+) pointer aligns with the **0.25-inch mark on the vertical ruler** and with the

(Project 6H–Ads continues on the next page)

(Project 6H–Ads continued)

6-inch mark on the horizontal ruler. Drag downward to the **0.5-inch mark on the vertical ruler** and to the right edge of the report. Click in the text box, and then type **=[Frequency]*[Cost per Placement]** Press Enter. Select the corresponding label control and delete it.

12. Click the **Label** button. Point to the **Page Header** section until the plus sign (+) pointer aligns with the **6-inch mark on the horizontal ruler** and with the bottom of the **Page Header** section bar. Click, and then type **Annual Cost:** Press Enter.

13. Select the **Cost per Placement label control** and the **Annual Cost label control**. **Align** to **Bottom** and **Size** to **Tallest**. Align the **Annual Cost label control** and the **text box control** to the **Left**, and then size them to the **Widest**. Format the calculated control to **Currency** with **0** decimal places.

14. Click the **Group & Sort** button to display the Group, Sort, and Total Pane. Add a

group for **Ad Size**, and then **Sort** by **Publication**.

15. In the **Detail** section, click the **Frequency text box control**. Click the **Totals** button, and then click **Sum**. In the **Ad Size Footer** section, insert a text box control, and then align it horizontally with the **Annual Cost: label control**. Click in the text box, and then type **=SUM([Frequency]*[Cost per Placement])** Press Enter. Delete the corresponding label control. Drag the top edge of the **Ad Size Footer section bar** up to the **0.5-inch mark on the vertical ruler**.

16. Switch to **Layout** view. Size all label and text box controls to just fit the data. If you are instructed to submit this result, create a paper or electronic printout. **Close** the report and **Save** changes.

17. Expand the **Navigation Pane**, **Close** the database, and then **Exit** Access.

End **You have completed Project 6H**

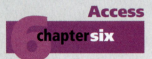

Access

Mastering Access

Project 6I — Supply Orders

In this project, you will apply all the skills you practiced from the Objectives in Projects 6A and 6B.

Maxine Hylton-Pert, Executive Chef for the Wild Islands Breeze restaurant franchise chain, places all of the supply orders for the chain. In the following project, you will create a form that can be used to order the supplies. You will also design a report to summarize the orders. Your completed form and reports will look similar to those in Figure 6.53.

For Project 6I, you will need the following files:

a06I_Supply_Orders
a06I_Logo
a06I_Pineapple

You will save your database as
6I_Supply_Orders_Firstname_Lastname

Figure 6.53

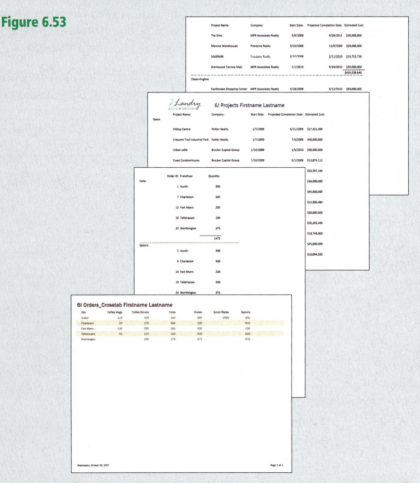

(Project 6I–Supply Orders continues on the next page)

Content-Based Assessments

Mastering Access

(Project 6I–Supply Orders continued)

1. **Start** Access. Locate and open the **a06I_ Supply_Orders** file. Save the database in the **Access 2007 Database** format in your **Access Chapter 6** folder as **6I_Supply_ Orders_Firstname_Lastname**

2. **Create** a form in **Form Design** view. For the **Record Source**, select the **6I Supply Orders** table. Add the following fields in order:
Franchise
Item
Quantity

   Drag the selected fields onto the design grid until the top of the arrow is aligned with the **1-inch mark on the horizontal ruler** and the **0.25-inch mark on the vertical ruler**. **Save** the form as **6I Supply Order Form Firstname Lastname**

3. Switch to **Layout** view. Widen all label and text box controls to display all field names and data.

4. Switch to **Design** view. Add a **Form Header** section and **Form Footer** section to the form. In the **Form Header** section, insert the **a06I_Logo**, and then align the right edge of it with the **1.5-inch mark on the horizontal ruler**.

5. In the **Form Header** section, insert a **Title label control**. Title the form **6I Supply Order Form** Size the **Title label control** to just fit the text. Center the control vertically.

6. In the **Form Footer** section, insert a label control. Align the control with the left edge of the form, the top and bottom of the **Form Footer** section, and the **3-inch mark on the horizontal ruler**. Type the following text in the label control: **Data Entry by Firstname Lastname** Adjust the width of the label control to fit the text.

7. Double-click the **Form** selector. On the **Property Sheet**, on the **Format tab**, click

in the **Picture** property setting box. Click the **Build** button. Locate and double-click **a06I_Pineapple** to insert the picture in the form. Click in the **Picture Tiling** property setting box. Click the **arrow**, and then click **Yes**.

8. In the **Detail** section, add a button to close the form. Align the button with the **3.5-inch mark on the horizontal ruler** and the **0.5-inch mark on the vertical ruler**. Select **Text: Close Form**. Name the button **btnCloseForm**

9. Switch to **Layout** view, and then select all label controls including the **Title** and **Button** controls. Apply **Bold** and **Italic** formatting.

10. If you are instructed to submit this result, create a paper or electronic printout of the first record. **Close** the form and **Save** changes.

11. **Create** a report in **Design** view. From the **6I Supply Orders** table, select all of the fields in the listed order. Drag the selection to the **Design** grid, aligning the plus (+) with the **1-inch mark on the horizontal ruler** and the bottom of the **Detail** section bar. **Save** the report as **6I Orders Firstname Lastname** Arrange in **Tabular** format. Add the **Report Header/Footer** to the report. In the **Report Header** section, insert the **a06I_Logo**, and then drag the right edge to the **1.5-inch mark on the horizontal ruler**. In the **Report Header** section, insert a **Title label control**. Accept the default name for the report. **Group** on the **Item** field, selecting **With a footer section** and **Keep whole group together on one page**. **Sort** in **Ascending** order by **Order ID**.

12. In the **Detail** section, select the **Item text box control**. **Copy** and **Paste** the control into the **Item Header** section, aligning it

(Project 6I–Supply Orders continues on the next page)

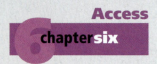

(Project 6I–Supply Orders continued)

with the left edge of the report. In the **Detail** section, select and delete the **Item text box control**. Drag the top edge of the **Item Footer** section bar upward to the **0.5-inch mark on the vertical ruler**.

13. Select the **Quantity text box control**, and then click the **Totals arrow**. Select the aggregate function **Sum**. In the **Report Footer** section, add a text box control aligned with the **1-inch mark on the horizontal ruler**, the top and bottom of the **Report Footer** section, and the **3-inch-mark on the horizontal ruler**. Delete the label control. In the text box control, type ="Orders placed on "& Date()

14. At the bottom edge of the **Item Footer** section, insert a line from the left edge of the report to the **5-inch mark on the horizontal ruler**. Format the line with a type of **Dots**, thickness of **2 pt**, and color of **Green5**.

15. Switch to **Layout** view, and then size the **Item text box controls** to just fit the data.

If you are instructed to submit this result, create a paper or electronic printout of both pages of the report. **Close** the report and **Save** changes.

16. **Create** a Crosstab Report using the **Report Wizard**. Select the **Query: 6IOrders_Crosstab**. Add all fields to the **Selected Fields** list. Do not specify a grouping. **Sort Ascending** by **City**. Select a **Tabular Layout** with **Landscape Orientation**. Be certain to **Adjust the field width so all fields fit on a page**. In the style box, select **Trek**. For the title of the report, type **6I Orders_Crosstab Firstname Lastname** Switch to **Layout** view, and then adjust all label and text box controls to just fit the data.

17. If you are instructed to submit this result, create a paper or electronic printout. **Close** the report and **Save** changes.

18. Expand the **Navigation Pane**, **Close** the database, and then **Exit** Access.

End **You have completed Project 6I** ─────────────

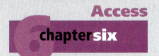

Business Running Case

Project 6J — Business Running Case

In this project, you will apply the skills you have practiced from the Objectives in Projects 6A and 6B.

From My Computer, navigate to the student files that accompany this textbook. In the folder **03_business_running_case**, locate and open the folder for this chapter. Open and print the instructions for this project, which are provided to you in Adobe PDF format. Follow the instructions and use the knowledge and skills you have gained thus far to assist the brother and sister team of Michael and Kristen Landry in meeting the challenges of owning and running their business.

 You have completed Project 6J _____

Access

chapter six

Rubric

The following outcomes-based assessments are *open-ended assessments*. That is, there is no specific correct result; your result will depend on your approach to the information provided. Make *professional quality* your goal. Use the following scoring rubric to guide you in *how* to approach the problem and then to evaluate *how well* your approach solves the problem.

The *criteria*—Software Mastery, Content, Format and Layout, and Process—represent the knowledge and skills you have gained that you can apply to solving the problem. The *levels of performance*—Professional Quality, Approaching Professional Quality, or Needs Quality Improvement—help you and your instructor evaluate your result.

	Your completed project is of Professional Quality if you:	Your completed project is Approaching Professional Quality if you:	Your completed project Needs Quality Improvements if you:
Software Mastery	Choose and apply the most appropriate skills, tools, and features and identify efficient methods to solve the problem.	Choose and apply some appropriate skills, tools, and features, but not in the most efficient manner.	Choose inappropriate skills, tools, or features, or are inefficient in solving the problem.
Content	Construct a solution that is clear and well organized, contains content that is accurate, appropriate to the audience and purpose, and is complete. Provide a solution that contains no errors of spelling, grammar, or style.	Construct a solution in which some components are unclear, poorly organized, inconsistent, or incomplete. Misjudge the needs of the audience. Have some errors in spelling, grammar, or style, but the errors do not detract from comprehension.	Construct a solution that is unclear, incomplete, or poorly organized, containing some inaccurate or inappropriate content; and contains many errors of spelling, grammar, or style. Do not solve the problem.
Format and Layout	Format and arrange all elements to communicate information and ideas, clarify function, illustrate relationships, and indicate relative importance.	Apply appropriate format and layout features to some elements, but not others. Overuse features, causing minor distraction.	Apply format and layout that does not communicate information or ideas clearly. Do not use format and layout features to clarify function, illustrate relationships, or indicate relative importance. Use available features excessively, causing distraction.
Process	Use an organized approach that integrates planning, development, self-assessment, revision, and reflection.	Demonstrate an organized approach in some areas, but not others; or, use an insufficient process of organization throughout.	Do not use an organized approach to solve the problem.

Problem Solving

Project 6K — Birthday Coupons

In this project, you will construct a solution by applying any combination of the skills you practiced from the Objectives in Projects 6A and 6B.

For Project 6K, you will need the following files:

a06K_Birthday_Coupons
a06K_Logo
a06K_Birthday

**You will save your database as
6K_Birthday_Coupons_Firstname_Lastname**

The Vice President for Marketing, Martin Famosa, encourages each of the individual restaurants of the Wild Islands Breeze franchise chain to offer birthday coupons to its customers as a promotional venture. Open the **a06K_Birthday_Coupons** database, and then save it as **6K_Birthday_Coupons_Firstname_Lastname** In this project, you will use some of the fields from the *6K Birthdates* table to create a form to enter the names, birthdates, and e-mail addresses of the customers who have visited one of the restaurants. Save this form as **6K Birthday Form Firstname Lastname** Add a control to print this form. Include the Wild Islands Breeze logo and title the form **6K Happy Birthday!** Using the form, add your own information to the underlying *6K Birthdates* table. If you are instructed to submit this result using the button control, create a paper or electronic printout of the record that contains your information only.

In addition to the form, create a report to display the birthdates grouped by month. The report should be sorted by date. Include a count of the birthdates per month. Add the **a06K_Birthday** image to the Report Header section. Title the report **6K Birthdays Firstname Lastname** Draw a line at the bottom of each group to separate each month. Save the report as **6K Birthdate Report** If you are instructed to submit this result, create a paper or electronic printout of the report.

End **You have completed Project 6K** ————————

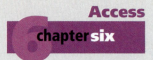

Problem Solving

Project 6L — Menu

In this project, you will construct a solution by applying any combination of the skills you practiced from the Objectives in Projects 6A and 6B.

For Project 6L, you will need the following files:

a06L_Menu
a06L_Logo

**You will save your database as
6L_Menu_Firstname_Lastname**

Maxine Hylton-Pert, Executive Chef for the Wild Islands Breeze restaurant chain, wants to know which menu items are most popular at the individual franchise locations. Open the **a06L_Menu** database and save it as **6L_Menu_Firstname_Lastname** In this project, you will create a form to be used by the managers of the different franchises to enter the most popular menu items. From the *6L Popular Item*s table, use all fields except the ID field. Save the form as **6L Popular Items Firstname Lastname** Format the form by changing the font type and font color of the label controls. Add **a06L_Logo** and title the form **6L Popular Menu Items** In the Form Footer section, insert a label control. In the label, type **Designed by: Firstname Lastname** Adjust the label controls and the text box controls to fit the data. If you are instructed to submit this result, create a paper or electronic printout of only the first record.

Create a crosstab report using the 6L Most Popular_Crosstab query. Select all fields from the query. Sort on the Franchise name. Choose an appropriate style. Title the report **6L Popular Items by Franchise** In the Report Footer section, add a label control that displays your name. Save the report as **6L Crosstab Report Firstname Lastname** Adjust all label and text controls to display all field names and data. If you are instructed to submit this result, create a paper or electronic printout.

End **You have completed Project 6L** ⎯⎯⎯⎯⎯⎯

Access

chapter six

Problem Solving

Project 6M — Vacation Days

In this project, you will construct a solution by applying any combination of the skills you practiced from the Objectives in Projects 6A and 6B.

For Project 6M, you will need the following files:

a06M_Vacation_Days
a06M_Logo

You will save your database as
6M_Vacation_Days_Firstname_Lastname

In this project, you will create a report to display the number of vacation days allotted and the number of vacation days taken by the employees of the Wild Islands Breeze franchise restaurant chain. Open the **a06M_Vacation_Days** database and save it as **6M_Vacation_Days_Firstname_Lastname** From the *6M Vacation Days* table, add the following fields to the report: Employee Name, Allotted Days, and Days Taken. Add a calculated text box control to display the number of vacation days each employee has remaining. Add an associated label control to describe this field. In the Report Header section, add the Wild Islands Breeze logo and a title that includes your Firstname Lastname. Sort on Employee Name. Adjust all label and text controls to display all field names and data. If you are instructed to submit this result, create a paper or electronic printout.

 End **You have completed Project 6M** ————————————

Problem Solving

Project 6N — Seasonal Items

In this project, you will construct a solution by applying any combination of the skills you practiced from the Objectives in Projects 6A and 6B.

> **For Project 6N, you will need the following files:**
>
> a06N_Seasonal_Items
> a06N_Logo

You will save your database as
6N_Seasonal_Items_Firstname_Lastname

The Executive Chef of the Wild Islands Breeze franchise restaurant chain, Maxine Hylton-Pert, adds seasonal items to the menu. In this project, you will open the **a06N_Seasonal_Items** database and save it as **6N_Seasonal_Items_Firstname_Lastname** You will create a crosstab report using the 6N Seasonal Items_Crosstab query. The query displays the menu item, the season in which it is offered, and the price of the item. The report should include all fields from the query. Sort on the menu item. Add the Wild Islands Breeze logo and a report title. In the Report Footer section, display your name and the date of the report. Adjust all label and text controls to display all field names and data. If you arc instructed to submit this result, create a paper or electronic printout.

End **You have completed Project 6N** ————————

Access

Problem Solving

Project 6O—New Franchises

In this project, you will construct a solution by applying any combination of the skills you practiced from the Objectives in Projects 6A and 6B.

For Project 6O, you will need the following files:

a06O_New_Franchises
a06O_Logo

You will save your database as
6O_New_Franchises_Firstname_Lastname

James McKinnon, Vice President of Franchising for the Wild Islands Breeze restaurant chain, is responsible for the costs analysis of new franchise proposals for the Wild Islands Breeze Corporation. In this project, you will open the **a06O_New_Franchises** database and save it as **6O_New_Franchises_Firstname_Lastname** You will create a form based on the *6O Startup Costs* table. Include all fields from the table. To the Form Header section, add **a06O_Logo** and title it **6O Costs Firstname Lastname** Add a background color to the form. Add a button control to close the form. Adjust all label and text controls to display all field names and data. If you are instructed to submit this result, create a paper or electronic printout of only the record that contains the Virginia Beach, Virginia franchise data.

Create a report using the *6O Startup Costs* table. Add all fields and use a tabular layout. Increase the height of the label controls so that you can decrease the width of the controls. Design the report to fit on one page in Landscape orientation. Group on Startup Date and sort by location. Add a total for every currency field. Adjust all label and text controls to display all field names and data. Save and title the report as **6O Total Costs Firstname Lastname** If you are instructed to submit this result, create a paper or electronic printout.

End **You have completed Project 6O** ——————

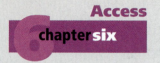
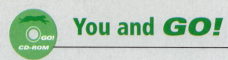
Project 6P — You and *GO!*

In this project, you will construct a solution by applying any combination of the Objectives found in Projects 6A and 6B.

From My Computer, navigate to the student files that accompany this textbook. In the folder **04_you_and_go**, locate and open the folder for this chapter. Open and print the instructions for this project, which are provided to you in Adobe PDF format. Follow the instructions to create a form and report for your personal inventory.

 You have completed Project 6P ———————————

GO! with Help

Project 6Q — *GO!* with Help

The Access Help system is extensive and can help you as you work. In this project, you will view information about adding aggregate functions to a report in Design view.

1 **Start** Access. On the right side of the Ribbon, click the **Microsoft Office Access Help** button. In the **Type words to search for** box, in the **Access Help** window, type **summing in reports** and then press Enter.

2 In the displayed **Search Results** pane, click **Summing in reports**. Maximize the Access Help window. Read the section titled **Add a total or other aggregate in Design view**.

3 If you want, print a copy of the information by clicking the **Print** button at the top of **Access Help** window.

4 **Close** the Help window, and then **Exit** Access.

 You have completed Project 6Q ———————————

7 chapterseven

Creating Advanced Forms and Reports

OBJECTIVES

At the end of this chapter you will be able to:

1. Create a Split Form
2. Create a Form and a Subform
3. Create a Multi-Page Form

OUTCOMES

Mastering these objectives will enable you to:

PROJECT 7A
Create Advanced Forms

4. Create and Modify a Subreport
5. Create a Report Based on a Parameter Query
6. Create an Alphabetic Index

PROJECT 7B
Create Advanced Reports

Southwest Gardens

The southwest style of gardening is popular in many areas of the country, not just in the yards and gardens of Arizona and New Mexico. The stylish simplicity and use of indigenous, hardy plants that are traditional in the southwest United States make for beautiful, environmentally-friendly gardens in any part of the country. Produced by Media Southwest Productions, the television show Southwest Gardens is broadcast nationwide. The show and its Web site provide tips and tricks for beautiful gardens, and highlight new tools and techniques; and the show's hosts present tours of public and private gardens that showcase the southwest style.

Creating Advanced Forms and Reports

Forms provide a way to enter, edit, and display data; reports display the data in a professional-looking manner. You have created and customized forms and reports. Access 2007 enables you to create a form, and also display the data inside the form in Datasheet view or to create forms that contain multiple pages. You have practiced creating relationships between tables and have seen that information from multiple objects can be presented in one object, such as a query that extracts data from multiple tables. If a one-to-many relationship exists between the underlying tables, forms can be used to manipulate data from multiple tables, and reports can display data from multiple tables. You have also practiced creating a parameter query, which, in turn, can be used to create a report based on the criteria entered when the report is opened.

Project 7A TV Shows

Toni Jones, president of Media Southwest Productions, wants the database forms to display related data. For example, she is interested in displaying the advertisers of the television shows on one form. In Activities 7.1 through 7.7, you will customize the company's forms to display data in two ways on the same form, to display data from multiple tables on one form, and to display data on multiple pages on a form.

For Project 7A, you will need the following files:

a07A_TV_Shows
a07A_Logo

You will save your database as
7A_TV_Shows_Firstname_Lastname
You will save your document as
7A_Tab_Control_Form_Firstname_Lastname

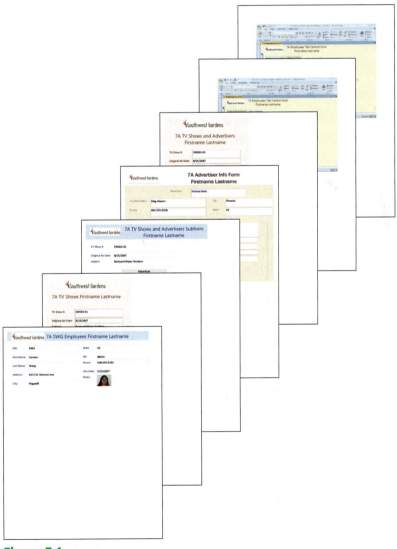

Figure 7.1
Project 7A—TV Shows

Objective 1
Create a Split Form

A *split form* displays data in two views—Form view and Datasheet view—on a single form. The two views display data from the same source, and are synchronized with each other at all times. When you select a field in one of the views, the same field displays in the other view. You can add, delete, or edit data in either view. An advantage of displaying data in a split form is the flexibility of finding a record in Datasheet view, and then editing the same record in Form view.

Activity 7.1 Creating a Split Form Using the Split Form Tool

In this activity, you will create a split form from scratch.

1 **Start** Access. Navigate to the location where the student data files for this textbook are saved. Locate and open the **a07A_TV_Shows** file. Click the **Office** button ![icon], point to **Save As**, and then click **Access 2007 Database**. In the **Save As** dialog box, navigate to the drive on which you will be saving your folders and projects for this chapter. Create a new folder named **Access Chapter 7** and **Save** the database as **7A_TV_Shows_Firstname_Lastname** in the folder.

2 Enable the content or add the Access Chapter 7 folder to the Trust Center. On the **Navigation Pane**, double-click **7A TV Show Advertisers** to open the table in Datasheet view. In the first record, in the **TV Show #** field, click the **arrow** to the right of *SWG01-01* to display a list of television show codes. In the first record, click in the **Advertiser** field, and then click the **arrow** to the right of *All Woods Lumber Supply* to display a list of advertisers.

Both of these fields are lookup fields. The TV Show # field looks up data in the *7A TV Shows* table. The Advertiser field looks up data in the *7A Advertiser Info* table. Because these fields look up data in specific tables, you will not change the names of the existing tables and forms in this database. If you did rename the tables, the lookup fields would not be able to locate the related tables.

3 Press [Esc] to close the list. If the small pencil displays in the record selector box, press [Esc] one more time. **Close** [×] the table.

4 On the **Navigation Pane**, double-click **7A SWG Employees** to open the table in Datasheet view. Take a moment to review the fields in the table. Scroll to the right until the **Attachment** field displays. In the **Attachment** field, double-click any record. In the displayed **Attachments** dialog box, click **Open** to display a photograph of the employee. **Close** [×] the window with the picture, and then **Close** [×] the **Attachments** dialog box.

5 Collapse [«] the **Navigation Pane**. On the Ribbon, click the **Create tab**. In the **Forms group**, click the **Split Form** button, and then compare your screen with Figure 7.2.

The split form displays in Layout view. The top section of the split form displays the data in Form view, and the bottom section of the split form displays the data in Datasheet view.

Figure 7.2

Split form in Layout view

Underlying table

Form section

Navigation Pane

Datasheet section

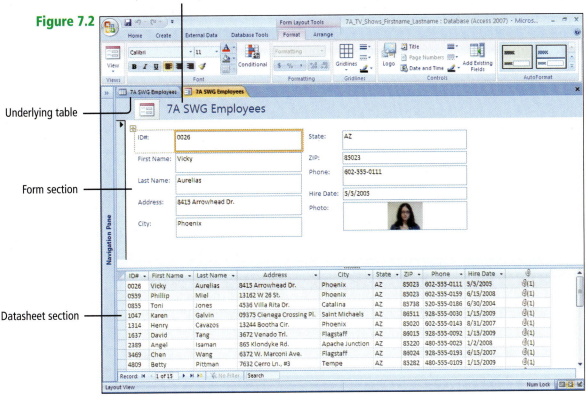

Another Way **To Create a Split Form**

The underlying table or query does not need to be open to create a split form. On the Navigation Pane, select the underlying table or query by clicking it. On the Create tab, in the Forms group, click the Split Form button.

6 In the datasheet section of the split form, click anywhere in the first record, and then press ⬇. Notice that the form section displays the data and photograph for the second record—the two sections are synchronized.

7 Save 🖫 the split form as **7A SWG Employees Split Form Firstname Lastname**

Activity 7.2 Formatting a Split Form

In this activity, you will enhance the split form by modifying the fields and form properties.

1 In the datasheet section of the split form, click anywhere in the first record. In the form section of the split form, click the **Photo** for *Vicky Aurelias*, and then compare your screen with Figure 7.3.

A Mini toolbar displays above Vicky's photograph. If the Mini toolbar does not display, point to the picture. A ***Mini toolbar*** is a miniature, semitransparent toolbar that is used to work with objects on the screen. In this case, the Mini toolbar displays a Previous button, a Next button, and an Attachment button. If there were multiple attachments for this record, clicking the Next button would display the next attachment, and clicking the Previous button would display the previous attachment.

Recall that the Layout Selector is used to select all of the fields in the column. Clicking any field in a column displays the Layout Selector for the column.

Figure 7.3

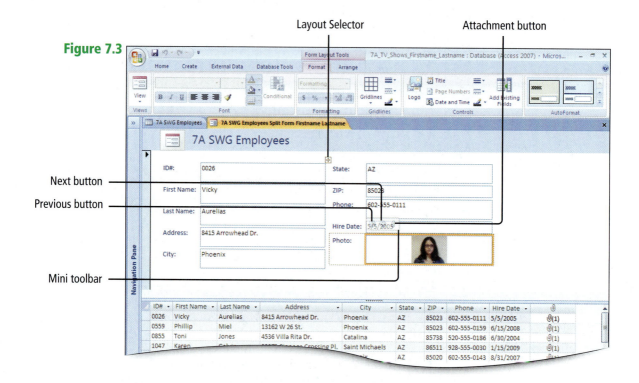

On the **Mini toolbar**, click the **Attachment** button to display the **Attachments** dialog box.

Display the Attachments dialog box when you have many attachments and do not want to scroll through them using the Previous and Next buttons on the Mini toolbar.

Close ✕ the **Attachments** dialog box. With the **Photo** field selected, on the Ribbon, click the **Arrange tab**. In the **Control Layout group**, click the **Remove** button. Notice that the Layout Selector no longer displays for the second column.

The Photo field is removed from the second column's stacked layout.

Click in the **Photo attachment control**—the box displaying the photograph. In the **Tools group**, click **the Property Sheet** button. Be sure the Property Sheet displays *Selection type: Attachment*. On the **Property Sheet Format tab**, click in the **Picture Alignment** property setting box—it displays *Center*—and then click the **arrow**.

From the displayed list, click **Top Left**, and then **Close** ✕ the **Property Sheet**.

Aligning the photograph at the left edge of the attachment control makes it easier to adjust the width of the control. Recall that you must remove a field from the predefined layout to resize only that field.

5 Point to the right edge of the **Photo attachment control** until the ⟷ pointer displays. Drag to the left until the border aligns with the right edge of the photograph, and then compare your screen with Figure 7.4.

Figure 7.4

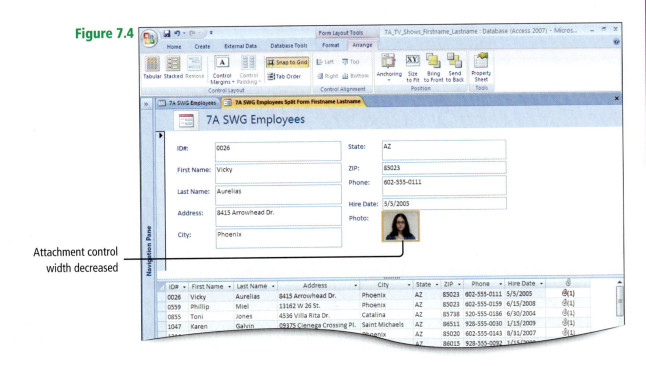

Attachment control width decreased

6 Press [PgDn] to display the second record, and notice that the width of the attachment control is also decreased for this record.

7 **Save** 💾 the split form. With the **Photo attachment control** selected, on the **Arrange tab**, in the **Tools group**, click the **Property Sheet** button. Alternatively, right-click the control and click Properties, or press [F4].

The property sheet for the Photo attachment control displays. If the property sheet for another field or section of the form displays, do not worry about it.

8 Click the **Selection type arrow**. Scroll until *Form* is displayed in the list, and then click **Form** to display the **Form Property Sheet**. On the **Property Sheet Format tab**, scroll down, if necessary, until the properties that relate to split forms display, and then compare your screen with Figure 7.5. Take a moment to study the six properties that directly relate to split forms, as described in the table in Figure 7.6.

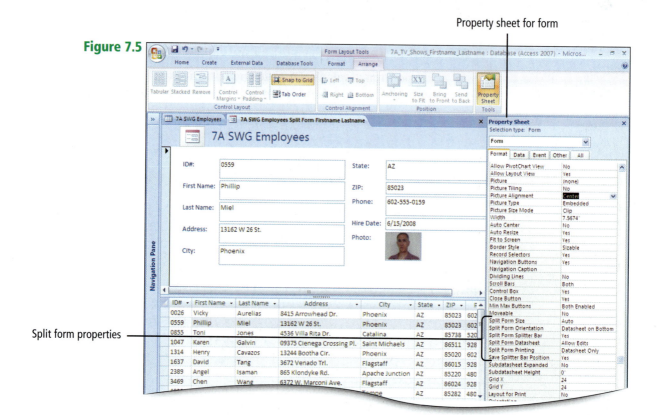

Property sheet for form

Figure 7.5

Split form properties

Split Form Properties

Property	Description	View(s) in Which the Property Can Be Set
Split Form Size	Specify an exact height or width, depending on whether the form is split vertically or horizontally, for the form section of the split form. For example, type *1″* to set the form height or width to 1 inch. Type *Auto* to set the size by other means, such as dragging the splitter bar in Layout view. The default is *Auto*.	Design or Layout
Split Form Orientation	Define whether the datasheet displays above, below, to the left, or to the right of the form. The default is *Datasheet on Bottom*.	Design
Split Form Splitter Bar	If set to *Yes*, the form and datasheet can be resized by moving the splitter bar that separates the two sections. If set to *No*, the splitter bar is hidden, and the form and datasheet cannot be resized. The default is *Yes*.	Design
Split Form Datasheet	If set to *Allow Edits* and the form's source can be updated, editing can be done in the datasheet section. If set to *Read Only*, editing cannot be done in the datasheet section. The default is *Allow Edits*.	Design or Layout
Split Form Printing	Define which section of the form is printed. If set to *Form Only*, only the form section is printed. If set to *Datasheet Only*, only the datasheet section is printed. The default is *Datasheet Only*.	Design or Layout
Save Splitter Bar Position	If set to *Yes*, the form opens with the splitter bar in the same position in which it was saved. If set to *No*, the form and datasheet cannot be resized, and the splitter bar is hidden. The default is *Yes*.	Design

Figure 7.6

9 On the **Property Sheet**, click in the property setting box for **Split Form Printing**, click the **arrow**, and then click **Form Only**. Notice that you can print either the Form or the Datasheet, but not both.

Does a message display, prompting you to change to Design view?

If you try to change a property that can only be changed in Design view, Access displays a message prompting you to change to Design view. If you then try to change a property that can only be changed in Layout view, Access will display the same message. If this happens, switch to Design view and then switch back to Layout view, or change to Design view, and then change the property settings. All split form properties can be changed in Design view.

10 On the **tab row**, right-click **7A SWG Employees Split Form**, and then click **Design View**. On the **Property Sheet** for the form, click in the **Split Form Orientation** property setting box, and then click the **arrow**. Compare your screen with Figure 7.7. If necessary, increase the width of the Property Sheet to display all four of the property settings.

Figure 7.7

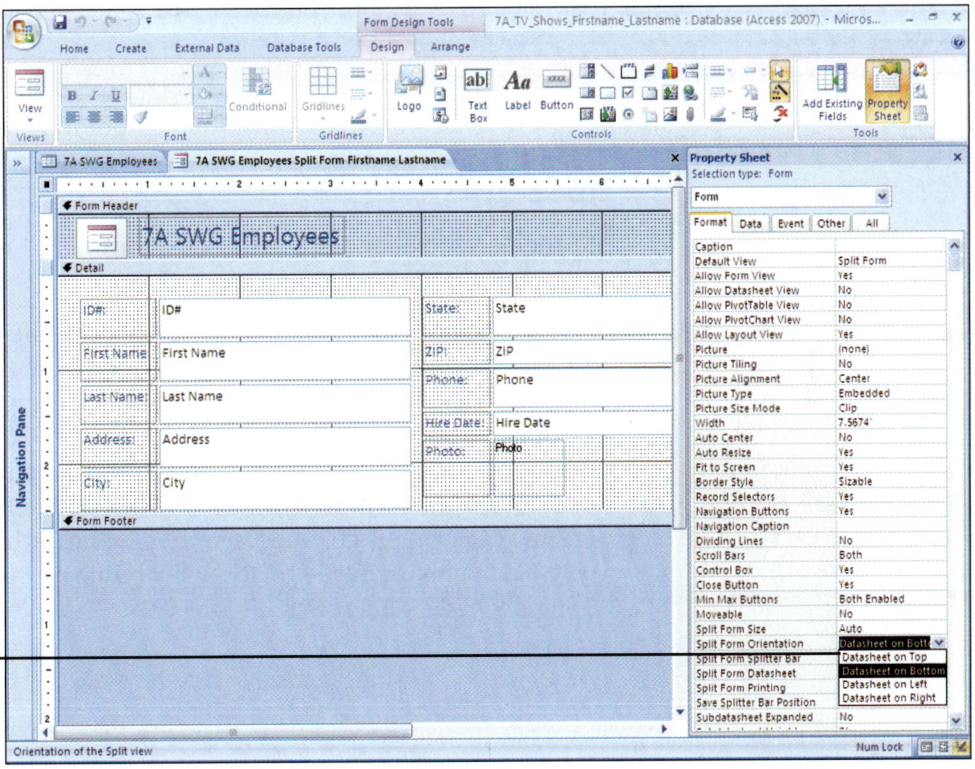

Split Form Orientation property settings

11 Click **Datasheet on Top**, and then **Close** the **Property Sheet**.

12 Switch to **Layout** view, and then compare your screen with Figure 7.8.

The datasheet section displays above the form section of the split form. A splitter bar divides the two sections.

Figure 7.8

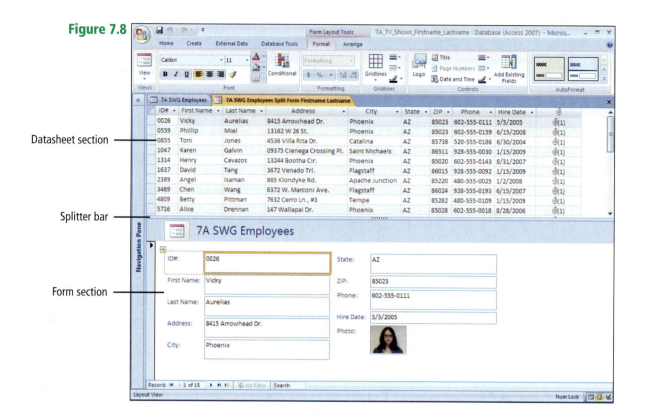

Datasheet section

Splitter bar

Form section

---

13 Point to the splitter bar until the ⊞ pointer displays. Drag upward until the dark horizontal line displays between the records with an **ID#** of **1047** and **1314**.

In the datasheet section, Records 1 through 4 display, and the height of the form section is increased.

14 On the **Format tab**, in the **Controls group**, click the **Logo** button. Navigate to the location where the student data files are saved, and then double-click **a07A_Logo**. Increase the width of the **logo control** approximately **two inches**, and then move the **label control** for the title to the right of the logo control. In the form section, click the **label control** for the form title, and then click to the right of **Employees**. Press Spacebar one time, and then using your own first and last name, type **Firstname Lastname** to add your name to the title of the form. Compare your screen with Figure 7.9.

Figure 7.9

Label control moved to the right

Logo inserted and resized

15 **Save** the form, and then switch to **Form** view. Press PgDn until **Record 8** displays as displayed in the navigation area. In the form section, change the **First Name** from *Chen* to **Carolyn** and then press Tab. Notice that in the datasheet section, the same record—*ID# 3469*—is selected and is in the editing mode. Also notice that the **First Name** field has been updated in the datasheet section.

Recall that you can only make changes to the data in the fields with the form displayed in Form view.

16 Press PgDn to move to the next record and to save the changes to Record 8. Press Page Up to display **Record 8**. In the form section, on the left side, click the **Record Selector** bar. If you are instructed to submit this result, create a paper or electronic printout of the selected record. On the **tab row**, right-click any tab, and then click **Close All**. Expand [»] the **Navigation Pane**.

The form section prints because you set the Split Form Printing property to Form Only.

More Knowledge
Adding or Deleting a Field

To add a field to a split form in Layout view, display the Field List—on the Format tab, in the Controls group, click the Add Existing Fields button. Drag the field from the Field List to the datasheet section or the form section. The field will be added to both sections of the split form.

To delete a field from a split form, you must delete it from the form section. The field will then be removed automatically from the datasheet section.

Activity 7.3 Converting an Existing Form into a Split Form

In this activity, you will convert *7A TV Shows Form* into a split form.

1 On the **Navigation Pane**, under **Forms**, right-click **7A TV Shows Form**, and then click **Design View**. Collapse « the **Navigation Pane**. On the **tab row**, click the **7A TV Shows Form tab**, and then press F4 to display the **Property Sheet** for the form. If the Property Sheet does not display *Selection type: Form*, click the Selection type arrow, and then click Form.

To convert an existing form to a split form, the form must be open in Design view.

2 On the **Property Sheet Format tab**, click in the **Default View** property setting box—*Single Form* is displayed. Click the **arrow**, and then click **Split Form**. **Close** × the **Property Sheet**, and then switch to **Layout** view.

The split form displays with the datasheet section on top; Access applied the same Split Form Orientation to this split form as the previous split form.

3 Switch to **Design view**, and then using the techniques you practiced in Activity 7.2, change the **Split Form Orientation** to display the **Datasheet on Bottom**. **Close** × the **Property Sheet**, display the split form in **Layout** view, and then compare your screen with Figure 7.10.

Figure 7.10

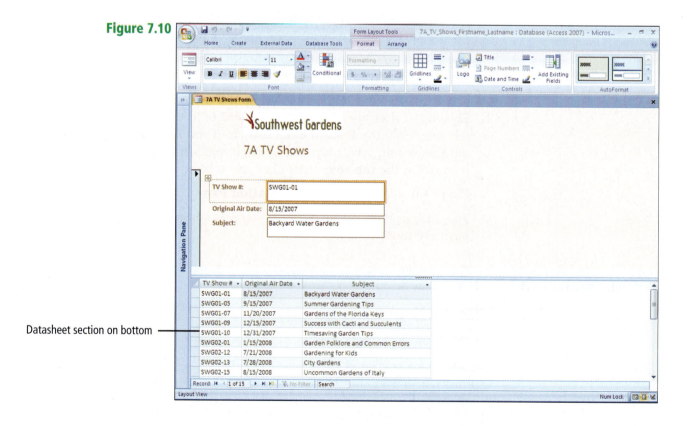

Datasheet section on bottom

4 In the form section, click the **title's label control**, and then click to the right of **7A TV Shows**. Press [Spacebar] one time. Using your own first and last name, type **Firstname Lastname** and then press [Enter].

5 Switch to **Design** view. Hold down [⇧ Shift], click the **title's label control**, and then click the **label control** for **TV Show #**. On the Ribbon, click the **Arrange tab**. In the **Control Alignment group**, click the **Left** button.

The left edge of the title's label control is aligned with the left edge of the TV Show # label control.

6 Click in an empty area of the design grid to deselect the controls, and then click the **title's label control**. Point to the right edge of the **title's label control** until the ↔ pointer displays. Drag to the right until the right edge of the label control aligns with the right edges of the text box controls in the Detail section. If your entire name does not display within the title's label control, click the **Home tab**; and in the **Font group**, reduce the font size of the text.

Even though the entire title displays in Layout view and in Form view, if the title is truncated in Design view, it will be truncated when you print the form.

7 **Save** 🖫 and **Close** ✕ the form. Expand ❯❯ the **Navigation Pane**. Under **Forms**, right-click **7A TV Shows Form**, and then click **Rename**. Type **7A TV Shows Split Form Firstname Lastname** and then press [Enter].

Recall that an object must be closed before you can rename it.

8 Double-click **7A TV Shows Split Form** to open it in Form view. Be sure that **Record 1** is displayed. In the form section, on the left side, click the **Record Selector** bar. If you are instructed to submit this result, create a paper or electronic printout of the selected record.

9 **Close** ✕ the form, and then collapse ❮❮ the **Navigation Pane**.

Objective 2
Create a Form and a Subform

In the previous activities, you created a split form that displayed the datasheet of the underlying table—the data in the form section was the same data as that displayed in the datasheet section. A **subform** is a form that is embedded within another form—the **main form**—and is used to view, enter, and edit data that is related to data in the main form. A subform is similar to a subdatasheet—the data in the related table is displayed without having to open another table or form.

Activity 7.4 Creating a Form and a Subform Using the Form Tool

If Access finds a single table that has a one-to-many relationship with the table used to create a form, Access adds the datasheet as a subform to display the related records. In this activity, you will create the main form using the *7A TV Shows* table. Because a one-to-many relationship has been created between this table and the *7A TV Show Advertisers* table, the datasheet for the *7A TV Show Advertisers* table will be inserted as a subform.

1 On the Ribbon, click the **Database Tools tab**. In the **Show/Hide group**, click the **Relationships** button. If the tables do not display in the Relationships window, on the **Design tab**, in the **Relationships group**, click the **All Relationships** button. If necessary, expand the table boxes and rearrange them so that it is easier to view the relationships as shown in Figure 7.11. Take a moment to study the established relationships.

This is an example of a ***many-to-many relationship*** between the *7A TV Shows* table and the *7A Advertiser Info* table. *Many* television shows can have *many* advertisers. Conversely, *many* advertisers can advertise on *many* television shows.

To create the *many-to-many relationship* between *7A TV Shows* and *7A Advertiser Info*, the *7A TV Show Advertisers* table was created. This table is known as a ***junction table***. It breaks down the many-to-many relationship into two *one-to-many relationships*. The data from the primary key fields—*TV Show #* and *Advertiser*—from the two tables are added to the junction table, which records each instance of the relationship. The primary key fields from the two tables are connected to the foreign key fields in the junction table.

2 **Close** ☒ the Relationships window, saving changes if prompted.

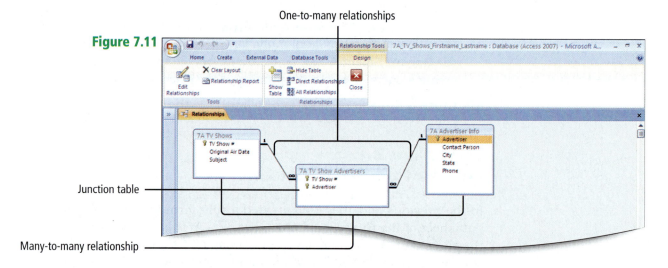

Figure 7.11

Note — Specifying Multiple Primary Key Fields

A junction table contains data from the primary key fields in two tables. The fields in the junction table are designated as primary key fields. In Design view, to specify multiple fields as primary key fields, hold down the ⌈Ctrl⌋ key, and then click the row selector boxes for each primary key field. On the Design tab, in the Tools group, click the Primary Key button. A junction table can include fields other than the common fields from the two related tables.

Expand 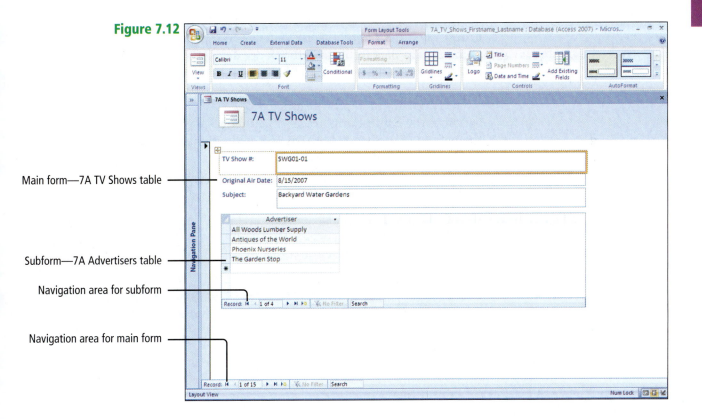 the **Navigation Pane**. Under **Tables**, click **7A TV Shows**. On the Ribbon, click the **Create tab**, and then in the **Forms group**, click the **Form** button. Collapse ◄◄ the **Navigation Pane**, and then compare your screen with Figure 7.12.

The main form—*7A TV Shows*—displays in Layout view. Because the table has a *one-to-many* relationship with the *7A Advertisers* table, the datasheet for the *7A Advertisers* table is automatically embedded as a subform. The main form has its own navigation area at the bottom of the screen, and the datasheet has its own navigation area in the middle of the screen.

Figure 7.12

Main form—7A TV Shows table

Subform—7A Advertisers table

Navigation area for subform

Navigation area for main form

3 In the main form, click the **TV Show # text box control**, and press PgDn until record **15** is displayed, observing changes in the subform and in the two navigation areas.

As you scroll through the records in the *7A TV Shows* table, the subform displays the related records for each television show. For example, in record 15, the TV Show # is *SWG03-06*, and three advertisers support this show.

4 In the main form, click the **Subject text box control**. Point to the right edge of the text box control until the ↔ pointer displays, and then drag the right edge of the text box control to the left until there is approximately **one inch** of space between *Devices* and the right edge of the text box control.

Because the controls are part of the same stacked layout, the widths of all of the text box controls is decreased.

5 Click anywhere in the subform. Notice that the Layout Selector displays above the upper left corner of the subform, and the datasheet is selected as indicated by the border around it.

6 Point to the right edge of the subform until the ↔ pointer displays, and then drag the right edge of the subform to the left until it aligns with the right edge of the **Advertiser** field. Point to the subform **Layout Selector** until the pointer displays, and then drag to the right until the subform is centered under the text box controls above the subform.

7 Edit the title of the form so it displays as **7A TV Shows and Advertisers Subform Firstname Lastname** On the **Format tab**, in the **Controls group**, click the **Logo** button. Navigate to the location where the student data files for this textbook are saved. Locate and double-click **a07A_Logo** to insert the logo in the form header.

8 If necessary, click the **logo control** to select it. Point to the bottom right corner of the control until the ↘ pointer displays. Drag downward to the bottom of the header section and to the right between the *S* and *h* in *Shows* as shown in Figure 7.13.

The logo size is increased, and it overlaps the title of the form.

Figure 7.13

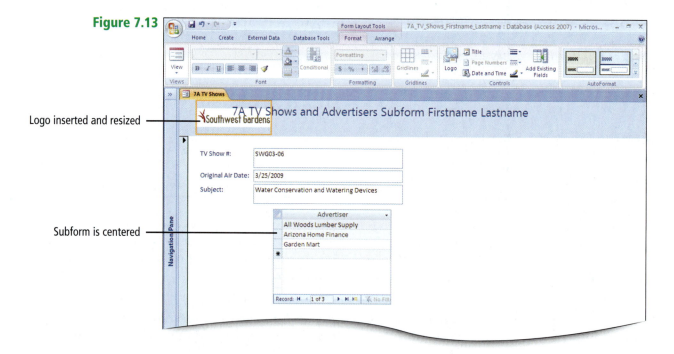

Logo inserted and resized

Subform is centered

9 Click the **title's label control**, and then click to the left of your **Firstname**. Press ⌫Bksp to delete the space between *Subform* and your *Firstname*. Hold down ⇧Shift, and then press Enter.

Your name displays on the second line in the label control.

10 Point to the left edge of the **title's label control** until the ↔ pointer displays. Drag to the right until the left edge of the label control aligns with the right edge of the logo control. Point to the right edge of the

title's label control until the ↔ pointer displays—the right edge may display at the very right side of your screen. Drag to the left until there is approximately **.25 inch** of space between *Subform* and the right edge of the label control. With the **title's label control** selected,

on the **Format tab**, in the **Font group**, click the **Center** button ▤.

11 Switch to **Design** view, and compare your screen with Figure 7.14. Notice that the subform control displays the related table's name— *Table.7A TV Show Advertisers*. Also, notice that the title's label control does not display the entire title.

Although you can make most adjustments to a form in Layout view, you should adjust the title's control in Design view to ensure the form's title will print as desired.

Title truncated   6.5-inch mark on horizontal ruler

Figure 7.14

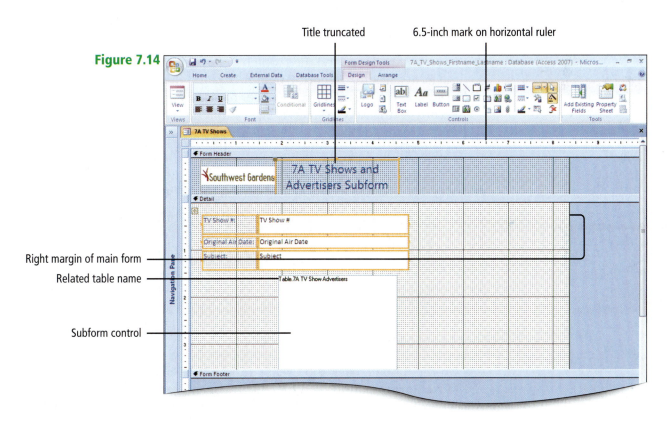

Right margin of main form

Related table name

Subform control

12 Click in an empty area of the design grid to deselect the controls, and then click the title's label control. Point to the right edge of the

title's label control until the ↔ pointer displays. Drag to the right until the right edge of the label control aligns with the **6.5-inch mark on the horizontal ruler**. Point to the right edge of the main form until

the ✛ pointer displays. Drag to the left until the right edge of the main form aligns with the **6.5-inch mark on the horizontal ruler**.

With narrow margins for a form and with Portrait orientation, the right edge of the form should not exceed 8 inches on the horizontal ruler; otherwise, pages will print with only the background color in the form header.

13 **Save** 💾 the form as **7A TV Shows and Advertisers Subform Firstname Lastname** and then switch to **Layout** view. Notice that the title displays in the center of the screen instead of centered over the form controls.

Centering the label control causes the label control to be centered between the logo and the right side of the screen. When you print, the title will be centered between the right side of the logo control and the right margin of the form.

14 Right-click the **title's label control**, and then click **Properties** to display the Property Sheet for the title. On the **Property Sheet Format tab**, scroll down until the **Horizontal Anchor** property displays, and then click in the property setting box. Click the **arrow**, and then click **Left**. **Close** ☒ the **Property Sheet**.

The title's label control is anchored at the left margin of the control in Layout view and in Form view.

15 **Save** 💾 the form, and then switch to **Form** view. On the left side of the form, click the **Record Selector** bar, and then if you are instructed to submit this result, create a paper or electronic printout of only Record 1—the selected record. Notice that both the main form and the subform print.

Close ☒ the form.

Activity 7.5 Creating a Form and a Subform Using the Form Wizard

Use the Form Wizard to create a form and a subform when you want to have more control over the design of the subform, or if the underlying table or query has more than one relationship established. If the underlying table or query that is on the *one* side of the relationship is related to more than one table or query on the *many* side of the relationship, the subform will not automatically be created when the form is created. The same technique can be used to create a split form between two tables that have a many-to-many relationship.

1 On the Ribbon, click the **Create tab**. In the **Forms group**, click the **More Forms** button, and then click **Form Wizard**. In the **Form Wizard** dialog box, click the **Tables/Queries arrow**, and then click **Table: 7A TV Shows**, which is on the *many* side of the relationship.

It does not matter which table you select first; in a later dialog box, you can select the table that displays in the main form and the table that displays in the subform.

2 Under **Available Fields**, click the **All Fields** button ⏵⏵ to add all of the fields to the **Selected Fields** box. In the same dialog box, click the **Tables/Queries arrow**, and from the displayed list, click **Table: 7A Advertiser Info**, which is on the *many* side of the relationship.

Add **All Fields** ⏵⏵ to the **Selected Fields** box. Click **Next**, and then compare your screen with Figure 7.15.

The second Form Wizard dialog box displays with a preview of how the data will be arranged. The order in which you select the tables or queries to be included in the main form and subform do not matter because you can change the way the data is displayed in this Form Wizard dialog box. If the relationship between the tables has not been established, this Form Wizard dialog box will not display.

Main form—fields from 7A TV Shows table

Figure 7.15

Subform—fields from
7A Advertiser Info table

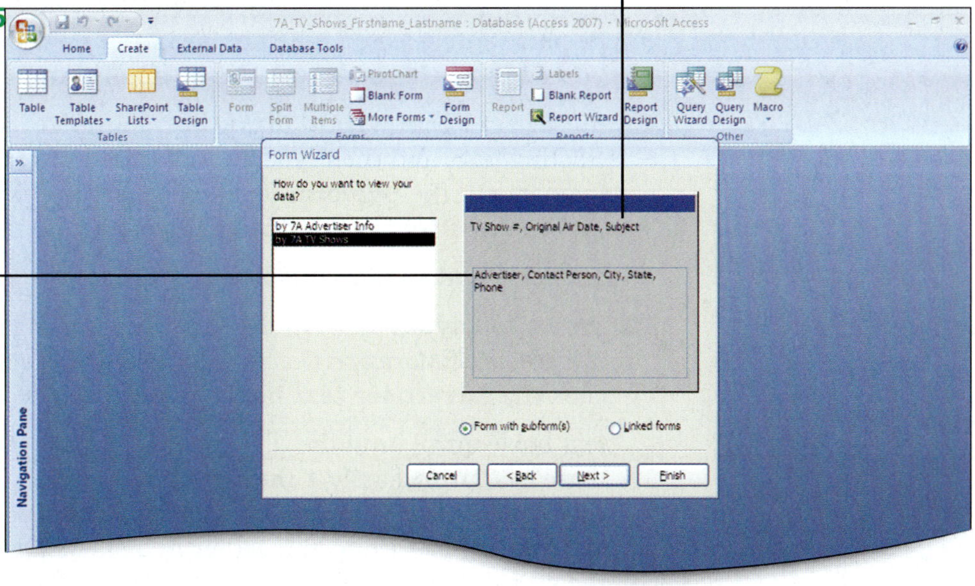

3 Under **How do you want to view your data?**, click **by 7A Advertiser Info**, and notice that the form will display with the *7A Advertiser Info table* as the main form and the *7A TV Shows* as the subform. Under the preview of the form, click **Linked forms**, and notice the preview displays two separate forms with a button on the main form that represents the link between the two forms.

A **linked form** is a related form that is not stored within the main form. To view the data in a linked form, click on the link that is displayed on the main form.

Note — Switching Main Form and Subform Tables

If the tables have a one-to-many relationship, and you switch the view to display the many side as the main form and the one side as the subform, the form will display as a single form instead of a main form with a subform. With a one-to-many relationship, the main form should display the table on the one side of the relationship, and the subform should display the table on the many side of the relationship.

4 Click **Form with subform(s)**, and then click **Next** to display the third **Form Wizard** dialog box, where you can select the subform layout. Notice the two layouts are **Tabular** and **Datasheet**, with Datasheet being the default layout.

Both layouts arrange the subform data in rows and columns, but the tabular layout is more customizable. You can add color, graphics, and other elements to a tabular subform. The subform you created in the previous activity used the datasheet layout, which is more compact than the tabular layout.

5 Click **Tabular**, and then click **Next** to display the fourth Form Wizard dialog box, where you can select the style for the form. Experiment by selecting several styles, noticing the preview of the form on the left side. When you are finished, click **Trek**, and then click **Next**.

Because you selected the Tabular layout on the previous Form Wizard page, this style will also be applied to the subform.

6 In the last **Form Wizard** dialog box, in the **Form** text box, select the existing text, and then type **7A Advertiser Info Form Firstname Lastname** In the **Subform** text box, select the existing text, type **7A TV Shows Subform Firstname Lastname** and then click **Finish**.

The form and subform display in Form view.

7 Switch to **Layout** view. In the main form, navigate to **Record 9**—*Advertiser* of *Maricopa County Stone and Marble*. In the main form, click the **Advertiser text box control**. Point to the right edge of the text box control until the ↔ pointer displays. Drag to the left until there is approximately **1 inch** of space between the data in the **Advertiser** field and the right edge of the text box control. Recall that the controls are grouped together in a stacked layout, so adjusting the size of one control adjusts the sizes of all of the controls. Do not be concerned if the data in the subform does not display.

8 Click the **Phone text box control**. Point to the **Phone text box control** until the ⌖ pointer displays. Drag upward until an orange horizontal line displays between the **Contact Person** field and the **City** field. Click the **City text box control**. Hold down ⇧ Shift, and then click the **State text box control** to select both controls. On the Ribbon, click the **Arrange tab**. In the **Control Layout group**, click the **Remove** button. Do not be concerned if the data in the subform does not display.

Recall that it is easier to have the fields that will be removed from a stacked layout at the bottom of the layout.

9 Point to the selected fields until the ⌖ pointer displays, and then drag upward and to the right until the **City** field aligns with the **Contact Person** field and there is approximately **.25 inch** of space between the *Contact Person text box control* and the *City label control*. With the two fields selected, in the **Control Layout group**, click the **Stacked** button. Point to the right edge of the **City label control** until the ↔ pointer displays. Drag the right edge of the **City label control** to the left until there is approximately **.5 inch** of space between the word *City* and the right edge of the *City label control*. Compare your screen with Figure 7.16.

After moving fields to a new column, you should group them as one layout for ease in making adjustments to the controls. The widths of the City and State label controls are decreased so that the text box controls will not exceed the printed page width.

Figure 7.16

Fields moved from first column

Widths of label controls
decreased

Main form—fields from
7A Advertiser Info table

Subform—fields from
7A TV Shows table

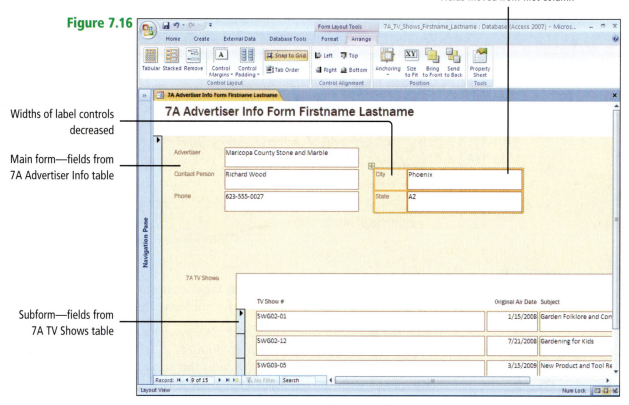

10 Using the techniques you have just practiced, select the **Advertiser text box control**, the **Contact Person text box control**, and the **Phone text box control**, and then **Remove** the controls from the stacked layout. Click in an empty area of the main form to deselect the controls, and then click the **Advertiser label control**. Hold down ⇧Shift, and then click the **Advertiser text box control** to select both controls. Point to one of the selected controls until the 🔲 pointer displays. Drag to the right until the controls are approximately centered between the controls on the left and the controls on the right. With the controls selected, on the **Arrange tab**, in the **Control Layout group**, click the **Stacked** button.

The Advertiser field is centered between the other controls and is contained in its own stacked layout. All three fields in the left stacked layout are removed from the stacked layout in order to keep the Advertiser field at the top of the column.

11 Click the **Contact Person label control**. Holding down ⇧Shift, click the **Contact Person text box control**, the **Phone label control**, and the **Phone text box control**. On the **Arrange tab**, in the **Control Layout group**, click the **Stacked** button. Compare your screen with Figure 7.17.

Figure 7.17

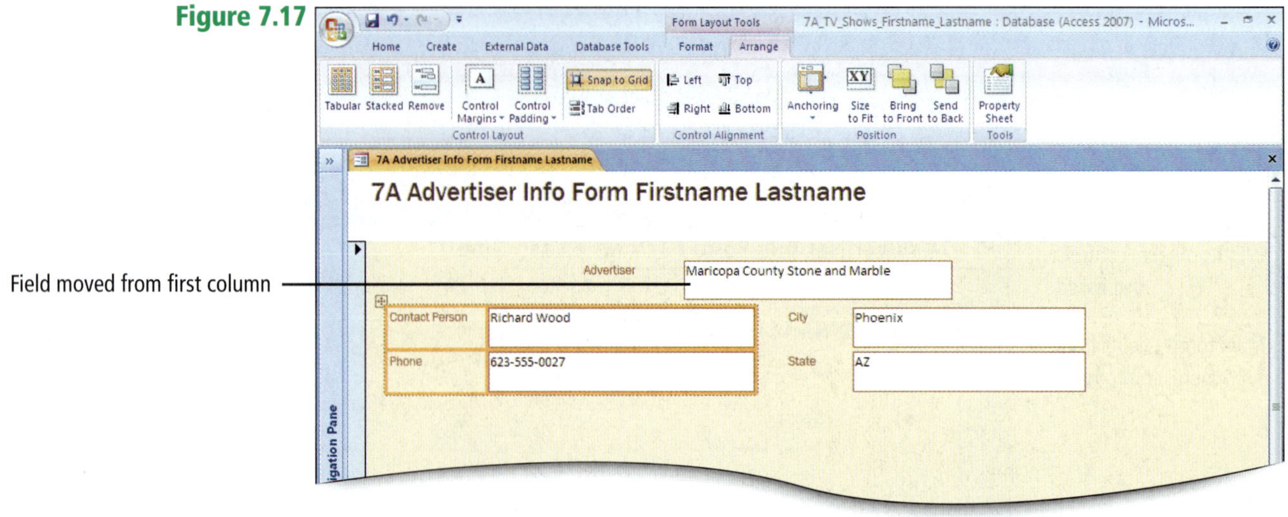

Field moved from first column

7A Advertiser Info Form Firstname Lastname

Advertiser	Maricopa County Stone and Marble
Contact Person	Richard Wood
Phone	623-555-0027
City	Phoenix
State	AZ

12 In the subform, click the **subform label control**—*7A TV Shows*—to display the **Layout Selector** for the subform. Point to the **Layout Selector** ⊞ until the ⌖ pointer displays. Drag the subform upward and to the left until there is approximately **.5 inch** of space between the **Phone** field and the subform, and the subform label control's left edge aligns with the left side of the main form.

The entire subform with tall and wide control boxes displays in tabular layout, and the horizontal scroll bar indicates that more of the subform can be displayed by scrolling to the right. After scrolling to the right, the vertical scroll bar indicates that more of the subform can be displayed by scrolling down.

13 With the subform selected, on the **Arrange tab**, in the **Tools group**, click the **Property Sheet** button. On the **Property Sheet**, click the **Selection type arrow**, and then click the *first* instance of **7A TV Shows Subform**. Compare your screen with Figure 7.18.

The first instance of *7A TV Shows Subform* is the entire subform. The second instance of *7A TV Shows Subform* is the subform label control. To be sure that you are selecting the correct item, click on the item from the list, and then view the item that is selected in the form or subform.

Figure 7.18

Property Sheet for subform

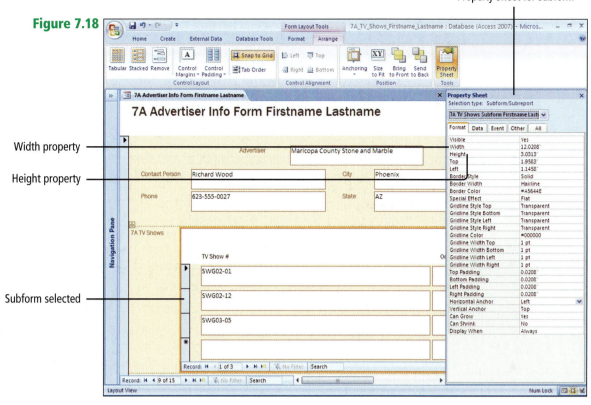

Width property

Height property

Subform selected

Navigation Pane

---

14 On the **Property Sheet Format tab**, select the **Width** property setting, type **6.5** and then press Enter.

Alert!

Did the property boxes disappear?

If the property boxes and settings disappear from the Property Sheet, on the Property Sheet, click the Data tab, and then click the Format tab. The property boxes and settings should redisplay.

15 Select the **Height** property setting, and then type **3** Press Enter, and then in the subform, click any **TV Show # text box control**. Notice that the **Property Sheet** displays for the **TV Show # text box control**. On the **Property Sheet Format tab**, change the **Width** property setting to **1** Change the **Height** property setting to **.25** and then press Enter.

The heights for all of the controls in the subform are adjusted, and the vertical scroll bar in the subform does not display.

16 In the subform, click any **Subject text box control**, and notice that the **Property Sheet** displays for the **Subject text box control**. On the **Property Sheet Format tab**, change the **Width** to **3.5** Press Enter, and then **Close** ✕ the **Property Sheet**.

The widths of the Subject controls are decreased, and the horizontal scroll bar in the subform does not display.

17 **Save** 🖫 the form. Using the techniques you practiced in the last activity, in the main form, add a **Logo** to the Form Header section using **a07A_Logo**, and then adjust the size of the logo so it is easily read. Move the form **title's label control** to the right of the logo, and display your name on the second line of the title. **Center** the text in the form title's label control, and, if necessary, align the right edge of the form title's label control with the right edge of the subform. **Horizontally anchor** the **title's label control** at the **left**. Compare your screen with Figure 7.19.

Title moved to right

Name displayed on second line of title

Figure 7.19

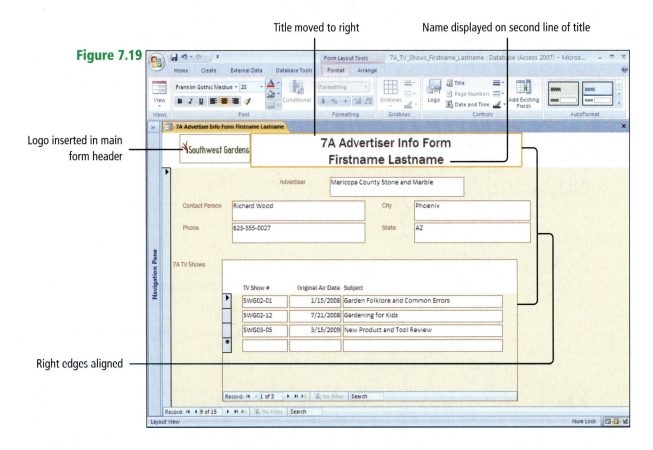

Logo inserted in main form header

Right edges aligned

18 **Save** the form, and then switch to **Design** view. Notice that the right margin of the form does not extend past 8 inches on the horizontal ruler; so there will be no extraneous pages printing. Also, notice that the entire title displays in the title's label control.

19 Switch to **Form** view. Press PgDn until the record for **Arizona Bank—**Record 4—displays. If you are instructed to submit this result, create a paper or electronic printout. only this record.

20 **Close** the form, and then expand the **Navigation Pane**. Under **Forms**, notice that **7A Advertiser Info Form** and **7A TV Shows Subform** display. Double-click **7A Advertiser Info Form** to open it in Form view. The subform is embedded in the form. Double-click **7A TV Shows Subform** to open it in Form view. This form displays the fields that were selected from the 7A TV Shows table that are used in the subform section of 7A Advertiser Info Form.

When a subform is created in a main form, a separate form object is created and displays on the Navigation Pane under Forms.

21 **Close All** forms.

More Knowledge

Adding the Table Name to the Subform

To add the name of the table used to create the subform at the top of the subform, add a label control to the Form Header section of the subform. Then type the name of the table. If the table name is added to the Form Header section, the label control with the table name that displays to the left of the subform should be deleted.

Activity 7.6 Creating a Subform by Dragging a Related Table Onto an Existing Form

In this activity, you will create a subform by dragging an existing table—*7A TV Show Advertisers*—that is on the *many* side of the relationship onto an existing form—*7A TV Shows Main Form*—that is on the *one* side of the relationship. If a form already exists, you do not have to re-create it using the Form Wizard to insert a subform. If a table has more than one relationship with other tables, this method is helpful in adding a subform to a form without using the Form Wizard. You can also drag a related form onto an existing form to create a subform.

1 On the **Navigation Pane**, under **Forms**, open **7A TV Shows Main Form** in Design view. On the **Design tab**, in the **Controls group**, be sure that the **Use Control Wizards** button is active.

The existing form must be open in Design view before dragging a related table onto it. If you try to drag a related table onto a form in Layout view, an error message displays.

2 In the form, point to the top of the **Form Footer section bar** until the pointer displays. Drag downward to the **3-inch mark on the vertical ruler** to create more space in the Detail section.

3 On the **Navigation Pane**, under **Tables**, drag **7A TV Show Advertisers** onto *7A TV Shows Main Form*—the main form—to the **1.75-inch mark on the vertical ruler** and even with the left edge of the form as displayed in Figure 7.20.

The first Subform Wizard dialog box displays, in which the fields are defined that link the main form with the subform. Notice at the bottom of the dialog box that Access will display records from the *7A TV Show Advertisers* table for each record in the *7A TV Shows* table using the *TV Show #* field—the common field.

Figure 7.20

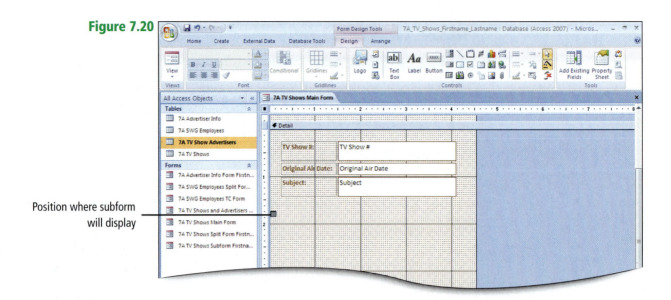

Position where subform will display

---

4 In the **Subform Wizard** dialog box, click **Define my own**.

The Subform Wizard dialog box changes to display list boxes in which you can select the fields that link the main form to the subform.

5 Under **Form/report fields**, in the **first list box**, click the **arrow**, and then click **TV Show #**. Under **Subform/subreport fields**, in the **first list box**, click the **arrow**, and then click **TV Show #**. Compare your screen with Figure 7.21.

The same field is used to link the form and the subform as when *Choose from a list* was selected. By default, Access uses the fields that are used to create the join line in the relationship between the tables. You should select *Define my own* when you want to use fields other than the common fields as defined in the relationship.

Figure 7.21

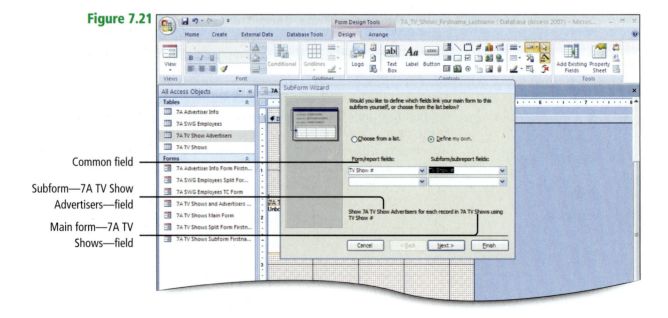

Common field

Subform—7A TV Show Advertisers—field

Main form—7A TV Shows—field

6 Click **Next**. Under **What name would you like for your subform or subreport?**, type **7A TV Show Advertisers Subform Firstname Lastname** and then click **Finish**. Compare your screen with Figure 7.22.

The subform displays under the label and text box controls of the main form, and a subform label control displays above the subform.

Figure 7.22

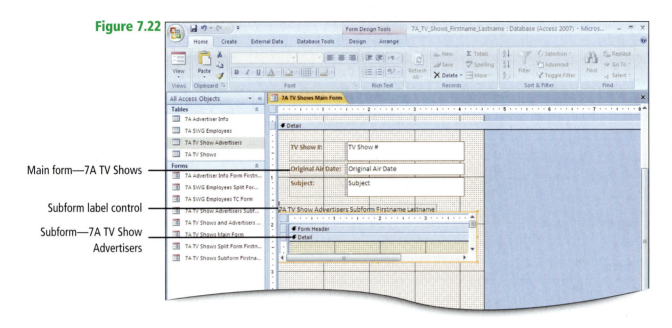

Main form—7A TV Shows

Subform label control

Subform—7A TV Show Advertisers

7 With the subform control selected, point to the **bottom middle sizing handle** of the subform control until the ⬍ pointer displays. If the subform is not selected, point to the bottom edge of the subform control, and then click to display the sizing handles. Drag downward to the **4-inch mark on the vertical ruler**. **Save** 🖫 the form, and then collapse « the **Navigation Pane**. Switch to **Layout** view. Press PgDn to display the record for each television show and the related record(s) in the subform. Notice that the **TV Show #** field displays in both the main form and in the subform.

8 In the navigation area for the main form, click the **First Record** button ◄. Switch to **Design** view. In the subform control, click the **TV Show # label control**, and then press Delete. Switch to **Layout** view.

The *TV Show* # field is removed from the subform.

9 Click the **subform control**. Point to the bottom edge of the **subform control** until the ⬍ pointer displays. Drag upward until the bottom edge of the subform aligns with the bottom edge of the blank row below the new record row. Point to the right edge of the **subform control** until the ↔ pointer displays. Drag to the left until the *right edge of the subform control* aligns with the *right edge of the Advertiser* text box controls, and then compare your screen with Figure 7.23.

Figure 7.23

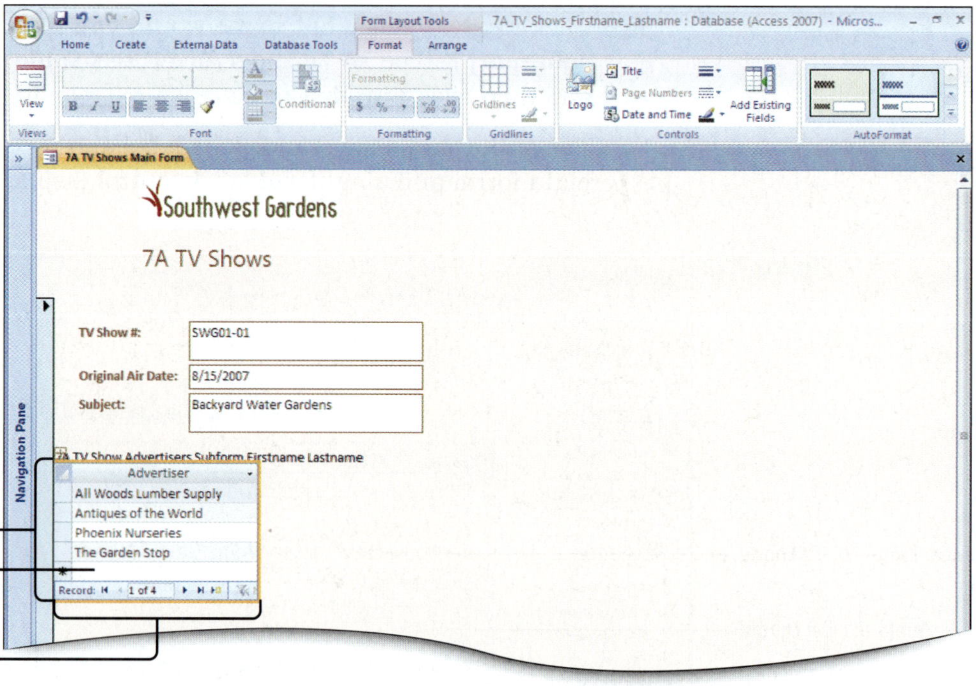

Subform height adjusted

New record row

Subform width adjusted

10 Click the **subform label control**, which displays *7A Show Advertisers Subform Firstname Lastname*, and then press Delete to remove the label control from the subform.

11 Click anywhere in the subform, and then point to the displayed **Layout Selector** until the pointer displays. Drag to the right until the subform is centered on the form.

12 **Horizontally anchor** the **label control** at the **left**. Change the title of the form to **7A TV Shows and Advertisers Firstname Lastname** and then place your name on the second line. Adjust the width of the **title's label control** so that the left edge of the label control aligns with the left edge of the field label controls, and the right edge of the title's label control aligns with the right edge of the field's text box controls. In the title's label control, **Center** the text, and then compare your screen with Figure 7.24.

Figure 7.24

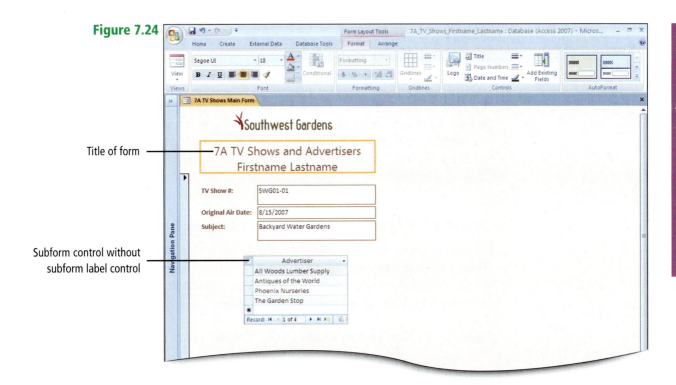

Title of form

Subform control without
subform label control

---

13 **Save** the form. If you are instructed to submit this result, create a paper or electronic printout of only the first record.

14 **Close** the form, and expand the **Navigation Pane**. Under **Forms**, **Rename** *7A TV Shows Main Form* to **7A TV Shows Main Form and Advertisers Subform Firstname Lastname**

More Knowledge

Creating a Form with Two Subforms or Nested Subforms

A form can contain more than one subform. The main form should have a one-to-many relationship with the first subform. The first subform should have a one-to-many relationship with the second subform. The main form would contain both subform controls. To create a form with two subforms, use the Form Wizard, selecting each table from the Tables/Queries drop-down list and each table's fields.

A form can also contain nested subforms. The main form should have a one-to-many relationship with the first subform. The first subform should have a one-to-many relationship with the second subform. Instead of the main form containing both subform controls, the first subform would contain the second subform control. You can have a maximum of seven levels of subforms. Create a form that contains a subform, and then in Design view, click the subform. On the Design tab, in the Tools group, click the Subform in New Window button. From the Navigation Pane, drag a form, table, or query to the subform and then link the fields between the first subform and the nested subform.

Objective 3
Create a Multi-Page Form

A *multi-page form* displays the data from the underlying table or query on more than one page. Creating a multi-page form enables you to divide a long form into sections that display on separate pages or to display subforms on different tabs within the main form. A multi-page form enables the user to display only the data that needs to be accessed, and displays the form in a more organized format.

Activity 7.7 Creating a Multi-Page Form Using the Tab Control

In this activity, you will modify a single form to create a multi-page form using the *tab control*. A tab control is used to display data on the main form on different tabs, similar to the way database objects, such as forms and tables, display on different tabs.

1 On the **Navigation Pane**, under **Forms**, open **7A SWG Employees TC Form** in Design view, and then collapse ⏩ the **Navigation pane**. Point to the top of the **Form Footer section bar** until the ⊕ pointer displays. Drag downward to the **3-inch mark on the vertical ruler** to increase the height of the Detail section.

2 On the **Design tab**, in the **Controls group**, click the **Tab Control** button 🔳. Move the 🔳 pointer into the **Detail** section until the plus (**+**) sign of the 🔳 pointer is aligned approximately with the **.25-inch mark on the horizontal ruler** and with the **.25-inch mark on the vertical ruler**. Click one time, and then compare your screen with Figure 7.25.

A tab control is inserted into the Detail section of the form. There are two tabs on the tab control. Each tab represents a separate page on the form. Do not be concerned if the page numbers on your tabs differ from those displayed in Figure 7.25.

Tab control button

Figure 7.25

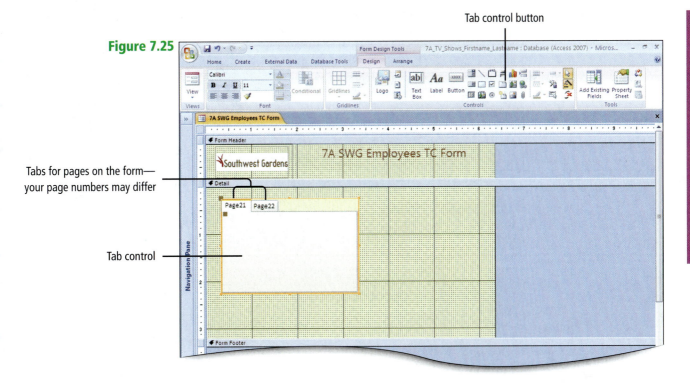

Tabs for pages on the form—
your page numbers may differ

Tab control

3 In the selected **tab control**, point to the **right middle sizing handle** until the ⟷ pointer displays. Drag to the right until the right edge of the tab control aligns with the **6-inch mark on the horizontal ruler**.

4 On the **Design tab**, in the **Tools group**, click the **Add Existing Fields** button.

The Field List for the *7A SWG Employees* table displays.

5 In the **Field List**, click **ID#**. Hold down ⇧ Shift, and then click **Last Name** to select three fields. Hold down Ctrl, click **Hire Date**, and then click **Photo** to select two additional fields. Point to a selected field, and then drag downward and to the left onto the first tab until the top of the arrow of the pointer aligns with the **1.5-inch mark on the horizontal ruler** and with the **.75-inch mark on the vertical ruler**. Compare your screen with Figure 7.26.

The controls for the fields are arranged in a stacked layout on the first tab in the tab control, and Access automatically adjusts the height of the tab control so that all of the controls display. The controls are not grouped together.

Figure 7.26

7A SWG Employees Field List

Fields dragged down to first tab

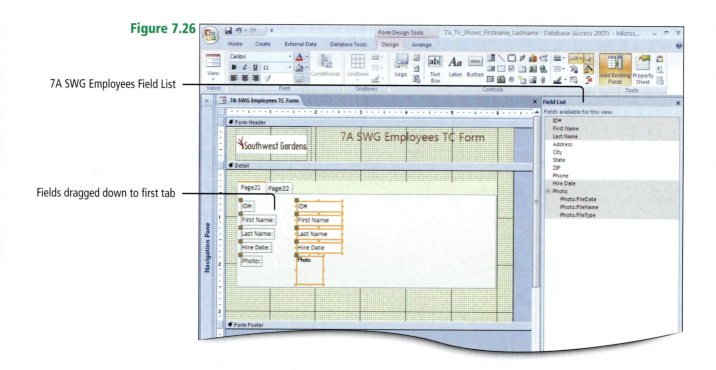

6 **Close** ✕ the **Field List**. Click in an empty area of the tab control to deselect the controls. Hold down ⇧ Shift, and then click the **label controls** and **text box controls** for the **Hire Date** and **Photo** fields.

Point to the selected controls until the ⇱ pointer displays. Drag to the right and upward until the *Hire Date* controls align with the *ID#* controls and there is approximately **.5 inch** of space between the two columns. Do not be concerned if the controls do not exactly align.

7 With the controls selected, on the Ribbon, click the **Arrange tab**. In the **Control Layout group**, click the **Stacked** button to group the controls together. Click the **ID# label control** to deselect the controls in the second column. Using the techniques you have just practiced, select all of the controls in the first column, and then group them together in a **Stacked** layout.

8 Click the **Layout Selector** ⊹ for the first column. Hold down ⇧ Shift, click the **Hire Date label control**, and then click the **Layout Selector** ⊹ above the second column to select both columns. On the **Arrange tab**, in the **Control Alignment group**, click the **Top** button, and then compare your screen with Figure 7.27.

Figure 7.27

Access | chapter 7

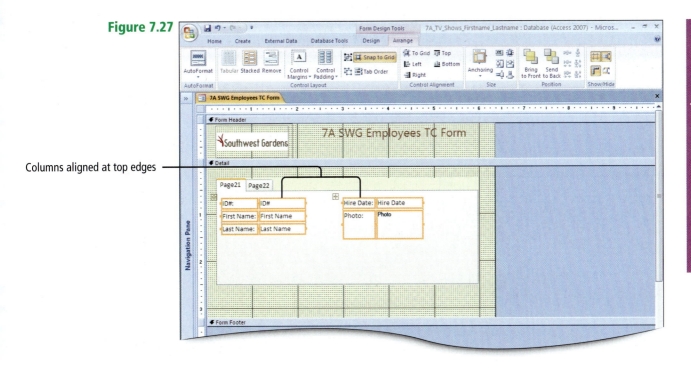

Columns aligned at top edges

9 **Save** 🖫 the form, and then switch to **Layout** view. Press [PgDn] several times to display the other records in the table, ensuring that all of the data displays in all of the fields.

10 Switch to **Design** view. In the **Detail** section, click the **second tab**, which has no controls added to it. On the **Design tab**, in the **Tools group**, click the **Add Existing Fields** button. In the **Field List**, click **Address**. Hold down [⇧ Shift], and then click **Phone** to select five fields. Point to the selected fields, and then drag downward and to the left

onto the second tab until the top of the arrow of the 🔲 pointer aligns with the **1.5-inch mark on the horizontal ruler** and with the **.75-inch mark on the vertical ruler**.

11 Using the techniques you have practiced, move the **Phone label control** and **Phone text box control** upward and to the right until the controls are aligned with the **Address** controls. Arrange the **Phone controls** in a **Stacked** layout. Arrange the eight controls in the first column in a **Stacked** layout. Align the tops of both

columns, **Close** ⊠ the **Field List**, and then compare your screen with Figure 7.28.

Figure 7.28

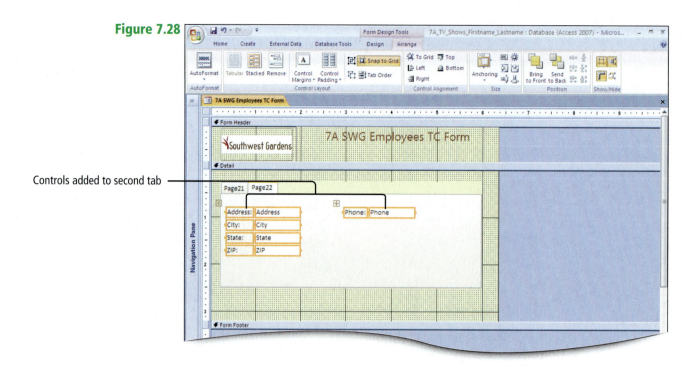

Controls added to second tab

12 **Save** 📅 the form, and then switch to **Layout** view. Click the **second tab** and notice that the data in the **Address** field is truncated. Press ⌨PgDn **three** times to display **Record 4**. Point to the right edge of the **Address text box control** until the ↔ pointer displays, and then drag to the right until the entire address displays in the text box control.

13 Right-click the **first tab**, and then click **Properties**. The Property Sheet displays *Selection type: Page*, and the Selection type box displays the page number of the tab. Click in the **Caption** property setting box, type **Employee Name and Photo** and then press ⌨Enter.

The first tab displays the text you entered in the Caption property setting box.

14 In the form, click the **second tab** to display the **Property Sheet** for the second tab. Click in the **Caption** property setting box, type **Address and Phone** and then press ⌨Enter to change the text on the second tab.

Close ✕ the **Property Sheet**. In the form, click the **Employee Name and Photo tab** to display the first page of the form.

15 Change the **title** of the form to **7A Employees Tab Control Form Firstname Lastname** and then place your first and last name on the second line of the title. Align the right edge of the title's label control with the right edge of the tab control, and then switch to **Form** view.

16 **Save** 📅 the form, and, if necessary, navigate to **Record 4**. Press ⌨Alt + ⌨PrtScr to place a copy of the screen into the Clipboard. Open **Microsoft Office Word 2007**. On the **Home tab**, in the **Clipboard group**, click the **Paste** button to place the screen shot in the Word document window. Press ⌨Ctrl + ⌨End to move to the end of the Word document, and then press ⌨Enter to insert a blank line at the bottom of the document. **Minimize** ➖ the Word window.

Because it takes a long time for Access to format a form that contains a tab control for printing, you are copying the screens displaying the data on the tabs into Word, and then printing the Word document.

17 In the **Access** window, on the form, click the **Address and Phone tab**. Press [Alt] + [PrtScr] to place a copy of the screen into the Clipboard. On the taskbar, click the **Document1 - Microsoft** button to display the Word document. In the **Word** window, on the **Home tab**, in the **Clipboard group**, click the **Paste** button to place the second copy of the screen in the Word document window.

18 In the **Word** window, on the **Quick Access Toolbar**, click the **Save** button 🖫. Navigate to the **Access Chapter 7** folder, and save the file as **7A_Tab_Control_Form_Firstname_Lastname** If you are instructed to submit this result, create a paper or electronic printout of the document.

The screen copy of the first tab prints on the first page, and the screen copy of the second tab prints on the second page.

19 **Close** ⊠ the **Word** window. If necessary, on the taskbar, click the **Access** button. In the **Access** window, **Close** ⊠ the form, and then expand ⊠ the **Navigation Pane**. **Close** the database, and then **Exit** Access.

End **You have completed Project 7A** —————————————

Project 7B Web Site Orders

Media Southwest Productions maintains a Web site where customers can order gardening supplies that are featured in the Southwest Gardens television show. Creating advanced reports will help the president and officers of the production company view the information in the database in a different way. In Activities 7.8 through 7.14, you will create advanced reports that display data from multiple tables and from a parameter query. You will also create an alphabetic index of garden suppliers. Your completed reports will look similar to those shown in Figure 7.29.

For Project 7B, you will need the following file:

a07B_Web_Site_Orders

You will save your database as
7B_Web_Site_Orders_Firstname_Lastname

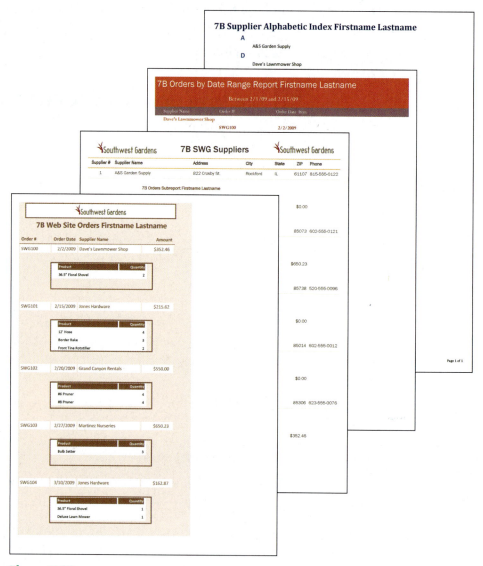

Figure 7.29
Project 7B—Web Site Orders

Objective 4
Create and Modify a Subreport

Reports can include information from more than one table in the database. For example, Media Southwest Productions wants to create a report listing all of the orders that were placed on the Web site, and then under each order number, the products and quantities that were included in the order. One way to accomplish this is to create a **subreport**. A subreport is a report that is embedded within another report—the **main report**.

Similar to forms and subforms, one report must serve as the main report, and another report is embedded within the main report. The main report is either bound or unbound. A **bound report** displays data from an underlying table, query, or SQL statement as specified in the report's Record Source property. An **unbound report** does not display data from an underlying table, query, or SQL statement and has an empty Record Source property setting. A **SQL statement** is an instruction using Structured Query Language. An example of an unbound report being used as the main form would be a report that displays a title, logo, and date, similar to a report header. A main report can also contain a subform instead of a subreport. A main report can contain up to seven levels of subforms and subreports.

Activity 7.8 Using the SubReport Wizard to Create a Subreport

In this activity, you will create a subreport using the SubReport Wizard. The main report will display the Web site orders, and the subreport will display the products that were ordered. Before creating a subreport using the SubReport Wizard, the underlying tables or queries should have established relationships.

1 **Start Access**. Navigate to the location where the student data files for this textbook are saved. Locate and open the **a07B_Web_Site_Orders** file. Save the database in the **Access 2007 Database** format in your **Access Chapter 7** folder as **7B_Web_Site_Orders_Firstname_Lastname**

2 If you did not add the Access Chapter 7 folder to the Trust Center, enable the content. Because some of the fields in the tables are lookup fields, you will not rename any of the tables. Collapse 《 the **Navigation Pane**.

3 On the Ribbon, click the **Database Tools tab**. In the **Show/Hide group**, click the **Relationships** button. Take a moment to review the relationships between the tables.

There is a *one-to-many* relationship between the *7B SWG Suppliers* table and the *7B Web Site Orders* table. There is a *one-to-many* relationship between the *7B Web Site Orders* table and the *7B Web Site Order Detail* table. There is a *one-to-many* relationship between the *7B Web Site Garden Supplies* table and the *7B Web Site Order Detail* table. The *7B Web Site Order Detail* table is a junction table that is used to create a *many-to-many* relationship between the *7B Web Site Orders* table and the *7B Web Site Garden Supplies* table.

4 **Close** ✕ the Relationships window, and then expand ⟩⟩ the **Navigation Pane**. Under **Reports**, right-click **7B Orders Report**, and then click **Copy**. On the **Home tab**, in the **Clipboard group**, click the **Paste** button. In the **Paste As** dialog box, under **Report Name**, and with the existing text selected, type **7B Orders Main Report Firstname Lastname** and then click **OK**.

On the Navigation Pane under Reports, the newly named copy of the *7B Orders Report* displays.

5 Open **7B Orders Main Report** in **Layout** view, and then collapse ⟨⟨ the **Navigation Pane**. Click the **small box** in the upper left corner of the report, where the top and left margins intersect. Recall that clicking this box selects the report. On the Ribbon, click the **Arrange tab**. In the **Tools group**, click the **Property Sheet** button.

The Property Sheet should display *Selection type: Report*.

6 Click the **Property Sheet Data tab**, and then compare your screen with Figure 7.30. Notice that the **Record Source** property setting is *7B Web Site Orders*.

7B Orders Main Report is bound to the *7B Web Site Orders* table.

Figure 7.30

Property Sheet for report ——

Report selector box ——

Report is bound to this table ——

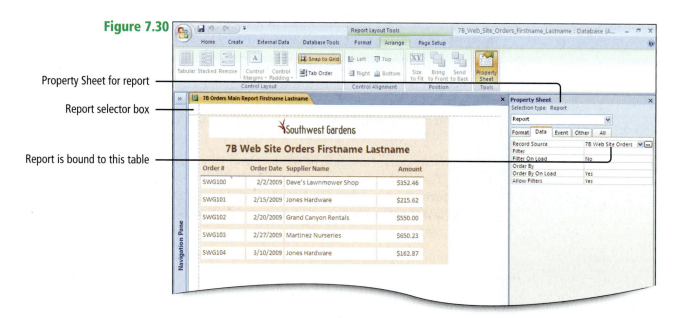

7 **Close** ✕ the **Property Sheet**, and then switch the report to **Design** view. In the **Report Header** section, click the **title's label control,** and then click one more time to enter into the editing mode. Change *Firstname Lastname* to your own first name and last name, and then press ⏎. In the report, point to the top of the **Page Footer section bar** until the ⊕ pointer displays. Drag downward to the **1-inch mark on the vertical ruler** to make room in the Detail section for the subreport.

8 On the **Design tab**, in the **Controls group**, be sure that the **Use Control Wizards** button ⬛ is active. In the **Controls group**, click the **Subform/Subreport** button ⬛. Move the mouse pointer down into the **Detail** section until the top of the plus (+) sign of the ⬛ pointer aligns with the **1-inch mark on the horizontal ruler** and with the **.5-inch mark on the vertical ruler**, and then click.

A subreport control is inserted into the Detail section of the report, and the SubReport Wizard dialog box displays. The control displays *Unbound* because the control has not yet been linked to a record source. In this first dialog box, select the existing table, query, report, or form to use as the source of data for the subreport.

9 In the **SubReport Wizard** dialog box, be sure that **Use existing Tables and Queries** is selected, and then click **Next**.

The second SubReport Wizard dialog box enables an individual to select the table or query and the fields to use in the subreport.

10 Click the **Tables/Queries** box **arrow**, and from the displayed list, click **Table: 7B Web Site Order Detail**. Under **Available Fields**, double-click **Product**, and then double-click **Quantity** to move the fields to the **Selected Fields** box. Click **Next**.

The third SubReport Wizard dialog box enables you to define the fields that link the main form to the subreport. Because there is a one-to-many relationship between the two tables, the default setting is to show the data in the *7B Web Site Order Detail* table for each record in the *7B Web Site Orders* table.

11 Click **Next**, name the report **7B Products Ordered Subreport Firstname Lastname** and then click **Finish**. Switch to **Report** view, and then compare your screen with Figure 7.31. Do not be concerned if your subreport labels are not in exactly the same location as Figure 7.31.

The subreport data displays under each record from the *7B Web Site Orders* table. For example, for *Order # SWG100*, two 36.5" Floral Shovels were ordered.

Figure 7.31

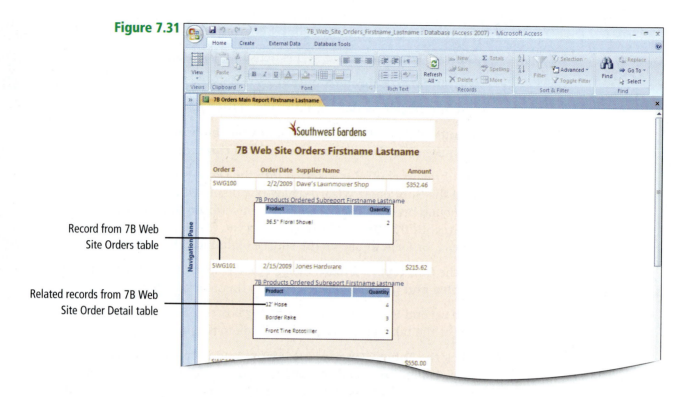

Record from 7B Web
Site Orders table

Related records from 7B Web
Site Order Detail table

Activity 7.9 Modifying a Subreport

Just like the main report, the subreport can be modified. In this activity, you will remove the name of the subreport, change the background color of the headings in the subreport, and change the border color of the subreport. You can modify the subreport in either Layout view or Design view.

1 Switch to **Layout** view. In any subreport control, click the **subreport label control**, which displays *7B Products Ordered Subreport*, and then press Delete.

The label control for the subreport no longer displays.

2 In any subreport control, click the **Product label control**. Hold down ⬆Shift and click the **Quantity label control** to select both controls. On the **Format tab**, in the **Font group**, click the **Fill/Back Color button arrow** ⬇. Under **Standard Colors**, on the sixth row, click the tenth color—**Brown 5**. With the label controls still selected, in the **Font group**, click the **Font Color button arrow** **A**⬇. Under **Standard Colors**, on the first row, click the first color—**White**. Click anywhere in the main form to deselect the label controls.

3 Click anywhere in the subreport, and then click the **Layout Selector** ⊞. On the **Format tab**, in the **Controls group**, click the **Line Color button arrow** ⬇. Under **Standard Colors**, on the sixth row, click the tenth color—**Brown 5**. In the **Controls group**, click the **Line Thickness button arrow** ≡⬇. In the displayed list, click the third line—**2 pt**—and then click anywhere in the main form to display the results of the formatting.

The subreport displays with a thicker brown border. Adding the thicker border decreased the area where the data displays, causing a horizontal scroll bar to display at the bottom of the subreport.

4 Click any **subreport control**—not a field label control or text box control in the subreport—and then point to the right edge of the subreport control until the ↔ pointer displays. Drag to the right approximately **.5 inch** to remove the horizontal scroll bar in the subreport. If the horizontal scroll bar still displays, drag the right edge of the subreport control to the right until the horizontal scroll bar no longer displays.

5 Using the techniques you have just practiced, add a **2 pt**, **Brown 5** border to the **logo control**, switch to **Report view**, and then compare your screen with Figure 7.32.

Figure 7.32

Border added to logo control

Font color and background color changed

Subreport control border changed

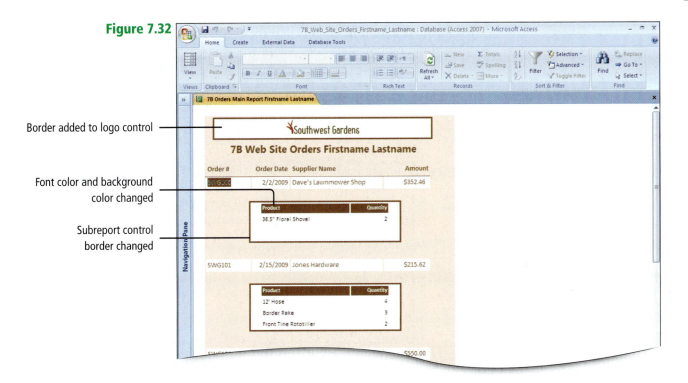

6 **Save** the report. If you are instructed to submit this result, view the report in **Print Preview**, be sure the **Margins** are set to **Narrow**, and then create a paper or electronic printout.

7 **Close** the Print Preview window and the report, and then expand the **Navigation Pane**.

Activity 7.10 Creating a Subreport by Adding an Object to an Existing Report

In this activity, you will drag the *7B Web Site Orders* table onto the *7B SWG Suppliers Report* to create a subreport. For the subreport to be linked to the main report, the underlying tables should have an established relationship. You can also create a subreport by dragging an existing form, subform, query, report, or subreport onto a report.

1 On the **Navigation Pane**, under **Reports**, locate **7B SWG Suppliers Report**, and then open the report in **Design view**. In the report, point to the top of the **Page Footer section bar** until the ⊞ pointer displays. Drag downward to the **1.75-inch mark on the vertical ruler** to make room in the Detail section for the subreport.

2 On the **Navigation Pane**, under **Tables**, click **7B Web Site Orders**, and then drag the table to the right onto the **Detail** section until the top of the ▦ pointer aligns with the **1-inch mark on the horizontal ruler** and the **.75-inch mark on the vertical ruler** as shown in Figure 7.33.

The SubReport Wizard dialog box displays, and suggests that the Supplier Name field in both tables be used as the field to link the *7B Web Site Orders* table and the *7B SWG Suppliers* table together. If you were dragging an existing report onto this report that had an established relationship between the underlying tables, the SubReport Wizard dialog box would not display.

Figure 7.33

1-inch mark on horizontal ruler

Indicates table is being dragged

.75-inch mark on vertical ruler

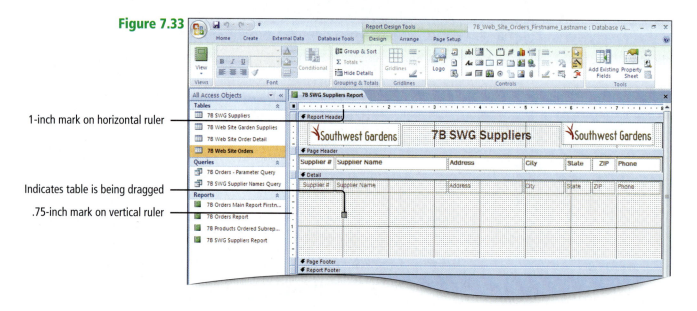

3 In the **SubReport Wizard** dialog box, be sure that **Choose from a list is selected**, and then click **Next**. Name the subreport **7B Orders Subreport Firstname Lastname** and then click **Finish**. On the **Navigation Pane**, notice that the newly created subreport displays under **Reports**.

4 Press `F4` to display the Property Sheet for the Subreport, and then collapse « the **Navigation Pane**. Click the **Property Sheet Data tab**, click in the **Link Master Fields** property setting box, and then click the **Build** button ▭. Compare your screen with Figure 7.34.

The Subreport Field Linker dialog box displays. The fields that are used to link the two underlying record sources together are displayed. The Master Fields property setting box displays the linked field in the main report. The Child Fields property setting box displays the linked field in the subreport. Access uses the two fields to display the related fields in both the main report and the subreport. Use the Subreport Field Linker dialog box to change the linked fields if the subreport does not display the data in the manner for which you intended. If you are unsure of which fields to link, click the Suggest button.

Figure 7.34

Field in subreport

Field in main report

Click to display suggested links based on relationships

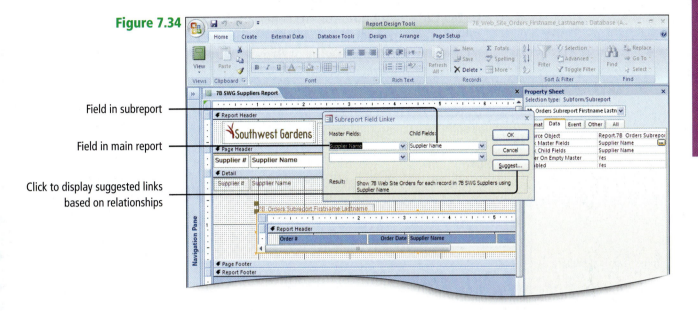

5 In the **Subreport Field Linker** dialog box, click **OK**. **Close** ✕ the **Property Sheet**, **Save** 🖫 the report, and then switch to **Layout view**. Notice that **Record 1** displays no data in the subreport; no orders have been placed with A&S Garden Supply. Notice that Record 2 displays one order in the subreport.

6 In the main report, locate Record 2—**Martinez Nurseries**. Notice that the subreport for this record also displays the name of the supplier in the third field. In the **subreport control** for **Record 2**, click **Martinez Nurseries**, and then press Delete to remove the label and text box controls and the redundant data.

7 Click the **subreport's Layout Selector** ✥, and then press F4 to display the Property Sheet for the Subreport. Click the **Property Sheet Format tab**, select the text in the **Width** property setting box, type **4.3** and then press Enter to change the width of the subreport control. **Close** ✕ the **Property Sheet**.

8 Click the **subreport label control**—*7B Orders Subreport Firstname Lastname*. Point to the selected label control until the 🔾 pointer displays, and then drag the control to the right until it is approximately centered between the margins of the subreport control. Change the **Font Color** of the text in the selected label control to **Brown 5**, and then add **Bold** formatting to the text.

The subreport has been modified, and the redundant field has been removed. A horizontal scroll bar displays in the subreport.

9 In the subreport control for Record 2, click the **Order # label control**.

Point to the right edge of the label control until the $\leftrightarrow$ pointer displays. Drag to the left until there is approximately **.5 inch** of space between *SWG103* and the right edge of the label control.

10 With the **Order # label control** selected, hold down ⇧Shift, click the **Order Date label control**, and then click the **Amount label control** to select all three label controls. Change the **Font Color** to **White**, change the **Fill/Back Color** to **Brown 5**, and then compare your screen with Figure 7.35.

Figure 7.35

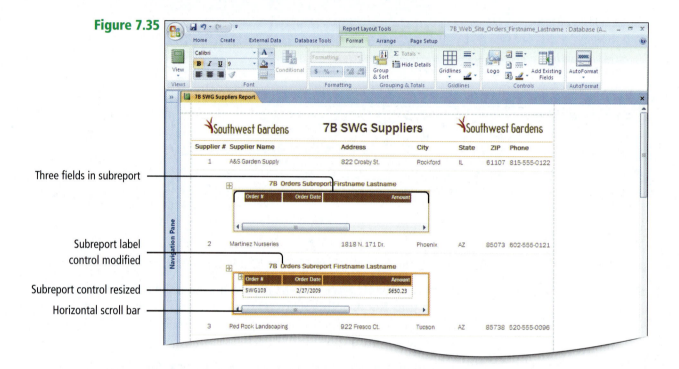

Three fields in subreport

Subreport label control modified

Subreport control resized

Horizontal scroll bar

11 Save the report, and then switch to **Design** view.

Activity 7.11 Displaying a Total from a Subreport on the Main Report

1 On the **Design tab**, in the **Tools group**, click the **Subreport in New Window** button.

The subreport displays on its own tab, and all of the controls are displayed, which makes it easier to edit.

2 On the **Design tab**, in the **Tools group**, click the **Property Sheet** button. Be sure that the Property Sheet displays *Selection type: Report*. On the **Property Sheet Format tab**, change the **Width** property setting to **4.3** and then **Close** the **Property Sheet**.

Recall that the subreport control displayed a horizontal scroll bar—this is because the actual subreport's width was wider than the size of the control. By making the width of the report the same as the width of the subreport control, the scroll bar will no longer display in the *7B SWG Suppliers Report*.

3 **Save** 🖫 *7B Orders Subreport*. In the **Detail** section, click the **Amount text box control**. On the **Design tab**, in the **Grouping & Totals group**, click the **Totals** button, and then click **Sum** to insert a calculated control into the Report Footer section.

4 **Save** 🖫 the subreport, and then **Close** ❌ *7B Orders Subreport*.

To view the results of the changes made to the subreport in the main report, you first must close the subreport.

5 Switch *7B SWG Suppliers Report* to **Report** view. Notice that the horizontal scroll bar no longer displays, and that in the subreport controls, **Record 1** displays a total Amount of **$0.00** and **Record 2** displays a total Amount of **$650.23**. Scroll down to display **Record 7**, which displays a total Amount of **$378.49**.

Adding a sum to a field in the subreport causes the sum to display in the subreport control on the main form.

6 Switch to **Design** view. On the **Design tab**, in the **Tools group**, click the **Subreport in New Window** button 🖳. Click the **Report Footer section bar**, and then press F4 to display the Property Sheet for the Report Footer section. On the **Property Sheet Format tab**, click in the **Visible** property setting box, which displays **Yes**. Click the **arrow**, and then click **No**.

The data in the Report Footer section will not display when the report is displayed in any view other than Design view. You will be displaying the calculated field in the main form, so it is being hidden from view.

7 In the **Report Footer** section, click the **calculated control**. The **Property Sheet** displays *Selection type: Text Box*, and the **Selection type** box displays *AccessTotalsAmount*. Click the **Property Sheet Other tab**, and then click in the **Name** property setting box. Select **AccessTotalsAmount**, type **Total Amount** and then press Enter. Compare your screen with Figure 7.36.

The Selection type box displays Total Amount, which is the new name of the text box control that displays the sum of the amount field. Rename controls to easily remember the name, especially if the control name is used somewhere else in the form. You will be using this control name to display the total of the amount field in the main form.

Figure 7.36

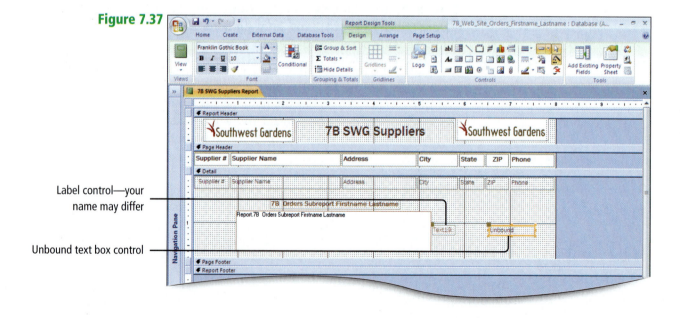

Name given to text box control

8 **Close** ✕ the **Property Sheet**, **Save** 💾 the report, and then **Close** ✕ *7B Orders Subreport*. Switch *7B SWG Suppliers Report* to **Report** view, and notice that the sum of the Amount field no longer displays in the subreport control.

9 Switch to **Design** view. On the **Design tab**, in the **Controls group**, click the **Text Box** button 🔲. Move the mouse pointer down to the **Detail** section until the top of the plus (+) sign aligns with the **6.5-inch mark on the horizontal ruler** and with the **1-inch mark on the vertical ruler**, and then click. Compare your screen with Figure 7.37.

A text box control with an associated label control displays in the Detail section. The text box control displays Unbound because the control is not linked to a field.

Figure 7.37

Label control—your name may differ

Unbound text box control

10 In the **Detail** section, click the **label control** that is associated with the unbound text box control, and then press `F4` to display the Property Sheet for the label control. Click the **Property Sheet Format tab**, select the text in the **Caption** property setting box, and then type **Total Amt:** Select the text in the **Width** property setting box, type **.75** and then press `Enter` to increase the width of the label control.

The Caption property setting controls the text that is displayed in the label control associated with the unbound text box control.

11 In the **Detail** section, click the **unbound text box control**. If the control is hidden behind the Property Sheet, decrease the width of the Property Sheet by dragging the left edge of the Property Sheet to the right. Click the **Property Sheet Data tab**, and then click in the **Control Source** property setting box. Click the displayed **Build** button ▣.

The Expression Builder dialog box displays. Although you can type the expression directly in the Control Source property setting box, the Expression Builder dialog box is similar to the Zoom dialog box, where you can see the entire typed expression. The Control Source property setting is used to link the text box control to a field.

12 In the **Expression Builder** dialog box, and using your own first name and last name, type **=IIf(IsError([7B Orders Subreport Firstname Lastname].[Report]![Total Amount]),0,[7B Orders Subreport Firstname Lastname].[Report]![Total Amount])** and then compare your screen with Figure 7.38.

You could have typed a more simple expression of =[7B Orders Subreport Firstname Lastname].[Report]![Total Amount]. The expression starts with an equal (=) sign and is followed by the name of the report enclosed in brackets. A period separates the report name with the object name—Reports—which is also enclosed in brackets. In this expression, you do not need [Report] because the name of the report is unique within the database. Many times, however, the name of the report is the same as the underlying record source, so you could have a table and a report with the same name. The exclamation (!) mark is called a *bang operator*. The bang operator tells Access that what follows it is an object that belongs to the object that precedes it in the expression. In this expression, Total Amount is an object in the 7B Orders Subreport Report. Recall that you renamed the calculated control in the subreport to Total Amount.

You typed a more complex expression. If the subreport does not contain any data, the control on the main report displays #Error when printed. To prevent this, use the IsError function within the IIf function, which will ensure that something other than #Error displays in the field; for example, display 0 if there is no data. The IIf function checks for the #Error message in the Total Amount field of 7B Orders Subreport. If #Error is found, 0 is displayed in the field. If #Error is not found, the data in the Total Amount field of 7B Orders Subreport is displayed.

Figure 7.38

Source report name

Source field name

Source object type

Bang operator

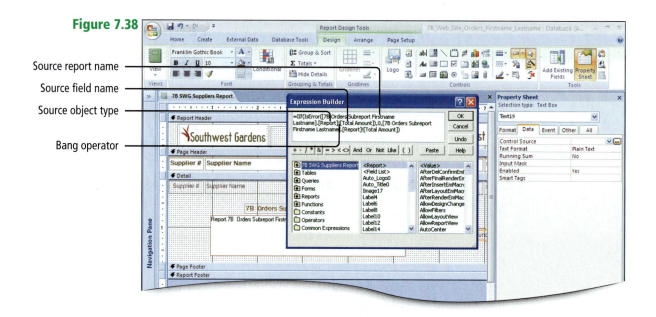

13 In the **Expression Builder** dialog box, click **OK**, and then press ⬇.

The expression displays in the Control Source property setting box.

Alert! **Does a message box display?**

If a message box displays stating that the expression contains invalid syntax, click OK. In the Control Source property setting box, click the Build button, and correct the expression. *Syntax* is the set of rules by which words and symbols in an expression are combined.

14 Click the **Property Sheet Format tab**. Click in the **Format** property setting box, click the displayed **arrow**, and then click **Currency**.

Close ☒ the **Property Sheet**.

The data that was typed in the Control Source property setting box displays in the text box control.

15 With the text box control selected, point to the small brown box that displays in the upper left corner of the text box control until the ⬉ pointer displays. Drag to the left until the left edge of the text box control aligns with the right edge of the label control that displays *Total Amt:*.

Dragging the small box that displays in the upper left corner of a control enables you to move only that control. If you point to any other part of the control before dragging, the control and its associated controls are moved.

16 **Save** 🖫 the report, and then switch to **Report** view. Scroll down to display **Record 7**, and then compare your screen with Figure 7.39.

The sum of the Amount field in the subreport is displayed in the main report and is formatted as Currency.

Figure 7.39

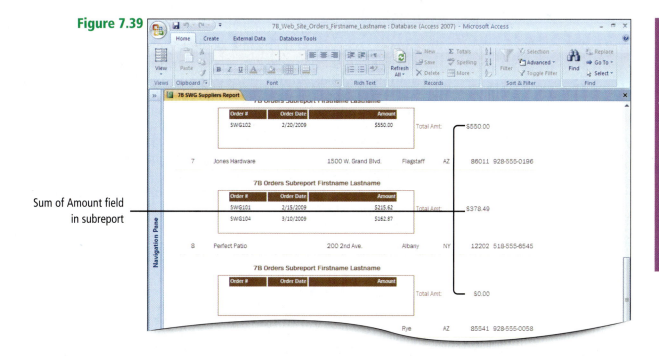

Sum of Amount field
in subreport

Alert!

Does an Enter Parameter Value message box display?

If an Enter Parameter Value message box displays, you probably typed the name of the subreport or the name of the field incorrectly. If this occurs, repeat Steps 11 and 12, ensuring that you type the expression correctly.

17 If you are instructed to submit this result, view the report in **Print Preview**, be sure the **Margins** are set to **Narrow**, and then create a paper or electronic printout.

18 **Close** ☒ the Print Preview window and the report, and then expand ☒ the **Navigation Pane**.

Objective 5
Create a Report Based on a Parameter Query

Recall that a *parameter query* prompts an individual for criteria before running the query. Using a parameter query as the record source for a report enables the user to set the criteria for the report when the report is opened. Recall that when a report is opened, the underlying table or query in the report is read to ensure that the report displays the most current data. Media Southwest Productions maintains a table to keep track of the Web site orders. A parameter query was created to display the orders between a range of dates.

Activity 7.12 Creating a Report Based on a Parameter Query

In this activity, you will view the design of the *7B Orders - Parameter Query*, and then create a report based on the parameter query.

1 On the **Navigation Pane**, under **Queries**, right-click **7B Orders - Parameter Query**, and then click **Design View**. In the design grid under **Order Date**, right-click in the **Criteria** row; and from the shortcut menu, click **Zoom**. In the **Zoom** dialog box, click anywhere in an empty area to deselect the expression. Compare your screen with Figure 7.40.

When the query is run, you are prompted to enter the first date in the range of dates, and then the ending date in the range. For example, you could display the order dates between February 1, 2009, and February 15, 2009. The order dates are obtained from the *7B Web Site Orders* table.

Figure 7.40

Zoom dialog box

Criteria for Order Date

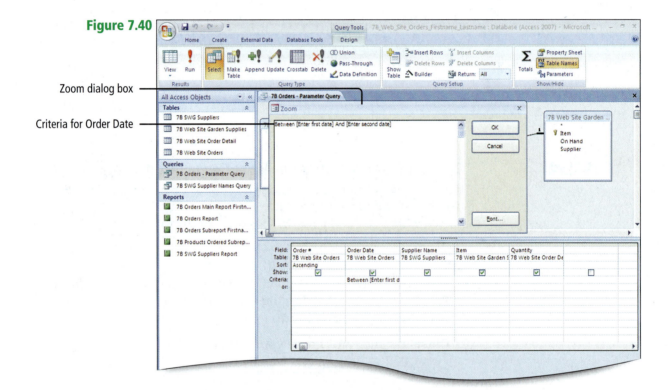

2 In the **Zoom** dialog box, click **OK. Close** ☒ the query. On the **Navigation Pane**, under **Tables**, double-click **7B Web Site Orders** to open the table in **Datasheet** view. Notice that the **Order Date** data ranges from 2/2/2009 to 3/10/2009.

When you run the parameter query, if you enter a range for which there is no data or if you enter the data incorrectly, the resultant fields will be empty.

3 **Close** ☒ the table. On the **Navigation Pane**, under **Queries**, double-click **7B Orders - Parameter Query**. In the **Enter Parameter Value** message box, under **Enter first date**, type **2/1/09** and then click **OK**. In the second message box, under **Enter second date**, type **February 15, 2009** and then click **OK**.

Because the Order Date field has a data type of Date, you can enter the date in several formats. The query is run and displays orders between February 1, 2009, and February 15, 2009.

Alert!

Did a message box display?

If a message box displays stating that the expression is typed incorrectly, you probably misspelled *February*. Open the query again and be sure you type the criteria correctly.

4 **Close** ☒ the query, and then collapse ◄ the **Navigation Pane**. On the Ribbon, click the **Create tab**. In the **Reports group**, click the **Report Wizard** button.

Because the query was selected on the Navigation Pane, the *7B Orders - Parameter Query* displays in the Tables/Queries box.

5 In the **Report Wizard** dialog box, click the **All Fields** button ⏭ to move all of the fields from the Available Fields box to the **Selected Fields** box, and then click **Next**.

6 In the second **Report Wizard** dialog box, under **How do you want to view your data?**, click **by 7B SWG Suppliers**, and then click **Next**. In the third **Report Wizard** dialog box, click **Next** to accept the current grouping level. In the fourth **Report Wizard** dialog box, **sort** the records by **Item** in **Ascending** order, and then click **Next**. In the fifth **Report Wizard** dialog box, click **Next** to accept the default Layout and Orientation.

7 In the sixth Report Wizard dialog box, in the style box, click **Equity**, and then click **Next**. Name the report **7B Orders by Date Range Report Firstname Lastname** and then click **Finish**.

An Enter Parameter Value message box displays. Because the report is based on a parameter query, you must enter the parameter values.

8 For the first date, type **2/1/09** and for the second date, type **2/15/09** and then compare your screen with Figure 7.41.

Four records are extracted from the underlying tables based on the parameter values entered. The Supplier Name data is truncated, and the Order Date for the second record displays as number or pound (#) signs, which indicates that the label control is not wide enough to display the numeric data.

Figure 7.41

Four items ordered between
2/1/09 and 2/15/09

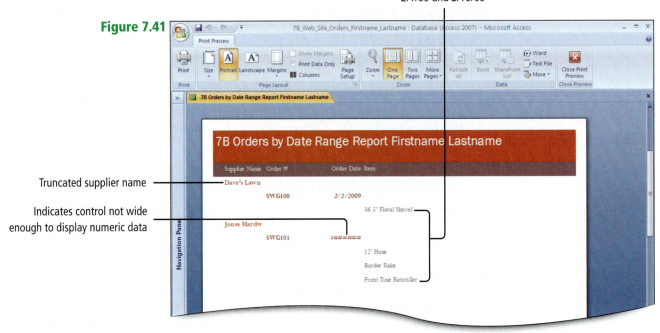

Truncated supplier name

Indicates control not wide
enough to display numeric data

9 On the **tab row**, right-click the **7B Orders by Date Range Report tab**, and then click **Layout View**. Click in the **text box control** that displays *Dave's Lawn*. Point to the right edge of the text box control until the ↔ pointer displays. Drag to the right until the entire supplier name—*Dave's Lawnmower Shop*—displays. Using this same technique, increase the width of the **Order Date text box control** to display all of the data.

10 **Save** the report, and then switch to **Design** view.

Activity 7.13 Printing the Parameters in the Report

The parameters used in the creation of the report can be printed as a part of the report by adding a text box control to a section. In this activity, you will add a text box control to the Report Header section to display the parameter values as a subtitle.

1 Point to the top of the **Page Header section bar** until the ⊕ pointer displays. Drag downward to the top of the **Supplier Name Header** section bar.

2 On the **Design tab**, in the **Controls group**, click the **Text Box** button. In the **Report Header** section, align the top of the plus (**+**) sign of the pointer with the **1-inch mark on the horizontal ruler** and **three dots** below the label control for the report title, and then click.

Recall that adding a text box control to the design also adds an associated label control that can be used to describe the data in the text box control.

3 Click the **label control** that is associated with the newly added text box control, and then press Delete.

4 Click the unbound **text box control**, and then press F4 to display the Property Sheet for the control. Click the **Property Sheet Data tab**, click in the **Control Source** property setting box, and then click the **Build** button. In the displayed **Expression Builder** dialog box, type **="Between "&[Enter first date]&" and "&[Enter second date]** and then compare your screen with Figure 7.42.

Recall that an expression must begin with an equal sign (=). The word *Between* and a space will print. The & symbol concatenates the string with the next part of the expression. *Enter first date* is enclosed in square brackets because it is part of the criteria that is retrieved from the parameter query. You must type the criteria exactly as it displays in the criteria of the parameter query. The criteria will be concatenated with the space, the word *and*, and another space. This is concatenated with the second criteria.

Figure 7.42

Type a space here

String expression

Criteria must be entered exactly as it displays in parameter query

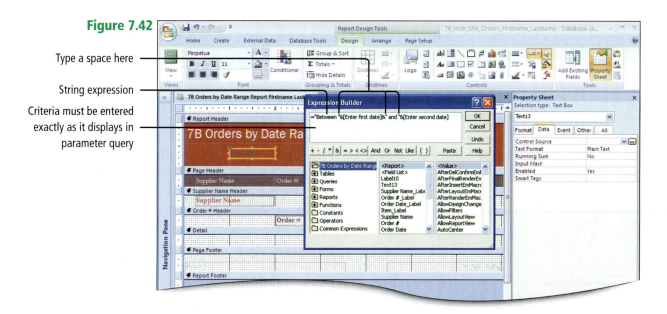

5 In the **Expression Builder** dialog box, click **OK**, and then press ↓ to save the property setting.

Alert!

Did a message box display?

If a message box displays stating that the expression you entered contains invalid syntax, click OK. Click the Control Source Build button, and then view Figure 7.42 to be sure that you typed the expression correctly. Common errors include not typing the equal sign, using parentheses instead of square brackets, leaving out the beginning or ending quotation marks, or leaving out one of the & symbols.

6 **Close** ☒ the **Property Sheet**. On the **Design tab**, in the **Font group**, click the **Font Color button arrow** ⬛. Under **Standard Colors**, on the first row, click the first color—**White**.

7 With the text box control selected, in the **Font group**, click the **Center** button ☰. In the **Font group**, click the **Font Size button arrow** ⬛, and from the displayed list, click **14**. Increase the width of the text box control until the entire expression displays.

8 On the Ribbon, click the **Arrange tab**. In the **Size group**, click the **To Fit** button.

The height of the text box control is increased to fit the size of the text, and the width of the text box control will adjust to fit the title that displays in Layout view, Report view, and Print Preview view.

9 **Save** ⬛ the report, and switch to **Report** view. For the first date, enter **2/1/09** and for the second date, enter **2/15/09**

The report displays with a subtitle of *Between 2/1/09 and 2/15/09*. When the criteria is displayed in the report, be sure to enter the criteria in a consistent manner. For example, do not enter 2/1/09 for the first date and February 15, 2009 for the second date. If you do, the subtitle will display as *Between 2/1/09 and February 15, 2009*.

Alert!

Did another message box display?

If an unexpected Enter Parameter Value message box displays when you try to print or preview a report, you may have misspelled one of the criteria or a field name in the expression. The parameter criteria in this report must match exactly to the parameter criteria used in the query. If this happens, click Cancel to return to Design view and correct the error.

---

10 Switch to **Print Preview** view. If you are instructed to submit this result, create a paper or electronic printout. **Close** ☒ the Print Preview window and the report, and then expand ≫ the **Navigation Pane**.

Objective 6
Create an Alphabetic Index

A report can display an *alphabetic index*, similar to the grouping of addresses in an address book. An alphabetic index groups items by a common first character. For example, all of your contacts can be sorted by last name in ascending order. All of the last names beginning with the letter *A* are grouped together under the letter *A*. All of the last names beginning with the letter *B* are grouped together under the letter *B*, and so on.

Activity 7.14 Creating an Alphabetic Index

In this activity, you will create an alphabetic index of the suppliers' names from *7B SWG Suppliers* table, using the *7B SWG Supplier Names Query*.

1 On the **Navigation Pane**, under **Queries**, double-click **7B SWG Supplier Names Query**. Take a moment to review the data in the query, and then switch to **Design view**.

The query displays the Supplier Name field in Ascending order from the *7B SWG Suppliers* table.

2 **Close** ⊠ the query, and then collapse «‖ the **Navigation Pane**.

3 On the Ribbon, click the **Create tab**. In the **Reports group**, click the **Report Wizard** button.

4 Because the query was selected on the Navigation Pane, in the **Report Wizard** dialog box, in the **Tables/Queries** box, **Query: 7B SWG Supplier Names Query** displays. If it does not display, click the **Tables/Queries arrow**, and then click **Query: 7B SWG Supplier Names Query**.

5 Under **Available Fields**, double-click **Supplier Name** to add the field name to the **Selected Fields** box, and then click **Next**.

Because the query sorts the Supplier Name in Ascending order, the field will automatically be sorted in the same manner in the report.

6 Click **Next**. Under **Layout**, be sure that the **Tabular** option button is selected. Under **Orientation**, be sure that the **Portrait** option button is selected, and then click **Next**.

7 In the style box, click **Office**, and then click **Next**. For the title of the report, type **7B Supplier Alphabetic Index Firstname Lastname** and then click **Finish**. Compare your screen with Figure 7.43.

The report displays in Print Preview. Because the column heading is difficult to see and some of the supplier names are truncated, the report needs some modifications.

Figure 7.43

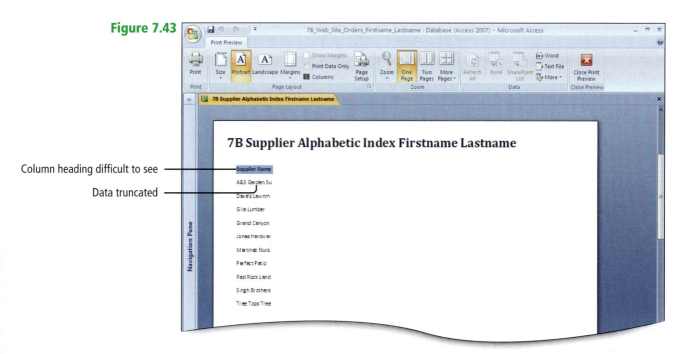

Column heading difficult to see

Data truncated

8 On the **Print Preview tab**, in the **Close Preview group**, click the **Close Print Preview** button. Switch to **Design** view. Click anywhere in an empty area of the design grid to deselect the controls, and then click the **Supplier Name label control**. Be sure that the orange border only displays around the Supplier Name label control. On the Ribbon, click the **Arrange tab**. In the **Control Layout group**, click the **Remove** button to remove the control from the form. Press Delete to remove the Supplier Name label control from the report.

9 **Save** 🖫 the report, and then switch to **Layout** view. Expand the width of the **Supplier Name text box control** so that all of the data displays for every record.

10 On the **Format tab**, in the **Grouping & Totals group**, click the **Group & Sort** button. In the **Group, Sort, and Total pane**, click **Add a group**. From the displayed list, click **Supplier Name**.

The report must be grouped by Supplier Name to create an alphabetic index of the names.

11 In the **Group, Sort, and Total pane**, on the **Group bar**, click the **More arrow**. Click the **by entire value arrow**, and from the displayed list, click the **by first character** option button. Click in an empty area of the report.

The first letter of the Supplier Name displays above the supplier names along with a label control that displays Supplier Name. You can select more than one character for the index.

12 In the **Group, Sort, and Total pane**, on the **Group bar**, to the right of **with title**, click the **Supplier Name** link. With Supplier Name selected, in the displayed **Zoom** dialog box, press Delete, and then click **OK**. Compare your screen with Figure 7.44.

The label control associated with the first character of the grouping is removed from the report. The first letter of the grouped Supplier Names displays above each grouping.

Figure 7.44

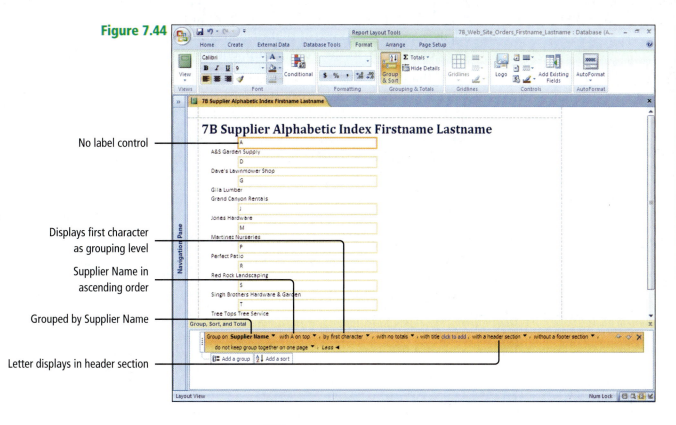

No label control

Displays first character as grouping level

Supplier Name in ascending order

Grouped by Supplier Name

Letter displays in header section

13 **Close** ☒ the **Group, Sort and Total pane**—do *not* click the Delete button.

14 Click the **Supplier text box control** for the first record—*A&S Garden Supply*. Point to the control until the 🖟 pointer displays. Drag to the right until the left edge of the text box control is approximately **.5 inch** to the right of the letter *A*. Change the **Font Size** to **11**, and then compare your screen with Figure 7.45.

Figure 7.45

Font size changed to 11

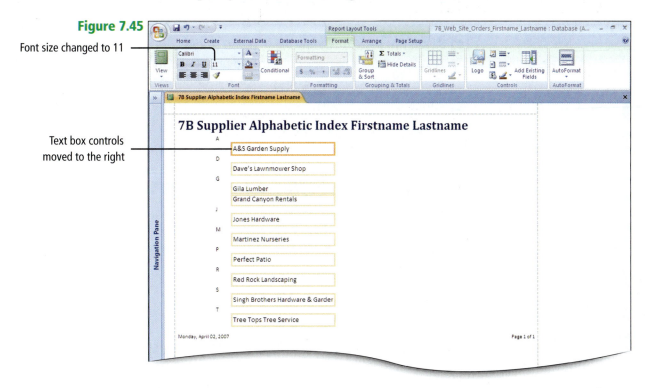

Text box controls moved to the right

15 Click the **text box control** that displays the letter *A*, and then on the **Format tab**, in the **Font group**, change the **Font Size** to **16**.

Click the **Font Color button arrow** 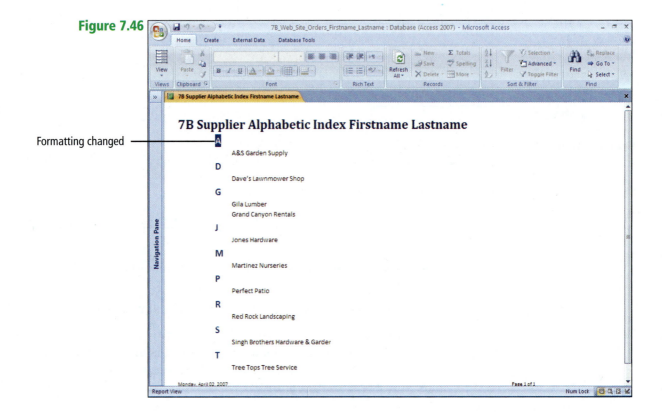. Under **Access Theme Colors**, on the first row, click the third color—**Dark Label Text** — and then add **Bold** formatting to the text.

16 **Save** the report, and then switch to **Report view**. Compare your screen with Figure 7.46.

Figure 7.46

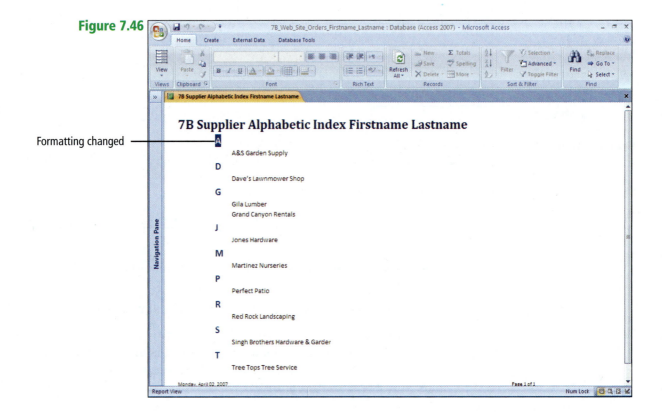

Formatting changed

17 Switch to **Print Preview** view. If you are instructed to submit this result, create a paper or electronic printout. On the **Print Preview tab**, in the **Close Preview group**, click the **Close Print Preview** button.

18 **Close** the report, and then expand the **Navigation Pane**.

Close the database, and **Exit** Access.

End **You have completed Project 7B** ————————————

There's More You Can Do!

From My Computer, navigate to the student files that accompany this textbook. In the folder **02_theres_more_you_can_do**, locate and open the folder for this chapter. Open and print the instructions for this project, which are provided to you in Adobe PDF format.

Try It! 1— Create a Nested Subform

In this Try It! project, you will add a subform to a form, and then add a second subform to the first subform.

Try It! 2—Create a Subreport that Displays Summary Data

In this Try It! project, you will add a subreport to a report that summarizes data.

Content-Based Assessments

Summary

Forms can be simple or complex. In this chapter, you created advanced forms that display data from one or more record sources. You created split forms that display data from one table in two different ways in the same form. You then created subforms using the Form Tool and the Form Wizard, and by dragging a related table onto an existing form. Subforms display data from related tables on one form. Forms can be displayed on multiple pages by using the Tab control.

Reports can also be simple or complex. You created advanced reports using some of the same techniques in creating advanced forms. You created subreports by using the SubReport Wizard and by dragging a related table onto an existing report. You then modified the reports to display the data in a professional-looking format. You created a report based on a parameter query and displayed the criteria as a subtitle in the report. Finally, you created a report that displayed an alphabetic index of supplier names.

Key Terms

The ⊙ symbol represents Key Terms found on the Student CD in the 02_theres_more_you_can_do folder for this chapter.

Content-Based Assessments

Matching

Match each term in the second column with its correct definition in the first column. Write the letter of the term on the blank line in front of the correct definition.

—— **1.** A form that displays data in two views—Form view and Datasheet view—on a single form.

—— **2.** A miniature, semitransparent toolbar that is used to work with objects on the screen.

—— **3.** A form that is embedded within another form and is used to view, enter, and edit data that is related to data in the main form.

—— **4.** A form that contains a subform.

—— **5.** A table that breaks down the many-to-many relationship into two one-to-many relationships.

—— **6.** A related form that is not stored within the main form.

—— **7.** A form that displays the data from the underlying table or query on more than one page.

—— **8.** An object inserted into a main form that displays data on different tabs.

—— **9.** A report that is embedded within another report—the main report.

—— **10.** A report that contains a subreport.

—— **11.** The exclamation (!).

—— **12.** The set of rules by which words and symbols in an expression are combined.

—— **13.** A query that prompts an individual for criteria.

—— **14.** A grouping of items by a common first character.

—— **15.** A subform that is embedded within another subform.

A Alphabetic index

B Bang operator

C Junction table

D Linked form

E Main form

F Main report

G Mini toolbar

H Multi-page form

I Nested subform

J Parameter query

K Split form

L Subform

M Subreport

N Syntax

O Tab control

Content-Based Assessments

Fill in the Blank

Write the correct word in the space provided.

1. The flexibility of finding a record in Datasheet view, and then editing the same record in Form view is an advantage of displaying data in a(n) _____ _____.

2. The property that defines whether the datasheet displays above, below, to the left, or to the right of the form is the split form _____ property.

3. A form similar to a subdatasheet—the data in the related table is displayed without having to open another table or form is a(n) _____.

4. You can also _____ a related form onto an existing form to create a subform.

5. A relationship between tables where one record in one table has many matching records in a second table, and a single record in the second table has many matching records in the first table is a(n) _____ _____ _____ relationship.

6. A third table containing the primary key fields from two tables in a many-to-many relationship is called a(n) _____ table.

7. To view the data in a linked form, click the _____ that is displayed on the main form.

8. A form that enables an individual to divide a long form into sections that display on separate pages or to display subforms on different tabs within the main form is a(n) _____ form.

9. An object inserted into a main form that displays data on different tabs is a(n) _____ control.

10. A report that displays data from an underlying table, query, or SQL statement as specified in the report's Record Source property is a(n) _____ report.

11. A report that does not display data from an underlying table, query, or SQL statement and has an empty Record Source property setting is a(n) _____ report.

12. A main report can contain up to seven levels deep of _____ and _____.

13. The operator that tells Access that what follows it is an object that belongs to the object that precedes it in the expression is a(n) _____ operator.

14. To enable an individual to set the criteria for the report when the report is opened, the record source should be a(n) _____ _____.

15. A report can display a grouping similar to that of addresses in an address book that is called a(n) _____ _____.

Project 7C—Historical Gardens

In this project, you will apply the skills you practiced from the Objectives in Project 7A.

Objectives: 1. *Create a Split Form;* **2.** *Create a Form and a Subform;* **3.** *Create a Multi-Page Form.*

David Tang, coordinator for cultural and historical events of Media Southwest Productions, wants the database forms to display related data. For example, he is interested in displaying the contacts for the historical gardens on one form. In this project, you will customize the company's forms to display data in two ways on the same form, to display data from multiple tables on one form, and to display data on multiple pages on a form. Your completed work will look similar to Figure 7.47.

> **For Project 7C, you will need the following files:**
>
> a07C_Historical_Gardens
> a07C_Logo
> A new blank Word document

You will save your database as
7C_Historical_Gardens_Firstname_Lastname
You will save your document as
7C_Tab_Control_Form_Firstname_Lastname

Figure 7.47

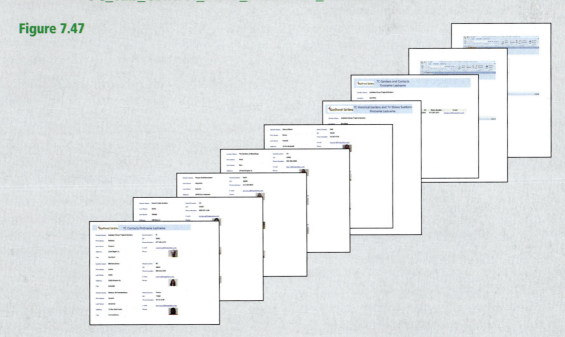

(Project 7C–Historical Gardens continues on the next page)

(Project 7C–Historical Gardens continued)

1. **Start Access**. Locate and open the **a07C_Historical_Gardens** file. Save the database in the **Access 2007 Database** format in your **Access Chapter 7** folder as 7C_Historical_Gardens_Firstname_Lastname

2. On the **Navigation Pane**, double-click **7C Contacts** to open the table in **Datasheet view**. Collapse the **Navigation Pane**. On the Ribbon, click the **Create tab**. In the **Forms group**, click the **Split Form** button. **Save** the split form as 7C Contacts Split Form Firstname Lastname

3. On the **Arrange tab**, in the **Tools group**, click the **Property Sheet** button. Click the **Selection type arrow**. Scroll until *Form* is displayed in the list, and then click **Form**. On the **Form Property Sheet**, click the **Format tab**. In the property setting box for **Split Form Printing**, click the **arrow**, and then click **Form Only**.

4. Switch to **Design view**. On the **Form Property Sheet Format tab**, click in the **Split Form Orientation** property setting box, and then click the **arrow**. Click **Datasheet on Top**, and then **Close** the **Property Sheet**.

5. Switch to **Layout view**. Point to the splitter bar until the ⬍ pointer displays. Drag upward until the dark horizontal line displays between the fourth and fifth records.

6. In the form section, click the **label control** for the form title, and then click to the right of **Contacts**. Press Spacebar one time, and then type your **Firstname Lastname** to add your name to the title of the form. On the **Format tab**, in the **Controls group**, click the **Logo** button. Navigate to the location where the student data files are saved, and then double-click **a07C_Logo**.

Increase the width of the **logo control** by approximately **two inches**. Center the **title label control** above the subform columns.

7. **Save** the form, and then switch to **Form view**. Press PgDn until **Record 4** displays. In the form section, change the **Phone Number** for *Alisha George* to 800-555-1136

8. Press PgDn to move to the next record and to save the changes to Record 4. Press Page Up to display **Record 4**. Unless you are required to submit your database electronically, in the form section, on the left side, click the **Record Selector** bar. If you are instructed to submit this result, create a paper or electronic printout of the selected record in **Landscape** orientation. On the **tab row**, right-click any tab, and then click **Close All**. Expand the **Navigation Pane**.

9. Under **Tables**, click **7C Gardens**. On the Ribbon, click the **Create tab**, and then in the **Forms group**, click the **Form** button. Collapse the **Navigation Pane**. In the main form, click the **Garden Name text box control**. Point to the right edge of the text box control until the ↔ pointer displays, and then drag the right edge of the text box control to the left until there is approximately **one inch** of space between *Gardens* and the right edge of the text box control.

10. Click anywhere in the subform. Point to the right edge of the subform until the ↔ pointer displays, and then drag the right edge of the subform to the left until it aligns with the right edge of the **Subject** field.

11. Edit the title of the form so it displays as 7C Historical Gardens and TV Shows Subform Firstname Lastname On the **Format tab**, in the **Controls group**, click the **Logo** button. Navigate to the location where the student

(Project 7C–Historical Gardens continues on the next page)

Content-Based Assessments

(Project 7C–Historical Gardens continued)

data files for this textbook are saved. Locate and double-click **a07C_Logo** to insert the logo in the form header.

12. If necessary, click the **logo control** to select it. Point to the bottom right corner of the control until the  pointer displays. Drag downward to the bottom of the header section and to the right between *Historical* and *Gardens*.

13. Click the **title's label control**, and then click to the left of your **Firstname**. Press ⟵Bksp to delete the space between *Subform* and your *Firstname*. Hold down ⇧Shift, and then press Enter.

14. Switch to **Design view**. Click in an empty area of the design grid to deselect the controls, and then click the title's label control. Point to the left edge of the **title's label control** until the ↔ pointer displays. Drag to the right until the left edge of the label control aligns with the right edge of the logo control.

15. Point to the right edge of the **title's label control** until the ↔ pointer displays. Drag to the right until the right edge of the label control aligns with the **7.5-inch mark on the horizontal ruler**. Point to the right edge of the main form until the ⊞ pointer displays. Drag to the left until the right edge of the main form aligns with the **7.5-inch mark on the horizontal ruler**. With the **title's label control** selected, on the **Format tab**, in the **Font group**, click the **Center** button.

16. **Save** the form as **7C Gardens and TV Shows Subform Firstname Lastname** and then switch to **Layout view**. Right-click the **title's label control**, and then click **Properties** to display the Property Sheet for the title. On the **Property Sheet Format tab**, scroll down until the

Horizontal Anchor property displays, and then click in the property setting box. Click the **arrow**, and then click **Left**. **Close** the **Property Sheet**.

17. **Save** the form, and then switch to **Form view**. On the left side of the form, click the **Record Selector** bar, and then if you are instructed to submit this result, create a paper or electronic printout of only Record 1—the selected record. Notice that both the main form and the subform print. **Close** the form.

18. On the **Navigation Pane**, under **Forms**, open **7C Gardens Main Form** in **Design view**. On the **Design tab**, in the **Controls group**, be sure that the **Use Control Wizards** button is active. In the form, point to the top of the **Form Footer section bar** until the ⊞ pointer displays. Drag downward to the **6-inch mark on the vertical ruler**.

19. On the **Navigation Pane**, under **Tables**, drag **7C Contacts** onto *7C Gardens Main Form* to the **1.75-inch mark on the vertical ruler** and even with the left edge of the form. In the **Subform Wizard** dialog box, click **Define my own**. Under **Form/report fields**, in the **first list box**, click the **arrow**, and then click **Garden Name**. Under **Subform/subreport fields**, in the **first list box**, click the **arrow**, and then click **Garden Name**. Click **Next**. Under **What name would you like for your subform or subreport?**, type **7C Gardens Contacts Subform Firstname Lastname** and then click **Finish**.

20. With the subform control selected, point to the **bottom middle sizing handle** of the subform control until the ↕ pointer displays. Drag downward to the **6-inch mark on the vertical ruler**. **Save** the form, and then collapse the **Navigation Pane**.

(Project 7C–Historical Gardens continues on the next page)

Content-Based Assessments

(Project 7C–Historical Gardens continued)

21. In the subform control, click the **Garden Name label control**, and then press ⌨Delete. Switch to **Layout view**.

22. Click the **subform control**. Point to the bottom edge of the **subform control** until the ↕ pointer displays. Drag upward until the bottom edge of the subform aligns with the bottom edge of the blank row below the new record row. Resize each field of the subform to just fit the data. Point to the right edge of the **subform control** until the ↔ pointer displays. Drag to the right until the *right edge of the subform control* aligns with the *right edge of the E-Mail* text box controls.

23. Click the **subform label control**, which displays *7C Gardens Contact Subform Firstname Lastname*, and then press ⌨Delete to remove the label control from the subform.

24. **Horizontally anchor** the **title's label control** at the **Left**. Change the title of the form to **7C Gardens and Contacts Firstname Lastname** and then place your name on the second line. Adjust the width of the **title's label control** so that the *left edge of the label control* aligns with the *left edge of the logo*, and the *right edge of the title's label control* aligns with the *right edge of the main form field's text box controls*. In the title's label control, **Center** the text.

25. **Save** the form. If you are instructed to submit this result, create a paper or electronic printout of only the first record in **Landscape** orientation. **Close** the form, and expand the **Navigation Pane**. Under **Forms**, **Rename** *7C Gardens Main Form* to **7C Gardens and Contacts Firstname Lastname**

26. On the **Navigation Pane**, under **Forms**, open **7C Contacts TC Form** in **Design view**, and then collapse the **Navigation Pane**. Point to the top of the **Form Footer**

section bar until the ⊕ pointer displays. Drag downward to the **3-inch mark on the vertical ruler**. On the **Design tab** in the **Controls group**, click the **Tab Control** button. Move the pointer into the **Detail** section until the plus (**+**) sign of the ⌖ pointer is aligned approximately with the **.25-inch mark on the horizontal ruler** and with the **.25-inch mark on the vertical ruler**, and then click.

27. In the selected **tab control**, point to the **right middle sizing handle** until the ↔ pointer displays. Drag to the right until the right edge of the tab control aligns with the **6-inch mark on the horizontal ruler**. On the **Design tab**, in the **Tools group**, click the **Add Existing Fields** button. In the **Field List**, click **Garden Name**. Hold down ⇧ Shift, and then click **Last Name** to select three fields. Hold down ⌨Ctrl, and then click **Photo**. Point to a selected field, and then drag downward and to the left onto the first tab until the top of the arrow of the ⌖ pointer aligns with the **1.5-inch mark on the horizontal ruler** and with the **.75-inch mark on the vertical ruler**.

28. **Close** the **Field List**. Press ⇧ Shift, and then click the **Photo control** to deselect it. With the remaining controls selected, point to the **right edge** of the text box controls until the ↔ pointer displays. Drag to the right until the right edge of the text box control aligns with the **4.5-inch mark on the horizontal ruler**. Click in an empty area of the tab control to deselect the controls. Click to select the **Photo label control** and press ⌨Delete. Click the **Photo** control and drag to the right and upward until the *Photo* control aligns with the *Garden Name* controls and there is approximately **.5 inch** of space between the two text box controls.

(Project 7C–Historical Gardens continues on the next page)

Content-Based Assessments

(Project 7C–Historical Gardens continued)

29. In the **Detail** section, click the **second tab**, which has no controls added to it. On the **Design tab**, in the **Tools group**, click the **Add Existing Fields** button. In the **Field List**, click **Address**. Hold down ⇧Shift, and then click **E-mail** to select six fields. Point to the selected fields, and then drag downward and to the left onto the second tab until the top of the arrow of the  pointer aligns with the **1.5-inch mark on the horizontal ruler** and with the **.75-inch mark on the vertical ruler**.

30. **Close** the **Field List**. Point to the right edge of the **E-mail text box control** until the ↔ pointer displays, and then drag to the right until the right edge of the text box controls aligns with the **5-inch mark on the horizontal ruler**. **Save** the form, and then switch to **Layout view**.

31. Right-click the **first tab**, and then click **Properties**. The Property Sheet displays *Selection type: Page*, and the Selection type box displays the page number of the tab. Click in the **Caption** property setting box, type **Contact Name and Photo** and then press Enter. In the form, click the **second tab** to display the **Property Sheet** for the second tab. Click in the **Caption** property setting box, type **Contact Info** and then press Enter to change the text on the second tab. **Close** the **Property Sheet**. In the form, click the **Contact Name and Photo tab** to display the first page of the form.

32. Change the **title** of the form to **7C Contacts Tab Control Form Firstname Lastname** and then place your first and last name on the second line of the title. Align the right edge of the title's label control with the right edge of the tab control, and then switch to **Form view**.

33. **Save** the form, and navigate to **Record 4**. Press Alt + PrtScr to place a copy of the screen into the Office Clipboard. Open **Microsoft Office Word 2007**. On the **Home tab**, in the **Clipboard group**, click the **Paste** button to place the screen shot in the Word document window. Press Ctrl + End to move to the end of the Word document, and then press Enter to insert a blank line at the bottom of the document. **Minimize** the Word window. In the **Access** window, on the form, click the **Contact Info tab**. Press Alt + PrtScr to place a copy of the screen into the Office Clipboard. On the taskbar, click the **Document1 - Microsoft** button to display the Word document. **Paste** the second screen in the Word document window. In the **Word** window, on the **Quick Access Toolbar**, click the **Save** button. Navigate to the **Access Chapter 7** folder, and save the file as **7C_Tab_Control_Form_Firstname_Lastname** If you are instructed to submit this result, create a paper or electronic printout of the document.

34. **Close** the **Word** window. If necessary, on the taskbar, click the Access button. In the **Access** window, **Close** the form, and then expand the **Navigation Pane**. **Close** the database, and then **Exit** Access. Submit your work as directed.

End **You have completed Project 7C**

Skills Review

Project 7D — Featured Gardens

In this project, you will apply the skills you practiced from the Objectives in Project 7B.

Objectives: 4. *Create and Modify a Subreport;* **5.** *Create a Report Based on a Parameter Query;* **6.** *Create an Alphabetic Index.*

Media Southwest Productions maintains a database of the historic gardens that are featured in the Southwest Gardens television show. Creating advanced reports will help the president and officers of the production company view the information in the database in a different way. In this project, you will create advanced reports that display data from multiple tables and from a parameter query. You will also create an alphabetic index of historic gardens. Your completed reports will look similar to those shown in Figure 7.48.

For Project 7D, you will need the following files:

a07D_Featured_Gardens
a07D_Logo

You will save your database as
7D_Featured_Gardens_Firstname_Lastname

Figure 7.48

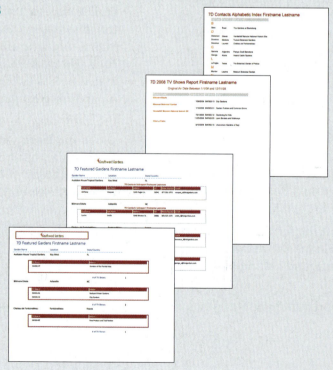

(Project 7D–Featured Gardens continues on the next page)

Content-Based Assessments

Skills Review

(Project 7D–Featured Gardens continued)

1. **Start Access**. Locate and open the **a07D_ Featured_Gardens** file. Save the database in the **Access 2007 Database** format in your **Access Chapter 7** folder as **7D_ Featured_Gardens_Firstname_Lastname**

2. Make a copy of the *7D Gardens Report*, name it **7D Gardens Main Report Firstname Lastname** and then open the report in **Design view**.

3. In the **Report Header** section, click the **title label control,** and then click one more time to enter into the editing mode. Change *Firstname Lastname* to your own first name and last name, and then press Enter. In the report, point to the top of the **Page Footer section bar** until the ⊕ pointer displays. Drag downward to the **1.75-inch mark on the vertical ruler** to make room in the Detail section for the subreport.

4. On the **Design tab**, in the **Controls group**, be sure that the **Use Controls Wizard** button is active. In the **Controls group**, click the **Subform/Subreport** button. Move the mouse pointer down into the **Detail** section until the top of the plus (+) sign of the ⊞ pointer aligns with the **1-inch mark on the horizontal ruler** and with the **.5-inch mark on the vertical ruler**, and then click.

5. In the **SubReport Wizard** dialog box, be sure that **Use existing Tables and Queries** is selected, and then click **Next**. Click the **Tables/Queries arrow**, and from the displayed list, click **Table: 7D TV Shows**. Under **Available Fields**, double-click **TV Show #** and **Subject** to move the fields to the Selected Fields box. Click **Next** two times. Name the report **7D Garden Shows Subreport Firstname Lastname** and then click **Finish**.

6. Switch to **Layout view**. In any subreport control, click the **subreport label control**, and then press Delete. In any subreport control, click the **TV Show # label control**. Hold down ⇧ Shift and click the **Subject label control** to select both controls. On the **Format tab**, in the **Font group**, click the **Fill/Back Color button arrow**. Under **Standard Colors**, on the sixth row, click the sixth color—**Maroon 5**. With the label controls still selected, in the **Font group**, click the **Font Color button arrow**. Under **Standard Colors**, on the first row, click the first color—**White**. Click anywhere in the main form to deselect the label controls.

7. Click anywhere in the subreport, and then click the **Layout Selector**. On the **Format tab**, in the **Controls group**, click the **Line Color button arrow**. Under **Standard Colors**, on the sixth row, click the sixth color—**Maroon 5**. In the **Controls group**, click the **Line Thickness button arrow**. In the displayed list, click the fourth line— **3 pt** —and then click anywhere in the main form to display the results of the formatting. Using the same procedure, add a **3 pt**, **Maroon 5** border to the **logo control**, and then **Save** your changes.

8. Click any **subreport control** and drag the right edge of the subreport control to the right until the horizontal scroll bar no longer displays. Switch to **Design view**. On the **Design tab**, in the **Tools group**, click the **Subreport in New Window** button. In the **Detail** section, click the **TV Show # text box control**. On the **Design tab** in the **Grouping & Totals group**, click the **Totals** button, and then click **Count Records** to insert a calculated control into the Report Footer section. **Save** and **Close** the subreport. Switch *7D Gardens Main Report Firstname Lastname* to **Report view**. Notice that in the subreport controls,

(Project 7D–Featured Gardens continues on the next page)

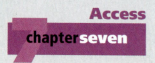

(Project 7D–Featured Gardens continued)

Record 1 displays a total count of **1** and **Record 2** displays a total count of **2**.

9. Switch to **Design view,** and then click any **subreport control**. On the **Design tab**, in the **Tools group**, click the **Subreport in New Window** button. Click the **Report Footer section bar**, and then press F4 to display the Property Sheet for the Report Footer section. On the **Property Sheet**, on the **Format tab**, click in the **Visible** property setting box, which displays **Yes**. Click the **arrow**, and then click **No**.

10. In the **Report Footer** section, click the **calculated control**. The **Property Sheet** displays *Selection type: Text Box*, and the **Selection type** box displays *Access TotalsTV Show #*. Click the **Property Sheet Other tab**, and then click in the **Name** property setting box. Select **AccessTotalsTV Show #**, type **Count of Shows** and then press Enter.

11. **Close** the **Property Sheet**, **Save** the report, and then **Close** *7D Garden Shows Subreport*. Switch *7D Gardens Main Report Firstname Lastname* to **Report view**, and notice that the count of the TV Shows # field no longer displays in the subreport control.

12. Switch to **Design view**. On the **Design tab**, in the **Controls group**, click the **Text Box** button. Move the mouse pointer down to the **Detail** section until the top of the plus (+) sign aligns with the **6.5-inch mark on the horizontal ruler** and with the **1.5-inch mark on the vertical ruler**, and then click. In the **Detail** section, click the **label control** that is associated with the unbound text box control, and then press F4 to display the Property Sheet for the label control. Click the **Property Sheet Format tab**, select the text in the **Caption** property setting box, and then type **# of TV Shows:** Select the text in the

Width property setting box, type **1** and then press Enter.

13. In the **Detail** section, click the **unbound text box control**. Click the **Property Sheet Data tab**, and then click in the **Control Source** property setting box. Click the displayed **Build** button. In the **Expression Builder** dialog box, and using your own first name and last name, type **=IIf(IsError([7D Garden Shows Subreport Firstname Lastname].[Report]![Count of Shows]),0,[7D Garden Shows Subreport Firstname Lastname].[Report]![Count of Shows])** In the **Expression Builder** dialog box, click **OK**, and then press ↓. **Close** the **Property Sheet**.

14. **Save** the report, and then switch to **Report view**. If you are instructed to submit this result, view the report in **Print Preview**, and then create a paper or electronic print-out of the first page of the report. **Close** the Print Preview window and the report, and then expand the **Navigation Pane**.

15. Make a copy of **7D Gardens Report**, name it **7D Featured Gardens Report Firstname Lastname** and then open the report in **Design view**. Point to the top of the **Page Footer section bar** until the ⊞ pointer displays. Drag downward to the **1.5-inch mark on the vertical ruler** to make room in the Detail section for the subreport. Switch to **Print Preview,** and then select **Landscape** orientation. **Close** Print Preview. On the **Navigation Pane**, under **Tables**, click **7D Contacts**, and then drag the table to the right onto the **Detail** section until the top of the ▦ pointer aligns with the **.5-inch mark on the horizontal ruler** and the **.5 -inch mark on the vertical ruler**. In the **SubReport Wizard** dialog box, be sure that **Choose from a list. Show 7D Contacts for each record in 7D Gardens using Garden**

(Project 7D–Featured Gardens continues on the next page)

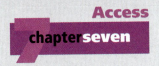

(Project 7D–Featured Gardens continued)

Name is selected, and then click **Next**. Name the subreport **7D Contacts Subreport Firstname Lastname** and then click **Finish**.

16. Press F4 to display the Property Sheet for the Subreport, and then collapse the **Navigation Pane**. Click the **Property Sheet Data tab**, click in the **Link Master Fields** property setting box, and then click the **Build** button. In the **Subreport Field Linker** dialog box, click **OK**. Click the **Format tab**, click in the **Width** property setting box, and then type **8.5** Close the **Property Sheet**. In the subreport, select and delete each of the following label controls: **Garden Name**, **City**, and **State/Country**. Switch to **Layout view**, and then adjust the widths of the text box controls for **Address**, **ZIP**, **Phone Number**, and **E-mail** fields to fit all data. **Save** the report.

17. Click the **subreport label control**. Point to the selected label control until the pointer displays, and then drag the control to the right until it is approximately centered between the margins of the subreport control. Change the **Font Color** of the text in the selected label control to **Maroon 5**, and then **Bold** the text. Switch to **Design view** and **Save** changes. In the subreport, select all six label controls. Change the **Fill/Back Color** to **Maroon 5**. Change the **Font Color** to **White**. **Save** the report, and then switch to **Report view**. If you are instructed to submit this result, view the report in **Print Preview**, be sure the **Orientation** is set to **Landscape**, and then create a paper or electronic printout of the first page of the report. **Close** the Print Preview window and the report.

18. On the Ribbon, click the **Create tab**. In the **Reports group**, click the **Report Wizard**

button. In the **Report Wizard** dialog box, **Select** the **Query: 7D TV Shows Parameter Query**. Click the **All Fields** button to move all of the fields from the **Available Fields** box to the **Selected Fields** box, and then click **Next**. In the second **Report Wizard** dialog box, click **Next** to accept the current grouping level. In the third **Report Wizard** dialog box, **Sort** the records by **Original Air Date** in **Ascending** order, and then click **Next**. In the fourth **Report Wizard** dialog box, click **Next** to accept the default Layout and Orientation. In the fifth Report Wizard dialog box, in the style box, click **Northwind**, and then click **Next**. Name the report **7D 2008 TV Shows Report Firstname Lastname** and then click **Finish**. For the first date, type **1/1/08** and for the second date, type **12/31/08**

19. On the **tab row**, right-click the **7D 2008 TV Shows Report tab**, and then click **Layout View**. Resize all label and text box controls to just fit the data. **Save** the report, and then switch to **Design view**.

20. Point to the top of the **Page Header section bar** until the ✛ pointer displays. Drag downward to the top of the **Featured Garden Header section bar**. On the **Design tab**, in the **Controls group**, click the **Text Box** button. In the **Report Header** section, align the top of the plus (**+**) sign of the ⊞abl pointer with the **1-inch mark on the horizontal ruler** and the **.5-inch mark on the vertical ruler**, and then click. Click the **label control** that is associated with the newly added text box control, and then press Delete. Click the unbound **text box control**, and then press F4 to display the Property Sheet for the control. Click the **Property Sheet Data tab**, click in the **Control Source** property setting box, and then click the **Build** button. In the

(Project 7D–Featured Gardens continues on the next page)

Content-Based Assessments

(Project 7D–Featured Gardens continued)

displayed **Expression Builder** dialog box, type ="Original Air Date Between "&[Enter first date]&" and "&[Enter second date] In the **Expression Builder** dialog box, click **OK**, and then press ↓ to save the property setting. **Close** the Property Sheet.

21. On the **Design tab**, in the **Font group**, click the **Font Color button arrow**. Under **Standard Colors**, on the sixth row, click the sixth color—**Maroon 5**. With the text box control selected, in the **Font group**, click the **Center** button. In the **Font group**, click the **Font Size button arrow**, and from the displayed list, click **14**. Increase the width of the text box control until the entire expression displays. On the Ribbon, click the **Arrange tab**. In the **Size group**, click the **To Fit** button.

22. **Save** the report, and switch to **Report view**. For the first date, enter **1/1/08** and for the second date, enter **12/31/08** Switch to **Print Preview view**. If you are instructed to submit this result, create a paper or electronic printout. **Close** the Print Preview window and the report, and then expand the **Navigation Pane**.

23. On the **Navigation Pane**, under **Queries**, double-click **7D Garden Contacts Query**. **Close** the query, and then collapse the **Navigation Pane**. On the Ribbon, click the **Create tab**. In the **Reports group**, click the **Report Wizard** button.

24. In the **Report Wizard** dialog box, in the **Tables/Queries** box, **Query: 7D Garden Contacts Query** should display. Under **Available Fields**, click the **Add All Fields** button, and then click **Next**. Click the **Remove Field** button to remove all grouping. Click **Next** two times. Under **Layout**, be sure that the **Tabular** option button is selected. Under **Orientation**, be sure that the **Portrait** option button is selected, and then click **Next**. In the style box, click

Northwind, and then click **Next**. For the title of the report, type **7D Contacts Alphabetic Index Firstname Lastname** and then click **Finish**.

25. **Save** the report, and then switch to **Layout view**. Adjust the width of all label and text box controls so that all of the data displays for every record.

26. On the **Format tab**, in the **Grouping & Totals group**, click the **Group & Sort** button. In the **Group, Sort, and Total pane**, click **Add a group**. From the displayed list, click **Last Name**. On the **Group bar**, click the **More arrow**. Click the **by entire value arrow**, and from the displayed list, click the **by first character** option button. Click in an empty area of the report.

27. In the **Group, Sort, and Total pane**, on the **Group bar**, to the right of **with title**, click the **Last Name** link. With *Last Name* selected, in the displayed **Zoom** dialog box, press Delete, and then click **OK**. **Close** the **Group, Sort and Total pane**.

28. Click the **text box control** that displays the letter *B*. Point to the control until the ⬚ pointer displays. Drag to the left approximately **.5 inch**. On the **Format tab**, in the **Font group**, change the **Font Size** to **16**. Click the **Font Color button arrow**. Under **Access Theme Colors**, on the first row, click the last color—**Highlight**—and then **Bold** the text.

29. **Save** the report, and then switch to **Report view**. If you are instructed to submit this result, switch to **Print Preview view**, and then create a paper or electronic printout of the report. On the **Print Preview tab**, in the **Close Preview group**, click the **Close Print Preview** button.

30. **Close** the report, and then expand the **Navigation Pane**. **Close** the database, and **Exit** Access. Submit your work as directed.

End **You have completed Project 7D** _____

Access

chapter seven

Mastering Access

Project 7E — Phone Orders

In this project, you will apply the skills you practiced from the Objectives in Project 7A.

Objectives: 1. *Create a Split Form;* **2.** *Create a Form and a Subform;* **3.** *Create a Multi-Page Form.*

Media Southwest Productions maintains a database where customers can place telephone orders for the gardening supplies that are featured in the Southwest Gardens television show. Toni Jones, president of Media Southwest Productions, wants the database forms to display related data. For example, she is interested in displaying the orders on one form. She also wants to display the CSR (Customer Service Representative) information in a tab control form. In the following project, you will customize the company's forms to display data in two ways on the same form, to display data from multiple tables on one form, and to display data on multiple pages on a form. Your completed forms will look similar to the ones in Figure 7.49.

> **For Project 7E, you will need the following files:**
>
> a07E_Phone_Orders
> a07E_Logo

You will save your database as
7E_Phone_Orders_Firstname_Lastname
You will save your document as
7E_Tab_Control_Form_Firstname_Lastname

Figure 7.49

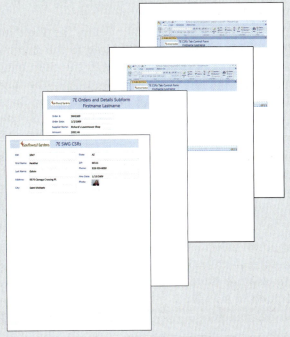

(Project 7E—Phone Orders continues on the next page)

(Project 7E–Phone Orders continued)

1. **Start Access**. Locate and open the **a07E_Phone_Orders** file. Save the database in the **Access 2007 Database** format in your **Access Chapter 7** folder as **7E_Phone_Orders_Firstname_Lastname**

2. On the **Navigation Pane**, double-click **7E SWG CSRs** to open the table in Datasheet view. Collapse the **Navigation Pane**. **Create** a **Split Form** and **Save** it as 7E SWG CSRs Split Form Firstname Lastname

3. In the form section of the split form, click the **Photo** for *Jane Hartigan* and **Remove** the **Photo** field from the second column's stacked layout. Click the **Photo control**.

4. In the **Property Sheet**, click the **Picture Alignment** property setting box **arrow**, and then click **Top Left**. **Close** the **Property Sheet**. Align the right edge of the **Photo attachment control** with the right edge of the photograph.

5. Switch to **Design view**. In the **Property Sheet**, click the **Selection type arrow**. Click **Form** to display the Form Property Sheet. Click the property setting box **Split Form Printing arrow**, and then click **Form Only**. Click the **Split Form Orientation** property setting box **arrow**, and then click **Datasheet on Top. Close** the **Property Sheet**.

6. Add the **a07E_Logo** to the form. Increase the width of the **logo control** approximately **two inches**, and then move the **label control** for the title to the right of the logo control. Click the **title's label control**, and then click to the right of **CSRs**. Press Spacebar one time, and then type **Firstname Lastname** to add your name to the title of the form.

7. Switch to **Form view**, and then select **Record 4**. In the form section, change the **First Name** from *Karen* to **Heather Save** the form. If you are instructed to submit this result, create a paper or electronic

(Project 7E–Phone Orders continues on the next page)

printout of only Record 4. On the **tab row**, right-click any tab, and then click **Close All**. Expand the **Navigation Pane**.

8. Click the **7E Orders** table. Click the **Create tab**, and then click the **Form** button. Collapse the **Navigation Pane**. In the main form, click the **Supplier Name combo box control**. Point to the right edge of the text box control until the ↔ pointer displays, and then drag the right edge of the combo box control to the left until there is approximately **one inch** of space between *Shop* and the right edge of the text box control.

9. Drag the right edge of the subform to the left until it aligns with the right edge of the **Quantity** field. Center the subform under the text box controls above it. Drag the right edge of the main form to the left to the **6-inch mark on the horizontal ruler**.

10. Add the **a07E_Logo** to the form. Drag the right bottom corner of the control downward to the bottom of the header section and to the right aligning it with the *Order # text box control.

11. Select the **Title label control box** and drag to the right until the left edge aligns with the right edge of the logo control. Edit the title of the form so it displays as **7E Orders and Details Subform Firstname Lastname** with your name on the second line of the **Title label control**. Switch to **Design view**. Drag the right edge of the **Title** label control to the **5-inch mark on the horizontal ruler**. **Center** the text of the title. Set the **Horizontal Anchor** property to **Left**.

12. **Save** the form as 7E Orders Firstname Lastname, and then switch to **Form view**. If you are instructed to submit this result, create a paper or electronic printout of only Record 1. **Close** the form.

Content-Based Assessments

Mastering Access

(Project 7E–Phone Orders continued)

13. Open **7E SWG CSRs TC Form** in **Design view**. Drag the **Form footer section bar** downward to the **3-inch mark on the vertical ruler**. On the **Design tab**, in the **Controls group**, click the **Tab Control** button. In the **Detail** section align the plus (+) sign of the  pointer with the **.25-inch mark on the horizontal ruler** and with the **.25-inch mark on the vertical ruler**. Click one time. Increase the size of the tab control by dragging to the right until the right edge of the tab control aligns with the **4-inch mark on the horizontal ruler**.

14. To the **first page** of the **tab control**, at the **1-inch mark on the horizontal ruler** and the top edge of the tab page, add the following fields: **ID#**, **First Name**, **Last Name**, **Hire Date**, and **Photo**. Expand the width of the **First Name** and **Last Name** text box controls to the **2.5-inch mark on the horizontal ruler**. Delete the **Photo label control**, and then position the left edge of the **Photo control** at the **3 inch mark on the horizontal ruler** and the top edge at the **1-inch mark on the vertical ruler**. In the first page of the tab control **Caption** property, type **Badge**

15. To the **second page** of the **tab control**, at the **1-inch mark on the horizontal** ruler and the top edge of the tab sheet, add the following fields: **Address**, **City**, **State**, **Zip**, and **Phone**. Expand the widths of all text box controls to the **3-inch mark on the horizontal ruler**. In the second page of the tab control **Caption** property, type **Contact Info**

16. Change the **title** of the form to **7E CSRs Tab Control Form Firstname Lastname** placing your name on the second line of the title. Align the right edge of the title's label control with the **4.5-inch mark on the horizontal ruler**. **Center** the text of the title. Set the **Horizontal Anchor** property to **Left**. Switch to **Form view**.

17. **Save** the form and navigate to **Record 3**. Using the Office Clipboard, **Copy** and **Paste** the first and second tabs into a Word document. Save this document as **7E_Tab_Control_Form_Firstname_Lastname**

18. If you are instructed to submit this result, create a paper or electronic printout of the **Word** document.

19. **Close** the **Word** window. If necessary, on the taskbar, click the **Access** button. In the **Access** window, **Close** the form, and then expand the **Navigation Pane**. **Close** the database, and then **Exit** Access. Submit your work as directed.

End You have completed Project 7E

Mastering Access

Project 7F—Phone Reps

In this project, you will apply the skills you practiced from the Objectives in Project 7B.

Objectives: 4. *Create and Modify a Subreport;* **5.** *Create a Report Based on a Parameter Query;* **6.** *Create an Alphabetic Index.*

Media Southwest Productions maintains a customer service order phone line where viewers can order gardening supplies that are featured in the Southwest Gardens television show. Creating advanced reports will help the president and officers of the production company study the information in the database in a different way. In the following project, you will create advanced reports that display data from multiple tables and from a parameter query. You will also create an alphabetic index of the last names of the customer service representatives. Your completed reports will look similar to those shown in Figure 7.50.

For Project 7F, you will need the following files:

a07F_Phone_Reps

a07F_Logo

**You will save your database as
7F_Phone_Reps_Firstname_Lastname**

Figure 7.50

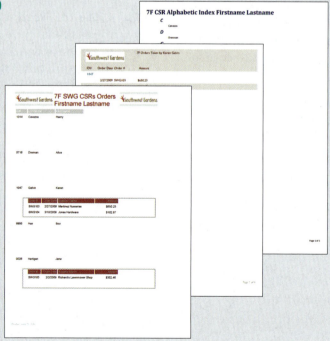

(Project 7F—Phone Reps continues on the next page)

Content-Based Assessments

Mastering Access

(Project 7F–Phone Reps continued)

1. **Start Access**. Locate and open the **a07F_Phone_Reps** file. Save the database in the **Access 2007 Database** format in your **Access Chapter 7** folder as **7F_Phone_Reps_Firstname Lastname**

2. Make a **Copy** of the **7F CSRs Report** and save it as **7F CSRs Orders Report Firstname Lastname Open** the **7F CSRs Orders Report** in **Design view**.

3. Edit the Title of the report by changing *Firstname Lastname* to your first name and last name.

4. Drag the **Page Footer Section bar** down to the **1.5-inch mark on the vertical ruler**. Click the **Subform/Subreport** button and align the top of the plus (+) sign of the [icon] pointer with the **.5-inch mark on the horizontal ruler** and with the **.5-inch mark on the vertical ruler**, and then click.

5. Using the **Subreport Wizard**, select **Use existing Tables and queries**. From the **7F Orders** table, select the following fields in this order: **Order #**, **Order Date**, **Supplier Name**, and **Amount**. **Show 7F Orders for each record in 7F SWG CSRs using ID#** Add your **Firstname Lastname** to the end of the default name for the subreport.

6. Switch to **Layout view**. Delete the **subreport label control**. Select the subreport and resize the label and text box controls to display all data. Change the **Back Color** of the label controls to **Maroon 5** and the **Font Color** to **Medium Gray 3**. Add a border of **Line Color Medium Gray 3** and **Thickness** of **2 pt** to the subreport. **Save** the report.

7. If you are instructed to submit this result, view the report in **Print Preview**, and then create a paper or electronic printout of only the first page of the report. **Close** the report, and then expand the **Navigation Pane**.

8. Click to select the **7F CSR Parameter Query**. Using the **Report Wizard**, add all **Available Fields** to the **Selected Fields** list. View the data by **7F Orders**. **Group** on the **ID#** field. **Sort Ascending** by **Order Date**. Use **Stepped** layout and **Portrait** orientation. Select the **Solstice** style. Add your first name and last name to the end of the default title. Select **Modify the report's design**, and then click **Finish**.

9. In the **Page Header section** of the report, select the label controls for the **First Name** and **Last Name** fields, and then press Delete.

10. Delete the report title's control box. To the **Report Header section**, add the **a07F_Logo**. Expand the width of the logo to the **2-inch mark on the horizontal ruler**. Add a text box control to the right of the logo, aligning it between the **2.5** and the **5.5 inch marks on the horizontal ruler**. Delete the text box label control. Click the unbound **text box control**. Click the **Property Sheet Data tab**, and then click in the **Control Source** property setting box. Open the **Expression Builder** dialog box. Type the following concatenated string in the text control box: **="7F Orders Taken by "&[First Name]&" "&[Last Name]**

11. In the **Page Footer section** of the report, click in the **Now() control box** to the right of the equal sign. Type **"Report prepared by Firstname Lastname on"&**

12. Switch to **Layout view**. In the **Enter Parameter Value** message box, under **Enter CSR#**, type **1047** Resize the label and text box controls to just fit the data. **Save** the report, and then switch to **Report view**.

13. If you are instructed to submit this result, create a paper or electronic printout. **Close** the report, and then expand the **Navigation Pane**.

(Project 7F–Phone Reps continues on the next page)

(Project 7F–Phone Reps continued)

14. Click **7F CSR Last Names Query**. **Create** a report using the **Report Wizard**. From the **Available fields list**, add **Last Name** to the **Selected Fields list**. No sorting is required. Use **Tabular** layout and **Portrait** orientation. Select the **Office** style. Title the report 7F CSR Alphabetic Index Firstname Lastname

15. Switch to **Layout view** to remove the **Last Name label control** from the stacked arrangement. Select the label control and delete it. Expand the width of the **Last Name text box control** so that all of the data displays for every record. In the **Group, Sort, and Total** pane, click **Add a group**, and then click **Last Name**. On the **Group bar**, click the **More arrow**. Click the **by entire value arrow**, and from the displayed list, click the **by first character** option button. Click in an empty area of the report. To the right of **with title**, click the **Last Name** link.

16. With *Last Name* selected, in the displayed **Zoom** dialog box, press Delete. Click the **text box control** that displays the letter *C*, and then on the **Format tab**, in the **Font group**, change the **Font Size** to **16**. Click the **Font Color button arrow**. Under **Access Theme Colors**, on the second row, click the last color—**Access Theme 10** — and then apply **Bold** and **Italic**.

17. Click the **Last Name text box control**, and then drag it to the right aligning the left edge of the control with the *A* in the title.

18. **Save** the report, and then switch to **Print Preview**. If you are instructed to submit this result, create a paper or electronic printout.

19. **Close** the report, and then expand the **Navigation Pane**. **Close** the database, and then **Exit** Access. Submit your work as directed.

End **You have completed Project 7F**

Mastering Access

Project 7G — Garden Tours

In this project, you will apply the skills you practiced from the Objectives in Projects 7A and 7B.

Objectives: 3. *Create a Multi-Page Form;* **5.** *Create a Report Based on a Parameter Query.*

Media Southwest Productions produces the television show Southwest Gardens. The show's hosts present tours of public and private gardens that showcase the southwest style. David Tang maintains an updated database about the tours of the featured historic gardens. In this project, you will design a multi-page form for the gardens and tour information that will be used to update this part of the production. You will also create a report based on a parameter query using the name of the garden. Your completed work will look similar to the form and report in Figure 7.51.

For Project 7G, you will need the following files:

a07G_Garden_Tours
a07G_Logo

**You will save your database as
7G_Garden_Tours_Firstname_Lastname
You will save your document as
7G_Garden_Tours_Tabs_Firstname_Lastname**

Figure 7.51

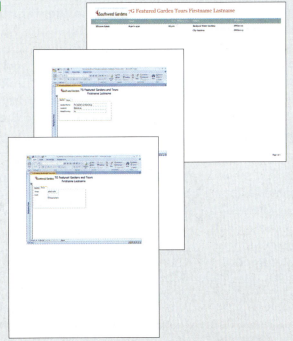

(Project 7G–Garden Tours continues on the next page)

Content-Based Assessments

Mastering Access

(Project 7G–Garden Tours continued)

1. **Start Access**. Locate and open the **a07G_Garden_Tours** file. Save the database in the **Access 2007 Database** format in your **Access Chapter 7** folder as 7G_Garden_Tours_Firstname_Lastname

2. Open **7G Featured Gardens and Tours Form** in **Design view**, and then collapse the **Navigation Pane**. Drag the top of the **Form footer section bar** downward to the **3-inch mark on the vertical ruler**. On the **Design tab** click the **Tab Control** button. In the **Detail** section align the plus (+) sign of the 🔲 pointer with the **.25-inch mark on the horizontal ruler** and with the **.25-inch mark on the vertical ruler**. Click one time.

3. Extend the right edge of the **tab control** to the **5-inch mark on the horizontal ruler**. To the **first page** of the **tab control**, from the **Property Sheet**, add a caption of **Garden** From the **Field List**, add the **Garden Name**, **Location**, and **State/Country** fields. Align the top of the arrow of the 🔲 pointer with the **1.5-inch mark on the horizontal ruler** and with the **.75-inch mark on the vertical ruler**. Extend the **text box controls** to the **4.5-inch mark on the horizontal ruler**. To the **second** page of the **tab control**, add a caption of **Tours** Add the **Times**, **Cost**, and **Reservations** fields to the same position as the first page.

4. To the **title** of the form, add a second line that contains your **Firstname Lastname** and then **Center** it in the control. **Save** the form. Use the Office Clipboard and Microsoft Word to create a document displaying both tab controls of **Record 10**. **Save** this document as 7G_Garden_Tours_Tabs_Firstname_Lastname

5. If you are instructed to submit this result, create a paper or electronic printout of the document. **Close** the **Word** window. If necessary, on the taskbar, click the **Access** button. In the **Access** window, **Close** the form, and then expand the **Navigation Pane**.

6. Click the **7G Garden Tours Query**. Collapse the **Navigation Pane**. **Create** a report using the **Report Wizard**. Use all of the fields. **View** your data by *7G Historical Gardens*. Do not add any grouping levels. **Sort** by **Subject** in **Ascending** order. Use **Block** layout and **Landscape** orientation. Select **Civic** style. Edit the title to display **7G Featured Garden Tours Firstname Lastname** Modify the report's design.

7. Add the **a07G_Logo** to the report and extend the control to the **2-inch mark on the horizontal ruler**. Move the **title control** to the left, aligning the left edge of the title control with the right edge of the logo control. Increase the size of the **Garden Name label control** by dragging the right edge of the control to the **2-inch mark on the horizontal ruler**. Decrease the size of the **Times label control** by dragging the right edge of the control to the **3.5-inch mark on the horizontal ruler**. Extend the right edge of the **Reservation label control** to the **5.5-inch mark on the horizontal ruler**. **Save** the report.

8. Switch to **Print Preview**. In the **Enter Parameter Value** message box, under **Enter Garden name**, type **estate** If you are instructed to submit this result, create a paper or electronic printout, adjusting the margins to fit the report on one page.

9. **Close** the Print Preview window and the report, and then expand the **Navigation Pane**. **Close** the database, and then **Exit** Access. Submit your work as directed.

End **You have completed Project 7G**

Mastering Access

Project 7H—Sweepstakes

In this project, you will apply the skills you practiced from the Objectives in Projects 7A and 7B.

Objectives: 1. *Create a Form in Design View;* **3.** *Format a Form;* **5.** *Create a Report in Design View;* **6.** *Add Controls to a Report;* **7.** *Group, Sort, and Total Records in Design View.*

Southwest Gardens offers three yearly sweepstakes to program viewers who have subscribed to the show's newsletter. The subscribers must register online to enter the sweepstakes. In the following project, you will create a form and a subform to enter the data for the sweepstakes participants. You will also create and modify a subreport based on the entries. You will create an alphabetic index of the entry participants. Your completed form and reports will look similar to those in Figure 7.52.

You will save your database as
7H_Sweepstakes_Firstname_Lastname

Figure 7.52

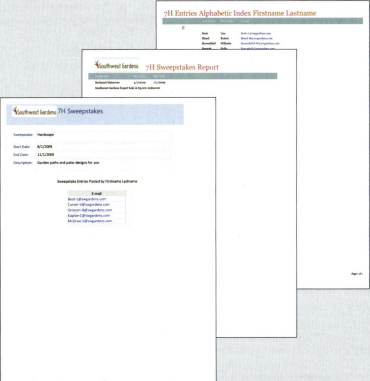

(Project 7H–Sweepstakes continues on the next page)

Content-Based Assessments

(Project 7H–Sweepstakes continued)

1. **Start Access.** Locate and open the **a07H_Sweepstakes** file. Save the database in the **Access 2007 Database** format in your **Access Chapter 7** folder as **7H_Sweepstakes_Firstname_Lastname** Collapse the **Navigation Pane.**

2. **Create** a form based on the **7H Sweepstakes** table. Switch to **Design view.** In the main form, add the **a07H_Logo** and extend the control to the **2-inch mark on the horizontal ruler.** Move the left edge of the **title's label control** to align with the right edge of the logo's label control and the right edge of the title's label control to align with the **6.5-inch mark on the horizontal ruler.** Drag the right edge of the text box controls to the **6.5-inch mark on the horizontal ruler.** Drag the right edge of the form to the **7-inch mark on the horizontal ruler.**

3. Select the **subform control**, and then drag the top edge of the control downward to the **2.5-inch mark on the horizontal ruler.** In the main form above the subform control insert a **label control** aligning the top of the plus (+) sign of the  pointer with the **2-inch mark on the horizontal ruler** and the **2-inch mark on the vertical ruler.** Type Sweepstake Entries Posted by Firstname Lastname

4. Switch to **Layout view.** Drag the right edge of the subform control to the right edge of the **E-mail text box control. Center** the subform below the subform's title label control in the main form.

5. **Save** the form as **7H Sweepstakes Form** If you are instructed to submit this result, create a paper or electronic printout of only **Record 2** of the main form. **Close** the form.

6. Make a **Copy** of the **7H Sweepstakes Report** and name it **7H Sweepstakes Main**

Report Firstname Lastname Open the **7H Sweepstakes Main Report** in **Design view.**

7. In the **Navigation Pane**, click and drag the **7H Sweepstakes Entries** table to the **Detail section** of the main report. Align it with the **.25-inch mark on the horizontal ruler** and the **.75-inch mark on the vertical ruler. Choose from a list** and **Show 7H Sweepstakes Entries for each record in the 7H Sweepstakes List.** Accept the default name for the subreport.

8. In the main report, select and delete the **subreports's label control.** Extend the lower edge of the subreport to the **2-inch mark on the vertical ruler.** In the subreport, select and delete the **Sweepstake label control** and **text box control.**

9. In the main report, in the **Page Footer section**, click the **Now() control box** to the right of the equal sign. Using your own first name and last name, type **"Prepared by Firstname Lastname on"&**

10. **Save** the report. If you are instructed to submit this result, create a paper or electronic printout of the first page of the report. **Close** the Print Preview window and the report. Expand the **Navigation Pane.**

11. Select the **7H Entries Query. Create** a report using the **Report Wizard.** Under **Available Fields**, add all fields to the **Selected Fields** box. Use **Tabular** layout and **Portrait** orientation. Select the **Civic** style. Edit the **title** of the report to 7H Entries Alphabetic Index Firstname Lastname

12. Switch to **Layout view.** Size all text box controls so that all of the data displays for every record. Add a **Group** on **Last Name, by first character**, with **no title.** Select the label and text box controls and move them to the right, aligning the left edge under the *A* in the title.

(Project 7H–Sweepstakes continues on the next page)

Access

chapterseven

Mastering Access

(Project 7H–Sweepstakes continued)

13. Click the **text box control** that displays the letter *B*. Change the **Font Color** to **Maroon**, change the **Font Size** to **12**, and then click the **Italic** button.

14. **Save** the report, and then switch to **Print Preview**. If you are instructed to submit this result, create a paper or electronic printout of the first page of the report. **Close** Print Preview.

15. **Close** the report, and then expand the **Navigation Pane**. **Close** the database, and **Exit** Access. Submit your work as directed.

End **You have completed Project 7H**

Mastering Access

Project 7I—Advertising

In this project, you will apply the skills you practiced from all the Objectives in Projects 7A and 7B.

Media Southwest Productions is funded by sponsors and advertisers. Toni Jones, president of the company, organizes the advertising in a database. In this project you will create advanced forms and subforms to help with the data entry. You will design reports and subreports to display the data in a useful manner. You will also design a report to display the advertisers in an alphabetical index. Your completed forms and reports will look similar to those in Figure 7.53.

For Project 7I, you will need the following files:

a07I_Advertising
a07I_Logo

You will save your database as
7I_Advertising_Firstname_Lastname
You will save your document as
7I_Advertiser_Contacts_Firstname_Lastname

Figure 7.53

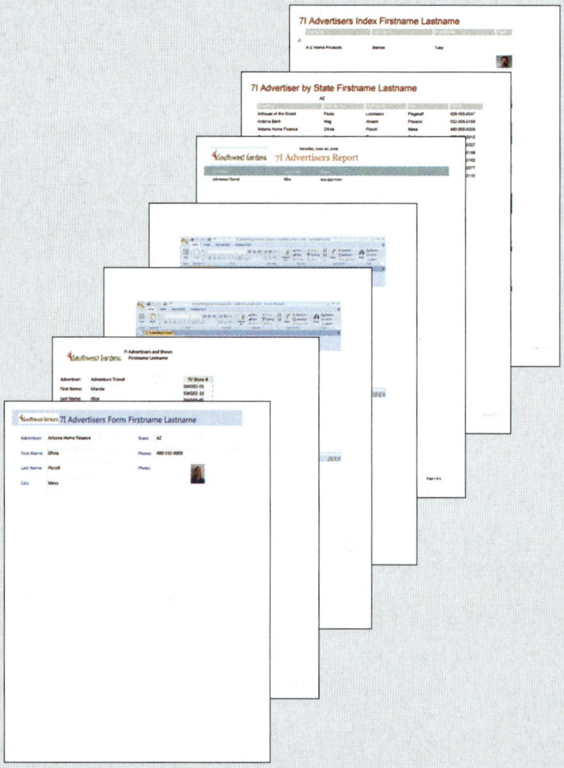

(Project 7I–Advertising continues on the next page)

Content-Based Assessments

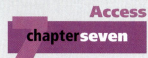
Mastering Access

(Project 7I–Advertising continued)

1. **Start Access**. Locate and open the **a07I_Advertising** file. Save the database in the **Access 2007 Database** format in your **Access Chapter 7** folder as 7I_Advertising_Firstname_Lastname

2. Using the **7I Advertisers Form**, **Create** a **Split Form**. Display the datasheet on the bottom. Choose to print the form only. Add your first and last names to the form title. Add the **a07I_Logo** to the form.

3. **Save** the form as **7I Advertisers Split Form Firstname Lastname** and then navigate to **Record 5**. In the form section, on the left side, click the **Record Selector** bar. If you are instructed to submit this result, create a paper or electronic printout of **Record 5** only. **Close** the form.

4. Select the **7I Advertisers** table and create a form in **Form Design**. Add the following fields to the design grid: **Advertiser**, **First Name**, **Last Name**, and **Phone**. Place the fields at the **1-inch mark on the horizontal ruler** and the **.25-inch mark on the vertical ruler**.

5. Select and drag the **7I TV Show Advertisers** table to the form design grid and align it with the **.5-inch mark on the horizontal ruler** and the **1.5-inch mark on the vertical ruler**. Choose from a list, showing **7I TV Show Advertisers**. Accept the default name for the subform. Delete the **subform label control**. In the subform, delete the **Advertiser label** and **text box controls**. Switch to **Layout view**. Adjust text box control widths to display all data and resize the subform to eliminate the scroll bars. Align the right edge of the subform with the right edge of the TV Show # field. **Save** the form as 7I **Advertisers and Shows Firstname Lastname**

6. Switch to **Design view**. Add the **a07I_Logo** and extend the label control to the **2-inch**

mark on the horizontal ruler. Add a **Title label control** at the right edge of the logo. Click, and then type **7I Advertisers and Shows** Place your first and last name on a second line of the title. **Center** the text. Move the subform control upward and to the right. Align it with the **4-inch mark on the horizontal ruler**, and align the top of the subform with the top of the **Advertiser text box control**. **Save** the form.

7. Switch to **Form view**. In the form section, on the left side, click the **Record Selector** bar. If you are instructed to submit this result, create a paper or electronic print-out of **Record 1** only. **Close** the form.

8. Open the **7I Advertisers TC Form** in **Design view**. Add a **tab control** to the design grid and align it at the **.25-inch mark on the horizontal ruler** and the **.25-inch mark on the vertical ruler**. Expand the right edge of the tab control to the **4-inch mark on the horizontal ruler**.

9. To the **first page** of the **tab control**, from the *7I Advertisers* table, add the following fields: **Advertiser**, **City**, **State**, and **Phone** Align the fields with the **1.5-inch mark on the horizontal ruler** and the **.75-inch mark on the vertical ruler**. Add the **Caption Advertiser** to the first tab. Switch to **Layout view**. Expand the **Advertiser text box control** to display the data in all records.

10. Switch to **Design view**. To the **second page** of the **tab control**, from the *7I Advertisers* table, add the **First Name**, **Last Name**, and **Photo** fields. Align the fields with the **1.5-inch mark on the horizontal ruler** and the **.75-inch mark on the vertical ruler**. Add the **Caption Contact**

11. Drag the right edge of the **title's label control** to the **5-inch mark on the horizontal ruler**. To a second line of the form

(Project 7I–Advertising continues on the next page)

Content-Based Assessments

(Project 7I–Advertising continued)

title's label control, add your first and last names. **Center** the title text. **Save** the form and switch to **Form view**. Navigate to **Record 7**.

12. Use the Office Clipboard and Microsoft Word to create a document displaying the contents of both tabs. Save the document as **7I_Advertiser_Contacts_Firstname_Lastname** If you are instructed to submit this result, create a paper or electronic printout of the document. **Close** the **Word** window. If necessary, on the taskbar, click the **Access** button. In the **Access** window, **Close** the form, and then expand the **Navigation Pane**.

13. Make a **Copy** of the **7I Advertisers Report** and **Paste** the copy as **7I Advertisers Main Report Firstname Lastname** and open the new report in **Design view**.

14. Click and drag the **7I TV Show Advertisers** table to the **Detail section** of the report, aligning it at the **2-inch mark on the horizontal ruler** and the **1-inch mark on the vertical ruler**. Choose the fields from a list so that **7I TV Show Advertisers for each record in 7I Advertisers using Advertiser** is shown. Change the **title** of the subreport to **7I TV Shows**

15. From the subreport, delete the **Advertiser label** and **text box controls**. **Remove** and delete the **TV Show # label control**. Reduce the width of the subreport to **1.5-inches**. In the main form, insert a **line** just above the **Page Footer section bar**. Extend the line from the left edge of the report to the **5-inch mark on the horizontal ruler**. Format the line in the color of **Maroon** and **Line Thickness** of **2 pt**.

16. Into the **Report Header section**, insert the **Date**. Use the **first format option** and

do not include the time. **Center** the **date's label control** over the title's label control. **Center** the date text. In the **Page Footer section**, delete the **Now() control** and replace it with a **label control**. Type your **Firstname Lastname** in the control.

17. Switch to **Layout view**. If necessary, resize the subreport control to eliminate all scroll bars. In the subreport label control, change the **Font Color** to **Maroon** and change the **Font Size** to **12**.

18. View the report in **Print Preview**, and then if you are instructed to submit this result, create a paper or electronic printout of the first page of the report. **Close** the Print Preview window and the report, and then expand the **Navigation Pane**.

19. Select the **7I Advertiser State Query**. Using the **Report Wizard**, create a report based on this parameter query. Select all fields for the report. Do not add any grouping or sorting. Use **Tabular** layout and **Portrait** orientation. Select the **Northwind** style. Title the report **7I Advertiser by State Firstname Lastname** Select **Modify the report's design**, and then click **Finish**.

20. Delete the **State label** and **text box controls**. Into the **Report Header section**, insert a **text box control** below the word *State* in the title. Delete the label control for this newly added text box control. In the text box control, type **=[State]**

21. Switch to **Layout view**. In the **Enter Parameter Value** message box, in the **Enter State Abbreviation** box, type **AZ** Resize the **Advertiser** field to display all of the data. **Save** the report.

22. View the report in **Print Preview**, and then if you are instructed to submit this result, create a paper or electronic printout. the

(Project 7I–Advertising continues on the next page)

Mastering Access

(Project 7I–Advertising continued)

report. **Close** the Print Preview window and the report, and then expand the **Navigation Pane**.

23. Select the **7I Advertisers** table. **Create** a report using the **Report Wizard**. Under **Available Fields**, add **Advertiser**, **First Name**, **Last Name**, and **Photo** to the **Selected Fields** box. Use **Tabular** layout and **Portrait** orientation. Select the **Northwind** style. Edit the **title** of the report to 7I Advertisers Index Firstname Lastname Select **Modify the report's design**, and then click **Finish**. Resize the **Photo control** to **Width** of **.5** inch and **Height** of **1** inch.

24. Switch to **Layout view**, Size all text box controls so that all of the data displays for every record. **Add a Group** on **Advertiser**,

by first character, with **no title**. Select the text box control that displays the letter A and then move it to the left, aligning the left edge with the left margin of the report. Click the **text box control** that displays the letter A. Change the **Font Color** to **Maroon**, change the **Font Size** to **12**, and then click the **Italic** button. **Save** the report.

25. View the report in **Print Preview**, and then if you are instructed to submit this result, create a paper or electronic printout of the first page of the report. **Close** the Print Preview window and the report.

26. Expand the **Navigation Pane**, **Close** the database, and then **Exit** Access. Submit your work as directed.

End **You have completed Project 7I**

Content-Based Assessments

 Business Running Case

Project 7J—Business Running Case

In this project, you will apply the skills you have practiced from the Objectives in Projects 7A and 7B.

From My Computer, navigate to the student files that accompany this textbook. In the folder **03_business_running_case**, locate and open the folder for this chapter. Open and print the instructions for this project, which are provided to you in Adobe PDF format. Follow the instructions and use the knowledge and skills you have gained thus far to assist the brother and sister team of Michael and Kristen Landry in meeting the challenges of owning and running their business.

End **You have completed Project 7J** ⎯⎯⎯⎯⎯⎯⎯

Outcomes-Based Assessments

Rubric

The following outcomes-based assessments are *open-ended assessments*. That is, there is no specific correct result; your result will depend on your approach to the information provided. Make *professional quality* your goal. Use the following scoring rubric to guide you in *how* to approach the problem and then to evaluate *how well* your approach solves the problem.

The *criteria* —Software Mastery, Content, Format and Layout, and Process—represent the knowledge and skills you have gained that you can apply to solving the problem. The *levels of performance* —Professional Quality, Approaching Professional Quality, or Needs Quality Improvement—help you and your instructor evaluate your result.

	Your completed project is of Professional Quality if you:	**Your completed project is Approaching Professional Quality if you:**	**Your completed project Needs Quality Improvements if you:**
Software Mastery	Choose and apply the most appropriate skills, tools, and features and identify efficient methods to solve the problem.	Choose and apply some appropriate skills, tools, and features, but not in the most efficient manner.	Choose inappropriate skills, tools, or features, or are inefficient in solving the problem.
Content	Construct a solution that is clear and well organized, contains content that is accurate, appropriate to the audience and purpose, and is complete. Provide a solution that contains no errors of spelling, grammar, or style.	Construct a solution in which some components are unclear, poorly organized, inconsistent, or incomplete. Misjudge the needs of the audience. Have some errors in spelling, grammar, or style, but the errors do not detract from comprehension.	Construct a solution that is unclear, incomplete, or poorly organized, containing some inaccurate or inappropriate content; and contains many errors of spelling, grammar, or style. Do not solve the problem.
Format and Layout	Format and arrange all elements to communicate information and ideas, clarify function, illustrate relationships, and indicate relative importance.	Apply appropriate format and layout features to some elements, but not others. Overuse features, causing minor distraction.	Apply format and layout that do not communicate information or ideas clearly. Do not use format and layout features to clarify function, illustrate relationships, or indicate relative importance. Use available features excessively, causing distraction.
Process	Use an organized approach that integrates planning, development, self-assessment, revision, and reflection.	Demonstrate an organized approach in some areas, but not others; or, use an insufficient process of organization throughout.	Do not use an organized approach to solve the problem.

Problem Solving

Project 7K — Host Itinerary

In this project, you will construct a solution by applying any combination of the skills you practiced from the Objectives in Projects 7A and 7B.

For Project 7K, you will need the following file:

a07K_Host_Itinerary
a07K_Logo

**You will save your database as
7K_Host_Itinerary_Firstname_Lastname**

Vicky Aurelias and Phillip Miel are co-hosts of the television show Southwest Gardens. The show includes some broadcasts from beautiful historic gardens around the world. The travel itineraries for the hosts have to be planned a year or more in advance. In this project, you will open the **a07K_Host_Itinerary** database and save it as **7K_Host_Itinerary_Firstname_Lastname**

Make a copy of the **7K SWG Employees Form**. Name the copy **7K SWG Employees Main Form** Using the copy as the main form, create a subform from the *7K Itinerary* table. Delete the *ID* and *Host* fields from the subform. Adjust all label and text box controls to display all data. Add your first name and last name to the subform's label control. Save the form as **7K Host Itinerary Subform**

Using the **7K Itinerary Parameter Query**, create two reports. The first one should list Vicky's Itinerary—7K Vicky's Itinerary. The second one should list Phillip's Itinerary—7K Phillip's Itinerary. Sort the reports by arrival date. Add the **a07K_Logo**. Add appropriate titles identifying the report by using the parameter in a report header text box control. In the report footer, add a text box control that displays the date and your first name and last name. If you are instructed to submit this result, create a paper or electronic printout of the forms for Vicky and Phillip. Create a paper or electronic printout of the itinerary reports for each host.

End You have completed Project 7K ———————

Access

chapter seven

Problem Solving

Project 7L — Special Programming

In this project, you will construct a solution by applying any combination of the skills you practiced from the Objectives in Projects 7A and 7B.

For Project 7L, you will need the following files:

a07L_Special_Programming
a07L_Logo

You will save your database as
7L_Special_Programming_Firstname_Lastname
You will save your document as
7L_Special_Programming_Firstname_Lastname

Toni Jones, president of Media Southwest Productions, has asked two of her employees—Karen Galvin and Henry Cavazos—to schedule special programming segments for the Southwest Gardens television show. These segments will focus on holiday and seasonal topics.

Open the **a07L_Special_Programming** database and save it as **7L_Special_Programming_Firstname_Lastname** In this project, you will use the **7L TV Shows Form** to create a multi-page form. To the first tab, add the TV Show # and the Original Air Date fields. Caption this tab **Show** To the second tab, add the Subject, Featured Garden, and Program fields. Caption this tab **Program** Adjust the tab controls and the label and text box controls to display all data. Create a Microsoft Word document to show the contents of both tabs. Save this document as **7L_Special_Programming_Firstname_Lastname** If you are instructed to submit this result, create a paper or electronic printout of this document.

Use the **7L TV Shows Query** to create a split form. Adjust label and text box controls to display all data. Display the data sheet on top. Select to print only the form. Add the **a07L_Logo** to the form. Add your first name and last name to a second line of the title. Save the form as **7L TV Shows Split Form** If you are instructed to submit this result, create a paper or electronic printout of only the first record.

Create an alphabetical index on special programs. Format the text box controls containing the letters. Arrange and adjust label and text box controls to display all data. Save this report as **7L Special Programming Index** If you are instructed to submit this result, create a paper or electronic printout of the report.

End **You have completed Project 7L**

Outcomes-Based Assessments

Problem Solving

Project 7M — Employees

In this project, you will construct a solution by applying any combination of the skills you practiced from the Objectives in Projects 7A and 7B.

> **For Project 7M, you will need the following file:**
>
> a07M_Employees

**You will save your database as
7M_Employees_Firstname_Lastname**

There are two hosts for the television show Southwest Gardens. They rotate their responsibilities. In this project you will open the **a07M_ Employees** database and save it as **7M_Employees_Firstname_Lastname** You will create and modify a subform to enter the TV show data for each host. Make a copy of the **7M SWG Employees Form**. Name the copy **7M TV Show Host** Open this form in Design view and drag the **7M TV Shows** table onto the form. Name the subform **7M TV Shows** Delete the Host label and text box controls. Adjust the label and text box controls to display all data. Eliminate scroll bars by resizing the subform. Center the subform label control over the subform. Edit the title of the main form by adding a second line of text that reads **designed by Firstname Lastname** Save the form. If you are instructed to submit this result, create a paper or electronic printout of only the form for Phillip Miel.

Make a copy of the **7M SWG Hosts Report**. Name the copy **7M Host Main Report** Open the **7M Host Main Report**. Onto this copy of the report, drag the **7M TV Shows** table. In the Subreport Wizard, select None for fields to link. From the subreport delete the Host label and text controls. Adjust the label and text controls to display all of the data. Delete the subreport label control. In the Report Footer of the main report, edit the date control to include **printed by Firstname Lastname** Save the report. If you are instructed to submit this result, create a paper or electronic printout of the report.

End **You have completed Project 7M** ——————

Problem Solving

Project 7N — Seminars

In this project, you will construct a solution by applying any combination of the skills you practiced from the Objectives in Projects 7A and 7B.

For Project 7N, you will need the following files:

a07N_Seminars
a07N_Logo

You will save your database as
7N_Seminars_Firstname_Lastname
You will save your document as
7N_Seminars_Tabs_Firstname_Lastname

Toni Jones, president of Media Southwest Productions, has tasked three of her employees with the responsibility of researching and lecturing on various seminar topics. These seminars are held at the television studio from where the Southwest Gardens show is broadcasted.

In this project you will open the **a07N_Seminars** database and save it as **7N_Seminars_Firstname_Lastname** Starting in Form Design view, you will create a multi-page form using fields from the **7N SWG Seminars** table and the **7N SWG Lecturer** table. Add the **a07N_Logo** and size the width to approximately 2 inches. Add a title that includes your first and last names. Display the lecturer information on one tab and the seminar information on the second tab. Add appropriate captions to the tabs. Resize the tab control as necessary. Adjust all label and text box controls to display all data. Save the form as **7N Seminar and Lecturer Form** Save the form. Select the first record. Use the Office Clipboard and Microsoft Word to save a copy of both tabs of the form. Save this document as **7N_Seminars_Tabs_Firstname_Lastname** If you are instructed to submit this result, create a paper or electronic printout of the document.

Create an alphabetic index report of the seminar topics presented through Southwest Gardens. Add the **a07N_Logo** to the report header and your first and last names to the report footer. Change the font color, font size, and font style of the text box controls that contain the letters. Adjust label and text box controls to display all data. If you are instructed to submit this result, create a paper or electronic printout of the report.

End You have completed Project 7N ————

Outcomes-Based Assessments

Problem Solving

Project 7O — Flowers

In this project, you will construct a solution by applying any combination of the skills you practiced from the Objectives in Projects 6A and 6B.

> **For Project 7O, you will need the following files:**
>
> a07O_Flowers
> a07O_Logo
>
> **You will save your database as**
> **7O_Flowers_Firstname_Lastname**

As a promotion for the Southwest Gardens television show, Toni Jones, president of Media Southwest Productions, is always looking for ways to increase the attendance of the live studio audience. She has decided to offer a featured plant to the guests in the audience.

Open the **a07O_Flowers** database and save it as **7O_Flowers_Firstname_Lastname** In this project, you will create a split form based on the *7O Flower/Plant* table. In the form, adjust label and text box controls to just display all data. Display the form above the data sheet. Delete the Photo label control and arrange the label and text box controls so that the first column contains the ID#, Photo, Common Name, and Scientific Name fields. The second column should display the other four fields. Add the **a07O_Logo** to the form header. Edit the form title to include your first and last names. Select the option to print the form only. Save the form as **7O Flower/Plant Split Form** If you are instructed to submit this result, create a paper or electronic printout of the form of record 8 only.

Open the **7O TV Shows Form** in Design view. Drag the *7O Historical Gardens* table to the design grid. Link Featured Garden to Garden Name. Drag the *7O Flower/Plant* table to the design grid below the Historical Gardens subform. Link Featured Plant to ID#. Save the form as **7O Shows/Gardens/Plants Form** Open each of the subforms and change the default view property to single form. Size the subforms to display all controls and eliminate any scroll bars. If you are instructed to submit this result, select record 4 of the main form. Create a paper or electronic printout of record 4 only.

End **You have completed Project 7O** —————————

 **Access**
chapterseven You and **GO!**

Project 7P—You and **GO!**

In this project, you will construct a solution by applying any combination of the Objectives found in Projects 7A and 7B.

From My Computer, navigate to the student files that accompany this textbook. In the folder **04_you_and_go**, locate and open the folder for this chapter. Open and print the instructions for this project, which are provided to you in Adobe PDF format. Follow the instructions to create forms and reports for your personal inventory.

End **You have completed Project 7P** —————————

GO! with Help

Project 7Q—**GO!** with Help

The Access Help system is extensive and can help you as you work. In this project, you will view information about adding aggregate functions to a report in Design view.

1 **Start Access**. On the right side of the Ribbon, click the **Microsoft Office Access Help** button. In the **Type words to search for** box, in the **Access Help** window, type **subreport** and then press .

2 In the displayed **Search Results** task pane, click **Create and use subreports**. Maximize the displayed window. Read the section titled **Display a total from a subreport on the main report**.

3 If you want to print a copy of the information. Select the text and click the **Print** button at the top of **Access Help** window. Under **Page Range**, select **Selection**, and then click **Print**.

4 **Close** the Help window, and then **Exit** Access.

End **You have completed Project 7Q** —————————

8 chaptereight

Creating Macros, PivotTables, and PivotCharts

OBJECTIVES

At the end of this chapter you will be able to:

1. Create a Standalone Macro with One Action
2. Add Multiple Actions to a Standalone Macro
3. Create a Macro Group
4. Associate a Macro with an Event
5. Create an Embedded Macro
6. Print Macro Details

7. Create a PivotTable from a Query
8. Create a PivotChart from a PivotTable

OUTCOMES

Mastering these objectives will enable you to:

PROJECT 8A
Create and Modify Macros

PROJECT 8B
Create and Modify PivotCharts and PivotTables

Providence and Warwick Hospital

Providence and Warwick Hospital serves the metropolitan area of Providence, Rhode Island, and the surrounding cities of Warwick, Rhode Island, and Fall River, Massachusetts. It is a world-class medical facility providing care to adults and children through the hospital as well as a number of social service and multidisciplinary facilities, such as the Asthma Center and Adult Metabolism Clinic. Scientists at the hospital conduct research and clinical trials of new drugs. The hospital's medical staff focuses on innovation and new technologies to provide quality patient care to patients at every stage of life.

Creating Macros, PivotTables, and PivotCharts

When working with Access, there are many tasks that you may need to perform repeatedly. You can automate a task by using a macro—a series of actions grouped together as a single command to accomplish a task or multiple tasks automatically. An action is a self-contained instruction that can be combined with other actions to automate tasks. For example, you may create a report or query that you open and print on a weekly basis. You can create a macro that prints the report when the user clicks a command button, or you can create a macro to add records to a second form.

Data in tables, queries, or forms can be displayed as a PivotTable or PivotChart to provide a more analytical view of the data. If you have worked with advanced features in Microsoft Excel, you may know how to create PivotTables and PivotCharts. A PivotTable is used to organize, arrange, analyze, and summarize data in a meaningful way. A PivotChart is a graphical view of the data in a PivotTable. In both PivotTables and PivotCharts, you can rearrange the data to display it with different row and column headings to perform a different analysis of the data.

Project 8A Benefits Info Sessions

Maria Benitez, Vice President of Operations for Providence and Warwick Hospital, wants to customize the database to display a form when the database is opened. She also wants to add buttons on the form to automate some of the most common tasks, such as displaying room information for an event or finding an event. In Activities 8.1 through 8.10, you will create macros to automatically display a form and message box when an individual opens the database. You will associate command buttons with a macro, group macros, and embed macros within a form, in addition to creating conditions that control whether a macro runs. Finally, you will display and print a report that documents the details of the macros you created. When completed, your results will look similar to Figure 8.1.

For Project 8A, you will need the following file:

a08A_Benefits_Info_Sessions

You will save your database as
8A_Benefits_Info_Sessions_Firstname_Lastname

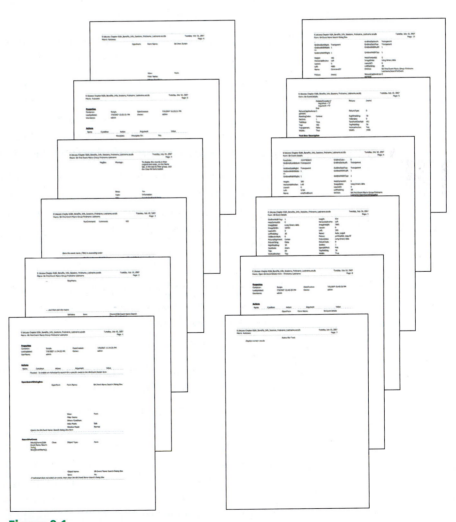

Figure 8.1
Project 8A—Benefits Info Sessions

Objective 1
Create a Standalone Macro with One Action

A *macro* is a series of actions grouped as a single command to accomplish a task or multiple tasks automatically. A *standalone macro* is a macro contained in a macro object that displays under Macros on the Navigation Pane. Some of the more commonly used actions are to open a report, find a record, display a message box, or apply a filter to a form or report. An *action* is a self-contained instruction that can be combined with other actions to automate tasks.

Before creating a macro, you should design it, listing the actions you want to occur and the order in which the actions should be executed. You should determine if an argument applies to the action. An *argument* is a value that provides information to the macro action, such as the words to display in a message box, or the control upon which to operate. You should also determine if any conditions should be specified. A *condition* specifies that certain criteria must be met before the macro action executes.

Activity 8.1 Creating a Standalone Macro

In this activity, you will create a standalone macro that will display the *8A Event Details* form when the macro is run.

1 Start Access. Navigate to the location where the student data files for this textbook are saved. Locate and open the **a08A_Benefits_ Info_Sessions** file. Click the **Office** button [icon], point to **Save As**, and then click **Access 2007 Database**. In the **Save As** dialog box, navigate to the drive on which you will be saving your folders and projects for this chapter. Create a new folder named **Access Chapter 8** and save the database as **8A_Benefits_Info_Sessions_Firstname_Lastname** in the folder.

2 If necessary, add the Access Chapter 8 folder to the Trust Center. On the **Navigation Pane**, under **Forms**, double-click **8A Event Details** to open the form in Form view. Notice that this form does not open automatically when the database is opened; you must double-click it to open it.

For this chapter, you must add the Access Chapter 8 folder to the Trust Center—you cannot just enable the content because some of the macros need to be trusted and will not execute properly if the database is not trusted.

3 Close [×] the form, and then collapse [«] the **Navigation Pane**.

4 On the Ribbon, click the **Create tab**. In the **Other group**, click the **Macro** button, and then compare your screen with Figure 8.2.

The Macro Builder displays, from which you can build the list of actions to be carried out when the macro runs. When the Macro Builder is first opened, the Action, Arguments, and Comment columns display. The Arguments column displays arguments that have been entered for an action. The Comment column displays a short description of the action and argument. The buttons on the Design tab are used to run, test, or modify a macro. The Show/Hide group displays buttons that are used to display columns in the Macro Builder or to display more actions.

Describe the action and argument

Figure 8.2

Macro Builder window

Select action

Argument for the action

Toggle buttons to display more columns

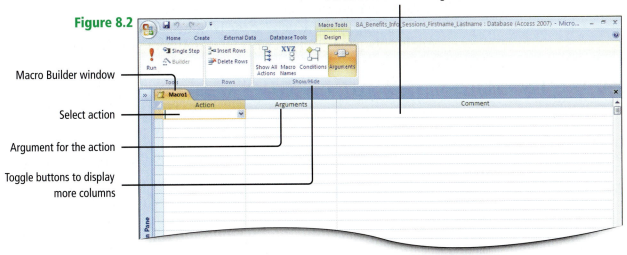

5 In the **Macro Builder**, under **Action**, in the first row, click the displayed **arrow**, and then compare your screen with Figure 8.3.

Because the Show All Actions button is not active, a shorter list of macro actions displays. These macro actions can be used in a database that has not been trusted. You can click the Show all Actions button to display a longer list of macro actions; however, if the database is not trusted and you select a macro action that requires the database to be trusted, the macro will not execute, and a message box will display.

Figure 8.3

Button not active

List of trusted macro actions

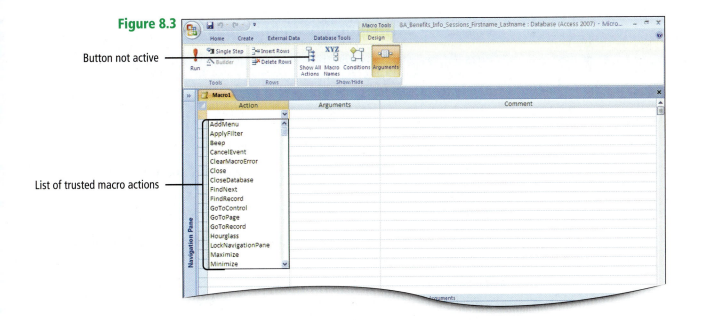

6 Scroll down the displayed list, and then click **OpenForm**. At the bottom right side of the screen, notice the description of the OpenForm action. Compare your screen with Figure 8.4.

The OpenForm action opens a form in Form view by default. The Arguments column displays the default arguments that are associated with the OpenForm action. At the bottom of the window, an Action Arguments pane displays, where the arguments can be entered.

Figure 8.4

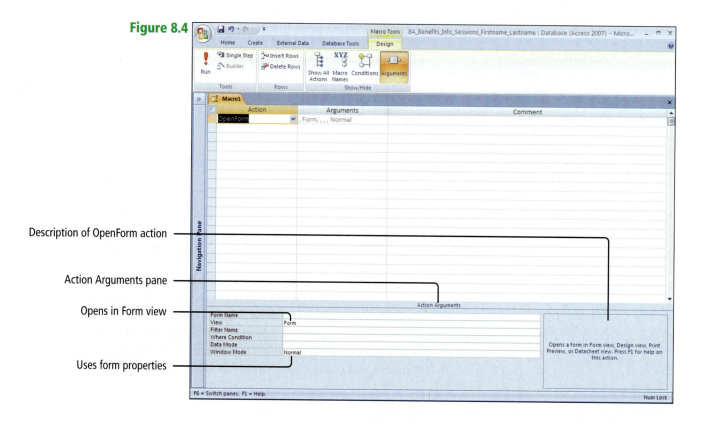

Description of OpenForm action

Action Arguments pane

Opens in Form view

Uses form properties

Note — Switching Between Panes

Press F6 to switch between the Macro Builder pane and the Action Arguments pane. Press F1 in an Action box or an Action Argument box to display the Access Help window.

---

7 Under **Action**, with **OpenForm** selected, press F1.

The Access Help window displays information about the OpenForm Macro Action.

8 Take a moment to scroll through the Access Help window to review the information. When you are finished, **Close** ⊠ the **Access Help** window.

9 Press F6 to switch to the **Action Arguments pane**. Alternatively, click in the Form Name box in the Action Arguments pane.

The insertion point is positioned in the Form Name box. At the bottom right side of the screen, the description of the action argument displays.

10 In the **Form Name** box, click the displayed **arrow**, and then click **8A Event Details**.

This is a required argument. After selecting the form, the name of the form displays in the Arguments column as the first argument.

11 Click in the **View** box, and then click the **arrow**. Notice that you can open the form in Form view, Design view, Print Preview, Datasheet view, PivotTable view, PivotChart view, or Layout view. Be sure that **Form** is selected.

12 Click in the **Filter Name** box, and then read the accompanying description. Click in the **Where Condition** box, and then read the accompanying description. Finally, click in the **Data Mode** box and read the description. Be sure that these arguments are left blank.

The Data Mode argument is used for forms that open in either Form view or Datasheet view. If left blank, Access opens the form in the data entry mode set in the form's Allow Edits, Allow Deletions, Allow Additions, and DataEntry property settings. Because these three arguments have no entries, the Arguments column displays three commas, one for each blank argument.

13 Click in the **Window Mode** box, and then read the accompanying description. Notice the options for displaying the form. Be sure that Window Mode setting is **Normal**. In the **Macro Builder**, point to the right column boundary of **Arguments** until the ⊕ pointer displays, and then double-click to resize the Arguments column. Compare your screen with Figure 8.5.

Arguments are entered in the Action Arguments pane, not the Arguments column. The commas in the Arguments column indicate that there was no argument entered for a property in the Action Arguments pane.

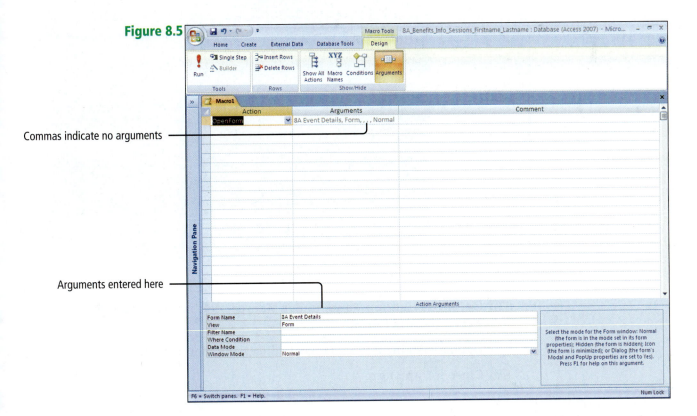

Figure 8.5

Commas indicate no arguments

Arguments entered here

14 In the **Macro Builder**, on the **first row**, click in the **Comment** box, and then type **Displays the 8A Event Details form when the macro is run - Firstname Lastname** and then press Enter.

You should always enter a description of a macro so that you and others can determine easily the actions that will occur when the macro runs.

15 On the **Design tab**, in the **Tools group**, click the **Run** button.

A message displays stating that you must save the macro before you run it.

16 In the displayed message box, click **Yes** to save the macro. In the **Save As** dialog box, under **Macro Name**, type **Open 8A Event Details Form - Firstname Lastname** and then click **OK**.

The macro is saved and runs. When the macro runs, it displays the *8A Event Details* form.

17 **Close** ☒ the *8A Event Details* form, and then **Close** ☒ the Macro Builder. Expand ☒ the **Navigation Pane**, and then compare your screen with Figure 8.6.

On the Navigation Pane, a new group—Macros—displays, and the newly created macro object displays under the group name.

Figure 8.6

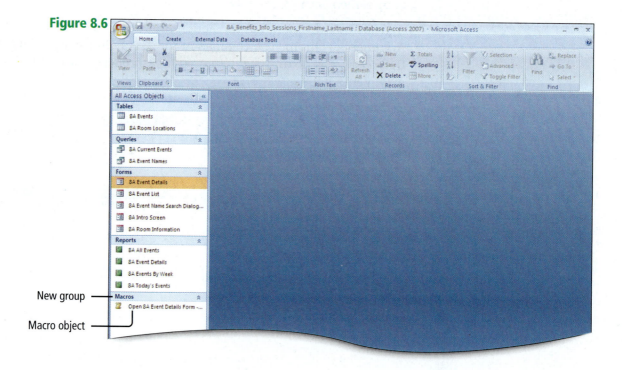

New group ——

Macro object ——

18 On the **Navigation Pane**, under **Macros**, double-click **Open 8A Event Details Form**.

Double-clicking a macro object causes the macro to run.

19 **Close** ☒ the form.

Activity 8.2 Opening a Form in Its Own Window

In this activity, you will modify the properties of a form to create a pop-up, modal window. A ***pop-up window*** suddenly displays (pops up), usually contains a menu of commands, and stays on the screen only until the user selects one of the commands. A ***modal window*** is a child (secondary window) to a parent window—the original window that opened the modal window—that takes over control of the parent window. A user cannot press any controls or enter any information in the parent window until the modal window is closed. Both pop-up and modal windows are commonly used when the database designer wants to direct a user's focus to the information in the window.

1 On the **Navigation Pane**, under **Forms**, double-click **8A Intro Screen** to open the form in Form view.

Like most of the objects you have opened, the form displays with its own tab.

2 Switch to **Design** view. On the **Design tab**, in the **Tools group**, click the **Property Sheet** button. If the Property Sheet does not display *Selection type: Form*, click the Selection type arrow, and then click Form.

3 On the **Property Sheet**, click the **Other tab**. Click the **Pop Up** property setting box **arrow**, and then click **Yes**. Click in the **Modal** property setting box, click the **arrow**, and then click **Yes**. Compare your screen with Figure 8.7.

The Pop Up property setting of Yes displays the object in its own window on top of all other opened objects. A setting of No displays the object as a tabbed object. Changing the Pop Up setting to Yes is most commonly used for objects that you want to get the attention of the individual using the database. The Modal property setting is used to keep the focus on the opened form. An individual cannot change the focus to another database object until the form is closed.

Figure 8.7

Modal property
setting changed

Property Sheet for form

Pop Up property
setting changed

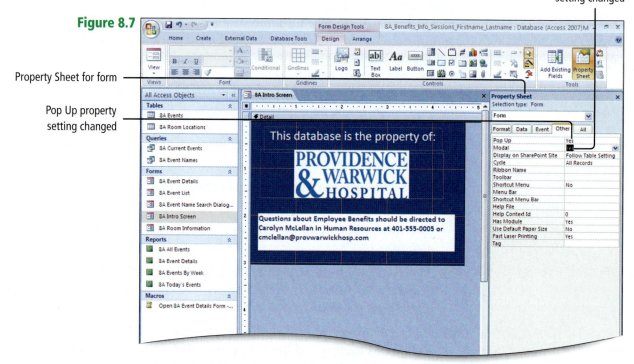

④ **Close** ✕ the **Property Sheet**, and then **Close** ✕ the form, saving changes when prompted. On the **Navigation Pane**, under **Macros**, double-click **Open 8A Event Details Form**, and then under **Forms**, double-click **8A Intro Screen** to open both forms in Form view. Notice the text in the title bar of the pop-up window. On the **Navigation Pane**, under **Forms**, double-click **8A Room Information**, and notice that the form does not open. Compare your screen with Figure 8.8.

8A Event Details opens as a default tabbed object, and *8A Intro Screen* opens in its own pop-up window. The pop-up window can be moved or closed. Until it is closed, the focus cannot be changed to another database object; that is why you cannot open the *8A Room Information* form. The *8A Intro Screen* form does not display Minimize or Maximize buttons, only a Close button. A form with the Modal property setting of Yes does not display the Minimize or Maximize buttons. A pop-up window with a Modal property setting of No can display the Minimize and Maximize buttons.

Figure 8.8

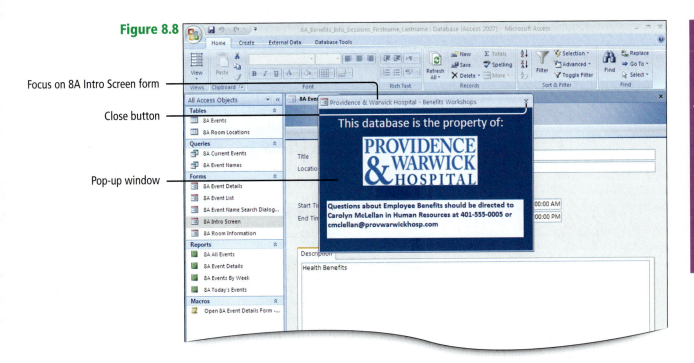

Focus on 8A Intro Screen form

Close button

Pop-up window

---

5 **Close** ☒ the **8A Intro Screen** form, and then **Close** ☒ the **8A Event Details** form. On the **Navigation Pane**, under **Forms**, right-click **8A Intro Screen**, and then click **Design View**.

6 On the **Design tab**, in the **Tools group**, click the **Property Sheet** button. Be sure that the **Selection type** box displays **Form**. On the **Property Sheet**, click the **Format tab**, and then take a moment to review some of the property settings for this form while comparing your screen with Figure 8.9.

The text entered in the caption property displays on the title bar of the form when it is displayed in Form view. The Allow Form View property setting is Yes, while all of the other views are disabled. Recall that you can click in a property setting box, and then press F1 to display the Access Help window for the property setting.

The Border Style property setting is Dialog, which is a thick border that can include a title bar with a Close button. The form cannot be resized, maximized, or minimized with this border style. Because this is a custom form that does not display any records from an underlying table or query, the Record Selectors, Navigation Buttons, and Scrolls Bars property settings have been set to No.

Figure 8.9

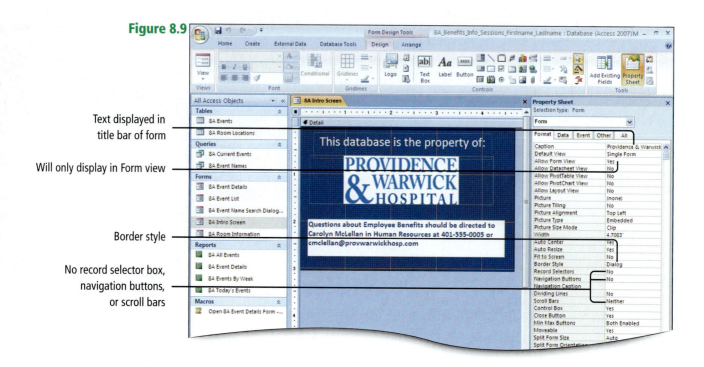

Text displayed in title bar of form

Will only display in Form view

Border style

No record selector box, navigation buttons, or scroll bars

7 Close ☒ the **Property Sheet**, **Close** ☒ the form, and then collapse ☒ the **Navigation Pane**.

Activity 8.3 Creating a Second Standalone Macro that Automatically Executes

In this activity, you will create another standalone macro that will open the *8A Intro Screen* form when the database is opened.

1 On the Ribbon, click the **Create tab**. In the **Other group**, click the **Macro** button to display the Macro Builder.

2 In the **Macro Builder**, under **Action**, on the **first row**, click the **arrow**, scroll down, and then click **OpenForm**. In the **Action Arguments pane**, click in the **Form Name** box, click the **arrow**, and then click **8A Intro Screen**.

3 In the **Macro Builder**, on the **first row**, click in the **Comment** box, and then type **Opens the 8A Intro Screen form - Firstname Lastname** Compare your screen with Figure 8.10.

Figure 8.10

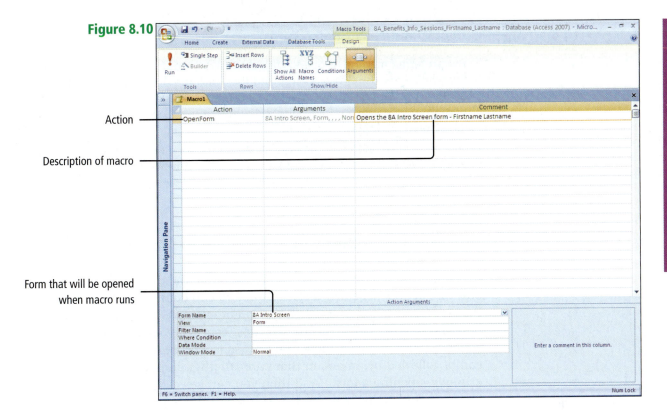

Action

Description of macro

Form that will be opened when macro runs

4 On the **Quick Access Toolbar**, click the **Save** button. In the **Save As** dialog box, under **Macro Name**, type **Autoexec** and then click **OK**.

When a macro is named *Autoexec*, Access automatically runs or executes the macro each time the database is opened. There can be only one macro in a database named *Autoexec*.

5 **Close** the Macro Builder, and then expand the **Navigation Pane**. Notice that on the **Navigation Pane**, under **Macros**, **Autoexec** displays. Double-click **Autoexec** to run the macro.

The *8A Intro Screen* form displays in its own pop-up, modal window.

6 **Close** the form. Click the **Office** button, and then click **Close Database**. In the **Getting Started with Microsoft Office Access** window, on the right side, under **Open Recent Database**, click **8A_Benefits_Info_Sessions**.

The macro automatically executes or runs when the *8A_Benefits_ Info_Sessions* database opens, and it displays the pop-up, modal *8A Intro Screen* form. Because this is a trusted macro action, the macro will execute even if the database has not been trusted or the content enabled.

7 **Close** the form.

To Automatically Open a Form

The preferred method to open an object when the database is opened is the following. Click the Office button, and then click the Access Options button. In the Access Options window, on the left side, click Current Database. Under Application Options, click the Display Form arrow, and then click the form that should be displayed when the database is opened.

Because you will add more actions to the standalone macro, it is appropriate to open the *8A Intro Screen* form as an auto executable action.

Objective 2
Add Multiple Actions to a Standalone Macro

In the previous activities, you created two macros that each contained only one action—opening a form. A macro can contain multiple actions that are executed in a specified order. For example, you can display an hourglass figure as the macro executes, especially macros with multiple actions, to let the user know that Access is working on a process. This can be followed by an action that runs another standalone macro—for example, opening a form. And then you can select the title bar on the form, maximize the form, and then turn off the hourglass figure.

Activity 8.4 Adding Multiple Actions to an Existing Standalone Macro

In this activity, you will modify the *Autoexec* macro and add more actions to the macro.

1 On the **Navigation Pane**, under **Macros**, right-click **Autoexec**, and then click **Design View**. Collapse « the **Navigation Pane**. In the **Macro Builder**, on the **first row**, point to the **Row Selector** box until the ➡ pointer displays. Right-click, and from the shortcut menu, click **Insert Rows** to insert a row above the OpenForm Action row.

2 On the **first row**, click in the **Action** box, click the displayed **arrow**, and then click **Hourglass**. Notice that the default argument is *Yes*. For the Hourglass action, click in the **Comment** box, and then type **Turn mouse pointer to an hourglass to show that the macro will take a few seconds to execute**

The Hourglass action changes the normal pointer to an hourglass to inform the user that some action is taking place. On a slower computer, the hourglass icon will keep the user from thinking that something is wrong with the database. If the computer is fast, the hourglass may not display. When the macro finishes running, the normal mouse pointer displays.

3 On the **second row**, point to the **Row Selector** box until the ➡ pointer displays. Right-click, and from the shortcut menu, click **Insert Rows** to insert a row between the Hourglass action row and the OpenForm action row.

4 On the **Design tab**, in the **Show/Hide group**, click the **Show All Actions** button.

Recall that the default list of macros displays trusted macro actions. The next macro action that you will add to the Macro Builder window is not a trusted macro action. For the macro to execute properly, you must add the location of the database to trusted locations or enable the content. Because this macro is used to open a pop-up, modal window, the database location must be trusted. The modal form will open automatically when the database is opened, and you cannot enable the content until the form is closed.

5 In the **Macro Builder**, on the **second row**, click in the **Action** box, and then click the **arrow**. From the displayed list, click **Echo**. In the **Comment** box, type **Hides the flickering screen as the macro actions execute** In the **Action Arguments pane**, click in the **Echo On** box, click the displayed **arrow**, and then click **No**. Click in the **Status Bar Text** box, type **Macro is running** and then compare your screen with Figure 8.11.

The Echo macro action hides or displays the results of the macro while it runs. Changing the Echo On argument to *No* hides the results. The Status Bar Text argument displays text on the status bar while the macro is running with Echo On set to No. The icon that displays in the Row Selector box indicates that the macro action is not trusted.

Figure 8.11

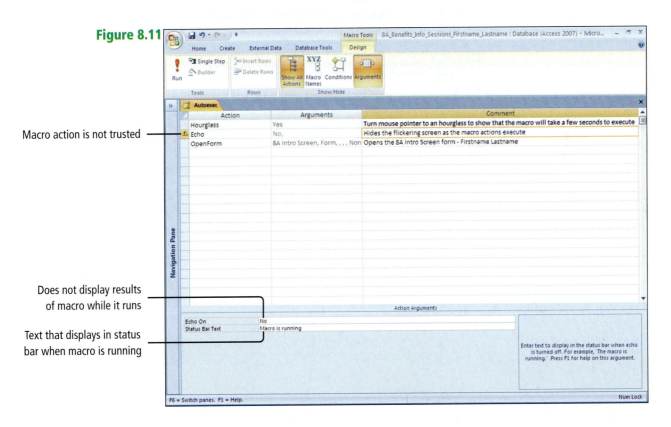

Macro action is not trusted

Does not display results of macro while it runs

Text that displays in status bar when macro is running

6 In the **Macro Builder**, on the **third row**, point to the **Row Selector** box until the ➡ pointer displays. Right-click, and from the shortcut menu, click **Insert Rows** to insert a row between the Echo action row and the OpenForm action row.

7 In the **Macro Builder**, on the **third row**, click in the **Action** box, and then click the **arrow**. Scroll down, and then click **RunMacro**.

The RunMacro action is used to run a macro from within another macro.

8 In the **Action Arguments pane**, click in the **Macro Name** box, click the **arrow**, and then click **Open 8A Event Details Form**. Click in the **Repeat Count** box, and then read the description. Click in the **Repeat Expression** box, and then read the description.

The Repeat Count and Repeat Expression action arguments are used when the macro should be run more than one time. Left blank, the macro will run only one time.

9 In the **Macro Builder**, on the **RunMacro row**, click in the **Comment** box, type **Opens the 8A Event Details form** and then press Enter.

10 In the **Macro Builde**r window, on the **fifth row**, click in the **Action** box, and then click the **arrow**. From the displayed list, scroll down, and then click **MsgBox**. In the **Comment** box, type **Displays a security message box**

The MsgBox macro action is a trusted action that displays a message box that contains a warning or informational message.

11 In the **Action Arguments pane**, click in the **Message** box, and then type **Only employees of Providence and Warwick Hospital are authorized to access this database. Unauthorized use will result in legal prosecution.**

12 Click in the **Beep** box, and on the lower, right side of the screen, read the description of the Beep argument. Be sure that the Beep argument is **Yes**, click in the **Type** box, click the **arrow**, and then click **Warning!**. Read the description of the Type argument and the different settings.

13 Click in the **Title** box, read the description of the argument, and then type **For Use by Providence and Warwick Employees Only!** Press Enter, and then compare your screen with Figure 8.12.

The MsgBox macro action can contain up to four arguments.

Figure 8.12

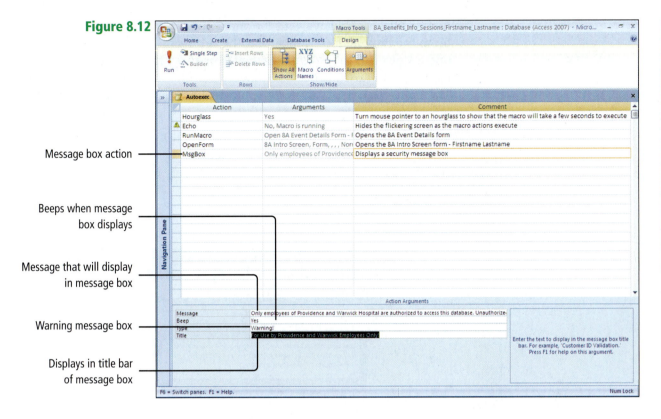

Message box action

Beeps when message box displays

Message that will display in message box

Warning message box

Displays in title bar of message box

14 In the **Macro Builder**, under **Action**, click in the **sixth row**, click the **arrow**, and then click **Hourglass**. Click in the **Comment** box, and then type **Restores the normal mouse pointer** In the **Action Arguments pane**, click in the **Hourglass On** box, click the **arrow**, and then click **No**.

The normal mouse pointer will be displayed to let the user know that the macro is finished executing.

15 In the **Macro Builder**, under **Action**, click in the **seventh row**, click the **arrow**, and then click **Echo**. Click in the **Comment** box, and then type **Displays screen results** Notice that in the **Action Arguments pane**, in the **Echo On** box, the setting is **Yes**.

Screen actions will no longer be hidden from the individual using the database.

Note — Turning Off Macro Actions

Access automatically restores the Hourglass and Echo to the default settings after a macro has finished running to protect inexperienced macro programmers from causing the system to continue displaying the hourglass icon, which might lead an individual to think that the database is operating incorrectly or is frozen. Even though Access restores these settings, it is good practice to always restore what you turn off. This will lead to better coding when you write Visual Basic code to execute commands.

16 On the **Quick Access Toolbar**, click the **Save** button. On the **Design tab**, in the **Tools group**, click the **Run** button. Point to the Access window title bar, and then compare your screen with Figure 8.13.

Access does not always wait for one action to complete before going on to the next action. Notice that the *8A Event Details* form is not yet open. However, the *8A Intro Screen* is open with a message box displayed on top of it. A beep sounded when the message box displayed. The hourglass displays, and the status bar displays *Macro is running*.

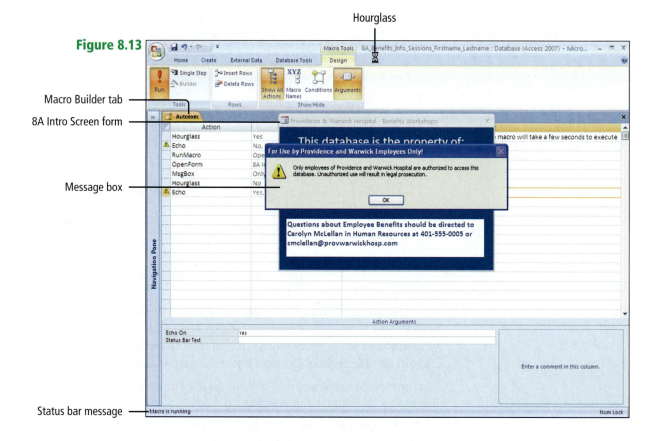

Figure 8.13

Hourglass

Macro Builder tab

8A Intro Screen form

Message box

Status bar message

17 In the displayed message box, click **OK**. The **8A Event Details** form displays underneath the **8A Intro Screen** form. **Close** the *8A Intro Screen* form. On the **tab row**, right-click any tab, and then click **Close All**.

18 Click the **Office** button , and then click **Close Database**. In the **Getting Started with Microsoft Office Access** window, on the right side, under **Open Recent Database**, click **8A_Benefits_Info_Sessions**.

The Autoexec macro automatically executes or runs when the 8A_Benefits_Info_Sessions database opens, and it displays the pop-up, modal *8A Intro Screen* form with the message box on top of it.

Alert! | **Did a message box display?**

If a message box displays stating that *The 'Echo' macro action cannot be run in disabled mode*, you did not add the Access Chapter 8 folder to Trust Center. The Echo macro action is not trusted by default. To correct this, click OK, click Stop All Macros, and then add the Access Chapter 8 folder to the Trust Center.

19 In the displayed message box, click **OK**. **Close** [X] the *8A Intro Screen* form, and then **Close** [X] the *8A Event Details* form. Expand [»] the **Navigation Pane**.

More Knowledge

Debugging a Macro

Debugging is using a logical process to find and reduce the number of errors in a program. To debug a macro, you can use ***single stepping***, which executes one action at a time. Single stepping enables you to observe the results of each macro action, which enables you to isolate any action that may be causing an error or that produces unwanted results.

To single step through a macro, open the macro in Design view. On the Design tab, in the Tools group, click the Single Step button. In the Tools group, click the Run button. The Macro Single Step dialog box displays information about the macro, including the macro name, the condition, the action name, the arguments, and an error number. An error number of 0 indicates that no error has occurred. In this dialog box, you can carry out the macro action by clicking Step. You can stop the macro and close the dialog box by clicking Stop All Macros, or you can turn off single stepping and run the rest of the macro by clicking Continue.

When the macro has fully executed, be sure to turn off single stepping on the Design tab in the Tools group by clicking the Single Step button.

Objective 3
Create a Macro Group

In the previous activities, you created a standalone macro with one action and another standalone macro with multiple actions. As you continue to create more macros, you may want to group related macros by creating a ***macro group***. A macro group is a set of macros grouped by a common name that displays as one macro object on the Navigation Pane. For example, you might want to create a macro group that opens several forms or reports in a database.

Activity 8.5 Creating the First Macro in a Macro Group

In this activity, you will create the first macro in the macro group that will open the *8A Event Name Search Dialog Box* form.

1 On the **Navigation Pane**, under **Forms**, double-click **8A Event Details**, and then double-click **8A Event Name Search Dialog Box** to open the forms in Form view. Point to the title bar of the **Event Name Search** dialog box until the [cursor] pointer displays. Drag the pop-up form downward and to the right until, on the **8A Event Details** form, the buttons under the title display. Compare your screen with Figure 8.14.

In this activity, you will create a macro group that executes and opens the *8A Event Name Search Dialog Box* form when a user clicks on the Find Event button on the *8A Event Details* form.

Figure 8.14

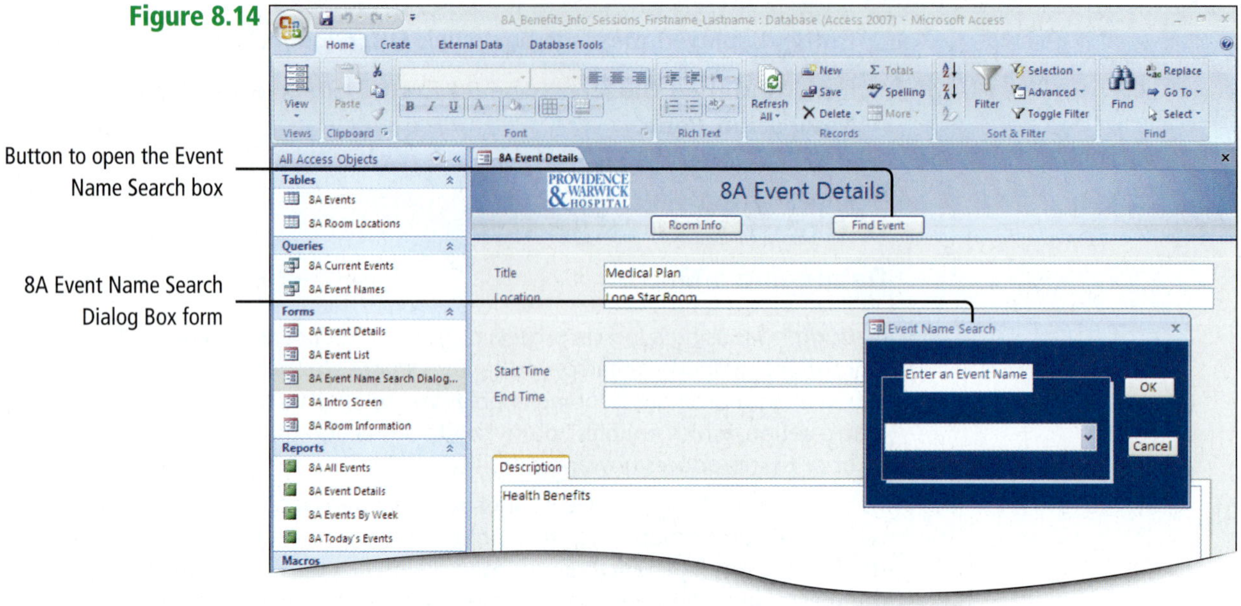

Button to open the Event Name Search box

8A Event Name Search Dialog Box form

2 **Close** ☒ the Event Name Search box, and then **Close** ☒ the *8A Event Details* form. Collapse ☒ the **Navigation Pane**.

3 On the Ribbon, click the **Create tab**. In the **Other group**, click the **Macro** button. On the **Design tab**, in the **Show/Hide group**, click the **Macro Names** button, and then click the **Show All Actions** button.

In macro groups, macro names are needed to distinguish the individual macros from one another. Within a macro group, the macro name is entered on the first line of the macro action. The macro name column is left blank for subsequent actions of the macro. The macro ends when the next macro name is encountered. Recall that the Show All Actions button displays trusted and untrusted macro actions.

4 In the **Macro Builder**, on the **first row**, click in the **Comment** box. Type **Purpose: To enable an individual to search for a specific event in the 8A Event Details form** and then press Enter.

It is a good practice to start a macro group with a description of the purpose of the macro group.

5 On the **third row**, click in the **Macro Name** box, and then type **OpenSearchDialogBox**

Macro names are limited to 64 characters. Because macros perform an action or actions, it is good practice to start the name of the macro with a verb—in this case, Open. Leaving a blank row between the purpose of the macro group and the first macro improves the readability of the Macro Builder.

6 On the same row, click in the **Action** box, click the **arrow**, and then click **OpenForm**. Click in the **Comment** box, and then type **Opens the 8A Event Name Search Dialog Box form** In the **Action Arguments pane**, click in the **Form Name** box, click the **arrow**, and then click **8A Event Name Search Dialog Box**. Click in the **Data Mode** box, click the **arrow**, and then click **Edit**. Compare your screen with Figure 8.15.

Editing is enabled so that the user can enter an event name in the combo box on the *8A Event Name Search Dialog Box* form. Because the form property has been set to open as a pop-up window, the Window Mode setting of Normal is appropriate.

Figure 8.15

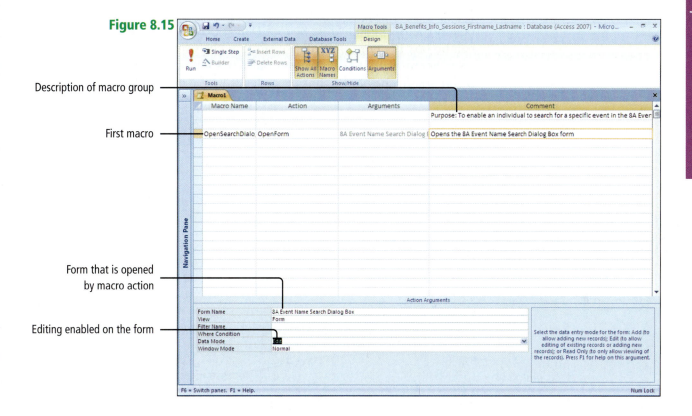

Description of macro group

First macro

Form that is opened by macro action

Editing enabled on the form

7 **Save** 🔲 the macro group as **8A Find Event Macro Group Firstname Lastname**

Activity 8.6 Creating a Second Macro in a Macro Group

In this activity, you will create a second macro in the macro group that will check to see if a value is entered for the event name in the *8A Event Name Search Dialog Box*, hide the *8A Event Name Search Dialog Box* form, change the focus to the *8A Event Details* form, select the title of the event on the *8A Event Details* form, sort the records by the event name, find the requested event, close the *8A Event Name Search Dialog Box* form, and display a message to the user with a reminder to display all of the records.

1 In the **Macro Builder**, on the **fifth row**, click in the **Macro Name** box, type **SearchForEvent** On the **Design tab**, in the **Show/Hide group**, click the **Conditions** button.

A Condition column displays between the Macro Name column and the Action column, and the insertion point displays in the Condition box. In some macros, an action should execute only under certain conditions. For example, if the user does not select a value in the combo box on the *8A Event Name Search Dialog Box* form, the macro should not execute. Recall that the warning symbol in the row selector box indicates that this Macro Action is not trusted.

2 In the Macro Builder, on the same row, right-click the **Condition** box, and then click **Zoom**. In the **Zoom** dialog box, type **IsNull([Forms]![8A Event Name Search Dialog Box]![EventName])** and then compare your screen with Figure 8.16.

The expression used for the condition checks the EventName combo box in the *8A Event Name Search Dialog Box* form to determine if the combo box is blank—IsNull. Recall that the exclamation (!) mark is a bang operator that tells Access that what follows it is an object belonging to the object that precedes it in the expression.

Figure 8.16

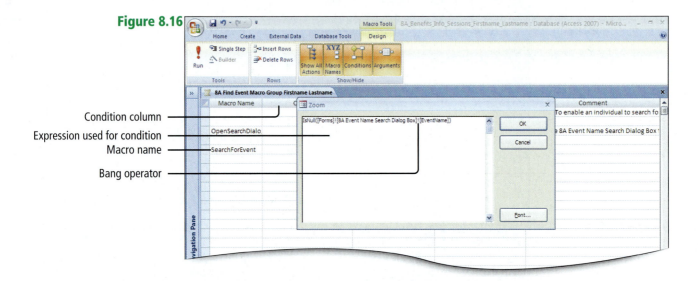

Condition column
Expression used for condition
Macro name
Bang operator

3 Be sure that you have typed the expression correctly. In the **Zoom** dialog box, click **OK**. On the same row, click in the **Action** box, click the **arrow**, and then click **Close**. In the **Action Arguments pane**, click in the **Object Type** box, click the **arrow**, and then click **Form**. Click in the **Object Name** box, click the **arrow**, and then click **8A Event Name Search Dialog Box**. Click in the **Save** box, click the **arrow**, and then click **No**. In the **Macro Builder**, click in the **Comment** box, type **If individual does not select an event, then close the 8A Event Name Search Dialog Box form** and then compare your screen with Figure 8.17.

If Access finds that the EventName combo box is blank, it will close the *8A Event Name Search Dialog Box* form and will not save any changes made to the form.

Figure 8.17

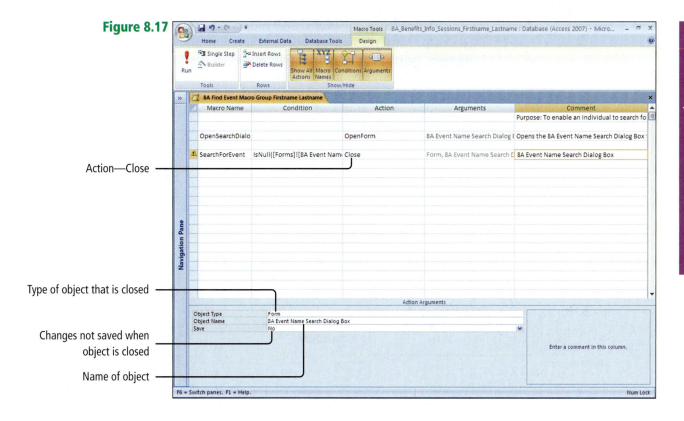

Action—Close

Type of object that is closed

Changes not saved when object is closed

Name of object

4 In the **Macro Builder**, on the **sixth row**, click in the **Condition** box, type three periods, and then press Tab to move to the Action box.

To execute a series of actions based on a single condition, enter the condition on the first action row, and then enter an *ellipsis* (...) in the Condition column for the subsequent action(s). Access tests the condition only once, with the first action, and then executes the additional actions if an ellipsis displays in the Condition column.

5 Click in the **Action** box, click the **arrow**, and then click **StopMacro**. Notice that there are no action arguments for the StopMacro action. On the same row, click in the **Comment** box, and then type **. . . and then exit the macro**

This macro first looks at the data in the EventName combo box. If the EventName combo box is blank, the form closes and the macro stops executing.

6 In the **Macro Builder**, on the **seventh row**, click in the **Action** box, click the **arrow**, and then click **SetValue**. In the **Action Arguments**

pane, click in the **Item** box, and then click the **Build** button ⊡ to open the Expression Builder. Compare your screen with Figure 8.18.

The SetValue macro action is an untrusted action that is used to set the value of a field, control or property on a form, a form datasheet, or a report. The item is the name of the field, control, or property whose value you want to set. You must use the full *syntax* to refer to the item—do not just type the field, control, or property name. Syntax refers to the spelling, grammar, and sequence of characters of a programming language. Access expects object names to be referred to in a specific manner, which is called the syntax.

The ***Expression Builder*** displays the expression as you build it. The operator buttons and list boxes help you build the expression using correct syntax. As you select an object in the first list box, the second and third list boxes will populate. In the first list box, the plus sign (+) next to an object indicates that there are more items to display under the object. The minus sign (−) indicates that the list under the object is fully expanded. Double-click the plus sign (+) or the object name with the plus sign to expand the list; double-click the minus sign (−) or the object name with the minus sign to collapse the list.

Figure 8.18

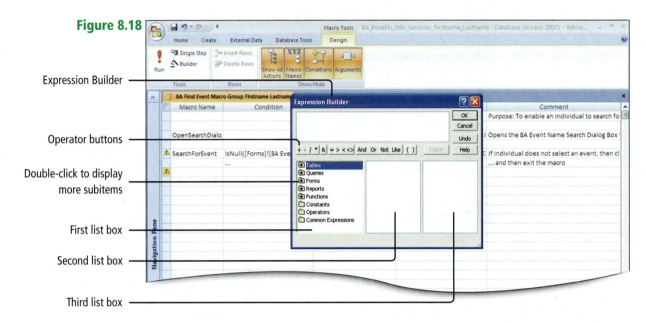

Expression Builder

Operator buttons

Double-click to display more subitems

First list box

Second list box

Third list box

7 In the **Expression Builder**, in the first list box, double-click **Forms** to expand the list. Under **Forms**, double-click **All Forms**. In the first list box, scroll down, and then click **8A Event Name Search Dialog Box**—use the horizontal scroll bar to display the entire name of the form.

The second list box displays controls on the form. The third list box displays property settings and ***events*** that can be associated with the form or the controls on the form. An event is any significant action that can be detected by a program or computer system, such as clicking a button or closing an object. Selecting an object in the second list box causes the values or events in the third list box to change because different objects have different property settings or events associated with them.

8 In the second list box, be sure that **<Form>** is selected. In the third list box, scroll down, double-click **Visible**, and then compare your screen with Figure 8.19.

The Expression Builder displays the correct syntax for the Visible property of the *8A Event Name Search Dialog Box*, which is a form. Instead of using the Expression Builder, you can type the expression in the Item box in the Action Arguments pane. An advantage of using the Expression Builder is that Access will insert square brackets and parentheses where they are required. Notice the only item that is enclosed in square brackets is the name of the form; the brackets are required because there are spaces in the name.

Figure 8.19

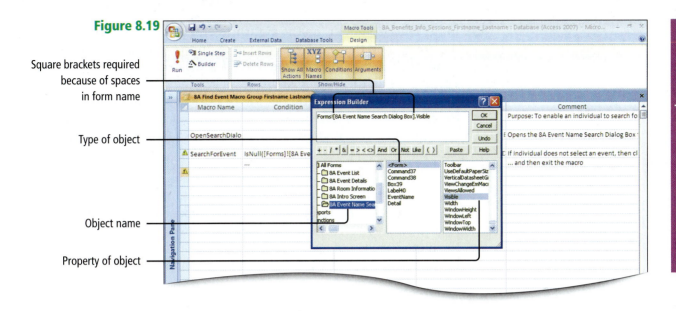

Square brackets required because of spaces in form name

Type of object

Object name

Property of object

▇9▇ In **the Expression Builder**, click **OK**. In the **Action Arguments pane**, click in the **Expression** box, and then type **False**

This macro action sets the Visible property setting of the *8A Event Name Search Dialog Box* form to false; in other words, it will hide the *8A Event Name Search Dialog Box* form.

▇10▇ In the **Macro Builder**, on the same row, click in the **Comment** box, and then type **Hides the 8A Event Name Search Dialog Box form** On the same row, click in the **Action** box, and then compare your screen with Figure 8.20.

Figure 8.20

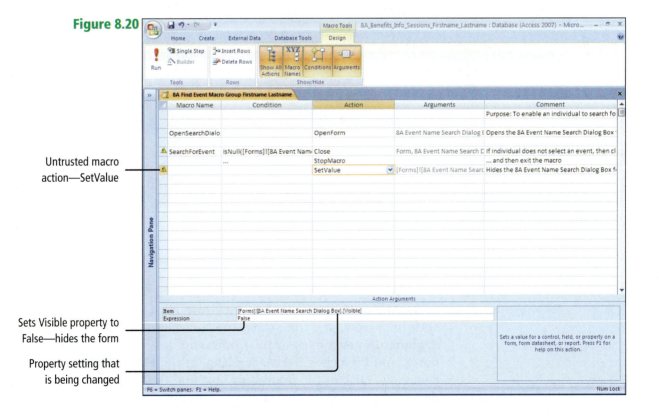

Untrusted macro action—SetValue

Sets Visible property to False—hides the form

Property setting that is being changed

11 In the **Macro Builder**, on the **eighth row**, click in the **Action** box, click the **arrow**, and then click **SelectObject**. In the **Action Arguments pane**, click in the **Object Type** box, click the **arrow**, and then click **Form**. Click in the **Object Name** box, click the **arrow**, and then click **8A Event Details**. Be sure that the **In Database Window** box displays **No**. In the **Macro Builder**, on the same row, click in the **Comment** box, and then type **Changes the focus to the 8A Event Details form** and then press Enter.

The SelectObject action is used to put the focus on a specified database object so that an action can be applied to that object. Recall that the *8A Event Details* form is automatically opened when the database is opened. Therefore, the In Database Window setting should be set to No. If the form is not open, Access needs to open it from the Navigation Pane, and the In Database Window setting should be set to Yes.

So far, the macro group will open the *8A Event Name Search Dialog Box* form, and then check to see if the EventName field displays data. If not, the macro stops executing. If data is displayed in the EventName field, the *8A Event Name Search Dialog Box* form will be hidden, and the focus will shift to the *8A Event Details* form.

12 In the **Macro Builder**, on the **ninth row**, click in the **Action** box, click the **arrow**, and then click **GoToControl**. In the **Action Arguments pane**, click in the **Control Name** box, and then type **Title** In the **Macro Builder**, on the same row, click in the **Comment** box, and then type **Places focus on Title field on the 8A Event Details form** and then press Enter. Compare your screen with Figure 8.21.

In the previous action, the focus was changed to the *8A Event Details* form. With this action, the focus is placed on a specific text box control named *Title* on that form.

Figure 8.21

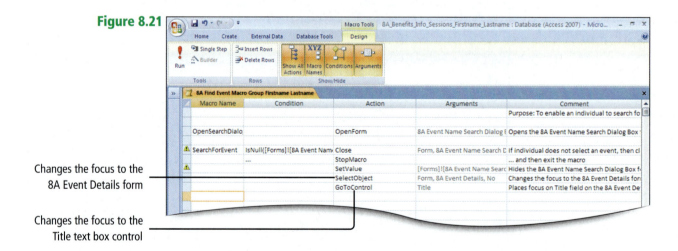

Changes the focus to the 8A Event Details form

Changes the focus to the Title text box control

13 In the **Macro Builder**, on the **tenth row**, click in the **Action** box, click the **arrow**, and then click **RunCommand**. In the **Action Arguments pane**, click in the **Command** box, click the **arrow**, scroll down, and then click **SortAscending**. In the **Macro Builder**, on the same row, click in the **Comment** box, and then type **Sorts the event name (Title) in ascending order** and then press Enter.

The RunCommand action is used to execute an Access command, such as Sort Ascending or Save a Record.

14 In the **Macro Builder**, on the **eleventh row**, click in the **Action** box, click the **arrow**, and then click **FindRecord**. In the **Action Arguments pane**, click in the **FindWhat** box, and then type **=Forms![8A Event Name Search Dialog Box]!EventName** Be sure that you have entered the data correctly. Click in the **Match** box, click the **arrow**, and then click **Start of Field**. Click in each of the other Action Arguments boxes, reading the description of each argument, and being sure not to change any of the settings. In the **Macro Builder**, on the same row, click in the **Comment** box, type **Finds the Title in the 8A Event Details form that matches the entry in the EventName combo box in the 8A Event Name Search Dialog Box form** and then compare your screen with Figure 8.22. Notice in the **Find What** box, that Access inserts square brackets around the object name and the control name.

The FindRecord action locates the first or next record that meets the specified search criteria; in this case, the data in the EventName field of the *8A Event Name Search Dialog Box* form must match the data in the Title field of the *8A Event Details* form. This macro action is similar to using the Find button on the Home tab.

Figure 8.22

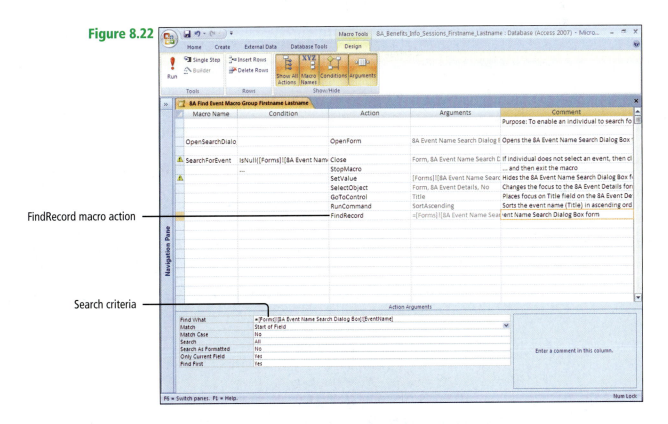

FindRecord macro action

Search criteria

15 In the **Macro Builder**, on the **twelfth row**, click in the **Action** box, click the **arrow**, and then click **Close**. In the **Action Arguments pane**, click in the **Object Type** box, click the **arrow**, and then click **Form**. Click in the **Object Name** box, click the **arrow**, and then click **8A Event Name Search Dialog Box**. In the **Macro Builder**, on the same row, click in the **Comment** box, and then type **Closes the 8A Event Name Search Dialog Box form** and then press Enter.

The Close action closes a specified object. If no object is specified in the Object Name box, the active object is closed.

16 In the **Macro Builder**, on the **thirteenth row**, click in the **Action** box, click the **arrow**, and then click **MsgBox**. In the **Action Arguments pane**, click in the **Message** box, and then type **To display the records in their original sort order, on the Home tab, in the Sort & Filter group, click the Clear All Sorts button** Click in the **Type** box, click the **arrow**, and then click **Information**. Click in the **Title** box, and then type **Search for Event Name** In the **Macro Builder**, on the same row, click in the **Comment** box, and then type **Displays a message telling individuals how to clear the sort method** Compare your screen with Figure 8.23.

Recall that if an individual filters or sorts records and closes the database, when the database is reopened, the filter or sort is still applied to the object.

Figure 8.23

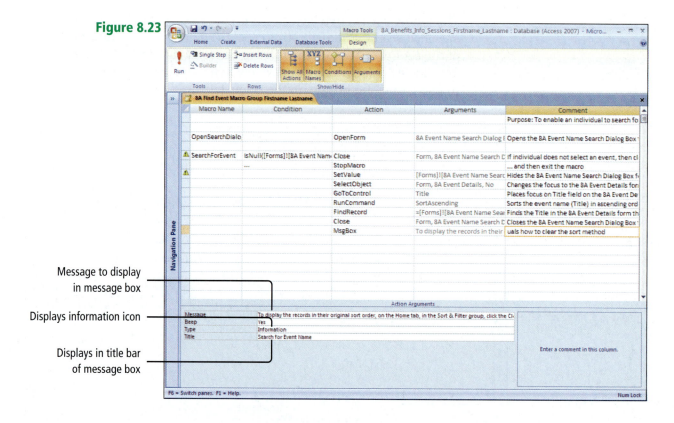

Message to display in message box

Displays information icon

Displays in title bar of message box

17 **Save** the macro group.

More Knowledge

Editing a Macro

To insert an action row in the Macro Builder, click in the row beneath where the new row will be inserted. On the Design tab, in the Rows group, click the Insert Rows button. To delete an action row, click in the row that you want to delete; and then on the Design tab, in the Rows group, click the Delete Rows button. To move an action row, click the row selector for the action row you want to move, and then drag the row selector to the new position.

Activity 8.7 Creating a Third Macro in a Macro Group

In this activity, you will create a third and final macro in the macro group that will close the *8A Event Name Search Dialog Box* form.

1 In the **Macro Builder**, on the **fifteenth row**, click in the **Macro Name** box, and then type **CancelSearch** On the same row, click in the **Action** box, click the **arrow**, and then click **Close**. In the **Action Arguments pane**, click in the **Object Type** box, click the **arrow**, and then click **Form**. Click in the **Object Name** box, click the **arrow**, and then click **8A Event Name Search Dialog Box**. In the **Macro Builder**, on the same row, click in the **Comment** box, and then type **Closes the 8A Event Name Search Dialog Box form** and then press Enter.

This macro will be used to close the *8A Event Name Search Dialog Box* form when the Cancel button on the form is clicked.

2 In the **Macro Builder**, on the **sixteenth row**, click in the **Action** box, click the **arrow**, and then click **SelectObject**. In the **Action Arguments pane**, click in the **Object Type** box, click the **arrow**, and then click **Form**. Click in the **Object Name** box, click the **arrow**, and then click **8A Event Details**. Be sure that the **In Database Window** box displays **No**. In the **Macro Builder**, on the same row, click in the **Comment** box, and then type **Changes the focus to the 8A Event Details form** and then compare your screen with Figure 8.24.

After the *8A Event Name Search Dialog Box* form is closed, the focus is placed on the *8A Event Details* form.

Figure 8.24

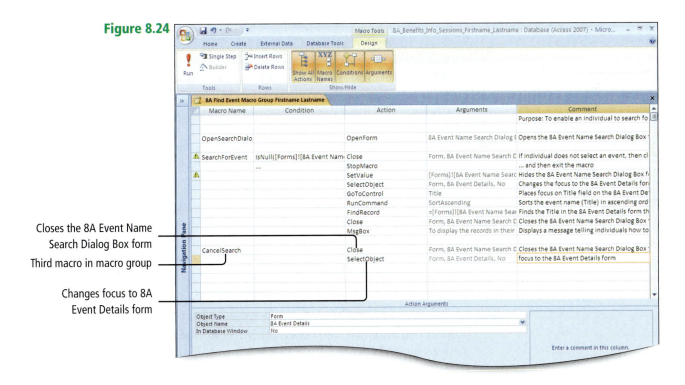

Closes the 8A Event Name Search Dialog Box form

Third macro in macro group

Changes focus to 8A Event Details form

3 Press Enter. **Save** 🖫 the macro group. **Close** ☒ the Macro Builder, expand ⧉ the **Navigation Pane**, and notice that under **Macros**, the macro group displays as one macro object.

Double-clicking the macro does not cause this macro to execute because the macro has not been associated with the buttons on the *8A Event Details* form or the *8A Event Name Search Dialog Box* form.

> ## More Knowledge
> ### Running a Macro that Is in a Macro Group
>
> On the Database Tools tab, in the Macro group, click the Run Macro button, and then, in the Macro Name list, click the macro. In the Run Macro dialog box, click OK. Keep in mind that some macro actions are dependent upon other macro actions that have previously executed, and independently, a macro action may not execute properly if run out of order.

Objective 4
Associate a Macro with an Event

Recall that an event is any significant action that can be detected by a program or computer system, such as clicking a button or closing an object. For example, clicking the Find Event button on the *8A Event Details* form causes a system event, upon which Access can execute a macro.

Activity 8.8 Associating a Command Button with a Macro

In this activity, you will associate clicking the Find Event button on the *8A Event Details* form with a macro—the *8A Find Event Macro Group* macro. Clicking the Find Event button will result in the macro executing.

1 On the **Navigation Pane**, under **Forms**, double-click **8A Event Details** to display the form in Form view. On the form, click the **Find Event** button, and notice that nothing happens because the button is not associated with any event.

2 Collapse ⧉ the **Navigation Pane**, and then switch the form to **Design** view. In the **Form Header section**, right-click the **Find Event** button, and then click **Properties**. Be sure that the **Property Sheet** displays *Selection type: Command button* and that the **Selection type** box displays *cmdFindEvent*.

3 On the **Property Sheet**, click the **Event tab**. Click the **On Click** property setting box, and then click the **arrow**. Notice that the complete names of some of the macros do not display. Point to the **left edge** of the **Property Sheet** until the ↔ pointer displays. Drag to the left to the **4.25-inch mark on the horizontal ruler** or until the complete names display. Click the **On Click** property setting **arrow**, and then compare your screen with Figure 8.25.

All of the macros that have been created display in the list. The macro group displays as *8A Find Event Macro Group*. The first macro in the macro group displays as *8A Find Event Macro Group. OpenSearchDialogBox*. The second macro in the macro group displays as *8A Find Event Macro Group.SearchForEvent*. The third macro in the macro group displays as *8A Find Event Macro Group. CancelSearch*.

Figure 8.25

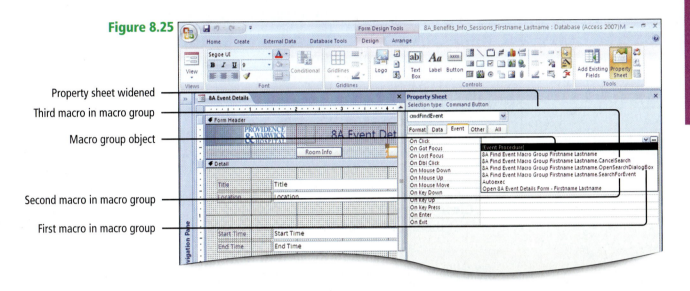

Property sheet widened

Third macro in macro group

Macro group object

Second macro in macro group

First macro in macro group

4 In the displayed list, click **8A Find Event Macro Group. OpenSearchDialogBox**.

When an individual clicks on the Find Event button in the *8A Event Details* form, the OpenSearchDialogBox macro in the *8A Find Event Macro Group* will execute.

5 On the **Property Sheet**, click the **Format tab**. In the **Caption** property setting box, click to the left of **Find Event**, and then type **&**

The ampersand (&) causes the letter that follows it to be underlined on the button, which will enable the user to use a shortcut key combination to access the button instead of clicking on the button. The user presses Alt + the letter to activate the button. For this button, the shortcut is Alt + F.

6 **Close** ✕ the **Property Sheet**, and then switch to **Form** view. Notice that on the **Find Event** button, the letter *F* is underscored, which indicates that pressing Alt + F is the same action as clicking on the button.

7 Click the **Find Event** button, and then compare your screen with Figure 8.26.

The Event Name Search dialog box displays, which is the *8A Event Name Search Dialog Box* form.

Figure 8.26

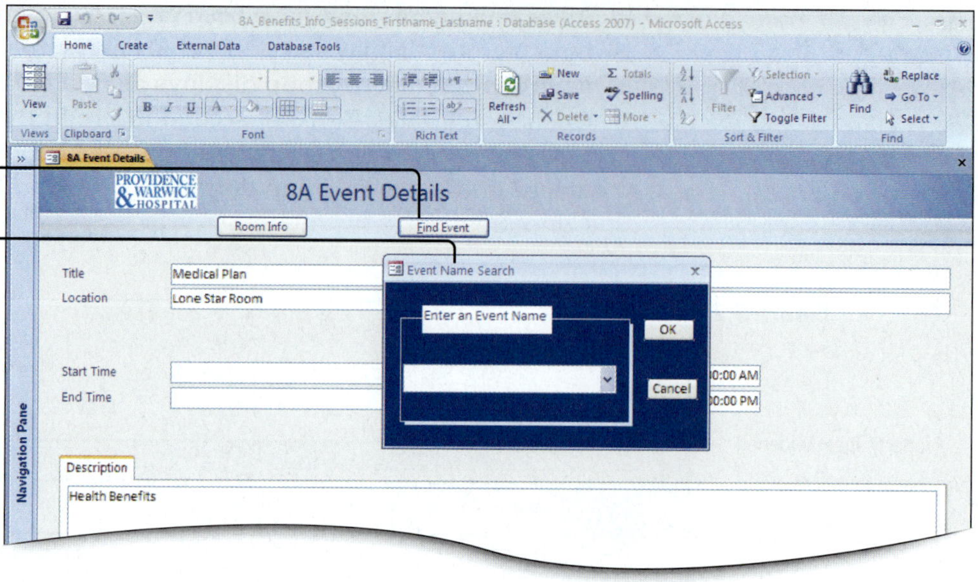

Shortcut key indicator

8A Event Name Search dialog box

8 **Close** ☒ the **Event Name Search** dialog box. Press ⌷Alt⌷ + ⌷F⌷. Notice that the **Event Name Search** box displays.

Alert! — **Did the Find and Replace dialog box display?**

If the Find and Replace dialog box displays instead of the Event Name Search box, you held down ⌷Ctrl⌷ instead of ⌷Alt⌷.

9 **Close** ☒ the **Event Name Search** dialog box, and then expand ⌷»⌷ the **Navigation Pane**. Under **Forms**, right-click **8A Event Name Search Dialog Box**, and then click **Design View**. Collapse ⌷«⌷ the **Navigation Pane**.

10 Right-click the **OK** button, and then click **Properties**. On the **Property Sheet**, click the **Event tab**. Click the **On Click** property setting **arrow**, and then click **8A Find Event Macro Group.SearchForEvent**. On the **Property Sheet**, click the **Format tab**. In the **Caption** box, click to the left of **OK**, and then type **& Close** ☒ the **Property Sheet**, and then switch the form to **Form** view.

When the OK button is clicked or the user presses ⌷Alt⌷ + ⌷O⌷, the second macro in the *8A Find Event Macro Group* executes.

11 **Save** 🖫 the form. In the **Enter an Event Name combo box**, click the **arrow**, and then click **Eye Care Plan**. Click **OK**, and then compare your screen with Figure 8.27.

The macro executes, the *8A Event Details* form displays the first record—Record 5—with an event name (Title) of Eye Care Plan, and a message box displays telling you to click the Clear All Sorts button to display the records in the original sort order.

Figure 8.27

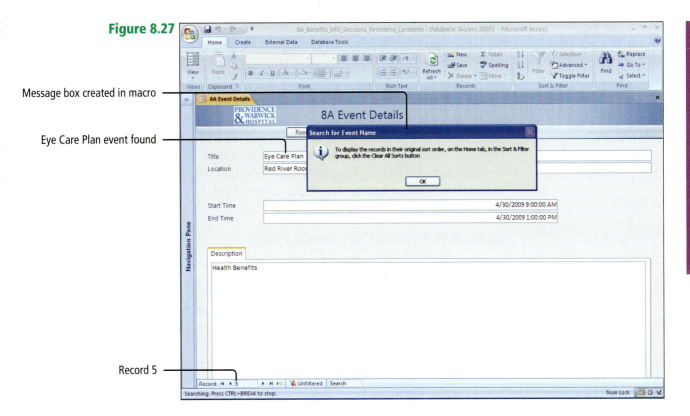

Message box created in macro

Eye Care Plan event found

Record 5

12 In the displayed message box, click **OK**. Press `Alt` + `F` to display the Event Name Search box. In the **Event Name Search** box, in the **Enter an Event Name combo box**, type **li** and notice that Access displays *Life Insurance Plan*. Press `Alt` + `O`. In the displayed message box, click **OK**.

Instead of selecting an item from the list, you can type the first few letters of the event name. If Access finds the event name in the list, it displays in the combo box. Record 7 is displayed.

13 On the **Home tab**, in the **Sort & Filter group**, click the **Clear All Sorts** button 🔲. Expand 🔲 the **Navigation Pane**. Under **Forms**, open the **8A Event Name Search Dialog Box** form in **Design** view, and then collapse 🔲 the **Navigation Pane**.

14 Right-click the **Cancel** button, and then click **Properties**. On the **Property Sheet**, click the **Event tab**, click the **On Click** property setting **arrow**, and then click **8A Find Event Macro Group.CancelSearch**. Click the **Property Sheet Format tab**. In the **Caption** property setting box, click to the left of **Cancel**, type **&** and then **Close** 🔲 the **Property Sheet**. **Save** 🔲 the form, and then switch the form to **Form** view.

Clicking the Cancel button on the *8A Event Name Search Dialog Box* form causes the third macro in the macro group to execute. The form closes, and the focus returns to the *8A Event Details* form.

15 In the **Event Name Search** box, click the **Cancel** button. Alternatively, press `Alt` + `C`.

The form closes, and the focus is placed on the *8A Event Details* form.

Objective 5
Create an Embedded Macro

An **embedded macro** is a macro that is stored in the event properties of forms, reports, or controls. They are not displayed on the Navigation Pane under Macros. Embedded macros are easier to manage because you do not have to keep track of the separate macro objects. Unlike standalone macros, when objects containing embedded macros are copied, imported, or exported, the macros are also copied, imported, or exported. Any standalone macro can be created as an embedded macro.

Activity 8.9 Creating an Embedded Macro

In this activity, you will create an embedded macro that will execute when the *Room Info* button is clicked on the *8A Event Details* form.

1 Switch the **8A Event Details** form to **Design** view. In the **Form Header section**, right-click the **Room Info** button, and then click **Properties**. Be sure that the **Property Sheet** displays *Selection type: Command button* and that the **Selection type** box displays *cmdRoomInfo*. Drag the left edge of the **Property Sheet** to the right to decrease the width of the Property Sheet.

2 On the **Property Sheet**, click the **Event tab**. Click the **On Click** property setting box **Build** button [...], and then compare your screen with Figure 8.28.

The Choose Builder dialog box displays, enabling you to select the Macro Builder, the Expression Builder, or the Code Builder. You have previously used the Macro Builder and the Expression Builder. The **Code Builder** is used to type programming code in Microsoft Visual Basic.

Figure 8.28

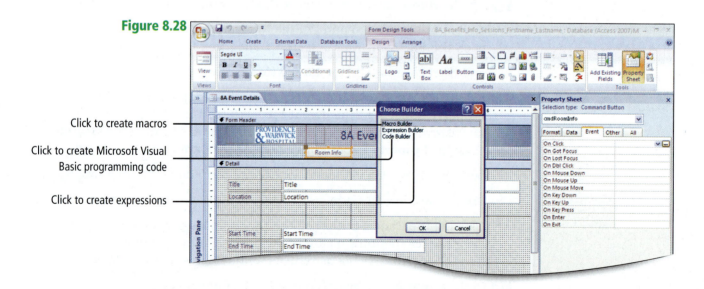

Click to create macros

Click to create Microsoft Visual Basic programming code

Click to create expressions

3 In the **Choose Builder** dialog box, click **Macro Builder**, and then click **OK** to display the Macro Builder.

4 In the **Macro Builder**, on the **first row**, click in the **Action** box, click the **arrow**, and then click **OpenForm**. In the **Action Arguments pane**, click in the **Form Name** box, click the **arrow**, and then click **8A Room Information**. Click in the **Where Condition** box, type **[Location]=[Forms]![8A Event Details]![Location]** and then compare your screen with Figure 8.29.

The Where Condition property selects the records from the *8A Room Information* form for the room Location displayed on the *8A Event Details* form.

Figure 8.29

Where Condition property ————

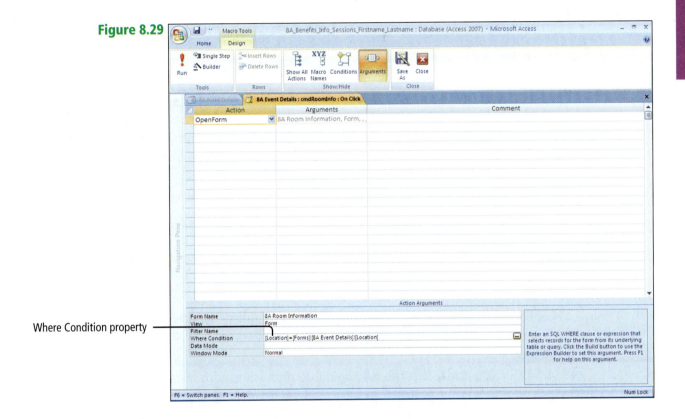

5 In the **Action Arguments pane**, click in the **Data Mode** box, click the **arrow**, and then click **Read Only** to enable the user to view only the data in the *8A Room Information* form. In the **Macro Builder**, on the first row, click in the **Comment** box, and then type **Opens the 8A Room Information form for room indicated on 8A Event Details form**

6 **Close** [×] the **Macro Builder**. In the displayed message box, click **Yes** to save the changes made to the macro and to update the On Click property. Compare your screen with Figure 8.30.

In the Property Sheet, the On Click property displays *[Embedded Macro]*. To display the macro, click the Build button.

Figure 8.30

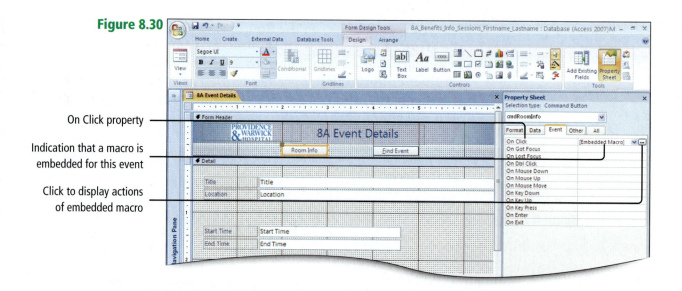

On Click property

Indication that a macro is embedded for this event

Click to display actions of embedded macro

7 On the **Property Sheet**, click the **Format tab**. In the **Caption** box, click to the left of **Room Info**, and then type **&** to create a shortcut key using the letter *R*. **Close** ☒ the **Property Sheet**, and then switch the *8A Event Details* form to **Form** view.

8 On the **8A Event Details** form, click the **Find Event** button. In the **Enter an Event Name** combo box, click the **arrow**, click **Eye Care Plan**, and then click **OK**. In the displayed message box, click **OK**. On the **8A Event Details** form, click the **Room Info** button. Alternatively, press ⌨Alt + ⌨R.

The *8A Room Information* form displays as a pop-up window and provides information about the Red River Room, the Location listed on the *8A Event Details* form.

9 **Close** ☒ the *8A Room Information* form. In the navigation area, click the **Last Record** button ▶|. In the **8A Event Details** form, click the **Room Info** button, and then compare your screen with Figure 8.31.

The pop-up window displays room information for the Lone Star Room, the same room location displayed on the *8A Event Details* form as indicated by the Filtered button in the navigation area of the *8A Room Information* form.

Figure 8.31

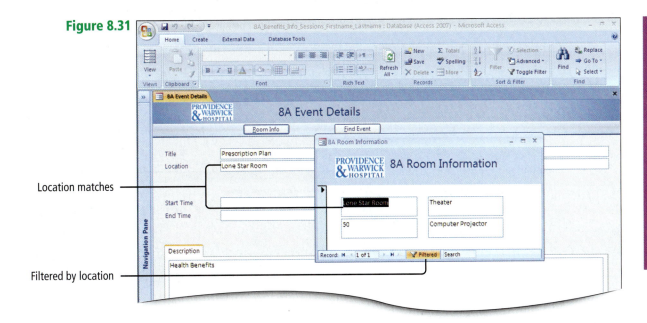

Location matches

Filtered by location

10 **Close** ☒ the *8A Room Information* form, and then **Close** ☒ the *8A Event Details* form, saving changes, if necessary. Expand ⟫ the **Navigation Pane**. Notice that under **Macros**, the macro you created to display the *8A Room Information* form does not display—embedded macros do not display on the Navigation Pane.

Objective 6
Print Macro Details

Use the ***Database Documenter*** to create a report that contains detailed information about the objects in a database, including macros, and to create a paper record.

Activity 8.10 Printing Macro Details

In this activity, you will use the Database Documenter to print out the details of the macros that you have created in this project.

1 Collapse ⟪ the **Navigation Pane**. On the Ribbon, click the **Database Tools tab**. In the **Analyze group**, click the **Database Documenter** button. In the displayed **Documenter** dialog box, click the **Macros tab**, and then compare your screen with Figure 8.32.

The Documenter dialog box displays tabs for each object type and a tab for the current database. Only standalone macros display on the Macros tab. Macros that are run are embedded with an object and will display as a property of the object.

Database Documenter button

Figure 8.32

Documenter dialog box

Macros tab

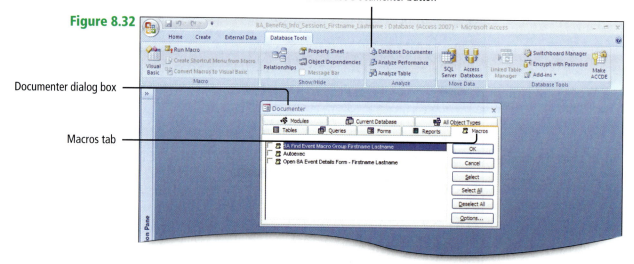

2 In the **Documenter** dialog box, click the **Options** button, and then compare your screen with Figure 8.33.

The Print Macro Definition dialog box displays. By default, properties, actions, arguments, and permissions by user and group display in the printed report.

Figure 8.33

Print Macro Definition dialog box

Click to deselect macro print option

Options button

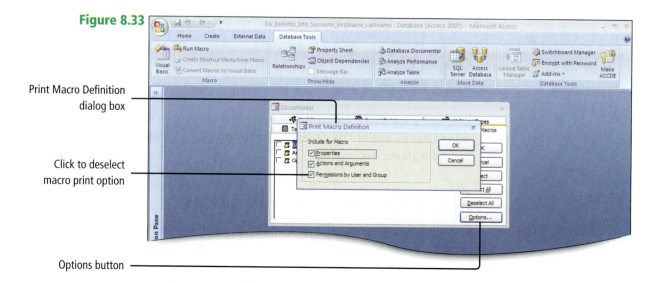

3 Click the **Permissions by User and Group** check box to clear it, and then click **OK**. In the **Documenter** dialog box, click **Select All**, and then click **OK**. Click in the middle of the document to zoom in, scroll up to display the top of the report, and then compare your screen with Figure 8.34.

The Object Definition opens in Print Preview, and displays the first page of information about the macro named *8A Find Event Macro Group*, including actions, arguments, conditions, and comments.

Figure 8.34

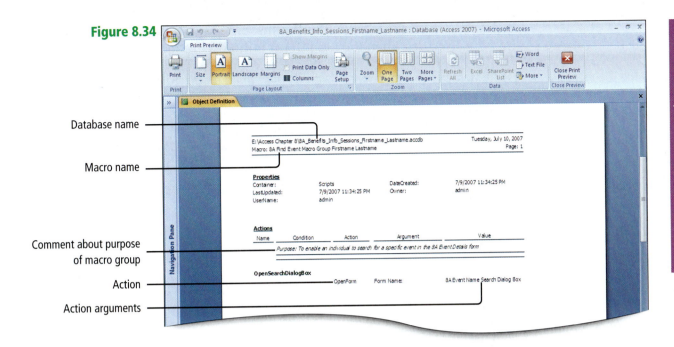

Database name

Macro name

Comment about purpose of macro group

Action

Action arguments

4 In the navigation area, click the **Next Page** button ▶ **four** times. Notice that the details of the **Autoexec** macro display. The name of the macro displays at the top of the document. Click the **Next Page** button ▶ **three** times to display the details of the **Open 8A Event Details Form** macro.

5 If you are instructed to submit this result, create a paper or electronic printout. Include the project, activity, and step number in the file name if you create an electronic printout. On the **Print Preview tab**, in the **Close Preview group**, click the **Close Print Preview** button.

6 On the **Database Tools tab**, in the **Analyze group**, click the **Database Documenter** button. In the **Documenter** dialog box, click the **Forms tab**. Click the **Options** button. In the **Print Form Definition** dialog box, clear the check boxes for **Code** and **Permissions by User and Group**, and then click **OK**.

7 In the **Documenter** dialog box, click the **8A Event Details** and **8A Event Name Search Dialog Box** forms.

These forms have macros associated with command buttons and an embedded macro.

8 In the **Documenter** dialog box, click **OK**. In the **Object Definition** print preview, zoom in, and then scroll up to display the top of the first page, noticing that the report displays properties of the **8A Event Details** form. In the navigation area, click the **Next Page** button ▶ **two** times, and then scroll down to display the bottom of Page 3.

The properties of the Find Event button—Command Button: cmdFindEvent—display.

9 In the navigation area, click the **Next Page** button ▶, scroll up to display the top of Page 4, and then compare your screen with Figure 8.35.

In the right column, the OnClick property displays the macro that executes when the Find Event button is clicked.

Figure 8.35

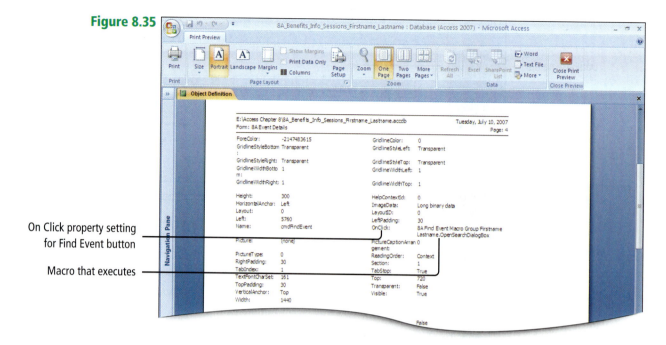

On Click property setting for Find Event button

Macro that executes

10 Scroll down to display the properties of **Command Button: cmdRoomInfo**—the Room Info button—and then compare your screen with Figure 8.36.

Clicking the Room Info button causes an Embedded Macro to execute. The embedded macro actions, arguments, conditions, and comments are displayed on the left side of the report next to OnClickEmMacro.

Figure 8.36

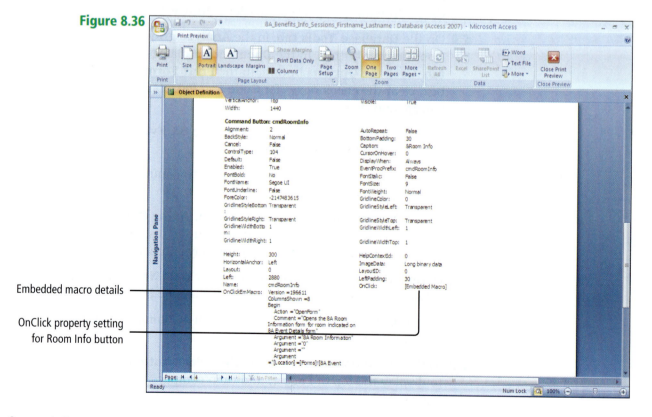

Embedded macro details

OnClick property setting for Room Info button

11 In the navigation area, click the **Next Page** button button until **Page 15** is displayed. Scroll through the page, noticing the **OnClick** property settings for the two buttons on the *8A Event Name Search Dialog Box* form.

12 If you are instructed to submit this result, create a paper or electronic printout of pages 3 to 5, and then create a paper or electronic printout of page 15. Include the project, activity, and step number in the file names if you create electronic printouts.

13 On the **Print Preview tab**, in the **Close Preview group**, click the **Close Print Preview** button. Expand ⟩⟩ the **Navigation Pane**. **Close** the database, and then **Exit** Access.

End **You have completed Project 8A** ——————————————

Project 8B **Nursing Salaries**

Maria Benitez, Vice President of Operations, wants to compare nursing salaries, including regular pay and overtime pay by department. In Activities 8.11 through 8.14, you will create a PivotTable and a PivotChart to analyze the nursing salaries by department and by quarter. Your completed PivotTable and PivotChart will look similar to those shown in Figure 8.37.

For Project 8B, you will need the following file:

a08B_Nursing_Salaries

You will save your database as
8B_Nursing_Salaries_Firstname_Lastname

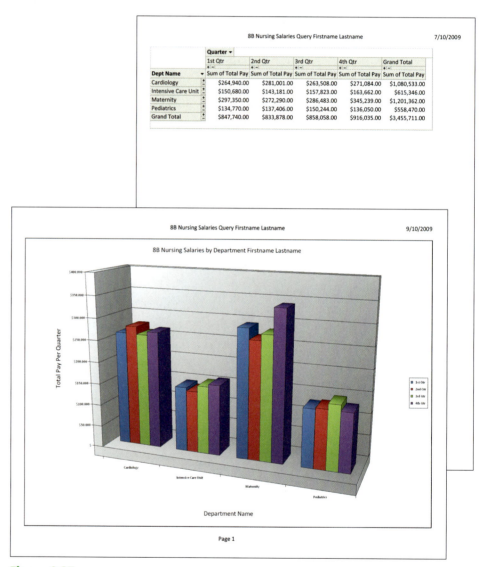

Figure 8.37
Project 8B—Nursing Salaries

Objective 7
Create a PivotTable from a Query

A *PivotTable* is used to organize, arrange, analyze, and summarize data in a meaningful way. A PivotTable displays trends and patterns at a glance for large amounts of data. In a PivotTable, rows can be categorized by different values, just as you did in the creation of a crosstab query; but you can also include multiple column categories and multiple calculated values. You can *pivot*, or rotate, the table to swap row headings with column headings to display the data in a different way.

A *PivotChart* is a graphical view of the data in a PivotTable.

Activity 8.11 Creating a PivotTable from a Query

In this activity, you will create a PivotTable to summarize nursing salaries per department by quarter.

1 **Start** Access. Navigate to the location where the student data files for this textbook are saved. Locate and open the **a08B_Nursing_Salaries** file. Save the database in the **Access 2007 Database** format in your **Access Chapter 8** folder as 8B_Nursing_Salaries_Firstname_Lastname

2 On the **Navigation Pane**, rename the two tables and the query by adding **Firstname Lastname** to the end of the object names. Under **Queries**, double-click **8B Nursing Salaries Query** to run the query.

The query displays department names, the quarter of the year, regular pay for all of the nursing staff in each department, overtime pay for all of the nursing staff in each department, and a calculated field for the total pay—regular pay plus overtime pay—for all of the nursing staff in each department. This query will be used in the creation of the PivotTable.

3 Collapse ⟪ the **Navigation Pane**. On the **tab row**, right-click **8B Nursing Salaries Query**, and then click **PivotTable View**. Compare your screen with Figure 8.38.

You can change to PivotTable view in either Datasheet view or Design view. A blank PivotTable design area displays, along with a PivotTable Field List that displays the field names in the *8A Nursing Salaries Query*. If the PivotTable Field List does not display, on the Design tab, in the Show/Hide group, click the Field List button.

The design area has several *drop zones* to which fields are dragged. The drop zones are outlined regions you see when you finish the steps of the PivotTable and PivotChart wizard. To lay out a PivotTable report, you drag fields from the field list window and drop them onto the drop zones. Generally, the Column Fields drop zone should have the fewest values to avoid having the user scroll horizontally through the values.

Figure 8.38

Field List button ——

Filter Fields drop zone ——

Column Fields drop zone ——

Row Fields drop zone ——

Totals or Detail Fields drop zone ——

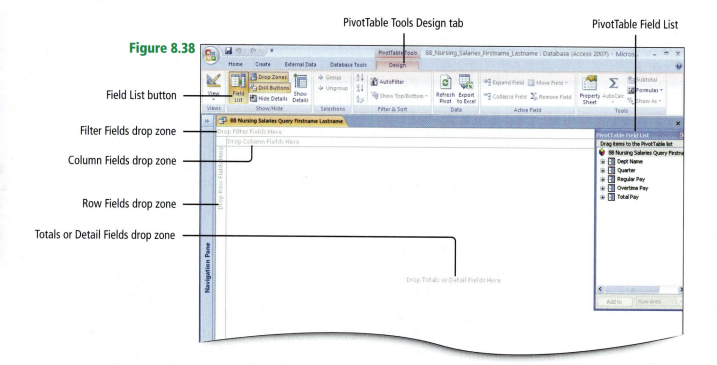

4 In the **PivotTable Field List**, drag the **Quarter** field to the **Drop Row Fields Here** area. Drag the **Dept Name** field to the **Drop Column Fields Here** area, and then compare your screen with Figure 8.39.

The four quarters display as row headings. In the PivotTable Field List, Quarter is bolded, indicating that the field is used in the PivotTable. A Grand Total row displays. Each row heading displays Drill Buttons, which are similar to expand and collapse buttons. Clicking the plus sign (+) expands or drills down to display more data. Clicking the minus sign (−) collapses or drills up to display less data.

The department names display as column headings with each department displaying Drill Buttons.

Bold formatting—fields used in PivotTable

Figure 8.39

Column headings ——

Row headings ——

Grand Total row ——

Drill buttons ——

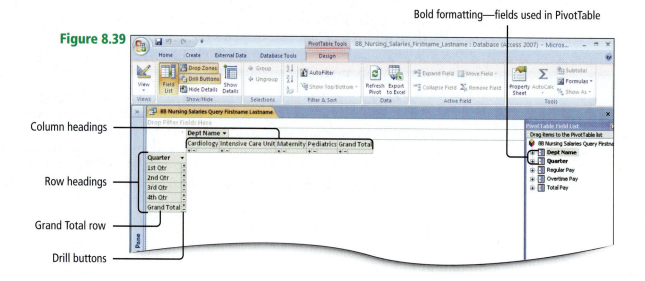

5 On the **PivotTable Field List**, drag the **Regular Pay** field to the **Drop Totals or Detail Fields Here** area, and then compare your screen with Figure 8.40.

The Regular Pay field for each quarter by department displays, enabling you to analyze the differences in nursing salaries for each department or within the same department by quarters.

Figure 8.40

Regular Pay per quarter by department

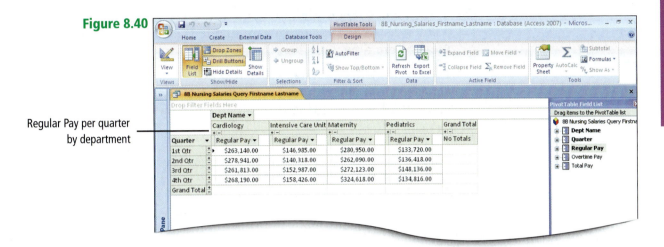

More Knowledge

Filtering a PivotTable

If this query contained a field with different hospitals, you could add the Hospital field to the Filter Fields drop zone. You could display all of the nursing salaries for each department by quarter for all of the hospitals, or you could select one or more hospitals to compare nursing salaries among the departments of those selected hospitals.

Activity 8.12 Pivoting the Data and Adding Totals

In this activity, you will pivot the table to swap row headings with column headings to display the data in a different way, and then you will sum the columns and rows.

1 In the **PivotTable design area**, point to **Quarter** until the ⬚ pointer displays. Drag upward and to the right and point to **Dept Name** until a dark blue line displays to the left of Dept Name, and then release the mouse button.

Quarter is changed to a column heading, and the data displays in a different manner.

2 In the **PivotTable design area**, point to **Dept Name** until the ![pointer] pointer displays. Drag downward and to the left to the **Drop Row Fields Here** area, and then compare your screen with Figure 8.41.

The departments are changed to row headings, and the data is displayed in a different manner. The flexibility in pivoting data in PivotTables makes this view a valuable tool for analyzing data.

Figure 8.41

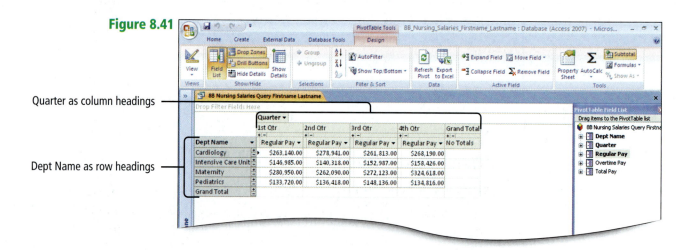

Quarter as column headings

Dept Name as row headings

3 In the **PivotTable design area**, click any one of the boxes that displays **Regular Pay**. On the **Design tab**, in the **Tools group**, click the **AutoCalc** button. From the displayed list, click **Sum**, and then compare your screen with Figure 8.42.

Every row and every column is summed, including the individual Dept Name rows, and a Sum function is added to the PivotTable Field List.

Figure 8.42

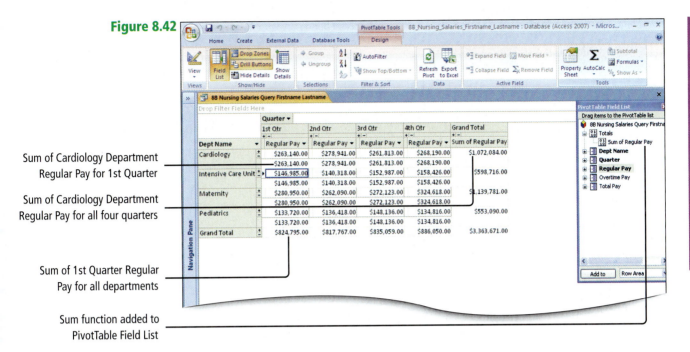

Sum of Cardiology Department
Regular Pay for 1st Quarter

Sum of Cardiology Department
Regular Pay for all four quarters

Sum of 1st Quarter Regular
Pay for all departments

Sum function added to
PivotTable Field List

4 In the **PivotTable design area**, under **Dept Name** and to the right of **Cardiology**, click the **Drill Up** button (−) to collapse the total row for Cardiology. Repeat the procedure for the **Intensive Care Unit** row, the **Maternity** row, and the **Pediatrics** row.

The PivotTable now displays the data in a more readable format.

5 **Close** ✕ the **PivotTable Field List**. To the right of **Quarter**, click the **arrow**. From the displayed list, click **3rd Qtr** and then click **4th Qtr** to clear the check boxes for these two quarters. Click **OK**. Notice that only data for the first two quarters displays, and the grand totals only sum the amounts for the two quarters. Also notice on the **Design tab**, in the **Filter & Sort group**, that the **AutoFilter** button is active, indicating that you are not viewing all of the data in the PivotTable.

6 On the **Design tab**, in the **Filter & Sort group**, click the active **AutoFilter** button.

The Filter—displaying only 1st and 2nd Qtr data—is removed, and all of the data is visible.

7 On the **Design tab**, in the **Filter & Sort group**, click the **AutoFilter** button.

The most recent filter is applied to the PivotTable, and only the 1st and 2nd quarter data displays.

8 To the right of **Dept Name**, click the **arrow**. From the displayed list, click **Intensive Care Unit**, and then click **Pediatrics** to clear the check boxes for these two departments. Click **OK**, and then compare your screen with Figure 8.43.

Only data for the Cardiology and Maternity departments for the first two quarters displays. PivotTables enable you to display only the data you want to see when you are analyzing and comparing data.

Figure 8.43

AutoFilter button

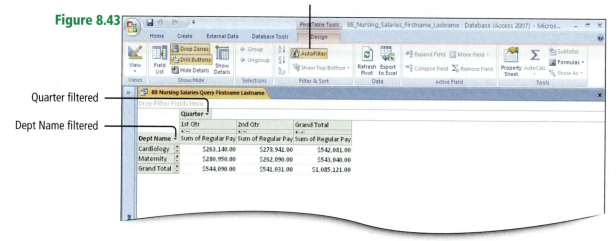

Quarter filtered

Dept Name filtered

9 On the **Design tab**, in the **Filter & Sort group**, click the active **AutoFilter** button to remove the filter. Collapse (-) the **Intensive Care Unit** row, and then collapse the **Pediatrics** row.

Activity 8.13 Removing and Adding Fields from and to the PivotTable

1 On the **Design tab**, in the **Show/Hide group**, click the **Field List** button to display the PivotTable Field List.

2 In the **PivotTable Field List**, right-click **Sum of Regular Pay**, and then click **Delete**. In the **PivotTable design area**, expand (+) the **1st Qtr**, **2nd Qtr**, **3rd Qtr**, and **4th Qtr** columns to display the Regular Pay data for each department.

3 In the **PivotTable design area**, click any box that displays **Regular Pay**. On the **Design tab**, in the **Active Field group**, click the **Remove Field** button. Alternatively, right-click one of the Regular Pay boxes, and from the shortcut menu, click Remove.

Only row headings and column headings display.

4 In the **PivotTable Field List**, drag **Total Pay** to the **Drop Totals or Detail Fields Here** area.

Total Pay is calculated by adding Regular Pay and Overtime Pay.

5 In the **PivotTable design area**, click any box that displays **Total Pay**. On the **Design tab**, in the **Tools group**, click the **AutoCalc** button, and then click **Sum**. Collapse (-) each of the **Dept Name row headings** so that the total for each department does not display, and then compare your screen with Figure 8.44.

Instead of just looking at Regular Pay statistics, you are now viewing the total pay, including overtime, for each department by quarter.

Figure 8.44

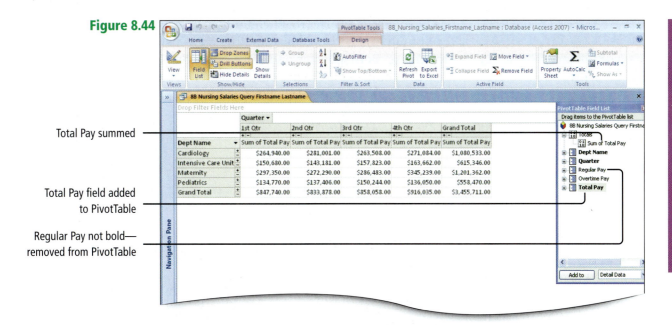

Total Pay summed

Total Pay field added to PivotTable

Regular Pay not bold—removed from PivotTable

6 On the **Design tab**, in the **Show/Hide group**, click the active **Drop Zones** button.

The Drop Filter Fields Here area no longer displays.

7 **Close** ☒ the **PivotTable Field List**, and then **Save** 🖫 the PivotTable. View the PivotTable in **Print Preview**, and then change the **Margins** to **Normal**. If you are instructed to submit this result, create a paper or electronic printout of the PivotTable. On the **Print Preview tab**, in the **Close Preview group**, click the **Close Print Preview** button, leaving the PivotTable open for the next activity.

Objective 8
Create a PivotChart from a PivotTable

A PivotChart is a graphical view of the data included in the PivotTable, although you can create a PivotChart without first defining a PivotTable. If you design a PivotChart, a PivotTable will automatically be created. To create a PivotChart from a PivotTable, the PivotTable must contain a calculated field.

Activity 8.14 Creating a PivotChart from a PivotTable

In this activity, you will create a PivotChart from the PivotTable you created in the previous activities.

1 On the **tab row**, right-click **8A Nursing Salaries Query**, and then click **PivotChart View**. **Close** ☒ the **Chart Field List**, and then compare your screen with Figure 8.45.

Because the PivotTable was already created, Access converts the data into a graphical representation of the data in the PivotTable. At the top of the PivotChart is the name of the field—Total Pay—that has been summed. The row headings—Dept Names—display at the bottom of the PivotChart, and the data displays within the PivotChart. Both Quarter and Dept Name display filter arrows to limit the chart to displaying only the data you want to analyze.

Figure 8.45

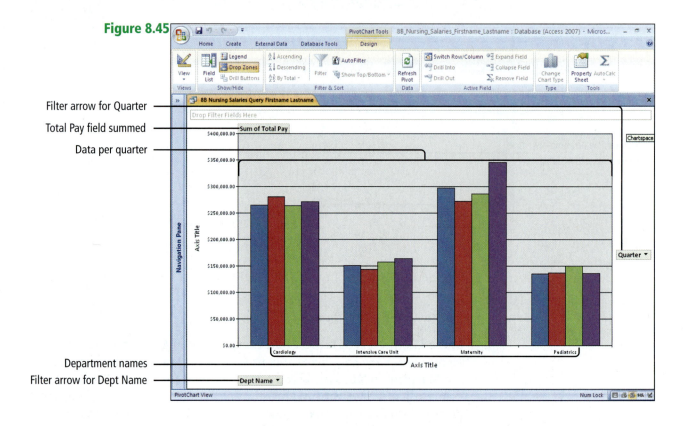

Filter arrow for Quarter
Total Pay field summed
Data per quarter

Department names
Filter arrow for Dept Name

2 On the right side of the **PivotChart design area**, click the **Quarter arrow**—scroll to the right, if necessary. Click **1st Qtr** and **2nd Qtr** to clear the check boxes, and then click **OK**.

Just as you did in the PivotTable view, you can filter the quarters or department names, making this a flexible tool for analyzing data.

3 Using the technique you just practiced, display the data for all four quarters. On the left side of the **PivotChart design area**, click **Axis Title**. On the **Design tab**, in the **Tools group**, click the **Property Sheet** button. In the **Properties** dialog box, click the **Format tab**. In the **Caption** box, select **Axis Title**, and then type **Total Pay Per Quarter**

4 At the bottom of the **PivotChart design area**, click **Axis Title** to display the **Properties** dialog box for this object. In the **Caption** box, select

Axis Title, and then type **Department Name Close** ✕ the **Properties** dialog box, and then compare your screen with Figure 8.46.

The axis titles have been changed to display a description of the data on the PivotChart.

Figure 8.46

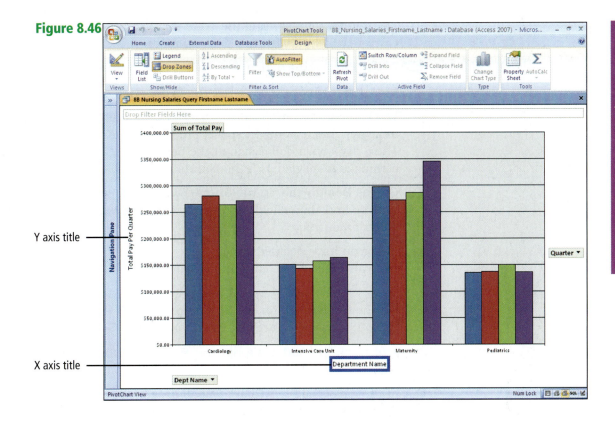

Y axis title

X axis title

5 On the **Design tab**, in the **Show/Hide group**, click the **Legend** button.

A *legend* displays under Quarter. A legend is text that describes the meaning of colors and patterns used in a chart.

6 Click in an empty area of the chart to deselect the axis title. On the **Design tab**, in the **Type group**, click the **Change Chart Type** button. In the displayed **Properties** dialog box, on the **Type tab**, notice that the chart type is a **Clustered Column** chart. On the second row, click the second chart type, which changes the chart to a **3D Column Clustered** chart type.

Column charts and bar charts are ideal for displaying varying values for different categories. Line charts are ideal for displaying changes in data over time, and pie charts are ideal for showing the percentages of a total figure.

7 **Close** ☒ the **Properties** dialog box. On the **Design tab**, in the **Active Field group**, click the **Switch Row/Column** button.

The row and column headings are pivoted to display the data in a different manner. The legend displays department names instead of quarters. If you keep this view, you would need to change the axis titles to reflect the changed column and row headings.

8 On the **Design tab**, in the **Active Field group**, click the **Switch Row/Column** button. On the left side of the PivotChart, click any of the numbers representing the Total Pay Per Quarter. In the **Tools group**, click the **Property Sheet** button. In the displayed **Properties** dialog box, click the **Format tab**. Click the **Number arrow**, and then click **Currency**.

The figures representing the Total Pay Per Quarter display with the Currency format with two decimal places.

9 In the **Properties** dialog box, click in the **Number** box, and then type **$###,###** Press Enter. **Close** ✖ the **Properties** dialog box.

You can enter an input mask to format the number. The # symbol indicates that a number, space, plus, or minus sign can be displayed. The $ displays a dollar sign at the beginning of the number, and a comma is displayed as a thousands separator.

10 On the **Design tab**, in the **Show/Hide group**, click the **Drop Zones** button, and then click in an empty area of the chart to deselect the dollar amounts.

After you have decided which departments and quarters to include, you can exclude the column and row heading filter arrows from the PivotChart.

11 On the **Design tab**, in the **Tools group**, click the **Property Sheet** button. In the **Properties** dialog box, on the **General tab**, under **Add**, click the **Add Title** button 📇. **Close** ✖ the **Properties** dialog box.

12 At the top of the **PivotChart design area**, right-click **Chart Workspace Title**, and then click **Properties**. In the **Properties** dialog box, click the **Format tab**. In the **Caption** box, select the text, type **8B Nursing Salaries by Department Firstname Lastname** and then press Enter. **Close** ✖ the **Properties** dialog box, and then compare your screen with Figure 8.47.

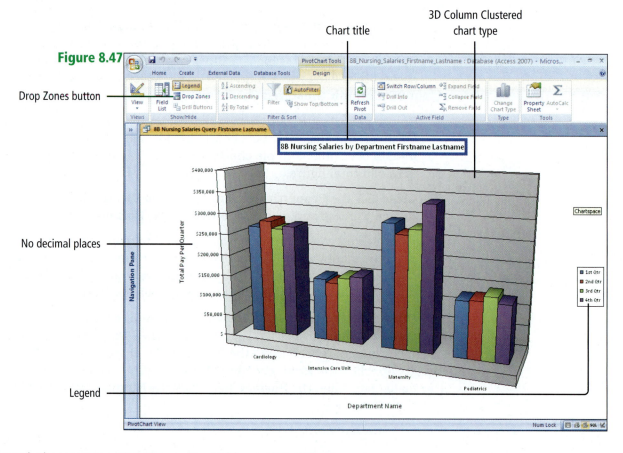

Figure 8.47

Chart title

3D Column Clustered chart type

Drop Zones button

No decimal places

Navigation Pane

Legend

13 **Save** [⊞] the PivotChart, and then view the PivotChart in **Print Preview**. If you are instructed to submit this result, create a paper or electronic printout of the PivotChart in **Landscape** orientation. Add the word *Chart* to the file name if you create an electronic printout. On the **Print Preview tab**, in the **Close Preview group**, click the **Close Print Preview** button, and then **Close** [×] the PivotChart.

14 **Expand** [»] the **Navigation Pane**. Under **Queries**, double-click **8B Nursing Salaries Query** to run the query. Collapse [«] the **Navigation Pane**. On the **tab row**, right-click **8B Nursing Salaries Query**, and then click **PivotTable View**.

The PivotTable displays as it was saved.

15 On the **tab row**, right-click **8B Nursing Salaries Query**, and then click **PivotChart View**.

The PivotChart displays as it was saved. To view a PivotTable or PivotChart, the underlying object must be open in either Datasheet view or Design view. You cannot display the PivotTable or PivotChart by right-clicking the underlying object on the Navigation Pane.

16 **Close** [×] the PivotChart, and then expand [»] the **Navigation Pane**. **Close** the database, and then **Exit** [×] Access.

Another Way

To Create a PivotChart

On the Navigation Pane, select the underlying object, and then collapse the Navigation Pane. On the Ribbon, click the Create tab. In the Forms group, click the PivotChart button. If the Chart Field List does not display, on the Design tab, in the Show/Hide group, click the Field List button—you may have to click it two times. Drag the fields onto the PivotChart design area, much like you dragged the fields onto the PivotTable design area.

End **You have completed Project 8B**

 There's More You Can Do!

From My Computer, navigate to the student files that accompany this textbook. In the folder **02_theres_more_you_can_do**, locate and open the folder for this chapter. Open and print the instructions for this project, which are provided to you in Adobe PDF format.

Try It! 1—Assign Values to Access Records Automatically

In this Try It! project, you will create a macro that automatically assigns values entered in one form to another related form.

Try It! 2—Cancel the Printing of a Report That Has No Data

In this Try It! project, you will create a macro that cancels the printing of a report when the report has no data.

Content-Based Assessments

Summary

Macros are created to automate database tasks. In this chapter you created standalone macros with one or more actions and action arguments. You created a macro group and added conditions to macro actions. You associated a macro with the clicking of a button and created an embedded macro. You printed documentation of the macro details using the Database Documenter.

PivotTables and PivotCharts display data in a different manner that is helpful when analyzing data. You created a PivotTable that summarized data by department and quarter and then pivoted the data to display it by quarter and then department. You created a PivotChart to display the same data in a graphical representation.

Key Terms

Content-Based Assessments

Matching

Match each term in the second column with its correct definition in the first column. Write the letter of the term on the blank line in front of the correct definition.

—— **1.** A series of actions grouped as a single command to accomplish a task or multiple tasks automatically.

—— **2.** A self-contained instruction.

—— **3.** A view of data that is used to organize, arrange, analyze, and summarize data in a meaningful way.

—— **4.** A graphical view of the data in a PivotTable.

—— **5.** A macro contained in a macro object that displays under Macros on the Navigation Pane.

—— **6.** A value that provides information to the macro action, such as the words to display in a message box, or the control upon which to operate.

—— **7.** A specification that certain criteria must be met before the macro action executes.

—— **8.** A window that suddenly displays, usually contains a menu of commands, and stays on the screen only until a user selects one of the commands.

—— **9.** A child (secondary window) to a parent window that takes over control of the parent window.

—— **10.** The action of using a logical process to find and reduce the number of errors in a program.

—— **11.** A debugging tool that executes one macro action at a time, enabling you to observe the results of each macro action and enabling you to isolate any action that may be causing an error or that produces unwanted results.

—— **12.** A set of macros grouped by a common name that displays as one macro object on the Navigation Pane.

—— **13.** Three dots (. . .) used in the Macro Builder Condition column to indicate an addition action that is to be executed based on a condition entered above.

—— **14.** A reference to the spelling, grammar, and sequence of characters of a programming language.

—— **15.** To rotate data in a PivotTable or PivotChart by changing row headings to column headings, and vice versa.

A Action

B Argument

C Condition

D Debugging

E Ellipsis

F Macro

G Macro group

H Modal window

I Pivot

J PivotChart

K PivotTable

L Pop-up window

M Single stepping

N Standalone macro

O Syntax

Fill in the Blank

Write the correct word in the space provided.

1. A series of actions grouped together as a single command to accomplish a task or multiple tasks automatically is a(n) _____.

2. Data in tables, queries, or forms can be displayed as a(n) _____ _____ or _____ _____ to provide a more analytical view of the data.

3. When designing a macro, you should decide if a value or _____ provides information to the macro action.

4. When the database designer wants to direct the user's focus to the information in the window, he may use either a(n) _____ window or a(n) _____ window.

5. A debugging tool that enables you to isolate any action that may be causing an error or produces unwanted results is _____ _____.

6. A set of macros grouped by a common name that displays as one macro object on the Navigation Pane is called a(n) _____ _____.

7. A window that displays the expression as you build it is the _____ _____.

8. Any significant action that can be detected by a program or computer system, such as clicking a button or closing an object is a(n) _____.

9. The ampersand (&) causes the letter that follows it to be underlined on a button, which will enable an individual to use a(n) _____ _____ combination to access the button instead of clicking on the button.

10. A macro that is stored in the event properties of forms, reports, or controls is a(n) _____ macro.

11. A window used to type programming code in Microsoft Visual Basic is the _____ _____.

12. A predefined procedure that performs calculations, returns a value, can accept input values, and can be used in building expressions is a(n) _____.

Fill in the Blank

13. A tool used to print a report containing detailed information about the objects in a database is the Database _____.

14. Outlined regions you see when you finish the steps of the PivotTable and PivotChart wizard are _____ _____.

15. Text that describes the meaning of colors and patterns used in a chart is a(n) _____.

Content-Based Assessments

Skills Review

Project 8C—Departments

In this project, you will apply the skills you practiced from the Objectives in Project 8A.

Objectives: 1. *Create a Standalone Macro with One Action;* **2.** *Add Multiple Actions to a Standalone Macro;* **3.** *Create a Macro Group;* **4.** *Associate a Macro with an Event;* **5.** *Create an Embedded Macro;* **6.** *Print Macro Details.*

Maria Benitez, Vice President of Operations for Providence and Warwick Hospital, wants to customize her database of department information to display a form when the database is opened. She also wants to add buttons to the form to automate some of the most common tasks, such as adding a new department and printing a record. In this project, you will create macros to automatically display a form and message box when the database is opened. You will associate command buttons with a macro, group macros, and embed macros within a form. Finally, you will display and print a report that documents the details of the macros you created. Your completed work will look similar to Figure 8.48.

> **For Project 8C, you will need the following file:**
>
> a08C_Departments
>
> **You will save your database as**
> **8C_Departments_Firstname_Lastname**

Figure 8.48

(Project 8C–Departments continues on the next page)

Skills Review

(Project 8C–Departments continued)

1. **Start** Access. Locate and open the **a08C_ Departments** file. Save the database in the **Access 2007 Database** format in your **Access Chapter 8** folder as 8C_ Departments_Firstname_Lastname and then collapse the **Navigation Pane**.

2. On the Ribbon, click the **Create tab**. In the **Other group**, click the **Macro** button. In the **Macro Builder**, under **Action**, in the first row, click the **arrow**. Scroll down the displayed list, and then click **OpenReport**. In the **Action Arguments pane**, in the **Report Name** box, click the **arrow**, and then click **8C Supervisors**. In the **View** box, be sure that **Report** is selected. The *Filter Name* box and the *Where Condition* box should be blank.

3. In the **Window Mode** box, be sure that the Window Mode setting is **Normal**. Point to the right column boundary of **Arguments** until the ⬌ pointer displays, and then double-click to resize the Arguments column.

4. In the **Macro Builder**, on the **first row**, click in the **Comment** box, and then type **Opens the 8C Supervisors report in report view - Firstname Lastname** and then press Enter. On the **Design tab**, in the **Tools group**, click the **Run** button. In the displayed message box, click **Yes** to save the macro. In the **Save As** dialog box, under **Macro Name**, type **Open 8C Supervisors Report - Firstname Lastname** and then click **OK**. **Close** the *8C Supervisors* report, and then **Close** the Macro Builder.

5. Expand the **Navigation Pane**. Under **Forms**, right-click **8C Intro Screen**, and then click **Design View**. On the **Design tab**, in the **Tools group**, click the **Property Sheet** button. On the **Property Sheet**, click the **Other tab**. Click in the **Pop Up** property setting box, click the **arrow**, and then click **Yes**. Click in the **Modal** property

setting box, click the **arrow**, and then click **Yes**. **Close** the **Property Sheet**, and then **Close** the form, saving changes when prompted. Collapse the **Navigation Pane**.

6. On the Ribbon, click the **Create tab**. In the **Other group**, click the **Macro** button. In the displayed **Macro Builder**, under **Action**, on the **first row**, click the **arrow**, scroll down, and then click **OpenForm**. In the **Action Arguments pane**, click in the **Form Name** box, click the **arrow**, and then click **8C Intro Screen**. In the **Macro Builder**, on the **first row**, click in the **Comment** box, and then type **Opens the 8C Intro Screen form - Firstname Lastname**

7. On the **Quick Access Toolbar**, click the **Save** button. In the **Save As** dialog box, under **Macro Name**, type **Autoexec** and then click **OK**. **Close** the Macro Builder, and then expand the **Navigation Pane**. On the **Navigation Pane**, under **Macros**, double-click **Autoexec** to run the macro. **Close** the form.

8. On the **Navigation Pane**, under **Macros**, right-click **Autoexec**, and then click **Design View**. **Collapse** the **Navigation Pane**. In the **Macro Builder**, on the first row, point to the **Row Selector** box until the ➡ pointer displays. Right-click, and from the shortcut menu, click **Insert Rows** to insert a row above the OpenForm Action row.

9. On the **first row**, click in the **Action** box, click the displayed **arrow**, and then click **Hourglass**. Notice that the default argument is *Yes*. For the Hourglass action, click in the **Comment** box, and then type **Turn mouse pointer into an hourglass**

10. On the **second row**, point to the **Row Selector** box until the ➡ pointer displays. Right-click, and from the shortcut

(Project 8C–Departments continues on the next page)

Skills Review

(Project 8C–Departments continued)

menu, click **Insert Rows** to insert a row between the Hourglass action row and the OpenForm action row.

11. On the **Design tab**, in the **Show/Hide group**, click the **Show All Actions** button. In the **Macro Builder**, on the **second row**, click in the **Action** box, and then click the **arrow**. From the displayed list, click **Echo**. In the **Comment** box, type **Hides the flickering screen as the macro actions execute** In the **Action Arguments pane**, click in the **Echo On** box, click the displayed **arrow**, and then click **No**. Click in the **Status Bar Text** box, type **Macro is executing**

12. On the **third row**, point to the **Row Selector** box until the ➡ pointer displays. Right-click, and from the shortcut menu, click **Insert Rows** to insert a row between the Echo action row and the OpenForm action row. In the **Macro Builder**, on the **third row**, click in the **Action** box, and then click the **arrow**. Scroll down, and then click **RunMacro**.

13. In the **Action Arguments pane**, click in the **Macro Name** box, click the **arrow**, and then click **Open 8C Supervisors Report**. The *Repeat Count* box and the *Repeat Expression* box should be blank.

14. In the **Macro Builder**, on the **RunMacro** row, click in the **Comment** box, type **Opens the 8C Supervisors report** and then press Enter.

15. In the **Macro Builder** window, on the **fifth row**, click in the **Action** box, and then click the **arrow**. From the displayed list, scroll down, and then click **MsgBox**. In the **Comment** box, type **Displays a security message box**

16. In the **Action Arguments pane**, click in the **Message** box, and then type **Only**

supervisors of Providence & Warwick Hospital are authorized to access this database. In the **Beep** box, be sure that the Beep argument is **Yes**. Click in the **Type** box, click the **arrow**, and then click **Warning!**. Click in the **Title** box, and then type **For Use by Providence & Warwick Hospital Supervisors Only!** Press Enter.

17. In the **Macro Builder**, under **Action**, click in the **sixth row**, click the **arrow**, and then click **Hourglass**. Click in the **Comment** box, and then type **Restores the mouse pointer** In the **Action Arguments pane**, click in the **Hourglass On** box, click the **arrow**, and then click **No**.

18. In the **Macro Builder**, under **Action**, click in the **seventh row**, click the **arrow**, and then click **Echo**. Click in the **Comment** box, and then type **Displays screen results** Notice that in the **Action Arguments pane**, in the **Echo On** box, the setting is **Yes**.

19. On the **Quick Access Toolbar**, click the **Save** button. On the **Design tab**, in the **Tools group**, click the **Run** button. In the displayed message box, click **OK**. Close the *8C Intro Screen* form. On the **tab row**, right-click any tab, and then click **Close All**.

20. On the Ribbon, click the **Create tab**. In the **Other group**, click the **Macro** button. On the **Design tab**, in the **Show/Hide group**, click the **Macro Names** button. In the **Show/Hide group**, click the **Show All Actions** button.

21. In the **Macro Builder**, on the **first row**, click in the **Comment** box, and then type **Purpose: To enable an individual to add a department to the 8C Dept Directors form** and then press Enter. On the **third row**, click in the **Macro Name** box, and then type **GoToNewRecord** On the same row, click in the **Action** box, click the **arrow**,

(Project 8C–Departments continues on the next page)

Skills Review

(Project 8C–Departments continued)

and then click **GoToRecord**. Click in the **Comment** box, and then type **Goes to new record** In the **Action Arguments pane**, click in the **Object Type** box, click the **arrow**, and then click **Form**. Click in the **Form Name** box, click the **arrow**, and then click **8C Dept Directors**. Click in the **Record** box; be sure that *New* is selected.

22. In the **Macro Builder**, on the **fourth row**, click in the **Action** box, click the **arrow**, and then click **GoToControl**. In the **Action Arguments pane**, click in the **Control Name** box, and then type **Department ID** Click in the **Comment** box, and then type **Moves focus from button to Department ID field** In the **Macro Builder**, on the **fifth row**, click in the **Action** box, click the **arrow**, and then click **SetValue**. In the **Action Arguments pane**, click in the **Item** box, and type **[Forms]![8C Dept Directors]![cmdAddNew].[Visible]** Click in the **Expression** box, and type **No** Click in the **Comment** box, and type **Hides the button** In the **Macro Builder**, on the **sixth row**, click in the **Action** box, click the **arrow**, and then click **SetValue**. In the **Action Arguments pane**, click in the **Item** box, and type **[Forms]![8C Dept Directors]![cmdShowAll].[Visible]** Click in the **Expression** box and type **Yes**. Click in the **Comment** box and type **Shows the button**

23. On the **eighth row**, click in the **Macro Name** box, and then type **ShowAll** On the same row, click in the **Action** box, click the **arrow**, and then click **ShowAllRecords**. Click in the **Comment** box, and then type **Show all records and exit data entry**

24. In the **Macro Builder**, on the **ninth row**, click in the **Action** box, click the **arrow**, and then click **GoToControl**. In the **Action Arguments pane**, click in the **Control Name** box, and type **Department ID**

Click in the **Comment** box, and then type **Moves focus from button to Department ID field** In the **Macro Builder**, on the **tenth row**, click in the **Action** box, click the **arrow**, and then click **SetValue**. In the **Action Arguments pane**, click in the **Item** box, and then click the **Build** button to open the Expression Builder. In the **Expression Builder**, type **[Forms]![8C Dept Directors]![cmdAddNew].[Visible]** Click in the **Expression** box, and type **Yes** Click in the **Comment** box, type **Shows the button** In the **Macro Builder**, on the **eleventh row**, click in the **Action** box, click the **arrow**, and then click **SetValue**. In the **Action Arguments pane**, click in the **Item** box, and type **[Forms]![8C Dept Directors]![cmdShowAll].[Visible]** Click in the **Expression** box, type **No** Click in the **Comment** box, type **Hides the button**

25. Press Enter. **Save** the macro group as **8C Add Dept Group Firstname Lastname Close** the Macro Builder, expand the **Navigation Pane**, and notice that under **Macros**, the macro group displays as one macro object.

26. On the **Navigation Pane**, under **Forms**, double-click **8C Dept Directors** to display the form in **Form** view. Collapse the **Navigation Pane**, and then switch the form to **Design view**. In the **Form Header section**, right-click the **Add Dept** button, and then click **Properties**. Be sure that the **Property Sheet** displays *Selection type: Command button* and that the **Selection type** box displays *cmdAddNew*. On the **Property Sheet**, click the **Event tab**. Point to the **left edge** of the **Property Sheet** until the ↔ pointer displays. Drag to the left to the **4.25-inch mark on the horizontal ruler**. Click the **On Click** property setting **arrow**.

(Project 8C–Departments continues on the next page)

Content-Based Assessments

(Project 8C–Departments continued)

27. In the displayed list, click **8C Add Dept Group Firstname Lastname.GoToNew Record**. On the **Property Sheet**, click the **Format tab**. In the **Caption** property setting box, click to the left of **Add Dept**, and then type **&**

28. On the **Property Sheet** display *Selection type: Command button* and in the **Selection type** box display *cmdShowAll*. On the **Property Sheet**, click the **Event tab**. Click in the **On Click** property setting box, and then click the **arrow**. In the displayed list, click **8C Add Dept Group Firstname Lastname.ShowAll**. On the **Property Sheet**, click the **Format tab**. In the **Caption** property setting box, click to the left of **Show All**, and then type **& Close** the **Property Sheet**.

29. Switch to **Form** view. Click the **Add Dept** button. In the **Department ID** field type **1236-D** Press ⇥ Tab, and type **Nutritional Services** Enter your information for all of the remaining fields except Supervisor ID: In the **Supervisor ID** field, type **417-Sup Save** changes and switch to **Design** view.

30. In the **Form Header section**, right-click the **Print** button, and then click **Properties**. Be sure that the **Property Sheet** displays *Selection type: Command button* and that the **Selection type** box displays *cmdPrintRec*. On the **Property Sheet**, click the **Event tab**. Click in the **On Click** property setting box, click the **Build** button.

31. In the **Choose Builder** dialog box, click **Macro Builder**, and then click **OK** to display the Macro Builder. In the **Macro Builder**, on the **first row**, click in the **Action** box, click the **arrow**, and then click **RunCommand**. In the **Action Arguments pane**, click in the **Command** box, click the **arrow**, and then click

SelectRecord. Click in the **Comment** box, and then type **Selects the current record**

32. In the **Macro Builder**, on the **second row**, click in the **Action** box, click the **arrow**, and then click **RunCommand**. In the **Action Arguments pane**, click in the **Command** box, click the **arrow**, and then click **PrintSelection**. Click in the **Comment** box, and then type **Prints the current record**

33. **Close** the Macro Builder. In the displayed message box, click **Yes** to save the changes made to the macro and to update the On Click property. On the **Property Sheet**, click the **Format tab**. In the **Caption** box, click to the left of **Print**, and then type **&** to create a shortcut key using the letter *P*. **Close** the **Property Sheet**, and then switch the *8C Dept Directors* form to **Form** view.

34. If you are instructed to submit this result, press PgDn until you display the record that contains your first and last names in the Director fields. Click in the **Department ID** field. Click the **Print** button to create a paper printout or create an electronic printout. **Close** the *8C Dept Directors* form.

35. On the Ribbon, click the **Database Tools tab**. In the **Analyze group**, click the **Database Documenter** button. If necessary, in the displayed **Documenter** dialog box, click the click the **Macros tab**. In the **Documenter** dialog box, click the **Options** button. Click the check box to deselect **Permissions by User and Group**, and then click **OK**. In the **Documenter** dialog box, click **Select All**. Click the **Forms tab**. Click the **Options** button. In the **Print Form Definition** dialog box, under **Include for Form**, select the **Properties** check box only. Under **Include for Sections and Controls**, select **Names and Properties**, and then click **OK**. In the **Documenter** dialog box, click the **8C Dept**

(Project 8C–Departments continues on the next page)

Skills Review

(Project 8C–Departments continued)

Directors check box, and then click **OK**. If you are instructed to submit this result, create a paper or electronic printout of pages 5 to 7. Create another paper or electronic printout of pages 20 to 26. Include the project number, 8C, and the page number range in the file names if you

create electronic printouts to overwriting any files. On the **Print Preview tab**, in the **Close Preview group**, click the **Close Print Preview** button.

36. Expand the **Navigation Pane**. **Close** the database, and then **Exit** Access.

End **You have completed Project 8C**

Skills Review

Project 8D—Gift Shop

In this project, you will apply the skills you practiced from the Objectives in Project 8B.

Objectives: 7. *Create a PivotTable from a Query;* **8.** *Create a PivotChart from a PivotTable.*

Maria Benitez, Vice President of Operations, wants to compare the prices of the items available in the hospital gift shop. In this project, you will create a PivotTable and a PivotChart to analyze the value of the inventory based on the quantity in stock and the selling price of the items. Your completed PivotTable and PivotChart will look similar to those shown in Figure 8.49.

For Project 8D, you will need the following file:

a08D_Gift_Shop

You will save your database as
8D_Gift_Shop_Firstname_Lastname

Figure 8.49

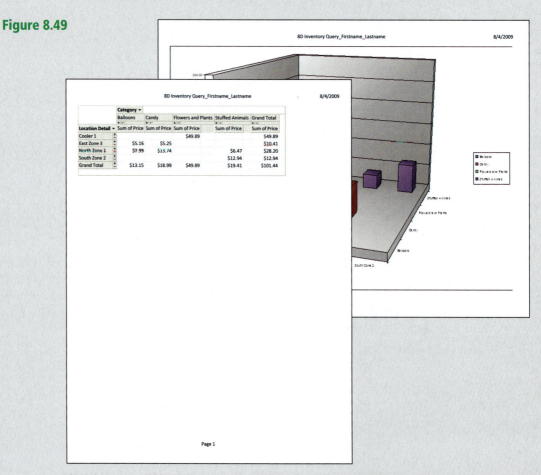

(Project 8D–Gift Shop continues on the next page)

Content-Based Assessments

(Project 8D–Gift Shop continued)

1. **Start** Access. Locate and open the **a08D_ Gift_Shop** file. Save the database in the **Access 2007 Database** format in your **Access Chapter 8** folder as **8D_Gift_Shop_ Firstname_Lastname**

2. On the **Navigation Pane**, **Rename** the two tables, the query, and the report by adding **Firstname Lastname** to the end of the object names. Under **Queries**, double-click **8D Inventory Query** to run the query.

3. Collapse the **Navigation Pane**. On the **tab row**, right-click **8D Inventory Query**, and then click **PivotTable View**. If necessary, on the Design tab, in the Show/Hide group, click the Field List button. In the **PivotTable Field List**, drag the **Category** field to the **Drop Row Fields Here** area. In the **PivotTable Field List**, drag the **Location Detail** field to the **Drop Column Fields Here** area. On the **PivotTable Field List**, drag the **Value** field to the **Drop Totals or Detail Fields Here** area.

4. In the **PivotTable design area**, point to **Category** until the pointer displays. Drag upward and to the right and point to **Location Detail** until a dark blue line displays to the left of Location Detail, and then release the mouse button. In the **PivotTable design area**, point to **Location Detail** until the pointer displays. Drag downward and to the left to the **Drop Row Fields Here** area.

5. In the **PivotTable design area**, click any one of the **Value** boxes. On the **Design tab**, in the **Tools group**, click the **AutoCalc** button. From the displayed list, click **Sum**.

6. In the **PivotTable design area**, under **Location Detail** and to the right of **Cooler 1**,

click the **Drill Up** button (−) to collapse the total row for Cooler 1. Repeat the procedure for the **East Zone 3** row, the **North Zone 1** row, and the **South Zone 2** row.

7. **Close** the **PivotTable Field List**. Click the **Category arrow**. From the displayed list, click **Candy**, and then click **Flowers and Plants** to deselect these two categories, and then click **OK**. Notice that only data for Balloons and Stuffed Animals displays, and the grand totals only sum the amounts for these two categories. Click the **Location Detail arrow**. From the displayed list, click **Cooler 1**, and then click **East Zone 3** to deselect these two Location Details, and then click **OK**.

8. On the **Design tab**, in the **Filter & Sort group**, click the active **AutoFilter** button to remove the filter. Collapse the **Cooler 1** row, and then collapse the **East Zone 3** row.

9. On the **Design tab**, in the **Show/Hide group**, click the **Field List** button to display the PivotTable Field List. In the **PivotTable Field List**, right-click **Sum of Value**, and then click **Delete**. In the **PivotTable design area**, expand the **Balloons**, **Candy**, **Flowers and Plants**, and **Stuffed Animals** columns to display the Value data for each category.

10. Right-click one of the **Value** boxes, and from the shortcut menu, click **Remove**. In the **PivotTable Field List**, drag **Price** to the **Drop Totals or Detail Fields Here** area. In the **PivotTable design area**, click any **Price** box. On the **Design tab**, in the **Tools group**, click the **AutoCalc** button, and then click **Sum**. Collapse each of the **Location Detail row headings** so that the detail for each Location Detail does not display.

(Project 8D–Gift Shop continues on the next page)

(Project 8D–Gift Shop continued)

11. On the **Design tab**, in the **Show/Hide group**, click the active **Drop Zones** button. **Close** the **PivotTable Field List**, and then **Save** the PivotTable. View the PivotTable in **Print Preview**, and then change the **Margins** to **Normal**. If you are instructed to submit this result, create a paper or electronic printout of the PivotTable. On the **Print Preview tab**, in the **Close Preview group**, click the **Close Print Preview** button, leaving the PivotTable open for the next step.

12. On the **tab row**, right-click **8D Inventory Query**, and then click **PivotChart View**. **Close** the **Chart Field List**. On the left side of the **PivotChart design area**, click **Axis Title**. On the **Design tab**, in the **Tools group**, click the **Property Sheet** button. In the **Properties** dialog box, click the **Format tab**. In the **Caption** box, select **Axis Title**, and then type **Total Price**

13. At the bottom of the **PivotChart design area**, click **Axis Title** to display the **Properties** dialog box for this object. In the **Caption** box, select **Axis Title**, and then type **Location Detail Close** the **Properties** dialog box. Click in an open area of the chart.

14. On the **Design tab**, in the **Show/Hide group**, click the **Legend** button.

15. On the **Design tab**, in the **Type group**, click the **Change Chart Type** button. In the displayed **Properties** dialog box, on the **Type tab**, notice that the chart type is a **Clustered Column** chart. On the second row, click the first chart type, which changes the chart to a **3D Column** chart type.

16. On the left side of the PivotChart, click any of the numbers representing the Total Price. In the displayed **Properties** dialog box, click the **Format tab**. Under Text format, Click the **B** to add bold to the currency values. **Close** the **Properties** dialog box.

17. On the **Design tab**, in the **Show/Hide group**, click the **Drop Zones** button.

18. **Save** the PivotChart, and then view the PivotChart in **Print Preview**. Click the **Landscape** button. If you are instructed to submit this result, create a paper or electronic printout. Add the word Chart to the file name if you create an electronic printout. On the **Print Preview tab**, in the **Close Preview group**, click the **Close Print Preview** button.

19. **Close** the PivotChart, and then expand the **Navigation Pane**. **Close** the database, and then **Exit** Access.

End **You have completed Project 8D**

Mastering Access

Project 8E — Orthopedic Supplies

In this project, you will apply the skills you practiced from the Objectives in Project 8A.

Objectives: 1. *Create a Standalone Macro with One Action;* **2.** *Add Multiple Actions to a Standalone Macro;* **3.** *Create a Macro Group;* **4.** *Associate a Macro with an Event;* **5.** *Create an Embedded Macro;* **6.** *Print Macro Details.*

Maria Benitez, Vice President of Operations for Providence and Warwick Hospital, wants to customize the orthopedic supplies database to display a form when the database is opened. She also wants to add buttons on the form to automate some of the most common tasks, such as adding a new department and printing a record. In this project, you will create macros to automatically display a form and message box when the user opens the database. You will associate command buttons with a macro, group macros, and embed macros within a form. Finally, you will display and print a report that documents the details of the macros you created. Your completed work will look similar to Figure 8.50.

For Project 8E, you will need the following file:

a08E_Orthopedic_Supplies

**You will save your database as
8E_Orthopedic_Supplies_Firstname_Lastname**

Figure 8.50

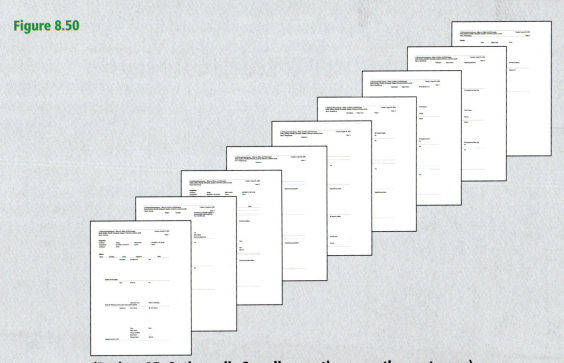

(Project 8E–Orthopedic Supplies continues on the next page)

Content-Based Assessments

(Project 8E–Orthopedic Supplies continued)

1. **Start** Access. Locate and open the **a08E_Orthopedic_Supplies** file. Save the database in the **Access 2007 Database** format in your **Access Chapter 8** folder as 8E_Orthopedic_Supplies_Firstname_ Lastname Collapse the **Navigation Pane**.

2. On the **Create tab**, click the **Macro** button. On the **Design tab**, in the **Show/Hide group**, click the **Show All Actions** button. Create a macro to open the *8E Intro Screen* form. In the **Macro Builder**, under **Action**, in the first row, click **OpenForm**. In the **Action Arguments pane**, for **Form Name**, select **8E Intro Screen**. Be sure the **View** box displays **Form** and the **Window Mode** box displays **Normal**. In the **Comment** box, type **Displays the 8E Intro Screen Run** the macro and **Save** it as **Autoexec**

3. Modify the **Autoexec** macro. Insert two rows above the **OpenForm** action row, and to the first row, add the action **Hourglass** with the **Comment Displays the hourglass** To the second row, add the **Echo** action. In the **Comment** box, type **Hides the flickering screen as the macro actions execute** In the **Action Arguments pane**, change the **Echo On** box to **No**. Click in the **Status Bar Text** box, and then type **Macro is executing**

4. On the **fourth row**, add a **MsgBox** action. Type a **Message** that displays **Purchases of orthopedic supplies in excess of $1,000 requires signature from Jennifer Lewis** Add a **Beep**, and change the **Type** box to **Information**. Title the **Message** box **Purchase Restrictions**

5. Click in the **fifth row**, click the **arrow**, and then click **Echo**. Click in the **Comment** box, and then type **Displays screen results** In the **Action Arguments pane**, be sure the **Echo On** box is set to **Yes**.

6. Click in the **sixth row**, click the **arrow**, and then click **Hourglass**. Click in the **Comment** box, and then type **Restores the normal mouse pointer** In the **Action Arguments pane**, change the **Hourglass On** box to **No**.

7. **Close** the Macro Builder and **Save** the macro.

8. Create a **Macro Group** to print the reports. Name this macro group **ReportGroup** In the first row, type **Developer: Firstname Lastname** as the **Commment**. The purpose of the macro group is to select report print options.

(Project 8E–Orthopedic Supplies continues on the next page)

Content-Based Assessments

(Project 8E—Orthopedic Supplies continued)

Macro Name	Condition	Action	Arguments	Comment
				Developer: Firstname Last Name-
				Purpose: Select report print options
Options		OpenForm	Form: 8E Report Options View: Form Data Mode:Edit Window Mode: Normal	Open report options form
PrintReport	1=[Forms]![8E Report Options]![Options]	RunMacro	Macro Name: ReportGroup. ReportAlpha	Option value 1
	. . .	StopMacro		
	2=[Forms]! [8E Report Options]! Options]!	RunMacro	Macro Name: ReportGroup.ReportID	Option value 2
	. . .	StopMacro		
	3=[Forms]! [8E Report Options]! [Options]	RunMacro	Macro Name: ReportGroup .ReportRep	Option value 3
	. . .	StopMacro		
ReportAlpha		Hourglass	Hourglass On: Yes	
		RunMacro	Macro Name: ReportGroup .Cancel	Close Report Options form
		OpenReport	Report Name: 8E Suppliers Alpha View: Print Preview Window Mode: Normal	Open report in print preview
		SelectObject	Object Type: Report Object Name: 8E Suppliers Alpha In Database Window: No	Switch focus
		Hourglass	Hourglass On: No	
ReportID		Hourglass	Hourglass On: Yes	
		RunMacro	Macro Name: ReportGroup.Cancel	Close Report Options Form
		OpenReport	Report Name: 8E Suppliers by ID View: Print Preview Window Mode: Normal	Open report in print preview

(Project 8E—Orthopedic Supplies continues on the next page)

(Project 8E–Orthopedic Supplies continued)

		SelectObject	Object Type: Report Object Name: 8E Suppliers by ID In Database Window: No	Switch focus
		Hourglass	Hourglass On: No	
ReportRep		Hourglass	Hourglass On: Yes	
		RunMacro	Macro Name: ReportGroup .Cancel	Close Report Options form
		OpenReport	Report Name: 8E Suppliers by Sales Rep View: Print Preview Window Mode: Normal	Open report in print preview
		SelectObject	Object Type: Report Object Name: 8E Suppliers by Sales Rep In Database Window: No	Switch focus
Cancel		Close	Object Type: Form Object Name: 8E Report Options	Close Report Options form
		GoToControl	Control Name:Supplier ID	Return focus to Suppliers form

9. Open the **8E Report Options** form in **Design** view. Right-click the **Print Report** button, and then click **Properties**. On the **Property Sheet**, click the **Event tab**. Click the **On Click** property setting box **arrow**, and click **ReportGroup.PrintReport**. Click the **Cancel** button. Click the **On Click** property setting box **arrow**, and then select **ReportGroup.Cancel**. **Close** the Property Sheet and **Close** the form. **Close** the **Macro Builder** and **Save** the group as **ReportGroup**

10. Double-click the **8E Suppliers** form. Click the **Print Report** button. Test each report option and **Close Print Preview**. **Close** the **8E Suppliers** form.

11. Collapse the **Navigation Pane**. On the Ribbon, click the **Database Tools tab**. In the **Analyze group**, click the **Database Documenter** button. In the displayed **Documenter** dialog box, click the **Macros tab**. In the **Documenter** dialog box, click the **Options** button. Clear the **Permissions by User and Group** check box, and then click **OK**.

(Project 8E–Orthopedic Supplies continues on the next page)

Content-Based Assessments

Mastering Access

(Project 8E–Orthopedic Supplies continued)

In the **Documenter** dialog box, click **Select All**, and then click **OK**. If you are instructed to submit this result, create a paper or electronic printout. Include the project number, 8E, in the file name if you create an electronic file. On the **Print Preview tab**, in the **Close Preview group**, click the **Close Print Preview** button.

12. Expand the **Navigation Pane**. **Close** the database, and then **Exit** Access.

End **You have completed Project 8E** _____

Access
chapter eight

Mastering Access

Project 8F — Yearly Supplies

In this project, you will apply the skills you practiced from the Objectives in Project 8B.

Objectives: 7. *Create a PivotTable from a Query;* **8.** *Create a PivotChart from a PivotTable.*

Parinder Salem, Community Relations Director, wants to compare the orthopedic supply orders over the past three years. In this project, you will create a PivotTable and a PivotChart to analyze the orders. Your completed PivotTable and PivotChart will look similar to those shown in Figure 8.51.

For Project 8F, you will need the following file:

a08F_Yearly_Supplies

**You will save your database as
8F_Yearly_Supplies_Firstname_Lastname**

Figure 8.51

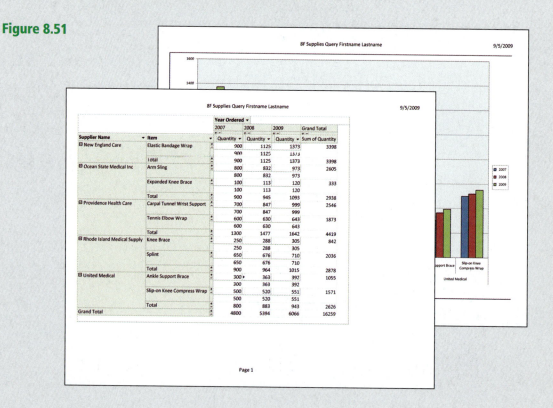

(Project 8F—Yearly Supplies continues on the next page)

(Project 8F–Yearly Supplies continued)

1. **Start** Access. Locate and open the **a08F_Yearly_Supplies** file. Save the database in the **Access 2007 Database** format in your **Access Chapter 8** folder as **8F_Yearly_Supplies_Firstname Lastname**

2. On the **Navigation Pane**, **Rename** the two tables and the query by adding **Firstname Lastname** to the end of the object names. Under **Queries**, double-click **8F Supplies Query** to run the query.

3. **Collapse** the **Navigation Pane**. On the **tab row**, right-click **8F Supplies Query**, and then click **PivotTable View**. If the Field List is not displayed, on the Design tab, in the Show/Hide group, click the Field List button.

4. In the **PivotTable Field List**, drag the **Item** field to the **Drop Row Fields Here** area. Drag the **Supplier Name** field to the left of **Item** until the dark blue line appears to the left of Item. Drag the **Year Ordered** field to the **Drop Column Fields Here** area. Drag the **Quantity** field to the **Drop Totals or Detail Fields Here** area.

5. In the **PivotTable design area**, click any one of the **Quantity** boxes. On the **Design tab**, in the **Tools group**, click the **AutoCalc** button. From the displayed list, click **Sum**. In the **Show/Hide Group**, click the **Drop Zones** button.

6. **Close** the **PivotTable Field List**, and then **Save** the PivotTable. View the PivotTable in

Print Preview, and then change the **Orientation** to **Landscape** and the **Margins** to **Normal**. If you are instructed to submit this result, create a paper or electronic printout of the PivotTable. On the **Print Preview tab**, in the **Close Preview group**, click the **Close Print Preview** button.

7. On the **tab row**, right-click **8F Supplies Query**, and then click **PivotChart View**. **Close** the **Chart Field List**. On the left side of the **PivotChart design area**, edit the **Axis Title** to display Quantity Ordered At the bottom of the **PivotChart design area**, edit the **Axis Title** to display Items by Supplier If necessary, **Close** the Properties dialog box. Add the **Legend** to the chart, and then click the **Drop Zones** button.

8. **Save** the PivotChart, and then view the PivotChart in **Print Preview**. If you are instructed to submit this result, create a paper or electronic printout of the PivotChart in **Landscape** orientation. Add the word Chart to the file name if you create an electronic printout. On the **Print Preview tab**, in the **Close Preview group**, click the **Close Print Preview** button, and then **Close** the PivotChart.

9. Expand the **Navigation Pane**. **Close** the database, and then **Exit** Access.

End **You have completed Project 8F**

Project 8G—Facility Expansion

In this project, you will apply the following Objectives found in Projects 8A and 8B.

Objectives: 5. *Create an Embedded Macro;* **6.** *Print Macro Details;* **7.** *Create a PivotTable from a Query.*

Paul Scheinman, CEO of the Providence and Warwick Hospital in Providence, Rhode Island, has proposed expanding one of the hospital's facilities. In this project, you will create a PivotTable to summarize the budgeted amounts for this expansion project. You will then build a macro embedded in a button on the 8G Projects form to open the PivotTable in Print Preview. Your completed PivotTable and Document Analyzer Form report will look similar to the table and report in Figure 8.52.

For Project 8G, you will need the following file:

a08G_Facility_Expansion

You will save your database as
8G_Facility_Expansion_Firstname_Lastname

Figure 8.52

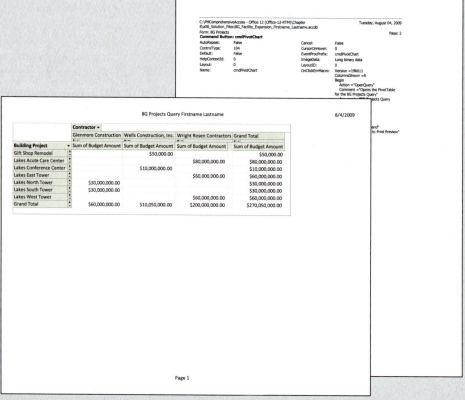

(Project 8G–Facility Expansion continues on the next page)

Content-Based Assessments

(Project 8G–Facility Expansion continued)

1. **Start** Access. Locate and open the **a08G_Facility_Expansion** file. Save the database in the **Access 2007 Database** format in your **Access Chapter 8** folder as **8G_Facility_Expansion_Firstname_Lastname Rename** the **8G Projects Query** by adding your **Firstname Lastname** to the end of the query name.

2. Open the **8G Projects Query** and switch to **PivotTable view**. From the **Field List**, drag the **Building Project** field to the **Drop Row Fields Here** area. Drag the **Contractor** field to the **Drop Column Fields Here** area. Drag the **Budget Amount** field to the **Drop Totals or Detail Fields Here** area. **Auto calculate** the **Sum** for the **Budget Amount**. **Hide Details** and **Drop Zones**. **Save** and **Close** the PivotTable.

3. Open the **8G Projects** form in **Design view**. Click the **Summary** button and open the **Property Sheet**. On the **Event tab**, click in the **On Click** build button, and then open the **Macro Builder**. In the **Action** box, select **OpenQuery**. Open the **8G Projects Query** in **PivotTable view**. Set the **Data Mode** to **Read Only**. Add a **Comment** Opens the PivotTable for the 8G Projects Query In the second **Action** box, add a **RunCommand** with a **Command** of **PrintPreview**, and a **Comment** Switch to Print Preview **Close** the **Macro Builder** and **Save** changes.

4. Switch the **8G Projects** form to **Form** view. Click the **Summary** button. Click the **Landscape** button. Set **Margins** to **Normal**. If you are instructed to submit this result, create a paper or electronic printout. Click the **Close Print Preview** button.

5. **Close** the query and the form. Run the **Database Documenter**. Select the **Forms tab**, and click **8G Projects**. Click the **Options** button and under **Include for Form**, select the **Code** check box only. Click the **Properties** button. Under **Print Categories**, select only **Other Properties**. Click **OK** three times. If you are instructed to submit this result, create a paper or electronic printout of only page 2 of the report. Include the project number, 8G, in the file name if you create an electronic printout. Click the **Close PrintPreview** button.

6. Expand the **Navigation Pane**. **Close** the database, and **Exit** Access.

End **You have completed Project 8G**

Mastering Access

Project 8H — Transcriptions

In this project, you will apply the following Objectives found in Projects 8A and 8B.

Objectives: 1. *Create a Standalone Macro with One Action;* **3.** *Create a Macro Group;* **4.** *Associate a Macro with an Event;* **5.** *Create an Embedded Macro;* **6.** *Print Macro Details;* **7.** *Create a PivotTable from a Query;* **8.** *Create a PivotTable.*

Maria Benitez, Vice President of Operations, is responsible for the transcriptionists employed by the hospital. In this project, you will create an autoexec macro that will open the 8H Transcriptionist form. You will create a macro group that will search for the record of a specific transcriptionist and associate macros of this group with an event. You will embed a macro into a button on the form. You will also prepare a PivotTable and PivotChart to display the number of lines each transcriptionist completes by document type. Your printed macro details, PivotTable, and PivotChart will look similar to those in Figure 8.53.

For Project 8H, you will need the following file:

a08H_Transcriptions

You will save your database as
8H_Transcriptions_Firstname_Lastname

Figure 8.53

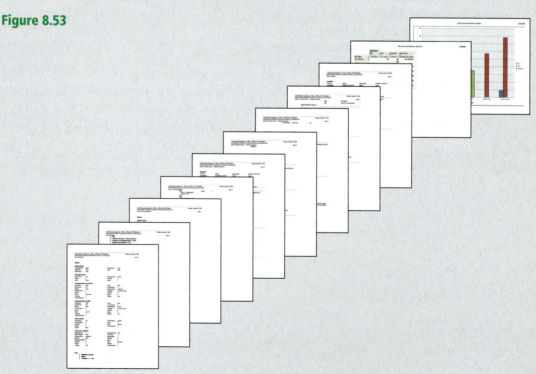

(Project 8H–Transcriptions continues on the next page)

Content-Based Assessments

(Project 8H–Transcriptions continued)

1. **Start** Access. Locate and open the **a08H_Transcriptions** file. Save the database in the **Access 2007 Database** format in your **Access Chapter 8** folder as 8H_Transcriptions_Firstname_Lastname

2. **Rename** the query by adding your **Firstname Lastname** to the end of the query name.

3. Create an **Autoexec** macro to **open** the **8H Transcriptionists** form in **Form view** and **Normal Window Mode**. Add a **Comment** that reads **Opens the 8H Transcriptionists form**

4. Create a macro group to locate a particular transcriptionist in the **8H Transcriptionists** form. Include the following Macro Names, Conditions, Actions, Arguments, and Comments:

Macro Name	Condition	Action	Arguments	Comment
				Developer: Firstname Lastname
				Purpose: To enable an individual to search for a specific transcriptionist in the 8H Transcriptionists form
OpenSearch Form		**OpenForm**	**Form: 8H Search View: Form Data Mode: Edit Window Mode: Normal**	**Opens 8H Search form**
SearchFor Trans	**IsNull([Forms]! [8H Search]! [LastName])**	**Close**	**Object Type: Form Object Name: 8H Search Save: No**	**If a transcriptionist is not selected, close the 8H Search form**
	. . .	**StopMacro**		
		SetValue	**Item: [Forms]! [8H Search].[Visible] Expression: False**	**Hides the 8H Search form**
		SelectObject	**Object Type: Form Object Name: 8H Transcriptionists In Database Window: No**	**Sets focus to 8H Transcriptionists form**
		GoToControl	**Control Name: Last Name**	**Sets focus to LastName field**

(Project 8H–Transcriptions continues on the next page)

(Project 8H–Transcriptions continued)

		RunCommand	Command: Sort Ascending	Sorts Last Names in Ascending order
		FindRecord	FindWhat: =[Forms]![8H Search]![LastName] Match: Whole Field Match Case: No Search: All Only Current Field: Yes Find first: Yes	Finds the Last Name in the 8H Transcriptionists form that matches the entry
		Close	Object Type: Form Object Name: 8H Search Save: No	Closes the 8H Search form
		MsgBox	Message: To display all records in original order, click Clear All Sorts button Type: Information Title: Search for Transcriptionist	Displays method to clear sort
CancelSearch		Close	Object Type: Form Object Name: 8H Search Save: No	Closes the 8H Search form
		SelectObject	Object Type: Form Object Name: 8H Transcriptionists In Database Window: No	Sets focus to 8H Transcriptionists form

5. **Save** the Macro group as **8H Search Group – Firstname Lastname Close** the **Macro Builder**.

6. Open the **8H Transcriptionists** form in **Design view** and select the **Find Transcriptionist** button. Display the **Property Sheet Event tab**, and from the **On Click arrow**, select **8H Search Group – Firstname Lastname.OpenSearchForm**.

7. Click the **Print Record** button, display the **Property Sheet Event tab**, and from the **On Click** build button, open the **Macro Builder**. Using the **Action** of **RunCommand**, create a two-step embedded macro to **Select** the record and to **PrintPreview** the record. **Save** and **Close** the macro. **Close** the form.

(Project 8H–Transcriptions continues on the next page)

Content-Based Assessments

(Project 8H–Transcriptions continued)

8. Open the **8H Search** form in **Design view**. Select the **OK** button. Click the **On Click arrow**, and then select **8H Search Group – Firstname Lastname.SearchForTrans**. Click the **Cancel** button. Click the **On Click arrow**, and then select **8H Search Group – Firstname Lastname.Cancel Search**. **Close** the form and **Save** changes.

9. Run the **Database Documenter**. Select the **Forms tab**, and select the **8H Search** and **8H Transcriptionists** check boxes. Click the **Options** button and under **Include for Form**, select the **Code** check box only. Click the **Properties** button. Under **Print Categories**, select only **Other Properties**. Click **OK** two times. Click the **Macros tab**, and then click **8H Search Group** and **Autoexec**. Include **Properties** and **Actions and Arguments**. If you are instructed to submit this result, create a paper or electronic printout. Include the project number, 8H, in the file name if you create an electronic printout and then click the **Close Print Preview** button.

10. Open the **8H Line Count** query in **PivotTable view**. Drag the **Doc Type** field to the **Drop Rows Here** area. Drag the **Last Name** field to **Drop Columns Here** area. Drag the **# of Lines** field to the **Drop Totals or Detail Fields** area.

11. Add an **Auto Calculation** for the **Average # of Lines** by **Doc Type**. Click the **Drop Zones** button.

12. Switch to **PivotChart view**. Edit the left **Axis Title** to display **Average # of Lines** and the bottom **Axis Title** to display **Document Type** Add a **Legend** and click **Drop Zones**.

13. View the PivotTable in **Print Preview**, and then change the **Margins** to **Normal** and **Orientation** to **Landscape**. If you are instructed to submit this result, create a paper or electronic printout of the PivotTable and the PivotChart. Add the word Chart to the file name if you create an electronic printout of the PivotChart. **Save** the query.

14. **Close** the query, and then expand the **Navigation Pane**. **Close** the database, and **Exit** Access.

End **You have completed Project 8H**

Mastering Access

Project 8I — Recruiting Events

In this project, you will apply all the skills you practiced from the Objectives in Projects 8A and 8B.

Parminder Salem, Vice President of Operations for Providence and Warwick Hospital, wants to customize the database to display a form when the database is opened. She also wants to add buttons on the form to automate some of the most common tasks, such as printing a form. In this project, you will create macros to automatically display a form and message box when a user opens the database. You will associate command buttons with a macro, group macros, and embed macros within a form, in addition to creating conditions that control whether a macro is run. Finally, you will display and print a report that documents the details of the macros you created. You will create a PivotTable and a PivotChart to analyze the number of applicants by semester and department. Your completed macros, PivotTable and PivotChart will look similar to those shown in Figure 8.54.

Figure 8.54

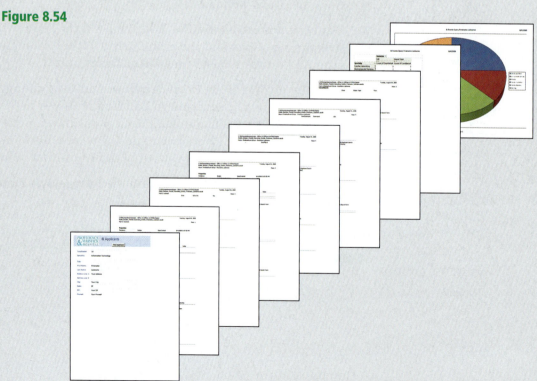

(Project 8I–Recruiting Events continues on the next page)

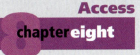

(Project 8I–Recruiting Events continued)

CancelSearch		Close	Object Type: Form Object Name: 8I Applicant Search Form Save: Prompt	Close the 8I Applicant Search Form
		SelectObject	Object Type: Form Object Name: 8I Applicants In Database Window: No	Set focus to 8I Applicants form

5. **Close** the **Macro Builder** and **Save** changes.

6. Open the **8I Applicants** form in **Design** view. Click the **Find Applicant** button. On the **Property Sheet**, on the **Event tab**, click the **On Click** box **arrow**, and then select **FindApplicant Group – Firstname Lastname.OpenApplicantSearch**. **Close** the form and **Save** your changes.

7. Open the **8I Applicant Search Form** in **Design view**. Click the **OK** button, and then display the **Property Sheet**. On the **Event tab**, in the **On Click** row, click the **arrow**, and then click **FindApplicant Group – Firstname Lastname.ExecuteSearch**. Click the **Cancel** button, click the **On Click** row **arrow**, and then click **FindApplicant Group – Firstname Lastname.Cancel Search**.

8. **Close** the form, saving your changes when prompted.

9. Open the **8I Applicants** table. Add a new record. In the **Specialty** field, type **Information Technology** Populate the remainder of the fields with your personal information. **Save** and **Close** the table.

10. Open the **8I Applicants** form and click the **Find Applicant** button. In the **Applicant Search** dialog box, enter your Last Name and click **OK**. Verify that the record contains your information and, if you are instructed to submit this result, create a paper or electronic printout of only this record. **Close** the form, and **Save** your changes.

11. Run the **Database Documenter**. If you are instructed to submit this result, create a paper or electronic printout of the **Properties** and the **Actions and Arguments** of the two macros. Include the project number, 8I, in the file name if you create an electronic printout.

12. Open the **8I Events Query** and switch to **PivotTable view**. If necessary, display the Field List. From the **Field List**, drag the **Specialty** field to the **Drop Row Fields Here** area. Drag the **Semester** field to the **Drop Column Fields Here** area. Drag the **Candidate#** field to

(Project 8I–Recruiting Events continues on the next page)

(Project 8I–Recruiting Events continued)

the **Drop Totals or Detail Fields Here** area. If the Candidate# field boxes do not display, click the Show Details button. Click any one of the **Candidate#** boxes. Click the **AutoCalc** button, and then click **Count**. Click the **Hide Details** button. Hide the **Drop Zones**, click the **Semester arrow**, and then clear the **Spring** check box.

13. **Close** the **PivotTable Field List**, and then **Save** the PivotTable. View the PivotTable in **Print Preview**, and then change the **Margins** to **Normal**. If you are instructed to submit this result, create a paper or electronic printout of the PivotTable. On the **Print Preview tab**, in the **Close Preview group**, click the **Close Print Preview** button.

14. On the **tab row**, right-click **8I Events Query**, and then click **PivotChart View**. **Close** the **Chart Field List**. Hide the **Drop Zones**, and then add a **Legend**. Be sure the chart is selected, click the **Change Chart Type** button, and then select the **3D Pie Chart**.

15. **Save** the PivotChart, and then view the PivotChart in **Print Preview**. If you are instructed to submit this result, create a paper or electronic printout of the PivotChart in **Landscape** orientation. Add the word Chart to the file name if you create an electronic printout. On the **Print Preview tab**, in the **Close Preview group**, click the **Close Print Preview** button, and then **Close** the PivotChart.

16. Expand the **Navigation Pane**, **Close** the database, and **Exit** Access.

 You have completed Project 8I ———————

Content-Based Assessments

Business Running Case

Project 8J — Business Running Case

In this project, you will apply the skills you practiced from the Objectives in Projects 8A and 8B.

From My Computer, navigate to the student files that accompany this textbook. In the folder **03_business_running_case**, locate and open the folder for this chapter. Open and print the instructions for this project, which are provided to you in Adobe PDF format. Follow the instructions and use the knowledge and skills you have gained thus far to assist the brother and sister team of Michael and Kristen Landry in meeting the challenges of owning and running their business.

 You have completed Project 8J ———————

Rubric

The following outcomes-based assessments are *open-ended assessments*. That is, there is no specific correct result; your result will depend on your approach to the information provided. Make *professional quality* your goal. Use the following scoring rubric to guide you in *how* to approach the problem and then to evaluate *how well* your approach solves the problem.

The *criteria*—Software Mastery, Content, Format and Layout, and Process—represent the knowledge and skills you have gained that you can apply to solving the problem. The *levels of performance*—Professional Quality, Approaching Professional Quality, or Needs Quality Improvement—help you and your instructor evaluate your result.

	Your completed project is of Professional Quality if you:	Your completed project is Approaching Professional Quality if you:	Your completed project Needs Quality Improvements if you:
1-Software Mastery	Choose and apply the most appropriate skills, tools, and features and identify efficient methods to solve the problem.	Choose and apply some appropriate skills, tools, and features, but not in the most efficient manner.	Choose inappropriate skills, tools, or features, or are inefficient in solving the problem.
2-Content	Construct a solution that is clear and well organized, contains content that is accurate, appropriate to the audience and purpose, and is complete. Provide a solution that contains no errors of spelling, grammar, or style.	Construct a solution in which some components are unclear, poorly organized, inconsistent, or incomplete. Misjudge the needs of the audience. Have some errors in spelling, grammar, or style, but the errors do not detract from comprehension.	Construct a solution that is unclear, incomplete, or poorly organized, containing some inaccurate or inappropriate content; and contains many errors of spelling, grammar, or style. Do not solve the problem.
3-Format and Layout	Format and arrange all elements to communicate information and ideas, clarify function, illustrate relationships, and indicate relative importance.	Apply appropriate format and layout features to some elements, but not others. Overuse features, causing minor distraction.	Apply format and layout that does not communicate information or ideas clearly. Do not use format and layout features to clarify function, illustrate relationships, or indicate relative importance. Use available features excessively, causing distraction.
4-Process	Use an organized approach that integrates planning, development, self-assessment, revision, and reflection.	Demonstrate an organized approach in some areas, but not others; or, use an insufficient process of organization throughout.	Do not use an organized approach to solve the problem.

Outcomes-Based Assessments

Problem Solving

Project 8K — Dictations

In this project, you will construct a solution by applying any combination of the skills you practiced from the Objectives in Projects 8A and 8B.

> **For Project 8K, you will need the following file:**
>
> a08K_Dictations

**You will save your database as
8K_Dictations_Firstname_Lastname**

Maria Benitez, Vice President of Operations, coordinates the dictation jobs from the physicians with the transcription jobs for the hospital. She needs to consider the number of lines per document and the length of the dictation. Open the **a08K_Dictations** file and save it as **8K_Dictations_Firstname_Lastname** In this project, you will create an autoexec macro to open the 8K Providers form in Form view. You will then create a macro group to open the 8K Search form and locate a particular provider by last name (Combo box Name is LastName). Name the macro group **FindProvider Group – Firstname Lastname** You will associate macros from the group with the OK and Cancel buttons on the 8K Search form. Create an embedded macro for the Print Record button on the 8K Providers form. If you are instructed to submit this result, create a paper or electronic printout of the details of the macros you created for this project.

Add your First and Last Name to the end of the 8K Dictated Minutes query name. Create a PivotTable using the data from the 8K Dictated Minutes query. Use the First and Last Name of the providers for the row headings and the Doc Type for the column headings. The Length of the dictation should be placed in the detail area. Use the AutoCalc feature to display average lengths of dictation. Create a PivotChart from the 8K Dictated Minutes query. Add a legend and appropriate axis titles. Save the PivotTable and the PivotChart. If you are instructed to submit this result, create a paper or electronic printout of both the table and chart.

End **You have completed Project 8K** ——————

Problem Solving

Project 8L — Length of Stay

In this project, you will construct a solution by applying any combination of the skills you practiced from the Objectives in Projects 8A and 8B.

For Project 8L, you will need the following file:

a08L_Length_of_Stay

**You will save your database as
8L_Length_of_Stay_Firstname_Lastname**

The Vice President for Operations at the Providence Warwick Hospital, Maria Beitez, must prepare a report on the length of patient hospital stays. She needs your help to present this data in a meaningful way. You have suggested creating a PivotTable and PivotChart. Open the **a08L_Length_ of_Stay** file and save it as **8L_Length_of_Stay_Firstname_Lastname** Create an Autoexec standalone macro to display the 8L Intro Screen form.

Add your First and Last Name to the end of the 8L Length of Stay query. Using this query, create a PivotTable to display the analysis of the average length of stay in a particular facility. Display only In-Patients in all facilities. Create a PivotChart in 3D Pie chart format. Add a legend to the chart.

If you are instructed to submit this result, create a paper or electronic printout of the PivotTable and PivotChart with Normal margins. If you are instructed to submit the macro details, create a paper or electronic printout.

End **You have completed Project 8L** ————————

Problem Solving

Project 8M — Patient Charges

In this project, you will construct a solution by applying any combination of the skills you practiced from the Objectives in Projects 8A and 8B.

For Project 8M, you will need the following file:

a08M_Patient_Charges

**You will save your database as
8M_Patient_Charges_Firstname_Lastname**

Paul Scheinman, CEO for Providence and Warwick Hospital, wants to study the patient charges accrued over the past few months at each of the individual facilities. Open the **a08M_Patient_Charges** database and save it as **8M_Patient_Charges_Firstname_Lastname** Create an Autoexec macro to open and display the 8M Intro Screen. Create a standalone macro to open the 8M Patient Charges report. Save this macro as **ChargeReport – Firstname Lastname** Use the P&W Asthma Center as the facility from which to generate the report. Open the 8M Patient Charges report in Design view and add a button to the header of the report. This button should embed a macro that will close the current report and open the 8M Patient Charges report to allow selection of a different facility. Give this button an appropriate name for this action. Add a second button to the report header to close the report and close the database. Name this button appropriately.

If you are instructed to submit this result, create a paper or electronic printout of the macro details and the reports for two of the facilities.

End **You have completed Project 8M**———————————

Outcomes-Based Assessments

Access
chaptereight

Problem Solving

Project 8N — Clinical Trials

In this project, you will construct a solution by applying any combination of the skills you practiced from the Objectives in Projects 8A and 8B.

> **For Project 8N, you will need the following file:**
>
> a08N_Clinical_Trials

You will save your database as
8N_Clinical_Trials_Firstname_Lastname

Parminder Salem, Community Relations Director, is very concerned about the health problems of the people living in the metropolitan area of Providence and the surrounding cities of Warwick and Fall River. She has requested the services of two of the doctors on the hospital staff to coordinate studies of these major health problems. In this project, you will open the **08N_Clinical_Trials** database and save it as **8N_Clinical_Trials_Firstname_Lastname**

Create an Autoexec macro to open the 8N Intro Screen and Beep when the database is opened. Create a PivotTable from the 8N Trials by Physician query. Use the medical record # as the field to count the number of patients in each study. Display these counts by study and physician. Create and format a PivotChart using the Stacked Pie chart type. Next, create a standalone macro to open the 8N Trials by Physician query in PivotTable view. Name this macro **8N PivotTable – Firstname Lastname** Create a second standalone macro to open the 8N Trials by Physician query in PivotChart view. Name this macro **8N PivotChart – Firstname Lastname**

If you are instructed to submit this result, create a paper or electronic printout of the macro details, the PivotTable, and the PivotChart.

End **You have completed Project 8N** ────────

Problem Solving

Project 8O — Patient Registration

In this project, you will construct a solution by applying any combination of the skills you practiced from the Objectives in Projects 8A and 8B.

For Project 8O, you will need the following file:

a08O_Patient_Registration

**You will save your database as
8O_Patient_Registration_Firstname_Lastname**

Patients who are scheduled for surgery at the Providence and Warwick Hospital in Providence, Rhode Island must be registered prior to the day of surgery. Maria Benitez, Vice President of Operations, needs a current list of those patients not registered for their surgical procedures. In this project, you will open the **a08O_Patient_Registration** database and save it as **8O_Patient_Registration_Firstname_Lastname** Open the 8O Provider form and add a new record. Enter your instructor as a Provider. Use Physician: **# 6000**, Status: **Resident**, Title: **M.D.**, Specialty: **Robotics** Open the **8O Patient** form and add yourself as a patient. Your Medical Record # is **2222-2222-22** Your Primary Physician is **6000** You have not expired!

Open the 8O PreAdmit query. You should see three patients who are not registered for surgery. Close the query and open the 8O PreAdmit form. Find your record and enter today's date as your Admit Date.

Create a group macro to print the selected record (Your information), requery (update the PreAdmit query), and Close the form and exit the database. Associate the three buttons on the 8O PreAdmit form with macros from this group.

If you are instructed to submit this result, create a paper or electronic printout of the macro group details and the record containing your medical registration.

End **You have completed Project 8O** ————————

You and *GO!*

Project 8P—You and *GO!*

In this project, you will construct a solution by applying any combination of the Objectives in Projects 8A and 8B.

From My Computer, navigate to the student files that accompany this textbook. In the folder **04_you_and_go**, locate and open the folder for this chapter. Open and print the instructions for this project, which are provided to you in Adobe PDF format. Follow the instructions to create a forms and reports for your personal inventory.

End You have completed Project 8P

GO! with Help

Project 8Q—You and *GO!*

The Access Help system is extensive and can help you as you work. In this project, you will view information about fixing a macro by stepping through it.

1. **Start** Access. On the right side of the Ribbon, click the **Microsoft Office Access Help** button. In the **Type words to search for** box, in the **Access Help** window, type **macro** and then press Enter.
2. In the displayed **Search Results** task pane, click **Fix a macro by stepping through it**. **Maximize** the Access Help window. Read the section.
3. If you want to print a copy of the information. Select the text and click the **Print** button at the top of **Access Help** window. Under **Page Range**, select **Selection**, and then click **Print**.
4. **Close** the Help window, and then **Exit** Access.

End You have completed Project 8Q

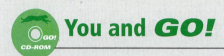

9 chapternine

Integrating Access with Other Applications

OBJECTIVES

At the end of this chapter you will be able to:

1. Import Data from a Word Table
2. Use Mail Merge to Integrate Access and Word
3. Import Data from an Excel Workbook
4. Insert an Excel Chart into a Report
5. Import from and Link to Another Access Database

OUTCOMES

Mastering these objectives will enable you to:

PROJECT 9A

Import Data from and Link to Data in Other Office Applications; Create Memos Using Mail Merge

6. Export Data to Word
7. Export Data to Excel
8. Export Data to an HTML File and an XML File

PROJECT 9B

Export Data to Office Applications, to HTML, and to XML Files

Penn Liberty Motors

Penn Liberty Motors has one of eastern Pennsylvania's largest inventories of popular new car brands, sport utility vehicles, hybrid cars, and motorcycles. Their sales, service, and finance staff are all highly trained and knowledgeable about their products, and the company takes pride in its consistently high customer satisfaction ratings. Penn Liberty also offers extensive customization options for all types of vehicles through its accessories division. Custom wheels, bike and ski racks, car covers, and chrome accessories are just a few of the ways Penn Liberty customers customize their cars.

Integrating Access with Other Applications

Although you can create tables by entering all of the data into the tables, the data may already exist in other files, such as a Word table, an Excel worksheet, another Access database, or other database application. You can either import data from another source, or link to the data in an external source. You can also use the data in an Access object to create individualized memos or letters.

Access enables you to export data from a database into a variety of different applications, such as Word, Excel, another Access database, or other database application. To share database information across different computer platforms or applications, you can export your tables, forms, queries, or reports using XML—a markup language similar to HTML, the markup language used to create Web pages.

Project 9A Penn Liberty Motors

Penn Liberty Motors maintains many of its records in Word, Excel, and Access files. Kevin Rau, President, and Marilyn Kellman, Finance Manager, want to bring the data from these files into an Access database to create queries and reports. In Activities 9.1 through 9.9, you will import data from Word, and then use the information in the Salespersons table to create a mail merge document in Microsoft Word. You will import data from Excel and another Access database, and also create links to data in these applications. Your completed files will look similar to those in Figure 9.1.

For Project 9A, you will need the following files:

New blank Access database
a09A_Employees.docx
a09A_Memo.docx
a09A_Used_Auto_Inventory.xlsx
a09A_Logo.jpg
a09A_Used_Auto_Chart.xlsx
a09A_SUVs_and_Motorcycles.accdb

You will save your files as
9A_Penn_Liberty_Motors_Firstname_Lastname.accdb
9A_Employees_Table_Firstname_Lastname.txt
9A_Custom_Memo_Firstname_Lastname.docx

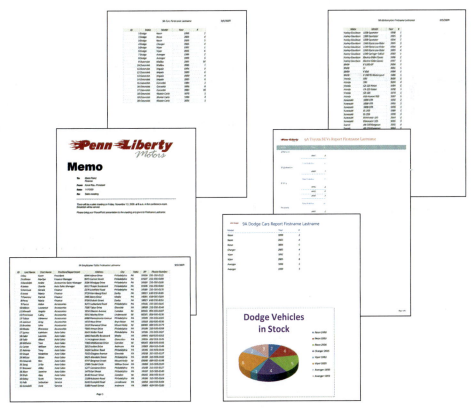

Figure 9.1
Project 9A—Penn Liberty Motors

Objective 1
Import Data from a Word Table

When you create a database, you can type the records directly into a table. You can also *import* data from a variety of sources. Importing is the process used to copy *in* data from one source or application to another application. For example, you can import data from a Word table or Excel spreadsheet into an Access database.

Activity 9.1 Prepare a Word Table for Importing

In this activity, you will create an empty database to store an imported Word table, and then prepare the Word table for the import process.

1 **Start** Access. In the **Getting Started with Microsoft Access** window, under **New Blank Database**, click the **Blank Database** button. On the right side of the screen, under **File Name**, select the text, and then type **9A_Penn_Liberty_Motors_Firstname_Lastname** Click the **Browse** button 📂, navigate to the drive on which you will be saving your folders and projects for this chapter, and then create a new folder named **Access Chapter 9** In the **Getting Started with Microsoft Access** window, click the **Create** button to create the database in the Access Chapter 9 folder. **Close** ⊠ the displayed table.

You have created an empty database to store the table that you will import from Word.

2 **Close** the database, and then **Exit** Access.

3 **Start** Word. Click the **Office** button 📘, and then click **Open**. Navigate to the location where the student data files for this textbook are saved. Locate and open the **a09A_Employees** file. Notice that employee data is saved in a table in this Word document.

4 On the Ribbon, click the **Layout tab**. In the **Data group**, click the **Convert to Text** button, and then compare your screen with Figure 9.2.

To import data from a Word table into an Access table, the data must be *converted* to a *delimited file*—a file where each record displays on a separate line, and the fields within the record are separated by a single character called a *delimiter*. A delimiter can be a paragraph mark, a tab, a comma, or another character.

Figure 9.2

Convert Table To Text
dialog box

Convert to Text
button

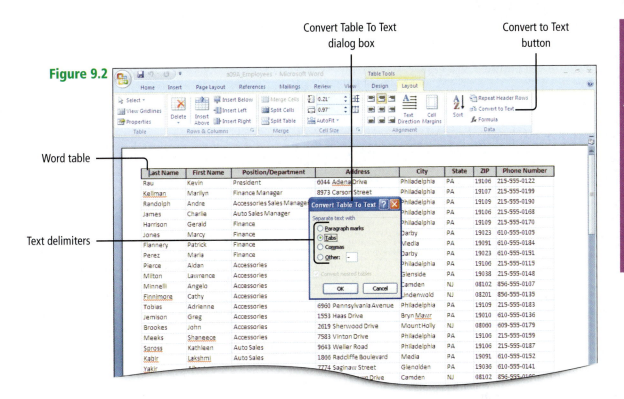

Word table

Text delimiters

5 In the displayed **Convert Table to Text** dialog box, be sure that the **Tabs** option button is selected—this is the delimiter character you will use to separate the data into fields—and then click **OK**.

6 Click anywhere to deselect the text. On the **Home tab**, in the **Paragraph group**, click the **Show/Hide** button ¶ to display formatting marks. Press Ctrl + End to move the insertion point to the end of the document, and then compare your screen with Figure 9.3.

Clicking the Show/Hide button enables you to see the tabs between the fields and the paragraph marks at the end of each line. Word also flags some proper names as spelling errors because they are not listed in the Word dictionary.

Figure 9.3

Tab character separates
fields

Show/Hide button

Paragraph mark at
end of lines

Word flags unrecognized
proper names

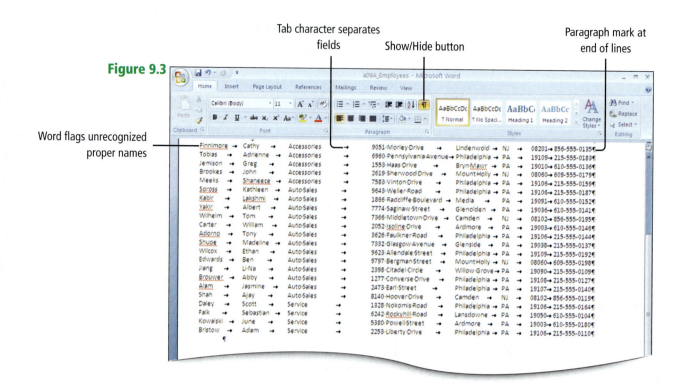

7 Click the **Office** button , point to **Save As**, and then click **Other Formats**. Navigate to the **Access Chapter 9** folder. In the **Save As** dialog box, in the **File name** box, select the existing text, and then type **9A_Employees_Table_Firstname_Lastname** Click the **Save as type arrow**, and from the displayed list, scroll down, and then click **Plain Text**. Compare your screen with Figure 9.4.

A Word table must be converted to a delimited text file and then saved as either *Plain Text* or Rich Text. Data stored in Plain Text format contains no formatting, such as bold or italics. Plain Text is also known as *ASCII*—American Standard Code for Information Interchange—text.

Figure 9.4

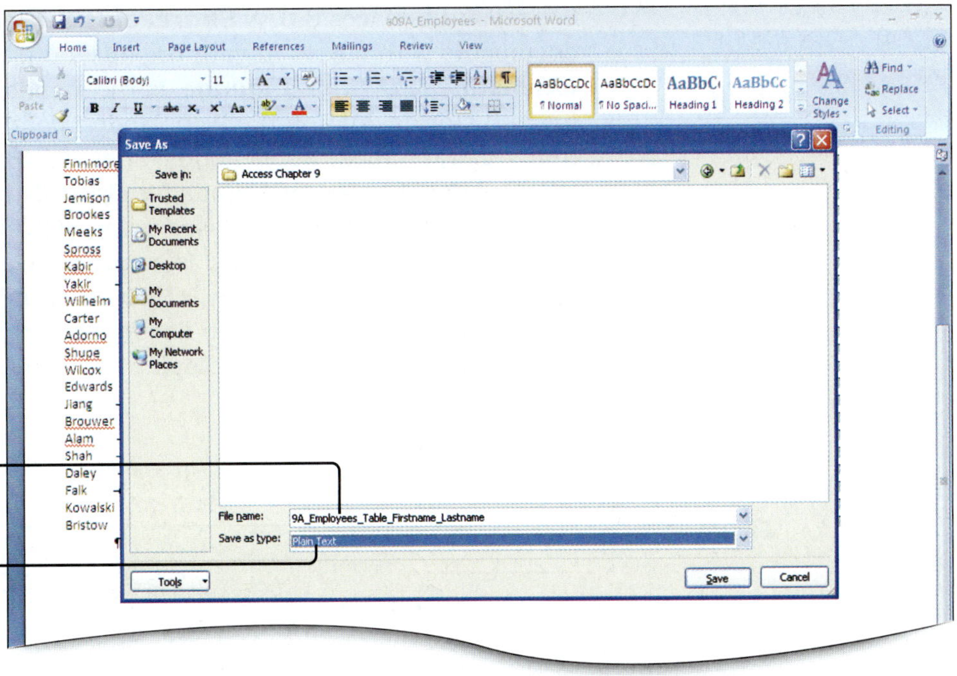

Name changed to
9A_Employees_Table

Format changed to Plain Text

8 In the **Save As** dialog box, click **Save**. In the displayed **File Conversion** dialog box, accept the default settings, and then click **OK**. **Exit** [X] Word.

Activity 9.2 Importing Data from a Word Table

In this activity, you will import the Word table data that is stored in a delimited text file into your 9A_Penn_Liberty_Motors database.

1 **Start** Access. In the **Getting Started with Microsoft Office Access** window, on the right side, under **Open Recent Database**, click **9A_Penn_Liberty_Motors** to open the empty database. Enable the content or add the Access Chapter 9 folder to the Trust Center. Notice that on the **Navigation Pane**, there are no tables in the database.

2 On the Ribbon, click the **External Data tab**. In the **Import group**, click the **More** button, and then compare your screen with Figure 9.5. Take a moment to study the applications from which you can import data or to which you can link data.

As you import data from the various applications, be sure to read what may happen to the data. Sometimes an existing table will be overwritten, and sometimes a number will be appended to the imported object if an object with the same name exists in the database. Sometimes you can change the data in the database, and the change will be synchronized to the source document and vice versa; sometimes the data will not be synchronized between the imported object and the source object.

A **SharePoint List** is a list of documents maintained on a server running Microsoft Office SharePoint Server 2007 or Windows

SharePoint Services 3.0. A **SharePoint Server** enables you to share documents with others in your organization. **XML**, which stands for **eXtensible Markup Language**, is the standard language for defining and storing data on the Web. Under *More*, you can import data from other database applications, such as dBASE, Paradox, and ODBC databases. **ODBC** stands for **Open Database Connectivity**, a standard that enables databases using SQL statements to interface with one another. Lotus 1-2-3 is a spreadsheet program. You can also import data or link to an **HTML—HyperText Markup Language**—document or Web document, or to an Outlook folder. HTML is a language used to display Web pages.

Most common applications from which to import data

Figure 9.5

Other applications from which to import data

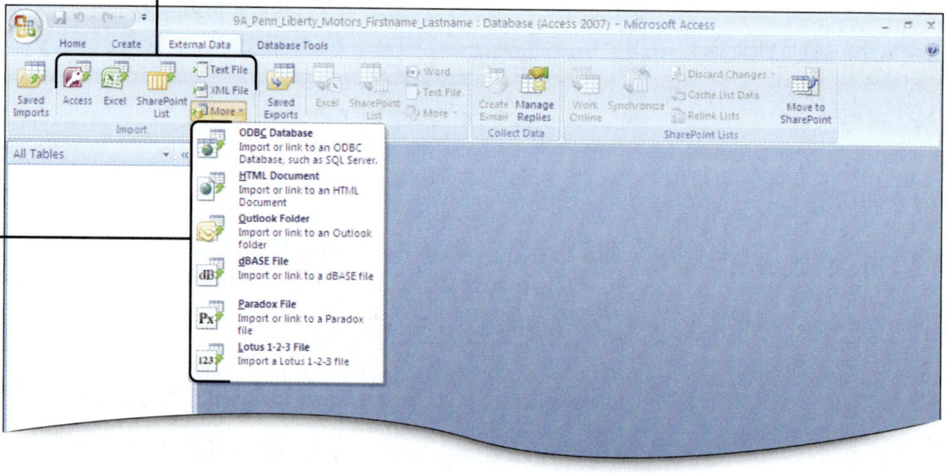

3 On the **External Data tab**, in the **Import group**, click the **Text File** button. In the displayed **Get External Data - Text File** dialog box, to the right of the **File name** box, click **Browse**. Navigate to the **Access Chapter 9** folder. In the **File Open** dialog box, double-click **9A_ Employees_Table**, and then compare your screen with Figure 9.6.

The source file—the one being imported—is listed in the File name box. When importing, if a table with the same name as the imported table does not exist, Access creates the object. If a table with the same name exists in the database, Access may overwrite its contents with the imported data. If you change data in the text file, the data will not be updated in the Access database.

A **link** is a connection to data in another file. When linking, Access creates a table that maintains a link to the source data. You cannot change or delete data in a linked table; however, you can add new records.

Figure 9.6

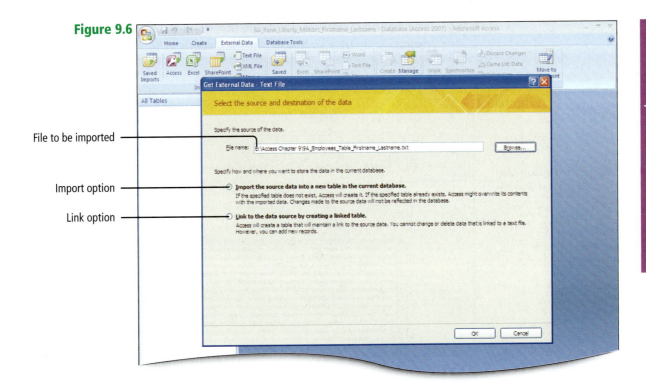

File to be imported

Import option

Link option

Note — Importing Versus Linking Database Files

Import when any of the following is true:

- The source file size is small and is changed infrequently.
- Data does not need to be shared with individuals using other database applications.
- You are replacing an old database application, and the data is no longer needed in the older format.
- You need to load data from another source to begin populating tables.
- You need the performance of Access 2007, while working with data from other database formats.

Link to a source when any of the following is true:

- The file is larger than the maximum capacity of a local Access database (2 gigabytes).
- The file is changed frequently.
- Data must be shared on a network with individuals using other database applications.
- The application is distributed to several individuals, and you need to make changes to the queries, forms, reports, and modules without changing the data already entered into the underlying tables.

4 In the **Get External Data - Text File** dialog box, be sure that the **Import the source data into a new table in the current database** option button is selected, and then click **OK**. Compare your screen with Figure 9.7.

The Import Text Wizard dialog box displays, indicating that the data seems to be in a Delimited format, using a comma or tab to separate each field.

Figure 9.7

Tab was used in source file as delimiter

File to be imported

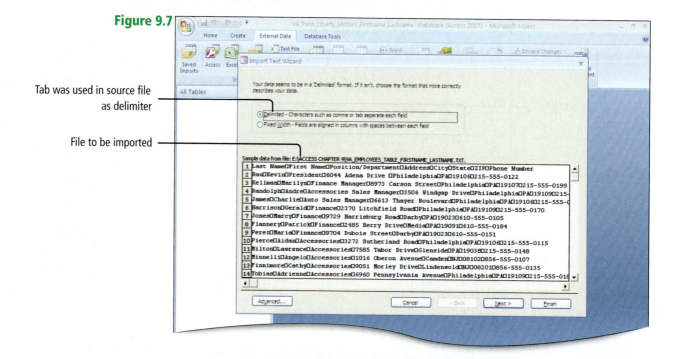

5 In the **Import Text Wizard** dialog box, be sure that the **Delimited** option button is selected, click **Next**, and then compare your screen with Figure 9.8.

In this Import Text Wizard dialog box, you select the delimiter that you used when you created the text file.

Choose delimiter used when text file was created

Click if text is surrounded by single or double quotation marks

Figure 9.8

Tab was used in source file as delimiter

Select if first row contains field names

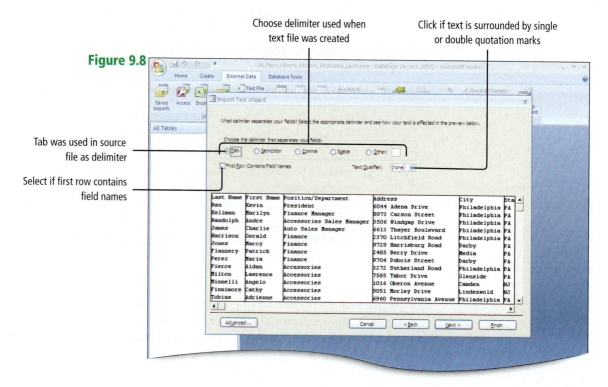

6 Click each delimiter option button, and then notice how the text is affected in the preview window. When you are finished, be sure that the **Tab** option button is selected. Select the **First Row Contains Field Names** check box to convert the field names to column headings instead of first record data. Click the **Text Qualifier arrow**, and notice that a single quotation mark and a double quotation mark display. If you are working with a file that includes text in quotation marks, you would indicate this by selecting either the single quotation mark or the double quotation mark. Be sure that **{none}** is selected.

7 Click **Next**, and then compare your screen with Figure 9.9.

In this Import Text Wizard dialog box, under Field Options, you can change the field name, set the data type, index the field, or skip the importing of the field.

Figure 9.9

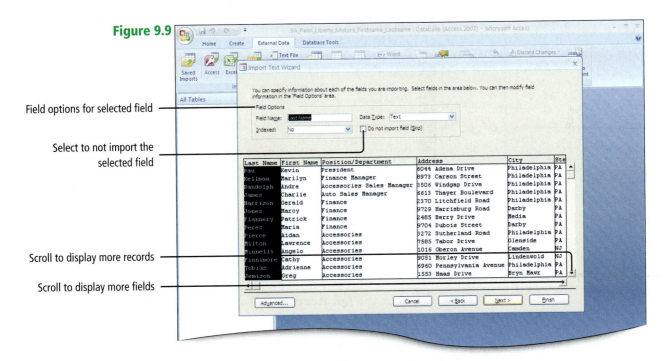

Field options for selected field

Select to not import the selected field

Scroll to display more records

Scroll to display more fields

Note — Saving Data as a New Table or Appending Data

If there is an existing table in the database, another Import Text Wizard dialog box displays before the one enabling you to change field options. This dialog box enables you to save the imported table as a new table or in an existing table. If you select the existing table, the data will be *appended*—added—to the end of the existing table.

8 The Field Options for the **Last Name** field are correct. Click anywhere in the **First Name** field; the Field Options are correct. Continue clicking in each field, noticing the Field Options. Use the horizontal scroll bar to display the fields on the right. Click in the

ZIP field to select the field. Under **Field Options**, click the **Data Type arrow**, and then click **Text**.

Because Access determined that the ZIP field contained all numbers, it assigned a data type of Long Integer. Recall that fields containing numbers that are not used in calculations should have a data type of Text.

9 Click **Next** to display primary key options, and then compare your screen with Figure 9.10.

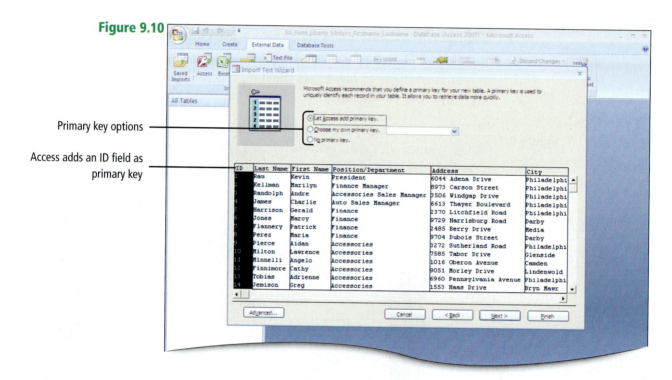

Figure 9.10

Primary key options

Access adds an ID field as primary key

10 Be sure that the **Let Access add primary key** option button is selected, and then click **Next**.

In this dialog box, you can accept the default name of the table or type a new name.

11 Click **Finish**. Because there are no errors in the imported file, the **Get External Data - Text File** dialog box displays, which enables you to save the import steps for future use.

When you import or export data in Access, you can save the settings you used so that you can repeat the process at any time without using the wizard. The name of the source file, the name of the destination database, primary key fields, field names, and all the other specifications you set are saved. You cannot save the specifications for linking or exporting only a portion of a table. Even though all of the specifications are saved, you can still change the name of the source file or destination file before running the import or export specification again.

Did an error message box display after clicking Finish?

If a message box displays, there may be extra blank lines at the end of the text file that causes blank records to be inserted into the database. If this occurs, click OK two times. Open the new table, delete any empty records, display the table in Design view, and then set the appropriate field as the primary key.

12 Select the **Save import steps** check box to display additional options. Click in the **Description** box, and then type **Imports a tab-delimited file that was a Word table** Notice that if you are using Outlook, you can create an Outlook Task to remind you when to repeat the import operation. Click **Save Import**, and notice that on the **Navigation Pane**, the **9A_Employees_Table** displays.

Access creates and saves the import specification in the current database. You cannot move or copy the specification to another database.

13 On the **External Data tab**, in the **Import group**, click the **Saved Imports** button, and then compare your screen with Figure 9.11.

The Manage Data Tasks dialog box displays with two tabs—one for Saved Imports, and one for Saved Exports. Clicking the Run button performs the operation using the selected specification. You can schedule an automatic execution of a specification at regular intervals by clicking the Create Outlook Task button or delete a specification by clicking the Delete button. You can change the name or description of a specification, change the source file in an import operation, or change the destination file in an export operation by clicking the appropriate section in the specification.

Changes the source file

Figure 9.11

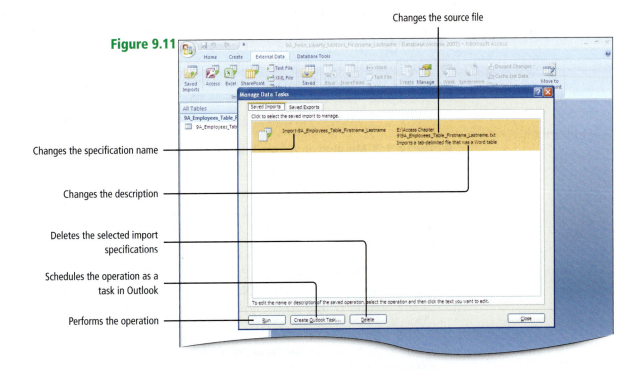

Changes the specification name

Changes the description

Deletes the selected import specifications

Schedules the operation as a task in Outlook

Performs the operation

14 In the **Manage Data Tasks** dialog box, click **Close**.

15 On the **Navigation Pane**, right-click **9A_Employees_Table**, and then click **Rename**. Type **9A Employees Table Firstname Lastname** to replace the underscores between the words in the table name with spaces, and then press Enter. Double-click **9A Employees Table** to open the table in **Datasheet** view, and then collapse « the **Navigation Pane**. Adjust the widths of all of the fields to display all of the data and the entire field name for each field.

All of the data from the Word table, which was converted to a delimited file, has been imported successfully into a table within the database, saving you from typing the data.

However, the table does not follow good design techniques—it is not *normalized*. In a normalized database, each field represents a unique type of data, each table has one or more primary key fields, the data is related to the subject of the table, and an individual can modify the data in any field—except the primary key field—without affecting the data in other fields. In the Position/Department, City, State, and ZIP fields, data is duplicated.

16 If you are instructed to submit this result, create a paper or electronic printout of the **first page** of the table in **Landscape** orientation, changing **Margins**, if necessary, to print all of the fields, and ensuring that the table name displays in the header. **Save** 🖫 the table, and then **Close** ✕ the table.

Objective 2
Use Mail Merge to Integrate Access and Word

Using Word's *mail merge* feature, letters or memos are created by combining, or *merging*, two documents—a *main document* and a *data source*. The main document contains the text of a letter or memo. The data source—an Access table or query—contains the names and addresses of the individuals to whom the letter, memo, or other document is being sent. Use the Mail Merge Wizard within Access to create a direct link between the table or query and the Word document.

Activity 9.3 Merging an Access Table with a Word Document

In this activity, you will create individual memos to the employees of Penn Liberty Motors to inform them of an upcoming staff meeting. You will create the memos by merging the individual names and position or department in the *9A Employees Table* with a memo created in Microsoft Word.

1 Expand » the **Navigation Pane**. Click the **Navigation Pane** title—**All Tables**—and then click **Object Type** to group the Navigation Pane objects by the object type instead of by Tables and Related Views.

2 If necessary, on the **Navigation Pane**, click **9A Employees Table** to select the table. On the Ribbon, click the **External Data tab**. In the

Export group, click the **More** button, and then click **Merge it with Microsoft Office Word**.

The Microsoft Word Mail Merge Wizard starts. In this first dialog box, you can link the data in the table to an existing Word document or create a new Word document, and then link the data in the table to the new document.

3 Be sure that **Link your data to an existing Microsoft Word document** is selected, and then click **OK**. In the **Select Microsoft Word Document** dialog box, navigate to the location where the student data files for this textbook are saved. Locate and open the **a09A_Memo** file, and then compare your screen with Figure 9.12. If the Word document does not display on the screen, click the a09A_Memo button on the taskbar.

Microsoft Word opens with the memo on the left and the Mail Merge task pane on the right.

Microsoft Word window   Maximize button

Figure 9.12

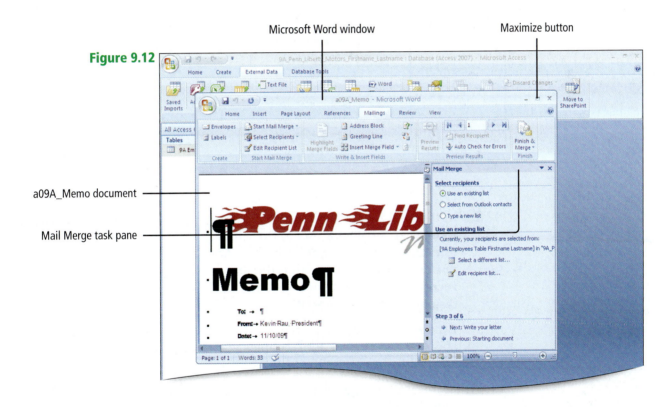

a09A_Memo document

Mail Merge task pane

4 On the **Microsoft Word** title bar, click the **Maximize** button. At the bottom of the **Mail Merge** task pane, notice that the wizard is on **Step 3 of 6**.

Because you are using an existing Word document, the first two steps are already defined.

5 In the **Mail Merge** task pane, under **Select recipients**, be sure that **Use an existing list** is selected. Under **Use an existing list**, click **Edit recipient list**, and then compare your screen with Figure 9.13.

The Mail Merge Recipients dialog box displays, enabling you to sort the list, filter the list, find duplicate entries, find a particular recipient or group of recipients, validate addresses, add recipients to the list, or remove recipients from the list.

Click to remove recipient from the list

List options

Figure 9.13

Mail Merge Recipients dialog box

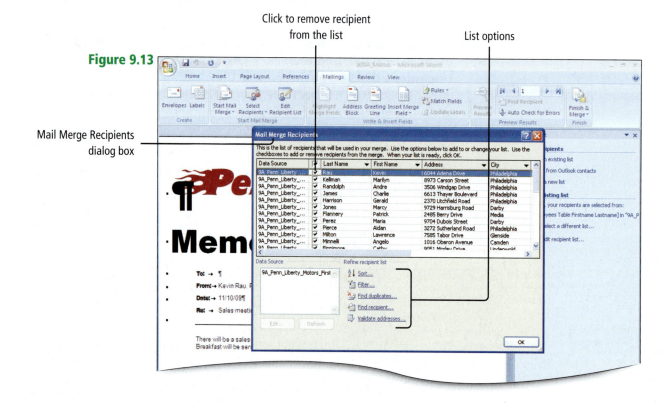

6 In the **Mail Merge Recipients** dialog box, on the first row for **Kevin Rau**, clear the **check box** to the left of **Rau** to remove this record from the list of recipients. Click the **Last Name arrow**, and then click **Sort Ascending**. Notice that the first record is empty. In this **empty record**, clear the **check box** to the left of where the last name would display, and then click **OK**.

Because the memo is from Kevin Rau, a memo should not be addressed to him. Sorting enables you to display any records that have no last name at the beginning of the list.

7 In the **Mail Merge** task pane, under **Step 3 of 6**, click **Next: Write your letter**. Take a moment to read the information in the **Mail Merge** task pane. When you are finished, on the left side of the screen in the memo, click to the right of **To** above the letter **K** in *Kevin*. In the **Mail Merge** task pane, under **Write your letter**, click **More items**, and then compare your screen with Figure 9.14.

The Insert Merge Field dialog box displays, which enables you to select a field from the database to insert into the memo. The Match Fields button enables you to map the fields in the table to the mail merge fields that are built into Word. For example, this table contains a field named Position/Department that could be mapped to the Word mail merge field entitled Job Title.

Fields that can be inserted into the memo

Figure 9.14

Insert Merge Field dialog box

Match Fields button

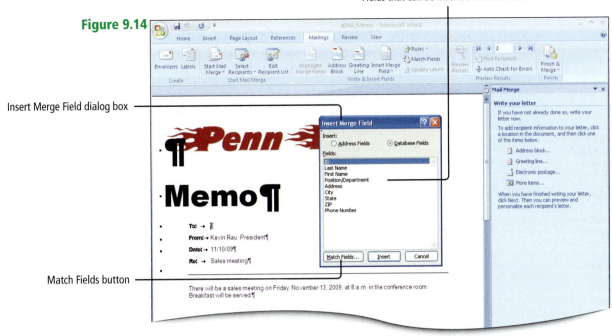

8 In the **Insert Merge Field** dialog box under **Fields**, click **First Name**, and then click **Insert**. Click **Last Name**, and then click **Insert**. Click **Position/Department**, and then click **Insert**. Alternatively, double-click the field. Click **Close**, and then compare your screen with Figure 9.15.

Word inserts each field name surrounded with the characters << and >>. There are no spaces between the field names. Instead of inserting all of the fields together, you can insert the First Name field, close the Insert Merge Field dialog box, type a space, reopen the Insert Merge Field dialog box by clicking More items in the Mail Merge task pane, and then insert the Last Name field.

Figure 9.15

Last Name field

First Name field

Position/Department field

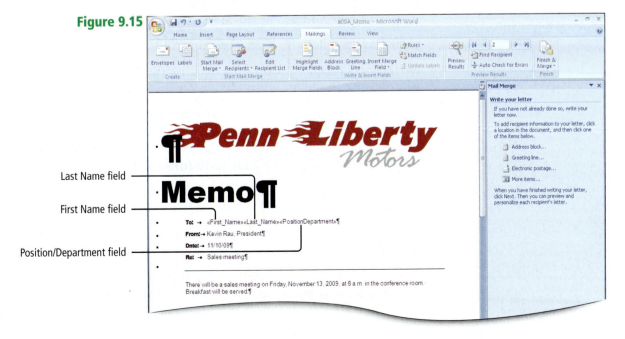

9 In the **memo**, click to the left of **<<Last_Name>>**, and then press `Spacebar` to insert a space between the First_Name and Last_Name fields. Click to the left of **<<PositionDepartment>>**, hold down `⇧ Shift`, and then press `Enter` to move the field to the next line. Compare your screen with Figure 9.16.

Because the memo has built-in formatting, you must press `⇧ Shift` + `Enter` to align the Position/Department field directly under the First Name field. If you press `Enter`, the Position/Department field will align at the left margin and a blank line will display above it.

Figure 9.16

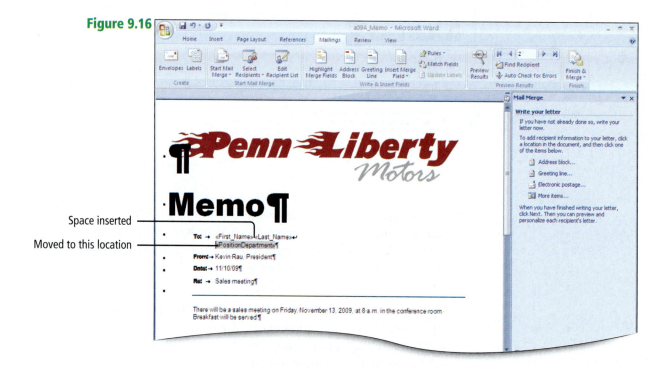

Space inserted

Moved to this location

10 In the **Mail Merge** task pane, under **Step 4 of 6**, click **Next: Preview your letters**. Notice that the first memo displays with a recipient name of **Tony Adomo**. In the **Mail Merge** task pane, under **Preview your letters**, click the **Next record** >> button to display the memo for the next recipient. Continue clicking the **Next record** >> button until the letter addressed to **Maria Perez** displays.

11 In the **Mail Merge** task pane, under **Step 5 of 6**, click **Next: Complete the merge**, and notice that in this step, you can either print the memos or personalize the memos. In the **Mail Merge** task pane, under **Merge**, click **Edit individual letters**.

By clicking *Edit individual letters*, you can customize one or more of the merged memos.

12 In the displayed **Merge to New Document** dialog box, click **Current record**, and then click **OK**.

The memo addressed to Maria Perez displays. At the end of the memo, a section break displays. The section break indicates where you can type a custom message.

13 Press Ctrl + End to move to the end of the memo after the section break. Using your own first name and last name, type **Please bring your PowerPoint presentation to the meeting and give it to Firstname Lastname** and then compare your screen with Figure 9.17.

Figure 9.17

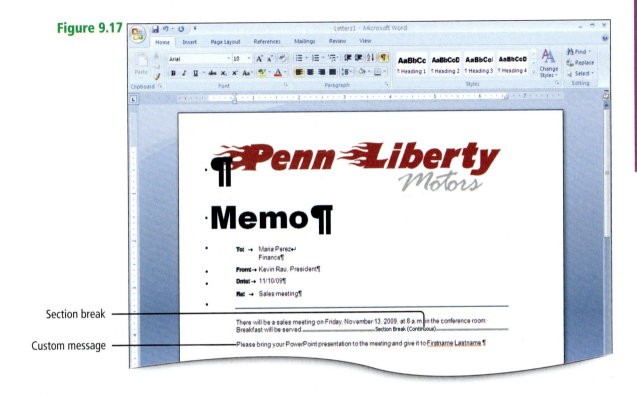

Section break

Custom message

14 On the **Quick Access Toolba**r, click the **Save** button. In the **Save As** dialog box, navigate to your **Access Chapter 9** folder, and then **Save** the Word document as **9A_Custom_Memo_Firstname_Lastname** If you are instructed to submit this result, create a paper or electronic printout.

15 **Close** Word to exit the custom document. Notice that the memo to Maria Perez without the custom message displays.

16 **Close** Word, and then in the displayed message box, click **No**. It is not necessary to save the original document. If the database is not displayed, on the status bar, click the **Microsoft Access** button to restore the database window to the screen.

Objective 3
Import Data from an Excel Workbook

Charlie James, the Auto Sales Manager, keeps an inventory of used cars, SUVs, and motorcycles in an Excel **workbook**. A workbook is an Excel file that contains one or more **worksheets**. A worksheet is the primary document used in Excel to save and work with data that is arranged in columns and rows. You can import the data from an Excel workbook into Access by copying the data from an open worksheet and pasting it into an Access datasheet, by importing a worksheet into a new or existing Access table, or by creating a link to a worksheet from an Access database. Within the Excel program, there is no way to save the workbook as an Access database. The worksheets within the workbook must be imported into an Access database.

Activity 9.4 Importing Data from an Excel Worksheet

In this activity, you will import an Excel worksheet containing the used car inventory, creating a new table in your database.

1 If necessary, on the Ribbon, click the **External Data tab**. In the **Import group**, click the **Excel** button.

The Get External Data - Excel Spreadsheet dialog box displays, indicating that you can import the source data into a new table, append a copy of the records to an existing table, or link to the Excel worksheet.

2 In the **Get External Data - Excel Spreadsheet** dialog box, to the right of the **File name** box, click the **Browse** button. Navigate to the location where the student data files for this textbook are saved. Locate and open the **a09A_Used_Auto_Inventory** file, and then notice that the name of the file has an **.xlsx** extension, which indicates the file is an Excel 2007 file.

3 In the **Get External Data - Excel Spreadshee**t dialog box, click **OK**, and then compare your screen with Figure 9.18.

The first Import Spreadsheet Wizard dialog box displays. A *spreadsheet* is another name for a worksheet. On this page you can select one worksheet—you can import only one worksheet at a time during an import operation. If you want to import several worksheets, save the import specification, and then change the source data. The first row displays column headings.

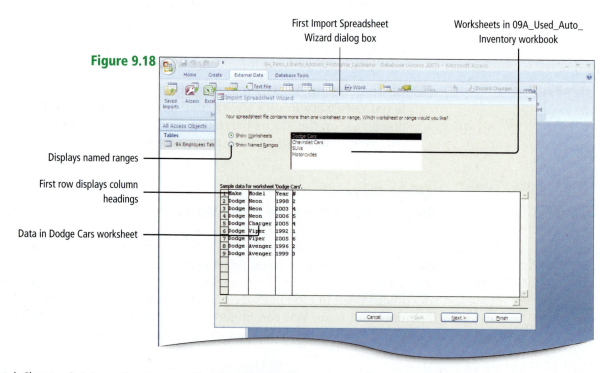

First Import Spreadsheet Wizard dialog box

Worksheets in 09A_Used_Auto_Inventory workbook

Figure 9.18

Displays named ranges

First row displays column headings

Data in Dodge Cars worksheet

4 In the **Import Spreadsheet Wizard** dialog box, click the **Show Named Ranges** option button, and then in the box, click **Dodge**.

This is the same data that displays in the *Dodge Cars* worksheet, but without the column headings. If the Excel worksheet contains *named ranges*, you can select the Show Named Ranges option button. A *range* includes two or more selected cells on a worksheet that can be treated as a single unit. A named range is a range that has been given a name, making it easier to use the cells in calculations or modifications. A *cell* is the small box formed by the intersection of a column and a row.

5 Click **Show Worksheets**, and be sure that **Dodge Cars** is selected. Click **Next** to display the second Import Spreadsheet Wizard dialog box. Notice that the wizard assumes that the first row contains column headings, and that Access uses the column headings as field names.

6 Click **Next** to display the third Import Spreadsheet Wizard dialog box.

Just as you did when importing a text file, you can change the field name, index the field, set the data type, or remove the field from the import operation.

7 In the bottom section of the dialog box, click each field—column—to display the **Data Type** for each field. Click **Next**. In the fourth **Import Spreadsheet Wizard** dialog box, be sure that **Let Access add primary key** is selected, and then click **Next**.

8 In the final **Import Spreadsheet Wizard** dialog box, in the **Import to Table** box, type **9A Cars Firstname Lastname** and then click **Finish**. Because you do not want to save the import steps, in the **Get External Data - Excel Spreadsheet** dialog box, click **Close**. On the **Navigation Pane**, the **9A Cars** table displays.

9 On the **Navigation Pane**, double-click **9A Cars** to open the table in **Datasheet** view, and then compare your screen with Figure 9.19.

The data from the *Dodge Cars* worksheet in the *a09A_Used_Auto_Inventory* Excel workbook has been imported into this new table. Further work is needed to normalize the data in this table.

Figure 9.19

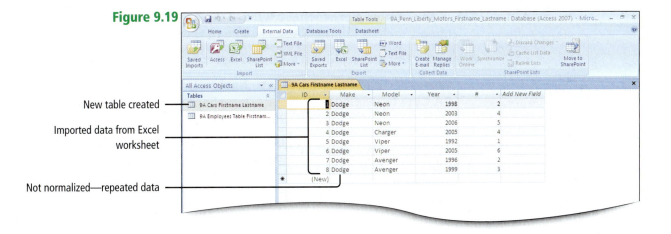

New table created

Imported data from Excel worksheet

Not normalized—repeated data

10 **Close** ✕ the table, and then collapse « the **Navigation Pane**.

> ## More Knowledge
> ### Importing from a Workbook that Contains a Chart
>
> If a workbook contains a chart on a separate worksheet, when you try to import any worksheet into Access, a message box displays stating that the wizard cannot access the information in the file, and that you should check the file you want to import to see if it exists and if it is in the correct format. You should make a copy of the workbook, open the copied workbook, and then delete the worksheet containing the chart or move the chart to the sheet with the related data. Save the workbook, close it, and then import the data from any of the worksheets.

Activity 9.5 Appending Data from Excel to a Table

In this activity, you will append data from an Excel worksheet to the *9A Cars* table. To append data, the table must already be created.

1 If necessary, on the Ribbon, click the **External Data tab**. In the **Import group**, click the **Excel** button. In the **Get External Data - Excel Spreadsheet** dialog box, click **Browse**. Navigate to the location where the student data files for this textbook are saved. Locate and **Open** the **a09A_Used_Auto_Inventory** file.

2 Under **Specify how and where you want to store the data in the current database**, click **Append a copy of the records to the table**. Click the **table name** box **arrow** to display the names of the two tables that are saved in the database. Be sure that **9A Cars** is selected, and then click **OK**.

3 In the first **Import Spreadsheet Wizard** dialog box, click **Chevrolet Cars**, and then click **Next**. In the second **Import Spreadsheet Wizard** dialog box, notice that Access has determined that the first row matches the field names contained in the existing table, and that you cannot clear the check box. Click **Next**.

4 In the **Import Spreadsheet Wizard** dialog box, click **Finish** to import the data to the *9A Cars* table in the current database.

5 In the **Get External Data - Excel Spreadsheet** dialog box, click **Close**, and then expand » the **Navigation Pane**. Double-click **9A Cars** to display the table in **Datasheet** view, and then compare your screen with Figure 9.20.

The data from the *Chevrolet Cars* worksheet in the *a09A_Used_Auto_Inventory* workbook is appended to the *9A Cars* table in your database.

Figure 9.20

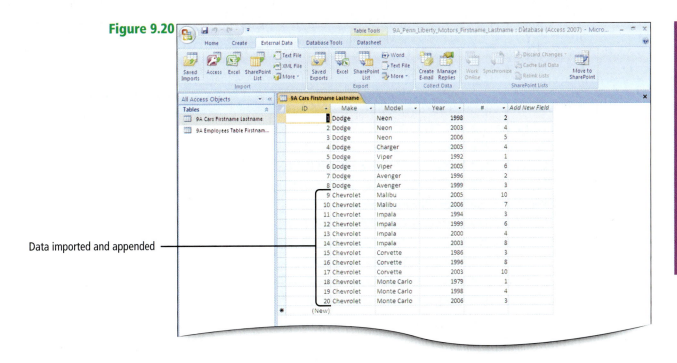

Data imported and appended —

6 If you are instructed to submit this result, create a paper or electronic printout of the table. **Close** ☒ the table, and then collapse « the **Navigation Pane**.

Objective 4
Insert an Excel Chart into a Report

A **chart** is a graphic representation of data. Data presented in a chart is easier to understand than a table of numbers. **Column charts** display comparisons among related numbers, **pie charts** display the contributions of parts to a whole amount, and **line charts** display trends over time. Excel is the best tool for creating a chart because there are a wide variety of chart types and formatting options.

Activity 9.6 Create a Query and a Report

In this activity, you will create a query. Using the query, you will create a report that will be used in the next activity.

1 On the Ribbon, click the **Create tab**. In the **Other group**, click the **Query Design** button. In the **Show Table** dialog box, double-click **9A Cars** to add the table to the Query Design workspace, and then in the **Show Table** dialog box, click **Close**.

2 Expand the field list to display the entire table name. In the field list, click **Make**. Hold down ⇧Shift, and then click **#** to select all four fields. Drag the selected fields down into the first column of the design grid, and then compare your screen with Figure 9.21.

Figure 9.21

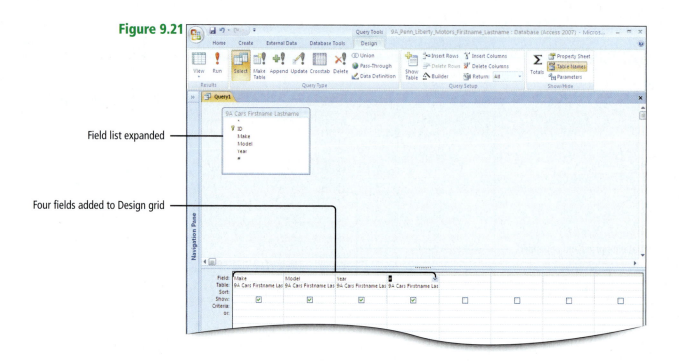

Field list expanded

Four fields added to Design grid

3 In the design grid, under **Make**, click in the **Criteria** box, and then type **dodge**

4 On the **Design tab**, in the **Results group**, click the **Run** button to display only the Dodge cars.

5 Switch the query to **Design** view. In the design grid, under **Make**, on the **Show** row, clear the check box, and then **Run** the query.

Recall that clearing the Show check box hides the field from the report. Because this report only displays Dodge cars, hiding this field is appropriate.

6 **Save** 🖫 the query as **9A Dodge Cars Query Firstname Lastname** and then **Close** ✕ the query. Expand ⟫ the **Navigation Pane**, and then notice that the query displays on the Navigation Pane.

7 On the **Navigation Pane**, under **Queries**, click **9A Dodge Cars Query** to select the query, and then collapse ⟪ the **Navigation Pane**.

8 On the Ribbon, click the **Create tab**. In the **Reports group**, click the **Report** button.

9 On the **Format tab**, in the **Controls group**, click the **Logo** button. Navigate to the location where the data files for this chapter are saved, and then double-click **a09A_Logo** to insert the logo into the header section of the report. Click anywhere in the **title**, double-click **Query** to select the word, type **Report** and then press Enter.

10 Switch to **Design** view. In the **Report Header** section, delete the **Date** and **Time text box controls**. In the **Page Footer** section, delete the **Page number text box control**. In the **Report Footer** section, delete the **Count calculated control**. Point to the bottom of the

Report Footer section until the ⊞ pointer displays, and then drag upward until the bottom edge of the section aligns with the bottom edge of the **Report Footer section bar**. Compare your screen with Figure 9.22.

The Report Footer section no longer displays, and controls have been removed from the report.

Figure 9.22

Controls removed from Report Header section

Control removed from Page Footer section

Report Footer section size decreased

11 **Save** 🖬 the report as **9A Dodge Cars Report Firstname Lastname**

Activity 9.7 Inserting an Excel Chart into a Report

In this activity, you will insert an Excel chart into *9A Dodge Cars Report*.

1 In the report, point to the top of the **Report Footer section bar** until the ⊞ pointer displays. Drag the section down to the **3-inch mark on the vertical ruler** to increase the size of the Page Footer section.

2 **Start** Excel. If necessary, maximize ⬜ the Excel window. Click the **Office** button 🔘, and then click **Open**. Navigate to the location where the data files for this chapter are saved, and then double-click **a09A_Used_Auto_Chart** to open the workbook. Compare your screen with Figure 9.23.

The workbook opens with the *Cars* worksheet displaying. A pie chart has been saved in the worksheet and displays the number of cars for each Model and Year of Dodge vehicles.

Figure 9.23

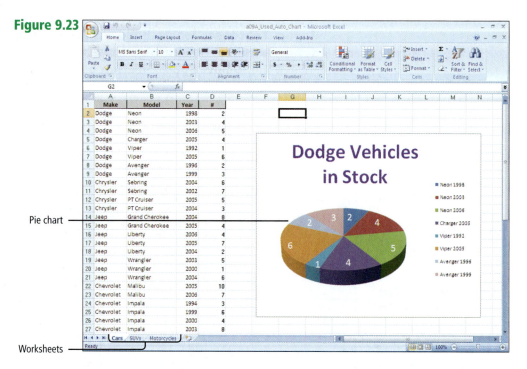

Pie chart

Worksheets

3 Click in an empty area of the **pie chart** to select the entire chart. Notice that in the worksheet a border displays around the **Model**, **Year**, and **#** fields. These fields were used to create the pie chart. On the **Home tab**, in the **Clipboard group**, click the **Copy** button to place a copy of the pie chart in the Office Clipboard. On the **Excel** title bar, click the **Close** button to close the workbook and to exit Excel.

4 In the **9A Dodge Cars Report**, right-click the **Page Footer section bar**, and then click **Paste**. Compare your screen with Figure 9.24.

The pie chart is pasted into the Page Footer section of the report.

Figure 9.24

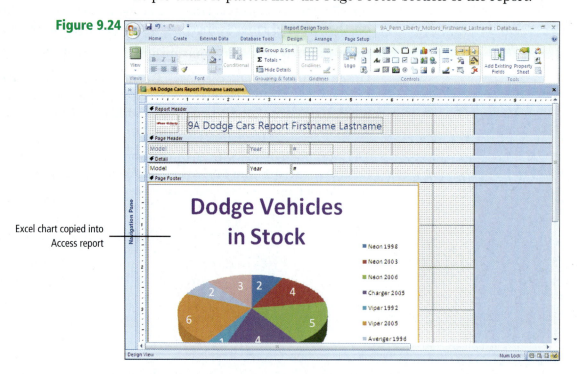

Excel chart copied into
Access report

5 **Save** 🖫 the report, and then switch to **Report** view. If you are instructed to submit this result, create a paper or electronic print out. **Close** ⊠ the report.

Objective 5
Import from and Link to Another Access Database

When you import data from another Access database, Access creates a copy of the source data without altering the source data. Import data from another database when you want to merge two databases by copying all of the objects in one database to another database. All of the tables, queries, forms, reports, macros, modules, and table relationships can be imported or copied to another Access database in a single operation. Import data from another Access database when you need to create similar tables, and want to use the structure of the source database tables. You should view the Access Help files if you are importing data from an older version of Access so that you can view the limitations of the import operation. Link to data in another Access database when the data is shared between various databases, or if someone else needs to have the ability to add records and use the data, but not change the structure of the table.

Activity 9.8 Importing Data from Another Access Database

In this activity, you will import the data contained in another Access database.

1 On the Ribbon, click the **External Data tab**. In the **Import group**, click the **Access** button. In the **Get External Data - Access Database** dialog box, click **Browse**. Navigate to the location where the data files for this chapter are saved, and then double-click **a09A_SUVs_and_Motorcycles**.

The source database must be closed before you can import data from it. The destination database must be open. To import the data into a new database, you must create a blank database that does not contain any objects before starting the import operation.

2 Be sure that the **Import tables, queries, forms, reports, macros, and modules into the current database** option button is selected, and then click **OK**. In the **Import Objects** dialog box, click the **Tables tab**.

The Import Objects dialog box displays the two tables contained in the a09A_SUVs_and_Motorcycles database. To choose multiple types of objects, first select one object, click the tab, and then click the object on that tab. To cancel a selected object, click the object again.

3 In the **Import Objects** dialog box, click **9A SUVs**, and then click **Options** to display additional import options. Compare your screen with Figure 9.25.

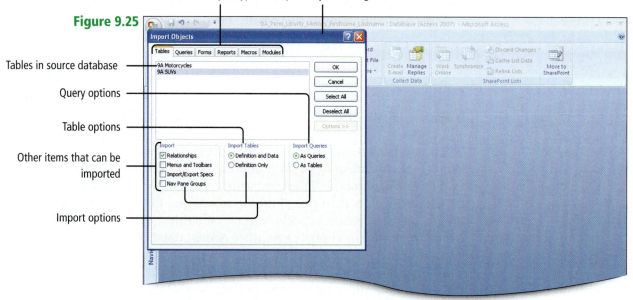

Figure 9.25

Tabs for object types

Import Objects dialog box

Tables in source database

Query options

Table options

Other items that can be imported

Import options

Note — Importing Queries, Forms, and Reports

You can import table relationships, custom menus and toolbars, saved import/export specifications, and custom Navigation Pane groups. For tables, you can import the table definition and data or only the table definition. The *definition* is the structure of the database—the field names, data types, and field properties. You can import queries as queries or as tables. If you import a query as a query, you must also import the underlying table or tables used to create the query.

Importing a query, form, report, subform, or subreport does not automatically import the underlying record sources. If you create one of these objects using the data in two related tables, you must also import those two tables; otherwise, these objects will not open properly.

4 In the **Import Objects** dialog box, click the **Queries tab**, and then click **9A Toyota SUVs Query**. Click the **Forms tab**, and then click **9A SUVs Form**. Click the **Reports tab**, click **9A Toyota SUVs Report**, and then click **OK**.

The Get External Data - Access Database dialog box displays, enabling you to save the import steps. If Access encounters any errors in the import operation, messages will display. During the import operation, to cancel the import operation, press Ctrl + Break.

5 In the **Get External Data - Access Database** dialog box, click **Close**.

6 Expand » the **Navigation Pane**, and then compare your screen with Figure 9.26.

A table, query, form, and report have been imported to the open database.

Figure 9.26

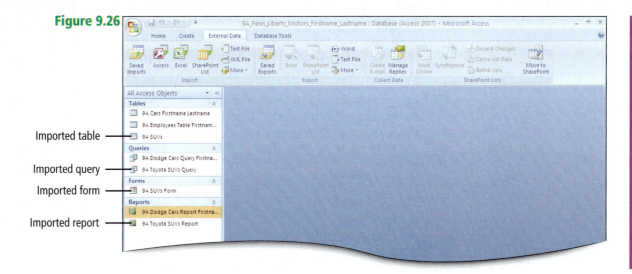

Imported table

Imported query

Imported form

Imported report

Alert!

Were all four objects not imported?

If all four objects were not imported, you may not have clicked the object in the Import Objects dialog box. To correct this, run the import operation again, and select the missing object or objects. Do not select objects that were imported correctly. For example, if you correctly imported the *9A SUVs* table, and then you import it again, a second *9A SUVs* table will be imported and will be named *9A SUVs1*.

7 On the **Navigation Pane**, under **Reports**, right-click **9A Toyota SUVs Report**, and then click **Layout View**. Click the title one time to select the title. Click to the right of **Report** to enter into editing mode, and then type **Firstname Lastname** On the **Format tab**, in the **Font group**, click the **Font Size button arrow** [11 ▾], and then click **16**.

8 **Save** 🖫 the report. If you are instructed to submit this result, create a paper or electronic printout.

9 **Close** [×] the report, and then collapse [«] the **Navigation Pane**.

Activity 9.9 Linking to a Table in Another Access Database

In this activity, you will link to the data in the *9A Motorcycles* table in the *a09A_SUVs_and_Motorcycles* database. You can link only to tables in another Access database; you cannot link to queries, forms, reports, macros, or modules.

1 If necessary, on the Ribbon, click the **External Data tab**. In the **Import group**, click the **Access** button. In the **Get External Data - Access Database** dialog box, **Browse** to the location where the data files for this chapter are saved, and then double-click **a09A_SUVs_and_Motorcycles**.

2 In the **Get External Data - Access Database** dialog box, click the **Link to the data source by creating a linked table** option button.

Changes made to the data in Access will be propagated to the source data and vice versa. If the source database requires a password, that password is saved with the linked table. You cannot make changes to the structure of the table in the linked table.

3 In the **Get External Data - Access Database** dialog box, click **OK**. In the **Link Tables** dialog box, on the **Tables tab**, click **9A Motorcycles**, and then click **OK**.

4 Expand ⟩⟩ the **Navigation Pane**, and then compare your screen with Figure 9.27.

The 9A Motorcycles linked table displays on the Navigation Pane under Tables. The arrow that displays to the left of the icon indicates that this is a linked object.

Figure 9.27

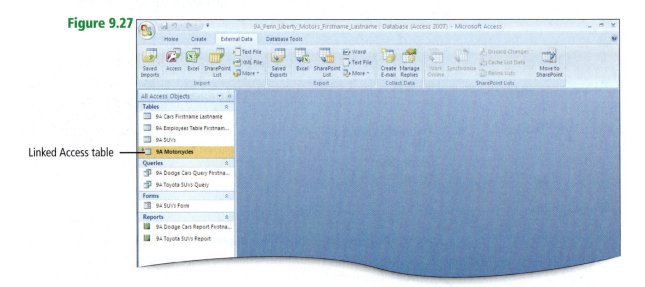

Linked Access table

5 On the **Navigation Pane**, under **Tables**, right-click **9A Motorcycles**, and then click **Rename**. Click to the right of **Motorcycles**, press [Spacebar], type **Firstname Lastname** and then press [Enter].

6 On the **Navigation Pane**, under **Tables**, double-click **9A Motorcycles** to display the table in **Datasheet** view. Adjust the widths of all of the columns.

7 If you are instructed to submit this result, create a paper or electronic printout. **Close** ✕ the table, saving changes when prompted. **Close** the database, and then **Exit** Access.

End **You have completed Project 9A** ————————

Project 9B Used Cars Inventory

Some of the salespersons at Penn Liberty Motors are uncomfortable working with Access, and they save their data in other applications. In addition, the Web master often asks for data to be included on the company's Web site. Access enables you to export data from an Access database into other applications, such as Word, Excel, another Access database, and other database applications. You can also export data to be used on a Web page. In Activities 9.10 through 9.15, you will export data to several types of applications. Your completed files will look similar to those shown in Figure 9.28.

For Project 9B, you will need the following file:

a09B_Used_Cars_Inventory.accdb

You will save your files as
9B_Used_Cars_Inventory_Firstname_Lastname.accdb
9B_Exported_Jeeps_Query_Firstname_Lastname.rtf
9B_Jeeps_Firstname_Lastname.docx
9B_Used_Vehicles_Firstname_Lastname.xlsx
9B_Jeeps_in_Stock_Firstname_Lastname.html
9B_Jeeps_in_Stock_Firstname_Lastname.rtf
9B_Jeeps_XML_File_Firstname_Lastname.htm
9B_Jeeps_XML_File_Firstname_Lastname.xml
9B_Jeeps_XML_File_Firstname_Lastname.xsl

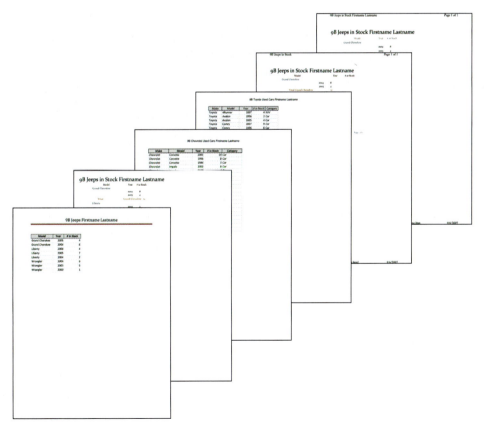

Figure 9.28
Project 9B—Used Cars Inventory

Objective 6
Export Data to Word

You can ***export*** a table, query, form, or report to Word 2007. Exporting is the process used to copy *out* data from one source or application to another application. You can then e-mail a single Word document rather than e-mailing the entire database. Exporting to Word is also helpful if you have a table that you want to format in a more formal way than you can by just printing an Access table. When you export an Access object, the Export Wizard creates a copy of the object's data in the Microsoft Word Rich Text Format file—an extension of .rtf is used. For tables, queries, and forms, hidden fields are not exported, and the visible fields and records display as a table in the Word document. When you export a report, the Export Wizard copies the report data and the design layout, making the Word document resemble the report as closely as possible.

Activity 9.10 Export an Access Query to Word

In this activity, you will export a query to Word 2007. The database must be open in Access to perform the export operation because there is no Access import feature in Word.

1 **Start** Access. Navigate to the location where the student data files for this textbook are saved. Locate and open the **a09B_Used_Cars_Inventory** file. Save the database in the **Access 2007 Database** format in your **Access Chapter 9** folder as **9B_Used_Cars_Inventory_Firstname_Lastname** Enable the content, or add the Access Chapter 9 folder to the Trust Center.

2 On the **Navigation Pane**, **Rename** the two queries and one report by adding **Firstname Lastname** to the end of the object names. Under **Queries**, double-click **9B Jeeps** to run and display the query results.

The query displays the model name, the year of the vehicle, and the number of Jeeps in stock.

3 Switch the query to **Design** view, and then compare your screen with Figure 9.29.

The underlying source of this query is the *9B Used Vehicles* query. In the design grid, in the last column, the criteria is *Jeep*, which extracts records with this criteria in the Make field. The field is hidden from the results because the data is redundant.

Figure 9.29

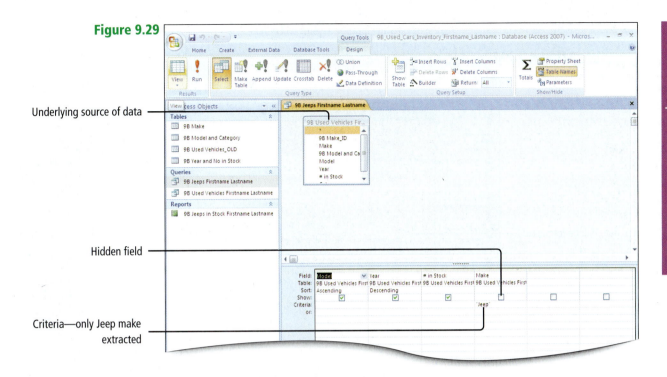

Underlying source of data

Hidden field

Criteria—only Jeep make
extracted

4 **Close** ⊠ the query. On the **Navigation Pane**, under **Queries**, right-click **9B Jeeps**, point to **Export**, and then click **Word RTF File**. Alternatively, on the Ribbon, click the External Data tab, and then in the Export group, click Word. Compare your screen with Figure 9.30.

The Export - RTF File dialog box displays, which enables you to select the destination for the data you want to export. Because the Export Wizard always exports formatted data, this option is selected and inactive. To display the Word document after the export operation is complete, select the check box for *Open the destination file after the export operation is complete*. The last selection—*Export only the selected records*—is inactive. If you want to export some of the records, before you begin the export operation, open the object and select the records.

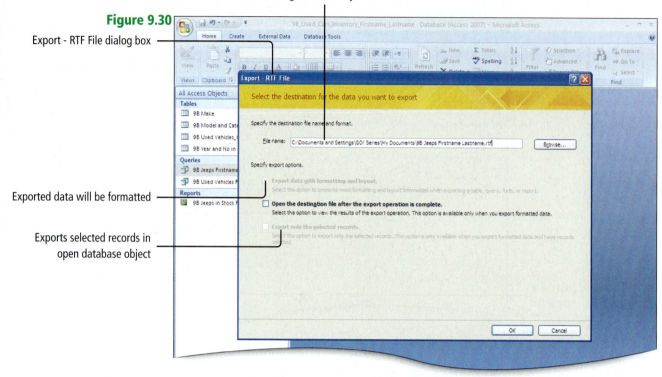

Figure 9.30

Export - RTF File dialog box

Default storage location—yours will differ

Exported data will be formatted

Exports selected records in open database object

5 In the **Export - RTF File** dialog box, click **Browse**. Navigate to the **Access Chapter 9** folder. In the **File name** box, select the existing file name, type **9B_Exported_Jeeps_Query_Firstname_Lastname** and then click **Save**.

Note — Merging Data with an Existing Word Document

When you export from Access to Word, the data is always exported into a new Word document. If you select an existing document, the Export Wizard overwrites the Word document with the new data. To insert the data into an existing Word document, export the data from Access into a new Word document, and then copy the data from the new Word document and paste it into the existing Word document. Alternatively, copy rows directly from an Access table, query, form, or report, and then paste them into the existing Word document.

6 In the **Export - RTF File** dialog box, under **Specify export options**, select the **Open the destination file after the export operation is complete** check box, and then click **OK**. If the Word document window does not fill the entire screen, click the Maximize button ⬚. Compare your screen with Figure 9.31. Do not be concerned if the paragraph symbols do not display.

The query data is exported to a Word document. Because the Word document did not exist, a new document was created. The data is displayed as a table in Word with the field names as column headings.

The hidden field—Make—does not display. In the title bar of the Word document, *[Compatibility Mode]* displays because this document has an .rtf extension instead of the standard .docx extension.

Word document name   Compatibility mode   Records

Figure 9.31

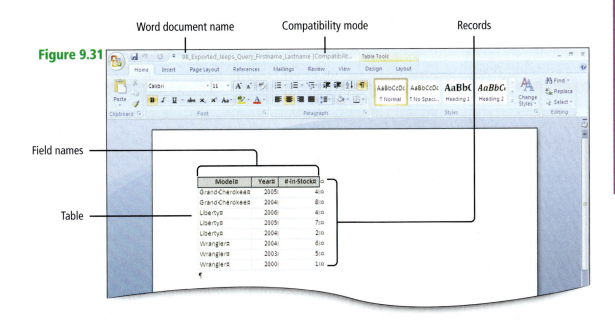

Field names

Table

7 On the Ribbon, click the **Insert tab**. In the **Header & Footer group**, click the **Header** button. In the **Built-In** gallery, click **Alphabet**, and then type **9B Jeeps Firstname Lastname** In the **Close group**, click the **Close Header and Footer** button.

8 On the **Quick Access Toolbar**, click the **Save** button, and then compare your screen with Figure 9.32.

A message displays stating that a feature in the document is not supported by earlier versions of Word, meaning that a document with an .rtf extension cannot display the data in the same manner as Word. Although the summary is cryptic, in this case, an .rtf document cannot display content controls. If you click Continue, Word converts the header data to static text.

Figure 9.32

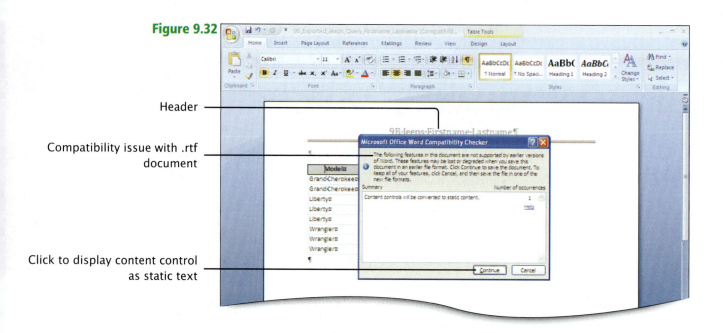

Header

Compatibility issue with .rtf
document

Click to display content control
as static text

9 In the message box, click **Cancel**. Click the **Office** button , point
to **Save As**, and then click **Word Document**. If necessary, navigate to
the **Access Chapter 9** folder. Change the file name to
9B_Jeeps_Firstname_Lastname Notice that the **Save as type** box displays **Word Document**, which means the file will be given a *.docx*
extension. In the **Save As** dialog box, click **Save**.

A message box displays stating that you are about to save your document to one of the new file formats and that changes may be made
in the layout of the document.

10 In the displayed message box, click **OK**. If you are instructed to submit this result, create a paper or electronic printout.

11 **Close** ☒ the Word window. In the **Export - RTF File** dialog box,
click **Close**.

Activity 9.11 Export an Access Report to Word

In this activity, you will export the *9B Jeeps in Stock* report to a Word
document.

1 On the **Navigation Pane**, under **Reports**, double-click **9B Jeeps in
Stock** to open the report. Switch to **Layout** view. Click the title—
9B Jeeps in Stock—**two** times to enter into editing mode. Click to the
right of **Stock**, press Spacebar, and then using your own first name and
last name, type **Firstname Lastname** Press Enter, and then **Save** 💾 the
report.

The report displays Jeep models, the year, and the number of vehicles in stock for each year of the model. Each model is summed, and
at the bottom of the report, the total number of Jeeps displays.

2 **Close** ☒ the report. On the **Navigation Pane**, under **Reports**,
right-click **9B Jeeps in Stock**, point to **Export**, and then click **Word**

RTF File. Be sure that the **File name** box displays the correct path to your **Access Chapter 9** folder. Replace the spaces in the file name—**9B Jeeps in Stock Firstname Lastname**—with underscores. Under **Specify export options**, click the **Open the destination file after the export operation is complete** check box, and then click **OK**. Compare your screen with Figure 9.33.

A message box displays, and then the document opens in Word. Although all of the data is exported, it is not aligned as nicely as it was in the Access report. You would probably want to do some further formatting in Word. All of the data is separated by tabs.

Underscores instead of spaces in file name

Figure 9.33

Indicates tab

Total rows need further formatting

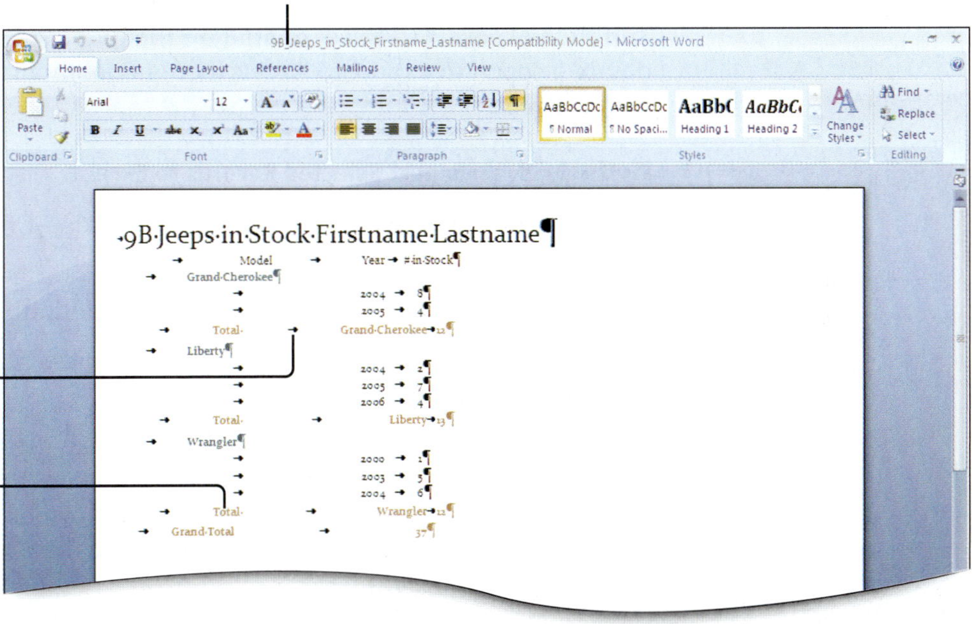

3 If you are instructed to submit this result, create a paper or electronic printout. **Close** ✕ the Word window. In the **Export - RTF File** dialog box, click **Close**.

More Knowledge

Exporting a Report as a Snapshot File

You can export a report as a *snapshot file*, which enables an individual to view an Access report without having Access installed on the computer. The extension for a snapshot file is .snp. To view a snapshot file, the Microsoft Snapshot Viewer program must be installed on the computer that will be used to open the snapshot file. In previous versions of Access, the Snapshot Viewer program was installed with Access. For Access 2007, you must download and install the free Microsoft Snapshot Viewer program from the Microsoft Download Center at **http://www.microsoft.com/downloads**. A benefit of exporting to a snapshot file is that the two-dimensional layout, graphics, and other embedded objects in the report are preserved.

Objective 7
Export Data to Excel

You can copy data from an Access database into a worksheet by exporting a table, form, or query to an Excel workbook; however, you cannot export reports, macros, or modules to Excel. When you export a table or form that contains subdatasheets or subforms, only the main datasheet or main form is exported. You can export only one database object in a single export operation; however, you can merge the data in multiple worksheets in Excel after completing the individual export operations.

Export data to Excel if individuals share the data, and some work with Access while others work with Excel. You can store the data in Access, and then export it to Excel to analyze the data. You must have the Access database open to export to Excel; there is no import operation for Access within Excel.

Activity 9.12 Export Selected Records to Excel

In this activity, you will export selected records—Chevrolet vehicle data—from an Access query to an Excel workbook.

1 On the **Navigation Pane**, under **Queries**, double-click **9B Used Vehicles** to run the query and to display the results. Collapse [«] the **Navigation Pane**.

2 In the **fifth record**—the first record displaying *Chevrolet* as the Make—click in the **Row Selector** box to select the record. Hold down [⇧ Shift], and then click in the **Row Selector** box for **Record 24**—the last record displaying *Chevrolet* as the Make. Compare your screen with Figure 9.34.

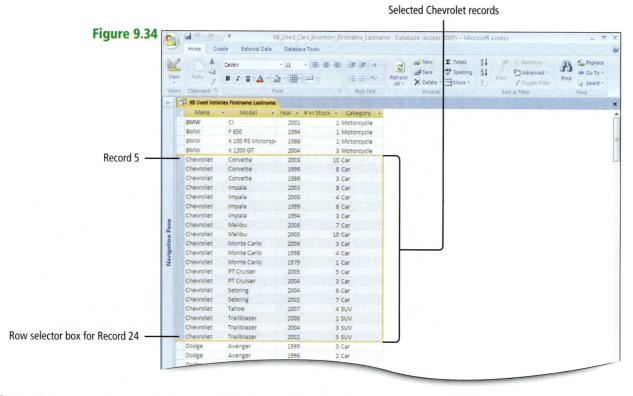

Figure 9.34

Selected Chevrolet records

Record 5

Row selector box for Record 24

3 On the Ribbon, click the **External Data tab**, and in the **Export group**, click **Excel**.

4 In the displayed **Export - Excel Spreadsheet** dialog box, in the **File name** box, be sure that the path to your **Access Chapter 9** folder is correct. In the file name—**9B Used Vehicles**—replace all spaces with underscores. Notice that in the **File format** box, the file will be saved as an Excel Workbook with an extension of .xlsx, which is the extension used for Excel 2007.

5 In the **Export - Excel Spreadsheet** dialog box, under **Specify export options**, select the **Export data with formatting and layout** check box. Select the **Open the destination file after the export operation is complete** check box, and then select the **Export only the selected records** check box.

Because you selected records in the query, the *Export only the selected records* option is active.

6 In the **Export - Excel Spreadsheet** dialog box, click **OK**, and then compare your screen with Figure 9.35.

Excel opens and displays the exported data in a worksheet within the workbook. The worksheet name is the same as the query from which the data was exported. The workbook name displays in the Excel window title bar.

Workbook name

Figure 9.35

Field names

Records

Worksheet name

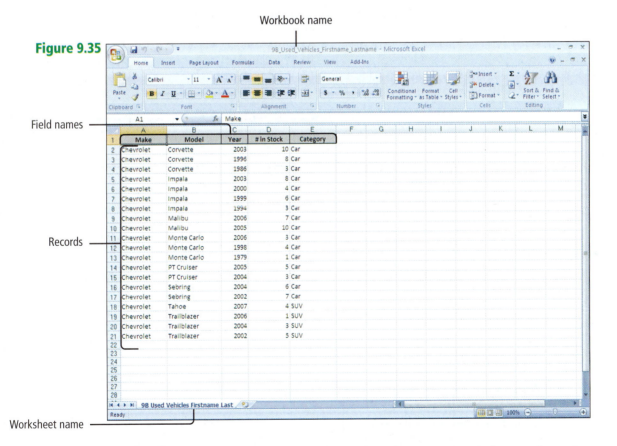

7 At the bottom of the worksheet, right-click the **Worksheet tab**, and then click **Rename**. Type **9B Chevrolet** and then press [Enter]. **Save** the workbook, and then **Minimize** the Excel workbook.

8 If necessary, click the **Microsoft Access** button on the taskbar to restore the Access window and display the query. Click anywhere in the datasheet to deselect the Chevrolet records.

Activity 9.13 Copying Selected Records to an Existing Excel Workbook

In this activity, you will export selected records—Toyota vehicle data—from an Access query to an Excel workbook by copying and pasting the records.

1 In the datasheet, scroll down until all of the **Toyota** records display. Using the techniques you practiced in the previous activity, select all of the records displaying a **Make** of **Toyota**.

2 On the Ribbon, click the **Home tab**. In the **Clipboard group**, click the **Copy** button. Alternatively, right-click in a blank area of the datasheet, and then click Copy; or press Ctrl + C.

3 On the taskbar, click the **Microsoft Excel** button to make the Excel window active.

4 At the bottom of the worksheet, to the right of the **9B Chevrolet tab**, click the **Insert Worksheet tab**. Compare your screen with Figure 9.36.

A blank worksheet is inserted to the right of the *Chevrolet* worksheet. A dark border displays around Cell A1.

Columns

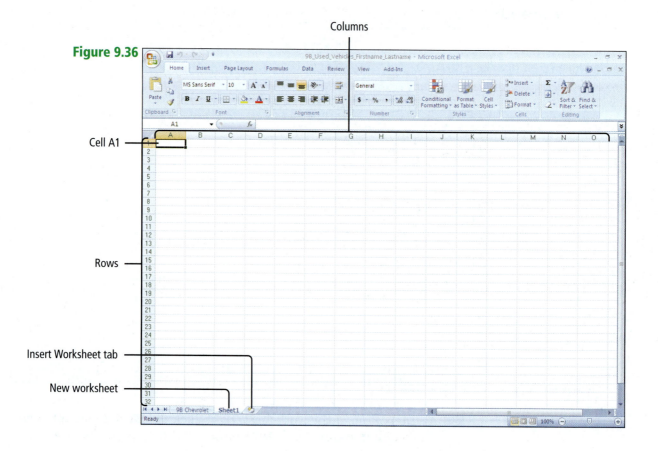

Figure 9.36

Cell A1

Rows

Insert Worksheet tab

New worksheet

5 With **Cell A1** selected, on the **Home tab**, in the **Clipboard group**, click the **Paste** button.

The selected records are copied into the *9B_Used_Vehicles* workbook on a separate worksheet.

Note — Exporting Data into an Existing Workbook

If you use the Export Wizard to export selected records into an existing workbook, the original data in the Excel workbook is overwritten.

---

6 Point to the Column border between **B** and **C** until the ⊕ pointer displays. Drag to the right until all of the data in **Cell B9**—*Highlander*—displays on one line.

7 Using the techniques you practiced in the previous activity, **Rename** the worksheet as **9B Toyota** and then compare your screen with Figure 9.37.

There are two worksheets in the *9B_Used_Vehicles* workbook—*9B Chevrolet* and *9B Toyota*. The *9B Toyota* worksheet is active.

Figure 9.37

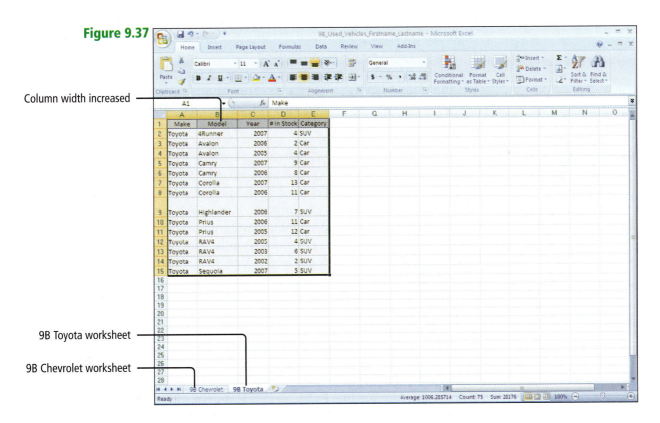

Column width increased

9B Toyota worksheet

9B Chevrolet worksheet

8 **Save** 🖫 the workbook. On the Ribbon, click the **Insert tab**. In the **Text group**, click the **Header & Footer** button. In the header box, type **9B Toyota Used Cars Firstname Lastname** Click anywhere in the worksheet to move the insertion point out of the header box.

9 At the bottom of the workbook, click the **9B Chevrolet tab**. Insert a **Header** of 9B Chevrolet Used Cars Firstname Lastname and then click anywhere in the worksheet to move the insertion point out of the header box.

10 Save 🖫 the workbook. Unless you are required to submit your files electronically, click the **Office** button 🗔 , and then click **Print**. In the **Print** dialog box, under **Print what**, click **Entire workbook**, and then click **OK**. If you are directed to submit an electronic printout of this workbook, from the **Office** menu 🗔 , point to **Save As**, and then click **PDF or XPS**. Click the **Options** button, and then select **Entire workbook**. Click **OK**, and then click **Publish**.

Both worksheets print with the header information at the top of the page.

11 Close ☒ the **Excel** workbook. In the **Access** window, **Close** ☒ the **9B Used Vehicles** query, and then expand ⟩⟩ the **Navigation Pane**.

Objective 8
Export Data to an HTML File and an XML File

If you need to display an Access object on a Web page, you can export the object to an HTML document. Web pages are text files that contain a mixture of text and codes that the Web browser interprets when it loads the Web page. The codes are known as *tags*. A tag begins with the < character and ends with the > character. For example, to add bold formatting to the word *Access*, you would surround the word with a beginning tag and an ending tag—<b>Access</b>. The <b> tag identifies where the bold formatting begins. The </b> tag identifies where the bold formatting ends.

XML, which stands for eXtensible Markup Language, is the standard language for describing and delivering data on the Web. In a manner similar to HTML, which uses tags to indicate how a Web browser should display text and graphics, XML uses tags to organize and present data. Unlike HTML, which has one set of standard tags, XML enables you to create your own set of tags for the types of data with which you work. By creating an XML document, the data can be displayed on a Web page, included in a Word document, analyzed in Excel, imported into a different database, or imported into many other programs that recognize XML files.

Activity 9.14 Export a Report to an HTML File

In this activity, you will export the *9B Jeeps in Stock* report to an HTML file.

1 On the **Navigation Pane**, under **Reports**, right-click **9B Jeeps in Stock**, point to **Export**, and then click **HTML Document**.

2 In the displayed **Export - HTML Document** dialog box, in the **File name** box, be sure that the file will be saved in the **Access Chapter 9** folder. In the file name, replace all of the spaces with underscores. Under **Specify export options**, select the **Open the destination file after the export operation is complete** check box, and then click **OK**.

3 In the displayed **HTML Output Options** dialog box, click **OK**, and then compare your screen with Figure 9.38.

The document displays in Microsoft Internet Explorer or in your default Web browser.

Microsoft Internet Explorer—your Web browser may differ

Figure 9.38

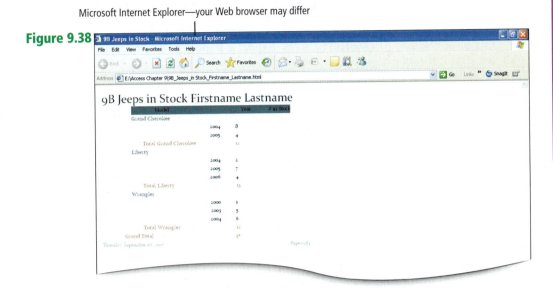

4 Right-click in an empty area of the Web page, and then click **View Source**. Compare your screen with Figure 9.39.

The HTML code displays in a new window. This is the actual document that was exported. The Web browser interprets the HTML tags and displays the text as a readable document. If you know HTML coding, you can format this document so that the column headings are more readable.

HTML code

Figure 9.39

Tags

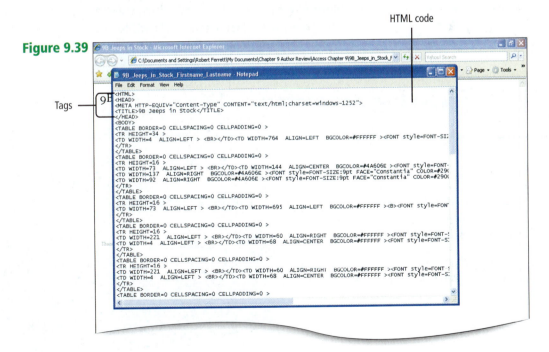

5 **Close** ❌ the window displaying the source code. If you are instructed to submit this result, create a paper or electronic printout of the Web page.

6 **Close** ❌ the Web browser window. In the **Export - HTML Document** dialog box, click the **Close** button.

Activity 9.15 Export a Report to an XML File

In this activity, you will export the *9B Jeeps in Stock* report to an XML file.

1 On the **Navigation Pane**, under **Reports**, right-click **9B Jeeps in Stock**, point to **Export**, and then click **XML File**.

2 In the displayed **Export - XML File** dialog box, in the **File name** box, be sure that the file will be saved in the **Access Chapter 9** folder. Select only the file name—*9B Jeeps in Stock Firstname Lastname.xml*—and then type **9B_Jeeps_XML_File_Firstname_ Lastname.xml** Click **OK**, and then compare your screen with Figure 9.40.

The Export XML dialog box displays. When you export data to XML, multiple files can be created. An **XML schema** is a document with an .xsd extension that defines the elements, entities, and content allowed in the document. It defines the tag names and defines the order, relationships, and data type you use with each tag. If you plan to import the XML data into another Access database, the schema is essential to ensure that all of the table relationships and data types are preserved when the data is imported.

An XML file cannot be viewed directly in a Web browser. Two additional files—**XML presentation files**—can be created so that the data can be viewed in a Web browser. A stylesheet (.xsl) transforms the generated XML data to HTML for presentation. The other file applies the stylesheet used by the Web server and creates an HTML document.

Figure 9.40

Data cannot be viewed in Web browser

Export schema check box

Create presentation files check box

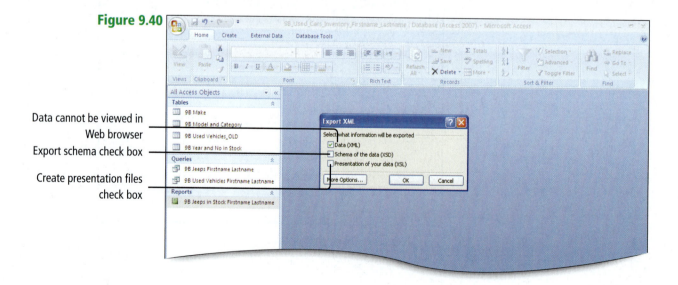

3 In the **Export XML** dialog box, be sure that the **Data (XML)** check box is selected, and then select the **Presentation of your data (XSL)** check box. Click **OK**. In the **Export - XML File** dialog box, click **Close**.

Because XML files are typically imported into other applications, there is no option to view the file after the export operation.

4 On the taskbar, click the **Start** button ![start], and then click **My Computer**. Navigate to the location where the **Access Chapter 9** folder is saved, and open the folder. Compare your screen with Figure 9.41.

Depending on your computer settings, the files contained in the Access Chapter 9 folder may display differently.

My Computer window   Maximize button

Figure 9.41

Views button

Access Chapter 9 folder

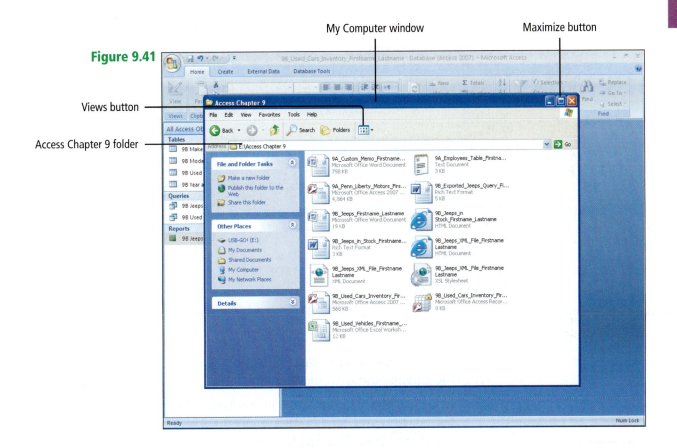

5 On the toolbar, click the **Views** button ![Views], and then click **Details**. **Maximize** ![Maximize] the window. In the column header row, point to the column border between **Name** and **Size** until the ![pointer] pointer displays, and then double-click to resize the Name column. Point to the column border between **Type** and **Date Modified** until the ![pointer] pointer displays, and then double-click to resize the Type column. Compare your screen with Figure 9.42.

In Details view, the name, size, and type of each file is displayed, in addition to the Date and Time the file was modified. Your dates and times will differ. Under Type, two HTML documents are displayed—*9B_Jeeps_in_Stock* and *9B_Jeeps_XML_File*. The *9B_Jeeps_in_Stock* file is the HTML file that you created when you exported to an HTML file. The *9B_Jeeps_XML_File* is an HTML presentation file that was created when you selected the *Presentation of your data (XSL)* check box while exporting to an XML file.

Under Type, there is an *XSL Stylesheet* file named *9B_Jeeps_XML_File*. This is the second presentation file that is used to create the HTML file. Finally, under Type, there is an XML document that stores the data that was exported.

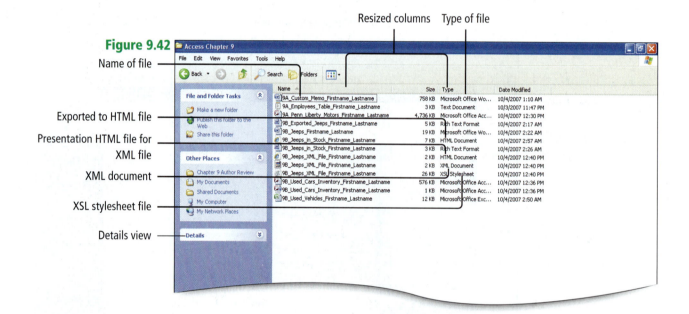

Figure 9.42

Name of file

Exported to HTML file

Presentation HTML file for XML file

XML document

XSL stylesheet file

Details view

Resized columns   Type of file

6 Locate the **9B_Jeeps_XML_File** that displays a **Type** of **HTML Document**, and then double-click it.

Because you created the two presentation files when you exported the report to an XML file, the report displays in your Web browser. If it does not, read the Alert that follows.

Alert!

Did an Information Bar message box display?

If an Information Bar message box displays, your Web browser is blocking content from displaying. In the dialog box, click OK. Click the Information bar, and then click Allow Blocked Content. In the Security Warning message box, click Yes. The procedure may differ depending upon your Web browser.

7 If you are instructed to submit this result, create a paper printout of the Web page, or submit your files electronically as directed.

8 **Close** ☒ the Web browser window, and then **Close** ☒ the Access Chapter 9 window. **Close** the database, and then **Exit** Access.

More Knowledge

Exporting Data to Another Access Database

You can copy data from an Access database into another Access database. Copying and pasting is easiest, but exporting offers you more options, such as exporting the table definition and the table, or exporting just the table definition, along with the option to save the export specification. You can export all of the database objects into another database. However, to export selected records, you must copy and paste the records.

Exporting an object to another database is similar to importing the object from the first database. Although you can import multiple objects in a single operation, you cannot export multiple objects in a single operation. So, if you want to export multiple objects, it is easier to open the destination database and perform an import operation. You cannot export table relationships, import and export specifications, custom menu bars, or custom toolbars. You cannot export a query as a table.

Export database objects when you want to copy the table structure to another database as a shortcut for creating a new table, when you want to copy the layout and design of a form or report as a shortcut for creating a new form or report, or when you want to copy the latest version of a table or form to another database at regular intervals using the export specification.

End **You have completed Project 9B** ——————————

  There's More You Can Do!

From My Computer, navigate to the student files that accompany this textbook. In the folder **02_theres_more_you_can_do**, locate and open the folder for this chapter. Open and print the instructions for this project, which are provided to you in Adobe PDF format.

Try It! 1—Import Data from a Previous Version of Access

In this Try It! project, you will import a table from an Access 2003 database.

Try It! 2—Export Data to a Text File

In this Try It! project, you will export a table from an Access database to a text file.

Summary

Importing is the process of copying *in* data from another application. Linking is the process of connecting to data in another application, and exporting is the process of copying *out* data to another application. In this chapter, you imported data from a Word table after converting the table to a text file. You saved the import specifications so that you could use the steps in another import operation. You created individual memos for the employees by using the Mail Merge feature within Access. You imported data from an Excel worksheet to a table in Access, and then used the import feature to append data from Excel to the same table. You linked an Excel chart to an Access report, imported data from another Access database, and linked to data in another Access database. You reversed the process by exporting a query and report to Word. You exported selected records to Excel, and copied and pasted records from Access to Excel. Finally, you exported an Access report to an HTML file and to an XML file, viewing both in a Web browser.

Key Terms

Content-Based Assessments

Matching

Match each term in the second column with its correct definition in the first column. Write the letter of the term on the blank line in front of the correct definition.

—— **1.** To copy *in* data from one source or application to another application.

—— **2.** To change data from one format to another.

—— **3.** A synonym for data stored without any formatting.

—— **4.** A connection to data in another file.

—— **5.** The acronym for the standard language for describing and delivering data on the Web.

—— **6.** The acronym for the standard that enables databases using SQL statements to interface with one another.

—— **7.** The acronym for a language used to display Web pages.

—— **8.** To combine a main document created in Microsoft Word with a data source created in Access.

—— **9.** The primary document used in Excel to save and work with data that is arranged in columns and rows.

—— **10.** An Excel file that contains one or more worksheets.

—— **11.** The small box formed by the intersection of a column and a row.

—— **12.** Includes two or more selected cells on a worksheet that can be treated as a single unit.

—— **13.** A graphic representation of data.

—— **14.** The process used to copy *out* data from one source or application to another application.

—— **15.** The extension for a snapshot file.

A ASCII

B Cell

C Chart

D Convert

E Export

F HTML

G Import

H Link

I Mail merge

J ODBC

K Range

L .snp

M Workbook

N Worksheet

O XML

Content-Based Assessments

Fill in the Blank

Write the correct word in the space provided.

1. Commas or tabs are commonly used to separate fields in a(n) _____ file.

2. A Microsoft server that enables you to share documents with others in your organization is a(n) _____ server.

3. When the data is added to the end of the existing table, it is _____ to the table.

4. In a(n) _____ database, each field represents a unique type of data, each table has one or more primary key fields, the data is related to the subject of the table, and an individual can modify the data in any field—except the primary key field—without affecting the data in other fields

5. In a mail merge operation, the Word document that contains the text of the letter or memo is the _____ _____.

6. In a mail merge operation, the Access table that contains the names and addresses of the individuals to whom the document is being sent is the _____ _____.

7. Another name for a worksheet is _____.

8. A chart that displays comparisons among related numbers is a(n) _____ chart.

9. A chart that displays the contributions of parts to a whole amount is a(n) _____ chart.

10. A chart that displays trends over time is a(n) _____ chart.

11. The table structure—field names, data types, and field properties—is the table _____.

12. A file format that enables an individual to view an Access report without having Access installed on the computer is a (n) _____ file.

13. Code used in HTML to format text is called a(n) _____.

14. A document with an .xsd extension that defines the elements, entities, and content allowed in the document is an XML _____.

15. Two XML files created when an Access object is exported to XML so that the data can be viewed in a Web browser are XML _____ files.

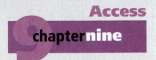

Access

chapter**nine**

Skills Review

Project 9C — Sports Cars

In this project, you will apply the skills you practiced from the Objectives in Project 9A.

Objectives: 1. *Import Data from a Word Table;* **2.** *Use Mail Merge to Integrate Access and Word;* **3.** *Import Data from an Excel Workbook;* **4.** *Insert an Excel Chart into a Report;* **5.** *Import from and Link to Another Access Database.*

Penn Liberty Motors maintains many of its records in Word, Excel, and Access files. Kevin Rau, President, and Marilyn Kellman, Finance Manager, want to bring the data from these files into an Access database to create queries and reports. In this project, you will import data from Word, and then use the information in the Customers table to create a mail merge document in Microsoft Word. You will import data from Excel and another Access database and create links to data in these applications. Your completed files will look similar to those in Figure 9.43.

You will save your files as
9C_Sports_Cars_Firstname_Lastname.accdb
9C_Customers_Table_Firstname_Lastname.txt
9C_Your_Letter_Firstname_Lastname.docx

Figure 9.43

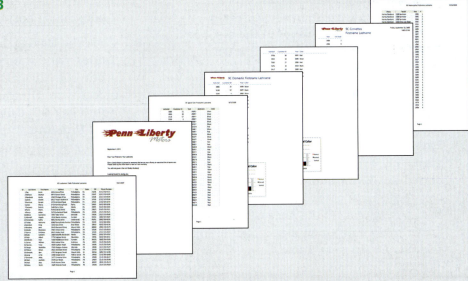

(Project 9C–Sports Cars continues on the next page)

Content-Based Assessments

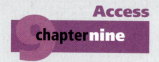

(Project 9C–Sports Cars continued)

1. **Start** Access. In the **Getting Started with Microsoft Access** window, under **New Blank Database**, click the **Blank Database** button. On the right side of the screen, under **File Name**, select the text, and then type **9C_Sports_Cars_Firstname_Lastname** Click the **Browse** button, navigate to the **Access Chapter 9** folder, and then click **OK**. Click the **Create** button. **Close** the displayed table, and then **Exit** Access.

2. **Start** Word. Click the **Office** button, and then click **Open**. Navigate to the location where the student data files for this text-book are saved. Locate and open the **a09C_Customers** file. On the Ribbon, click the **Layout tab**. In the **Data group**, click the **Convert to Text** button. In the displayed **Convert Table to Text** dialog box, be sure that the **Tabs** option button is selected, and then click **OK**. Click any-where to deselect the text.

3. Click the **Office** button, point to **Save As**, and then click **Other Formats**. Navigate to the **Access Chapter 9** folder. In the **Save As** dialog box, in the **File name** box, select the existing text, and then type **9C_ Customers_Table_Firstname_Lastname** Click the **Save as type arrow**. From the displayed list, scroll down, click **Plain Text**, and then click **Save**. In the displayed **File Conversion** dialog box, click **OK** to accept the default settings. **Exit** Word.

4. **Start** Access. Under **Open Recent Database**, click **9C_Sports_Cars** to open the empty database. On the Ribbon, click the **External Data tab**, and then in the **Import group**, click the **Text File** button. In the dis-played **Get External Data - Text File** dialog box, to the right of the **File name** box, click **Browse**. Navigate to the **Access Chapter 9** folder. In the **File Open** dialog box, double-click **9C_Customers_Table**.

5. Be sure that the **Import the source data into a new table in the current database** option button is selected, and then click **OK**. In the **Import Text Wizard** dialog box, be sure that the **Delimited** option button is selected, and then click **Next**. Be sure that the **Tab** option button is selected. Select the **First Row Contains Field Names** check box. In the **Text Qualifier** box, be sure that {**none**} is selected. Click **Next**.

6. Click in the **ZIP** field to select the field. Under **Field Options**, click the **Data Type arrow**, and then click **Text**. Click **Next** to display primary key options. Be sure that the **Let Access add primary key** option button is selected, and then click **Next**. Click **Finish**.

7. Select the **Save import steps** check box to display additional options. Click in the **Description** box, and then type **Imports a tab delimited text file that was a Word table** Click **Save Import**, and notice that on the **Navigation Pane**, the **9C_Customers_ Table** displays. On the **External Data tab**, in the **Import group**, click the **Saved Imports** button and confirm that your import file is there. In the **Manage Data Tasks** dialog box, click **Close**.

8. Click the **Navigation Pane** title—**All Tables**—and then click **Object Type** to group the Navigation Pane objects by the object type. On the **Navigation Pane**, right-click **9C_Customers_Table**, and then click **Rename**. Type **9C Customers Table Firstname Lastname** to replace the under-scores between the words in the table name with spaces. Double-click **9C Customers Table** to open the table in **Datasheet** view, and then collapse the **Navigation Pane**. To **record 34**, add your-self as a customer. Adjust the widths of all

(Project 9C–Sports Cars continues on the next page)

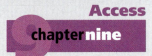

Skills Review

(Project 9C–Sports Cars continued)

of the fields to display all of the data and the entire field name for each field.

9. If you are instructed to submit this result, create a paper or electronic printout of the **second page** of the table in **Landscape** orientation, changing **Margins**, if necessary, to print all of the fields. **Save** the table, and then **Close** the table.

10. Expand the **Navigation Pane**. On the Ribbon, click the **External Data tab**. In the **Export group**, click the **More** button, and then click **Merge it with Microsoft Office Word**. Be sure that **Link your data to an existing Microsoft Word document** is selected, and then click **OK**. In the **Select Microsoft Word Document** dialog box, navigate to the location where the student data files for this textbook are saved. Locate and **Open** the **a09C_Ad** file.

11. In the **Mail Merge** task pane, under **Select recipients**, be sure that **Use an existing list** is selected. In the **Mail Merge** task pane, under **Step 3 of 6**, click **Next: Write your letter**. Click to the right of **Dear**, and then press ⎵Spacebar. In the **Mail Merge** task pane, under **Write your letter**, click **More items**. In the **Insert Merge Field** dialog box under **Fields**, click **First Name**, and then click **Insert**. Click **Last Name**, click **Insert**, and then click **Close**. In the letter, click to the left of **<<Last_Name>>**, and then press ⎵Spacebar to insert a space between the First_Name and Last_Name fields. Type a **colon** after the Last Name field.

12. In the **Mail Merge** task pane, under **Step 4 of 6**, click **Next: Preview your letters** box, and notice that the first memo displays with a recipient name of **Kevin Rau**, President of Penn Liberty Motors. Under **Make changes** in the Mail Merge task

pane, click the **Exclude this recipient** button.

13. In the **Mail Merge** task pane, under **Step 5 of 6**, click **Next: Complete the merge**, and notice that in this step, you can either print or personalize the letters. In the **Mail Merge** task pane under **Merge**, click **Edit individual letters**. In the displayed **Merge to New Document** dialog box, click **From** and type **34 To: 34** Click **OK**. In the letter, click at the end of the paragraph that begins *Penn Liberty Motors*, and then press ⎵Enter **two** times. Type **You will look great in that red Shelby Mustang!**

14. On the **Quick Access Toolbar**, click the **Save** button. In the **Save As** dialog box, navigate to your **Access Chapter 9** folder, and then **Save** the Word document as **9C_Your_Letter_Firstname_Lastname** If you are instructed to submit this result, create a paper or electronic printout of the **current page**, and then click **OK**.

15. **Close** Word to exit the merged document. **Close** Word again, and in the displayed message box, click **No**. It is not necessary to save the original document. If the database is not displayed, on the status bar, click the Microsoft Access button to restore the database window to the screen.

16. On the **External Data tab**, in the **Import group**, click the **Excel** button. In the **Get External Data - Excel Spreadsheet** dialog box, to the right of the **File name** box, click the **Browse** button. Navigate to the location where the student data files for this textbook are saved. Locate and open the **a09C_Sports_Car_Sales** file. In the **Get External Data - Excel Spreadsheet** dialog box, click **OK**. Be certain **Import the source data into a new table in the current database** is selected, and then

(Project 9C–Sports Cars continues on the next page)

(Project 9C–Sports Cars continued)

click **OK**. In the **Import Spreadsheet Wizard** dialog box, be certain that **Show Worksheets** is selected and **In Stock** is highlighted. Click **Next**. Be certain that the **First Row Contains Column Headings** check box is selected. Because the data types are correct, click **Next**. Select **Choose my own primary key**. Click the **table name** box **arrow**, click **Vehicle#**, and then click **Next**. In the final **Import Spreadsheet Wizard** dialog box, in the **Import to Table** box, type **9C Sports Cars Firstname Lastname** and then click **Finish**. In the **Get External Data - Excel Spreadsheet** dialog box, click **Close**.

17. On the **External Data tab**, in the **Import group**, click the **Excel** button. Locate and open the **a09C_Sports_Car_Sales** file. Under **Specify how and where you want to store the data in the current database**, click **Append a copy of the records to the table**. Click the **table name arrow**, select **9C Sports Cars**, and then click **OK**. In the **Import Spreadsheet Wizard** dialog box, be certain that **Show Worksheets** is selected. Click **Special Order**, and then click **Next**. Click **Next**. In the **Import Spreadsheet Wizard** dialog box, click **Finish** to import the data to the *9C Sport Cars* table in the current database. In the **Get External Data -Excel Spreadsheet** dialog box, click **Close**, and then expand the **Navigation Pane**. Double-click **9C Sport Cars** to display the table in **Datasheet** view. If you are instructed to submit this result, create a paper or electronic printout of the table. **Close** the table, and then collapse the **Navigation Pane**.

18. On the **Create tab**, in the **Other group**, click the **Query Design** button. In the **Show Table** dialog box, double-click **9C Sports Cars**, and then in the **Show Table**

dialog box, click **Close**. In the field list, click **Vehicle#**. Hold down (⇧ Shift), and then click **Color** to select all five fields. Drag the selected fields down into the first column of the design grid, In the design grid, under **Domestic**, click in the **Criteria** box, type **Y** and then on the **Show** row, clear the check box. On the **Design tab**, in the **Results group**, click the **Run** button. **Save** the query as **9C Domestic Firstname Lastname** and then **Close** the query.

19. Expand the **Navigation Pane**, under **Queries**, click **9C Domestic** to select the query, and then collapse the **Navigation Pane**. On the **Create tab**, in the **Reports group**, click the **Report** button. On the **Format tab**, in the **Controls group**, click the **Logo** button. Navigate to the location where the data files for this chapter are saved, and then double-click **a09C_Logo**. Switch to **Design** view. In the **Report Header** section, delete the **Date** and **Time text box controls**. Move the title control so the right edge of the control aligns with the **1.5-inch mark on the horizontal ruler**. Drag the right edge of the logo control to the **mark on the horizontal ruler**. In the **Page Footer** section, delete the **Page number text box control**. In the **Report Footer** section, delete the **Count calculated control**. Point to the bottom of the **Report Footer** section until

the ![pointer icon] pointer displays, and then drag upward until the bottom edge of the section aligns with the bottom edge of the **Report Footer section bar**. **Save** the report as **9C Domestic Report Firstname Lastname** In the report, point to the top of the **Report Footer section bar** until the

![pointer icon] pointer displays. Drag the section down to the **3-inch mark on the vertical ruler** to increase the size of the Page Footer section.

(Project 9C–Sports Cars continues on the next page)

Content-Based Assessments

(Project 9C–Sports Cars continued)

20. **Start** Excel. If necessary, maximize the Excel window. Click the **Office** button, and then click **Open**. Navigate to the location where the data files for this chapter are saved, and then double-click **a09C_Domestic_Chart** to open the workbook. Click in an empty area of the **column chart** to select the entire chart. On the **Home tab**, in the **Clipboard group**, click the **Copy** button to place a copy of the chart in the Office Clipboard. On the **Excel** title bar, click the **Close** button to close the workbook and to exit Excel. In the **9C Domestic Report**, right-click the **Page Footer section bar**, and then click **Paste**. **Save** the report, and then switch to **Report** view. If you are instructed to submit this result, create a paper or electronic printout. **Close** the report.

21. On the **External Data tab**, in the **Import group**, click the **Access** button. In the **Get External Data - Access Database** dialog box, click **Browse**. Navigate to the location where the where the data files for this chapter are saved, and then double-click **a09C_Used_Cars_Inventory**. Be sure that the **Import tables, queries, forms, reports, macros, and modules into the current database** option button is selected, and then click **OK**. In the **Import Objects** dialog box, click the **Tables tab**, and then click **9C Used Vehicles**.

22. In the **Import Objects** dialog box, click the **Queries tab**, and then click **9C Corvettes**. Click the **Reports tab**, click **9C Corvettes in Stock**, and then click **OK**. In the **Get External Data - Access Database** dialog

box, click **Close**. Expand the **Navigation Pane**.

23. On the **Navigation Pane**, under **Reports**, right-click **9C Corvettes in Stock**, and then click **Layout View**. Click the title *9C Corvettes* one time to select the title. Click to the right of **Corvettes**, press [Shift] + [Enter], and then type **Firstname Lastname Save** the report. If you are instructed to submit this result, create a paper or electronic printout of the report. **Close** the report, and then collapse the **Navigation Pane**.

24. On the **External Data tab**, in the **Import group**, click the **Access** button. In the **Get External Data - Access Database** dialog box, **Browse** to the location where the data files for this chapter are saved, and then double-click **a09C_Motorcycles**. Click the **Link to the data source by creating a linked table** option button, and then click **OK**. In the **Link Tables** dialog box, on the **Tables tab**, click **9C Motorcycles**, and then click **OK**. Expand the **Navigation Pane**. On the **Navigation Pane**, under **Tables**, right-click **9C Motorcycles**, and then click **Rename**. Click to the right of **Motorcycles**, press [Spacebar], type **Firstname Lastname** and then press [Enter]. On the **Navigation Pane**, under **Tables**, double-click **9C Motorcycles** to display the table in **Datasheet** view. Adjust the widths of all of the columns. Unless you are required to submit your database electronically, **Print** the table. **Close** the table, saving changes when prompted. **Close** the database, and then **Exit** Access.

End **You have completed Project 9C**

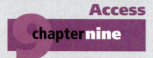

Skills Review

Project 9D—Sport Vehicles

In this project, you will apply the skills you practiced from the Objectives in Project 9B.

Objectives: 6. *Export Data to Word;* **7.** *Export Data to Excel;* **8.** *Export Data to an HTML File and an XML File.*

Some of the employees of Penn Liberty Motors are not comfortable working with Access. They save their data in Word and Excel. Access enables you to export data from an Access database into these applications. You can also export data to be used on a Web page. In this project, you will export data to several types of applications. Your completed files will look similar to those shown in Figure 9.44.

For Project 9D, you will need the following file:

a09D_Sport_Vehicles

You will save your files as
9D_Sport_Vehicles_Firstname_Lastname.accdb
9D_Imports_Query_Firstname_Lastname.rtf
9D_07-08_Models.xlsx
9D_Corvettes_in_Stock.html
9D_Corvettes_XML_File_Firstname_Lastname.htm
9D_Corvettes_XML_File_Firstname_Lastname.xml
9D_Corvettes_XML_File_Firstname_Lastname.xsl
9D_Imports_Firstname_Lastname.docx
9D_Imports_RTF_Firstname_Lastname.rtf

Figure 9.44

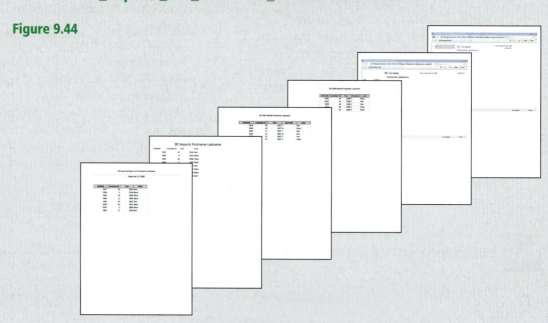

(Project 9D–Sport Vehicles continues on the next page)

Content-Based Assessments

(Project 9D–Sport Vehicles continued)

1. **Start** Access. Navigate to the location where the student data files for this textbook are saved. Locate and open the **a09D_Sport_Vehicles** file. Save the database in the **Access 2007 Database** format in your **Access Chapter 9** folder as **9D_Sport_Vehicles_Firstname_Lastname** Enable the content or add the Access Chapter 9 folder to the Trust Center.

2. On the **Navigation Pane**, under **Queries**, right-click **9D Imports**, point to **Export**, and then click **Word RTF File**. In the **Export - RTF File** dialog box, click **Browse**. Navigate to the **Access Chapter 9** folder. In the **File name** box, select the existing file name, type **9D_Imports_Query_Firstname_Lastname** and then click **Save**.

3. In the **Export - RTF File** dialog box, under **Specify export options**, select the **Open the destination file after the export operation is complete** check box, and then click **OK**. On the Word Ribbon, click the **Insert tab**. In the **Header & Footer group**, click the **Header** button. In the **Built-In** gallery, scroll down and click **Conservative**, and then type **9D Imported Sports Cars Firstname Lastname** Click **Pick the Date** down **arrow**, and click **Today**. In the **Close group**, click the **Close Header and Footer** button. On the **Quick Access Toolbar**, click the **Save** button. In the message box, click **Cancel**. Click the **Office** button, point to **Save As**, and then click **Word Document**. If necessary, navigate to the **Access Chapter 9** folder. Change the file name to **9D_Imports_Firstname_Lastname** Notice that the **Save as type** box displays **Word Document**, which means the file will be given a *.docx* extension. In the **Save As** dialog box, click **Save**. In the displayed message box, click **OK**. If you are instructed to submit this result, create a paper or electronic

printout. **Close** the Word window. In the **Export - RTF File** dialog box, click **Close**.

4. On the **Navigation Pane**, under **Reports**, double-click **9D Imports** to open the report. Switch to **Layout** view. Click the title—**9D Imports**—two times to enter into editing mode. Click to the right of **Imports**, press Spacebar, and then using your own first name and last name, type **Firstname Lastname** Press Enter, and then **Save** the report.

5. **Close** the report. On the **Navigation Pane**, under **Reports**, right-click **9D Imports**, point to **Export**, and then click **Word RTF File**. Be sure that the **File name** box displays the correct path to your **Access Chapter 9** folder. Rename the file **9D_Imports_RTF_Firstname_Lastname** Under **Specify export options**, select the **Open the destination file after the export operation is complete** check box, and then click OK. If you are instructed to submit this result, create a paper or electronic printout. **Close** the Word window. In the **Export - RTF File** dialog box, click **Close**.

6. On the **Navigation Pane**, under **Queries**, double-click **9D 07-08 Models** to open the query in Datasheet view. Collapse the **Navigation Pane**. In the **first record**, click in the **Row Selector** box to select the record. Hold down ⇧Shift, and then click in the **Row Selector** box for **Record 6**—the last record displaying *2007* as the Year. Click the **External Data tab**, and in the **Export group**, click **Excel**.

7. In the **Export - Excel Spreadsheet** dialog box, in the **File name** box, be sure that the path to your **Access Chapter 9** folder is correct. In the file name—**9D 07-08 Models**—replace all spaces with underscores. Notice that in the **File format** box,

(Project 9D–Sport Vehicle continues on the next page)

(Project 9D–Sport Vehicles continued)

the file will be saved as an Excel Workbook with an extension of .xlsx, which is the extension used for Excel 2007. In the **Export - Excel Spreadsheet** dialog box, under **Specify export options**, select the **Export data with formatting and layout** check box. Select the **Open the destination file after the export operation is complete** check box, and then select the **Export only the selected records** check box. Click **OK**. At the bottom of the worksheet, right-click the **Worksheet tab**, and then click **Rename**. Type **9D 2007** and then press Enter. **Save** the workbook, and then **Minimize** Excel.

8. If necessary, on the taskbar, click the **Microsoft Access** button to restore the Access window and to display the query. Click anywhere in the datasheet to deselect the 2007 records. In the datasheet, using the techniques you practiced in the previous steps, select all of the records displaying a **Year** of **2008**. Right-click in the selected area of the datasheet, and then click **Copy**. On the taskbar, click the **Microsoft Excel** button to make the Excel window active. At the bottom of the worksheet, to the right of the **9D 2007**, click the **Insert Worksheet tab**.

9. With **Cell A1** selected, on the **Home tab**, in the **Clipboard group**, click the **Paste** button. Point to the Column border between **B** and **C** until the ⊹ pointer displays. Drag to the right until all of the data in **Cell B1**—*Customer ID*—displays. Using the techniques you practiced in the previous steps, **Rename** the worksheet to **9D 2008** **Save** the workbook. On the Ribbon, click the **Insert tab**. In the **Text group**, click the **Header & Footer** button. In the header box, type **9D 2008 Models**

Firstname Lastname Click anywhere in the worksheet to move the insertion point out of the header box.

10. At the bottom of the workbook, click the **9D 2007 tab**. Insert a **Header** of **9D 2007 Models Firstname Lastname** and then click anywhere in the worksheet to move the insertion point out of the header box.

11. **Save** the workbook. Unless you are required to submit your files electronically, click the **Office** button, and then click **Print**. In the **Print** dialog box, under **Print what**, click **Entire workbook**, and then click **OK**. If you are directed to submit an electronic printout of this workbook, on the Office menu, point to **Save As**, and then click **PDF or XPS**. Click the **Options** button, and then select **Entire workbook**. Click **OK**, and then click **Publish**. **Close** the **Excel** workbook. In the **Access** window, **Close** the **9D 07-08 Models** query, and then expand the **Navigation Pane**.

12. On the **Navigation Pane**, under **Reports**, right-click **9D Corvettes in Stock**, and open the report in **Design** view. Add your **Firstname Lastname** as the second line of the title. **Save** and **Close** the report. Right-click **9D Corvettes in Stock**, point to **Export**, and then click **HTML Document**. In the **Export - HTML Document** dialog box, in the **File name** box, be sure that the file will be saved in the **Access Chapter 9** folder. In the file name, replace all of the spaces with underscores, and then click **OK**. Under **Specify export options**, select the **Open the destination file after the export operation is complete** check box, and then click **OK**. In the **HTML Output Options** dialog box, click **OK**.

13. If you are instructed to submit this result, create a paper or electronic printout of the

(Project 9D–Sport Vehicles continues on the next page)

(Project 9D–Sport Vehicle continued)

Web page. **Close** the Web browser window. In the **Export - HTML Document** dialog box, click the **Close** button.

14. On the **Navigation Pane**, under **Reports**, right-click **9D Corvettes in Stock**, point to **Export**, and then click **XML File**. In the **Export - XML File** dialog box, in the **File name** box, be sure that the file will be saved in the **Access Chapter 9** folder. Select only the file name—**9D Corvettes in Stock.xml**—and then type **9D_Corvettes_ XML_File_Firstname_Lastname.xml** Click **OK**. In the **Export XML** dialog box, be sure that the **Data (XML)** check box is selected, and then click the **Presentation of your data (XSL)** check box. Click **OK**. In the **Export - XML File** dialog box, click **Close**.

15. On the taskbar, click the **Start** button, and then click **My Computer**. Navigate to

the location where the **Access Chapter 9** folder is saved, and open the folder. On the toolbar, click the **Views** button, and then click **Details**. **Maximize** the window. In the column header row, point to the column border between **Name** and **Size** until the pointer displays, and then double-click to resize the *Name* column. Point to the column border between **Type** and **Date Modified** until the [⊹] pointer displays, and then double-click to resize the *Type* column. Locate the **9D_Corvettes_ XML_File** that displays a **Type** of **HTML Document** and double-click it. If you are instructed to submit this result, create a paper or electronic printout of the Web page. **Close** the Web browser window, and then **Close** the Access Chapter 9 window. Collapse the **Navigation Pane**. **Close** the database, and then **Exit** Access.

End **You have completed Project 9D**

Content-Based Assessments

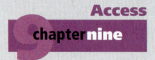

Project 9E—Custom Features

In this project, you will apply the skills you practiced from the Objectives in Project 9A.

Objectives: 1. *Import Data from a Word Table;* **2.** *Use Mail Merge to Integrate Access and Word;* **3.** *Import Data from an Excel Workbook;* **4.** *Insert an Excel Chart into a Report;* **5.** *Import from and Link to Another Access Database.*

Penn Liberty Motors offers extensive customization options for all types of vehicles through its accessories division. In this project, you will import a Word table as a plain text file. You will use this imported table to merge the customization packages to a flyer created in Word. You will import data from an Excel worksheet and create a report with an imported Excel chart. Your completed work will look similar to Figure 9.45.

> ### For Project 9E, you will need the following files:
>
> New blank Access database
> a09E_Custom_Features.docx
> a09E_Flyer.docx
> a09E_Package_Sales.xlsx
> a09E_Employees.accdb
> a09E_Logo.jpg
>
> **You will save your files as**
> **9E_Customization_Firstname_Lastname.accdb**
> **9E_Custom_Features_Firstname_Lastname.docx**
> **9E_Flyer_Firstname_Lastname.docx**

Figure 9.45

(Project 9E–Custom Features continues on the next page)

Content-Based Assessments

Mastering Access

(Project 9E–Custom Features continued)

1. **Start** Access. Create a new blank database called **9E_Customization_Firstname_Lastname** and save it in your **Access Chapter 9** folder. **Close** the displayed table. **Exit** Access.

2. **Start** Word. Locate and open the **a09E_Custom_Features** document. On the **Layout tab**, in the **Data group**, click the **Convert to Text** button. Separate the text with **Tabs**, and then click **OK**.

3. Click the **Office** button, point to **Save As**, and then click **Other Formats**. Navigate to the **Access Chapter 9** folder. Change the name of the file to **9E_Custom_Features_Firstname_Lastname** Save the file as **Plain Text**. In the displayed **File Conversion** dialog box, accept the default settings, and then **Exit** Word.

4. **Start** Access, and then open the **9E_Customization_Firstname_Lastname** empty database. On the **External Data tab**, in the **Import group**, click the **Text File** button. **Browse** to the **Access Chapter 9** folder, and then open **9E_Custom_Features**.

5. Be sure that the **Import the source data into a new table in the current database** option button is selected, and then click **OK**. In the **Import Text Wizard** dialog box, be sure that the **Delimited** option button is selected, click **Next**. Be sure that the **Tab** option button is selected. Select the **First Row Contains Field Names** check box. In the **Text Qualifier** box, be sure that **{none}** is selected, and then click **Next**.

6. Change the **Data Type** in the **Customer Rating (1-5)** field to **Text**. Click **Next**. Be sure that the **Let Access add primary key** option button is selected, and then click

   Next. Edit the table name by replacing the underscores with spaces. Click **Finish**.

7. Select the **Save import steps** check box to display additional options. Click in the **Description** box, and then type **Imports a tab delimited text file that was a Word table** and then click **Save Imports**.

8. Group the **Navigation Pane** objects by the **Object Type**. Open the **9E Custom Features** in **Datasheet** view, and adjust the widths of all of the fields to display all of the data and the entire field name for each field.

9. If you are instructed to submit this result, create a paper or electronic printout of the table in **Landscape** orientation. **Save** the table, and then **Close** the table.

10. Select the **9E Custom Features** table. In the **Export group**, click the **More** button, click **Merge it with Microsoft Office Word**. Be sure that **Link your data to an existing Microsoft Word document** is selected, and then click **OK**. Locate and open the **a09E_Flyer** file.

11. In the Word **Mail Merge** task pane, under **Select recipients**, be sure that **Use an existing list** is selected, and then click **Next: Write your letter**. One at a time, click to the right of **Package Deal**, **Custom Feature**, and **Warranty**, inserting the appropriate field name. Click **Close**. At the bottom of the flyer, replace **Firstname Lastname** with your first and last names. **Preview your letters**. **Complete the merge**. Save your document in the **Access Chapter 9** folder as **9E_Flyer_Firstname_Lastname** Unless you are required to submit your files electronically, **Print** the **Current page**.

(Project 9E–Custom Features continues on the next page)

Access

chapternine

Mastering Access

(Project 9E–Custom Features continued)

12. **Close** Word to exit the merged document. **Close** Word again, and do not save the original document. Restore the database window to the screen.

13. In the **Import group**, click the **Excel** button. Locate and open the **a09E_Package_Sales** file. In the **Get External Data - Excel Spreadshee**t dialog box, click **OK**. Be certain **Import the source data into a new table in the current database** is selected. Click **OK**. In the **Import Spreadsheet Wizard** dialog box, be certain that **Show Worksheets** is selected and **Packages** is highlighted. Click **Next**. Select the **First Row Contains Column Headings** check box. Click **Next** two times. **Let Access add primary key**, and then click **Next**. Name the table **9E Package Sales Firstname Lastname** and then click **Finish**. In the **Get External Data - Excel Spreadsheet** dialog box, click **Close**.

14. Select the **9E Package Sales** table and create a new **Report**. Add the **a09E_Logo** into the header section of the report. Switch to **Design** view. In the **Report Header** section, delete the **Date** and **Time text box controls**. Move the title control so the left edge of the control aligns with the **2-inch mark on the horizontal ruler**. Drag the right edge of the logo control to the **1.5-inch mark on the horizontal ruler**. In the **Page Footer** section, delete the **Page number text box control**. In the **Report Footer** section, delete the **Count calculated control**. Close the **Report Footer** section. Increase the size of the Page Footer section to the **3-inch mark on**

the **horizontal ruler**. **Save** the report as **9E Package Sales Firstname Lastname**

15. **Start** Excel. **Open** the **a09E_Package_Sales** workbook. In the **Package Totals** worksheet, select the entire chart. **Copy** the chart to the Office Clipboard. **Exit** Excel. In the **9E Package Sales** report, **Paste** the chart in the Page Footer. **Save** the report, and then switch to **Report** view. If you are instructed to submit this result, create a paper or electronic printout. **Close** the report.

16. In the **Import group**, click the **Access** button. Locate and open the **a09E_Employees** database. Click the **Link to the data source by creating a linked table** option button, and then click **OK**. In the **Link Tables** dialog box, on the **Tables tab**, click **9E Employees**, and then click **OK**.

17. In the **Import group**, click the **Access** button. Locate and open **a09E_Employees**. Be sure that the **Import tables, queries, forms, reports, macros, and modules into the current database** option button is selected, and then click **OK**. In the **Import Objects** dialog box, click the **Queries tab**, click **9E Accessory Staff**, and then click **OK**. Click **Close**. **Rename 9E Accessory Staff** by adding your **Firstname Lastname** to the end of the query name.

18. Double-click **9E Accessory Staff**. If you are instructed to submit this result, create a paper or electronic printout. **Close** the query, and then **Exit** Access.

 End **You have completed Project 9E**

Mastering Access

Project 9F—Custom Features

In this project, you will apply the skills you practiced from the Objectives in Project 9B.

Objectives: 6. *Export Data to Word;* **7.** *Export Data to Excel;* **8.** *Export Data to an HTML File and an XML File.*

Some of the accessory sales staff of Penn Liberty Motors are not comfortable working with Access. They save their data in Word and Excel. Access enables you to export data from an Access database into these applications. You can also export data to be used on a Web page. In this project, you will export data to several types of applications. Your completed files will look similar to those shown in Figure 9.46.

For Project 9F, you will need the following file:

a09F_Custom_Features

You will save your files as
9F_Custom_Features_Firstname_Lastname.accdb
9F_Accessory_Staff_Firstname_Lastname.docx
9F_Accessory_Staff_Firstname_Lastname.rtf
9F_Luxury_Features_Firstname_Lastname.xlsx
9F_Package_Sales.html
9F_Package_Sales_XML_Firstname_Lastname.xml
9F_Package_Sales_XML_Firstname_Lastname.htm
9F_Package_Sales_XML_Firstname_Lastname.xsl

Figure 9.46

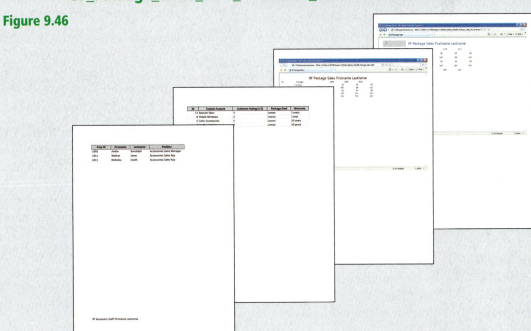

(Project 9F–Custom Features continues on the next page)

(Project 9F–Custom Features continued)

1. **Start** Access. Locate and open the **a09F_Custom_Features** file. Save the database in the **Access 2007 Database** format in your **Access Chapter 9** folder as **9F_Custom_Features_Firstname_Lastname**

2. On the **Navigation Pane**, under **Queries**, right-click **9F Accessory Staff**, point to **Export**, and then click **Word RTF File**. Navigate to the **Access Chapter 9** folder. In the **File name** box, select the existing file name, type **9F_Accessory_Staff_Firstname_Lastname** and then click **Save**.

3. Under **Specify export options**, select the **Open the destination file after the export operation is complete** check box, and then click **OK.** On the Word Ribbon, click the **Insert tab**. In the **Header & Footer group**, click the **Footer** button. In the **Built-In** gallery, click **Blank**, and then in the **Type text box**, type **9F Accessory Staff Firstname Lastname** Click the **Close Header and Footer** button. Using the default file name, save the document as a **Word Document** in the **Access Chapter 9** folder. In the displayed message box, click **OK.** If you are instructed to submit this result, create a paper or electronic print-out. **Close** the Word window. In the **Export - RTF File** dialog box, click **Close**.

4. On the **Navigation Pane**, under **Tables**, double-click **9F Custom Features** to open the table in **Datasheet** view. **Sort** the data sheet by **Package Deal** in ascending order. Select the records from the *Luxury Package Deal.* In the **Export group**, click **Excel.**

5. **Save** the file in your **Access Chapter 9** folder as **9F_Luxury_Features_Firstname_Lastname** Under **Specify export options**, select all three check boxes, and then click **OK.** At the bottom of the worksheet,

right-click the **Worksheet tab**, and then click **Rename**. Type **9F Luxury** and then press ⏎. Click in cell **B6** and type **Luxury Package Sales Rep: Firstname Lastname Save** the workbook. If you are instructed to submit this result, create a paper or electronic printout. **Close** the **Excel** work-book. In the **Access** window, **Close** the **9F Custom Features** table, but do not save the changes.

6. On the **Navigation Pane**, under **Reports**, open the **9F Package Sales** report in **Design** view. Add your **Firstname Lastname** to the end of the title. **Save** and **Close** the report. Right-click the **9F Package Sales** report, point to **Export**, and then click **HTML Document**. Navigate to the **Access Chapter 9** folder. In the file name, replace all of the spaces with underscores. Under **Specify export options**, select the **Open the destination file after the export operation is complete** check box, and then click **OK.** In the **HTML Output Options** dialog box, click **OK.** Click **OK** if you are prompted about the section width.

7. If you are instructed to submit this result, create a paper or electronic printout of the Web page. **Close** the Web browser window. In the **Export - HTML Document** dialog box, click the **Close** button.

8. On the **Navigation Pane**, under **Reports**, right-click **9F Package Sales**, point to **Export**, and then click **XML File**. Save the file in the **Access Chapter 9** folder as **9F_Package_Sales_XML_Firstname_Lastname.xml** and then click **OK.** In the **Export XML** dialog box, be sure that the **Data (XML)** check box is selected, and then select the **Presentation of your data (XSL)** check box. Click **OK.** In the **Export - XML File** dialog box, click **Close**.

(Project 9F–Custom Features continues on the next page)

Access
chapter nine

Mastering Access

(Project 9F—Custom Features continued)

9. Locate the **9F_Package_Sales_XML** file that displays a **Type** of **HTML Document** and double-click it. If you are instructed to submit this result, create a paper or electronic printout of the Web page. **Close** the Web browser window, and then **Close** the Access Chapter 9 window.

10. **Exit** Access.

 You have completed Project 9F ————————————————

Access
chapter**nine**

Mastering Access

Project 9G—Promotions

In this project, you will apply the following Objectives found in Projects 9A and 9B.

Objectives: 1. *Import Data from a Word Table;* **2.** *Use Mail Merge to Integrate Access and Word;* **3.** *Import Data from an Excel Workbook;* **8**. *Export Data to an HTML File.*

Andre Randolp, Accessories Sales Manager, and Charlie James, Auto Sales Manager, at Penn Liberty Motors have teamed up to offer special monthly promotions to encourage the customers to revisit the showroom. In this project, you will import an Excel worksheet that contains the customer list and a Word table that contains the promotion details. You will use mail merge to inform the customers about the promotions. You will export a form created from the promotions table to an HTML file so it can be viewed as a Web page. Your completed files will look similar to those shown in Figure 9.47.

For Project 9G, you will need the following files:

New blank Access database
a09G_Promotions_Letter.docx
a09G_Customers.xlsx
a09G_Monthly_Promotions.txt
a09G_Logo.jpg

You will save your files as
9G_Promotions_Firstname_Lastname.accdb
9G_Monthly_Promotions_Firstname_Lastname.html
9G_Promotions_Firstname_Lastname.docx

Figure 9.47

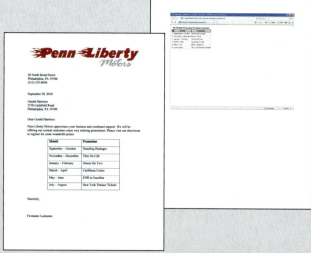

(Project 9G–Promotions continues on the next page)

(Project 9G–Promotions continued)

1. **Start** Access. **Create** a new blank database and save it in the **Access Chapter 9** folder as **9G_Promotions_Firstname_Lastname Close** the table. **Close** the database, and then reopen it.

2. Import **External Data** from the **a09G_Customers** Excel file into a new table in the **9G_Promotions** database. The **first row contains column headings**. Verify that the data type for the **ZIP** field is **text. Let Access add primary key**. Import to table **9G Customers Firstname Lastname** It is not necessary to save the import steps.

3. Select the **9G Customers** table. Merge it with the existing Microsoft Word Office **a09G_Promotions_Letter**. The recipients will be selected from the existing list in the **9G Customers** table. Write your letter by inserting the following fields from the table as displayed. Place your insertion point at the beginning of the second blank line after the current date. Add the **Address Block**.

4. Insert the **First Name** and **Last Name** fields after the space in the salutation line. Place a space between these fields. In the closing of the letter, replace Firstname Lastname with your **Firstname Lastname**

5. **Preview your letters** and **Complete the merge. Save** the Word document in your **Access Chapter 9** folder as **9G_Promotions_Letter_Firstname_Lastname** Unless you are required to submit your files electronically, **Print** the **fifth record** only. **Close** the Word window, and then **Exit Word.**

6. **Import External Data** from the Text file **a09G_Monthly_Promotions**. Import the source data into a new table in the current database. Use the **tab delimiter**. The **first row contains field names**. The data types are correct. **Let Access add primary key**. Import this text to **9G Monthly Promotions Firstname Lastname** Do not save Import Steps.

7. From the **9G Monthly Promotions** table, **Create** a form. Add the **a09G_Logo** to the form header. In the **Title** of the form, move your Firstname Lastname to a second line. Move the left edge of the **title control** to the **2-inch mark on the horizontal ruler**. Drag the right edge of the **title control** to the **5-inch mark on the horizontal ruler**. Drag the right edge of the **logo control** to the **1.75-inch mark on the horizontal ruler. Save** the form as **9G Monthly Promotions Firstname Lastname** and then **Close** the form.

8. On the **Navigation Pane**, right-click the **9G Monthly Promotions** form. **Export** the form as an **HTML document**. **Save** the document in your **Access Chapter 9** folder as **9G_Monthly_Promotions_Firstname_Lastname** Open the destination file after the export operation is complete. In the **HTML Output Options** dialog box, click **OK.**

9. If you are instructed to submit this result, create a paper or electronic printout of the Web page. **Close** the Web browser window. In the **Export - HTML Document** dialog box, click the **Close** button.

10. **Exit** Access.

End You have completed Project 9G

Access

Mastering Access

Project 9H—Service

In this project, you will apply the following Objectives found in Projects 9A and 9B.

Objectives: 4. *Insert an Excel Chart into a Report;* **5.** *Import from and Link to Another Access Database;* **6.** *Export Data to Word;* **7.** *Export Data to Excel.*

Kevin Rau, President of Penn Liberty Motors, is very interested in customer satisfaction. Surveys to indicate level of satisfaction are taken at various steps in the process of purchasing a vehicle. In this project, you will import an Excel chart that illustrates the level of customer satisfaction into an Access report. You will import from and link to a table in the customer database. You will export the data from the surveys to a Word document and an Excel worksheet. Your completed files will look similar to those shown in Figure 9.48.

For Project 9H, you will need the following files:

a09H_Service.accdb
a09H_Survey.xlsx
a09H_Penn_Liberty_Motors.accdb

You will save your files as
9H_Service_Firstname_Lastname.accdb
9H_Survey_Results_ Firstname_Lastname.rtf
9H_Survey_Firstname_Lastname.xlsx

Figure 9.48

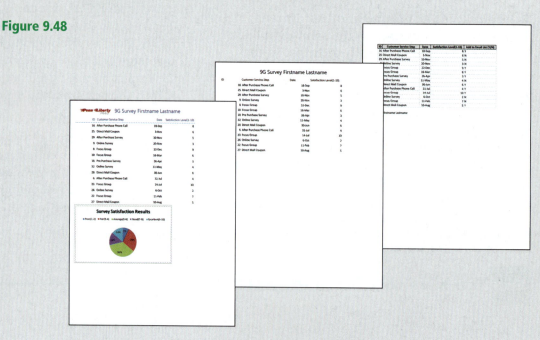

(Project 9H–Service continues on the next page)

Content-Based Assessments

Mastering Access

(Project 9H–Service continued)

1. **Start** Access. Locate and open the **a09H_Service** file. Save the database in the **Access 2007 Database** format in your **Access Chapter 9** folder as **9H_Service_Firstname_Lastname**

2. **Rename** the objects by adding your **Firstname Lastname** to the end of each object name.

3. **Create** a **linked 9H Customers** table from the **a09H_Penn_Liberty_Motors** database.

4. Open Microsoft Excel and open the **a09H_Survey** workbook. Click the **Chart tab**, right-click anywhere in the pie chart area, and then click **Copy**. **Close** the workbook and **Close** Excel.

5. In the **9H_Service** database, open the **9H Survey Results** report in **Design** view. **Paste** the chart in the Report Footer area. Add your **Firstname Lastname** to the end of the report title. **Save** the report. Unless you are required to submit your database electronically, **Print** the report, adjusting the report width as needed to print one page. **Close** the report.

6. Right-click the **9H Survey Results** report. Point to **Export**, and then click **Word RTF File**. Navigate to your **Access Chapter 9**

folder, and **Save** the exported file as **9H_Survey_Results_Firstname_Lastname.rtf Open the destination file after the export operation is complete**. Notice that the chart does not export to an RTF file. If you are instructed to submit this result, create a paper or electronic printout. **Close** the document, and then **Exit** Word. Do not save the export steps.

7. Right-click the **9H Survey** table. Point to **Export**, and then click **Excel**. Save the table with formatting and layout in your **Access Chapter 9** folder as **9H_Survey_Firstname_Lastname.xlsx Open the destination file after the export operation is complete**. Click in cell **B17** and type your **Firstname Lastname** Press Ctrl + A to select all of the worksheet. Point to the line between column A and column B until the ⟷ pointer displays, and then double-click to display all column headings and data.

8. **Save** the worksheet. Unless you are required to submit your files electronically, **Print** the worksheet. **Exit** Excel, and do not save the export steps.

9. **Exit** Access.

End **You have completed Project 9H** —————————

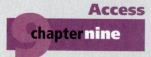

Mastering Access

Project 9I — Sponsored Events

In this project, you will apply all the skills you practiced from the Objectives in Projects 9A and 9B.

Penn Liberty Motors of Philadelphia, Pennsylvania prides itself on its service to the community. The employees organize and host several charitable and community activities. In this project, you will import data from a Word document and an Excel worksheet. You will use the mail merge option to integrate Word and Access. You will insert an Excel chart into an Access report and link this database to another Access database. You will then export data back to Word, Excel, and an HTML file. Your complete files will look similar to those shown in Figure 9.49.

For Project 9I, you will need the following files:

a09I_Sponsored_Events

a09I_Event_Chart.xlsx

a09I_5K_Event.docx

a09I_10K_Event.xlsx

a09I_Annual_Run.docx

a09I_Penn_Liberty_Motors.accdb

You will save your files as

9I_Sponsored_Events_Firstname_Lastname.accdb
9I_Annual_Run_Firstname_Lastname.docx
9I_5K_Event_Firstname_Lastname.txt
9I_Sponsors_Firstname_Lastname.html
9I_Employees_Firstname_Lastname.rtf
9I_5K_Event_Firstname_Lastname.xlsx

Figure 9.49

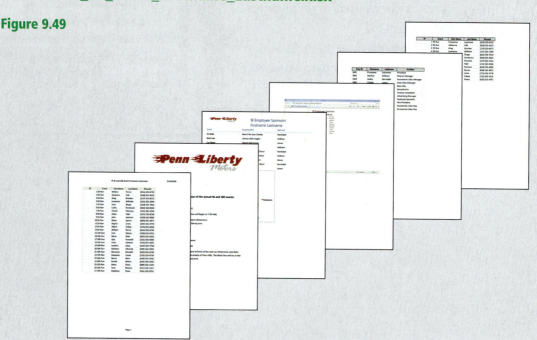

(Project 9I–Sponsored Events continues on the next page)

Mastering Access

(Project 9I–Sponsored Events continued)

1. Start Access. Locate and open the **a09I_Sponsored_Events** file. Save the database in the **Access 2007 Database** format in your **Access Chapter 9** folder as **9I_Sponsored_Events_Firstname_Lastname Rename** the **9I Events** table and **9I Sponsors** report by adding your **Firstname Lastname** to the end of the object name.

2. Start Word. Locate and open the **a09I_5K_Event** file. Convert the displayed table to text. **Save** this converted text file in your **Access Chapter 9** folder in **Plain Text** format as **9I_5K_Event_Firstname_Lastname** and then **Exit** Word.

3. Locate and **Import** the text file **9I_5K_Event** as a new table into the **9I_Sponsored_Events** database. Note that tabs are used as the delimiter character and that the first row of the table contains field names. Verify the data types as text and **Let Access add primary key**. Name the table **9I 5K and 10K Event Firstname Lastname** Do not save the import steps. Open the table and **delete** the blank **record 14** from the table. **Close** the table.

4. Locate the **a09I_10K_Event** workbook and **Append** a copy of the records to the **9I 5K and 10K Event** table. Do not save the import steps. Open the table to view the data. Unless you are required to submit your work electronically, **Print** the table. **Close** the table.

5. Locate and **Import** from the **a09I_Penn_Liberty_Motors** database the **9I Employees** table. **Create** a **linked** table using the **9I Customers** table.

6. Select the **9I Customers** table. **Merge** this table with the **a09I_Annual_Run** Word

document. Be certain that the insertion point is at the beginning of the first blank line. Click **Address block**. In the **Insert Address Block** dialog box, click **OK**. Scroll to the end of the document and replace **Firstname Lastname** with your first and last names. Complete the merge. Click **Save As** and save your document as **9I_Annual_Run_Firstname_Lastname** If you are instructed to submit this result, create a paper or electronic printout of the first record only. **Exit** Word.

7. Locate and open the **a09I_Event_Chart** workbook. On the **Event Chart** worksheet, **Copy** the chart, and then **Close** the workbook. Open the **9I Sponsors** report in **Design** view. To the title of the report, on a second line, add your **Firstname Lastname Paste** the chart in the Report Footer area. **Save** the report. If you are instructed to submit this result, create a paper or electronic printout. **Close** the report.

8. On the **Navigation Pane**, right-click the **9I Sponsors** report. Point to **Export**, and then click **HTML Document**. **Save** the file in your **Access Chapter 9** folder as **9I_Sponsors_Firstname_Lastname.html** If you are instructed to submit this result, create a paper or electronic printout of the Web page.

9. Select the **9I Employees** table. **Export** the table to a **Word RTF** file in your **Access Chapter 9** folder as **9I_Employees_Firstname_Lastname** Open the file. Replace **Emp ID 1001**—Kevin Rau—with your **Firstname Lastname** You now have the Position of President. **Save** the file. If you are instructed to submit this result, create

(Project 9I–Sponsored Events continues on the next page)

Content-Based Assessments

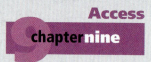
(Project 9I–Sponsored Events continued)

a paper or electronic printout. **Exit** Word. Do not save the export steps.

10. Open the **9I 5K and 10K Event** table. Select **records 1 through 13**—5K Run. **Export** these records to an Excel workbook in your **Access Chapter 9** folder. Name the Excel file to which you are exporting **9I_5K_Event_Firstname_Lastname** Select all three export option check boxes. In **cell C2**, type your **Firstname** and in **cell D2** type your **Lastname** If you are instructed to submit this result, create a paper or electronic printout of the worksheet. **Close** and **Save** the workbook, and then **Exit** Excel.

11. **Close** the table, **Close** the database, and **Exit** Access.

End **You have completed Project 9I**

Content-Based Assessments

 Business Running Case

Project 9J — Business Running Case

In this project, you will apply the skills you have practiced from the Objectives in Projects 9A and 9B.

From My Computer, navigate to the student files that accompany this textbook. In the folder **02_theres_more_you_can_do**, locate and open the folder for this chapter. Open and print the instructions for this project, which are provided to you in Adobe PDF format. Follow the instructions and use the knowledge and skills you have gained thus far to assist the brother and sister team of Michael and Kristen Landry in meeting the challenges of owning and running their business.

End **You have completed Project 9J** ⎯⎯⎯⎯⎯⎯⎯⎯⎯⎯

Outcomes-Based Assessments

Access

chapternine

Rubric

The following outcomes-based assessments are *open-ended assessments*. That is, there is no specific correct result; your result will depend on your approach to the information provided. Make *professional quality* your goal. Use the following scoring rubric to guide you in *how* to approach the problem and then to evaluate *how well* your approach solves the problem.

The *criteria*—Software Mastery, Content, Format and Layout, and Process—represent the knowledge and skills you have gained that you can apply to solving the problem. The *levels of performance*—Professional Quality, Approaching Professional Quality, or Needs Quality Improvement—help you and your instructor evaluate your result.

	Your completed project is of Professional Quality if you:	Your completed project is Approaching Professional Quality if you:	Your completed project Needs Quality Improvements if you:
1-Software Mastery	Choose and apply the most appropriate skills, tools, and features and identify efficient methods to solve the problem.	Choose and apply some appropriate skills, tools, and features, but not in the most efficient manner.	Choose inappropriate skills, tools, or features, or are inefficient in solving the problem.
2-Content	Construct a solution that is clear and well organized, contains content that is accurate, appropriate to the audience and purpose, and is complete. Provide a solution that contains no errors of spelling, grammar, or style.	Construct a solution in which some components are unclear, poorly organized, inconsistent, or incomplete. Misjudge the needs of the audience. Have some errors in spelling, grammar, or style, but the errors do not detract from comprehension.	Construct a solution that is unclear, incomplete, or poorly organized, containing some inaccurate or inappropriate content; and contains many errors of spelling, grammar, or style. Do not solve the problem.
3-Format and Layout	Format and arrange all elements to communicate information and ideas, clarify function, illustrate relationships, and indicate relative importance.	Apply appropriate format and layout features to some elements, but not others. Overuse features, causing minor distraction.	Apply format and layout that does not communicate information or ideas clearly. Do not use format and layout features to clarify function, illustrate relationships, or indicate relative importance. Use available features excessively, causing distraction.
4-Process	Use an organized approach that integrates planning, development, self-assessment, revision, and reflection.	Demonstrate an organized approach in some areas, but not others; or, use an insufficient process of organization throughout.	Do not use an organized approach to solve the problem.

Problem Solving

Project 9K — Sales Data

In this project, you will construct a solution by applying any combination of the skills you practiced from the Objectives in Projects 9A and 9B.

> **For Project 9K, you will need the following files:**
>
> New blank Access database
> a09K_Sales_Data.xlsx
> a09K_Congratulations.docx
> a09K_Logo.jpg

You will save your files as
9K_Sales_Data_Firstname_Lastname.accdb
9K_Congratulations_Firstname_Lastname.docx

Charlie James, auto sales manager for Penn Liberty Motors, prefers to use Microsoft Excel as a tool for calculating the sales and commissions for his staff. However, because the president of the company would prefer to have all of the data in one database, he has asked for your help to import the files. Create a new, blank Access database. Save it as **9K_Sales_Data_Firstname_Lastname** From the **a09K_Sales_Data** workbook, import the Excel worksheet **9K Qtr Sales** as a table into your blank database. Do not import the field(skip) Total. Name the table **9K Qtr Sales Firstname Lastname** Delete the blank and Total rows from the table. Create a report from the *9K Qtr Sales* table. Add the **a09K_Logo**. Insert the **9K Qtr Sales** worksheet chart into the report footer. Unless you are required to submit your work electronically, print the report.

Import a second worksheet **9K Qtr Commissions** as a table into your database. Name this table **9K Qtr Commissions Firstname Lastname** Use this table to merge with the Word document **a09K_Congratulations**. Insert the Salesperson field after the word *Salesperson*. Insert the **1st Qtr** sales field at the end of the next line after *Your 1st Qtr Sales for 2009 were*. Replace Firstname Lastname with your name. Save the congratulations letters as **9K_Congratulations_Firstname_Lastname** If you are instructed to submit this result, create a paper or electronic printout of Mr. Hartigan's letter of congratulations.

End **You have completed Project 9K**

Problem Solving

Project 9L — Advertisements

In this project, you will construct a solution by applying any combination of the skills you practiced from the Objectives in Projects 9A and 9B.

For Project 9L, you will need the following file:

a09L_Advertisements.accdb

You will save your files as
9L_Advertisements_Firstname_Lastname.accdb
9L_Advertisements_Workbook_Firstname_Lastname.xlsx
9L_Cost_Analysis_Firstname_Lastname.html

Kevin Rau, President of Penn Liberty Motors, explores many different venues to advertise his business. Most of the data for the advertisements is kept in a database. Some of his employees would like to see the data arranged in a worksheet to create a what-if analysis. In this project, you will export the data from the database tables into an Excel worksheet. Open the **a09L_Advertisements** database, and then save it as **9L_Advertisements_Firstname_Lastname** Export the *9L Advertisements* table to an Excel workbook. Save the workbook as **9L_Advertisements_Workbook_Firstname_Lastname** Rename the sheet tab **Data** Export the 9L Cost Analysis Query to a second sheet in the same workbook. Rename this sheet **Analysis** Type your Firstname Lastname in an empty cell in each of the sheets. Unless you are required to submit your files electronically, **Print** both worksheets.

Add your **Firstname Lastname** to the end of the 9L Cost Analysis Summary 1 query. Export this query to an HTML file. Save the file as **9L_Cost_Analysis_Firstname_Lastname.html** Unless you are required to submit your files electronically, **Print** the Web page.

 End **You have completed Project 9L** ————————

Problem Solving

Project 9M — Recognition

In this project, you will construct a solution by applying any combination of the skills you practiced from the Objectives in Projects 9A and 9B.

For Project 9M, you will need the following files:

a09M_Recognition.accdb
a09M_Birthday_List.docx
a09M_Birthday_Card.docx

You will save your files as
9M_Recognition_Firstname_Lastname.accdb
9M_Birthday_List_Firstname_Lastname.txt
9M_My_Card_Firstname_Lastname.docx

Penn Liberty Motors is a friendly workplace, and the employees treat each other as family. The management staff wants all employees to feel special and appreciated. You have been asked to help with an employee recognition project. Some records are in a Word file, and other records are kept in a database. You will import the data from the Word table into a database table and then merge this table with certificates created in Word.

Open **a09M_Recognition** and save it as **9M_Recognition_Firstname_Lastname** Open the **a09M_Birthday_List.docx**, and then convert the table to text. Save this text file as **9M_Birthday_List_Firstname_Lastname** Import this text file into your Access database, saving it as table named **9M Birthday List Firstname Lastname** Open this file and add your name and birthday to the data. Merge this table with the **a09M_Birthday_Card** file. Adjust the spacing as necessary. Locate your card and save it as **9M_My_Card_Firstname_Lastname** If you are instructed to submit this result, create a paper or electronic printout of your birthday card.

End **You have completed Project 9M** ———————————

Access

chapternine

Problem Solving

Project 9N — Service Records

In this project, you will construct a solution by applying any combination of the skills you practiced from the Objectives in Projects 9A and 9B.

For Project 9N, you will need the following files:

New blank Access database
a09N_Service_Records.docx
a09N_Logo.jpg

**You will save your database as
9N_Service_Records_Firstname_Lastname.accdb**

Penn Liberty Motors takes great pride in its service department. The community knows that the mechanics employed by Penn Liberty Motors are the best in the area. It is important that accurate service records are maintained in a database. Many of the mechanics are more comfortable completing the service forms and reports in a Word table. You have been asked to import this information into an Access table, and then create a report to be used to display the activities of the service department.

Create a new database and save it as **9N_Service_Records_Firstname_ Lastname** Convert the table in the **a09N_Service_Records** document to a text file. Save this file as **9N_Service_Records.txt** Import this text file and save the table as **9N Records Firstname Lastname** Create a report from this table. Add the **a09N_Logo** to the report. Unless you are required to submit your database electronically, **Print** the report.

End **You have completed Project 9N** ————————

Problem Solving

Project 9O — Financing

In this project, you will construct a solution by applying any combination of the skills you practiced from the Objectives in Projects 9A and 9B.

For Project 9O, you will need the following files:

New blank Access database
a09O_Financing.xlsx
a09O_Logo.jpg

You will save your files as
9O_Financing_Firstname_Lastname.accdb
9O_Options_Firstname_Lastname.html

Customers at Penn Liberty Motors are offered a variety of financing options. In this project, you will assist the finance manager, Marilyn Kellman, by exporting the financial options from an Excel workbook into an Access database. You will create a report from the data and insert a chart displaying the financing.

Create a new database in your **Access Chapter 9** folder and name it **9O_Financing_Firstname_Lastname** Import the *9O Options* and *9O Depreciation* worksheets from the **a09O_Financing** workbook. Save the worksheets in two different tables. Name the tables to match the names of the worksheets. Add your **Firstname Lastname** to the end of each table name.

Create a report from the **9O Depreciation** table. Insert the chart from the 9O Depreciation Chart sheet in the a09O_Financing Excel workbook into the report footer. Save the report in your **Access Chapter 9** folder as **9O Vehicle Depreciation Firstname Lastname** If you are instructed to submit this result, create a paper or electronic printout.

Export the **9O Options** table as a Web page. Save this file in your **Access Chapter 9** folder as **9O_Options_Firstname_Lastname.htm** If you are instructed to submit this result, create a paper or electronic printout.

End You have completed Project 9O —————————

Access

chapter**nine**

 You and *GO!*

Project 9P—You and *GO!*

In this project, you will construct a solution by applying any combination of the Objectives found in Projects 9A and 9B.

From My Computer, navigate to the student files that accompany this textbook. In the folder **04_you_and_go**, locate and open the folder for this chapter. Open and print the instructions for this project, which are provided to you in Adobe PDF format. Follow the instructions to import and export files for your personal inventory.

End **You have completed Project 9P** _____

GO! with Help

Project 9Q—*GO!* with Help

The Access Help system is extensive and can help you as you work. In this project, you will view information about fixing a macro by stepping through it.

1 Start **Access**. On the right side of the Ribbon, click the **Microsoft Office Access Help** button. In the **Type words to search for** box, on the **Access Help** window, type **export** and then press Enter.

2 In the displayed search results, click **Export data to a text file**. Maximize the displayed window. Read the section.

3 If you want to, print a copy of the information. Select the text, and then click the **Print** button at the top of **Access Help** window. Under **Page Range**, select **Selection**, and then click **Print**.

4 **Close** the Help window, and then **Exit** Access.

End **You have completed Project 9Q** _____

10 chapterten

Administering Databases

OBJECTIVES

At the end of this chapter you will be able to:

OUTCOMES

Mastering these objectives will enable you to:

1. Compact and Repair a Database
2. Back Up a Database
3. Use the Database Splitter
4. Convert Databases to Other Versions
5. Replicate and Synchronize a Database

PROJECT 10A
Manage Access Files

6. Use Microsoft Access Analysis Tools
7. Add Smart Tags
8. Modify Access Views and Behaviors

PROJECT 10B
Improve Performance and Customize Access

Image Medtech

Located in the northern part of the greater New York metropolitan area, Image Medtech develops, manufactures, and distributes medical imaging equipment for the diagnosis and research of conditions and diseases. The equipment records images, processes and stores these images, and provides a means for printing and distributing them electronically. The company is a leader in state-of-the-art noninvasive diagnostic methods such as measurement of body temperature and blood flow. The company's products are used in a variety of healthcare environments, including hospitals, doctors' and dentists' offices, imaging centers, and pharmaceutical companies.

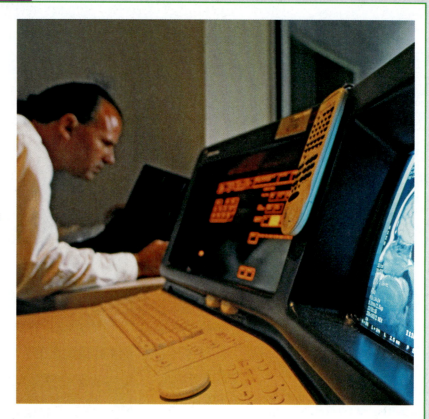

Administering Databases

After a database is created, a database administrator works to keep the database useful and efficient. Throughout the life of a typical organization's database, tables are added; design changes are made to queries, forms, and reports; and data is constantly added. Eventually, database performance can degrade. Fortunately, Access provides several tools to keep databases healthy. Analysis tools enable the administrator to identify potential problems and then fix them. File management tools rebuild databases into smaller, more efficient files. Often, database tables are moved to a separate, faster server, and then custom databases are designed for different work groups and individuals. Understanding how to maintain a database is critical to the success of the individuals who rely on its data.

Project 10A Customers

In Activities 10.1 through 10.8 you will use several tools in Access to manage database files. A file structure can be optimized, the file can be backed up, or the database can be split into two separate files. Access 2007 supports many different file formats, and you may need to convert from one file format to another. Access also provides a tool that enables users to work with portable copies of the database that keep in synch with each other. Image Medtech needs you to administer their databases by applying several of these file management tools. As you work, you will create screen shots. Your finished screen shot document will look similar to Figure 10.1.

For Project 10, you will need the following files:

a10A_Customers
a10A_Customers_97

**You will save your files as 10A_ACCDE_Firstname_Lastname
10A_Customers_2003_Firstname_Lastname
10A_Customers_2007_Firstname_Lastname
10A_Customers_Firstname_Lastname
10A_Customers_Firstname_Lastname_2009-02-02 (Your date
   will differ)
10A_Customers_Firstname_Lastname_be
10A_Replica_Firstname_Lastname
10A_Screens_Firstname_Lastname**

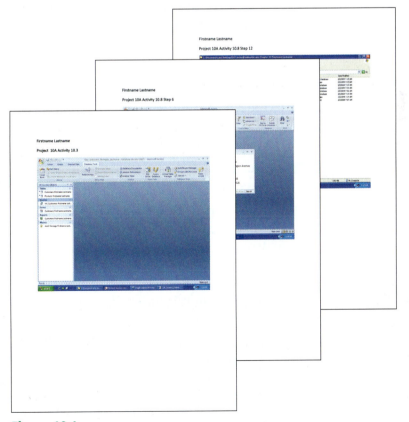

Figure 10.1
Project 10A—Customers

Objective 1
Compact and Repair a Database

Database files should be routinely rebuilt to ensure optimal performance. When working with a database, file sizes increase rapidly, especially as forms, queries, or reports are modified or deleted. Unlike most application files, when objects or records are deleted, the database file size does not decrease. Access provides a tool that rewrites database files so that the data and objects are stored more efficiently.

Activity 10.1 Compacting and Repairing a Database

Compact and Repair is a process where an Access file is rewritten to store the objects and data in more efficiently. Image Medtech has a database that has just gone through a development process. New forms, queries, and reports were created, and several old objects need to be removed from the database. In this project, you will delete the old objects, and then use the Compact and Repair tool to rebuild the Image Medtech database file.

1 **Start Access**. Navigate to the location where the student data files for this textbook are saved. Locate and then open the

a10A_Customers file. Click the **Office** button 🖼, point to **Save As**, and then click **Access 2007 Database**. In the **Save As** dialog box, navigate to the drive on which you will be saving your folders and projects for this chapter. Create a new folder named **Access Chapter 10** and save the file as **10A_Customers_Firstname_Lastname** in the folder.

2 If necessary, enable the content or add the Access Chapter 10 folder to the Trust Center.

3 In the **Navigation Pane**, under **Queries**, click **Products Query**, and then press Delete. In the displayed message, click **Yes**. Using the technique just practiced, delete the **Products** form and **Products** report.

4 At the end of each remaining database object name, add your first and last names.

5 Using either the **Start** menu or the **Desktop**, open **My Computer**. In the displayed **My Computer** window, open your **Access Chapter 10** folder.

Alert!

Viewing files in Windows Vista

Throughout this chapter, you will need to view files using Windows Explorer. If your computer is running Windows Vista, to view the files, click the Start menu 🟦, and then click Computer. In the Computer folder window, open your Access Chapter 10 folder. If necessary, in the Access Chapter 10 folder window toolbar, click the Views arrow, and then click Details. As you work with the chapter, keep in mind that any references to *My Computer* should be replaced with *Computer folder window* in Windows Vista.

6 If necessary, from the View menu, click Details. **Maximize** 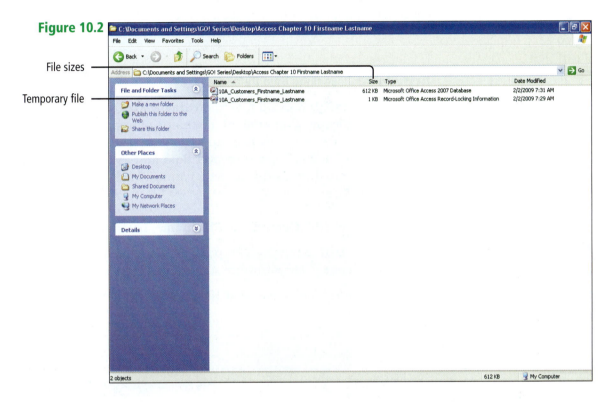 the **My Computer** window, and then compare your screen with Figure 10.2.

Access database file sizes are commonly measured using bytes. The file size for the database is about 600 MB. **MB** is the abbreviation for megabyte. A single **megabyte** stores 1,048,576 bytes. A **byte** typically stores a single character, such as a digit or letter, and is used to measure storage sizes on disks or in computer memory. The other file is a temporary file that Access creates whenever a database file is open. Access deletes this temporary file when the database is closed.

Figure 10.2

File sizes

Temporary file

7 Leave My Computer open and switch to the **Access** window. Click the **Office** button, point to **Manage**, and then click **Compact and Repair Database**.

8 Switch to the **My Computer** window, and then observe the smaller file size.

9 Leave the My Computer window and the Access window open for the next activity.

More Knowledge

Repairing an Access File

Compact and Repair is also used to repair files with certain problems such as a corrupt form or report. To repair a database using Compact and Repair, start Access, but do not open the corrupted database. Start the Compact and Repair tool. In the displayed Database to Compact From dialog box, navigate to the corrupt file, select it, and then click Compact. In the Compact Database Into dialog box, type a new name for the database, and then click *Save*. Access creates a copy of the original database and in the copy, corrects as many errors as it can.

Objective 2
Back Up a Database

Organizations often invest important resources to prevent the loss of their data. **Data loss** is the unexpected loss of data caused by such actions as hardware failure, accidental deletion of records, theft, or natural disaster. When data is lost, it is usually recovered using a copy of the database. **Back up** refers to the process of creating a copy of a file or files. Organizations typically back up their databases at least once a day, and before making design changes or performing maintenance tasks. The collection of backup copies is used to recover data and provide a useful historical record of the organization's transactions.

Activity 10.2 Backing Up a Database

Microsoft Access provides a tool to create backup copies of its databases. A **backup** is a copy of an original file that is stored in an alternative location. Medtech needs a daily backup of its database. The company will use its set of daily backups to recover data and as a historical record of its business activities. In this activity you will back up the Image Medtech database.

1 Display the **10A_Customers_Firstname_Lastname** database window.

2 Click the **Office** button 🔵, point to **Manage**, and then click **Back Up Database**. Compare your screen with Figure 10.3.

The current date is placed at the end of the file name.

Figure 10.3

Current date appended to file name—yours will differ

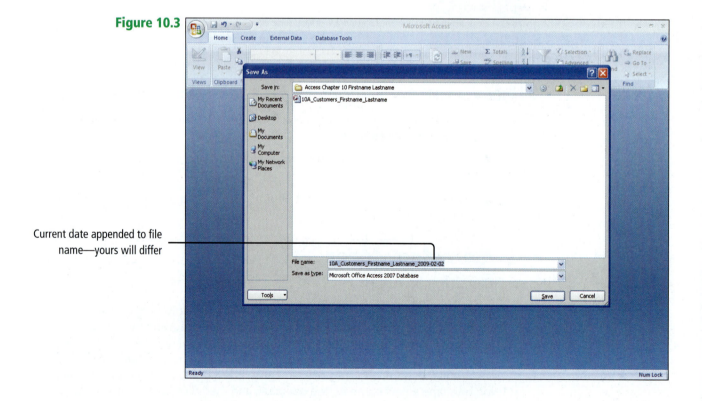

3 In the displayed **Save As** dialog box, click the **Save** button.

4 Switch to the **My Computer** window. Point to the line to the right of the **Name** column header. With the ⊕ pointer, double-click so that the entire file name for the backup displays.

5 Point to the line to the right of the **Type** column header. With the ⊕ pointer, double-click so that all of the text in the Type column displays.

6 Compare your screen with Figure 10.4. Be sure that the text in the Name, Size, Type, and Date Modified columns is not truncated.

If you are using Windows Vista, the order of your columns may be different.

Figure 10.4

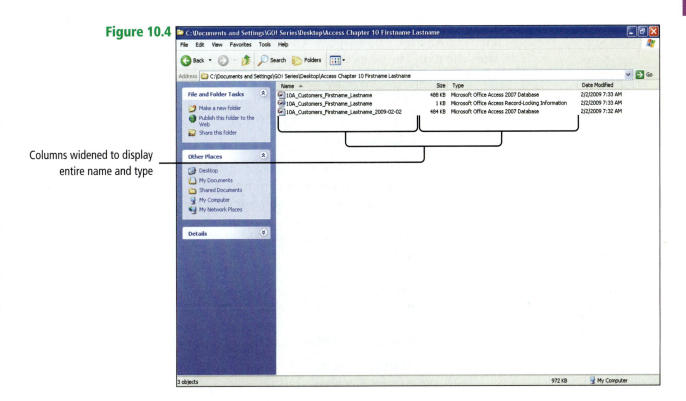

Columns widened to display entire name and type

7 Leave My Computer and the Access database open for the next activity.

Note — Back Up to an Alternative Location

In a business application, storing backup copies on the same computer is not recommended. If a data loss event happens, the backup copy would probably be lost along with the original. Many organizations store their backup copies on removable media such as magnetic tapes and optical discs, and then store the media in a location that is safe from theft or natural disaster. Many organizations store their backup copies on a separate hard drive located in another building.

Objective 3
Use the Database Splitter

Business databases are often divided into two parts—a back-end and a front-end. The **back-end** consists of the database tables and their data. The back-end is typically placed on a server and is not directly seen by the end-user. In Access, the **front-end** comprises the database forms, queries, reports, and macros. The end-users open the front-end to work with the data stored in the back-end tables. Dividing the database enables the database administrator to design multiple front-ends while maintaining a single source of data.

Activity 10.3 Splitting a Database

A **split database** is an Access database that is split into two files—one containing the back-end, and one containing the front-end. Several departments at Image Medtech need their own forms, reports, and queries. Instead of trying to coordinate separate databases, the company would like to place all of the database tables on a network server. Each department will then have its own custom front-end that links to the tables in the back-end file. In this activity, you will use the Split Database tool to create two separate files—one for the back-end, and one for the front-end.

1 Switch to the **10A_Customers_Firstname_Lastname Access** window.

2 Click the **Database Tools tab**, and then in the **Move Data group**, click the **Access Database** button.

3 In the displayed **Database Splitter** dialog box, read the message, and then click the **Split Database** button.

4 In the **Create Back-end Database** dialog box, be sure your **Access Chapter 10** folder is open. Notice the suggested file name, and then click the **Split** button. Read the displayed message, click **OK**, and then compare your screen with Figure 10.5.

In the Navigation Pane, the two tables display the linked table icon and the other objects display as before. Recall that a linked table is a table that resides in a separate database file.

Figure 10.5

Linked tables

5 Press PrtScr. **Start Word** to create a new, blank document. In the **Word** document, type your first and last names, and then press Enter. Type **Project 10A Activity 10.3** press Enter, and then **Paste** the screenshot. **Save** the file in your **Access Chapter 10** folder as **10A_Screens_ Firstname_Lastname**

6 Switch to the **Access** window, and then **Exit** ☒ Access. Switch to the **My Computer** window. Double-click **10A_Customers_ Firstname_Lastname_be**. Click the **Navigation Pane arrow**, click **Object Type**, and then compare your screen with Figure 10.6.

The two linked tables reside in this back-end database file. Typically, the file containing the back-end would reside on a network server that all departments can access. Notice that none of the front-end objects in the Customers database were copied to this back-end file.

Figure 10.6

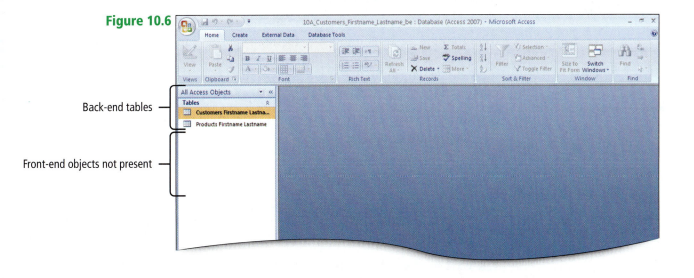

Back-end tables

Front-end objects not present

7 Leave the Word and My Computer windows open for the next activity.

More Knowledge

Moving the Back-End to a Microsoft SQL Server

Instead of moving the back-end into a separate Access database file, it can be placed on a Microsoft SQL Server. *Microsoft SQL Server* is a database application designed for high-end business uses. If a database contains thousands of records, or if it will be accessed by multiple users at the same time, moving the back-end files to a Microsoft SQL Server will dramatically improve performance. To move the tables to a Microsoft SQL server, in the Move Data group, click the SQL Server button. To move the back-end to a Microsoft SQL Server, Microsoft SQL Server must be installed and running on a networked computer. A username and password will be required before the tables can be moved. Once moved, the front-end can be created using Access. In this manner, Access links to the tables located on the Microsoft SQL Server.

Objective 4
Convert Databases to Other Versions

Microsoft Access 2007 supports databases that are saved in several different formats. Database files versions prior to Access 2003 must be converted to the new Access 2007 file format before they can be opened. The Access 2007 file format, however, does not support all of the features found in the older Access 2002 - 2003 file format. If those features are needed, the database will need to be converted from the Access 2007 file format to the Access 2002 - 2003 file format. When working with an Access 2002 - 2003 file, Microsoft Access 2007 opens the file directly and adds the features supported by the older file format to the Ribbon.

Activity 10.4 Creating a Secure ACCDE File

An *ACCDE file* is an Access 2007 file format that prevents individuals from making design changes to forms, reports, and macros. Image Medtech wants to provide a locked-down version of its database so that individuals cannot make any design changes. In this activity, you will create and test an ACCDE file.

1 **Start** Access, and then **Open** the **10A_Customers_Firstname_ Lastname** database.

2 Click the **Database Tools tab**. In the **Database Tools group**, click the **Make ACCDE** button.

3 In the **File name** box, change the file name to **10A_ACCDE_Firstname_ Lastname** Be sure that the path for your **Access Chapter 10** folder displays, and then click **Save**.

4 **Exit** Access. Switch to the **My Computer** window, and then compare your screen with Figure 10.7.

The Type description for the ACCDE file is Microsoft Access ACCDE Database. A padlock is added to the icon to indicate the file's "locked-down" status.

Figure 10.7

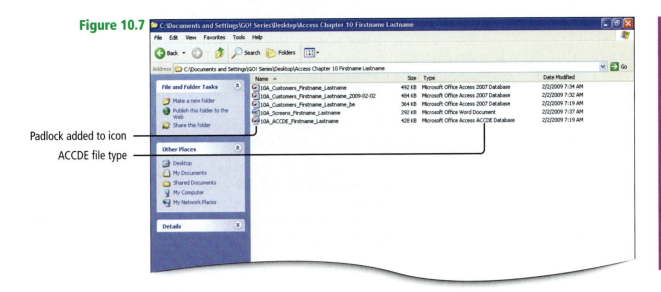

Padlock added to icon

ACCDE file type

5 In **My Computer**, double-click **10A_ACCDE_Firstname_Lastname**. If the Microsoft Office Access Security Notice displays, click Open.

6 Click the **Create tab**, and then compare your screen with Figure 10.8.

The forms and reports creation tools are dimmed, indicating that new forms and reports cannot be created.

Figure 10.8

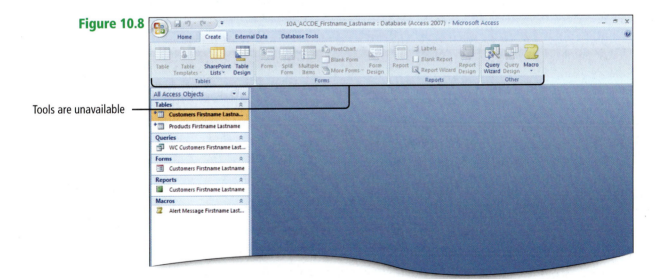

Tools are unavailable

7 In the **Navigation Pane**, under **Forms**, right-click **Customers**, and notice that the Design View command is dimmed. Design changes cannot be made in an ACCDE file.

8 Click the **Office** button , and then click **Close Database**. Leave Access, Word, and My Computer open for the next activity.

Activity 10.5 Converting an Access 97 Database

Image Medtech has several customer records stored in a database that was created with Microsoft Office Access 97. The company no longer has this version of Access, and it needs to work with the database using Access 2007. In this activity, you will convert the Access 97 file into the Access 2007 file format.

1 In Access, click the **Office** button 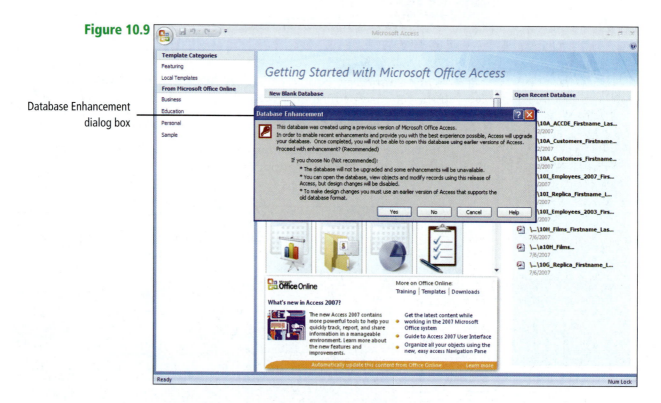, and then click **Open**. Navigate to the location where the student data files for this textbook are saved. Locate the **a10A_Customers_97** file, click it, and then click **Open**. Compare your screen with Figure 10.9.

In the Database Enhancement dialog box, if the No button is clicked, Access 2007 will open the Access 97 file; however, design changes are not supported. Other features will also be disabled. If the Yes button is clicked, the database will be converted to the Access 2007 file format.

Figure 10.9

Database Enhancement dialog box

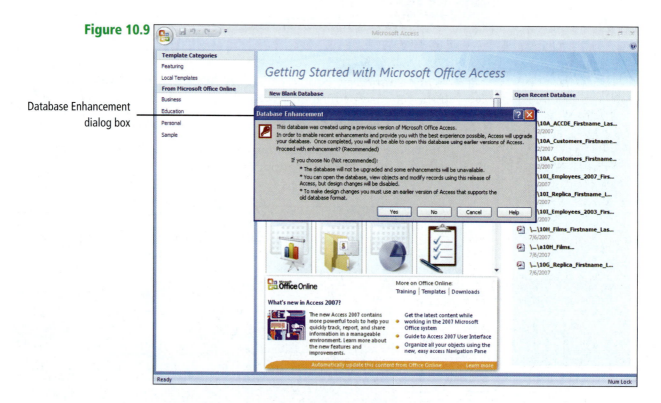

2 In the displayed **Database Enhancement** dialog box, read the message, and then click the **Yes** button.

3 In the displayed **Save As** dialog box, navigate to your **Access Chapter 10** folder. In the **File name** box, type **10A_Customers_2007_Firstname_Lastname**

4 In the **Save as type** box, be sure that Microsoft Office Access 2007 Database displays, and then click **Save**.

5 Read the displayed message, and then click **OK**. Read the second displayed message, and then click **OK**.

6 Click the **Navigation Pane arrow**, and then click **All Access Objects**.

7 In the **Navigation Pane**, under **Tables**, double-click **Conversion Errors**.

8 Increase the width of the **Error Description column** so that it fills the empty space given in the table window.

9 Increase the height of the rows so that all of the text in the **Error Description** field displays. Compare your screen with Figure 10.10.

The table displays as an overlapping window instead of a tabbed document. Later in this chapter, you will practice changing the window back to a tabbed document.

The error description was produced because the Access 2007 file format does not support user-level security. This error description is generated for all databases converted from Access 97, even when user-level security was not being used. Image Medtech will not use this feature, so the conversion error message should be ignored.

Figure 10.10

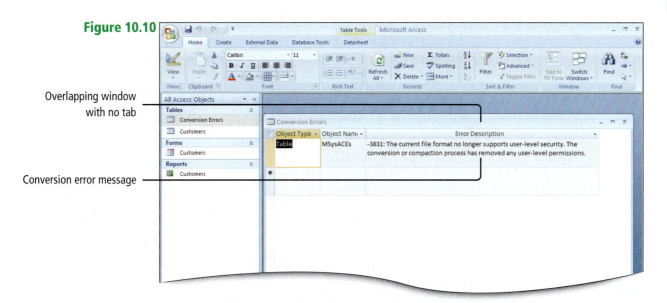

Overlapping window with no tab

Conversion error message

Note — Your Title Bar May Display Differently

When converting databases, the Access title bar may or may not display the file name in the title bar after it is converted. Keep this in mind as you compare your screen with the figures in this text.

10 In Access, click **Save** , and then **Close** the table. If you maximized the table, in the upper left corner of the Access window, the table's Close button is located directly below the Access Close button. Leave the database open for the next activity.

More Knowledge
Converting a Microsoft Access 95 Database

Databases saved in the Microsoft Access 95 file format cannot be directly converted to an Access 2007 file. To convert an Access 95 file, create a new 2007 database, and then use the Import tool to import the objects into the Access 2007 database.

Activity 10.6 Converting to a 2002 - 2003 Database

Access 2007 can work directly with the Access 2002 - 2003 and Access 2007 file formats. The file format used by Access 2007 supports many features not found in older file formats. Conversely, the Access 2002 - 2003 file format supports several features that are not available when the database is saved in the Access 2007 file format. A summary of features for the two file formats is shown in Figure 10.11. Image Medtech would like to use a feature that is available only for databases saved in the 2002 - 2003 file format. In this activity, you will convert a database to the 2002 - 2003 file format.

Comparison of Supported Features

Feature	2002 - 2003 File Format	2007 File Format
File Extension	.mdb	.accdb
Locked-down version	MDE file	ACCDE file
Replication	Yes	No
User-Level Security	Yes	No
Data Access Pages	Yes	No
Password Protection	Yes	Yes (Enhanced)
Multivalued Lookup Fields	No	Yes
Attachment Data Type	No	Yes
History Tracking for Memo Fields	No	Yes
Rich Text Formatting in Memo Fields	No	Yes
Integration with Windows SharePoint Services	No	Yes
Integration with Outlook	No	Yes

Figure 10.11

1 If necessary, open 10A_Customers_2007_Firstname_Lastname.

2 Click the **Office** button , point to **Save As**, and then click **Access 2002 - 2003 Database**.

Note — Attempting to Convert a Database with Access 2007 Features

Access will not convert a database to an older version if it contains features supported only with the Access 2007 file format. The features must be removed before converting the database.

3 In the displayed **Save As** dialog box, if necessary, navigate to your Access Chapter 10 folder. Change the file name to **10A_Customers_2003_ Firstname_Lastname** and then click **Save**. If a message displays, click OK.

The application title bar displays *(Access 2002 - 2003 file format)*.

4 Delete the **Conversion Errors** table.

5 Click the **Navigation Pane arrow**, and then click **All Access Objects**.

6 Click the **Database Tools tab**, and then compare your screen with Figure 10.12.

The Administer group displays two buttons: *Users and Permissions* and *Replication Options*. These two features are not supported in the Access 2007 file format. Microsoft Access 2007 displays these buttons only when an Access 2002 - 2003 file is open.

7 Leave the database open for the next activity.

Access 2002 - 2003 file format

Figure 10.12

Administer group

More Knowledge

Converting an Access 2002 - 2003 File to the Access 2007 File Format

To convert a 2002 - 2003 file to the Access 2007 file format, use the Save As command and select Access 2007 for the file type. If the older version contains features that are not supported by the Access 2007 file format, Access will remove those features.

Objective 5
Replicate and Synchronize a Database

Access provides a method to enable multiple individuals to work with multiple copies of a single database, and then share their changes with the original database and each other. A *replica* is a special copy of a database where changes made in the replica are sent to the original database and any other replicas that may exist. **Replication** is the process of creating a replica. Replication enables several individuals to work with the database without connecting to their organization's network. When they do connect to the original database, they can send their changes to the master database.

Activity 10.7 Creating a Replica of a Database

An employee at Image Medtech needs to work on the database while she is on a business trip. She will not be able to access the company database while away, so she will need to update the original database when she returns. In this activity, you will replicate the database, and then test the replica set. A **replica set** is composed of the original database and all replica copies. Replication is not supported with the Access 2007 file format, so you will use the Access 2002 - 2003 database that you created earlier.

1 If necessary, open 10A_Customers_2003_Firstname_Lastname, and then click the Database Tools tab.

2 In the **Administer group**, click the **Replication Options** button, and then click **Create Replica**.

3 Read the displayed message that the database must be closed, and then click **Yes**.

In a replica set, design changes can be made to the Design Master only. A **Design Master** is the original database in a replica set. Design changes made in the design master are passed on to each replica.

4 The database closes, and a conversion message displays. Read the conversion message, and then click **No**.

You already have another copy of the database that can be used as a backup. Creating another backup is not necessary.

5 In the displayed **Location of New Replica** dialog box, be sure that your **Access Chapter 10** folder is open. In the **File name** box, type **10A_Replica_Firstname_Lastname**

6 Select the **Prevent deletes** check box.

Selecting the Prevent deletes check box prohibits others from deleting records.

7 Click **OK**. The database opens and a message with information about the replica displays. Read the displayed message, and then click **OK**. Compare your screen with Figure 10.13.

In the title bar, *Design Master* displays next to the file name to indicate that the Design Master is currently open. In the Navigation Pane, the Replication icon displays next to each database object name.

Figure 10.13

Design Master

Replication icons

8 Open the **Customers** form. Click the **New (blank) Record** button, and then enter the following record:

ID	9
Name	Flora Stone
Address	788 Washington Avenue
City	Uttica
State	NM
Postal Code	24012
Phone	(505) 555-0121
Active?	Checked

9 Switch to **Layout** view. If necessary, close the Property Sheet. In the **AutoFormat group**, apply the **Metro** Autoformat—the third choice in the third row.

The form's background changes to white, and the font changes to the font used by the Metro AutoFormat. Because this form has no open header, most of the AutoFormat features do not display. Files saved in the Access 2002 - 2003 file format cannot display all of the AutoFormat features typically placed in form and report headers.

10 Click **Save** , **Close** the form, click the **Office** button , and then click **Close Database**.

11 Open **10A_Replica_Firstname_Lastname**, and then open the **Customers** form.

The replica does not yet reflect the two changes that you made to the original. These changes will be updated in the next activity.

12 In the first record, select the **Active?** check box.

13 **Close** ✕ the form. Leave the database open for the next activity.

Activity 10.8 Synchronizing a Database

Replicas enable Access to synchronize changes made to the Design Master and replicas. To *synchronize* is to update each member of a replica set by exchanging all updated records and design changes. In the previous activity, you added a record and made a design change using the Design Master. You then opened the replica and changed the first record. In this activity, you will synchronize all of the changes that you made.

1 If necessary, open 10A_Replica_Firstname_Lastname.

2 Click the **Database Tools tab**. In the **Administration group**, click the **Replication Options** button, and then click **Synchronize Now**.

3 In the displayed **Synchronize Database** dialog box, click **OK**.

4 Read the displayed message, and then click **Yes**. In the displayed message, click **OK**.

The database closes, synchronizes the replica set, and then reopens.

5 Open the **Customers** form. Click the **Last Record** ▶| button, and then compare your screen with Figure 10.14.

The AutoFormat applied in the Design Master has been applied to the form in the replica copy. The record for Flora Stone, which was added in the Design Master, has been added to the replica.

Figure 10.14

Record for Flora Stone added

Formatting applied

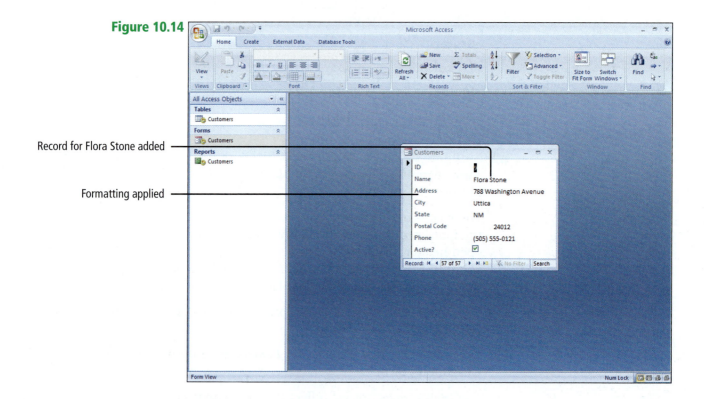

6 Press [PrtScr]. In the **Word** document, press [Enter], and then press [Ctrl] + [Enter] to insert a page break. Type your first and last names, press [Enter], and then type **Project 10A Activity 10.8 Step 6** Press [Enter], **Paste** the screen shot, and then click **Save** 🖫 .

7 In **Access**, **Close** ☒ the form, and then **Exit** Access.

8 **Open 10A_Customers_2003_Firstname_Lastname**, and then open the **Customers** form. In the first record, confirm that the *Active?* check box is selected.

9 **Close** ☒ the form, and then **Exit** Access.

10 Return to the **My Computer** window. In your **Access Chapter 10** folder, be sure that you are still in **Details** view and that all the files created in this project display. Be sure that the columns are wide enough to display all of the Name and Type descriptions.

11 Press [PrtScr], and then **Close** ☒ **My Computer**.

12 In the **Word** document, press [Enter], and then press [Ctrl] + [Enter] to insert a page break. Type your first and last names, press [Enter], and then type **Project 10A Activity 10.8 Step 12** Press [Enter], **Paste** the screen shot, and then click **Save** 🖫 . If you are instructed to submit this result, create a paper or electronic printout of the Word document.

13 **Exit** Word.

End **You have completed Project 10A**

Project 10B **Invoices**

Microsoft Access 2007 has several tools that analyze the database to help the administrator improve performance. Another feature enables you to work directly with Microsoft Outlook 2007 from within Access. Database designers also customize the way Access looks and operates by modifying database options. In Activities 10.9 through 10.17, you will help Image Medtech to optimize database performance, integrate its customer data with Outlook, and provide its end-users with a custom look and feel. As you work, you will document your work by creating screen shots. Your completed screen shots document will look similar to the printout shown in Figure 10.15.

For Project 10B, you will need the following files:

a10B_Invoices
a10B_Icon

You will save your files as
10B_Invoices_Firstname_Lastname
10B_Screens_Firstname_Lastname

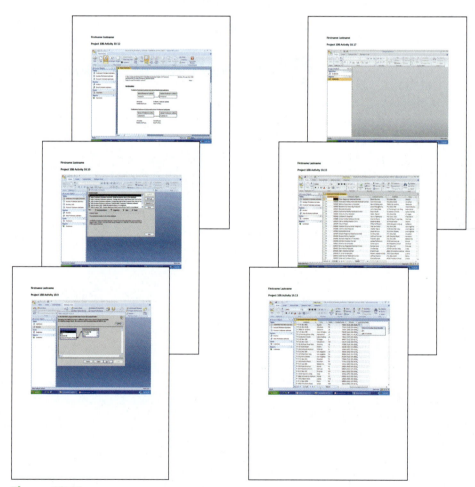

Figure 10.15
Project 10B—Invoices

Objective 6
Use Microsoft Analysis Tools

Microsoft Access provides several analysis tools that provide useful information to the database administrator. One tool scans tables for redundant data, and then provides a mechanism to split them into smaller, related tables. Another tool analyzes all database objects and lists possible design flaws that decrease performance. Another analysis tool creates a highly detailed report listing the attributes for the entire database. These analysis tools are used to improve database performance and increase data reliability.

Activity 10.9 Using the Table Analyzer

The **Table Analyzer** searches for repeated data in a table, and then splits the table into two or more related tables. The process of breaking a single table into smaller, related tables is called **normalization**. Employees at Image Medtech notice that when they enter invoices into the database, they spend a significant amount of time typing the same product names, product descriptions, and prices into each record. In this activity, you will use the Table Analyzer to see if the table needs to be split into two or more related tables.

1 **Start Access**. Navigate to the location where the student data files for this textbook are saved. Locate and then open **a10B_Invoices**.

Click the **Office** button , point to **Save As**, and then click **Access 2007 Database**. In the **Save As** dialog box, navigate to your **Access Chapter 10** folder, and then save the file as **10B_Invoices_Firstname_ Lastname**

2 Open the **Invoices** table. Click the **Product ID column arrow**, and then click **Sort Smallest to Largest**.

3 Scroll through the table, observe the duplicate entries in the Description and Price columns, and then **Close** the table without saving any changes.

4 Click the **Database Tools tab**. In the **Analyze group**, click the **Analyze Table** button. If the wizard displays a screen called *The Table Analyzer: Looking at the Problem*, click the Next button two times. Be sure that the **Invoices** table is selected, and then compare your screen with Figure 10.16.

If the *Show introductory pages?* check box is selected, two extra screens will display the next time the Table Analyzer is started. These two screens explain the normalization process.

Figure 10.16

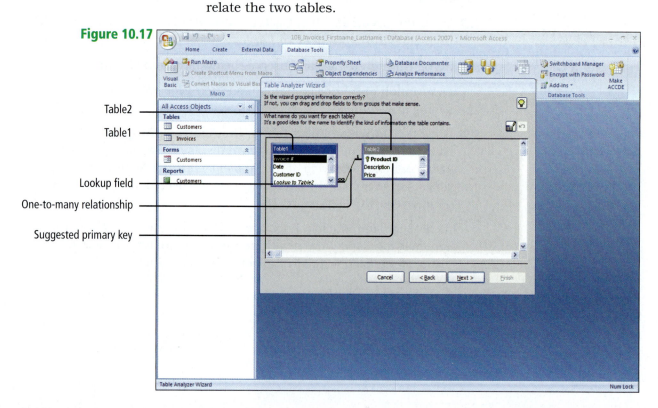

5 Click the **Next** button. In the displayed wizard dialog box, read the directions. Be sure that the **Yes, let the wizard decide** option button is selected, and then click **Next**.

6 In the displayed Wizard dialog box, read the directions, and then compare your screen with Figure 10.17.

The wizard suggests placing the product data into a related table currently named Table2. It suggests using Product ID as its primary key. In the proposal for Table1, a lookup field will be inserted to relate the two tables.

Figure 10.17

Table2
Table1

Lookup field
One-to-many relationship
Suggested primary key

7 Double-click the **Table1** title bar. In the displayed dialog box, in the **Table Name** box, type **Invoices Firstname Lastname** and then click **OK**.

8 Double-click the **Table2** title bar. In the displayed dialog box, in the **Table Name** box, type **Products Firstname Lastname** and then click **OK**.

9 Click the **Next** button, and then read the directions displayed in the Wizard dialog box. In the **Invoices** table, click **Invoice #**, and then click the **Set Unique Identifier** button.

10 Press PrtScr. Create a new, blank Word document. In the **Word** document, **Paste** the screen shot. Type your first and last names, press Enter, and then type **Project 10B Activity 10.9** Press Enter, and then **Paste** the screen shot. **Save** the document in your **Access Chapter 10** folder with the name **10B_Screens_Firstname_Lastname** Leave the Word document open.

11 Switch to the **Access** window. Click **Next**, and then read the directions displayed in the Wizard dialog box. Be sure that the **Yes, create the query** option button is selected, and then click **Finish**.

12 **Close** the displayed **Access Help** window, and then compare your screen with Figure 10.18.

The two tables are created, and the original table is renamed Invoices_OLD. A query named Invoices is created and is opened in Datasheet view. This query is used so that the reports and forms that relied on the old Invoices table will still work.

Figure 10.18

Query in Datasheet view ——

New Invoices table ——
Original table ——
New Products table ——
New query ——

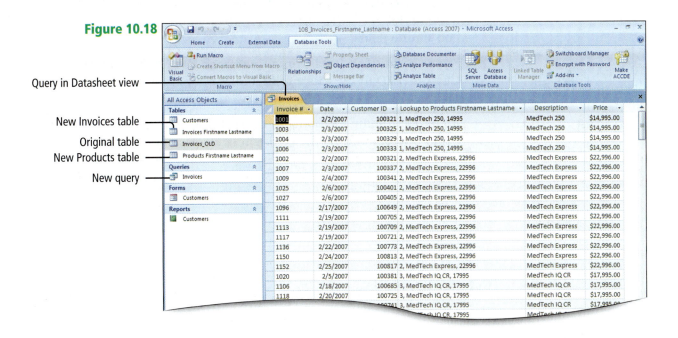

13 **Close** the query. In the **Show/Hide group**, click the **Relationships** button. If necessary, in the Relationships group, click the All Relationships button.

14 Right-click the **Relationship** line, and then click **Edit Relationship**. Notice that the Cascade Delete Related Records check box is not selected. This prevents accidental deletion of records during the conversion process. Click the **Cancel** button to close the dialog box without making any changes.

15 Close ⊠ the **Relationships** window. Leave the database open for the next activity.

Activity 10.10 Using the Performance Analyzer

Poor database design impairs performance, especially when the database is used to store large amounts of data. Access provides a tool that assists the database administrator to locate and fix problems that might hinder performance. Image Medtech needs to analyze their database to increase its performance. In this activity, you will use the Performance Analyzer to identify and fix problems with their database. The **Performance Analyzer** is a wizard that analyzes database objects, and then offers suggestions for improving them.

1 If necessary, open 10B_Invoices_Firstname_Lastname.

2 At the end of the **Customers** table name, add your first and last names.

3 Click the **Create tab**. In the **Other group**, click the **Query Design** button. Add the **Invoices** table that you created in the previous

activity, add the **Customers** table, and then **Close** the **Show Table** dialog box.

4 From the **Invoices** table, add the **Invoice #** and **Date** fields to the design grid. From the **Customers** table, add the **Company Name** and **Phone** fields.

5 From the **Invoices** table, drag **Customer ID** and drop it over **Customer ID** in the **Customers** table. Compare your screen with Figure 10.19.

An indeterminate relationship between the two tables is established using Customer ID as the common field. Recall that an indeterminate relationship is one that does not enforce referential integrity. The relationship applies to this query only and is not defined for the entire database.

Figure 10.19

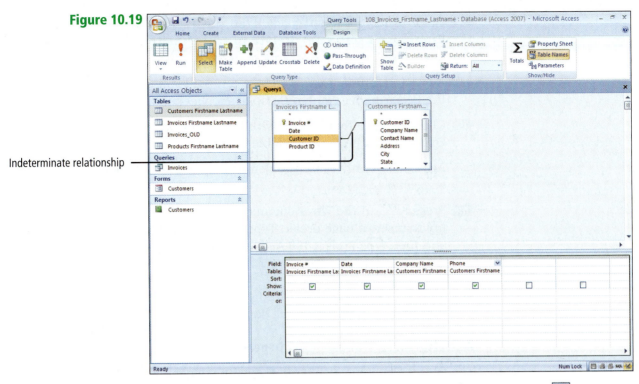

Indeterminate relationship

---

6 In the **Results group**, click the **Run** button. Click **Save** ☐ , type

Sales Firstname Lastname and then click **OK**. **Close** ☒ the query.

7 Click the **Database Tools tab**. In the **Analyze group**, click the **Analyze Performance** button.

8 In the displayed **Performance Analyzer** wizard, click the **All Object Types tab**. Click the **Select All** button, and then click **OK**. Compare your screen with Figure 10.20.

The Performance Analyzer provides three levels of suggestions: Recommendations, Suggestions, and Ideas. For this database, the Performance Analyzer has no recommendations, one suggestion, and several ideas.

Figure 10.20

Ideas

Suggestion

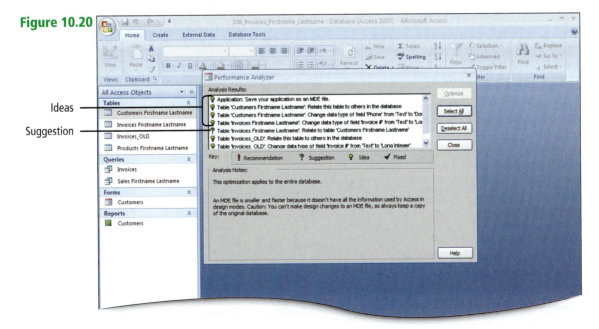

9 Under **Analysis Results**, click the suggestion **Table 'Invoices Firstname Lastname'. Relate to table 'Customers Firstname Lastname'**. Click the **Optimize** button.

A one-to-many relationship between the two tables is defined, and the Performance Analyzer displays a check mark next to the item.

10 Click the first item labeled with the **Idea** icon. Notice that the Optimize button is unavailable.

Access fixes only those problems identified as a recommendation or suggestion.

11 Press PrtScr. In the **Word** document, press Enter, and then press Ctrl + Enter to insert a page break. Type your first and last names, press Enter, and then type **Project 10B Activity 10.10** Press Enter, **Paste** the screen shot, and then click **Save** 🖫 .

12 Return to **Access**. Read through the remaining ideas, and then click the **Close** button. Leave the database open for the next activity.

Activity 10.11 Viewing Object Dependencies

The Object Dependencies pane shows the dependencies between database objects. A ***dependency*** is an object that requires, or is dependent on, another database object. For example, several forms, reports, and queries may rely on a single table. Deleting that table would "break" those dependent objects. The Invoices_OLD table may have no other database objects depend on it. In this activity, you will use the Object Dependencies pane to determine if any objects depend on the Invoices_OLD table. If not, you will delete the table.

1 If necessary, open 10B_Invoices_Firstname_Lastname, and then click the Database Tools tab.

2 In the **Show/Hide group**, click the **Object Dependencies** button. If a message displays, click **OK**. On the right side of the Access window, notice that the Object Dependencies pane displays.

3 If necessary, in the Navigation Pane, click the Customers table, and then in the Object Dependencies pane, click Refresh.

4 If necessary, click the *Objects that depend on me* option button. Compare your screen with Figure 10.21.

The Invoices table, Sales query, Customers form, and Customers Report all depend on the Customers table.

Figure 10.21

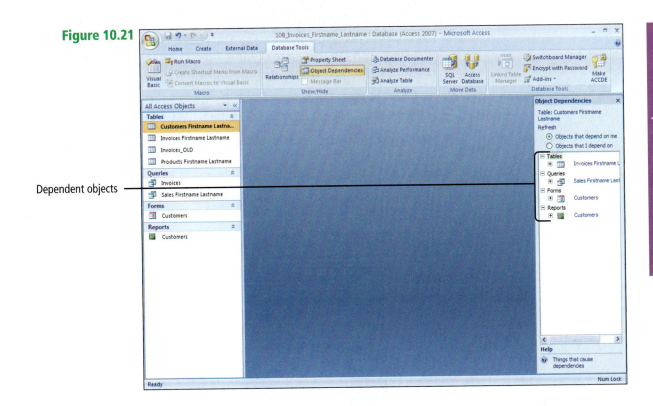

Dependent objects

5. In the **Navigation Pane**, click the **Invoices_OLD** table, and then in the **Object Dependencies** pane, click **Refresh**. Notice that no database objects depend on the Invoices_OLD table.

6. **Close** ✕ the **Object Dependencies pane**, and then **Delete** the **Invoices_OLD** table.

7. In the **Analyze group**, click the **Analyze Performance** button. In the displayed **Performance Analyzer** wizard, click the **All Object Types tab**, click the **Select All** button, and then click **OK**.

With the deletion of the Invoices_OLD table, only three ideas are given by the Performance Analyzer. The MDE file referred to in one of the ideas is now called an ACCDE file, which you practiced making in an earlier activity.

8. In the **Performance Analyzer** dialog box, click the **Close** button, and then leave the database and Word document open for the next activity.

Activity 10.12 Using the Database Documenter

The **Database Documenter** builds a report with detailed information about all of the objects in a database. This detailed report is often referred to as a **data dictionary**. The data dictionary created by the Database Documenter should be printed periodically and stored in a secure location. Image Medtech needs to document certain database features. In this activity, you will create a report using the Database Documenter.

1. If necessary, open 10B_Invoices_Firstname_Lastname, and then click the Database Tools tab.

2 In the **Analyze group**, click the **Database Documenter** button. In the displayed **Documenter** dialog box, click the **All Object Types tab**, click the **Select All** button, and then click **OK**.

The Database Documenter displays the data dictionary report in Print Preview. This report cannot be saved.

3 In the **Zoom group**, click the **Zoom** button, and then compare your screen with Figure 10.22.

Figure 10.22

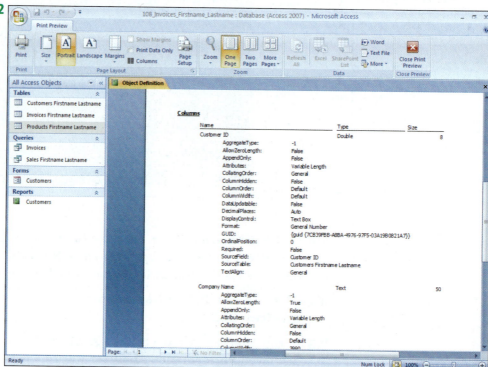

4 Scroll as needed and click the **Next Page** ▶ button to skim through a few of its 55 pages.

In an organization, this report would be printed, bound, and stored in a secure location.

5 Click the **Close Print Preview** button. Click the **Database Tools tab**. In the **Analyze group**, click the **Database Documenter** button.

6 In the displayed **Documenter** dialog box, click the **Options** button. Under **Include for Table**, click so that only the **Relationships** check box is selected.

7 Under **Include for Fields**, click the **Nothing** option button. Under **Include for Indexes**, click the **Nothing** option button.

8 Compare your screen with Figure 10.23, and then click **OK**.

Figure 10.23

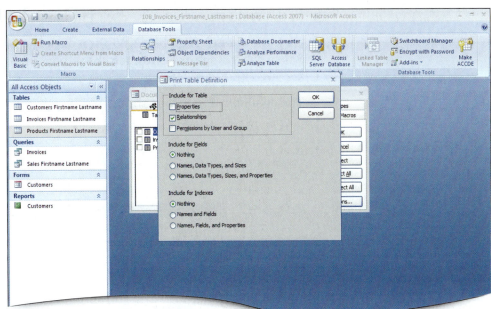

9 In the **Documenter** dialog box, select the **Invoices** table check box, and then click **OK**.

10 Click the **Zoom** button, and then scroll as needed so that all of the report text displays in the window. Some of the table names may be truncated.

11 Press ⟨PrtScr⟩. In the **Word** document, press ⟨Enter⟩, and then press ⟨Ctrl⟩ + ⟨Enter⟩ to insert a page break. Type your first and last names, press ⟨Enter⟩, and then type **Project 10B Activity 10.12** Press ⟨Enter⟩, **Paste** the screen shot, and then click **Save** 🖫 .

12 In **Access**, click the **Close Print Preview** button. Recall that this report cannot be saved. Leave the database open for the next activity.

Objective 7
Add Smart Tags

Smart tags enable the end-user to perform tasks from Access that would usually require another program, such as Outlook, to be open. Smart tags are assigned in a table's Design view by changing the field's Smart Tags property. With smart tags in place, the user can perform tasks within Access such as automatically adding a phone number to their Outlook Contacts.

Activity 10.13 Adding Smart Tags

The Marketing Department at Image Medtech would like to integrate the customer data in its database with Microsoft Outlook 2007. Outlook is a personal information management program that manages e-mail, contacts, tasks, and appointments. In this activity, you will assign a smart tag to the *Phone* field in the *Customers* table.

1 If necessary, open 10B_Invoices_Firstname_Lastname.

2 In the **Navigation Pane**, right-click the **Customers** table, and then click **Design View**.

3 In the **Field Name** column, click **Phone**. Under **Field Properties**, click the **Smart Tags** box, and then click the **Build** button ⊡. Select the **Telephone Number** check box, and then compare your screen with Figure 10.24.

The available smart tags that could be applied to this field display.

Figure 10.24

Available smart tags ———

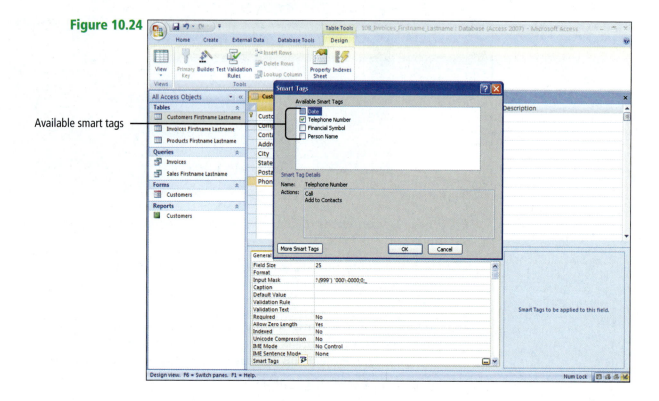

The Telephone Number smart tag is not available

Outlook 2007 must be installed on your computer for the Telephone Number smart tag to display as an option.

4 Click **OK** to close the dialog box.

5 **Save** 🖫 your changes, and then switch to **Datasheet** view.

6 Scroll so that the **Phone column** displays. Place the pointer over any cell containing a phone number, but do not click.

A small, purple triangle indicates that a smart tag is available. When you point to the field, the Smart Tags Actions button displays.

7 Click the **Smart Tags Actions button arrow** ⓘ, and then compare your screen with Figure 10.25.

If your computer is connected to a phone, Outlook will dial the number when the Call command is clicked. When the Add to Contacts command is clicked, Outlook starts and opens a new, untitled contact with the phone number already entered. Unless you have configured Outlook to work on your computer, do not try using any of the smart tag actions.

Figure 10.25

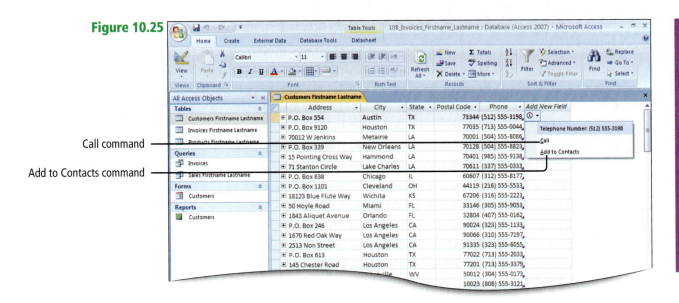

Call command

Add to Contacts command

8. With the Smart Tag Actions menu still displayed, press PrtScr. In the **Word** document, press Enter, and then press Ctrl + Enter to insert a page break. Type your first and last names, press Enter, and then type **Project 10B Activity 10.13** Press Enter, **Paste** the screen shot, and then click **Save** 🖫.

9. In **Access**, **Close** ☒ the table, and then leave the database open for the next activity.

More Knowledge

Finding More Smart Tags

Smart tags can be created to perform specialized tasks. You will find more smart tags by clicking the More Smart Tags button in the Smart Tags dialog box. These tags are created by Microsoft, third-party companies, and other developers.

Objective 8
Modify Access Views and Behaviors

Access has many options that affect database views and behaviors. These options are changed using the Access Options dialog box. For example, there are options to alter the colors and border, options for how text is formatted, and settings that alter how windows display. The Access Options dialog box is also used to add and remove commands from the Quick Access Toolbar. A custom interface is provided by changing the options for Navigation Pane. There are literally hundreds of option settings available to the database designer.

Activity 10.14 Modifying Access Options

Image Medtech would like their database to have a unique look and feel. They also want the Smart Tags Action button to display in Forms and Reports, but not in a table datasheet. In this activity, you will use the Access Options dialog box to apply a custom color scheme and alter where smart tags display.

1 If necessary, open 10B_Invoices_Firstname_Lastname.

2 Click the **Office** button 🗐, and then click the **Access Options** button. If necessary, click **Popular**. Compare your screen with Figure 10.26.

The left pane displays several option groups that when clicked, display their settings in the larger pane. The settings for the Popular option group currently display.

Figure 10.26

Option groups

Popular settings

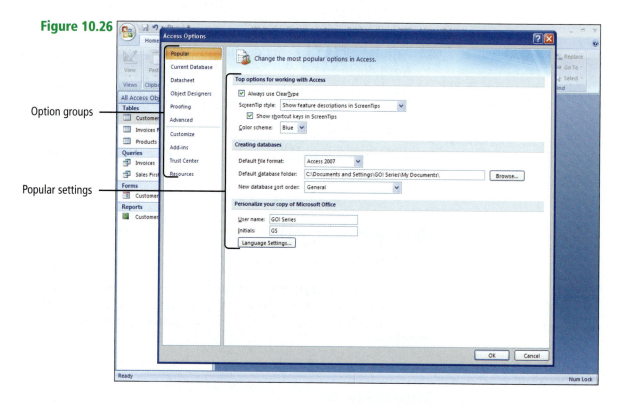

3 Under **Top options for working with Access**, click the **Color scheme arrow**, and then click **Silver**.

4 Under **Personalize your copy of Microsoft Office**, in the **User name** box, type your first and last names. In the **Initials** box, type your first, middle, and last initials.

5 Click **OK**, and then observe the changes to the database color scheme.

These changes will affect every database opened on this computer. You will change them back their original settings later in this chapter.

6 Click the **Office** button 🗐, and then click the **Access Options** button. In the left pane, click **Datasheet**.

7 Under **Default colors**, click the **Font color button arrow**. In the displayed gallery, click **Access Theme 10**—the last color in the second row.

8 Under **Gridlines and cell effects**, clear the **Horizontal** check box.

9 Under **Default font**, click the **Font arrow**, and then click **Arial Narrow**.

10 In the left pane, click **Object Designers**. Under **Table design**, in the **Default text field size**, replace the existing value with **50**

The default field size for new text fields will be 50 instead of 255.

11 In the left pane, click **Advanced**. Scroll down to view the options under **Display**. Clear the **Show Smart Tags on Datasheets** check box.

12 Click **OK**. Open the **Customers** table in Datasheet view. Scroll so that the Phone field displays. Place the pointer over any phone number and notice that the Smart Tag Actions button does not display.

13 **Close** ⊠ the **Customers** table. Leave the database open for the next activity.

Activity 10.15 Customizing the Quick Access Toolbar

Any Access command, including those not available on the Ribbon, can be added to the Quick Access Toolbar. Image Medtech would like to add their commonly used commands to the Quick Access Toolbar. In this activity, you will use two different methods to customize the Quick Access Toolbar.

1 If necessary, open 10B_Invoices_Firstname_Lastname.

2 Click the **Office** button 🔲, and then click the **Access Options** button. Click **Customize**. Alternatively, click the Customize Quick Access Toolbar arrow, and then click More Commands. Compare your screen with Figure 10.27.

Under *Choose commands from*, the commands from the Popular Commands group display. Under *Customize Quick Access Toolbar*, the commands on the current Quick Access Toolbar are listed. The *Customize Quick Access Toolbar* menu provides two options—the Quick Access Toolbar can be modified for all databases, or just the current database.

Figure 10.27

Changes all databases or
current database
Available Popular Commands

Current commands on the
Quick Access Toolbar

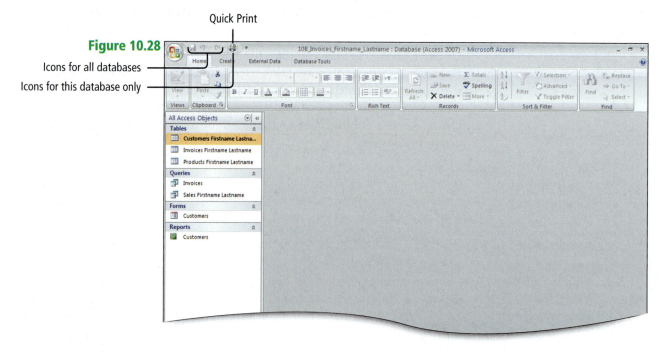

3 In the upper right corner, click the **Customize Quick Access Toolbar arrow**, and then click the path to the currently open database.

Image Medtech wants these changes for this database only.

4 In the list below **Popular Commands**, scroll down. Click **Quick Print**, and then click the **Add** button.

5 Click **OK**, and then compare your screen with Figure 10.28.

The Quick Print icon has been added to the Quick Access Toolbar. Icons added to just one database are placed in a separate area to the right of the other icons.

Quick Print

Figure 10.28

Icons for all databases
Icons for this database only

6 Click the **Office** button ⊞, point to **Save As**, and then right-click **Access 2007 Database**. In the displayed shortcut menu, click **Add to Quick Access Toolbar**.

The icon displays with the group of permanent commands. Commands added using the right-click method are added to all databases.

7 Open the **Customers** table in Datasheet view. Press PrtScr. In the **Word** document, press Enter, and then press Ctrl + Enter to insert a page break. Type your first and last names, press Enter, and then type **Project 10B Activity 10.15** Press Enter, **Paste** the screen shot, and then click **Save** ⊟.

8 In **Access**, **Close** ☒ the **Customers** table. Leave the database open for the next activity.

Activity 10.16 Setting Current Database Options

When changing options, the Current Database group provides several useful options. These options enable the database designer to create a look and feel of a custom application. Image Medtech would like their database to have a unique look and feel, and the company does not want end-users to make design changes. In this activity, you will create a custom application title and application icon for the database, and then disable Layout view.

1 If necessary, open 10B_Invoices_Firstname_Lastname.

2 Click the **Office** button ⊞, click the **Access Options** button, and then click **Current Database**.

3 Under **Application Options**, in the **Application Title** box, type **Image Medtech**

The *Application Title* is the text that displays in the Access title bar when that database is open. If the Application Title is blank, the file name and application name display instead.

4 To the right of **Application Icon**, click the **Browse** button. In the displayed **Icon Browser** dialog box, change the file type to **Bitmaps (*.bmp)**.

5 In the displayed **Icon Browser** dialog box, navigate to where the student files for this project are stored. Locate and click **a10B_Icon**, and then click **OK**.

6 Select the **Use as Form and Report Icon** check box.

7 Under **Application Options**, select the **Compact on Close** check box.

With this option selected, the database will be compacted and repaired each time that it is closed.

8 Clear the **Enable Layout View for this database** check box.

9 Click **OK**, read the displayed message, and then click **OK** again.

10 Close the database, and then reopen **10B_Invoices_Firstname_Lastname**.

11 Open the **Customers** report in Report view, and then compare your screen with Figure 10.29.

The application title displays in the title bar. The application icon displays in the report's tab and also in the application's taskbar button. If the database file or icon image file is renamed or moved to another location, the icon will no longer display.

Application title

Figure 10.29

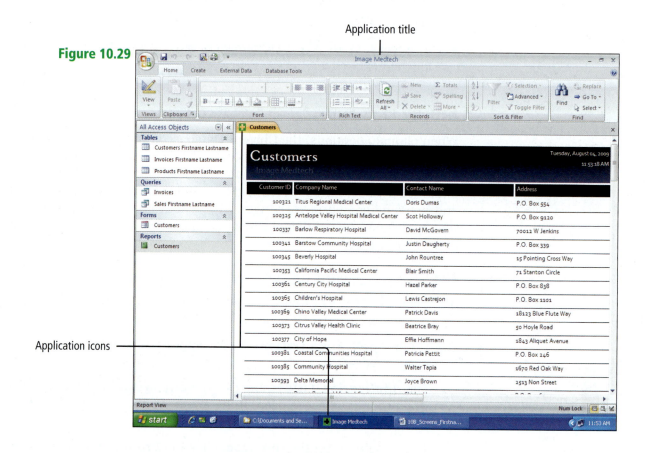

Application icons

12 Close ✕ the report, and leave the database open for the next activity.

Activity 10.17 Customizing the Navigation Pane

To create a custom interface for the end-user, the database designer may choose to customize the Navigation Pane instead of creating a switchboard. Image Medtech would like their users to see only forms and reports in the Navigation Pane. In this activity, you will add a custom category and two groups to the Navigation Pane. You will then add the form and report their respective groups.

1 If necessary, open 10B_Invoices_Firstname_Lastname.

2 Click the **Office** button 🔘 , click the **Access Options** button, and then, if necessary, click **Current Database**.

3 Under **Navigation**, click the **Navigation Options** button, and then compare your screen with Figure 10.30.

The existing categories for the Navigation Pane display on the left and the groups for each existing category display on the right. Categories and Groups are edited using the buttons below the two columns.

Figure 10.30

Existing Categories

Groups for Tables and Related Views

Editing buttons

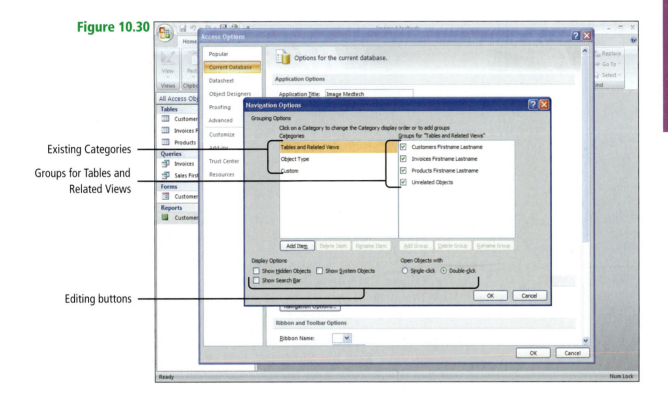

4 Click the **Add Item** button, type **Image Medtech** and then press Enter.

Image Medtech displays as a category. A ***Navigation Pane category*** is a top-level listing that displays when the Navigation Pane arrow is clicked.

5 With the **Image Medtech** category selected, click the **Add Group** button. Type **Data Entry** and then press Enter.

Data Entry displays as Group. A ***Navigation Pane group*** is a second-level listing that display when a Navigation Pane category is selected.

6 Click the **Add Group** button. Type **Reports** and then press Enter.

7 Click **OK** two times. Click the **Navigation Pane arrow**, and then click **Image Medtech**.

8 In the **Navigation Pane**, under **Unassigned Objects**, drag the **Customers** form and drop it over the **Data Entry** group.

9 In the **Navigation Pane**, under **Unassigned Objects**, drag the **Customers** report and drop it over the **Reports** group. Compare your screen with Figure 10.31.

The objects display as shortcuts within their respective Navigation Pane groups, and they are no longer listed under Unassigned Objects.

Figure 10.31

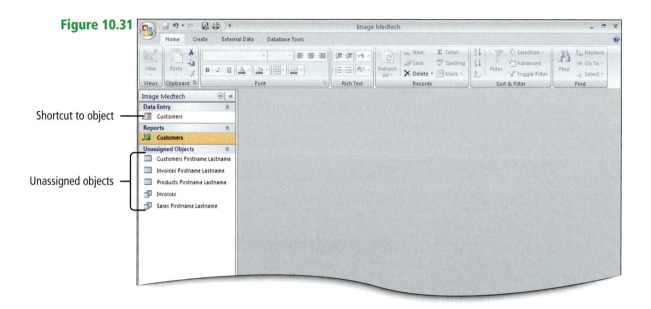

Shortcut to object

Unassigned objects

10 Click the **Office** button , click the **Access Options** button, and then under **Navigation**, click the **Navigation Options** button.

11 In the **Categories** column, click **Image Medtech**. In the **Groups** column, clear the **Unassigned Objects** check box, and then click **OK** two times. Notice that only the two objects that you assigned earlier display in the Navigation pane.

12 Right-click the **Customers** form, and in the displayed shortcut menu, click **Rename Shortcut**. Add your first and last names at the end of the object name. Use this same technique to add your first and last names to the Customers report name.

13 Press PrtScr. In the **Word** document, notice that the Silver color scheme has been applied.

14 Press Enter, and then press Ctrl + Enter to insert a page break. Type your first and last names, press Enter, and then type **Project 10A Activity 10.17**

Press Enter, **Paste** the screen shot, and then click **Save** . If you are instructed to submit this result, create a paper or electronic printout of the Word document.

15 **Exit** Word and return to **Access**. In the **Quick Access Toolbar**, right-click the **Save As Access 2007** button, and then click **Remove from Quick Access Toolbar**.

16 Click the **Office** button , click the **Access Options** button, and then click **Popular**. Click the **Color scheme arrow**, and then click **Blue**.

17 Click **Datasheet**. Click the **Font color button arrow**, and then click **Automatic**. Under **Default gridlines showing**, select the **Horizontal** check box. Under **Default**, click the **Font arrow**, and then click **Calibri**.

18 Click **Object Designers**, and then set the **Default text field size** back to **255**

19 Click **Advanced**, scroll down, and then under **Display**, select the **Show Smart Tags on Datasheets** check box.

20 Click **OK** to close the **Access Options** dialog box, and then **Exit** Access.

More Knowledge

Displaying a Switchboard Form on Startup

Customizing the Navigation Pane is meant to replace the Switchboard form used in previous versions of Access. Access 2007 still supports switchboards, and some designers may choose to use a switchboard instead of customizing the Navigation Pane. If a switchboard is used, in the Current Database options, set the Display Form option to the switchboard form, and then clear the Display Navigation Pane check box. When the database is started, the Switchboard form will open and the Navigation Pane will not display.

 You have completed Project 10B

 There's More You Can Do!

From My Computer, navigate to the student files that accompany this textbook. In the folder **02_theres_more_you_can_do**, locate and open the folder for this chapter. Open and print the instructions for this project, which are provided to you in Adobe PDF format.

Try It! 1—Convert a Replicated Database to Access 2007

In this Try It! project, you will convert a replicated 2002 - 2003 database into the Access 2007 format.

Content-Based Assessments

Summary

As databases collect more and more data, and database objects are added, modified, and deleted, performance begins to degrade. Access provides several analysis tools designed to improve database performance. Splitting the databases into two files enables several different database front-ends to be built using a single source of data. Multiple copies of a database can be replicated so that individuals can work with the database away from work, and then synchronize their changes with the design master when they return. You have practiced creating databases using several different file types, each with a specific purpose such as creating a secure ACCDE file or backup. Finally, you practiced customizing Access views by adding commands to the Quick Access Toolbar and by creating a custom Navigation Pane.

Key Terms

Content-Based Assessments

Access
chapter ten

Matching

Match each term in the second column with its correct definition in the first column. Write the letter of the term on the blank line in front of the correct definition.

_____ **1.** The process where an Access file is rewritten to store objects and data more efficiently.

_____ **2.** The abbreviation for a megabyte.

_____ **3.** A unit used to measure computer storage sizes; it typically stores a single character, such as a digit or letter.

_____ **4.** The unexpected loss of data caused by actions such as hardware failure, accidental deletion of records, theft, or natural disaster.

_____ **5.** The process of creating a copy of a file or files.

_____ **6.** The database tables and their data stored in a separate file.

_____ **7.** The database forms, queries, reports, and macros stored in a separate file.

_____ **8.** A database application designed for high-end business uses.

_____ **9.** An Access 2007 file format that prevents users from making design changes to forms, reports, and macros.

_____ **10.** A special copy of a database where any changes made are sent to the original database.

_____ **11.** To update each member of a replica set by exchanging all updated records and design changes.

_____ **12.** A wizard that analyzes all database objects, and then offers suggestions for improving their design.

_____ **13.** A tool that builds a report with detailed information about all of the objects in a database.

_____ **14.** The text that displays in the Access title bar when that database is open.

_____ **15.** A top-level listing that displays when the Navigation Pane arrow is clicked.

A ACCDE

B Application Title

C Back up

D Back-end

E Byte

F Compact and Repair

G Data loss

H Database Documenter

I Front-end

J MB

K Navigation Pane category

L Performance Analyzer

M Replica

N SQL Server

O Synchronize

Content-Based Assessments

Fill in the Blank

Write the correct word in the space provided.

1. A unit used to measure storage sizes that stores 1,048,576 bytes is called a(n) _____.

2. A copy of the database that is stored in an alternative location is called a(n) _____.

3. The database tables and their data, when stored in a separate file, is called a(n) _____.

4. An Access database that is stored in two files—one containing the back-end and one containing the front-end—is called a(n) _____ database.

5. The process of creating a replica is called _____.

6. The original database and all replica copies is called a(n) _____ _____.

7. The original database in a replica set is called the _____ _____.

8. A wizard that looks for repeated data in a table, and then splits the table into two or more related tables is called the _____ _____.

9. The process of breaking a single table into smaller, related tables is called _____.

10. An object that requires, or is dependent on, another database object is called a(n) _____.

11. A tool that builds a report with detailed information about all of the objects in a database is called the _____ _____.

12. A detailed report with information about every aspect of a database is called a(n) _____ _____.

13. A field property that enables the end-user to perform tasks from Access that would usually require another program such as Outlook to be open is called a(n) _____ _____.

14. A top-level listing that displays when the Navigation Pane arrow is clicked is a(n) _____ _____ _____.

15. A second-level listing that displays when a Navigation Pane category is selected is a(n) _____ _____ _____.

Skills Review

Project 10C—Administration

In this project, you will apply the skills you practiced from the Objectives in Project 10A.

Objectives: 1. *Compact and Repair a Database;* **2.** *Back Up a Database;* **3.** *Use the Database Splitter;* **4.** *Convert Databases to Other Versions;* **5.** *Replicate and Synchronize a Database.*

Image Medtech needs to protect its database files and build several front-end databases using a single set of back-end tables. The company also needs to work with a database saved in Access 97. One worker will need to work with that database at home and then synchronize the changes when he is at work. In this project you will optimize the company database, and then split it into two files. You will convert an old database, and then create a replica of the design master. You will document your work by creating screen shots. Your completed screen shots will look similar to the printout shown in Figure 10.32.

For Project 10C, you will need the following files:

a10C_Administration
a10C_QC_97

You will save your files as
10C_Administration_Firstname_Lastname
10C_Administration_Firstname_Lastname (ACCDE file)
10C_Administration_Firstname_Lastname_2007-07-01 (your date will differ)
10C_Administration_Firstname_Lastname_be
10C_QC_2003_Firstname_Lastname
10C_QC_2007_Firstname_Lastname
10C_Replica_Firstname_Lastname
10C_Screens_Firstname_Lastname

Figure 10.32

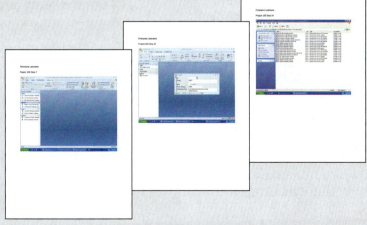

(Project 10C–Administration continues on the next page)

Skills Review

(Project 10C–Administration continued)

1. **Start Access**. Locate and then open the **a10C_Administration** file. Click the **Office** button, point to **Save As**, and then click **Access 2007 Database**. Save the database in your **Access Chapter 10** folder as **10C_Administration_Firstname_Lastname**

2. In the **Navigation Pane**, under **Queries**, click **Salary Group C**, and then press Delete. In the displayed message, click **Yes**. Repeat this technique to delete the **Salary Group D** and **Salary Group E** queries.

3. Delete the following reports: **Salary Group C**, **Salary Group D**, and **Salary Group E**.

4. For the remaining database objects, add your own first and last names at the end of each object's name.

5. Open the **Office** menu, point to **Manage**, and then click **Back Up Database**. Save the backup in your **Access Chapter 10** folder using the name provided in the **Save As** dialog box.

6. Click the **Database Tools tab**. In the **Move Data group**, click the **Access Database** button. In the **Database Splitter** dialog box, click the **Split Database** button. In the **Create Back-end Database** dialog box, be sure your **Access Chapter 10** folder is open, click the **Split** button, and then click **OK**. Read the message, and then click **OK**.

7. Press PrtScr. Open a new, blank **Word** document. In the **Word** document, type your first and last names, press Enter, and then type **Project 10C Step 7** Press Enter, and then **Paste** the screen shot. **Save** the Word document in your **Access Chapter 10** folder as **10C_Screens_Firstname_Lastname**

8. Return to **Access**. In the **Database Tools group**, click the **Make ACCDE** button. In

the **Save As** dialog box, be sure that your **Access Chapter 10** folder is open, and then click **Save**.

9. From the **Office** menu, point to **Manage**, and then click **Compact and Repair Database**.

10. From the **Office** menu, click **Close Database**. From the **Office** menu, click **Open**. Navigate to where the student files for this project are stored, click **a10C_QC_97**, and then click **Open**. In the displayed **Database Enhancement** dialog box, click **Yes**.

11. In the **Save As** dialog box, name the file **10C_QC_2007_Firstname_Lastname** and then save it in your **Access Chapter 10** folder. In the two message that display, click **OK**.

12. Open the **Conversion Errors** table, and then read contents of the **ErrorDescription** field. **Close** the table, and then delete the **Conversion Errors** table.

13. From the **Office** menu, point to **Save As**, and then click **Access 2002 - 2003 Database**. Name the file **10C_QC_2003_Firstname_Lastname** and then save it in your **Access Chapter 10** folder. In the displayed message, click **OK**.

14. Click the **Navigation Pane arrow**, and then click **All Access Objects**.

15. Click the **Database Tools tab**. In the **Administer group**, click the **Replication Options** button, and then click **Create Replica**. In the first displayed message, click **Yes**. In the second displayed message, click **No**. Name the file **10C_Replica_Firstname_Lastname** and then save it in your **Access Chapter 10** folder. Click **Save**, and then in the displayed message, click **OK**.

(Project 10C–Administration continues on the next page)

(Project 10C–Administration continued)

16. Open the **QC Input** form in Layout view. Apply the **Origin AutoFormat**—the fourth choice in the fourth row. Click **Save**, and then **Close** the form.

17. From the **Office** menu, click **Close Database**. From the **Office** menu, click **Open**. Navigate to your **Access Chapter 10** folder, and then double-click **10C_Replica_Firstname_Lastname**.

18. Open the **QC Input** form. For the first record, change the **Serial Number** to **2981B** and then **Close** the form.

19. Click the **Database Tools tab**. In the **Administer group**, click the **Replication Options** button, and then click **Synchronize Now**. In the displayed dialog box, click **OK**, and then in the next two messages, click **Yes** and then **OK**.

20. Open the **QC Input** form. Press PrtScr. **Close** the form and then **Exit** Access.

21. In the **Word** document, press Enter, and then press Ctrl + Enter to insert a page break. Type

your first and last names, press Enter, and then type **Project 10C Step 21** Press Enter, and then **Paste** the screen shot.

22. Open **My Computer**, and then open your **Access Chapter 10** folder. If necessary, maximize the My Computer window and switch to Details view. Be sure that all the files created in this project display. Be sure that the columns are wide enough to display all of the Name and Type descriptions.

23. Press PrtScr, and then **Close** My Computer.

24. In the **Word** document, press Enter, and then press Ctrl + Enter to insert a page break. Type your first and last names, press Enter, and then type **Project 10C Step 24** Press Enter, **Paste** the screen shot, and then click **Save**. If you are instructed to submit this result, create a paper or electronic printout of the Word document.

25. **Exit** Word. If you are submitting files electronically, submit the files as directed by your instructor.

End **You have completed Project 10C**

Skills Review

Project 10D — Marketing

In this project, you will apply the skills you practiced from the Objectives in Project 10B.

Objectives: 6. *Use Microsoft Access Analysis Tools;* **7.** *Add Smart Tags;* **8.** *Modify Access Views and Behaviors.*

Image Medtech needs to improve the performance of their marketing database. In this project, you will use the Access analysis tools to make several improvements to the database. You will then add smart tags and change several Access options. You will document your work by creating screen shots. Your screen shots document will look similar to the print-out shown in Figure 10.33.

For Project 10D, you will need the following file:

a10D_Marketing

**You will save your document as
10D_Marketing_Firstname_Lastname**

Figure 10.33

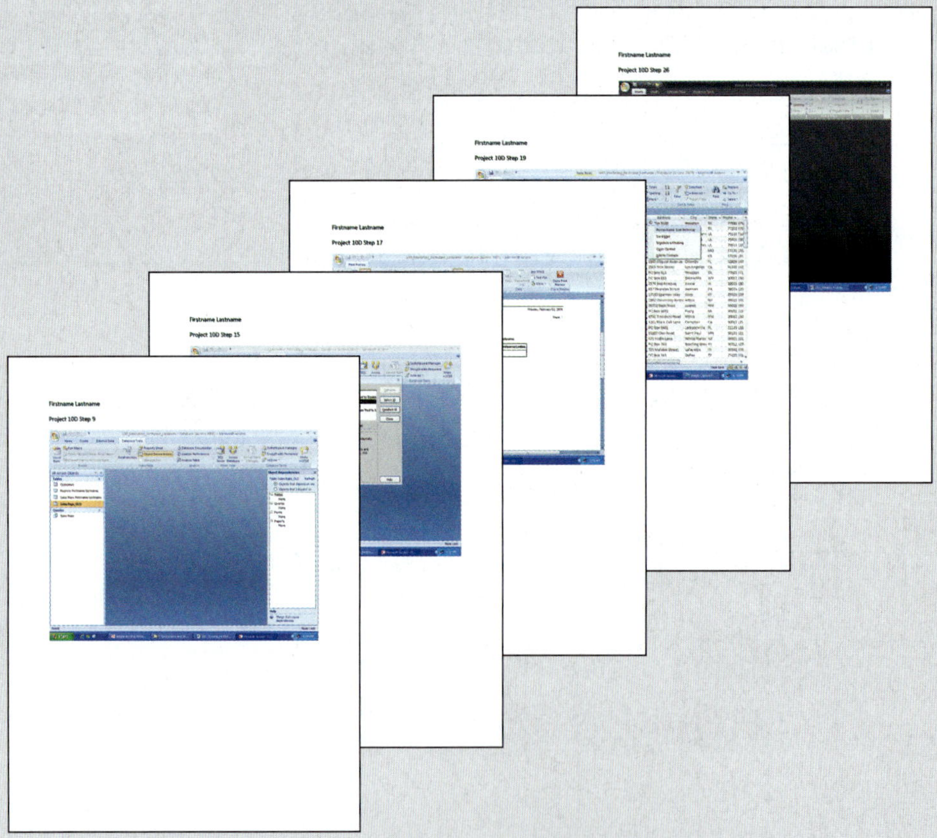

(Project 10D–Marketing continues on the next page)

Content-Based Assessments

Skills Review

(Project 10D–Marketing continued)

1. **Start Access**. Locate, and then open the **a10D_Marketing** file. Click the **Office** button, point to **Save As**, and then click **Access 2007 Database.** Save the database in your **Access Chapter 10** folder as 10D_Marketing_Firstname_Lastname

2. Click the **Database Tools tab**, and in then the **Analyze group**, click the **Analyze Table** button. If the introductory page displays, click **Next** two times.

3. Under **Tables**, click **Sales Reps**, and then click **Next**. Be sure that **Yes, let the wizard decide** is selected, and then click **Next**.

4. Double-click the **Table1** title bar, type **Sales Reps Firstname Lastname** and then click **OK**. Double-click the **Table2** title bar, type **Regions Firstname Lastname** and then click **OK**.

5. Click **Next**. With the **Regions** table still selected, click the **Add Generated Key** button—the button with the green plus sign and yellow key. In the **Sales Reps** table, click **Sales Rep ID**, and then click the **Set Unique Identifier** button.

6. Click **Next**, and then click **Finish**. **Close** the **Access Help** window, and then **Close** the **Sales Reps** query.

7. Be sure that **Sales Reps_OLD** table is selected, and then in the **Show/Hide group**, click **Object Dependencies**. In the displayed message, click **OK**.

8. In the **Object Dependencies** pane, check that no database objects depend on the **Sales_Reps_OLD** table. Press PrtScr, and then **Close** the **Object Dependencies** pane.

9. Open a new, blank **Word** document. In the **Word** document, type your first and last

names, press Enter, and then type **Project 10D Step 9** Press Enter, and then **Paste** the screen shot. **Save** the Word document in your **Access Chapter 10** folder as 10D_Screens_Firstname_Lastname

10. Return to **Access**, and then delete the **Sales Reps_OLD** table. Rename the **Customers** table, adding your first and last names at the end the object's name.

11. Click the **Create tab**. In the **Other group**, click the **Query Design** button. Add the **Customers** and **Sales Reps** tables to the query, and then **Close** the **Show Table** dialog box.

12. From the **Customers** table, add the **Company Name** field, and then from the **Sales Reps** table, add the **Firstname** and **Lastname** fields. Scroll to the bottom of the **Customers** table. Relate the two tables by dragging the **Sales Rep** field and dropping it on the **Sales Rep ID** field in the **Sales Rep** table.

13. Click **Save**, type **Customer Query Firstname Lastname** and then click **OK**. **Close** the query.

14. Click the **Database Tools tab**, and in then the **Analyze group**, click the **Analyze Performance** button. Click the **All Object Types tab**, click the **Select All** button, and then click **OK**.

15. Under **Analysis Results**, click the **Suggestion** with the green question mark, and then click the **Optimize** button. Press PrtScr, and then click the dialog box **Close** button. In the **Word** document, press Enter, and then press Ctrl + Enter to insert a page break. Type your first and last names, press Enter, and then type **Project 10D Step 15** Press Enter, **Paste** the screen shot, and then click **Save**.

(Project 10D–Marketing continues on the next page)

Content-Based Assessments

(Project 10D–Marketing continued)

16. Return to **Access**. In the **Analyze group**, click the **Database Documenter** button. In the **Documenter** dialog box, check the **Customers** table, and then click the **Options** button. Under **Include for Table**, only **Relationships** should be checked. The **Include for Fields** option and the **Include for Indexes** option should be set to **Nothing**. Click **OK** two times.

17. In **Print Preview**, **Zoom** in and then scroll so that all of the report text displays. Press PrtScr, and then click the **Close Print Preview** button. In the **Word** document, press Enter, and then press Ctrl + Enter to insert a page break. Type your first and last names, press Enter, and then type **Project 10D Step 17** Press Enter, **Paste** the screen shot, and then click **Save**.

18. Open the **Customers** table in Design view. Click the **Contact Name** field name, click the **Smart Tags** box, and then click the **Build** button. Check **Person Name**, and then click **OK**.

19. Click **Save**, and then switch to Datasheet view. In the first record, place the pointer over Scot Holloway, and then click the **Smart Tag Actions** button. Press PrtScr, and press Esc. In the **Word** document, press Enter, and then press Ctrl + Enter to insert a page break. Type your first and last names, press Enter, and then type **Project 10D Step 19** Press Enter, **Paste** the screen shot, and then click **Save**.

20. Return to **Access**, and then **Close** the **Customers** table. From the **Office** menu, click the **Access Options** button. If necessary, click Popular. Click the **Color scheme arrow**, and then click **Black**.

21. Click **Current Database**, and then in the **Application Title** box, type Image

Medtech Marketing Clear the **Display Status Bar** check box.

22. Under **Navigation**, click the **Navigation Options** button. Click the **Add Item** button, type **Marketing**, and then press Enter. Click the **Add Group** button, type **Customers** and then press Enter. Click **OK** two times.

23. Read the displayed message, and then click **OK**. From the **Office** menu, click **Close Database**, and then reopen the database.

24. Click the **Navigation Pane arrow**, and then click **Marketing**. Drag the **Customers** table and drop it into the **Customers group**. Drag **Customer Query** and drop it into the **Customers** group.

25. From the **Office** menu, click the **Access Options** button. Click **Customize**, click the **Customize Quick Access Toolbar arrow**, and then click the path for the current database. In the list below **Popular Commands**, click **Open**, and then click the **Add** button.

26. Click **OK**. Press PrtScr. In the **Word** document, press Enter, and then press Ctrl + Enter to insert a page break. Type your first and last names, press Enter, and then type **Project 10D Step 26** Press Enter, **Paste** the screen shot, and then click **Save**. If you are instructed to submit this result, create a paper or electronic printout of the Word document.

27. **Exit** Word. From the **Office** menu, click the **Access Options** button. Click **Popular**, and then change the **Color scheme** back to **Blue**. Click **OK**, and then **Exit** Access. If you are submitting your files electronically, submit the files as directed by your instructor.

End **You have completed Project 10D**

Mastering Access

Project 10E — Management

In this project, you will apply the skills you practiced from the Objectives in Project 10A.

Objectives: 1. *Compact and Repair a Database;* **2.** *Back Up a Database;* **3.** *Use the Database Splitter;* **4.** *Convert Databases to Other Versions;* **5.** *Replicate and Synchronize a Database.*

Image Medtech needs to protect its database files and build a front-end database using a single set of back-end tables. The company also needs to work with a database saved in Access 97. One worker will need to work with that database while on a trip, and then synchronize the changes when she returns. In the project, you will optimize the company database, and then split it into two files. You will convert an old database, and then create a replica set. You will document your work by creating screen shots. Your completed screen shots will look similar to the printout shown in Figure 10.34.

For Project 10E, you will need the following files:

a10E_Management
a10E_Tubes_97

You will save your files as
10E_Management_Firstname_Lastname
10E_Management_Firstname_Lastname (ACCDE file)
10E_Management_Firstname_Lastname_2007-07-01 (your date
will differ)
10E_Management_Firstname_Lastname_be
10E_Replica_Firstname_Lastname
10E_Screens_Firstname_Lastname
10E_Tubes_2003_Firstname_Lastname
10E_Tubes_2007_Firstname_Lastname

Figure 10.34

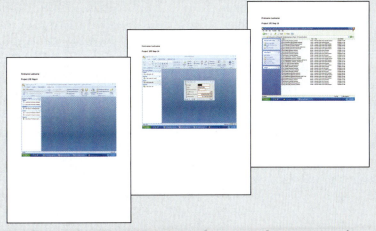

(Project 10E–Management continues on the next page)

(Project 10E–Management continued)

1. **Start Access**. Open **a10E_Management** located with the student files for this text. Click the **Office** button, point to **Save As**, and then click **Access 2007 Database.** Save the database in your **Access Chapter 10** folder as **10E_Management_Firstname_ Lastname**

2. Delete the following queries: **FL Customers**, **HI Customers**, **VA Customers**, and **WA Customers.** Delete the following reports: **FL Customers**, **HI Customers**, **VA Customers**, and **WA Customers**. Do not delete the *State Query* or *State Report.*

3. For the remaining database objects, add your own first and last names at the end of each object's name.

4. Create a backup copy of the database. Save the backup in your **Access Chapter 10** folder with the name suggested by Access.

5. Split the database into a back-end and front-end file. Save the back-end file in your **Access Chapter 10** folder with the name suggested by Access.

6. Press PrtScr. Open a new, blank Word document, type your first and last names, press Enter, and then type **Project 10E Step 6** Press Enter, and then **Paste** the screen shot. **Save** the Word document in your **Access Chapter 10** folder as **10E_Screens_ Firstname_Lastname**

7. Create a secure **ACCDE** version of the database file. Save the ACCDE file in your **Access Chapter 10** folder with the name suggested by Access.

8. **Compact and Repair** 10E_Management_ Firstname_Lastname.

9. **Close** the database. Convert **a10E_ Tubes_97**, located with the student files that came with your text, into an Access 2007 file. Name the converted file **10E_ Tubes_2007_Firstname_Lastname** and save it in your **Access Chapter 10** folder. Delete the **Conversion Errors** table.

10. Save the database in the **Access 2002 - 2003** file format. Name the file **10E_Tubes_ 2003_Firstname_Lastname** and save it in your **Access Chapter 10** folder. In the **Navigation Pane arrow**, display **All Access Objects**.

11. Replicate the current database. Do not create a backup, name the replica **10E_Replica_ Firstname_Lastname** and then save it in your **Access Chapter 10** folder.

12. Open the **X-Ray Tubes (97)** form in Layout view. Apply the **Equity** AutoFormat—the fourth choice in the second row. Click **Save**, and then **Close** the form.

13. **Close** the database, and then open **10E_ Replica_Firstname_Lastname**. Open the **X-Ray Tubes (97)** form. In the first record, change the **Coefficient** to **1.68** and then **Close** the form.

14. Synchronize the replica and Design Master databases. Open the **X-Ray Tubes (97)** form. Press PrtScr. **Close** the form, and then **Exit** Access. In the **Word** document, press Enter, and then press Ctrl + Enter to insert a page break. Type your first and last names, press Enter, and then type **Project 10E Step 14** Press Enter, **Paste** the screen shot, and then click **Save**.

15. Open **My Computer**, and then open your **Access Chapter 10** folder. If necessary, maximize the My Computer window and

(Project 10E–Management continues on the next page)

(Project 10E–Management continued)

switch to Details view. Be sure that all the files created in this project display. Be sure that the columns are wide enough to display all of the Name and Type descriptions. Press PrtScr, and then **Close** My Computer.

16. In the **Word** document, press Enter, and then press Ctrl + Enter to insert a page break. Type your first and last names,

press Enter, and then type **Project 10E Step 16** Press Enter, **Paste** the screen shot, and then click **Save**. If you are instructed to submit this result, create a paper or electronic printout of the Word document.

17. **Exit** Word. If you are submitting files electronically, submit the files as directed by your instructor.

End **You have completed Project 10E**

Content-Based Assessments

Project 10F — Sales Reps

In this project, you will apply the skills you practiced from the Objectives in Project 10B.

Objectives: 6. *Use Microsoft Access Analysis Tools;* **7.** *Add Smart Tags;* **8.** *Modify Access Views and Behaviors.*

Image Medtech needs to improve the performance of their Sales database. In this project, you will use the Access analysis tools to make several improvements to the database. You will then add smart tags and modify the database by changing several of its options. You will document your work by creating screen shots. Your screen shots document will look similar to the printout shown in Figure 10.35.

For Project 10F, you will need the following file:

a10F_Sales_Reps

You will save your files as
10F_Sales_Reps_Firstname_Lastname
10F_Screens_Firstname_Lastname

Figure 10.35

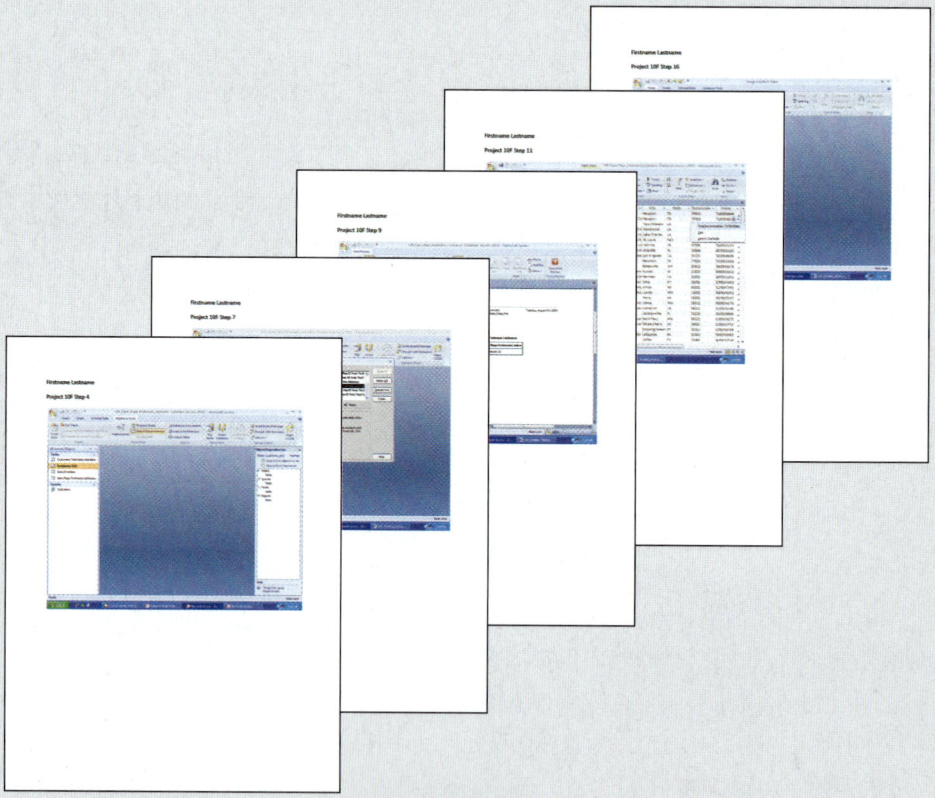

(Project 10F–Sales Reps continues on the next page)

(Project 10F–Sales Reps continued)

1. **Start Access**. Locate, and then open the **a10F_Sales_Reps** file. Click the **Office** button, point to **Save As**, and then click **Access 2007 Database.** Save the database in your **Access Chapter 10** folder as **10F_Sales_Reps_Firstname_Lastname**

2. Use the **Table Analyzer** wizard to analyze the **Customers** table. Have the wizard decide how to split the table, and then rename the suggested tables as follows:

Suggested Table	New Name
Table1	Customers Firstname Lastname
Table2	Sales Reps Firstname Lastname

3. After renaming the tables, click **Next**. In the **Customers** table, set **Customer ID** as the primary key. In the **Sales Reps** table, set **Sales Rep ID** as the primary key. Choose the option to create the query, and then **Finish** the wizard.

4. Close all open objects, open the **Object Dependencies** pane, and then display all database objects that depend on the **Customers_OLD** table. Press PrtScr, and then **Close** the **Object Dependencies** pane. Open a new, blank Word document, type your first and last names, press Enter, and then type **Project 10F Step 4** Press Enter, and then **Paste** the screen shot. **Save** the Word document in your **Access Chapter 10** folder as **10F_Screens_Firstname_Lastname**

5. Delete the **Customers_OLD** table. For the **Sales Directors** table, add your first and last names at the end the object's name. Rename the **Customers** query to **Old Customers Firstname Lastname**

6. Start a new query in **Query Design** view, and then add the **Sales Directors** and **Sales Reps** tables to the query. From the **Sales Directors** table, add the **Region** field, and then from the **Sales Reps** table, add the **Firstname** and **Lastname** fields. Click **Save**, type **Regions Firstname Lastname** and then click **OK**. **Close** the query.

7. Run the **Performance Analyzer** wizard for **All Object Types**. **Optimize** the item with the **Suggestion** icon. Press PrtScr, and then **Close** the wizard. In the **Word** document, press Enter, and then press Ctrl + Enter to insert a page break. Type your first and last names, press Enter, and then type **Project 10FD Step 7** Press Enter, **Paste** the screen shot, and then click **Save**.

8. Start the **Database Documenter**. In the **Documenter** dialog box, select the **Sales Directors** table. Select the following options: under **Include for Table**, only **Relationships** should be checked. The **Include for Fields** option and the **Include for Indexes** option should be set to **Nothing**. Generate the report.

9. In **Print Preview**, zoom in and then scroll so that all of the report text displays. Press PrtScr, and then click the **Close Print Preview** button. In the **Word** document, press Enter, and then press Ctrl + Enter to insert a page break. Type your first and last names, press Enter, and then type **Project 10F Step 9** Press Enter, **Paste** the screen shot, and then click **Save**.

10. Open the **Customers** table in Design view. For the **Phone** field, assign the **Telephone Number** smart tag.

(Project 10F–Sales Reps continues on the next page)

(Project 10F–Sales Reps continued)

11. Click **Save**, and then switch to **Datasheet** view. In the first record, display the **Smart Tag Actions** for the phone number. Press PrtScr, and then **Close** the table. In the **Word** document, press Enter, and then press Ctrl + Enter to insert a page break. Type your first and last names, press Enter, and then type **Project 10F Step 11** Press Enter, **Paste** the screen shot, and then click **Save**.

12. Open the **Access Options** dialog box. Under **Object Designers**, change the default text field size in tables to **75**

13. Change the **Application Title** to Image Medtech Sales For the **Application Icon**, assign **a10F_Icon**, a bitmap file located within the student files. For the current database, disable Layout view.

14. Edit the following Navigation Pane options: add a new category named **Sales** and then add a new group named **Sales Reps** In the **Navigation Pane**, display the **Sales** category. Drag the **Sales Reps** table and drop it into the **Sales Reps** category. Using the Navigation Pane options, do not display **Unassigned Items** in the Navigation Pane when the **Sales** category is selected.

15. For the current database only, add the following commands to the **Quick Access Toolbar**: **Import Access database**, **Import Excel spreadsheet**, and **Open**.

16. Close all open dialog boxes and database objects. Press PrtScr. In the **Word** document, press Enter, and then press Ctrl + Enter to insert a page break. Type your first and last names, press Enter, and then type **Project 10F Step 16** Press Enter, **Paste** the screen shot, and then click **Save**. If you are instructed to submit this result, create a paper or electronic printout of the screen shots document.

17. **Exit** Word. Reset the default text field size in tables back to **255** and then **Exit** Access. If you are submitting your files electronically, submit the files as directed by your instructor.

End **You have completed Project 10F**

Mastering Access

Project 10G — Products

In this project, you will apply all the skills you practiced from the Objectives in Projects 10A and 10B.

Objectives: 3. *Use the Database Splitter;* **4.** *Convert Databases to Other Versions;* **5.** *Replicate and Synchronize a Database;* **6.** *Use Microsoft Access Analysis Tools;* **7.** *Add Smart Tags;* **8.** *Modify Access Views and Behaviors.*

Image Medtech needs to make various improvements to two of its databases. In this activity, you will use analysis tools, change options, and split a database into two files. You will then convert an old database and replicate it. You will document your work by creating screen shots. Your screen shots document will look similar to the printout shown in Figure 10.36.

> ### For Project 10G, you will need the following files:
>
> a10G_Products
> a10G_Rad_Levels_97

You will save your files as
10G_Products_Firstname_Lastname
10G_Products_Firstname_Lastname_be
10G_Rad_Levels_2003_Firstname_Lastname
10G_Rad_Levels_2007_Firstname_Lastname
10G_Replica_Firstname_Lastname
10G_Screens_Firstname_Lastname

Figure 10.36

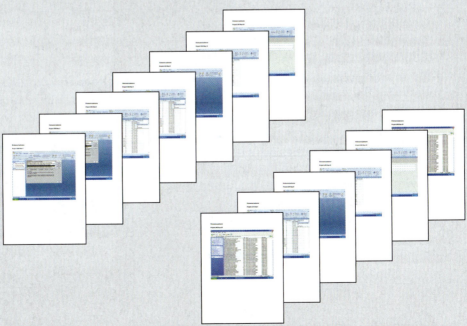

(Project 10G–Products continues on the next page)

(Project 10G–Products continued)

1. **Start Access. Open a10G_Products** located with the student files for this text. Click the **Office** button, point to **Save As**, and then click **Access 2007 Database**. Save the database in your **Access Chapter 10** folder as **10G_Products_Firstname_Lastname** For all of the database objects, add your own first and last names at the end of each object's name.

2. In the **Navigation Pane**, double-click the **Product Line** query to open the query in datasheet view. Click **Save**, and then close the query.

3. Run the **Performance Analyzer** wizard for **All Object Types**. **Optimize** the item with the **Suggestion** icon. Press PrtScr, and then **Close** the wizard. **Start** Word to open a new, blank document, type your first and last names, press Enter, and then type **Project 10G Step 3** Press Enter, and then **Paste** the screen shot. **Save** the Word document in your **Access Chapter 10** folder as **10G_Screens_ Firstname_Lastname**

4. Start the **Database Documenter**. In the **Documenter** dialog box, select the **Products** table. Select the following options: under **Include for Table**, only **Relationships** should be checked. The **Include for Fields** option and the **Include for Indexes** option should be set to **Nothing**. Generate the report.

5. In **Print Preview**, zoom in and then scroll so that all of the report text displays. Press PrtScr, and then click the **Close Print Preview** button. In the **Word** document, press Enter, and then press Ctrl + Enter to insert a page break. Type your first and last names, press Enter, and then type **Project 10G Step 5** Press Enter, **Paste** the screen shot, and then click **Save**.

6. Open the **Employees** table in Design view. For the **Phone** field, assign the **Telephone Number** smart tag.

7. Switch to **Datasheet** view. In the first record, place the pointer over the phone number, and then click the **Smart Tag Actions** button. Press PrtScr, and then **Close** the table. In the **Word** document, press Enter, and then press Ctrl + Enter to insert a page break. Type your first and last names, press Enter, and then type **Project 10G Step 7** Press Enter, **Paste** the screen shot, and then click **Save**.

8. Split the database into a back-end and front-end file. Save the back-end file in your **Access Chapter 10** folder with the name suggested by Access.

9. For the current database only, add the following commands to the **Quick Access Toolbar**: **Print Preview** (located in *Popular Commands*) and **Table Design** (located in *Commands Not in the Ribbon*). Click **OK**, and then press PrtScr. In the **Word** document, press Enter, and then press Ctrl + Enter to insert a page break. Type your first and last names, press Enter, and then type **Project 10F Step 9** Press Enter, **Paste** the screen shot, and then click **Save**.

10. **Close** the database. Convert **a10G_Rad_Levels_97**, located with the student files that came with your text, into an Access 2007 file. Name the converted file **10G_Rad_Levels_2007_Firstname_Lastname** and save it in your **Access Chapter 10** folder. Delete the **Conversion Errors** table.

11. Save the database in the **Access 2002 - 2003** file format. Name the file **10G_Rad_Levels_2003_Firstname_Lastname** and save it in your **Access Chapter 10** folder.

(Project 10G–Products continues on the next page)

Content-Based Assessments

Mastering Access

(Project 10G—Products continued)

12. Open the **Access Options** dialog box, and then click **Current Database**. Under **Document Window Options**, click **Tabbed Documents**. **Close** and then re-open the database. Open the **CR1001** table in Datasheet view. Press [PrtScr] and then close the table. In the **Word** document, press [Enter], and then press [Ctrl] + [Enter] to insert a page break. Type your first and last names, press [Enter], and then type **Project 10G Step 12** Press [Enter], **Paste** the screen shot, and then click **Save**.

13. Replicate the current database. Do not create a backup, name the replica **10G_Replica_Firstname_Lastname** and then save it in your **Access Chapter 10** folder.

14. With the **CR1001** table selected, click the **Create tab**. In the **Forms group**, click the **Form** button. Apply the **Northwind AutoFormat**—the last choice in the third row. Click **Save**, type **CR1001 Firstname Lastname** and then press [Enter].

15. **Close** the form, and then **Close** the database. Open **10G_Replica_Firstname_Lastname**. Synchronize the replica and Design Master databases. Open the **CR1001** form. Press [PrtScr]. **Close** the form,

and then **Exit** Access. In the **Word** document, press [Enter], and then press [Ctrl] + [Enter] to insert a page break. Type your first and last names, press [Enter], and then type **Project 10G Step 15** Press [Enter], and then **Paste** the screen shot.

16. Open **My Computer**, and then open your **Access Chapter 10** folder. If necessary, maximize the My Computer window and switch to Details view. Be sure that all the files created in this project display. Be sure that the columns are wide enough to display all of the Name and Type descriptions. Press [PrtScr], and then **Close** My Computer.

17. In the **Word** document, press [Enter], and then press [Ctrl] + [Enter] to insert a page break. Type your first and last names, press [Enter], and then type **Project 10G Step 17** Press [Enter], **Paste** the screen shot, and then click **Save**. If you are instructed to submit this result, create a paper or electronic printout of the Word document.

18. **Exit** Word. If you are submitting files electronically, submit the files as directed by your instructor.

End **You have completed Project 10G**

Access
chapter ten

Mastering Access

Project 10H — Films

In this project, you will apply all the skills you practiced from the Objectives in Projects 10A and 10B.

Objectives: 1. *Compact and Repair a Database;* **2.** *Back Up a Database;* **3.** *Use the Database Splitter;* **4.** *Convert Databases to Other Versions;* **6.** *Use Microsoft Access Analysis Tools;* **8.** *Modify Access Views and Behaviors.*

Image Medtech needs various improvements made to its database. In this activity, you will use analysis tools, change options, and split a database into two files. Before making changes, you will create a backup. When you are done, you will save the database as a secure ACCDE file. You will document your work by creating screen shots. Your screen shot document will look similar to the printout shown in Figure 10.37.

> ### For Project 10H, you will need the following file:
>
> a10H_Films

You will save your files as
10H_Films_Firstname_Lastname
10H_Films_Firstname_Lastname (ACCDE file)
10H_Films_Firstname_Lastname_2007-07-06 (your date will differ)
10H_Films_Firstname_Lastname_be
10H_Screens_Firstname_Lastname

Figure 10.37

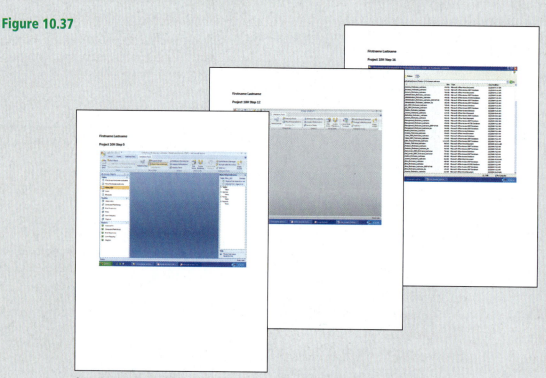

(Project 10H–Films continues on the next page)

Content-Based Assessments

Mastering Access

(Project 10H–Films continued)

1. **Start Access**. Open **a10H_Films**, located with the student files. Click the **Office** button, point to **Save As**, and then click **Access 2007 Database**. Save the database in your **Access Chapter 10** folder as **10H_Films_Firstname_Lastname**

2. Create a backup copy of the database. Save the backup in your **Access Chapter 10** folder using the name suggested by Access.

3. Use the **Table Analyzer** wizard to analyze the **Films** table. Let the wizard decide how to split the table, and then rename the suggested tables as follows:

Suggested Table	New Name
Table1	Films Firstname Lastname
Table2	Film Series Firstname Lastname

4. After renaming the tables, assign **Product ID** as a primary key, and then finish the wizard using the wizard's suggested options.

5. Close all open objects, and then in the **Object Dependencies** pane, display all database objects that depend on the **Films_OLD** table. Press PrtScr, and then **Close** the **Object Dependencies pane**. Open a new, blank Word document, type your first and last names, press Enter, and then type **Project 10H Step 5** Press Enter, and then **Paste** the screen shot. **Save** the Word document in your **Access Chapter 10** folder as **10H_Screens_Firstname_Lastname**

6. Delete the **Films_OLD** table.

7. Open the **Access Options** dialog box, and then change the **Color Scheme** to **Silver**. Change the **Application Title** box to **Image Medtech**

8. Change the Navigation Pane options as follows: add a new category named **Products** and then add a new group in that category named **Films**

9. For the current database only, add the following commands to the **Quick Access Toolbar**: **Open**, **Print Preview**, and **Quick Print**.

10. Close all dialog boxes, and then delete all of the database reports and queries. For the two remaining database tables, add your own first and last names at the end of each object's name. **Compact and Repair** the database file.

11. Split the database into a back-end and front-end file. Save the back-end file in your **Access Chapter 10** folder with the name suggested by Access.

12. In the **Navigation Pane**, display the **Products** category. Drag the **Film Series** and **Films** tables and drop them into the **Films** group. Press PrtScr. In the **Word** document, press Enter, and then press Ctrl + Enter to insert a page break. Type your first and last names, press Enter, and then type **Project 10H Step 12** Press Enter, **Paste** the screen shot, and then click **Save**.

13. Create a secure **ACCDE** version of the database file. Save the ACCDE file in your **Access Chapter 10** folder with the name suggested by Access.

14. Change the Access color scheme back to **Blue**, and then **Exit** Access.

(Project 10H–Films continues on the next page)

Access

chapter ten

Mastering Access

(Project 10H–Films continued)

15. Open **My Computer**, and then open your **Access Chapter 10** folder. If necessary, maximize the My Computer window and switch to Details view. Be sure that all the files created in this project display. Be sure that the columns are wide enough to display all of the Name and Type descriptions. Press PrtScr, and then **Close** My Computer.

16. In the **Word** document, press Enter, and then press Ctrl + Enter to insert a page break. Type your first and last names, press Enter, and then type **Project 10H Step 16** Press Enter, **Paste** the screen shot, and then click **Save**. If you are instructed to submit this result, create a paper or electronic printout of the Word document.

17. **Exit** Word. If you are submitting files electronically, submit the files as directed by your instructor.

End You have completed Project 10H

Content-Based Assessments

Access
chapter ten

Mastering Access

Project 10I—Employees

In this project, you will apply all the skills you practiced from the Objectives in Projects 10A and 10B.

The Image Medtech Human Resources Department needs to work with an old database that was used to store records for employees. In this activity, you will convert the database to Access 2007, use several analysis tools, and then customize the database by changing several options. You will create several versions of the database, including a backup, a secure ACCDE file, a split database, and a replica set. You will document your work by creating screen shots. Your screen shot document will look similar to the printout shown in Figure 10.38.

For Project 10I, you will need the following file:

a10I_Employees_97

You will save your files as
10I_Backup_Firstname_Lastname
10I_Employees_2003_Firstname_Lastname
10I_Employees_2007_Firstname_Lastname
10I_Employees_2007_Firstname_Lastname (ACCDE file)
10I_Employees_2007_Firstname_Lastname_be
10I_Replica_Firstname_Lastname
10I_Screens_Firstname_Lastname

Figure 10.38

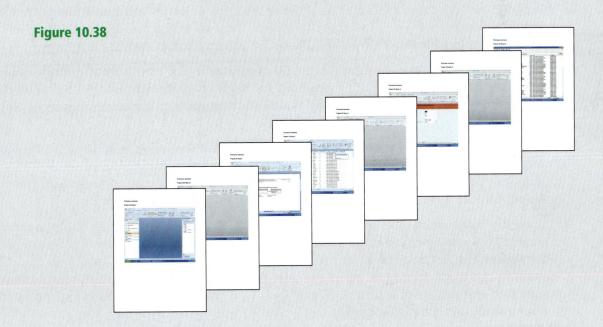

(Project 10I–Employees continues on the next page)

Mastering Access

(Project 10I–Employees continued)

1. **Start Access**. Convert **a10I_Employees_97**, located with the student files that came with your text, into an Access 2007 file. Name the converted file **10I_Employees_2007_Firstname_Lastname** and save it in your **Access Chapter 10** folder. Delete the **Conversion Errors** table.

2. Use the **Table Analyzer** wizard to analyze the **Employees** table. Let the wizard decide how to split the table, and then rename the suggested tables as follows:

Suggested Table	New Name
Table1	Employees Firstname Lastname
Table2	Positions Firstname Lastname
Table3	Departments Firstname Lastname

3. In the **Table Analyzer**, set **ID** as the primary key for the **Employees** table. In the next wizard screen, click **Next**, and then click **Yes**. In the next screen, click **Next**, and then click **Yes**. On the last wizard screen, click **Finish**.

4. Close all open objects, and then in the **Object Dependencies pane**, display all database objects that depend on the **Employees** query. Press [PrtScr], and then **Close** the **Object Dependencies pane**. **Start** Word to open a new, blank document, type your first and last names, press [Enter], and then type **Project 10I Step 4** Press [Enter], and then **Paste** the screen shot. **Save** the Word document in your **Access Chapter 10** folder as **10I_Screens_Firstname_Lastname**

5. Delete the **Employees_OLD** table, the **Employees** query, the **Employees** form, and then the **Employees** report.

6. Run the **Performance Analyzer** wizard for all database objects. **Optimize** the item with the **Suggestion** icon. Press [PrtScr], and then **Close** the wizard. In the **Word** document, press [Enter], and then press [Ctrl] + [Enter] to insert a page break. Type your first and last names, press [Enter], and then type **Project 10I Step 6** Press [Enter], **Paste** the screen shot, and then click **Save**.

7. Open the **Database Documenter**. In the **Documenter** dialog box, select the **Employees** table. Select the following options: under **Include for Table**, only **Relationships** should be checked. The **Include for Fields** option and the **Include for Indexes** option should be set to **Nothing**. Generate the report.

8. In **Print Preview**, zoom in, and then scroll so that all of the report text displays. Press [PrtScr], and then click the **Close Print Preview** button. In the **Word** document, press [Enter], and then press [Ctrl] + [Enter] to insert a page break. Type your first and last names, press [Enter], and then type **Project 10I Step 8** Press [Enter], **Paste** the screen shot, and then click **Save**.

9. Open the **Employees** table in Design view. For the **Phone** field, assign the **Telephone Number** smart tag. **Save** the changes, and then switch to **Datasheet** view. In the first record, display the **Smart Tag Actions** menu for the phone number. Press [PrtScr], and then press [Esc]. **Close** the table. In the **Word** document, press [Enter], and then press [Ctrl] + [Enter] to insert a page break. Type your first and last names, press [Enter], and then type **Project 10I Step 9** Press [Enter], **Paste** the screen shot, and then click **Save**.

(Project 10I–Employees continues on the next page)

Content-Based Assessments

(Project 10I–Employees continued)

10. Open the **Access Options** dialog box, and then change the **Color Scheme** to **Silver**. Change the **Application Title** box to Image Medtech

11. For the current database only, add the following commands to the **Quick Access Toolbar**: **Export to Excel Spreadsheet**, **Spelling**, and **Toggle Filter**.

12. Change the following Navigation Pane options: add a new category named **Human Resources** and then in that new category, add a new group named **Employees** Close the dialog box, and then in the **Navigation Pane**, display the **Human Resources** category. Place the **Employees** table in the **Employees** group.

13. In the **Navigation Pane**, rename **Lines**, **Products**, and **Product Line** to include your first and last names at the end of each object name. Press [PrtScr], and then press [Esc]. In the **Word** document, press [Enter], and then press [Ctrl] + [Enter] to insert a page break. Type your first and last names, press [Enter], and then type **Project 10I Step 13** Press [Enter], **Paste** the screen shot, and then click **Save**.

14. Create a backup copy of the database. Save the backup in your **Access Chapter 10** folder using the name a10I_Backup_Firstname_Lastname

15. **Compact and Repair** the current database.

16. Create a secure **ACCDE** version of the database file. Save the ACCDE file in your **Access Chapter 10** folder with the name suggested by Access.

17. Save the database in the **Access 2002 - 2003** file format. Name the file 10I_Employees_2003_Firstname_Lastname and save it in your **Access Chapter 10** folder.

18. Replicate the current database. Do not create a backup, name the replica 10I_Replica_Firstname_Lastname and then save it in your **Access Chapter 10** folder.

19. In the **Navigation Pane**, display **All Database Objects**. Select the **Employees** table, click the **Create tab**, and the in the **Forms group**, click the **Form** button.

20. Apply **Civic AutoFormat**—the last choice in the first row. Decrease the width of the data grid so that the text boxes are about 2.5 inches wide. Click **Save**, click **OK**, and then **Close** the form.

21. **Close** the database. Open **10I_Replica_Firstname_Lastname**. Synchronize the replica and Design Master databases. Open the **Employees** form. Press [PrtScr]. **Close** the form, and then **Close** the database. In the **Word** document, press [Enter], and then press [Ctrl] + [Enter] to insert a page break. Type your first and last names, press [Enter], and then type **Project 10I Step 21** Press [Enter], and then **Paste** the screen shot.

22. Open **10I_Employees 2007_Firstname_Lastname**. Split the database into a back-end and front-end file. Save the back-end file in your **Access Chapter 10** folder with the name suggested by Access. Press [PrtScr]. In the **Word** document, press [Enter], and then press [Ctrl] + [Enter] to insert a page break. Type your first and last names, press [Enter], and then type **Project 10I Step 22** Press [Enter], and then **Paste** the screen shot.

(Project 10I–Employees continues on the next page)

(Project 10I–Employees continued)

23. In **Access**, reset the **Color Scheme** to **Blue**, and then **Exit** Access.

24. Open **My Computer**, and then open your **Access Chapter 10** folder. If necessary, maximize the My Computer window and switch to Details view. Be sure that all the files created in this project display. Be sure that the columns are wide enough to display all of the Name and Type descriptions. Press ⌈PrtScr⌉, and then **Close** My Computer.

25. In the **Word** document, press ⌈Enter⌉, and then press ⌈Ctrl⌉ + ⌈Enter⌉ to insert a page break. Type your first and last names, press ⌈Enter⌉, and then type **Project 10I Step 25** Press ⌈Enter⌉, **Paste** the screen shot, and then click **Save**. If you are instructed to submit this result, create a paper or electronic printout of the Word document.

26. **Exit** Word. If you are submitting files electronically, submit the files as directed by your instructor.

End **You have completed Project 10I**

 ## Business Running Case

Project 10J—Business Running case

In this project, you will apply the skills you have practiced from the Objectives in Projects 10A and 10B.

From My Computer, navigate to the student files that accompany this textbook. In the folder **03_business_running_case**, locate and open the folder for this chapter. Open and print the instructions for this project, which are provided to you in Adobe PDF format. Follow the instructions and use the skills you have gained thus far to assist the brother and sister team of Michael and Kristen Landry in meeting the challenges of owning and running their business.

 End You have completed Project 10J————————

Outcomes-Based Assessments

Rubric

The following outcomes-based assessments are *open-ended assessments*. That is, there is no specific correct result; your result will depend on your approach to the information provided. Make *Professional Quality* your goal. Use the following scoring rubric to guide you in *how* to approach the problem and then to evaluate *how well* your approach solves the problem.

The *criteria*—Software Mastery, Content, Format and Layout, and Process—represent the knowledge and skills you have gained that you can apply to solving the problem. The *levels of performance*—Professional Quality, Approaching Professional Quality, or Needs Quality Improvement—help you and your instructor evaluate your result.

	Your completed project is of Professional Quality if you:	Your completed project is Approaching Professional Quality if you:	Your completed project Needs Quality Improvements if you:
Software Mastery	Choose and apply the most appropriate skills, tools, and features and identify efficient methods to solve the problem.	Choose and apply some appropriate skills, tools, and features, but not in the most efficient manner.	Choose inappropriate skills, tools, or features, or are inefficient in solving the problem.
Content	Construct a solution that is clear and well organized, contains content that is accurate, appropriate to the audience and purpose, and is complete. Provide a solution that contains no errors of spelling, grammar, or style.	Construct a solution in which some components are unclear, poorly organized, inconsistent, or incomplete. Misjudge the needs of the audience. Have some errors in spelling, grammar, or style, but the errors do not detract from comprehension.	Construct a solution that is unclear, incomplete, or poorly organized, containing some inaccurate or inappropriate content; and contains many errors of spelling, grammar, or style. Do not solve the problem.
Format and Layout	Format and arrange all elements to communicate information and ideas, clarify function, illustrate relationships, and indicate relative importance.	Apply appropriate format and layout features to some elements, but not others. Overuse features, causing minor distraction.	Apply format and layout that does not communicate information or ideas clearly. Do not use format and layout features to clarify function, illustrate relationships, or indicate relative importance. Use available features excessively, causing distraction.
Process	Use an organized approach that integrates planning, development, self-assessment, revision, and reflection.	Demonstrate an organized approach in some areas, but not others; or, use an insufficient process of organization throughout.	Do not use an organized approach to solve the problem.

Problem Solving

Project 10K — Pipeline

In this project, you will construct a solution by applying any combination of the skills you practiced from the Objectives in Projects 10A and 10B.

For Project 10K, you will need the following file:

a10K_Pipeline_97

**You will save your database as
10K_Pipeline_Firstname_Lastname**

Image Medtech has an old database with a single table that needs to be converted into an Access 2007 database with related tables. To start, convert **a10K_Pipeline_97** into an Access 2007 file, with the name **10K_Pipeline_Firstname_Lastname** Delete the Conversion Errors table. For the *Sales Pipeline* table, add your first and last names at the end of its name.

Use the Table Analyzer to convert the *Sales Pipeline* table into several smaller, related tables. For each suggested table, assign an appropriate name, and include your first and last names in the table name. Modify the suggestions for each table's primary key as appropriate. For example, make sure each table is assigned a primary key, and *do not* use phone extensions for the primary keys. Ignore the wizard's suggestions for correcting typographical errors, and *do not* have the wizard create a query.

After creating the new tables, open the Relationships window. Rearrange the displayed tables so that the relationships display clearly. Save the layout of the Relationships window. Submit the project as directed by your instructor.

End **You have completed Project 10K** ───────────

Problem Solving

Project 10L — Replication

In this project, you will construct a solution by applying any combination of the skills you practiced from the Objectives in Projects 10A and 10B.

For Project 10L, you will need the following file:

a10L_Replication

You will save your files as
10L_Replication_Firstname_Lastname
10L_User1_Firstname_Lastname
10L_User2_Firstname_Lastname

Two workers at Image Medtech need to work with the company database from remote locations. You need to replicate the database so that all the changes that they make can be synchronized. To start, open **a10L_Replication**, and then save it as a 2003 database with the name **10L_Replication_Firstname_Lastname** For each database object, add your own name to the end of each object name.

Create two replicas of 10L_Replication_Firstname_Lastname. For the first replica, do not create a backup copy, and save it in your Access Chapter 10 folder with the name **10L_User1_Firstname_Lastname** For the second replica, do not create a backup copy, and save it in your Access Chapter 10 with the name **10L_User2_Firstname_Lastname**

In the Design Master, create a form using all of the fields in the *Invoices* table. Format the form as needed, and apply the AutoFormat of your choice. Save the form as **Invoices Firstname Lastname** Synchronize the changes made to the Design Master with the replicas for *User1* and *User2*. Submit the project as directed by your instructor.

End **You have completed Project 10L** ——————————

Problem Solving

Project 10M — Design

In this project, you will construct a solution by applying any combination of the skills you practiced from the Objectives in Projects 10A and 10B.

For Project 10M, you will need the following file:

a10M_Design

**You will save your database as
10M_Design_Firstname_Lastname**

Image MedTech would like you to redesign their database. To start, open **a10M_Design**, and then save it as a 2007 database with the name **10M_Design_Firstname_Lastname** For each database object, add your first and last names at the end of its name.

Change the following options for the current database. Create an appropriate application title, and then assign the icon name *aM10_Icon* located with the student files. Set the icon to display in all forms and reports. Set the database to compact each time it is closed, and disable Layout view.

Create a custom Navigation Pane with at least one category and at least two groups. Place each database object in the appropriate group. After organizing the Navigation Pane, change the setting so that the *Unassigned Objects* group does not display. On the Quick Access Toolbar, add five tools that you think will be frequently used. Be sure to add the tools to the current database's Quick Access Toolbar and not to all Quick Access Toolbars. Submit the project as directed by your instructor.

End **You have completed Project 10M** ——————————

Outcomes-Based Assessments

Access

chapter ten

Problem Solving

Project 10N — Front-Ends

In this project, you will construct a solution by applying any combination of the skills you practiced from the Objectives in Projects 10A and 10B.

For Project 10N, you will need the following file:

a10N_Front-Ends

**You will save your databases as
10N_Back-End_Firstname_Lastname
10N_Marketing_Firstname_Lastname
10N_RandD_Firstname_Lastname**

Two departments at Image Medtech need different databases that share the same tables. In this project, you will split the database, and then create two different front-ends. To start, open **a10N_Front-Ends**, and then save it as a 2007 database with the name **10N_Marketing_Firstname_Lastname** For each database object, add your name at the end, and then split the database using **10N_Back-End_Firstname_Lastname** for the back-end file name.

With the *Marketing* database open, create a form for each database table. Format the forms to display effectively on the screen, and then save each form with the name provided by Access.

Start a new database named **10N_RandD_Firstname_Lastname** Close the displayed *Table 1* without saving it. Use the Get External Data dialog box to link the *Lines* and *Products* tables from the **10N_Back-End** database. Create a form for each of the two tables. Format the forms to display effectively on the screen, and save each form with the name provided by Access. Submit the project as directed by your instructor.

End **You have completed Project 10N**

Problem Solving

Project 10O — Optimize

In this project, you will construct a solution by applying any combination of the skills you practiced from the Objectives in Projects 10A and 10B.

For Project 10O, you will need the following file:

a10O_Optimize

You will save your databases as
10O_Optimize_Firstname_Lastname
10O_ACCDE_Firstname_Lastname

Image Medtech needs to improve the speed of its database. In this project, you will use the Performance Analyzer to improve the database. To start, open **a10O_Optimize**, and then save it as a 2007 database with the name **10O_Optimize_Firstname_Lastname**

Run the Performance Analyzer for all database objects. For all items marked Suggested, optimize the database. Run the Performance Analyzer a second time and optimize all suggested items. Ignore the suggestions for those items marked as ideas. For each database object, add your first and last names at the end of its name. Make an ACCDE version of the database using the name **10O_ACCDE_Firstname_Lastname** Open the ACCDE version, and run the Performance Analyzer again. Submit the project as directed by your instructor.

End You have completed Project 10O ——————

Outcomes-Based Assessments

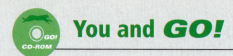 You and *GO!*

Project 10P—You and *GO!*

In this project, you will construct a solution by applying any combination of the Objectives found in Projects 10A and 10B.

From My Computer, navigate to the student files that accompany this textbook. In the folder **04_you_and_go**, locate and open the folder for this chapter. Open and print the instructions for this project, which are provided to you in Adobe PDF format. Follow the instructions to create a form to enter records for a database of personal music.

 You have completed Project 10P

GO! with Help

Project 10Q—*GO!* with Help

The Access Help system is extensive and can help you as you work. The Access Options dialog box is often used to create an application that prevents others from viewing all database objects or from using Layout view. These options can be bypassed to gain full access to the database.

1. **Start Access**, and then click the **Help** button.
2. In the **Search** box, type **bypass startup options** and then click **Search**.
3. In the **Access Help** window, from the **Results** list, click **Bypass startup options when you open a database**.
4. Read how to bypass startup options.
5. If you want to print a copy, click the **Print** button at the top of Access Help window.
6. **Close** the **Help** window, and then **Exit** Access.

 You have completed Project 10Q

chaptereleven

Securing Databases and Writing SQL Statements

OBJECTIVES

At the end of this chapter you will be able to:

1. Encrypt and Decrypt Databases
2. Secure the Access Administrator Account
3. Create an Access Administrative User
4. Create Users and Groups
5. Change Ownership and Assign Permissions to Database Objects
6. Test and Reset Default Security Settings
7. Create and Modify Workgroups Using the Security Wizard

8. Modify a Query in SQL View
9. Create a Query in SQL View
10. Create a Union Query Using SQL
11. Create Calculated Fields and SQL Aggregate Functions

OUTCOMES

Mastering these objectives will enable you to:

Project 11A
Secure Access Databases

Project 11B
Write SQL Statements

DeLong Grant Law Partners

Attorneys at DeLong Grant Law Partners counsel their clients on a wide variety of issues including contracts, licensing, intellectual property, and taxation, with emphasis on the unique needs of the sports and entertainment industries. Entertainment clients include production companies, publishers, talent agencies, actors, writers, artists—anyone involved in creating or doing business in the entertainment industry. Sports clients include colleges and universities, professional sports teams, athletes, and venue operators. Increasingly, amateur and community sports coaches and organizations with concerns about liability are also seeking the firm's specialized counsel.

Securing Databases and Writing SQL Statements

Organizations that store information in databases often wish to limit who can view the data. Typically, only a small set of individuals are allowed to view reports, enter new records, alter records, or delete records. An even smaller group should be allowed to make design changes to the database. Design changes include adding and removing fields from a table; adding tables; and designing queries, forms, and reports. Access provides a mechanism whereby users must enter their user name and password before opening a database. Different privileges can then be assigned to each user as needed.

Access provides a view for creating and modifying the SQL, or Structure Query Language, that makes all of its queries work. Certain types of queries must be designed using this view. For example, by writing SQL commands, the results of two or more queries can be combined into one query. Database designers also use this view to learn how SQL works.

Project 11A **Lawyers**

Delong Grant Law Partners has a database that contains lawyer data, corporate client data, and corporate case data. To maintain attorney-client confidentiality, the partners must be sure that the data is seen only by authorized lawyers. In Activities 11.1 through 11.11, you will secure three versions of this database so that the partners can evaluate which security method will work best. You will encrypt and decrypt a database saved in the Access 2007 file format. Using databases saved in the Access 2002 - 2003 file format, you will create accounts for lawyers and staff and set different levels of security. You will also generate security reports that will look similar to the reports shown in Figure 11.1.

For Project 11A, you will need the following files:

a11A_Lawyers
a11A_2007

You will save your files as
11A_2003_Firstname_Lastname
11A_Encoded_Firstname_Lastname
11A_Lawyers_Firstname_Lastname
11A_Screens_Firstname_Lastname
11A_System_Firstname_Lastname
11A_WIF_FML (Access file, Windows shortcut, workgroup
information file, Snapshot file)
11A_WIF_Unsecured_FML

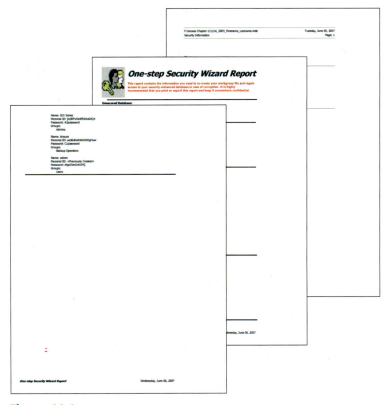

Figure 11.1
Project 11A—Lawyers

Objective 1
Encrypt and Decrypt Databases

The data stored in any company's database is one of that company's most valuable assets. If proprietary knowledge is made public, the company could lose its competitive advantage. Further, personal information stored in the database needs to be protected from unauthorized access. For these reasons, the data needs to be hidden until the correct password is entered. Only authorized users should know what that password is.

Activity 11.1 Encrypting a Database with a Password

DeLong Grant Law Partners have a moral and legal responsibility to keep the data they collect hidden from unauthorized individuals. If one of the company computers or laptops is ever lost or stolen, the data should be unreadable to anyone outside of the company. In this activity, you will make an Access 2007 database unreadable until a password is entered.

1 **Start** Access. Navigate to the location where the student data files for this textbook are saved. Locate and then open the **a11A_Lawyers** database. Click the **Office** button 📇, point to **Save As**, and then click **Access 2007 Database**. In the **Save As** dialog box, navigate to the drive on which you will be saving your folders and projects for this chapter. Create a new folder named **Access Chapter 11** and then save the file as **11A_Lawyers_Firstname_Lastname** in the folder.

Alert!

Access asks me to log in

If the previous student at your computer did not remember to reset the Access security settings on your computer, they will need to be reset before you can continue with this project. Complete the steps to reset user security found in Activity 11.9, "Copying and Resetting Default Security Settings."

---

2 If necessary, add the Access Chapter 11 folder to the Trust Center. In the **Navigation Pane**, rename each table by adding **FML** using the first, middle, and last initials of your own name to the end of each object name. Do not use any spaces in the table names.

Note — Table and Field Naming Conventions

Recall that in this chapter, you will be creating queries by writing SQL. To simplify the SQL statements, database designers usually choose a naming convention where table and field names are kept short and do not contain any spaces. For this reason, all of the projects in this chapter follow what is known as the Upper Camel Case naming convention, and you will add your initials to the table names instead of your first and last name.

---

3 Click the **Office** button 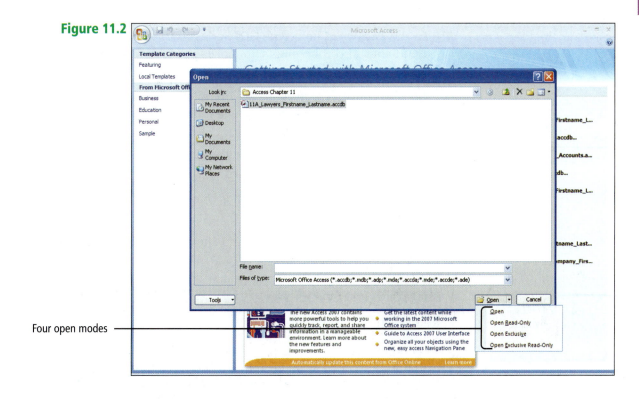, and then click **Close Database**. Click the **Office** button , and then click **Open**. In the **Open** dialog box, open the **Access Chapter 11** folder, and then click **11A_Lawyers_ Firstname_Lastname** one time. In the lower right corner of the **Open** dialog box, click the **Open button arrow**, and compare your screen with Figure 11.2

Three additional open modes display. ***Open Read-Only*** opens the database so that all objects can be opened and viewed, but data and design changes cannot be made. ***Open Exclusive*** opens the database so that changes can be made, but no one else may open the database at the same time. ***Open Exclusive Read-Only*** opens the database in both Exclusive and Read-Only modes.

Figure 11.2

Four open modes

4 Click **Open Exclusive**.

The database must be opened in exclusive mode before it can be encrypted. To ***encrypt*** means to hide data by making the file unreadable until the correct password is entered.

5 Click the **Database Tools tab**, and in the **Database Tools group**, click the **Encrypt with Password** button. Compare your screen with Figure 11.3.

Figure 11.3

6 In the **Password** box, type **GO! Series** In the **Verify** box, type **GO! Series** and then click **OK**. Access passwords are case sensitive, so be sure to capitalize exactly as shown.

Special characters and spaces are allowed in Access password names. In this password, a space follows an exclamation mark.

7 **Close** and then reopen the database. In the displayed **Password Required** dialog box, type **GO! Series** and then click **OK**. Alternatively, type the password, and then press Enter.

With encrypted Access 2007 files, individuals must enter a password to work with the database.

8 Click the **Office** button 📋, and then click **Close Database**.

More Knowledge

Removing Encryption

Entering the correct password for an encrypted file enables you to work with the database, but the file remains encrypted. If you no longer desire that a password be required to open the database, the file must be permanently decrypted. To *decrypt* is remove a file's encryption. To decrypt an Access database saved in the 2007 file format, use the Decrypt Database button located in the Database Tools group. After entering the correct password, the file will no longer be encrypted.

Activity 11.2 Encoding and Password Protecting a 2003 Database

DeLong Grant Law Partners need more control over who can view and work with their database. The Access 2002 - 2003 file format provides more options for securing databases than the 2007 file format. In this activity, you will encode a database saved in the 2002 - 2003 file format, password protect the database, and then test these security settings.

1 Click the **Office** button 📋, and then click **Open**. Navigate to the location where the student data files for this textbook are saved, and then open **a11A_2007**.

2 Click the **Office** button 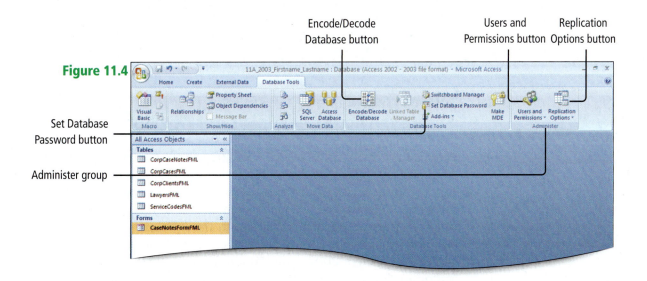, point to **Save As**, and then click **Access 2002 - 2003 Database**. In the **Save As** dialog box, navigate to the **Access Chapter 11** folder and **Save** the file as **11A_2003_Firstname_Lastname**

3 Click the **Navigation Pane arrow**, and then under **Filter by Group**, click **All Access Objects**. On the **Navigation Pane**, rename each object by adding your first, middle, and last initials to the end of each object name. Do not use any spaces in the table names.

4 Open **CaseNotesForm** in Design view. Display the properties for the form. In the **Property Sheet Data tab**, click the **Record Source arrow**, and then click **CorpCaseNotes**. Click **Save**, and then **Close** the form.

5 Click the **Database Tools tab**, and then compare your screen with Figure 11.4.

In the Database Tools group, two buttons display—*Encode/Decode Database* and *Set Database Password*. A new group displays, the *Administer group*, with two buttons—*Users and Permissions* and *Replication Options*. These buttons display only when the database is saved in the 2002 - 2003 file format.

Figure 11.4

Encode/Decode Database button

Users and Permissions button

Replication Options button

Set Database Password button

Administer group

6 In the **Database Tools group**, click the **Encode/Decode Database** button.

Files in the 2002 - 2003 format use the terms encode and decode. To **encode** means to encrypt a 2002 - 2003 database without requiring a password to open it. To **decode** a database means to remove a file's encoding.

7 In the displayed **Encode Database As** dialog box, under **Save in**, be sure that your **Access Chapter 11** folder displays. In the **File name** box, type **11A_Encoded_Firstname_Lastname** and then click **Save**.

A new encrypted file is created, but is not opened. The current database remains unencrypted.

8 Click the **Office** button 🔲, and then click **Close Database**. Use the technique practiced in earlier activities to open **11A_Encoded_ Firstname_Lastname** using the **Open Exclusive** command.

Although the file is encrypted, Access did not prompt you for a password.

9 Click the **Database Tools tab**, and then in the **Database Tools group**, click **Set Database Password**.

10 In the displayed **Set Database Password** dialog box, in the **Password** box, type **GO! Series** In the **Verify** box, type **GO! Series** and click **OK**.

11 Click the **Office** button 🔲, and then click **Close Database**. Open **11A_Encoded_Firstname_Lastname** using the **Open** command. Type the password **GO! Series** and then click **OK**.

12 Click the **Office** button 🔲, and then click **Close Database**.

More Knowledge

Securing Databases in the 2002 - 2003 File Format

Databases in the 2002 - 2003 file format are password protected, but the file is not encrypted. In this case, software other than Access could be used to view the data. For this reason, databases in this file format should be password protected and encoded.

Objective 2
Secure the Access Administrator Account

Saving an Access database in the 2002 - 2003 file format enables user-level security. *User-level security* enables administrators to grant different permissions to different users or groups of users. The *administrator* is the person who has full permissions to all database objects and manages all users and groups. By default, the administrator's account is not secured and anyone could be given administrator permissions. The first step in securing a 2002 - 2003 database is to secure the default administrator account.

Activity 11.3 Securing the Administrator Account

Access comes with a built-in administrator account. This account is unsecured, and Access does not require the administrator to enter a user name and password. DeLong Grant Law Partners do not want to leave this account unsecured. In this activity, you will secure the built-in administrator account.

1 Locate and open the **11A_2003_Firstname_Lastname** database.

2 Click the **Database Tools tab**. In the **Administer group**, click the **Users and Permissions** button, and then click **User and Group Accounts**. Compare your screen with Figure 11.5.

Under User, one user is listed—*Admin*. A **user** is a person who will need to use the database. **Admin** is the name of the default user in Access. *Admin* is a member of two groups—Admins and Users. A **group** is a collection of users who will use the database in similar ways.

Figure 11.5

User's name

Users groups

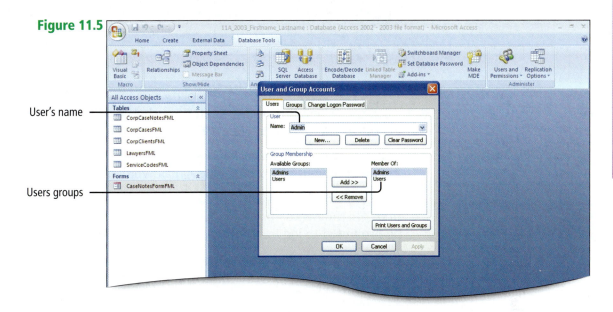

3 Click the **Change Logon Password tab**. Click in the **New Password** box, type **A1password** and then press Tab. In the **Verify** box, type **A1password** and then click **OK**.

When opening a database, users usually must log in. To **log in** means to enter a user name and password. By default, the *Admin* password is blank.

4 Click the **Office** button , and then click **Exit Access**. **Start** Access, open **11A_2003_Firstname_Lastname**, and then compare your screen with Figure 11.6. If necessary, in the Name box, type **Admin**

Access displays the Logon dialog box. A **logon** is the user name and password used to log in; however, the terms *log in* and *logon* are often used interchangeably.

Figure 11.6

Users logon

Access did not prompt me to log in

If you did not exit Access and then start it again, you will not be prompted to log in. Exit Access, and then reopen the database. If Access still does not ask you to log in, the security settings on your computer may not be saving your security settings. In this case, you may need to complete Activities 11.1 through 11.9 in one session.

5 In the **Password** box, type **A1password** and then press Enter.

6 Click the **Office** button 🔘, and then click **Exit Access**. **Start** Access again, and then open **11A_Lawyers_Firstname_Lastname**.

7 In the displayed **Logon** dialog box, if necessary, in the Name box, type **Admin** In the **Password** box, type **A1password** and then press Enter.

The User and Groups Account dialog box changes your security settings for the Access program, not the current database. You will now be prompted to log in when you open any of your databases.

8 In the displayed **Password Required** dialog box, click **Cancel**.

Access prompts you for the *GO! Series* password that you set for 11A_Lawyers_Firstname_Lastname. This password is required for this database only.

9 Locate and open the **11A_2003_Firstname_Lastname** database.

You did not need to log in this time because you did not exit Access and were still logged in as *Admin*.

10 Leave the database open for the next activity.

Objective 3
Create an Access Administrative User

Access allows more than one administrator account. Two or more administrators can share administrative tasks or cover for each other if one is unable to work with the database. Providing separate administrative accounts also enables each administrator to keep his or her password private.

Activity 11.4 Adding an Administrative User Account

An Access database may have more than one administrator account. DeLong Grant Law Partners would like to add a second Access administrator for their databases. In this activity, you will add and then secure a second administrative user account.

1 Click the **Database Tools tab**. In the **Administer group**, click the **User and Permissions** button, and then click **User and Group Accounts**.

2 In the displayed **User and Group Accounts** dialog box, under **User**, click the **New** button.

3 In the displayed **New User/Group** dialog box, in the **Name** box, type **Admin2** In the **Personal ID** box, type **Asdfgh2**

The *Personal ID*, or *PID*, is a unique identifier that Access needs to manage a user's ability to work with database objects. The Personal ID must be between 4 and 20 characters long. The Personal ID is not the account password.

4 Click **OK**, and compare your screen with Figure 11.7.

The new user's name displays in the Name box. Access has included *Admin2* as a member of the *Users* group because all users must be a member of the *Users* group.

Figure 11.7

New user

Member of the Users group

5 In the **User and Group Accounts** dialog box, click the **Add** button.

The *Admin2* user is now a member of the *Admins* group.

6 Click **OK**, click the **Office** button , and then click **Exit Access**. **Start** Access, and then open **11A_2003_Firstname_Lastname**.

7 In the displayed **Logon** dialog box, in the **Name** box, type **Admin2** Leave the **Password** box blank, and then click **OK**.

To secure the *Admin2* account, you must log in as *Admin2*. Only the *Admin2* user is authorized to change the password for that account.

8 Click the **Database Tools tab**. In the **Administer group**, click the **User and Permissions** button, and then click **User and Group Accounts**.

9 In the displayed **User and Group Accounts** dialog box, click the **Change Logon Password tab**. Notice that the User Name displays as *Admin2*.

10 In the **New Password** box, type **A2password** and then in the **Verify** box, type **A2password** Leave the **Old Password** box blank, and then click **OK**.

11 Click the **Office** button ![Office button], click **Exit Access**, and then reopen **11A_2003_Firstname_Lastname**.

12 In the displayed **Logon** dialog box, in the **Name** box, type **Admin2** In the **Password** box, type **A2password** and then click **OK**. Leave the database open for the next activity.

Objective 4
Create Users and Groups

Only administrators are allowed to create new users and groups. Each user and group needs to be named and assigned a unique ID. Typically, groups are created first. Users are then created and added to the appropriate groups. Assigning users to groups simplifies the process of managing the users. Each user's account is unsecured and must be secured using techniques similar to securing the administrative accounts.

Activity 11.5 Creating a Group and Adding Users

DeLong Grant Law Partners wants each lawyer to be able to log in using a unique logon for each lawyer. Because all of the lawyers will use the database in the same way, the database administrator would like to manage all of the lawyers as a single group. In this activity, you will create a Lawyers group, and then create a new user account for one of the company lawyers. You will place the new user into the Lawyers group. After securing the new user account, you will print a report listing user and group settings.

1 Click the **Database Tools tab**. In the **Administer group**, click the **User and Permissions** button, and then click **User and Group Accounts**.

2 In the displayed **User and Group Accounts** dialog box, click the **Groups tab**, and then click the **New** button.

3 In the displayed **New User/Group** dialog box, in the **Name** box, type **Lawyers** and then in the **Personal ID** box, type **Ladfgh1**

4 Click **OK**, and then click the **Users tab**. Compare your screen with Figure 11.8.

Lawyers displays under Available Groups.

Figure 11.8

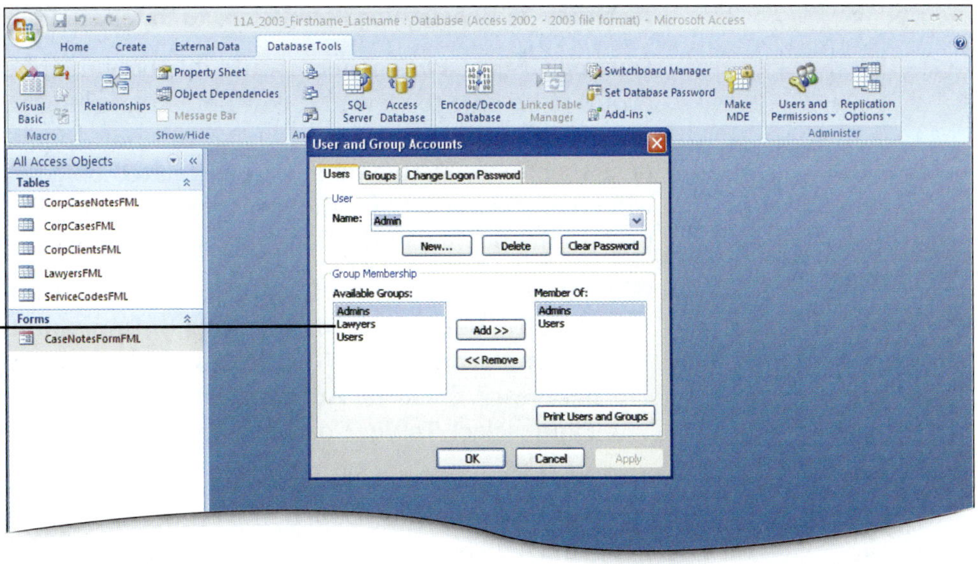

Access | chapter 11

Lawyers group

5 Under **User**, click the **New** button. In the displayed **New User/Group** dialog box, in the **Name** box, type **LDeLong** and then in the **Personal ID** box, type **Ladfgh2** Click **OK**.

LDeLong is a member of the *Users* group. Recall that all users must be a member the *Users* group.

6 If necessary, display *LDeLong* in the Name box. Under **Available Groups**, click **Lawyers**, and then click the **Add** button.

The user *LDeLong* is added to the *Lawyers* group.

7 Under **User**, click the **New** button. In the displayed **New User/Group** dialog box, in the **Name** box, type **HGrant** and then in the **Personal ID** box, type **Ladfgh3** Click **OK**.

8 If necessary, display *HGrant* in the Name box. Under **Available Groups**, be sure that **Lawyers** is selected, and then click the **Add** button.

9 Click the **Print Users and Groups** button. If you are instructed to submit this result, with the **Both Users and Groups** option button selected, click **OK**, and then create a paper or electronic printout. Otherwise, click **Cancel**.

10 Click **OK** to close the **User and Group Accounts** dialog box. Leave the database open for the next activity.

Objective 5
Change Ownership and Assign Permissions to Database Objects

With users assigned to groups, the administrator grants permissions to users or groups. A **permission** is the level of access to a database object granted to a user by an administrator. There are several levels of access that can be granted, such as viewing data; entering new records; or changing the design of tables, queries, reports, or forms. When permission is granted to a group, each member of the group inherits those permissions.

Activity 11.6 Assigning Permissions to Database Objects

DeLong Grant Law Partners would like only members of the Lawyers group to be able to view and edit notes regarding their corporate cases. Further, the partners want *Admin2*, but not *Admin*, to be able to make design changes to this table and its related objects. In this activity, you will change several user and group permissions for database objects to protect the privacy of the company's corporate case notes.

1 If necessary, click the Database Tools tab. In the **Administer tab**, click the **Users and Permissions** button, and then click **User and Group Permissions**. Next to **List**, select the **Groups** option button. If necessary, click the **Admins** group name, and then under **Object Type**, select **Table**. Compare your screen with Figure 11.9.

The List option button group is used to switch between user names and group names. Depending on the selected option, user or group names display on the left. A list of database objects displays on the right. The *Object Type* arrow is used to select different object types, such as queries, forms, and reports. The group permissions for the currently selected object are selected. The Current User box indicates that you are logged in as the *Admin2* user.

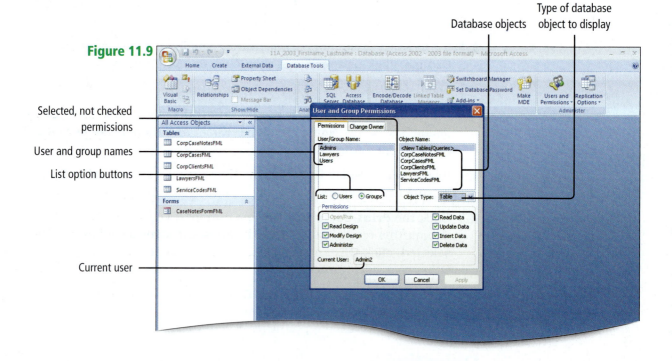

Figure 11.9

2 Under **Object Name**, click each table and observe the permissions for each object.

The Admins group has full privileges for every object in the database. The various permission levels are described in the table shown in Figure 11.10.

Access Permission Levels

Permission	Description
Open/Run	Users can open the database and run macros and VBA code.
Read Design	Users can open the object in Design view but cannot make any changes to the object's design.
Modify Design	Users can change the object's design.
Administer	Users can assign permissions for other groups and users even when the administrative user does not own the object.
Read Data	Users can view the data in a table or query but cannot change the data or table design.
Update Data	Users can view and make changes to the existing data, but cannot alter the object's design.
Insert Data	Users can insert new records.
Delete Data	Users can delete records.

Figure 11.10

3 Under **User/Group Name**, click **Users**. Under **Object Name**, click **CorpCaseNotes**. Clear the **Read Design** check box, and then click the **Apply** button. Press PrtScr.

Without Read Design permission, no other permissions are possible and are removed. The *Users* group and all of its members no longer have permission to view the *CorpCaseNotes* table. *Users* will not be able to view any queries, forms, or reports if those objects depend on the data in the *CorpCaseNotes* table.

4 Create a new, blank document in **Word**. In your **Access Chapter 11** folder, **Save** the file as **11A_Screens_Firstname_Lastname** In the **Word** document, **Paste** the screen shot.

5 Switch to **Access**. Click the **Object Type arrow**, and then click **Database**. Under **Permissions**, clear the **Open Exclusive** and **Administer** check boxes, and then click the **Apply** button. Compare your screen with Figure 11.11.

All users are members of the *Users* group. The company does not want all users to have administrative rights or be able to open the database using the Open Exclusive command.

Figure 11.11

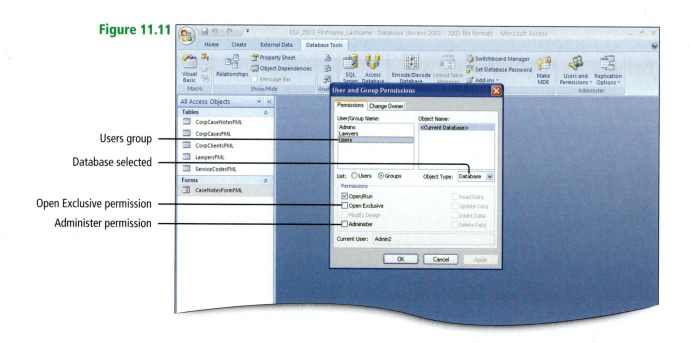

Users group

Database selected

Open Exclusive permission

Administer permission

6 Press PrtScr, and then in the **Word** document, **Paste** the screen shot.

7 Switch to **Access**. Click the **Object Type arrow**, and then click **Table**. Under **User/Group Name**, click **Lawyers**. Under **Object Name**, click **CorpCaseNotes**. Select each of the following check boxes: **Read Data**, **Update Data**, **Insert Data**, and **Delete Data**. Click the **Apply** button. Press PrtScr, and then in the **Word** document, **Paste** the screen shot.

Access selected the Read Design permission for you. Members of the *Lawyers* group will be able to view and change data in the *CorpCaseNotes* table. Only administrators will be able to edit the table's design.

8 Under **Object Name**, click **CorpCases**, and then select each of the following check boxes: **Read Data**, **Update Data**, **Insert Data**, and **Delete Data**. Click the **Apply** button. Press PrtScr, and then in the **Word** document, **Paste** the screen shot.

Members of the *Lawyers* group will need permission to read and write data in the *CorpCases* table because this table is related to the *CorpCaseNotes* table.

9 In **Access**, under **Object Name**, click **Lawyers**, and then select each of the following check boxes: **Read Data**, **Update Data**, **Insert Data**, and **Delete Data**. Click the **Apply** button. Press PrtScr, and then in the **Word** document, **Paste** the screen shot.

The *Lawyers* table is also related to the *CorpCaseNotes* table.

10 In **Access**, click the **Object Type arrow**, and then click **Form**. Under **Object Name**, click the **CaseNotesForm**. Under **Permissions**, select the **Open/Run** and **Read Design** check boxes, and then click the **Apply** button. Press PrtScr, and then in the **Word** document, **Paste** the screen shot.

Members of the *Lawyers* group will be able to use the form to read, edit, delete and enter new corporate case notes. They will not be able to change the design of the form.

11 **Save** 💾 the Word document and leave it open for the next activity. Leave the **Users and Group Permissions** dialog box open for the next activity.

Activity 11.7 Changing Ownership of Database Objects

Recall that DeLong Grant Law Partners would like *Admin2* to be the sole administrator of the Corporate Case Notes table. Because this table was created by *Admin*, that administrator is the current owner of that table. An owner of an Access object is allowed to change his or her permissions for that object. As owner of the object, *Admin* could change the permissions that you set in the previous activity. In this activity, you will change the ownership of the Corporate Case Notes table to *Admin2*.

1 In the **Users and Group Permissions** dialog box, click the **Change Owner tab**. If necessary, under Object Type, click Table. Compare your screen with Figure 11.12.

Each database table displays and lists its current owner.

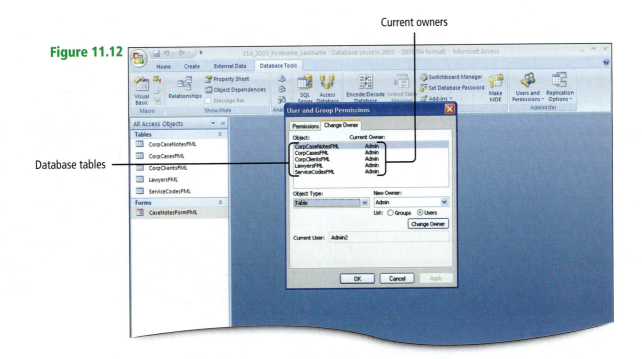

Figure 11.12

Current owners

Database tables

2 Click the **CorpCaseNotes** table. Click the **New Owner arrow**, click **Admin2**, and then click the **Change Owner** button. Press PrtScr, and then in the **Word** document, **Paste** the screen shot.

If ownership had been transferred to *LDeLong*, she would be allowed to change her permissions for that table.

3 In Access, click the **Object type arrow**, and then click **Form**. With **Admin2** still displayed under **New Owner**, click the **Change Owner**

button. Press PrtScr, and then in the **Word** document, **Paste** the screen shot.

4 In Access, click the **Permissions tab**. Under **User/Group Name**, click **Admins**. Click the **Object Type arrow**, and then click **Table**. Under **Object Name**, click the **CorpCaseNotes** table. Clear the **Read Design** check box, and then click the **Apply** button. Press PrtScr, and then in the **Word** document, **Paste** the screen shot.

Members of the *Admins* group no longer have any permissions to use the table.

5 In Access, next to **List**, select the **Users** option button. If necessary, select Admin and CorpCaseNotes. Under **Permissions**, clear the **Read Design** permission, and then click the **Apply** button. Press PrtScr, and then in the **Word** document, **Paste** the screen shot.

Admin will no longer be able to view the corporate case notes.

6 Switch to **Access**. Under **User/Group Name**, click **Admin2**. Under **Permissions**, click the **Administer** check box, and then click the **Apply** button. Compare your screen with Figure 11.13.

Admin2 is granted full permissions to the table. *Admin2* is the only user with administrative rights to this table.

Figure 11.13

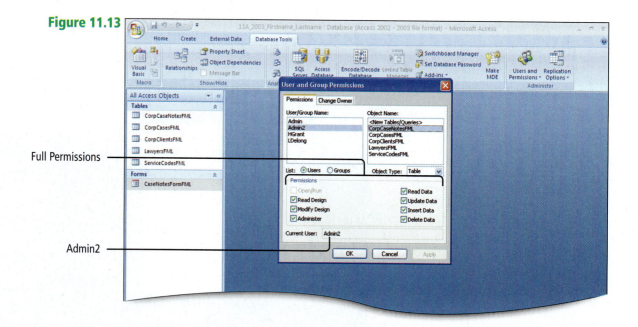

Full Permissions

Admin2

7 Press PrtScr, and then in the **Word** document, **Paste** the screen shot.

8 If you are instructed to submit this result, create a paper or electronic printout of **11A_Screens_Firstname_Lastname**.

Save 💾 the Word document, and then **Exit** ✕ Word.

9 In Access, click **OK** to close the dialog box, click the **Office** button 🔘, and then click **Exit Access**.

Objective 6
Test and Reset Default Security Settings

The user-level security changes that you have made so far will affect every database opened or created on your computer. These settings need to be tested and then reset so that the databases created in other projects will not be affected by the changes that you made.

Activity 11.8 Testing Default Security Settings

In this activity, you will test the security settings for two of the users at Delong Grant Law Partners. You will test that *Admin* cannot view the Corporate Case Notes, and then log in as *LDeLong* and enter a test corporate case note. You will then check that *LDeLong* cannot alter the design of the Corporate Case Notes form.

1 **Start** Access, and then open **11A_2003_Firstname_Lastname**. Log in using **Admin** and **A1password** as the logon.

2 On the **Navigation Pane**, double-click **CaseNotesForm**, and then compare your screen with Figure 11.14.

You are logged in as *Admin*. In previous activities you removed this user's permission to work with the CorpCaseNotes table. *Admin* will not be able to use any objects related to the table, including the forms, reports, or queries that use this table.

Figure 11.14

3 Read the displayed message, and then click **OK**. Click the **Office** button, and then click **Exit Access**.

4 **Start** Access, and then open **11A_2003_Firstname_Lastname**. In the displayed **Logon** dialog box, in the **Name** box, type **LDeLong** Leave the **Password** box blank, and then click **OK**.

To secure the account, you must log in using the new user's logon.

5 Click the **Database Tools tab**. In the **Administer group**, click the **User and Permissions** button, and then click **User and Group Accounts**. Compare your screen with Figure 11.15.

The New, Delete, and Clear Password buttons are unavailable, and the Groups tab does not display. You must be logged in as one of the administrators to be able to create and delete users and groups.

Figure 11.15

Groups tab does not display

Disabled buttons

6 Click the **Change Logon Password tab**. Leave the **Old Password** box blank. In the **New Password** and **Verify** boxes, type **L1password** and then click **OK**.

7 On the **Navigation Pane**, double-click **CaseNotesForm**. Use the form to enter the following data:

CCase_ID	CC000001
Date	Enter the current date
Lawyer_ID	L001
Note	This is a test record.

8 Click the **Next record** ▶ button.

The record is saved because all members of the *Lawyers* group have the necessary permission to insert new records.

9 Click the **Design View** button. Read the displayed message, and then click **OK**. Increase the width of the **CorpCaseID** text box approximately 1 inch, and then **Close** ✕ the form.

10 In the displayed message, click **Yes**. Read the next displayed message, and then click **OK**. The form is closed without saving the change that you made.

Members of the *Lawyers* group do not have permission to make changes to the design of this form.

11 Click the **Office** button 📋, and then click **Exit Access**.

More Knowledge

Using Strong Passwords

A *weak password* is a password that is easy to guess. Weak passwords may lead to costly losses of valuable data. A *strong password* is a password that is very difficult to guess. Strong passwords include at least seven characters and avoid using actual words. These passwords also include special characters such as !, #, and ;, and a mix of upper and lowercase letters. If the databases that you work with in these projects contained real data, then stronger passwords would be needed.

Activity 11.9 Copying and Resetting Default Security Settings

The default security settings for Access are stored with your program settings. In Windows XP, these settings are usually stored in the Documents and Settings folder. In Vista, these settings are usually found in the Users folder. In this activity, you will locate the file where your default security settings are stored, and then copy that file to your *Access Chapter 11* folder. You will then delete the original file so that Access will use the security settings that were in place before you began this project.

1 If your computer is running Windows Vista, start with Step 6. Otherwise, start with Step 2.

2 Open **My Computer**. Double-click **Local Disk (C:)**, and then double-click the **Documents and Settings** folder.

3 In the **Documents and Settings** folder, locate the folder with the same name that you used to log in to this Windows session, and then double-click that folder.

4 Double-click the **Application Data** folder. Double-click the **Microsoft** folder, and then double-click the **Access** folder. Compare your screen with Figure 11.16.

Access stores the default security settings in a file called System. This file has the *.mdw* file extension.

System

Figure 11.16

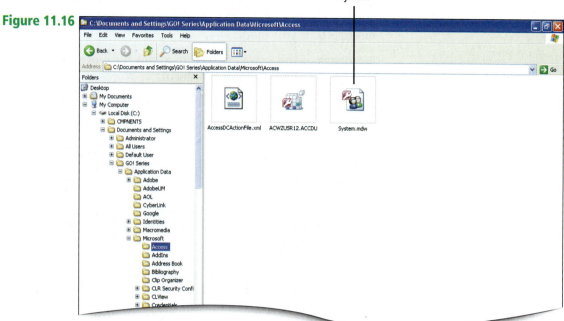

Alert!

I cannot open the folders described in this activity.

The Application Data folder may not be listed because it is a hidden system folder. To view hidden system folders, from the Tools menu, click Folder Options. In the Folder Options dialog box, click the View tab, and then click the *Show hidden files and folders* option button. Click OK. If your Windows security settings prevent you from viewing any of the folders in this activity, you will need to skip this activity.

---

5 Right-click the **System** file, and from the displayed shortcut menu, click **Cut**.

Access will re-create this file the next time Access is opened. Skip to Step 10.

6 If your computer is running Windows Vista, open the **Computer** folder window. For the rest of this chapter, whenever you are asked to work with *My Computer*, you will need to work with the *Computer* folder window instead.

7 Double-click **Local Disk (C:)**, and then double-click the **Users** folder. In the **Users** folder, locate the folder with the same name that you used to log in to this Windows session, and then double-click that folder.

8 Double-click the **AppData** folder, and then double-click the **Roaming** folder. Double-click the **Microsoft** folder, and then double-click the **Access** folder. Compare your screen with Figure 11.17.

Access stores the default security settings in a file called System. This file has the *.mdw* file extension.

Figure 11.17

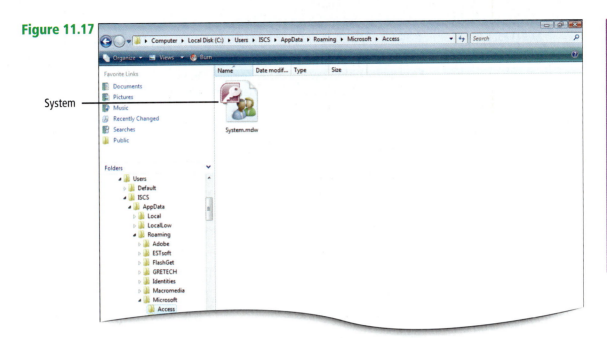

System

9 Once you have located the *System* file, right-click the **System** file, and then from the displayed shortcut menu, click **Cut**. Access will re-create this file the next time Access is opened.

10 **Close** the **My Computer** window. Open a new **My Computer** window, and then navigate to your **Access Chapter 11** folder. In the **Access Chapter 11** folder, right-click a blank area, and then from the displayed shortcut menu, click **Paste**.

11 Right-click the pasted file, and from the displayed shortcut menu, click **Rename**. Type **11A_System_Firstname_Lastname** and then press Enter. **Close** the **My Computer** window.

System.mdw is a database that can be opened and viewed in Access. It contains queries that list all of the users and groups that you created in this project.

Objective 7
Create and Modify Workgroups Using the Security Wizard

Access stores security settings in workgroup information files. A **workgroup information file** is a separate file in which Access stores the user and group security settings. Each workgroup information file stores settings for a workgroup. A **workgroup** is a collection of groups and users that can be applied to a single database or shared among several databases. New workgroups can be created using the Security Wizard, which is also known as the User-Level Security Wizard. The Security Wizard is used to create new workgroup information files, which can be applied to a single database.

Activity 11.10 Adding Users and Groups in a New Workgroup Information File

DeLong Grant Law Partners would like a member of their clerical staff to be able to open and create backup copies of this database, but not be able to view or change any data. In this activity, you will create a new workgroup information file and then add the new backup user.

<table>
<tr><td>

Alert!

</td><td>

Move your Access 11 folder to the root of your storage area

Your security settings may not work correctly if your Access Chapter 11 folder is located within several other folders. On your storage drive, move your Access Chapter 11 folder outside of any other folders.

</td></tr>
</table>

■1 **Start** Access. Locate and then open the **11A_2003_Firstname_ Lastname** file. Click the **Office** button 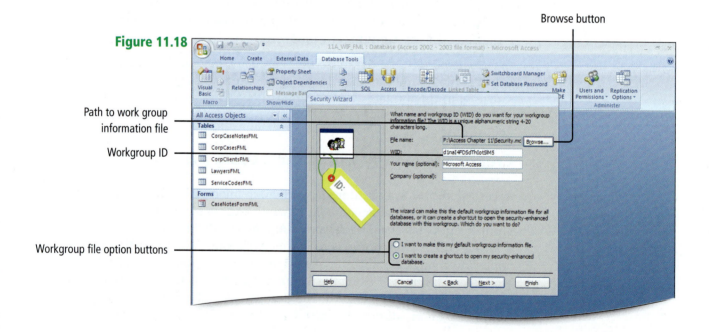, point to **Save As**, and then click **Access 2002 - 2003 Database**. In the **Save As** dialog box, navigate to your **Access Chapter 11** folder, and then save the file as **11A_WIF_FML** Be sure to replace *FML* with your initials.

When creating new workgroup information files, the file names need to be kept as short as possible.

■2 Click the **Database Tools tab**. In the **Administer group**, click the **Users and Permissions** button, and then click **User-Level Security Wizard**.

■3 In the **Security Wizard** dialog box, with the **Create a new work- group information file** option button selected, click **Next**, and then compare your screen with Figure 11.18.

The Browse button defines the path to the new workgroup informa- tion file that will be created. The wizard generates a Workgroup ID. The **Workgroup ID**, or **WID**, is a unique identifier that Access needs to manage each workgroup. The two option buttons determine if this new workgroup will apply to this database only, or to all databases.

Browse button

Figure 11.18

Path to work group information file

Workgroup ID

Workgroup file option buttons

■4 Click the **Browse** button. In the displayed **Select a workgroup file** dialog box, navigate to your **Access Chapter 11** folder. In the **File name** box, substituting your own initials, type **11A_WIF_FML** and then click **Select**.

The workgroup information file will be saved with the *.mdw* file extension.

5 In the **Company** box, type **DeLong Grant Law Partners** Be sure that the **I want to create a shortcut to open my security-enhanced database** option button is selected, and then click **Next** two times.

A list of Pre-built user groups display. A **Pre-built user group** is a group provided by Access that has its permissions already configured to perform specific types of tasks.

6 Select the **Backup Operators** check box, and then click **Next** two times. Under **<Add New User>**, click the user name listed on your screen, and then compare with Figure 11.19.

Because you are no longer using the default workgroup information file, none of the groups and users that you created earlier should be listed. By default, the only user listed has the same name as the user name you used to log in to your Windows computer. This user will be the default administrator for this database and has been assigned a blank password.

Figure 11.19

Windows user name—yours will be different
Blank password

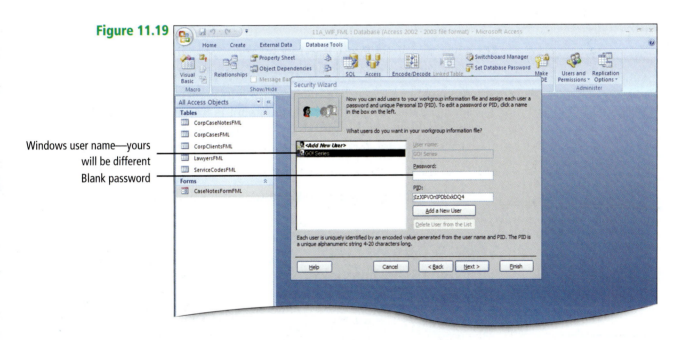

7 In the **Password** box, type **A3password** Verify that you typed the password correctly, and then click the **Add a New User** button.

The administrator account for this database is now secure.

8 In the **User name** box, type **khouse** In the **Password** box, type **C1password** Verify that you typed the password correctly, and then click the **Add This User to the List** button.

Many system administrators prefer to use lowercase for all user names.

9 Click **Next**. Click the **Group or user name arrow**, and then click **khouse**. Click the **Backup Operators** check box, and then click **Next**.

khouse now has the same permissions as the *Backup Operators* group.

10 Click the **Browse** button, and then navigate to your **Access Chapter 11** folder. In the **File name** box, type **11A_WIF_Unsecured_FML** where *FML* is your first, middle, and last initials. Click the **Select** button.

11 Click **Finish**. If you are instructed to submit this result, create a paper or electronic printout of the displayed One-step Security Wizard Report.

The One-step Security Wizard Report lists all of your users, groups, and passwords. For security reasons, this report cannot be not saved. In the next step, an electronic version of this report will be created.

Alert!

The wizard displays a message that an error occurred

The information that links the database to the new workgroup information file is stored in a shortcut on the desktop. If your Access Chapter 11 folder is located within several other folders, the path to your database and workgroup information file may be too long for this shortcut to work correctly. In this case, delete the shortcut, move your Access Chapter 11 folder outside of any other folders on your storage drive, and then repeat this activity.

---

12 Click the **Close Print Preview** button. In the displayed message, click **Yes** to create a Snapshot file for the report.

A Snapshot Viewer document is saved in the same directory as your secure database. A Snapshot document is like a screen capture except that in this case, it captures the report printout. The Snapshot Viewer views Snapshot documents without having to open Access.

13 Read the displayed message, and then click **OK**. Click the **Office** button [icon], and then click **Exit Access**.

More Knowledge

Using the Snapshot Viewer

To view Snapshot files, the Snapshot Viewer program must be installed on your computer. The Snapshot Viewer does not come with Office 2007, but the program can be downloaded from Microsoft's Web site.

Activity 11.11 Testing the New Workgroup Security Settings

In this activity, you will open a database using the security settings in a new workgroup information file. You will then test that *khouse* has no permissions to the database other than to make a backup copy.

1 Close any open windows so that the desktop displays.

2 On the **Desktop**, locate the shortcut starting with the text *11A_WIF_FML*. Right-click the **11A_WIF_FML** shortcut, and then from the displayed shortcut menu, click **Properties**. Compare your screen with Figure 11.20.

In the Target box, the text instructs Windows to open the 11A_WIF_FML database and apply the security settings in the workgroup information file that you created. The database can no longer be opened directly and must be opened using this shortcut.

Figure 11.20

Target property

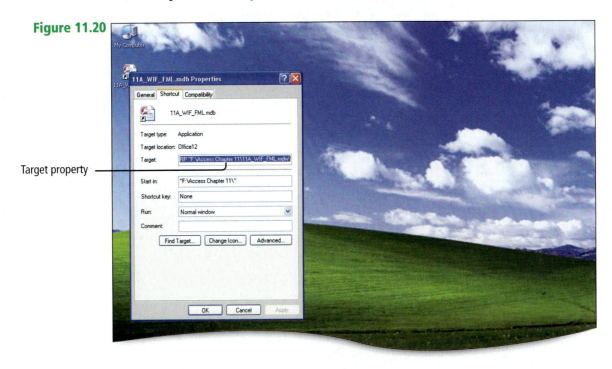

3 Click **Cancel** to close the **Properties** dialog box without making any changes.

4 Double-click the **11A_WIF_FML** shortcut.

5 In the displayed logon dialog box, in the **Name** box, type **khouse** In the **Password** box, type **C1password** and then press Enter.

Alert!

The database could not be opened by double-clicking the shortcut

Your Access Chapter 11 folder may be inside too many folders. See the Alert! at the beginning of the previous activity.

If you copy or move a database that has an associated workgroup information file, the shortcut file that opens the database no longer points to the database and its associated workgroup information file. When this happens, you will need to return to your original computer. You can also copy the original shortcut and then edit the shortcut's Target property so that it points to the correct files.

6 On the **Navigation Pane**, double-click the **ServiceCodes** table. Read the displayed message, and then click **OK**.

khouse does not have permission to view any data.

7 Click the **Office** button ![Office button], point to **Save As**, and then click **Access 2002 - 2003 Database**. In the **Save As** dialog box, click **Cancel**.

khouse does have permission to make a backup copy of the database.

8 Click the **Office** button [icon], and then click **Exit Access**.

9 If you are to turn in your work electronically, **Cut** and **Paste** the **11A_WIF_FML** shortcut to your **Access Chapter 11** folder, and then submit all files listed at the beginning of this project as directed by your instructor.

End **You have completed Project 11A** ――――――――――

Project 11B Overdue Accounts

Delong Grant Law Partners store billing information in two unrelated tables. They need queries that combine the data from both tables so that they can call those clients that need to pay their bill. The only way to combine these two queries is to work in SQL view. The partners have given you several tables from their database, each with a small sample of data. Once the queries are working properly, they can be applied to the full data set. In Activities 11.12 through 11.17, you will write queries in SQL view. Using this view, you will be able to create queries that cannot be created in Design view. Your completed queries and report will look similar to the printouts shown in Figure 11.21.

For Project 11B, you will need the following file:

a11B_Overdue_Accounts

You will save your database as
11B_Overdue_Accounts_Firstname_Lastname

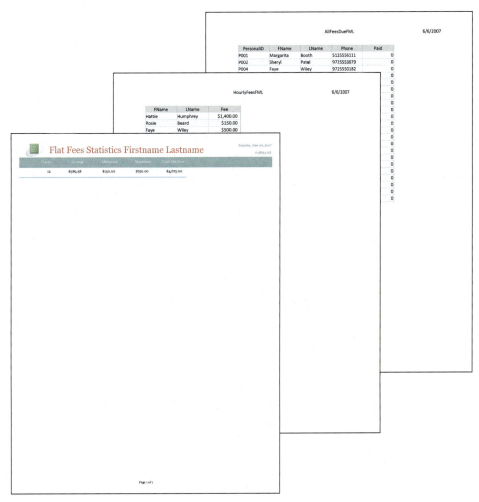

Figure 11.21
Project 11B—Overdue Accounts

Objective 8
Modify a Query in SQL View

All Access queries use SQL. **SQL**, or **Structured Query Language**, is a language used by many database programs to view, update, and query data in relational databases. In Access, queries can be created in Design view and then modified in SQL view. Starting in Design view saves time and is a good way to become familiar with writing SQL.

Activity 11.12 Modifying a Query in SQL View

Delong Grant Law Partners need a query that lists each client who was charged a flat fee and has not yet paid that fee. In this activity, you will create that query in Design view and then modify it in SQL view.

1 **Start** Access. Navigate to the location where the student data files for this textbook are saved. Locate and then open the **a11B_Overdue_ Accounts** database. Click the **Office** button, point to **Save As**, and then click **Access 2007 Database**. In the **Save As** dialog box, navigate to your **Access Chapter 11** folder, and then save the file as **11B_Overdue_Accounts_Firstname_Lastname** in the folder.

2 Rename each table by adding **FML** to the end of each object name. Be sure to replace *FML* with your own initials, and do not use any spaces in the table names.

3 Click the **Create tab**, and then in the **Other group**, click the **Query Design** button. Using the techniques you have practiced, add the **PersonalClientsFML** and **FlatFeeBillingFML** tables to the query design workspace. **Close** the **Show Table** dialog box.

4 From the **PersonalClientsFML** table, add the following fields to the design grid: **PersonalID**, **FName**, **LName**, and **Phone**. From the **FlatFeeBillingFML** table, add the **Paid** field to the design grid. In the **Criteria** box for the **Paid** column, type **No**

5 Click **Save**, type **FlatFeesDueFML** using your own initials, and then click **OK**.

6 Locate the status bar in the lower right corner of the database window, and then click the **SQL View** button. Click any blank area in the SQL workspace, and then compare your screen with Figure 11.22.

When you work in Query Design view, Access builds the equivalent SQL statement. An **SQL statement** is an expression that defines the SQL commands that should be performed when the query is run. SQL statements typically contain several SQL clauses that begin with keywords. **Keywords** are commands built into the SQL programming language. Keywords are typically written using uppercase letters. In SQL View, statements are edited in the design grid.

Figure 11.22

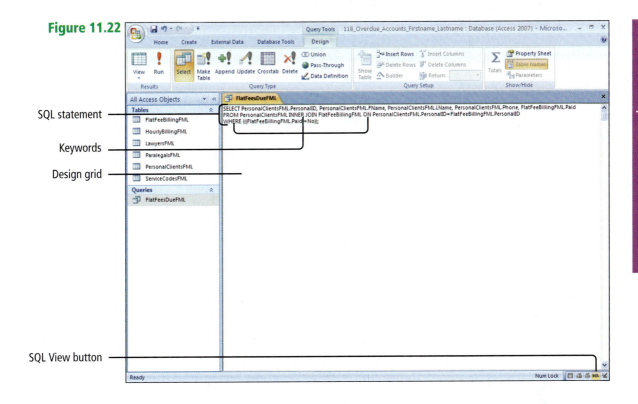

SQL statement

Keywords

Design grid

SQL View button

7 In the SQL statement, click to the left of the keyword *FROM*, and then press Enter.

This SQL statement starts with a SELECT clause. A **SELECT clause** lists which fields the query should display. The second clause in this SQL statement is a FROM clause. A **FROM clause** lists which tables hold the fields used in the SELECT clause.

8 Click to the left of the keyword *INNER*, and then press Enter **two** times.

A **JOIN clause** defines the join type for a query. Recall that an inner join displays only those records that have a corresponding record in both of the related tables. A **WHERE clause** defines the criteria that should be applied when a query is run.

9 In the **WHERE** clause, remove all six parentheses.

These parentheses would be needed only if a more complex WHERE clause was written. Often, the SQL generated while in the Design view will not be as efficient as the SQL written by a database designer in SQL view.

10 Click **Save**. In the **Results group**, click the **Run** button. Click the **LName column arrow**, and then click **Sort A to Z**. Compare your screen with Figure 11.23.

Brandi Dorsey and Faye Wiley are each listed two times. This type of duplication may lead to duplicate phone calls being made to the client.

Figure 11.23

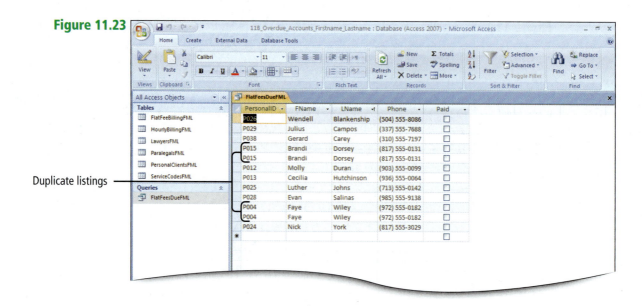

Duplicate listings

11 In the status bar, click the **SQL View** [SQL] button. Click to the right of the keyword SELECT, press [Spacebar] and then type **DISTINCT**

The **DISTINCT** keyword removes duplicates from query results. It always follows the SELECT keyword, and is added only in SQL View.

12 **Run** the query and notice that duplicate records no longer display. Click **Save** [📷], and then **Close** [×] the query.

Objective 9
Create a Query in SQL View

Many database designers find it easier to design their queries in SQL view. The typical SQL query uses the same three-step sequence. Understanding this sequence removes much of the complexity of the typical SQL statement. Working in SQL view enables the designer to write more efficient SQL, and also provides more control than Design view. Many types of queries can be created only when working in SQL view.

Activity 11.13 Creating an SQL Statement

Delong Grant Law Partners need a query that lists each client who was charged an hourly rate and has not yet paid the fee. Due to the nature of this query, you will need to work in SQL view to write a query not available in Design view. In this activity, you will create that query in SQL view.

1 Click the **Create tab**, and then in the **Other group**, click the **Query Design** button. Close the displayed **Show Table** dialog box, and then in the status bar, click the **SQL View** [SQL] button.

Because you started with a select query, the SELECT keyword displays followed by a semicolon. Semicolons are used to mark the end of SQL statements.

2 Click before the semicolon, press [Spacebar] and then type the following, substituting FML with your own initials: **PersonalClientsFML. PersonalID, PersonalClientsFML.FName, PersonalClientsFML.LName, PersonalClientsFML.Phone, HourlyBillingFML.Paid** Compare your screen with Figure 11.24.

In a SELECT clause, both the table name and field name are included and are separated by a period. Multiple fields must be separated by commas.

Figure 11.24

Period separates table and field name

Comma separates fields

Semicolon

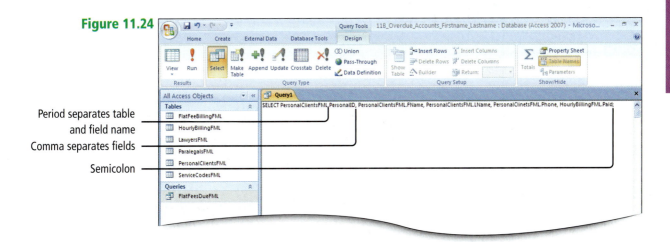

3 Press [Enter], and then type the following FROM clause, substituting your own initials: **FROM PersonalClientsFML, HourlyBillingFML**

All tables used in the SELECT clause must be listed in the FROM clause and are separated by commas.

4 Press [Enter], and then type the following WHERE clause, substituting your own initials: **WHERE HourlyBillingFML.Paid=No**

Recall that in the WHERE statement, the criteria for the query is defined.

5 Click **Save** [icon], and then, substituting your own initials, type **HourlyFeesDueFML** Click **OK**.

6 Be sure that the semicolon is at the end of the query. Click the **Run** button, and then compare your screen with Figure 11.25. If you receive a message that the query has errors or the Enter Parameter Value dialog box displays, go back and check your typing very carefully.

The result of this query is a cross join query. Recall that in a cross join query, every possible combination of records between two related tables will be returned. If no join type is defined or if there is a mistake in the WHERE clause, SQL returns a cross join query. When tables contain a large number of records, cross join queries will take a very long time to run. In this query, the join type needs to be defined.

Figure 11.25

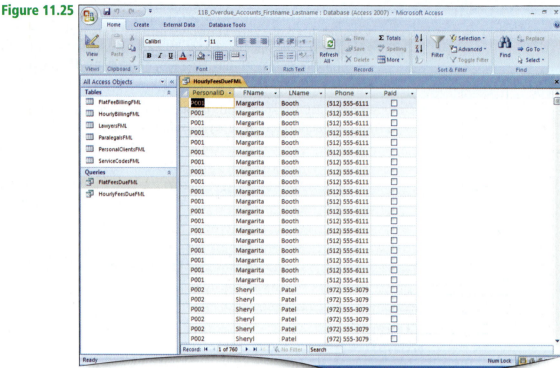

7 **Save** 💾 your query, and then return to **SQL view**. Leave the query open for the next activity.

Activity 11.14 Specifying the Join Type in SQL

The Hourly Billing Due query currently returns a cross join. Once a join type is specified in the query, it will display one record per customer. In this activity, you will add an SQL clause so that the two tables used in the query use an inner join.

1 In **SQL** view, in the **FROM** clause, click between *PersonalClientsFML* and the comma, and then press Enter.

2 Press Delete to remove the comma and *Hourly_Billing*.

3 Type the following JOIN clause, using your own initials:
INNER JOIN HourlyBillingFML

The **INNER JOIN** keyword instructs the query to use an inner join between two tables.

4 After *HourlyBillingFML*, press Spacebar, and type the following ON clause:
ON PersonalClientsFML.PersonalID = HourlyBillingFML.PersonalID

The **ON** keyword is used to specify which field is common to two tables. The combination of INNER JOIN and ON keywords creates a relationship between the two tables. In this query the Personal_ID field is used to join the tables.

5 Click **Save** 💾, and then **Run** the query. Sort the **LName** column in alphabetical order, and then compare your screen with Figure 11.26.

The tables are joined correctly, but customers with more than one outstanding bill are listed two or more times.

Figure 11.26

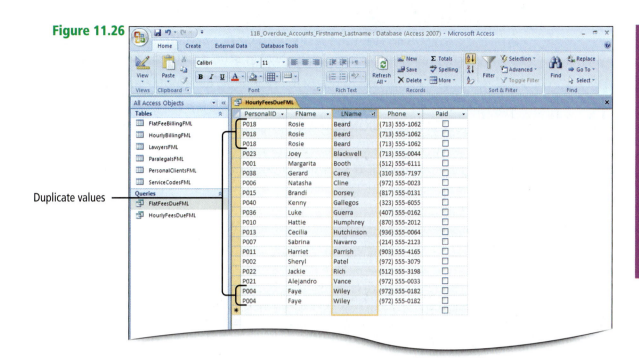

Duplicate values

6 Return to **SQL View**. After the **SELECT** keyword, press ⌴Spacebar⌴, and then type **DISTINCT**

7 **Run** the query. Check that no customer is listed more than once. Click **Save** 🖫, and then **Close** ✕ the query.

Objective 10
Create a Union Query Using SQL

Using SQL, the results of two or more queries can be displayed in one query. A **union query** combines the results of two or more similar select queries. The combined queries must have the same number of columns and the same data types in each corresponding column. Union queries are created only in SQL view.

Activity 11.15 Creating a Union Query in SQL View

Recall that Delong Grant Law Partners need a list of all personal clients with amounts owed. In earlier projects, you built two separate queries, one for flat fees and the other for hourly fees. In this activity, you will use SQL to combine the results of both queries into a single query.

1 Click the **Create tab**, and then in the **Other group**, click the **Query Design** button. **Close** the displayed **Show Table** dialog box.

2 In the **Query Type group**, click the **Union** button. Notice that the query switches to SQL view.

3 Open the **FlatFeesDueFML** query, and then in the status bar, click the **SQL View** 🆂🆀🅻 button. With the entire SQL statement selected, right-click anywhere in the design grid, and then click **Copy**.

4 **Close** ⌧ the **FlatFeesDueFML** query. In the union query, right-click anywhere in the design grid, and then click **Paste**.

5 At the end of the SQL statement, delete the semicolon, and then press Enter **two** times.

6 Type **UNION** and then press Enter **two** times. Compare your screen with Figure 11.27.

The *UNION* keyword is used to combine one or more queries in a union query.

Figure 11.27

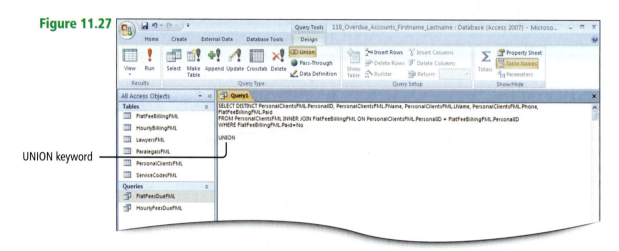

UNION keyword

7 Open the **HourlyFeesDueFML** query, and then in the status bar, click the **SQL View** button. With the entire SQL statement selected, right-click anywhere in the design grid, and then click **Copy**.

8 **Close** ⌧ the **HourlyFeesDueFML** query. In the union query that you are building, right-click next to the insertion point, and then click **Paste**.

9 Click **Save** 📷, type **AllFeesDueFML** using your own initials, and then click **OK**.

10 On the **Navigation Pane**, notice the union query icon to the left of the query's name. In the **Results group**, click the **View button arrow**, and notice that Design view is not available for this query.

11 **Run** the query, and then compare your results with Figure 11.28.

Figure 11.28

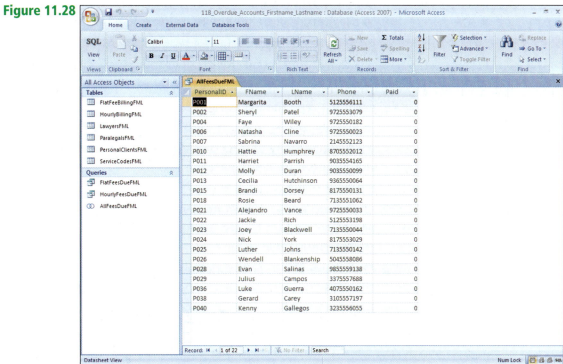

12 If you are instructed to submit this result, create a paper or electronic printout of the query.

Click **Save** 💾, and then **Close** ❌ the query.

Objective 11
Create Calculated Fields and SQL Aggregate Functions

SQL is a powerful language that does far more than create select queries. SQL provides commands to create calculated fields and summarize data using aggregate functions. Recall that an aggregate function performs a calculation on a column of data and returns a single value. When creating calculated fields, many developers prefer to work in SQL view because long expressions can be viewed without having to use the Zoom feature.

Activity 11.16 Creating Calculated Fields in SQL

Delong Grant Law Partners need a list of total amounts due for the clients who were billed at an hourly rate. In this activity, you will write an SQL statement with a field that calculates fees by multiplying the number of hours by the hourly rate.

1 Click the **Create tab**, and then in the **Other group**, click the **Query Design** button.

2 Use the displayed **Show Table** dialog box to add the **PersonalClientsFML** and **HourlyBillingFML** tables, and then **Close** the dialog box.

3 From the **PersonalClientsFML** table, add the **FName** field, and then add the **LName** field.

4 In the status bar, click the **SQL View** 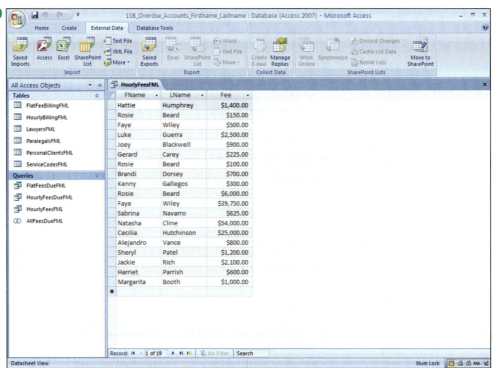 button.

> Starting this query in Design view saves you from having to type the SELECT, FROM, and INNER JOIN clauses.

5 To the right of the entire SELECT clause, type a comma, press Spacebar, and then type the following:
HourlyBillingFML.Hours * HourlyBillingFML.Rate AS Fee

> A calculated field with the caption *Fee* will display the product of the Hours and Rate fields for each record. The **AS** keyword creates captions for fields.

6 At the end of the SQL statement, click to the left of the semicolon, press Enter, and then type the following WHERE clause:
WHERE HourlyBillingFML.Paid = No

7 Click **Save** , type **HourlyFeesFML** using your own initials, and then click **OK**.

8 **Run** the query, and then compare your screen with Figure 11.29.

Figure 11.29

FName	LName	Fee
Hattie	Humphrey	$1,400.00
Rosie	Beard	$150.00
Faye	Wiley	$500.00
Luke	Guerra	$2,500.00
Joey	Blackwell	$900.00
Gerard	Carey	$225.00
Rosie	Beard	$100.00
Brandi	Dorsey	$700.00
Kenny	Gallegos	$300.00
Rosie	Beard	$6,000.00
Faye	Wiley	$39,750.00
Sabrina	Navarro	$625.00
Natasha	Cline	$54,000.00
Cecilia	Hutchinson	$25,000.00
Alejandro	Vance	$800.00
Sheryl	Patel	$1,200.00
Jackie	Rich	$2,100.00
Harriet	Parrish	$600.00
Margarita	Booth	$1,000.00

9 If you are instructed to submit this result, create a paper or electronic printout of the query.

Close the query.

Activity 11.17 Writing SQL Aggregate Functions

Delong Grant Law Partners need a report showing summary statistics for the amounts due from clients paying flat fees. In this activity, you will use SQL aggregate functions to calculate summary statistics and then create a report based on the query.

1 Click the **Create tab**, and then in the **Other group**, click the **Query Design** button. **Close** the displayed **Show Table** dialog box. In the status bar, click the **SQL View** 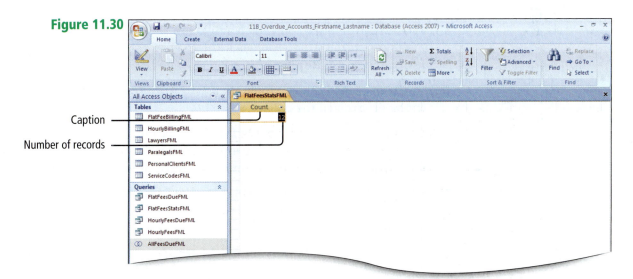 button.

2 In the design grid, delete the semicolon, press ⌴Spacebar, and then, substituting *FML* with your own initials, type the following:
Count(FlatFeeBillingFML.Fee) AS Count

Count is an SQL aggregate function.

3 Press Enter, and then type the following FROM clause:
FROM FlatFeeBillingFML

4 Press Enter, and then type the following WHERE clause:
WHERE FlatFeeBillingFML.Paid=No;

5 Click **Save** 💾, type **FlatFeesStatsFML** using your own initials, and then click **OK**.

6 Click the **Run** button, and then compare your screen with Figure 11.30.

The number of records in the query displays in a column that has *Count* as its caption.

Figure 11.30

Caption

Number of records

7 Return to **SQL View**. Click to the right of the entire **SELECT** clause, and then type a comma. Press Enter, and then type the following:
Avg(FlatFeeBillingFML.Fee) AS Average,

8 Continue adding to the SELECT clause as follows:

| Min(FlatFeeBillingFML.Fee) AS Minimum, |
| Max(FlatFeeBillingFML.Fee) AS Maximum, |
| Sum(FlatFeeBillingFML.Fee) AS [Total Flat Fees] |

Because Total Flat Fees contains spaces, it must be enclosed in square brackets. In Access SQL statements, any table name or field name, that has spaces must be enclosed in square brackets. If there are no spaces, then the square brackets are optional. After [Total Flat Fees], no comma is needed because it is the end of the SELECT clause.

9 Compare your screen with Figure 11.31, click **Save** , and then **Run** the query.

Figure 11.31

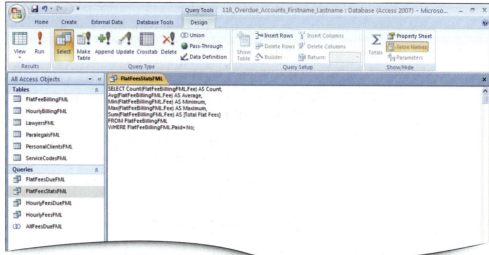

10 **Close** ✕ the query. On the **Navigation Pane**, click to select the **FlatFeesStatsFML** query. Click the **Create tab**, and in the **Reports group**, click the **Report** button.

11 In the displayed report, apply the **Civic AutoFormat**—the last choice in the first row of the gallery.

12 Click anywhere in the **Total Flat Fees** column to select the column. In the **Grouping & Totals group**, click the **Totals** button, and then click **Sum** to remove the second displayed total for that column.

13 Change the report's **Title** text box to **Flat Fees Statistics Firstname Lastname** If you are instructed to submit this result, create a paper or electronic printout.

14 Click **Save** , and then accept the **Report Name** by clicking **OK**.

15 **Close** ✕ the report, click the **Office** button , and then click **Close Database**.

End **You have completed Project 11B** ————————

There's More You Can Do!

From My Computer, navigate to the student files that accompany this textbook. In the folder **02_theres_more_you_can_do**, locate and open the folder for this chapter. Open and print the instructions for this project, which are provided to you in Adobe PDF format.

Try It! 1—Write SQL to Create a Full Outer Join

In this Try It! project, you create a query that joins two tables with a full outer join, which is accomplished only by writing SQL.

Try It! 2—Digitally Sign an Access 2007 Database

In this Try It! project, you will create a certificate of authority and use it to digitally sign an Access 2007 database.

Content-Based Assessments

Summary

In this chapter, you practiced securing databases and writing SQL. Databases saved in the 2007 file format protect data by encrypting the database, which makes the data unreadable to anyone who does not possess the correct password. Databases saved in the 2002 - 2003 file format also offer user-level security. You practiced setting default security settings by managing permissions for administrators, groups, and users. You also practiced creating workgroup information files using the Security Wizard.

Writing your own SQL in SQL view provides options not available in query Design view. You used the SQL view to write SQL to join two queries in a union query, create calculated fields, and provide aggregate statistics. Knowing how to modify SQL directly gives you greater control and flexibility when designing queries. The same SQL statements that you wrote in this chapter can also be used to query databases other than Access, such as Microsoft SQL server or MySQL.

Key Terms

Admin 959	**Group** 959	**Signed package** ●
Administrator 958	**INNER JOIN (SQL)** 984	**SQL or Structured**
AS 988	**IS NULL** ●	**Query Language** 980
Asterisk (*) ●	**JOIN clause** 981	**SQL statement** 980
Certificate Authority	**Keyword** 980	**Strong password** 971
(CA) ●	**Log in** 959	**UNION** 986
Decode 957	**Logon** 959	**Union query** 985
Decrypt 956	**ON** 984	**User** 959
Digital certificate	**Open Exclusive** 955	**User-level security** 958
●	**Open Exclusive**	**Weak password** 971
Digital signature	**Read-Only** 955	**WHERE clause** 981
●	**Open Read-Only** 955	**Workgroup** 973
DISTINCT 982	**Permission** 963	**Workgroup ID or**
Encode 957	**Personal ID or PID** 961	**WID** 974
Encrypt 955	**Pre-built user**	**Workgroup**
FROM clause 981	**groups** 975	**information file** 973
Full outer join ●	**SELECT clause** 981	

The ● symbol represents Key Terms found on the Student CD in the 02_theres_more_you_can_do folder for this chapter.

Matching

Match each term in the second column with its correct definition in the first column. Write the letter of the term on the blank line in front of the correct definition.

—— **1.** A mode that opens the database so that all objects can be opened and viewed, but data and design changes cannot be made.

—— **2.** To hide data by making the file unreadable until the correct password is entered.

—— **3.** To remove the encoding from a database in the 2002 - 2003 file format.

—— **4.** A database that grants different permissions to different users or groups of users has this type of security.

—— **5.** A collection of users who will use the database in similar ways.

—— **6.** The user name and password used to log in to an account.

—— **7.** The level of access to a database object granted to a user by an administrator.

—— **8.** A password that is easy to guess.

—— **9.** A separate file in which Access stores the user and group security settings for one or more databases.

—— **10.** Groups provided by Access that have their permissions already configured to perform specific types of tasks.

—— **11.** An expression that defines the SQL commands that should be performed when the query is run.

—— **12.** The SQL clause that defines which fields should display.

—— **13.** An SQL keyword that removes duplicates from query results.

—— **14.** The SQL keyword used to combine one or more queries.

—— **15.** An SQL keyword that creates a caption for a field.

A AS

B Decode

C DISTINCT

D Encrypt

E Group

F Logon

G Open Read-Only

H Permission

I Pre-built user groups

J SELECT

K SQL statement

L UNION

M User level

N Weak password

O Workgroup information file

Fill in the Blank

Write the correct word in the space provided.

1. To encrypt a database, the database must first be opened using the _____ _____ command.

2. To remove encryption is to _____ the database.

3. To hide data in a database saved in the 2002 - 2003 file format without requiring a password to open it is to _____ the database.

4. The person who has full permissions to all database objects and manages all users and groups is called the _____.

5. The default administrator is named _____.

6. To enter a user name and password is to _____ _____.

7. The unique identifier that Access needs to manage a user's ability to work with database objects is the _____ _____ or _____.

8. A password that is hard to guess is called a(n) _____ password.

9. A collection of groups and users that can be applied to a single database or shared among several databases is called a(n) _____.

10. A programming language used by many database programs to view, update, and query data in relational databases is _____ or _____ _____ _____.

11. The SQL clause that specifies which tables are used is the _____ clause.

12. A command built into the SQL programming language is called a(n) _____.

13. The SQL clause that defines the criteria that should be applied when a query is run is the _____ clause.

14. The SQL clause used to define which field is the common field between two related tables is the _____ clause.

15. A query that combines the results of two or more similar select queries is called a(n) _____ query.

Skills Review

Project 11C — Paralegals

In this project, you will apply the skills you practiced from the Objectives in Project 11A.

Objectives: 1. *Encrypt and Decrypt Databases;* **2.** *Secure the Access Administrator Account;* **3.** *Create an Access Administrative User;* **4.** *Create Users and Groups;* **5.** *Change Ownership and Assign Permissions to Database Objects;* **6.** *Test and Reset Default Security Settings;* **7.** *Create and Modify Workgroups Using the Security Wizard.*

DeLong Grant Law Partners want to secure the database tables used by their paralegals. You will create new accounts and add a paralegals group. You will assign permissions, and then test your security settings. You will also create a new workgroup information file for the database used by Human Resources. Your completed security reports will look similar to those shown in Figure 11.32.

For Project 11C, you will need the following files:

a11C_Paralegals
a11C_Personnel

You will save your files as
11C_2007_Firstname_Lastname
11C_Encoded_Firstname_Lastname
11C_HR_FML (Access 2003 file and Snapshot file)
11C_Paralegals_Firstname_Lastname
11C_Screens_Firstname_Lastname
11C_System_Firstname_Lastname
11C_Unsecured_Firstname_Lastname 11C_WIF_FML

Figure 11.32

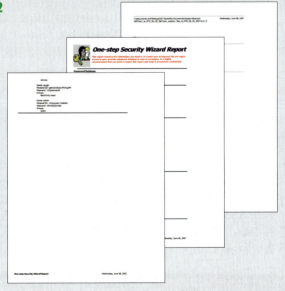

(Project 11C–Paralegals continues on the next page)

(Project 11C–Paralegals continued)

1. **Start** Access. Locate and then open the **a11C_Paralegals** file. If prompted to log in, click Cancel, and then reset the default security settings as directed later in Step 24.

2. Click the **Office** button, point to **Save As** and click **Access 2002 - 2003 Database**, and then save the database in your **Access Chapter 11** folder as **11C_Paralegals_ Firstname_Lastname Rename** the database tables by adding **FML** to the end of each table name using your own initials. Do not use any spaces in the table names.

3. Click the **Database Tools tab**. In the **Administer group**, click the **Users and Permissions** button, and then click **User and Group Accounts**. In the displayed **User and Group Accounts** dialog box, click the **Change Logon Password tab**. In the **New Password** and **Verify** boxes, type **11Cpassword1** and then click **Apply**.

4. Click the **Users tab**, and then click the **New** button. In the displayed **New User/Group**, under **Name**, type **ParalegalAdmin** Under **Personal ID**, type **11cdfgh3** and then click **OK**. Click the **Add** button to add *ParalegalAdmin* to the *Admins* group.

5. In the displayed **User and Group Accounts** dialog box, click the **Groups tab**, and then click the **New** button. In the displayed **New User/Group**, under **Name**, type **Paralegals** Under **Personal ID** type **11cdfgh4** and then click **OK**.

6. In the displayed **User and Group Accounts** dialog box, click the **Users tab**, and then click the **New** button. Under **Name**, type **MAyers** Under **Personal ID** type **11cdfgh4** and then click **OK**. In the displayed **User and Group Accounts** dia-log box, under **Available Groups**, click **Paralegals**, and then click the **Add** button.

7. If you are instructed to submit this result, click the Print Users and Groups button, create a paper or electronic printout. Click **OK** to close the User and Group Accounts dialog box.

8. In the **Administer group**, click the **Users and Permissions** button, and then click **User and Group Permissions**. Click the **Change Owner tab**, and then under **Object**, click the **PersonalCaseNotes** table. Click the **New Owner arrow**, click **ParalegalAdmin**, and then click the **Change Owner** button.

9. Click the **Permissions tab**. Next to **List**, select the **Groups** option button. Under **User/Group Name**, click **Users**. Under **Object Name**, click **PersonalCaseNotes**, and then under **Permissions**, clear the **Read Design** check box. Click the **Apply** button.

10. Press PrtScr. Start a new **Word** document, and then **Paste** the screen shot. **Save** the Word document as **11C_Screens_Firstname_Lastname**

11. In Access, under **Object Type**, click **Database**. Under **Permissions**, clear the **Administer** check box, and then click the **Apply** button. Press PrtScr, and then **Paste** the screen shot into the Word document.

12. Under **User/Group Name**, click **Paralegals**. Under **Object Type**, click **Table**, and then under **Object Name**, click **PersonalCaseNotes**. Under **Permissions**, select the following check boxes: **Read Data**, **Update Data**, **Insert Data**, and **Delete Data**. Click the **Apply** button. Create a screen shot, and then **Paste** it into the Word document.

(Project 11C–Paralegals continues on the next page)

(Project 11C–Paralegals continued)

13. Under **Object Name**, click **PersonalCases**. Under **Permissions**, select the following check boxes: **Read Data**, **Update Data**, **Insert Data**, and **Delete Data**, and then click the **Apply** button. Create a screen shot, and then **Paste** it into the Word document.

14. **Save** the Word document. If you are instructed to submit this result, create a paper or electronic printout of 11C_Screens_ Firstname_Lastname **Exit** Word.

15. **Close** the **User and Group Permissions** dialog box. In the **Database Tools group**, click the **Encode/Decode Databas**e button. **Save** the encoded file in the **Access Chapter 11** folder as **11C_Encoded_ Firstname_Lastname**

16. **Exit** Access. **Start** Access, and then locate and open the **11C_Paralegals_Firstname_ Lastname** database. In the displayed **Logon** dialog box, in the **Name** box, type **MAyers** Leave the **Password** box blank, and then click **OK**.

17. Click the **Database Tools tab**. In the **Administer group**, click the **Users and Permissions** button, and then click **User and Group Accounts**. In the displayed **User and Group Accounts** dialog box, click the **Change Logon Password tab**. In the **New Password** and **Verify** boxes, type **11Cpassword3** and then click **OK**.

18. On the **Navigation Pane**, double-click the **PersonalCaseNotes** table, and then enter the following test record:

PCaseID	Date	NoteAuthor	Note
PC00001	Enter current date	Melody Ayers	This is a test note.

19. **Close** the table, and then **Exit** Access. **Start** Access, and then locate and open the **11C_Paralegals_Firstname_Lastname** database. In the displayed **Logon** dialog box, in the **Name** box, type **ParalegalAdmin** Leave the **Password** box blank, and then click **OK**.

20. Click the **Database Tools tab**. In the **Administer group**, click the **Users and Permissions** button, and then click **User and Group Accounts**. In the displayed **User and Group Accounts** dialog box, click the **Change Logon Password tab**. In the **New Password** and **Verify** boxes, type **11Cpassword2** and then click **OK**.

21. Click the **Office** button, point to **Save As**, and then click **Access 2007 Database**. **Save** the file in your **Access Chapter 11** folder as **11C_2007_Firstname_Lastname** Read the displayed warning, and then click **OK**.

22. **Close** the database. Click the **Office** button, click **Open**, and then locate your **Access Chapter 11** folder. Select **11C_2007_Firstname_Lastname**, click the **Open button arrow**, and then click **Open Exclusive**.

23. When prompted to log in, in the **Name** box, type **ParalegalAdmin** In the **Password** box, type **11Cpassword2** and then click **OK**.

24. Click the **Database Tools tab**, and in the **Database Tools group**, click the **Encrypt with Password** button. In the displayed **Set Database Password** dialog box, in the **Password** and **Verify** boxes, type **11Cpassword4** and then click **OK**.

25. **Exit** Access. In **My Computer**, navigate to **Local Disk (C:)\Documents and Settings***User Name***\Application Data\Microsoft\Access**, where *User Name* is your current Windows logon name. If your computer is running

(Project 11C–Paralegals continues on the next page)

Content-Based Assessments

(Project 11C–Paralegals continued)

Windows Vista, open the Computer folder window, navigate to Local Disk (C:)\Users*User Name*\AppData\ Roaming\Microsoft\Access. Right-click the **System** file, and from the displayed shortcut menu, click **Cut**.

26. In your **Access Chapter 11** folder, right-click, and then from the displayed shortcut menu, click **Paste**. Right-click the pasted file and then from the displayed shortcut menu, click **Rename**. Type **11C_System_Firstname_Lastname** and then press Enter. **Close** the **My Computer** window.

27. **Start** Access. Locate and open the **a11C_Personnel** database. Click the **Office** button, point to **Save As** and click **Access 2002 - 2003 Database**, and then save the database in the **Access Chapter11** folder as **11C_HR_FML** using your own initials.

28. Click the **Database Tools tab**. In the **Administer group**, click the **Users and Permissions** button, and then click **User-Level Security Wizard**. Be sure that the **Create a new workgroup information file** option button is selected.

29. Click **Next**, and then click the **Browse** button. In the displayed **Select a workgroup file** dialog box, navigate to your **Access Chapter 11** folder. In the **File name** box, type **11C_WIF_FML** using your own initials, and then click **Select**. Be sure the **I want to create a shortcut to open my**

security-enhanced database option button is selected, and then click **Next** two times.

30. Select the **Read-Only Users** check box, and then click **Next** two times. Click the only user listed, which should be the user name you used to log in to your computer. In the **Password** box, type **11Cpassword5** and then click the **Add a New User** button.

31. In the **User name** box, type **apugh** In the **Password** box, type **11Cpassword6** and then click the **Add This User to the List** button.

32. Click **Next**. Click the **Group or user name arrow**, and then click **apugh**. Click the **Read-Only Users** check box, and then click **Next**.

33. Click the **Browse** button and navigate to your **Access Chapter 11** folder. Name the backup **11C_Unsecured_FML** using your own initials, and then click **Select**.

34. Click **Finish**. If you are instructed to submit this result, create a paper or electronic printout of the One-step Security Wizard Report. **Close** Print Preview. In the displayed message, click **Yes**. In the next displayed message, click **OK**.

35. **Exit** Access. If you are submitting this project electronically, submit all the files listed at the beginning of this project as directed by your instructor.

End **You have completed Project 11C**

Content-Based Assessments

Skills Review

Project 11D — Top Accounts

In this project, you will apply the skills you practiced from the Objectives in Project 11B.

Objectives: 8. *Modify a Query in SQL View;* **9.** *Create a Query in SQL View;* **10.** *Create a Union Query Using SQL;* **11.** *Create Calculated Fields and SQL Aggregate Functions.*

DeLong Grant Law Partners want a report that lists their top accounts. To build the report, you will create two queries using SQL view. You will join the two queries into single query. You will then create a query that summarizes the data in the union query and build the report from this query. Your completed report will look similar to the report shown in Figure 11.33.

> ### For Project 11D, you will need the following file:
>
> a11D_Top_Accounts

**You will save your database as
11D_Top_Accounts_Firstname_Lastname**

Figure 11.33

(Project 11D–Top Accounts continues on the next page)

(Project 11D–Top Accounts continued)

1. **Start** Access. Locate and open the **a11D_Top_Accounts** file. Click the **Office** button. Point to **Save As**, click **Access 2007 Database**, and then save the database in the **Access Chapter 11** folder as 11D_Top_Accounts_Firstname_Lastname **Rename** the database tables by adding **FML** to the end of each table name using your own initials.

2. Click the **Create tab**, and then in the **Other group**, click the **Query Design** button. In the displayed **Show Table** dialog box, with **CorpAccounts** selected, click the **Add** button. In the dialog box, double-click **FlatFees**, and then click the **Close** button.

3. From the **CorpAccounts** table, add the **CorpName** field to the design grid. From the **FlatFees** table, add the **Fee** field to the design grid.

4. In the **Show/Hide group**, click the **Totals** button. In the **Total** row for the **Fee** column, change **Group By** to **Sum**. **Save** the query with the name **FlatFeesQuery** using your own initials.

5. In the status bar, click the **SQL View** button. After the *AS* keyword, replace the text *SumofFee* with **Totals**

6. In the **Results group**, click the **Run** button. View the results, and then click the **SQL View** button. Click **Save**.

7. Click the **Create tab**, and then in the **Other group**, click the **Query Design** button. **Close** the **Show Table** dialog box, and then click the **SQL View** button.

8. Replace the existing text with the following SELECT clause using your own initials: **SELECT CorpAccountsFML.CorpName, Rate * Hours AS Totals**

9. On a new line, enter the following FROM clause using your own initials: **FROM CorpAccountsFML INNER JOIN HourlyFeesFML ON CorpAccountsFML.CorpID = HourlyFeesFML.CorpID;**

10. Click the **Run** button to test the query so far. **Save** the query as **HourlyFeesQueryFML** using your own initials.

11. Click the **SQL View** button. In the SELECT clause, replace the text *Rate * Hours* with **Sum(Rate * Hours)**

12. At the end of the SQL statement, delete the semicolon, press Enter, and then type the following clause: **GROUP BY CorpAccountsFML.CorpName**

13. Click the **Run** button, view the results, and then click **Save**.

14. Click the **Create tab**, and then in the **Other group**, click the **Query Design** button. In the displayed **Show Table** dialog box, click the **Close** button, and then in the **Query Type group**, click the **Union** button.

15. Display the **FlatFeesQuery** query in SQL view. Select the entire SQL statement, right-click, and then from the displayed shortcut menu, click **Copy**. Display the union query that you are building, right-click, and then click **Paste**. Delete the semicolon, press Enter **two** times, and then type **UNION**

(Project 11D–Top Accounts continues on the next page)

Content-Based Assessments

(Project 11D–Top Accounts continued)

16. Display the **HourlyFeesQuery** query in SQL view, and then **Copy** the entire SQL statement. Display the union query, press Enter **two** times, and then press Ctrl + V.

17. **Save** the query with the name **FeesUnionFML** using your own initials, and then click the **Run** button. View the results, and then **Close** all three open queries.

18. Click the **Create tab**, and then in the **Other group**, click the **Query Design** button.

19. In the displayed **Show Table** dialog box, click the **Queries tab**, and then click the **FeesUnionFML** query. Click the **Add** button, and then click the **Close** button. Add the **CorpName** field to the design grid, and then add the **Totals** field.

20. In the **Show/Hide group**, click the **Totals** button. In the **Total** row for the **Totals** column, change **Group By** to **Sum**.

21. Click in the **Sort** row for the **Totals** column. Click the displayed arrow, and then click **Descending**.

22. **Save** the query with the name **TopAccountsFML** using you own initials. Click the **Run** button and view the results.

23. Click the **SQL View** button. After the SELECT keyword, press Spacebar, and then type: **TOP 10**

24. **Run** the query and view the results. Click **Save**, and then **Close** the query.

25. On the **Navigation Pane**, click to select the **TopAccounts** query. Click the **Create tab**, and then in the **Reports group**, click the **Report** button. Click the **AutoFormat** button, and then click the **Paper** style—the second choice in the second row.

26. Change the report **Title** text box to **Top Accounts Firstname Lastname** Change the **CorpName** label to **Corporation Name**

27. At the top of the **Totals** column, change the **SumofTotals** label to **Totals** At the bottom of the **Totals** column, click the text box that calculates the grand total, and then apply the **Currency** format.

28. **Save** the report with the name suggested by Access. If you are instructed to submit this result, create a paper or electronic printout of the report. **Close** the report, and then **Exit** Access.

End **You have completed Project 11D**

Mastering Access

Project 11E—Accountants

In this project, you will apply the skills you practiced from the Objectives in Project 11A.

Objectives: 1. *Encrypt and Decrypt Databases;* **2.** *Secure the Access Administrator Account;* **3.** *Create an Access Administrative User;* **4.** *Create Users and Groups;* **5.** *Change Ownership and Assign Permissions to Database Objects;* **6.** *Test and Reset Default Security Settings;* **7.** *Create and Modify Workgroups Using the Security Wizard.*

DeLong Grant Law Partners want to secure the databases used by their accounting and marketing departments. You will create new user accounts and add an Accountants group. You will assign permissions, and then test your security settings. You will also create a new work-group information file for the database used by the marketing depart-ment. Your completed security reports will look similar to those shown in Figure 11.34.

For Project 11E, you will need the following files:

a11E_Accountants
a11E_Clients

You will save your files as
11E_2007_Firstname_Lastname
11E_Accountants_Firstname_Lastname
11E_Clients_FML (Access 2003 file and Snapshot file)
11E_Encoded_Firstname_Lastname
11E_Screens_Firstname_Lastname
11E_System_Firstname_Lastname
11E_Unsecured_Firstname_Lastname
11E_WIF_Firstname_Lastname

Figure 11.34

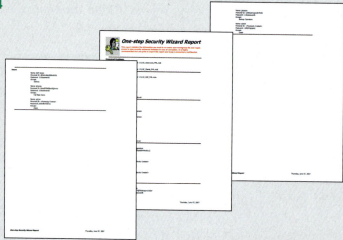

(Project 11E–Accountants continues on the next page)

chapter eleven Access

Mastering Access

(Project 11E–Accountants continued)

1. **Start** Access. Locate and open the **a11E_Accountants** file. If asked to log in, click Cancel, exit Access, and then reset the default security settings.

2. Click the **Office** button, point to **Save As**, click **Access 2002 - 2003 Database**, and then save the database in your **Access Chapter11** folder as **11E_Accountants_Firstname_Lastname** Add **FML** to the end of each table name using your own initials. Do not use any spaces.

3. Change the logon password for the default administrative account, *Admin*, to **11Epassword1** Create a new user with the **Name AccountAdmin** and a **Personal ID** of **11edfgh1** Add *AccountAdmin* to the *Admins* group.

4. Add a new group with the **Name Accountants** and a **Personal ID** of **11edfgh2** Add a new user with the **Name MRush** and a **Personal ID** of **11edfgh3** Add *MRush* to the *Accountants* group. If you are instructed to submit this result, click the Print Users and Groups button to create a paper or electronic printout.

5. For the **Users** group, remove the **Administer** permission for the **Database** object. Apply the change, capture the screen, and then **Paste** the screen shot into a new, blank **Word** document. Save the Word document as **11E_Screens_Firstname_Lastname**

6. For the **FlatBilling** and **HourlyBilling** tables, remove the **Read Design** permission for the **Users** group. After applying each change, make a screen capture that shows the permissions for that table, and then **Paste** the screen shot into the Word document.

7. For the **Accountants** group, add the following permissions to all four database tables: **Read Data**, **Update Data**, **Insert Data**, and **Delete Data**. As you apply the changes for each table, capture each screen, and then **Paste** the screen shot into the Word document.

8. For the **FlatBilling** and **HourlyBilling** tables, change the owner to *AccountAdmin*. Capture the screen, and then **Paste** it into the Word document. If you are instructed to submit this result, create a paper or electronic printout of the Word document.

9. **Save** the Word document, and then **Exit** Word. In Access, encode the open database. **Save** the encoded file in your **Access Chapter 11** folder as **11E_Encoded_Firstname_Lastname**

10. **Exit** Access, and then open **11E_Accountants_Firstname_Lastname** using the *AccountAdmin* logon. Recall that the default password is blank. Change the password for *AccountAdmin* to **11Epassword2**

11. Click the **Office** button, point to **Save As**, click **Access 2007 Database**, and then in the **File name** box, type **11E_2007_Firstname_Lastname** Click **Save**, read the displayed message, and then click **OK**.

12. Open **11E_2007_Firstname_Lastname** using the **Open Exclusive** command. Encrypt the database using the password **11Epassword2** and then **Exit** Access.

13. In **My Computer**, navigate to **Local Disk (C:)\Documents and Settings***User Name***\Application Data\Microsoft\Access**, where *User Name* is your current Windows logon name. If your computer is

(Project 11E–Accountants continues on the next page)

Access

chapter eleven

Mastering Access

(Project 11E–Accountants continued)

running Windows Vista, navigate to Local Disk (C:)\Users*User Name*\AppData\Roaming\Microsoft\Access. **Cut** the **System** file, and then **Paste** it into your **Access Chapter 11** folder. **Rename** the file **11E_System_Firstname_Lastname**

14. **Start** Access, and then open the **a11E_Clients** database. Click the **Office** button, point to **Save As** and click **Access 2002 - 2003 Database**, and then save the database in the **Access Chapter11** folder as **11E_Clients_FML** using your own initials.

15. Start the **User-Level Security Wizard**. Use the **Browse** button to name the new workgroup information file **11E_WIF_FML** in your **Access Chapter 11** folder.

16. In the wizard, add the **Backup Operators** group, and then change the administrator

password to **11Epassword5** Add a new user with the name **jdodson** and a password of **11Epassword6** Add **jdodson** to the **Backup Operators** group.

17. **Save** the backup file that will be created as **11E_Unsecured_FML** in your **Access Chapter 11** folder, and **Finish** the wizard.

18. If you are instructed to submit this result, create a paper or electronic printout of the One-step Security Wizard Report. **Close** Print Preview. In the displayed message, click **Yes**. In the next displayed message, click **OK**. **Close** the database, and then **Exit** Access. If you are submitting this project electronically, submit all the files listed at the beginning of this project as directed by your instructor.

End **You have completed Project 11E**

Access
chapter eleven

Mastering Access

Project 11F—Services

In this project, you will apply the skills you practiced from the Objectives in Project 11B.

Objectives: 8. *Modify a Query in SQL View;* **9.** *Create a Query in SQL View;* **10.** *Create a Union Query Using SQL;* **11.** *Create Calculated Fields and SQL Aggregate Functions.*

DeLong Grant Law Partners want a report that describes the various services that they provide to corporations and organizations. To build the report, you will create two queries using SQL view. You will join the two queries into a single query. You will then create a query that summarizes the data in the union query and build the report from this query. Your completed report will look similar to the report shown in Figure 11.35.

For Project 11F, you will need the following file:

a11F_Services

You will save your database as
11F_Services_Firstname_Lastname

Figure 11.35

(Project 11F–Services continues on the next page)

Access

chapter eleven

Mastering Access

(Project 11F–Services continued)

1. **Start** Access. Locate and open the **a11F_Services** file. **Save** the database in the **Access Chapter 11** folder as **11F_Services_Firstname_Lastname** At the end of each table name, add **FML** using your own initials and no space.

2. Start a new query in **Design** view. **Add** the **Services** and **FlatFees** tables to the query. From the **Services** table, add the **Service** field to the design grid. From the **FlatFees** table, add the **Fee** field.

3. In the **Show/Hide group**, click the **Totals** button. In the **Total** row for the **Fee** column, change **Group By** to **Avg**.

4. In SQL view, adapt the *SELECT* statement so that the calculated field's caption will display as **Average Run** the query and view the results. **Save** the query as **FlatServicesFML** using your own initials.

5. Start a new query in **Design** view, and then switch to **SQL** view. Add a **SELECT** statement that displays the **Service** field from the **Services** table.

6. Add a calculated field to the *SELECT* statement that multiplies the **Rate** and **Hours** fields. Write the SQL needed so that the calculated field's caption displays as **Average**

7. Add a **FROM** clause that joins the **Services** table to the **HourlyFees** table with an inner join that uses the **ServiceCode** fields from each table. If needed, use the FROM clause in the query created earlier in this project as your reference.

8. For the calculated field, add an SQL aggregate function that calculates the average of the *Rate* field multiplied by the *Hours* field. Add a **GROUP BY** clause that groups the query by each **Service** If needed, use the query created earlier in this project as your reference.

9. **Run** the query and view the results. **Save** the query as **HourlyServicesFML** using your own initials.

10. Create a new **Union** query. **Copy** and **Paste** the SQL from the two queries created earlier and join them using the **UNION** keyword. **Run** the query, view the results, and then **Save** the query as **ServicesUnionFML** using your own initials.

11. Create a new query in **Design** view. In the displayed **Show Table** dialog box, click the **Queries tab**, add the **ServicesUnion** query, and then **Close** the dialog box. Add the **Service** field to the design grid, and then add the **Average** field.

12. In the **Show/Hide group**, click the **Totals** button. In the **Total** row for the **Average** column, change **Group By** to **Avg**. **Save** the query with the name **ServicesQueryFML** using your own initials. Click the **Run** button, view the results, and then **Close** all open queries.

13. On the **Navigation Pane**, click to select **ServicesQuery**. Click the **Create tab**, and then in the **Reports group**, click the **Report** button. Click the **AutoFormat** button, and then click the **Opulent** style—the second choice in the fourth row.

14. Change the **Title** text box to **Services Firstname Lastname** Click the **AvgofAverage** label, and then change the label text to **Average** At the bottom of the **Average** column, click the text box that calculates the column total, and then press ⌧Delete. If you are instructed to submit this result, create a paper or electronic printout.

15. **Save** the report with the name suggested by Access. **Close** the report, and then **Exit** Access. If you are submitting this project electronically, submit the database as directed by your instructor.

End **You have completed Project 11F**

Content-Based Assessments

Mastering Access

Project 11G — Bonuses

In this project, you will apply the skills you practiced from the Objectives in Projects 11A and 11B.

Objectives: 1. *Encrypt and Decrypt Databases;* **2.** *Secure the Access Administrator Account;* **4.** *Create Users and Groups;* **5.** *Change Ownership and Assign Permissions to Database Objects;* **6.** *Test and Reset Default Security Settings;* **8.** *Modify a Query in SQL View;* **9.** *Create a Query in SQL View;* **10.** *Create a Union Query Using SQL;* **11.** *Create Calculated Fields and SQL Aggregate Functions.*

The two lead partners, DeLong and Grant, need a confidential query listing the four lawyers who have generated the most business. You will secure the database so that Lawrence Delong can access the tables and create the necessary queries. You will create two queries using SQL view, join them in a union query, and then build another query summarizing the union query. Your completed security report and query will look similar to Figure 11.36.

For Project 11G, you will need the following file:

a11G_Bonuses

You will save your files as
11G_Bonuses_Firstname_Lastname
11G_Encoded_Firstname_Lastname
11G_Screens_Firstname_Lastname
11G_System_Firstname_Lastname

Figure 11.36

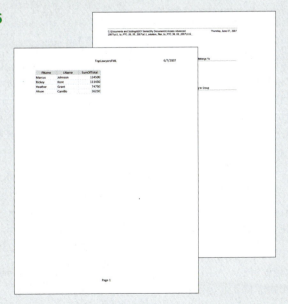

(Project 11G–Bonuses continues on the next page)

Content-Based Assessments

chapter eleven Access

Mastering Access

(Project 11G–Bonuses continued)

1. **Start** Access. Locate and then open the **a11G_Bonuses** database. **Save** the database as an **Access 2002 - 2003 Database** in your **Access Chapter 11** folder as **11G_Bonuses_Firstname_Lastname** At the end of each table name, add **FML** using your own initials and no space.

2. Change the password of the default administrative account, *Admin*, to **11Gpassword1**

3. Encode the database. **Save** the encoded copy in your **Access Chapter 11** folder with the name **11G_Encoded_Firstname_Lastname**

4. Add a new group with the **Name Partners** and a **Personal ID** of **11gdfgh1** Add a new user with the **Name LDeLong** and a **Personal ID** of **11gdfgh2** Add *LDeLong* to the *Partners* group. If you are instructed to submit this result, click the Print Users and Groups button, and then create a paper or electronic printout.

5. Change the ownership of the **FlatFees** and **HourlyFees** tables to **LDelong**. Capture the screen, and then **Paste** the screen shot into a new, blank **Word** document. **Save** the Word document as **11G_Screens_Firstname_Lastname**

6. For the *Partners* group, add the following permissions to the **FlatFees** and **HourlyFee** tables: **Read Data**, **Update Data**, **Insert Data**, and **Delete Data**. For each table, capture the screen showing its permissions, and then **Paste** them into the Word document.

7. If you are instructed to submit this result, create a paper or electronic printout of the Word document. **Save** the Word document, and then **Exit** Word.

8. Start a new query in **Design** view. Add the **Lawyers** and **FlatFees** tables to the query.

From the **Lawyers** table, add the **FName** and **LName** fields to the design grid. From the **FlatFees** table, add the **Fee** field.

9. In the **Show/Hide group**, click the **Totals** button. In the **Total** row for the **Fee** column, change **Group By** to **Sum**.

10. In **SQL** view, change the caption for the calculated field to **Total Run** the query and view the results. **Save** the query as **FlatFeesQueryFML** using your own initials.

11. Start a new query, and then switch to **SQL** view. Using the earlier query as your guide, write a SELECT statement that displays the **FName** and **LName** fields from the **Lawyers** table.

12. Add a calculated field to the *SELECT* clause that multiplies the **Rate** and **Hours** fields. Write the SQL needed so that the calculated field's caption displays as **Total**

13. For the calculated field, add an SQL aggregate function that calculates the total of the **Rate** field multiplied by the **Hours** field.

14. Add a **FROM** clause that joins the **Lawyers** table to the **HourlyFees** table with an inner join that uses the **LawyerID** fields from each table.

15. Copy the *GROUP BY* clause from **FlatFeesQuery** and **Paste** it into the current query. **Run** the query and view the results. **Save** the query as **HourlyFeesQueryFML** using your own initials.

16. Create a new **Union** query. **Copy** and **Paste** the SQL statements from the two queries created earlier and join them using the **UNION** keyword. **Run** the query, view the results, and then **Save** the query as **UnionFML** using your own initials. **Close** all open queries.

(Project 11G–Bonuses continues on the next page)

(Project 11G—Bonuses continued)

17. Create a new query in **Design** view, add the **Union** query, and then add the **FName**, **LName**, and **Total** fields to the design grid. Add the **Total row** to the design grid, and then in the **Total row** for the **Total** column, change **Group By** to **Sum**.

18. In the **Total** column, change the **Sort** row value to **Descending** In SQL view, after *SELECT*, add the **TOP 4** keyword.

19. **Save** the query as **TopLawyersFML** using your own initials. **Run** the query. If you

are instructed to submit this result, create a paper or electronic printout. **Close** the query and **Exit** Access.

20. Locate the default workgroup information file, named **System**, on your computer. **Cut** the **System** file, and then **Paste** it into your **Access Chapter 11** folder. **Rename** the file **11G_System_Firstname_Lastname**

21. If you are submitting this project electronically, submit all the files listed at the beginning of this project as directed by your instructor.

End **You have completed Project 11G** —————

Access
chapter eleven

Mastering Access

Project 11H — Annual Dinner

In this project, you will apply the skills you practiced from the Objectives in Projects 11A and 11B.

Objectives: 2. *Secure the Access Administrator Account;* **4.** *Create Users and Groups;* **5.** *Change Ownership and Assign Permissions to Database Objects;* **7.** *Create and Modify Workgroups Using the Security Wizard;* **8.** *Modify a Query in SQL View;* **9.** *Create a Query in SQL View;* **10.** *Create a Union Query Using SQL.*

DeLong Grant Law Partners hold an annual dinner for their corporate clients. In this project, you will create a report that displays the invitation list to this event. The report will be based on a union query that combines results into two queries. You will also secure the database using the Security Wizard and then test your security settings. Your completed security report and Dinner Invitations report will look similar to the reports shown in Figure 11.37.

For Project 11H, you will need the following file:

a11H_Annual_Dinner

You will save your files as
11H_Dinner_FML (Access database and Snapshot file)
11H_Unsecured_FML
11H_WIF_FML

Figure 11.37

(Project 11H–Annual Dinner continues on the next page)

Content-Based Assessments

(Project 11H–Annual Dinner continued)

1. **Start** Access. Locate and open the **a11H_Annual_Dinner** database. **Save** the database as an **Access 2002 - 2003 Database** in your **Access Chapter 11** folder as **11H_Dinner_FML** At the end of each table name, add **FML** using your own initials and no space.

2. Start a new query in **Design** view. Add the **CorpAccounts** and **FlatFees** tables to the query. From the **CorpAccounts** table, add the following fields to the design grid: **CorpName**, **Street**, **City**, **State**, and **PostalCode**. From the **FlatFees** table, add the **Date** field.

3. In the **Criteria row** for the **Date** field, add the following criteria: **>12/31/2007** In the **Show row** for the **Date** field, clear the check box. **Save** the query as **FlatFeesQueryFML** using your own initials.

4. Switch to **SQL** view, and leave the query open as a reference for the next query. Start a new query and switch to SQL view. Write a SELECT statement that displays the following fields from the **CorpAccounts** table: **CorpName**, **Street**, **City**, **State**, and **PostalCode**.

5. Add a **FROM** clause that joins the **CorpAccounts** table to the **HourlyFees** table with an inner join using the **CorpID** field from each table.

6. Add a **WHERE** clause that returns only those records where the date is after **12/31/2007 Save** the query as **HourlyFeesQueryFML** using your own initials.

7. Create a new **Union** query. **Copy** and **Paste** the SQL from the two queries created earlier and join them using the **UNION** keyword. **Run** the query, view the results, and then **Save** the query as

DinnerInvitesFML using your own initials. **Close** all open queries.

8. On the **Navigation Pane**, click to select the **DinnerInvites** query. Click the **Create tab**, and then in the **Reports group**, click the **Report** button. Resize each column to better fit its contents. Be sure all of the report displays on a single page.

9. Change the **Title** text box to **Dinner Invitations Firstname Lastname Save** the report with the name suggested by Access, and then **Close** the report.

10. Start the **User-Level Security Wizard**, and then create a new workgroup information file. In the wizard, **Save** the workgroup information file in your **Access Chapter 11** folder with the name **11H_WIF_FML** using your own initials.

11. In the wizard, use the option to create a shortcut to the database, and then add the **Full Data Users** pre-built group to the workgroup information file. Use the wizard to add the following password to the default administrative account: **11Hpassword1**

12. Add a new user with a **User name** of **kmorse** and a **Password** of **11Hpassword2** Add **kmorse** to the **Full Data Users** group. In the final step of the wizard, in your **Access Chapter 11** folder, **Save** the unsecured backup as **11H_Unsecured_FML**, using your own initials.

13. **Finish** the wizard. If you are instructed to submit this result, create a paper or electronic printout of the One-step Security Wizard Report. **Close** the report, and then click **Yes** to create a Snapshot document.

14. Open **11H_Dinner_FML** using the new workgroup information file that you cre-

(Project 11H–Annual Dinner continues on the next page)

Mastering Access

(Project 11H–Annual Dinner continued)

ated. Recall that you need to double-click the desktop shortcut that was created by the wizard. Log in with the **Name kmorse** and the **Password 11Hpassword2**

15. Open the **Dinner Invites** report. As a member of the *Full Data User* group, *kmorse* has permission to view the data displayed in the report. If you are

instructed to submit this result, create a paper or electronic printout of **Close** the report.

16. **Exit** Access. If you are submitting this project electronically, submit all the files listed at the beginning of this project as directed by your instructor.

End **You have completed Project 11H** ————————————————

Mastering Access

Project 11I—Seminar

In this project, you will apply the skills you practiced from all of the Objectives in Projects 11A and 11B.

DeLong Grant Law Partners need a list of personal clients to invite to a seminar where they can inform the clients about their services. They wish to invite just the clients who have been billed less than $500 dollars in services. You will use SQL to create four queries to generate the desired list of clients. You will then edit the Access default security settings by creating new users and groups and then assigning permissions and ownership to database objects. You will also create a new workgroup information file and add a new backup operator for the database. Finally, you will encrypt a database saved in the 2007 file format. Your completed security reports and final query will look similar to Figure 11.38.

For Project 11I, you will need the following files:

a11I_Seminar
a11I_2007

You will save your files as
11I_2007_Firstname_Lastname
11I_Encoded_Firstname_Lastname
11I_Screens_Firstname_Lastname
11I_Seminar_Firstname_Lastname (database and Snapshot file)
11I_System_Firstname_Lastname
11I_Unsecured_Firstname_Lastname
11I_WIF_FML

Figure 11.38

(Project 11I–Seminar continues on the next page)

(Project 11I–Seminar continued)

1. **Start** Access. Locate and open the **a11I_Seminar** database. **Save** the database as an **Access 2002 - 2003 Database** in your **Access Chapter 11** folder with the name **11I_Seminar_Firstname_Lastname** At the end of each table name, add **FML** using your own initials and no space.

2. Encode the database. **Save** the encoded copy in your **Access Chapter 11** folder with the name **11I_Encoded_Firstname_Lastname**

3. Change the default administrative account—*Admin*—to **11Ipassword1** Add a new group with the **Name Clerks** and a **Personal ID** of **11idfgh1** Add a new user with the **Name PVelez** and a **Personal ID** of **11idfgh2** Add *PVelez* to the *Clerks* group.

4. Add a new user with the **Name HSheppard** and a **Personal ID** of **11idfgh3** Add *HSheppard* to the *Admins* group. If you are instructed to submit this result, click the Print Users and Groups button and then create a paper or electronic printout.

5. For the **Users** group, remove all permissions to the **PersonalClients** table. After applying the change, capture the screen, and then **Paste** the screen shot into a new, blank **Word** document. **Save** the Word document as **11I_Screens_Firstname_Lastname**

6. For the **Clerks** group, add the following permission to the **PersonalClients** table: **Read Design**, **Read Data**, **Update Data**, **Insert Data**, and **Delete Data**. Apply the changes, capture the screen, and then **Paste** it into the **Word** document.

7. Change the ownership of the **PersonalClients** table to **HSheppard**. Apply the changes, capture the screen, and then **Paste** it into the **Word** document. If you are instructed to submit this result, create a paper or electronic printout of the

Word document. **Save** the Word document, and then **Exit** Word.

8. **Exit** Access, and then open **11I_Seminar_Firstname_Lastname** using the **HSheppard** logon. Recall that the password is blank. Change the password for **HSheppard** to **11Ipassword2**

9. Start a new query in **Design** view. **Add** the **PersonalClients** and **FlatFees** tables to the query. From the **PersonalClients** table, add the **FName** and **LName** fields to the design grid. From the **FlatFees** table, add the **Fee** field.

10. In the **Show/Hide group**, click the **Totals** button. In the **Total** row for the **Fee** column, change **Group By** to **Sum**. In the **Criteria** row for the **Fee** column, type **<500**

11. In SQL view, after the *AS* keyword, change *SumofFee* to **Total Save** the query as **FlatFeesQueryFML** using your own initials.

12. **Copy** the query's SQL statement to the Office Clipboard. Start a new query, and then switch **SQL** view. **Paste** the SQL statement from the Office Clipboard.

13. Edit the *FROM* clause so that the **PersonalClients** table is joined with an inner join to the **HourlyFees** table. Use the **PersonalID** fields from each table to link the two tables.

14. In the new query's *SELECT* clause, change the SQL aggregate function *Sum(FlatFeesFML.Fee)* to an aggregate function that finds the sum of the **Rate** field multiplied by the **Hours** field.

15. Edit the *HAVING* clause to calculate the sum of the **Rate** field multiplied by the **Hours** field. **Save** the query as **HourlyFeesQueryFML** using your own initials.

(Project 11I–Seminar continues on the next page)

(Project 11I–Seminar continued)

16. Create a new **Union** query. **Copy** and **Paste** the SQL from the two queries created earlier, and then join them using the **UNION** keyword. **Run** the query, view the results, and then **Save** the query as **SeminarUnionFML** using your own initials.

17. Create a new query in Design view, **Add** the **SeminarUnion** query, and then add the **FName**, and **LName** fields to the design grid. **Save** the query as **InviteesFML** using your own initials.

18. In **SQL** view, after the keyword *SELECT*, add the **DISTINCT** keyword. **Run** the query, and then sort the results by **LName**. If you are instructed to submit this result, create a paper or electronic printout of the query. Click **Save**, and then **Close** all open queries.

19. **Exit** Access. Locate the default workgroup information file, named **System**, on your computer. **Cut** the **System** file, and then **Paste** it into your **Access Chapter 11** folder. **Rename** the file **11I_System_Firstname_Lastname**

20. Open **11I_Seminar_Firstname_Lastname**. Start the **User-Level Security Wizard**, and then create a new workgroup information file. In the wizard, **Save** the workgroup information file in your **Access Chapter 11** folder with the name **11I_WIF_FML** using your own initials.

21. In the wizard, use the option to create a shortcut to the database, and then add the **Backup Operators** pre-built group to the workgroup information file. Use the wizard to add the following password to the default administrative account: **11Ipassword3**

22. Add a new user with a **User name** of **aweeks** and a **Password** of **11Ipassword4** Add **aweeks** to the **Backup Operators** group. In the final step of the wizard, save the unsecured backup as **11I_Unsecured_Firstname_Lastname** in your **Access Chapter 11** folder.

23. If you are instructed to submit this result, create a paper or electronic printout of the One-step Security Wizard Report. **Close** the report, and then click **Yes** to create a Snapshot document.

24. **Exit** Access. Open **11H_Seminar_Firstname_Lastname** using the new workgroup information file that you created earlier. Log in with the **Name aweeks** and the **Password 11Ipassword4**

25. Attempt to open one of the database tables. From the **Office** menu, point to **Save As**, and then click **Access 2002 - 2003 Database**. In the displayed **Save As** dialog box, click **Cancel**.

26. **Exit** Access. Open a **11I_2007**. From the **Office** menu, point to **Save As**, and then click **Access 2007 Database**. Name the database **11I_2007_Firstname_Lastname** and then **Save** it in your **Access Chapter 11** folder.

27. **Close** the database, and the **Open** it in **Exclusive** mode. Encrypt the database with the password **GO! Series**

28. **Close** the database, and then **Exit** Access. If you are submitting this project electronically, submit all the files listed at the beginning of this project as directed by your instructor.

End **You have completed Project 11I**

 Access

 Business Running Case

Project 11J—Business Running Case

In this project, you will apply the skills you have practiced from the Objectives in Projects 11A and 11B.

From My Computer, navigate to the student files that accompany this textbook. In the folder **03_business_running_case**, locate and open the folder for this chapter. Open and print the instructions for this project, which are provided to you in Adobe PDF format. Follow the instructions and use the skills you have gained thus far to assist the brother and sister team of Michael and Kristen Landry in meeting the challenges of owning and running their business.

 You have completed Project 11J ——————————

Outcomes-Based Assessments

Rubric

The following outcomes-based assessments are *open-ended assessments*. That is, there is no specific correct result; your result will depend on your approach to the information provided. Make *Professional Quality* your goal. Use the following scoring rubric to guide you in *how* to approach the problem and then to evaluate *how well* your approach solves the problem.

The *criteria*—Software Mastery, Content, Format and Layout, and Process—represent the knowledge and skills you have gained that you can apply to solving the problem. The *levels of performance*—Professional Quality, Approaching Professional Quality, or Needs Quality Improvement—help you and your instructor evaluate your result.

	Your completed project is of Professional Quality if you:	Your completed project is Approaching Professional Quality if you:	Your completed project Needs Quality Improvements if you:
Software Mastery	Choose and apply the most appropriate skills, tools, and features and identify efficient methods to solve the problem.	Choose and apply some appropriate skills, tools, and features, but not in the most efficient manner.	Choose inappropriate skills, tools, or features, or are inefficient in solving the problem.
Content	Construct a solution that is clear and well organized, contains content that is accurate, appropriate to the audience and purpose, and is complete. Provide a solution that contains no errors of spelling, grammar, or style.	Construct a solution in which some components are unclear, poorly organized, inconsistent, or incomplete. Misjudge the needs of the audience. Have some errors in spelling, grammar, or style, but the errors do not detract from comprehension.	Construct a solution that is unclear, incomplete, or poorly organized, containing some inaccurate or inappropriate content; and contains many errors of spelling, grammar, or style. Do not solve the problem.
Format and Layout	Format and arrange all elements to communicate information and ideas, clarify function, illustrate relationships, and indicate relative importance.	Apply appropriate format and layout features to some elements, but not others. Overuse features, causing minor distraction.	Apply format and layout that does not communicate information or ideas clearly. Do not use format and layout features to clarify function, illustrate relationships, or indicate relative importance. Use available features excessively, causing distraction.
Process	Use an organized approach that integrates planning, development, self-assessment, revision, and reflection.	Demonstrate an organized approach in some areas, but not others; or, use an insufficient process of organization throughout.	Do not use an organized approach to solve the problem.

Problem Solving

Project 11K — Contracts

In this project, you will construct a solution by applying any combination of the skills you practiced from the Objectives in Projects 11A and 11B.

For Project 11K, you will need the following file:

a11K_Contracts

**You will save your database as
11K_Contracts_Firstname_Lastname**

DeLong Grant Law Partners need a list of each client that has asked for assistance with contracts. Because the clients are listed in two tables, in this project you will need to use SQL to return only one record per client, and then combine the two queries in a union query. To start, open **a11K_Contracts**, and then save it as a 2007 database with the name **11K_Contracts_Firstname_Lastname** At the end of each table name, add **FML** using your own initials and no space.

Using SQL, create a query that lists personal clients who have cases listed in the *Cases* table. List only the clients where the *ServiceCode* is equal to SC03. Include the *Name*, *Street*, *City*, *State*, and *PostalCode* fields. Add the necessary SQL command so that clients are not listed more than one time in the query's results. Save the query as **PersonalQueryFML** using your own initials.

Using SQL, create a query that lists corporate clients who have cases listed in the *Cases* table. List only the clients where the *ServiceCode* is equal to SC03. Include the *CompanyName*, *Street*, *City*, *State*, and *PostalCode* fields. Add the necessary SQL command so that clients are not listed more than one time in the query's results. Save the query as **CorporateQueryFML** using your own initials.

Create a union query that combines the two queries. Save the query as **AllClientsFML** using your own initials. Create a report based on the union query. Format the report to effectively present the results. Save the report as **AllClientsFML** Encrypt the database using the password **GO! Series** and then submit the project as directed by your instructor.

End You have completed Project 11K —————

Problem Solving

Project 11L — Workgroup

In this project, you will construct a solution by applying any combination of the skills you practiced from the Objectives in Projects 11A and 11B.

For Project 11L, you will need the following file:

a11L_Workgroup

**You will save your files as
11L_Workgroup_Firstname_Lastname**

DeLong Grant Law Partners need to secure the database containing a list of past cases. In this project, you will use the Security Wizard to create a workgroup information file to manage user-level security for the database. To start, open **a11L_Workgroup**, and then save it as a 2002 - 2003 database with the name **11L_Workgroup_Firstname_Lastname** At the end of each table name, add **FML** using your own initials and no space.

Use the security wizard to create a new workgroup information file in your Access Chapter 11 folder named **11L_WIF_FML** using your own initials. Add the Backup Operators, Full Data Users, and Full Permissions security group accounts. Secure the default administrative account by assigning the password **11Lpassword1** Add the following users and assign them to the groups as shown in the following table:

User Name	Password	Assigned Group
wcamacho	11Lpassword2	Full Permissions
bbean	11Lpassword3	Full Data Users
rbarron	11Lpassword4	Full Data Users
glivingston	11Lpassword5	Backup Operators

Save the unsecured backup copy in your Access Chapter 11 folder with the name **11L_Unsecured_Firstname_Lastname** If you are instructed to submit this result, create a paper or electronic printout of the One-step Security Wizard Report. When you close the report, create the Snapshot Viewer document. Log in as each user and test that each user has the correct permissions. Submit the project as directed by your instructor.

End You have completed Project 11L ——————————

Outcomes-Based Assessments

Access
chapter eleven

Problem Solving

Project 11M — Phone List

In this project, you will construct a solution by applying any combination of the skills you practiced from the Objectives in Projects 11A and 11B.

For Project 11M, you will need the following file:

a11M_Phone_List

**You will save your database as
11M_Phone_List_Firstname_Lastname**

DeLong Grant Law Partners want a list of all names and phone numbers of clients with open cases. To start, open **a11M_Phone_List**, and then save it as a 2007 database with the name **11M_Phone_List_Firstname_Lastname** At the end of each table name, add **FML** using your own initials and no space.

Using SQL, create a query that lists the names and phone numbers of personal clients who have open cases listed in the *Cases* table. Add the necessary SQL command so that clients are not listed more than one time in the query's results. Save the query as **PersonalQueryFML** using your own initials.

Using SQL, create a query that lists the names and phone numbers of corporate clients who have open cases listed in the *Cases* table. Add the necessary SQL command so that clients are not listed more than one time in the query's results. Save the query as **CorporateQueryFML** using your own initials.

Create a union query that combines the two queries. Save the query as **AllClientsFML** using your own initials. Create a report based on the union query. Format the report to effectively present the results. Save the report as **AllClientsFML** using your own initials. Encrypt the database using the password **GO! Series** and then submit the project as directed by your instructor.

End **You have completed Project 11M**

Access

chapter**eleven**

Problem Solving

Project 11N — Hourly Fees

In this project, you will construct a solution by applying any combination of the skills you practiced from the Objectives in Projects 11A and 11B.

> **For Project 11N, you will need the following file:**
>
> a11N_Hourly_Fees

You will save your database as
11N_Hourly_Fees_Firstname_Lastname

DeLong Grant Law Partners would like a report with summary statistics for the Hourly Fees table. To start, open **a11N_Hourly_Fees**, and then save it as a 2007 database with the name **11N_Hourly_Fees_Firstname_Lastname** At the end of each table name, add **FML** using your own initials and no space.

Create a new query in SQL view that calculates the following summary statistics for the *HourlyFees* table: Count, Minimum, Maximum, Average, and Total. For each statistic, you will also need to include the SQL command to calculate the amount charged, which is the *Hours* field multiplied by the *Rate* field. For each of the five fields, include SQL that will display the following captions in each column: Count, Minimum, Maximum, Average, and Total. Save the query as **HourlyStatisticsFML** using your own initials.

Create a report based on the query. Format the report to effectively present the results. Save the report as **HourlyStatisticsFML** using your own initials. Encrypt the database using the password **GO! Series** and then submit the project as directed by your instructor.

End **You have completed Project 11N** ———————————

Access
chapter eleven

Problem Solving

Project 110 — Law Library

In this project, you will construct a solution by applying any combination of the skills you practiced from the Objectives in Projects 11A and 11B.

For Project 110, you will need the following file:

a110_Law_Library

You will save your files as
110_Law_Library_Firstname_Lastname
110_Screens_Firstname Lastname
110_System_Firstname_Lastname

DeLong Grant Law Partners wish to set user-level security and then set permissions for their new law library database. To start, open **a110_Law_Library**, and then save it as a 2002 - 2003 database with the name **110_Law_Library_Firstname_Lastname** At the end of each table name, add **FML** using your own initials and no space.

Add a new group named **Librarians** with a PID of **Osdfg1** Add the following users and assign add them to the following groups:

User Name	PID	Group
APrince	Osdfg2	Admins
GMiddleton	Osdfg3	Librarians
KSpears	Osdfg4	Librarians

Secure the following accounts with these passwords:

User Name	Password
Admin	110password1
APrince	110password2
GMiddleton	110password3
KSpears	110password4

(Project 110–Law Library continues on the next page)

Access

chapter eleven | ## Problem Solving

(Project 11O–Law Library continued)

Set the following permissions and place a screen capture for each in a Word document:

Group	Object Type	Granted Permissions
Users	Database	Open/Run
Users	Law Library table	Read Design, Read Data
Librarians	Law Library table	Administer
Librarians	Services table	Read Design, Read Data, Update Data, Insert Data, Delete Data

If you are instructed to submit this result, create a paper or electronic printout of the Users and Groups report and the Word screen shot document. Save the Word document as **11O_Screens_Firstname Lastname** Exit Access, and then locate the default workgroup information file on your computer. Cut and paste the file into your Access Chapter 11 folder. Rename the workgroup information file **11O_System_Firstname_Lastname**. Submit the project as directed by your instructor.

End You have completed Project 11O ———————

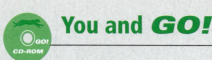 You and *GO!*

Project 11P — You and *GO!*

In this project, you will apply the skills you have practiced from the Objectives in Projects 11A and 11B.

From the student files that accompany this textbook, open the folder **04_you_and_go**. Locate the You and *GO!* project for this chapter and follow the instructions to create a form to enter records for a database of personal music.

End You have completed Project 11P

GO! with Help

Project 11Q — *GO!* with Help

The Access Help system is extensive and can help you as you work. There are several SQL aggregate functions that you have not yet used in this chapter, such as First, Last, StDev, and Var. The Access Help system provides a help page for each SQL aggregate function. Each help page provides definitions and examples of each function written in SQL.

1 Start **Access**. Click the **Microsoft Office Access Help** button.

2 In the **Search** box, type **SQL** and then click **Search**.

3 In the **Access Help** window, from the **Results** list, click **SQL Aggregate Functions**. In the displayed help page, click each of the SQL Aggregate Functions to learn how each is written in Access.

4 If you do not understand any of the terms displayed as red text, click the term and a definition displays. Use the **Back arrow** to return to the list of SQL aggregate functions.

5 If you want, print a copy of any of the SQL Aggregate Functions help pages by clicking the Print button at the top of Access Help window.

6 **Close** the Help window, and then **Exit** Access.

End You have completed Project 11Q

chaptertwelve

Customize Access Using Visual Basic for Applications

OBJECTIVES

At the end of this chapter you will be able to:

1. Modify an Existing VBA Module
2. Debug and Test VBA Code
3. Write an Event Procedure
4. Use Variables, Properties, and Methods

5. Prompt for User Input
6. Write Control Structures
7. Perform Calculations and Make Comparisons
8. Add a Subroutine to Trap Errors

OUTCOMES

Mastering these objectives will enable you to:

Project 12A
Modify, Write, and Debug VBA Code

Project 12B
Write an Interactive VBA Application

Cross Oceans Music

Cross Oceans Music produces and distributes recordings of innovative musicians from every continent in genres that include Celtic, jazz, new age, reggae, flamenco, calypso, and unique blends of all genres. Company scouts travel the world attending world music festivals, concerts, and small local venues to find their talented roster of musicians. These artists create new music using traditional and modern instruments and technologies. Cross Oceans customers are knowledgeable about music and demand the highest quality digital recordings provided in state-of-the-art formats.

Customize Access Using Visual Basic for Applications

In earlier projects, you customized Access databases by adding switchboards and creating macros. An even more powerful way to control how forms, queries, and reports function is to use a programming language called Visual Basic for Applications (VBA). Visual Basic for Applications is used to create custom interfaces and to automate tasks. For example, you can prompt for information, and then based on that input, have Access perform one of several complex tasks. Visual Basic for Applications is a structured, high-level programming language. Learning to write code in Visual Basic for Applications provides a much greater understanding of how to write code in any programming language. In this chapter, you will customize databases using Visual Basic for Applications.

Project 12A Compact Discs

Cross Oceans Music needs a way to browse their catalog of compact discs. They want to click a compact disc title, and have the songs on that compact disc automatically display. Another coworker searched the Internet and found a solution that relies on Visual Basic for Applications. When they click a title in a combo box, all the song information for that disc displays in a list box. The VBA code writes and executes several SQL queries. In Activities 12.1 through 12.8, you will complete the custom interface. Your finished code will look similar to the code shown in Figure 12.1.

For Project 12A, you will need the following file:

a12A_Compact_Discs

You will save your files as
12A_Compact_Discs_Firstname_Lastname
12A_Code_Firstname_Lastname

```
Option Compare Database

Private Sub cboCDs_AfterUpdate()
'Sends an SQL subquery to qrySongListFML
'Query results display in lstTracks
'Written by Firstname Lastname
'02/02/2009

'Declares variables
    Dim strSQL As String
    Dim strSelectedItem As String

'Assigns the title selected in the combo box to strSelectedItem
    strSelectedItem = cboCDs.Value

'Assigns an SQL query statement to strSQL
    strSQL = "SELECT qrySongListFML.CDTitle, qrySongListFML.Track, " & _
    "qrySongListFML.Title, qrySongListFML.Length " & _
    "FROM qrySongListFML " & _
    "WHERE qrySongListFML.CDTitle = '" & strSelectedItem & "';"

'Updates the list box Row Source and runs the query
    lstTracks.RowSource = strSQL
    lstTracks.Requery
End Sub

Private Sub Form_Load()
'Writes an SQL subquery in the query named qrySongListFML
'Populates the combo box named cboCDs
'Adapted by Firstname Lastname
'02/02/2009

'Writes the SQL query statement
    Dim strSQL As String

    strSQL = "SELECT DISTINCT qrySongListFML.CDTitle " & _
    "FROM qrySongListFML " & _
    "ORDER BY qrySongListFML.CDTitle;"

'Displays the query results in the combo box
    With cboCDs
        .RowSource = strSQL
        .RowSourceType = "Table/Query"
        .BoundColumn = 1
    End With

End Sub
```

Figure 12.1
Project 12A—Compact Discs

Objective 1
Modify an Existing VBA Module

Visual Basic for Applications (VBA) is a high-level programming language built into Microsoft Office. VBA is a subset of *Visual Basic*, an easy-to-learn, yet powerful programming language commonly used to build business applications. The code written in Visual Basic for Applications is usually referred to as Visual Basic. A coworker at Cross Oceans Music has created a form with a combo box and list box that will provide a custom interface for viewing compact discs. The Visual Basic code has been placed in the form's module. A *module* is a collection of Visual Basic code. In Access, each form or report that uses Visual Basic code will have its own module. You will view and edit the existing code by opening the form's module.

Activity 12.1 Opening and Viewing an Existing VBA Module

To work with VBA code, a module must be opened using the Visual Basic Editor. The *Visual Basic Editor (VBE)* is the program used to edit VBA code. In this project, you will open and view an existing module in the Visual Basic Editor.

1 **Start** Access. Navigate to the location where the student data files for this textbook are saved. Locate and then open the

a12A_Compact Discs file. Click the **Office** button [icon], point to **Save As**, and then click **Access 2007 Database**. In the **Save As** dialog box, navigate to the drive on which you will be saving your folders and projects for this chapter. Create a new folder named **Access Chapter 12** and save the file as **12A_Compact_Discs_Firstname_ Lastname** in the folder.

2 If necessary, enable the content or add the Access Chapter 12 folder to the Trust Center. Compare your screen with Figure 12.2.

Three of the database objects are named using Hungarian notation. *Hungarian notation* is a naming convention where programming objects are given a prefix that identifies what type of object they are. Hungarian notation is optional and typically used with Visual Basic and Visual Basic for Applications. A table of common prefixes is shown in Figure 12.3.

Figure 12.2

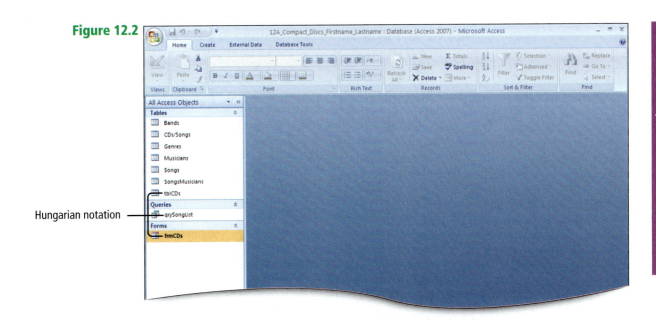

Hungarian notation

Common Object Prefixes

Object	Prefix
Check box	chk
Combo box	cbo
Command button	cmd
Form	frm
Label	lbl
List box	lst
Option button	opt
Query	qry
Report	rpt
Table	tbl
Text box	txt

Figure 12.3

3 Rename the database tables so that each begins with the **tbl** prefix and ends with your initials. For example, rename **Bands** to **tblBandsFML** using your own initials. Rename the query and form by adding your initials to the end of each name without using spaces.

In this chapter, you will be writing Visual Basic and SQL statements. For this reason, all of the projects in this chapter follow the Upper Camel Case naming convention, and you will add your initials to the table names instead of your first and last name.

4 In the **Navigation Pane**, double-click the **qrySongListFML** query. Scroll through the query and familiarize yourself with the company's compact discs. When you are finished, **Close** ☒ the query.

5 In the **Navigation Pane**, double-click the **frmCDsFML** form, and then compare your screen with Figure 12.4.

At the top of the form, a combo box lists the company's current compact discs. Below the combo box, a list box with multiple columns lists the songs in the *Cross the Ocean* CD. Because you changed the name of the query that this combo box uses as its data source, clicking the combo box would cause an SQL error message to display.

Figure 12.4

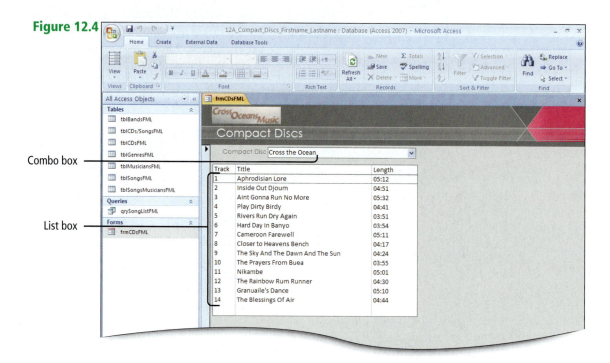

6 In the status bar, click the **Design View** button ⬛, and then double-click the list box. In the displayed **Property Sheet**, click the **Data tab**. Right-click the **Row Source** property, and then click **Zoom**.

The displayed Zoom dialog box contains an SQL query statement. This query runs inside the qrySongListFML query as an SQL subquery. An **SQL subquery** is an SQL SELECT statement nested inside another query. The WHERE statement in this subquery returns just the songs from the *Cross the Ocean* compact disc.

7 Click **Cancel** to close the **Zoom** dialog box. Click the **Database Tools tab**, and in the **Macro group**, click the **Visual Basic** button. Alternatively, press ⌨Alt + ⌨F11. Compare your screen with Figure 12.5. If your screen looks different, refer to the Alert! that follows Figure 12.5.

The **Visual Basic window** is the window that displays the Visual Basic Editor program. Below the menu bar, the VBE Standard toolbar displays. In the upper left corner, the **Project Explorer** displays the modules for the database. In the lower left corner, the **Properties window** displays the properties for each database object. The existing VBA code for the form displays in the Code window. The **Code window** is used to write and edit the VBA code.

Visual Basic window   Code window

Microsoft Visual Basic window maximized

Figure 12.5

VBE Standard toolbar

Project Explorer (Your list may differ)

Properties window (Your list may differ)

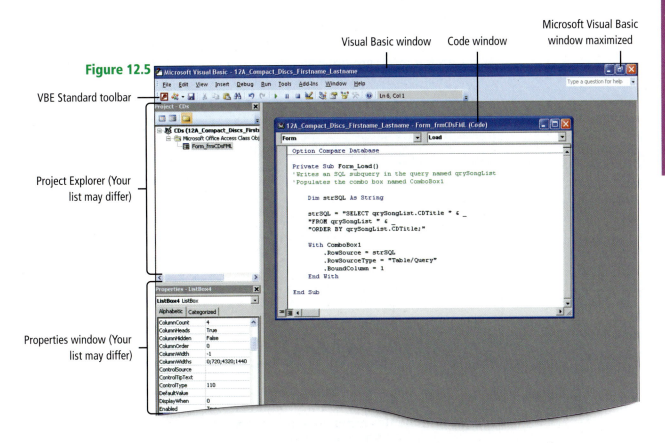

```
Option Compare Database

Private Sub Form_Load()
'Writes an SQL subquery in the query named qrySongList
'Populates the combo box named ComboBox1

    Dim strSQL As String

    strSQL = "SELECT qrySongList.CDTitle " & _
    "FROM qrySongList " & _
    "ORDER BY qrySongList.CDTitle;"

    With ComboBox1
        .RowSource = strSQL
        .RowSourceType = "Table/Query"
        .BoundColumn = 1
    End With

End Sub
```

Alert!

Does your screen look different?

Depending on your computer's settings, some of the VBE screen elements may not display as shown in Figure 12.5. If necessary, maximize 🔲 the Microsoft Visual Basic window.

To display the Project Explorer, from the View menu, click Project Explorer. To display the Properties window, from the View menu, click Properties Window. To display the Code window, in Project Explorer, expand ⊞ the CDs (*12A_Compact_Discs_Firstname_Lastname*) VBA project. Expand ⊞ the *Microsoft Office Access Class Objects* folder, and then double-click the displayed *Form_frmCDsFML*.

8 Leave the Visual Basic window open for the next activity.

Activity 12.2 Documenting Code with Comments

A **programming comment** is an embedded remark written by the programmer. Programming comments are used to document and explain the code in simple, human language. Comments are useful when working with modules that contain lengthy code or when more than one person will work with the code. In this project, you will view the comments left by a coworker at Cross Oceans Music, and then add your own comments.

1 If necessary, in the displayed Code window, click the Maximize button [image]. Compare your screen with Figure 12.6.

In the Code window, the two green lines that start with a single quotation mark are programming comments. In VBA, all comments must begin with a single quotation mark.

Figure 12.6

Programming comments

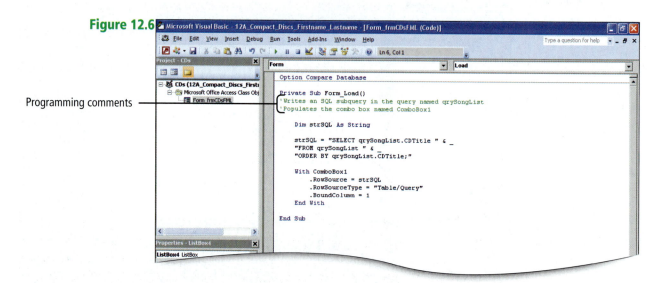

2 Read the two comments, and then in the second comment, click after the word *ComboBox1*. Press Enter, and then type the following comment: **'Adapted by Firstname Lastname** Use your own name, and be sure to include the single quotation mark at the beginning of the line.

3 Press Enter. Notice that the line displays in green.

Alert! | **A "Compile Error" message displays**

All VBA comments must start with a single quotation mark. Click OK to close the message, and then place a single quotation mark at the beginning of the line.

---

4 Type a single quotation mark, type the current date using the mm/dd/yyyy format, and then press ↓.

5 Press Enter, and then add the following comment: **'Writes the SQL query statement**

6 Click in the blank line above the text *With ComboBox1*, press Enter, and then type the following comment: **'Displays the query results in the combo box**

7 Click in any other line of code so that the comment text displays as green, and then compare your screen with Figure 12.7.

Figure 12.7

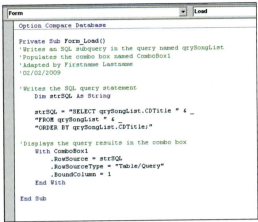

```
Form                                          ▼  Load

Option Compare Database

Private Sub Form_Load()
'Writes an SQL subquery in the query named qrySongList
'Populates the combo box named ComboBox1
'Adapted by Firstname Lastname
'02/02/2009

'Writes the SQL query statement
    Dim strSQL As String

    strSQL = "SELECT qrySongList.CDTitle " & _
    "FROM qrySongList " & _
    "ORDER BY qrySongList.CDTitle;"

'Displays the query results in the combo box
    With ComboBox1
        .RowSource = strSQL
        .RowSourceType = "Table/Query"
        .BoundColumn = 1
    End With

End Sub
```

8 From the **File** menu, click **Close and Return to Microsoft Office Access**. Alternatively, press Alt + Q.

9 Leave the form open for the next activity.

Activity 12.3 Editing an Existing VBA Procedure

Programmers often edit existing code to adapt that code for their own purposes. Even without examining how all of the code works, programmers can make changes to produce the desired results. In this project, you will edit the code so that the CD titles display properly in the Compact Disc combo box.

1 In the **frmCDsFML** form, switch to **Form** view, and then click the **Compact Disc** combo box **arrow**. Read the displayed error message, and then click **OK**.

2 Press Alt + F11. In the first comment, change *qrySongList* to **qrySongListFML** using your own initials.

The Visual Basic window opens with the panes and Code window displayed as they were when you last closed the window.

3 Using the comments that you wrote in the previous activity, locate the section of code that writes the SQL statement.

4 In the SQL statement, change the three instances of *qrySongList* to **qrySongListFML** using your own initials.

5 Press Alt + Q to return to the form. Click **Save** 🖫, and then **Close** ✕ the form.

6 Open **frmCDsFML**. Click the **Compact Disc arrow**. Scroll down and notice that each CD title is listed multiple times, one time for each song in the compact disc.

7 Click any blank area of the form, and then press Alt + F11.

8 Locate the lines where the SQL query is written. After the word *SELECT*, add a space, and then type **DISTINCT** Be sure there is a space before and after the word, and be sure to type the keyword using all capital letters.

Recall that the SQL keyword DISTINCT removes duplicate values from the query's results.

9 Compare your code carefully with Figure 12.8 and fix any errors.

Figure 12.8

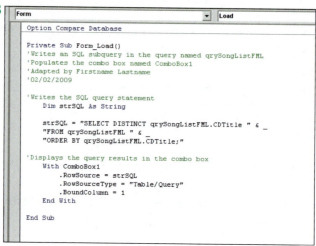

```
Form                                        ▼  Load

Option Compare Database

Private Sub Form_Load()
'Writes an SQL subquery in the query named qrySongListFML
'Populates the combo box named ComboBox1
'Adapted by Firstname Lastname
'02/02/2009

'Writes the SQL query statement
    Dim strSQL As String

    strSQL = "SELECT DISTINCT qrySongListFML.CDTitle " & _
    "FROM qrySongListFML " & _
    "ORDER BY qrySongListFML.CDTitle;"

'Displays the query results in the combo box
    With ComboBox1
        .RowSource = strSQL
        .RowSourceType = "Table/Query"
        .BoundColumn = 1
    End With

End Sub
```

10 Press Alt + Q to save your changes and return to the form. Click the **Compact Disc** combo box **arrow**, and then notice duplicate titles still display.

The SQL query that you edited runs only when the form is opened.

11 Click **Save** 🖫, and then **Close** ✕ the form.

12 Open **frmCDsFML** in Form view. Click the **Compact Disc** combo box **arrow**, and notice that each title is listed one time. If you received an error, return to the code and repeat Steps 9 through 11.

13 Leave the form open for the next activity.

Objective 2
Debug and Test VBA Code

Studies have shown that on average, programmers spend about half of their time writing code and the other half testing and debugging that code. To **debug** is to find and fix errors in the code. To reduce the amount of time spent debugging, experienced programmers test their code early and often. This means that they test the code while it is being written instead of trying to type all of the code before testing it. Testing early makes it much easier to locate the cause of errors.

Activity 12.4 Debugging and Testing VBA Code

Access provides two methods of locating errors—using a compiler, and testing in the form or report. The **VBA compiler** translates the VBA code written by the programmer into another language that can be interpreted by the computer. In this project, you will practice debugging using the VBA compiler and by testing the code in the form.

1 Click the **Database Tools tab**. In the **Macro group**, click the **Visual Basic** button.

2 In the displayed **Code** window, at the beginning of the first comment, remove the single quotation mark. Press the ⬇, and then compare your screen with Figure 12.9.

The comment with the error displays as red text. Omitting the single quotation mark at the beginning of the comment is an example of a syntax error. A *syntax error* is an error that breaks one of the rules of the VBA programming language. The VBA compiler locates many syntax errors as you type them and displays the compile error message.

Figure 12.9

Error displays in red

Compile error message

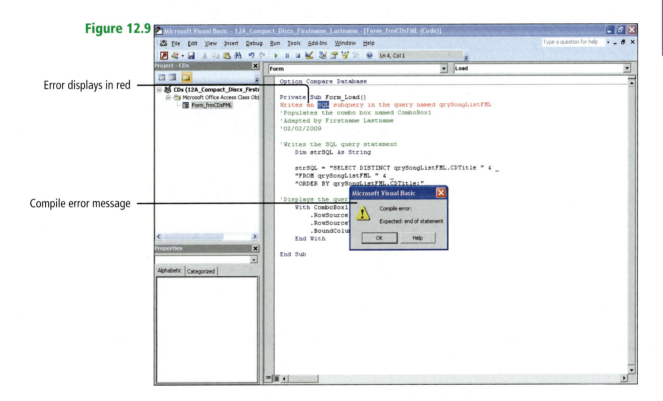

3 In the displayed message, click **OK**. At the beginning of the first comment, insert a single quotation mark.

4 From the **Debug** menu, click **Compile CDs**.

Compiling the code before running it increases the speed at which the code will run. Before VBA code can run, it must be compiled. If you do not compile the code yourself, Visual Basic for Applications will compile it before running the code.

5 Below the comment *Writes the SQL query statement*, change the word *FROM* to **FORM** and then click any other line.

Because this is not a syntax error, no error message displays.

6 From the **Debug** menu, click **Compile CDs**.

7 From the **File** menu, click **Close and Return to Microsoft Office Access**.

8 Save ![save icon], and then **Close** ![close icon] the form. **Open** the form in **Form** view.

The VBA code ran without any syntax errors.

9 Click the **Compact Disc** combo box **arrow**, and then compare your screen with Figure 12.10.

The VBA code has generated an SQL error because Access cannot perform the subquery using the word *FORM*. This is an example of a logical error. A ***logical error*** is an error where the code performs exactly what is written, but it does not return the expected results. Logical errors are much harder to discover and fix than syntax errors.

Figure 12.10

SQL error message

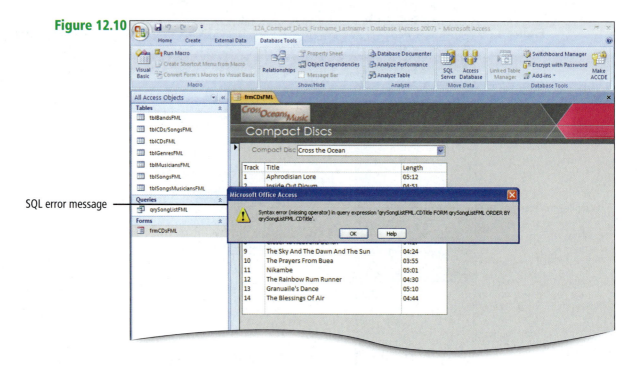

10 Click **OK**, and then open the **Visual Basic** window by pressing ⎗Alt⎗ + ⎗F11⎗. In the line that writes the SQL query, change the word *FORM* to **FROM**

11 From the **File** menu, click **Close and Return to Microsoft Office Access**. **Save** ![save icon], and then **Close** ![close icon] the form.

12 **Open** the form, and then click the **Compact Disc arrow**.

Because the VBA code executed a proper SQL statement, each title displays.

13 Leave the form open for the next activity.

Activity 12.5 Debugging Run-Time Errors

A ***run-time error*** is an error that occurs when the code attempts to perform an invalid operation. When this happens, the Visual Basic Editor provides a way to pause and then debug the code. In this activity, you will rename the combo box and list box, and then debug the code.

1 With the form open, in the status bar, click the **Design View** button [image].

2 Click the list box to display its properties. In the **Property Sheet**, click the **Other tab**, and then in the **Name** box, replace the existing text with **lstTracks** Recall that *lst* is the Hungarian notation for a list box. Be sure to use the lowercase letter "l", not the number one.

You will use the name *lstTracks* in a later activity. Programmers often start by renaming the form's controls using meaningful names. Controls with meaningful names are easier to identify and remember during the coding process.

3 Click the combo box, and in the **Property Sheet,** change the **Name** property to **cboCDs**

4 Click **Save** [image], and then click the **Form View** button.

The run-time error message states that an object is required and provides three active buttons. Because you renamed the combo box, you will need to update the VBA code.

5 In the displayed message, click the **Debug** button, and then compare your screen with Figure 12.11.

On the toolbar, the Run/Continue, Break, and Reset buttons display. The code is currently in *Break mode*, a temporary suspension in the execution during which you can debug the code. In the gray area to the left of the Code window, a margin indicator points to the place in the code where the invalid operation was attempted and the line of code is highlighted in yellow. In the Visual Basic Editor, a *margin indicator* provides visual clues in the left margin while you edit code.

Figure 12.11

Run/Continue button

Break button

Reset button

Highlighted code

Margin indicator

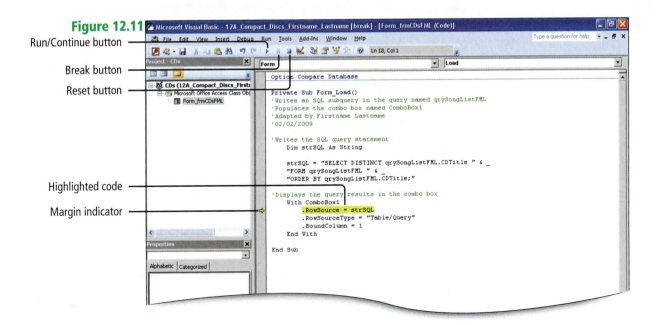

6 Point to the word *strSQL* and read the displayed ScreenTip message.

Pausing the mouse over certain words in the code reveals a ScreenTip displaying the values that are assigned to that word. Knowing these values helps the programmer locate errors in the code. When debugging, often the code containing the error is one line above the margin indicator.

7 In the line above the margin indicator, point to *ComboBox1*, and then in the displayed ToolTip, read the value assigned to it.

The ComboBox1 value is *Empty*. This value is *Empty* because the form no longer has a control named *ComboBox1*.

8 In the upper portion of the code, in the second comment, replace the word *ComboBox1* with **cboCDs**

9 In the lower portion of the code, after the word *With*, replace the word *ComboBox1* with **cboCDs**

10 On the toolbar, click the **Continue** button. Read the displayed message, and then click **OK**.

11 Click **Save** 🖫, and then **Close** ⊠ the form. Open **frmCDsFML** in Form view. Be sure that the form opens without any run-time errors. If necessary, return to the Code window, check your typing, and then open the form again.

12 Leave the form open for the next activity.

Objective 3
Write an Event Procedure

VBA is an event-driven language. An *event-driven language* is code that is run in response to user actions rather than running from beginning to end. In VBA, event-driven code must be placed in procedures. A *procedure* is a named group of programming statements that run as a unit. The current code for the frmCDsFML form populates the combo box when the form is opened, but it does not update the list box when a different title is selected. Another procedure is needed so that the list box is updated whenever a compact disc title in the combo box is clicked.

Activity 12.6 Writing an Event Procedure

Recall that Cross Oceans Music wants the compact disc song data to display whenever they click a title in the Compact Disc combo box. In this activity, you will add a procedure that runs whenever the one of the titles listed in the combo box is clicked.

1 With the form open, in the status bar, click the **Design View** button 🖾. In the **Property Sheet**, click the **Selection type arrow**, click **Form**, and then click the **Event tab**.

The Event tab displays the events available for the form. An *event* is a user action such as typing, using the mouse, or updating a record.

Different types of controls have different types of events available to them. Common events are listed in the table in Figure 12.12.

Common Events

Event	Trigger
On Click	The user clicks the control.
After Update	The user updates data.
On Change	The user changes the text in a text box or combo box.
On Got Focus	The control gains focus. For example, when the insertion point is placed in a text box, the text box has the focus.
On Lost Focus	The control loses focus.
On Dbl Click	The user double-clicks the control.
On Key Press	The user presses and releases a key while the control has focus.
On Load	The user opens the form or report.
On Close	The user closes the form or report.
On Current	The user displays a different record on a form.
On Error	The procedure creates an error when it runs.

Figure 12.12

2 In the **Property Sheet**, click **On Load**, and then click the displayed **Build** button ⬛.

The procedure that populates the combo box is linked to the form's On Load property.

3 **Close** ⬛ the Visual Basic Window.

4 Click the **Compact Disc** combo box. In the **Property Sheet**, click **After Update**, and then click the displayed **Build** button ⬛.

5 In the displayed **Choose Builder** dialog box, click **Code Builder**, click **OK**, and then compare your screen with Figure 12.13.

The module for the form displays, and a new sub named cboCDs_AfterUpdate is created. In VBA, a **sub procedure**, also called a **sub**, is a procedure that executes code without returning a value. The statements in a sub procedure must be enclosed by the Sub and End Sub statements. This sub procedure will run every time a new CD title in the combo box is clicked.

Figure 12.13

New sub procedure

End Sub statement

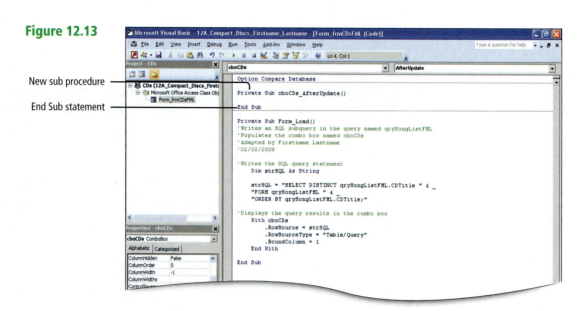

6 Click to the right of *cboCDs_AfterUpdate()*, press Enter, and then add the following comments:

'Sends an SQL subquery to qrySongListFML (Use your own initials)
'Query results display in lstTracks
'Written by Firstname Lastname (Use your own name)
'mm/dd/yyyy (Enter current Date)

7 Click **Save** 🖫, and leave the **Visual Basic** window open for the next activity.

Objective 4
Use Variables, Properties, and Methods

VBA procedures contain statements that are executed when the procedure is run. These statements store values in the computer's memory, change properties for a form's controls, and execute procedures that are built into the VBA programming language. The event procedure that you are writing will do all three of these when a compact disc title in the combo box is clicked.

Activity 12.7 Declaring Variables and Assigning Values to Variables

The event procedure that you are writing will use two variables. *Variables* are programming objects used to store values in the computer's memory. Variables require a unique name, and the type of data the variable will store should also be defined. A *data type* is the type of value that a variable will store, such as text, a whole number, or a decimal value. In this activity, you will declare two variables, define their data types, and then assign values to the variables.

1 After the date comment, press Enter **two** times, and then type the following comment: **'Declares variables**

2 Press Enter, press Tab, and then type the following: **Dim strSQL As String** As you type, notice that the Visual Basic Editor

AutoComplete feature provides a menu of suggestions that are based on what you are currently typing.

In VBA, variables are typically declared using the Dim statement. The As statement defines the variable's data type. When variables are declared, VBA reserves the computer memory needed to store any values that may be assigned to the variable. In this case, the variable will be a **string**—a sequence of alphanumeric characters. When using Hungarian notation, variables with the string data type are usually given the *str* prefix. The common VBA data types are described in the table in Figure 12.14.

Common Data Types in Visual Basic for Applications

Data Type	Description	Corresponding Field Data Type	Required Memory (Bytes)	Hungarian Notation Prefix
Boolean	Can only be two values: True and False.	Yes/No	2	bln
Currency	A number with up to 15 digits to the left of the decimal point and up to 4 digits to the right of the decimal point.	Currency	8	cur
Date	Stores dates and times.	Date/Time	8	dtm
Double	Stores extremely small negative numbers and extremely large positive numbers.	Number/Double	8	dbl
Integer	Any whole number between -32,768 and 32,767.	Number/Integer	2	int
Long	Any whole number between -2,147,483,648 and 2,147,483,647.	Number/Integer AutoNumber	4	lng
Object	Refers to an object, such as an ActiveX component.	Not applicable	4	obj
Single	Stores very small negative numbers and very large positive numbers.	Number/Single	4	sng
String	A sequence of alphanumeric characters that contain approximately 2 billion characters.	Text or Memo	varies	str
Variant	Stores any type of data; if no data type is assigned, it will be assigned the variant data type.	Not applicable	16 or 22	vnt

Figure 12.14

3 Press Enter, and then type the following: **Dim strSelectedItem As String**

4 Press Enter **two** times, press ←Bksp, and then type the following comment: **'Assigns the title selected in the combo box to strSelectedItem**

5 Press Enter, press Tab, and then type the following:
strSelectedItem = cboCDs

6 After *cboCDs*, type a period, and then compare your screen with Figure 12.15.

The Visual Basic Editor's Auto List Members displays a list of available properties and methods that can be applied to the combo box named *cboCDs*.

Auto List Members box

Figure 12.15

Available property

Available method

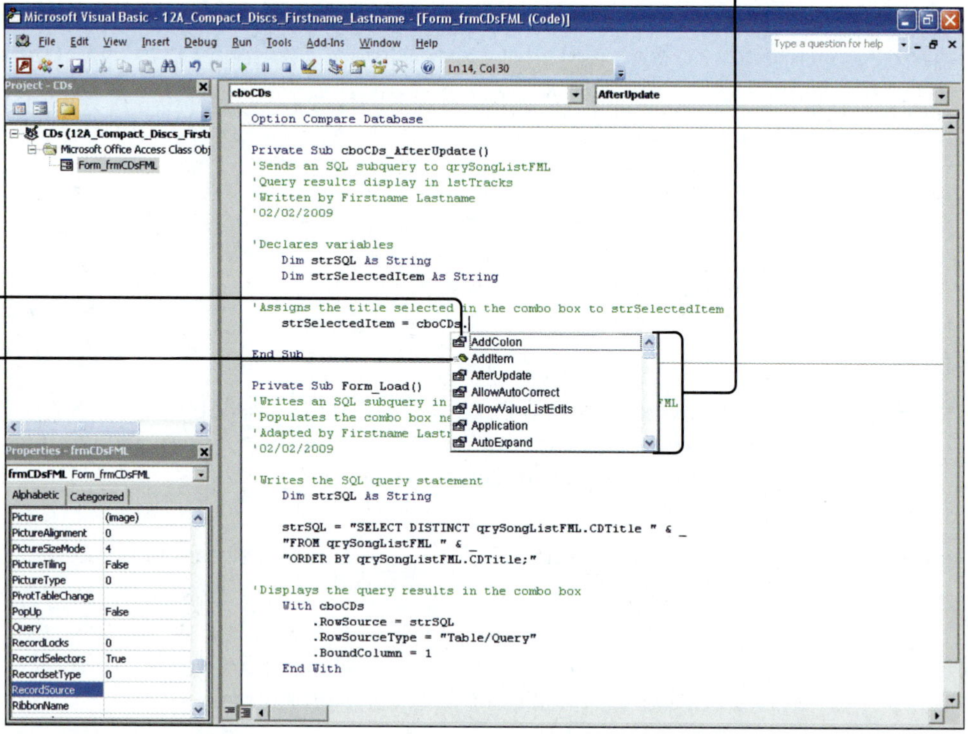

7 Type **valu** Notice that the word *Value* is selected in the Auto List Members box, and then press Tab.

The Auto List Members box completed the rest of your typing and capitalized the word *Value*. The Value property in a combo box is equal to whichever item is selected in the combo box. In this case, when a compact disc title is clicked, the variable *strSelectItem* will store the name of the selected title.

8 Press Enter **two** times, press ←Bksp, and then type the following comment: **'Assigns an SQL query statement to strSQL**

9 Press Enter, press Tab, and then type the following substituting your own initials where appropriate:
strSQL = "SELECT qrySongListFML.CDTitle, qrySongListFML.Track, " Use a single line and be sure to include the space before the closing quotation mark.

This statement assigns the characters between the quotation marks to the variable *strSQL*. String values must be enclosed within quotation marks.

10 After the double quotation mark, add a space, type the following: **& _** and then press Enter. Be sure to include a space between the ampersand and the underscore.

In Visual Basic, a statement must be written as a single line of code. If a line becomes too long to fit on the screen, it can be divided into several lines by placing an underscore character at the end of a line. The underscore tells Visual Basic that the statement continues on the next line.

11 Type the following substituting your own initials: **"qrySongListFML.Title, qrySongListFML.Length "** Be sure to include a space before the ending quotation mark.

The ampersand, &, tells Visual Basic to concatenate. To **concatenate** means to combine two or more strings together into a single string. In this case, the string that you just entered will be combined with the string that you entered on the previous line.

12 Add a space, and then type the following: **& _** Press Enter, and then type the remaining two lines as shown:

"FROM qrySongListFML " & _

"WHERE qrySongListFML.CDTitle = '" & strSelectedItem & "';"

At the end of this statement, be sure to type a double quotation mark, single quotation mark, semicolon, and then another double quotation mark.

13 Compare your screen carefully with Figure 12.16. Notice that after *Title =*, there is a single quotation mark followed by a double quotation mark. Notice that after the second ampersand (&), there is a double quotation mark followed by a single quotation mark.

Figure 12.16

Single quotation followed by a double quotation

Double quotation followed by a single quotation

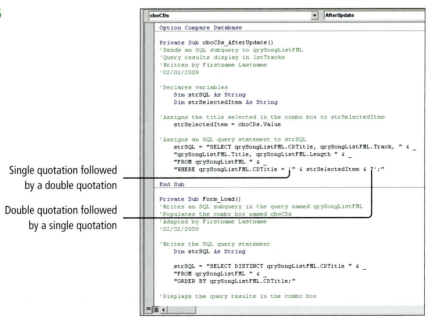

14 Press [Alt] + [Q], and then switch to **Form** view. Click the combo box **arrow**, and then click a different CD title. If no error messages display, continue to the next step. If an error message displays, return to the Code window, correct your typing mistakes, and then test again.

15 Click **Save** 🖫 and leave the form open for the next activity.

Activity 12.8 Changing Form Properties and Using Methods

VBA code is often used to change the properties for controls on a form or report. These are the same properties you have edited in the Property Sheet in previous projects. VBA code can also perform actions on a control using methods. A *method* is a function that is built into the VBA language. A *function* is a named group of programming statements that run as a unit, but unlike a sub procedure, a function returns a value. In this activity, you will change the Row Source property of the list box, and then write a method to run the SQL query.

1 Press [Alt] + [F11] to return to the Visual Basic window. In the **cboCDs_AfterUpdate** sub, click in the blank line above *End Sub*, press [Enter], and type the following comment:
'Updates the list box Row Source and runs the query

2 Press [Enter], press [Tab], and then type the following:
lstTracks.RowSource = strSQL

To change a control's property using VBA, the control name is separated from the property name by a period. In this case, the Row Source property for the list box is assigned the value stored in the strSQL variable.

3 Press [Enter], and then type the following: **lstTracks.Requery**

To run a method on a control, the control name and method name are joined with a period. The *requery* method runs the SQL query stored in the list box's *Row Source* property without having to reopen the form. The methods used in this chapter are described in Figure 12.17.

Common Visual Basic for Applications Methods

Method	Description
Close	Closes the form or report.
DSum	Calculates the sum for a field in a specific set of records.
Exit	Terminates the application, a sub, a loop, or a function.
InputBox	Displays a prompt inside a dialog box and waits for the user to type a response. The function returns whatever the user typed as a string.
Left	Returns the specified number of characters in a string starting from the left—for example, the first five characters in the string.
OpenForm	Opens a form.
OpenReport	Opens a report.
MsgBox	Displays a message box with several options for different buttons and returns a value based on which button is clicked.
Requery	Reapplies a control's Row Source property without having to reopen the form or report.
RGB	Used to define a color when changing a property such as Back Color or Border Color.
Right	Returns the specified number of characters in a string starting from the right—for example, the last five characters in the string.
Str	Converts a number value into a string value.
Trim	Removes any leading and trailing spaces from a string.
Val	Converts a string value into a number value.

Figure 12.17

4 From the **Debug** menu, click **Compile CDs**.

5 Compare your code carefully with the code shown in Figure 12.18.

Be sure that you typed the lowercase letter "l" in *lstTracks*, not the number 1.

Figure 12.18

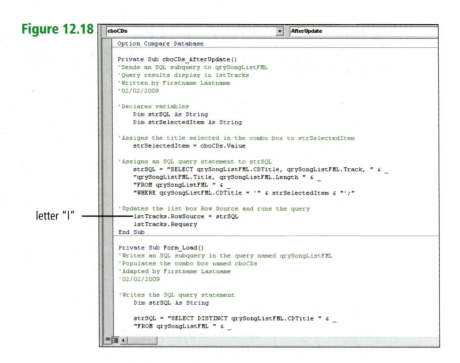

letter "l" ——

Figure 12.18

6 Press [Alt] + [Q]. If necessary, switch to Form view. Click the **Compact Disc** combo box **arrow**, and then click **Air Time**. Compare your screen with Figure 12.19.

The tracks for the *Air Time* compact disc display.

Figure 12.19

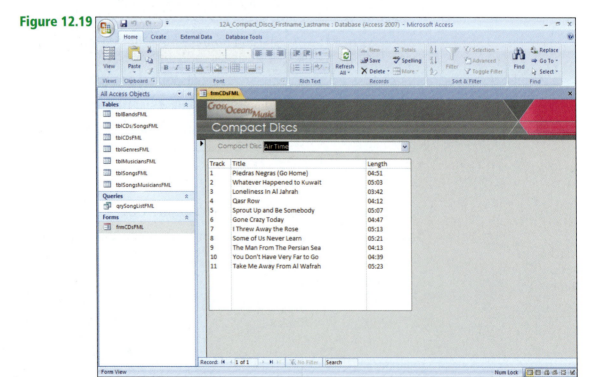

7 Test the code by clicking other compact disc titles.

8 Press [Alt] + [F11]. Press [Ctrl] + [A] to select all of the code, and then press [Ctrl] + [C] to copy the code to the Office Clipboard.

9 Click **Save** 💾, and then **Close** ❌ the Visual Basic window. Click **Save** 💾, **Close** ❌ the form, and then **Exit** Access.

10 Start a blank document in **Word**. In the **Styles group**, click the **No Spacing** button. Change the **Font** to **Courier**.

11 Click the **Page Layout tab**. In the **Page Setup group**, click the **Margins** button, and then click **Narrow**.

12 Type **12A_Code_Firstname_Lastname** substituting your own name, and then press [Enter] **two** times. Press [Ctrl] + [V] to paste the code. **Save** the document as **12A_Code_Firstname_Lastname** If you are instructed to submit this result, create a paper or electronic printout.

13 **Exit** Word.

End **You have completed Project 12A** ————————————

Project 12B Shipping

Cross Ocean Music charges for shipping based on three criteria. First, the shipping rate depends on the method used to ship the item. Second, shipping is capped at $18.00 for any single order. Third, when the correct code is entered, the shipping method will be 2nd Day Ground, but the shipping charge is free. In this project, you will add a button to the Cross Ocean Music Invoices form that calculates the total shipping when it is clicked. In Activities 12.9 through 12.14, you will need to write Visual Basic code to calculate and then display the total shipping. Your completed code will look similar to the printout shown in Figure 12.20.

For Project 12B, you will need the following file:

a12B_Shipping

You will save your files as
12B_Shipping_Firstname_Lastname
12B_Code_Firstname_Lastname

```
12B_Code_Firstname_Lastname
Private Sub cmdUpdateShipping_Click()
On Error GoTo errorMessage
'Calculates shipping in frmInvoicesFML
'Written by Firstname Lastname
'02/02/2009

'Declares variables
Dim strInputCode As String
Dim strShippingMethod As String
Dim curRate As Currency
Dim intItemCount As Integer
Dim curTotalShipping As Currency

'Prompts the user for the free shipping code
strInputCode = InputBox("Enter the free shipping code or click Cancel.", _
"Free Shipping Code")

'Determines shipping method
If strInputCode = "KDNE3" Then
    strShippingMethod = "Free"
Else
    strShippingMethod = cboShippingMethod.Value
End If

'Determines shipping rate
Select Case strShippingMethod
    Case "Ground"
        curRate = 1.5
    Case "2nd Day Ground"
        curRate = 3.5
    Case "Overnight"
        curRate = 7.5
    Case "Free"
        curRate = 0
    Case Else
        MsgBox ("Please choose a shipping method.")
End Select

'Calculates the final shipping charge
'Writes the charge into txtShipping
intItemCount = frmLineItems!txtItemCount.Value
curTotalShipping = curRate * intItemCount
If curTotalShipping < 18 Then
    Forms!frmInvoicesFML!txtShipping = curTotalShipping
Else
    Forms!frmInvoicesFML!txtShipping = 18
End If
Exit Sub
errorMessage: MsgBox ("Unable to calculate shipping.")
End Sub
```

Figure 12.20
Project 12B—Shipping

Objective 5
Prompt for User Input

VBA procedures often require that the end-user type a response or click a choice. When a procedure needs to prompt for input, the InputBox method is often used. The InputBox method displays a prompt in a dialog box, and then waits for a typed response or a button to be clicked.

Activity 12.9 Prompting the User for Input

Cross Oceans Music needs to type a code in order to assign free shipping. In this activity, you will create a button, and then add an event procedure that prompts the user to type the free shipping code.

1 **Start** Access. Navigate to the location where the student data files for this textbook are saved. Locate and open the **a12B_Shipping** file.

Click the **Office** button 🔘, point to **Save As**, and then click **Access 2007 Database**. In the **Save As** dialog box, navigate to your **Access Chapter 12** folder, and then save the file as **12B_Shipping_Firstname_Lastname** in the folder.

2 Add **FML** to the end of each database object name. Use your own initials and do not add any spaces to the object names.

3 Open **frmInvoicesFML** in Design view. If necessary, close the Property Sheet. In the **Controls group**, click the **Button** button.

Place the ⊞ pointer one grid dot below the top of the **Detail** section and over the **6-inch vertical gridline**, and then click.

4 In the displayed **Command Button Wizard** dialog box, click the **Cancel** button, and then compare your screen with Figure 12.21.

Figure 12.21

Command button (Your caption may vary)

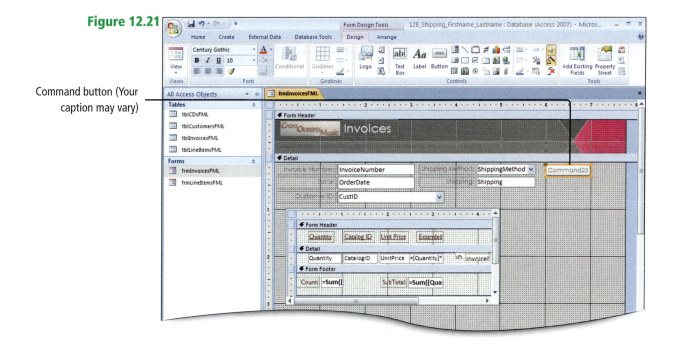

5 Click a blank area of the form, and then double-click the **Command** button. In the **Property Sheet**, click the **Format tab**, and then change the **Caption** property to **Update Shipping**

6 In the **Property Sheet**, click the **Other tab**, and then change the **Name** property to **cmdUpdateShipping**

7 In the **Property Sheet**, click the **Event tab**, and then for the **On Click** property, click the **Build** button ⬚. In the displayed **Choose Builder** dialog box, click **Code Builder**, and then click **OK**.

Recall that an event procedure for a control can be created by changing one of the control's Event properties. This procedure will run when the button is clicked.

8 Between the **Sub** and **End Sub** statements, add the following comments on three lines as shown:

'Calculates shipping in frmInvoicesFML (Use your own initials)
'Written by Firstname Lastname (Use your own name)
'mm/dd/yyyy (Enter current Date)

9 Press Enter **two** times, and then type the following comment: **'Declares variables**

10 Press Enter, and then type the following: **Dim strInputCode As String**

The variable *strInputCode* will store the free shipping code that will be entered by the user. In the previous project, you indented the statements that declared variables. Indenting is optional and does not affect how the code is run.

11 Press Enter **two** times, and then type the following comment: **'Prompts the user for the free shipping code**

12 Press Enter, and then type the following: **strInputCode = InputBox(** Compare your screen with Figure 12.22.

As you type, the Visual Basic Editor often displays context-sensitive help. In this case, the displayed help shows the required and optional arguments for the InputBox method.

Figure 12.22

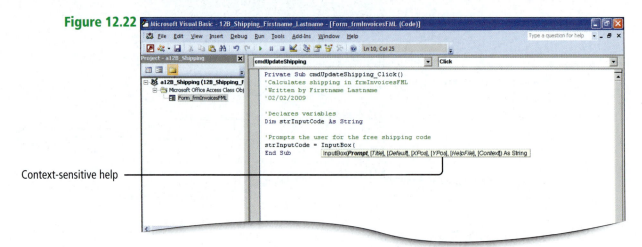

Context-sensitive help

13 After *InputBox(*, type the rest of the statement on two lines as shown:

"Enter the free shipping code or click Cancel.", _
"Free Shipping Code")

The variable *strInputCode* is assigned whatever value is typed into the input box.

14 Leave the Visual Basic window open for the next activity.

Activity 12.10 Testing User Input

Recall that methods are functions that return values. The InputBox method returns a string based on user actions. In this activity, you will test that the InputBox works correctly and returns a string based on responses to the prompt.

1 In the gray area next to the **End Sub** statement, click one time, and then compare your screen with Figure 12.23.

The red dot in the margin indicates that a breakpoint has been set. A **breakpoint** is a location in the code, set by the programmer, where the procedure will stop running and enter Break mode.

Figure 12.23

Breakpoint margin indicator ——

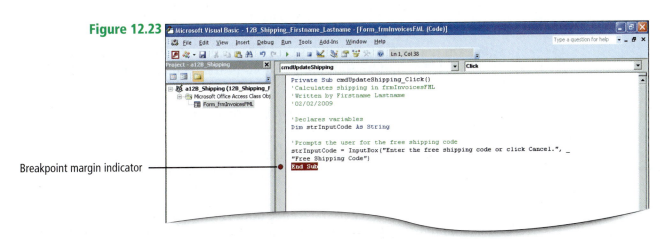

2 Click **Save**. From the **File** menu, click **Close and Return to Microsoft Office Access**.

3 **Close** the **Property Sheet**. Increase the width of the **Update Shipping** button on the form so that the entire caption displays.

4 Switch to **Form** view, and then click the **Update Shipping** button on the form.

The dialog box title and prompt match the text that you typed in the InputBox method. If the prompt does not display, return to the code, fix any typing mistakes, and then test again.

5 In the displayed **Free Shipping Code** dialog box, substituting your own name, type **Firstname Lastname** and then click **OK**.

The procedure enters Break mode, and you are returned to the Visual Basic Editor.

6 Point to the text *strInputCode*, and then compare your screen with Figure 12.24.

Whatever you typed in the InputBox should display as the variable's value. Setting a breakpoint enables you to stop and test that the programming is assigning the correct values to its variables.

Figure 12.24

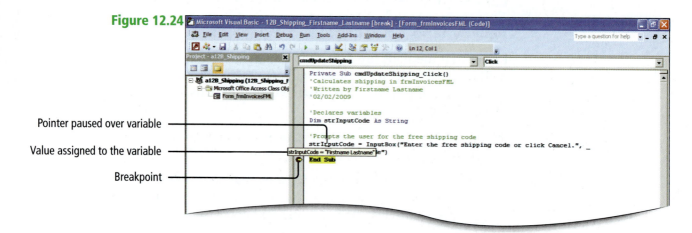

Pointer paused over variable

Value assigned to the variable

Breakpoint

7 On the toolbar, click the **Reset** □ button. Press Alt + Q, and then click the **Update Shipping** button. In the displayed prompt, click the **Cancel** button.

8 Point to the text *strInputCode*, and then observe that the value is two double quotation marks, " ".

The string returned by the InputBox method is empty. An empty string is represented by two quotation marks with no space between them.

9 On the toolbar, click the **Reset** button □. In the gray margin, click the red **Breakpoint margin indicator** to remove it. Leave the Visual Basic window open for the next activity.

Objective 6
Write Control Structures

A **control structure** is a programming method that controls how statements in a procedure are run. In programming, control structures are used to decide whether statements should run or be ignored, whether statements should be repeated, or whether the order statements are run in should change. To calculate the shipping on the Cross Oceans Music invoices form, two common control structures will be used.

Activity 12.11 Writing an If Then Statement

In VBA, the *If Then Else* statement is a control structure used to decide which statements should run based on whether a condition is true or false. In this activity, you will add an *If Else* control structure to the *cmdUpdateShipping* procedure. *If* the correct code is entered, *then* shipping will be free. Otherwise (*else*), the shipping rate will be determined from the rate selected in the combo box on the selected form.

1 Click after the statement *Dim strInputCode As String*, press Enter, and then type **Dim strShippingMethod As String**

2 Click to the right of *"Free Shipping Code")*, and then press Enter **two** times. Type the following comment: **'Determines shipping method**

3 Press Enter, and then type the following *If Then* statement: **If strInputCode = "KDNE3" Then**

4 Press Enter, press Tab, and then type the following: **strShippingMethod = "Free"**

5 Press Enter, press ←Bksp, and then type following: **Else**

6 Press Enter, press Tab, and then type the following: **strShippingMethod = cboShippingMethod.Value**

If the *KDNE3* is entered into the prompt, the shipping method will be *Free*. In all other cases, the shipping method will equal whichever item is selected in the combo box.

7 Press Enter, press ←Bksp, and type the following: **End If**

The *End If* statement signals the end of the *If Then Else* control structure.

8 In the gray area next to *End If*, click to place a breakpoint. Compare your code carefully with Figure 12.25.

Figure 12.25

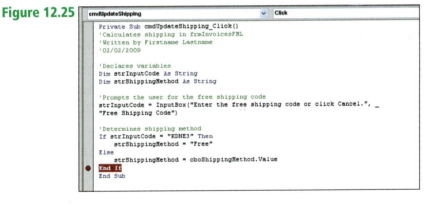

```
cmdUpdateShipping                                          Click

Private Sub cmdUpdateShipping_Click()
'Calculates shipping in frmInvoicesFML
'Written by Firstname Lastname
'02/02/2009

'Declares variables
Dim strInputCode As String
Dim strShippingMethod As String

'Prompts the user for the free shipping code
strInputCode = InputBox("Enter the free shipping code or click Cancel.", _
"Free Shipping Code")

'Determines shipping method
If strInputCode = "KDNE3" Then
    strShippingMethod = "Free"
Else
    strShippingMethod = cboShippingMethod.Value
End If
End Sub
```

9 Click **Save**, press Alt + F11, and then click the **Design View** button.

10 Double-click the **Shipping Method** combo box. In the displayed **Property Sheet**, click the **Other tab**, and then change the control **Name** to **cboShippingMethod**

The Name property must match the name that you used in the code.

11 Click the **Form View** button, and then click the **Update Shipping** button. In the displayed dialog box, type **KDNE3** and then click **OK**.

12 In the displayed Code window, point to the text *strShippingMethod*, and check that it was assigned the value *Free*.

13 On the toolbar, click the **Reset** ☐ button, and then press (Alt) + (Q). Be sure that **Ground** is selected in the combo box, and then click the **Update Shipping** button. In the displayed dialog box, click **Cancel**. Check that the value of *strShippingMethod* is equal to *Ground*.

14 Click the **Reset** ☐ button, and then press (Alt) + (Q). In the **Shipping Method** combo box, select **2nd Day Ground**. Click the **Update Shipping** button again. In the displayed dialog box, type **wrong1** and then press (Enter). Check that the value of *strShippingMethod* is equal to *2nd Day Ground*.

15 On the toolbar, click the **Reset** ☐ button. In the gray margin, click to remove the breakpoint.

16 Click **Save** 🖫, and then **Close** ☒ the Visual Basic window. Click **Save** 🖫, and leave the form open for the next activity.

Activity 12.12 Writing a Select Case Statement

A **select case statement** is a control structure that evaluates a single expression, and then executes one of several groups of statements depending on what that value is. Select case statements work much like a long series of *If Then Else* statements. They are useful when several possible conditions exist, and you want a different action to be performed for each. For example, the shipping method at Cross Oceans Music will have one of four different values—one of the three shipping methods or the free option. In this activity, you will write a Select Case statement to assign the shipping rate that corresponds with the shipping method selected in the combo box.

1 In the form, click the **Shipping Method arrow** and observe the values. Compare your screen with Figure 12.26.

Figure 12.26

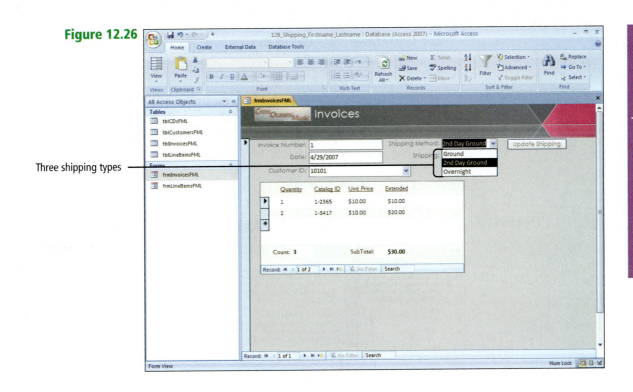

Three shipping types

2 Click the **Database Tools tab**, and from the **Macro group**, click the **Visual Basic** button.

3 Click at then end of the statement *Dim strShippingMethod As String*, press Enter, and then type the following: **Dim curRate As Currency**

The variable *curRate* will store the shipping rate.

4 Click the right of *End If*, press Enter **two** times, and then type the following comment: **'Determines shipping rate**

5 Press Enter, and then type the following: **Select Case strShippingMethod**

6 Press Enter, press Tab, and then type the following: **Case "Ground"**

7 Press Enter, press Tab, and then type the following: **curRate = 1.5**

This statement will run only when *strShippingMethod* is equal to *Ground*. The indentation is used to make the code more readable.

8 Press Enter, press ←Bksp, and then continue typing the Select Case statement using the lines and indentation as shown:

Case "2nd Day Ground"

   curRate = 3.5

Case "Overnight"

   curRate = 7.5

Case "Free"

   curRate = 0

Case Else

   MsgBox ("Please choose a shipping method.")

End Select

9 Click **Save** ![save icon], and then compare your code carefully with Figure 12.27.

The Select Case statement must begin with *Select Case* and end with *End Select*. The Case Else group will execute only when *strShippingMethod* does not equal any of the values given in the four Case Is groups. The MsgBox method will display a message asking that a shipping method be selected.

Case group   Case Else group

Figure 12.27

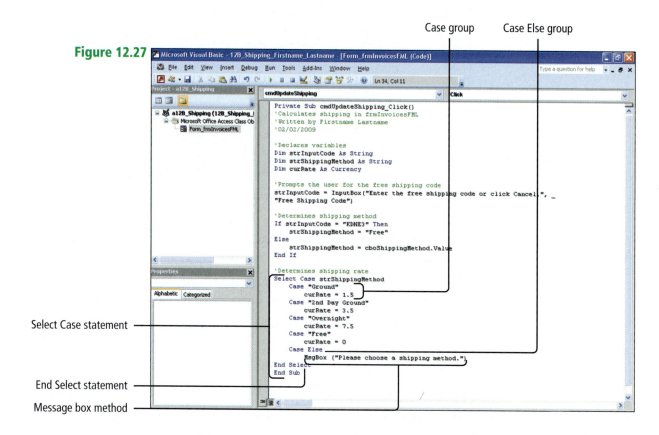

Select Case statement

End Select statement
Message box method

10 Press ⌤Alt⌤ + ⌤Q⌤, to return to the form. If necessary, click the Form View button.

11 In the **Shipping Method** combo box, replace the current value with **wrong** Click the **Update Shipping** button.

12 In the displayed **Free Shipping Code** dialog box, click **OK**.

Because a correct shipping method was not selected, the MsgBox method was executed. Well-written code handles every possible response, such as typing the wrong shipping method into the combo box.

13 Read the displayed message, and then click **OK**. Click the **Shipping Method arrow**, and then click **Ground**. Click the **Update Shipping** button, and then click **OK**.

If there are no mistakes in your code, nothing more happens.

14 Click **Save** ![save icon], and leave the form open for the next activity.

More Knowledge

Loop Control Structures

A *loop* is a control structure that repeats statements until a certain condition is met. Common loops are shown in the table in Figure 12.28.

Common Visual Basic for Applications Loop Control Structures

Common Loop	Example
Do While Loop	Do While i < 5 i = i + 1 *Statements* Loop
For Next	For x = 0 To 5 *Statements* Next
For Each	For Each ctrControl In Application.Forms.myForm *Statements* Next

Figure 12.28

Objective 7
Perform Calculations and Make Comparisons

Often, values need to be changed by performing calculations. In Visual Basic, calculations are very similar to the expressions that you have used to create calculated fields. The same mathematical operators that you have used in other projects are also used in VBA. Recall that operators are also used to compare values. Common Visual Basic operators are listed in the table shown in Figure 12.29.

Common Visual Basic for Applications Operators

Mathematical Operators	Description
&	Concatenate
+	Add
–	Subtract
*	Multiply
/	Divide
%	Modulus (Returns the remainder after dividing two numbers)
Comparison Operators	
=	Equal to
<>	Not equal to
<	Less than
>	Greater than
<=	Less than or equal to
>=	Greater than or equal to

Figure 12.29

Activity 12.13 Performing Calculations and Comparing Values

Recall that Cross Oceans Music shipping is calculated using one of four rates and that the maximum shipping charge is $18.00. In this activity, you will calculate the shipping charge and use comparison operators to cap shipping charges at $18.00.

1 Click the **Design View** button, and then click the **Shipping** text box.

2 In the **Property Sheet**, click the **Other tab**, and then change the **Name** property of the control to **txtShipping**

3 In the subform, display the properties for the calculated control to the right of the **Count:** label. Change the **Name** property of the control from *Text12* to **txtItemCount**

4 Click **Save** . Click the **Database Tools tab**, and in the **Macro group**, click the **Visual Basic** button.

5 In the upper portion of the Code window, click to the right of *Dim curRate As Currency*, press Enter, and then type the following: **Dim intItemCount As Integer**

6 Press Enter, and then declare the following variable: **Dim curTotalShipping As Currency**

7 At the bottom of the Code window, click to the right of *End Select*, press Enter **two** times, and then type the following comments:

> 'Calculates the final shipping charge
>
> 'Writes the charge into txtShipping

8 Press Enter, and assign the following value:
intItemCount = frmLineItems!txtItemCount.Value

Because there are two forms, a main form and a subform, the form name must be included. In VBA, form names and their controls are separated by exclamation marks.

9 Press Enter, and then assign the following calculated value:
curTotalShipping = curRate * intItemCount

10 Press Enter, and then type the following *If Then Else* control, substituting your own initials in the form name:

> **If curTotalShipping < 18 Then**
>
>   **Forms!frmInvoicesFML!txtShipping = curTotalShipping**
>
> **Else**
>
>   **Forms!frmInvoicesFML!txtShipping = 18**
>
> **End If**

11 Compare your code carefully with Figure 12.30.

Before *frmInvoicesFML*, the *Forms* object is given—as in *Forms!frmInvoicesFML*—so that Access can locate the correct form.

Figure 12.30

Forms object

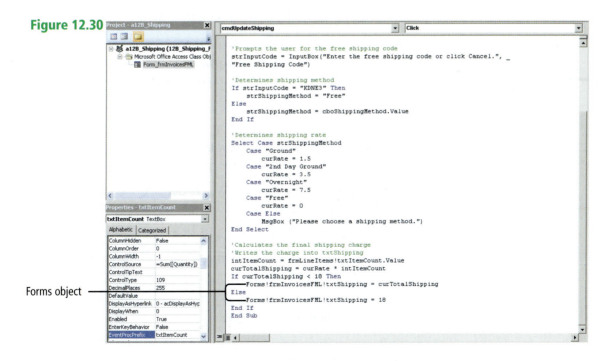

12 Click **Save** 🖫. From the **File** menu, click **Close and Return to Microsoft Office Access**.

13 Click the **Form View** button. Click the **Shipping Method arrow**, click **2nd Day Ground**, and then click the **Update Shipping** button. In the displayed **Free Shipping Code** dialog box, click **Cancel**. Check that the *Shipping* text box displays $10.50.

14 Change the **Shipping Method** to **Overnight**, and then click the **Update Shipping** button. Click **Cancel**, and then check that the *Shipping* text box displays $18.00.

15 Click the **Update Shipping** button again. In the displayed **Free Shipping Code** dialog box, type **KDNE3** and then press ⏎. Check that the *Shipping* text box displays $0.00.

16 Click **Save** 🖫, and leave the form open for the next activity.

Objective 8
Add a Subroutine to Trap Errors

The possibility that a procedure will create an error always exists because no programmer can predict every possible end-user response. A common approach to handling unpredicted errors is to create a subroutine that runs if an error occurs. A ***subroutine*** is code that resides within a procedure, to perform a specific task independent from the procedure. Subroutines run only when called by the procedure.

Activity 12.14 Adding a Subroutine to Trap Errors

Cross Oceans Music does not want to see the run-time error message should an error occur. ***Error trapping*** is the process of controlling how a program responds to run-time errors. In this activity, you will create a subroutine that provides a message in the event a run-time error occurs.

1 Press ⎇ + F11 to open the Visual Basic Editor. Click to the right of the statement *Private Sub cmdUpdateShipping_Click( )*, press ⏎, and then type the following: **On Error**

On Error is a type of event. When On Error is placed in the procedure, this line will respond to an error event.

2 After *On Error*, add a space, and then type **GoTo errorMessage**

The GoTo method instructs the procedure to go directly to a subroutine named *errorMessage*.

3 Scroll to the *End Sub* statement, and then insert a new line above it. In the new line, type **Exit Sub**

If the procedure gets to this point without any errors, it will stop executing code.

4 Press ⏎, and then type the following subroutine:
errorMessage: MsgBox ("Unable to calculate shipping.")

This line of code is often called an event handler. When an error occurs, the program skips to this subroutine, displays an error message, and then moves to the *End Sub* statement.

5 Press Alt + Q to return to the form. Test the code by choosing various shipping options and clicking the **Update Shipping** button. If you typed your code correctly, no errors should occur.

6 Press Alt + F11. Locate the statement *strShippingMethod = cboShippingMethod.Value*. Change the spelling of the combo box by removing the first letter: **boShippingMethod.Value**

This will cause an error when the procedure is run.

7 Press Alt + Q, and then click the **Update Shipping Button**. Click **OK**, and then compare your screen with Figure 12.31.

Figure 12.31

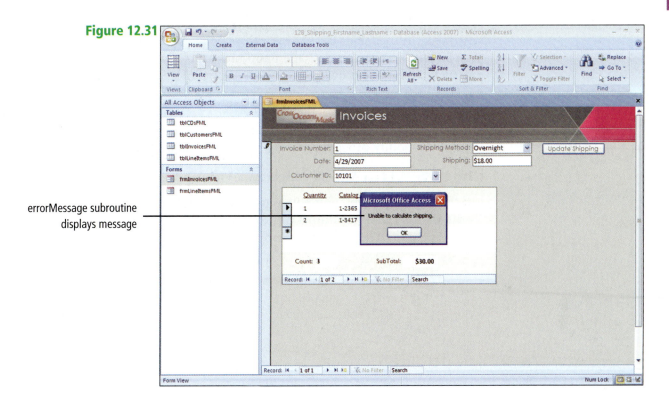

errorMessage subroutine
displays message

8 In the displayed message, click **OK**. Press Alt + F11. Change the spelling of the combo box name back to **cboShippingMethod.Value**

9 Press Ctrl + A to select all of the code. Press Ctrl + C to copy the code to the Clipboard.

10 Click **Save** , and then **Close** the Visual Basic window. Click **Save** , **Close** the form, and then **Exit** Access.

11 Start a blank document in **Word**. In the **Styles group**, click the **No Spacing** button. Change the **Font** to **Courier**.

12 Click the **Page Layout tab**. In the **Page Setup group**, click the **Margins** button, and then click **Narrow**.

13 Type **12B_Code_Firstname_Lastname** substituting your own name, and then press Enter **two** times. Press Ctrl + V to paste the code. **Save** the document as **12B_Code_Firstname_Lastname** If you are instructed to submit this result, create a paper or electronic printout.

14 **Exit** Word.

End You have completed Project 12B ──────────────

 There's More You Can Do!

From My Computer, navigate to the student files that accompany this textbook. In the folder **02_theres_more_you_can_do**, locate and open the folder for this chapter. Open and print the instructions for this project, which are provided to you in Adobe PDF format.

Try It! 1—Convert a Macro to Visual Basic

In this Try It! project, you will convert a macro to Visual Basic code, and then modify procedure using the Visual Basic Editor.

Try It! 2—Add an ActiveX Web Browser to a Form

In this Try It! project, you will add a Web browser to a form, and then write Visual Basic to control the Web browser.

Content-Based Assessments

Summary

Visual Basic for Applications is a powerful way to control how forms, queries, and reports function. In this chapter, you customized forms by writing Visual Basic code. You have used many of the techniques common to any programming language. For example, you declared variables and assigned values to them. You have prompted for input, and then, based on that input, controlled which statements the Visual Basic program should execute. You have practiced debugging code, and written a subroutine to trap errors. Learning to write code in Visual Basic for Applications provides almost unlimited possibilities to customize the Access database experience.

Key Terms

Break mode 1037	**Margin indicator** 1037	**String** 1041
Breakpoint 1051	**Method** 1044	**Sub procedure**
Code window 1031	**Microsoft ActiveX**	(sub) 1039
Concatenate 1043	control .... 🟢	**Subroutine** 1060
Control structure ..1052	**Microsoft Web**	**Syntax error** 1035
Data type 1040	Browser .... 🟢	**Variable** 1040
Debug 1034	**Module** 1028	**VBA compiler** 1034
Error trapping 1060	**Procedure** 1038	**Visual Basic** 1028
Event 1038	**Programming**	**Visual Basic**
Event-driven	comment 1031	Editor (VBE) 1028
language 1038	**Project Explorer** 1030	**Visual Basic for**
Function 1044	**Properties window** 1031	Applications
Hungarian notation 1028	**Run-time error** 1036	(VBA) 1028
If Then Else 1052	**Select case**	**Visual Basic**
Logical error 1036	statement 1054	window 1030
Loop 1057	**SQL subquery** 1030	

The 🟢 symbol represents Key Terms found on the Student CD in the 02_theres_more_you_can_do folder for this chapter.

Content-Based Assessments

Access

chapter twelve

Matching

Match each term in the second column with its correct definition in the first column. Write the letter of the term on the blank line in front of the correct definition.

____ **1.** A programming language built into Microsoft Office applications.

____ **2.** The name of the program used to view and write VBA code.

____ **3.** A naming convention where programming objects are given a prefix that identifies what type of object they are.

____ **4.** An SQL SELECT statement nested inside another query.

____ **5.** In the Visual Basic window, this lists the database modules.

____ **6.** This translates the code written by the programmer into another language that can be interpreted by the computer.

____ **7.** An error where the code runs, but the program does not return the expected results.

____ **8.** A temporary suspension in the execution of code during which you can debug the code.

____ **9.** A type of programming language in which code is run in response to user actions.

____ **10.** A procedure that executes code without returning a value.

____ **11.** A programming object used to store values.

____ **12.** A procedure or function that is already built into the VBA language.

____ **13.** A control structure used to decide if a statement should run based on whether a condition is true or false.

____ **14.** A control structure that evaluates a single expression, and then executes one of several groups of statements depending on what that value is.

____ **15.** Code that resides within a procedure, to perform a specific task independent from the procedure.

A Break mode

B Event-driven

C Hungarian notation

D If Then Else

E Logical error

F Method

G Project Explorer

H Select Case

I Sub

J Subquery

K Subroutine

L Variable

M VBA Compiler

N Visual Basic Editor

O Visual Basic for Applications

Fill in the Blank

Write the correct word in the space provided.

1. VBA is a subset of a high-level programming language developed by Microsoft called _____ _____.

2. A collection of Visual Basic code is called a(n) _____.

3. The window that displays the Visual Basic Editor is called the _____ _____ _____.

4. An embedded remark written by the programmer to document the code is called a(n) _____.

5. The process of finding and fixing errors in the code is to _____ the code.

6. An error that breaks a VBA programming language rule is called a(n) _____ error.

7. An error that occurs when the code attempts to perform an invalid operation is called a(n) _____ error.

8. Visual clues in the left margin of the Code window are called _____ _____.

9. A named group of programming statements that run as a unit, such as a sub or function, is called a(n) _____.

10. User actions such as typing, clicking the mouse, or updating a record are all examples of a(n) _____.

11. A data type that holds a sequence of alphanumeric characters is called a(n) _____.

12. A procedure that returns a value is called a(n) _____.

13. A point in the code, set by the programmer, where the procedure will stop running and enter Break mode is called a(n) _____.

14. A programming method that determines how statements in a procedure are run is called a(n) _____ _____.

15. The process of controlling how a program responds to run-time errors is called _____ _____.

Access

chapter twelve

Skills Review

Project 12C—Bands

In this project, you will apply the skills you practiced from the Objectives in Project 12A.

Objectives: 1. *Modify an Existing VBA Module;* **2.** *Debug and Test VBA Code;* **3.** *Write an Event Procedure;* **4.** *Use Variables, Properties, and Methods.*

Cross Oceans Music would like you to build a form that automatically lists each band in a combo box. A list box needs to display the members of any band selected in the combo box. In this project, you will adapt the VBA code module that lists the bands in the combo box, and then add an event procedure that updates the list box whenever the selection in the combo box changes. Your completed VBA code module will look similar to the code shown in Figure 12.32.

For Project 12C, you will need the following file:

a12C_Bands

You will save your files as
12C_Bands_Firstname_Lastname
12C_Code_Firstname_Lastname

Figure 12.32

```
12C_Code_Firstname_Lastname

Option Compare Database

Private Sub cboBands_AfterUpdate()
'Sends an SQL subquery to qryBandsFML
'Displays results in lstMembers
'Created by Firstname Lastname
'02/02/2009

'Declares variables
Dim strSelectedItem As String
Dim strSQLQuery As String

'Assigns the band selected in the combo box
strSelectedItem = cboBands.Value

'Assigns the SQL statement
strSQLQuery = "SELECT qryBandsFML.[Band Name], qryBandsFML.Name,
qryBandsFML.Country " & _
"FROM qryBandsFML " &
"WHERE qryBandsFML.[Band Name] = '" & strSelectedItem & "';"

'Updates the list box Row Source property and runs the query
lstMembers.RowSource = strSQLQuery
lstMembers.Requery

End Sub

Private Sub Form_Load()
'Writes an SQL subquery in the query named qryBands
'Populates the combo box named cboBands
'Adapted by Firstname Lastname
'02/02/2009

'Declares variables
    Dim strSQL As String

'Writes the SQL statement
    strSQL = "SELECT DISTINCT qryBandsFML.[Band Name] " & _
    "FROM qryBandsFML " &
    "ORDER BY qryBandsFML.[Band Name];"

'Displays the results of the SQL query in the combo box
    With cboBands
        .RowSource = strSQL
        .RowSourceType = "Table/Query"
        .BoundColumn = 1
    End With

End Sub
```

(Project 12C–Bands continues on the next page)

(Project 12C–Bands continued)

1. **Start** Access, and then locate and open the **a12C_Bands** file. Click the **Office** button, point to **Save As** and click **Access 2007 Database**, and then **Save** the database in your **Access Chapter12** folder as **12C_Bands_Firstname_Lastname** For each database object, add **FML** at the end of its name using your own initials and no spaces.

2. In the **Navigation Pane**, double-click **qryBandsFML**, and then familiarize yourself with the query results. Observe that each band name displays multiple times, and then **Close** the query.

3. In the **Navigation Pane**, double-click **frmBandsFML**. Press [Alt] + [F11] to display the Visual Basic window. In the **Project Explorer**, locate the **Form_frmBandsFML** module, and then double-click it.

4. In the displayed **Code** window, read the five comments. After the second comment, create a new line, and then add the following comments on two lines as shown:

'Adapted by Firstname Lastname (Use your own name)
'mm/dd/yyyy (Use the current date)

5. In the SQL Statement, after the keyword *SELECT*, add a space, and then type **DISTINCT**

6. Locate the lines that assign the SQL statement to the *strSQL* variable. For the three instances of *qryBands*, change each to **qryBandsFML** using your own initials.

7. Press [Alt] + [Q]. Click **Save**, and then **Close** the form. Open **frmBands** in Form view, and then, in the combo box, check that each band is listed one time.

8. Click the **Design View** button. In the **Detail** section, double-click the form's combo box. In the displayed **Property Sheet**, click the **Event tab**.

9. Click in the **After Update** row, and then click the row's displayed **Build** button. In the displayed **Choose Builder** dialog box, click **Code Builder**, and then click **OK**.

10. In the event procedure that displays, add the following comments on four lines as shown:

'Sends an SQL subquery to qryBandsFML (Use your own name)
'Displays results in lstMembers
'Created by Firstname Lastname (Use your own name)
'mm/dd/yyyy (Use the current date)

11. After the last comment, press [Enter] **two** times, add the following comment, and then declare the two variables:

'Declares variables
Dim strSelectedItem As String
Dim strSQLQuery As String

(Project 12C–Bands continues on the next page)

Access
chapter twelve
Skills Review

(Project 12C–Bands continued)

12. Press [Enter] **two** times, add the following comment, and then assign the following value to the *strSelectedItem* variable:

> 'Assigns the band selected in the combo box
>
> strSelectedItem = cboBands.Value

13. Press [Enter] **two** times, add the following comment, and then assign the following value to the *strSQLQuery* variable. Substitute your own initials where appropriate:

> 'Assigns the SQL statement
>
> strSQLQuery = "SELECT qryBandsFML.[Band Name], qryBandsFML.Name, qryBandsFML.Country " & _
>
> "FROM qryBandsFML " & _
>
> "WHERE qryBandsFML.[Band Name] = '" & strSelectedItem & "';"

14. Press [Enter] **two** times, add the following comment, and then assign the following property to the list box. Be sure to use the lowercase letter "l" in *lst*, not the number one:

> 'Updates the list box Row Source property and runs the query
>
> lstMembers.RowSource = strSQLQuery

15. Press [Enter], and then apply the following method:

> lstMembers.Requery

16. From the **File** menu, click **Close and Return to Microsoft Office Access**. Click **Save**, and then **Close** the form. Open **frmBands** in Form view.

17. Test your code by clicking different band names in the Band combo box. If a run-time error occurs or you get unexpected results, return to the code, carefully check your typing, and then test the form again.

18. Press [Alt] + [F11]. With the insertion point in the Code window, press [Ctrl] + [A], and then press [Ctrl] + [C]. Close the Visual Basic window. Click **Save**, **Close** the form, and then **Exit** Access.

19. Start a blank document in **Word**. In the **Styles group**, click the **No Spacing** button. In the **Font group**, click the **Font button arrow**, and then click **Courier**. Click the **Page Layout tab**. In the **Page Setup group**, click the **Margins** button, and then click **Narrow**.

20. Type **12C_Code_Firstname_Lastname** substituting your own name, and then press [Enter] **two** times. Press [Ctrl] + [V] to paste the code. **Save** the document as **12C_Code_Firstname_Lastname** If you are instructed to submit this result, create a paper or electronic printout.

21. **Exit** Word.

End **You have completed Project 12C**

Access
chapter twelve

Skills Review

Project 12D — Musicians

In this project, you will apply the skills you practiced from the Objectives in Project 12B.

Objectives: 5. *Prompt for User Input;* **6.** *Write Control Structures;* **7.** *Perform Calculations and Make Comparisons;* **8.** *Add a Subroutine to Trap Errors.*

Cross Oceans needs to protect the data in their musicians table from unauthorized access. In this project, you will set up the Musicians form to prompt any users who open the form for a password. The form will not open until the correct password is entered. You will also use VBA to apply a custom input mask when the musician is from Canada. Your completed VBA code module will look similar to the code shown in Figure 12.33.

For Project 12D, you will need the following file:

a12D_Musicians

You will save your files as
12D_Musicians_Firstname_Lastname
12D_Code_Firstname_Lastname

Figure 12.33

```
12D_Code_Firstname_Lastname

Private Sub Form_Current()
'Applies Canadian Postal Code input mask
'Written by Firstname Lastname
'02/02/2009

If txtCountry.Value = "Canada" Then
    txtPostalCode.InputMask = ">L0>L 0>L0;;#"
Else
    txtPostalCode.InputMask = ""
End If
End Sub

Private Sub Form_Load()
On Error GoTo CloseForm
'Prompts for a password
'Written by Firstname Lastname
'02/02/2009

'Declares variable
Dim strInput As String

'Prompts for password
strInput = InputBox("Confidential data:" & vbCrLf & _
"Please enter a password.", "Logon")

'If correct, form loads; if canceled, form closes; else ask for input again
Select Case strInput
    Case "GO! Series"
        Exit Sub
    Case ""
        DoCmd.Close acForm, "frmMusiciansFML"
    Case Else
        Call Form_Load
End Select

Exit Sub
CloseForm: DoCmd.Close acForm, "frmMusiciansFML"
End Sub
```

(Project 12D–Musicians continues on the next page)

Skills Review

(Project 12D—Musicians continued)

1. **Start** Access. Locate and open the **a012D_Musicians** file. Click the **Office** button. Point to **Save As**, click **Access 2007 Database**, and then **Save** the database in the **Access Chapter 12** folder as **12D_Musicians_Firstname_Lastname** For each database object, add **FML** at the end of its name using your own initials and no spaces.

2. In the **Navigation Pane**, double-click **frmMusicians** and familiarize yourself with the form. Click the **Design View** button, and then in the **Tools group**, click the **Property Sheet** button. Click the **Selection type arrow**, and then click **Form**.

3. Click the **Property Sheet Event tab**, click the **On Load** row, and then click the row's displayed **Build** button. In the displayed **Choose Builder** dialog box, click **Code Builder**, and then click **OK**.

4. In the **Form_Load** sub that you just created, type the following comments on three lines as shown:

'Prompts for a password
'Written by Firstname Lastname (Use your own name)
'mm/dd/yyyy (Use the current date)

5. Press ⟨Enter⟩ **two** times, add the following comment, and then declare the variable:

'Declares variable
Dim strInput As String

6. Press ⟨Enter⟩ **two** times, add the following comment, and then add the following prompt as shown:

'Prompts for password
strInput = InputBox("Confidential data:" & vbCrLf & _
"Please enter a password.", "Logon")

7. Press ⟨Enter⟩ **two** times, and then add the following comment and select case control structure. Substitute your own initials in the form name:

'If correct, form loads; if canceled, form closes; else ask for input again
Select Case strInput
Case "GO! Series
Exit Sub
Case ""
DoCmd.Close acForm, "frmMusiciansFML"
Case Else
Call Form_Load
End Select

(Project 12D—Musicians continues on the next page)

Access

Skills Review

(Project 12D–Musicians continued)

8. Press [Enter] **two** times, and then add the following statement and subroutine substituting your own initials:

Exit Sub
CloseForm: DoCmd.Close acForm, "frmMusiciansFML"

9. In the upper portion of the procedure, insert a new line above the first comment, and then add the following error trapping statement in the new line: **On Error GoTo CloseForm**

10. From the **File** menu, click **Close and Return to Microsoft Office Access**. Click **Save**, and then **Close** the form.

11. Open **frmMusiciansFML** in Form view. In the displayed **Logon** dialog box, type **GO! Series** and then click **OK**. The form and all of its fields should display. If you encounter run-time errors, or encounter unintended results, return to the code and carefully check your typing.

12. **Close** and then open **frmMusiciansFML**. In the displayed **Logon** dialog box, type **yyy** and then press [Enter]. In the displayed **Logon** dialog box, click the **Cancel** button.

13. Open **frmMusiciansFML** in Design view. Display the properties for the form. Click the **On Current** row, and then click the row's displayed **Build** button. In the displayed **Choose Builder** dialog box, click **Code Builder**, and then click **OK**.

14. In the new *Form_Current* sub, type the following comments:

'Applies Canadian Postal Code input mask
'Written by Firstname Lastname (Use your own name)
'mm/dd/yyyy (Use the current date)

15. Press [Enter] **two** times, and then write the following If Then Else control structure:

If txtCountry.Value = "Canada" Then
txtPostalCode.InputMask = ">L0>L 0>L0;;#"
Else
txtPostalCode.InputMask = ""
End If

16. From the **File** menu, click **Close and Return to Microsoft Office Access**. Switch to Form view, and then enter **GO! Series** as the password.

17. In the first record, press [Tab] **five** times, and then test your input mask by typing the following: **Y2Y 5R8**

18. Press [Alt] + [F11]. With the insertion point in the Code window, press [Ctrl] + [A], and the press [Ctrl] + [C]. **Close** the Visual Basic window. Click **Save**, **Close** the form, and then **Exit** Access.

(Project 12D–Musicians continues on the next page)

(Project 12D–Musicians continued)

19. Start a blank document in **Word**. In the **Styles group**, click the **No Spacing** button. In the **Font group**, click the **Font button arrow**, and then click **Courier**. Click the **Page Layout tab**. In the **Page Setup group**, click the **Margins** button, and then click **Narrow**.

20. Type **12D_Code_Firstname_Lastname** substituting your own name, and then press Enter **two** times. Press Ctrl + V to paste the code. **Save** the document as **12D_Code_Firstname_Lastname** If you are instructed to submit this result, create a paper or electronic printout.

21. **Exit** Word.

 End   You have completed Project 12D ————————————————————————

Mastering Access

Project 12E — Print Form

In this project, you will apply the skills you practiced from the Objectives in Project 12A.

Objectives: 1. *Modify an Existing VBA Module;* **2.** *Debug and Test VBA Code;* **3.** *Write an Event Procedure;* **4.** *Use Variables, Properties, and Methods.*

Cross Oceans Music would like two buttons to control which form a split form will print—the Form view or the Datasheet view. In this project, you will adapt the VBA code module that prints the Form view, and then write an event procedure that prints the Datasheet view. Your completed VBA code module will look similar to the code shown in Figure 12.34.

For Project 12E, you will need the following file:

a12E_Print_Form

You will save your files as
12E_Print_Form_Firstname_Lastname
12E_Code_Firstname_Lastname

Figure 12.34

```
12E_Code_Firstname_Lastname

Option Compare Database

Private Sub cmdPrintDatasheet_Click()
On Error GoTo Cancel
'Prints the datasheet in a split form
'Created by Firstname Lastname
'02/02/2009

Forms!frmSongsFML.SplitFormPrinting = acGridOnly
DoCmd.RunCommand acCmdPrint
Exit Sub
Cancel: Exit Sub
End Sub

Private Sub cmdPrintForm_Click()
On Error GoTo Cancel
'This procedure prints the Form view in a split form
'Adapted by Firstname Lastname
'02/02/2009

Dim strMessage As String

strMessage = "In the Print dialog box, click Selected Records(s)!"
MsgBox strMessage, vbOKOnly, "Alert!"

Forms!frmSongsFML.SplitFormPrinting = acFormOnly
DoCmd.RunCommand acCmdPrint

Exit Sub
Cancel: Exit Sub
End Sub
```

(Project 12E–Print Form continues on the next page)

(Project 12E–Print Form continued)

1. **Start** Access. Locate and open the **a012E_Print_Form** file. Click the **Office** button. Point to **Save As**, click **Access 2007 Database**, and then **Save** the database in the **Access Chapter 12** folder as **12E_Print_Form_Firstname_Lastname** For each database object, add **FML** at the end of its name using your own initials and no spaces.

2. Open the **Visual Basic** window, and then open the **Code** window for **frmSongsFML**. Click to the right of sub's comment, press Enter, and then the following comments:

   > 'Adapted by Firstname Lastname (Use your own name)
   >
   > 'mm/dd/yyyy (Use the current date)

3. After the last comment, press Enter **two** times, and then declare a variable named **strMessage** with the **String** data type.

4. Press Enter **two** times, and then add a statement that assigns the following value to *strMessage*: **"In the Print dialog box, click Selected Record(s)!"**

5. Press Enter, and then add following method: **MsgBox strMessage, vbOKOnly, "Alert!"**

6. Locate the line of code that prints the form, and then change the form name to **frmSongsFML** using your own initials.

7. Test your code in the form by clicking the **Print Form** button. Be sure that the warning message displays, followed by the Print dialog box. Do not print; click the **Cancel** button.

8. Click **Save**, and then switch to **Design** view. Below the **Print Form** button, insert a new button. In the displayed **Command Button Wizard**, click **Cancel**.

9. For the new command button, assign the following properties:

Caption	Print Datasheet
Name	cmdPrintDatasheet

10. If needed, resize the button so that all of the caption text displays.

11. For **cmdPrintDatasheet**, create a new event procedure for its **On Click** event.

12. In the new procedure, add the following comments.

    > 'Prints the datasheet in a split form
    >
    > 'Created by Firstname Lastname (Use your own name)
    >
    > 'mm/dd/yyyy (Use the current date)

13. Press Enter **two** times, and type the following statements using your own initials in the form name:

    > Forms!frmSongsFML.SplitFormPrinting = acGridOnly
    >
    > DoCmd.RunCommand acCmdPrint

(Project 12E–Print Form continues on the next page)

Content-Based Assessments

(Project 12E–Print Form continued)

14. Click **Save**, return to the form, and then switch to **Design** view. Click the **Print Datasheet** button, but do not print. In the displayed **Print** dialog box, click **Cancel**. Clicking Cancel in the Print dialog box creates a run-time error. In the displayed **Microsoft Visual Basic** dialog box, click the **Debug** button.

15. Click the **Reset** button. Above the first comment, insert a blank line, and then add the following error trapping event: **On Error GoTo Cancel**

16. Above **End Sub**, create a blank line, and then type **Exit Sub** Press ⏎, and then add the following subroutine: **Cancel: Exit Sub**

17. In the form, test the **Print Datasheet** button. In the **Print Dialog** box, click **Cancel**. If no run-time errors occur, the error trapping sub-routine is working.

18. **Copy** all of the code in the **Code** window, and then **Close** the Visual Basic window. Click **Save**, **Close** the form, and then **Exit** Access.

19. Start a blank document in **Word**. Apply the **No Spacing** style, the **Courier** font, and then set the margins to **Narrow**. Type **12E_Code_Firstname_Lastname** substituting your own name, press ⏎ **two** times, and then **Paste** the code. **Save** the document as **12E_Code_Firstname_Lastname** If you are instructed to submit this result, create a paper or electronic printout.

20. **Exit** Word.

 You have completed Project 12E

Mastering Access

Project 12F—Clear Form

In this project, you will apply the skills you practiced from the Objectives in Project 12B.

Objectives: 5. *Prompt for User Input;* **6.** *Write Control Structures;* **7.** *Perform Calculations and Make Comparisons;* **8.** *Add a Subroutine to Trap Errors.*

Cross Oceans Music would like a button that clears the data in a form. In this project, you will write an event procedure that clears the data on the Songs form. Your completed VBA code module will look similar to the code shown in Figure 12.35.

You will save your files as
12F_Clear_Form_Firstname_Lastname
12F_Code_Firstname_Lastname

Figure 12.35

```
12F_Code_Firstname_Lastname

Private Sub cmdClearForm_Click()
On Error GoTo Quit
'Asks if user wants to clear the form
'If Yes, form is cleared; Else a message displays
'Written by Firstname Lastname
'02/02/2009

Dim strResponse As String
Dim objControl As Object

strResponse = MsgBox("Are you sure you want to clear this form?", vbYesNoCancel,
"Caution!")

Select Case strResponse
    Case 6 'Yes button returns 6 when clicked
        GoTo ClearForm
    Case 7 'No button return 7 when clicked
        MsgBox "Form not cleared.", vbOKOnly
        GoTo Quit
    Case Else
        Exit Sub
End Select

ClearForm:
For Each objControl In Forms!frmSongsFML.Controls
    If TypeOf objControl Is TextBox Then
        objControl.SetFocus
        objControl.Text = ""
    ElseIf TypeOf objControl Is CheckBox Then
        objControl.SetFocus
        objControl.Value = False
    ElseIf TypeOf objControl Is ComboBox Then
        objControl.SetFocus
        objControl.Text = ""
    End If
Next
Exit Sub
Quit: Exit Sub
End Sub
```

(Project 12F–Clear Form continues on the next page)

(Project 12F–Clear Form continued)

1. **Start** Access. Locate and open the **a012F_Clear_Form**. Click the **Office** button. Point to **Save As**, click **Access 2007 Database**, and then save the database in the **Access Chapter 12** folder as **12F_Clear_Form_Firstname_Lastname** For each database object, add **FML** at the end of its name using your own initials and no spaces.

2. In the **Navigation Pane**, double-click **frmSongs** and familiarize yourself with the form.

3. Switch to **Design** view, and below the **Genre** list box, insert a new command button. In the displayed **Command Button Wizard**, click **Cancel**.

4. For the new command button, assign the following properties:

Caption	Clear Form
Name	cmdClearForm

5. If needed, resize the button so that all of the caption text displays.

6. For **cmdClearForm**, create a new event procedure for its **On Click** event.

7. In the new procedure, add the following comments.

'Asks if user wants to clear the form
'If Yes, form is cleared; Else a message displays
'Written by Firstname Lastname (Use your own name)
'mm/dd/yyyy (Use the current date)

8. Press Enter two times, and declare a new variable named **strResponse** that will store **String** values.

9. Press Enter, and then declare the following variable: **Dim objControl As Object**

10. Press Enter two times. For the *strResponse* variable, use the *MsgBox* method to assign the following value as shown:

strResponse = MsgBox("Are you sure you want to clear this form?", _vbYesNoCancel, "Caution!")

11. Press Enter two times, and write the following Select Case control structure. Because the two case statements end with comments, be careful to include the single quotation mark as shown:

Select Case strResponse
Case 6 'Yes button returns 6 when clicked
Call ClearForm
Case 7 'No button returns 7 when clicked
MsgBox "Form not cleared.", vbOKOnly
GoTo Quit
Case Else
Exit Sub
End Select

(Project 12F–Clear Form continues on the next page)

Access

Mastering Access

chapter twelve

(Project 12F–Clear Form continued)

12. Press Enter **two** times, and then type the following subroutine. In the form name, use your own initials:

ClearForm:
For Each objControl In Forms!frmSongsFML.Controls
If TypeOf objControl Is TextBox Then
objControl.SetFocus
objControl.Text = ""
ElseIf TypeOf objControl Is CheckBox Then
objControl.SetFocus
objControl.Value = False
ElseIf TypeOf objControl Is ComboBox Then
objControl.SetFocus
objControl.Text = ""
End If
Next

13. In the upper portion of the procedure, create a new line above the first comment, and then add the following error trapping event: **On Error GoTo Quit**

14. Above *End Sub*, insert a new line, and then add the following statement and subroutine:

Exit Sub
Quit: Exit Sub

15. **Save** the code, and then return to the form. Switch to **Form** view, and then click the **Clear Form** button. In the displayed **Caution!** dialog box, click the **Yes** button. The form should clear. Press Esc to return the data to the current record.

16. Click the **Clear Form** button. In the displayed **Caution!** dialog box, click the **No** button. The message box should display, and the form is not cleared. Click **OK**. Click the **Clear Form** button. In the displayed **Caution!** dialog box, click the **Cancel** button. Nothing more should happen.

17. **Copy** all of the code in the **Code** window, and then **Close** the Visual Basic window. Click **Save**, **Close** the form, and then **Exit** Access.

18. Start a blank document in **Word**. Apply the **No Spacing** style, the **Courier** font, and then set the margins to **Narrow**. Type **12F_Code_Firstname_Lastname** substituting your own name, press Enter **two** times, and then **Paste** the code. **Save** the document as **12F_Code_Firstname_Lastname** If you are instructed to submit this result, create a paper or electronic printout.

19. **Exit** Word.

End **You have completed Project 12F** ————————————————

Mastering Access

Project 12G — Song Length

In this project, you will apply the following Objectives found in Projects 12A and 12B.

Objectives: 2. *Debug and Test VBA Code;* **3.** *Write an Event Procedure;* **4.** *Use Variables, Properties, and Methods;* **5.** *Prompt for User Input;* **6.** *Write Control Structures;* **7.** *Perform Calculations and Make Comparisons;* **8.** *Add a Subroutine to Trap Errors.*

Cross Oceans Music needs the length of each song to be stored as both a text value and a number. The text value, such as 4:24, is used when displaying song times on CD jackets. The total seconds, 264, is used when calculating the total time on a CD. In this project, you will write an event procedure that calculates the total number of seconds. Your completed VBA code module will look similar to the code shown in Figure 12.36.

For Project 12G, you will need the following file:

a12G_Song_Length

You will save your files as
12G_Song_Length_Firstname_Lastname
12G_Code_Firstname_Lastname

Figure 12.36

```
12G_Code_Firstname_Lastname

Private Sub cmdCalcSeconds_Click()
On Error GoTo ErrorMessage
'Writes the total seconds into the LengthInSeconds field
'Written by Firstname Lastname
'02/02/2009

Dim strMinutes As String
Dim strSeconds As String

strMinutes = InputBox("How many minutes?", "Enter Number")
strSeconds = InputBox("How many seconds?", "Enter Number")

If strMinutes <> "" And strSeconds <> "" Then
    LengthinSeconds.Value = strMinutes * 60 + strSeconds
End If
Exit Sub
ErrorMessage: MsgBox "Cannot convert song length! The value will not be changed."
End Sub
```

(Project 12G–Song Length continues on the next page)

Access

chapter twelve

Mastering Access

(Project 12G–Song Length continued)

1. **Start** Access. Locate and open the **a012G_Song_Length**. Click the **Office** button. Point to **Save As**, click **Access 2007 Database**, and then **Save** the database in the **Access Chapter 12** folder as **12G_Song_Length_Firstname_Lastname** For each database object, add **FML** at the end of its name using your own initials and no spaces.

2. Open **frmSongsFML** in Design view. For the **cmdCalSeconds** button, create a new event procedure for its **On Click** event.

3. In the new event procedure, add the following comments:

'Writes the total seconds into the LengthInSeconds field
'Written by Firstname Lastname (Use your own name)
'mm/dd/yyyy (Use the current date)

4. Press [Enter] **two** times, and then declare the following variables:

Variable Name	Data Type
strMinutes	String
strSeconds	String

5. Press [Enter] **two** times, and then assign these values to the following variables:

Variable	Assigned Value
strMinutes	InputBox ("How many minutes?", "Enter Number")
strSeconds	InputBox ("How many seconds?", "Enter Number")

6. Press [Enter] **two** times, and then write the following *If Then* statement

If strMinutes <> "" And strSeconds <> "" Then
LengthinSeconds.Value = strMinutes * 60 + strSeconds
End If

7. Click **Save**, and then return to the form. Switch to **Form** view, and then click the **Calculate Seconds** button. In the displayed prompts, type **2**, press [Enter], type **30** and then press [Enter]. The *Length in Seconds* field should display *150*.

8. Click the **Calculate Seconds** button. In the displayed prompt for minutes, type **four** and then click **OK**. In the prompt for seconds, type **three** and then click **OK**. Because you typed words, not numbers, a run-time error occurs. Click the **End** button, and then return to the code window.

9. Above the procedure's first comment, insert a blank line, and then type the following event handler: **On Error GoTo ErrorMessag**e

(Project 12G–Song Length continues on the next page)

(Project 12G—Song Length continued)

10. After the *End If* statement, add the following:

> **Exit Sub**
>
> **ErrorMessage: MsgBox "Cannot convert song length! The value will not be changed."**

11. Click **Save**, and then return to the form. Click the **Calculate Seconds** button. In the displayed prompt for minutes, type **four** and in the prompt for seconds, type **three** Instead of a run-time error, the message from the ErrorMessage subroutine should display.

12. In the current record, use the **Calculate Seconds** button to calculate the value for **5** minutes and **8** seconds.

13. **Copy** all of the code in the **Code** window, and then **Close** the Visual Basic window. Click **Save**, **Close** the form, and then **Exit** Access.

14. Start a blank document in **Word**. Apply the **No Spacing** style, the **Courier** font, and then set the margins to **Narrow**. Type **12G_Code_Firstname_Lastname** substituting your own name, press Enter **two** times, and then **Paste** the code. **Save** the document as **12G_Code_Firstname_Lastname** If you are instructed to submit this result, create a paper or electronic printout.

15. **Exit** Word.

 You have completed Project 12G ———————————————

Content-Based Assessments

Mastering Access

Project 12H — CD Length

In this project, you will apply the following Objectives found in Projects 12A and 12B.

Objectives: 1. *Modify an Existing VBA Module;* **2.** *Debug and Test VBA Code;* **4.** *Use Variables, Properties, and Methods;* **6.** *Write Control Structures;* **7.** *Perform Calculations and Make Comparisons;* **8.** *Add a Subroutine to Trap Errors.*

Cross Oceans Music has a form that they use to decide which songs should be placed on a new CD. A coworker has written a VBA module that calculates the total time for each CD, which cannot exceed 74 minutes. In this project, you will adapt the VBA module so that the total time is formatted red if the value is greater than 74 minutes and add an error trapping subroutine. Your completed VBA code module will look similar to the code shown in Figure 12.37.

> **For Project 12H, you will need the following file:**
>
> a12H_CD_Length
>
> **You will save your database as**
> **12H_CD_Length_Firstname_Lastname**
> **12H_Code_Firstname_Lastname**

Figure 12.37

```
12H_Code_Firstname_Lastname

Option Compare Database

Public Function SecondsToText(intTotalSeconds As Integer) As String
'Converts any time in seconds into a string (mm:ss)
'Written by Hugh Chapman
'Modified by Firstname Lastname
'02/02/2009

'Declare variables
Dim intMinutes As Integer
Dim intSeconds As Integer
Dim strMinutes As String
Dim strSeconds As String

'Calculate the minutes and seconds
intMinutes = Val(intTotalSeconds / 60)
intSeconds = intTotalSeconds Mod 60

'Convert integers to strings
strMinutes = Str(intMinutes)
strSeconds = Str(intSeconds)

'Remove leading spaces
strMinutes = LTrim(strMinutes)
strSeconds = LTrim(strSeconds)

'Return the final value (mm:ss)
SecondsToText = strMinutes & ":" & strSeconds
End Function

Private Sub cmdCalcTotalTime_Click()
On Error GoTo ErrorMessage
'Calculates the total time for the CD
'Written by Hugh Chapman
'Modified by Firstname Lastname
'02/02/2009

'Declare variables
Dim intTotal As Integer
Dim strTime As String
Dim strMessage As String

strMessage = "Unable to calculate time due to error."

'Add the Total Length_In_Seconds using DSum method
intTotal = DSum("LengthInSeconds", "qrySongsFML", _
"CDTitle=Forms!frmCDsFML!CDTitle")

'Call function and display answer in text box
strTime = SecondsToText(intTotal)
txtTotalTime.Value = strTime

'Apply conditional formatting
If intTotal > 4440 Then
    txtTotalTime.ForeColor = RGB(200, 0, 0)
Else
    txtTotalTime.ForeColor = RGB(0, 200, 0)
End If

Exit Sub
ErrorMessage: MsgBox strMessage, vbOKOnly
End Sub
```

(Project 12H—CD Length continues on the next page)

(Project 12H–CD Length continued)

1. **Start** Access. Locate and open the **a012H_CD_Length**. Click the **Office** button. Point to **Save As**, click **Access 2007 Database**, and then **Save** the database in the **Access Chapter 12** folder as **12H_CD_Length_Firstname_Lastname** For each database object, add **FML** at the end of its name using your own initials and no spaces.

2. Display the **Code** window for the **frmCDsFML**. Familiarize yourself with the code. Notice that a function and a sub procedure have already been written.

3. In the sub procedure, locate the statement that uses the DSum method. In the statement, change the query name to **qrySongsFML** using your own initials. Change the form name to **frmCDsFML** using your own initials.

4. Click **Save**, return to **frmCDsFML**, and then switch to **Form** view. Click the form's **Calculate Total Time** button. If necessary, debug the code.

5. In the main form, click the **Next Record** button until the songs for *Jambalaya*, record 9 of 15, display. Click the **Calculate Total Time** button, and then notice that this CD is too long.

6. In the *cmdCalcTotalTime* event procedure, after *'Written by Hugh Chapman*, add the following comments:

'Modified by Firstname Lastname (Use your own name)
'mm/dd/yyyy (Use the current date)

7. Add a new line above *End Sub*, and then add the following *IfThenElse* control structure:

'Apply conditional formatting
If intTotal > 4440 Then
txtTotalTime.ForeColor = RGB(200, 0, 0)
Else
txtTotalTime.ForeColor = RGB(0, 200, 0)
End If

8. **Save** your code, and then test the code in the form. If the total time is greater than 74 minutes, the text should display in red. If not, the text should display in green. Check several records.

9. Click the **New (blank) record** button, and then click the **Calculate Total Time** button. In the displayed run-time error message, click **Debug**, and then click the **Reset** button.

10. In the *cmdCalcTotalTime* sub procedure, create a new line above the first comment, and then add the following error event handler: **On Error GoTo ErrorMessage**

11. Click to the right of *Dim strTime As String*, press Enter, and then declare a new variable with the name **strErrorMessage** and the **String** data type.

12. Press Enter **two** times. For the **strMessage** variable, assign the following value: **"Unable to calculate time due to error."**

(Project 12H–CD Length continues on the next page)

(Project 12H–CD Length continued)

13. After the *End If* statement, press Enter **two** times, and then add the following statement and subroutine:

> Exit Sub
>
> ErrorMessage: MsgBox strMessage, vbOKOnly

14. **Save** your code and return to the form. In the blank record, click the **Calculate Total Time** button. Your error message should display instead of a run-time error.

15. **Copy** all of the code in the **Code** window, and then **Close** the Visual Basic window. Click **Save**, **Close** the form, and then **Exit** Access.

16. Start a blank document in **Word**. Apply the **No Spacing** style, the **Courier** font, and then set the margins to **Narrow**. Type **12H_Code_Firstname_Lastname** substituting your own name, press Enter **two** times, and then **Paste** the code. **Save** the document as **12E_Code_Firstname_ Lastname** If you are instructed to submit this result, create a paper or electronic printout.

17. **Exit** Word.

End **You have completed Project 12H** ──────────────────────────

Mastering Access

Project 12I — Genres

In this project, you will apply all the skills you practiced from the Objectives in Projects 12A and 12B.

Cross Oceans Music would like to password protect the form used to manage personnel records. The company also has a form that lists all of the songs when a genre is selected in a combo box. The form needs to be debugged and also needs to display the number of songs for the selected genre. In this project, you will write VBA code for the two forms. Your completed VBA code modules will look similar to the code shown in Figure 12.38.

For Project 12I, you will need the following file:

a12I_Genres

You will save your files as
12I_Genres_Firstname_Lastname
12I_Personnel_Code_Firstname_Lastname
12I_Genres_Code_Firstname_Lastname

Figure 12.38

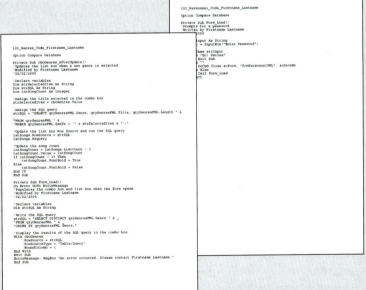

(Project 12I–Genres continues on the next page)

(Project 12I–Genres continued)

1. **Start** Access. Locate and open **a012I_Genres**. Click the **Office** button. Point to **Save As**, **Access 2007 Database**, and then **Save** the database in the **Access Chapter 12** folder as **12I_Genres_Firstname_Lastname** For each database object, add **FML** at the end of its name using your own initials and no spaces.

2. Open **frmPersonnel** in **Design** view. Add a procedure for the form's **On Load** event.

3. In the *Form_Load* procedure, add the following comments:

'Prompts for a password
'Written by Firstname Lastname (Use your own name)
'mm/dd/yyyy (Use the current date)

4. Press [Enter] **two** times, and then declare the following variable:

Variable Name	Data Type
strInput	String

5. Press [Enter], and then assign the *strInput* variable the value from returned from an *InputBox* method. For the InputBox arguments, type **"Enter Password"**

6. Press [Enter] **two** times, and then write a *Select Case* control structure that evaluates the *strInput* variable.

7. In the *Select Case* control, write three *Case* statements with the following values and actions. In the form name, use your own initials:

Case Value	Action if true
"Go! Series"	Exit Sub
""	DoCmd.Close acForm, "frmPersonnelFML", acSaveNo
Else	Call Form_Load

8. **Save** the code. In the form, test each of the following scenarios: 1. If the wrong password is entered, then another prompt should display; 2. If the correct password is entered, the form should open; 3. If the Cancel button is clicked, then no more prompts should display and the form should not open.

9. In the **Code** window, **Copy** all of the code for the **frmPersonnelFML** form, and then **Close** the Visual Basic window. Click **Save**, and then **Close** the form.

10. Start a blank document in **Word**. Apply the **No Spacing** style, the **Courier** font, and then set the margins to **Narrow**. Type **12I_Personnel_Code_Firstname_Lastname** substituting your own name, press [Enter] **two** times, and then **Paste** the code. **Save** the document as **12I_Personnel_Code_Firstname_Lastname** If you are instructed to submit this result, create a paper or electronic printout.

(Project 12I–Genres continues on the next page)

(Project 12I–Genres continued)

11. Open **frmGenresFML** in Design view, and then open the code module for the form. In the sub *cboGenres_AfterUpdate*, click to the right of the first comment. Press Enter, and then add the following comments:

> 'Modified by Firstname Lastname (Use your own name)
>
> 'mm/dd/yyyy (Use the current date)

12. In the sub *cboGenres_AfterUpdate*, locate the statement where *strSQL* is assigned a value. Change each occurrence of *qryGenres* to **qryGenresFML** using your own initials.

13. In the sub *Form_Load*, click to the right of the first comment. Press Enter, and then add the following comments:

> 'Modified by Firstname Lastname (Use your own name)
>
> 'mm/dd/yyyy (Use the current date)

14. In the sub *Form_Load*, locate the statement where *strSQL* is assigned a value. Change each occurrence of *qryGenres* to **qryGenresFML** using your own initials.

15. Click **Save**, and then test that selecting a Genre in the combo box results in all of the songs for that genre displaying in the list box. If necessary, debug your code.

16. In **frmGenresFML,** switch to **Design** view. Use the **Property Sheet** to assign the **Unbound** text box the **Name txtSongCount**

17. In the sub *cboGenres_AfterUpdate*, click to the right of *Dim strSQL AS String*, and then press Enter. Declare a new variable named **intSongCount** and assign it the **Integer** data type.

18. In the sub *cboGenres_AfterUpdate*, click to the right of *lstSongs.Requery*, and then press Enter **two** times. Add the following comment: **'Update the song count**

19. Press Enter, and then calculate the number of songs listed by typing the following: **intSongCount = lstSongs.ListCount – 1**

20. Press Enter, and then write the song count to the form by typing the following: **txtSongCount = intSongCount**

21. Press Enter, and then add the following *If Then Else* control structure:

> If intSongCount < 15 Then
>
>   txtSongCount.FontBold = True
>
> Else
>
>   txtSongCount.FontBold = False
>
> End If

22. In the form, test that the count of each genre's song list changes whenever the combo box is updated and that the **Calypso** genre count displays bold text.

(Project 12I–Genres continues on the next page)

Access

chapter twelve

Mastering Access

(Project 12I–Genres continued)

23. In the *Form_Load* procedure, insert a new line above the first comment, and then add a statement that creates an error event handler. If an error occurs, the program should skip to a subroutine named **ErrorMessage**

24. At the end of the *Form_Load* procedure, create a subroutine named **ErrorMessage** that displays a message box with the following message: **"An error occurred. Please contact Firstname Lastname."** In the message, use your own name.

25. Before the *ErrorMessage* subroutine, add the statement **Exit Sub**, and then test your code.

26. **Copy** all of the code in the **Code** window, and then **Close** the Visual Basic window. Click **Save**, **Close** the form, and then **Exit** Access.

27. Start a blank document in **Word**. Apply the **No Spacing** style, the **Courier** font, and then set the margins to **Narrow**. Type **12I_Genres_Code_Firstname_Lastname** substituting your own name, press Enter **two** times, and then **Paste** the code. **Save** the document as **12I_Genres_Code_Firstname_Lastname** If you are instructed to submit this result, create a paper or electronic printout.

28. **Exit** Word.

End **You have completed Project 12I**

Content-Based Assessments

Project 12J—Business Running Case

In this project, you will apply the skills you practiced from all the Objectives in Projects 12A and 12B.

From My Computer, navigate to the student files that accompany this textbook. In the folder **03_business_running_case**, locate and open the folder for this chapter. Open and print the instructions for this project, which are provided to you in Adobe PDF format. Follow the instructions and use the skills you have gained thus far to assist the brother and sister team of Michael and Kristen Landry in meeting the challenges of owning and running their business.

End **You have completed Project 12J** ——————————

Rubric

The following outcomes-based assessments are *open-ended assessments*. That is, there is no specific correct result; your result will depend on your approach to the information provided. Make *Professional Quality* your goal. Use the following scoring rubric to guide you in *how* to approach the problem and then to evaluate *how well* your approach solves the problem.

The *criteria*—Software Mastery, Content, Format and Layout, and Process—represent the knowledge and skills you have gained that you can apply to solving the problem. The *levels of performance*—Professional Quality, Approaching Professional Quality, or Needs Quality Improvement—help you and your instructor evaluate your result.

	Your completed project is of Professional Quality if you:	Your completed project is Approaching Professional Quality if you:	Your completed project Needs Quality Improvements if you:
1-Software Mastery	Choose and apply the most appropriate skills, tools, and features and identify efficient methods to solve the problem.	Choose and apply some appropriate skills, tools, and features, but not in the most efficient manner.	Choose inappropriate skills, tools, or features, or are inefficient in solving the problem.
2-Content	Construct a solution that is clear and well organized, contains content that is accurate, appropriate to the audience and purpose, and is complete. Provide a solution that contains no errors of spelling, grammar, or style.	Construct a solution in which some components are unclear, poorly organized, inconsistent, or incomplete. Misjudge the needs of the audience. Have some errors in spelling, grammar, or style, but the errors do not detract from comprehension.	Construct a solution that is unclear, incomplete, or poorly organized, containing some inaccurate or inappropriate content; and contains many errors of spelling, grammar, or style. Do not solve the problem.
3-Format and Layout	Format and arrange all elements to communicate information and ideas, clarify function, illustrate relationships, and indicate relative importance.	Apply appropriate format and layout features to some elements, but not others. Overuse features, causing minor distraction.	Apply format and layout that does not communicate information or ideas clearly. Do not use format and layout features to clarify function, illustrate relationships, or indicate relative importance. Use available features excessively, causing distraction.
4-Process	Use an organized approach that integrates planning, development, self-assessment, revision, and reflection.	Demonstrate an organized approach in some areas, but not others; or, use an insufficient process of organization throughout.	Do not use an organized approach to solve the problem.

Problem Solving

Project 12K — Producers

In this project, you will construct a solution by applying any combination of the skills you practiced from the Objectives in Projects 12A and 12B.

For Project 12K, you will need the following file:

a12K_Producers

You will save your database as
12K_Producers_Firstname_Lastname

Cross Oceans Music has a form that should list each producer in a list box. When a producer's name is clicked, the songs produced by that producer should display in a second list box. In this project, you will need to fix several problems with the form and its code module in order for it to work correctly. Open a12K_Producers, and then save it as a 2007 database with the name **12K_Producers_Firstname_Lastname** For each database object, add **FML** at the end of its name using your own initials and no spaces.

Open the code module for *frmProducersFML*. For the two event procedures, update the first comment so that it describes what the procedure should do. The second comment should include your first and last names, and the third comment should give the current date. From the code, determine what names should be assigned to the form's two list boxes, and then assign those names. For each procedure, determine what variables are used, and under the appropriate comment, declare those variables with the correct data type. Update the code to reflect updated database object names.

Debug the code so that the form works as intended. In the Form_Load procedure, modify the SQL query string so that each producer is listed only one time in the list box. Test your code and correct any run-time or logical errors. For both procedures, add error trapping. If an error does occur, have a subroutine display the message *Sorry, an error occurred.* Test the code again. If you are instructed to submit this result, create a paper or electronic printout.

End **You have completed Project 12K** —————

Outcomes-Based Assessments

Problem Solving

Project 12L — Navigation

In this project, you will construct a solution by applying any combination of the skills you practiced from the Objectives in Projects 12A and 12B.

For Project 12L, you will need the following file:

a12_Navigation

**You will save your file as
12L_Navigation_Firstname_Lastname**

Cross Oceans Music needs a single form that can navigate their database. They would like the form to display buttons that open each item. To start, open **a12L_Navigation**, and then save it as a 2007 database with the name **12L_Navigation_Firstname_Lastname** For each database object, add **FML** at the end of its name using your own initials and no spaces.

In the form frmNavigationFML, copy the existing command button, and then Paste it eight times. Arrange the nine buttons in an easy to navigate manner. For four of the command buttons, add a caption and name each based on the form that it will open. To open each form, create an On Click event procedure for each button that adapts the following VBA code: *DoCmd.OpenForm "frmBandsFML", "", "", , acNormal.*

For four of the other command buttons, add a caption and name based on the report that each will open. To open each report, create an On Click event procedure for each button that adapts the following VBA code: *DoCmd.OpenReport "rptBandsFML", acViewReport, "", "", acNormal.*

For the last button, provide the caption, *Close Database*, and name it cmdExit. Create an On Click event procedure that adapts the following VBA code: *DoCmd.Quit acPrompt.* If necessary, adjust the arrangement of the buttons on the form. Test that each button works as intended. If you are instructed to submit this result, create a paper or electronic printout.

End You have completed Project 12L _____

Problem Solving

Project 12M — Customers

In this project, you will construct a solution by applying any combination of the skills you practiced from the Objectives in Projects 12A and 12B.

For Project 12M, you will need the following file:

a12M_Customers

**You will save your database as
12M_Customers_Firstname_Lastname**

Cross Oceans Music would like to prevent unauthorized personnel from viewing the data in the Customers table. They would like the form for this table to be protected by a password. To start, open **a12M_Customers**, and then save it as a 2007 database with the name **12M_Customers_Firstname_Lastname** For each database object, add **FML** at the end of its name using your own initials and no spaces.

For *frmCustomersFML*, add an event procedure that will run each time the form is opened. In the procedure, use comments to describe what the procedure will do, list your name, and also list the current date. Declare all variables that will be used in the procedure and assign each the appropriate data type. When the form opens, prompt for the correct password. If the correct password is entered, the form should open and no more prompts should display. If an incorrect password is entered, the prompt should display again. If the password is left blank or the Cancel button is clicked, the form should close. Add error trapping so that in case of an error, the form closes. If you are unsure how to create this code, use the code from Project 12D as your reference.

Test and debug your code, making sure that the form opens only when the correct password is entered. In all other cases, it should close. If you are instructed to submit this result, create a paper or electronic printout.

End You have completed Project 12M ⎯⎯⎯⎯⎯⎯

Outcomes-Based Assessments

Access
chapter twelve

Problem Solving

Project 12N — Studio Fees

In this project, you will construct a solution by applying any combination of the skills you practiced from the Objectives in Projects 12A and 12B.

> **For Project 12N, you will need the following file:**
>
> a12N_Studio_Fees

You will save your database as
12N_Studio_Fees_Firstname_Lastname

Cross Oceans Music has started renting out its recording studios to other groups and musicians. The company would like a form to enter information about the groups who rent the studios. To start, open **a12N_Studio_Fees**, and then save it as a 2007 database with the name **12N_Studio_Fees_Firstname_Lastname** For each database object, add **FML** at the end of its name using your own initials and no spaces.

In *frmStudio_FeesFML*, create a new procedure for the *Total_Hours* After Update event. The procedure needs to calculate the rental fee based on a sliding scale and then write that value into the *RentalFee* field. In the procedure, add comments describing what the procedure does and include your name and the current date as comments. Use either a *Select Case* or *If Then Else* control structure to calculate the Rental Fee according to this scale:

If the value in TotalHours is 5 or less, then the rate is $500 per hour.
If the value in TotalHours is from 6 to 15 hours, then the rate is $350 per hour.
If the value in TotalHours is more than 15 hours, then the rate is $250 per hour.

Declare all variables used in the procedure and assign each the correct data type. After calculating the value, the code should place the results in the *RentalFee* field. Test your code in the form. After fixing any run-time errors, use the form to check that the correct fees are applied in all situations. If you are instructed to submit this result, create a paper or electronic printout.

End **You have completed Project 12N** ————————————

Problem Solving

Project 12O — Debug

In this project, you will construct a solution by applying any combination of the skills you practiced from the Objectives in Projects 12A and 12B.

> **For Project 12O, you will need the following file:**
>
> a12O_Debug
>
> **You will save your database as**
> **12O_Debug_Firstname_Lastname**

A coworker at Cross Oceans Music needs help debugging a form. To start, open **a12O_Debug**, and then save it as a 2007 database with the name **12O_Debug_Firstname_Lastname** For each database object, add **FML** at the end of its name using your own initials and no spaces.

The coworker first noticed a problem when ground shipping always came out as $20.00. At $2.00 per item, ground shipping should be much cheaper than the results she was getting. Then she noticed that if the Cancel button was clicked in the prompt for the free code, the shipping charges would not be displayed. When trying to fix these problems, the prompt for the free code stopped displaying. She tried to write an error trapping event, but the error message that she wrote displayed every single time. Now, she is unable to get the program to run without displaying a run-time error. Debug the code module to correct all of these problems. If you are instructed to submit this result, create a paper or electronic printout.

End **You have completed Project 12O** ———————————

 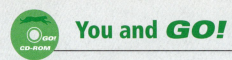

Access

chapter **twelve**

You and *GO!*

Project 12P — You and *GO!*

In this project, you will construct a solution by applying any combination of the Objectives found in Projects 12A and 12B.

From My Computer, navigate to the student files that accompany this textbook. In the folder **04_you_and_go**, locate and open the folder for this chapter. Open and print the instructions for this project, which are provided to you in Adobe PDF format. Follow the instructions to create a form to enter records for a database of personal music.

End You have completed Project 12P ———————————

GO! with Help

Project 12Q — *GO!* with Help

There are many events supported by Visual Basic. One useful event for forms is the On Current event. The Visual Basic Editor has its own help system, separate from the help system used by Access. In this activity, you will use Help for Visual Basic.

1 **Start** Access. Open one of the student files for Chapter 12 that came with your text.

2 Press Alt + F11 to open the Visual Basic Editor.

3 In the **Visual Basic Editor**, click the **Help** button.

4 In the **Search** box, type **OnCurrent** and then click **Search**.

5 In the **Access Help** window, from the **Results** list, click **Current Event (Help > Access Object Model Reference > Form Object > Events)**.

6 Read about the Current event. Scroll down to see an example event procedure for the Current event.

7 If you want to print a copy, click the **Print** button at the top of Access Help window.

8 **Close** the Help window, **Close** the Visual Basic Editor, and then **Exit** Access.

End You have completed Project 12Q ———————————

Glossary

ACCDE file An Access 2007 file format that prevents users from making design changes to forms, reports, and macros.

Action A self-contained instruction that can be combined with other actions to automate tasks.

Action query A query that lets you create a new table or change data in an existing table.

Admin The name of the default administrator in Access.

Administrator The person who has full permissions to all database objects and manages all users and groups.

Aggregate functions Functions, such as sum, average, count, maximum, minimum, standard deviation, or variance, used to perform a calculation on a column of data and return a single value.

Alphabetic index Grouping of items by a common first character.

Append To add on.

Append query An action query that adds new records to an existing table.

Appended When importing, data is added to the end of an existing table.

Application Title The text that displays in the Access title bar when that database is open.

Argument A value that provides information to the macro action.

Arithmetic operators Mathematical symbols used in creating expressions, such as +, −, *, /, ∧, \, and Mod.

AS An SQL keyword that creates a caption for a field.

Ascending order Sorts text alphabetically (A to Z) and sorts numbers from the lowest number to the highest number.

ASCII American Standard Code for Information Interchange. A synonym for plain text.

Asterisk (*) In an SQL statement, this will select all fields from the tables listed in the FROM clause.

Back up The process of making a copy of a database or other files to prevent data loss.

Back-end The database tables and their data.

Backup A copy of the database that is stored in an alternative location.

Bang operator An exclamation mark used in an expression that tells Access what follows it is an object that belongs to the object that precedes it in the expression.

Blank Form tool A tool used to create a simple form without any special formatting.

Blank Report tool A tool used to create a simple report without any special formatting.

Bound Tied to. A term used to describe the relationship between data in a form and data in the underlying table or query—when a record is updated in either the table or form, the related objects will be updated.

Bound control A control that obtains its data from an underlying table or query.

Bound report A report that displays data from an underlying table, query, or SQL statement as specified in the report's Record Source property.

Break mode A temporary suspension in the execution of code during which you can debug the code.

Breakpoint A point in the code, set by the programmer, where the procedure will stop running and enter Break mode.

Button control A control that enables an individual to add a command button to a form or report that will perform an action when the button is clicked.

Byte A unit used to measure computer storage sizes; it typically stores a single character, such as a digit or letter.

Calculated control A control that obtains its data from an expression or formula.

Calculated field A field that obtains its data by performing a calculation or computation, using a formula.

Cascade Delete An option used when referential integrity is enforced that enables an individual to delete a record in a table and delete all of the related records in related tables.

Cascade options Options, such as Cascade Delete and Cascade Update, that enable an individual to update records in related tables when referential integrity is enforced.

Cascade Update An option used when referential integrity is enforced that enables an individual to change the data in the primary key field and update the fields in related tables.

Cell In Excel, the small box formed by the intersection of a column and a row.

Certificate Authority (CA) A commercial organization that verifies the validity of signed certificates.

Chart A graphic representation of data.

Clipboard In Windows, a temporary storage area that can store up to 24 items.

Code Builder A window used to type programming code in Microsoft Visual Basic.

Code window The window used to write and edit VBA code.

Column chart A chart that displays comparisons among related numbers.

Combo box A combination of list box and text box; a control that enables an individual to select from a list or to type in a value.

Common fields Fields that contain the same data in more than one table.

Compact and Repair A process where an Access file is rewritten to store the objects and data more efficiently.

Comparison operators Symbols that Access uses to compare the value in the field with the value given after the comparison operator, for example, =, >, <.

Compound criteria More than one condition—criteria—in a query. Uses logical operators to create compound criteria.

Concatenate To combine two or more strings together into a single string.

Condition Specifies that certain criteria must be met before the macro action will be executed.

Contextual tab A tab that displays with contextual tools that contain related groups of commands that you may need while working with an object.

Contextual tools Enable you to perform specific commands related to the current or selected object. Contextual tools only display when needed for the current or selected object.

Contiguous Located next to one another.

Control layout A guide that aligns the controls on a form or report horizontally and vertically to give the form or report a uniform appearance.

Control structure A programming method that controls how statements in a procedure are run.

Controls Objects on a form or report in Design view that display data, perform actions, and let you enhance the form or report.

ControlTip Text that displays when an individual pauses the mouse pointer over an object.

Convert To change data from one format to another, such as converting a Word table to a delimited text file.

Copy The action of sending a duplicate version of a selected item to the Clipboard, leaving the original item intact.

Criteria Conditions that identify the specific records for which you are looking.

Cross join A type of join where each row from one table is combined with each row in a related table. Cross joins are usually created unintentionally when you do not create a join line between related tables and can result in many records being displayed in the query results.

Crosstab query A query that uses an aggregate function for data that is grouped by two types of information and displays the data in a compact, spreadsheet-like format.

Crosstab report A report that uses a crosstab query as the record source and displays calculated data grouped by two different types of information.

Current field The field in which you are ready to enter data. The field is white with a blinking insertion point.

Data Facts about people, events, things, or ideas.

Data dictionary A detailed report with information about all of the objects in a database.

Data entry The process of typing the records.

Data loss The unexpected loss of data caused by such actions as hardware failure, accidental deletion of records, theft, or natural disaster.

Data source In a mail merge operation, the Access table that contains the names and addresses of the individuals to whom the document is being sent.

Data type A characteristic that defines the kind of data that can be entered into a field, such as numbers, text, or dates. Each field can contain only one data type.

Data validation Rules that help prevent individuals from entering invalid data.

Database A collection of data related to a particular topic or purpose.

Database Documenter A tool used to print a report containing detailed information about the objects in a database.

Database structure Includes field names, data types, data formats, and other settings that define the database.

Datasheet view A window that displays data in rows and columns.

Debug To find and fix errors in the code.

Debugging Using a logical process to find and reduce the number of errors in a program.

Decode To remove a file's encoding.

Decrypt To remove a file's encryption.

Default value A value that displays in a field for a new record. This value can be changed unless a validation rule prohibits it.

Definition The table structure—field names, data types, and field properties.

Delete query An action query that removes records from an existing table in the same database.

Delimited file A file containing data where each record displays on a separate line and the fields within the record are separated by a single character called a delimiter.

Delimiter A character used in a delimited file to separate the fields. Common delimiters are commas or tabs.

Dependency An object that requires, or is dependent on, another database object.

Descending order Sorts text in reverse alphabetical order (Z to A) and sorts numbers from the highest number to the lowest number.

Design grid The lower portion of the query window used to specify the field names and the criteria for the query.

Design Master The original database in a replica set.

Design view A more detailed view of the structure of the form or report where the form or report is not running—you cannot see the data from the underlying table or query while making modifications.

Destination table The table that will be affected by an append, update, or delete query.

Detail section A section of a form or report that displays data from the underlying table or query. In a form, one record is displayed at a time.

Digital certificate A digital means of providing identity and authenticity.

Digital signature An electronic signature that can be used to authenticate the identity of the sender of a message or the signer of a document; the identity of the person or company who wrote a macro or VBA code in an Access database.

DISTINCT An SQL keyword that removes duplicates from query results.

Double-click Clicking the left mouse button two times in rapid succession.

Drag Clicking an object, holding down the left mouse button, and moving the mouse in a specified direction.

Drop zones The outlined regions you see when you finish the steps of the PivotTable and PivotChart wizard. To lay out a PivotTable report, you drag fields from the field list window and drop them onto the drop zones.

Dynamic Changing.

Ellipsis Three dots—. . .—used in the Macro Builder Condition column to indicate an addition action that is to be executed based on a condition entered above.

Embedded Another word for *inserted*.

Embedded macro A macro that is stored in the event properties of forms, reports, or controls. They are not displayed on the Navigation pane under Macros.

Encode To encrypt a 2002–2003 database without requiring a password to open it.

Encrypt To hide data by making the file unreadable until the correct password is entered.

Error trapping The process of controlling how a program responds to run-time errors.

Event Any significant action that can be detected by a program or computer system, such as clicking a button or closing an object.

Event-driven language Code that is run in response to user actions rather than running from beginning to end.

Export To create a file in a format that another application understands, enabling the two programs to share the same data; the process used to copy out data from one source or application to another application.

Expression A combination of functions, field values, constants, and operators that brings about a result.

Expression Another term for formula.

Expression Builder A feature used to create formulas (expressions) in query criteria, form and report properties, and table validation rules.

eXtensible Markup Language See *XML*.

Extracting Locating specific information in a database by using a query.

Field Each column in a table that contains a category of data.

Field box The intersection of a column and row.

Field list A box listing the field names in a table.

Field properties Characteristics or attributes of a field that control how the field will display and how the data can be entered in the field.

Filtering Displays a subset of the total records.

Find Duplicates Query Wizard A query wizard used to locate duplicate records in a table.

Find Unmatched Query Wizard A query wizard used to locate unmatched records in a related table.

Flagged Highlighted.

Focus The object that is selected and currently being acted upon.

Footer Information that displays at the bottom of every form or the bottom of every page in a report.

Foreign key field The field that is included in the related table so it can be joined with the primary key field in another table. It links the two tables together.

Form A database object that can be used to enter or modify data in a table. A form can also be used to view data from a table or query.

Form Footer section A section of the form that displays information in the footer.

Form Header section A section of a form that displays information in the header.

Form selector In Design view, the box in the upper right corner of a form where the rulers meet; used to select the entire form.

Form tool A tool used to instantly create a form in a simple top-to-bottom layout with all the fields lined up in a single column with a preformatted style.

Form view A view used to view, add, delete, or modify *records* using a form.

Form Wizard A step-by-step guide used to create a form where you can select the fields from one or more tables or queries, select a form layout, and select a style.

FROM clause An SQL keyword that lists which tables hold the fields used in the SELECT clause.

Front-end The database forms, queries, reports, and macros.

Full outer join A join type that displays all records from two related tables, even when there is no matching record in the other table.

Function A predefined procedure—one that Access has already built for you—that performs calculations, returns a value, can accept input values, and can be used in building expressions.

Global options Options that affect multiple items; for example, setting global options for the Navigation Pane affects every category and group on the Navigation Pane.

Group A collection of users who will use the database in similar ways.

Header Information that displays at the top of every form or the top of every page in a report.

HTML Stands for *HyperText Markup Language*, a language used to display Web pages.

Hungarian notation A naming convention where programming objects are given a prefix that identifies what type of object they are.

HyperText Markup Language See *HTML*.

If Then, If Else, or If Else If Control structures used to decide which statements should run based on whether a condition is true or false.

Image control A control that enables an individual to insert an image into any section of a form or report.

Import To copy data *in* from one source or application to another application.

Index A special list created in Access to speed up searches and sorting—for example, the index at the back of a book.

Information Data that has been organized in a useful manner.

INNER JOIN (SQL) An SQL keyword that instructs the query to use an inner join between two tables.

Inner join The default type of join. When a query with an inner join is run, only the records where the common field exists in both related tables are displayed in the query results.

Input mask A field property that determines the data that can be entered, how the data displays, and how the data is stored.

Insertion point A blinking vertical line that indicates where text will be typed.

Instance A term used to describe the number of times Access is simultaneously running.

Is not null Not empty.

IS NULL An SQL statement that signifies that the field is empty.

Join The relationship between tables or queries based upon common fields, which is displayed as the join line in the Query Design workspace. A join helps to extract the correct records from the related tables and queries when a query is run.

JOIN clause An SQL keyword that defines the join type for a query.

Join line The line connecting a primary key field to a foreign key field.

Junction table A third table containing the primary key fields from two tables in a many-to-many relationship.

Keyword A command built into the SQL programming language.

Label control A control on a form or report that displays text that is not bound to an underlying table or query. A title or field name is contained in a label control.

Label Wizard A step-by-step guide used to create labels for a wide variety of standard label sizes.

Landscape orientation The printed page is wider than it is tall.

Layout The arrangement of controls on a form or report.

Layout view A view used when modifying a form or report when the form or report is running—you can see the data as it displays in Form view or Report view.

Left outer join A type of outer join that displays all of the records on the *one* side of the relationship, whether or not there are matching records in the table on the *many* side of the relationship.

Legend Text that describes the meaning of colors and patterns used in a chart.

Line chart A chart that displays trends over time.

Line control A control that enables an individual to insert a line in a form or report.

Link A connection to data in another file.

Linked form A related form that is not stored within the main form. To view the data in a linked form, click the link that is displayed on the main form.

List box A control that enables an individual to select from a list.

Log in To enter a user name and password.

Logical error An error where the code runs, but the program does not return the expected results.

Logical operators Used in compound criteria to enter criteria for the same field or different fields. Includes AND, OR, and NOT.

Logo A graphic or picture used to identify a company or organization.

Logon The user name and password used to log in.

Lookup field A field that restricts the data entered because the person entering the data must select the data from a list that is retrieved from another table, from a query, or from a list of values that you enter.

Loop A control structure that repeats statements until a certain condition is met.

Macro A series of actions grouped as a single command to accomplish a task or multiple tasks automatically.

Macro group A set of macros grouped by a common name that displays as one macro object on the Navigation pane.

Mail merge To combine a main document created in Microsoft Word with a data source created in Access, resulting in a group of form letters or memos.

Main document In a mail merge operation, the Word document that contains the text of the letter or memo.

Main form A form that contains a subform.

Main report A report that contains a subreport.

Make table query An action query that creates a new table by extracting data from one or more tables.

Many-to-many relationship A relationship between tables where one record in one table has many matching records in a second table, and a single record in the second table has many matching records in the first table.

Margin indicator Visual clues in the left margin provided by the Visual Basic Editor while you edit code.

MB The abbreviation for megabyte.

Megabyte A unit used to measure storage sizes; it stores 1,048,576 bytes.

Merging Combining two documents to create one document.

Method A function that is built into the VBA language.

Microsoft ActiveX control A pre-built program designed to run inside of multiple programs.

Microsoft SQL Server A database application designed for high-end business uses.

Microsoft Web Browser An ActiveX control that displays a Web page inside another application.

Mini toolbar A miniature, semitransparent toolbar that helps you work with objects.

Modal window A child (secondary window) to a parent window—the original window that opened the modal window—that takes over control of the parent window. A user cannot press any controls or enter any information on the parent window until the modal window is closed. Commonly used when the database designer wants to direct the user's focus to the information in the window.

Module A collection of Visual Basic code.

Multi-page form A form that displays the data on more than one page.

Multivalued field A field that holds multiple values, such as a list of people to whom you have assigned a task.

Named range In Excel, a range that has been given a name, making it easier to use the cells in calculations or modifications.

Naming convention A set of rules that an organization uses to standardize the naming of objects.

Natural primary key Data that cannot be used more than one time, such an employee number or license plate number.

Navigation Pane category A top-level listing that displays when the Navigation Pane arrow is clicked.

Navigation Pane group A second-level listing that displays when a Navigation Pane category is selected.

Nested subform A subform that is embedded within another subform.

Normalization The process of breaking a single table into smaller, related tables.

Normalized Well designed. Refers to databases where each field represents a unique type of data, each table has one or more primary key fields, the data is related to the subject of the table, and an individual can modify the data in any field—except the primary key field—without affecting the data in other fields.

Null value Refers to a field that has no data or is empty.

Objects The components in the database, such as tables, forms, and reports.

ODBC Stands for *Open Database Connectivity*, a standard that enables databases using SQL statements to interface with one another.

ON An SQL keyword used to specify the field that is common to two related tables.

One-to-many relationship One field—usually the primary key field—in a table is related to many fields—the foreign key field—in the related table.

One-to-one relationship A relationship between tables where a record in one table has only one matching record in another table.

Open Database Connectivity See *ODBC*.

Open Exclusive Opens the database so that changes can be made, but no other user may open the database at the same time.

Open Exclusive Read-Only Opens the database in both Exclusive and Read-Only modes.

Open Read-Only Opens the database so that all objects can be opened and viewed, but data and design changes cannot be made.

Orphan records Records that reference deleted records in a related table.

Outer join A type of join used to display records from both related tables, regardless of whether there are matching records.

Override Take the place of.

Page Footer section A section of a report that displays information that will print at the bottom of every page.

Page Header section A section of a report that displays information that will print at the top of every page.

Parameter A value that can be changed.

Parameter query A query that prompts you for criteria before running the query.

Paste The action of moving the selected item from the Clipboard into a new location.

Path The location of a folder or file on your computer or storage device.

PDF See Portable Document Format.

Performance Analyzer A wizard that analyzes database objects, and then offers suggestions for improving their design.

Permission The level of access to a database object granted to a user by an administrator.

Personal ID or PID A unique identifier that Access needs to manage a user's ability to work with database objects.

Picture Alignment property A property that determines where the background picture for a form or report displays.

Picture Size Mode property A property that determines the size of a picture in a form or report.

Pie chart A chart that displays the contributions of parts to a whole amount.

Pivot To rotate data in a PivotTable or PivotChart by changing row headings to column headings, and vice versa.

PivotChart A graphical view of the data in a PivotTable.

PivotTable A view of data that is used to organize, arrange, analyze, and summarize data in a meaningful way.

Placeholder An object that can be replaced with another object.

Plain text Text that does not contain formatting information, such as bold, italic, or fonts.

Point A measurement equal to 1/72 of an inch.

Pop-up window A window that suddenly displays (pops up), usually contains a menu of commands, and stays

on the screen only until an individual selects one of the commands. Commonly used when the database designer wants to direct the user's focus to the information in the window.

Populate Fill a table with data.

Portable Document Format (PDF) A common format for shared documents that was created by Adobe Systems. When a PDF file is viewed online or printed, it retains the original format; the data in the file cannot be easily copied or changed.

Portrait orientation The printed page is taller than it is wide.

Pre-built user groups Groups provided by Access that have their permissions already configured to perform specific types of tasks.

Primary key field A special field that contains unique data that can never be used again within the same field.

Print Preview Displays how a table or form will look when printed. Even though the table is hard to read, you can see how all the fields and data will display on the printed page.

Procedure A named group of programming statements that run as a unit.

Program tab Replaces the standard set of tabs when you switch to certain authoring modes or views.

Programming comment An embedded remark written by the programmer.

Project Explorer The pane that displays the modules for the database.

Propagate To spread, disseminate, or apply. For example, when you make a change to a table, you can propagate the changes to objects that were created using the table as a record source.

Properties Characteristics that determine the appearance, structure, and behavior of an object.

Properties window The window that displays the properties for each database object.

Property Sheet A list of properties for an object.

Property Update Options button A button that enables an individual to update the Property Sheet for a field in all objects that use this table as the record source.

Queries Database objects used to sort, search, and limit the data that displays.

Query A question formed in a manner that Access can interpret.

Query Datasheet view Displays the *results* of a query.

Query Design view Displays *how* a query was formed, including the tables/queries and the fields used and the criteria specified.

Query design workspace The top portion of the query window, where tables and queries are added.

Range In Excel, two or more selected cells on a worksheet that can be treated as a single unit.

Record Each row in a table that contains all of the data pertaining to one person, place, thing, event, or idea.

Record Source property A property setting that enables you to specify the source of the data for a form or a report. The property setting can be a table name, a query name, or an SQL statement.

Referential integrity A set of rules that prevents orphan records in related tables.

Relational database The tables in the database relate to or connect to other tables through common fields.

Relationship An association that is established between two tables using common fields.

Replica A special copy of a database where any changes made using the replica are sent to the original database and any other replicas that may exist.

Replica set The original database and all replica copies.

Replication The process of creating a replica.

Report A database object that can be used to summarize and present data in a professional-looking format from a table or query.

Report Footer section A section of a report that displays information that will print at the bottom of the last page.

Report Header section A section of a report that displays information that will print at the top of the first page.

Report tool A tool used to instantly create a report in a tabular layout with a preformatted style.

Report view A view used to display records as they will print in a report.

Report Wizard A step-by-step guide used to create a report where you can select the fields from one or more tables or queries, select a record layout, select a style, and specify how the data is grouped and sorted.

Required Mandatory. A setting for a field requiring that the field be populated with data.

Rich text Text that contains formatting information, such as bold, italic, or fonts.

Right outer join A type of outer join that displays all of the records on the *many* side of the relationship, whether or not there are matching records in the table on the *one* side of the relationship.

Right-click Clicking the right mouse button one time.

Run The process of Access looking at the records in a table or tables included in a query, finding the records that match specified conditions (if any), and displaying those records in Datasheet view.

Run-time error An error that occurs when the code attempts to perform an invalid operation.

Running Showing the data from an underlying table or query in a form or report displayed in Layout view.

ScreenTip A short description that displays when you hold the mouse pointer over an object.

Section bar In Design view, the bar that divides the sections of a form or report.

Select case statement A control structure that evaluates a single expression, and then executes one of several groups of statements depending on what that value is.

SELECT clause An SQL keyword that lists which fields the query should display.

Select query A query that obtains its data from one or more tables, from existing queries, or from a combination of the two. The results of the query are displayed in Datasheet view. The select query is a subset of data that is used to answer specific questions.

SharePoint List A list of documents maintained on a server running Microsoft Office SharePoint Server 2007 or Windows SharePoint Services 3.0.

SharePoint Server A Microsoft server that enables you to share documents with others in your organization.

Shortcut An icon with an arrow in it.

Shortcut menu A list of context-related commands that displays when you right-click a screen element or object.

Signed package An encoded database with a digital certificate included in the file.

Significant digit A number other than 0 on the right side of a decimal point.

Single stepping A debugging tool that executes one macro action at a time, enabling you to observe the results of each macro action and enabling you to isolate any action that may be causing an error or that produces unwanted results.

Sizing handles Small boxes around the edge of a control that are used to resize a control and to indicate when a control is selected.

Smart Tag A field property that enables the end user to perform tasks from Access that would usually require another program such as Outlook to be open.

Snapshot file A file format that enables an individual to view an Access report without having Access installed on the computer. The extension for a snapshot file is .snp.

Sorting The process of arranging data in a specific order based on the value in a field.

Source table The table from which records are being extracted.

Split database An Access database that is split into two files—one containing the back-end, and one containing the front-end.

Split form A form that displays data in two views—Form view and Datasheet view.

Spreadsheet Another name for a worksheet.

SQL (Structured Query Language) A language used by many database programs to view, update, and query data in relational databases.

SQL statement An expression that defines the SQL commands that should be performed when the query is run.

SQL subquery An SQL SELECT statement nested inside another query.

Stacked control layout The controls in a form are arranged vertically with the label control to the left of the text box control.

Standalone macro A macro contained in a macro object that displays under Macros on the Navigation pane.

Static data Data that does not change.

Status Bar Text property A property that enables an individual to add descriptive text that will display in the status bar for a selected control.

String A sequence of alphanumeric characters.

String expression A formula that looks at a sequence of characters and compares them to the criteria in a query.

Strong password A password that is very difficult to guess.

Sub procedure (sub) A procedure that executes code without returning a value.

Subdatasheet Related records that display when clicking the plus sign (+) next to a record in a table on the *one* side of a relationship.

Subform A form that is embedded within another form.

Subreport A report that embedded within another report.

Subroutine Code that resides within a procedure, to perform a specific task independent from the procedure.

Subset A portion of the total records.

Synchronize Compare records in database objects and update changes; to update each member of a replica set by exchanging all updated records and design changes.

Syntax The set of rules by which words and symbols in an expression are combined.

Syntax error An error that breaks one of the rules of the VBA programming language.

System table A table created by Access to keep track of data. An individual cannot view or work with a system table.

Tab control An object inserted into a main form that displays data on different tabs.

Tab order The order in which the fields on a form are selected when the Tab key is pressed.

Table Analyzer A wizard that looks for repeated data in a table, and then splits the table into two or more related tables.

Tables The foundation on which an Access database is built because all of the data in an Access database is stored in one or more tables. Each table contains data about only one subject.

Tables and Related Views On the Navigation Pane, a view that groups the objects by tables and their related objects. For example, a query that is based upon a table will be grouped with that table.

Tabular control layout The controls in a form are arranged in columns and rows, like a datasheet, with label controls—usually field names—across the top and text box controls—usually containing data from the underlying table or query—under the related label controls.

Tag Code used in HTML to format text.

Template A ready-to-use database that has been created by Microsoft to help you quickly create your own database. A template gives you a starting point for your database. You can use the template database as it is or customize it to suit your needs.

Text box control A control on a form or report that displays data that is bound to an underlying table or query. The data from a field is contained in a text box control.

Tiling A 1-inch square of a picture that is repeated across and down a form or report.

Toggle buttons Buttons that are used to perform a task and then cancel the same task.

Totals query A query used to calculate subtotals across groups of records.

Truncated A condition that occurs when a control in a form or report is not wide enough to display the data, causing some of the ending characters to be cut off.

Trust Center A security feature that checks documents for macros and digital signatures.

Trusted source A person or organization that you know who will not send you databases with malicious code.

Unbound control A control that does not obtain data from an underlying table or query.

Unbound report A report that does not display data from an underlying table, query, or SQL statement as specified in the report's Record Source property.

Unequal join A type of join used to combine rows from two data sources based on field values that are not equal. An unequal join can only be created in SQL view.

UNION An SQL keyword used to combine one or more queries in a union query.

Union query A query that combines the results of two or more similar select queries.

Unique Only one of its kind.

Unmatched records Records in one table that have no matching records in a related table.

Update query An action query that is used to add, change, or delete data in fields of one or more existing records.

User A person who will need to use the database.

User-level security Allows administrators to grant different permissions to different users or groups of users.

Validation rule An expression that precisely defines the data that will be accepted in a field.

Validation text The error message that displays when an individual enters a value prohibited by the validation rule.

Variable A programming object used to store values in the computer's memory.

VBA compiler Translates the VBA code written by the programmer into another language that can be interpreted by the computer.

Visual Basic An easy-to-learn, yet powerful programming language commonly used to build business applications.

Visual Basic Editor (VBE) The program used to edit Visual Basic code.

Visual Basic for Applications (VBA) A programming language built into Microsoft Office.

Visual Basic window The window that displays the Visual Basic Editor program.

Weak password A password that is easy to guess. Weak passwords may lead to costly losses of valuable data.

WHERE clause An SQL keyword that defines the criteria that should be applied when a query is run.

Wildcard characters Serve as a placeholder for one or more unknown characters in your criteria. Examples are * and ?

Wizard A guide that presents each step as a dialog box in which you choose what you want to do and how you want the results to look.

Workbook An Excel file that contains one or more worksheets.

Workgroup A collection of groups and users that can be applied to a single database or shared among several databases.

Workgroup ID or WID A unique identifier that Access needs to manage each workgroup.

Workgroup information file A separate file in which Access stores the user and group security settings for one or more databases.

Worksheet The primary document used in Excel to save and work with data that is arranged in rows and columns.

XML Stands for *eXtensible Markup Language*, the standard language for describing and delivering data on the Web.

XML Paper Specification (XPS) A common format for shared documents that was uses XML code. When an XPS file is viewed online or printed, it retains the original format; the data in the file cannot be easily copied or changed.

XML presentation files Two XML files created when an Access object is exported to XML so that the data can be viewed in a Web browser.

XML schema An XML document that defines the elements, entities, and content allowed in the document. It defines the tag names and defines the order, relationships, and data type you use with each tag.

XPS See *XML Paper Specification*.

Zero-length string Two quotation marks with no space between them, indicating no value exists for a required field.

Zoom To increase or to decrease the viewing area of the screen.

Zoom in Decreases the viewing area of the screen to look closely at a particular section of a document.

Zoom out Increases the viewing area of the screen to see a whole page on the screen.

Index

SINGLE PC LICENSE AGREEMENT AND LIMITED WARRANTY

READ THIS LICENSE CAREFULLY BEFORE OPENING THIS PACKAGE. BY OPENING THIS PACKAGE, YOU ARE AGREEING TO THE TERMS AND CONDITIONS OF THIS LICENSE. IF YOU DO NOT AGREE, DO NOT OPEN THE PACKAGE. PROMPTLY RETURN THE UNOPENED PACKAGE AND ALL ACCOMPANYING ITEMS TO THE PLACE YOU OBTAINED THEM. *THESE TERMS APPLY TO ALL LICENSED SOFTWARE ON THE DISK EXCEPT THAT THE TERMS FOR USE OF ANY SHAREWARE OR FREEWARE ON TH E DISKETTES ARE AS SET FORTH IN THE ELECTRONIC LICENSE LOCATED ON THE DISK:*

1. GRANT OF LICENSE and OWNERSHIP: The enclosed computer programs ("Software") are licensed, not sold, to you by Prentice-Hall, Inc. ("We" or the "Company") and in consideration of your purchase or adoption of the accompanying Company textbooks and/or other materials, and your agreement to these terms. We reserve any rights not granted to you. You own only the disk(s) but we and/or our licensors own the Software itself. This license allows you to use and display your copy of the Software on a single computer (i.e., with a single CPU) at a single location for academic use only, so long as you comply with the terms of this Agreement. You may make one copy for back up, or transfer your copy to another CPU, provided that the Software is usable on only one computer.

2. RESTRICTIONS: You may not transfer or distribute the Software or documentation to anyone else. Except for backup, you may not copy the documentation or the Software. You may not network the Software or otherwise use it on more than one computer or computer terminal at the same time. You may not reverse engineer, disassemble, decompile, modify, adapt, translate, or create derivative works based on the Software or the Documentation. You may be held legally responsible for any copying or copyright infringement which is caused by your failure to abide by the terms of these restrictions.

3. TERMINATION: This license is effective until terminated. This license will terminate automatically without notice from the Company if you fail to comply with any provisions or limitations of this license. Upon termination, you shall destroy the Documentation and all copies of the Software. All provisions of this Agreement as to limitation and disclaimer of warranties, limitation of liability, remedies or damages, and our ownership rights shall survive termination.

4. DISCLAIMER OF WARRANTY: THE COMPANY AND ITS LICENSORS MAKE NO WARRANTIES ABOUT THE SOFTWARE, WHICH IS PROVIDED "AS-IS." IF THE DISK IS DEFECTIVE IN MATERIALS OR WORKMANSHIP, YOUR ONLY REMEDY IS TO RETURN IT TO THE COMPANY WITHIN 30 DAYS FOR REPLACEMENT UNLESS THE COMPANY DETERMINES IN GOOD FAITH THAT THE DISK HAS BEEN MISUSED OR IMPROPERLY INSTALLED, REPAIRED, ALTERED OR DAMAGED. THE COMPANY DISCLAIMS ALL WARRANTIES, EXPRESS OR IMPLIED, INCLUDING WITHOUT LIMITATION, THE IMPLIED WARRANTIES OF MERCHANTABILITY AND FITNESS FOR A PARTICULAR PURPOSE. THE COMPANY DOES NOT WARRANT, GUARANTEE OR MAKE ANY REPRESENTATION REGARDING THE ACCURACY, RELIABILITY, CURRENTNESS, USE, OR RESULTS OF USE, OF THE SOFTWARE.

5. LIMITATION OF REMEDIES AND DAMAGES: IN NO EVENT, SHALL THE COMPANY OR ITS EMPLOYEES, AGENTS, LICENSORS OR CONTRACTORS BE LIABLE FOR ANY INCIDENTAL, INDIRECT, SPECIAL OR CONSEQUENTIAL DAMAGES ARISING OUT OF OR IN CONNECTION WITH THIS LICENSE OR THE SOFTWARE, INCLUDING, WITHOUT LIMITATION, LOSS OF USE, LOSS OF DATA, LOSS OF INCOME OR PROFIT, OR OTHER LOSSES SUSTAINED AS A RESULT OF INJURY TO ANY PERSON, OR LOSS OF OR DAMAGE TO PROPERTY, OR CLAIMS OF THIRD PARTIES, EVEN IF THE COMPANY OR AN AUTHORIZED REPRESENTATIVE OF THE COMPANY HAS BEEN ADVISED OF THE POSSIBILITY OF SUCH DAMAGES. SOME JURISDICTIONS DO NOT ALLOW THE LIMITATION OF DAMAGES IN CERTAIN CIRCUMSTANCES, SO THE ABOVE LIMITATIONS MAY NOT ALWAYS APPLY.

6. GENERAL: THIS AGREEMENT SHALL BE CONSTRUED IN ACCORDANCE WITH THE LAWS OF THE UNITED STATES OF AMERICA AND THE STATE OF NEW YORK, APPLICABLE TO CONTRACTS MADE IN NEW YORK, AND SHALL BENEFIT THE COMPANY, ITS AFFILIATES AND ASSIGNEES. This Agreement is the complete and exclusive statement of the agreement between you and the Company and supersedes all proposals, prior agreements, oral or written, and any other communications between you and the company or any of its representatives relating to the subject matter. If you are a U.S. Government user, this Software is licensed with "restricted rights" as set forth in subparagraphs (a)-(d) of the Commercial Computer-Restricted Rights clause at FAR 52.227-19 or in subparagraphs (c)(1)(ii) of the Rights in Technical Data and Computer Software clause at DFARS 252.227-7013, and similar clauses, as applicable.

Should you have any questions concerning this agreement or if you wish to contact the Company for any reason, please contact in writing:

Multimedia Production
Higher Education Division
Prentice-Hall, Inc.
1 Lake Street
Upper Saddle River NJ 07458